Dig

David Nichols tells the story of Australian rock and pop music from 1960 to 1985 – formative years in which the nation cast off its colonial cultural shackles and took on the world.

Generously illustrated and scrupulously researched, *Dig* combines scholarly accuracy with populist flair. Nichols is an unfailingly witty and engaging guide, surveying the fertile and varied landscape of Australian popular music in seven broad historical chapters, interspersed with shorter chapters on some of the more significant figures of each period. The result is a compelling portrait of a music scene that evolves in dynamic interaction with those in the United States and the UK, yet has always retained a strong sense of its own identity and continues to deliver new stars – and cult heroes – to a worldwide audience.

Dig is a unique achievement. The few general histories to date have been highlight reels, heavy on illustration and short on detail. And while there have been many excellent books on individual artists, scenes and periods, and a couple of first-rate encyclopedias, there's never been a book that told the whole story of the irresistible growth and sweep of a national music culture. Until now . . .

'The droll and often delightfully irritated David Nichols brings a savoury palate to this tasting of Australian sounds . . . It will be a brave writer indeed who intends to top *Dig* as an entertaining version of what happened in Australian rop and pock between 1960–85.'
— JEN JEWEL BROWN

'Thank you, comrade. From a player.
Someone had to wrestle this shit down.'
— DAVE GRANEY

'Nichols possesses one of the best bullshit detectors around.'
— SOPHIE CUNNINGHAM

ALSO BY DAVID NICHOLS

The Go-Betweens

The Bogan Delusion

Pop Life
(with Marc Andrews and Claire Isaac)

Trendyville
(with Renate Howe and Graeme Davison)

Dig

Australian Rock and Pop Music 1960-85

DAVID NICHOLS

Foreword by Dave Graney

VERSE CHORUS PRESS   PORTLAND   MELBOURNE   LONDON

This book is dedicated to my parents, Jane Miller and Graham Nichols,
and to the memory of Katherine Spielmann

Published by Verse Chorus Press | versechorus@gmail.com
2nd revised printing, November 2017
© 2016 David Nichols
Foreword © 2016 Dave Graney
Cover art © Ben Montero
Book design and layout by Steve Connell/Transgraphic Services

All rights reserved. No part of this book may be reproduced, stored in or introduced into a retrieval system, or transmitted in any form or by any means (digital, electronic, mechanical, photocopying, recording, or otherwise) without the prior written permission of the publisher, except by a reviewer, who may quote brief passages in a review.

The author and the publishers wish to thank all those who supplied illustrative material and gave permission to reproduce copyright material in this book. Every effort has been made to contact all copyright holders, and the publishers welcome communication from any copyright owners from whom permission was inadvertently not obtained. In such cases, we will be pleased to obtain appropriate permission and provide suitable acknowledgment in future printings.

Country of manufacture as stated on the last page of this book

Library of Congress Cataloging-in-Publication Data

Names: Nichols, David, 1965-
Title: Dig : Australian rock and pop music, 1960-85 / David Nichols.
Description: Portland, OR : Verse Chorus Press, 2016 | Includes bibliographical references and index.
Identifiers: LCCN 2015034550 | ISBN 9781891241260 (pbk.) | ISBN 9781891241611 (ebook)
Subjects: LCSH: Popular music--Australia--1961-1970--History and criticism. | Popular music--Australia--1971-1980--History and criticism. | Popular music--Australia--1981-1990--History and criticism.
Classification: LCC ML3504.N53 2016 | DDC 781.640994/09046--dc23
LC record available at http://lccn.loc.gov/2015034550

This project has been assisted by the Australian Government through the Australia Council, its arts funding and advisory body.

Contents

Foreword by Dave Graney vii

INTRODUCTION – Ascension 1

1 Wild Beat Overture 9

2 A Funny Buzz – THE EARLY TO MID SIXTIES 16

3 I Feel as Good As If I Were Dead – THE BEE GEES 48

4 We Weren't Exactly Keeping a Low Profile – THE MISSING LINKS . . . 58

5 The Snap and Crackle of Pop – THE MID TO LATE SIXTIES 66

6 Falling off the Edge of the World – THE EASYBEATS 122

7 Knights in Yellow Armour – PIP PROUD 134

8 It's a Flash! – THE EARLY TO MID SEVENTIES 144

9 Million Dollar Riff – DADDY COOL / SKYHOOKS 216

10 We Aren't Here to Confuse People – AC/DC 236

11 Bending Corners – THE MID TO LATE SEVENTIES 246

12 Five Years of Fancy Cars – DRAGON 354

13 Happy/Sad Is a Really Fantastic Emotion – THE REELS 372

14 We Were 60 Years Old When We Were 19 – THE TRIFFIDS 390

15 There's Absolutely No Art in the Moodists – THE MOODISTS 402

16 The Modern Song – THE EARLY TO MID EIGHTIES 410

AFTERWORD – What's It Like Out There? 542

Acknowledgments 549

Notes 551

Index 577

Foreword

I first met David Nichols when he was a teen music fan in early 80s Melbourne. He was too young to get into the pubs my band the Moodists were mostly playing in but had started a fanzine and wrote about music and drew cartoons for it. If truth be told, having a teenage fanzine writer and illustrator on your case is a pretty cool situation to be in. He made us authentic, in a way.

In the intervening years he has continued to write about and engage with popular and unpopular music as a community radio broadcaster, an artist manager (very briefly) and as a musician himself. His writing was published in actual pop monthlies like *Smash Hits* and successful lifestyle advertising cultural wraparounds such as *Rolling Stone Australia*. He has experienced the limitations and constraints of the scene on the island and has continued to chase down rumours and will-o'-the-wisp reputations that occasionally spawn mad fevers in the compound and he's brought a lot of them down to earth and into play here.

As he says in the introduction, it's a large book and it obeys no logic other than what chance and the weather have given him to use, just this one time he has everything and everyone in his sights. He has given himself the power and conceit to set a grid and tempo to a larger story than anybody has attempted before. He also became an actual historian along the way too. A made guy.

This book has been years – decades – in the making. Stories you had to really get a feel for, otherwise they'd just come out all wrong. Just pale shadows of American or British stories. Mad characters like Johnny O'Keefe getting right up in your face and bellowing out of tune about how great they were. Just listen to the digital files now and it sounds all blustering and off-key, but if a writer could take you somewhere close to the race-track and you could smell the fumes on the audience's breath too...

So many details that jump out at you in each chapter. Young British emigrés traveling on the same ships to Australia in the late 50s who emerge a decade later as flaming pop stars from different cities, still looking back at the world they'd been dragged away from. The Bee Gees in the dusty cowtown that was early 60s Brisbane and their precocious child talent contest rivals, Billy Thorpe and Lobby Loyde.

There's also the endlessly repeated struggles for authenticity as "real" music is posited against "pop pap". People fight that battle in the late 50s and the early 60s. Trad jazzers and folkies versus rock'n'roll barbarians. People making their own instruments and clothes. Art vs. money. The technology dragging the floor out from under the players feet – constantly. The wider world flooding in and washing through the whole picture. The regional variations, the radio pumping out sounds as soon as the vinyl was baked in the pressing plants. Then TV opening up the pipelines as well. People mad for new shit! Then the New Zealanders coming in with their weird vowels – their poise and their brains and their drugs!

This text is dense and full of mad detail. David Nichols is deeply and widely interested in the characters and the choices they make or have to make in the scenes here. He's got empathy and his own prejudices balancing all the while too. He admits at the start – it's a Melbourne-centric story in many ways, but why not? If that's the spot you were watching, reading and listening from for the most part?

I had a friend who was from the UK alternative 80s music world and he'd ended up happily in Melbourne and working in the scene in a music distribution admin type gig. He was a real music fan though. He continued to proudly love the most vegetable of prog, even when it stank to high heaven, at least in the knowing nostrils of the general music snobs that he had surrounded himself with. If the prog scene was a section of a Royal Botanic Gardens, he especially loved what would be known in lay terms as The Stinking Penis Plant Of That Peculiar World. Yes, King Crimson. We were talking upon matters musical one day and the theme was the relative merits of various books on the subject. By this time, the mid 90s, the field was growing by the day and you would have been right to wonder if the story was in danger of being told one too many times. It was getting to be all hearsay and rote tale telling. My friend James opined that for a music book to be considered good – in his not so humble opinion – the writer had to champion at least ONE act in it that just defied all known streams of thought as to what was considered to be good taste. The story or argument had to be built around one massive, gushing column of totally strange material. Some hopelessly untrendy, unknown, forgotten, degraded, weak and basically unstable piece of stuff. Past its use-by date. Uncultured, unpasteurized, unmediated junk. If that presence was held to be there, in the mind of the writer – and he used that presence to illuminate the dense jungle surrounds he was guiding us through – well it was an argument that was at the least worth giving an audient posture toward.

In this book, David Nichols has summoned many emanations of such a presence for us to give our attention to. A great piece of work in itself.

Thank you comrade. From a player. Someone had to wrestle this shit down. It will be a great challenge for someone in the future to pick up the trail for Volume Two.

Dave Graney,
Melbourne 2015

Introduction

ASCENSION

This book is an attempt to make sense of events, people, places and recordings that emerged under the banner of Australian popular music between 1960 and 1985. The time frame is somewhat arbitrary; it is the product of conceiving a fifty-year history (from 1960 to 2010), only to realise that fifty years was too much to take on if I was to do the material justice, and consequently splitting the period in half (the second half of what is now a two-volume survey can be expected sometime in the third decade of this century). Like any history should, it tries to challenge assumptions – in this case, assumptions about the culture, the times and the outcomes of Australian pop – and re-evaluate its subject.

One thing I did not want to do is write a book that strings together all the previously published anecdotes about pop musicians to create a smug, comfortable bedtime story for baby boomers. I also hoped to avoid writing one of those point-and-laugh books about historical 'fashion crimes', which try to calm fears about change and experiment by poking fun at the past and people who can't answer back (because even if they're still alive and interested, they're not that person anymore). Both these approaches are no more than lazy historical window-shopping; they don't ask any difficult questions about the politics, places of consumption and production, interactions and conversations, power structures or beliefs within pop music.

The process of writing this book was, as a result, complicated and arduous, though often rewarding and enjoyable. It is founded on documentary evidence, drawn primarily from the Australian music press, augmented by published and unpublished memoirs, films and television programs, and of course actual records (that is, 7- and 12-inch vinyl, or CD re-releases). These are combined with interviews and a small amount of internet research. Sources are supplied in the endnotes for every statement made in the book, aside from interviews which I conducted myself; the reader can assume that if no source is given for a quote, it is one I obtained from my informants. I appreciate that there is an inherent weakness in using the music press so extensively: on a number of occasions, while seeking clarification on a particular statement from decades ago, I was told by a musician that they were actually teasing, joking with, or lying to the journalist in question. Even when that's not happening overtly, the music press is notoriously full of boasts and promotional puff. Yet I contend – particularly as I am one of those people who has trouble recalling what he did last week *and* twenty years ago – that when writing history there is a potentially greater weakness in depending too heavily on people's memories of past events. I have also been told often enough by many of my informants that their memories are obscured by whatever drugs and alcohol they were using at the time; this confirms for me that my approach is probably the best one.

This book is enormous – not an assertion of its excellence, incidentally, just a statement of fact. It could have been twice as big. It is structured in chapters of vastly different sizes, the larger of which are subdivided into smaller sections. The shorter chapters concentrate on particular artists, with the aim of presenting a number of historical 'slices' in the form of a case study. The 'cases' are all valid and important artists, but they are not necessarily the *most* valid and important; indeed, that's a judgment I don't want to have to try to make.

I have tried to be user-friendly and provide some kind of overarching framework to help my reader stay focused, but at the same time both you, my reader, and I have to remember that to 'focus' the story necessitates being restrictive, and perhaps even deceptive. It is *easier* to regard history as a story of leaders and followers, or people magically drawn by irresistible, pervasive ideas (in the case of a history of music from the early 60s to the mid 80s, 'the Beatles', 'the Stones', 'psychedelia', 'counterculture', 'the new wave'). Unfortunately for history books, though fortunately for real life, this is simply not how the world works. The history of any cultural phenomenon is of people jostling – for supremacy, or just a livelihood, or a number of different things at once – and these people's paths cross or they don't, and they become successful in the eyes of others, or they don't, and they produce great work or terrible work or, in the case of most people, work that lies somewhere in between.

I should say, too, that I am of the belief, though it is entirely unprovable, that talent does not carve its own path: if the Easybeats hadn't met a Dutch doorman at a Sydney club in the early 60s, they may not have become Australia's biggest pop group of the mid 60s (or they *may* have, by some other means, but the point is merely that they may *not* have; the genius of George Young and Harry Vanda was not a irresistible force that would inevitably discover gold). In one sense this attitude masks a degree of card-shuffling; I would, however, trot out the old adage that describes success as 'one percent inspiration, ninety-nine percent perspiration' – and add that luck has to be considered a huge part of the whole shebang as well. In short, there is no inevitability to any of these stories. Ian Meldrum probably *was* wrong to overspend his production budget on 'The Real Thing', and because it went on to become a hit, and an iconic song, does not vindicate that decision; it's merely harder to come by stories of people who overspent Meldrum-style and produced a megaflop, because no-one wants to remember that, or they fudge the issue, or apply creative accounting, or it just doesn't mean as much because it happened to nobodies – but it certainly happens. On a related point, the Models' single 'On' is, I am certain to the point of declaring it an indisputable fact, at least a thousand times better by almost any standard than their later release 'Out of Mind, Out of Sight', and the reality that the first was not a hit, while the second was, proves nothing about either record's intrinsic value, though it does perhaps prove something about marketing and how the record-buying public feels about aspiring pop bands wielding chain saws in their videos. All art relates to commerce on some level; pop music seems to have done so more than most art forms, though this might just be a perception. Writing commercial pop music requires great talent, but the greatest pop groups in the world – the Reels, for instance – were often barely able to eke out a living. Only the most ardent free-market advocate would suggest that the craft of pop music is entirely about creating music that is more popular than any other music, and even popularity is hard to gauge exactly: Hunters and Collectors' 'Throw Your Arms Around Me' was not a hit at the time of its release, but twenty-five years later it was the most popular karaoke song in Australia.

Some may feel I pay insufficient attention to questions of culture, gender, and race in this book; others may feel I pay too much attention to these issues simply by mentioning them in this sentence. I grew up in the 1970s as part of quite possibly the first generation of non-indigenous Australians to be relieved of the idea that Australian culture was inherently inferior and that any pursuit of culture per se was to be found in other, older countries. Which is not to say we were unaware of this idea, and indeed in many ways it still persists. But we did not suffer under the weight of it in the way our predecessors might have. What is more, my childhood encompassed the years when Australia embraced multiculturalism. I was born as the country approached a milestone – twenty years of immigration from continental Europe – and was shifting toward an ostensibly merit-based (rather than racially oriented) immigration policy. Australian multiculturalism is a Canadian concept taken to its logical extreme; one outcome is that over a third of Australians today have a parent or a grandparent who was born outside the country. An equally important aspect of ethnic difference – policy towards and treatment of Australian Aboriginal people – also began to be addressed, haltingly, awkwardly – and often badly, as it still is at time of writing. I mention all these issues here in order to explain some of the opinions expressed in this book and some of the decisions I made in prioritising certain elements, people and artefacts over others. Briefly, my attitude is that I know there was a 'cultural cringe'; I know there was (and is) racism in Australia; I know women were (and are still) oppressed. I don't shy away from these things in this history; I want you, as a reader, to take them as a given. What I don't want to do is to return continually to these essential, central elements of Australian society during the period I am analysing as to an unscratchable itch. They are undeniable truths. Anyone who dismisses my attitude as 'politically correct' is, I contend, an anti-historical crank who won't get much out of this book (or, for that matter, life): such people should write their own books to read. Having said all that, I am troubled by the lack of marginalised voices in this volume: my explanation for this is simply that many of the people who might have been discussed under this rubric were uncontactable or unwilling to talk. I feel particularly the lack of a large number of female performers who are difficult to write about in the context of a work like this because, in the main, they were vocal interpreters of others' music: pretty mastheads fronting a showband. Print media advertising from the early 60s shows a huge parade of such young women, whose careers were almost certainly brief and exploitative. I don't wish to diminish performers such as these; I do pay closer attention to some (for instance, Adelaide's April Byron, who was a songwriter as well) but I feel that ultimately the focus has to be on musicians who either write their own music or who strongly and decisively reinterpret others' work in a challenging way. Given the horrifically sexist, indeed in many ways misogynist, times, this was exceptionally more difficult for women to achieve than it was for men. Women, or rather girls, were assigned the role of appropriate *consumers* of popular music, particularly 'pop' music. Fortunately for everyone (except talented female musicians of the 60s and 70s, many of whom can and do feel cheated), the idea that a successful songwriter and/or instrumentalist might be female is almost – *almost* – unremarkable in popular music today.

At the same time, I feel no need to justify the high concentration of New Zealanders present in this history; all I can really say is, firstly, that my New Zealand-born informants (I use two, in particular, when discussing the 60s and early 70s: Brian Peacock and Mike Rudd) have a good perspective on the Australia they encountered, and secondly, that there's an argument to be made that New Zealand punches above its weight as a creative society, in pop music and other areas. To leave out that delightful nation close to Australia's east would, in any case, both pander to nationalism and skew the work to the point of inaccuracy. I have not, it should be noted, tried to tell New Zealand's own pop music story (which John Dix relates in his remarkable *Stranded in Paradise*).

Incidentally, in mentioning my awareness of various prejudices in Australia's past and present, I do not mean to suggest that I am some kind of cross between Buddha and a blank slate: I can't not be affected by my own experiences. All any of us can do is recognise our possible biases. Many may feel there is a distinct Melbournist tinge to this work: certainly, I have lived in Melbourne for three-quarters of my life, including the years I was working on this book. However, all evidence suggests that Melbourne was the centre of Australian music in the 60s and through to the early 80s; while there's no particular reason why this was the case, once it became so, the culture naturally expanded on itself. To investigate the smaller capitals and other regions in detail would have been fascinating. But concentrating too much on peripheral places, which took from the wider world but did not have input back, would be detrimental to the overall narrative.

I have tried to avoid some of the usual pitfalls of music history and criticism (including, I hope, irritating and clichéd expression). I consider many music writers have shown a lazy dependence on the idea of 'influence', and this harks back to my earlier gripe about the notion of a 'second-rate' Australia of the past in which people are beholden to ideas delivered by boat from London. The notion of 'influence' strikes me as nothing more than a convenient way of pigeonholing people, and one which hides more important truths. Billy Green, guitarist/songwriter in the group Doug Parkinson and the Questions (later retitled Doug Parkinson In Focus) between 1966 and 1970, may well have devoured every Beatles album when it came out; he would have been a little marginalised if he hadn't. But if he did, I don't see this as any justification for talking about the Beatles' influence on Billy Green, because to do so obscures the reality that a number of factors were at work here: Billy Green was surely at least as influenced by the group's record company saying 'Be at the recording studio on Friday to record a hit single'; by the opportunity to write for Doug Parkinson's extraordinary voice, much more powerful and versatile than any of the Beatles'; by his own experimentation with new instruments and non-Anglo-American music; by the desire to create new music in a pop context; by competition with other groups; by the spirit of the times; by a desire to continue to work in the music industry; and so on. That this group's best-known hit was a cover of 'Dear Prudence' neither negates nor proves this assertion, incidentally. Billy Green's best songs for In Focus, such as 'Without You', are unique.

It also perturbs me that so many writers seem to use the term 'influenced by' as a polite way of saying 'copied', or implying some similar value judgement about the capacity of artists for original thought. Going beyond this, it needs to be said that even when groups or artists *do* copy the style and sound of more famous artists, there are numerous reasons why they might do so, including for instance a commercial imperative, or an artisanal impulse, or the wish to pay homage or contribute to the general musical culture in a style people will easily recognise. 'Influence' covers and hides anything; if the 70s Tasmanian group Beathoven mimicked the sound of the early Beatles, were they 'influenced' by the Beatles or were they influenced by the idea of taking a recognisable retro sound, selling records, and launching careers by it? Daddy Cool may have been 'influenced' by 1950s doo-wop in a manner of speaking, but the *impetus* for the group was surely the idea of playing doo-wop in a 'head' music environment. The idea of 'influence' hangs out with all of these possibilities, and explains absolutely nothing. It is worth noting, too, that artists – particularly when they are looking back over decades – are often extremely keen to describe their work in terms of influences, possibly in part as a convenient shorthand but also possibly because artists are typically the worst judges of their own work and often think of it largely in terms of what they and others were (or could have been) listening to at the time. Many also hope to simply diminish their earlier work as juvenilia.

I have also tried to move away from the illustration mode usually adopted in pop-culture histories. The internet will soon enter its third decade of mass popularity; almost any depiction of a given artist, as well as their music, can now be summoned up in an instant, and I imagine most of my readers have access to this delightful mess. What then would be the point of reproducing conventional photographs of the people cited in the text? Whatever promo picture I might choose to illustrate what Australian Crawl looked like, you can not only find that image online, you can also view a dozen or more other photos, along with many videos and much more besides, that will collectively give you a greater understanding of the group's line-ups and styles. Instead, I have drawn on images that are still largely hidden from the web, which I hope provide something of the flavour of the times rather than merely highlighting some celebrities. There is a far more extensive world of knowledge, opinions and images out there now to follow up, should you be so inspired, and I hope you are.

Finally, a word about errors. It might appal anyone who hasn't written a book to find a historian conceding error in a work before it is even published. When you're making assertions twenty to a page, and throwing in the odd bad-tempered criticism or high five, some things are bound to get out of whack. Sometimes – perhaps without realising it – a writer sacrifices a narrow, strict truth in pursuit of a broader one. I have tried not to do this, but I also try to write concisely and appropriately – and entertainingly, too, if I can. The documents I've used sometimes conflict with one another, and people's memories sometimes conflict with the documents, so in some cases I've had to make a captain's pick. If I have put two and something that looked like two together and come up not with four, but with 4.1 or 7, I hope the reader can forgive me and the libelled keep their lawsuits to a minimum.

Music, like any art, provokes strong responses, of course, and there are times when I am no doubt unreasonably harsh, or unreasonably glowing, in my assessment of some work or another. Readers should take my meanderings in the spirit they are intended; I welcome correspondence on any subject. My ultimate aspiration is that this work inspires others to tease out more of this history, in new ways and revelatory interpretations.

David Nichols
Melbourne, 2015

1 Wild Beat Overture

> 'Rock' meant SHOCK in Australia. It came crashing in like a wild-beat overture to a massive new morality – or rather immorality – play. It stirred complacent aldermen to apoplexy, sent the record industry into an uncontrollable spin – and produced a species of Australian never before observed – the 'real mad' popsters and their 'real gone' audiences of screaming young girls.[1]

Conventional rock music history would have us believe Johnny O'Keefe was the Australian initiator of rock music in Australia. In fact, what he did was far less innovative: he was one of a group of men and women who personified this particular strand of youth culture, and guided the Australian public's understanding of rock 'n' roll. The celebration, even deification, of O'Keefe continues in unusual places: vintage footage of an audience reacting to O'Keefe and his group the Dee Jays (O'Keefe said it stood for 'doovenile jelinquents'[2]) as they perform 'Shout' has since 1987 led off every episode of *Rage*, ABC-TV's long-running late-night video-clip show, while on the soundtrack Iggy Pop sings his version of O'Keefe's 'Real Wild Child'. O'Keefe, who is discussed comprehensively in the next chapter, has two major records in his legend. The first is his version of 'Shout', which Festival Records' Ken Taylor remembered as:

> the first record ever established on the popular market by TV alone. Every radio station banned it because it was a 'screamer' – an extremely noisy and (some station managers thought) offensive form of Rock and Roll. But by that time Johnny had been appearing on an ABC teenage television show called *Six O'Clock Rock* and TV had no inhibitions about 'Shout'. It took off like a rocket.[3]

O'Keefe's second iconic release was 'Wild One', a 1958 song he purportedly wrote but which has been more accurately attributed jointly to O'Keefe, John Greenan and Dave Owens.[4] It was raucous, fun rubbish, but Buddy Holly and Jerry Lee Lewis were sufficiently taken by its vigour to record versions of it.[5] Taylor remembered O'Keefe as 'a cocky, square-cut, jaunty guy with an earnest air under his confident grin'[6] and, intriguingly, as 'a comet in the milky way of Australian pop stardom.'[7] O'Keefe appears to have coerced Taylor into signing him to Festival by announcing that it had happened, though it is hard to imagine – particularly at a time when a typical recording contract was strongly in a record label's favour – why Festival would have considered signing O'Keefe a risky move.[8] O'Keefe had already established himself most effectively and lucratively as a rock and roll performer, jumping on a bandwagon at the same time that noted composer and pianist Percy Grainger, at the end of his rich and disturbing life, was predicting rock's future via his forays into electronic instruments and 'free music'.

In many respects Grainger's output is peripheral to the story of late-20th century popular music. His life, however, is very relevant indeed: he was a popular international artist who made his reputation (and money) mostly as a performer rather than a composer; he showed – as so many Australians have since – that his Australianness, rather than being a handicap, gave him an awareness of international cultures and a unique perspective that was to his benefit. Additionally, but perhaps not unrelatedly, many aspects of Grainger's character would be reflected in the attitudes and behaviour of popular Australian musicians of this period, particularly the penchant for outrageous public declarations and international re-making of the self. Though Grainger was an elderly man in the 1950s, he enjoyed rock music, which he experienced – appropriately – via films, and which he considered to be a branch of the type of modern music also exemplified by the experimental, electronically powered noise generators he helped to create.[9] It is perhaps for this reason that Peter Duncan, in his film about Grainger, *Passion,* has the Grainger character (played by Richard Roxburgh) proclaim: 'By the end of the 20th century people will be listening to African music . . . they'll be dancing to African music'. Duncan's Grainger also presciently claims that the future of music lies with 'delicately controlled machines', though he makes one claim too many when he adds that he would 'one day invent' them.[10]

The real Percy Grainger was born in 1882 in the Melbourne suburb of North Brighton,[11] the same general beachside area that 60 years later would nurture popular music talents like Keith Glass, Hans Poulsen and Ross Wilson, and some decades later Mick Turner. That Grainger was born into a family of bigots[12] was not particularly unusual; bigotry was par for the course at the time. His obsession with racial distinction[13] (which included strong elements of Aryan romanticism), his refusal to kowtow to conventional attitudes to incest, and his delight in sado-masochism[14] were unsavoury facets of a refracted display of extraordinary, creative, passionate spirit. His tendency towards vegetarianism,[15] his passion for folk and 'free' music, his frankness and openness were among the more pleasant aspects of his complicated personality. A piano virtuoso, Grainger toured the world from an early age playing the works of others, transcribing and adapting traditional and classical works, and collecting folk music and tangible musical memorabilia.

Grainger's attitude to his own more conventional compositions (the most famous of which is the jaunty and faintly revolting 'Country Gardens') seem to summon up within him the kind of language often used by the more dramatic rock star: for instance, his statement, late in life, that:

> The object of my music is not to entertain, but to agonize – to make mankind think of the agony of young men forced to kill each other against their will & all other thwartments and torturings of the young.[16]

Similarly, and once again evoking passion as a prime motivator, Grainger 'believed and preached the idea that mere technical skill and excellence were barriers to fine performances.'[17] He also sought to blur distinctions between 'serious' and popular musics, often incorporating ragtime or folk tunes into his concert repertoire. Teaching at New York University in 1932, he invited Duke Ellington and his band to perform for a class.[18] One of his NYU students was Bernard Herrmann, later to become Hollywood's greatest mid-20th-century film soundtrack composer.[19]

PERCY GRAINGER
Thrived on Contradictions

His biographer John Bird tells us that some of Grainger's ideas were 'so crass and mulishly stupid as to make his friends and colleagues want to run and hide with embarrassment.'[20] However, his much laboured over, but sadly underdeveloped, 'free music' was in many ways his boldest and most intriguing contribution to Australian music. According to Bird:

> The roots of Grainger's Free Music... went back to his childhood, the rolling hills of South Australia which he saw from the train that took him from Melbourne to Adelaide, the water which lapped at the sides of the rowing boat in Albert Park lake and, above all, the sounds of the wind as it howled through the telegraph wires on the Australian country roads. Often he thought to himself that just as the sounds and shapes of nature knew no arbitrary scales or metres so there should be no reason why in its search for full emotional expressiveness music should not enjoy a similar freedom. Just as a painter could move from one colour to another by either a gradual blending of tints or an abrupt transition, so should a composer be able to move from one note to another by a gliding tone as well as by a leap if he so wished...[21]

Grainger's interest in music made by telegraph wires found reflection in Alan Lamb's field recordings of such sounds in the Australian outback in the 60s, then in the piano wire music made by New Zealander Alastair Galbraith and American

Matt De Gennaro in the 1990s. Grainger wrote that his free music would be 'more soulrevealing, more melodious, more truly tender and lovely than any music yet'; he was also excited by the idea that, through it, 'Australian musical life can be freed from the absurdities, falseness, ignorance & good-for-nothingness that plagues European & American musical life.'[22]

Grainger worked on free music from 1945 onwards, via a number of carefully constructed 'pretty machines.' They employed all kinds of cast-off junk, including cotton reels, children's toy records, carpet rolls, a vacuum cleaner, strong brown paper and string. He gave them deliberately silly names, such as 'the Crumb-catcher and Drain Protector Disc' and 'the Cross-Grainger Double-decker Kangaroo-pouch Flying Disc Paper Graph Model for Synchronizing and Playing 8 Oscillators'.[23] Though Grainger was intrigued by sound that was generated purely electronically, his machines were distinct from what we would now understand as synthesizers. The Cross-Grainger Kangaroo-pouch system, for instance:

> consisted of two huge vertically mounted carpet rolls around which had been wound two strips of strong coloured paper whose specially cut "hill-and-dale" upper contours corresponded to the pitch and dynamic needs of the music. The two carpet rolls, graphically termed by the inventors the "Feeder" and "Eater" revolving turrets, took the rolls of "hill-and-dale" paper through two metal cages wherein mechanical means were provided to track the undulations and activate the pitch and volume of eight oscillators.[24]

In the late 1950s, as Professor Loughlin, Ormond Professor of Music at the University of Melbourne, was professing the controversial opinion that 'the higher forms of music, rock 'n' roll not forgotten . . . occupy their own necessary niche in the musical world,'[25] the Grainger Museum was still being developed – a work in progress since 1938 – in its specially constructed quarters.

There is no direct evidence that Grainger's example inspired Australians to explore their own forms of national pop or experimental or electronic music, or for that matter their own tonal compositions. Nevertheless it should be noted that in 1956 the national news and comment magazine *The Bulletin* could make jokes about '"Waltzing Matilda" being played in rock 'n' roll time by Billy Bong and his Jumbucks'[26] at the same time as – relatively seriously – it evoked bizarre imagery of the ordinary middle-aged man working on his home-made noise generator to create an 'electronic symphony composition'[27], thus implying this was a respectable suburban hobby for Australians, and one recognisable to its readers.

Like Grainger, Ken Taylor found his inspiration at the cinema, albeit as a rock and roll entrepreneur rather than as a composer or performer. This, at least, was Taylor's claim in his 1970 memoir *Rock Generation*. After seeing *Blackboard Jungle*, Taylor relates with sly, tabloidish humour, he felt like 'a reluctant but overstimulated witness of a rape – which, come to think of it, I was.'[28]

I almost shed a tear for poor, violated Miss Conventional Music. After such a treatment by Haley and his Comets, could she ever be the same again? I was certain that some remarkable children would be coming from her defloration – and my plans were already made to be doctor and midwife to them. THEY WOULD BE THE FIRSTBORN OF AUSTRALIA'S OWN AGE OF POP.[29]

Similarly, Taylor (who was, it must be remembered, writing for a permissive late-60s audience) saw rock 'n' roll as gender-bending:

What we actually experienced in the 1950s was the emergence of the male animal to seize his moment of glory from females in the eternal war of the sexes. Rock music was his weapon, his instrument. He used it ruthlessly to knock mid-twentieth century woman from her traditional role of Seductress. *MAN* became the coquette![30]

Grainger's ethnic folk music collecting and his obsession with his own racial imprint find reflection not only in the work of later musicians and performers but also in the response they met internationally. Rolf Harris was an entertainer from the Perth suburb of Bassendean (he was known, indeed, as 'the Boy from Bassendean') who sought to support his pursuits as an artist by forays into show business in Britain in the early 1950s. 'I don't try to push it,' he said twenty years later and surely tongue-in-cheek, 'but my roots are all-Australian.'[31] Over the next fifty years he was probably the best-known Australian in Britain, Kylie Minogue notwithstanding; he never lost his accent – indeed, it would have been a professional disaster for him if he had. Though he became better known later in life as a painter – and was ultimately defined by his 2014 trial and conviction as a serial sexual predator – he had several hit singles from the 1950s onwards. 'Two Little Boys' was a campy World War I–themed folk song, 'Tie Me Kangaroo Down Sport,' a jovial singalong, and 'Jake the Peg' a curiously dirty piece of (apparently) Dutch humour that involved Harris balancing on a life-sized third leg. He created his hit single 'Sun Arise' from a traditional Aboriginal song together with Harry

"*Play your didgeridoo, Blue* . . . ."

"*Tie that kangaroo down, lady, tie that kangaroo down!*"

Butler, an environmentalist who became famous in Australia as a television documentary presenter in the mid 1970s. There were two versions, one closer to the original; the song's original producer, George Martin, persuaded Harris to write a middle eight.[32] Harris later said:

> So many people think it is an old aboriginal song, and I could shake them, because anything less like an aboriginal song I can't imagine. What actually happened was I met a chap called Ted Egan working for the aboriginal welfare department up at Gove in Arnhem Land, and we stayed with him on our last trip around Australia, he sang a lot of songs to me and this was one of them... He said it was a song that he had learnt from his Dad...[33]

The list of Australians who made an impact on the international pop scene in the early days of rock and rock-influenced pop is extensive. However, from the perspective of the early 21st century, it would appear that too much effort was expended in the years following the 1950s – perhaps as individuals like Johnny O'Keefe attempted to reinvent themselves on the comeback trail, and books like Taylor's *Rock Generation* were published – to make that decade seem like a vibrant and individualistic era in Australian music. If it was, and certainly there were some remarkably good musicians working in the field at this time, particularly those with a jazz background but also others with 'hillbilly' or country and western precedents, most recordings that survive from the period do not tend to show it. Perhaps this is merely an indication of the difficulties inherent in recording and the cautious nature of the industry at the time. Slim Dusty's remark that 'some of the engineers' he worked with in the 1950s 'were real bastards'[34] supports this notion.

In addition to O'Keefe, there are a few names that come to mind when people think of pre-60s rock and pop music in Australia. Clinton Walker and Peter Doyle have written about Les Welch, 'Australia's great anticipator of rock 'n' roll'[35], whose first record was 'Elevator Boogie Blues'[36] in 1949; six years later Welch recorded an EP, *Saturday Night Fish Fry*, which 'blurred the genre boundaries'.[37] Welch was quoted in 1955 as saying that rock and roll was 'the purest form of jazz – the real jazz...

Actually it is nothing new – we have been recording and playing rock and roll for the past twelve years.'[38] Musicians like John 'Catfish' Purser, who joined O'Keefe's group, had a jazz background; forty years later he described himself and his band as 'just raw rock 'n' roll people'.[39] John Sangster's memoir *Seeing the Rafters* mentions his swing band the Mouldie Fygges[40] and the conviction of one of Sangster's friends that jazz had given way to a 'watered-down descendant',[41] swing, in 1929. Torres Strait Islander Vic Sabrino (born George Assang – a variation of this Chinese-derived surname was later given to Wikileaks founder Julian Assange through his adopted father) was, according to Clinton Walker, 'the only man in Australia in the 1950s who could really sing the blues.' Sabrino played with jazz musician Graeme Bell's band.[42] Other rock 'n' roll groups with jazz forbears, such as the Thunderbirds, 'packed out local dancehalls in Melbourne' in the late 1950s.[43] The aforementioned Slim Dusty (born Gordon Kirkpatrick) had a major hit record in 1957 with 'A Pub with No Beer', written by Gordon Parsons but with lyrics unwittingly purloined from a poem published thirteen years previously.[44] Dusty relates in his memoir that the song sold 30,000 copies, 'compared with some rockers' sales of 500', before 'city radio' would deign to play what was seen as a superseded form – country pop. The song was later a success in Britain and Ireland, and in parts of Canada affected, in a development coincidentally useful to Dusty, by a brewery strike.[45]

Col Joye came from a boxing background; he lived in the Sydney suburb of East Hills, and appropriately when he moved into musical performance it was originally to play hillbilly music, from where it seemed 'a normal extension' to go into rock 'n' roll.[46] Col and his brother Kevin were actually named Jacobsen; their stage surname came about on the advice of a clairvoyant. They worked out a business plan for Col's rock 'n' roll career on the family kitchen table, made their own guitars and amplifiers, and played a sped up form of American country music. Col Joye, a 'non-smoking, non-drinking, yet fun-loving individual,'[47] became renowned for 'polychromatic showmanship', including 'that little shuffling jig-step of Col's that actually comes from the shadow-sparring routine he used in his amateur boxing days.'[48] Like the Shadows, the Joy Boys made albums without Joye when they weren't backing him.

Along with performing, the Jacobsens became tour bookers, inspired by the example of Lee Gordon.[49] Gordon was an American promoter who brought a number of well-known American stars to Australia in the late 1950s and early 60s

– he has been referred to as 'just the go-between Australia needed to connect' with America[50] – as well as promoting a very limited amount of Australian talent (and recording at least one single of his own, a very strange, self-parodying piece entitled 'She's the Ginchiest'). It was Gordon who brought Little Richard to Australia; the star threw his jewellery into the Hunter River (not Sydney Harbour, as is often suggested), so frazzled was he by seeing *Sputnik 1* in the night sky.[51] Gordon also promoted acts such as the 'Satin Satan', New Zealander Johnny Devlin – 'the next best thing to Elvis.' Presley himself would never be seen in Australia; notoriously he refused to tour outside the USA.[52] Stories abound regarding Gordon's eccentricity: for example, the time when, believing he would soon die, he partied with a coffin in his flat.[53] Ken Taylor both celebrated and mourned Gordon in his 1970 memoir:

> In his first dynamic years he had suave, smooth Italian good looks, a persuasive manner which won response from everyone he met and an enthusiasm that few artists or financiers could resist. Later he became withdrawn, rather gnome-like, taking risks with his health that characteristically matched the other great gambles of his life.[54]

There are many stories of local performers being drafted into performing rock 'n' roll just because it was the newest fad: some of them stayed in the scene, others moved into other fields or disappeared entirely. Bobby Bright sang at a basketball social at the age of thirteen under the potent influence of crème de menthe; the following week he appeared on *Woody's Teen Time*. 'I stayed at television and started working for a guy called Ivan Dayman running dances round Adelaide.'[55] Bright's was just one of hundreds of stories of a happy accidental rise to fame and a performing career of varying value.

UNIQUE!
Robuk Pressmatic has three separate motors — one for each speed! It's the only fully-equipped high-quality tape recorder at a sensible price . . .
ONLY 89 GNS.

Robuk
PRESSMATIC TAPE RECORDER

Guaranteed by
AMALGAMATED WIRELESS (AUSTRALASIA) LIMITED

What all this indicates is that the rock'n'roll scene in Australia in the mid to late 1950s was confused, scattered and in many ways ineffectual. There were undoubtedly some important players in the music industry, and some of them – like Dayman, the Jacobsens, or even O'Keefe – would go on to play an entrepreneurial and/or performing role well beyond these early days. But what the late 1950s show most clearly is that time spent trying to pin down what the first rock 'n' roll record in Australia was, or who the rock 'n' roll icons of that decade were, is, in the overall scheme of things, time wasted. At this time, rock 'n'

WILD BEAT OVERTURE

roll was essentially just one form of popular music across the world, and a rather annoying, bratty one, at that. It was also viewed by many as a novelty form with a limited shelf life. Considering the simplistic and often inferior records produced under the rock 'n' roll banner in these early days, such an assessment was actually reasonable. It was not until the early 60s that this amalgam of blues, rhythm and blues, skiffle and pop began to get experimental and interesting on a regular basis, and this was as true in Australia as anywhere else.

In January 1960, *Australasian Post* predicts the year ahead.

2 A Funny Buzz

THE EARLY TO MID SIXTIES

> *'Why don't you teach her "Botany Bay"?' said Ruth,*
> *sticking her head round the door.*
> *'I don't know it.'*
> *'You've been culturally imperialised.'*
> *'I know,' he said. 'I bet I have more fun than you do.'*
> – Helen Garner, 'Other People's Children' (1980)[1]

To those who were born in the middle decades of the 20th century and immersed in Western culture and pop music, the coming of British groups such as the Rolling Stones and the Beatles seem to have made 1960 and 1965 as distinct from one another as desert and jungle. Just as the early to mid 1970s are often characterised as a period in which bored teenagers sat around waiting for punk to 'break', the early 1960s are generally seen – even by people who lived through those years – as a time of musical and even social stasis. This is a subjective view; it holds sway because history is written by the winners – rock and rollers, in this case – rather than those who followed other types of music. Certainly, Western popular music of the early 60s owes much more to a white European tradition than to an African-American one, and it therefore often sounds far more pallid, low-key, pedestrian and 'sing-song' to 21st-century ears than the music that came after mid-decade. Advances in recording and reproduction served to sharpen this distinction. Ultimately, we can only hear the past strained through the sieve of the present, and the thin gruel which results in this case is not always easy to stomach. Most of us – as well as those who did the choosing for our canon – are coming from a very different aesthetic position. The first hundred pages of Bob Stanley's excellent overview of British pop, *Yeah Yeah Yeah*, demonstrate this many times over.

Rock and roll – whenever it began and whatever it ultimately is – had briefly come to the fore in the mid 1950s, of course, but at that time it seemed to most listeners merely an extremist novelty. Along with its milder associate, pop music, it had jostled with folk, jazz and other forms as one of a number of appropriate teen enthusiasms. The early rock and roll musicians did not spring fully formed into this performance mode: they had started out as jazz or country players, working in what we would now understand as a swing style. American-British record producer Joe Boyd, discussing the London scene of the early 60s, observes:

> Some jazz clubs had already started programming folk singers and comedians while others would soon be taken over by rock entrepreneurs. Jazz had comfortably coexisted with R&B and rock 'n' roll, but the Birth of Rock elbowed it out of the way.[2]

If this was true in the UK and in Boyd's other hangouts, such as New York, it was not necessarily so in Australian cities, where jazz and folk were a conjoined force, often 'against' rock and roll, although rock and roll in the early 60s did not seem a terribly potent force. The big names of 50s rock – Col Joye, Johnny O'Keefe, Dig Richards, and others who made their names early – had by now become established entertainers, compelled by professional requirements to broaden their palette and demonstrate they were more than just rockers. Just as, twenty years later, many young or otherwise unknown musicians saw punk as a way to break into the music industry, 'rock and roll' in the mid 1950s was – accidentally or deliberately – a starting point for men and women who quickly became entertainers in a variety of styles. A post-rocker might sing ballads on television variety shows, or take on older standards so as to appeal to a broader demographic. The many covers of show tunes released in the early 60s – Billy Thorpe's 'Over the Rainbow' and Normie Rowe's 'Que Sera Sera (Whatever Will Be, Will Be)', for example – might be seen as attempts to appeal across markets.

Christopher Koch's 1985 novel *The Doubleman* (a story Koch himself describes as a 'fairy tale') presents a sensitive portrait of post-war Australia's cultural touchstones (in this case, Hobart in the 50s and Sydney in the 60s). Koch worked for the ABC, the national broadcaster, in the 60s and presents a credible account of the way entertainers – and through them specific cultures – might gain a hold on the population. The book's narrator, Richard Miller, tells a story about a folk-rock group called Thomas and the Rhymers, who take Australia by storm with a unique and complex sound that acknowledges both traditional balladry and psychedelia. This last element does not sound particularly plausible, but everything surrounding it does, particularly the importance of media (notably television) and the transition the band undergoes from playing crowd-pleasing country and western in regional towns to performing in the elitist folk clubs of the gentrifying inner city.

Prominent modernist architect Robin Boyd coined the term 'Austerica' to describe what he saw as Americanised modern Australia; he was talking about streetscapes and buildings – design styles rather than cultural ones, either popular or high – but the concept can readily be extended, and many critics believe that Austerica also reigned in the cultural sphere in the mid 20th century. Lawrence Zion has claimed that Australians of the late 1950s did not understand the 'cultural origins of rock 'n' roll'.[3] By this he appears to mean that Australia, lacking a visible, oppressed non-European population at this time and with much of its population still in many ways embracing the repulsive concept of 'white Australia', was unable to comprehend rock and roll as the product of the losing end of a social/ethnic imbalance. Yet he also suggests that 'most rock 'n' roll performers [appropriated] "America" as the source of their style ... distilled through records, radio, magazines [and] Hollywood films,' and through visiting American performers.

For all his strengths as a cultural commentator, Zion is entirely wrong even to imply that there was one 'Australia' in the late 50s, let alone that it was some kind of Austerica. Nigel Buesst's glorious 1963 short film, *Fun Radio*, is a red-blooded critique of the kind of Americanisation that Zion claims to detect – and its very existence demonstrates that Austerica was hardly an all-pervasive phenomenon. The Australian-raised Buesst, a creative and often whimsical left-of-centre filmmaker, supported himself as a photographer and a stringer for television news for most of this decade. When he came back to Australia in the early 60s from Britain (where he had worked on Ealing comedies), he was horrified by what he saw as a new and (at least in comparison with Britain) crass commercialism. *Fun Radio* is his filmic response, a highly structured and often very funny composite of news images from his own camera, set to the hysterical banter of commercial radio DJ Don Lunn. Lunn himself appears (apparently unwittingly) in the film, as do the accoutrements of contemporary teen life in all their hollow horror, including beach and surf culture and an absurd competition in which young women are compelled to trot alongside a Volkswagen being driven slowly around Melbourne's Albert Park Lake – when the car's tank runs dry, one of the contestants wins it. There are also scenes of American pop stars, such as the Beach Boys and Roy Orbison, landing at Melbourne's Essendon Airport and clips of international touring artists in concert, wittily juxtaposed with boxing footage. All of this set to a soundtrack of forcedly jolly and 'modern' surf music.

As this chapter will show, the reality of Australia in the early 60s is very different from any fantasy of a hyper-Americanised 'Austerica'. The documentary evidence points instead to the dominance of a particular strain of Australian pop star. Young Australians certainly worshipped some American idols – such as Johnny Ray, whom Johnny O'Keefe had impersonated professionally before working under his own name – and there were also very popular British stars, like Cliff Richard. Numerous movements and trends existed in youth culture at the time, however, both within and outside the various cultural styles that we have come to understand as 'rock and roll'. Whether Australians saw these movements – and the Australian celebrities who promoted them and worked within them – as uniquely local, or as part of the local branch of a wider scene, depended on the individual and his or her world view, as we will see.

YOUNG MODERN: ONE CITY'S POP CULTURE IN THE EARLY SIXTIES

Looking in detail at the scene in one city can deepen our understanding of all of them: in his study 'Rock 'n' Roll, Youth Culture and Law 'n' Order', Raymond Evans claims that a focus on one city's youth culture in the 50s enables a 'closer-grained regional analysis' which captures 'additional texture, detail and nuance' that a wider perspective might miss.[4] I will take a similarly closer-grained approach here, using the Adelaide magazine *Young Modern* to assess the way popular music was represented to teenagers in Australia in the early 60s.

Young Modern in 1965, with a young Twilights on the cover (courtesy Ron Tremaine/State Library of South Australia)

During this period, Australian cities were more likely to celebrate their own performers than would be the case later in the decade. State capitals had their own television and radio stations, which promoted local and international (rather than national and international) entertainers. Adelaide briefly even had its own pirate radio station;[5] it was operated by John Woodruff, who would later become an important figure in music management, beginning with Adelaide group the Angels. Similarly, there were local specialist magazines. Fondly remembered by those who grew up in Adelaide in the 60s (John Dowler named his late-70s proto-new-wave group after it, though silverchair probably *didn't* name their 2007 album after it), *Young Modern* lasted for four years. It had a number of owners, though some measure of control was usually exercised by one Ron Tremaine, who claimed in 1964 (by which time he was its managing editor, at the age of 23) to have come to the magazine after working on the Adelaide *News*, followed by *Stock and Station Journal*, a position playing piano with a group called the Del-Aires, and management of a club called the Princeton 'running casual dances for young people'. Tremaine eventually became the magazine's proprietor.[6]

Whether because it was desperate to increase sales, or just because it had the freedom to do so, *Young Modern* experimented with different styles and ideas, showcasing youth culture in numerous forms. It even delved into politics, an area few of its readers may have felt directly connected to, given that the voting age at this time was still 21. Nevertheless, the youthful and cultured future Premier of South Australia, Don Dunstan, was featured in the magazine, writing about the questionable fairness of long-established patrician Premier Thomas Playford's ability to retain power in the state through the support of independents.[7] Perhaps this was, for some *Young Modern* readers, a significant contribution to their rising political consciousness.

JAZZ, FOLK AND POP AROUND AUSTRALIA

Those *Young Modern* readers who did see political change in the air may have thrilled to the words of local folk singer Paul Brand, who told the magazine:

> Life should be regarded as a comprehension of all the body can see and do. In suburbia, however, it seems man is content with married life, a family, and a home. They are in a rut – a great unthinking rut.'[8]

Brand was a popular proposition in Adelaide in 1962. He released an LP, *Feeling Folk Blues*, and like many of his folk cohort he also sang trad jazz with a local band, Dick Frankel's Jazz Disciples.[9] His 'only future plans' in 1962 were 'to learn all I can about jazz in any way possible, and to convey these feelings back to people.'[10] When he played his own version of folk music, at the 'beaty'[11] Catacombs Coffee Lounge in the tiny inner-eastern suburb of Hackney, for instance,

> There was virtually no sound from the audience – no conversation, no shuffling of feet, just an occasional clinking of a coffee cup. Occasionally the door leading from the street opened, and more people entered, quietly finding themselves a seat at the crowded tables. When he had finished, the applause was quite outstanding – exuberant and sustained.[12s]

Brand's back and forth between jazz and folk might seem unusual today, but this pairing was a major drawcard for young Australians in the early 60s. The Brisbane Folk Centre at the Geographical Society Hall, with its 'twelve largish tables' and 'dim lighting (candles)', featured numerous acts playing a range of music from traditional songs to classical guitar; attendees also played chess or dominos or sang along with the performers.[13] Evening events – such as singer Paul Marks's shows with the Melbourne New Orleans Jazz Band – might involve a solo singer performing folk and blues songs to their own guitar accompaniment, and then a second set with the jazz band behind them. Marks, who worked as a hospital theatre orderly, a labourer and a postman, had begun Paul Marks's Blues Band in 1956, and recorded for the Swaggie label in 1958.[14]

As we will see, certain pop or rock groups, like the Seekers and the Loved Ones, would evolve from the Melbourne branch of this scene. One of the more unlikely success stories was that of Sydneysider Gary Shearston, who went from the protest folk scene of the 60s – and a commercial TV show – to a top ten hit in Britain in 1975 with a version of Cole Porter's 'I Get a Kick out of You'.[15] Back in Adelaide at the dawn of the 60s, however, Paul Brand saw no value in striving for crossover between folk, pop and rock and roll; indeed, he was withering about what he (or perhaps *Young Modern*) called 'r and r', telling the magazine, 'I fail to see how the average-minded person can absorb all this r and r, much less even try to appreciate it.'[16] A similar attitude is expressed from a different angle by Christopher Koch's fictional Brian Brady: 'I just want to dig those old bush songs up and sing them, and travel the country. Pop music's nothing but concocted crap.'[17] The real folk singer Martyn Wyndham-Reade had a similar attitude, sympathising with people he was sure were 'sick and tired of being belted over the head with rock and roll and the other garbage they hear.'[18]

The contrast between jazz 'beatniks' and rock was plain to most, and jazz was seen as a more cultured pursuit, as one writer to *TV Week*, signing themselves 'Intellectual', suggested:

> You should go to a rock 'n' roll dance and see some of the rough types that get there. Then you should go to a beatnik gathering. They are peaceful and intellectual. Perhaps their fashions are different, but weren't rock 'n' roll fashions also different when they were first introduced?[19]

The Red Onions, from Melbourne, are a perfect example of a trad jazz band with youth appeal, a sense of humour, and an approach that would later seem to fit perfectly with mid-60s rock; indeed, a breakaway section of the group would go on to form the Loved Ones. The Red Onions' star was Englishman Gerry Humphrys (also spelt Humphreys and Humphries), who was profiled thus in *Young Modern*:

> Clarinet ... 22 years ... shaved off his beard to a wigmaker, received 7/6, then bought a Modigliani postcard print, copied it, and sold it as an original for 15 gns, for which he promptly purchased a clarinet for 2/6 and an old pair of wellington boots. Likes ... old faces and opportunity shops.[20]

Some of the content of this profile may be true, as indeed may be the assertion that tuba player Kim Lynch 'was left an estate which included a tuba captured from the Comanches during the Battle of Agincourt.'[21]

Nigel Buesst's film *Gerry Humphrys – The Loved One*, completed in 2000, included interviews with Humphrys (who by this time had returned to his native England, where his Australian fame meant nothing and where he opted not to use his musical talents) and with those who had witnessed his achievements. Buesst comments that Humphrys 'entered

"And I'll bet they waste all their time painting pictures and writing poetry."

our world, blew up a storm and seemingly disappeared.'²² Humphrys said he had relocated to Australia in his late teens because:

> I wasn't getting on very well with my stepfather ... My father was killed during the war, there was a certain amount of friction [at home] at the time ... We used to receive regular food parcels after the war ... Billie Bluegum was my favourite teddy bear ... I was always in touch with Australia, very fond of it. April 1 1957, I left for Australia.²³

Humphrys' circle included Gordon Dobie, who remembered Humphrys as owning nothing but 'the clothes he stood up in and his clarinet,'²⁴ and Adrian Rawlins, who reminisced about spending time with Humphrys in 1959 when 'he'd only fairly recently arrived in Melbourne ... Gerry seemed to me a typical kind of jazzo.'²⁵ Another informant on the Buesst film about Humphrys, Sue Ford, recalled a café called Reata which, true to the stereotype of this era, featured 'glittering sort of candles in Chianti bottles', where she listened to Humphrys' 'wonderful improvisations' on clarinet.²⁶ Ross Hannaford, who would be an even bigger pop star than Humphrys within a decade as the guitarist in Daddy Cool, was 'in love with the Red Onions' and was lucky enough to find himself a day job assembling planet lamps with Humphrys ('a very funny man') and other band members.²⁷ The Red Onions Jazz Band played southern suburban Melbourne middle-class haunts such as Ormond RSL and Beaumaris Yacht Club (Humphrys was known to sleep on the beach at Beaumaris).²⁸ Humphrys was the band's raconteur,²⁹ and while the group was promoted as New Orleans jazz, it also had a darker, Celtic or medieval tinge.³⁰ An unidentified interviewee in Buesst's documentary tells us:

> There was a distinctive Melbourne bohemian push ... they were true bohemians, they were folk singers, they were artists and musicians ... there was a gallery in East St Kilda that had a party every week at midnight.

Koch's fictionalised assessment of the folk scene is typified by 'the Loft', whose atmosphere combines a nascent form of patriotism and identification with the working classes' lot – presumably the province of a young middle-class clientele –with a faked nostalgia for the 19th century:

> Three storeys above the Darling Harbour docks, it really had been a grain loft, years ago. Gordon Cartwright, the middle-aged ex-carnival man who ran it, had leased the top floor of one of the old brick warehouses here to cash in on the folk phenomenon ... A heavily symbolic sack of wheat hung near the stage. Nearby, in the western wall, a door opened onto space. Its old loading platform and beam-and-tackle were still suspended three floors above the lane, and an appropriate nineteenth century portscape glimmered out there, like Doré's

London: the lamps and stone mushrooms of the Pyrmont Bridge; the lights of wharves and ships.'[31]

Posters of famous folk artists like the Seekers are to be found here (though their inclusion in this pen-picture may have been to assure any sceptical readers that Thomas and the Rhymers were *not* based on the Seekers). Koch's slightly acid outlook, and the enlistment of a former carny as the person profiting financially from the scenario, might seem more typical of the rock world, but there was surely crossover between the impresarios of the two scenes.

As indicated earlier, jazz clubs intersected with the folk scene in Adelaide. *Young Modern* reported that 'Jazzwise, some eminent authorities say that in a few months Adelaide will be the centre of modern gear in Australia.' These clubs included La Cantina (which by the 1980s had become a rock venue called Lark and Tina's), Black Orchid ('definitely for people who wear big pearl cufflinks', according to *Young Modern*), the Cellar, the aforementioned Catacombs ('where the music was folksy sort of stuff but good'), Las Vegas, and The Tavern.[32] It is often suggested that the appearance in Australia of non-English speaking migrants, especially those from Italy, revolutionised coffee consumption in the nation, inducting many Australians into the world of the espresso machine and, of course, coffee snobbery. A consumer culture naturally evolved around a mood-enhancing drug such as caffeine, and the coffee club needed a music to go with it. Both jazz and folk extended into this realm, but also into regular suburban dances, generally referred to by the name of the church or civic hall which hosted them. In Melbourne, Keith Barber from Glenroy had played in a jazz band called the Soul Agents; they changed into a bluesy rock group, the Wild Cherries, playing in a coffee lounge in the inner Melbourne suburb of South Yarra 'which had survived on jazz but was rapidly changed in 1963 into one of the country's first discotheques, the Fat Black Pussy Cat.'[33]

There were other Australian jazz musicians soon to convert to rock and pop who had already gone overseas. The most notable – though an anomaly – is Christopher 'Daevid' Allen, who as a child had been a radio actor on 3DB. In his late teens he attended Melbourne's National Art Gallery School, while at the same time studying electric guitar ('mainly chords')[34] with the jazz player, composer, and writer of television and commercial music, Bruce Clarke (Clarke also worked in television set design, and later taught both the Birthday Party's Mick Harvey and I'm Talking/Essendon Airport's Robert Goodge). At the age of 22 Allen moved to London, where his career as a musical performer began in earnest.[35] He additionally became, in writer Ian Peel's words, 'a prolific tape-loop composer.'[36] Allen met Robert Wyatt and also Kevin Ayers, who convinced Allen he should abandon jazz for rock music by playing him records by the Yardbirds. Allen later told Richie Unterberger he was 'really grateful' to Ayers:

Because what he brought to me was the possibility to go out of rather a strict music and poetry that I was practicing, and show me a way that I could actually get involved in the rock scene, without really particularly changing what I was doing. And he encouraged me to do that. He was the prime mover in getting me to do that, I think. It was he and I that started Soft Machine.[37]

Allen's tenure in the band he and Ayers began with Wyatt was short, because he was banned from re-entering Britain from France by UK immigration authorities in 1967 – 'ostensibly because I am by birth Australian' (not usually a barrier at that time) 'but actually because I was playing in a psychedelic band promoting hallucinogens. Stopped at Dover with the band, singled out and sent back to Paris with only my guitar.'[38] Not only did this halt Allen's involvement in Soft Machine (his work with this brilliant band is captured on an often-reissued album of demos recorded by Giorgio Gomelsky, though Allen's own song from the sessions, 'Fred the Fish', has disappeared), it also prevented him from fulfilling plans he had made with Paul McCartney to collaborate on tape loops.[39] He went on to lead numerous incarnations of his band Gong, and did not return to Australia until 1981. (As an aside, Soft Machine had several unusual Australian connections, the most interesting of which after Allen was the exceptional, enigmatic and unavoidably 'centre stage' drummer Phil Howard. Howard's Australian origins were known to all around him, yet he seems to have made little impact in Australia itself before his British work. He replaced Wyatt in 1971 and played on half of Soft Machine's fifth album before being fired. He has since disappeared.)

The correct mode of dress in Australia's jazz and folk worlds was generally considered to involve a duffle coat; in Melbourne this might be accompanied by some item of red clothing – socks, for instance. The duffle coat in particular, however, seemed to become a symbol simply of slightly – one might say safely – transgressive youth. Take this complaining letter, for instance, published in *Young Modern* in June 1963:

> DEAR EDITOR:
> Last week at St. Clair dance, I saw a youth dressed in suit, collar and duffle coat try to enter. He was told to remove his coat, yet he was a regular, not a foreigner. To top this, two girls entered the dance wearing black stockings. Is St. Clair getting soft on girls and hard on boys?
> DUFFLE COAT'S BROTHER, Adelaide.[40]

'Melbourne is most fortunate in having a number of excellent folk-singers within its city walls,' mused *Young Modern* in April 1963; having just extended its distribution into the eastern states, the magazine was probably eager to emphasise its newly widened focus:[41]

These include Glen Thomasetti, Martyn Wyndham-Reade, Brian Mooney, Trevor Lucas, David Lumsden and Peter Laycock . . . These singers are to be heard on records, at concerts, and in particular in coffee lounges . . . For the coffee lounge is the stronghold of the Melbourne folk singer.[42]

Thomasetti, a contributor to *Australian Tradition*, the Melbourne folk magazine co-edited by Wendy Lowenstein, subsequently took a different course: she became a brilliant novelist. Lowenstein herself became a historian (she is also the mother of film director Richard Lowenstein). The evocatively named Wyndham-Reade has already been mentioned; Lucas relocated to London in the mid 60s, where he became a member of Fairport Convention and the husband of Sandy Denny (a relationship her producer Joe Boyd has described as damaging to her work).[43] Lucas would produce the very FM-radio friendly (but highly political) bands Goanna and Redgum in the 80s. In 1970, Lucas told *Go-Set*:

> I used to sing with a traditional jazz band in Melbourne. I was very young. I started playing guitar when I was 13 or 14. Then I got into folk music, playing and singing. I made a folk LP back in Australia . . . Australia is a very stimulating place to work in because of the middle-class oppression. It helps people to be a little more creative, it makes them fight that much harder, like in Ireland. You don't get this so much in London.'[44]

In a 1962 issue of the small magazine *Jazz Notes*, it was proclaimed that 'Melbourne, whether you like it or not, IS the jazz centre of Australia and has been for the past 17 years or so' (that is, since the end of the Second World War), though this statement was made in the context of the Australian Jazz Convention being held in Adelaide.[45] The greatest commercial success of the folk and jazz scenes in Melbourne – or anywhere else – at this time was not particularly class-conscious or even broadly challenging, however. Judith Cock,[46] a secretary at the Eye and Ear Hospital in Melbourne, began singing in public, covering Bessie Smith songs with the University Jazz Band.[47] She'd been playing piano and dabbling in trad jazz since the early 60s.[48] Understandably, but to her regret, she changed her surname to Durham when she began making public performances. Three decades later she recalled her jazz days as a bit of a romp:

> Jazz was so incredibly popular, there was a real cult movement in those days. Town halls were literally packed to the rafters every weekend with teenagers. It was crude entertainment in a way, but it had a real character of its own. It had its own fashion – corduroys, sloppy joes and desert boots. You'd knit yourself a jumper, using very big needles and a special stitch to end up with a fisherman's rib. [You wore] very tight corduroys . . . as tight as you could stand, with the big jumper over them. Then you'd top it all off with a duffle coat!

> The jazz shows were very uplifting and we'd stomp and cake-walk all over the joint. When they were over, everybody went off to a coffee lounge. You maybe had a beatnik boyfriend, and went off for coffee and a toasted cheese sandwich after the dance. It was the in thing to do.[49]

The Seekers formed in 1962. Keith Potger and Athol Guy had both been in rock and roll bands in the late 1950s – the Trinamics and the Ramblers, respectively. When these broke up, the two of them, along with Ken Ray and Bruce Woodley, started a doo-wop group called the Escorts,[50] which evolved into the folk group the Seekers. The initial line-up fractured when Ray left the group to get married;[51] unknowingly, Durham was debuting for the Seekers as Ray's replacement when she performed at the Treble Clef.[52] According to the account she gave official biographer Graham Simpson, she was asked to join the group in a very vague manner, so that her full membership was henceforth assumed by everyone but her. She continued to sing jazz as a solo artist after she had joined the band which would make her internationally famous, including a massively successful rendition of 'The Lord's Prayer' at Melbourne's Myer Music Bowl.[53]

In 1963 the Seekers (including Durham) signed to the W&G label, a recording concern operated by two families, the Whites and the Gillespies, with the redoubtable Ron Tudor as its A&R man and publicity director. Tudor, as it happened, offered to release a 7" EP of Durham as a solo artist.[54] Durham, meanwhile, assumed that Seekers' records would be credited to 'Judith Durham and the Seekers', but the paternalistic and single-minded Athol Guy opposed this[55] (his paternalism and single-mindedness would be useful to him later in the decade, when he became a conservative politician). Durham correctly saw the Seekers as daggy and herself 'as very hip and a bit off-beat' in a way that 'didn't fit with the image'.[56] The group recorded *Introducing the Seekers* for W&G, but were only mildly successful in Australia; it took a trip to the UK and a series of happy accidents to make them million-selling stars. Foremost among these accidents was their encounter with Dion O'Brien, better known as Tom Springfield of highly successful group the Springfields. O'Brien's sister and bandmate, Dusty Springfield, claimed that the Springfields broke up when they saw 'what was coming'[57] – that is, the Beatles. She was probably wrong about their own unsustainability in the mid 60s, though: the Seekers, for whom Tom Springfield then wrote a series of exceptional hit songs, were strong challengers to the Beatles, and Springfield herself as a solo artist was a marvel.

Young Modern uncovered more folk stars who would go on to great pop things; in early 1962, the magazine spotlighted a young family man from Para Hills,[58] in the city's north-east, who by the end of the decade would be one of the country's best-known pop producers:

> One of the finest jazz voices in South Australia may be heard every Saturday night at the Boomerang Club coming from the vocal cords of Pat Aulton.
> The visitors' first impression of Pat is that he is a wild "rocker", but give him his guitar, put him in a coffee lounge, and the true artist in him comes out.[59]

Late the same year, Aulton won the *Young Modern* Songwriting Competition with song called 'Our Love of Long Ago'. The magazine had a relationship with the local television program *Woodies Teentime*, and Aulton appeared on the show to receive his award.[60]

YOUNG ELIZABETHANS

In the mid 1950s South Australia had been the site of a bold new experiment by the Playford government. The 'new town' of Elizabeth, constructed in a rural area north of Adelaide, was intended primarily as a domicile for immigrants from northern Europe who worked in manufacturing. Elizabeth is where later commercial pop/rock stars like Jimmy Barnes, his brother John Swan, Bernard 'Doc' Neeson, Doug Ashdown, Glenn Shorrock (who later reported that 'the first electric guitar I ever saw was Doug Ashdown's'),[61] and other fine musicians such as Martin Armiger and Pip Proud were to begin the long process of honing their skills for the wider world.

Barnes became one of Australia's best-loved singers as a member of Cold Chisel and later as a solo artist; John Swan ("Swanee") had a successful solo career in the 80s; Neeson would be the singer in the Angels; Ashdown became a well-respected folk musician and singer-songwriter; Shorrock was first a teen idol as a member of the Twilights in the late 60s, and then in the 70s the voice of the international million-selling Little River Band; Armiger was a member of the Sports and later a writer, producer, and co-ordinator of soundtracks, while Proud was an innovator who enjoyed (or didn't) a brief period of prominence in the late 60s and a revived career in the early 21st century. In short, this new town was a hotbed of talent and ambition.

Elizabeth had its own major venue, the Octagon, where in the late 60s the teenaged Barnes and Swan could thrill to such groups as the Masters Apprentices.[62] Between Elizabeth and Adelaide proper lies Salisbury, and here the youth of the two cities could mix. Dances held there – sometimes under the name of the Matelot Club – attracted up to 700 people.[63] The young Doc Neeson booked shows there.[64] The readers of *Young Modern* first encountered Glenn Shorrock as part of Salisbury Youth Centre's attraction the Twilights, who at this early stage were represented rather confusingly as a sub-set of another band, the Vectormen, because the three singers of the original Twilights performed in tandem with other groups. Shorrock had heard Elvis Presley's 'Heartbreak Hotel' while he was living in the Elder Park Hostel, and was a bodgie 'from then on.'[65]

It seems, from this angle, that Elizabeth and Salisbury were much more rock-oriented than Adelaide itself. In October 1962, an enthused reader yelled from *Young Modern*'s letters page:

> Not many teenagers in Adelaide have heard of the dance at the Salisbury District Youth Centre. This is a well patronised dance, with attendance of over 500 . . . The resident band is the Vectormen who have a tremendous sound . . . They are from Elizabeth and have played at many local dances. Kevin Steele and Don Parsons are the two male vocalists and are backed [sic] by three terrific boys, the TWILIGHTS, Mike, Glen [sic] and Paddy, who have appeared on *Seventeeners*.[66]

The Twilights went on to become one of the biggest Australian groups of the sixties, and recorded one of the decade's best albums, *Once Upon a Twilight*. But Adelaide's dance scene had many other stars too. Barry McAskill was the leader of Levi Smith's Clefs (he was also, notably, arrested for leading a conga line from the Whisky disco along Sydney's William Street, causing a three-hour traffic jam).[67] He had 'sung his way to the top' in Adelaide in 1963; as well as being the 'compere-vocalist' of the TV show *Teensville*, he performed with his own group on Wednesday nights at the "Drifter's Casual Club."[68] Doug Ashdown, like many of his colleagues, was born in the UK. On arriving in Adelaide, he formed the Sapphires; he returned to the UK in the early 60s and joined a band called Rommel and the Desert Rats, then went back to Adelaide to play alongside Bobby Bright in the Beaumen (or Bowmen) until, at the end of 1964, he remade himself as a solo folk artist. 'I was sort of the underground in Adelaide', he claimed ten years later, writing songs about 'heavy things like why is there air?'[69] The second half of the 60s would see him record and release excellent albums on a regular basis.

APRIL IN ADELAIDE, PATTI IN MAROUBRA

Adelaide, however vibrant, was a small city, and Ron Tremaine was adamant that *Young Modern*, which at this time was still completely focused on Adelaide, was by and for its audience:

> We couldn't run a teenage magazine and keep the kids out, and, of course, we didn't want to. They got in our chairs, tables, tea trays and hair, and we never knew whether it'd be some interstate name or Fred Nerk from Snake Gully who'd be sidling round the end of the counter.[70]

So it was perhaps not surprising that in 1962, when a young girl from the Adelaide suburb of Tranmere – April Potts, soon to be known as April Byron – gave Johnny O'Keefe a song she had written, this in itself would be newsworthy to *Young Modern*. That she was then involved in some uproar within its pages is also unsurprising. Potts had shown O'Keefe the song, 'He's My Michael', assuming he would somehow help her to record and release it. Instead, he 'gave' it to his protégé Laurel Lea, much to Potts's displeasure. As *Young Modern* told its readers, 'she was most adamant... "NOBODY BUT ME RECORDS MY SONG!"'[71]

It is difficult in hindsight to establish whether this was a beat-up; soon enough, 'April Byron' signed a contract with O'Keefe, and Sydney singer Kevin Todd recorded her song after it received 'top treatment by one of Sydney's leading arrangers' and 'the backing of one of the best bands.'[72] Two years later she was being described as 'Girl of the Moment' in 'Victoria and Melbourne' when 'Heart' was released on the Leedon label;[73] her 'Make the World Go Away' was a minor hit the same year, and she later received some songs from the Bee Gees for a single. But despite her talent and charisma, she did not have a genuine hit record.

For Australia as a whole, the girl of the moment was Little Pattie, née Patricia Amphlett, from the southeastern suburbs of Sydney (Eastlakes, where the local beach is Maroubra). She was her school's star pupil and aspired to a career as a neurosurgeon – something her parents were willing to support her in and which was clearly not beyond her – but was sidetracked by singing at a young age. She was not some kind of Gidget figure: she was originally nicknamed 'Little Pattie' by schoolfriends because she had two taller friends with the same name.[74] Winning a talent contest ('because nobody else entered', she said later[75]) launched Amphlett on a pop career and she scored early with her exceptional 'He's My Blonde-Headed, Stompie Wompie, Real Gone Surfer Boy', backed with 'Stompin' at Maroubra'. The record reached no. 2 late in 1963, and Amphlett was thrown into a pop tempest which took the unglamorous form of endless touring, often by train, with her manager Philip Jacobsen and his brother, Col Joye. It must have required enormous stamina to cope with being an intelligent teenager and yet routinely treated as 'a bit of fairy floss.'[76] She has since claimed that one of the few times she was taken seriously was the night she spent with the Beatles in Sydney, celebrating Paul McCartney's 22nd birthday at their hotel.[77] By the mid 60s she was doing panto – *The Ugly Duckling*, with Johnny O'Keefe[78] – but her career had not devolved into fluffy irrelevance. She also found herself literally on the front line, when she and Col Joye performed in Vietnam for Australian troops and were unwilling witnesses to the battle of Long Tan. This was not what politicised her, though; it was more the casual way in which she had been treated by the industry as a young girl in show business. She later lent her name and talents to left-wing causes and has become prominent in arts and entertainment union organisation.

MY FUTURE – "LITTLE" PATTIE

Hit records – nightclubs – tours – more records – what does the future hold for the brightest young star on the Australian entertainment horizon

Little Pattie, who is fifteen, made her professional singing debut just 12 months ago when your sleeve, and although Pattie may only have a short sleeve she is carrying the four aces.

OLD WAVE

Another surf music success story was the Atlantics, named not after the ocean (which doesn't touch Australian shores) but after a briefly popular brand of fuel. The group members met on a bus travelling between a Sydney beach and their home suburb of Randwick in Sydney in the summer of 1960-61.[79] Their biggest and best-remembered hit was 1963's 'Bombora', written by guitarist Jim Skiathitis and drummer Peter Hood before surf music had become big but released to capitalise on the craze. 'Bombora' sold half a million copies in twelve countries.[80] Sven Libaek, later known as a composer of remarkable film and television soundtracks, was an A&R man for CBS at the time and the group's producer. Instrumental rock/pop in the surf music and/or 'Shadows' style enjoyed broad but brief popularity, but the Atlantics would move away from their instrumental base to back the established singer Johnny Rebb. They would never recapture their early success, though Peter Hood's song 'Come On', released by the Atlantics in 1967, is an acknowledged classic. Guitarist/keyboard player Theo (Thaao) Penglis, guitarist and collector (perhaps metaphorically) of empty whiskey bottles[81] would go from surf music to Hollywood success; he played Andre DiMera in the American television soap *Days of Our Lives* from 1981.

The Exciting Summer Sound of Sydney is 2SM

Every weekend and public holidays this summer, 2SM will broadcast shark patrols from their eye in the sky.
"Murf the Surf" in Surfline '64.
It's "Good Guy" Tony Murphy with the surfingest sound on radio — Saturday, 5-8 p.m. The latest in music from the Top 100, surfing results, surfing news—all on "Surfline '64"—plus *all* weekend and holidays, too the "Good Guys" spin discs from the 2SM Top 100.
Mr. Surf joins 2SM.
Yes! Australia's Mr. Surf, Bob Evans, joins the exciting 2SM summer line-up. Bringing you expert, up-to-the-minute reports on surfing conditions from Palm Beach to Cronulla—7.45 a.m. to 5 p.m.— Saturday, Sunday and Public Holidays.
Join the "Good Guys"—you'll be in good company!   TOP OF THE DIAL

Instrumental groups everywhere could see the writing on the wall. The Mustangs, a popular Adelaide dance band, advertised for a singer in late 1965: 'They had to catch up or fade away',[82] writes Jim Keays; he saw the group as 'virtually from the old wave.'[83] Keays, who had arrived in Adelaide's comfortable eastern suburbs from Scotland with his adoptive parents at the age of five,[84] joined the Mustangs and helped transform them into a different group, the Masters Apprentices. Whether he had a vision of what they would become is uncertain; what he was armed with was the memory of a genuine vision – an apparition – from his early adolescence, which had told him unequivocally that he would go on to lead the biggest band in Australia.[85]

ROCK AND ROLL'S SENSIBLE PROFESSIONALS: THE JACOBSENS

Colin and Kevin Jacobsen, the sons of cabinet makers in a family of five, jumped on rock and roll at the appropriate time and, while it might have seemed in the early 60s that they offered a less interesting shadow version of the extravagant and rambling exploits of Johnny O'Keefe (of whom more later), they were without doubt the greater success story in the long term.

Both Jacobsens played in the jazz group the KJ Quintet in the late 1950s (Kevin on piano, Colin on guitar and vocals), then discovered that rock and roll was simply 'country music with a backbeat'. Interviewed for the television show *Talking Heads* in 2006, Joye declared 'I was in the right place at the right time.'[86]

My brother started a band and they played for the local football club, weddings, and things like that. Then I came to sit in with them, and sing songs and play guitar. So Kevin Jacobsen became – he was KJ, so it was the KJ Quintet. But we had to get out of the name of KJ Quintet when we were booked to do a big show, because that sort of didn't work. And we had to get a good name because all the names were Elvis Presley, Gene Vincent, roll-off-the-tongue names. And Colin Jacobsen didn't roll off the tongue. So we had a meeting with a clairvoyant lady and she came up with the name of Col Joye and the Joy Boys. We got into show business, I suppose, inadvertently in a way, because we were playing dances and weddings and cabarets and things like that. And one day Brian Henderson had *Bandstand* running, and he said, 'I've been getting letters in about Col Joye and the Joy Boys, but I don't know how to find them, but they tell me they're pretty good.' So from that we played other shows, and we were asked to record for Festival Records, and then we had a number one record.[87]

Joye makes it sound easier than it probably was: the group had gone through a number of incarnations and unsuccessful records before 'Bye Bye Baby' made the top five in both Sydney and Melbourne midway through 1959. Joye would go on to become known as a gentle, reasonable, pleasant star – in sharp contrast to Johnny O'Keefe, with whom he would have considerable conflict.

In terms of drama, O'Keefe's story is more compelling – he certainly hurt more people, including himself. But Joye and the Jacobsen management/recording/touring empire were a consistent presence on the Australian scene for decades.

ROCK AND ROLL'S IGNORANT, ARROGANT PIGS

An argument could be made that the most significant difference between folk, jazz, and rock and roll stars was the way they conducted themselves. Rock stars – with the possible exception of Johnny O'Keefe, who had to have a finger in every possible pie – had not yet begun to project themselves in an intellectual, social-commentary framework. Rockers like Dig Richards, who would not shine as a creative performer until the 70s and his *Harlequin* album, seemed to be cartoon characters, more Flintstonian than anything else. 'I'm beginning to wonder if I have the evil eye on me,' Richards joked to *TV Week* in 1961. Not only was his career at a standstill – echoes therein of Peter Sellers's comedy record 'I'm So Ashamed' – but he was forever having car accidents (he was 'branded "the worst teenage driver in show business"') and made news for trivial clumsiness, such as when he hit his head in a swimming pool.[88] The early rock and roll singing stars, young and reckless, often played up to the goofy light the press shone on them.

Whatever the fascinations of his particular story, his (questionable) status as an innovator, and the undoubted talents of his backing musicians, Johnny O'Keefe's real talent lay in self-promotion. This is a rare and important knack, but it does not necessarily make one's recorded music legacy pleasant listening. The mid-80s telemovie *Shout! The Story of Johnny O'Keefe* presents the whole O'Keefe story in telling ways: O'Keefe, as played by Terry Serio, is bratty, cocksure, and always doing first in Australia what others had done a few years previously in the rest of the world. Curiously, in casting Serio as O'Keefe the show's producers chose someone who was better looking and a much better singer than the man he was portraying, presumably on the grounds that, thirty years on, Australians expected more from their stars than the original could muster.

O'Keefe appears to have long held an urge to take centre stage; he appeared as an actor in amateur theatre in the early 1950s (a production of *Death of a Salesman* in 1952, for instance),[89] and he would later be a driving force behind a branch of the community group the Younger Set's drama activities on behalf of the Spastic Centre.[90] He became associated with the controversial American promoter Lee Gordon, undermining Gordon's assumption that only American acts would attract Australian crowds: O'Keefe went on to tour Australia with Little Richard, Gene Vincent and Eddie Cochran in 1957; with Buddy Holly and the Crickets in 1958;[91] and with Chuck Berry and Bobby Darin in 1959.[92] In 1958, he facilitated the creation of the song 'The Wild One', arguably his longest lasting legacy (though he is also remembered for his boisterous version of 'Shout' as well as other hits). His contribution to 'The Wild One', on which he is credited as a co-writer, was the absurd, sexual line 'Shake it till the meat comes off the bone'. Sydney DJ Tony Withers was also credited as a co-writer – purely as an incentive for him to play 'The Wild One' on his program on 2SM – which he naturally did.[93] Long after O'Keefe's death, Iggy Pop would cover the song, having heard Albert Lee's 1982 version while on David Bowie's yacht, on a tape compiled by the painter George Underwood. The song was known in the USA as 'Real Wild Child'; Lee's version added, in brackets, 'Wild One'. Pop would re-record it with the Melbourne group Jet in 2008 to celebrate its fiftieth anniversary, and praised it for what he saw as its immutable value – its 'tiny idea' and 'simple premise.'[94]

O'Keefe worked with musicians of a high standard, but his records are generally dull. He knew his abilities lay elsewhere. In the early 60s, as he moved towards a damaging series of nervous breakdowns and prescription drug dependency, O'Keefe travelled throughout the United States to further his career while simultaneously making a statement about Australian talent and ability. 'Anyone can see that Johnny O'Keefe is the king of Australian rock 'n' roll,' a *TV Week* reader calling him or herself 'OK O'Keefe' wrote in 1960. 'He has more personality and is a better singer than pudgy-faced [New Zealander Johnny] Devlin will ever be.'[95] His ostentatious tastes were also a thrill for many: 'Johnny doesn't look sloppy like most rock 'n' roll artists, either,' cooed two of his biggest Adelaide fans, teenagers Kaye Stewart and Joan Kennett in *Young Modern*:

> 'With that cute hairdo and sophisticated suits, he looks really SOPHISTICATED and SMOOTH.
> 'Mmmm... did you know he bought a pair of 8-carat gold shoes worth £50?
> 'Ohhhh... GORGEOUS!'[96]

Part of his decadence, however, might also have been that he was rumoured to be 'a pig socially,' as a 1962 *Young Modern* piece put it.[97] Popular rock and roll singer Betty McQuade also called him an 'ignorant, arrogant pig.'[98] His first wife, who suffered appallingly at his hands, described him as 'horribly untidy,' – probably one of the lesser of his unpleasant characteristics that she experienced.[99]

Combining delusion with berserk optimism, O'Keefe constantly advertised his far-reaching plans; to a degree, rock and roll seemed as much his franchise as his career. He manufactured his own publicity.[100] When it was reported that he was Australia's highest-paid entertainer, his answer: 'Those reports are way out, man', may have been a denial – or else a clever use of beat-speak.[101] He planned an alcohol-free restaurant for teenagers in 'down town' Sydney.[102] He put some old green gloves from the ABC prop room on John Hurley for *Six O'Clock Rock*, thus creating Jade Hurley.[103] The same show gave Noelene Batley to Australia: her song 'Barefoot Boy' was a hit.[104] Batley had won a talent quest at Ling Nam's Chinese Restaurant in Sydney[105] and – according to one of its organisers, Festival A&R man Ken Taylor – was 'a most docile and co-operative young artist, and one of the loveliest human beings that this industry has ever produced.'[106] She would go on to work in cabaret in Japan and the US.

Six O'Clock Rock began in 1959, and had a jazz element;[107] each instalment began with the Paddington Town Hall clock striking six,[108] and ended with O'Keefe and his manager Peter Page vomiting (off camera) from nerves and relief.[109] In

Koch's *The Doubleman*, for which the author no doubt drew on his experiences working at ABC, a show called *Eight O'Clock Rock* is the locus of a decadent, sexually exploitative and simmeringly gay party scene; O'Keefe's environment was possibly less sophisticated and camp, but probably just as venal.[110] 'Before it erupted on our screens,' remembers one viewer, the writer Denise Young, 'parents and kids watched more or less the same movies and listened to more or less the same songs.' The emergence of 'the first oppositional show', *Six O'Clock Rock*, saw the creation of a public rebel: 'Johnny O'Keefe yawped our barbaric yawp.'[111]

O'Keefe wanted to translate his yawp into American[112] by recrafting *Six O'Clock Rock* as 'a big budget international show' and pitching it to television stations in the US; *TV Week* reported O'Keefe saying 'he has made negotiations with "certain people."'[113] He certainly thought big: 'Biographies of O'Keefe and about 100,000 wallet-sized give-away photographs' were, it was said, 'distributed among America's 4,000 radio stations' during his promotional blitz there in early 1960. O'Keefe was promoted as 'Boomerang Boy',[114] having obtained rudimentary skills in boomerang throwing from residents of the urban Aboriginal settlement of La Perouse, in Sydney's south.[115] He appeared on the TV show *American Bandstand*[116] and also 'sent 200 three-minute colour film clips to theatres and TV stations'; gave 'boomerangs to every U.S. radio station'; and hired 'rock and roll pioneer, Bill Haley, as his manager'. It was announced that 'as a gimmick – he plans to stand on the ledge of the 80th floor of the Empire State Building and threaten to jump off, unless every New York disc jockey plays his records.'[117] One sarcastic *TV Week* reader suggested that someone give him a push – to help him find 'the only smash hit he will ever make.'[118] Yet the last of these soundbite-style claims actually suggested a desperate and perhaps ailing man. In April 1960 he was reported to be suffering from nervous tension.[119] There are conflicting reports of how many copies his American single "She's My Baby," on Liberty, sold: a few hundred, two thousand,[120] or a hundred thousand.[121] He later claimed to have sold many records in New Orleans by pretending to be black[122] (that is, he limited publication of his photograph in the media, thus keeping his whiteness a secret), and that the reason he was dumped by Liberty was because he'd been fraternising with black musicians[123] in that city. It is clear that the truth of these assertions is entirely secondary to the value they had in promoting Johnny O'Keefe.

A car accident outside the NSW town of Kempsey in June 1960 led to operations (reputedly, twenty-seven) to restore his face,[124] which he nevertheless stated was not important in a career sense.[125] Guitarist Johnny Greenan, and his wife Jan, were also injured in the accident; O'Keefe's defence counsel tried to imply that Johnny Greenan had been driving O'Keefe's Plymouth Belvedere. O'Keefe made his facial operations a feature of *Six O'Clock Rock*, inviting viewers to observe his changing visage over the months. His next album was called *I'm Still Alive,* and its cover showed the wreck O'Keefe and the Greenans had emerged from.

Later, pursuing his dreams of fame in Britain, O'Keefe found himself in a mental institution in Tooting Bec, having overdosed on his numerous prescription drugs (and others); on regaining consciousness O'Keefe, virtually a walking cliché by this time, told doctors he was Christ.[126] Returning to Sydney, he heard Martians' voices in his head.[127] In 1961 he moved to commercial television with *The Johnny O'Keefe Show*;[128] a title that was later changed to *Sing, Sing, Sing* to downplay its identification with a figurehead who was often too unwell to compere. His frequent replacement – who had once told O'Keefe to 'stick his show in his fucking arse' when faced with a demand that he have his hair cut for television[129] – was the young Billy Thorpe, who would go on to much greater things.[130] By 1964 O'Keefe was described as 'aggressive and abusive' as a result of nervous breakdowns, drugs and possibly his car accident.[131] He was given shock treatment,[132] which exacerbated his paranoia and delusions. He nevertheless maintained his career for more than another decade, often as a nostalgia act. In 1977 he unveiled a commemorative grotto to Elvis Presley in Melbourne General Cemetery; by the following year, O'Keefe too was dead.

TEENAGE, MY FOOT! POP ON TV

O'Keefe was many things in one package, and a particularly prominent part of his identity for Australians was his role as a TV host. His overreaching self-promotion should not obscure the fact that, even by the standards of the time, his televisual style was very rough. This may have been why the teenagers thought he was, if not one of them, at least genuine and honest; in Australian society there can be two sides to being 'a pig socially'. A letter writer to *TV Week* in March 1960, spoke damningly of Melbourne's 'so-called teenage shows':

> Teenage, my foot! They are all ('Cool Cats', 'Teenage Hour' and the revolting 'HI Fi Club') arranged, designed and compered by adults, who have barely an idea of what teenagers want in rock 'n' roll. We, the teenagers, don't want sponsors, commercials, prizes, competitions, clubs, elaborate sets and the stiff, unnatural little dolls trying to jive in shiny suits, well-oiled hair and ballerina dresses. We don't want formality. We want these shows to slam on the entertainment, and slam it on good. But all we ever see is the occasional carefully rehearsed item inserted among a lot of trivial drivel. Sydney has the right idea in 'Six O'Clock Rock'. You could not call it uncouth or unsuitable, it is good, clean fun for all kids, and it wastes no time with unnecessary talking. Melbourne tries to make up for its lack of talent with the sugary artificial jazz which is so unbearable. To think that the 'Hi Fi Club' is being transmitted all over Australia makes me shudder.[133]

Hi-Fi Club was compered by Bert Newton, a DJ who was already well on his way to becoming one of Australia's most beloved television personalities.[134] The show purported to offer 'Modern music designed for moderns'. Col Joye and the Joye Boys were regular guests,[135] though Joye was generally critical of television as a medium; he told *TV Week* in 1960 that it did not give 'local artists a "fair go"'. The magazine continued:

> Col, who earns as much as the Prime Minister, Mr. Menzies, said television was his worst form of income ... 'I regard it only as a means of entertaining crippled children and other unfortunate people who normally are not able to see me perform.'[136]

Joye later recalled:

> There was no rehearsals, you just went on and sung your things. But in those days, we did things that no television station in the world would have attempted. We did outdoor shows and our equipment was pretty bad, pretty basic – even our recording equipment. But we got by.[137]

Other shows abounded; the Australian incarnation of *American Bandstand* began as *Accent on Youth* and was then called *TV Disk Jockey* before becoming *Bandstand* in 1958.[138] The Allen Brothers – Peter Allen and Chris Bell, who were neither brothers nor truly surnamed Allen – were regulars on the show between 1960 and 1963[139] and – in a bizarre story often marveled at even today – went on to be managed by Judy Garland after they appeared in cabarets in Tokyo.[140] *Bandstand*, helmed by the straightlaced but apparently fun-loving Brian Henderson, who soon found his niche in a much longer career as a newsreader, seems to have been cosy and lacking in surprise.

Though its title seems strange from a post-1977 perspective, the November 1965 TV show *The New Wave on Stage* perfectly encapsulates the way popular rock music was performed and presented at this time. Presented at the Capitol Theatre in Perth, the show begins with Max Merritt and the Meteors, introduced as a New Zealand group, performing a jovial, jaunty 'Dizzy Miss Lizzy'. The constant presence of a particular whistling noise in the audience response suggests that the enthusiastic crowd response heard on the soundtrack is actually a tape loop. Merritt's Meteors also provide backing for the next song, Lynne Randell's 'It's Alright', which is almost impressive in its lyrical banality and repetitiveness; Randell performs careful, stilted dance moves, but the song is rousing. Jade Hurley's 'How I Lied' is an impressively dramatic pop tune; Hurley collapses at his piano while introducing another song – the victim, we are told, of an old knee injury. Stepping in, Max Merritt and the Meteors present an invigorated 'Hold On'. Ray Brown and the Whispers, a Leedon signing from Sydney and a successful chart act in 1965, then perform 'Gloria' and three more of their hits from that year, all covers. Brown, like Randell, periodically waves to certain audience members; by this portion of the show the audience, having been provided with streamers and large balloons, are rambunctious. While it might be safe to assume that the show was sanitised and streamlined for the sake of a televisual hour, it nevertheless demonstrates the raw abilities and focused showmanship of Australian pop/rock musicians in the mid 60s.

INDIGENOUS VS. LOCAL

The rise of Aboriginal singer Jimmy Little as a country and western balladeer in the early 60s is one of those exceptions that proves a rule. There were few Aboriginals in the mainstream media then – as now – and with all due respect to Little and his considerable abilities, it could certainly be argued that he served white Australian prejudice as, through no fault of his own, he became the *one* well-known Aboriginal pop singer. His popularity allowed the majority of Australians to rest assured that they were not as racist as was sometimes declared. This, of course, was hardly Little's problem, much less his doing. His biggest hit was 'Royal Telephone', a glib country and western ballad which would be remembered by no-one if Little had not sung it. His rise to fame came at the same time the *Bulletin*, Australia's pre-eminent weekly journal, controversially dropped its banner slogan 'Australia for the White Man' (although it is worth noting that its use of this phrase was historically more complicated – tangled up with the issue of exploitation of imported non-white labour – than it seems at first glance).

Jimmy Little saw himself as a peacemaking example:

> I had a freedom that excluded me from being prejudiced against. Because I was non-threatening. I was an ally of everybody. Wanting to be an interpreter, a communicator and a person who can explain situations. I didn't want to jeopardise that by saying, I belong to this [ethnic and/or political] group.
>
> I felt that if they can break the egg that I'm in then they can destroy me if they like, you know. What I was doing, I was promoting Aboriginal Australia. Promoting to the hilt. [141]

He praised his fellow Australian performers – the vast majority of whom were non-indigenous – as versatile and necessarily able: 'Countries like the USA have such a wide circuit that many entertainers can use the same routine for years and build up a big reputation for themselves,' he reasoned. 'In Australia entertainers have to vary their method of presentation, their songs and even their dress regularly. This means that artists out here are more original in their routines.' [142]

Australian consumers occasionally agreed with this broad assessment. Less than a year before Little's claim, three Australian singles had taken up the top three positions in Melbourne's top forty: Col Joye's "Yes Sir, That's My Baby", Lonnie Lee's "I Found a New Love" and O'Keefe's "Come On and Take My Hand." [143] While student journalists complained that record sales might only reflect sales of 400 copies in key 'record bars' (so that 'shop girls and office tea boys . . . are determining what the rest of the population is hearing all day'),[144] it does indicate a certain grass-roots interest in, and support for, local artists.

Australia was to America as New Zealand was to Australia: when rocker Max Merritt relocated to Sydney in November 1963[145] – one stage in a journey that would eventually take him on to London in the 70s and later, to the USA – he felt like a 'veteran of music and show business. I had been doing it about two years when I got to Sydney.' Yet Australia made him feel like 'a grain of salt in the bottom of a bucket. It seemed so huge after living in Christchurch and Auckland.'[146]

Australia itself was gradually becoming more accessible and networked. In 1964, groovy *Oz* magazine entrepreneurs and enfants terribles Richard Neville and Martin Sharp were generating publicity and flying around the country visiting universities to raise money towards court costs resulting from an obscenity prosecution (discussed further in chapter 4).[147] At the same time, novel ways were being found to cross great distances economically: a 22-year-old javelin thrower named Reg Spiers illicitly flew from London to Perth in a C.O.D. crate marked 'synthetic polymer emulsion', then hitched home to Adelaide.[148]

References to the USA – and comparisons between the talent and ability of Australian and American performers – were evidently a constant. In a nation supposedly dominated by the cultural cringe, the public pronouncements were very often on Australia's side, even if it only took the form of Mouseketeer Cheryl Holdridge's reputed declaration in 1960 that she was 'in love with' local pop singer Lucky Starr.[149] The American success of Melbournite Diana Trask was a matter of fascination for the celebrity magazines. Trask, who was reported glibly opining that 'all young Australian artists should go to America if they want to get on',[150] was represented by *TV Week* as living out a kind of tawdry show-business life in which she was 'constantly surrounded by the wealthiest stage-door Johnnies in America', playing places like Harrah's in Lake Tahoe,[151] and starring on TV shows like *Sing Along with Mitch*. *TV Week's* breathless accounts made even the 'minor virus' Trask caught during a 'Mexican engagement' seem glamorous.[152]

It is important to note, however, that the Australian acts mentioned above saw America largely in terms of their own ambition – as a place where they could show a wider audience what they could do. *TV Week* mused in 1961 that the USA was the Australian artist's 'land of failure,'[153] stage-door Johnnies or no. However, the cultural cringe rhetoric that is supposed to have been so ubiquitous at this time is far less evident when Australians were talking about Britain or the US than might have been assumed. If Australian audiences were in thrall to international artists, they were – and are – just as likely to turn against them, or at the very least consider them ripe for parody.

Rolf Harris and Frank Ifield were both enormously successful in Britain (and Canada) by the early 60s. Harris had no particular performance background in Perth, where he had been born and raised; he had relocated to Britain in the early 1950s to pursue an art career and became an entertainer, recording a series of comedy pop hits produced by George Martin. His musical successes were executed in tandem with a growing reputation as a popular children's television performer.

Ifield had three million-selling hits around the world in the early 60s. The son of an inventor, he grew up in the New South Wales town of Dural, where he subsequently claimed that he discovered yodelling to the family cow (Betsy) resulted in a higher milk yield.[154] He would later credit the country and western music he heard on Sydney radio, along with the discovery of his own singing voice as a companion on his three-mile walk to school, as his most critical musical impetus. His first concert performance was at the Dural Memorial Hall. Like Harris, however, he had ambitions to become a visual artist; musical entertaining seemed to simply carry him along in its wake. His singing career, which had already been fostered by radio, really took off in 1956 when television was introduced to Australia at the time of the Melbourne Olympics. Ifield was soon a star on a program called *Campfire Favourites*. The sleevenotes to his early 60s *Greatest Hits* proclaim that it was 'the challenge of tackling and conquering a new audience which drove him to leave Australia, where as a top-line entertainer his future was secure.'[155] Decamping for Britain in late 1959, he released his iconic and best-remembered single, the breezy 'I Remember You' (top ten in America, Britain and elsewhere) followed by 'Lovesick Blues' and 'The Wayward Wind'. Unlike Harris, Ifield rarely made much of his Australianness, beyond the rather unusual insinuation that yodelling was an appropriately rural activity, such as might be practiced by a young man from the rugged outback (although it isn't). Rubbish like 'She Taught Me How to Yodel' attempted to capitalise on this fiction; his speedy, syncopated reading of the early-20th-century 'unofficial national anthem' of Australia, 'Waltzing Matilda', was a stab at another aspect of his legend. His own songwriting – for instance, his single 'I Listen to My Heart' – was of the same standard as the songs procured for him.

1964 saw many Australians fall in line with the rest of the world's adulation of the Beatles. Jan Smith's novel *An Ornament of Grace*, published in 1966 but written two years earlier, is a stunningly cruel novel about a populist journalist in Sydney. Here she describes an unnamed group who are plainly the Beatles on what would prove to be their only collective visit to Australia. She depicts 'a bright, hot room with flushed faces and wet feet, trying to think of something no one else will ask and knowing it's impossible.'[156]:

> "Don't tell me they wrote that song themselves?"
> "Did you see what they did at the airport?"
> "Ask them about the film and how much money they're getting."

Everybody will, if someone else doesn't get in first. At least the television people have gone, so we're spared one misery, listening to those cute bastard-American idiots in their cute suits asking about their sex lives and making ten minutes stretch into twenty... Already it's started, the big fish like Heath and Sarah zooming in with how much money are you making and what do you think of Australia? Tell us we're as loud and noisy and appreciative as people anywhere else, or better. There's nothing worse than being different.[157]

Smith's cynical assessment of the Beatles and Australia was not unusual at the time. *Oz* reported that the Beatles' Sydney shows were underattended, and in the initial burst of their fame the group were regarded by many in Australia (as elsewhere) as manufactured and/or exploitative commercial rubbish. Col Joye said of the group many years later that 'I didn't like them much 'cause they cut the

The Beatles' 1964 tour of Australia, while inspirational for many, drew scorn from young and old fogeys alike (left: *Oz* 9, May 1964; above: *Nation*, May 14, 1964).

legs from underneath me, and O'Keefe as well,'[158] though – as previously stated – Joye has nevertheless enjoyed an impressive fifty-year career.

Although the impact of the Beatles in Australia would turn out to be considerable, it is simplistic to suggest that they pressed a 'reset' button for Australian pop and rock music. The country already had many stars, and more were emerging.

BILLY THORPE SCREWS HIS HEAD OFF

Billy Thorpe was virtually born into show business, and he would make much of his early 60s experiences. Thorpe grew up in Brisbane – he had first appeared on children's TV in that city in 1957, when he was 11 years old.[159] He had been friends there with two Barrys: Gibb and Lyde (the latter later became known as guitar player and producer Lobby Loyde).[160] Thorpe sometimes performed under the name Little Rock Allen[161] and had worked with his idols[162] O'Keefe and Joye as part of a show known as the Rockin' Roll Train, travelling to and playing regional areas on a train.[163]

Thorpe moved to Sydney to further his career. In the first of two sensationalist memoirs he wrote in the 1990s, he reminisces:

> With all the amazing surf beaches in and around Sydney, surf music and dances, known as 'stomps', were huge. Surf clubs all over Australia, and particularly those around Sydney, were havens for live music and bands. Some of the local surf groups, such as Roland Storm and the Statesmen, had big local followings on this circuit.[164]

Roland Storm and the Statesmen featured Billy Green, who will be a name to contend with throughout the next fifteen years of this narrative; he is discussed further at the end of this chapter. Another impressive local group was Ray Brown and the Whispers, a Sydney group who released five successful singles and no less than three albums in 1965.

In the early 70s, talking with Lee Dillow from *Daily Planet,* Thorpe was effusive about the early 60s:

> I was really digging Surf City, consequently I was there quite a bit. One night a band came in. They were playing there, it was Vince Melouney, John Watson, Col Baigent and another couple of guys ... The Aztecs.

The Aztecs had started out as an instrumental group called the Vibratones; they had a recording agreement with a label known as Linda Lee (there was clearly something about this kind of alliterative name in the early 60s: Lonnie Lee and Laurel Lea were stars during this period, and it might even have had an impact on Barry Lyde's decision to become Lobby Loyde). The Aztecs' manager John Harrigan operated Surf City and another venues such as Stomp City and the Beach House. Writing in 1996 of his first – unrehearsed – show with the Aztecs backing him, Thorpe described it as a synergistic success that marked a new chapter in the development of rock: 'the unstoppable rolling excitement of something new.'[165] Thorpe told Dillow:

> They didn't have a singer at that stage so Harrigan informed them that if we could get together he could probably record us ... We put down a thing called 'Blue Day'. It was shithouse, but it got to about No. 10 in Sydney. A funny buzz.[166]

Second guitarist Tony Barber had joined the new group around the same time as Thorpe, and had written 'Blue Day'; by 1996 Thorpe had revised his opinion of the song to 'a great first record.'[167] Through its relationship with the distributor/label Festival, the new group including Thorpe was able to record at the larger company's studio.[168]

Later, while Harrigan was on an overseas trip, his mother signed the group to Alberts. Though this publishing house-cum-production company was later to prove very important to Australian music, Alberts were not yet a label in their own right and – not to put too fine a point on it – the Aztecs were no Missing Links (though they did have much greater commercial success). Thorpe continues the story: since 'Blue Day' had been a 'moderate success',

> we recorded again. This time it was "Poison Ivy". I don't know to this day what happened. One week we were virtually unknown – the next week we were being chased down the street ... I was only 16, you dig, and there I was, meeting all these incredible people, travelling around the country. Staying in the best hotels, drinking booze, screwing my head off.[169]

Barber was a creditable songwriter, but Billy Thorpe and the Aztecs' biggest early hits were pedestrian covers, the unsurprising 'Poison Ivy', 'Mashed Potato' and, most dismally from an artistic perspective, the string-laden horror that was their 'Over the Rainbow'. 'Sick and Tired', however, is a good demonstration of the group's dynamism. Though they were based in Sydney, they were also exceptionally popular in both Melbourne and Perth.[170] The group released its first album on Parlophone in 1965; it did not contain any originals.[171] There were strains, as Thorpe told Dillow: 'At the time we were all young kids. There was so much stress and we were so important in the business. So many offers being made to us individually – I guess that's what happened.'[172]

Tony Barber was the first to quit the Aztecs because, he told Dean Mittelhauser twenty years later, 'It got tedious... We met people that we'd never meet again, and had to be on our best behaviour... ALWAYS! Nicely dressed because in those days all the bands were smartly dressed.'[173] Barber's subsequent solo career was patchy, but nevertheless artistically greater than Thorpe's in the same period. Thorpe, who died in 2007, is held in high regard in the early 21st century because of his work in the late 60s and early 70s, when he reinvented himself for the alternative festival circuit; in his earlier days he was little more than an eager performer and, not unrelatedly, a sexual colossus, if his memoirs are to be believed.

Other stars comparable to Thorpe began to emerge. Normie Rowe was a trainee telephone technician who sang on the Melbourne dance circuit, usually with the band the Thunderbirds. 3KZ DJ Stan Rofe encouraged him to go professional.

> He said, "Do you have any aspirations of being a singer?" And I didn't know what an aspiration was. He explained it to me, invited me off to some of the bigger dances in Melbourne. I met some of my idols. And then I started working in these places, and it gave me the background. From the dances, people saw me and invited me to appear on shows like *The Go Show* and *Teen Scene*.[174]

Rowe's early hits, like Thorpe's, were often notionally updated versions of old chestnuts such as 'Que Sera Sera' or 'It Ain't Necessarily So' – great records, but hardly creative milestones. Rowe's career, like Col Joye's, would become that of a performer in a light entertainment/cabaret style; Rowe's was arguably ruined by his own Vietnam experience – mirroring Elvis Presley, he was required to be a member of the armed forces. As will be seen in later chapters, Johnny Young would have a major impact, as the writer of what was far and away Rowe's best song, 'Hello' (not a huge hit, for the usual inexplicable reasons), and of a truly masterful song *about* Rowe – 'Smiley', sung by Ronnie Burns. Rowe would also give the world, via his transformed backing band the Playboys, one of the great and (relatively) unsung experimental pop groups of the late 60s, Procession.

MOVERS AND SHAKERS

Much is made of the British or other overseas origins of Australian pop stars of the 1960s, particularly in non-Australian accounts. This connection between migrant status and success as an entertainer is easily explained by reviewing the biographies of popular performers from all over the world: the ability and willingness to entertain is a valuable skill for any child whose family is new in a neighbourhood, and particularly for those who regularly move around. Families whose parents are in the military, or the public service, and so on have a high proportion of children with the skill to entertain. The mobility of the Gibb family is almost certainly the formative element of the Bee Gees' success, for instance. The country of birth of an Australian pop star is no indication of anything; the fact that they were migrants at a young age was in many cases the impetus that drove them to be entertainers.

Consider, for instance, a major talent like Wilhelmus Arnoldus Maria Francis Groenewegen. Though fondly remembered in some quarters, he left Australia for the USA in the mid 1970s – and left rock for jazz soon afterwards. As a result, his contribution to Australian pop music has been marginalised in the collective memory. He had moved from the Netherlands to the regional NSW town of Orange in the late 1950s with his three brothers, three sisters and widowed mother, and picked up a guitar at the age of 14. Through his job as a chemist's delivery boy, he was able to buy an acoustic Nightingale Jackaroo from a pawn shop; 'it had a stencil of a Jackaroo,' he recalls, 'with a hat with corks – he was sitting against a tree with a billy boiling.' Soon, Groenewegen was playing top-forty songs by ear.

After the family moved to Sydney's north shore, Groenewegen began to play Friday night dances in the suburb of Brookvale with Bix Bryant and the Raiders. The group was evidently a hoot; he recalls a prank they played, pretending the house they lived in was haunted, that was written up in the Sunday papers and made them famous to the extent that tourists would pass by to stare at it.

Groenewegen's bands morphed from Roland Storm and the Statesmen, mentioned above as playing at Surf City, to the Epics and the Questions; he saw Doug Parkinson play at a talent quest and 'blow everybody's mind'. The creative relationship between Groenewegen – who would soon go by the name Billy Green, for commercial reasons – and the powerful singer Parkinson will be outlined in chapter 4.

Joe Camilleri's early musical experiments are similarly interesting, both because Camilleri would later become a major star in Australia with Jo Jo Zep and the Falcons and subsequently the Black Sorrows, but also because his experiences, like Groenewegen's, show that rock and pop music was a good way for a recent immigrant to become socially accepted. Camilleri was born in Malta in 1948; his family came to Australia when he was two.[175] His early life in music reads like a script for a poignant film:

> Rock & roll singing was always what I wanted to do, even when I was very young. Our family didn't have a gramophone but this lady down the road did, and we'd go down to her place and listen to the rock & roll records and then get out on the median strip ... and sing to the cars.[176]

Camilleri started playing music in 1964:

> I bought a bass guitar from Suttons, a white Fender bass. I was working at Australian Motor Industries, getting parts for cars, and I started to take lessons

in bass guitar. You always start with your friends. I was going out with fellow countrymen – all Maltese – and a guy had bought a beautiful set of drums, all sparkly, red and white, and I got the white bass. It was all colour and movement. So we just tried to play – all very unusual stuff, very weird.

The band was called the Drollies: 'Remember how we used to have little troll dolls on our pencils and they used to dangle off the F.J.s? They were the days, squire, I tell you.'[177]

> We finally got seven songs together ... we were the worst band in the world for all time ... We were on first, supporting the Wild Colonials, Normie Rowe, Spinning Wheels, Lyn Randell, Bobby and Laurie and the Rondells and a band called the King Bees which I finally joined ... It really would have been great if it had been 1971 or 1972. I reckon we sounded like Captain Beefheart doing Little Richard songs, which is fantastic. I had a tambourine. I had all the movements ... We got things made, we all had blue suits with purple lining, it was just ridiculous – all for this one job. The band broke up after the job because we were so awful.[178]

Before and after Beatlemania, there were hundreds of groups around the country like the Drollies. Some were closer to getting a bite of the cherry than others, and the process of success and failure owed far more to chance than it did to ability, of course: John Finlay, manager of Channel Nine's talent booking subsidiary Southern Talent Services, told *Young Modern* seven big names to watch out for in

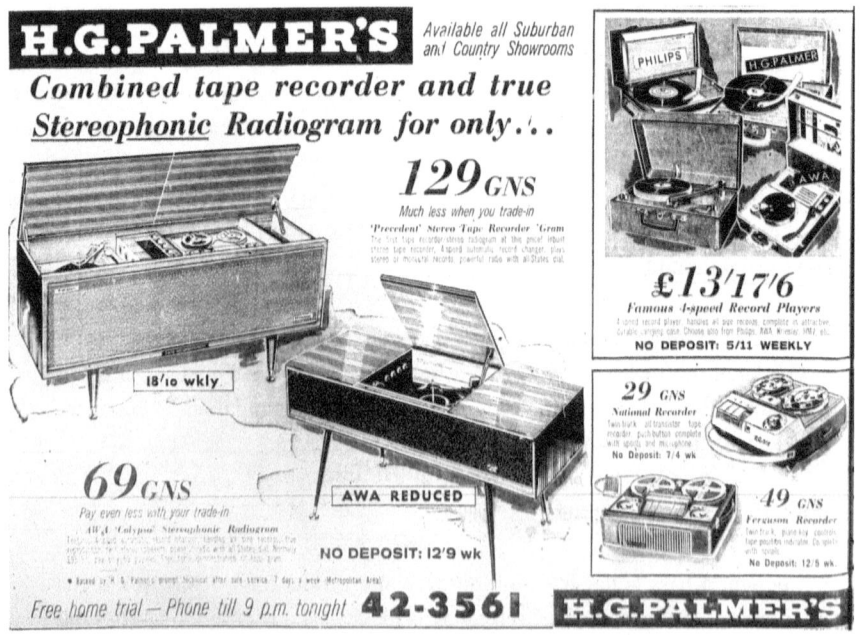

1964. These included Johnny Ioannou, a Greek singer 'not long in this country'; Tina Lawton, a folk singer; Toni Hendry and Janice Kaye; the Folk Three; and the Del Rios.[179] None of these acts made any great impact; neither did the Four Tones, whose 'Tennessee Stomp' was issued on *Young Modern*'s own record label. This was similar in concept to the label started by *Everybody's* magazine in Sydney, though it predated it; the YM label was only distributed in Adelaide.[180]

FRESH, ORIGINAL, DYNAMIC AND DEFUNCT

In 1964 *Young Modern* was trumpeting itself as 'a fresh, original and dynamic magazine for youth – the teens AND twenties – who are the spearhead of our nation.'[181] It announced its transition from fortnightly to weekly production in what appears to have been its final issue, in mid 1965.[182] With hindsight, this was clearly the passing of a great institution. Had it survived a little longer it surely would have provided a valuable ongoing account of the rise of the many talented Adelaide and other Australian musicians of the late 60s. Along with the increasingly exciting local scene, Beatlemania – which *Young Modern* was belatedly beginning to notice – would probably have sustained it for years; the magazine's publisher Ron Tremaine was instrumental in bringing the Beatles to Adelaide. Adelaideans had been lucky in the early 60s, whether they realised it or not (some, like John Dowler, obviously did); they'd had their own magazine, which spoke directly to them on a number of important issues.

It may seem a banal generalisation, but it is no less true for that: the 1960s were a time of enormous change for pop music and youth culture. Any objective observer at the time, lacking our hindsight, would surely have been convinced that rock and roll – that primitive, slightly silly and slapdash form – was a fad that would pass, albeit too slowly, and the serious and deep popular music of the 60s would be based in folk and jazz. There might even be some who still feel this was the case.

The evidence assembled in this chapter shows that, even at this early stage in modern rock/pop music, Australian artists were not passive recipients of international sounds, and did not necessarily merely fabricate local versions of the work of artists from the northern hemisphere (that is, from Britain or North America). The 'indigenous' (Anglo working-class) element in folk music, the experimental aspects of jazz, the locally relevant aspect of surf music – these and other strains of popular music were all at work on local pop and rock and roll. Few Australians would have demanded *only* to hear local artists play local music, but equally few Australians would have denied the ability of Australian artists to entertain their own people. By various means, new bands and artists would come forth in the second half of the sixties to express youth and social issues, either directly and overtly, or simply in radical sounds and styles. As the Seekers, Frank Ifield and Rolf Harris had already done, some of them would go on to make a mark on the wider world; others would make their biggest mark in Australia itself.

From *The Legend: The Illustrated Story of the Bee Gees*, written by David English and illustrated by Alex Brychta, ©1979 The Legend Company.

3 I Feel As Good As If I Were Dead
THE BEE GEES

As the mammoth, five-author, bone-dry 'biography' published in 2000 attests, the Bee Gees' story is much bigger than a short chapter in this book can or should even try to cover. In any case, the most revealing account of their career – for its vivacity and, for that matter, its semi-official status – remains *The Legend*, David English and Alex Brychta's comic-strip version of the group's story up to 1979, in which the Gibb brothers are depicted as animals: Barry as a lion, Robin a red setter and Maurice an ('eager') beaver. English, the president of their 1970s label, RSO, was close to the Gibbs both professionally and personally.

There is no doubt, however, that the Bee Gees' story is integral to the development of Australian pop and rock music. Even if it is accepted that the Bee Gees were not *really* an Australian group ('British, of course,' decrees English rock historian Vernon Joynson, a little too gleefully[1]), their impact on the Australian scene was multifaceted and emphatic, as was its effect on them. The Bee Gees' Australian period encompassed their most formative years; Australia allowed the brothers contact with the mainstream media, more time in small but functional studios than they would otherwise have enjoyed, and access to a range of artists through whom they developed their writing, performing and production skills. Such a wealth of experience would not have been readily available to them if they had continued to live in Manchester, let alone on the Isle of Man, where they were born. That the Gibbs recognised this is born out by the fact that in the early 70s they arranged for their younger brother Andy to work for an extended time on the Australian pop/tour circuit. They seem to have wanted him to replicate their own experience, probably as a prelude to his induction into the Bee Gees, though Andy's successful solo career in the late 70s and his death a decade later ensured this did not take place.

For the Gibbs, Australia was a proving ground. Barry Gibb said as much in 1969:

> The nine years' struggle was the best thing that could happen to us. Our success now is probably due to the experience we gained throughout that period. If we had've had success in Australia right from the beginning we probably would not have developed our song-writing ability, and have just rested on our laurels.[2]

It should also be borne in mind that the Bee Gees who had their first international hits in the late 60s – the band which included guitarist Vince Melouney and drummer Colin Peterson – were two-fifths Australian born, and every band member had spent most of his life in Australia. Peterson was a sufficiently integral member of the group that his presence as a Bee Gee no doubt kept the band intact after the temporary departure of Robin Gibb in 1969, and his later sacking probably precipitated, or perhaps merely confirmed, the demise of the original group.

By the late 1950s the Gibb family were Brisbaneites (they apparently lived in Cribb Island, or in Redcliffe, or both of these lower-class suburbs) when the brothers' performing career began in earnest. Initially, Barry was the most comfortable and accomplished performer, and the only songwriter. By the late 60s Robin's songs would come to equal, and sometimes surpass, Barry's in quality; he also developed a distinctive, tremulous singing style (within the family it was jokingly referred to as 'the quavering Arab').[3] Maurice was always a minor force as a songwriter, providing additional material for albums and complementary instrumentation and arrangement, such as the crucial piano riff for 'Spicks and Specks', their first big Australian hit.

Part of the Bee Gees' official story is that Australia did not recognise them until it was too late – that is, until they had decided to return to the UK in 1967. Erroneous claims abound on the sleeve notes of reissues, such as a mid-70s Pickwick cash-in collection of the group's early 60s material, whose notes assert that 'I Was a Lover, a Leader of Men' was a number one hit in Australia in 1965, and in quickie bios, for example that 'when the Bee Gees left Australia, they'd already gotten three of their songs on the Australian charts in the number one position.'[4] Tony Brady, a Festival Records employee in the 1960s, opines in the first episode of the series *Long Way to the Top* that Barry Gibb's music was 'so far ahead' of local artists.[5] But this is hindsight talking, and he's wrong (at least, the recorded output does not support his statement). Australians, like mass consumers everywhere, have never lacked a desire to purchase music of remarkably low quality, but nonetheless the story of the Bee Gees being underappreciated in Australia in the 60s glosses over the inferior and derivative nature of much of their early work. Which is to say: the early Bee Gees weren't a success and didn't deserve to be. The novelty factor of a weird-looking, fraternal folk-pop threesome who wrote (most of) their own songs – and, in fact, songs for a considerable number of other artists – may have been compelling when it came to filling up the schedules of television and live variety shows, but there are simply very few songs from the Bee Gees' early years that shine forth as original or interesting. This is true even within the often unexciting framework of early 60s pop music. 'It is no wonder that the Bee Gees never had a vast send-up [sic] when they left Australia', wrote 'Irene' in a letter to *Go-Set* magazine:

Before they left, their music was mediocre to say the least, except their last record 'Spicks and Specks' . . . How are newspapers supposed to acclaim a pathetic group? . . . Although the Bee Gees are now an excellent group, they should realize their position when they left us.[6]

The group's migration history is relatively well known. The Gibb family had lived both on the Isle of Man and in Manchester in the 1940s and 50s and by the time they relocated to Queensland in the late 1950s, the brothers had already made tentative forays into the field of public performance. Some sources, including the group's own lighthearted comic-strip story, suggest the family's relocation was due in part to the desire to avoid reform school punishment for Maurice and Robin, who habitually committed 'Grand Arson' in Manchester.[7] Curious connections extend across the group's early days: they travelled to Australia on the same ship as Red Symons, later Skyhooks' lead guitarist,[8] and they knew Lobby Loyde and Billy Thorpe as teenagers in Brisbane. Loyde and Thorpe were not just friends, but also competitors, as Loyde told the authors of *Wild About You*:

> We were all buddies when we were young. It was the eternal talent quest thing. Every time you'd walk in, if Gibby and the two little dribblers were there, you were just wasting your time because you knew they'd take [the prize] away. Even if they were rotten, they'd still get the vote, because Barry was about four foot tall and they [Robin and Maurice] were about two foot tall, and they used to get up there and sing harmonies and it'd be all over for everyone else. And if they didn't win, Thorpe did. So if those two started, you wouldn't have a shot![9]

The number of 'BGs' in their life at this time is also peculiar – and was clearly impossible to resist when it came to choosing a name. Local impresario Bill Good had organised a racing meeting at Brisbane's Redcliffe Speedway and invited the Gibbs to perform, presumably during a break in the main event; disc jockey Bill Gates was driving in a stock car race and was impressed enough to offer his services as manager. Legend has it that the group's remarkably hokey name emerged from a combination of these two and Barry Gibb, although Glenn A. Baker has countered this with his own claim that the group was already known, very ungrammatically, as the Brother Gibbs.[10] English and Brychta's suggestion that Gates 'tried to encourage sister Leslie to join the group as singer' renders Baker's assertion problematic.[11]

Gates had a radio show, *Midday Platter Chatter*, and in the innocently nepotistic spirit of the times, would play Bee Gees songs on his program. The group soon anchored a variety show on local Brisbane television on Friday nights. A new management team – the Jacobsen brothers – tried to get Festival interested, and Jacobsen 'sacrificed' one of his recording acts, Judy Cannon, for the sake of the Gibbs (Cannon was leaving the country anyway).

The Bee Gees grew up in public, and were both outgoing and impulsive. Jacobsen later recalled that mainstream television producers saw them as 'cheeky little bastards, young upstarts. It was almost impossible to get *Bandstand* to take them.'[12] They nevertheless had a profile: Jacobsen persuaded Lee Gordon to let them support Chubby Checker.[13] The group's (or more accurately, at this early stage, Barry's) songwriting ability was notable from an early age, even if at this point it manifested itself most notably as a simple capacity for high output, and a ballad by the 17-year-old Barry, 'They'll Never Know', was covered by Wayne Newton. Baker states that over sixty Gibb songs were recorded by Australian artists in the 60s.

In an era before it was de rigueur for groups to generate most or all of their own material, this ability to write was very important; the contents of the group's first album was very clearly spelt out in its title: *The Bee Gees Sing and Play 14 Barry Gibb Songs*.

Soon they were being extensively recorded by yet another mentor, Ossie Byrne, in his St Clair Recording Studio, located behind a butcher's in the Sydney suburb of Hurstville.[14] It is important to note that the Bee Gees might well have been unable to find and utilise a studio in the way they did Byrne's had they been living anywhere but in Sydney (where the family had moved in early 1963 with the boys' career in mind). The Bee Gees became a group who could work up their releases, as well as backing tracks for songs intended for others, on tape – as opposed to bringing fully realised songs to the studio. The Gibbs would later joke that their popularity with Byrne was primarily due to a sexual attraction they held for him, though there is no evidence for this, any more than there is regarding their relationship with their manager of the 60s and 70s, Robert Stigwood.

The group was plainly highly regarded in the pop industry at the time, as is evidenced by the strong support that Fred Marks of Festival Records gave them[15] and by their ongoing relationship with songwriter/entrepreneur Nat Kipner, who co-wrote songs with Maurice and other group members and whose son Steve was also involved in some of their projects. Nat Kipner issued Bee Gees records on his Everybody's label, which was tied to the well-known gossip/glossy magazine (Lilian Roxon was perhaps its most notable contributor); this later morphed into the Spin label and booking agency, secretly co-owned and operated by Clive Packer (so secret even Packer's wife was unaware of the connection).[16] The Packers are a powerful media and, more recently, gambling family; Clive was the patriarch Frank's 'outsider' son. Kipner arranged distribution for Spin with Festival, and this company retained rights to the Spin label and held an extended contract for Bee Gees recordings following their international success, a contract that continued into the 70s. Kipner also produced the hit 'Spicks and Specks'.[17]

Other musical Bee Gee friends of the early-to-mid 60s included Trevor Gordon (a former schoolfriend and TV show host in Brisbane), Colin Stead, Lori Balmer, Ronnie Burns and Cheryl Grey, née Sang. A decade later, after she had reputedly sustained a singing career for some years in Yugoslavia, Stigwood and Barry Gibb renamed the Melbourne-born Cheryl as Samantha Sang (the 'Samantha' came from one of Gibb's cats), and the Gibbs wrote and produced the international hit 'Emotion' for her.[18]

The Bee Gees' abilities as producers and writers were developed in their Hurstville days. Their song 'Coalman,' which was a hit for Ronnie Burns,[19] is a good example of the 'three I's' approach of most of their Australian pop material. It is simultaneously idiotic, infectious and inspired, and its jolly, working-class tone owes much to ditties like 'My Old Man's a Dustman' (which the Gibbs had recorded for Jacobsen and Joye in 1958)[20] and the George Formby-esque forays of Herman's Hermits. It is also patronising in the way only a bunch of aspirationals like the Gibbs could be: of course, the Gibb boys yearned for stardom, but their family's move to Australia from England in the 50s is indicative of that immigrant 'improvement' spirit. 'Coalman' is also lyrically so simplistic that it must surely have been written in minutes, without pause to think of the possible subtexts to a song about a boy who tells his romantic troubles to a young coalman who 'takes my hand' and 'understands'. Of course, this is also an indication of a historical period which was not so much innocent as adept at compartmentalisation and denial: only a few listeners are likely to imagine that the singer was enjoying the coalman's soothing touch and empathy in itself, and *they* weren't going to discuss this openly. But even if one can explain away the gay interpretation – or rather, the way its possibilities were ignored in the 1960s – while acknowledging and enjoying, even admiring, its existence, that still leaves the song's perverse assertion that the 'coalman' is a 'soul man'. If we assume the coal man is white (the undoubtedly white Burns in fact applied burnt cork to his face for promotional photos), then the melting-pot of ridiculous stereotypes – the simple, working-class, dirty but caring labourer with the heart of an African-American (or Aboriginal?) man – is complete.

What were the Bee Gees saying about the boy in the song's relationship with the coalman? They weren't saying anything, of course. They were merely running together every rhyme for 'coalman' (a reasonably rare profession in itself in Australia in the 60s, incidentally) they could think of, fitting the words to a catchy tune, and giving Ronnie Burns a hit single. Like many of their songs from their Australian period, the result was childlike and flippant, the product of three outsider siblings with a knack for attention-getting, whose life experience derived in large part from listening to other people's music. David N. Meyer, author of a 2013 history of the group, observes insightfully that the Gibbs 'grew up as performers with no real sense of themselves'. Even truer is this critique: 'The Bee Gees would forever suffer from not being able to tell their best material from their worst.'[21]

The Bee Gees released 'Spicks and Specks' – a classic pop song of the once-heard-never-forgotten variety, based on Maurice's bold and resonant keyboard riff played on the St Clair pianola[22] – on Barry's birthday, 1 September, 1966. They performed the song that night at a Sydney Town Hall show at which they shared the bill with a panoply of talents including Vince Melouney. Dinah Lee,[23] who was also performing that night, was offered 'Spicks and Specks' by the Gibbs, who were not yet convinced of its value.[24] Quite different from the rich, dramatic ballads they would begin to produce in London only six months later, 'Spicks and Specks' is charged and rollicking; it was accompanied by a film clip of the group mugging and clowning around a Cessna. The origins of the song's title are very obscure, though one suggestion at the time was that it had originally been intended as the name for a pop group.[25] If this was so, it offers further evidence of cognitive disconnect ('spick' is, or was, a charged racial epithet).

The Gibbs had already decided to leave Australia and return to Britain at the time 'Spicks and Specks' was released. There are a number of possible reasons for this decision, not all of them commercial. It has been suggested that the boys' Murry Wilson-esque father, Hugh Gibb, was worried that Barry would be conscripted to fight in the Vietnam War, which Australia had entered in 1965 in support of US involvement.[26] The relocation to Britain may have been intended to be temporary; Barry reputedly bid farewell to his friend Colin Stead, Baker later reported, with the words, 'I'll see you in 12 months'.[27] Other sources also suggest that they did not intend to return to Britain permanently;[28] in keeping with the group's approach to recording, they were probably playing it by ear. There was nothing promising on the horizon, and while 'Spicks and Specks' might arguably have been seen as a song with which to conquer the world (it was a hit in some European countries, but was essentially a parting gift for Australia), the Bee Gees' future was unknowable.

Soon after their arrival, the Gibbs were lucky enough to make a connection in London with Robert Stigwood, a fellow Australian who was at that stage in controversial negotiations to take over the running of Brian Epstein's NEMS organisation. The Bee Gees were able to sign with Polydor internationally as a result of Stigwood's intervention, while remaining on the Spin label in Australia. Someone talked them out of jumping on the temporarily popular bandwagon of 'world' bands and renaming themselves Rupert's World (it may have been Stigwood, wanting to avoid confusion with a rockier group from Sydney, Lloyd's World, which he was briefly interested in; Johnny Young, of whom more anon, had previously named *his* group Danny's World).

The Bee Gees' third album was entitled *Bee Gees 1st*. It was an instant hit. The sleevenotes to the album accidentally mentioned that they had spent some time in Australia but firmly ignored the existence of the band's previous LPs: this was a rebirth. Lillian Roxon neither praised nor derided the group when she described them in her 1969 *Rock Encyclopedia* as sounding "more like the Beatles than the Beatles ever did."[29] *Bee Gees 1st* contains some brilliant songs, most notably the superb evergreen 'To Love Somebody', the propulsive 'Red Chair Fade Away', the plaintive 'Holiday', and the completely bizarre, heavy, Gregorian chant-infused 'Every Christian Lion Hearted Man Will Show You'. This last song, as well as the one that follows it on the album, 'Craise Finton Kirk Royal Academy of Arts', were singles for Johnny Young; the first of them – released in the UK as 'Every Christian' and credited to 'Johnnie Young' – was notoriously one of those songs that might have been a hit in Britain if pirate radio hadn't been scuttled.

Most important for Bee Gees' future career was the hit single 'New York Mining Disaster, 1941', reportedly inspired by their visit to the Welsh mining village of Aberfan in the company of Ossie Byrne, who remained their producer for *Bee Gees First*. Aberfan had been the scene of a tragic accident the previous year, when a coal tip collapsed onto houses and a school, killing 116 children and 28 adults:[30] certainly, the switching of the date to exactly a quarter century earlier, as well as the relocation to a setting as different from regional Wales as possible without being wilfully obscure, supports this idea. Yet perhaps another story about the song's origins – that the group were inspired by the claustrophobic feelings induced by a power outage in a demo studio in London – is more in keeping with their common state of detachment from the real world.[31] In late 1967, Robin and his wife Molly were in a serious rail accident, and bravely assisted in rescuing other passengers from the wreckage.[32] This brush with real tragedy – many of the passengers Robin pulled from the wreckage were dead – inspired him to write the ballad 'Really and Sincerely' the following day.

The Bee Gees were still an Australian group, and they hung out with other young Australian men in London in their early days there, as the provenance of the Johnny Young single suggests. Former Aztecs guitarist Vince Melouney – who had played on a few of the Bee Gees' Sydney recordings on a freelance basis – benefited financially from this cameraderie: having relocated to England at the end of 1966, he first found a job with Simca Motors; then, he told Lee Dillow in 1971, the Easybeats 'introduced me around to quite a few people, one of whom was Long John Baldry. He had a band together and the guitar player was leaving and I was going to take his place ... That all fell through, of course ... Right after the Baldry thing [the Gibbs] arrived in town – I rang them up to say hello and that's how it started. We did a session that night and from that time I was in the band.'[33]

Melouney has the distinction of being the only Bee Gee not named Gibb to have a song recorded and released by the band ('Such a Shame', on *Idea*). Additionally, his playing was singled out on occasion – for instance, for its 'slightly subdued Hendrix style'.[34] Despite this success and the financial reward, he was frustrated by the incessant touring and the restrictions placed on him by the Gibbs. His account to Dillow of the Bee Gees' activities in the late 60s is telling:

We never really got to see or do much. I mean we were there and it was like working all the time. Doing concerts to incredible crowds of people. Quite a bit of television as well. Ed Sullivan, Hollywood Palace, that sort of thing . . . All of a sudden I had a Bentley and so much money. Wow. So much money. I just don't know what happened. From there on in I forgot about everything. Money became the ruler of my life. It was really a sad scene.

The whole thing was really getting me down . . . I was seeing people like Clapton and Beck, people I really respected. I just wasn't doing anything like this. With the Bee Gees I was playing G major chords and G minor chords – in the key of C all the time. I wasn't allowed any solos. I wasn't allowed anything bigger than a 100 watt Marshall and if I played it any louder than the two setting there was trouble. There were so many restrictions . . .[35]

Even though Melouney had been permitted a song on *Idea*, he could have little doubt that the Bee Gees were a Gibb vehicle. He left in November 1968 and formed a new band, Fanny Adams, which is discussed in a later chapter:

I told the guys I wanted to leave and they said cool.

I really wanted to write songs and no matter how many I wrote, whether they were good, bad or otherwise, I just couldn't do a thing with them. I couldn't play them with the band, I couldn't record them myself, I couldn't even give them to other people so I just became completely stationary . . .[36]

The Bee Gees' balladry was the antithesis of much of the heavy rock of the late 60s, but while the Gibbs insisted on Melouney restraining himself when he was playing in the band, they were nonetheless enthusiastic about such groups. When they arrived on a visit to Australia at Christmas 1967, Barry enthused about 'the' Cream as 'fantastic! They are the greatest group that ever has been or will be! . . . They just turn the audience on with their tremendous music.' Some would have noted that this group shared a manager in Stigwood with the Bee Gees themselves; Robin Gibb – slightly more left-of-centre musically, yet affectedly reserved – chipped in: 'I detest the guitar smashing antics of some groups . . .'[37] Shortly afterwards, these two brothers would, it was reported, 'collapse in Turkey . . . due to strain of Australian fans following them around.[38]

There is surely no mystery to the temporary demise of the Bee Gees in the late 60s. They had extraordinary success around the world in a short period of time at a very young age – the twins, in fact, were still in their late teens. For the ludicrous reason that every other band was inflicting overextended would-be meisterwerks on their audiences, the Bee Gees were told by their management that their next album would be a double. They rose to the challenge with the exceptional *Odessa*, but it caused problems within the group politically, particularly as Robin was starting to challenge Barry as a songwriter. Barry Gibb and Colin Peterson returned to Australia in January 1969 to holiday, and announced that 'Odessa' would be their next single. Aside from claiming that he was about to star in a Western, 'which I have always wanted to do' (but he did not: his film roles to date have been *Sergeant Pepper's Lonely Hearts Club Band* and his own execrable 1984 'video album' *Now Voyager),* Barry announced that Peterson was like a 'fourth' brother.[39] Soon afterwards, in a dispute over whether a Robin song ('Lamplight') or a Barry song ('First of May') would be the next Bee Gees single, Robin left the group. Barry and Maurice – and Peterson – began work on the album *Cucumber Castle* and its associated TV special; during that time Peterson was sacked from the band (he would later work in the Australian music industry).[40] The dispute between Barry and Robin persisted; Barry claimed that Robin and Molly were accusing him of 'foul things, well below the belt, you couldn't print them.'[41] In an unusual one-off, the oldest Gibb sibling, sister Lesley, sat in for Robin in a television appearance.

There is no definite point at which the Bee Gees ceased to regard themselves – or even ceased being – Australians; Barry visited in 1969 and 1970 and undertook low-key media commitments.[42] The group reformed without Melouney or Peterson after a lengthy break in late 1970; they would produce some of their best work in the early 70s, including Maurice's remarkable Moog experiment, 'Sweet Song of Summer,' and the almost-perfect album *Trafalgar.*

They toured Australia in 1972.[43] The country had changed, and this was the time when Australians seem to have felt ready to acknowledge the problematic status of the relationship between the group and their adopted country. Alistair Jones damned them in *Planet*:

> The brothers Gibb descend like some jet-setting relative you've always secretly resented but like being seen with; the way Princess Margaret can look when placed against her stolid sister, or with her dull nephews and nieces.
>
> It's not all that difficult to believe that they were once our very own; the haircuts have turned into coiffures, the jewels are gaudy and showy, and the colours too co-ordinated; the style is that tasteless swank of the nouveau [sic] riches – crystal palaces, gold fleur de lis [sic] and the cleaning lady on Wednesdays.
>
> The music is a commercial success but it's as bland as American food.[44]

By the time the group achieved its biggest and most lasting success in the late 70s, in association with the disco era, there was little discussion of their Australian legacy. What's more, the humour and quirky melodrama that had made their music interesting in the 60s and early 70s was far more muted. After 1975 the Gibbs were based in Miami.

TEENAGE RHYTHM 'N' BLUES DANCE
LIVERPOOL TOWN HALL, FRIDAY, 28th MAY

THE PLEAZERS

2 GREAT GROUPS
The Exciting
MISSING LINKS
7.30 — 9 P.M.

PLUS
The Sensational
PLEAZERS
9 — 11.30 P.M.

PLEASE NOTE!! IMPROPERLY DRESSED TEENAGERS WILL NOT BE ADMITTED—NO JEANS, NO SHORTS, ETC.

ADMISSION **7/-**

MISSING LINKS BLAST OFF AT 7.30 —   BE EARLY

H.G. PALMER'S
Special Announcement!
PERSONAL APPEARANCE
SEE and HEAR the latest musical sensation from Sydney
THE FIVE
'MISSING LINKS'
The new Rock and Roll Group with the 'Rolling Stones Sound.'
at H. G. Palmer's Newcastle Showrooms
297 HUNTER STREET
TO-DAY
THURSDAY, 1st OCT.
12.30 pm to 2 pm
Plus Guest Visit by
PAUL MICHAEL
ZANY MASKED DJ FROM U.S.A.
(Appeared recently on Dave Allen show)

BITING EYE..
fri.. STEVE and THE BOARD
       MISSING LINKS
sat.. PURPLE HEARTS
sun.. 2-6 pm THE 5
DISCO 56 Little Bourke St. (Paris End)

4 We Weren't Exactly Keeping a Low Profile
THE MISSING LINKS

The Missing Links were an anomaly for their time: they were a band – two bands, actually – that functioned as an umbrella for a range of outstanding, fiery, reckless free spirits who rapidly, yet apparently artlessly, bashed out a very fine recorded legacy. They were not typical of their day, but they were exactly the kind of band that had to exist at a time when Australians were grappling with that question of what the strengths of Australian music could be.

The idea of 'Missing Links' was a knowing nod to the popular perception of long-haired youth and primitive behaviour, something anyone could get. There was also a particularly Australian aspect to the name, if one wanted to make a crass analogy with Aboriginal people who were so often criticised as being primitive throwbacks and a quickly perishing connection to the past – though the Missing Links themselves did not make this comparison and, in fairness to them, were obviously claiming to *be* the links in question. Strangely though, the art department at Phonogram, for whom the Links made their one and only album, saw a historical Australian connection: the LP cover depicted the group shackled to an enormous ball and chain. a reference to convictism. Their final, posthumous EP kept an aspect of this metaphor going; its title was *Unchained*.

The Missing Links concept – essentially, loud and frantic R&B – was so strong that it survived a complete line-up change (all the more unusual because there was no strong manager figure in their orbit, eager to rationalise such changes for the purpose of retaining a commercially vibrant brand). A Sydney group, the Missing Links were important in the early to mid 1960s music scene for their vibrancy and their extreme outlook.

R&B was becoming a passion for a minority of young men around Australia; they included Keith Glass, Ross Wilson, Gulliver Smith and Kerryn Tolhurst in Melbourne, and Matt Taylor and Lobby Loyde in Brisbane, all of whom would be notable in the scene for decades. Most of these devotees began as enthusiastic magpies, and Peter Anson was no different. Anson's father had introduced him to jazz, and he'd been listening to it from an early age: 'I collected books about it, and records. All those books mentioned the origins of jazz in early black music.'[1] More extraordinarily. in a time of institutionalized racism, he was a beneficiary of the US government's generosity in spreading the blues message:

> There was a record shop in Sydney called Edels. They had Sonny Terry, Brownie McGee, Lightnin' Hopkins. Then I found out, through a bass player I knew, about Alan Lomax's blues recordings put out by the Library of Congress. We didn't know where we'd find these records and he said, 'Why don't we try the American embassy?' Off we went. And they said, 'Oh, we've got all these recordings – you can take 'em home and have a listen.'

This was only part of the Missing Links' inspiration, though. Anson claims to have been more directly motivated by Ray Hoff, a Sydney musician who, with his group the Off Beats, was a regular live favourite in the early sixties. Hoff later relocated to Perth, where most of his recording was done and where he was a strong favourite of another 60s icon, Johnny Young. Perth had a blues scene that filled some with awe; it offered, as one commentator put it, 'escape from the convention-ridden and practical-minded world of today ... a dark, eerie sort of a world.'² For Anson, Hoff was 'the Sinatra of the blues in this country, and I could get to see him regularly; he was one of the guys I used to talk to.'

> I don't know where he got his stuff, but he knew all about the blues – and Chuck Berry and Jerry Lee Lewis, too. He used to do a solo gig with just an electric guitar at a folk club in Kings Cross. He was featured there, and live he meant more to me than those early Stones things.

Still, Anson's wish to avoid a day job was probably the strongest motivating force in the creation of the group in early 1964. His brother, Cliff, was working as a roadie for Billy Thorpe:

> He said, 'These guys are making a bit of dough – why don't you get a band together, play some tunes, get something going, I can get you some work.'
> So I put an ad in the *Herald* for musicians, and various people turned up. Then, through contacts my brother had, we got auditioned around the place ... I gave up my job as a public-service clerk. It was 1970 the next time I had a day job.

Coincidentally, many of the Missing Links came from northern New South Wales, specifically the Port Macquarie area. Guitarist (and later well-known Sydney recording engineer) Dave Boyne was one of them, Ronnie Peel was another. Peel had learnt piano from an 'old time piano teacher who'd been a bit of a gay girl in her time and knew all about boogie'.³ One day, Peel saw a new kind of 'big long guitar' on TV and 'it fucking freaked me right out'; he discovered it was a bass. Acquiring one, he played it in a group called the Mystics which, like Port Macquarie itself, featured a few future Missing Links. They played surf music at what were known as Sound Lounges – discotheques with live bands, often operated by Ivan Dayman

– some in Sydney suburbs like Dee Why and Parramatta. Peel met a young man with 'the longest hair I'd ever seen in my life': this was Anson. Another core early member was singer Bob Brady, from all reports a perspicacious character. After initially considering the name Fang, the new group became the Missing Links.

Anson remembers the group taking off quickly, though he is equivocal about their level of success. 'There was a bit of screaming from the audience – it was part of the thing to scream, wasn't it? They'd just scream for the sake of it. Sometimes you couldn't hear yourself too well.' As Mike Rudd explains more fully in the next chapter, Anson says this meant less than it might seem because of the minimal power of rock equipment at the time: 'The biggest amplifier was about 30 watts!'

The Missing Links were then living in the middle ring suburb of Top Ryde, sharing a flat with two brothers whose parents were their landlords. This was an advantage, because the group's 'wild' appearance might have counted against them when it came to mundanities like finding a place to live. Anson says the flat had another advantage: it was 'in the middle of a shopping centre. At night, you could make all the noise you wanted.'

The group had a lot of work. 'My dad knew the entertainment director for Miller's Pubs, so we got work on that circuit,' says Anson. They were also associated with John Harrigan's agency (see chapter 2) and played at his venues. They had some high profile engagements, such as playing at a benefit for *Oz* magazine in November 1964; its editors were being prosecuted for a satirical cartoon by Martin Sharp about a yob's night out. An engagement that fell through perhaps brought them more kudos than it would if it had gone ahead: the promoter of the Rolling Stones' 1964 tour, Harry M. Miller, threw them off the bill of the Sydney show, reputedly because they looked too scruffy. This would be enough in itself to earn them a badge of honour, but the legend has further developed that the Missing Links were dropped because they presented too much competition to the Stones in terms of their wild and rugged sound: they blew the Stones off the stage.

> I didn't make a brilliant living, but I certainly managed to pay my rent. If you look at the top ten and top forty of that time, there was a lot of Australian stuff on the charts. A hell of a lot more than there is now. And we got plenty of gigs – just local dances, sound lounges, but they were all paid . . . We didn't end up playing much blues, though we always featured a couple of Leadbelly songs in the stage repertoire. We always did 'Midnight Special.'

Suzie Wong's was a Sydney club that served as the hub of the blues-rock scene in the mid 60s. Anson remembers it as a great place:

> Once we started working there, we were meeting other musicians – there was music seven nights a week. It was a meeting place for people who'd go hang out there in the daytime. And we'd be working there at night. It was a trad-jazz

place originally, and then slowly it changed over. It had a fabulous atmosphere. It was underground, downstairs, in an arcade. You went down and there was a bar, and a dance floor; it probably held a hundred people.

The guy that owned Suzie Wong's, Jim Harris, was Greek. I think they had a Chinese cook – but he only cooked spaghetti!

Suzie Wong Restaurant

The Missing Links recorded one single for Alberts (via the Harrigan connection). 'I don't think we were trying to do anything much,' says Anson of the recording session for the single.

> Alberts was trying to start up a stable of recording people. They signed us and when the time came to record they suggested we do some originals. So we sat down and wrote those songs. Not because we wanted to write songs . . . but we had a recording contract and we were expected to do it! I didn't have much vision at that stage.

It was the only record the first Missing Links made, a tuneful Anson composition called 'We 2 Should Live.' It was released in early 1965 on Parlophone, which had a special relationship with Alberts' music publishing company; the two companies were a couple of months away from hitting gold with the Easybeats. In the Missing Links, however, Alberts were confronted with a group who, whatever they did have, certainly had no sense of a collective direction. Anson, sick of being forced to play Beatles covers (presumably by svengalis like Harrigan), had ideas for a new group; he eased himself out of the Missing Links soon after the release of 'We 2 Should Live'. He was soon a core member of Jeff St John and the Id, having 'met the guys who ended up being the Id hanging out' at Suzie Wong's during the day. 'I'd left the Links and was hanging around the scene. I met these guys who said "Yeah, we want to form a blues band."'

Andy Anderson remembers Anson as 'a purist, an original – I liked him a lot. Pete Anson loved R&B, jazz, blues . . .' Anderson was known in his Missing Link days as Andy James (the name change came about, he says, because he ran away from home in New Zealand in 1965 at the age of 16, and didn't want his parents to find him); he came to the Missing Links via an ad in the paper placed by guitarist John Jones.

Anderson joined the Missing Links in mid 1965. By this stage it was not so much a group in flux, more a name looking for some people to embody it. The one connection between the later Links and the earlier one was Jones, who replaced Anson shortly before the end of the original band's life. Anderson had filled in once for original drummer Danny Cox, and believes that 'they were on the verge of breaking up when I first saw them – I helped to patch things as a drummer, but then they broke completely. I remember backing Bob Brady [in a solo performance]; he kicked someone in the head at Bankstown, which caused a huge ruckus. I thought we'd never get out of there alive. He was a hard boy. Very hard boy.'

Once the new Links were under way, the original group made themselves scarce, says Anderson. Over a few months in mid 1965 the entire line-up was replaced.

Doug Ford was born in Casino, NSW (not far from Port Macquarie) and went to Sydney to attend the Radio and Television School, where he was hassled and eventually dismissed from his apprenticeship because of his long hair. John Jones approached him and 'said they were reforming the Missing Links.'[4] (In 1970, Ford claimed to have spent six months of 1965 at the Conservatorium of Music where he was 'taught basic jazz' in 1965 before he joined the Missing Links.)[5] Ford recalls that the Links would go to extremes in their stage act, with outfits made from chaff bags dyed pink or red, with holes cut out for their arms and heads, hessian trousers and cowboy boots: 'Nobody else was doing anything like that'.

The Missing Links have a 13-month recording history: from March 1965 to April 1966. One single by the original line-up; four singles, a covers EP and an album by the second version. In mid 1965, the Links were signed to Philips, whose staff were clearly open to unusual sounds: it would soon be Pip Proud's label too. Anderson remembers visiting their offices:

> I remember going in there one day after I'd had my first taste of grass ... I squatted down – there was nowhere to sit, with albums on all the chairs in this guy's office – so he sat at his desk and I squatted down on the rug. The next minute he was saying, 'Are you all right?' I was still in the squat position, but I'd fallen onto my back and I was staring up at him. People were looking into the office and he was looking down and going, 'Are you all right?' That might be the reason we only did one album for them!

What is actually surprising – and possibly further evidence of Philips's adventurousness during this brief period – is that the Missing Links got to make an album at all. This was a period in which many groups were denied the opportunity to produce an album until they had chalked up a number of chart successes with singles. Even a major live drawcard with chart successes, like Doug Parkinson In Focus, was not given this opportunity – and it was clear that group, unlike the Missing Links, had a large repertoire, thanks to their peerless songwriter/guitarist Billy Green. Add to this unusual situation the fact that various members of the Missing Links believe that Philips manufactured only small quantities (hundreds of copies) of the group's releases, and it seems likely that Philips either did not know what it was doing, or was doing something other than trying to make a hit group out of the Missing Links.

The Missing Links is an uneven album, with crazy covers ranging from Dylan ("On the Road Again") to Chris Montez, off-the-cuff originals and a couple of R&B standards – and a backwards-played "Mama Keep Your Big Mouth Shut" for good measure, alongside an orthodox forwards version. Anderson sees the backwards song – which was released, improbably, over two sides of a single – as an attempt to recreate the improvisational insanity and unearthly quality of the Links live: "We heard the tape playing backwards as it rewound, and I said 'That's our sound, man, that's what we sound like live! Release that!' They said 'You've got to be kidding' and I said 'That's what people like!' When we'd end up smashing instruments, all that shit." Of the rest of the album, Anderson says:

> It was just microphones hanging from the roof of the studio. The fastest, loudest noise to get to the mike won. I think we sounded a hell of a lot better live, a lot gruntier and more menacing. Sometimes that sound comes through, but it was pretty primitive recording. Pretty basic.
>
> But we didn't know we were doing an album! I know I wrote 'Wild About You' and 'Speak No Evil' at the time. 'Driving Me Insane', I always loved that song. When Hutch [drummer Baden Hutchens] brought it in he was like, 'You sing it!' and I was, 'No, you sing it, man!' And when you listen to his drumming... that was our sound. A lot happened on that track that was just like we were. Yeah, I loved that.
>
> 'Some Kind of Fun' is more or less done the way Chris Montez did it, just a bit rougher. It was just a matter of, 'Oh, let's put that down' – I don't even know if we thought we'd recorded it, because it didn't take long to put something down. All of a sudden it was 'That's enough, we've got enough for an album.'

Anderson understandably sees this as a pity because, as he remembers it, the band had more potential than could be translated to record:

> There was something happening musically in that band that was... you'd get carried away. We used to break things up and stuff, but it was contained within the music, it wasn't a matter of [we're] gonna run out and hurt someone...
>
> But it might have seemed quite scary. Like when you're riding a motorbike, it's not scary to you, but when you ride past someone really fast they go... 'Shit!' If you look across at someone else doing a hundred miles an hour, when you're going the same speed, it doesn't matter – you're on the same wavelength. You can reach over and touch the other person.
>
> I didn't smoke a lot or drink a lot onstage in those days, it was definitely the music... Oh, there were pills, the methedrine gets you going... but I just loved the music, and being free of those limits like 'twelve bars and then back to the chorus,' you know. I loved it, there was a real freedom going on.

The Missing Links split for the last time in late 1966, because, Maggie Makeig claimed in *Everybody's*, their 'producers and managers all want to make them sound like Normie Rowe'.[6] This seems unlikely, if only because it would have been impossible. Realising as so many did at this time that Sydney was not the place to do the things they were doing, Ford and Anderson relocated to Melbourne to start a band that was initially known as the New Missing Links and then the Running Jumping Standing Still.

The Missing Links' legend was revived early – appropriately, though, for a group that seemed bigger than the sum of its parts, this was not because of the activities of its former members. Ross Wilson, who had never made any bones about his garage-rock roots, was involved in the Missing Link record label with Keith Glass and David Pepperell in the mid 70s: the name was a direct reference to the group. Wilson also masterminded the soundtrack to *Oz*, Chris Löfvén's 'rock and roll road movie', and arranged for the singer-turned-actor Graham Matters – he'd been a member of the Adderley Smith Blues Band in Melbourne – to sing the Missing Links' 'You're Driving Me Insane' for it. Meanwhile, unbeknown to almost anyone, Brisbane's Saints had been playing 'Wild About You' in their live set since 1974.

Individual Missing Links benefited little from this (particularly as a dogsbody at EMI listed the songwriting credit for the Saints' record version of 'Wild About You' on their first album as 'Unknown'). Former Links went on to seemingly mundane and 'straight' day jobs – aside from Anderson, who has become a well-known television actor, and Doug Ford, who joined the Masters Apprentices and, with Jim Keays, wrote some of their biggest hits.

It is distinctly possible that the Missing Links remain so highly regarded and beloved largely because they were able to record an album and they took to the task of making it with devil-may-care gusto. Certainly, their outsider status was a major part of what Anderson and Ford thought they were about, as Anderson recalls:

> 'Long haired poofters' is what you'd get called . . . 'animals'. There was the sharpies, and in Melbourne there was the mods and whatever, surfers and mods and everyone hated bloody longhairs. It was pretty dangerous.
>
> It was fine during the day, walking round the city. Doug and I used to taunt people. One day we went to a department store and I pretended to be blind . . . He led me round and I'd pretend to speak this stupid language and he'd pretend to be translating for me. We had a lot of games. We weren't exactly keeping a low profile.

As much as the band may have been an anomaly, the Missing Links' legacy has been pervasive over the intervening fifty years. As we shall see, many later groups similarly refused to keep a low profile – with often spectacular results.

GO-SET   WEDNESDAY, MARCH 12, 1969

GO-SET DISCO GUIDE
8 days a week

SOONER OR LATER YOU'LL BE SEEN AT **SWINGER**
MELBOURNES BIGGEST SATURDAY NIGHT DANCE
COBURG CITY HALL

KNOW WHERE

TUESDAY:
FRANK TRAYNORS
Margaret Roadknight, John Graham
VICTORIA AND ALBERT
Theatre Restaurant Club — Browns

WEDNESDAY:
PRINCE ALBERT GEORGE SEBASTIANS
Closed
FRANK TRAYNORS
Danny Spooner and Guests
VICTORIA AND ALBERT
Groop

THURSDAY:
IMPULSE (Ormond Hall)
Dave McCallum Power Set, Qld. Avengers, Tony Shepp compere, Groovy Rooftop Garden, Thursday Dancers
PRINCE ALBERT GEORGE SEBASTIANS
Browns
THUMPIN' TUM
Valentines
FRANK TRAYNORS
Chris Duffy, Peter Dickie and guests
VICTORIA AND ALBERT
Billy Thorpe and Aztecs, Floor Show. Bobby and Laurie

FRIDAY:
54321
(Cnr. Foster and Langhorne Sts., Dandenong)
Jeff St. John and the Copper Wine
431
(St. Kilda Road)
Graduate, Michelle Kennedy, City Stompers, Compere Tony Shepp
LIFE
Closed due to other commitments. Watch out for our big Friday night spectacular coming soon
PRINCE ALBERT GEORGE SEBASTIANS
Groop, Valentines
FRANK TRAYNORS
Margaret Smith, David Howard, Declan Affley, Bruce Stuchbery
THUMPIN' TUM
Campact, Billy Thorpe and Aztecs
UNCLE JOHN'S CABIN
Valentines, Issus, Compere Ian Simpson, Janine
VICTORIA AND ALBERT
Groop, Campact

SATURDAY:
CAESARS
(Mornington Civic Centre)
Zoot, Peeling
COWES OLD POST OFFICE
Re-opens Good Friday
COLAC DANCELAND
Dave McCallum Power Set, Wanderers, Brendon Scanlon your host, Saturday Swingers
DOLLYS
(Masonic Hall, Brighton)
Valentines, Plum, Jeff Crozier and his Magic Band, fee t shirts.
431
(St. Kilda Road)
Jigsaw, Spice of Life, Tony Shepp compere
GAS
Daisy Clover, Leprechauns, plus surprise group
IMPULSE (Ormond Hall)
Mixtures, Nova Express, Jeff St John and the Copper Wine, Peter Bond compere Thursday Dancers, Groovy rooftop garden.
SEEPOUT
Closed for renovations
THE LANE
Natures Own, Zoot, Dream

54321
a special announcement

DUE TO THE OVERWHELMING CROWDS WHO, SINCE OUR RE-OPENING HAVE ENJOYED 54321 EVERY FRIDAY, WE ARE NOW FORCED TO OPEN UP ON **SATURDAY NIGHTS** AS WELL, TO CATER TO THE DANDENONG EXTRA IN SET

SO ON SATURDAY, MARCH 22 WE OPEN UP WITH AUSTRALIA'S TOP TALENT

MEANWHILE THIS FRIDAY CATCH JEFF ST. JOHN AND COPPER WINE, NATURES OWN AND OUR SPECIAL SURPRISE GROUP

CNR. FOSTER and LANGHORNE STREETS, DANDENONG

THE LANE — SAT.

ZOOT
DREAM
NATURES OWN
MECHANICS HALL EX-PENNY LANE HALL
FRANKSTON

FUZZ IS BORN

Rank
NOW AVAILABLE FOR BOOKINGS THROUGH
NORTHSIDE PROMOTIONS 809 2195
or JOHN RYAN PROMOTIONS 50 3108 ALSO BOOKING
BARRY AND JILL, GENE PIERSON, CARNIVAL, CHELSEA SET, SEBASTIAN, CHESTNUT ST QUARTET, CAMPACT

Musical instruments
TO SELL — Electric Piano Hohner imported, in excellent condition. Contact 88 9494.
SITAR for sale 398 1879 A H

Miscellaneous
EAR PIERCING, girls and guys Leo Tabb, 427 Sydney Road, Brunswick 38 5417
FOR HIRE — Liven up your party with flashing fluorescent and coloured lights Ideal for atmospheric lighting at parties, dances Ring 85 6059

GRECH SOUND SYSTEMS
SOUND EQUIPMENT HIRING SPECIALISTS
P.A. SYSTEMS   GUITAR AMPS
ALL DISCO EQUIPMENT
5 Menana Rd., Glenroy
Phone: 9 a.m.-4.30 p.m. — 306 8097
4.30-6.30 p.m. — 306 4675
A.H.: 309 2738

GIGANTIC HENDRIX POSTERS

THESE FANTASTIC 60" x 40" POSTERS ARE AVAILABLE AND ARE PROBABLY THE FINEST OF THEIR TYPE PRICE $2.95 ea.

SEND ORDERS WITH REMITTANCE TO
54321
2 STUART STREET
DANDENONG
3175

5 The Snap and Crackle of Pop
THE MID TO LATE SIXTIES

> 'There's a new age dawning this year, he told me. 'An old cycle's ending and a new one begins, in 1966. Did you know that, Dick? The earth-forces will come into their own, and people will be liberated.'
> – C. J. Koch, *The Doubleman*[1]

The story of the counterculture that developed in the western world in the late 60s is, like that of any mythological era, riddled with half-truths crossed with untruths. As we shall see, the notion often expressed at this time that all was now opportunity and possibility – from the breaking down of rigid, millennia-old institutions to the radical act of releasing a single that was more than three minutes long – amounted in fact to one step forward, three steps in another direction entirely.

Visceral and showy, it is easy to imagine the period as boldly painted in illusory deep patterns of ultra-sensation. 'Somehow with the optimism of the sixties,' the film director Peter Weir claimed two decades later, 'there was a feeling that everything was going to work out, that you didn't need to plan.'[2] Of course, this is only a very small segment of the cultural mix, inseparable from the rest. Pip Proud claimed that the best way to typify the late 60s in Sydney was as a time when special inspectors had the power to measure women's bathing costumes at Sydney beaches – which is to say that it was a time of prudery thrown into stronger contrast by a small number of 'liberated' minds. Certainly the Australian government remained conservative throughout this period, during which three Prime Ministers – Menzies, Holt and the slightly more interesting Gorton – presided over a persistently strong 'lucky country' economy.

Similarly, even though the counterculture was sold by means of rhetoric that invoked anti-commercial, even anti-capitalist values, a general cynicism prevailed in many quarters as to whether particularly 'out there' artists were genuine and their work valid, or if consumers were not so much going on a trip as being taken for a ride. This scepticism extended even into the alternative scene(s). Essentially, there were very few people throughout the world, including Australia, who didn't think that the action – where the beautiful people were making free decisions based purely on their own enlightenment – was happening somewhere else. Barry Miles, a self-proclaimed insider in the London 'underground', has discussed the way his small, select gang felt that the Move, a group from Birmingham, had demonstrated hypocrisy by suddenly experiencing an 'overnight conversion to hippiedom' when they released 'I Can Hear the Grass Grow' in early 1967. 'The point,' says Miles, 'is that psychedelic music grew from an environment, a very specific London one...'[3]

In fact there are quite a few 'points', and the most pertinent one is that while many, indeed most, kowtowed to London as the centre of the counterculture universe during this time, there is no reason to assume that London's psychedelic explosion was any more exciting than anyone else's. Miles is presumably speaking only from his own experience at what seemed like the pumping heart of a movement. For that matter, when Proud ventured to London at the very end of that decade he found that his few Sydney friends who'd made good didn't want to know him, and the scene, in general terms, was dismal. In any case it is quite possible that the interpretations of that cultural style that were created in other places were more impressive than the original – whatever that original actually was. Russell Morris's 'The Real Thing' may be 'a dog of a song' without 'much there melody-wise and lyric-wise', as Dave Mason of the Reels once put it.[4] But as a studio experiment allowed to run riot in the form of a 7" single, it was a stunning leap in a new direction, and its similarly chart-topping follow-up, 'Part Three: Into Paper Walls)', went twice as far again.

Many others talk of this period as one in which technology (especially those mundane matters of amplification and multi-track recording) could never match their own vision or ambition; at the same time, tape recording was becoming more convenient and compact: a 'new boom in electronics' was announced in 1967, as the cassette tape was readied for launch.[5] Similar advances at both the home and public music production level were made rapidly in the later 60s and into the 70s.

Very few people of any stripe trust art, or their responses to it, and art – pop music included – often goes out of its way to be untrustworthy. Towards the end of Patrick White's 1970 novel *The Vivisector*, a life of the fictional modern artist Hurtle Duffield, White gives over more than five pages to snatches of dialogue from the vain, trivial, pretentious and foolish glitterati of Sydney responding (or not) to a retrospective of the artist's work. The themes of the babble include whether or not Duffield sells largely to Americans, how rich he must be, and how little the attendees actually understand the work in question. It's an extended riff on the same type of hollow chatter Jan Smith relates from the Beatles press conference (see chapter 2). White, as one of Australia's most celebrated and yet most misunderstood writers, is in part bemoaning his own fate (he even includes a dig at himself[6]), but he is also reflecting on the fate of creators in the marketplace, as indeed his character's life itself is an extended reflection on the 20th century in Australian art. The point White makes, writing as he is on the cusp of what would turn out to be non-indigenous Australia's greatest leap to date in terms of artistic flowering, is that art and commerce are inseparable, that commerce's blunt, mulish desire leads art wherever it wants it to go. Even in the case of Duffield – who comes (through adoption) from a wealthy background but whose interest in money goes no further than its power to free him to paint pictures when he pleases – materialism, the dictates of fashion, and the petty lives of the miserable rich women he courts are bound up with his life as an artist.

In 1970 Marty Rhone – a Dutch-Indonesian Australian with handsome, apparently Asian features and a string of very fine, but for the most part commercially unsuccessful singles behind him – released a self-penned parody song, 'So You Want To Be a Pop Singer'. In it, he mimicked and satirised three vocalists who are rarely, for all their good qualities, spoken of in the same sentence: Russell Morris, Bob Dylan and Johnny Farnham. Rhone's record focused particularly on the 'manager' operating the star (Ian Meldrum, Morris's manager and Farnham's manager Daryl Sambell were both referred to by their nicknames, 'Molly' and 'Sadie'). Rhone was holding the pushy hand of the industry up for examination, and while he delivered the song with a smile on his face, its humour bordered on viciousness.

Rhone was vicious because the pop scene was tough, particularly for Australian artists. Only a small percentage of consumers would have failed to make a distinction between locally made and international records and acts. Increasingly, fans of Australian musical stars came to see international acceptance as, if not the raison d'etre of local performers, then certainly something worth grabbing at any opportunity. Record companies were, of course, complicit in this. Australia could be a proving ground for numerous artists, just as the Bee Gees or the Easybeats had honed their skills there. By the 1980s, groups like INXS were readily peddling the nonsense that their hardiness as a band was forged in the fabled 'beer barns' of the Australian suburbs. Yet it was also true that any Australian group which had experienced success in its homeland potentially offered the best of both worlds to a British or American record company – it was both new (at least to audiences outside Australia) *and* polished. Thus Bee Gees' *1st*, or Procession's remarkably assured, crafted, and tasteful second take at a debut LP; or the Masters Apprentices'

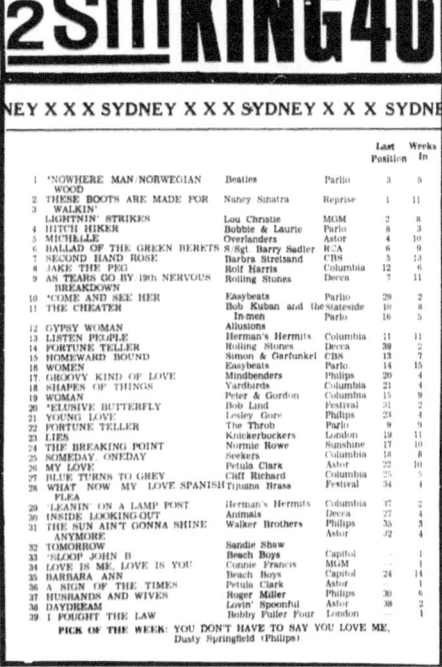

third album, *Choice Cuts,* their first release in Britain after numerous Australian hits. The La De Das, the Twilights, Johnny Young, the Easybeats, Olivia Newton-John, MPD Ltd and many others were able to reinvent themselves in the northern hemisphere. But while Australian impresario Robert Stigwood's willingness to take on an Australian group called the Bee Gees made it possible for them to land on their feet overseas, most Australian acts suffered as a result of the insularity and provincial nature of the 'scenes' they were trying to break into. This may well have been a result of outright prejudice in some cases, but more often – as we shall see – the networks that mattered simply weren't available to new arrivals.

The internationalists nevertheless made inroads – although this in no way diminishes the worth and importance of those who stayed behind, many of whom were making even better records than their peers who'd been drafted to the UK by dint of having achieved everything they were supposed to achieve in Australia. The Australian-in-Europe professionals were often producing bland work in order to compete in the mainstream, whereas their former colleagues were relegated to the margins, where the greatest art is usually found. By definition, those at the margins usually don't have the wherewithal to leave a very visible legacy; as a result, the official histories are riddled with gaps. Thus, for example, we have the account offered in the 90s by British rock journalist Martin Huxley, who dismisses Australian music of the 60s apparently because of its lack of international commercial success:

> Such Melbourne-based acts as the Loved Ones, the Groop, Ronnie Burns, Normie Rowe and Bobby and Laurie, along with Adelaide transplants the Masters Apprentices and the Twilights (not to mention Bon's old Perth pal Johnny Young) would never really figure out how to process their influences into anything authentic or personal and would never really produce music of sufficient merit to cause any sleepless nights for their overseas contemporaries.[7]

Huxley is attempting here to create a context for AC/DC, the subject of his biography, and (as non-Australian writers of books about Nick Cave have also discovered) it is easy to talk up your subject by deriding their contemporaries or context on the basis of their supposed obscurity. It's even easier when you have evidently done no research. Huxley's central premise, that groups like the Loved Ones or the Twilights were in the business of 'process[ing] influences', along with his assumption that the only success is commercial success, is ludicrous and beneath contempt. Try to imagine Pete Townshend in 1967 feeling nervous upon discovering that the Loved Ones, based in Melbourne, are a truly superb rock band.

When it comes to processing 'influences', journalist/social commentator Craig McGregor offers a more accurate picture of young Australians in the mid 60s:

> The process of borrowing from overseas can be quite random. Duffle coats, winkle-picker shoes, drain-pipes, Beatle hairstyles and black stockings betray

the English influence; whitewall tyres, Bermuda shorts, swept-back motorcycle handlebars, surf shirts and sneakers betray the American. But often there is an astute selectivity at work. Young Australians seem to have rejected the sentimentality of many US films and TV shows, but have accepted the American talent for self-criticism; it seems to fit in well with the sardonic tradition of local humour.[8]

OUTSIDERS AND INSIDERS

At least since the 1960s, New Zealanders have seen Australia as the next step up the ladder; a few have made the next step, beyond their greater neighbour (greater, at least, in size) and into the wider world's consciousness. Max Merritt, for instance, was a figure to reckon with in Australia in the 70s, and his various incarnations of Max Merritt and the Meteors were famously inspirational to Australians who saw them play live.

This section introduces two important individuals who travelled from New Zealand to Australia in the mid 60s with their respective bands. Mike Rudd and Brian Peacock would both go on to play important roles as songwriters – and in other areas of the music industry – in Australia. Their stories are of great interest in themselves within the context of Australian music, and each of them, in a different way, also provides an invaluable take on the Australian scene from 1966 onwards. One significant difference between them concerns their outlook and approach: Peacock, who played in and wrote for the Librettos, Normie Rowe's Playboys, and Procession, saw his time in Sydney, and later Melbourne, as an interlude; he was always en route to London. Rudd, who was a member of the Party Machine, then formed Spectrum and was simultaneously in Ross Wilson's Sons of the Vegetal Mother, had rather different ambitions, and fitted into the Melbourne scene very early in his career. One important element in both men's stories is Melbourne-born Ross Wilson, another remarkable and multi-faceted figure who will also appear at many points throughout this story.

Like so many of the strands in this history, beginnings, ends and definitive intersections can be hard to pinpoint. A motley assortment of private schoolboys in Melbourne's bayside suburbs of Brighton and Beaumaris coalesced in the mid 60s into groups such as the Fauves, including Ross Hannaford; the Rising Sons, with Keith Glass; and the Pink Finks, with Ross Wilson.

Hannaford recalled in 1971 that the Fauves "only knew two numbers":

> We thought it would be funny to start a rock band and we played at this church dance and Ross Wilson sat in with this other band that played there. The guys used to live in the same street where we practiced. It was Keith Glass's band. We've known Keith a long time. Ross started with them and played a bit of harp...[9]

Keith Glass – yet another figure who will play important roles in this story – went on to be guitarist and songwriter in the great Melbourne pop groups 18th Century Quartet (which also featured Hans Poulsen as singer-songwriter) and Cam-Pact; in the mid 70s, together with Wilson, he would also start (and go on to run with his wife Helena) the Missing Link label (the record shop with the same name was a continuation of Archie and Jugheads, which Glass opened with David Pepperell early in that decade).

In 1972, the fortunes of relative newcomer TV broadcaster the 0-10 network would be saved by the scandalous soap opera *Number 96*; alongside topless women and storylines involving drug use and adultery, the show famously introduced sympathetic gay characters – reputedly for the first time in mainstream television anywhere. Homosexuality was, nonetheless, illegal throughout Australia until the individual states and territories began a piecemeal process of decriminalization starting in 1973. It was therefore a brave, if not foolhardy, move for the Melbourne group Cam-Pact – who identified, in the main, as heterosexual – to flirt with a homosexual 'image' several years earlier. It came in the form of, firstly, their name (they were originally the Camp Act), and secondly a mouth-to-mouth kiss between bassist Mark Barnes and guitarist Chris Stockley in the film clip for their first single, 'Something Easy' (1967). Such 'shock tactics' paved the way for other groups – the Zoot, for instance – to make an impression with similar attention-grabbing ideas. Cam-Pact themselves were impressive and unusual; they were predominantly a soul group, but they also delved into psychedelic pop.

By the time Mike Rudd's group Chants R&B arrived in Melbourne from Christchurch towards the end of 1966, individuals like Wilson, Hannaford and Glass had graduated from school dances and very local venues like the Beaumaris Community Centre's venue, Stonehenge, to become players on the Melbourne scene. Hannaford had joined Wilson in the Pink Finks, and in early 1967 they formed a new band together, Party Machine. Rudd heard Party Machine playing, 'maybe it was at Tenth Avenue and I thought, "this actually sounds like a really good band, I really love what they're doing"... I just stored that away, and then I heard they were looking for a bass player, and auditioned.' The group were unusual for the time, not necessarily because they played their own material for the most part, but because they played Ross Wilson's material, which was provocative and didactic, and also on occasion personal. Wilson's songs were as unique to his experience and worldview as, for instance, those of Ray Davies. Rudd, who at this stage did not write songs himself, remembers the group was 'successful to a degree':

> In the early stages we were doing fifty-fifty covers and Ross's material, and it expanded from there. I think I had something to do with the discussions in the van on the interminable drives from Sydney, saying, 'Look, we may as well just go for broke and hope to impress industry people – i.e. musicians – with what we're doing', because I felt quite strongly that what Ross was writing and what we were playing was so different. And when I look back on it now, it still is. Everyone else was going in one particular direction, a very UK-oriented thing, and Ross was in a different area, probably more towards the States. But it was very different for here. If you listen to it now it's cute, you'd almost call it psychedelic bubblegum.

Robert Wolfgramm, a schoolboy in the late 60s, and raised as a Jehovah's Witness, experienced a debauched (in comparison to his usual existence) weekend to which the Party Machine contributed when he attended a show at Piccadilly's, a club based at Ringwood in Melbourne's outer east:

> First on stage was the Party Machine featuring Ross Hannaford, Ross Wilson and Mike Rudd, followed by the highlight for the outer urban 'heavy', 'progressive' set, Lobby Loyde's Wild Cherries. What with mostly mod girls and sharpie boys, 20-minute jams, and throwing-up, I knew this was 'happening'. I might have been the only brave hippie there, but this really was 'the scene'. And I was in it. Of course, I couldn't keep my mouth shut and once the stories of my 'wild' weekend in Ringwood reached back to the power centre of the Academy, that was the end of weekends away. I'd been let off the leash to be 'a witness' in the big smoke, but had been trashed by it. As it turned out, I didn't need another Piccadilly's experience; one was sufficient to cast my reputation among my peers as a hippie-druggie. On the sniff of a vomitus handkerchief, I became famous.[10]

Another incident in the Party Machine's life – as described by Hannaford in 1971 – shows the kind of aggression a band might encounter when trying to confront and provoke an audience, rather than merely pander to them. This remains, of course, a working hazard in entertainment:

> A fight we had when we played in this nasty place ... this joint, like Tenth Avenue. There were sharpies and all these nasty little girls. They kept putting

shit on Mike, saying he was dirty; it was stupid, because he's a clean guy. Also my amp, which I used to put on a chair, the whole thing fell over while I was playing and everyone laughed. This made me angry, like I didn't show it, but it was pent up anger. The tune we saved for last, had a long randy solo in it and they were pissing around and rolling on the floor and all that. I was facing my amp and playing guitar, and sort of walking backwards, with my back to the audience, known [sic] there was a mike standing behind me, but making it look accidental-like, when I was walking backward I knocked the mike stand into the audience. You might think that's an aggressive thing to do, but they were nasty people. There was just a little stage and I was standing on the floor. I was really angry and I was bumping people accidentally. I knew they would get in the way. So they bashed me back and at one stage they had me on the ground and were kicking me and stuff. I got up and swung my guitar around. We finished and although I'd started all the trouble they didn't pick on me when we were taking out the gear, they bashed up Mike and Russell. Mike got a really big black eye out of it. Nasty. Yes, that is a highlight I suppose. [11]

The Party Machine leant towards a multimedia approach. 'The days of four musicians walking on stage and merely playing are fast disappearing,' *Go-Set* lectured its readers in early 1968. 'The emphasis now is on the visual side with the sound playing a supporting, and complementing role.'[12] Pip Proud's withering assessment of 1960s prudery is confirmed by the response to the Party Machine's most notorious act, the publication of their 'songbook', which included two sets of lyrics, 'I Don't Think All Your Kids Should Be Virgins' and 'Don't It Make You Sick' ('First I got an axe and I split her in two ...'). The typeset, photocopied 'books' were seized by the Vice Squad and the band was attacked in the tabloid press. 'It sounds so incredibly quaint nowadays', says Rudd.

The Party Machine broke up in April 1969. David Elfick wrote in *Go-Set* that Ross Wilson was moving to Britain to join the well-known Melbourne group Procession:

> This shock decision came just as the group are receiving the recognition they deserve. Last year their songbook caused a sensation but after that died down, their popularity waned ... Lead guitarist Ross Hannaford has decided to return to art school. The two remaining members of the group, Mike Rudd, bass guitarist, and Peter Curtin, drummer, will keep together and form another group. They will be joined by David Skewes (ex Mantra) who will be on a Hammond organ ...[13]

This last assemblage was to be the beginning of Spectrum, who will be discussed in greater detail in chapter 8.

Procession, the band Wilson left the Party Machine and Melbourne to join, has a long and involved history that begins with Brian Peacock, guitarist and singer in New Zealand's biggest mid-60s group, the Librettos, flying into Sydney. It is best told in his words:

> I have a vivid impression of arriving in Sydney at night time and seeing the city from the air, which was mind-boggling. We spent the next year, at least, living in abject poverty in Sydney, keeping up the image in New Zealand. Trying to live this double life of successful pop stars when in reality we were doing second jobs like car washing and so on in Kings Cross. We basically became a backing band, guns for hire in the Sydney leagues clubs. I remember working with Lucky Starr, who was hot on the heels of his 'I've Been Everywhere' hit.
>
> We were pretty amazed about the industry built up around the leagues clubs of NSW and Queensland. We were in Sydney, so we could earn really good money in the leagues clubs, but we were also playing the rock venues of the time, from Surf City at Kings Cross down to tiny little bars like Suzie Wong's, which a lot of the pop groups of the time were working. The money was really poor, the conditions were really poor. But we loved it, money was really just a means to an end in those days, and the Australian industry was pretty grass roots, there was no infrastructure for popular music at that time.
>
> The Librettos were lucky enough to get into some of the Normie Rowe tours, and they went on forever, they'd be three or four months long, typically, he'd do one-nighters in every town throughout the outback. Apart from the major cities, you'd do the Dubbos, Waggas, it was a never-ending slog from one end of the country to the other. We thrived on it. We thought it was great. We were like the opening act on a bill of twenty artists – it seemed like twenty – the Sunshine Review, all the artists that worked on the same label Normie was released through.

Normie Rowe was the biggest star of his kind in Australia in the mid 1960s. He had been discovered by Ivan Dayman; Dayman introduced him to one-time *Young Modern* songwriting competition winner Pat Aulton, who would become his producer.[14] Handsome, with a fine voice and a jovial approach, many of Rowe's song choices at this time – like those of so many of his peers – now seem stodgy and unimaginative. He certainly got the breaks, even starring in a film made in New Zealand called *Don't Let it Get to You*.[15] One early band who backed Rowe was the King Bees, which also featured Joe Camilleri.[16] Rowe soon created his own permanent outfit, the Playboys.

Dayman managed both Rowe and Marcie Jones, a singer who featured heavily on Dayman's *Go!! Show* and played at many of his suburban dances. Rowe and Jones became romantically involved, and Dayman dealt with the situation by booking them tours on opposite sides of the country.[17] Later, when Rowe was in the UK, Dayman persuaded his manager there, David Joseph, to withhold Jones's letters to Rowe, so as to damage their relationship.[18]

Peacock continues:

> Ivan Dayman was the promoter. He was based in Brisbane but Sunshine was a Festival Records imprint so it was all run out of Sydney. Pat Aulton was the main producer. It was like a mini-Motown set-up, we were like the house band for a lot of recordings.
>
> Pat Aulton liked us as musicians, and started using us doing backing tracks for some of the artists on Sunshine. There was Peter Doyle, Marcie Jones, there was a whole lot . . . Mike Furber, though he had a band called the Bowery Boys. I can't remember which ones we played on and which ones we toured with. We used to back some of those artists live on Ivan Dayman's shows. I think the link with Sunshine came out of us working for Ivan at his clubs. He had what were called sound lounges all around the country.
>
> They were known as sound lounges, which I think probably originally started with recorded music [being] played in them, but increasingly they had live acts as he built up his roster of artists, and we were probably one of the main ones, because we would go anywhere and do anything in our eagerness to work. Ivan used to take full advantage of it! But we were willing participants.
>
> It was really very ad hoc. For instance, he had a venue up in Brisbane called Cloudlands Ballroom, which was this beautiful old ballroom up on top of a hill, legendary. It actually had some accommodation in the basement below it, and we used to live there when we were up in Brisbane. We played these big shows in the ballroom, and then we'd go down to our little dive of an apartment down below! That used to be our base in Queensland, and Ivan would wander in some day and say 'I want you to do Toowoomba, then Sydney, then Melbourne', he'd give us some folded bills, and he'd say – he had this saying we always used to send up – 'Take the Valiant, father'. He had this old station wagon; we used to throw all our equipment in the back of it, three amps and a drumkit, and we'd fit in the back of a Valiant station wagon and drive from Brisbane to Melbourne in one hit, without thinking anything of it. We'd do a week in Melbourne at one of his venues, then up to Sydney to one of his clubs there and you'd play there the whole week. You'd do these really long sets, starting about eight or nine till three in the morning. So it was a great experience for a bunch of young kids.
>
> We had a radio hit here in Australia – that song 'Rescue Me' by Fontella Bass, which we'd been playing for years in New Zealand. During that era the nightclub scene in Sydney was really big, the real true traditional Vegas-style nightclubs, and I remember getting somehow into Chequers free to see Shirley Bassey. This was the mid 60s, and this was the kind of manager we had . . . old-school show business, someone like Shirley Bassey was seen as the epitome of show business. Those things were still an influence on us even though we were taking

a completely different path musically. It was still that mixture of putting on a show, a consciousness of that. Then we graduated up the ladder in the Sunshine thing, we became more important, and we got onto the big Normie Rowe tours. That was luxury for us, we were touring in a proper coach, the artists were in a coach, staying in motels, instead of scrabbling round in people's apartments and on couches.

The Librettos occasionally achieved broad exposure, for example when they supported the Seekers' second major Australian tour in 1966.[19] This may have been where Peacock first made the connections that would result in his becoming road manager and occasional songwriter for the New Seekers in the early 70s. In the mid 60s, however, the Librettos' lifestyle was still hand-to-mouth.

We'd go back every six months or so to do a tour of New Zealand to restock the coffers. We were living a pretty tough life at the time, eating bread and jam, all sharing one flat in Kings Cross. It was around the time of Max Merritt and the Meteors, and Dinah Lee was doing pretty well around here, and the Invaders – they were the New Zealand acts who were over here trying to break into the Australian scene. So that led on to the Normie Rowe tours, then eventually Normie's management being taken over by David Joseph, who was a television producer from Melbourne. We were asked to join Normie's backing group, myself and another guy from the Librettos. By that stage the Librettos got pretty close to the end of their path, a couple of the members had left and we'd replaced them, then we went from being a quartet to being a trio. So the two of us who were original members of the Librettos got asked to join Normie's band, and that meant our chance to get to England so we decided to do it.

David Joseph had lined up a record deal for Normie with Polydor in the UK so we thought it was well worth while taking up the offer. But it was a couple of the members of Normie's old Playboys and us, it was never really a great matching up because we were worlds apart . . . we had no ties really to Australia, whereas they wanted to get back to their girlfriends, back to Melbourne.

It was a very interesting time to be in London, we got to see some great artists because of the link with Polydor. Polydor UK distributed the Stax-Volt label amongst others, and we were doing a lot of demos and rehearsal work in the Polydor studios right in the middle of London and as a result of that when the Stax-Volt tour came through the UK, Otis Redding, Sam and Dave, Eddie Floyd, Booker T and the MGs, all those artists, they kicked off the tour with a week's rehearsals at the Polydor studios in London, So I got to sit in on the rehearsals with those guys for a week. Experiences you'd never dream of – Booker T and the MGs, just incredible! Polydor also had the Who, so I used to bump into Keith Moon all the time going up in the lift, I remember standing side-stage at the Hammersmith Odeon . . . the artists we saw in those years!

Joseph's schemes for Normie Rowe's international success fell in a heap when Rowe was called up for national service in September 1967; the tide of public opinion had not yet turned regarding the Vietnam war, as it soon would, and the decision was made that Rowe should serve. Glenn A. Baker postulates that this was a government public relations exercise, and the fact that Rowe was singled out was a secret even to the pop star himself.[20] Rowe's best singles came late in his pop career, with Peacock's irresistible 'Penelope' (1968) and Johnny Young's remarkable 'Hello' (1970). Ronnie Burns's 1970 hit 'Smiley' ('Off to the Asian war . . . '), writing of which was credited to Johnny Young (though Ian Meldrum claims that both he and John Farrar were involved in the song's creation),[21] was a mournful paean to Rowe. Burns had, presumably, changed his attitude to Rowe by the time he sang 'Smiley'; in early 1968 he had been quoted musing cruelly about his rival: 'Normie Rowe the singer is . . . a manufactured product of excessive promotion, it works but it doesn't last.'[22]

In Rowe's absence, Joseph and Peacock decided to remake the Playboys (who now had two British members, Trevor Griffin and Mick Rogers) as a new band. Local content regulations, and the launch of a new television channel by air travel magnate Reg Ansett, meant an opportunity for a Saturday morning pop show on which the group – now renamed Procession – could perform regularly. This entailed returning to Australia (Melbourne, this time, where Peacock soon got married and started a family) and a chance to relaunch for the international market:

> David, being the smart guy that he was, had come up with this idea of what he was going to do after the Normie Rowe thing had fallen through, which was to go back to what he knew – TV production – and he'd come up with this concept which he couldn't see missing, in that the Australian channels needed it more than anything else. And that was a 4-hour Saturday morning music show which cost bugger all to produce . . .
>
> It was really shoestring – he had a little office in Fitzroy Street in St Kilda, in the building where [artist] Charles Blackman's studio was, up towards the corner of Grey Street. We were in Armstrong's most of the week doing the backing tracks for the artists and they would record them and then mime to them . . . that gave us enormous freedom in the recording studio to do our own stuff. We used to knock off all the Channel Ten stuff as quick as we could and then we'd use the nights and early mornings to work on our own stuff. Channel Ten were paying for all the studio time, or David's production company, I can't remember which.

Joseph had arranged for a Brisbane pop singer he'd seen supporting Rowe to host the show: the singer was Ross D. Wyllie (it rhymed with 'smiley') and the show *Uptight*; a title which no-one involved seemed to realise was somewhat angsty for a programme of unrehearsed, knockabout pop miming and chat. Wylie was paid a pittance ($60 a week, he later recalled), but his pop career subsequently flourished, as will be seen later in this chapter. He also made an album, *Uptight Party Time*, credited to Ross D. Wyllie and the Uptight Party Team via 'four separate recording sessions and countless cans of Fosters.' A medley of 31 songs (from 'Satisfaction' to 'Flowers in the Rain' to 'You Are My Sunshine'), the LP was 'A Procession Production' and demonstrated yet again the versatility of Peacock's group. David Joseph 'basically saw the two things' – band and TV show – 'working hand in hand', Peacock says:

> He knew we wanted to get back to England as soon as we could, and was encouraging us to get as much writing and demoing done as we could. Which is what we did. We put together a whole lot of demos, and then he flew off to the US and the UK and put together a record deal with Philips in England and Mercury in the US. Those labels were allied — all owned by Philips... Our sole intent was to get back overseas.

The readers of *Go-Set* were worried about an air of 'hype' surrounding Procession. Canberran Paul Culnane – later a music historian of some note and co-founder of the exceptional *Milesago* website – wrote a barbed letter to the magazine in 1968 about Ian Meldrum's overly rapturous review of the group:

> Dear Go-Set.
> I was appalled at the giving away of 'instant fame' to the Procession. Granted I haven't heard 'Anthem', nor experienced what is hailed as 'sensational' by *Go-Set* writers; but aren't Procession getting the easy way out, when we, the actual people who make groups what they are, haven't seen or heard them yet?
> Surely it is up to us to like who we like or don't like without it being pumped into our brains by know-alls like Mr. Meldrum, who is so sure of himself he can pass a judgement without us even having heard of the Procession.[23]

Meldrum's response was that 'A certain Canberra-ite should get his facts right and get with it by joining the Procession.'[24]

Procession's debut album was *Procession Live at Sebastian's*, recorded on 3 April, 1968 – probably before the *Uptight* record, which was issued the same year. It was 'the first stereophonic 'LIVE' performance album ever produced in Australia', proclaimed Anthony Knight's sleevenotes. The album, says Peacock, 'was to show that we were a good live band, because we knew from our time over there that you had to be able to cut it live, not just be a studio band.'

> The idea of making a live album first was part of that plan to get the record deal that we wanted. And to his credit, David pulled it off. We had one of the first major advance record deals signed for an artist that had never left the country... And that enabled us to go, when we did go to England, we rented this grand house in Chester Square which is just behind Buckingham Palace in Chelsea. The house was owned by the British Ambassador to Brazil, Lord Russell, and it was very grand – which I think was partly to meet David's requirements. We all moved in — David and his wife and child, and then the band members. It was a four- or five-storey London townhouse. Grand. The full bit, with the servants' quarters in the basement. So the multi-thousand dollar advance that we got went a long way towards paying for that lifestyle for the first six months or a year.

The group had signed to Mercury, for whom they recorded their self-titled debut studio album; in the US, the album was released on Mercury subsidiary Smash, home to Jerry Lee Lewis, It was produced by Mike Hugg, the drummer from Manfred Mann. Peacock remembers:

> We always thought we were one step away from making it. You always have that hope. And we were doing things, to the best of our knowledge, in the way that we needed to do them. But it just shows that it doesn't matter how much money you spend on something, if it's not in the groove... I don't think we ever really made the right record. I don't blame anyone for it not working. It can be a very random thing.
>
> In some ways it was frustrating... I think part of the problem was that we really allowed ourselves to be moved away from our original intentions, in the effort to get commercial success. In Australia we'd been really pretty progressive. We set the agenda creatively. Then we went to the UK and we fell into being pushed around a lot more by the record company and the requisites of the commercial pop world. So I think we lost a bit of direction.

Peacock and Ross Wilson had no doubt crossed paths before (Rudd remembers the Party Machine appearing on *Uptight* in pyjamas, though this presumably was not the reason the group were temporarily banned from the show). Wilson was, in any case, a well-known figure in Melbourne and Peacock decided he might be Procession's future.

David eventually gave up and brought his family back to Australia. We then went back to our gigging, just being a real rock group in the back of a transit van up and down the M1 and playing wherever we could get a gig. That's when we started reigniting the passion that we'd had before. That led to re-looking at the realities of what the group was. I knew about Ross Wilson's Party Machine, and I was really keen on bringing Ross over to join the band.

I rang him up and told him what we were doing and asked him if he was interested in joining us. I don't think it was too much of a surprise that he leapt at the chance and came over. I think he was feeling, at the time, that he was banging his head against a brick wall, and the idea of getting away and going to London for a while appealed to him.

Wilson's decision meant the end of the Party Machine, says Rudd: 'Automatically. And I don't think we were that injured – we may have had our noses out of joint for a week but we could see it was an opportunity for Ross and then I saw it perhaps as a possible stage of evolution for myself.' Peacock picks up the story:

Ross came over and got married. I'd found this fantastic old country mansion at Reigate, outside London, in Surrey. So when he came over I'd already moved the band into this country estate. That was quite fun in itself. It was a beautiful house, really impeccably furnished with a Steinway grand piano in the drawing room and antique furniture throughout. We had to maintain the pretence that it was a couple – myself and my wife and kids – living there. When in fact we had about ten people living there – band members, roadies, girlfriends. Whenever the agent and the owner used to come around to inspect it, we had to bundle everyone into the transit van and pop down to the local pub while my wife and I went through the charade of showing them through the house.

This house featured in Australian director Philippe Mora's first feature film, *Trouble in Molopolis*, which starred Richard Neville, Germaine Greer and Martin Sharp. Peacock felt himself a part of the Australasian expat scene, and he was where the action was – London:

During that era we were playing clubs in London which were really upmarket discos. Places like Revolution Club. Just on weeknights, it wouldn't start until two in the morning, and you'd play a couple of one-hour sets. The A list of London pop society on any given night would be out in those clubs. You'd have McCartney and Lennon and Eric Clapton and people like that turning up to your gigs. Not because *we* were there, we happened to be *playing* there, but these were the kind of people who were walking around in the clubs at two or three in the morning. It was a whole other world.

> We were basically working to get another record deal. The Philips deal had come to an end. We were out of contract and looking to start over. But the problem was that there was Ross and I and the other half of the band – as it turned out later, it wasn't obvious at the time – was a bit begrudging of the fact that this guy had been parachuted in from Australia and made the lead singer, when we had Mick Rogers, who was a great singer. I had been doing all the lead vocals before that . . . We had a regular weekly spot at the Marquee, which was pretty big-time in those days –we had a Tuesday night residency there with Yes. So we were doing pretty well live, we were certainly no slouches, but it never really gelled properly. It was like a strange mishmash of Ross's songs with the much more pop approach that I had to writing.
>
> But I remember some of his songs that we used to do were more [like] Party Machine and Sons of the Vegetal Mother, like 'Papa's in the Vice Squad' and 'Make Your Stash'.

This last song would later feature on albums by both Spectrum and Daddy Cool.

> That tells you were they were coming from. It was a pretty heavily drug-related culture at the time. Acid was prevalent in London. I think the last thing we did together as a band before Ross came back – and this is the desperation state we'd reached – we did this boat trip from Southampton to New York and back on this little Italian steamer, ferrying American students back from their European vacations and then bringing another load over. It was a pretty interesting trip. But when we got to New York Ross and I were — it really illustrated the split in our band — Ross and I went off to Greenwich Village and looked up all the landmarks that we wanted to see and that's when we discovered macrobiotics . . . when we got back our wives were all astounded when we announced we were only going to be eating brown rice from now on. And we proceeded to do that. But that then led to Sons of the Vegetal Mother and where all that came from.

Not only did Wilson have his macrobiotic philosophy when he returned to Australia, he also had a wife – Pat, who had gone with him to Britain – and a song, 'Eagle Rock', which had come to him in a dream and will be associated with him for ever after. Ross (and Pat) Wilson's next phase is discussed in chapter 9.

CLEVES

Another important trans-Tasman story, this one involving the then-unusual scenario of a woman playing a role as an instrumentalist within a group, was that of the Cleves, who had begun in New Zealand as the Clevedonaires. Unlike Rudd's or Peacock's groups, the Cleves did not make a significant impact on the charts, or even sustain a high media profile, but they were present at a number of significant moments in the history of the period, particularly in the presentation of rock/

pop music in other media. Gaye Harmon, who played in the band with two of her brothers, recalls that the group decided to relocate to Sydney after they had been swept up in media interest in New Zealand regarding a tour to Vietnam for the purpose of entertaining troops there – a tour they pulled out of when they discovered they'd only been given one-way tickets.

> We must have got the travel bug, so with Vietnam a non-starter we settled for going to Australia instead . . . Work had been arranged for us at Cooma in the Snowy Mountains. The day we arrived, we had to play a four-hour set until midnight, then we were told to pack up all our gear and set it up in a nightclub down the road, where we were expected to play until 3 a.m. This was to be a nightly arrangement. Naturally, we weren't too thrilled about it, so we got in touch with our New Zealand agent, Benny Levin, and he got us out of the deal and found alternate work for us as resident band at the Hume Hotel in Yagoona. So we moved to Sydney.
>
> The Hume is now sheltered accommodation, I believe, but it was a great venue in those days. We loved it there. We played to packed houses, fronting under our new, shortened name 'the Cleves' and also backing guest stars like Eden Kane and Dinah Lee. Dinah Lee enjoyed working with us and introduced us to a friend of hers, Bobbie, who was PA to the head of the Cordon Bleu agency, Harry Widmer. It was a great piece of luck, as Harry became our agent and then the work just kept coming.

Harmon recalls that Widmer was key to the group providing music for the soundtrack to Peter Weir's short film *Michael*, part of *Three to Go*, a trilogy exploring individual (fictional) young people's stories. The songs they wrote for the film were released as an EP, *Music from Michael*; they also recorded a scintillating self-titled album that ran between prog and pop. The Cleves were versatile in the extreme: in the early 70s, they recorded a single 'Bonnie, Bonnie, Bonnie – Na, Na, Hey, Kiss Him Goodbye' with Donnie Sutherland, the ex-jockey who had become a DJ and *Go-Set* writer; they also recorded jingles and other sessions. Their story in the 70s will be resumed later in this narrative.

THE TELEVISION'S HUNGRY

In subsequent chapters, the power and value of the mid-70s television show *Countdown* will be discussed, as will the strange misconception in many music and popular culture histories that *Countdown* was the first 'real' Australian rock program, arriving in what had been a music-television desert. Putting aside the fact that music television is, in most of its incarnations, barely something to celebrate, it should be pointed out – if this chapter hasn't already provided enough evidence – that pop and rock music was very much a part of Australian television by the late 60s. It seems to have been almost de rigueur to give a star his or her own TV show, in fact. Ronnie Burns's hit with 'Smiley' coincided with the announcement of his clip and mime show *Now Sound*.[25] Earlier in the decade, in April 1966, Laurie Allen and Bobby Bright – as Bobby and Laurie – had a number one hit with 'Hitchhiker'. The pair were then given their own show, *It's a Gas*, which first aired in July 1966.[26] The program – its name was later changed to the more compelling *Dig We Must*[27] – featured comedy as well as music.

Another beneficiary of television's embrace of pop was Billy Thorpe, who was briefly discussed in chapter 2 and will feature heavily in chapter 9. In 1965 he had split the original Aztecs and put together a new line-up:

> Firstly I got Johnny Dick and Teddy Toi from [Max Merritt and] the Meteors... They were pissed off with the lack of recognition they were getting, I guess, so they decided to join me. Also a band from Western Australia called Ray Hoff and the Offbeats were playing in Sydney at the time. So I got the two guitar players from there. Firstly Mike Downs and then Col Risby.[28]

Thorpe's live television show, *It's All Happening*, was from all reports a vibrant and sensational program featuring not only local acts like the Easybeats but also international visitors such as Neil Sedaka. A few years later, Thorpe griped to *Planet*'s Lee Dillow that the show's demise was caused by network politics:

> BT: Political scenes by Channel 7 down here which I'd dig you to print.
> LD: How do you mean political?
> BT: Well they had a teen show of their own in mind with Ian Turpie and all those cats. So if Sydney wouldn't take that, they wouldn't take ours. So that was that. An incredible disillusionment for us. Our ratings were so good.[29]

The show in question was presumably *The Go!! Show*, which was hosted first by Ian Turpie and then by Johnny Young. The following year, Thorpe acted as fill-in host for *The Go!! Show* while Young was overseas, and told his audience he was going to drop acid on air. The Minister for Health – via talkback host Mike Walsh – informed Thorpe that he would go to jail if he did. The threat no doubt ruffled feathers and delighted viewers, but it appears Thorpe did not go ahead with it.[30]

THE WAY THEY PLAYED

In 1966 journalist Maggie Makeig travelled to Hobart with the ambition of finding out how the teenagers of that city were catered for musically. She visited Beachcomber, 'a big teenage dance centre in Hobart' – and saw the bands the Falcons, the Silhouettes, the Avantis: 'Some were good, some were rank amateurs'. She also listed other bands, such as Chaos + Co ('a basically English group'), the Kravats, the Trolls, the Bitter Lemons, and the Beat Preachers. There were two music shows on local TV, *Saturday Stomp* and *Saturday Party*.[31]

Perth-born songwriter Brian Cadd had recently left Hobart – where he was playing in the Planets – for Melbourne, where Ian Meldrum persuaded him it would be a good idea to change his name to Brian Caine (this didn't last).[32] Later in the decade the Van Diemen label issued records by a number of Tasmanian artists, including Clockwork Oringe[33] and Sweaty Betty.[34]

Each Australian city had its particular scene and style, as well (of course) as its rip-offs and frauds. In 1970, the poet Andrew Jach published a piece in the small press magazine *Holocaust* called 'Brisbane your balls have burnt off'. In it he replicates the visceral and to his mind hollow world of Brisbane nightlife, where one might find:

> some vain semblance of enjoyment from the
> vast array of In places, such as the red orb
> > the reD ORB
> > the rED ORB
> > the RED ORB
> > thE RED ORB
> > tHE reD ORB
> > THE RED ORB
> > and also
> > the municipal library
> OPEN MONDAY TO FRIDAY TILL TEN
> > > > can be obtained[35]

Jim Keays writes convincingly about the late-60s live music circuit in his memoir *His Master's Voice*, describing Brisbane as 'run by [a] cartel',[36] Ivan Dayman operating a bus with the Sunshine logo on its side, in which he would 'ferry artists up and down the vast Queensland coast.'[37] Brisbane was also oppressive, in Lobby Loyde's memory: 'You used to get raided for having long hair, playing loud music, walking sideways and looking bad on a Sunday afternoon.'[38] Brisbane had its own TV pop show, *Countdown*; in October 1967, Dayman's Sunshine label issued a various artists album called *T.V.'s "Countdown"*, which preceded *Uptight Party Time* by a year. The *Countdown* album featured tracks from future *Uptight* compère Ross D. Wyllie.[39]

Any touring band would have to play Sydney, but groups from outside were often ambivalent, even apprehensive, of the venues it offered. 'Sydney was different,' according to Keays, who was from Adelaide but lived in Melbourne, the heart of music in Australia at this time: 'The criminal element ran the strip clubs, the nightclubs and most other venues.'[40] *Go-Set's* publisher Philip Frazer saw Sydney as 'old school': 'In Sydney the venues tended to be controlled by old time entrepreneurs and record companies.'[41]

THE SNAP AND CRACKLE OF POP

Twice in two years, Sydney's august *Bulletin* went out to local clubs to try and whip itself into a state of shock at the goings-on of contemporary youth. In 1968 it exposed the main hives:

> In Sydney, at lunch-time, the Op Pop, a cavernous blue-black cellar in Castlereagh Street, with mirrors, harsh bands, and teenagers in what appear to be cast-offs lurking in every corner, is packed solid, and on Saturday nights 600 or more will be found slumped on the steps or milling round the dance floor. North Sydney's sober purlieus have been enlivened of late by Here, a brash discotheque that is open until well past midnight; the Manly Pacific Hotel is crammed on Saturdays for the Questions, and the P.A. Club at Prince Alfred Hospital jumps to the Castaways group; along the North Shore a string of wine bars and discotheques

rivals the more urban attractions of the Hawaiian Eye, the Whisky a Go Go, the Vibes, and Beethoven's. None of these places can match the Melbourne discotheques, headed by Sebastian's and Bertie's, which have superb bands and facilities and feature the liveliest singers in the country.[42]

In 1970, the *Bulletin* returned to the Whisky a Go Go, which it declared to be Sydney's most successful disco, 'a fitting place for the rhythmic pulsations to be shared in the no-touch, do-your-own-thing that has become the disco job pattern.' Jonathan's, an old cinema on Broadway (a road south of the city centre which turns into George Street, central Sydney's main thoroughfare) with silver walls, 'plush lounges, shaped Perspex lighting and a sound system of infinite complexity.' Its 'ten-man resident group, the Complex, threw away its Sergio Mendes bag and delved deep into the eclectic cornucopia of the "new" rock. The ties and jackets rule was relaxed.' Other discos, at this time, were Stagecoach, Caesar's Palace (which Keays describes as 'a seedy late-night dive in the heart of downtown Sydney.'[43] It was the venue where Chain recorded their debut album, *Chain Live*[44]), and Caesar's In Place.[45] The Masters Apprentices were also welcomed at Ward Austin's Jungle 'and countless suburban dances from Hunters Hill to St Ives and Clovelly.'[46]

For Keays, Melbourne similarly presented 'an endless procession of suburban dances. These were held in Mechanic's Institute Halls, Masonic Halls, Scout halls, town halls – in fact any hall that would allow rock 'n' roll music.'[47] Halls would take on temporary names as venues: Broadmeadows Town Hall was the 'Palace'[48] and later the White Elephant and (as mentioned earlier) Beaumaris Civic Centre was 'Stonehenge'. Keays later adds Lion's Clubs to the list of potential venues.[49] The large number of venues around the city and its hinterland meant there was plenty of work for bands; however, it also meant that bands had to travel widely – and fast – between shows:

> We would do three gigs a night most Fridays and Saturdays no matter what state we were in – stoned or Queensland ... It was a mad dash to make them all. Each dance featured three bands and there was no margin for error.[50]

Mike Rudd, who saw enough of this life in his own professional career in the Party Machine and others, can also stand back and critique the practice:

> When I first went as Joe Public to Sebastian's and saw the Loved Ones, I was just knocked out. I thought they were the best thing I'd ever seen. But they'd do the same thing – they'd do half an hour at Sebastian's, and then off they went, and they'd do maybe two or three spots a night. And that actually killed that band. They cite that as the reason, because they had half an hour's worth of material, that's all they did.

The groups' equipment was, by necessity, relatively portable, according to Rudd:

> They'd be using their own equipment, but it'd be tiny. It'd be very similar to what bands are doing today, mostly, which is carrying a little portable amp. The PAs were even portable, but the PAs would be there because they'd be act one or two or three on the night, and they wouldn't mic anything up. Those were the days! . . . I actually enjoyed those days. Soundwise it was at a reasonable level, you couldn't get above a hundred watts anywhere, doing anything, so audiences and musicians weren't being deafened as a matter of course.
>
> Well the Thumpin' Tum was a tiny place, Sebastian's was tiny, the Catcher was reasonably large and they probably had a slightly bigger PA than most places, but the technology just wasn't there, you didn't have three-way or four-way PAs, it was just column speakers – that was it, that was as dangerous as it got.

THE LOVED ONES AND 'THE LOVED ONE'

The late 1960s – hippiedom, psychedelia and associated elements – remain iconic and fascinating to many members of the generation which experienced them first-hand and many who have come to them since then. The era has, not surprisingly, been the focus of numerous books and films, both fiction and factual. Iain McIntyre's *Tomorrow Is Today* is a particularly valuable and in-depth overview of Australian pop in its wider social context between 1966 and 1970, and is strongly recommended for anyone with a particular interest in that scene. This chapter strives to avoid replicating material from that book, but it is so good that some duplications cannot be avoided. McIntyre's praise for the Loved Ones – shared by Mike Rudd, whose late-70s band, Instant Replay, did a version of the Loved Ones' 'Everlovin' Man'[51] – as an undeniably original and irresistible Australian group of the 60s – is one of these.

The Red Onions Jazz Band was briefly discussed in chapter 2 as an example, perhaps, of a jazz collective that walked and talked like a pop group, with its Dadaist humour and unique personality. In October 1965, with their second album, *Wild Red Onions*, still unreleased, three members of the group – Gerry Humphrys, Kim Lynch, and the orchestrator of the coup, relative newcomer Ian Clyne[52] – went into the studio with former Wild Cherries guitarist Rob Lovett for what was ostensibly another Red Onions recording session.[53] To the surprise of their label, W&G, they emerged as the Loved Ones, with a new sound and a new song – 'The Loved One'. 'I suddenly found that to me, quite realistically, my roots were in blues,' Humphrys told Nigel Buesst, 'so I rapidly learnt to play the harmonica . . . it was R'n'B with baroque classical influences I find it very hard to put a tag on.'[54] 'The Loved One', patched together in the studio and a perfect example of seemingly artless high complexity in music, was perfect. Humphrys included handclaps in the verse because he felt that without them 'people are going to get lost'.[55]

The unusual and non-intuitive nature of the Loved Ones' material is best demonstrated by Humphrys' obvious inability to mime to it during the group's many television appearances: he anticipates exultations that aren't there and consistently mouths the wrong words.[56] Yet it's clear that Humphrys was the heart and soul of the group, which peaked quickly and died within two years, the victim of its own inexperience and overwork. Clyne had been sacked early in the piece, for being too organised and ambitious, while W&G's unwillingness to invest in the band, along with the various demands of fame and fortune, proved to be a drag on the group's creativity, to name but three bummers. In Nigel Buesst's 2000 film about Humphrys, Lynch complains of having 'no time to refresh or write new material, half-hour spots . . . the band was stagnating, frankly.'[57]

> Many a time with the Loved Ones, the original inspiration just sounded so much better. That's why, in the end, we used to compose in the studio. That's the way I find I can work, personally, Of course it's a bit of a bind for the musos, because they like to be a little more secure.[58]

'The Loved Ones was basically a revivalist group', Humphrys told *Daily Planet* in 1971. At one stage we had three records in the top ten. Once we had become successful, we were obliged to play only our records. It was all too commercial, and I got out. It took me two years to recover from that incredible scene.[59]

The Loved Ones split in October 1967, though they reformed briefly in early 1968 for a 3XY 'pop happening' where, it was reported, they wore 'clothes designed by up and coming gear designer Helen Hooper' and attended 'a select orgy in her honour.'[60]

Writer Barry Dickins met Humphrys in 1969, by which time he was working as a set designer for TV's Channel 7. He remembered him as 'a man who made me laugh as soon as I looked at him . . . a Cockney bloke with enormous black eyes and remarkable long black hair and dimples. Gerry Humphreys [sic] and I started working immediately, making a papier maché walnut some 70 feet in length. It was wanted urgently for the Channel Seven Ballet. The stroppy, overweight girls had to emerge from this prop for a scene in *The Nutcracker Suite.*' Dickins says Humphries had a cooker and a bar fridge inside the walnut and invited women into it for sexual activities.[61] This was only part of Humphrys' hijinks:

> One sunny June day outside the loading bay, Gerry found an old had-it wooden recorder that some musician had turfed in the drain. He patiently repaired it with wire and sticky tape and played jazz on it. Immediately. 'Far out, man!' he said to me, and to my surprise he disrobed and got on the top of the rubbish cart and we wheeled him nude into the workshop.[62]

This story is both wonderful and somehow terrible, because it seems to mark the way in which Humphrys was exchanging his creative role for that of a mere showman. As we will see in chapter 8, he remained a figure in early 70s Melbourne before returning to Britain, more or less permanently, in 1977.

TWO POP EXPOSÉS

There were pop shows, and there were also shows *about* pop on television. At least two one-off productions from the mid to late 60s enlighten us about this phenomenon in great detail, and set the agenda for this chapter with their rapid montages of exotic cynicism and flamboyant glibness. One is the 1967 television pilot *Approximately Panther*, directed by Tony L. Lamb. It provides a perfect picture of mid-60s Australia and where it positioned itself as part of the world, and more particularly a portrait of Melbourne, 'the Mecca of Australian music' at this time according to Jim Keays.[63] *Approximately Panther* was founded on the vibe generated by the Melbourne-based music magazine *Go-Set*, though it pushed a little further than the 'teens and twenties paper' (of which more later). The program begins with an over-the-top montage of soldiers, people farewelling an ocean liner, a headline trumpeting 'girl in space'; it then switches to footage of young people, Gerry Humphrys, the Rolling Stones, the edifice of Melbourne's major railway station in Flinders Street, a violin on a chair, a guitar in a tree, an old car, a new car, a ticking clock, people in a club, and a pinball machine. The show's host is typing at a table in a small room with books in the background. 'I'm Douglas Panther,' he announces, '*Go-Set's* drunken reporter.'

The show juggles the probably impossible task of delivering an exposé of 1960s youth while at the same time catering to the same youth. Lamb also flags various marketing possibilities for an *Approximately Panther* TV series, as Panther asks about the spending power of an eighteen-year-old and explores possibilities of cars, fashion and guitars. One of the strangest elements of the film is the inclusion of the Beatles' clip for 'Penny Lane' with occasional and seemingly random bursts of teenage screaming on the soundtrack – another example of Australian ambivalence towards international pop success.

We see Normie Rowe going to London, and the girls who saw him off at Essendon Airport; Panther tells the viewer that Melbourne has become Australia's 'teen mecca', an excuse to segue into the Loved Ones' 'Everlovin' Man' being played by a 3AK DJ hamming it up in the studio and a montage of DJ faces with a monkey's face thrown in. Panther is next seen atop a rubbish tip writing his genius work on a portable typewriter. The Loved Ones' filmclip for 'The Loved One' follows, blended into footage of a DJ playing it on the radio and Gerry Humphrys' excruciatingly poor miming covered up slightly by tree foliage in front of his face. We're then given a brief tour of Melbourne 'discotheques' (pronounced 'discotheek' on the soundtrack), including the Garrison and the Thumpin' Tum. The group Running Jumping Standing Still (with Andy Anderson, once of the

Missing Links) is seen, while an unidentified person claims mysteriously on the soundtrack that 'you can pick up girls, there's always girls there . . . there are even some of them that are licensed.' The film ends with footage of people at a party in a Victorian-era house drinking from the bottle and dancing to a stop-start pop song. Tellingly, if you want to see all this frenzied decadence as some kind of furious romp raging against the Vietnam war and the last flickering moments of innocent delight, a candle is burning down.

The Snap and Crackle of Pop was an exposé in Sydney TV station ATN-7's documentary series *Seven Days*. Broadcast in June 1968, it's an hour-long report that reveals the kinds of resistance pop musicians faced in the 60s. *Seven Days* attacks on a number of fronts, shocked at Lobby Loyde's Wild Cherries and their preference for improvisation, shocked at Max Merritt and the Meteors' hair, shocked at how easy it is to film a woman's sequined underpants when she is dancing and your camera is on the floor. It's the usual mixture of prurience, squeamishness and jealousy. That said, it provides a multi-faceted overview of the pop scene at that moment in time, from the far-out to the very staid, and to that extent it seems truthful.

A narrative thread that runs throughout the program is the story of a group, the Climax 5, who are temporarily under the wing of Pat Aulton, now transformed from the folk songwriter of early-60s Adelaide into a producer of quick and snappy 45s for Festival. Aulton is himself reasonably dismissive, if not of the Climax 5 themselves, at least of the pop process and his own 'ears' when it comes to picking a hit. The progress of the song is followed from two of the group's members – Nick and Mick – playing it to both Aulton and Jack Arthur at Leeds Music. 'We use a group sound for the teenyboppers . . . it's not raucous and noisy, it's just a happy little song,' says Aulton.

The Climax 5's record 'is one of the 200-odd records released in Australia last month', our host, writer-director Lance Peters, tells us as he stands, looking slightly appalled, in Edels record shop. The Climax Five are just another of those pop groups with 'kidney- or heart- or pelvis-shaped guitars . . . occasionally one of the members is a girl . . . she's the one with the short hair.' The groups are dressed by 'that well-known tailor, St Vincent de Paul' (a second-hand shop) and the music is 'made up of 90 percent exploitation and 10 percent hallucination.' The groups, Peters persists, are 'motivated by such components as sexual frustration, parental neglect, war, despair and occasionally even talent.'

'Individualism is out, collectivism is in', according to Peters, and we see some brief footage of the appropriately named group Unknown Blues. The process, we are told, is to 'buy a guitar, learn a few chords, write a few songs, and then try them out on a music publisher.' In this scene, like many in the film, the camera performs a loving close-up on every participant's cigarette.

Flash to the Executives, at this stage a highly successful club group, and more loving camera work on their cigarettes. One year previously, we are told, an industrial designer named Harry Widmer made a bet he could promote a new group (an 'unknown industrial product', *The Bulletin* suggested),[64] and the fresh-faced youngsters we see before us are currently enjoying the outcome of this boast. 'Every group that's got a top record, we copy it,' claims one band member. The Executives' philosophy seems to be: 'Doing so much material, you must eventually end up with material that's your own'. The group toured the US in 1968.[65] Ten years later former Executive Ray Burton would confess that he didn't really like the rest of the band 'as people'. But, he noted, 'it was a ticket to America, after all.'[66] The song 'My Aim Is to Please You' is the Executives' greatest pop moment; much later, a version of the group would contribute the lively theme song to the soap opera *The Young Doctors*. Burton's songwriting work is discussed in chapter 8.

The Snap and Crackle of Pop shows us the Executives playing at Cronulla Surf Club in Sydney's south, a venue run by their manager. A teenage dance, we are informed, brings them $150 a night; a one-night club date nets $200 and a school function $80. So the group make between $80 and $1800 a week, split – after deducting costs – between performers, manager and road manager. 'It's no bonanza', we are told, 'and popularity is a fickle mistress.'

The film offers a midway proposition between the Climax 5 and the ultra-commercial Executives in the form of Doug Parkinson and the Questions, whose loud amps – 'almost to distortion level' – are clearly an issue for Peters. 'You've got to have volume and punch and drive and a feel,' comments Parkinson, 'and transmit it to the audience.' Another member of the Questions – who were, at this time, on the very brink of changing the name of their group to Doug Parkinson In Focus, following a court case over their name – suggests that 'at the rate we're going, about 90 percent of the pop musicians today are going to be deaf in five years, either from the band they're playing in or the in-between discotheque music'. There were, plainly, new issues in the style and power of pop music.

Parkinson and the Questions had previously existed separately from one another. Parkinson's first group had been Strings and Things, who rose to prominence in 1964 at the Narrabeen Antler, on Sydney's northern beaches. He then went on to the A Sound, a high school band featuring the siblings Helen and Syd Barnes on bass and guitar; this group recorded a single for Festival in 1966.[67] Parkinson was a cadet reporter with the *Daily Telegraph* at the time. Meanwhile the Questions, who included Duncan Maguire and Billy Green, were playing at the Caropus Room at another northern Sydney suburb, Manly; they had recorded an instrumental album with the imaginative title *What Is a Question*.

The national 'Battle of the Sounds' competition, run by the chocolate manufacturer Hoadley's from 1966 to 1972, was hotly contested; Parkinson's group tried three times to win what *Planet's* Lee Dillow called 'Hoadley's Battle of the Rip-offs'. Parkinson recalled: 'Winning on our third attempt [in 1969] was unbelievable. I honestly feel that when the Groop won [in 1967] we were robbed. I know we had no presentation but F . . . ! Surely it's music.' Parkinson and In Focus, wearing 'stunning black and red uniforms', eventually won in competition with the Valentines, Aesop's Fables (from Sydney), the Brisbane Avengers, and Chain.[68] As well as scoring a national hit with a raucous version of the Beatles' recent album track 'Dear Prudence', they received a 'very exciting film festival award for our Coke commercial.'[69] A greatly superior record to 'Dear Prudence' was its follow-up, the Billy Green original composition 'Without You'. In 1971, Parkinson reflected bitterly on the dictates of the market: 'We now observe the graph as it descends. We put "Hair" on the flip side and it was about here that the crack started to widen. We were bowing to pressure, trying to be popular at the expense of our music.'[70]

The group produced a number of remarkable, edgy and creative singles, mostly written by Green. The band's line-up was, unfortunately, erratic. Green, who had threatened to leave the band during its Questions period to become a producer,[71] and who later did leave to form another, short-lived group called Rush, says now:

> In Focus really split up because of Duncan's inability 'to put up with Johnny Dick's sense of groove'. That was it really. Those two were always fighting. I was the glue, the PR person to put them back together again, magically. Sometimes, backstage, Duncan would be making Johnny Dick feel like a heel, right before going on stage. I would jump in there and do a quick repair job so we could do a good show.
>
> Duncan could be a bastard sometimes . . . hard to believe. Eventually, and inevitably, Johnny quit! He couldn't stand it anymore. That's when Doug and Johnny split to England . . .

The story of the band they formed with Vince Melouney, Fanny Adams, is told in chapter 8.

The Snap and Crackle of Pop also covers Melbourne group the Wild Cherries, and its report on this outfit opens a new can of worms: the issue of improvisation and its impact on a professional performance. The Wild Cherries – seen here in their second incarnation featuring Lobby Loyde, who had recently defected from Brisbane-Melbourne group the Purple Hearts – claim in the show that they improvise a lot and play more for themselves than the audience. Author and journalist Craig McGregor, who appears in the film in a boxing ring with, amongst others, Sven Libaek and DJ Bob Rogers, claims to have heard the Wild Cherries many times and opines that 'they're a very good pop group indeed,' adding that – contrary to what

Purple Hearts, ca. 1965

many viewers may have believed – 'you can improvise on an electric guitar just as a jazz musician can improvise on the sax.'

Loyde had first played onstage at the age 17 at Cloudland. As he told Iain McIntyre, his first band was the Devil's Disciples in 1963 in his native town of Brisbane. As mentioned, his friends and competitors in local talent shows back then were the Bee Gees ('Gibby and the two little dribblers')[72] and Billy Thorpe. Late in life, Loyde remembered Brisbane – particularly its Blues Club – as being as progressive as Melbourne in the early to mid 60s, possibly more so. His Purple Hearts bandmate Mick Hadley remembers 'one venue, the Primitif', but also enough shows in halls and ad hoc spaces to make it 'pretty vibrant, really.'[73]

The Purple Hearts were a nationwide sensation; *Everybody's* appears to have considered them bad boys, running a photograph of them captioned: 'Normally they are not to be found on demolished building sites, but we took them to one anyway, because we felt the bricks and steel and mortar suited their uncompromising attitude to blues, and their clunky gear.'[74]

Loyde claims in *The Snap and Crackle* that the Wild Cherries' set is 'almost totally' improvised, because the alternative is 'boring, bores the people, bores us.' He went on to show his ongoing interest, which he would continue to display in different ways through the 1980s and his SCAM management organization, in the contrasts between art and profit:

> If you're going to play the same old stale thing the same way every night you get pretty sick of it, especially when you're lazy like us and you don't learn that many new songs... Even the most successful pop groups, that claim they make a fortune, don't. There's no money in this country. If you got a number one record you'd be lucky to get $600 out of it, even if you sold 50,000 copies.

From the boxing ring, Libaek commends Max Merritt and the Meteors, in part for their jazz inflections: band members Stewie Speer and Bob Birtles (not to be confused with Beeb Birtles, who hit it big in the 70s with the Little River Band) both have a jazz background. The *Snap and Crackle* take on Merritt and the Meteors is that they're the 'oldest pop group in Sydney,' with an average age of 33; Speer was forty at the time.[75] It is unclear when this interview snippet was filmed but it seems likely to have been before a major car accident near Bunyip, east of Melbourne, in June 1967, during which Merritt lost an eye, Speer suffered damage to his hands and had his legs crushed (Merritt joked: 'Stewie had what they called scrambled legs'), and Birtles acquired a permanent limp. Only bassist Yuk Harrison was relatively unscathed.[76] The group continued valiantly, and were even given the prize, in 1969, of a four-part ABC-TV concert series, just before they relocated to Britain, identified by Merritt as 'an easy place to lose bread'.[77]

The program goes on to state that 'the pop world today is a mini-matriarchal society' – by dint of the young girls who, as consumers, ostensibly control it. When it comes to girl singers – Lynne Randell and Cheryl Gray (later known as Samantha Sang) are held up as examples) – we are told that they are 'small, cute and plain'.

The Snap and Crackle then profiles Johnny Farnham, shown being interviewed on the new northern NSW television station ECN8 while out touring with the still ubiquitous Col Joye. Farnham speaks in quotable quotes that acknowledge both the extremely surreal lot of the pop star and his gratitude at being so loved:

> Last night we played Tamworth and I got the sleeve of my shirt ripped out ... the fans made me and I love every one of them ... I haven't been mobbed very often – I've been in the business just since the record's come out – but I, confidentially, love it ... I was a plumber for two years before I was a singer – even now I don't have the nerve to go up to a girl and ask her to dance with me.

We see Farnham and a scratch band rollicking through 'the record' in question, 'Sadie (The Cleaning Lady)' which, of all the records and songs dismissed as wanting in this book, is probably the worst: it is shallow, smarmy and snide, a sub-George Formby music hall dud without even a redeeming double entendre. A novelty song poking fun at a woman who works in a dreary and unpleasant job, it rather undermines the 'matriarchal society' tag, though in his live rendition Farnham does at least veer away from the record to declare 'I love you though you'll always be a cleaning lady' (!).

Farnham has been smoking since he was five;[78] he migrated to Australia with his family at the age of ten. He was at school when he joined the Mavericks, and a plumber's apprentice when his second band, Strings Unlimited, began playing.[79] A show of theirs in country Victoria got them attention from accountant-turned-manager Daryl Sambell, while an EP they recorded got them noticed by an advertising executive hoping to find a distinctive voice for a television advertisement for Trans-Australian Airlines. In both cases, the attention was really directed at Farnham, who went solo in 1967 and released 'Sadie' towards the end of that year. The current affairs program *4 Corners* devoted a programme to showing – much like *The Snap and Crackle*'s coverage of the Climax 5 – 'how a record company promotes an unknown.'[80] This, along with manufactured outrage from DJ Stan Rofe, who insisted he hated the single,[81] helped 'Sadie' become the biggest selling Australian record of 1968.

Daryl Sambell, who would also manage the Masters Apprentices and others, is described by Jim Keays as 'overtly gay . . . he flitted around like Nureyev and was quintessentially high camp.'[82] Sambell has also been described as 'Rasputin',[83] while inside the industry (and, as mentioned, in Marty Rhone's 'So You Want To Be a Pop Singer') Sambell was known as 'Sadie'. Farnham was chosen to sing 'Sadie', and the use of the tag to refer to Sambell was surely as a result of the song being a hit, but Sambell *was* reputed to personally launder Farnham's clothes.[84] Keays claims that his fellow Masters Apprentice Glenn Wheatley's fictionalised memoir, *Who the Hell is Judy in Sydney*, would never 'pass the lawsuit test . . . The Daryl Sambell-Johnny Farnham stories alone would have tipped the bucket, and half the industry would have come down like a ton of bricks.'[85] The fact that Wheatley went on to manage Farnham from the late 70s onwards, and is credited with reinventing his career, only adds intrigue to this statement.

After 'Sadie', Farnham had a string of hits including the absurd 'Jamie', written by Hans Poulsen; a version of 'Raindrops Keep Falling on My Head', the possibly humorously titled 'Looking through a Tear' and the marvellous Vanda and Young composition 'Things to Do'. Peter Dawkins, who will feature in future chapters, produced *JP Farnham Sings* in July 1975, the singer's last album for five years[86] and the final element in the first stage of his career, during which he was overworked and the strategy behind his management seemed primarily one of exploitation.

Wherever there's a pop group, Lance Peters informs us in *The Snap and Crackle of Pop*, there's a manager. Harry Widmer, Carol West (Lynne Randell's manager), and Peter Conyngham ('who's almost as young as all the groups he manages') are all mentioned. Conyngham is seen on screen railing against unethical practices in the industry; similarly, West critiques 'little agents starting up that don't even have a hundred dollars to back themselves.'

A record which retails for a dollar, we are told, will earn the artist four or five cents; top-forty lists are compiled by phoning record stores, but they are not done very comprehensively. Pop, it would seem, 'floats on a sea of promotions'. A group of DJs from Sydney's 2UW, including Ward Austin and Baby John Burgess, are shown discussing – and dismissing – numerous records. 'Climax 5,' exclaims one contemptuously. 'What a name to have!' Another ponders:

> Why do they release these records with this simple little backing . . . and then say, 'Oh you don't play Australian records' – You can't play this in competition with what the Town Criers come up with in Melbourne, which is a good production sound [because] they've spent money on it.

The Climax 5 are given the thumbs down, though those present claim – perhaps for the benefit of the television cameras – to be interested in seeing whether the kids 'vote' for it. It is fairly safe to assume they did not.

PRINT MEDIA REPORTING, AND CREATING, THE COUNTERCULTURE

> *Despite, or perhaps because of, Australia's remote and unexciting image, the You Beaut land is compulsively tuned in to the rest of the world, thirstily absorbing the pop products of its culture and society.*—Richard Neville, *Playpower* (1970)[87]

Richard Neville ('an acid munching, jumped up ex-public schoolboy',[88] according to a joking character assassination in *The Living Daylights*, the Australian counterculture newspaper edited by his former colleague on *Oz*, Richard Walsh, in 1973-4) was being disingenuous here – or, more accurately, unusually modest – when he typified Australians as merely 'thirstily *absorbing* . . . pop products'. He was one of the many Australians who had also been busily *producing* such products, in the form of the original Sydney incarnation of *Oz* magazine and more particularly its London-based successor, and through his part in its media fallout. Writing his examination/exhortation of the alternative society, *Playpower* ('a quasi revolutionary document for the contentment of crème caramel–slurping rich kid armchair revolutionaries')[89] in his London domicile, he was pitching his plea for clemency to the Western world, which was yet to sit in judgment (via its representatives drawn from propertied Britons over forty) on London *Oz* for its 'Schoolkids' issue.[90]

Neville had left Walsh to continue publishing the satirical *Oz* in Sydney, and relocated to London:

> The genesis of London *Oz* was due more to the enthusiasm of a Fleet Street newspaper than the determination of its founder. Shortly after arriving in the UK from Australia I was interviewed by the *Evening Standard*. The idea of launching a London *OZ*, at that time barely a passing fancy, somehow ended up a headline: 'Rebel Aussie whizz-kid to publish here.' Telephones began buzzing with eager contributors, printers extended lunch invitations . . . and what was once merely my exhibitionistic impulse to impress a friendly gossip columnist soon gathered its own momentum and hit the streets a few months later with a resounding thud.[91]

Australia had a whirlwind revolutionary 60s like other western nations, in some ways more so, and in the mid 60s individual Australians abroad contributed to – in some cases, led – contemporary debates in the countries where they were living. Readers of the thoughtful Sydney journal *Nation*, for instance, were informed that Germaine Greer was 'the biggest figure on the London Other-Culture scene' alongside Mary Quant and Mick Jagger.[92] Neville's involvement in the international 'scene' also justifiably lent him the status of a counterculture hero. The charge that he was a pornographer (because of 'Schoolkids' *Oz*) or someone merely along for the ride – he certainly entertained the latter possibility – was bolstered by an Australian critic in London who saw Neville as a 'half-phoney... playing to the gallery, cashing in on other people's genuine craziness'.[93] It might be contended that Australians could only be this innovative when they left Australia; Lillian Roxon, the *Everybodys* journalist who redefined music criticism in New York in the early 70s, is another example. There may be some truth to all this, but in any case it would not detract from the status of these individuals as role models for younger Australians.

In Australia itself, the standard pop press was not big on surprises. The early 60s had *Young Modern*, a concerted attempt by 'straight' publishing to make something of interest to the still rather ill-formed teenage audience. Philip Frazer's *Go-Set*, which began publishing in 1966, was every bit as cynical in its motivation, but arguably more adventurous and even countercultural.

In 1965 Frazer had edited Melbourne's Monash University's student paper, *Lot's Wife*, with Tony Schauble. 'We'd changed it into quite a good political, liberal conscience paper,' he told *Planet's* Lee Dillow in 1972, 'as opposed to the lairy style that had been uni papers up until then.'[94] Frazer and Schauble then started thinking about other publications they might produce:

> We had a whole series of ideas that we'd thought up purely as a diversion. One of them was a teenage paper. Normie Rowe was happening at the time. This seemed to be the ultimate – a pop paper for the manipulated teenage populat[ion]. We thought up the whole format in a morning, including the name – which was the corniest name we could think of – that being what the whole game was about. That afternoon we went to 3UZ with our idea. It was incredible. The reaction was fantastic... It was just a whole trip that took off without anyone having any motivation at all.[95]

Go-Set began in February 1966 in Melbourne, and brought the writing of Lily Brett, Douglas L. Panther, David Elfick, Wendy Saddington, Greg Quill, amongst others, to prominence (the last two listed were also well-known musicians). It is described by historian Seamus O'Hanlon as a 'manifestation of a very vibrant youth culture in Melbourne in the 1960s' and, indeed, as confirming Melbourne as the 'centre of the pop scene' from the mid 60s.[96] By the end of its first year, there were three versions of *Go-Set*, aimed at pop fans and advertisers in Victoria-Tasmania, NSW-Queensland, and Western and South Australia.[97] The paper's form and style was exactly what its audience required, and its most unusual aspect, from an early 21st century viewpoint, is that it aimed to cater for both teenagers and readers in their 20s – demographics that many would see as quite different (though teenagers have never objected to reading something for an older age group, of course). The magazine offered up photographs of, and gossip and interviews with, stars of the moment and would-be stars, record reviews, advice and fashion tips. Advertising was largely but not exclusively for music-related items – records, instruments, live shows and the like. Early in its existence the magazine had a cross-promotional, mutually beneficial relationship with television's similarly titled *Go!! Show*.

Keays says the Masters Apprentices read the magazine 'avidly in Adelaide'; he describes it as 'a crazy, unorganized mess, but it worked.'[98] Later, the publishers were to launch a subsidiary, more pop-oriented version called *Gas* and a more adult, political publication, *Revolution*.[99] *Go-Set* continued on into the 70s with, it claimed, a circulation of 57,000 per week.[100] Its format had implications for the way the Australian music press would operate for at least two decades after its demise in 1974. *Juke*, which was initially edited by former *Go-Set* chart compiler (and critic, writer and ultimately editor) Ed Nimmervoll, was arguably a direct successor to *Go-Set*, particularly in its post-Nimmervoll era, when it became a much more uncritical reporter on the music industry, unlike the relatively partisan and left-field *Rock Australia Magazine* (better known as *RAM*). Ian Meldrum – who will be discussed further anon – joined the staff of *Go-Set* early in its existence; his original job was to clean the house the magazine was run from.[101] He was soon writing for them, with a story about Ronnie Burns meeting the (flamboyant and gay) thespian Frank Thring.[102] It is possibly true that Meldrum was the magazine's greatest gift to Australian music – and like the magazine itself, it was a gift with both positive and negative implications.

MOLLY

Ian Meldrum was born in the regional Victorian town of Orbost, near the holiday beach settlement Lakes Entrance, in 1946.[103] He has always been relatively secretive about his background, and it is plain that he did not fit in. He learnt piano from an early age, then did musical comedy at school; he liked 'classical music and musical comedy and all of that' and experienced pop music through the Tarax jukeboxes in Kyabram, a town north of Melbourne[104] – 'I liked it, but it didn't move me.'[105] He relocated to Melbourne for his final years of schooling, attending the prestigious Wesley College. In 1962, while studying law at the University of Melbourne, he was billeted with some aunts in St Kilda. In a strange and audacious move, he asked their neighbours across the road – the Burns family, whose son Ronnie was a singer – if he could live with them instead.[106] What was even more extraordinary was that Meldrum did go on to live with the Burnses – for almost a decade.[107]

Another turning point for Meldrum was hearing the Beatles on a transistor radio 'in the sand dunes' at yet another regional Victorian pleasure spot, Point Leo.[108] And in a happy accident for his future career, he once tripped over singer Lynne Randell on the beach 'and we became great friends.'[109]

A friend from school, Max Ross, had gone on to be a member of the Groop, a hit band which began as the Wesley Trio and which, Meldrum later recalled, 'was the first band I could get into because it was Australian music.' It was late 1965.

> I knew some people in the industry like Stan Rofe and Ken Sparkes ... I said I'd try to get their record "Ol' Hound Dog" on air. I never looked at it then as even publicity, because I was being the regular band moll.'[110]

The 'moll' tag, which Meldrum happily applied to himself with all its sexually subservient connotations,[111] possibly led to Rofe's dismissive nickname for him: 'Molly'. Within six months – in tandem with his *Go-Set* activities – Meldrum was not only a reporter on the TV show *Kommotion*, he was also miming international hits for the show (a briefly popular practice until it was banned by Actors Equity in 1967).

Go-Set, August 30, 1969.

Meldrum's involvement in Russell Morris's career included his first acknowledged production job, 'The Real Thing'. The song was supposedly written by Johnny Young for Ronnie Burns. The story goes that when Meldrum heard the demo tape as he was passing by Young's dressing room at *Uptight*, he cajoled a copy from Young and insisted to EMI that the song be given to Morris, whom he was now managing. On the recording, the song, which is in three distinct parts, was played by the Groop; Meldrum impulsively urged them to play for twice as long as was originally intended, speeding up as they went. He then added an overkill of sound effects and overdubs – everything including the kitchen sink *and* a Hitler speech and a nuclear explosion – as well as Groop member Brian Cadd reading the 'conditions of sale' wording from the back of a tape box:

> 'I said, "Just read part of that." So where you hear the talking it is in fact Brian reading and then he and I going into hysterical laughter.'[112]

Howard Gable, who had recently come to Melbourne from New Zealand as resident A&R/producer for EMI (he had produced 'Sadie'), saw no commercial potential in the recording, and initially refused to release it, at which Meldrum 'really kicked up a stink . . .'[113] The battle to see the record become Morris's solo debut, and to have it available nationwide, was possibly as arduous as the recording process itself, if not more so. But by April 1969, *Go-Set* was reporting that 'The Real Thing' was 'a real hit': 'Record bars are finding it hard to keep the record in stock. In Sydney you can't buy a copy of "The Real Thing" anywhere.'[114]

Achieving a number one single allowed Meldrum, Morris and Young to have a free hand in creating its follow-up, which was a Morris and Young collaboration in the way that 'A Day in the Life' was a Lennon-McCartney song – it was two separate tunes jammed together. Former Missing Link Doug Ford played on 'Part Three Into Paper Walls' as well as its flipside, 'The Girl That I Love'.[115] The A side – which is seven minutes long, forty seconds longer than its predecessor – starts up where 'The Real Thing' ends (and then ends with the beginning of 'The Real Thing'!); it's as if the team were making a concept album in instalments. Meldrum was, incidentally, never paid for his production work, as this would have been seen as a conflict of interest.[116] Twenty-five years later, he remarked with his usual candor and garbled syntax, 'I'd be the last person to hire myself to do a record production.'[117] His meticulous muddle-headedness – 'he only ever understood passion', according to engineer Ern Rose[118] – might have been the reason that Brian Cadd, when he was 'going through a period of slight disenchantment' with his friend, recorded a song about Meldrum called 'Handyman.'[119]

WINGS OF AN EAGLE

Meldrum's ascent as a record producer is one way to look at the success of 'The Real Thing'; another is through the career of the 19-year-old whose name was on the single's label, Russell Morris. In early 1968, Meldrum had written in *Go-Set* that 'the biggest threat to Ronnie is the golden wonder boy, Johnny Farnham, who with his first record "Sadie" has reached the coveted No. 1 position in most states.'[120] Ronnie Burns's biggest hit, 'Smiley', was still ahead of him, but as we have already seen his status as 'golden wonder boy' would be usurped not only by Farnham but by Russell Morris – and as a result of Meldrum's own efforts.

Russell Morris may have seemed like the flipside (substantial, 'with-it', sensitive) to the jovial showman Johnny Farnham in 1968, but he was still in many ways the same kind of product. Indeed, 'The Real Thing' was just as much a novelty record as 'Sadie', though its bombast and good-natured pretentiousness certainly made it more listenable. And Morris felt obliged to defend Farnham in the early 70s: 'He really likes what he's doing . . . he must be to keep going. That's what he is, it's what he wants to do.'[121]

Russell Morris had left his group, Somebody's Image, with whom he had achieved minor chart success, in 1967. 'Everyone wanted to be in a band,' he later recalled, 'some of the bands were just hopeless.'[122] Thirteen years after leaving Somebody's Image he told Toby Creswell:

> We were up in Sydney after we'd had two hit singles, and we were living on bananas and yoghurt with five dollars each in our pockets, and sleeping on the floor of a friend's house in Stanmore. My manager, who also managed Ronnie Burns, was in town at the time and I came in to see him at the Sheraton to get some more money. We were desperate and here he was staying in a real hotel . . . I thought, 'Fuck this, I gave up a diploma in accounting to be in a rock & roll band and these are the guys with all the money' . . . I decided to leave the band and go solo.[123]

As related, Meldrum took up the cudgels on Morris's behalf, acting as his manager and the producer of his first two solo singles (they parted ways just before Morris travelled to the UK). The acknowledged top-flight songwriters at the time, Johnny Young and Hans Poulsen, both submitted songs. Along with 'The Real Thing' and 'Part Three Into Paper Walls', there was Poulsen's 'The Girl That I Love', a sparkling ballad. As mentioned above, 'Part Three' also incorporated a song by Morris himself, and his subsequent hits – such as 'Wings of an Eagle', about a dying Aboriginal man[124] – were self-penned. Morris was a key participant, often outshining more established acts, in Operation Starlift – a package tour that included the Masters Apprentices, Zoot, Ronnie Burns, the Valentines, the Kinetics and Farnham, as well as local artists in each state.[125]

By 1971 Morris was recreating himself as a sensitive artist (he wrote some remarkable hits at this time) – the opposite of Farnham, who played with scratch bands and toured constantly: 'I won't work without a good band to work with me,' Morris said. 'I refuse to work in hotels, which my manager can't understand, 'cause that's where the bread is . . . I want people to listen to what I'm doing, plus, of course, I'm still trying to overcome my pop star image.'[126] Possibly the best of his singles was the relatively bombastic 'Mr. America', an exploration of his possible future as an international star.

Morris was sensitive about his public image. 'I can walk down the street,' he told Lee Dillow in 1971, 'and some thirteen-year-old chick will say: "Oh, look. There's Russell Morris. Isn't he a prick. What a shit."'[127] 'At that time,' he later told Creswell, 'Thorpie was king and I was a big poofta.'[128] He took up karate for self-defence, because 'guys seem to take exception to me' and it cleared his head: 'I've written some of my best songs while I was training'.[129] He spent five years in the US, beginning in 1973. While Morris's songwriting and much of his output was original and sophisticated (his late-70s/early-80s career as part of Russell Morris and the Rubes a little less so), he did not manage to reinvent himself as a megastar the way John Farnham did in the 80s. He did, however, enjoy one of the biggest selling albums of his career – *Sharkmouth* – in 2013.

SONGWRITERS WITH A GOLDEN TOUCH

In the mid to late 60s it became possible – and credible – to be both a songwriter and a performer, and some young men from diverse backgrounds achieved this distinction and record-selling status. Hans Poulsen – born Bruce Gordon Poulsen, in 1945 in the Melbourne bayside suburb of Chelsea – started a group in 1965 that he called the 18th Century Quartet and recorded 'The World Goes On.'[130] Rock promoter Ian Oshlack tried to turn the band into a supergroup with a revised line-up including Keith Glass: 'They describe their sound as baroque beat.'[131] Glass later described the group as like 'an electrical Seekers. We were a pretty innovative band.'[132] Poulsen, who claimed he lived 'on my own or with gentle chicks that looked after me.'[133] wrote hits for New Zealand groups Larry's Rebels and the Fourmyula ('Lady Scorpio' was co-written with Bruce Woodley, who considered Poulsen 'a quirky little character');[134] for Zoot ('Monty and Me', also written with Woodley); and for Russell Morris ('It's Only a Matter of Time' and 'You on my Mind'). His 1970 solo hit 'Boom Sha La La Lo' was another Woodley co-write; the two – along with Billy Green – also put together a soundtrack for a surfing film, *Getting Back to Nothing*. Like Poulsen's two solo albums (*Natural High* and *Lost and Found, Coming Home the Wrong Way Round*), these were released on Fable. Considered by some to have been the standout performer at the 1970 Ourimbah festival,[135] Poulsen left Australia in 1972 for pastures new and wrote songs for the New Seekers, who became something of a repository for Australasian expat songwriters. Along with Captain Matchbox, Poulsen is a star of the pivotal party scene in Tim Burstall's rousing 1971 film *Stork*. In the mid 80s, eight of his songs appeared in Dave Clarke's *Time the Musical* and on the soundtrack album sung by Stevie Wonder, Cliff Richard and Dionne Warwick.[136] Poulsen's star diminished in the 80s, and his whimsy increasingly fell on deaf ears (for instance, the publicity surrounding his cassette-only album *Sacred Games* which proclaimed that its title track was written 'after contact with the dolphin Holy Fin.'[137])

Johnny Young was well-known as a pop performer, first in Perth and then nationwide, before he took on the additional role of hit songwriter. Born John de Jong in Rotterdam, he was part of the Dutch diaspora to Australia in the late 1940s, where his family settled in Kalamunda, an outer suburb of Perth. (Young came to Australia much earlier – and at a younger age, it should be noted, than other well-known Dutch-born Australian musicians like Billy Green or Harry Vanda.) By the age of twenty, he was working as a DJ, as a television compere (for *Club 17*), and releasing singles. His first hit, the following year, was 'Step Back', released on the Clarion label. It was donated to him by the Easybeats, who he met when they were passing through Perth. Angus Young (no relation, obviously) has suggested that in the early 60s Bon Scott played drums in a band backing Young, which is possible but unsubstantiated.[138] Moving to the eastern states, Johnny Young hosted the pop show *Too Much*, then took over *The Go!! Show* from Turpie. In early 1968, Young told *Go-Set* that his success was due to 'lucky circumstances':

> 'I was not talented', he said, 'just fortunate.'
> 'Johnny O'Keefe was the genius who helped me originally,' he said. 'Most people think I'm big-headed.'[139]

It's not clear what role O'Keefe played in Young's success, but it is clear that Young was both astute and very conscious of his place in the industry – he added as much as he could to his armoury of abilities throughout the 60s, just as O'Keefe had (and more). In the space of a few years he went from performer to TV compere to songwriter, journalist, DJ and producer. Perhaps to counter the impression that their writers and the musicians they wrote about constituted a mutually backscratching elite, in the late 60s/early 70s *Go-Set* flirted with hostility between its columnists. Ian Meldrum and Young were both contributors to the magazine when Meldrum wrote:

> Who can forget the times when Johnny Young played King pop star? The innocent, wide-eyed little boy who projected his adolescent body on stage, hand over mouth, completely overcome by the occasion, and awkwardly hand clapping through every number, and at the same time the obnoxious little terror off stage who ruthlessly trod on people to fulfil his ambitions.[140]

One can only speculate on what Meldrum meant by this; other sources suggest that Young was particularly well-liked in the music industry, either because of or despite his good-natured blandness. It was apparently an act of generosity – he paid for Barry Gibb to fly from Queensland to Sydney for a television appearance, when Gibb had been facing a gruelling drive – that cemented the friendship between the two men. The Bee Gees and/or Gibb were to write a number of songs with Young in mind. During Young's time in London Barry Gibb gave him some lessons in songwriting, at which point Young seemingly effortlessly added this string to his bow. Returning to Australia in early 1968 'in a state of exhaustion after six months' intensive work' in Europe, Young claimed expansively that he was making $2,000 dollars a week; that 'When people say that Johnny Young was a flop as a pop singer in England, I readily agree with them'; and, most importantly, that he was about to release an album of his own songs, *Surprises*.[141]

Young's pop singing success diminished at the same time his writing successes began. His biggest hit was undoubtedly 'The Real Thing' for Russell Morris, as discussed above. His 'I Thank You', written for the Aboriginal boxer-turned-singer Lionel Rose, is little more than a ditty, though it did reputedly sell 50,000 copies and led to 'thousands of teenagers screaming their groovy heads off for their latest idol, Lionel.'[142] The Lionel Rose phenomenon deserves wider study as an extraordinary outpouring of affection for an indigenous Australian shortly after a referendum in which Australians voted overwhelmingly to allow the Commonwealth to legislate for all indigenous people: an act which is often seen as an invitation to Aboriginal people to become part of mainstream Australia.

The best Johnny Young composition is a tie between 'Smiley', sung by Ronnie Burns and a number one hit in 1970, and 'The Star', recorded by Ross D. Wyllie, which had enjoyed chart success a year earlier. Like 'The Real Thing', these songs were sugar-coated subversion, though the first may have been accidentally so; Young and others have given varying explanations of the connection between the song 'The Real Thing' and the 'It's the real thing' slogan used to promote Coca-Cola in the same year (1969). It has been posited that Young heard the phrase in London and decided to satirise it, and through it capitalism and advertising. Another version has it that the song was offered to Coca Cola as a jingle, that the song was rejected but the *phrase* taken on by the company worldwide.[143] In the 1970 film *The Naked Bunyip*, an exploration of sexuality in Australia, Morris (a symbol in the film for all teen idols) is seen singing 'The Real Thing' in front of a large Coca-Cola banner. Perhaps Young's parody was co-opted by the company, but in the final analysis it seems most likely that 'the real thing' as a phrase was merely a manifestation of the late-60s zeitgeist, just as Morris's band had called themselves Somebody's

Image. The globally famous New Seekers song – 'I'd Like to Teach the World to Sing', from 1971 – began life as a Coke commercial, incidentally.

'Smiley', a song about Normie Rowe, was curious for a number of reasons, not least that Colin Peterson – the drummer in the Bee Gees during their early UK years – had played a character called 'Smiley' in a film of the same name in the late 1950s. Young also wrote a brilliant song, 'Hello', for Rowe to sing – this and Brian Peacock's 'Penelope' were Rowe's two best tracks of the period. 'The Star' was a hit for Wyllie, who had formerly been a member of Brisbane group the Kodiaks[144] but, as mentioned earlier, was best known as the host of *Uptight*. The song was a reflection on the loneliness of the popular performer. Even at a time when the Australian pop press was impressed by almost anything, it was not particularly besotted with Wyllie. Meldrum – admittedly the Australian journalist who was keenest to whip up controversy – wrote in *Go-Set* that Wyllie 'walks with a limp, has had numerous flop records, is certainly no Davy Jones.'[145] Wyllie's limp was the result of childhood polio; his doctor had recommended music tuition as therapy.[146] Meldrum continues:

> He readily admits that he hasn't the voice of Tom Jones nor the sex appeal of Elvis Presley, but Ross D. Wyllie should be more than happy with the talent he has.'[147]

Presumably he was. 'The Star' was also a top-forty hit in Britain for Herman's Hermits in late 1969; the group first heard it while touring Australia in the middle of that year.[148]

Young had teamed up with Kevin Lewis, formerly of Festival Records, to take over David Joseph's television shows (the *Happening* series) and produce a new one, *Young Talent Time*. That his subversiveness had been a mere blip is shown by a 'Lewis-Young production' LP released under Young's name and entitled *A Young Man and his Music*; here Young presents insipid readings of songs he had written for others that seem to suggest an artist who does not even realise, much less take pleasure in, the quality of his own work (astutely, he did not attempt to sanitise 'The Real Thing'). *Young Talent Time*, a show which would bring performers such as Jamie Redfern, Debbie Byrne, Dannii Minogue and Tina Arena to the world, was often grotesque high kitsch. Young chose to avoid any reference to his songwriting past, and indeed since the earliest period of *Young Talent Time* has been happy to use as his signature tune his 1967 ballad version of the Beatles' 'All My Loving'.

POP AND BUBBLE . . .

Bubblegum, as a form, has been derided widely since its creation. Indeed, the backlash against bubblegum began almost as soon as the term was coined, and came in tandem with resistance to what was seen as its campy and crassly commercial qualities; some listeners undoubtedly felt that bubblegum was overly calculated, almost scientifically catchy. Yet in many instances this scornful dismissal of bubblegum was unfair, especially when contrasted with the ways in which other extremely simple, repetitive and instant forms of popular music, such as heavy rock, have been lionised.

Zoot began in Adelaide in the early 1960s, and were originally named Down the Line, after a Hollies song. One mainstay of the group was Beeb Birtles, born Gerard Birtlekamp, whose family arrived from Holland in 1958, when he was 10.

Like many scenes of the time, the Adelaide live music industry seems to have been run rather like a sport. The 'opposition' band to Down the Line was the Mermen, featuring singer Darryl Cotton and guitarist Rick Brewer. Cotton switched sides, or was otherwise transferred to Zoot, in early 1965, and Brewer moved over soon after.[149] Their name change to 'something short and punchy' was a gift from budding entrepreneur Doc Neeson,[150] who would become lead singer of the Angels in the 70s. Paddy McCartney, one of the two singers in the Twilights, alerted EMI to Zoot's potential, and the group travelled to Melbourne in mid 1968 to be immersed in a marketing plan that would prove to be a short-term success but also bring about their undoing. Birtles later recalled:

> There was a guy in Melbourne who was a manager, called Wayne De Gruchy. Wayne came over to see the group and saw a lot of potential in us becoming a very popular young band in Australia. And when they brought us over to Melbourne, he and another guy that owned the Bertie's disco in Melbourne decided that they needed a gimmick of some sort, to really get the band going. And the image that was decided on was: 'Think pink, think Zoot'! It was this outrageous thing where the band dressed up in all-pink clothes, which of course ... all the young girls loved us in these ridiculous outfits and all their boyfriends hated our guts, y'know? And that's really how the whole thing came about ... I always felt very very uncomfortable dressing that way, 'cos it wasn't me. But, at the same time ...[151]

Later that year, Zoot appeared at the Melbourne Velodrome alongside the Twilights, the Masters Apprentices, Johnny Young, the Iguana and the Wild Cherries. The event was broadcast on television and radio; this may have been a factor in their success. Within six months, Zoot had switched managers – to Daryl Sambell – and released 'Monty and Me', a song written by Hans Poulsen and Bruce Woodley and produced by Ian Meldrum, to considerable success. Signing with Sambell was a strange move for a group who would soon become so sensitive about their perceived sexuality; Cotton told the student press in early 1969 that 'there are a helluva lot of camps in the business. These blokes can break you if you don't sleep with them. They could stop any group in Australia.'[152] Zoot were immersed in a Think Pink ad campaign: invitations to its launch took the shape of a big pink heart, the group wore pink suits, and Rick Brewer played a pink drum kit.[153] Jim Keays claimed two decades later that his group, the Masters Apprentices, had decided at the time that 'we wouldn't have what we considered a pansy sort of look, like the Zoot in their pink outfits and stuff.'[154] In fact, Keays bought his sexually ambiguous clothing in women's clothing stores, despite his professed anti-'pansy' stance.

Having arrived in a flash, Zoot seemed quickly on the wane, perhaps because of the gimmickry associated with their popularity. The always loud-mouthed and judgmental Stan Rofe commented:

> I don't disadmire the Zoot, nor do I have any personal grudge agin' them. As predicted by all in the industry, they were the big bubblegum group of 1969 and even their staunchest fans won't deny on the eve of another year the Zoot's star is fading.[155]

The group received a new lease on life when they attracted a hot new talent to their ranks in Rick Springfield, a Sydney guitarist/songwriter who had toured Vietnam with Mike Brady's MPD Ltd and, under the name of Wickedy Wak, released a single written by Johnny Young and produced by Meldrum, the rousing 'Billie's Bikey Boys'. Springfield attempted to extract Zoot from pink stigma by means of riff-rock, beginning with a single, 'Mr. Songwriter'/'Flying', the latter having all the elements that characterised the classic sound of his international hit career in the 80s. Zoot's next single, 'Hey Pinky', was accompanied by a ritual burning of their pink clothes on the show *Happening '70*; the visceral effect of which was presumably somewhat muted by the fact that it took place on black-and-white television. 'We keep telling people our musical style has changed,' whined an unidentified Zoot member to *Go-Set's* Jean Gollan, adding that 'more people are listening to us and agreeing. They're realizing that we're not quite the pink poofters that they thought.'[156]

Springfield was the first Zoot member to maintain a strong songwriting presence, and the group's sound shifted radically. He also initiated the band's cover of the Beatles' 'Eleanor Rigby',[157] which sounded more like Black Sabbath's 'Paranoid'. This was the sum total of its genius, unfortunately; it is almost a novelty record, and whatever novelty it had was somewhat undermined by the fact that Doug Parkinson In Focus had done something very similar, though slightly better, the previous year. It is a shame, considering the high quality of the other material released by Zoot at this time – for instance, the epic 'Turn Your Head', or the show-business psychodrama of 'The Freak' – that, like Parkinson's band, they are generally remembered not for their excellent original material but for a

tossed-off and ineffectual Beatles cover.

Zoot split in mid 1971. Springfield went on to become a star in the US, as an actor and performer; Rick Brewer was to see major chart success again in the Ferrets; while Birtles and Cotton remained together as a duo under the name Frieze, discussed below.

Zoot's career ran parallel to – and, in some respects, in competition with – that of Perth's Valentines; indeed, the Valentines' break up (on 1 Aug 1970)[158] occurred shortly after they were embroiled in a brief public argument with Zoot (and the Masters Apprentices) about which of the bands was the first to wear a specially designed band uniform.

The Valentines brought joint vocalists Bon Scott and Vince Lovegrove to Australia's attention. The group had come together in 1966 as a merger of Perth's two top acts, the Spektors and the Winztons (Scott was from the former, Lovegrove the latter). Scott would go on to sing in Fraternity and AC/DC; Lovegrove would become known as a manager, promoter and journalist. Other members would have extensive careers in a number of top groups, drummer Doug Lavery for instance, would become a member of Axiom.

Whatever qualities the Valentines may have possessed, like Zoot before Springfield (or, for that matter, the Masters Apprentices between Mick Bower and Doug Ford, as we shall see below), the group lacked a songwriter. Although rhythm guitarist Ted Ward provided some strong material, the fact that three of the Valentines' seven singles came via the Easybeats is testament to this deficiency. They also lacked focus, as they were well aware. Scott admitted late in the group's career: 'We can do anything from heavy rock to bubblegum, but there's nothing that could be called distinctively the Valentines. But when we find our bag, baby, we'll be sticking to it!'[159]

Like Johnny Young, they became Clarion recording artists; their most interesting single was a cover of the Soft Machine's brilliant 'Love Makes Sweet Music'; like the original, it was not a hit. (There is no evidence that Soft Machine founder Daevid Allen's Australian origins played any part in the decision to cover this song.) In late 1967 the Valentines moved to Melbourne, which they made their base for the next three years. They also switched labels, from Clarion to Philips, at the instigation of Ron Tudor, formerly of W&G and soon to launch his own Fable label. Their 1969 single 'My Old Man's a Groovy Old Man' – a genuine bubblegum record, though nowhere near Vanda and Young's best work – was a top-forty hit. In March of that year members of the group were prosecuted for marijuana possession, an event which *Go-Set* claimed 'shook the pop world', but far from adversely affecting their status, this seemed to have boosted it: 'They even gained in popularity.' The Valentines subsequently came out in favour of pot legalisation. *Go-Set* asked: 'Was this when they first realised that they could be honest with their fans?'[160]

Late in the Valentines' career, their music was reported to be 'getting heavier (and better) all the time – now with their own arrangements of Jeff Beck and

Chicago's plus their own compositions.'[161] Their last single, 'Juliette', was probably their best, but they split four months after its release.

Other practitioners of bubblegum in Australia found it expedient to move into fresh fields. Sydney group Flying Circus had two hits written by the American song writing duo, Buzz Cason and Mac Gayden: 'Hayride' and 'La La'. They toured with the Valentines (and Johnny Farnham and Mike Furber), whom they considered 'gas guys', saying: 'They really turned us on to the simple things in life, picnics on the roadside and such. We really dig that group.' Flying Circus's live set included some country rock songs,[162] and this was to become their stock in trade. In the early 70s they relocated to Canada, where they achieved no little success in a larger market.

MASTER KEAYS

In chapter 2 we briefly encountered the Mustangs as they ambivalently accepted a vocalist in the form of Jim Keays. The group had auditioned Keays in late 1965 at their rehearsal space in an old stables;[163] Keays had just given up on learning the bass; his tutor had been the Twilights' John Bywaters.[164] The augmented line-up became the Masters Apprentices. 'The Masters and the Easybeats,' David Day and Tim Parker write in their 1987 history of Adelaide rock and pop, 'were probably the two major bands to actually start what has now become known as the Australian sound', adding rather needlessly that 'the Masters were really a band that created their own sound ... It was an Australian sound.'[165]

The new group covered Adelaide in advertising stickers[166] and had a residency in a café over a fish and chip shop in Glenelg. They then found a venue that was arguably more appropriate: the Beat Basement, a club with a 'rounded ceiling, so it was much like a tunnel.'[167] Other bands playing there – according to Keays – included a slew of intriguingly named outfits such as the Others, Blues Rags 'N' Hollers, Dust and Ashes, Y?4, 5 Sided Circle, and the Syssys.[168] The next major venue for the Masters was the Octagon in Elizabeth, where they became the 'biggest drawcard.'[169] They would then move on to regional tours in South Australia, including the industrial town of Whyalla and the 'Cornwall of the south', the Yorke Peninsula.[170]

In 1966 the Masters' Mick Bower and Rick Morrison made up a song in the studio, possibly at the suggestion of engineer/producer Max Pepper. They called it 'Undecided', and it brought together all the tricks they'd learned as an R&B pop band. Pepper, an Adelaide personality, was remembered decades later for having sold posters of James Dean's mangled car at rock and roll parties[171] and for his Gamba studio, which included a Moog synthesiser and became a 'centre for experimentation.'[172] at night. Pepper achieved the echo effect on Keays's vocal from what he called the 'government garage across the road' from his studio;[173] the crickets that can be heard on the song were, however, unintentional. In a story that seems quite common amongst groups at this time (the same thing supposedly happened to Zoot), however extraordinary it may seem, the band were unaware that 'Undecided' had been released until they heard it on the radio.

The Masters moved to Melbourne, living at first in an unromantic caravan park in Sunshine.[174] 'When we went to Melbourne eventually,' Keays recalled in Parker and Day's book, 'we were branded a new wave sort of band because of our looks.'[175] Their record label, Astor, sent them to Armstrong's in Albert Park Road to record:[176] amongst his other achievements, house engineer Roger Savage had recorded the Rolling Stones' debut single 'Come On'. Here, he was set to work as engineer on Bower's turgid 'Living in a Child's Dream',[177] though Ian Meldrum may have been the actual producer on the song.[178] For a brief period in the mid 1960s Bower was turning out the most powerful and pointed R&B pop singles in Australia, if not the world: 'Wars or Hands of Time', the B side to 'Undecided', was an early anti-Vietnam pop song that packed a considerable punch, and 'Buried and Dead', the Masters Apprentices' second single, was a vibrant gem. It is a shame that the juvenile psychedelia of 'Living in a Child's Dream' was

Bower's last major hit: the mounting pressure of the group's increasing celebrity became too much for him. He suffered a nervous breakdown[179] and was compelled to leave the band, who were now in need of a songwriter. Another great writer, the iridescent Brian Cadd – a rival to Poulsen and Young, who is discussed further in chapter 8 – gave the group a song called 'Silver People' which they turned into one of their best tracks, the compulsive 'Elevator Driver'.[180]

Like the Missing Links before them, the Masters Apprentices had two very different line-ups. Two years into their ascendancy, the entire band aside from Keays had been replaced for various reasons (health, competence, a wish to stay in Adelaide rather than relocate to Melbourne). 'Essentially, the Masters were two entities,' Keays writes in his autobiography; the first version 'ceased to exist at about New Year's Eve 1967.'[181] The difference between the Masters Apprentices and the Missing Links, of course, is that the Masters had one constant in Keays (with the exception of the band's final, short-lived incarnation in Britain).

The early 1968 line-up of the Masters featured Doug Ford, formerly of the Missing Links and Running Jumping Standing Still, Colin Burgess, later AC/DC's first drummer, and guitarist Peter Tilbrook. True to the spirit of 1968, the band wore 'clothes which Jim designs and we all wear,' huffed Burgess, 'except for Peter [Tilbrook], who's commercial and buys off the rack.'[182] Keays had hoped to get

Beeb Birtles into the group as bassist; instead, a chance airplane seat assignment found him talking with Daryl Sambell, who suggested Glenn Wheatley,[183] then playing in the Brisbane group Bay City Union.

In late 1969 the group recorded 'Turn up Your Radio': 'It screams and tears thru your trannie,' yelled the ever-modern Meldrum from the pages of *Go-Set*, 'like a JUMBO JET taking off from KENNEDY airport.'[184] Having exhausted all avenues (and themselves) in becoming the biggest group in Australia in the late 60s, the Masters Apprentices journeyed to the UK in May 1970;[185] Glenn Wheatley and Marcie Jones, who was working there with her group the Cookies, pretended to be married in order to rent a house in London.[186] The group would later record at Abbey Road; at least one of their last singles, 'Because I Love You', was a very good song.[187] Keays claims that the Bronze label, home of Manfred Mann's Earth Band (featuring Mick Rogers, previously of Procession) and Uriah Heep, wanted to sign them – but that EMI wouldn't let them out of their contract.[188] Their Masters Apprentices' legacy and Keays's subsequent activities will be discussed in later chapters.

SUPERDROOP'S SUPERGROUPS

Jim Keays recalls that in the mid 1960s he and other Masters would go and see the Twilights at Adelaide's Oxford Club: 'They were fantastic', he says, while adding: 'We didn't want to be like them.'[189] Indeed, the Masters' story was that of a group always chasing a decent songwriter and songs; the Twilights were immensely versatile and scintillating and also had at least one brilliant songwriter in Terry Britten. Like many of the abovementioned groups, however, most of their best-known hits are covers; Britten's contributions are the exceptions.

The Twilights (who were discussed briefly in chapter 2 in their earliest, vocal-only incarnation) moved to Melbourne in 1965 after recording their first single, 'I'll Be Where You Are', at Vi-Sound Studios on Hindley St. They had a hit, 'If She Finds Out', the following year and won Hoadley's National Battle of the Sounds in 1966. In order for them to take part, one of their vocalists (McCartney) had to exit the band temporarily, because the competition required a five-piece group; the prize was a trip to the UK, and the other band members

The Twilights depicted as puppets of their manager, Garry Spry

worked their passage on the liner that took them to Britain so as to raise the money for his fare. Terry Britten's '9.50' was recorded at Abbey Road in early 1967. Drummer Laurie Pryor contributed a song called 'Young Girl', and the group also played a Hollies cover, 'What's Wrong with the Way I Live'. Whereas Jim Keays's memory of Abbey Road is glimpsing John Lennon playing piano through a studio door, Glenn Shorrock had the distinction of standing next to Paul McCartney at a urinal.

The Twilights were an unusual bag. Shorrock, for all his vocalising and other musical skills, seemed happiest when dressed up as 'Superdroop', a fat superhero character the group introduced into their live performances towards the end of their career as they tried to spark up their act; Superdroop is also featured in the video they made to promote their single 'Cathy Come Home'. Twenty years later – after his dream run with Little River Band – Shorrock returned to this kind of cabaret when he concocted *Two for the Show* for the Sydney nightclub Kinselas, where he performed impressions of Joe Cocker, Easybeats, the Bee Gees, Billy Thorpe, Ross Wilson and Johnny O'Keefe.[190]

The Twilights' first, self-titled album had been almost entirely covers; 'Needle in a Haystack' had been a particularly big hit for them. Their second (and final) album, *Once Upon a Twilight*, is probably one of the best psychedelic pop records of the 1960s, replete with an unlistenable comedy number ('The Cocky Song') and Britten gems such as 'Mr. Nice', 'Blue Roundabout', 'Take Action' and 'Paternosta Row'.

Cliff Richard covered a song from the LP, Britten's 'Mr Nice' (Britten would go on to spend much of the 70s as Richard's guitarist/songwriter); at approximately the same time, Britten released a solo single, '2000 Weeks', named for Tim Burstall's film and written on commission from Columbia Pictures.[191] *Once Upon a Twilight* had the same name as a TV pilot made in 1967 that starred the group (as themselves), comedian Mary Hardy and Ronnie Burns (indeed, the show is an origins story for Burns, in which the hick mummy's boy from Gumnut Gully, 'Alphonse,' becomes a pop star). Shorrock's new year's resolution for 1968 was 'for the TV show to be a success, and for the group to make it in America.'[192] They went to the UK instead and, facing the possibility of success – a *Top of the Pops* appearance and pirate radio exposure – they bailed. In his memoir, *From This Side of Things*, the Groop's Brian Cadd muses on the fate his band and Shorrock's both suffered there:

> The Twilights and the Groop were typical of so many of the acts that went to London and failed. We experienced enough once we got there to realise that no-one from Australia at that point really understood how it all worked. The Groop had taken a manager over who was spectacularly out of his league in an industry that was huge and powerful and that swallowed up acts like ours, virtually on sight.[193]

Reputedly the Twilights could earn a thousand dollars for a half-hour appearance in Australia; in many of their performances they chose to recreate a famous album of the time – such as *Ogden's Nut Gone Flake* or *Sgt. Pepper's Lonely Hearts Club Band* – on stage, though little evidence remains of the effectiveness of these imitations. They announced their breakup in 1969, giving the highly unlikely explanation that Pryor had 'told the other members of the six-member group he wanted to concentrate on jazz' (it's possible that he wanted to, but he didn't). They played their farewell performance at the Sydney Trocadero at the beginning of February that year.[194]

Shorrock almost immediately went into management, taking on one of two bands known at the time as the Avengers – the one from Brisbane, rather than the one from New Zealand.[195] The Brisbane Avengers were set to record two Terry Britten compositions for their single; Shorrock later claimed, wistfully, that the group was 'like a "little Twilights" to me.'[196] Ian Meldrum 'hurriedly made my exit' from an interview with them, 'because strains of the N. Z. Avengers' current single wafted through the air' from a nearby radio. The battle of the Avengers was clearly going to be fierce, although the Brisbane group seemed good-natured about the situation: 'They also said that if their current name doesn't work out and the NZ Avengers take the glory they will seriously consider joining up with the Valentines to make an 11-piece group . . . the VALENVENGERS.'[197]

Shorrock's retirement from performance was extremely temporary. Ian Meldrum had a knack for being on the spot when major splits were announced; he appears to have been the first journalist to be told the Beatles were breaking up, though it didn't really register with him until he read the transcript of his interview in *Go-Set*. He was in the studio with the Groop (their 'Woman You're Breaking Me', an early Brian Cadd songwriting venture, was a huge hit in 1967, kept out of the top spot only by Procol Harum's 'A Whiter Shade of Pale' and the Beatles' 'All You Need is Love'),[198] when he was told by Ronnie Charles that the band were 'splitting up for all time and that Brian and Donnie were forming a new group.'

> 'Don't be ridiculous', I said.
> 'It's true,' said Ronnie.
> 'What are you going to do?' I asked.
> 'Well I haven't had much time to think about it,' said Ron, 'considering I only found out about it an hour ago.'[199]

Meldrum goes on to say that he has heard from the manager of Melbourne band the Iguana that Shorrock has quit as manager of the Brisbane Avengers, and from Vince Lovegrove that Doug Lavery is leaving the Valentines 'to join a supergroup.' Allegations then flew thick and fast – that Don Mudie and Brian Cadd had facilitated the breakup of the Groop to form Axiom, drawing members from the Valentines and Cam-Pact, and 'immediately hailed as a supergroup'. The shake-up that led to the creation of Axiom was so intense that *Go-Set* created a table for its readers showing what the ramifications would be.[200]

For his part, Doug Lavery claimed he hadn't enjoyed being in the Valentines because he didn't like the music. Cam-Pact's Chris Stockley stated that 'Keith Glass and I had already decided to leave the Cam-Pact long before I heard from Brian. We were on the verge of forming a new group with Paddy from the Twilights – we still needed an organist. But that fell through when Keith went to Sydney to do *Hair*.'

Cadd announced that the scene needed 'more groups working together, supergroups . . . intergroup performances' and in one rumination he virtually wrote the Fable label/Bootleg Family Band manifesto:

> There should be pop festivals. One thing I've noticed – there's very little pop world social life. In Sydney they try, at places like Caesar's and the Here, but all you end up [with] is a conglomeration of new groups . . . There's so much unexploited talent around. Australia is probably the most talented country in the world . . . The best thing that would help Australia would be radio stations playing 90 percent Australian records, regardless of their quality . . . It'd be bad at first, but the standard would have to improve.[201]

Axiom retreated to the northern Victorian town of Nathalia, where Don Mudie's family lived, and rehearsed in the local football club's changing rooms for two weeks.[202] They were initially uncertain whether to record or not, because they didn't want to be tied into a contract that would spoil their international chances. If they were able to get a one-record deal, they were looking to record two songs. One of these would be a signature hit – Cadd's lilting, hippie-ish 'A Little Ray of Sunshine'.[203]

Shorrock's departure from the Avengers' management seemed a fait accompli; he had almost joined the group Ram Jam, 'but they weren't after the international acclaim and prestige so I decided against it'. Axiom's attraction was 'the fact that they wanted to go to England as much as I did.'

> Plus, of course, the fact that they're all known in their own right. I wouldn't have been prepared to go through all that getting known again. I mean why should I? – I've been through enough of it. [204]

In hindsight it seems amusing that *Go-Set* felt the 26-year-old Shorrock was too old for the 'limelight'.[205]

If Axiom's Australian contemporaries Mississippi had an American name, Axiom had a contentiously 'American' song as their debut single: 'Arkansas Grass', a veiled critique of the Vietnam War in the guise of an American Civil War story. Its follow-up, the top-five hit 'A Little Ray of Sunshine', remains an Australian classic, and its quality was apparent even in 1970, when Jean Gollan wrote in *Go-Set* that 'If ever a single seemed aimed at number one, this is it.'[206] Ed Nimmervoll concurred, lauding Shorrock's rendition of 'a plaintive, caressing lyric to just bass and a growing string arrangement which builds into a full, thumping climax, only to grow soft again. Everything is just SO right.'[207] Shorrock brought an element of comedic performance to Axiom's live shows, just as he had done for the Twilights, and the band claimed 'the progressive groups criticize them for the comedy aspect of their stage act', which a *Go-Set* reporter described as 'nearly always hilariously funny.'[208] Shorrock was still playing Superdroop onstage (in fact, he won a talent contest during Axiom's sea voyage to Britain).[209]

With his time as hit writer for the Groop under his belt, Cadd in particular was a name to be reckoned with at this time, and big things were expected of Axiom. *Go-Set* reported that 'Axiom intend to play the whole English scene very cool – they regard it as the first step in their real ambition, which is to get to America with some sort of name behind them, and perhaps a couple of English records.'[210] Their album *Fools Gold* was accompanied by a 20-minute colour film 'made for the overseas market'.[211]

There were two warning signs, though neither seemed terribly ominous at the time. One was the lone dissenting voice of critic Ed Nimmervoll, who wrote that 'Axiom lack just one thing – a something which is pure, unmistakable Axiom.'[212] The other was the insistence by Sitmar, the shipping line which took them to Britain, that they strike a nautical pose on the cover of their album: for Cadd the cover 'remains one of the truly great mockeries of a rock band.'[213] The group lasted long enough to return to Australia once, but their second trip to London saw them break up almost immediately, in March 1971.[214]

Axiom's story was that of the Twilights and the Groop all over again. Cadd returned to Australia and produced a vast and impressive body of work in the early to mid 70s, including advertisements, hit singles, television themes and film soundtracks; he was immortalized in 1974 after writing the theme song to the film *Alvin Purple* – but also by being discussed in the film itself, which was at the time the most commercially successful Australian movie ever released.[215]

Shorrock remained in Britain after Axiom's demise and joined a British-Belgian orchestral jazz-rock outfit called Esperanto, which released three albums; this band recorded at least one Shorrock song ('Statue of Liberty') which would also be released by the Little River Band, and reputedly also performed (but did not release) Shorrock songs that are now seen as LRB standards, including 'Help Is on Its Way' and 'Emma'. He also released solo singles, including the strangely meta 'Let's Get the Band Together'.

Shorrock's star would not shine in the USA the way he hoped until an unusual combination of celebrity musicians came together in Little River Band in the early 70s; this process is described in chapter 8. In the meantime, future bandmate Beeb Birtles was suffering the indignity of being sponsored by the Frieze clothing company. After the breakup of Zoot, Birtles and Darryl Cotton formed a duo that was forced to take the name Frieze, and the company – perhaps unable to get over the Think Pink days – insisted they adopt silly, clothing-related names, though of course only Birtles needed to do so. 'Darryl Cotton was okay, he was Cotton, right?' Birtles told Parker and Day in 1987. 'But they wanted to call me something like Terry Lene. and I was supposed to have a brother called Crepe Lene...'[216] The duo played shows in department stores to a pre-recorded backing track; they had a genuinely grotesque song, 'Why Do Little Kids Have To Die'. Not long after their album was issued, credited to both 'Frieze' and 'Birtles and Cotton', Birtles joined up with Mississippi, whose members included Graeham Goble. LRB was slowly being assembled.

SWINGING IN THE BREEZE

In 1968 Doug Ashdown made a superb album, *Source*, which included a composition called 'Something Strange', which he explained was 'written with me singing into a tape recorder. I don't know what the words meant... It's all quite ridiculous.'[217] After recording three albums on his own, Ashdown formed a songwriting and production relationship with Jimmy Stewart; their first album working together, *The Age of Mouse*, was a double. It was also released in the USA (as a single disc), where it sold 'a few thousand copies.' The two went to New York in 1972 and hated it; they were advised to go to Nashville. Ashdown assumed the southern city would feature 'everyone sitting on porches with corn-cob pipes and guitars – wholesome beautiful country and nice houses', but it turned out to be 'full of insurance companies and printers [and] office buildings'.[218] Within a year, Ashdown had written a country hit single.

After he and Stewart returned to Australia in 1974, Ashdown had this message for his musical compatriots:

> Every single person who makes a record in this country... must be made to realise that our market isn't Australia, it's the entire English-speaking world.[219]

It is clear from memoirs, memories and recordings that the Australian pop scene was diverse and vibrant in the late 1960s – most particularly, though not by any means exclusively, in Melbourne. When the Seekers completed their successful Australian tour, which included playing to 200,000 people at Melbourne's Myer Music Bowl in March 1967 (a controversially brief twenty-minute set!)[220] many might well have taken the group's international success as a sign of the future for Australian music. Indeed, as we will see, when the Seekers split in 1968 some of that band's members used their international contacts to introduce other Australasians to the world market, and the Bee Gees did the same: Maurice Gibb not only introduced Tin Tin (Steve Groves and Steve Kipner) to the British charts, but also maintained contact and offered opportunities to such Australian stars as Ronnie

Burns. *Go-Set* broke the news in a way that highlights the occasional ambivalence in Australia to the possibility of losing favourite musicians to the wider world:

> 'What?' I hear the anguished cry of many Burns fans – 'Our all-Australian Ronnie can't do it to us, even if it does mean an L.P. with Maurice Gibb!' But you can relax – Ronnie is only going to be away for four weeks – 2½ weeks in England to make the L.P., three days in Germany to promote his single, and a week in the states.[221]

The album was to be made up of Maurice Gibb and Johnny Young compositions, but was later called off because of 'costing difficulties'.[222] However, when Barry Gibb subsequently lined up more sessions Burns cancelled because he wanted to promote 'Smiley'. 'This could be my first chance at an Australian gold record,' Burns reasoned, 'and I value that more than rushing into English recording.'[223]

There are so many examples of Australians relocating to Britain for long or short periods during this period that the music press seemingly had to redefine 'success' constantly so as to make each new departure notable. The Seekers had set the bar very high, so that even though their major success was as a pop group, it became necessary to categorise them as something else, in order that each new pop hopeful could be 'Australia's first' pop or rock artist to make waves internationally.

The rising star of Olivia Newton-John is an example. Newton-John, the daughter of a noted Melbourne academic, was a *Go!! Show* regular in the mid 60s. By the end of that decade, she was chosen to join Don Kirshner's post-Monkees group Toomorrow (not to be confused with the British pop group with the more conventional spelling), who starred in a film of the same name.[224] 'Two good years out of my life wasted', she was later to tell *TV Week*,[225] but soon afterwards she had her first big hit with 'If Not for You'. Like that of the Bee Gees, Newton-John's Australian career is the familiar story of an artist gaining all the professional experience necessary to launch herself fully formed, yet 'new', on the international market.

The mid-60s Newton-John was a bubbly innocent whose career arc was the one aspired to by so many teenage girl TV stars; the rich irony being that in Newton-John's case, ambition was the only thing she lacked. Indeed, that lack was a considered policy: 'I wasn't at all ambitious,' she told Debbie Kruger in 1994, adding that 'it' (success) 'just kept happening to me,' but also pointing out that in Australia in the 1960s an ambitious woman was seen as 'grasping' and, presumably, self-promoting to an amoral degree.

Newton-John won a contest on Johnny O'Keefe's show *Sing Sing Sing* in 1964; the prize, as was common, was a trip to England. Like Little Pattie a few years previously, Newton-John's education was lost to music and television. The people of Melbourne chipped in to the debate between Newton-John and her mother, who won: she 'kind of dragged me ... She said I needed to broaden my horizons.'

By the end of 1965, the two were living in Perrins Court, two blocks from the Hampstead tube station, with Newton-John plotting for many months to return to Australia and rejoin her boyfriend, *Go!! Show* host Ian Turpie. At a certain point – unlike her singing partner Pat Carroll, who had a genuine desire for success but was unable to extend her visa – Newton-John's career took on a life of its own. Her first major hit – a cover of a song she disliked, Bob Dylan's 'If Not for You' (previously covered by George Harrison), set her on a country-rock course in the early 70s, and she gained a public profile which soared to megastar status later in the decade.

The La De Das also enjoyed an international profile for a brief period. The group had been formed by Kevin Borich and Phil Key in New Zealand in 1965; they initially recorded 'in a guy called Eldridge Stebbing's garage'[226] (Stebbing would later become a legendary Auckland producer). They moved to Australia in 1967, and first played at radio DJ Ward Austin's Jungle discotheque, then supported the Easybeats for their final shows (according to Phil Key, 'Kevin did a whole set with his fly down. The girls yelled at him and we tried to do our thing and no one knew who the hell we were.')[227] The La De Das achieved some notoriety by taking on a concept album project: a song cycle based on Oscar Wilde's *The Happy Prince*, narrated by poet, scenester, and self-styled friend to the Stones and Dylan (and in the real world, associate of the Red Onions and Loved Ones) Adrian Rawlins. Though pretentious, this album is musically marvelous; nevertheless, the group disowned it almost immediately. Phil Key berated his group's commitment to the record by admitting, 'We weren't here to promote it . . . but we wanted to go to England, and we had some money and we didn't care.'[228] The La De Das toured France; in one more story of almosts to throw on the rock history pile, they reputedly failed to attend an audition with Led Zeppelin manager Peter Grant because their truck broke down.[229] They also 'almost' had a hit with the Beatles' song 'Come Together', which they had recorded on the understanding that the Beatles would not release theirs in the near future – then they did.[230] The group entered a period of disarray, but reconvened in Australia in the early 70s and recorded some excellent material; their *Rock and Roll Sandwich*, produced by Rod Coe (of whom more later) is fast, loud and fun.

HEADING FOR THE SEVENTIES

Joe Camilleri, whom we have already encountered as a member of the short-lived Drollies, was one of thousands of young Melbournians hopping between bands, developing his musical versatility and style, throughout the 60s. At the time, he says, 'I was living in North Altona and I wanted to live in St Kilda'[231] – in other words, he was a suburban boy who longed for bohemia. In 1986, Camilleri gave an extensive overview of his early career to Wendy Milsom and Helen Thomas:

> I was fortunate that the band called the King Bees were desperate for a singer. They came from the other side. I came from Altona and I was a bit of a wild dog in those days. They were all Melbourne Grammar boys [and] Glen Waverley High kids. They taught me a lot, I couldn't speak English before I met them. They were doing a job in Footscray. I auditioned for them and we went through about forty songs... They used to back Normie Rowe... So I would do Normie Rowe songs, and 'I Belong With You' and all the Easybeats songs.
>
> We were really young. We were fifteen or sixteen years old and we were supporting the Easybeats, and we were playing at the Catcher when it used to go until 6 a.m. We would get something like $32 for the night and we would be there from 9 p.m. to 6 a.m. We had to play between all the main groups. It was pretty outrageous stuff... Ross Wilson's band the Pink Finks, Little Gulliver.[232]

If the King Bees had a job in Warrnambool: 'we would put everything in the Dodge; the PA, the amps, ourselves, guitars... It was just a sedan. Dave Flett was a genius, he could make it fit. His motto is: if it doesn't fit, cut it in half. We would have a little spot for Peter Starkie in the back seat, because he was the skinniest'.[233]

Flett, Starkie and Camilleri all went on to have varying degrees of success in Melbourne music in the 70s – Camilleri would become the most famous of the three; by the end of the decade he would lead one of the country's most prominent live bands, who were also a pop chart act.

The spirit of the late sixties as the times crept slowly into the early 70s is probably best exemplified by Wendy Saddington. Like so many of the great Australian musicians (especially female musicians) of this time, Saddington was under-recorded, and while she had her fervent fans – not least Renée Geyer – she remained a minority taste when she could quite appropriately have been a superstar. John Topper, an informant on the early 70s who will feature heavily in chapter 8, remembers seeing Saddington around his local area (the government housing estate of West Heidelberg) before she became famous. Saddington left school at fifteen. 'I've had about

25 jobs since I left school, they were all bomb-outs,' she moaned in 1968. 'The only thing I can do besides sing is type and that doesn't really grab me.'[234] She was 'discovered' in 1966 at a coffee shop in Carlton called the Love In.

> This guy from a group called the Revolution got in contact with me and before long I was singing with them at a few gigs. Then I became involved with the James Taylor Move, who I put up with for four months. We just didn't suit each other, I mean to say – they wanted to wear their creepy thin suits when I wanted to sing. I guess you could put it down to a mild clash of personality.

She went on to perform with the long-lasting, much beloved Chain (as well as giving them a new name to replace Beat 'n' Tracks[235]), though she later dismissed this experience by saying: 'You can take so much of working your guts out five lousy nights a week for some pathetic amount of money which when split five ways becomes even worse.'[236]

Saddington was an unusual type; her attitude was forthright and her preference – to sing live and to perform covers of songs she loved ('Nobody Knows You (When You're Down and Out)', as done by Jimmy Cox, Bessie Smith, Odetta, Otis Redding, etc.); Robert Parker's 'Barefootin''; the Beatles' 'Tomorrow Never Knows'; Bob Dylan's 'Just Like Tom Thumb's Blues'; and Nina Simone's 'Backlash Blues'), rather than concentrating on original composition and a stream of records – was considered commercial suicide. 'Some admire me, some think I'm the opposite – rubbish', she told a *GTK* reporter in 1970. 'Melbourne's slowing down,' she told *Go-Set*, 'because the discos are unlicensed and the kids are too young.'[237] She would shortly begin work as a *Go-Set* journalist, noted most particularly for her work as an advice columnist. The punchline of this 1969 interview resonates with her spirit, a kind of down-at-heel larrikinism that serves as both an epitaph and a provocative poke in the eye to the whole of the 1960s, not *just* young female singers:

> Before you go Wendy, any words of wisdom to aspiring young female singers?
> 'Yeah, give it up 'cos you're no good.'[238]

Perhaps some did, and of course many young performers of both sexes gave up, or were given up on, many of them justifiably. Yet the 1970s would in fact see a flowering of Australian popular music, and a whole new outpouring of something which, while it might have seemed at times dangerously close to patriotism, could more correctly be characterised as the unlocking of creativity and activity in live and recorded music, in songwriting, in broadcasting and in political awareness.

6 Falling off the Edge of the World
THE EASYBEATS

> *'Easyfever was a disease. Everybody in the pop scene contracted it as the sound of our greatest ever group swept the country in 1966.*
>
> *The Easys were churning out number one hits faster than any other artist could even make records. Every Easybeats performance was the scene for riots on a scale unknown before on the Australian pop scene.'*
> – David Elfick, 1969[1]

Like the Gibb brothers, the members of the Easybeats were migrants, though not all of them were from England: they were variously of Scottish, Dutch and English origin. Nevertheless, the Easybeats were unquestionably an Australian band. Unlike the Bee Gees, they had their greatest success in Australia and have continued to identify as Australian – although not without caveats, as a recent comment from Harry Vanda indicates:

> We always wanted to relate to Australia; we called ourselves an Australian band, although there were no Australians in it to speak of. But yeah, we felt Australian by that time already. Maybe because of the acceptance we'd had here, all the help, all the people on our side. To us this was an absolutely wonderful country. The alternative to pumping petrol in Glasgow or The Hague. So we were Australians and we remained Australians ever since.[2]

Not unnaturally, a large number of Australians continue to regard the group with great affection; 'Friday on My Mind', their biggest hit internationally and a number one in Australia over the summer of 1966-7, is often cited as the best of all Australian pop records. It is certainly close to perfect within its genre, but it is far from unique in the group's remarkable and brilliant catalogue.

The Easybeats came together in 1964 at Villawood Migrant Hostel in Sydney's south-western suburbs. One of the band's songwriting masterminds, guitarist George Young, has said the various members were living 'in or around' the hostel at the time.[3] Not only were they a mix of European ethnicities; they also varied in age, from late teens to mid-twenties. Drummer Gordon 'Snowy' Fleet had been a member of Liverpool band the Nomads (not, as frequently stated, the Mojos); he was 24 (an advanced age, to some) and married with a child. He named his new band the Easybeats after another he had previously played in, and was also its first manager.[4] Bass player Harry Vanda – he'd shortened his name to four easy syllables from the difficult six of Hendrickus Vandenberg – was 18, and had been in Australia a year;[5] in the Netherlands he'd had a band called the Starfighters. Guitarist Dingeman Vandersluys (rendered in some quarters as van der Sluijs), who took the stage name Dick Diamonde, was also Dutch by birth, and married. Teenage vocalist 'Little' Stevie Wright had 'come through the ranks of local clubs, dances and talent shows'[6] and was known to many as Chris Langdon when Vanda and Diamonde first met him. He had played in a band called the Outlaws (or was playing in this band when the rest of the Easybeats met him – accounts differ), followed by another called Chris Langdon and the Langdells, which some sources suggest briefly included Vanda and Diamonde. The three of them heard about 'this shit-hot little bloody guitarist,'[7] the Scottish-born George Young. Wright reverted to his real name for the new group after edging out a competitor, John Bell, who was deemed 'a bit shy' for the projected image (Bell went on to perform with the Throb).[8] Never ones to waste names, the new group initially called themselves the Starfighters.[9]

'George could busk his way through a bit of piano, guitar', his younger brother Angus has recalled, adding that all his brothers 'were players, which is strange, I suppose, because my mother and father never played.'[10] The oldest of the Young brothers, Alex, was a working musician who'd stayed in Britain when the family emigrated and settled in the Sydney suburb of Burwood; his two younger brothers, Malcolm and the aforementioned Angus would also become highly successful and distinctive guitarists. Like the Bee Gees, the oldest sibling in the family was a sister; Margaret Young had an R&B record collection that included Chuck Berry, Little Richard and Fats Domino. These classics are often credited with influencing all the boys, though – like the Gibbs' sister, Lesley – Margaret was not a performer.

Vanda says that as a displaced person, he – along with the rest of his family – had 'a bit of an "us and them" mentality.

> I think a lot of the way we expressed ourselves – talking, looking, the attitude – would also have been very much a part of the music. But maybe not from an intellectual point of view, just from an attitude point of view.'[11]

In his early days in the group, it is often suggested, Vanda's limited English kept him in the background – or, rather, meant he expressed himself primarily via his music and goofy facial expressions. Yet Young's thick Scottish accent was a similar hindrance, and their common eagerness to experiment with sound might well have come from a desire to express their individuality without inviting ridicule by actually saying – or singing – anything.

The new group arrived in a hurry. A casual Dutch-related connection – a bouncer they met on the street – led to a late-night residency at a notorious establishment in Sydney's Kings Cross called Beatle Village. A more lucrative deal lured them from there to the Bowl then on to John Harrigan's venues Surf City and the Beach Hut. Through their manager, real-estate agent Mike Vaughan ('probably one of THE great characters ever', according to Lillian Roxon),[12] the group met the 26-year-old Ted Albert, who became their producer and publisher. Ultimately the Alberts' and Youngs' family businesses would collaborate on one of the great showbiz success stories of the late 20th century. Alberts was a long-established and highly successful family music publishing business, and in the early 60s had forged a relationship with EMI to release various 'Albert Productions' on the Parlophone label; it would set up its own label in the early 70s. Alberts' biggest commercial successes during its Parlophone days were the Easybeats and Billy Thorpe and the Aztecs, though from an artistic perspective the success of early Missing Links and Throb singles should not be discounted.

Ted Albert usually recorded his bands at pop radio station 2UW's Radio Theatre in George Street, Sydney and it was here he took his new signings to record the reputed 45 songs in their repertoire, most of which were original Wright/Young or, less frequently, Wright/Vanda/Young compositions. George Young later recalled that Albert 'was so scared that he would miss a possible hit that he took us into the studio and had us put down every song we had, finished or not. Most of it was dreadful, although the first single came from those sessions.'[13]

Other recollections by Young contradict this in detail but not in spirit. Their debut, 'For My Woman', was certainly dynamic; the second, 'She's So Fine', was a number one hit around Australia in mid 1965 – a considerable feat for a group which had barely toured and did not have the advantage of network television exposure. Vaughan martyred himself for the cause, selling his Jaguar to buy a station wagon so the Easybeats could go on tour. They did so on wages so low that they were living, the possibly apocryphal story goes, on soup made from potato peelings. Certainly, semi-starvation appears to have been the reason Wright collapsed on *The Go!! Show* and was hospitalised. However weakened they may have been, however, the Easybeats were young men with a guppy spark: their self-defence-motivated fight with a group of labourers in Windsor Hotel is said to have made them a favourite with Melbourne DJs. 'Easyfever' meant 300 fans invaded the Youngs' family home when their address was published in a magazine; it meant a Brisbane Festival Hall show was cut short by police after 17 minutes because of the mass hysteria that broke out. A *Bulletin* columnist was witness to the phenomenon, describing Easyfever as though it were some kind of cult or mass-hypnosis exercise. Girls would frantically attack security guards or beat themselves up in their anguish; some 'tugged at their own hair or just sat there with three or four fingers in their mouths...'[14] Of course, it wasn't really a 60s phenomenon – it was a mass-media phenomenon. Similar episodes of mass hysteria half a century earlier focused on movie stars. But it was unusual for an Australian group to attract such a response.

'Wedding Ring' is a beautiful document of early-60s male and female roles: all Wright wants is 'love'; all his woman 'wants wants wants is a wedding ring' (the group tried to keep it a secret that three of them were married, but Wright, who wrote and sang these words, was a bachelor). It was a top-ten hit nationally, as was 'Sad and Lonely and Blue'. In his fine history of the Vanda and Young relationship, John Tait relates a perfect example of crude humour in the kind of audience participation that would reach its apex with the 'no way, get fucked, fuck off' response chanted at the Angels in the 1970s: the audience's response to the 'call' of the Easybeats' 'Come and See Her' was 'gonorrhea, gonorrhea.'[15] Their audiences were not immune to genuine emotional manipulation, though; 'In My Book' was written as a tearjerker, and in performance Wright would surreptitiously poke his fingers in his eyes to produce real tears.[16] After 'Women (Make You Feel Alright)', which Young has said was 'knocked out... in about ten minutes',[17] reached number one – 'we still don't like it much', Wright said at the time[18] – the group started to get used to being at the top of the Australian charts. The next step, as their fans well understood, would have to be the world:

> Dear Go-Set
> I am a regular "Go-Set" reader and a fan too... but I am upset about a comment on the Easybeats by Stan Rofe. He said the Easybeats will have to brush up a little on their act if they hope to do well in America. I think they are by far Australia's No. 1 group, and will soon be the world's. I think their act is great and Little Stevie is fantastic the way he goes on, but George is my favourite. It is just unfortunate that Little Stevie's pants split...
>
> Good luck, Easybeats, for when you go overseas... I'm sure you have plenty of fans who wish you the same!'
> Dissatisfied Easybeat Fan Forever, Northcote.[19]

According to Vanda, the group feared they would reach a point where audiences might respond with '"Oh shit, not them again!" So we felt [we should] leave on a high note and let's see if we can duplicate the whole experience over there.'[20] 'Over there' was to be Britain; they recorded 'Sorry', another extraordinary, classic single, to keep Australia satisfied while they were gone and set 14 July, 1966 as the date on which they would leave Australia. In the first week of July, the newlywed Vanda's young wife, Pam, committed suicide – apparently out of anguish at the prospect of being left behind in Australia. He became a widower with a five-month-old son, Johan.

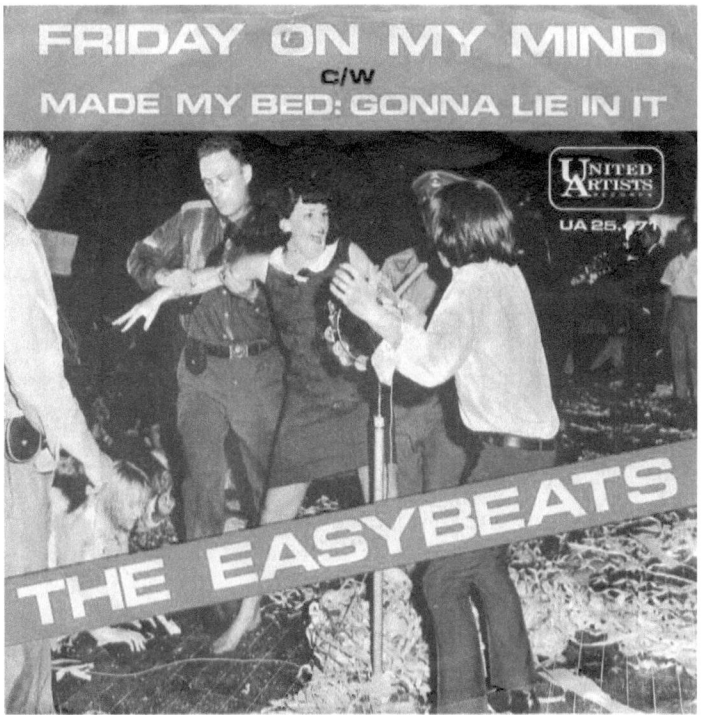

The Easybeats did not change their plans; Vanda's parents stepped in to take care of their infant grandson. Vanda has always sought to downplay the importance of this event in the Easybeats story – a tragedy that surely damaged all the lives it touched. He told Debbie Kruger in 2005 that 'it was a private thing,' adding that if it had come out in any of his songs, it was only 'from sheer carelessness.' It was not his desire to 'bore the world shitless with my pain.'[21] That may be so, but Vanda, who remarried, has written countless songs about desertion and loneliness in the last forty years.

Easyfever riots continued when the group touched down in Perth en route to the UK; screaming fans prevented their aeroplane from taking off again by surrounding it on the tarmac. The group's Australian earnings meant they were no longer starving by this stage ('we took a lot of money', Vanda said in 1969)[22] but naturally on arriving in London they were keen to make further progress. It didn't help that, as Wright later recalled, the band were treated by the British 'with the contempt they usually reserve for those from a European country.'[23] Ted Albert, who had produced their records to date, came to London, where they recorded 'Baby I'm A Comin',' a funny, catchy, bizarre tearaway of a song.[24] Their British label United Artists had no faith in its hit potential, and instead put Chicagoan Shel Talmy – who'd already worked wonders on the Who and the Kinks – in charge. The first session with Talmy produced four tracks which formed the core of the

US album *Good Friday:* 'Remember Sam', 'Made My Bed, Gonna Lie in It', 'Pretty Girl' and the first notable song written by Vanda and Young *without* Wright, 'Friday on My Mind'. The two had been inspired to write the song after seeing a short film about French vocal group the Swingle Singers, who specialized in largely a capella vocalized versions of famous classical pieces such as Bach's "Air on the G String".[25] The only evident similarity between the Swingle Singers' sound and 'Friday on My Mind' is the frantic, staccato, wordless backing vocals in the song's chorus which – like a lot of the best ideas – started out seeming hilarious, then became a key feature of something new and marvellous. Young has described 'Friday on My Mind' as 'real working class rock 'n' roll', adding: 'Being Hostel boys, that's what you dream about, Friday.' As he goes on to explain, the record was not an instant hit in Britain:

> It was practically a repetition of the same situation with our first record in Australia. Not many people were interested – not because we were an Australian band or anything, it's just that they weren't into the record.
>
> But then the pirate radio stations got a hold of it. Caroline, London, even Luxembourg, all these stations had Australian disc jockeys, and all the guys would slip in the record even though it wasn't programmed. It was due to these guys that the record broke. . . . we were very pleased. It was one in the eye to everyone who thought we wouldn't make it.[26]

As mentioned, in Australia 'Friday on My Mind' is generally regarded as a classic – if not *the* classic – Australian pop song. It is not particularly local in theme – except that it's putatively anti-authoritarian (Stevie tells us that though he's working for 'the rich man', he'll 'change that scene one day', though there's no more to the manifesto than that, and Simon Reynolds points out that a song like the Specials' 'Friday Night, Saturday Morning' from 1981 makes it seem somewhat hollow in comparison),[27] and it's anti-work, too. In November 1966, while the equally magnificent, rapid-fire 'Sorry' was at the top of the Australian charts, 'Friday on My Mind' was released and became an enormous hit, reaching #1 by the end of the year. Many saw it as consummate British beat pop: sharp, powerful, provocative. The Easybeats, for a moment, had the world at their feet.

The next single, 'Who'll Be the One', was every bit as melodic and inventive as 'Friday', but without the power-pop attack; it was not a success. Young described it later as 'rubbish, crap'.[28] A group as marvelous as the Easybeats could, however, have clawed their way back from this: it was the industry – and, according to Young, 'the dope thing'[29] – that was the real problem. Yet while drugs may have been a factor, Vaughan was perhaps the real stumbling block; he had entangled the group in a number of unwieldy contracts, and then absented himself. In 1976, George Young recalled the Easybeats' situation in the late 60s:

[We'd] start recording for one company and halfway through we'd find that the money had run out so we'd stop, start all over again two or three months later with another company and then the same thing would happen, it got so confusing.

But we kept on writing. So we had a regular thing going where we would go down to the Central Sound Studios in Denmark Street, London, every week to demo the latest tunes we had written. We got to the stage where we could get down a pretty complete demo in about an hour, with overdubs, effects and everything else.[30]

Australia still offered uncomplicated love. On 13 May, 1967 the Easybeats returned, the glow of 'Friday' all about them, for a tour, supported by the Twilights, Ronnie Burns and Larry's Rebels; conquering heroes, the group received a civic reception at Sydney Town Hall. A *Bulletin* correspondent found Stevie 'drinking beer out of a can and wearing a saffron-colored shirt with white sleeves' and noted, in the non sequitur style of the times, 'The same color is worn by novice Buddhist monks and it is also painted on the tails of airliners to warn away other airliners.'[31] Wright related the ubiquitous groupie tales: of a girl who delivered herself to the band at Lennons Hotel in Brisbane in a parcel, the Perth girls who crawled through their hotel fanlight.[32] The reporter went to the show and saw what excited girls, though s/he remained personally unmoved:

The greatest excitement came during the playing of 'Friday on My Mind'. Little Stevie was enormously impressive. Not only did he sing, he shook, he vibrated, he shuddered and with his hands and fingers extended he made high-speed quivering movement, like someone suffering from electric shock or on the farthest extremity of delirium tremens.[33]

The only major line-up change in the band's history occurred on this tour when, suffering from fractured and strained family relationships, Snowy Fleet left the group. He became a successful builder in Perth, not touching a drumkit again until the Easybeats' brief 1986 reunion; in the 21st century he ran Fleet Studios in the Perth suburb of Jandakot. Back in Britain, the band began recording a new album, to be titled *Good Times*, with producer Glyn Johns and makeshift drummer Freddy Smith. UK record company support fell through, however, and the *Good Times* album was not released; five of its tracks surfaced in 1977 on the Easybeats compilation, *The Shame Just Drained*, and its title was recycled for a definitive quarter-century Alberts compilation in 1988. The Purple Hearts' drummer Tony Cahill – who had previously played with Screamin' Lord Sutch in London and would later be the bassist in Python Lee Jackson – became a permanent replacement for Fleet and the first Australian-born Easybeat. The group's epic next single, 'Heaven and Hell', was recorded and released soon afterwards. Young recalls:

> We, as a band, weren't worldly-wise like other bands around us... We were still kids and there was nobody, no producer, no record company people, looking over our shoulder and pointing us the right way. We were more or less left to blow with the wind, with no conception of the business, marketing or musical policy, we were just writing music for music's sake – not a bad thing, I suppose.
>
> At that time we were very anti-nonoriginal, so to speak. The ultimate as far as we were concerned was to be totally original and get hits. Original in the sense of finding new drumbeats, new guitar styles, new melodies, new chord changes, that sort of thing.[34]

'Heaven and Hell' was original, and also vibrant and ambitious; it had a good chance of being a hit around the Western world except for a very clearly articulated line about 'discovering someone else in your bed' which led to it being banned by some radio stations; European radio didn't touch it either. Young has since said that the failure of 'Heaven and Hell' was disillusioning for him and Vanda, who were now in the most experimental phase of their time in the Easybeats, though they would write more 'three-minute operas', notably 'Falling off the Edge of the World' and the inferior 'The Music Goes Round My Head' (which Young has described, for no obvious reason, as being in a ska/bluebeat style).[35] The brilliant 'Come In, You'll Get Pneumonia' was the latter's B side, with orchestral contributions courtesy of the Bee Gees' arranger Bill Shepherd and backing vocals from Olivia Newton-John and Pat Carroll, but it would have been another masterful Easys moment even without the all-star cast; it accomplished the improbable feat of being a funky weepy.

There is a story that Paul McCartney heard one of these late-period Easybeats singles on his car radio and was so besotted that he pulled over and called the BBC to find out who was singing it – and to ask the station to play it again. Some (including Young) say this was their later single 'Good Times.'[36] Even this kind of support, however, wasn't enough.

Young has said the duo's response to their failure to chart was 'bugger it, let's turn out any old muck to get a hit!'[37] Vanda concurs that 'we came up with tunes like "Hello How Are You" and real maudlin shit, because we were trying to get on the radio.'³⁸ 'Hello How Are You' simply shows that the Easybeats' 'maudlin shit' is anyone else's magnificent, lush pop. It was mildly successful, making the top twenty in Britain (and 23 in Australia). Vanda, incidentally, puts one of the team's greatest songs – the complex, funny and brilliant ballad 'Falling in Love Again' – in the same 'cornball' bag, and calls it 'our BBC period'³⁹; it was later recorded by Ted Mulry with lashings of what sounded like sitar, but was probably Billy Green's treated guitar, for a top-three hit in 1971.

By 1969, Vanda and Young – at this point jointly the Brian Wilson of the group – were holed up in a flat in Moscow Road that had previously been a jingle studio for pirate radio. They were concentrating on making demos, often for other artists, with a view to restoring the group's fortunes. Somehow – it now seems bizarre that such a thing could happen – the last proper Easybeats album, *Friends*, was made up almost completely of Vanda and Young demos, sung mainly by Young, with the addition of two group tracks, 'St Louis' and the regrettably titled 'Rock and Roll Boogie'. Composer credits on almost all tracks are given to one 'Russell', though whether this is record company error or a ploy devised by Vanda and Young to negotiate their way through the complications of being exclusively signed to more than one label is difficult to judge.⁴⁰ In his comprehensive 1977 interview with Glenn A. Baker, Young described this record succinctly as 'a fuckup that came from changing labels . . . Harry and I played the drums and just about everything else.'⁴¹

'St Louis' offers an early example of Vanda and Young's tendency to reference American place names in their songs, though as Vanda conceded to Debbie Krueger: 'I wouldn't know what bloody St Louis was like; I've never been there.'⁴² Another peculiar habit of theirs is to begin songs with the information that the singer/narrator is walking down the street. 'Walking in the Rain', famously covered by Grace Jones, is perhaps the best of these, though 'Yesterday's Hero' offers strong competition. It had to be a strategy, and it certainly served them well in the following decades.

The group was petering out, and there are many suggestions that Stevie Wright's heroin use, which was to dog him throughout the 70s and 80s and make him an embarrassment to his former bandmates and many in the industry, had begun (Tony Cahill was already hooked). They returned to Australia in October 1969 to make some money, recording an *Easybeats Special* for Channel 7 and performing 35 live shows. Vanda announced his engagement to Melbournite Robyn Thomas. The support act for the group's shows was the Valentines, for whom Vanda and Young had written some songs. It seems clear in hindsight that, although there was no official announcement, this was the end. 'Eventually we'll come home,' Vanda told the press, suggesting that he and Young would be working behind the scenes with a range of artists.⁴³

Tait puts forward the tantalizing notion of a plan to relaunch the Easybeats in London in the early 70s involving Harry Vanda, George Young and his brother

Alex, plus drummer Eddie Sparrow, who worked extensively with former Soft Machine guitarist Kevin Ayers.[44]

Python Lee Jackson, with Tony Cahill, would have a freak international hit in 1972 with 'In a Broken Dream', largely because they'd happened to employ Rod Stewart, at the time a relatively unknown session singer, when they recorded it in 1970. Dick Diamonde did nothing musically significant after the Easybeats. Wright, described by Vanda in 1969 as a 'novelist, an actor, and "an all-round show-biz person,"' took on menial jobs, joined the cast of *Jesus Christ Superstar*, consolidated his aforementioned heroin habit, and began working on a solo album. But as he told Ed Nimmervoll in 1975, it 'just wasn't coming together' – he'd never written music before and hadn't written lyrics for years – and so he 'went to the boys and they saw the basis of something good in what I'd done.' Essentially, 'the boys' (Vanda and Young, of course) took over the project; they 'played practically everything on the album between the two of them', as well as writing almost all the songs.[45] The resulting *Hard Road* (1974) – and its 1975 successor, *Black Eyed Bruiser* – followed a similar formula; they are ersatz Easybeats albums, indicators of where the group might have gone had they stayed together. They also form the best 'missing link' argument for the theory that AC/DC was essentially a continuation of the Easybeats.

It was reported in 1974 that the multiple contracts in which Mike Vaughan had entangled the band made it impossible for Wright to do what he wanted him to do (with Vanda and Young's approval), which was to form his own new Easybeats, aided by agent Michael Chugg[46]: the name was effectively 'unusable'.[47] Wright's early solo forays were highly successful, but his addiction would soon ruin his chance of becoming the vocalist with Mott the Hoople[48] – and, most likely, with AC/DC. Certainly, Bon Scott came across like a parallel-universe Stevie, as well he might have done, given the predilection his Valentines had for Vanda/Young compositions.

The continuing partnership of Vanda and Young is covered in further detail in chapter 8. Like the Easybeats, it appears to have gone into abeyance without any fanfare; a 2006 John Paul Young album, *In Too Deep*, features a picture of chief composer/producer Harry Vanda at the controls with a very empty seat beside him. When 'Friday on My Mind' was voted "Best Australian Song" by the Australian Performing Rights Association in 2001, it was Harry Vanda who served as spokesman for the duo (and the band), as George Young was living in apparent seclusion in Portugal, Stevie Wright made no sense, and the others were now absent from the industry. But the Easybeats' legacy was already assured, without the need for any industry kowtowing; in fact, Alberts themselves had begun the process of enshrining the Easybeats' legacy with the release of a 1977 compilation with the aforementioned ridiculous title *The Shame Just Drained*: it only scratched the surface of the previously unreleased material. A 2-LP career retrospective, *Absolute Anthology*, emerged the following year. Repackaging has long been Alberts policy: the teen-oriented various artists compilation *Rocka* was soon joined by 'collector'-oriented releases such as *Alberts Archives,* featuring obscure Vanda/Young productions and early 60s tracks from Billy Thorpe, the Throb and, of course, the Easybeats.

For better or worse (probably worse, given the awfulness of the record), INXS and Jimmy Barnes gave the canonization of Vanda and Young perhaps its biggest boost when they covered 'Good Times', the Easybeats' worst single, in 1987. The Barnes/INXS version appeared on the soundtrack of Joel Schumacher's film *The Lost Boys* and thereby became a top-fifty hit in the US.[49] Barnes, in particular, slaughtered the song (though at least he didn't replicate guest backing vocalist Steve Marriott's pig squeals on the original). But whatever its artistic value (essentially none), the record showed that when Australia's most successful pop/rock artists of the late 80s wanted to represent the best of Australian commercial rock music, they turned to the Easybeats. There was something in their work for everyone, and almost all of it was magnificent.

bass. An interesting set for blues enthusiasts.

to repeat the successes of '64-'65.

● Spooky Tooh, alias Art.

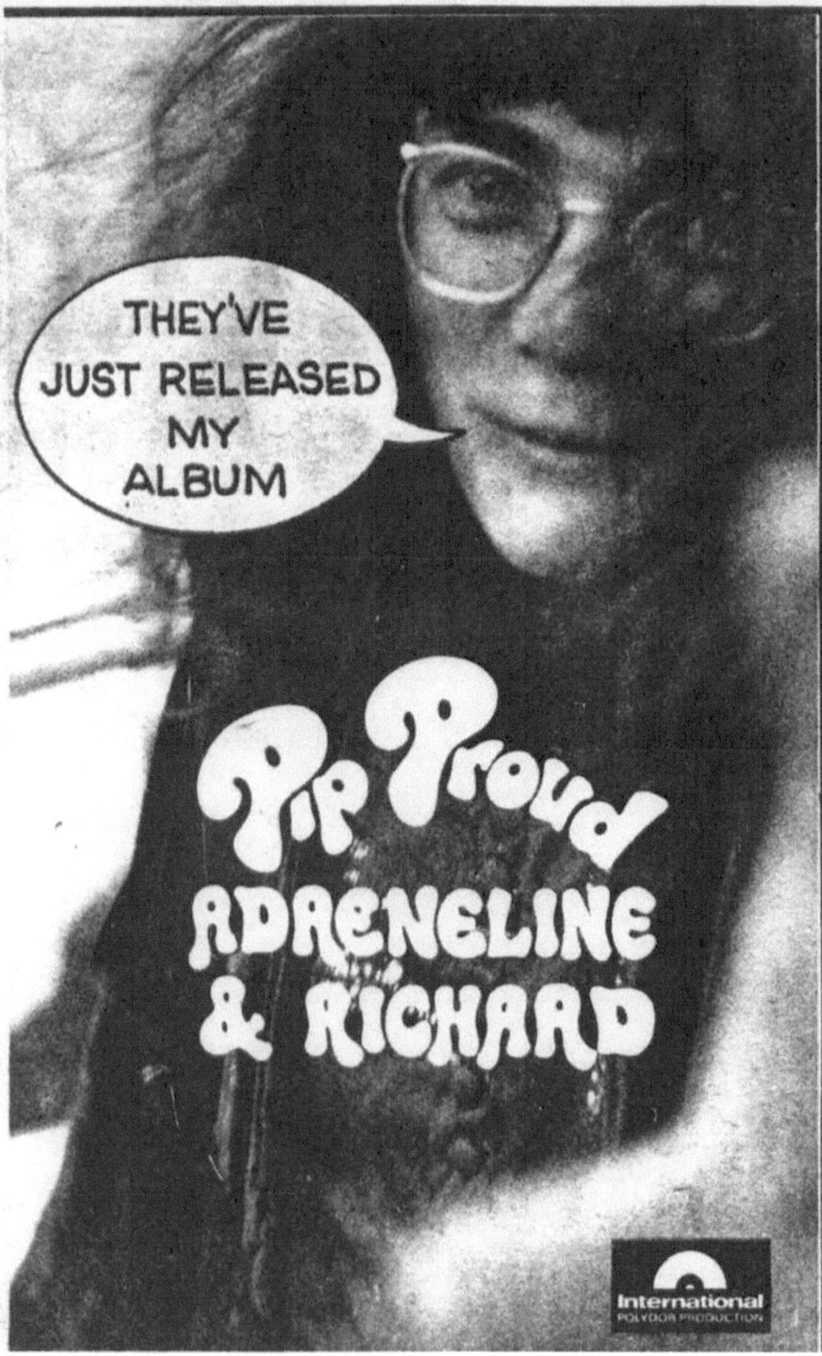

SUPE
FAIRY
ART

When
album
England
the writ
is actu
is nov
Tooth,
tined to
known

The fe
sound
guitar
really
number
Going
Spooky
under
"What's
track
Thing"
ing bo
holds o
of thre
between
drums
are son
slanted

A rea
venturo
music,
original
and tw
in such
are ind
the gr
materia

CH

"HURT
CHRIS
rod)

You'v
guy cre
do som
materia
worth
across
tics'
wrote)
when
bourne
cord-pl
was too
plastic
thing o

7 Knights in Yellow Armour
PIP PROUD

> *my music has brought young people to tears, to exclaims of 'genius', yet, still, there are these incredible people who think im a child. Gosh, i was screwed up too, i used to cry at night, but i got out of it, i created my self out of the mess my parents manufactured, but it seems theres not many like me. isnt there anyone who values truth before pleasure? i have no resentment, only a rather compassionate repulsion, and hence, a lonliness.*[1]
> – Pip Proud, circa 1967

In 2006 Lobby Loyde described Australian music of the 1960s and 70s as 'bloody sissy pop. The worst elements of pop.'[2] This view, coloured by insider experience, has its merits. Sissy pop – a valid form in itself, with Johnny Young's song 'The Girl That I Love' perhaps a prime and marvelous example of it – certainly thrived in this place and time (the alert reader may also have noticed that Adelaide even had a group in the mid 60s called the Syssys). But it is also undeniably true that some of the best pop music ever made came about in this era. If Pip Proud was pop (folk pop?), then he proves it.

While much of the flowery and celebratory puff which seems unavoidable in writing about the 60s should be viewed with some scepticism, the short public career of Pip Proud between 1967 and 1969 demonstrates, at the very least, that major record companies of the period were happy, even eager, to release experimental and entirely original Australian-made music, however possibly harrowing and uncomfortable (or, for that matter, valid and rich) it might have been for some listeners. Such companies were no doubt operating on the principle that the hippie and/or rock market was too difficult for them to understand, and that therefore anything might sell (the punk/new wave market was treated in much the same way a decade later), and this included albums of strange, surreal, whimsical-cum-scary songs sung in a hesitant yet eloquent way to the accompaniment of a solitary unplugged electric guitar.

Philip Proud was born in 1947 in South Australia; his father was a state public servant whose work required that the family – Pip, his parents, older brother Geoffrey and a number of Aboriginal foster children who would now mostly be classed as members of the 'stolen generation' – move around the state. He introduced himself to the readers of *Australian Poetry Now!*, an anthology of work by new poets that included his friend Michael Dransfield (through whose influence he was included in the book) thus:

> My name is Phillip John Proud, and this was naturally shortened to Pip Proud a few years ago ... My parents are middle class and so on, and so on.[3]

The 'middle class' admission might indicate a desire to avoid the kind of exposé Bob Dylan underwent in 1963 when *Newsweek* revealed he was merely 'a Jewish kid from the suburbs'.[4] Though Proud had not made the outlandish claims about his origins that Dylan had, like many others he had reinvented himself as transcending considerations of class, time and material status. As mentioned in chapter 3, the Proud family had lived for some time in Elizabeth, so Pip had lived there at the same time as the likes of Glenn Shorrock, Doc Neeson and Jimmy Barnes, though he did not know them.

Pip and his brother Geoffrey were creative types; Geoff would go on to become an extremely well-known and successful painter. Pip, diagnosed with motor coordination difficulties at a young age, prescribed guitar for himself as therapy – and it worked. As a teenager he was anti-authoritarian (he enticed an early girlfriend to run away from home with him; the experience is explored in a masked fashion in one of his early songs, 'Latin Version'), but he was never anti-learning; he had a strong interest in both the theoretical and practical aspects of science and left school to become an electrical apprentice and/or radio technician in his mid-teens. He spent some time as an apprentice in that line of work for the Federal Government's extensive and wide-ranging Snowy Mountains hydroelectric scheme, then abandoned this to live with Geoff in Sydney, where the brothers endured Gothic poverty for some time until the elder Proud began to receive some recognition and find supporters for his art. Forty years later, Pip wrote:

> All this lugging my guitar around trying to figure an E chord from an A chord. My brother trying to paint pictures. Once we rented a laundry to live in. It had a sloping cement floor with a big old cement laundry tub and a bunsen burner for a stove, but somehow we didn't mind. We had our dreams of fame and wealth one day, but the pleasure was from the sheer iconoclasm of it all. It was bloody hard and cold but each day seemed new ... It was cool to see how many days we could stay awake without sleep. We used to compete like that. I think five was our record though I'm not sure who won. My brother painting and me trying to figure out how a damn guitar works.

Geoff's rising star aided Pip in another way, as two men stepped in to further the younger artists' careers. One of Geoff's patrons, a stockbroker named Michael Hobbs, purchased a tape recorder for Pip and then, on hearing the songs Pip produced, paid for 50 (some sources say a mere 20) copies of an album, *De Da De Dum*, to be pressed on a pretend label called Grendel. Garry Shead, a painter like Geoff but also a cartoonist (for *Oz*) and maker of experimental short films, directed a 20-minute film called *De Da De Dum*, which was essentially a documentary about Pip Proud.

Pip wrote many letters to Hobbs, primarily to reinforce Hobbs's Medici-like patronage. He assumes throughout that Hobbs has his best interests at heart, but does not wish to draw on his goodwill more than necessary. He also, plainly, intends to use Hobbs's monetary gifts and/or loans to secure an 'in' with the conventional pop industry in Australia; the letters refer to important industry figures of the day, such as Ivan Dayman, Jim Sharman and Harry M. Miller. Hobbs was apparently not interested solely in Proud's musical career but rather in his overall development as an artist, so the letters also refer to books he is writing (Proud completed numerous novels, most of which he destroyed in the early 70s), film scripts, and a play, *Almond*, which was performed in Sydney in 1968. One letter reads (typing errors, aside from idiosyncrasies of capitalisation, corrected):

> My latest book will be finished in a few weeks. i showed it to Garry and his friend today and they were most impressed, as have been every one who has looked thru it. It is in two parts, describing the developments of a young man and his friend thru five years. the first part describes their meeting and relationship and the tentative changes L.S.D. has on them near the end of that section, and the second part is simply of a picnic they both have five years later, their thoughts and reminiscences.[5]

Usually, though, the letters are about Proud's music. They begin at the time Garry Shead embarked on the *De Da De Dum* film (Shead also wrote to Hobbs with a recommendation, saying 'I think Pip's music is so authentic and good that he is potentially the most original pop musician in Australia.'[6]) and occasionally refer to recent phone calls or interactions between Proud and Hobbs. One letter discusses the kinds of records Proud might go on to make, including an option in which he appears to place himself in a writer/producer position rather than a performer role:

> Well, Mr Hobbs, i have two kinds of music that are possibly capable of getting the success we want.
>
> the first kind of music is the kind on the film, and this is very simple to produce in all respects, but, as it is, if i am to continue with the sole guitar and my voice, nothing much can come from this, save a small name and following. to escape this nothingness and still keep the words to this type of song, i must orchestrate that the music has a beauty of its own, with the words and their feeling still guiding the melody this would require harpsichords and the like. there is no hope, and indeed, i feel, very little point in doing this, as i would produce only a

> very weird and beautiful sound. i think people would have to be led to like it, and
> i would have nothing to lead them with, except the film-type songs, but as i said,
> the following would be too small to bother leading. of course, business would
> improve as the word spread, but i am too impatient to wait for that sort of thing.
>
> the other type of music i have is a gentle but earthy sort of pop music. this
> would be very lucrative from near the beginning, after i had made the necessary
> adjustments to my self and thinking, which would be no trouble. the difficulties
> in doing this are these. firstly, i would need a very obedient group who were paid
> a regular wage, and this would be fairly impossible to get, as well as bringing
> many new problems such as where to practice etc.
>
> the second difficulty is brought with the second possibility, and this concerns
> musicians also. for, i could write out each song in full detail, hire musicians from
> their union for an initial charge of $20 a piece, and get them to play it whilst it was
> recorded. there are a few singers who do this. of course money is the problem.[7]

In *De Da De Dum*, Proud holds up the record of the same name, so it (or at least its sleeve, complete with track listing) plainly existed prior to filming. However, the versions of the songs that are heard in the film differ from those on the album; some of songs are not on the album at all. A letter to Hobbs claims that EMI had the 'record of the film music' though whether this refers to *De Da De Dum*, to the recordings in the film, or to something else is unclear. The same letter suggests the promoter Ivan Dayman as a possible industry contact, and Proud indicates he is on the verge of hitchhiking to Brisbane to introduce himself to Dayman.[8]

During the short and heady period in which he began his musical forays (probably around August 1967) Proud met Alison Burns. 'She had on a purple, woven dress and a hat, with thick, long, dark hair, and purple stockings. We started talking and she showed me her poetry,' he told *Australian Women's Weekly*.[9] The two of them (with another friend) appear on the cover of the album and in extensive scenes in the film, strolling along and exploring the beauty and horror of late-60s Sydney to the backdrop of Proud songs like 'An Old Servant' and 'De Da De Dum' itself. In a short interview segment, Proud claims as his inspiration 'knights in yellow armour'.

It is clear that the film – which was made available via the Ubu Collective, an experimental and low-budget filmmaking and distribution group – brought no little publicity to Proud, though whether it was seen by a broad audience is uncertain. Unlike many short films of the time, for instance, it does not appear to have been shown on television. Bob Cooley, an A&R man at Philips (and/or Phonogram; the company was transitioning at this stage, its parent having merged with Deutsche Grammophon),[10] was alerted to the Proud phenomenon by the film and arranged to re-record the material on the *De Da De Dum* album with a slightly altered track listing, to be released on the Polydor International imprint. In 1968 magazine writer James Oram quizzed Cooley on Proud and reported thus:

'He is,' said Cooley, 'either a genius or an oddball.'

'I am,' said Pip Proud, 'a romanticist, an idealist, a writer of fantasy.'

Whatever he is, Pip Proud is in danger of becoming one of Australia's biggest singing sensations. I shouldn't use the word 'singing', for he recites rather than sings and does it to a badly played guitar and a cowbell tinkled by his girlfriend.'[11]

It may be that Cooley anticipated hiring session musicians to back Proud on these new recordings, but Pip's erratic timing and inability to record his guitar and vocal separately would in any case have made this impossible. In the end, only two tracks were given additional instrumentation: the feminist parable 'Adreneline and Richard' (which became the title for this new version of the album) and 'Purple Boy Gang', which Proud had originally written for the Aboriginal singer Black Allen Barker and was transformed here into a rollicking R&B number. Proud did not hear these transformed tracks until after the album was released.

Philips/Phonogram allowed – indeed, required – him to appear on television, where he was often ridiculed by smarmy hosts and where the freedom of live TV allowed him to turn the tables on producers and cameramen who tried to make him stay in shot and play particular songs. In July 1968 he wrote to Hobbs from Melbourne, where he may have travelled specifically to appear on *Uptight*. 'If you wish to see the fulfillment of your ambitions concerning my abilities then you could tune into channel 10 on saturday morning on the 5th of July at 10 AM I do not know precisely at what time "I" shall be on.'[12]

Proud was in some respects an early example of a music phenomenon better suited to television than live performance, since he was soft-spoken and needed strong, separate amplification on his vocals. He did not shy from performing in front of an audience, however, particularly at the anti-war Arts Vietnam concerts in Sydney, and at his own series of concerts which he dubbed 'The Best in the World'.

The press coverage from this time displays an undeniable ambivalence with regard to Proud's unique style of half-spoken, half-sung, often absurdist and wry but never absurd or clichéd, guitar-based songs. Gil Wahlquist, music writer for Sydney's *Sun Herald* (also widely available in Melbourne, which lacked its own Sunday papers at this time) praised the album, concluding rousingly: 'If he can keep it up (he's only 21) he'll go places. If he doesn't, his contribution so far is considerable.'[13] *Go-Set*, on the other hand, would only refer to the album at arm's length as 'described as the most poetic disc ever made in Australia.'[14] Proud clearly felt that *Go-Set* should support him; given the general sycophancy and uncritical outlook that characterised most of its editorial coverage, he certainly could feel unjustly singled out when it did not. David Elfick, who ran the Sydney edition of *Go-Set*, was less than thrilled, in Proud's view. He wrote to Hobbs:

> The man from the *Go-Set* magazine simply doubted his own judgement with the songs it seems. we were foolish in that we mentioned andrew loogold ham

[sic] and his rejection of us, and the go set man brought a tired looking beatnick around to listen to the songs, he undoubtedly didnt like it, and so Mr david elfick simply became shy with us . . .

The reference to Andrew Loog Oldham is curious – it is probably connected to the Paul Jones/Who/Small Faces concert that took place in January 1968, when Proud met the Small Faces[15] – but the wider meaning is clear: Elfick was kowtowing to someone he saw as an international arbiter of opinion. On the other hand, says Proud:

Some people who came to our house on friday heard the music and began exclaiming and laughing, they said i had a 'whole metaphysical complex', what ever that means, and they became quite elated, so isn't that good?

He continues, baffled:

People who meet us seem to get initially very excited, as david elfick, who then suddenly withdraw, and im not sure what this is. we think it may be due to the personal neurosis of inadequacy with some, whilst with others its perhaps a contempt derived from their inabilities they discover from comparing.[16]

Proud told Oram that if the public decided 'it's a send-up . . . well, all right. I will be disappointed, but there's nothing I can do about it.'[17] At the same time, he mixed an insistent dedication to success with despondency: 'there is no market that can be easily reached. i do not wish to spend this year cultivating one.'[18] Similarly, he schemed:

There are probably 50 people just like me in Australia, all saying the same things in different ways, and so how I am to succeed is by working into areas where they would not go. – The first album was a good example of this.[19]

And . . .

For, you see, the artist sets the fashion in music and so people buy his music, which has made itself fashionable. If i cannot succeed in making myself fashionable, then some one else will make me unfashionable.[20]

'I am already regarded as Australia's top underground singer,'[21] he told Hobbs. Proud was in his early twenties at this time, and it's possible his arch personal style was working against him (even more so than his unconventional musical style) in a scene which prided itself on being both mellow and unassuming. Penniless – he often did not have enough to eat – he boasted of a largesse that was plainly beyond his wildest dreams. David Elfick reported in *Go-Set* that Proud had 'tried to go into the Sydney Public Library last week but was barred because he had no shoes on' and quoted Proud declaring he had 'decided to offer the director of the library $1,000 if he would allow bare feet into libraries.'[22]

As we have seen from the Missing Links' experience (see chapter 4), Philips/Phonogram was one label that did not seem to object to fairly low record sales. In any case, *Adreneline and Richard* must have been extremely cheap to make – the product of less than a day's recording, and very little mixing. While it is uncertain how well it sold, it was evidently enough for the company to request further product. Proud wrote to Hobbs that he had written a song he thought appropriate for a single: 'We took a tape to Philips – they liked the song very much but will not record it until we get a drummer. This could be recorded privately for about $50...'[23] Elfick wrote that the song was 'one of a series of songs that Pip wrote on the Titanic disaster'[24] – an unintentionally amusing slip, but telling nonetheless, although there are no songs on the second album, *A Bird in the Engine*, that would seem to fit this description. In March 1969, the *Bulletin* told its readers that 'his new record will have the music of bass, drums, and even a cello, so perhaps some musicianship will be managed without the pretentiousness he says he dreads so much. Certainly, if he's only feigning his dread, he's taking a lot of trouble to maintain the pose.' (Of his fans, Proud apparently said: 'I think half of them come along to see how bad I am.')[25]

The short-lived Pip Proud Group featured two young men he met at a party: John Black on bass and Peter Fairlie on drums. 'Tomorrow,' wrote Michael Symons in the *Australian*, 'he spends five hours at another studio recording four possible singles and a fifth if he has learnt piano in time.'[26] He might have done so, and he might have involved Black and Fairlie, but no single or Pip Proud Group recording emerged.[27] In 1969 Proud recorded a second album accompanying himself on guitar in a small cheap studio in the inner-city Sydney suburb of Darlinghurst. Most of the tracks on this album were in the same vein as the first; there was, however, a truly extraordinary title track in which Proud was accompanied by a friend, Harry Johnson, banging a microphone on a cardboard box to create a thunderous, evil sound which anticipated art-punk by a decade.

Proud played very few live shows in Sydney in the late 60s. His debut was at one of a series of anti-war concerts presented by Arts Vietnam at Paddington Town Hall on 3 October 1968, along with Nutwood Rug and Peter Anson's group, the Id. The following February, Proud presented his play, *Almond*, 'involving four characters. They are Ellis, who is the protagonist, a girl named Madrid, her sister Ruth and another character of doubtful definition called Osborne.'[28] By all accounts this production was not a major success; audience members booed during its performance. In April 1969, he organised two concerts under the title "The Best in the World". This was the name of a new song he had written (not about himself), but his use of the title in this context was, of course, typical Proud.

He told Hobbs that 'over a thousand people attended both concerts.'[29] One of these people was Michael Dransfield, an up and coming poet who was besotted by Proud's music and introduced himself backstage. The two men would become inseparable for a time: Dransfield went out with Alison Burns's sister Hilary, and the four of them shared a flat in the six months before Proud and Alison Burns left Australia.

In October 1968, with no obvious impetus from Proud himself, *Go-Set* had used a picture of the singer in a competition they were running, which rather irresponsibly for a 'teens and twenties newspaper' offered one lucky reader the chance to 'win a one way ticket anywhere.' Even more ridiculously than usual for *Go-Set*, the competition – for which a winner was never announced – was described as 'for people who want to pursue their groove. Once you find your groove, you probably won't want to come back.'[30] A year later, Proud was working to find his groove, mending washing machines and saving money to go to Europe.[31] In November 1969, *Go-Set* readers were told:

> Pip has left for England where he hopes to crack the big time. He already has a couple of people interested in his work and has a contact in Apple Records. Pip has become very interested in Archeology and hopes to do some field work on the subject when he goes to Abyssinia.[32]

London was, however, a disappointment. Apple were, of course, deluged with tapes from hopefuls. The BBC DJ John Peel was more encouraging; he had a label, Dandelion, at this time. Accessing a golfball typewriter with only capital letters, Proud wrote to Alison Burns's mother:

> I WENT AND SAW JOHN PEEL, AND HE IS VERY KEEN ON MY MUSIC AND ONLY APOLOGISED THAT HE COULDN'T GIVE ME A RECORD CONTRACT STRAIGHT OFF, BUT HE SAID HE'D SEE WHAT HE CAN DO, AND I'LL RING HIM TOMORROW. NOT WISHING TO SOUND TOO CASUAL, ACTUALLY IM IN UTTER EXCITEMENT.'[33]

'I AM REALLY TRYING FOR A HIT SINGLE,' he bellowed across two continents and an ocean. 'IF I GET THAT, JUST ONCE, WE CAN ALL RETIRE... THIS ISNT AUSTRALIA.'[34]

Burns joined him in London, but the experience was profoundly unhappy. Proud finished a novel, *The White Forest*, which Dransfield was going to publish (but didn't). Starving in London is much like starving in Sydney, only much colder – the pair began their return to Australia by traveling across Europe and Asia (no Abyssinian archaeology is known to have been undertaken). Whilst they were in India, they learned that Proud's adopted sister had killed herself; his parents flew him back to Australia.

Until this point, most Australian artists who had travelled overseas for fame were funded by record sales, perhaps even record companies, and had at least the slightest hope of hitting a chord with an existing industry: Proud, his major label experience notwithstanding, had nothing comparable behind him. Back in Sydney he wrote some more songs – recorded at home – and by the mid 70s was writing poetry and radio plays for 2JJ (amongst them a series called *Vlort Phlitson*), but his initial reach for the stars was concluded.

Some years afterwards, in the late 70s, Proud wrote to Michael Hobbs after he'd just heard the Clash on the radio:

> '"I have no will to survive, i cheat if i can't win" . . . That's a line out of a "punk rock" song I'm listening to. You know, I'm starting to get this feeling of "what are the young coming to?" I say all of this to you because you thought maybe I was worth encouragement or something.'[35]

Pip Proud was an unusual, in some ways unique artist (and he would be again; his revived career in the 1990s is just as extraordinary). Many have dismissed him on the basis of their mistaken estimation of his idiosyncratic style (although few with a more evident display of ignorance than British 'psychedelia' expert Vernon Joynson, who – typically for a writer who has no issue appropriating the ideas of others as his own – offers a cursory 'Both albums are reputedly awful.')[36] It would also be far too simple to write off his work from this time as being of interest merely as an example of how 'out there' major record labels were willing to go in the late 60s, even though this is true as far as it goes. The more important thing to note about Proud's work is that, regardless of when it happened, he was reinventing pop with an injection of artistic and literary experiment and a brash, rebellious attitude. The story of Pip Proud in the late 60s demonstrates one of the core truths of not just Australian music history but the history of all art, everywhere – great visionaries are not always recognised in their time, and great art is not always rewarded, yet this fact should neither enhance nor diminish the value of the art itself. Proud's biggest error – though it is an entirely understandable one – was to quit music so early in the piece and let circumstances, together with others' ignorant low estimation of his abilities and his own self-doubt, define the narrative.

In his provocative 1970 'bio' for *Australian Poetry Now!* Proud had taunted its readers, whom he assumed to be eggheads. 'Any displeasure,' he wrote, 'is due to your blindness or illusion.'[37] This statement could serve as an epitaph to his 1960s career.

AZTEC ENERGY

AZTECS LIVE SUPPORTED BY WARREN MORGAN 25TH JULY — 6TH AUG.

AZTECS LIVE SUPPORTED BY LOBBY LOYDE COLOURED BALLS 20TH–23RD JULY

with GERRY HUMPHRIES · compere

AND SUNBURY
POP FESTIVAL ON FILM

featuring—
Max Merrit & The Meteors
Greg Quill & The Country Radio
Sera, Chain, Pirana,
and many more.

"This brilliant piece of work captures better than actually being there just what Australian rock festivals and Australian films are on about" — Review.

Thursday 20th: Brisbane Festival Hall
Friday 21st: Armidale Town Hall
Saturday 22nd: Lismore City Hall
Sunday 23rd: Dubbo Civic Centre
Tuesday 25th: Canberra Theatre
Wednesday 26th: Woolongong – Vista Theatre

Thursday 27th: Sydney – Hordern Pavilion
Friday 28th: Griffith – Woodside Hall
Saturday 29th: Orange – Amoco Centre
Sunday 30th: Melbourne – Festival Hall
Tuesday 1st: Geelong Palais
Wednesday 2nd: Colac – Regent Theatre

Thursday 3rd: Hamilton – Regent Theatre
Friday 4th: Adelaide – Thebarton Town Hall (Barton)
Saturday 5th: Elizabeth – Octagon
Sunday 6th: Mt. Gambier – Odeon Theatre

8 It's a Flash!
THE EARLY TO MID SEVENTIES

> Australian rock is probably the most advanced in the music world because this country has never known success, that perverter of truth and destroyer of progress. By the very virtue of its separateness and isolation Australian rock has weaved itself into its own thing; it has a distinction, an original and exciting dimension so totally its own. Even our pop-hype groups are so much better than many so-called 'International-Heavy-Super-Hype' bands, our pop-hypes have to achieve on stage the same sounds English and American bands achieve in a million dollar studio. Put them in good studios with open-minded technicians and you get LPs like 'the Masters" English LP, a very good LP for a band that musically is still learning what it's about. Put the Aztecs, Chain, Spectrum etc. into the same studios and watch out ears.'[1]

Lobby Loyde was expressing a minority view when he trumpeted these forthright, insider opinions on the state of Australian music in 1971 in the high-quality weekly Melbourne music paper *Daily Planet*. He appears to have forgotten about his childhood rivals the Bee Gees, along with other Australians who'd had major success in the 1960s (though these omissions can perhaps be explained by his definition of 'rock').

Within the next few years Australian groups and artists such as AC/DC, Rick Springfield, Olivia Newton-John and Little River Band would experience major international success. None of them was obviously Australian in sound or style, but all emerged quite organically from within the Australian pop/rock industry, even if only the first was likely to have met with Loyde's approval – appropriately so, since AC/DC owed a significant debt to his own work.

Loyde was already a well-known player when he wrote these words. He had gravitated from Brisbane to Melbourne in the late 60s, had joined and then left the Aztecs, and was currently playing with a final, ad hoc line-up of the Wild Cherries, who had an extraordinary single on the Havoc label, 'I'm the Sea (Stop Killing Me)', the B side of which also bore the title 'Daily Planet'. Loyde would shortly move on to form the Coloured Balls, a group that grew out of his solo experiments. In this 1971 diatribe he went on to declare 'war on Schmaltz' on behalf of 'Australian rock players':

We think Australian audiences deserve the music we can hear in our heads; not the sell out crap that recording company producers hear in their cash register un-heads.'[2]

Like a number of his contemporaries, including Billy Thorpe, Loyde's condemnation of the mainstream music industry derived from bitter experience. His rejection of the economics of the business was fashionably simplistic, but it stands to reason that Australian record companies would ignore Australian acts as long as they could profit by concentrating primarily on promoting their parent companies' British and American artists, whose recording costs they didn't have to pay and who they only had to deal with in person on the rare occasion those artists came to Australia on tour.

The early 70s would see the overturning of this cosy arrangement, as the national culture quickly, if unevenly, came into bloom. The development of a consciously Australian popular music was a key element in this broader flowering. The next two chapters – one an overview of the period, the other focusing specifically on Daddy Cool and Skyhooks – explore its different aspects.

NEW SOCIETY

The decade of the 70s is typified for many Australians by the gospel-pop song 'It's Time', which was the campaign theme of the victorious Labor Party in the watershed election of August 1972. The song's vocalist was Alison McCallum, who in the late 60s had been a member of Dr Kandy's Third Eye (along with Gulliver Smith). McCallum had recently made the national top ten with Vanda and Young's song 'Superman'; given her participation in 'It's Time,' listeners might well have felt invited to compare Labor's visionary leader Gough Whitlam with that same superhero.

There was nervous anticipation, both optimistic and pessimistic, about the new society that would take shape after the expected Labor victory; the question of the future appearance and feel of the new Australian culture was foremost for Australians. Australians (particularly but not solely young Australians) seem to have known that something was about to happen as soon as the 1970s rolled around. The nation had been prosperous for so long that almost no one under 35 had any memory of what it was like to be anything other than securely employed; this was largely true even among people who considered themselves working class and/or downtrodden. Consequently, society's elders – whose fears and conservative habits (or in some cases radical left-wing politics) had been shaped by the Depression and the Second World War – seemed alien to them.

Its relative prosperity notwithstanding, Australia was plainly a morally and spiritually frazzled nation ready for some kind of cultural revolution. Billy McMahon, the new Liberal Prime Minister who had come to power via a backroom coup in 1971, was neither liked nor trusted even by those in his own party and government, and his promotion was clearly a mistake.³ (Time would show that his greatest legacy, aside from making Whitlam's victory easier, was the fathering of the Hollywood actor Julian.)

It seemed highly unlikely that the electorate – even if most of it had happily tolerated two decades of oppressively staid federal government under the patrician Menzies, the stilted Holt, and the cocky and genially gnarled Gorton – would elect McMahon: a Labor government in 1972 was closer to certain than it had been for decades, and had indeed almost happened in 1969. The youth vote – there were adults with no memory of a government other than the Liberal/Country Party conservative coalition – was one important sector of the population agitating for change; Gough Whitlam had also courted other elements of the community, such as postwar migrants and residents of the underresourced outer suburbs of the major cities. What's more, the Liberals' entanglement of Australia in the Vietnam war had become widely unpopular, perhaps because, as journalist and activist Pete Steedman has put it, 'mummy middle class' had begun to see 'sonny middle class coming back in a fucking bag'⁴; Australian women, led by Jean McLean, organised the Save Our Sons Movement. The rise of this organisation made it plain that protest against government policy was not *merely* the province of overstimulated, rebellious-for-the-sake-of-it young people; there were also others who (albeit more cautiously) rejected not only the war but the 'straight' yet hypocritical society from which it had sprung. While protest against the Vietnam war, rapacious urban development, and racism was no longer only the province of youth, however, rock and pop music was still primarily for the under-25s who had grown up with it.

The early 70s saw an upsurge in political activism which embraced the Aboriginal Land Rights movement⁵ and other protests by and on behalf of Aboriginal people in Australia, including the Aboriginal embassy that was erected three times outside Parliament House in Canberra, and pulled down by the authorities twice.⁶ The Aboriginal Black Panther movement shone briefly, with leading activist Denis Walker thrilling and frightening the Anglo-Australian media with statements such as: 'It would give me a lot of pride to walk down the street carrying a gun to make sure no pig could touch me.'⁷ Walker's Anglo-Australian girlfriend, Lindy Morrison, was a social worker in Brisbane, although she would soon abandon that profession for the theatre and later for music – all of these pursuits were appropriate within the world of protest and activism. In the country that had been in the forefront of enfranchising women 80 years earlier but then became mired in adherence to textbook gender roles, women's liberation marches were now frequent and effective. Merely the activism inherent in leading a radical lifestyle was liberating for many women *and* men. Most prominent – probably because they were the most inclusive – were the seminal Vietnam moratoriums of 1970 and 1971,⁸ mass demonstrations that are still regarded as a crucial element in the development of not only a radical Australia but also a motivated middle Australia. Ian Turner wrote of the first moratorium in Melbourne in May 1970:

There had been nothing like it in Melbourne since V-E day; a concourse of people so vast that the city centre was wholly occupied. The traffic stopped, the shops closed; for a whole afternoon the city returned to one of its traditional functions – a place where pedestrians could define their own needs and purposes... The people of my generation made at most one in ten of those who filled the streets. The ninety per cent were young. For the first time even children had taken to the streets of their own volitions... telling the oldies that the world would soon be theirs... This was the counter-culture on the march...[9]

In Sydney, Greg Quill reported, 'A very human anger hurled itself down wintry city blocks and stamped into cold pavements.'[10]

For once, the vast majority of Australia's pop stars let it down; none of these potential role models seemed to think change would come about through protest, though Wendy Saddington assured *Go-Set* readers that 'the Vietnam War stinks'. Ronnie Burns – still in the public's mind the star who sang the first anti-Vietnam pop song, 'Smiley' – said he'd be marching in the moratorium parade 'because I believe the war's wrong' but said he felt it would only be a gesture. Mike Rudd, always cynical, didn't think the Moratorium 'will really succeed'.[11] Jeremy Noone of Company Caine coined the term 'plastic wombats' to refer to his country's soldiers in Vietnam (the Australian cousins of the 'Yankee paper tigers').[12] The Arts Vietnam festival staged in Sydney in October 1968 had been by all reports a major success in raising consciousness about the war; Pip Proud and Nutwood Rug Band were there, but it is plain that many were sceptical about young people's involvement in these causes.

Tim Burstall's wonderful comedy *Stork* shows the confusion these ideas often generated. Eleven minutes into the film, a montage of protest posters introduces a scene in which Bruce Spence, in the title role, disrupts a Monash University lecture. The showy music that plays over these posters seems to suggest a cavalcade of craziness, or perhaps a collection of consumable, but ephemeral, protest 'products': it's yet another example of the non sequitur approach to the representation of political activism in the early 70s. In early 1972, Anarchist draft resister Michael Matteson came out of hiding to appear on the cutting-edge current affairs show *This Day Tonight*, with every expectation of being arrested afterwards. Instead, he escaped through a small window at the back of the ABC's Sydney studios.[13] The police ended up looking stupid and *TDT* looked refreshingly countercultural; the real radicals looked brave and principled (as indeed they were); and activism was seen to be effective, whatever Ronnie Burns might believe.

There were numerous other changes in the air. In his book on glam rock, Barney Hoskyns quotes *Esquire* journalist Tom Hedley to the effect that the early 70s were 'the homosexual time... The faggots were our [i.e., Americans'] new niggers.'[14] 'Homosexuality was chic,' Hedley says, and in Australia too, gay liberation was a hot topic. In one sense, of course, this was old news in Australian pop – Keith Glass's soul-pop group Cam-Pact's flirtation with a homosexual 'style' had already challenged convention in the late 1960s. Jim Keays writes that in the late 60s Daryl Sambell 'quite frequently' booked the Masters Apprentices into 'camp dances ... in out-of-the-way venues that only those in the know could find'.[15] There was clearly a whole vocabulary of camp behaviour in the music hall styles of are-they-or-aren't-they-gay celebrities of Australian television such as Graeme Kennedy, Stuart Wagstaff, Frank Thring,[16] Ian Meldrum, and a host of lesser lights. At the same time, everyday life featured often horrific violence against gay men, which in many ways can be interpreted as sanctioned by the wider society. Unsurprisingly for the times, there were also macho groups like the Zoot (discussed in chapter 5 in their late 60s context), who saw the writing on the wall for their former non-threatening bubblegum image and were quick to deny any 'pink poofter'[17] tag. There is also, of course, Johnny Farnham's infamous line (no doubt a reaction to rumours about his close relationship with his manager): 'If poofters come near me, I'll kill 'em'.[18] A Gay Lib demonstration against the ABC's decision – apparently at the last minute – not to screen a report on

homosexuality[19] appears to have been an important spark for the gay rights rallies which took place in mid 1972. In July of that year, the organisation C.A.M.P. proclaimed a 'Sexual Liberation Week'.[20]

Few would disagree that Melbourne remained the centre of Australia's music scene in the early 70s, as it had been in the late 60s. When the decade began, clubs like Sebastian's and Bertie's (both brainchildren of Michael Browning, soon to be manager of AC/DC), and the Thumpin' Tum, all located in the central business district, reigned supreme. Weekend dances in the middle-to-outer suburbs – such as the Q Club in Kew, Pepper's in Box Hill, the White Elephant at Broadmeadows, and the Purple Spirit in Sunshine – would host name bands like the La De Das, the Aztecs, and Chain. Establishments like the T. F. Much Ballroom (in Fitzroy, walking distance from the city centre, and the natural place for Peter Weir to document Australia's emerging pop/rock acts) and Toorak's Regent Theatre augmented the scene by featuring markets and art as well as innovative new bands.

Melbourne was famously the most staid and wowserish of the nation's state capitals, but it nevertheless (or perhaps for that very reason) had a thriving art-rock underbelly. It had the nation's premier 'import' record shop, Archie and Jugheads; located 'in a tiny lane off Collins Street' and owned and operated by Keith Glass and David Pepperell, the shop offered British and American releases for sale before the Australian branches of the major record labels had issued them locally.²¹ That Melbourne boasted the country's best newspaper (*The Age*), and that after 1971 the state of Victoria had an unusually liberal Liberal government under the benign and democratic Rupert Hamer, did not hurt matters.

In January 1970 the *Age* tossed out some apparently zany predictions about the decade ahead. Many of them proved to be correct. It suggested the Labor party would win the next federal election, in 1972, and serve two terms – which it did, even if its second term was cruelly curtailed by political conspiracy at the highest levels. The paper also suggested 'TV, movies, pop music, color, art and good design' would free young people's minds from an 'obsession with the printed word', and:

> Young people... will be bored and dissatisfied... Young fashions – as usual – will outrage the oldies. The more sartorially adventurous young men will probably be wearing codpieces, while bared breasts and scantily-girt buttocks will be de rigueur for the trendier (skinnier?) young women.²²

Out-of-town weekend rock festivals were providing places for young people to congregate, and even if they didn't actively conspire against the mainstream, but rather maintained a sullen lack of interest in it, such gatherings made them realize just how many they were in number.

PILGRIMAGES FOR POP

As will be seen, *where* people experienced their rock and pop would become very important. Festival events were quickly embraced by Australians – already well acquainted with various versions of an outdoor lifestyle. Tully and Billy Thorpe and the Aztecs starred at the 'Pilgrimage for Pop' festival at Ourimbah. Here, in February 1970, a natural amphitheatre near Gosford in NSW²³ saw '8,000 people who like pop and individuality' congregating in a 'green valley'. The event had been organized by the Nutwood Rug Band, a group of US draft dodgers from California. Plainly, there was great apprehension amongst law enforcers about the event, but as *Go-Set* reported: 'The local police gazed at the thousands of colorful "pilgrims" and got used to the idea that long hair, beards, beads and no-bras don't spell trouble.'²⁴ *Age* journalist Robert Drewe – later to become a very good novelist – noted 'short back-and-sides young constables' looking 'frankly envious as young semi-naked couples emerged from the shady Ourimbah Creek.'²⁵ Wendy

Saddington, who wrote regularly for *Go-Set* in the early 70s, presented a report on Ourimbah that presented it as a genuine communal experience:

Ourimbah was simply a flash, a quick look at how life should be and a brilliant weekend proving that one can be so much happier without the ridiculous restrictions and conventions which society insists upon. A place, a time where policemen could be people and people could be humans, not just indoctrinated representatives of ammunition or targets. [26]

The Fairlight Festival near Mittagong the following year was a disaster due to weather and organizational problems;[27] Myponga, with a smaller group of attendees (estimated at 5,500), was not a success either: heavy rain and icy winds no doubt made the experience unpleasant even before the Draft Resisters' Union tried to break down the fence, distributed pamphlets condemning the festival as a money-making concern, and at one point marched onto the stage chanting 'out, pigs' and 'free concert'.[28] Another 'pop concert', sponsored by the T. F. (the 'T. F.' did indeed stand for 'Too Fucking') Much Ballroom and planned for the outer Melbourne township of Launching Place, was washed out and a compensatory event was staged five weeks later at Burnley Oval in inner Melbourne, where the musical exponents joined forces with the long-running Ashton's Circus.[29] Anticipation of Launching Place inspired two marvelous songs recorded at the sessions for (and added to the reissue of) Spectrum's first album, *Spectrum Part*

One, though Mike Rudd's bleak description of 'children making love to children' hardly evoked feelings of bliss. The organisers of the Lothlorien festival arranged not only for the presence of the Nutwood Rug Band, but also displayed an Australian flag appropriated from atop the Sydney GPO; 'Friends', the *Planet's* correspondent announced, 'the Commonwealth patches its flags.'[30]

It is distinctly possible that even for those who did not attend these regional festivals – some of which were day trips from major cities, others camping forays only available to dropouts (or the wealthy or frugal or otherwise 'free') – the image of rock 'n' roll in the countryside, rather than in small clubs or halls in cities and towns, was part of a nascent environmentalist ethos, as exemplified by poet Charles Buckmaster, writing in 1970:

> There is no retreat – you thrust your obscenities beneath my feet and tell me that
> I soil *your* earth!
> I scrape at the bitumen of your carnal streets – the soil in which no thing could grow for a thousand years. So much destruction![31]

Midway between the rock festival experience and countercultural lifestyle celebration was the Aquarius Festival, which the Australian Union of Students had organised every two years since 1967. The 1971 iteration of this arts and music festival, held in Canberra, was in retrospect deemed to have been 'a good example of bourgeois culture at its worst', so it was decided to move the 1973 event away from 'the university scene' to a location in northern NSW. The small town of Nimbin was chosen by co-directors 'Kaptain Kulture and Superfest' (Johnny Allen and Graeme Dunston of the NUAUS),[32] who ruminated: 'The big if is whether the locals would take kindly to an inundation of heads.'[33] Many of them didn't, but within a relatively short time the 'heads' *became* the locals – Nimbin was soon known in Australia as the epitome of an 'alternative lifestyle' town, though today it is perceived as a bastion of elderly hippies and hard drugs. Another festival in northern NSW, the Tamworth Country Music Festival – now a national institution – began as a low-key and very traditional affair, also in 1973.[34]

For most Australians old enough to remember the early 70s, the most important rock festivals were the four Sunburys, staged by Odessa Promotions, which was headed by promoter John Fowler. The first was in January 1972; all took place in a 'natural amphitheatre' by a stream just outside Melbourne. Not only were many of the performances legendary (particularly those by Chain, Billy Thorpe and the Aztecs, and the Coloured Balls), there were also – importantly – films and records made of at least some of the Sunbury shows, which greatly increased their impact. At Sunbury '73, Paul Hogan – 'everybody's favourite clown' for his TV work and witty cigarette ads – entertained the crowd.

Skyhooks, in only their first year of existence, and with original singer Steve Hill, were notoriously a major event at Sunbury '74. They were booed off stage;

Hill quit after seeing film of himself from the day. The group would triumph with new singer Graeme 'Shirley' Strachan at next year's Sunbury. Sunbury '74 also saw 'one of England's up-and-coming name groups, Queen,[35] perform twice and get pilloried by the crowd despite – or because of? – Michael Chugg's appearance beforehand to 'bawl everybody out before they started, with an order for indulgence or good manners or shut up or piss off'.[36] Queen vowed never to return to Australia (though their moral rectitude didn't prevent them playing Sun City under apartheid, and evidently what they meant was that they would not come back to Australia until the nation embraced them commercially.) The four Sunburys were not all momentous debuts and presentations of 'the ripe raspberry' to British pretenders; Australian *Rolling Stone* blithely reported (with its usual mix of poor writing and obliquity) of 1974's event that 'someone drowned on the last day, and there were a couple of casualties';[37] while Sunbury '75 has been described as a 'shit fight in the mud'.[38]

Deep Purple were the only band who played Sunbury '75 and got paid, apparently because they were the only band paid *up front*. When the show was less lucrative than expected (torrential rain meant that less than half the expected number turned up), there was no money left to pay anyone else; of the Australians, only Jim Keays – who'd done a deal with Colonial Jeans to present his *Boy from the Stars* – made money at the time. When Deep Purple returned to Australia later that year, the musicians union brokered a levy on their fee to provide recompense to the other bands. Nevertheless, the unfairness of the original situation understandably raised the ire of many participants – Billy Thorpe suggested it was the reason he left Australia for America.[39]

Unsurprisingly, drugs were a major feature of these events. Two youths were charged with selling LSD at Sunbury '73[40] and gaoled for three months. Another attendee was remanded for riotous assembly and hindering and assaulting police.[41] Drugs, of whatever stamp, were of course an ongoing issue. Johnny Young philosophised that 'If marijuana were legalized, nobody would be interested in smoking it ... It is like underground music – as soon as it becomes a commercial success, underground freaks lose interest in it.'[42] At the same time, self-proclaimed 'prude' and 'teetotaller'[43] Moss Cass – the Labor MP for Maribyrnong and just under two years away from becoming Minister for the Environment and Conservation in the Federal Labor government – was promoting the legalization of marijuana and claiming that nicotine and alcohol users were hypocrites for resisting such a move.[44]

The T. F. Much's successor, the Much More Ballroom, had been closed in 1972 'because of a complaint that marijuana was smoked there' (presumably, on more than one occasion) and Wendy Arnott in the *Age* opined that 'without it, the picture of places to go and enjoy rock in pleasant conditions is quite desolate.'[45]

By mid 1974 the dichotomy between festivals and smaller venues had become a major issue: the former, it was argued, offered mellow, introspective music for the intellect, in contrast with the harsh, loud, dance music for the feet provided in the latter. Having only just established rock music as an art form, of sorts, some observers were out to pillory "pub rock" and its main promoter, booker Bill Joseph. In *The Rock Scene 1974*, a documentary begun by Bert Deling and Gary Martyn but seemingly never finished, Captain Matchbox's Mic Conway suggests that Joseph's bands are 'practically all heavy rock bands... the music itself is innately aggressive which I'm not saying is a bad thing' unless 'it's the *only* thing that is happening...'[46] Few groups straddled the two scenes, though one worthy of further investigation is the pointedly camp Cranberry Junglepuss's Fourteenth Tree Group, a band which used its exceptional two-drum-kit line-up to resounding effect live in both intimate and festival settings. The group's one album, *Jumbo's Tea Party*, attests to a rowdy combination of funk, grooves and general hedonism.[47]

As we will see, pub rock – a form no-one thought of as anything but throwaway in its early days, when larger, outer-suburban pubs were experimenting with ways to bring in clientele – would come to be a genre all its own. Usually thunderous music with chanted vocals and catchy choruses, it was instantly appealing, anti-intellectual, also often good-humoured. Its musical originals may have come from garage rock and R&B; its roots might also be in the foot-stomping boogie of Billy Thorpe or Lobby Loyde's Coloured Balls. In its initial phase it meant bands like Buster Brown, a group described by its vocalist, Gary 'Angry' Anderson, as 'a real tiger on the end of a rope.'[48] From 1973 to 1975 he trumpeted that band as a voice of the downtrodden working class; he would then transfer that rather ill-defined but apparently heartfelt spirit to Rose Tattoo. In *The Rock Scene 1974*, former T. F. Much proprietor John Pinder criticises the nascent pub scene, talking of 'giant drinking farms where people can only come in their Holden Monaros to listen to that very aggro, negative sort of music which is popularised by that environment;' what Pinder wanted to see, on the other hand was a 'discotheque-y kind of venue' that could operate as a workshop. Underlying this was apparently a desire to see greater experimentation and less professionalism: Pinder felt that mistakes were important: 'There's nowhere for people to be *bad* anymore.'[49]

Drugs and religion seemed to mix in strange ways – although both promoted a higher consciousness, after all. Megan Sue Hicks visited Australia from the US in 1970, and made her own impact, albeit small. She was twenty years old:

> I came to Australia in 1970, when my father's company transferred him to Sydney. He worked in the oil industry, and the South Pacific was booming at the time. I had a one-year work visa... In some respects Sydney was so sophisticated and so cosmopolitan. In other respects, in terms of the music business, it seemed like everyone was trying to invent it and no one knew what the thing would look like when it was done. There was a lot of squabbling, and jockeying for position and posing, and it seemed like kids trying to find a grown up way to behave, and when you think of it most of us *were* kids – I didn't know anyone over 30.

> Through my mother's involvement in one of the churches in Sydney, I met Clelia Adams...⁵⁰ She was the office manager for the Sydney bureau of *Go-Set*... She was hanging round with a bunch of Christadelphians at that time, a strange little sect. One of the guys at *Go-Set* was a Cristadelphian, I think he was trying to date Clelia, or convert her – if he couldn't do one, he'd do the other. My mother was very religious, she'd dragged me along I think it was the Methodist mission. They had youth groups and services but it was pretty much a snore.

Hicks was soon working as a 'gofer' at *Go-Set's* Sydney office. Her Christian beliefs would have stood her in good stead at this period. Agitation for change – in a different direction – was coming in the form of the so-called Jesus Rock fad of the early 70s. The most infamous local product of this phenomenon was Sister Janet Mead's 1974 hit recording of 'The Lord's Prayer'; Mead was a teacher (at Adelaide's St. Aloysius College) who had been invited to record Donovan's 'Brother Sun, Sister Moon' at Festival Records in Sydney with producer Martin Erdman; for the B side, she bashed out a version of the Lord's Prayer with music arranged by Arnold Strals. 'I simply sang a prayer I use daily to a new tempo,' she explained.⁵¹ The song was a worldwide hit; it is rumoured to be the first Australian recording (as opposed to a recording made outside Australia by an Australian artist) to sell a million copies in the USA.

Less well-known today, although it was a phenomenon at its inception, is *Rock Mass for Love*, which began in Perth in 1970 under the sponsorship of the Very Rev. John Hazlewood. Claiming that 'people had been alienated from Christ too long by narrow expressions of itchy-bitchy love,' Hazlewood arranged for music written by 25-year-old Bruce Devenish to be performed by Perth's top group, Bakery.⁵² They recorded a live album at a mass at St George's Cathedral in Perth on 21 March 1971 that almost made the national top twenty.⁵³ Bakery would go on to record one of the great progressive rock albums of the era, *Momento*, a 1972 recording which, sadly, has been largely forgotten. A film, *Alpha and Omega*, was made of the 'Rock Mass'.⁵⁴

Soon afterwards, impresario Harry M. Miller was conducting auditions for the Australian production of Andrew Lloyd Webber and Tim Rice's *Jesus Christ Superstar* in the basement of Melbourne's Metro Theatre.⁵⁵ Many who were chosen would soon be big names, notably Jon English (as Judas), John Paul Young (as Annas) and Marcia Hines (an American who had come to Australia to appear in the stage production of *Hair* and replaced Michelle Fawdon as Mary Magdalene in *Jesus Christ Superstar* a year into the show's run).⁵⁶ Hines later became a well-loved pop star in Australia, with numerous hit singles between 1975 and 1981. English, who had been a member of Sydney band Sebastian Hardie, went on to be a television actor as well as scoring a run of hit singles.⁵⁷ Less distinguished was the career of Trevor White, who went from playing Jesus to releasing possibly the best dance-pop single of the 70s, 'All You Want to Do Is Dance' (1977), to... very little else.

Planet's Sydney correspondent was blown away by the spectacle of *Jesus Christ Superstar*:

> Visually the set is too much, too much altogether. The object which dominates is a 15-foot duodecahedron (I didn't know either . . . anyway it's a 12-sided figure). The top half lifts off . . . the five sides open like petals and there is a centre plate which acts as a lift and sinks down to become a trapdoor . . . and it rotates, the whole damn thing rotates . . . The duodecahedron reminded me of a cross between a lunar module, a water lily and a venus fly trap. The set is a massive distraction. It appears to be audience-orientated instead of concept-orientated.'[58]

Miller, whose career as a manager, publicist and entrepreneur has made him infamous in Australia for decades, began promoting international touring acts in 1961 with the Kingston Trio. He'd brought *Hair: The American Tribal Love-Rock Musical* to Australia in 1969.[59] His success as a promoter in the early 70s notwithstanding, he was happy to describe Australian society at this time as a sandwich with a 'strange soggy filling . . . an awful spaghetti in the middle.'

> What's happening now is that the person I call the man in the street, who does a damn hard day's work, is reacting against the spaghetti filling because he's becoming more informed . . . On the other side of the sandwich, are the true leaders.'[60]

Hair is often lauded as an icebreaker, perhaps even a groundbreaker, in Australia for the nudity and hippie politics it brought to the stage, but also for the stars it created. Many loved it; some were less than impressed; one of the unimpressed, Adrian 'Avatar' Linden, decided to create a rock musical of his own, *Grass*, for which Sven Libaek wrote the music. The show was about a girl, Janet Ant, who is prosecuted for smoking marijuana, and the mock-trial created by her friends.[61]

In a time of upheaval and dissent, confusers abounded. The so-called 'Wonderful Wizard of Aussie', Ian Channell, inaugurated ALF – the Australian Liberation Front for Action, Love and Freedom, and, in the early 70s, became 'official resident merlin of the University of New South Wales.'[62] Channell attacked student activists and suggested their issues were 'poisonous bullshit'.[63] He later saw the attractions of a wider realm and moved to New Zealand to become wizard of an entire dominion.

AIR PLAY

The 1970 'Radio Ban' proved to be a watershed in the history of Australian popular music. The vagaries of the music industry and the corresponding unpredictability of chart success make it hard to state anything with certainty, but the ban might well have killed off some careers prematurely (or justifiably) and boosted a number of others. Examples of pop stars whose careers might have been very different without the ban include late 60s performers such as Johnny Young, Issi Dy, Ronnie Burns and Ross D. Wyllie; those who benefited included the group later known as Mississippi but at the time called Allison Gros, as well as other Fable label artists. Paul Conn, in his *2000 Weeks,* sees a direct relation between the radio ban and a 'stimulus given to non-commercial music'.[64] Certainly by the time the dispute ended in October, with the radio stations retaining their right to play music without paying record companies for the privilege, a reset button had been pushed on the music scene.

Since the mid 50s, record companies had agreed to accept as 'payment' for allowing their recordings to be played on the radio a mandatory (short) period per day during which their new releases would be played – something that amounted to free advertising for all the major labels.[65] But these internationally owned labels, along with Rupert Murdoch's label Festival, had grown dissatisfied with the arrangement, arguing that they were essentially providing free content to radio stations. Through their organization, the Australian Performing Rights Association, they attempted to negotiate a new deal with the Federation of Australian Radio Broadcasters, pushing for financial compensation based on airplay. The radio stations rejected this on the grounds that they were providing promotion, thus spurring sales; the *Bulletin* described the dispute as a question of 'just who is doing whom a service.'[66]

Negotiations broke down in late May 1970,[67] and the big labels imposed a six-month freeze on the supply of new records to radio; the broadcasters in return imposed a ban on playing new releases by those labels, as well as excluding them from the regional top-forty charts which they compiled. Consequently, many records released at this time did not get airplay – others, such as Spectrum's 1971 hit 'I'll Be Gone', were held back until the dispute was resolved. With his usual poor spelling Stan Rofe announced:

> The ban effects new records by Russell Morris, Doug Parkinson, Ross D. Wyllie, Normie Rowe, Jeff St John, Ronnie Charles, Issi Dy and the Sect.

'I've waited months to put this one out,' rued Issi Dy of his new single, 'now it'll probably die, without airplay.'[68] (It did, whatever the reason.) Russell Morris, who already had two chart-toppers under his belt, was conciliatory: 'The only good thing that may come out of it is the new labels which will spring up (such as the Fable label), which won't be involved in the dispute. Artists who normally wouldn't be given a chance by the larger companies could get on this way, and the scene will gain some new acts.'[69]

The Fable label – under the aegis of Ron Tudor, formerly of W&G – certainly benefited from the radio ban, most specifically through their middle-of-the-road singer Liv Maessen, who made number one in mid-May with a version of Mary

Hopkin's 'Knock, Knock Who's There' (the original, like many UK hits of that period, had fallen victim to the ban), and the Mixtures, who covered Mungo Jerry's 'In the Summertime' and hit number one in August. Within a year the Mixtures would have a number two single in Britain with their own, very similar 'The Pushbike Song'.[70] The band's Mick Flynn would be back in Australia a few years later touring as half of Pussyfoot, with a revoltingly coy number one single entitled 'The Way That You Do It'.[71] An ad for Fable in *Go-Set* featured not only Maessen but also folksinger John Williamson's 'Old Man Emu' (top ten in July); the Strangers and their new single 'Melanie Makes Me Smile' (number 14 the same month); and Hans Poulsen's 'Boom-Sha-La-La-Lo' (top ten in May).[72]

Tudor let Fable bask in the glory, flying his artists to the Kings Cross Hotel to present them to the Sydney public, where one reporter marveled at Poulsen's 'white pyjama suit and love beads'.[73] Poulsen's cachet at this time can be deduced from his appearance in *Stork*, where he performs in the extended party scene, backed by Captain Matchbox Whoopee Band. Carrl and Janie Myriad (née Conway, sister to Captain Matchbox's Conway brothers), who played mandocello and 'dolcema'[74] respectively, were described by a journalist as 'a tall blond boy looking like Louis Hayward as Captain Blood [and] a girl with long dark hair and a face that would not have been out of place in a Renaissance painting.' They advocated a form of music they called 'ragtime progressive bluegrass', releasing 'Last Saturday (We Fell in Love)' on the label – it did not chart.[75] However, they appear to have been an exception to Fable's run of diverse hits at that time.

This brief period of great success allowed Fable to make investments in a number of other acts including Allison Gros, who had a number one hit in mid 1971 under the name Drummond with a cover of the Rays' 1957 hit (written by Frank Slay and Bob Crewe), 'Daddy Cool'. Ron Tudor is interviewed in *The Rock Scene 1974*, and pinpoints as the major drawback to operating in the Australian record industry the difficulty of reaching critical mass:

> We've had a few handicaps – one of them being . . . the size of our domestic market, which is the one we have to live and survive in, and we have to gear our productions to survive in our market of 13 million people . . . we can't run to making the kind of productions that'll make a big impression overseas.
>
> Tudor professed himself mildly heartened, however, by the links his label had made internationally:
>
> A few years ago I would have been appalled at spending more than $4,000 on producing an album. Recently we spent $15,000 dollars on the new Brian Cadd album that's coming out . . . We've placed Cadd's album overseas, so we get advance moneys . . .

As well as pursuing an international solo career (largely American-based, through Chelsea Records),[76] Cadd managed a Fable subsidiary label, Bootleg,[77] and the Bootleg Family Band – originally formed with Cadd at the helm to back the label's various artists – had their own top-ten hit in early 1973, a cover of Loggins and Messina's 'Your Mama Don't Dance'. Bootleg also released Mississippi's hit records and a commercially successful LP by Kerrie Biddell in 1973, and generated sufficient revenue, it would seem, for Cadd to convincingly sue the label for $10,000 in royalties in the mid 70s.[78]

Fable's achievements provided encouragement for other 'minor' or independent labels that soon followed, including Havoc, which showcased the production talents of Aztecs drummer Gil Mathews. The most prominent and longest lasting of these new 'minors' was Mushroom, established by Michael Gudinski with Ray Evans in 1973; some journalists claim that Mushroom 'blurred the lines between independents and majors,'[79] though this is probably most true for those who would *like* to see those lines blurred, or who never really understood the distinction between major and independent in the first place. Certainly Mushroom had a distribution relationship with a 'major' record company (Festival) from the outset, which disqualifies it as a truly independent label ('Without the backing of an established label like Festival there would have been no Mushroom Records', Stuart Coupe writes in his biography of Gudinski).[80]

MAGIC MUSHROOM

Of course, the music scene was influenced by the wider society, and in turn had an effect on it. Beyond any doubt, the explosion of new underground or pseudo-underground press reinforced and informed a more questioning and radical sector in society, on that was more influential than its small numbers might suggest. Though his international idol was initially Chris Blackwell of Island Records,[81] Gudinski could probably best be typified as an Australian version of Richard Branson (although, unlike Branson, he has kept his interests primarily in entertainment and media). As a young Melbourne entrepreneur who had overcome his initial traumatic rock and roll experience of roadying for the Valentines,[82] Gudinski learnt the ropes in the multi-manager agency AMBO and joined in a merger with two other agencies, the Masters Apprentices' Drum, operated by Adrian 'Ada' Barker, and Michael Browning's Australian Entertainment Exchange,[83] to form Consolidated Rock.[84] Browning had moved into artist management from booking bands for the big Melbourne discotheques, and would later manage AC/DC. The Tasmanian Michael Chugg, who briefly operated a Consolidated Rock office in Sydney, formed the Sunrise agency with Roger Davies which entered a partnership with Philip Jacobsen's Let it Be; Chugg went on to manage Stevie Wright and would be a constant presence on the Australian touring/promotion scene for forty years.

Gudinski and Browning now set up a weekly paper called the *Daily Planet* (later just the *Planet*).[85] 'Molly would bag us every week in *Go-Set* for having a monopoly,' Gudinski recalls in Ian Meldrum's autobiography. 'I thought "Fuck you, Molly, we'll start our own newspaper and put you out of business.'[86] Another account suggests Gudinski and Browning were merely annoyed by another 'article' or 'weekly column'; what was perhaps more important was the entrenched nature of *Go-Set* itself.[87] The new publication was high-quality, less 'teen' and more 'serious' (instead of 'albums' and 'singles' charts, it had 'albums' and 'sellouts' charts, for instance).[88] The *Planet* was a financial disaster over its two year run but an artistic triumph; this history draws extensively on its writing. Significant figures involved in its production include top-notch editor/journalist Lee Dillow, who became John Paul Young's tour manager[89] and later organiser of the 1983 Narara festival;[90] the exceptional Jenny Brown was also given freedom to write long, probing and thoughtful articles. Gudinski used contacts he made at this time to expand his touring and recording interests further after *Planet's* demise in March 1972. Although they did not stage the actual event, Gudinski and Evans booked the bands for Sunbury in 1972 through their agency, once again under the AEE name; Gudinski also sold watermelons there.[91]

Other papers were created at this time: they included *The Living Daylights*, which can be seen as an Australian offshoot of London *Oz* by dint of the involvement of Richard Neville and cartoonist Martin Sharp, who had already achieved international fame via his album covers for Cream (see chapter 4) and was soon to achieve art world fame with his 'Yellow House' installation-cum-gallery in Sydney. *The Living Daylights* (it was originally to have been called *Flash*) was a short-lived, hybridised challenge to the sensationalist *Truth* – as envisaged by hippies.[92] The *Nation Review* came out of a merger of two excellent journals, the staunch, challenging and established (but graphically limited) *Nation* and the much younger *Review*; it was edited by Richard Walsh, who had been involved with Sydney *Oz* its entire life.[93]

Although *Go-Set* limped on into the second half of 1974, its publishers had essentially abandoned it – in part because they now considered it to be 'nauseating to a lot of people'[94] but also because they owed their printer too much money – in favour of the radical and exotic *Digger*, whose many notable achievements include publishing the article for which reporter Helen Garner was sacked from her day job as a schoolteacher. Garner's dismissal was for a frank article about her forays into sex education, and education's loss was fiction's gain: she would go on to write brilliant novels, such as *Monkey Grip* and the magnificent *The Children's Bach*, that evoke the free and conflicted scene of the 70s.

Funding for *Digger*, which proclaimed complete equality among its staff, came in part from a deal with 'the American hip-capitalist rock magazine *Rolling Stone*,' under which *Digger* would produce an 'Australian Flyer' segment for the local edition.[95] At an earlier point, the Australian magazine *Revolution* had merged with or otherwise been consumed by *Rolling Stone*[96] in much the same way the British magazine *Friends* aka *Frenz* was devoured by the voracious American brand. Unlike *Rolling Stone* itself, *Digger* was rightly seen as a cornerstone of the counterculture, and bands – such as Daddy Cool, Captain Matchbox and the Pelaco Brothers in August 1975 – rallied to support it.[97] Other magazines included *Dingo*, which had an aggressively "underground" image and was produced by Fitzroy anarchists,[98] and *Rats*, which was edited by Piotr and Laurel Olszewski and took a less forgiving, unfunny, satirical line. The December 1970 issue of *Thorunka*, an offshoot of the University of New South Wales student magazine *Tharunka*, was prosecuted for obscenity; Germaine Greer was called as a witness.[99] Wendy Bacon, a courageous journalist and activist, spent eight days in jail in the name of free speech.[100]

These magazines were not only radical in outlook, they followed (perhaps by osmosis) the credo of the aforementioned Pete Steedman, editor at different times in the 1960s of the student papers *Lot's Wife* and *Farrago* and later of *Broadsheet* (he was also occasionally on staff at *Go-Set*). Steedman, who had also spent a short time in London leading conservation groups for the preservation of Piccadilly Circus and Covent Garden,[101] was dedicated to diversity in his journalistic endeavours: it was not a question of merely offering a 'right of reply', let alone subscribing to the nonsensical idea that all readings of events/history have equal value, but simply that anyone who cared sufficiently should be allowed a voice. Steedman's papers, and many that followed, were full of *arguments*.[102] The new countercultural papers were not just about rock music, and in some cases they weren't about music at all; nevertheless, various permutations of popular music were clearly the soundtrack to everything in their pages; music was bound up in the politics of the time as well as the recreational philosophy – the lifestyle – of young Australians.

IT'S TIME

When Germaine Greer moved to Britain in 1964 she quickly made an impact, not least with her work for London *Oz* (most prominently, though not exclusively the women's liberation issue), *Private Eye* and then her revolutionary 1970 book *The Female Eunuch* (which Steedman claims to have copyedited).[103] She came to be regarded with awe by some Australians. Patrick Flanagan, writing in *Nation*, saw her as 'a contemporary intellectual guru', who, unlike her fellow expats Richard Neville and Barry Humphries, was 'known to lapse into coherence'.[104] Greer, who notoriously posed with Vivian Stanshall of the Bonzo Dog Doo Dah Band as a 'groupie' for issue 19 of the UK *Oz*, had dedicated her book to Lillian Roxon,[105] more because of Roxon's effusive, embracing personality than her status as a groundbreaking advocate/music journalist and encyclopedist. But Greer approved of the rock world, seeing in rock 'new possibilities in the imagery of womanhood.'[106] Her celebrity, chic and radical outspokenness was embraced by Labor's opposition leader Gough Whitlam, who took her 'to tea'[107] when she returned to Australia for a visit in 1971.

Whitlam marked himself out as different to many previous Prime Ministers – even the staunch and principled previous leaders of his own party – by his urbanity and his interest in the arts. In 1967 Harry Widmer had exploited an election campaign to promote the popular, fun, mixed-gender pop showband he managed by printing up 9,000 posters urging passers-by to 'Vote for the Executives'.[108] In 1972, Labor stood this concept on its head: instead of selling pop through politics, it sold itself through pop. The party's election slogan, 'It's Time', was embodied in Alison MacCallum's song, written by Pat Aulton and Paul Jones. For the first time an Australian political campaign was defined by a pop song. Little Pattie, Judy Stone, and Col Joye were joined by TV stars Bert Newton and Bobby Limb and other celebrities in the associated TV ad.

Gough Whitlam and Little Pattie modelling the Labor Party's 1972 election campaign t-shirts

Whitlam's government lasted only three years, but it left Australia entirely changed, particularly in terms of its cultural self-confidence. In his first weeks in power, before parliament reconvened, he and deputy Lance Barnard operated as a two-person government, instituting reforms to social policy that progressive-minded Australians had advocated for decades; they officially ended the country's involvement in the Vietnam War, freed conscientious objectors from jail, and pardoned draft evaders.[109] While many Australians under forty, pressure-cooked by conservative state and federal governments for decades, might have felt justified in rejecting *all* conventional government, few could deny that Whitlam appealed to the young and recognised their importance in Australia's future.

Given that Whitlam's entrée into government is associated in popular memory with pop, it's appropriate that many songs owe their existence to his government. Under Labor, the Industries Assistance Commission held an inquiry into the practices of the recording industry, in the course of which Fable's Ron Tudor railed against the domination of local 'musical culture and heritage' by 'people whose community interest and spirit run counter to the majority of Australians', by which he presumably meant those who did not support a locally based music industry.[110] Among the specific issues raised were a restriction on miming that applied only to Australian artists (international artists, so often seen in film clips, were exempt). In response to the spirit rather than the letter of these objections, the quota of Australian music (by composition and/or performance) played on radio was doubled from 5 to 10 percent in 1973. In 1976 it was doubled again.

Mike Rudd is enthusiastic about Whitlam's effect on the national music culture:

> It's reflected in the charts. There was suddenly an acceptance of the Australian voice. If you look at the charts at that time, it's all Australian bands clustering

at the top of the charts. There's two reasons for that, but the political one was very strong, and there was a very strong feeling that voice was acceptable. But there was also the situation with the birth of the PVCA ... the radio ban on international record companies which gave birth to "The Pushbike Song" and other things, where Australian bands were covering hits from the UK charts on the Fable label.
And that got the factory going, if you like. That was what got Armstrong's studio going, so the groundwork was there for [the time after the ban], when it all opened up again.

Whitlam makes a brief appearance in the second Barry McKenzie film, *Barry McKenzie Holds His Own,* playing himself (although his voice on the soundtrack is obviously dubbed by someone else); he's shown giving Edna Everage a damehood – something that would substantially define her, and Barry Humphries', subsequent career). The *Barry McKenzie* films, better remembered now than the superior comic strip which spawned them, were themselves liberating for Australians. Though they are chiefly embraced today for promoting an extraordinary range of metaphors, invented dialect, and vomiting, they were fiercely critical of both Australians and their traditional rivals, the British. Bob Ellis wrote of the first collection of strips that it should be memorialised by 'a brazen statue' of McKenzie, 'chilled Fosters in fist, hurtling towards the urinal ... erected in Chifley Square.'[111] Others saw the McKenzie strip as 'anti-feminine ... unreadable rubbish ... an insult to humanity'.[112] There may well be some truth in the last of these accusations but this was a time of enormous change and drama. Parody, trenchant protest, and gossamer-winged escapism rubbed shoulders and vied for acceptance as the most valid expression of Australian culture.

SEEK AND YE SHALL FIND

The origins of folk music as a youth movement, and its close association with trad jazz, were discussed in chapter 2. The Seekers, who were amongst the most successful pop manifestations of that scene in the 60s, re-emerged in two forms in the 70s, neither of them heavy on substance (with all the good and bad implications of that word).

To Judith Durham's disgust, Keith Potger had formed a pop group he called the New Seekers in London in 1969; he performed with the group only briefly then opted to retire from the line-up and manage it together with Procession's manager, David Joseph. The five-piece – 'more entertaining than the Seekers ever were', according to *Go-Set,* which was always about what was happening that moment[113] – featured Australian performers Peter Doyle and Marty Kristian, who had cut their teeth in their home market in the 60s (the German-born Kristian had been an architecture student in Melbourne; Doyle had been a popular solo artist, a *Go!! Show* regular, and a member of the popular Virgil Brothers between

1968-70). The New Seekers extruded high-quality pop with mass appeal. Brian Peacock was involved with them as a songwriter (he penned their British hit 'When There's No Love Left'; they also covered Procession's 'Anthem') and also as their road manager. The group was a natural continuation of Peacock's professional relationship with David Joseph, but was marketed largely as Keith Potger's concept[114] – an early album was titled *Keith Potger and the New Seekers*. Curiously, the band also contributed to a grave spiritual dilemma for Peacock:

> It very much had David's brains behind it . . . David had scored a record deal for the concept, then they set out to recruit a group, and they used some of my songs for the first album . . . I did all the touring behind those first couple of albums for the New Seekers. To the point where, eventually, I just got really burnt out from it.
>
> I remember one of those life-changing moments. I was in the Warwick Hotel in New York with the New Seekers doing their American tour, and I just had one of those dreadful nights . . . It wasn't drug-induced, just a total paranoia that I was doing completely the wrong thing, and whole music industry was doomed and riddled with corruption. It was around the same time as I discovered that Warner Bros was owned by the Kinney Corporation, who were basically car-park operators and were a heavily mobbed-up, mafia-riddled company.
>
> It was around the time of spiritual awakening . . . I'd been going for some time to this meditation teacher in London with Terry Britten and a couple of other music friends. Kevin Peek was another one. We were all part of this little group of like-minded people who were into meditation . . .
>
> I just decided that night I was going to get out of the music industry forever. It was really black doom. All my passion and love for it had been soaked up and misused and ended up going totally the wrong way. [The New Seekers were] like an *Australian Idol* group. But totally stuck together, and in the middle of it was an Australian guy called Peter Doyle who I'd worked with way back in the Sunshine years. And he was a wonderful guy, but he got completely caught up — he was friends with Joe Walsh, hanging out with those kind of people. It didn't look good, the way some parts of it were going. I think it all got too much for me.
>
> So I went back to England and told David and Keith that was it, I was retiring from the music scene – and they were just aghast. I said, 'But don't worry, I've found someone else to take over,' which was Glenn Wheatley. He started the week I finished. I knew Glenn from the Masters days.

Another *Go!! Show* stalwart, Buddy England, was involved in another Seekers spin-off – the mid-70s revival of the original band under the original name, but without Durham. 'I would love to see Judith with us,' mused Bruce Woodley at the time, 'but if she was really against the idea . . . frankly, I wouldn't care too much.'[115] Athol Guy, at that stage still the Liberal MP for Gisborne, had asked England to find the group a new singer. He saw Louisa Wisseling singing with a group in a restaurant called the Swagman, in Melbourne's eastern suburbs, 'took Athol to have a listen ... made Louisa an offer and there you are.'

> I was also asked to vet material for the group to record their return [album] and also to write the charts for the vocals as well as the charts for the orchestrations. I signed them to the Astor label ... The album was a success. Bruce left a year later and I joined the group.[116]

An ongoing, revolving-cast version of the Seekers, with Julie Anthony and then Karen Knowles singing, would continue periodically throughout the 70s and 80s, and had major hit singles, yet the Seekers – who resumed their 'original' line-up (with Durham) in the 90s – and their fans seem content to forget the Wisseling era. Like the New Seekers, the 70s ('Old'?) Seekers were closer to melodic pop than they were to folk.

Folk continued to be a music of choice for some in the 70s, however, and it gained a local, radical edge as well. Folk, folk-rock and its variants had as good a shot as any at becoming the national music, though many of the folk/acoustic groups ended up leaning more towards rock as the decade wore on. Country folk suited many of them. Megan Sue Hicks, working at *Go-Set's* Sydney office and writing her own songs, was a folkie, 'and not a very gritty folkie at that, so rock 'n' roll wasn't really my music of choice.'

> So when we went to review bands it was deafening, it was just an assault on my ears. I did go to a lot of clubs and listen to bands and show up – I guess they wanted *Go-Set* staff to be seen at the clubs and be thought to be involved.
>
> I had played guitar (abysmally) and sung (sweetly) through high school and my first two years of college – at parties and school talent shows, but nothing like professionally. I was a folkie of the Peter, Paul & Mary stripe, acoustic but not gritty. But for a person who wants to perform, this seemed like a way to do it.
>
> One evening Cleli dragged me and my guitar across the road to where her friend Doug Rowe lived in a cavernous old rowhouse with a bunch of guys who made inflatable furniture – they called their company "Plosions," as in 'im-' and 'ex-', I suppose. She told me to sing one of my songs for Doug. Doug was taken with the song and the way I sounded (waif-like) and asked if I had written others. I sang my other two or three original songs, and he told me he'd like to produce an album if I could come up with enough original material for two sides of an LP. I got right to work.

The album, *Maranatha*, was recorded in studio down time with Doug Rowe's country rock band Flying Circus, who had already had 'bubblegum' hits in the late 60s but were aiming for something higher and would shortly head for Canada.

Maranatha is a classic of its time, and features not only remarkable songs from Hicks herself but fine playing from the group. The first song, 'Hey, Come Out and Play', touches (perhaps accidentally) on Nico and the Doors but remains wholly Megan Sue Hicks; other tracks are lighter and less ominous, but still retain a poppy feel, with mild Christian overtones. By the time *Maranatha* was released, Hicks had moved back to the USA, and with no promotion, it disappeared quickly. The publicity department at Warner Brothers – who had somehow come into possession of the album from EMI – may not have felt confident about promoting Megan Sue Hicks particularly because, in one of those bizarre truths stranger than fiction, there were two other performers called Megan Hicks in the Australian entertainment industry at the time.[117]

Other folk singers depended, in their balladic form and protest-themed lyrics, on Australian traditions. John Schumann's lecturer at Flinders University, Brian Medlin, had been arrested at a Vietnam moratorium demonstration, a moment Schumann saw as key to his own political development and his birth as a performer:

> If I hadn't been doing philosophy and hadn't been taught by Brian Medlin . . . and hadn't had my perceptions kicked out from the inside, and if I hadn't come to a realization that we in Australia were being lumbered with cultural and geographical references from America and England and it was about time we began to talk about our own backyard, perhaps I wouldn't have written songs at all. My view was then, and still is, that Australians should write songs about Australia.[118]

Schumann formed Redgum in 1975. Another university-oriented folk group, the Original Bushwackers and Bullockies Bush Band (later simply the Bushwackers), formed in 1971, aiming to make Australian folk music once again relevant to the contemporary mainstream – an ambition in which the band was largely successful: 'to take the Australian folk music tradition by the scruff of the neck and make it a living, breathing contemporary musical experience.'[119] The original band was primarily made up of people from Latrobe University, an institution that was only a few years old and very radical.[120] Dobe Newton, the longest lasting member by the end of the group's existence, joined in 1973; he later co-wrote Bruce Woodley's claim for a new national anthem 'I Am Australian'.[121]

Groups like the Bushwackers and Redgum presented hearty songs from the Australian folk tradition with touches of radical politics,[122] but also deviated from the puritan re-creation ethic in their use of modern instruments such as mellotron and electric guitar. The Bushwackers have at different times included Freddy Strauks, better known as the drummer from Skyhooks, and Pete Drummond, drummer in the 21st-century incarnation of Dragon, showing if nothing else that the band has a long commercial currency. It should also be mentioned, if only to avoid any impression that he was himself Australian, that the Bushwackers briefly included British world traveller and itinerant musician Pete Farndon. He went back to the UK with the band in 1976 to record an album and then, having got home, quit. Soon afterwards he met Chrissie Hynde and mused prosaically, 'Am I gonna be in a band with this *cunt?*'[123] He was, before being sacked in 1982. He died the following year.

JUG A LUG

A complement to the bush band phenomenon was the jug band. We've already witnessed the emergence on the late-60s Adelaide scene of Doc Neeson (the 'Doc' came from 'Doc Holliday'; his given name was Bernard), who'd arrived from Belfast with his family. He was soon running local dances; when a band called Down the Line signed up to play in 1968, he suggested they adopt a groovier, retro name: Zoot. Later, while attending Flinders University (like Schumann), Neeson met John and Rick Brewster and the three formed the self-styled 'surreal' Moonshine Jug and String Band in Nov 1971. The group released an EP and a single, and then made the decision to go electric, at which point they lost most of their fans: they became a 50s/60s retro band called the Keystone Angels. It would still be some time before they reached their peak state as, simply, the Angels, via the guidance of Vanda and Young and their forward-thinking manager, John Woodruff. Another band from Adelaide at this time, the more radical Red Angel Panic, featured one Chris Bailey who later joined the Angels, though there seems to have been no direct link in naming between the two angelic groups (nor did this Chris Bailey have any connection to the Saints' singer of the same name).

The early to mid 70s were certainly full of Captains. Internationally, former Deep Purple singer Rod Evans was recording under the name Captain Beyond. In Australia, the Groop's former singer, Ronnie Charles (real name Ron Boromeo) helmed Captain Australia and the Honky Tonk between 1970 and 71.[124] Tony Edwards's comic character Captain Goodvibes was a popular feature of *Tracks*, the surfing magazine started by David Elfick of *Go-Set*. The Mixtures' 'Captain Zero' was a top-ten hit in December, 1971. And there was also a Captain running a jug band: Melbourne's Captain Matchbox Whoopee Band, who used 1930s popular music as their source material and were seen

A
HEARTFELT
APOLOGY

PETER ANDREWS
&
GINELD
DEEPLY REGRET TO
ANNOUNCE THAT THE
BIG MAMA THORNTON
WILLIE DIXON &
FURRY LEWIS

FESTIVAL
OF BLUES

IS NOW
CANCELLED

DUE TO A FUCK UP
THAT WAS AS
UNAVOIDABLE AS
IT IS A PAIN IN
THE ARSE TO US ALL.
TICKETS WILL BE REFUNDED
AT THE AGENCIES WHERE
THEY WERE PURCHASED.

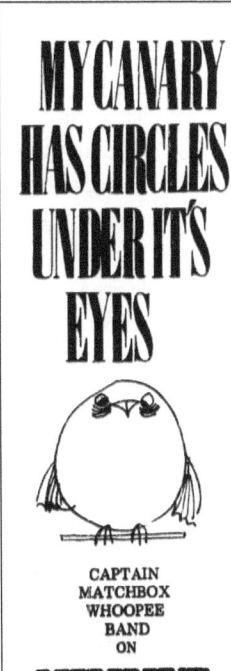

MY CANARY
HAS CIRCLES
UNDER IT'S
EYES

CAPTAIN
MATCHBOX
WHOOPEE
BAND
ON
image
IS..119

by many as representative of a genuine Australianness.

Though vaguely similar in some ways to Britain's Bonzo Dog Doo Dah Band (whom they hadn't heard), Captain Matchbox didn't see themselves as 'part of any particular movement, we were really working against the trend and taking the micky out of the fashion in the music industry.'[125] 'Good times are deeply imbedded in Captain Matchbox's approach to music', writes David Bland in his boisterous sleevenotes to their *Smoke Dreams* album. Production is credited to Rhett H. Walker: in the *Rock Scene 1974* documentary Mic Conway explains to Bert Deling that Walker was the program manager at 3AK, 'at that time a very hip rock station', and that he ensured they received airplay for their single 'My Canary Has Circles under His Eyes' so that it became a hit. He adds that the respect that was suddenly accorded the band once they'd received radio play 'must be the greatest joke of all time'.[126]

Captain Matchbox also added, or highlighted, the earthy universality of the wisecracking, sleazy pop song of the interwar period – their rendition of 'Who Walks Out When I Walk In' is prefaced on *Smoke Dreams* by theatrical sounds of lovemaking. In Peter Weir's wonderful short film *3 Directions in Australian Pop Music*,[127] the group play this song in a proto-punk style: the vigour and hilarity make the whole shebang both flippant and furious. They are also seen in a backyard performance in Chris Löfvén's 1971 film, *Part One – 806*, and, as mentioned earlier, in *Stork*,[128] where they are very clearly a vigorous, colourful, and central element of house party revelry, rather than a retro curiosity.[129] *Stork's* director Tim Burstall was reputedly a 'party-goer par excellence',[130] and a group like Captain Matchbox evidently represent part of the general cultivated and/or cultured mayhem.

Like many around them, the group's core components, the Conway brothers, came from the middle-ring, middle-class suburb of Camberwell, although the group became established as a mainstay of the inner-city Melbourne suburb of Carlton. An interview from 1975 – by which time the 'poised, proud and patriotic flat-footed'[131] group had incorporated Chris Worrall from the Pelaco Brothers (of whom more anon) – gives a taste of what is clearly an ebullient, aggressive, comedic, pretension-busting group:

> Q. What sort of music was the original band playing?
> TIM: Jug band music!
> MIC: The original members were Jim, me . . .
> TIM: That's not what he asked!
> MIC: That *is* what he asked.
> TIM: No, he asked what sort of material was . . .
> MIC: Jug band fucking music!
> [. . .]
> Q. Why pick jug band music when rock 'n' roll is the main thing happening?
> TIM: Coz we like it

DAVE: We can't play rock 'n' roll.
CHRIS: We've all tried and failed. This band is well known as the end of the line. You try for a few years to be a star . . .
MIC: That's enough, Chris.

The group were also happy to take a sacrilegious potshot at the biggest group in Australia at the time:

Q: Do you aim for or appeal to a particular sort of audience, say as in Skyhooks' teenybopper audience?
DAVE: Don't you like Skyhooks?
TIM: They're my favourite band.
CHRIS: I reckon they're a pile of shit.
DAVE: No, they're intellectuals who have adopted a certain attitude to their job and succeeded at it.
CHRIS: Whereas we've failed.[132]

Later in the interview Chris fantasises that Mic 'had to make love' to daytime TV talk show host, Mike Walsh, in order to get exposure for the group, to which Dave responds, 'Mike Walsh is a cunt'.[133] This is obviously not the funniest, cleverest or most insightful thing to say about a beloved television personality, but it does indicate an iconoclastic attitude, and is certainly in keeping with the band's later forays. Just as late-70s punks took on a style of music that was regarded, by the mid 70s, as a retro form (we tend to call the earlier music 'garage punk' now, or '60s punk') as a means of bypassing the pretensions and excesses of prog rock and its associated forms, in the early 70s jug bands like Captain Matchbox took an archaic music and made it fast, sexy and relevant. This was not old music recreated; it was old music *reactivated* to reject poseurs and pretentious wankers; it paralleled that 1930s pornographic comic phenomenon in the USA ('Tijuana bibles') and Robert Crumb's throwback style, or even Peter Lillie and Johnny Topper's suave comic book character, After Dinner Moose. Indeed, 'After Dinner Moose' himself was to conduct 'the world's first JUG BAND BIG BAND, a thirty piece orchestra'[134] in an event that was advertised in *Planet* in March 1972 and perhaps even took place.

Alistair Jones wrote tongue in cheek in *Planet* of Captain Matchbox's 'corrupting influence' – something in which they colluded with Carlton's Australian Performing Group (the two entities would eventually join together to create an event known as *Soapbox Circus*).

It is easy to detect a Jug Band freak. They have little red darting eyes, dissipated bodies, demented grins, debauched leers and a tendency to blurt a furtive 1, 2, 1, 2, 3, 4 on first waking . . .

In the smokey backroom of a deserted lolly shop I spoke to the Matchbox about their 'corrupting influence'. One performance, a 'deluge of eroticism' at Montsalvat, prompted the prim conscience for Melbourne's guilt-ridden to make accusations of 'sex on stage'. (The Tribe, with a touch of traditional buffoonery, run amok with phallic symbols).

Jones also mentioned a non-human member, Whoopee the Wonder Dog, whose 'contribution is the occasional turd'.[135]

When they toured as part of *Soapbox Circus*, the members of Captain Matchbox became increasingly involved in political comment and theatre.[136] In the spirit of the times, expressed in the desire to progress, challenge and innovate, many musicians tried to add a extra-musical, dramatic element to their performances. *Planet* told the world that Wendy Saddington had recreated herself:

> The fierce Afro hair style has been pruned into a cut not unlike Gough Whitlam turned rocker. Her new performing face is that of a tragic clown, slightly evil and totally impenetrable. By removing all signs of being approachable, she is able to communicate entirely on her own terms. With one black leg and one white leg she might well be the jester from a very black comedy.[137]

Rock and jazz singer Jeannie Lewis played in 1972 accompanied by a 'mime and tap' artist, Jewellion;[138] Wendy Saddington had her own mime, Morris Spinetti, performing as 'Teardrop'; he is seen in Saddington's performance (sporting her new 'tragic clown' look) in 3 *Directions in Australian Pop Music*.

Groups like Captain Matchbox, and singers like Saddington, made up part of the passing show at Much More Ballroom, 'the unchallenged centre of the new New Society' to the 'second generation freaks'.[139] Its core value, if David Pepperell's effusive description is anything to go by, was variety. The Much More was the successor to the T. F. Much Ballroom: both were art- and theatre-oriented, and gave music an extra dimension that reflected the counterculture. John Pinder, a central figure in the running of these venues, later managed comedy clubs. The theatre-comedy-Carlton crossover is captured on the 1975 album *Buried Treasure* credited to Captain Rock, which was comedian/musician Bob Brown supported by members of Skyhooks, Captain Matchbox, Daddy Cool and other luminaries.

Daddy Cool, who emerged in 1970 and provided a refreshing, immediate and (it would transpire) commercially successful side to this cavalcade of art-rock, were nevertheless deeply immersed in this scene.

DIVERGING PATHS

The Coloured Balls, on the other hand, were not. This group went through numerous line-ups from 1972 to 1973 under the direction of Lobby Loyde. Just as much as Daddy Cool, they were a breath of fast, furious fresh air, conjuring up sensational glam/power pop – like their brilliant single 'Flash', which appeared on the superlative *Ball Power* album. Listened to with hindsight, this is music that sounds as if it is referencing 1977 punk, rather than 1973 rock.

The Coloured Balls were adopted by the retooled Sharpie movement – Australia's most notorious youth fashion group, which may have been reminiscent in some respects of 60s skinheads and/or 50s teddy boys, but which was distinctively and self-consciously Australian without being jingoistic.[140] One assessment of the Coloured Balls in the mid 70s suggested that the fact they received 'no media' prevented them becoming 'something like the phenomenon Skyhooks have become.'[141] Wendy Arnott summed up their place in the scene in 1972 when she wrote:

> Lobby Loyde's Colored Balls[142] appear to be filling the gap left by the Aztecs, and Sherbet and Blackfeather have both emerged as tremendously popular teeny-bopper groups. Carson, the Indelible Murtceps and especially Miss Universe have put up good performances and the M[a]cKenzie Theory have won themselves a strong following with their highly individualistic style.[143]

Carson (originally Carson County Band) were a diverse and talented Melbourne band who released two LPs in 1972 and 1973. Miss Universe was a short-lived group featuring Tim Gaze and Nigel Macara, of whom more anon. Sydney's Blackfeather were briefly very successful with the single 'Boppin' the Blues' (not the Carl Perkins song), a number one hit in 1972. Blackfeather had come to prominence with 1971's 'Seasons of Change', co-written by John Robinson and Neale Johns, guitarist and singer respectively. The two fell out, and each, for a short time, had their own Blackfeather (manager Peter Conyngham owned the name, and supported Johns's version of the band). Johns (it was his Blackfeather which had the 1972 hit) would later put together a band called, bizarrely and appallingly, Homicidal Idol.[144]

A *Planet* writer stumbled across It Flew Away in the seaside town of Ocean Grove, and was surprised to find a group 'completely decked out like "Monashites" (that is, habitués of Monash University). He didn't expect them to be any good: 'They were a few years older than what would be expected as well, so I settled back to listen to some bad music without much potential among the individual players. If they were younger I would have waited for the potential.' As it turned out, the group's performance excited him; he found they had 'no direct influences but do draw inspiration from bands such as Co. Caine, Spectrum and Langford Lever. They feel that these bands are just about the only ones they've heard that are not going backwards into the simple blues format.' The group's songs, many of them written by organist Ian Clarke, were inspired by his life outdoors: 'He chases wasps!' [145]

Though it oversimplifies what was clearly a rich tapestry of different musics and approaches, it is not entirely inaccurate to typify the scene at this time as being, effectively, two scenes. There were the art-rockers, the progressives who hoped to lift Australians out of mundane reality and onto another plane with virtuosity and challenging, epic work – bands like It Flew Away (who did not release anything during their existence) and MacKenzie Theory. Then there were groups who engaged with Australian themes in a jokey but also in some respects aggressive way: Captain Matchbox and the Pelaco Bros were of this ilk. Playing rockabilly and old-time swing, they were fellow travelers on the road from Daddy Cool to Skyhooks, as we shall see in the next chapter. They were anti-progressives, in a sense, but they were not retro acts; rather, they were theatrical deflaters of pretension.

Both kinds of group – progressive *and* ocker – were sustainable at this time, as the examples of MacKenzie Theory and the Pelaco Brothers will show.

MacKenzie Theory were peak amongst the experimental groups of the era, and one of the most commercially successful. They were led by Rob MacKenzie, who had previously played with the Virgil Brothers, Leo and Friends (also known simply as Friends), and King Harvest – these last two bands were interlinked and their members later formed the jazz-rock group Ayers Rock, the first Mushroom act to be signed to a label outside Australia.[146] In 1970 MacKenzie was hired as a temp to play with the Aztecs after Billy Thorpe broke his wrist. He was also part of the short-lived instrumental group Great Men – an interesting experience, he later said, but one which he also hated;[147] the band fired him. He invited a young Tasmanian, Cleis Pearce, to form MacKenzie Theory soon after they met at the Sydney Arts Factory in 1971; the group went through two different rhythm sections. American-born Mike Leadabrand explains how he came to be the group's first bass player:

> I was living at John Pinder's house in Fitzroy when Company Caine were in town. I had heard they were having a rough time with their guitarist, Russell Smith, and would be interested in trying me out. I did a gig with them and it went well and just before they left to return home to Sydney they said they were interested and would let me know in a couple of days. My own opinion was that swapping Russell for me was like trading in your Porsche for a 120Y, but if they were crazy enough I was keen. After a couple of weeks of waiting, I hitchhiked to Sydney to ask them what they'd decided, and they said 'Oh, sorry. We patched things up with Russell and forgot to tell you.'

So, depressed, I stayed at their place that night contemplating my future. Two people arrived... and introduced themselves as Rob and Cleis. We talked all night and decided to go back to Melbourne and start a band. We could not find a bass player so I made the switch, and soon after we found Andy [Majewski, the band's first drummer], who was a fresh faced 18-year-old. I would say it was one of the luckiest breaks of my life, getting to play with Rob and Cleis...

It Flew Away were on our wavelength. Few others. It was never a drug-oriented band. I met a guy a few years ago who, upon hearing I was in the band, said 'You used to play on acid every gig.' He was heartbroken when I told him we had never played on acid and rarely even had a joint. Such was the myth of the band and how people compartmentalise things that are new. I have heard people say that Cleis was a crazed druggy because she doesn't talk very much – and that makes me angry. She is, and always was, clean-living and unassuming. She just plays like she walks, in strange, wonderful dimensions.

The mere fact that ethereal, highly structured and high-concept jazz-rock, revolving around a guitarist and a (female) viola player, could make the scene – and the charts – shows a remarkable change in Australian audiences' tastes. Pearce told Margo Huxley of the *Daily Planet* that she 'never thought about the novelty of being a chick in a band – if some people like to see it as that, then perhaps that's all they're capable of seeing.'[148] She quickly added this was not a put-down (!).

MacKenzie Theory really *were* espousing a theory: they were 'a band for people to be thinking by, an event in thinking.'[149] The group's name had come from a chance – sarcastic – comment made by John Pinder about MacKenzie's pontificating; aside from wryly co-opting Pinder's dig, MacKenzie also saw the opportunity to guarantee this new group was one that wouldn't be able to fire him.

His explanation of the 'theory' to the readers of *Go-Set* suggests an interesting take on pacifism, Marxism and environmentalism. He was against war, the exploitation of workers, and waste:

> If we look at things in terms of evolution, evolution of individuals, evolution of whole populations or of a piece of music... For example take one of our songs. Say a song that starts with a single piece violin doesn't know about them. The violin becomes swamped at this point, and for it to be heard it has to fit into the rest of the band, or remain swamped.
>
> It does fit in, and what it enters into then, as a patriotic group, a social group. But it's only one social group of many.
>
> So now we develop the song and it becomes more intense... The band then enters the 'war' phase, where individual members are trying to override each other. This builds up till the number reaches a state of chaos (remember all this is in about seven minutes), a survive or die situation.

> Then the guitar starts playing chords, and the chaos stops, and the band starts together in a symphonic way.
> That was about a thousand years in seven minutes, so I hope people will look for that sort of thing when they listen to our music.[150]

This is both funny and clever, though it's probably not intended to be funny; there also may well be errors in the original transcription. Pearce points out that it was all a very serious venture for MacKenzie:

> His ideas on the consumer society, and the political situation in the world and profit, the idea of how selling things for a higher price to make profit was leading to the collapse of the Earth – environmental ideas. It was a ferment of continual conversation. We were very fired up with what was going on in the world and music could influence things. It was a very passionate feeling that drove the musical ideas, the technique of the music and the form, all the nitty gritty of the music was subservient to the emotion, the politics, the environmental stuff, the whole Vietnam thing. We ended up being an incredibly successful university band, what was happening in the universities then was so powerful in the anti-Vietnam movement. The music we were playing was fired up by all these things happening at the same.
>
> Lyrics just didn't enter the picture. People were always saying 'what's wrong with you, why don't you have a vocalist?' Rob is quite different, he had his own mind, his own way; he thought words got misinterpreted too easily. He thought music was a more direct way of expressing what we were about.
>
> We tried to *play* like voices, especially Rob, he was very much like a voice, and I developed this technique, this way of playing where I was echoing him, doing harmonies, and that was very strong. I was playing by feel and inspiration. It was many years later that I became conscious enough to know what I wanted to do technically with my playing. At that age, I'd come out from a very sheltered family, like a jail, I was incredibly naïve, so naïve it was like I was walking around in a dream. My mind wasn't conscious of technical things – it's hard to explain – I didn't really know the difference between thinking and feeling.

Some of their pieces were meant to be stories, if not epics; one, according to MacKenzie, was 'meant to sound just like you've turned the radio onto one station and then gone onto another'[151] – a major challenge in live music. Pearce and MacKenzie, both classically trained, were utterly committed. Pearce had essentially run away from her Hobart home and university studies; 'My family were very left-wing, and I was always going on peace marches and demos, that was my background', she recalls. When she met MacKenzie, 'We just came together and I never questioned it.'

Ray Evans and Michael Gudinski then stepped into the picture with their new record label. They originally planned to call it Consolidated Rock Records, after the booking agency Gudinski co-ran with Michael Chugg,[152] but ended up naming it after the 'Magical Mushroom Mansion', a 'groovy disco'[153] Gudinski operated for two weeks in St Kilda.[154] MacKenzie Theory would be the second chart success for Mushroom Records (Madder Lake's 'Goodbye Lollipop' was the first) and the first album hit for the label, even though, as Pearce recalls, 'they thought it was ridiculous not having a singer and me not being up the front like a star.' Of course, 'you'd expect that of the industry,' she says; she believes Gudinski 'respected' MacKenzie 'as a player . . . but I don't think he was very impressed by the direction Rob was going in.'

> However, gradually he realised we were doing quite well, especially at universities, and we might sell records, so he said he'd help us get gigs . . . So we had this sort of relationship with Gudinski. At one stage we were managed by Ray Evans and he gave us gigs at Sunbury, which was OK – we went over really well.

> I remember recording *Out of the Blue*, I was very nervous because I felt very insecure, I felt quite under-confident, like they were putting a spotlight on my playing and I was very defensive, I had to do a solo, there was some criticism – from [engineer] John Sayers – I got very upset! It felt really disappointing, the whole thing, just being in this room. I remember Rob – you know how the red light comes on when you're recording, he put green paper around it – 'I don't want a red light when I'm recording, I want green light'. He had such high standards...

The group were photographed by Graeme Webber on infra-red film posed on Olinda Golf Course one evening for a mystical, charged album cover.[155] Pearce remembers some journalists 'got' MacKenzie Theory:

> Jenny Brown... was really into our band – she was really enthusiastic about it. Some people were excited. It was all part of the ongoing flow of the time. The album wasn't a huge deal – the live gigs were much more important.

Perhaps the best description of a MacKenzie Theory show appeared in the University of Queensland magazine *Semper*. Its uncredited writer recalled:

> I have this memory of Rob's long gold brown hair flinging through an arc of 360 degrees from down his bare back up and over and down his face, synchronized with the rhythm and with a massive male in the crush of dancing bodies whose hair was the same length and color and moving in the same way in conscious answer. Having set up these conduits, the massive assault of the music charges along with ear-splitting force. One feels that somewhere, something is being broken down, some consciousness, some resistance is being destroyed or created. But what?[156]

This may have been the show that Mike Leadabrand recalls as 'probably the most memorable event of my life.'

> It was as if the music came through us from somewhere else, and we were along for the ride as much as the audience. When it was over, everyone knew that something had happened that we had no way to talk about. We were second billed that night to a popular Brisbane band called Shepherd; they were going to go on after us, but when we finished the set they said they could not go on after what had happened. Nobody complained or wondered why. This happened about three or four times in my three years with the band, and those times formed the person I would be to this day.

Richard Lee, then violinist for the group Isaac Aaron and later a member of Sidewinder and Dragon, reviewed the first album, *Out of the Blue*, for Melbourne University's *Farrago*. His description of the band live also rings true:

> The first time I heard MacKenzie Theory was at a function in Wilson Hall [at Melbourne University]. Within five minutes I knew I was listening to a top rate performance and that Rob MacKenzie was a fantastic guitarist, but that was as far as my comprehension went that night . . . I came away from the performance with a mind full of sudden rhythm changes, violent volume changes, weird screaming guitar, wailing, moaning viola and incomprehensible riffs. I was muddled, confused and slightly unimpressed . . . The next time I heard them I was very impressed and the time[s] after that I have never failed to be excited by this strange and original group . . . I love the music. It can really take you away.[157]

The album had been recorded live in the studio 'in front of a paltry audience',[158] with overdubs added later. Perhaps comparing the album to the group's live shows, many listeners at the time seemed to regard *Out of the Blue* as a disappointment; in the early 21st century it sounds remarkable and exotic. Its successor, the live album *Bon Voyage*, is arguably an even more confident and engaging work.

Rob MacKenzie's audacity, and his progressive approach, had been acknowledged when he was amongst the first people to receive a travel grant from the Australia Council for the Arts ('they seem to be backing all the wrong horses, people who have never been successful in any way', grumbled hit songwriter Kevin Johnson in the pages of *Rolling Stone*, almost confirming the value of the choice).[159] MacKenzie, Pearce and the group's second drummer, Greg Sheehan, played a few shows in London in the mid 70s before disbanding. In the late 70s Pearce returned to Australia to a long and creative music career – including playing in former Great White Noise saxophonist Sandy Evans's mid-80s group Women and Children First, which also included Sheehan[160]; MacKenzie moved to the US and, later, spent a decade playing guitar in Sha Na Na.

MacKenzie Theory's sound and style was so far removed from that of a group like the radical rockabilly/country and western–playing Pelaco Brothers that it's hard to imagine an early 70s scene that had room for both. Peter Lillie derided them equally at first; he continued to deride MacKenzie Theory but soon revised his opinion of the Pelaco Brothers, asked to join the band, and became one of its main songwriters. They were one of those relatively short-lived groups whose members would go on to distinguish themselves for decades afterwards. Joe Camilleri would be a presence on the Australian music scene for five decades (and counting) through Jo Jo Zep and the Falcons and the Black Sorrows; Stephen Cummings would hit it big, first as singer with the Sports and then as a well-loved and respected songwriter and solo performer. Lillie, a masterfully witty songwriter, would only ever achieve cult status, despite some amazing solo recordings, and later in his career published poetry. Johnny Topper ('I have tried to get people to call me by my real name, but it's too much bother now') played bass in the Pelaco Brothers and went on to play in their natural continuations, the Autodrifters and the Relaxed Mechanics. He remembers the group emerging – like Skyhooks' Red Symons and Steve Hill – from musical theatre, at venues such as La Mama and the Pram Factory, which also provided much of the raw material for the film renaissance that took place at this time:

> We did plays there which we wrote and starred in, like *Gone to See a Man about a Dog* which Jane Clifton was in, she was a narrator. She was a member of Tribe, too, who were precursors to Circus Oz. We also did a play called *Mechanics in a Relaxed Manner*, with ten people in the cast, on orchestra, elaborate sets. After the plays Peter and I did T. F. Much – we'd play after Captain Matchbox or between their sets, I remember doing some recording with them, something that involved tearing up newspapers.

Topper and Lillie met Cummings. Cummings and a friend were jealous of the two young men and had, according to a Lillie poem, 'seen us in their car/ Had joked, "lets run them over/ So that we can be more famous!"'[161] Topper and Cummings planned to launch a magazine called *Hound*, of which Topper remembers:

> We actually had an office but we didn't have any money to print it, and we hit on the idea of selling subscriptions beforehand to fund it. We were hopeless at selling subscriptions but I think we got enough money ... to buy a guitar and a bass at a pawn shop in Russell Street. Peter Lillie taught us a few chords, and we played at Pram Factory, and then we started playing as the Pelaco Brothers.

The idea may in fact have been to operate a band to raise money for the magazine. Camilleri was asked to join as saxophonist; Cummings had been in Camilleri's audiences since his days with the King Bees and the Adderley Smith Blues Band (featuring Broderick Smith and Kerryn Tolhurst, later of the Dingoes), which had begun in 1964, years before Camilleri's involvement, and 'lasted right up to the very first show of T. F. Much'.[162] But it was Camilleri's subsequent band, Lipp and the Double Decker Bros, that was probably closest to the spirit of Topper, Lillie, and Cummings. Topper continues:

> We soon became a part of this thing called Culture in the Workplace, run by some trade union organisation, and we used to play at the railways and the factories to all these people who hated us, ignored us, had no interest in county and western and rockabilly, and were bored out of their heads – miserable Italian and Greek migrant workers down at the docks! Occasionally they'd say 'Why don't you get a girl in your act?' Ted Bull, the famous trade union figure said to

us, one day, 'Whatever you do, if you attain some show-business heights, lads, never forget your working class origins.'

Pelaco is a well-known shirt brand, famously manufactured in the Melbourne suburb of Richmond where its factory building remains. A later Lillie band, the Leisuremasters, referenced a brand of trousers. The play *Gone to See a Man about a Dog*, the only surviving Topper-Lillie dramatic piece, is obsessively concerned with clothing and style. The narrator – played by Jane Clifton – enthuses in her description of the show's main characters, Jake and Jackie:

> As they walk, the discerning Thomastown taste, superb cut, and excellence of design in their lower garments becomes more apparent. As one follows the ripple in the crisp King Gees upward onto the magnificent terylene togas draped delicately over their tuberculosis infected torsos ... a special C. S. I. R. O. blend of Merino houndstooth, native wolf fur, and black jacket tarpaulin, and of course, elbow patches from an army surplus water-bag naturally ... It's as if they were walking the catwalk at the Leviathan menswear store ... An elegantly spruced and be-hatted hound flanks the two men's bib-and-brace knee-high to their slide-rule pockets.[163]

The hound in question is a 'pedigreed Preston Piss Pointer.' No doubt one had to be there to fully unpack the humour in this work, but just as Skyhooks' lyrics were so often commented on for their inclusion of Melbourne place-names, a device Barry Humphries had excelled with decades previously, Topper and Lillie were discovering the poetry in simple recognition. Australian audiences, so long used to hearing references to place names from everywhere in the world but their own country, were now enjoying the novelty.

The local nature of the name Pelaco Bros might be deduced from the fact that Sydney-based Australian *Rolling Stone* couldn't understand it, or rather, appears to have been under the impression there was a Melbourne band called 'Captain Pelaco'.[164]

The shirt company's mascot was a grinning Aboriginal man crying the slogan 'Mine tink it dey fit'. The brand was sufficiently a part of the culture to be a television sponsor – hence a program screening on television in the early 60s, *Pelaco Inquest* (!).[165] The Pelaco sign is very visible in a number of scenes in the film *Dogs in Space* (in which Joe Camilleri, incidentally, has a small role as an irate neighbour). Topper says applying the name to the band was his idea:

> We were interested in writing songs about Australian things. I don't know if we consciously did it in the sense of having to do things *for Australia* – but we had no need to write about other things. Stuff here intrigued us. I don't think we

consciously thought of it as a manifesto or to prove ourselves as Australians, although people said that afterwards.

The group acquired managers in Tim Stobart and Laurie Richards; Richards would later play an important part in late 70s Australian punk music thanks to two venues he ran, the Tiger Lounge (sufficiently established by late 1976 that AC/DC would do an anonymous 'warm-up' gig there prior to a homecoming tour)[166] and the Crystal Ballroom, showcasing many soon-to-be-famous names on the 'scene', not least the Boys Next Door. Topper says:

> Laurie and Tim were our managers. Having managers had a certain professional thing about it. The next thing they did was send us on a tour to Perth, which was insane. Just before we went we played Sunbury, in the secondary tent. There was us, and the Salvation Army rock band! It was the Sunbury where no-one got paid except Deep Purple.
>
> Peter Lillie had this Rambler and we drove to Adelaide. It was 2 o'clock in the morning and it was really hot. Peter knew Adrian Rawlins and he wanted to hang out at his place for a day. Peter wrote off the Rambler and we caught a bus to Perth. They had booked us at a place called Gobbles, in between sets by this black DJ. They got these hay bales into Gobbles . . .
>
> It was torture. It was like an actual discothèque, and it was half an hour of us, and half an hour of this dj who'd play the Commodores, 10 pm to 4 am four nights a week. A rockabilly group was completely incongruous, but they wouldn't let us out of the contract, we had to stay there. It was incredibly low pay. We couldn't afford to stay anywhere, it was insane. We had to knock on people's doors . . . we'd heard about these alternative groups and somehow we got their addresses – they didn't know us. We just said, 'Can we stay at your place for six weeks?' They were really nice people.

One of these bands was Last Chance Café, who were the biggest Perth group of their brief era (along with another, less traditional band known as Pus, of whom

more later). They would soon become a favourite of Dragon's Paul Hewson and provide Dragon with a vocalist, Billy Rogers, in the late 70s.

Topper continues the story of the Pelaco Brothers' Perth adventure:

> I don't know why Joe Camilleri had joined the band, and I'm sure he regretted it. He got a cleaning job – because he was married; he couldn't go back to Melbourne and his wife with no money! We'd go out to these stupid places for other gigs and not get paid for those either. Peter Lillie and I went round to this big booking agent and said, you're going to have to pay us actual money, or change the times, it's impossible for us to do the gigs, and they said, 'You have to do them'. We ended up telling them to get fucked. They said we'd never work in Perth again, which of course we greeted with derisive laughter. It was just ridiculous.

Camilleri later said he 'couldn't believe it. We had $5 a day to live on and we used to have to walk home.'[167] Towards the end of the Pelaco Brothers' time in Perth, Ross Wilson hired Camilleri to play a one-off show with Daddy Cool when they came through Perth.[168] On their return to Melbourne, Topper recalls, the group continued to play the conventional industry game for their booking agents Premier, playing 'places like the Village Green, supporting Ariel. You'd have to carry the headline group's P.A. in.' They had a conference with Gudinski, and were on the verge of signing to Mushroom – MacKenzie Theory's label – to make an album. 'But before we recorded we broke up. Stephen Cummings and Joe Camilleri had had enough; they had their own plans by then.' Camilleri claimed Cummings was working on new songs in a 'style with a definitely Australian flavour to it.'[169]

Cummings and Camilleri's plans may not have included signing with Mushroom as the lead singers in *other* bands, but both the Sports and Jo Jo Zep and the Falcons did end up recording for the label. Meanwhile, Topper and Lillie created a number of variations on the Pelaco Brothers theme, including the Autodrifters, the Pelaco Playboys (who supported Split Enz at an early Melbourne show at the St Kilda Sea Baths), and the Relaxed Mechanics. Topper then went on to form bands without Lillie in a similar vein, such as the Fabulous Nudes, the North 2 Alaskans, the Armchairs (with Ian Stephen) and the Pete Best Beatles in which every band member was named Pete Best except the drummer – he was 'Beat Pest'. The group wore 'wigs' made of footballs. Topper's music and performing career was never going to make him a pop star – that was plainly not where his interests lay – but he did manage the very popular Dynamic Hepnotics for a time in the early 80s.

Other groups in this vein saw themselves either as essentially live performers, or as operating too far outside the industry to make records. Though they incorporated theatre in the same way as Captain Matchbox and the Pelaco Brothers did, their appeal was perhaps unable to survive onto record without a visual element. One of these was Rock Granite and the Profiles, whom Pat Wilson came to sing with. Her husband Ross appeared ungracious about her abilities in the *Daddy Cool* documentary:

> Most of the time Pat just stays home and cooks, minds the kid and waits around for me to come back from tours. Except when she used to nag me about singing with DC – she always wanted to do a number with DC, she's always on our back to do that, but I always said no, mainly because I didn't think she could sing that well. But her brother John... he had all these art student [Prahran Art College] friends. They got a band together after a long time of messing around; it's just basically really a good time fun band, I guess it was influenced by DC's ideals. They're called Rock Granite and the Profiles, and they were looking for a... they had this really greasy number, they needed a girl to sing who had a really slick nightclub-type dress, and Pat had one so they gave her a test and it turned out she could sing OK, I was wrong all the time. So she does this number with them, and I think she's going to do some more with them from now on.[170]

This song is included in the documentary, where Wilson is introduced as 'Lady Slick'; the tune itself is a bizarre ballad in which Wilson describes washing her jeans and dropping 'a few beans' as a prelude to romance.[171] Jenny Brown labeled Rock Granite's songs as 'upper cheesey-grin, grabbable stuff... melodies you can hum nostalgically while submerged in a bubble bath.'[172]

Wayne Burt was the songwriter and guitarist in Rock Granite[173] and later in the decade would co-found Jo Jo Zep and the Falcons with Joe Camilleri; the early Jo Jo Zep single 'Beating around the Bush' had been a Rock Granite song.[174] Rock Granite broke up in mid 1975 because, it was announced, some of the Profiles believed Pat Wilson was getting too much attention; Wilson herself announced that Gulliver Smith, Gunther Gorman, Greg Macainsh and Ross Wilson, among others, would be writing an album of songs for her.[175] So many terrible albums have been made, and this one would probably have been wonderful, but it never emerged. Pat was equivocal: 'I might just buy myself a color TV set and watch a few mid-day movies,' she told Stephen Maclean from *Juke*.[176] The following decade she topped the charts with 'Bop Girl', a song written by Ross, promoted with a video that featured the screen debut of Nicole Kidman.

Prior to his experience with the Pelaco Brothers, Camilleri sang, played saxophone and provided what *Planet* described as 'foreign language translations' in Lipp and the Double Decker Brothers, a group which also featured former/future Skyhook Peter Starkie; 'Janie' (Jane) Clifton, who would later be the singer in Stiletto; and the 'Lippettes' Babs Daley and Avril Bell. The group refused to go into the recording studio[177] yet remained audience favourites. They followed Billy Thorpe and the Aztecs at one of their Sunbury shows with a parody version of what 'Anna Keys' (actually, Jenny Hunter-Brown, here writing in the third person, a few years later) called their 'Suck More Piss Youth Rally'.

> She remembered seeing the roadies set up these huge two-dimensional cardboard 'amps' whose 'volume knobs' the band adjusted by climbing up ladders. The crowd had instantly split into two – one faction ... pissing themselves laughing: the other, whose dreams were being heavily trod upon, erupting with abuse. The scene, lit in heavy white floods, seems a crystallisation of Australia's music scene.[178]

Writing at the time (as Jenny Brown), she eulogised them:

> Who could resist lifting a toe, dropping a tear, during that classic melody 'Seagull Jobbies' ... When we laugh at the 'Brothers' we are laughing at ourselves. (Wa ha ha).[179]

Bands like Lipp and the Double Decker Brothers are remembered – and documented in print at the time – as marvellous local antidotes to pretension and bombast in the music business, but it was part of their approach to stay apart from the mainstream industry (perhaps this was also part of their appeal). For that reason, not only can they not be properly judged by historians, but neither did they properly engage with the scene at the time (except as commentators on it). They disbanded in 1972, shortly after mounting a Much More Ballroom musical, *Godburst*.[180] By most accounts they were remarkable, which makes their absence from the body of recorded work from this period regrettable.

POP MUSIC IS DEAD

The distinction between a band like the Aztecs and Lipp and the Double Decker Brothers (both were 'good time' bands, but the latter satirical, the former bombastic) was different to that between MacKenzie Theory and the Pelaco Brothers (the first was complex and meaningful, the second retro-flavoured deconstruction).

Another dividing line was also clear: Jim Keays recalls the attitude he faced when he returned to Australia a second time in the early 70s – that 'pop music is dead and you won't fit in here.'[181] His band, the Masters Apprentices, had a long slow death themselves. They'd recorded two exceptional albums in the UK, *Choice Cuts* in 1971 and *A Toast to Panama Red* the following year; the first of these included 'Because I Love You', deservedly a hit single and a song that acquired iconic status in subsequent decades. Their Victorian country tour under the banal title 'Stateside 70', which began in Colac,[182] was the beginning of their end.[183] Their campus experiences must have been a sign, as Keays says:

> At Monash Uni in Melbourne they sat cross-legged on the refectory floor, stoned out of their heads, and grooved to our music like no audience of ours had done before. This became the norm at our gigs and these new, musically aware fans helped us to adjust our perspective on both performance and stage presentation. If they thought you were cool, they'd throw bags of dope on to the stage in appreciation.[184]

That final touch is hard to imagine, given that marijuana possession was at the height of its illegality, and didn't come cheap; but Keays's underlying point still stands.

New Masters songs. such as the bizarre 'Future of Our Nation' from their live album *Nickleodeon,* flopped everywhere except Tasmania and Adelaide. 'It apparently didn't receive much airplay in Melbourne,' mused Glenn Wheatley in late 1971; and 'Sydney of course never did play our records.'[185]

Wheatley and Keays quit the band. A new version of the Masters featuring Doug Ford and Colin Burgess, joined by Colin's brother Denny, were reported to be 'really getting things together' in Britain.[186] Wheatley moved definitively into management having been offered 'a good job by David Joseph' – Brian Peacock's, as mentioned earlier; he was philosophical about his former group: 'If the album that we did does any good when it is released in England on Dec. 6th . . . it will help them on their way, because as far as England is concerned they will be the Masters Apprentices.'[187] Keays, now a father, intended to live in Adelaide: 'I've had several offers from magazines, radio and television', he said portentously, 'and I will try to incorporate a couple of them into my art.'[188] In fact, Keays would have a major success in 1975 with the bizarre concept album *The Boy from the Stars,* after briefly reconvening with the Burgess brothers in Adelaide in 1973 for an ill-fated group called Hard Rock Theatre.[189]

The Masters Apprentices had been a notoriously unstable band, but it is hard to imagine that they could have survived long into the 70s in any case – the suburban dance scene which had fostered them was no more. Rock had moved into other spheres. and was now as much an adult pursuit as a teen enthusiasm. Thus, Madder Lake – who had two 1973 top-forty hits, 'Goodbye Lollipop' and '12 lb Toothbrush', that were later declared to be 'classic' rock, and were a mainstay of the Mushroom label in its early days – made their live *debut* at a festival (Sunbury '72).[190] Other groups, now largely forgotten, included Michael Turner in Session, who appeared on the Havoc Records' compilation of Australian rock bands put together by Lobby Loyde and who, Jenny Brown claimed, 'take you back to the blood level with music based on the heartbeat.'[191]

One collective that clearly needs to be documented in greater detail in its own right is Company Caine. Singer Gulliver Smith already had a CV which, apart from anything else, brimmed with imaginative names: Little Gulliver and the Children, Dr. Kandy's Third Eye, Time and the Forest Flower, Ripped

Family Marches; later, during a break from Company Caine, he briefly formed the Dead End Kids, who became the Bad Companions. Smith even created his own first name (to replace 'Kevin') and a mythical land to live in, Slatzilvania.[192] Company Caine's album *A Product of a Broken Reality* was innovatively futuristic and featured some extraordinary cover art from Ian McCausland – the group appear to have been exceptional. Smith told *Planet* he had written a book, *Sex, Dope and Violence in Everyday Life* (this announcement came in the same month that Daddy Cool released their album *Sex, Dope, Rock 'n' Roll: Teenage Heaven*), which would 'expose the rock scene'; the magazine also announced that the group's 'skinhead single "Now I'm Together" looks like being banned by Sydney radio stations for the violence contained within the lines "punching up pussy cats" and "choking white hens".'[193] Company Caine were also writing (rock) operas, one of which was called *A Stone of Class Distinction* – 'a story about a roady who starts a fight at a disco and starts throwing chicks around, then someone hands him a trip.'[194] Another, *What the F**k is Happening on Planet Earth?*, was about Poison Cyanide Gas Mafalda, a prostitute in love with Vishdungarius, an intergalactic visitor. The group broke up, moved to Sydney, considered reforming as Metropolis and then returned to their original name, which – despite many lazy, misguided or adventurous promoters' attempts, was never (they said) *really* meant to be spelt 'Co. Caine'. David Pepperell and Keith Glass, alerted to their commercial possibilities particularly by the number of people who eagerly snapped up old copies of *Product of a Broken Reality* at their shop, Archie and Jugheads, reissued it on their Real label, and Pepperell became almost-their-manager.[195] Glass (in particular) would hereby enter two decades of record production and distribution using his import record shop knowledge of a cultivated, definable market.

Sydney had its own rock legends, and Tamam Shud, Kahvas Jute and Tully all deserve acknowledgement. All three groups – the first two connected by a common member and friendship, the first and third by spiritual and/or experimental, progressive leanings – are responsible for stunningly original and compelling work. Tamam Shud had a five-year career starting in Newcastle in

1968 when they emerged as a progressive rock group from a surf pop band called the Sunsets. Sixteen-year-old guitarist Tim Gaze joined the group for their second album, *Goolutionites and the Real People,* then left almost as quickly to join Kahvas Jute. *Goolutionites,* released in 1970, is undoubtedly one of the best albums of that year: it's orchestral, melodic, impassioned, and imaginatively and smartly played. Tamam Shud enjoyed a high profile at this time and contributed most of the songs – in various permutations – to the soundtrack of the surf film *Morning of the Earth.* Whereas Tamam Shud's name was Persian, Kahvas Jute chose theirs by blindly sticking a pin in an encyclopedia then perverting a Turkish word for 'policeman'. They shone for a brief moment in 1971-72 as exponents of progressive rock. Their one album, *Wide Open,* produced by Pat Aulton, was a textured and melodic work ('for young lads, we nailed it', says bassist Bob Daisley). The group (without Gaze, who went back to Tamam Shud) moved to London, where Davey O'List – in between his tenure in the Nice and his brief moment in Roxy Music – was a member. Shedding a few members (Daisley stayed in Britain, joining Chicken Shack and then Mungo Jerry, after which he was somehow sentenced to play in Ozzy Osbourne's Blizzard of Ozz, Black Sabbath and Uriah Heep in the 80s), singer/guitarist Dennis Wilson and latter day bass player Peter Roberts got back together in Sydney in 1974 as Chariot, where they were part of the Trafalgar stable with Radio Birdman but disbanded before their debut album's release.

Like Tamam Shud, Tully emerged in 1968: some members had been in Levi Smith's Clefs. They became the house band for Jim Sharman's production of *Hair,* which had been funded largely by television star Graeme Kennedy[196] and which also featured the 'scrawny, sexy' Keith Glass (prior to his Archie and Jugheads foray; he was in the production only for its first six months)[197] and later the 'gifted and delightful' Marcia Hines.[198] Tully recorded the *Morning of the Earth* soundtrack album in 1969 with guests including jazz drummer John Bamford. Later that same year they featured in their own ABC-TV show, *Fusions;* they heralded 1970 by starring at Ourimbah and, weeks later, playing with the Sydney Symphony Orchestra as part of 'classical' composer Peter Sculthorpe's *Love 200.*

As should be clear from even this schematic account, Tully were brilliant progressive musicians; they took subtle cues from surf music itself, just as they appealed to 'head' surfies on Sydney beaches. The group's name – shared with a small town in Queensland – was obscure, except that it came from a philosophy (and/or a novel) by its drummer, Robert Taylor. 'As far as I know,' flautist/keyboard player Richard Lockwood said in 2012, 'it was kind of a philosophy that he had that he called "Life Is the Blood of Tully" – you'd have to ask him but he's not around to ask. Tully's not the town [in Queensland, pop. 2400] – just something he dreamed up, I'd say. When we put up those posters [reading] "Life Is the Blood of Tully", some character came along and took them all down and made them into "Life is Life". We all thought that was very good, and also a bit of a wakeup call. But I have no idea, seriously. Definitely not the town. We never went that far north. I know that it wasn't the town. Whether it was a *man* ...'

By the end of 1970, the group's unfortunate practice of shedding old members and acquiring new ones had accelerated; religious differences seem to have played a part in this (Krishna and Meher Baba being the main culprits). Tully merged with their 'sister band' Extradition in 1971. 'Tully was a very different creature to Extradition,' Lockwood recalled:

> Tully was a wild sort of creature, whereas Extradition was ethereal and very beautiful in my opinion, so when I first heard it, Extradition, I was just blown away. We liked one another enough to form one band out of the two bands. I think it was a very happy – well, whether it was happy or not, it was a lovely marriage of the two bands for the short period it lasted. Pity it didn't last longer.[199]

Their second album, *Sea of Joy*, was the soundtrack to Paul Witzig's surfing film of the same name. Their final album, 1972's *Loving Is Hard*, is superb; its first side, in particular, exemplifies everything that was golden about early 70s progressive pop.

Aspiring young musicians took their breaks where they found them. Bendigo-born Ian Rilen's first 'real' band (he tended to discount his first, Lotus, even though they featured at the 1971 Myponga Festival) was Space, in 1971. They are often referred to in historical accounts as 'Tully in Space', which is a great name but not the name the group went by. Space was an entirely new band with some former Tully members, singer Terry Wilson and drummer Robert Taylor. According to Rilen:

> I was friends with the keyboard player [Bobby Gebert], who was a fucking genius ... He got me in on bass and we went on tour to Perth. They were all great musicians – like, Dave Kain was the guitar player, and he was sort of a guitar hero of ten years ago, and I was this idiot young guy who couldn't play ... Then I lived in a house with Lee Hamilton ... and Lee and myself got this band together ... One night Phil Key, who'd been in the La De Das, and Norm Roue came around and said they were getting this band together and for me and Dallas [Royall] to come around ... That band turned out to be Band of Light.'[200]

Rilen's involvement with Band of Light lasted from late 1972 though 1973, and gave him his first brush with the pop charts. The group made a sharp, trippy single and album in 1973; the single, 'The Destiny Song', was a national top-thirty hit while the album, *Total Union*, made the top twenty. According to Rilen, Key's wife Pam 'wrote the lyrics, really atrocious stuff', including those of the single; he also claimed that he and Roue left the band because Key refused to let them contribute songs themselves.[201] Key reconfigured the group to record a second album, *The Archer*, in 1974.

It was to be the very definition of a long, strange trip for Rilen, who would next play briefly in the delightfully titled Hot Cock with Ray Goodwin, then co-found Rose Tattoo with slide guitarist Peter Wells, then form X with Steve Lucas, and then Sardine V with Stephanie Rilen; the latter bands would have a lot to do with Lobby Loyde, who was at this time recording wildly diverse albums under his own name, some of which went unreleased for decades.

Roue joined Buffalo, a notoriously heavy group which had begun in 1970 when Dave Tice and Peter Wells moved from Brisbane to Sydney as part of a band called Head. Buffalo was the first Australian band signed to Phonogram's progressive label Vertigo; they produced four albums between 1972 and 1976, all with provocative contents behind sex-and-death-themed cover art: *Dead Forever*, *Volcanic Rock*, *Only Want You for Your Body* and *Mother's Choice*. Roue joined in 1974[202] but had a breakdown at the end of that year and quit. Following Buffalo's split, Wells was – early and often – a member of Rose Tattoo, while Tice would become the singer for British pub-rock band the Count Bishops.

For these musicians and many others, there was clearly a growing chasm between rock and pop, although there was – as always – the possibility of a pop hit for certain rock bands (it would be more accurate to say that 'pop music' was not the only music on the 'pop' charts). With Australian blues rock on the rise in the early 70s, its practitioners were frustrated: Billy Thorpe, by this time the heaviest blues rocker in the country, claimed 'We need about half a dozen big concerts to show people blues. When enough kids see what's going on they'll really dig it.'[203] He had his head screwed on, though, and neither he nor his people had any qualms about releasing a virtually spontaneous and straightforward rehash of 'Over the Rainbow', from his 1974 Sunbury show.[204]

Thorpe's biggest hit of the early 70s, amongst some lethargically boogie-led albums, had come a couple of years earlier: 'Most People I Know Think That I'm Crazy' was basically a pop song, with the vocals up loud and the tunefulness accentuated. While they were recording it at T.C.S. studios at television's Channel 9 in Melbourne, the *Planet* reported that Thorpe and the Aztecs upset 'the Italian residents of Richmond' by 'blowing so loud that they brought a chorus of howls and bangings from the families in the houses opposite – a good one hundred yards away!'[205] It was to become far and away the Havoc label's best-selling release, and a quarter of a century later also the name of Thorpe's second book, its title moulded into the shape of a youthful buttock, a reference no doubt to his 1974 album with the Aztecs *More Arse than Class*. A 1975 hit 'It's Almost Summer' is a similar example of the remarkable mellow pop which Thorpe did so well, but which is rarely associated with his name today. Soon afterwards, he was touring the US on the back of a significant hit album, *Children of the Sun*, which enjoyed major success on FM radio.

PARTY MACHINES

Ross Wilson, Mike Rudd and Ross Hannaford played as Party Machine between 1967 and 1969; Rudd formed Spectrum in 1969 when Wilson left for Britain to join Procession (see chapters 6 and 8), and his new group had a number one hit in early 1971, 'I'll be Gone', with a video directed by Chris Löfvén, later to direct the excellent and extraordinary film *Oz*. Rudd recalls:

> 'I'll Be Gone' was held up for six months; it was ready to be released, and the [radio] ban came into effect. So there was an unnaturally long time between our recording it and it being released, in which time we'd evolved into something which I hadn't anticipated when I started writing songs . . . we didn't have that many songs, so we stretched them out and we became a prog-rock band.

The group had been signed to the Australian incarnation of the recently launched British progressive label Harvest, whose UK arm issued records by Little River Band, the Saints, and Ariel, Rudd's post-Spectrum group. Rudd has no idea why he was on Harvest; it seems this was never explained to him:

> I'm sure it was mentioned as being a prestigious thing – but no-one had really much of an idea. I think was pretty much at the beginning of the Harvest label as well. And look, bitching about the record company is traditional, but EMI had openly said to us that records were only part of their business. White goods were a much bigger part of their business.

'I'll Be Gone' is a winning example of Australian blues rock-pop of the early 70s (alongside Madder Lake's 'Goodbye Lollipop' and Chain's 'Black and Blue'). It is instantly recognisable to millions of Australians to this day (and, like Daddy Cool's 'Eagle Rock', which hit number one a few months later, it chugs along on an apparently simple, but actually rather complex, rhythm). Rudd, who has described Spectrum as 'serious . . . serious to po-faced',[206] believed the song was too commercial to appear on the group's incredibly fine debut album, *Spectrum Part One*,[207] which does however feature Wilson's very catchy 'Make Your Stash' (initially written for Spectrum,[208] this song also appears on the second Daddy Cool album, *Sex, Dope, Rock 'n' Roll* . . .) and other close-to-pop hits such as 'Drifting'. Spectrum's second album, *Milesago*, was a double and allowed the group to take their possibilities even further. Just as Wilson had Sons of the Vegetal Mother (of which Rudd had been an early member) as well as its 'dance band' flipside Daddy Cool, Rudd created a parallel-universe Spectrum, the Indelible Murtceps, in October 1971.[209] Spectrum was, in Rudd's words, 'dyin' at the box office'.

> It was a fairly elaborate setup to present Spectrum, especially if you included the light show, which we wanted to do. But of course in pubs there was no way you

could do that, so we made the whole thing more mobile and actually had two drumkits, one for Spectrum and one for Murtceps; and Murtceps didn't use the organ, they just used the piano. We kept it small deliberately, in case we had to do more than one gig a night.

They were Murtceps because that was Spectrum spelled backwards, and they were 'indelible' because they 'refused to be rubbed out',[210] though they also played a few shows as the Inedible Crumpets, according to an announcement in *Planet*:

> Murtceps also known as 'Inedible Crumpets Workshop' playing at Sebastian's with Spectrum, Langford Lever, It Flew Away, Captain Matchbox... Workshop number Two, at a time and place yet to be discovered, is sure to be an innovator. It is inspiringly entitled A Brick Veneer Evening and features the Sounds of the Suburbs. It is hoped that many creative bands will take a hand in the invention of this night. MacKenzie Theory are to be amongst them.[211]

It is Murtceps rather than Spectrum who are captured (along with Wendy Saddington and Captain Matchbox) in Peter Weir's 3 *Directions in Australian Pop Music*. On that night, Rudd recalls, the group were trying out a now forgotten replacement keyboard player for the recently-departed Lee Neale. Because Rudd and bass player Bill Putt performed again under the name Spectrum from the late 80s (and Rudd has continued the band after Putt's death in 2013), it is worth noting that the original group only existed for three and a half years, breaking up due to line-up difficulties after drummer Ray Arnott left to join Wilson's shortlived Mighty Kong. The original Spectrum's last concert took place on April 15, 1973; it was 'the end of the best group Australia has ever had,' said *Farrago*.[212] Almost immediately Ariel formed around Rudd and Putt, along with Tim Gaze and Nigel Macara, initially of Tamam Shud and then Miss Universe; the new group had a top-forty single with 'Jamaican Farewell' later in the year.

> Ray Arnott had had enough in a big way, and so we said, OK that's been one change too many, we'll stop. And [manager] Phil Jacobsen, bless him, said – 'Hmm, I wish this could keep going.'

Ariel was a good excuse to clear the boards and do something radically different. You've got to do that every now and again . . . the life expectancy of a band is four years, end of story. I mean – two years, you're pushing it, and four years, that's it, that's the end. The absolute, you've got to stop and start again or do something.

'Ariel is not only a band but a personality contributed to by all members,' mused Richard Lee, who found the group's music 'exciting and weird.'[213] The group's first album, *A Strange Fantastic Dream*, 'provoked controversy from the moment it was released', according to Rudd. 'I mean, there was a dirty great hypodermic needle dominating the front cover, for Christ's sake.'[214] Three tracks were all but banned by the Broadcasting Control Board ('I'd figured that the stations might get into trouble if they did play "Chickenshit",' Rudd told *Go-Set's* Helen Barrett; 'I can understand it . . . then again I *can't!*'[215]

The original line-up disbanded on a Western Australian tour but, on the strength of John Peel's enthusiasm on Radio 1, EMI in Britain were keen for Ariel to visit London and record a new album at Abbey Road, Rudd recalls:

> All the kudos was for the first Ariel album, mainly from John Peel. But there were other people that were probably not as well documented as John Peel. And so Phil was in the position of having an offer to take that band over to the UK to record – and we went to WA and imploded in a huge way. There was no way back, really. There probably was, but we never were in the money-earning category, so we could never grease the situation with money, which is what bands do if that sort of situation arises. So we couldn't see any way around it, and in fact at that stage I'd had enough of everything.

Nevertheless, they soon reassembled to record demos for a new album, *The Jellabad Mutant*, 'because rock operas were the go.'[216] Guitarist Harvey James and drummer John Lee were new members. Rudd again:

> I went off with my wife down the coast and started tooling round with the *Jellabad Mutant* idea, which I thought was just something to keep me entertained. I got in touch with Bill again – so *Spinal Tap!* . . . I said, 'Why don't we get that John Lee bloke that used to play with the Dingoes, he was a loud drummer'. I had a penchant for loud drummers at that stage. Then John said, 'why don't we get this other guitarist' . . . That's how Harvey got in the band, they knew each other pretty well . . . and Phil said, 'Oh, well we can reactivate this'. It's still Ariel. We demoed the *Mutant* and I think that probably put paid to it really, but Phil managed to keep things grinding, so we ended up [in the UK]. But instead of the doors being open for us, we had a week to record the album. So it was, 'you can't

record *that* any more, what the fuck are we going to record?' We backtracked a bit, and had a week to mix it.

Scrabbling for a replacement to *The Jellabad Mutant*, Ariel brought forth *Rock & Roll Scars*, a 'pushy, funky album'[217] largely made up of old Spectrum material with three new tracks.[218] Unsurprisingly, the sound and style of the album is marvelous, though the inclusion of so much old material – a reworked 'I'll Be Gone', the Indelible Murtceps's 'We are Indelible', and the like – is a matter of regret to anyone who believes groups can only progress with new material. One new track, recorded before they went to London, the (non-album) single 'Yeah Tonite', is remarkable and delightful for its shallow, pop hipness, more suitable for a boy band like the Bay City Rollers than a head outfit. Two British visits later, Ariel ended its days broke and despondent, pushing slight music like the single 'Disco Dilemma'. Rudd and Putt, like many of their cohort, finished the 70s in a miasma of rehashed and underfunded attempts at maintaining a music career.[219]

The new sophisticated rock scene came in all shapes and forms. The Executives, who had seen success in the 60s, changed with the times, grabbed a coy new name, Inner Sense, and relocated to the US.[220] When things failed to work out to their satisfaction, the group split. Guitarist Ray Burton's biggest moment (to date) was his co-write with Helen Reddy of her international smash hit, 'I Am Woman'. Back in Australia, Carol and Brian King were recruited for Rodney Stewart's musical *Nuclear* alongside Erl Dalby, known for his 1970 northern-hemisphere hit 'Can't Wait for September', written by Vanda and Young. Writing in the *Sun-Herald* Gil Walhquist lauded the show's album for offering, among other things, sensuousness 'amidst the atomic fusion'.[221] The Executives were playing again in the mid 70s, for instance at Gatties in Double Bay ('the gateway to Sydney's new scene for the wonderful ones'[222]), and they achieved one last great moment, the instrumental theme to the TV soap *The Young Doctors*, in 1976.

Max Merritt moved to Britain in 1971 with the Meteors, including legendary drummer Stewie Speer. The touring Masters Apprentices and their guide Brian Peacock decided not to stay with them in the 15-bedroom mansion they were renting for £25 a week, so daunted were they by the sight.[223] After line-up changes, Merritt and the Meteors signed to Arista in 1975. Their 1976 single 'Slipping Away' was plaintive pop, markedly different to their 60s output; it became a signature song for the group in Australia, and a minor hit in Britain. Their manager, Peter Raphael, fled to Spain after using the insurance settlements the Meteors received from their earlier car crash as leverage for bank loans. In the late 70s Merritt moved to Los Angeles and became a set designer; he worked on the clip for Madonna's 'Material Girl'.[224] Between the lines of these minutiae (a polite word for 'trivia') one can discern the diminished dreams of a band who were by all reports one of the greatest of the 60s, but whose potential was hardly rewarded with recording or commercial success commensurate with their abilities.

ROCKA

As songwriter/producers, Harry Vanda and George Young were a world unto themselves in Australia in the 1970s. Their home base, Alberts, was always a publisher of songs as well as a record company, and was keen to foster new writers as well. Ted Mulry was a relatively recent British immigrant (he was 21 when he arrived in 1968); legend had it he was driving a tractor for the NSW Main Roads Department when he submitted some songs to Alberts – solely because they were the first music publisher listed in the phone book.

Mulry's first career success was as a balladeer, singing two very impressive pop songs: 'Julia', which he wrote, and 'Falling in Love Again', a gift from Vanda and Young, left over from their attempts to deliver another hit for the Easybeats. George Young now says the song was 'deliberately schmaltzy';[225] in fact it's cunningly self-referential, as it makes a very good case for the celebration of falling in love being a suitable subject for a song. A sumptuous romp with glorious sitar sounds (as mentioned, reputedly the clever guitar work of Billy Green), 'Falling in Love Again' was accompanied by one of the most inadvertently funny (or perhaps just amusingly flippant?) music videos ever made. Mulry's first two albums, *Falling in Love Again* (1971) and *I Won't Look Back* (1973) are enigmatic. The first features a slew of Mulry originals – not all of them great – and odd covers like the Beatles' 'Let It Be' and Joni Mitchell's 'Circle Game'.[226] The second, which features his rendering of his own 'snappy, grinding little rocker'[227] titled 'You're All Woman', which had been a big hit for Sherbet in 1972, sees Mulry gain further confidence as a performer – something he had never really expected to become. The title track – his first real rock recording, and clearly something he'd been pushing to do for some time[228] – is over seven minutes long. *I Won't Look Back*'s cover shows Mulry sitting in a canvas folding chair that has the word 'composer' affixed to it with (surely) unintentionally visible masking tape – and looking back(wards).

Mulry would later claim 'I hated me when I was solo',[229] in which case he was fortunate to inherit bandmates Herm Kovacs and Les Hall when the Velvet Underground, their group with Malcolm Young, split up. The Ted Mulry Gang began in September 1972, with Mulry playing bass.[230] In 1976 he explained the change in direction he'd wanted to make:

> I wrote a lot of songs and had a boy-next-door image. I never really liked it and the songs were OK only if somebody else sang them. I got out of that image by going rock and starting from the bottom again. I suffered for a while, but was determined not to go back to ballads and to stick it out or give it up.[231]

His fully fledged boogie-stomp period was just around the corner.

Mulry will always be fondly remembered for the cheeky glam-rock hits he had with TMG. These included 1975's legendary 'Jump in My Car', which has been demonized by some as glorifying sexual assault – 'about picking up random girls and raping them'[232] – when literally speaking it was just peculiar; the narrator didn't want sex, he really *did* just want to drive a girl to her home.[233] This record's success was by no means a foregone conclusion (Mulry later claimed it was 'out six months' before it began to sell).[234] Chris Spedding covered it soon afterwards[235] but it was David Hasselhoff who achieved the highly unlikely feat of taking the song into the UK top five in 2006, without any 'retro' sentimentality to power it – it was unknown to most of his audience. TMG also had hits in 1976-77 with 'Darktown Strutters' Ball' (the 1917 trad jazz hit rejigged as Status Quo–style boogie), 'Crazy' (the best ever Rod Stewart hit that wasn't by Rod Stewart) and the cod-reggae carry-on of 'Jamaica Rum'.

Alberts' chief money-spinners were nonetheless still the Young brothers and Harry Vanda. Vanda and Young's relationship survived long after the demise of the Easybeats, and their talent for metamorphosis led to continued success. They spent most of their time in the early 70s in the UK, doing what they'd already been doing for a while: cloistering themselves in the studio, experimenting with pop music and drugs, of which their favourite seems to have been alcohol. 'If we'd stuck to a formula like the Hollies, we could have lasted forever,' said Vanda in 1974.[236] They released unsuccessful singles in the UK and Europe under various names including Haffy's Whiskey Sour (an advertising tie-in,[237] the song was called 'Shot in the Head'), Tramp ('Vietnam Rose'), Paintbox ('Get Ready For Love'), Moondance ('Lazy River'; in Australia this record was credited to Vanda & Young) and Band of Hope (although the single 'Working Class People' remained unreleased; Johnny O'Keefe later covered it). They also had a group called the Marcus Hook Roll Band, which released a grotesque song called 'Louisiana Lady'; the interest generated by that record led to an album recorded under that group name – and to greater things, as will be seen.

George Young had an ongoing chess game he played by telephone with Ted Albert in Sydney, and the duo continued to provide Alberts with material: 'Falling in Love Again', for instance; and a less successful Mulry single, 'Ain't it Nice'; as well as John Paul Young's first hit, 'Pasadena', which they had co-written with actor David Hemmings, and which was somehow recorded under the aegis of British manager Simon Napier-Bell (Mulry also covered the song). While he was in Australia Napier-Bell also took an interest in Alison McCallum; he produced her hit single 'Superman', another Vanda-Young composition.

In 1973 Albert decided it was time to lure his star players back home. Clinton Walker, setting the scene for the birth of AC/DC in his biography of Bon Scott, tells us that 'Ted promised Harry and George ... that he would build them a studio, and that they could run it as they chose. Harry and George, in return, promised to get down to some serious work.'[238] As it transpired, the initial studio would be in George Young's back yard,[239] although Albert opened the King Street Studio soon afterwards. Vanda and Young's work was primarily for the Alberts label, for which the company had arranged distribution through EMI, having extracted itself from its previous licensing deal with Parlophone.

The seriousness of this work can best be measured by the Alberts compilation album *Rocka,* released in 1975 and spanning the previous six years. Its cover, by the wonderful Alan Puckett, features a green lizard coveting a rock improbably wrapped in an Australian flag, while a frog, some ants and a stag beetle look on; the names of the artists on the record are chiseled on another rock and the album title is graffitied on another. Just in case the Australianness of the album is not entirely clear, the Southern Cross is depicted in the night sky above. A coupon inside the sleeve encourages the consumer to mail it in, stating: 'I love the "Rocka" Album and now I'd love the "Rocka" Souvenir Song Book...' The album was reported to have achieved sales of a hundred thousand within the year;[240] its promotional copy proclaimed: '*Rocka* has been carefully programmed and produced to achieve the same impact, mood, flow and feel as a successful rock radio station. With *Rocka* you don't just pick out your favourite tracks, you just let the whole album flow right on through... there ain't no ads!'[241]

With one exception (Little River Band's slick 'Everyday of My Life', presumably included as a sop to distributor EMI) everything on *Rocka* is directly traceable to Vanda and Young as producers or writers, or both. The album contains four AC/DC songs, including top-twenty hits 'High Voltage', 'It's a Long Way to the Top' and 'Jailbreak'; the Angels' classic (though never a chart hit except much later, in a live version) 'Am I Ever Gonna See Your Face Again', which Vanda and Young produced; TMG's 'Jump in my Car' and 'Crazy' (the first hits recorded at King Street). There are also three tracks Vanda and Young wrote and produced for Stevie Wright's patchy solo career, including his largely forgotten – but genuinely marvelous – 'Black Eyed Bruiser', which is a template for AC/DC's career if ever there was one, even if it leans closer to glam than to boogie. There is also the overrated and overwrought nonsense of Wright's 'Evie', the most commercially successful of the Vanda/Young productions for Wright, but hardly essential. Side two of the album opens with a very creditable version of the duo's 'St. Louis' belted out by John Paul Young, and closes with the Easybeats' ostentatious 'Good Times', the B side to 'Land of Make Believe', which had been a top-thirty hit in August 1968. For no clear reason, there are also two tracks from the Marcus Hook Roll Band's album *Tales of Old Grand-Daddy*, an early 70s studio experiment between Vanda, Young and ex-Pretty Things bassist Wally Allen that saw Angus and Malcolm Young recording for the first time; these songs are far more funky than anyone involved now seems willing to admit. Tracks segue into each other, and there's a poppy 'Rocka' ID inserted on each side, all in simulation of a radio station, one specially set up as testament to the genius of Harry and George.

Harry Vanda told *Juke's* Andy Bradley in 1977 that 'We're more or less trying to cover the whole spectrum of music ... We don't have to stick to the one thing because we write so many songs...'[242] They continued as studio gurus and hitmakers, producing and writing on an ambitious scale throughout the 70s – and beyond, although their last major success was Mark Williams's gaudy 'Show No Mercy' in 1990. Vanda and Young produced the first six AC/DC albums and would nurture and shape the band's career throughout the early 70s (an excellent memoir by Mark Evans reveals the prominence of their role in this process) and brought the same intelligent, straightforward production style to Rose Tattoo's debut album and the first album by the Angels, for instance, thus setting a standard for the 70s Australian rock sound.

Vanda and Young's best contributions played to what had been their forte from the start, guitar pop. The Scottish-born (but somehow accent-free) John Young had been a member of Elm Tree, a Sydney band of the late 60s, and the single 'Pasadena' was a top-ten hit for him in 1972. Subsequent singles on the Alberts label hadn't been successful, although he'd kept working, as a cast member of the long-running *Jesus Christ Superstar*. Vanda and Young then took him on as a project. (Whatever European-penned or otherwise ignorant AC/DC books might assume, 'John Young' was not related to George, Malcolm and Angus Young – nor, for that matter, was Johnny Young.)

While John Young was certainly trying to bounce back after a couple of flops, it's hard to believe that Vanda and Young actually wrote 'Yesterday's Hero', his next single, about him. It's tempting to imagine that they envisaged the track as a single for Stevie Wright, who was by all accounts a mess at this point (Stephen Phillips, writing in *Juke* in 1984, also thinks this was the case).[243] John Young's testimony from the time suggests the song was written on the spot: 'George sat there and wrote the words. We waited until we had the lyric line off him and then we did the song.'[244] It's hard to debate the memory of an eyewitness, yet it's still hard to believe Wright was not the song's true inspiration. It's another of Vanda and Young's 'three minute operas', though they cheat a little – the implication that the song's subject has suicided or otherwise brought calamity on himself and others comes only from a spoken intro in the style of a newsreader. Vintage Australian rock and roller Dig Richards had released a record in 1965 titled 'I Was Yesterday's Hero, Today I'm a Heartbroken Clown', but whatever its origins, the strident, if not bombastic, attack of the Vanda and Young song made it compellingly catchy: it couldn't have been better. The single was originally released under the name 'John Young', but a decision was made at this time to insert the middle name 'Paul' to avoid any confusion with Johnny Young, who was by then a well-known TV personality.

The follow-ups to 'Yesterday's Hero, like 'I Hate the Music', were equally provocative, and 'Standing in the Rain', a disco boogie, suggests that Vanda and Young's strategy for 'JPY' was to cast him as an unwitting loser. His best-known and best-loved song, though, was 1977's 'Love Is in the Air', similar musically to 'Standing in the Rain' but far more schmaltzily merry; it was a hit around the world at the time and later revived and remixed, on Ted Albert's initiative, for Baz Luhrmann's 1992 film *Strictly Ballroom*. Under the wing of manager Wayne de Gruchy,[245] Young was a success for Alberts because he was both good-looking

– some might even have said sexy – and content to have his career effectively controlled by the best svengalis in the business.

William Shakespeare is generally put forward as the joke end of the Vanda/Young oeuvre (or ignored completely as an embarrassment), but the two singles that reached number one in 1974 for William Shakespeare – aka Johnny Cave, Caves or Cabe, formerly a hard-rock vocalist[246] – were pop gold. His album, with the not very Shakespearian title *Can't Stop Myself from Loving You*, is divided into two 'acts' rather than sides; on the cover, Cave is dressed in some kind of theatre-restaurant conception of 'Shakespeare the poet' who, he said, would have worn those 'sort of costumes' had he lived 'in the rock and roll age.'[247] Barely articulate but quite genial, Cave was the subject of a long, sardonic piece on *GTK* in early 1975, in which much time was devoted to his own recounting of the sad tale of his house burning down after he fell asleep with a cigarette in his hand.

Some (perhaps all) of the William Shakespeare oeuvre was recorded before Cave was recruited to sing vocals. 'Can't Stop Myself from Loving You' is once heard, never forgotten; an essential ingredient in any glam-rock collection. 'My Little Angel' is a different breed of song, syrupy and 'cornball' in the extreme; it is also unfocused – the listener is left in some doubt as to the present whereabouts of the 'angel' in question. She is clearly the singer's daughter and has plainly disappeared; it's almost as if half of another song's lyrics has crept in at the end, but perhaps that's part of the general knocked-out ambience of the whole. Watching Cave stumble through his miming to 'My Little Angel' on *Countdown* is an uneasy experience forty years later,[248] even without the knowledge that he would shortly after be charged with carnal knowledge of a 15-year-old girl ('a lot of hogwash' he told *GTK*),[249] receiving a conviction that would

end his pop career decisively. Twenty five years later, homeless, he was essentially rescued and installed in government housing by the former Go-Betweens drummer Lindy Morrison in her role as a case worker for Support Act Limited; Morrison was later to describe Cave as 'the sad face of glam rock in Australia.'[250] His two singles – undoubtedly the highlights of the album – are further examples of Vanda and Young's genius for pop music, which they have tended to underplay now that AC/DC looks like becoming their most lasting legacy.

1977 was a great year for Vanda and Young. In a rare press interview three years earlier Vanda had proclaimed that if he and Young ever formed another band, 'it will be absolutely outrageous.'[251] Their 'solo' project Flash and the Pan was launched with the sublime single 'Hey, St. Peter'. The single came with a zany video ('conceived by David from [TV show] *Flashez*... He knows what goes with what'[252]) in which Harry and George ham it up in classic 60s Easybeat style; the witty clincher of the video – and a canny piece of product placement – is that St Peter has come to dispense ice cream from Peters, Australia's best-known ice cream company ('the health food of a nation'). It made the top five (Grace Jones later covered its B side, 'Walking in the Rain').

Employing mostly spoken-word vocals (they claimed Pip Proud as an influence), Flash and the Pan encompassed numerous sounds and styles, all of them distinctively Vanda and Young. Their third album, 1982's *Headlines*, saw Stevie Wright briefly included in the group's line-up, though what he actually did is difficult to tell – presumably, he was largely there to draw a wage and continue his downward spiral, though he spun an interesting story for *Rolling Stone* that when he 'ended up in hospital' (for unexplained reasons), his vocals were fed into a computer with the result that George Young's voice dominated on the finished record.[253] More sensibly, he noted that he, Vanda and Young had all had their 'downs': 'They've had bouts with alcohol and tragedies in their families and they've had a down probably equal to mine, so they know pretty well where I'm coming from.'[254] It was at this time that Flash and the Pan's 'Waiting for a Train', a Teutonic disco song plainly not sung by Wright (in fact, not really 'sung' at all), went top ten in Britain. The duo continued to release records under the Flash and the Pan name until 1992.

Another inspired, though perhaps ultimately underdone Vanda/Young project was the hard-rock album *Rock & Roll Women* by the group Cheetah. Cheetah was essentially comprised of Chrissie and Lyndsay Hammond, London-born sisters who had emigrated to Melbourne at a young age in the late 1950s. Chrissie Hammond had played Mary Magdalene in *Jesus Christ Superstar* and had a stint in an early line-up of Air Supply. The sisters formed Cheetah in 1977 and had a top-ten hit the following year with an Ian Meldrum-produced cover of the Ronettes' song, 'Walking in the Rain'. Unhappy with their careers since then, they were preparing to depart for Europe when George Young forestalled them with a contract. Chrissie said that Alberts 'asked us what we wanted to do – the first time anyone has done that.'[255] Vanda and Young's songs for the duo are often curiosities at best; the opening 'Bang Bang (Shot Full of Love)' sets the tone, and the miming of fellatio in the video to the chugging minor hit 'Spend the Night' illustrates the depth of meaning.

RAVE ON

Many artists from the 60s came back for a second go in the first half of the 70s; Gerry Humphrys, a popular compere at dances and festivals, returned to recording with Gerry and the Joy Band on Sparmac in 1971; his reading of Buddy Holly's 'Rave On' utilised the talents of Warren 'Pig' Morgan from the Aztecs, three quarters of Daddy Cool, the ubiquitous Billy Green,[256] Margaret RoadKnight, and 'Inga (ex-Captain Matchbox)' on violin,'[257] though in Buesst's documentary on

Humphrys he is seen singing the song backed by Daddy Cool,[258] and his group from this period also often featured Brian Peacock on bass.[259] Peacock now says that Green 'took me in like I was a peer of his. I'd never considered myself to be in the same class as a musician like him. And he got me in session work, doing Coke ads — because I came back on the bones of my arse, with a young family to support.' Mike Edwards recalled the Joy Band as being a 'zany whacky act' who appeared regularly on *Uptight* as well as at clubs like Bertie's and Sebastian's. 'The sort of material we did was varied, it was often thematic'; it could even be provocative, as when the group 'dressed up as Anzacs' and performed war songs.[260]

Humphrys' pacifist, free-love politics were a major part of his persona by now:

> I suppose I am more of a showman than a strict musician. On *Uptight* I was permitted to do my own raves. That was in the beginning. After a while I was given regulations – don't mention politics, religion or sex; that sort of thing... And then I learnt that many of the groups on the show were not being paid. They were told that television exposure was sufficient recompense. It was all rather disgusting, so I left.[261]

He became more of a fellow traveler on the music scene than a major contributor of new work; he designed posters for the T. F. Much Ballroom, and acted as compere at benefits for the Vietnam Moratorium, Sunbury and the Q Club. He told the *Planet*:

> To a certain extent I fulfil my part in the revolution when I am on stage at concerts, or at the Q Club. If you are honest with people, if you can make them laugh, then you are helping them; you are making the world just that little bit better. The Q Club is important to me; the people who got here are generally simple people; they are just as sophisticated as those you might find at some of the bigger places in the city. They are also younger; most of them would be apprentices or shop workers, people of that sort. For those reasons, I think they need more help than those who are into thinking about social matters. I like to think I am helping by showing them a good time.[262]

ADELAIDE

Humphrys also acted as an occasional correspondent for the *Planet*. He went to Adelaide for a short promotional tour, and wrote back that it was a tiny city packed with talent:

> Yet that small city with a telephone book half the size of Melbourne's, containing the pink and white pages in one, has produced over the years the Twilights, through to Fraternity.

Local groups work their arses off playing from 8 till 12 and they told me it was always the thirty minutes on and ten off thing. That's why most Adelaide groups have a repertoire of 50,000 tunes which vary from rock 50/50 and top forty.

All this is due to the new S.A. licensing act which allows teenage entertainment in hotels. Though it was obvious to me that no birth certificate was needed for proof of age and there was a handful of kids at each venue that should have been in bed at 8.30. One of the stipulations of the new law was that all such venues must be promoted by charitable organisations such as the local life-saving club etc. The hassle with this was that the law has given birth to a new breed of promoter. This means that their inexperience tends to cause a few teething problems like lack of advertising and no free passes.

However, he said, some members of his generation – a good five years older than the average punter – like 'Jim Keayes [sic] and Vince Lovegrove are trying to do things like Town Hall concerts etc.'[263]

At the same time, Adelaide was hosting some unusual spectres. As we have seen, Bon Scott had a long career already (in pop terms) as a vocalist in the Valentines ('I admit now that I'm not a musician's arsehole', his bandmate Vince Lovegrove said in 1970, 'but Bon is a musician.')[264] Scott subsequently found himself a position as singer in Fraternity. This group had formed from the ashes of Levi Smith's Clefs, and according to Clinton Walker, were waiting for the world to come to their 'antipodean Nashville'[265] in the Adelaide Hills, once it intuitively deduced their brilliance. Their first album, *Livestock*, was co-produced by Doug Ashdown. Fraternity's Bruce Howe explained that Adelaideans 'dig us for what we are – we don't have to sacrifice our principles.'[266] Described by Walker as producing 'pompous, ponderous art rock'[267] though their music was often far more up-tempo and celebratory than such a description suggests, Fraternity were largely funded by an entrepreneur/Medici figure, Hamish Henry, using an inheritance. After winning the Hoadley Battle of the Sounds, the band travelled to the UK, where they were an ignominious failure (even after temporarily changing their name to Fang). Soon after they returned to Australia at the end of 1972, Scott left and John Swan replaced him; sometimes the group would perform with Swan's younger brother Jim Barnes instead. Born in Glasgow and transplanted to Adelaide's industrial satellite 'new town' of Elizabeth in 1961 when he was 'about 5',[268] Barnes would become one of Australia's most famous and treasured singing stars. His first band was called Tarkus;[269] neither that group nor Fraternity were going places.

Fairly or otherwise, today we see Fraternity's direction as rapid and inevitable movement towards a dead end; the era of the communal rural musical collective was drawing to a close. It was also around this time that Les Kaczmarek began advertising around Adelaide for people to form a band, although there was no indication then, of course, that he was assembling something that would still be having an impact on Australian music forty years later. Kaczmarek brought a sensational Northern Territory guitarist, Ian Moss, and a serious pianist, Don Walker, together with Phil Small (bass) and Steve Prestwich (drums)[270] in a group called Orange. They rehearsed in the Women's Liberation Hall in Adelaide for a few months[271] before auditioning singers. The descriptor 'punk' gets thrown around a lot when discussing the early 70s, as people try to search for precursors to punk rock: Jimmy Barnes was by some definitions a 'tough Elizabeth punk' when he auditioned successfully to be the group's singer.[272] The band were sufficiently tight-knit by 1974 that they decamped en masse to the other side of the country (just as INXS were to do a few years later to stay tight with their youngest Farriss brother). Don Walker was moving to Armidale to pursue an honours degree in quantum mechanics, and the entire group followed him to northern New South Wales, where – apparently unaware that the era of the communal rural musical collective was drawing to a close as outlined above – they lived on a farm outside Glen Innes. By this time they were called Cold Chisel.

Walker would subsequently be lauded as one of late-20th-century Australia's great literate songwriters, but by his own estimation his efforts for early-70s Chisel were 'total shit'; presumably, then, the other members must have just liked him.[273] As we shall see in a later chapter, the band's rise to prominence in the second half of the decade, like that of Midnight Oil, would make Australian mainstream guitar music – which was denigrated or praised as 'pub rock' – interesting.

A SPIRITUAL EXPERIENCE

In Sydney too, groups emerged at this time whose members would go on to cause greater waves later in the decade. Reg Mombassa, denigrating Radio Birdman's lead singer Rob Younger, claimed in the mid 1980s that he had first set eyes on Younger in 1971: 'He was walking up from French's, and he had knee-high boots on. I thought, "What a horrible-looking bloke".'[274] Younger was 19, Mombassa 20. In her history of Radio Birdman, Vivien Johnson observes that 1972 groups the Rats and TV Jones were 'engaging in that high energy musical anarchy which Johnny Rotten five years later made definitive of punk. They were punk bands before there were punk bands.'[275] Fifteen-year-old Rick Grossman, who was part of that scene, had an epiphany when he saw Led Zeppelin in Sydney in 1972:

> It sounds corny, but it was like a spiritual experience. I walked out a completely different person... Soon after I saw Led Zeppelin, I met Mark Kingsmill... and he and I and Deniz Tek... and Anthony Vitale, who looked like Keith Richards and was as obsessed with punk rock as me, formed a band. We practiced at nights in a school in Paddington and made a horrendous noise.[276]

Like Pus in Perth, Chris Walsh and Garry Gray's band Judas Iscariot and the Traitors in Melbourne, JAB in Adelaide, and Kid Galahad and the Eternals in Brisbane, these were early 70s pre-'punk explosion' punk bands, whose very existence is now unavoidably seen through the prism of what came afterwards, in 1976 and 77. It is undeniable that they existed, though, even if they only appealed to a very select few. It is hard to be certain where they thought their music would lead them – the instigators now seem unsure themselves. Many of them would soon be famous, or notorious, or both.

POP ON TV

Pop music was (and remains) relatively cheap filler for television, even back in the days when the miming was filmed in a studio rather than arriving prepackaged in the form of video, production costs paid for by the artist via its record label. When the 70s began, there was a slew of pop music TV shows, including the long-running *Bandstand,* on which Australian celebrities sang current hits. *Uptight*

was also apparently going strong, though its host Ross D. Wyllie was searching for, or on the verge of being sent to, fresh pastures; it was rumoured he would be replaced by John Farnham.[277] January 1970 saw six hours of pop TV served up for Melbourne teens and twenties each Saturday,[278] though local 'scenes' were often seen as a problem, and in early 1972 the *Daily Planet* bemoaned the fate of 'the ill-fated "Wrinkly" show', which aired only in Victoria – 'cancelled because of being a "local product" and not suitable for National viewing.'[279] The unusual title of this show was related to a highly successful publicity campaign for Melbourne radio station 3AK, featuring, for instance, a blurry photograph of a topless man and woman and the legend 'Where No Wrinklys Fly.'[280]

The few fragments of *Uptight* footage preserved in the National Film and Sound Archive show that it was a very loose, unscripted piece of cheap morning television filler. Kids yelled and screamed off-camera, Wyllie stumbled through his non-scripts, bands mimed badly, in-jokes abounded. Certainly it had its critics, such as the always forthright Wendy Saddington, who wrote in *Go-Set* about the show's treatment of the band she had named and then quit:

> Ross D. Wyllie said on *Uptight* the day the Chain appeared, 'See, Wendy Saddington, we do have blues groups on the show'. Immediately after the Chain's appearance they were barred from *Uptight*. Does Ross D. Wyllie contradict himself or does his wife do it for him?[281]

This cryptic last line was a reference to Eileen Wyllie, the show's producer.[282]

Chain were, incidentally, a formidable underground group who did actually hit the top of the charts in Melbourne – and top ten nationally – with 'Black and Blue', described by Ian McFarlane as 'one of the first (if not *the* first) blues-based singles of the modern rock era to reach #1 anywhere in the world'.[283] Matt Taylor, the group's singer, and its guitarist Phil Manning have long been iconic in Australian music generally and particularly within their own milieu of blues rock.

Pop still seemed healthy, even in the face of the radio ban or a certain *Go-Set* writer's irritation. In March of 1970, Johnny Young negotiated a new show, which he would co-produce, to replace *Uptight*. *Happening '70* made some concessions to the swinging new decade: 'Many groups have complained of having to dress up for *Uptight*, or being banned because they wore jeans. From now on the only rule will be that the groups are "normally hygienic".'[284] In practice, the differences in terms of content appear to have been minimal.

Wendy Milsom, assessing the new program at the end of 1970, saw it as out of touch and retrograde. She wrote:

> *Happening 70*, the only large-scale pop show on television, is one of the major reasons why pop music has been so far behind this year ... The type of people promoted on the show are not the pop stars of today – they are has-beens who should be left alone to become nobodys ... This backward, unthinking, attitude is a product of the power elite of pop establishments. It controls the pop media and dances, and by holding new people back it has done more damage this year than at any other time.[285]

Nonetheless, *Happening 70* (rebadged every year, naturally) continued for three years. Like Milsom, neither the *Daily Planet* nor Billy Thorpe thought it was an adequate representation of any 'happening' they knew of. *Happening '71* was referred to as *Haphazard 69* by the *Planet* for its slapdash presentation – for instance, screening half of (the apparently forgiven – or perhaps not) Chain's video for 'Judgement' followed by the announcement that it would be screened soon.[286] Perhaps this kind of media treatment ground Chain down; within six months they were recording their 'farewell LP', though the breakup was to be temporary (the group formally ended – again – in 2014).[287] Thorpe, meanwhile, called *Happening '71* 'a bag of shit':

> It don't know what it is – it's not a TV show – maybe it's a very bad 1962 ... What they're doing is what QTQ9 in Brisbane were doing when I was 14. I know, 'cos

I was doing it ... On the Australian music scene as I know it man, the change is coming.[288]

The show persisted, with a limited budget and seemingly keeping no-one happy. *Happening '72* was compered by Jeff Phillips with Ian Meldrum,[289] rather than by Wyllie, who (like Issi Dy) was to become a late-night movie 'host' later in the decade. By January 1973 the *Happening* had disappeared, and so had that rambling style of pop TV, at least for the time being. In early 1974, shows dedicated to particular 'all-rounder' pop stars, such as Colleen Hewett, and Johnny Farnham's series *It's Magic* were being developed.[290] Farnham was also a presence in the pervasive move of pop music into TV and radio advertising: 'I'm sick to death of his voice telling me to eat this bread, fly that airline or drink a particular soft drink', wrote *Go-Set* reader Janice Morton in early 1974.[291]

ABC-TV's long-running *GTK* (the title stood for 'Get to Know') was also available, a ten-minute daily show which covered a multitude of 'youth' topics, had no presenter, and often featured specially recorded studio performances or live shows captured around town (for instance, touring artists Gary Glitter and Led Zeppelin). *Go-Set* described it as 'the most advanced and intelligent discourse on pop culture life styles produced in Australia'.[292] *GTK* guests the Masters Apprentices were happy to play live on TV for the first time since their early days in Adelaide; all the TV work they'd done in between had involved miming.[293] GTK sometimes ran interviews, too – for some reason (probably that she was cool), Germaine Greer spoke to Led Zeppelin on a Sydney Harbour ferry for *GTK* in 1972. As was the style at the time, the show (if it can be called a show; it was more like an interlude) was more comfortable with a shoulder-shrugging non

sequitur than a forthright attack; within those limitations, however, it managed to be thought-provoking – the ABC has often done this kind of thing well – and put a range of left-field groups on national television. The ABC saw its mandate as being to deliver programming to all demographics; it was also, at roughly the same time, producing the sketch comedy series *Aunty Jack,* Rory O'Donoghue and Graeme Bond's show that 'threatened you'[294] and which gave rise to the hit single 'Farewell Aunty Jack.' (The 'threat' in question was the title character's catchphrase: 'And remember, if you don't tune into the show next week I'll come round your house and rip yer bloody arms off! And I will too.')

In its success at airing new Australian pop in a live-in-the-studio setting, *GTK* can be seen as one of a number of precursors to *Countdown,* which began in late 1974 and is discussed in detail in chapter 11. Its interview/issue component can be seen as a forerunner of teen shows such as *Flashez,* hosted by Mike Meade and minor pop star Ray Burgess;[295] Burgess hoped that the show would 'have a similar effect to 2JJ on musical tastes.'[296]

There were other rock shows, late-night ones, mainly on the ABC. *Rock 'n' Roll Ballroom of the Air* featured ballroom dancers 'twisting, bopping' in 'incredible free form' to acts like Ayers Rock, Renée Geyer, Doug Parkinson and Daddy Cool.[297] *Radio with Pictures* (not the New Zealand institution) kicked off in early 1975 with a show by Rory O'Donoghue's new – and very short-lived – band Dapto.[298]

FOUR-LANE HIGHWAY

Writing at the start of 1971, Wendy Milsom proclaimed that 'out of the 1970 pop scene jumble something healthy has emerged, which should set the pattern for 1971. Talented artists are writing and developing a purely Australian sound with a feeling not used overseas.'[299] If anyone seemed to have a good chance of success, it was Fanny Adams, a group put together by Vince Melouney, the former Aztecs and Bee Gees guitarist. Having left the highly successful but somewhat rigid Gibb brothers' enterprise and secured a solo record deal in Britain, Melouney recruited Doug Parkinson, fresh from a very successful late-60s Australian career, and two former members of the second Aztecs line-up, Johnny Dick and Teddy Toi ('Teddy and JD were good buddies back from the New Zealand days,' recalls Billy Green) to join him in this new band. Quite different to Melouney's Bee Gees work, Fanny Adams played heavy, bluesy, progressive rock, and its members were instantly filled with a sense of their own perfection. They wrote their self-titled album together, with Melouney producing; there were songs with audacious titles like 'Sitting on Top of the Room', 'They're All Losers, Honey' and – strangely self-referentially, given Melouney's recent history – 'Got to Get a Message to You'. On a short trip back to Australia, Parkinson told a reporter he wished he wasn't there:

> It's like flying back into a cloud. I'm inspired by nothing now. We're really here to get the band ready for America, and that's all . . . It would be really incredible

to fall over one day and float upwards because you hit a rock nobody had yet found.³⁰⁰

As beautiful and bizarre as these images were, Fanny Adams had only weeks to live. Parkinson's old colleague Billy Green recalls:

> Coming back from a year of rehearsal and recording in England, Fanny Adams got a big write-up before a performance in Melbourne Town Hall. Doug, forgetting how much Australians dislike boasters, said in the interview that 'Fanny Adams was the best band in the world' !!!!! I was there at that concert, I liked them, but they were not very exciting at all, and certainly not the best band in the world. All the critiques they got were pretty bad ...

The group disbanded shortly afterwards when a fire in Sydney discotheque Caesar's Palace destroyed all its equipment, but that was, it seems, only the last straw.³⁰¹ A year later, Parkinson was still licking his wounds:

> It looked good for a while – the Rolls Royce, the town house, the genuine antiques, Vince looking like a million dollars. I thought to myself, Christ, you've been a good boy, maybe this is what you've been working for. This is it. The band started to shape up well ... But we got into the studio and the truth came out. In my opinion Vince just couldn't play. Personal hang-ups. The 'land of milk and honey' disintegrated. There were five of us living in one hotel room ... Fucking bummer. We all got the crabs. The whole thing more or less fell to bits. It was all done for Vince's production company. We felt like employees. There was no musical freedom. Bad vibes all the way along. We were offered a tour of the States to coincide with the release of the record. So we thought we'd come here first and knock off the rough edges. Up to this stage we hadn't washed before a live audience. We got here and played at Wallacia – heard everyone else, then ourselves, and I realised I'd put myself on the biggest bum trip of my life. It was just a bad band.'³⁰²

Melouney, while disputing Parkinson's assessment of his abilities, essentially agreed: the album, he told Lee Dillow of *Planet,* was 'really shithouse'. Australian musicians had advanced considerably since he left: 'I didn't realise there were so many good players here. I guess my attitude was a kind of we'll show "them".'³⁰³

Parkinson and Melouney were wrong: the Fanny Adams album is a choice slice of bluesy rock, well performed by fine players. Melouney's next step was to join the Cleves, initially to fill in for Gaye Harmon, who had been temporarily laid low by illness. According to Harmon, he quit when the group decided to press on to Britain. Parkinson and Green then resumed their working relationship. When In Focus had disbanded, Green recalls:

Duncan and I formed a group called Rush, with Malcolm McGee singing, Kevin Murphy on drums, Steve Yates on keys. We had some gigs up in Sydney... We got fired from all of them because the band sucked, and because the drummer, who was still recovering from ODing [on] heroin, looked pretty bad when he was playing, like he would do a drum fill and miss the toms he was aiming for. The Drug Squad were watching us in one club in North Sydney we were performing at, and told the boss to fire us immediately. I was very unhappy in that group anyway... talk about lack of groove.

It hardly needs to be said that this Rush bore no connection whatsoever to the Toronto group of the same name. After Fanny Adams played their few Australian shows and fell apart, says Green:

That's when I got a call from Doug, asking if I would be interested in putting the band together again... and could I talk Duncan into it? After our own failure with Rush, Duncan said he'd be up for it but not with Johnny Dick on drums... that's when Mark Kennedy (ex-Spectrum) came into the picture.
That combination was not successful either, to my mind. The group with JD was magic! And with Mark Kennedy it was not. It wasn't to last too long. That's when Doug got JD and myself with Les Stacpool (ex-Browns) and Mick Rogers (he had just come back from the UK and saw himself as a kinda Eric Clapton), and the three guitar players would take turns on the bass... toooooo weird... That didn't last too long either.

Once more, the lesson for the likes of Fanny Adams seems to have been reinforced: Don't bother trying to become world-famous. However huge you may have been in Australia or anywhere, you will undoubtedly disappear into some kind of bizarre London, LA or New York music industry time-warp, so that when you return home, with your tail between your legs, no-one will remember you well enough to know *why* your tail was between your legs. But if you simply hung around your home town continuing to produce and perform, people would start to wonder why you lack ambition.

Billy Green was an exception. He'd been a major part of renegade director Sandy Harbutt's bikie film, *Stone*, one of the classics of its generation and a production rife with realistic, real and extraordinary violence and grandeur. Green played a bikie called 69 but more importantly he wrote and recorded the film's remarkable soundtrack. He had some prior experience – alongside Hans Poulsen and, of all people, Bruce Woodley – recording songs for a surf film called *Getting Back to Nothing*; Harbutt's film, however, was in part moulded by Green's musical vision. By 1975 he was writing music for commercials and plotting his next move. He recalled this period in 2008:

> In that time I was already writing for the *Stone* movie and heavy into full-time session work at Armstrong's... There was a lot of shuffling going on... It was the time of 'supergroups' and after I recorded the *Stone* soundtrack that's when I put together a true supergroup called Sanctuary. The ones that were lucky enough to catch that very short-lived ensemble could testify to the amazing talent contained therein. That group was on fire and burned out in a matter of months.

Sanctuary featured Graham Morgan on drums, Mal Logan and Peter Jones on keyboards, Barry Sullivan on bass, Green on guitar (he also composed all the music), and Renée Geyer on vocals. 'Everyone in the band realises that the old rock 'n' roll beat isn't enough anymore. We all want to express what we have inside,' Green told *Go-Set*. While he freely admitted being indebted to some jazz influences, he also confirmed that his music 'would progress if I was living in a cave.' He was, it was clear, a genuinely motivated artist:

> The lack of challenge has held back the Australian music scene... You must not let the audience rule you... The trouble is, if you get praised for a certain level, you stay at that level, because everyone in the world wants to be loved...'[304]

In 1973, Adrian Rawlins wrote a letter to the *Nation Review* in response to harsh criticism of Australian rock music as a generic form. Rawlins sang the praises of Billy Green, as 'a songwriter as potentially fertile and inventive as Bob Dylan' with hundreds of songs 'as good as anything written by the Beatles.'[305] Green's subsequent story – like so many in this book – deserves room to breathe in a longer narrative of its own. He departed for the USA in 1975, 'just to look', and was aided in a number of his forays there by former Valentines and In Focus drummer Doug Lavery, who now had a rock and roll showband in Houston.

Another Australian legend, Rob MacKenzie, played a part in yet another big change in Green's life. While living in LA in 1984, Green had made contact with him:

> I brought my broken Gibson Les Paul to him and he took it off my hands and I swapped it for a Fender Strat...
>
> Funny little memories. I was rehearsing to record with Louise Goffin (Carole King and Jerry Goffin's daughter) and in the middle of the rehearsal my guitar strap lock came undone and the guitar hit the concrete floor. For me that was a very clear message to stop playing the guitar and get serious about the sax. I still have the Strat but never play it... I never stopped playing the sax.

Green's saxophone was generously purchased for him by the director of *Stone*, Sandy Harbutt, as a token of Harbutt's esteem for the composer who had contributed so much to his extraordinary film. When Green switched from guitar to sax, he changed focus to jazz and is now a successful musician in New York under the name Wil Greenstreet, using a more literal translation of his Dutch name while also paying homage to Hollywood character actor Sydney Greenstreet.

Green's mid-70s experience was perhaps a happy exception. The Australian music industry – at least as represented in the very mainstream-oriented music and news media of the time – was like an animal that chased its offspring away at the first opportunity. Easily the best of these was the Dingoes (named, it has to be noted, over a decade before the world heard Meryl Streep, as Lindy Chamberlain, utter the line about the dingo who 'took my baby'). The group 'quietly slipped out of the country on July 13' 1976, according to Australian *Rolling Stone*, heading first for Ontario, Canada, from where they would plan their attack on the USA.[306] Much of the band's career would play out in the United States, where it bears many similarities to that of New Zealand's Hello Sailor: both were courted by famous heroes (Mick Jagger, in the Dingoes' case; Ray Manzarek, in Hello Sailor's) and were ultimately let down by their record company. In 1992 INXS's Jon Farriss wrote a letter to *Rolling Stone* expressing his 'disappointment in the lack of recognition given to a true group of originators in Oz rock, the Dingoes'.[307] That said, the Dingoes had been a well-loved Melbourne institution by the time they left Australia, not least for their performances at the Station Hotel in Prahran, captured on the *Live at the Station* album and their first, self-titled LP. In early 1975 they had experimented with new ways to put themselves in front of an audience, like the "Eliminate the Middle Man" concert they put on along with Greg Quill and Captain Matchbox. This show was rumoured to have netted $40 – hardly a fortune – but the groups could perhaps console themselves that no 'middle man' had profited. Their manager, Phillip Jacobsen, told *Rolling Stone* of his hopes for the band, who played a highly appealing and intelligent country-themed rock: 'What I want to do is branch them out into their true market – which is *anybody*.'[308] The group's bass player, John Bois, has written a witty extended memoir of their experiences, *The Dingoes' Lament* (named after a track he wrote on their debut).

The Dingoes in Greville Street, Prahran

The two best-known Australian groups who departed for, and made their names in, the USA, honing their talents and filing down any rough edges to become as soft and friendly as possible, were Little River Band and Air Supply. Both tailored themselves to an overseas template: if any group could be said to encapsulate the direction of Australian popular music and the music industry in general in the mid 70s, it was the smooth and conformist Little River Band.

At the beginning of the 70s, international success for Australian acts was rare. By the end of the decade, while it was still deemed worthy of comment, it was nevertheless seen as a much more realizable dream, at least for some. Singer Colleen Hewett trumpeted her deal with Atlantic Records in the pages of *Go-Set* in early 1974, featuring a host of covers of songs by Led Zeppelin, the Who and Gordon Lightfoot.[309] Melbournite Helen Reddy's colossal 1972 success, 'I Am Woman' (co-written, as mentioned earlier, with the Executives' Ray Burton), was a single that defined a time and a set of ideals.

The Cleves were not really an Australian group, though they now had an Australian manager in professional hairdresser Barry Earl, and had added Ace Follington – formerly of Chain and Country Radio – as their drummer. Like Fraternity, who had changed their name to Fang for the British market, they decided the Cleves was hardly the right name with which to attack Britain in the 70s. Gaye Harmon remembers they 'needed something that people would be shocked enough to remember first time they heard it and that fitted our image':

> Barry came up with 'Bitch', a fairly daring name in the early 70s. It had a raw sound to it and, with a woman in the band, suited us well. Later, when we were signed to Warner Brothers, we had publicity photos of the band done with me dressed head to foot in tight black leather, complete with hand painted psychedelic snakes, clutching a bull-whip. Not really my style, to be honest, but it fitted the bill.

Gaye Harmon was not one to be exploited or duped. But it is stating the obvious to say that her experience was the rule for women in music in the 60s and 70s: she was either an anomaly to be highlighted, or an absurdity to be demeaned. She says now that it was not in the supposedly backward Antipodes, but in the ostensibly progressive United Kingdom that she encountered the most problems—in Britain she faced questions about the suitability of a woman playing music in a group at all: "I never found it odd to be a girl in a band. I was just the bass player, who later became the keyboard player. It seemed very normal to me . . . When we got to England in the early 70s, girls playing in a band were looked upon as something of a novelty." The crunch came for Bitch when the group was asked to become part of a new configuration featuring Mike Harrison, once of Spooky Tooth; Harrison and his manager refused to countenance a woman playing music with them. This was the last straw, and the various Bitch components drifted back to New Zealand.

The Moir Sisters, who John Paul Young considered 'one of the most underrated talents in the country'[310] – for him, being 'underrated' was apparently consistent with having a top-forty hit with their own composition 'Good Morning (How Are You?)' – were signed internationally by Elton John. A three-piece vocal group, the Moirs wrote the material on their extremely impressive first album *Lost Somewhere Beyond Harmony* themselves; it is a spacious and attractive combination of folk and blues with a hint of progressive rock, and featured a number of Melbourne luminaries including the ubiquitous Billy Green. The sisters were unhappy with the way they were treated by their arranger, whose ideas were 'just so straight . . . We still haven't achieved the sound we want yet.'[311]

Queenslander Kevin Johnson, who started his career in the northern city of Rockhampton and leapt from the Registrar General's Department into another noble establishment, the Col Joye organisation, was notable: his single 'Rock & Roll (I Gave You the Best Years of my Life)' was corny country roll, and millions loved it, whether sung by Johnson, by absurdist pop impresario and criminal Jonathan King, or by Terry Jacks, who made it top ten in Canada.[312] Additionally, Mac Davis had a hit with the song in 1974 – sugared with a happy ending.

Rick Springfield, an ex-member of the Zoot, was another international success story. His strong songwriting skills and pop-star looks helped him achieve a hit in the USA with 'Speak to the Sky' in 1971. The next single, 'What Would the Children Think', was less successful. Interviewed by Garry Hyde for *GTK* at the time, Springfield said his follow-up was 'just too different', explaining that 'when "Speak to the Sky" was released I was getting letters from these kids', but for its successor 'I was getting letters from housewives'.[313] His career tainted by apparently undeserved accusations of payola, Springfield would not have another major hit until the early 80s, but he was the star of an educational cartoon series, *Mission: Magic* in 1973. His album of the following year, *Comic Book Heroes,* was an example of a performer attempting to hedge his bets – a pop star striving to keep his teen audience while hoping he looked ironic enough to ensnare an older fanbase, too. Anticipating the real or imagined issues faced by the management and record companies of groups like Johnny Diesel and the Injectors and silverchair in the 90s, Springfield was faced with the dichotomy between pop success and 'validity'. 'When I first went over there', he told Hyde, 'the magazines asked if I could do a few things. We've tried to keep it like no yucky stuff . . . the first album was played on underground stations, so there's a chance . . .'[314] One can only imagine what teenage fans – and those in the 'underground' – thought of Springfield's decision to cohabit with the 15-year-old actress Linda Blair; his later career, played out in America, saw him become an unlikely 'new wave' pop star at the same time he played the playboy Dr Noah Drake on *General Hospital*.

In the early 70s, Hyde put a question to Springfield that would be asked again and again throughout that decade.

> Hyde: There's a lot of rhubarb around at the moment, people proclaiming that as far as Australia's concerned our day is coming musically. How do you feel about it?'
> Springfield: Yeah I agree, because in America . . . I've found they're just becoming more aware that we play music down here on guitar, not just didgeridoo.[315]

Beeb Birtles, Springfield's old bandmate in Zoot, was nowhere near as much of a hunk, but he too had his sights set on America. In the mid 80s, his current bandmate in the Little River Band, drummer Derek Pellicci, claimed that LRB had forged 'a nice bitumen four-lane highway in the U.S. for other bands to follow.'[316] This dry, slightly whingeing statement contains a certain amount of truth – ultimately, it was just a changing of the guard to institute a set of Australian gatekeepers rather than international ones – but it is also indicative of the central problem LRB poses. They were all about being *as good as* and *as popular as* existing groups, and Australianness was *not going to get in their way*.

In one sense LRB can be seen as a supergroup, self-improving via natural selection over ten years, the distilled essence of a number of groups who almost but didn't quite have the necessary mass appeal of the band who finally *did* make it. Paul Conn suggests a 'positive effect' from musicians who had 'gained experience with different styles . . . better players tended to join together to produce a high quality result'. While 'high quality' has to be taken with a grain of salt here, this theory, applied to LRB, can extend to include LRB's manager Glenn Wheatley and his experience as a member of the Masters Apprentices: if Wheatley did not actually hand-pick the members of LRB he was definitely there from the outset. Wheatley's opinion of the Masters' time in Britain in the early 70s was that 'both band and management were very naïve about the music and the selling process.' He claims that he used the experience to absorb 'as much as I could' and came back to Australia to create a band good 'enough' to take on the world.[317] Unfortunately, the often thoroughly mediocre work released under the Little River Band name demonstrates that the axiom of experience leading to excellence is simply not tenable in LRB's case, their commercial potency notwithstanding.

In the 1979 short film about LRB, *Never Ending Apprenticeship* – a title which, consciously or unconsciously, flags their connection with the Masters Apprentices' former bass player – main songwriter Graeham Goble suggests a direct line from Allison Gros through Mississippi to Little River Band: to him, they are the same band under different names, although clearly they have only one common element – Goble himself.[318] For many, however, the 'classic' LRB line-up (Birtles left in 1983) contains not only Goble and Birtles but also Glenn Shorrock. Birtles and Goble had a history together in a group called Mississippi, which, to judge by its preposterous name, clearly had its sights set on going global. Goble had arrived in Melbourne from Adelaide as a member of a band with a bizarre if not terrible name, Allison Gros. Allison Gros had a hit, but not as themselves: they were commissioned by Ron Tudor to record a cover of the 1957 hit by American band the Rays, 'Daddy Cool', under his studio-band name Drummond. Thus they cashed in on Daddy Cool the band (which kicked off its *Daddy Who? Daddy Cool* album with a version of the same song) *and* the public's eternal love of novelty hits (the track features speeded up 'chipmunk'-style vocals).[319] Allison Gros was then rebranded as Mississippi and had a huge hit in 1972[320] with the Goble composition

'Kings of the World'. This remarkable blend of Cat Stevens, proto-glam and the Beach Boys with a gothic lyric shows that Goble was a songwriter of enormous potential; unfortunately, the potential – and all the drama of his music[321] – would be sacrificed to the creation of LRB's international-appeal artisanal approach.[322]

Goble sought out Birtles as a bass player but included him in Mississippi as rhythm guitarist on the strength of his ability to harmonise within the band; drummer Derek Pellicci, who would become another LRB mainstay, was brought in at the same time. Mississippi toured with the Jackson 5 in 1973; Charlie Tumahai – previously of the much-lauded supergroup Healing Force (whose 'Golden Miles' was a sensational hit in 1971), then Chain, then Alta Mira, and later a member of Be Bop Deluxe and (for ten years) the Herbs– was also in the group at this time. Mississippi left Australia for Britain in mid 1974 and, like the Twilights and Axiom before them, broke up. Birtles, Goble and Pellicci returned to Australia, recruited Glenn Shorrock and began their next campaign.

The nascent LRB kept using the name Mississippi, for want of anything better, but only as a temporary measure. On the way to a show in Geelong, Shorrock noticed the turn-off to the town of Little River and decided, first that it would be a great name for a song and then – of course! – a band.[323] There must have been some humour intended in changing the name from one of the largest rivers in the world to a self-confessed small one, but it has of course long outlasted the witty reference; the new name was simply plain and sounded down-home and noncommittal. (The group later insisted that jokes about 'Little River Bland' didn't bother them.[324])

They had now added a layer of concerted and profound meaninglessness over a bedrock of untruthfulness: they weren't from Little River; they simply drove past it. One wonders if the present-day members of LRB, none of whom belonged to the original group – the original members sold the rights (they say accidentally) to Steve Housden in the 1990s; 'The current band has all rights to use the LRB logos et cetera', Pellicci told an interviewer in 1997[325] – could even explain its name, much less point out Little River on a map. For all that, it's apt that the name persists in the hands of a group of American musicians who still tour, peddling old LRB hits, and even produce new records under the LRB name. It's the logical conclusion of Birtles, Goble and Shorrock's success.

'We always aimed at a world market,' Goble said in the 80s:

> from the very beginning we wanted to be more than just a local band, but we never actually designed the band to sound American. I guess we've been labeled American because our harmony style could have come out of the West Coast quite easily, but I put that down to the fact that we're a band with a lot of good singers ... I don't think our music is uniquely Australian.[326]

Marc Hunter's rhetorical question of the late 70s – whether Americans needed LRB 'when they've got the Eagles'[327] – was asked, in different ways, by many Australians. Dave Warner had a song called 'The Monster's Back' in which he decried 'Little River Band, the great pretenders / Glen Shorrock thinks he got brought / Up in California, the stupid bastard.'[328] Shorrock was an easy target, but Warner (who is discussed in chapter 11) was saying pretty much what many had been feeling for a while.

Early LRB projects demonstrated the group's industry-friendly approach; an advertisement for the Witchery clothing chain, for instance, which was later configured into a moderate hit single.[329] LRB's hits in the mid 70s were not always – as popular imagination would have it – as smooth as silk and twice as shiny; 'Happy Anniversary' and 'Help is On its Way' touch on disco, the first emerging from ace bassist George McArdle's audition (!) with the band[330] and the second from a jam between McArdle and Shorrock 'mucking around with some chords' during recording.[331] 'Witchery' itself is as good as good Dragon. 'Emma', for all its posturing, is rapid-fire and very hooky. 'Home on Monday' is fast, punchy, even Jimmy Webbish. The languid and decadent 'Reminiscing', with its soft-shoe jazz inflection and its pseudo–honky tonk piano is one of those songs that you can't believe hadn't always existed, it sounds so natural (Goble, the song's author, reputedly saw it as evoking 'a guy and a girl walking hand in hand past white picket fences'). Frank Sinatra thought it was *the* song of the 70s.[332] Though 'Curiosity (Killed the Cat)' is harrowingly staccato and awkward, the outro – with its shades of 'Kings of the World', though nowhere near as sweet – at least shows the craft of their work. Their December 1976 epic 'It's a Long Way There' nicely rounded off a year that had begun with AC/DC's strident and funny 'It's a Long Way to the Top': both songs were about the same thing.[333]

LRB were created to go about the *business* of making music, and in that regard they were a manufactured group. There was, Birtles has said, 'a lot of tension between us' at the best of times.[334] They achieved commercial success in the main by ignoring rather than exploiting their Australianness; the joke of the *Diamantina Cocktail* album sleeve, containing a recipe for a drink containing an emu egg, resonated for Australians, but the album's sleeve was in fact different in different international territories. At their best they were a good, slick pop band, but what LRB contributed to music in a creative sense was in no way commensurate with their staggering record sales. As has so often happened, by the time the group 'made it' they had lost everything but the cutthroat desire not to let their previous decade (and more) in music have been a waste of time. Thousands of far more talented people from the Australian scene circa 1974 lacked the tenacity, backing, luck or desire to make such leaps of fame: MacKenzie Theory's Rob MacKenzie ended up playing in Sha Na Na – not an embarrassment in itself, but no musical tour de force, either – and his former partner Cleis Pearce makes limited-run albums with Celtic themes from her Byron Bay home; Pelaco Brothers' Peter Lillie became a minor cult hero – a long history of heroin use contributed to his death from liver disease in 2012; Stephen Cummings and Joe Camilleri were to become major stars locally. There was no room for anything as superb as 'Kings of the World' in LRB; it would have been thrown out in rehearsal as too quirky for Dubuque.

Fortunately for the members of Little River Band, they were able to sell their wares in the international marketplace; though they were never regarded as innovative figures, there was recognition of the strengths of three very competent songwriters within one superslick band that saw them capture wide interest, particularly in the USA.

Fortunately for music audiences in Australia, the development of a distinctively Australian music and attitude was proceeding apace. The second half of the 70s would see not only the development of iconic groups such as Skyhooks, Midnight Oil and AC/DC, but also the metamorphosis of pub rock into Australian new wave music, which was often literate, smart and witty, among other things. There is no great mystery behind this: part of the basis for these successes was a sophisticated music industry complex which required artists to front it. At the same time, lesser lights would shine valiantly and briefly, and a number of truly excellent groups would kick against the dominant modes of the day ... and many would opt for the byways and back streets rather than Little River Band's four-lane highway.

9 Million Dollar Riff
DADDY COOL / SKYHOOKS

> Australia is no longer the lucky country or the swagman at the billabong – this is a New Place with a new way of looking at things, a country stretching out and looking at itself. It is extremely pretentious to compare Macainsh with Henry Lawson, but if you can compare Bob Dylan with Rimbaud and Lorca then I can't see why not. Lawson's work was the first true Australian writing and Macainsh's is the first look at Australia as a modern, vibrant country and his view of Australia is much more to be desired than those of Slim Dusty, Reg Lindsay and their ilk. Most of us drive Valiants not brumbies.[1]

With these words, from an early issue of the proud, hopeful (and, in this author's opinion, soon to be terrible) new music magazine *Juke*, 'Dr. Pepper' (David Pepperell) was trumpeting a new Australian culture, and Skyhooks, whose chief songwriter Greg Macainsh he's praising here, were the source of a lot of that pride and hope. Skyhooks' precursors – because they negotiated a path for Australian groups to lead the way in the Australian scene – were Daddy Cool. The two bands were very different, with no overlap in membership nor even any similarity of style, yet they had a lot in common, from their birthplace – at the collision point of Melbourne's outer suburbs with its inner city – to their status as groundbreaking groups in terms of impact on the industry as well as musical significance.

Looking back at the various groups and movements the hip young things of Australia would have been exposed to in the early 70s, it's clear this was a time when the underground diverged spectacularly from the mainstream; smarmy types like Johnny Farnham and Ronnie Burns could not compete – in hip quotient and perhaps even in star quality – with cool alternaheads like Mike Rudd or, for that matter, with any enlightened individual's own personal trip. Of course, those who espoused a genuinely 'underground' line of self-fulfilment, dismissing material concerns as irrelevant and stressing the importance of spiritual wholeness, were unlikely to be championing *themselves* as the next big thing. But it should come as no surprise that it was from the underground, rather than the entertainment industry, that the next big things emerged. Daddy Cool would spring fully formed from the fun side of the portentous Sons of the Vegetal Mother, and Skyhooks – who slipped into Daddy Cool's space the minute the original vacated it – had their origins in the same kinds of theatrical, countercultural places, though they were from geographically quite distinct parts of Melbourne.

As we have seen, Glenn Wheatley took what he learnt with the Masters Apprentices to make Little River Band a success internationally; and as we will shortly see, Harry Vanda and George Young used their experience with the Easybeats to concoct AC/DC's winning formula. Ross Wilson similarly distilled certain elements of his Daddy Cool recipe to armour-plate the success of Skyhooks in Australia through his production work for and general mentoring of the younger band. As the primary singer, guitarist and songwriter for Daddy Cool, Wilson took that band to a position of prominence that no previous Australian group had occupied in Australia. Surprisingly, the group was a hit even though their image and sound ran completely counter to those of the teen heartthrob bands – and, for that matter, to the sounds of the international scene. When he came across Skyhooks, Wilson quickly appreciated where the marriage of his custodianship and the innate talents of Greg Macainsh might lead. He was right.

We left Ross Wilson in London in 1969, after he had been invited by Brian Peacock to participate in what turned out to be the very last days of Procession. The group recorded with Wilson ('it was really bad', he said in 1970)[2] and nothing was issued; visa problems and a general air of despondency put an end to the experiment. It was in the UK that Wilson wrote the first version of a song called 'Eagle Rock' which – once he'd assured himself he hadn't accidentally copied it from someone else[3] – he realised was 'going to be a hit straight away'. Pat Wilson, his wife at the time, later recalled that 'it just exploded'.[4]

Wilson's forte is pop of various stripes, and his successful songwriting has always leaned in that direction. But he did not return to Australia with the intention of making it big on the strength of 'Eagle Rock'. He flirted with the idea of joining Company Caine,[5] who briefly backed him doing 'real primitive versions'[6] of his songs, including 'Eagle Rock', but weren't interested in taking him on full time. He went on to create Sons of the Vegetal Mother, a band 'about macrobiotic food'[7], with Trevor Griffin, Mike Rudd (sometimes), Ross Hannaford, Wayne Duncan, Gary Young and four brass players. Bassist Duncan had played in a group called Cashbox with pop singer Issy Dy, Rick Brewer and Michelle Kennedy.[8] Duncan and Young, a drummer, had a professional relationship that stretched back some years, including work with groups like Bobby and Laurie, until the radio ban meant that 'all of a sudden, there's no work'.[9] Young had met Wilson at a paperback book warehouse where they'd both been forced to get a job – Wilson because he was back in Australia with a young family to support, and Young because the showband/session musician work which sustained him throughout the 60s had dried up.

Sons of the Vegetal Mother were heavy, and though there was humour in their ludicrous name, they were fervent believers in the benefits of a macrobiotic diet. Wilson went to the pages of *Revolution* to publicise his cause, and published not only articles such as 'Rice Revival' but also the lyrics to the band's song 'Brown Rice', half of which (two of four lines) were the title.[10]

One of the venues at which the Sons were often seen was the T. F. Much Ballroom in Brunswick Street, Fitzroy, which 'represented what was going on in the inner city' amongst 'a certain clique of people'[11]. Although Wilson took the concept seriously, and no doubt other members did too, they were also enthused about another project based on Wilson's love of 50s doo-wop, which in his view was largely unknown in Australia, and which led to the core of the band playing a separate set of material under the name Daddy Cool. The debut of this alter-ego group was forced when Sons of the Vegetal Mother arrived to play at Glenelg, one of Adelaide's most rugged and boisterous seaside suburbs, and a support band failed to show up – Daddy Cool burst forth ready made.[12]

Daddy Cool were 'something anybody could understand', according to Wilson[13]; in their initial phase they were about good times, mild silliness and adolescent longing.[14] Young and Duncan were a tight and intelligent rhythm section (Skyhooks' Greg Macainsh would later credit two influences on his playing: Duncan and 'Shirley Douglas's bass tutor book'[15]), and Hannaford was a guitar great. Hannaford, apparently painfully shy in everyday life[16] but an extrovert in performance, now claims that 'we were stoned all the time'.[17] Daddy Cool's approach to 50s vocal harmonies and rock was integrated into a genuinely modern group; the music's roots were American, but at the same time the band tracked the story of Australian engagement with American culture in the 50s under the benign (and sterile, and gaudy) moon of Robert Menzies' post-war consumer culture. Milk bars, drive-ins, premarital sex, surfing and dancing were all that mattered in the songs that made up the first DC album, and if you were under twenty in 1971, that was a world you had known, at least via thrilling rumour.

Daddy Cool fitted in with the progressive bands who played venues like T. F. Much; they were as zany as Captain Matchbox and as musically varied and interesting as It Flew Away. It didn't hurt that some of their covers, like 'Baby Let Me Bang Your Box', possessed the gritty, rude humour beloved of the baby boomers which – again like Captain Matchbox – confirmed that there was a sexy core to all human interaction throughout history; that is, it undermined the oppressive older generation, humanizing them by proving that everyone experiences the same longings and thrills in their youth.

A decade later, Adrian Ryan remembered Daddy Cool as shining in 'the darkest days of hippie boogie', bringing back 'joie de vivre and showmanship to Australian rock ... the doo-wop cum Philly/New York r and b moves that DC dealt so brilliantly were a world removed from anything that had previously gone down in local music.'[18] This is revisionism history – after all, Cam-Pact had explored similar territory years before Daddy Cool, and hippie boogie was just one of the many musical styles around in 1971 – but Daddy Cool's huge impact should nevertheless not be underestimated.

The red centre of Daddy Cool's appeal was 'Eagle Rock', which wasn't in fact anything like doo-wop but did nevertheless have a fundamental earthiness – not to mention a very unusual rhythm for a pop song – that made it seem not so much vintage rock and roll (whatever that might have meant in 1971) as something from a parallel universe. 'Eagle Rock' was not overtly Australian either; Australia has three indigenous eagles, but obviously the eagle is best known as an American symbol, and the phrase 'eagle rock' has been documented as early-20th-century American sexual slang.

Wilson had picked up the term from a magazine caption to a picture showing African Americans dancing. The song harked back to a universal pre-rock time, appearing to reference some kind of mythical hillbilly music. Twenty years later, the Reels recorded a hoedown version that was probably the best comment on the song's appeal and impact; the Wiggles brought it to a worldwide audience in 2003. Daddy Cool's original was also similar to 'Woman of the World', an earlier song of Wilson's which he performed with Party Machine, and in which Wilson refers to himself as 'Daddy'. The syncopation was the principal musical difference.

The group was hurriedly signed to Ken Sparkes and John McDonald's label Sparmac by Robie Porter, who had enjoyed hits of his own (as steel guitar player Rob E. G.) in the previous decade, as well as working as an actor – he had just been seen alongside Charlotte Rampling in *Three*.[19] Porter produced their debut album, *Daddy Who? Daddy Cool!* in a week at Bill Armstrong's Studio, which struck Gary Young as being like Sun Studio.[20] They spent the most time on 'Eagle Rock', which the label had such high hopes for that they paid for it to be mastered on hi-tech equipment in Los Angeles. Amongst the youngsters who queued up to buy a copy of the single on its release in May 1971 was the young Greg Macainsh, a self-professed 'big fan'.[21]

Daddy Cool didn't look like pop stars; they were hairy and shabby. Ross Wilson really *was* a daddy, with a wife (the glamorous Pat, who wrote an advice column for *Go-Set* as 'Mummy Cool'[22]) and baby son (Daniel, born in 1972).[23] Ian McCausland, *Go-Set*'s art designer and a whiz with an airbrush, created a graphic for the album cover of the group looking waywardly ridiculous, but at the same time as they seemed on the way to becoming a cross between the Archies and some cartoon beatniks, their good-natured enjoyment of a somewhat obscure but clearly extremely infectious genre shone through. As a university newspaper critic put it in mid 1971:

> It has been the year of Daddy Cool all right, bringing to some of us the rock and roll we never had and to some of us, the rock and roll we had had and had long forgotten, and to the rest of us the rock and roll we never wanted.
>
> But what we all got was a glorious send-up of the fifties rock styles, and underlining it all the satirization of a whole life style mixed with a nostalgia for an uncomplicated rock and roll and for a life that was all rock, chicks and school.[24]

Daddy Cool's career trajectory from their inception to reaching number one – 'Eagle Rock' entered the charts in late May and spent almost six months in the top forty – was unprecedented amongst Australian bands; the band's subsequent life was, if not predictable, then certainly a template for many groups since. Their second single, 'Come Back Again', was a little reminiscent of 'Eagle Rock', but slowed down into country blues, with a less instant hook and maximised plaintiveness. Their third, 'Hi Honey Ho', was 'Come Back Again' speeded up with a different hook and horns; all three are ingrained into the consciousness of anyone over 50 who grew up in Australia. The group toured the USA three times supporting – amongst many others – Captain Beefheart, Fleetwood Mac, and Little Feat. Their first visit even saw Kim Fowley involved in some typical hype: Fowley accosted Wilson at the airport from a wheelchair and then leaped out of it, claiming to have been cured by Wilson's miraculous healing power.

Another foray to the USA inspired band insider Peter Andrew to hold forth on the comparative nature of venues in Los Angeles and the larger Australian cities:

> The Whisky A-Go-Go is a cunt of a place – it's probably ruined more bands than it's helped.
>
> It's sort of like Chequers and those other places in Sydney; and a bit like Bertie's, here in Melbourne. It caters to record executives, Beverley Hills hippies and tourists![25]

The group quickly appreciated that whatever it was that made them special in Australia, and however great they were as players (which they were), and however superb many of their songs were, trying for a hit in America was a coals-to-Newcastle effort that was unlikely to pan out. Of course, Elton John's homage, 'Crocodile Rock' – directly inspired by 'Eagle Rock'[26] – was just as much of an impostor; but John had brand power on his side (his lyricist Bernie Taupin wore Daddy Cool promotional items on John's record covers). Robie Porter went as far as producing an American version of 'Eagle Rock' – under the ridiculous band name the Hot Mummas.

Perhaps Wilson didn't even want 'Eagle Rock' to be a worldwide success; recognizing the danger of being pigeonholed as a one-hit wonder, he was eager to move forward into 'serious' contemporary rock. The group recruited Jerry Noone on saxophone and piano; he had previously been in the groups Battersea, Mabel's Dream, Kite and most importantly Company Caine.[27] Noone was only a member for five months but it was long enough to make his mark on the second Daddy Cool album, *Sex, Dope, Rock 'n' Roll: Teenage Heaven*. The LP was a hit on its release in January 1972, and featured a much more up-to-the-moment group on tracks like 'Make Your Stash' and

'Please Please America (Hear My Plea)', which would have sounded a lot more at home on a Sons of the Vegetal Mother album, had one ever materialised.

Daddy Cool played the final show of their first incarnation in August 1972 at the Much More Ballroom.[28] The group was clearly struggling under the weight of its own success and also from the restraints its chosen concept placed on it stylistically; drummer Gary Young performed a set of his own songs at this show, many of them country-tinged and introduced in a parodically smooth, cabaret style. Young was emerging as a strong songwriter and the last Daddy Cool single, 'Rock 'n' Roll Woman' (a song nowhere near as bad as its title), was his composition.

Wilson and Hannaford then formed Mighty Kong, a group whose potential would never be fully realised. It was born out of a project initially planned with Company Caine's Gulliver Smith, who left before it came to fruition. Mighty Kong's one album, *All I Wanna Do Is Rock*, seems to lack heart and vigour, although its sound – contemporary guitar-based rock with vocals high in the mix – provided a template for Wilson's production work for Skyhooks. When all the members of Mighty Kong apart from Wilson and Hannaford quit,[29] the two of them reassembled Daddy Cool in 1974, first for a one-off Sunbury show and then to tour and release a couple of singles that were commercially unsuccessful – far closer to contemporary country rock – but very catchy.

Recruiting Ian 'Gunther' Gorman (the 'European-type' nickname came from a schoolteacher)[30] as a second guitarist, the revamped Daddy Cool planned to wait out their recording contract with Sparmac and sign a better one[31], but they broke up again in late 1975.

A near-reformation of Daddy Cool in the form of Young's early-80s band the Rocking Emus featured all the original members except Wilson, along with Jeff Burstin of Jo Jo Zep and the Falcons, the group Young had only recently quit after five years.[32] Like a scrambled jigsaw puzzle, the highly employable and engaged Young, Duncan, and Hannaford would occupy a particular place in the Melbourne music scene for the next thirty years and more, backing various ephemeral or important musicians on projects both valid and foolish, while at the same time working up their own long- or short-lived projects. Hannaford's groups Lucky Dog – a reggae outfit with songs dedicated to his interest in mysticism – and later Dianna Kiss would enjoy ongoing popularity on the Melbourne scene without making any significant impact on mainstream music.

By the time the original Daddy Cool finally disbanded, Wilson had added a second string to his bow: he had become daddy to a new breed of rock musician. Hannaford remembers playing a show – probably as part of Mighty Kong at Melbourne University in July 1973 – at which the group essentially failed to connect with its audience. He then saw Skyhooks come out to tumultuous applause, and interpreted it as an unwitting passing of the baton to the only slightly younger crew (Wilson was just over three years older than Skyhooks' leader Greg Macainsh).[33] Wilson took them under his wing:

> Mighty Kong was where I first saw Skyhooks. They played a gig with us, and then as time went by we were nurturing that and I was getting involved in rehearsals with them and then the line-up was changing, so over a period of about a year it all gradually came together.[34]

Wilson signed Macainsh as a songwriter to his Doo Dah Music[35] and celebrated his acquisition by performing the Skyhooks song 'Saturday Night' with Daddy Cool on the TV show *GTK* in 1974. For most who saw it, this would have been their first experience of the song, which Skyhooks did not record until the following year, for their second album.[36] Aside from a jokey spoken-word section, it was not typical DC fare.[37]

In 2007, Macainsh described Skyhooks to an American interviewer as:

> An eclectic bunch of young men from Melbourne . . . heavily influenced by British glam rock and Captain Beefheart and blues and Gary Glitter . . . quite a theatrical presence.[38]

Macainsh was a new breed; he came from the Melbourne suburb of Eltham, of all places. Jazz musician John Sangster recalls 'Eltham and the Artists' Colony, where everything was built of mud-brick except for the Great Hall, which had bodgie-tudor beams made of gumtree logs painted black'. In his memoir, Sangster is mildly withering about this Melbourne outer suburb, not least 'the soft weathered blues and purples and pinks of the sun-dried cow-shit wash they put on the walls.'[39] More involved and committed members of the Eltham community have described it as 'a rural Bloomsbury'[40] and the first attempt to create what they saw as a genuinely 'Australian way of life.'[41] Macainsh's mother was a librarian, and his father Noel was an academic[42] who distinguished himself as a poet in the 1950s and after.

Macainsh made his first forays into rock music in 1965, playing bass in the covers band Spare Parts.[43] The group featured a drummer, Imants ('Freddie') Strauks, who would be the other half of Macainsh's rhythm section in almost all his groups for the next fifteen years, including Claptrap, Sound Pump[44] and Frame,[45] and of course Skyhooks. Jenny Brown, who gradually became an intimate of the group during their heyday, believes Strauks was the best musician in Skyhooks; he and Macainsh had a kind of Hannaford-Wilson relationship. Macainsh also played briefly in a long-running group called the Reuben Tice Memorial Band, supposedly named for a 'Canadian scientist who was found dead in his lab after a final unsuccessful attempt to invent a machine to de-wrinkle prunes.'[46] At the 2014 launch of a collection of 'Carlton' music of the mid 70s, Johnny Topper described the band as 'the Grateful Dead of Hurstbridge'; Macainsh's first (known) song was 'I Went Down to Eltham to Get Me a Job in a Band.'

Frame and Reuben Tice were mainstays of a series of 'Super Shows' organized by 'the Tice' at the Fire Brigade Hall in the neighbouring suburb of Research, 30 km from central Melbourne.[47] Reuben Tice were inheritors of Eltham's artisan ethic[48] and the *Daily Planet* reported that 'the idea of these Super Shows is to raise enough money to build a bigger and better hall at Research so that they can fit more people and put on bigger and better shows so that they can make more money and build an even bigger hall'.[49] More likely they were simply non- or minimal-profit events, 'full of cheerful freaks who cavorted and got loose with friends and family on weekend afternoons.' Captain Matchbox were often an attraction, alongside very local outfits,[50] and Peter Lillie and Johnny Topper performed comedy. A teenage Stephen Cummings was also involved, operating a film projector to screen vintage episodes of the locally made police drama *Division 4* on the walls.

Frame featured not only Macainsh and Strauks but also vocalist Graeme Strachan, a carpenter's apprentice from Mount Waverley.[51] Strauks had met Strachan at a Max Merritt show at the Village Green Hotel,[52] and Strachan would soon be drawn to Eltham on a regular basis because of the ready access there to marijuana 'and other drugs and parties . . . a few people would be drawn from the suburbs to make the trip to Eltham.'[53] Though they'd occasionally venture into inner Melbourne to play a show in Carlton,[54] Frame was 'sorta really happy' staying outside the music industry, according to Strachan: 'Anything to do with a big scene we just said no.'[55]

Strachan quit Frame in late 1972; Macainsh, who was by this time studying film at Swinburne College of Technology (where he made the bones of a moving and funny documentary about the Sharpie movement, later assembled into an impressionistic short film by others), engaged additional guitarists in the form of Peter Starkie (from Lipp and the Double Dekker Brothers, and the King Bees) and Peter Ingliss, who had recently left Captain Matchbox, and they began playing as Skyhooks. Though neither of these early recruits would make it into the 'classic' line-up of the band – Peter Starkie's younger brother Bob (known as 'Bongo') was the Starkie who became the best-known Hook – the pool of earthy inner-city bands drawn on for the first version of the group is telling. Skyhooks would have underground arty roots, an original approach, *and* – most surprisingly given these facts – become extremely famous. Macainsh had three albums' worth of songs ready to roll out over the next two years.

Steve Hill, a 'Trotskyist cook',[56] had been part of Tribe,[57] a 'Carlton mime/theatre group who for a brief period stepped out of the counter culture dives of Carlton and into the spotlight at rock concerts.'[58] He'd met Macainsh and Strauks at Arlberg, a ski resort on Mt Buller, where Frame had played some shows while Hill was working in the kitchen. Hill and Macainsh were both Captain Beefheart fans, and schemed to create a new band which would 'send up' glam rock in its appearance and presentation,[59] although it's uncertain whether this was based on a love or a hate relationship with that musical form.[60] He had never performed as a singer before, but Hill joined the group, which he expected would sound like Captain Beefheart.[61] It really didn't.

Macainsh considered a number of names for the new band, including – extraordinarily, since this would later, purely coincidentally, be the name of one of the biggest Australian groups of the 80s – Icehouse.[62] Whatever the origin of the Skyhooks name – a short film called *Sky Hook*, about the use of a helicopter to source oil in New Guinea, was made in the late 1950s, for example[63] – the group made its debut on April 16, 1973 at St Jude's Church Hall in Carlton.[64] Jenny Brown, a friend of Ross Wilson's, saw the group early in their career:

> I think the first time I saw them ... it was at Sebastian's, and I was really knocked out, I thought they were just terrific. They were tight, they were musically a strong punchy band and they had a real up-yours satirical side to them, and they were dressed in a way that was really absurdist, they sent up the whole notion of glam, quite strongly, so they were never actually a glam band, the satirical angle was so strong. I loved the theatricality and the way they embraced all that ...

The original line-up didn't last long. When he saw them at the Mighty Kong show that July, Ross Wilson was impressed, but he also remembers perceiving the band as two distinct halves: Hill, Macainsh and Strauks were 'outlandish . . . leaping around a lot', while the two guitarists were 'working away like ditch-diggers in the corner'.[65] Peter Starkie left Skyhooks to join Roger Rocket and his Millionaires,[66] backing Paul Madigan's wife, a stripper named Mary 'Doody' Scott Pilkington;[67] Ingliss left to form his own band, but at the time of writing has yet to do so.[68] Their replacements were Bob 'Bongo' Starkie, who had been a student at Melbourne High with Michael Gudinski of Mushroom Records,[69] and then at Swinburne with Macainsh; and Redmond ('Red') Symons, who had been 'on the fringes' of the Carlton-based Australian Performing Group,[70] which operated in a famous space known as the Pram Factory. Symons had appeared in the plays *A Night in Rio* and *Africa*.[71] He eagerly broke up his own band, Scumbag[72] – which included his girlfriend, Jenny Keath, and Jane Clifton[73] – when he was asked to join Macainsh's:

> At the start of the Seventies it was the golden age of social services. If you'd finished university you could be on the *professional* dole . . . it fomented an interest in the arts. I was living in Carlton, there were things like the Pram Factory theatre . . . a theatrical environment that fed ultimately into the music, and it was a perfectly simple transition from that, when I joined the Skyhooks, to television, which is the perfect vehicle for vaudeville.[74]

Symons later recalled of his early involvement in Skyhooks that 'Macainsh already had the songs and the whole Skyhooks concept planned. At first he directed it and told us what to do, which is only right. It was his music.'[75]

Skyhooks' new line-up appeared at the third Sunbury Festival in 1974, and two songs from their performance, 'Love on the Radio' and 'Hey What's the Matter?', were included on the live album of the event released by Mushroom. After seeing TV footage of himself at Sunbury, an embarrassed Hill quickly made plans to quit.[76] Symons later claimed partial responsibility for a 'covert undermining' of Hill: 'We white-anted him basically'.[77]

A new singer was needed. Ross Wilson apparently 'considered joining' the band himself,[78] but Graeme Strachan – relinquishing his given name for the prettier 'Shirley' (the name, relating to his curly blond hair, was reputedly first applied during a 'verbal spar with some of his mates from the Phillip Island Board Riding Club'),[79] and often abbreviated to 'Shirl' – was contacted. He auditioned and was accepted.[80]

One largely unsung associate of both Mighty Kong and Skyhooks (and other bands from this time and place), who contributed significantly to the legacy of Skyhooks in particular, is Uschi (Ursula) Flett. From an artistic background, Flett was inspired by theatre, dolls' clothes and Fellini's *Satyricon*, as well as her experience designing stage costumes for her brother Dave during his time in Lipp and the Double Deckers.[81] The first costume she created for Skyhooks was a gold shirt for Peter Starkie; ultimately she was responsible for a multitude of

the band's extraordinary costumes; some of them were one-offs, but others achieved iconic status. Macainsh would often wear a white suit; Symonds would be at turns adorned with curlicues under his eyes, a ruffle and/or a vampire-style cape; Bongo Starkie was often seen in a frightwig, elaborate face paint and oversize collar arrangements which made him look sometimes like an evil rodent, at others like a 17th-century Eastern European prince.

Skyhooks were signed to Mushroom and managed by Michael Gudinski, who claimed to have had an 'instant flash' of inspiration (to sign them to his label, presumably) when he saw them.[82] Wilson was ready to produce the band, contributing his own hit-making renegade experience, a pecuniary interest and a determination to preserve what he called their 'cheeky edge'.[83] The members offered a good mixture of the new (Starkie), the semi-new (Strachan and Symonds) and the tried and true (Macainsh and Strauks). Wilson prepared them thoroughly, and the songs were reworked and shaped with his guidance in rehearsal and the studio. Brown says that Wilson 'obviously had the trust and respect of the band through the background, he's a good guy, you know, he's not a rip off merchant . . . That connection with Ross really raised the stakes and the vibe and the energy that was around with other booking agents and people that were seeing them and getting excited . . .' Macainsh later recalled that the album was completed 'in a hundred hours . . . I think it took us two weeks to make that record.'[84]

Remarking on its selection in 2004 by a group of music industry representatives and fans as the best Australian album ever made – no doubt still a common opinion today – Greg Neighbour described *Living in the 70's* as 'Australia's equivalent to *Never Mind the Bollocks* . . . so profoundly did it shake up the rock industry, excite the fans and inflame certain conservative corners of the population.'[85] It was very different to the Sex Pistols album in that *Never Mind the Bollocks* actually *upset* the music industry, whereas Skyhooks' debut was cause for widespread rejoicing. That said, some in the neurotic mid-70s media did become hot and bothered by a group that sang about 'going to bed together'; certainly the fact that Australian *Rolling Stone* took eight months (!) to review the album suggests it must have had a distasteful whiff of radicalism to it.[86] Six of the songs on *Living in the 70's* were banned by the Australian Broadcasting Authority because of references to sex and drugs; this fact is often cited as having been a recipe for commercial success, although in hindsight it was in Skyhooks' case merely the exciting garnish to an already appealing dish. The unprecedented sales of *Living in the 70's* (at the time it was the biggest-selling Australian album ever, and it spent 16 weeks at number 1) also meant the salvation of Mushroom Records: until the success of Skyhooks, the label that described itself as 'Australia's progressive record company' seems to have been on the verge of bankruptcy, or at least this is the way Gudinski likes to dramatise it. Its future was assured for some time to come because of the band.

Niels[87] Hutchinson's cover art for *Living in the 70's*, while captivating, is the most inappropriate thing about the album. The inner sleeve is a sensational piece of mid-70s collage: an audience of creepy egg-ball heads views the band watching themselves *mirrored in the audience*. The back cover – nine identical men and nine identical women queuing up across a road to pay money for some kind of performance, with Carlton's familiar high-rise Housing Commission towers in the background – is at the very least agreeably stylised and oblique (Macainsh apparently believes these figures represent sharpies).[88] But why on earth does the front cover show the group arriving at an airport in their own private plane!?

This is not an album about being rock stars, or big shots, or jetsetters; it is famously an album about being a local, Australian – in fact utterly *Melbournian* – observer of city life. Melbourne suburbs are mentioned in three of the ten song titles, 'Balwyn Calling', 'Carlton (Lygon Street Limbo)' and 'Toorak Cowboy' – a remarkably high proportion, given that Australian songwriters had generally abandoned local place names around the time of Little Pattie's 'Stomping at Maroubra' in 1963. The hostile (and in hindsight somewhat misogynist) Balwyn references were unfair, considering that Frame's 'biggest weekend' as a band had been, in Strachan's memory, 'one night at Vintner Girls School in Balwyn and two gigs at the Balwyn Boys Club.'[89]

While the album's themes were largely universal, the names and notions were primarily white Australian, political, and socially aware, most notably 'Whatever Happened to the Revolution?' with its soundbites from the 1970 Vietnam moratorium protest. As a songwriter Macainsh was a bit of an outsider (Eltham crossed with Carlton was the perfect mix), bright and wry. Symons contributed one song, 'Smut', about masturbating in a cinema and ejaculating into an empty Twisties packet – extraordinarily, this song was chosen to be performed live on *GTK*; during the broadcast Symons took time out from singing the song to ask the television audience if they understood it. The Alice Cooper-ish second single, with opening chords that paid homage to the Purple Hearts, was 'Horror Movie.' It was hardly a work of genius,[90] unless you are of the opinion that anything that gets to number one in the charts is by definition a work of genius.

The band was able to take advantage of the new TV show *Countdown*. Their first *Countdown* appearance was without Macainsh, who had hepatitis; Jenny Keath pretended to be him.[91] Macainsh would soon be too famous for the group to get away with such light-hearted deception, and part of the reason was the subsequent rise of *Countdown*; when they went on tour their exposure on the show meant 'everyone had heard of you.'[92]

Notably, Skyhooks managed to appeal to a new, teenage audience – and thus compete with other 'teenybopper' bands like Sherbet and Hush – while retaining their older, more sophisticated fans. 'Our fans are the young boppers,' Strachan said in 1975, 'and you get the university crowd which doesn't scream but does appreciate what you're doing. In fact we're lucky with the universities that we can pull it off. The material appeals, relates.'[93]

The group's second album, *Ego Is Not a Dirty Word*, was again produced by Wilson; it provided two more top-ten hits (the title track and 'All My Friends Are Getting Married') and cover art which parodied – almost taunted – their teenage fans in rather grisly fashion. The back cover, depicting a letter from a fan with a severed finger attached, implied that groupies would mutilate themselves for their favourite Hook; it was a cunning way of acknowledging the teenyboppers while denigrating them in typically withering camp fashion.

Macainsh, who didn't do interviews during the initial phase of Skyhooks' success, later claimed that the most important thing the group did 'was demonstrate it was commercially viable' to be an Australian rock group singing Australian songs and selling records primarily in Australia: *Living in the 70's* sold a quarter of a million copies. 'So people in the business went "wow – this is serious money..." I think it gave local musicians and people in the music business a sense of pride...'[94] The new gay monthly, *Campaign*, celebrated them as court jesters for a jaded society that was a democracy in name only:

> Skyhooks are a lot more than just a pretty face. Or a pretty flash of thigh, for that matter. They are the diarists of a generation, no less. They are plastic disposable

poets. They are Clowns, distorted and decadent, pointing the Finger at the rat race, the consumer gorging orgy, Vietnam and anything else at which an impudent finger can be entertainingly be pointed.[95]

Macainsh is reported to have claimed that Skyhooks 'couldn't have risen under a Liberal government'.[96]

Like Daddy Cool before them, the sensible (or at least inevitable) next step for Skyhooks after two hugely successful albums was to travel to the USA. They did so in March 1976, though jobbing country-music bassist Tom Robb filled in for an ailing Macainsh on the first part of the tour.[97] Perhaps unsurprisingly, the group didn't like America.[98] America didn't care much for them, either: their garish costumes and make-up were particularly offensive to the mainstream concertgoer. Symons later recalled that Skyhooks were met with 'a mixture of confusion and revulsion by the rather more Dionysian American audiences';[99] it was reported in the Australian press that American audiences believed the group were prostitutes, though what this actually *meant* is unclear.[100] One American critic wrote that 'their idea of cool was your idea of cool a few years ago,'[101] which was ridiculous – and superficial – considering how outside, not behind, 'cool' the group was. As with many Australian travellers, exposure to other cultures made Symons understand what it meant to be an Australian artist: it was on this tour, he says, that the notion of 'a national identity started to make sense to me'.[102] It also showed Symons how *art-ridden* Skyhooks were: he compared Skyhooks' American experience with that of Roxy Music, with whom they shared a bill in New Orleans: 'We were both Swinburne Tech art bands . . . terribly clever and lateral and Swinburne Tech.'[103] At one point a girl in the front row asked Symons if the band would play Roxy Music's hit from the previous year, 'Love Is the Drug'.[104] (Swinburne Technical College – where the Boys Next Door would soon play their infamous second show – was where Macainsh had gone to film school; Symonds on the other hand has a Bachelor of Science from the University of Melbourne.)

Most of Skyhooks' shows on their first US tour were opening for Uriah Heep, often unadvertised: Jenny Brown, who accompanied them as a reporter, wrote that it might well have been a 'classic drag to suddenly become Nobody Foreign and the Unknowns after experiencing the fab privileges and gas adulation showed upon those who adorn ganz en farben [sic] the front covers of *RAM*'.[105] Freddy Strauks put it most succinctly:

> The music is unfamiliar to the crowds and the stage act has got them bamboozled. It seems that Americans are at the mercy of the media and other organizations out of their control. They only latch on to something that has been fed to them in the greatest quantity. Our morale is high, but it looks like a long hard climb.[106]

While the rejection of a marvellous Australian icon like 'the 'Hooks' might have been distressing for the band and their machine (and their fans), it is in some respects understandable, and it's not merely a matter of the band's songs being 'too local'. If the image of the band walking across the tarmac from the 'Skyhooks' jet on the cover of *Living in the 70's* was confusing to Australians (though it no doubt seemed to make more sense to audiences elsewhere in the world), their costumes and posturing didn't really make sense to *anyone* watching them. It was evident that even the band members weren't sure if they were putting forward a satire of what a rock group looked like, or actually behaving like a rock group should. Symons suggested that 'we're superficially horrible, we're weird, we're like vampires, like children's monsters of some sort.'[107] But multiple time changes and pealing guitar solos aside, this was music with lyrics that spoke to ordinary, sensitive, intellectual and/or cynical Australian people. So why was it being performed by outlandish fruitcakes? If Australians nevertheless accepted this aspect of Skyhooks, it was presumably because they were used to encountering detached flotsam from around the world: coming across a snippet of Roy Wood and a pinch of Randy Newman, why not combine them? Even today international commentators whose understanding is purely superficial, and for whom the visual aspect is virtually everything, will pigeonhole Skyhooks as an Australian version of Kiss, whereas in fact no two 70s rock/pop bands were less alike. It is worth repeating: Skyhooks may have *looked* like a glam rock band, but they were not one, in any sense.

It suited many Australians that Skyhooks didn't set the world on fire. It suggested they were clearly unique to the nation, 'our own'. When they returned for their 'The Brats are Back' tour they played up the Australian angle and went on stage at the Melbourne Town Hall to the country's unofficial national anthem, 'Waltzing Matilda': never had the 'play' button on a tape recorder been pressed with such knowing irony.[108]

While a *Campaign* writer found a good percentage of the third Skyhooks album, *Straight in a Gay Gay World*, which they recorded with Wilson in San Francisco at the end of their US tour, to be 'about as satisfying as instant mashed potato'[109] (which, incidentally, can be quite satisfying, at least in the short term), it was a top-ten hit in September 1976[110] and produced a breezy top-twenty single in 'Blue Jeans'. But for a group which had essentially had it remarkably easy almost from the start, any setback – such as a failure to expand its popularity into other territories – was likely to be blown out of proportion everywhere, including in its members' own minds. Symons was later to claim that in early 1977 he was ejected from the band by devious means (they broke up, he says, then reformed without him).[111] His replacement was Bob Spencer, formerly of the harder rock group Finch. Finch had supported Skyhooks in mid 1975, at which time Spencer was still at school.[112] He was introduced to Skyhooks fans from the stage by Strachan as a 'shit hot little cunt' – it was a term of praise.[113]

Another album followed in 1978, *Guilty until Proven Insane*. Macainsh's music was now moving in a straight-ahead rock direction, although still nothing like Kiss; Spencer complained that 'everyone says our music these days is American punk.'[114] 'Women in Uniform,' later a top-forty hit in the UK for Iron Maiden,[115] was Skyhooks' last major Australian success for twelve years. Strachan, who Symons has described as not 'even remotely an artistic person'[116] also had a couple of solo hits with maudlin cover versions (such as 'Tracks of My Tears'); however, he had his heart set on television. He quit the band in June 1978, explaining to *Juke* readers the following year that he was hoping for job security: 'Look at people like Bert Newton who have worked their arses off and served their time . . . they'll be quite secure for the rest of their lives.'[117] Gudinski was, it appears, negotiating on his behalf for the children's TV show that would become *Shirl's Neighbourhood*.[118] Best of all for Strachan, it seemed, was that he no longer had the constant grind of tours and promotion, of having to 'jump into a radio show and talk to some fucking turkey out in the middle of Shit Creek or whatever.'[119]

After considering Peter Garrett of Midnight Oil[120] as a possible replacement (Garrett was not actually offered the job and it's unlikely he would have taken it), as well as an unidentified woman (perhaps Jane Clifton)[121], and teasing *RAM* about 'a character named "George"',[122] Macainsh recruited Tony Williams of the old Research Super Show band Reuben Tice.[123] Williams may have been a contender some years earlier, when Strachan got the job.[124] 'Tony's good nature made him a favorite with many fans,' says one observer of the group with Williams, 'though the general public found it hard to embrace a Shirley-less Skyhooks.'[125] Williams, who had quit music and was working in a sawmill, was a much less flamboyant front man than Strachan, but the group had always been Macainsh's vehicle, in any case.

Skyhooks' next single, 'Over the Border', was a response to the reactionary politics of the Queensland state government. It contained some ghastly rhymes – perhaps in homage to the bang-it-out spirit of punk – but the sentiment and the riff were both gold. Joh Bjelke-Petersen, the state premier, observed of the high chart placing of the single in Queensland that the group's 'cheap little gimmick has worked,'[126] but in fact, even though the departure of Strachan had freed the group up and given it a new artistic lease on life – they had also quietly abandoned the costumes and make-up by this stage – on balance nothing really worked at all from then on. Reported new songs 'Yeah Howard' (about Howard Hughes) and the reputedly 'reggaeish' 'The Sporting Life' did not emerge on record.[127] Subsequent singles, 'This Town is Boring', a definite dip of the lid to punk, and 'Keep the Junk in America' – sung by Starkie – were as unsuccessful as the album they came from, the ludicrously titled yet nevertheless underrated *Hot for the Orient*, which was full of bizarre ruminations on fatuous *NME* readers who only *pretended* to like XTC (as an example of a 'new wave' flash in the pan), and sexy yet vampiric women.

Mushroom had not really helped the band, releasing a 'greatest hits' compilation of the type that often emerges when a record company wants to squeeze the last out of a group.[128] On 16 June 1980, Skyhooks played their last show – in the regional West Australian town of Kalgoorlie – and broke up, petulantly announcing as much with an ad in *Juke* in which they quoted one of their lesser songs, 'Why don't you all get fucked'.[129] 'At the time,' Macainsh later reflected, 'we felt we'd become the victims of . . . the tall poppy syndrome'.[130] It was the end of an era, although Macainsh and Starkie briefly harboured hopes of continuing the Skyhooks name with new members and material.[131] So much had changed, even in the five years since their biggest hits, that not too many saw the end of the group as a tragedy.

Reformations are, naturally, the time to reap the adulation you'd forgotten you ever received by the time your band split. Daddy Cool remained legendary. 'Eagle Rock' – the success of which Gary Young has described as 'a bit embarrassing',[132] though it can't be unpleasant embarrassment – increased in popularity over time to the extent that it was a hit all over again in 1982, with nothing but Chris Löfvén's old black-and-white video to promote it. The core of the group reformed in 1994 for *The Ballad of Oz*, a joint CDEP – a bizarre format that fools no-one – to which they and Skyhooks each contributed two tracks. More importantly, Daddy Cool had a fully fledged reunion in 2005, initially at an Indian Ocean Tsunami benefit in Melbourne, then to promote a double DVD set *The Complete Daddy Cool* featuring that concert and some early 70s footage, and to make a new album.

Skyhooks' and Daddy Cool's stars burned bright and hot long after their initial demise, and because it was such a curious 'retro' exercise their incarnations after the 1980s are worth detailing here, rather than later in this narrative. The 'classic' Skyhooks, with Strachan and Symons, reformed in 1983,[133] playing 16 shows around Australia to unprecedented adulation and record crowds. Thus was initiated an intermittent existence for Skyhooks which peaked in 1990 when a new single, 'Jukebox in Siberia' reached number one. It sounded like the band of old, though the lyrics were unworthy of Macainsh in his heyday. Subsequent singles – like 'Tall Timber' (1991), which did not sound a bit like Skyhooks, and the abovementioned *Ballad of Oz* – were not as well received, and the band went back into limbo. Somewhat uniquely, considering his great importance in the music industry, Macainsh has not launched a solo career and has rarely even been associated with other bands, other than playing with John Farnham following the singer's success with his *Whispering Jack* album in the mid 80s.[134] This in itself was a perverse act, considering the way Farnham's smooth and pallid productions – even if, or rather, partly thanks to the fact that he typically included a Ross Wilson song as a cornerstone of his huge-selling 80s/90s albums – ran so counter to the fancy, sardonic rocking of Macainsh's own work. Macainsh has also played live with Dave Warner's From the Suburbs (see chapter 11) – perhaps a better match with the sound and style of Macainsh's musical history.

Of all the former Skyhooks, Red Symons has probably achieved the longest lasting fame, as a regular on the progressively more dreadful comedy-variety show *Hey Hey its Saturday* in the 1990s, where he played himself as a sour curmudgeon. When that show was thankfully axed (a brief 2009 return notwithstanding), he continued to work as a 'personality', popular on Melbourne radio, and as a successful newspaper columnist and author.

Freddie Strauks and Gary Young had both followed their initial success with time in well-known and respected Melbourne groups, the Sports and Jo Jo Zep and the Falcons respectively. A group featuring Bongo Starkie, Strauks (now using the first name Imants), Ross Hannaford, Wayne Duncan, Frankie J. Holden and Wilbur Wilde – the last two former members of Ol' 55 – began playing shows under the name Ol' Skydaddys in the mid 90s.[135]

Strachan, a television star on a home improvement program in the 90s, was killed flying a helicopter in 1998. A private show celebrating a 'thirtieth anniversary' (of the release of Skyhooks' debut album) in 2005 saw Ross Wilson assume vocal duties for one night; they all did it again in 2015. Soon after the first of the shows with Wilson, a 'one-off' public show in Sydney was a chance for original singer Steve Hill to perform one more time with the initial Skyhooks line-up – Macainsh, Strauks, Ingliss and Peter Starkie; Hill died of cancer soon afterwards. Macainsh qualified as a lawyer in November 2006.[136]

Emerging from a landscape of trippy, near-psychedelic early 70s experiments, both Daddy Cool and Skyhooks inspired a much larger and, importantly, more confident cohort of musicians and other artists in the mid to late 70s. It could be convincingly argued that the move both bands made from a world of free, spontaneous, 'head' music to a world of mega-sales, line-up changes and support staff caused them – particularly Skyhooks – to lose whatever unique elements they had in the first place, though of course the aging process will do this naturally. Skyhooks' last big hit, 'Jukebox in Siberia', is the most glib boogie rock imaginable. Of the members of Daddy Cool, Hannaford, Duncan and Young appear to have remained relatively pure, perhaps because they have been denied sufficient opportunity to be otherwise (though for their sins they all played on Shirley Strachan's undeniably diabolical solo album, *It's All Rock 'n' Roll to Me*, in the mid 70s). Most of Wilson's music crimes, meanwhile, have been committed under the Mondo Rock name.

Daddy Cool reformed in 2005 for a benefit concert in aid of Aceh tsunami victims, and stayed together to record a third album, *The New Cool*, released in late 2006. The first featured track delighted Peter Lillie, who might have been forgiven for thinking he was languishing forgotten: it was a cover of his song 'They Built the Ute', originally recorded in 1978 by the Autodrifters in what Wilson claims was 'by far the best version'.[137] Wilson was Lillie's music publisher; he had produced demos for the Pelaco Bros and also Lillie's 1978 solo single 'Hanging Round the House', on which Strauks played drums. Old Carlton links can be strong.

Daddy Cool and Skyhooks were two bands that shaped the Australian cultural and social landscape in the last third of the twentieth century in the direction of an appreciation (albeit abstract) of the value of local music and musicians, and their impact is still being felt. If it's difficult at this point to see their legacy in the everyday music world, it's only because – like so many innovators whose timing was just perfect – their impact was total. Daddy Cool's casual aplomb was a model for the way Australian musicians would tend to carry themselves thereafter: cool, good-humoured, but craftsmanlike. As for Skyhooks, even groups who publicly derided them, like Radio Birdman, were acknowledging their importance. The fact that much of their work holds up less well today, having been superseded by less blunt, more subtle, less wacky music – is irrelevant: these bands, and the songs of Wilson and Macainsh, made all those subsequent forays more possible. In that sense (and a few others), these were the two most important Australian bands in the Australia of the early-to-mid 1970s. But they were, of course, only a weave in the fabric.

10 We Aren't Here to Confuse People
AC/DC

> As far as I'm concerned, when Malcolm and Angus started the band in 1973, '74, they had a vision of what they wanted to do. We haven't changed, aside from a few fine-tunings here and there, from that vision. – Brian Johnson, 1992[1]

AC/DC and the Bee Gees are the two Australian groups among the world's five most successful pop/rock acts. It would be fatuous to omit a thorough account of such a supremely important and worthy group from this history, though it is undeniably true that AC/DC's trajectory is very well known and, like the group's music, ludicrously easy to follow. It is also rather dull without AC/DC's music being played loudly in the background for context, or illustration, or just because. So this chapter, while necessary, is somewhat snarky – not because AC/DC aren't brilliant at what they do, but because those who have sought to celebrate them in history are, with a few notable exceptions, so inept. Like INXS and Nick Cave, AC/DC have been the subject of numerous histories, the majority of which are poorly written, culled almost entirely from press interviews (and, more recently, from ill-directed web research), and riddled with howlers born of the authors' own ignorance and presumably their eagerness to claim the final chunk of their advance from their publishers. As much as anything, this chapter is an attempt to sift the misinformation out of these works.

Anyone who purchased Martin Huxley's *AC/DC: The World's Heaviest Rock* (1996), should be entitled to a refund; more effort surely went into the mildly clever title and the arresting cover image (an amp knob turned up to 11, only 11 is titled 'AC/DC') than into research for the contents of the book. All journalists and historians make mistakes, but Huxley's suggestion that Malcolm Young's first band came from Newcastle, England to Australia[2] (they actually formed in the town of Newcastle, north of Sydney), and his offhand confusion of the Sydney suburb of Burwood with the Melbourne suburb of the same name, merely because the Young family lived in the former and Bon Scott's 1960s bubblegum band the Valentines briefly (according to Huxley) sequestered themselves in the latter,[3] reveal *The World's Heaviest Rock* as a quickie career survey extrapolated from poorly copied notes. Even more embarrassing than these howlers are Huxley's previously mentioned putdowns of Australian music of the 60s, music he obviously has not heard but is nonetheless happy to condemn out of hand.[4] These displays of stupidity would be enough to annoy even slightly knowledgeable readers, but they also deserve the contempt of those interested only in learning about AC/DC, because they so blithely dismiss the importance of the band's context. AC/DC emerged from a milieu that included, for example, Coloured Balls, Buster Brown, the La De Das, Buffalo, and Billy Thorpe and the Aztecs. These were groups of whose output Stella (president of the AC/DC fan club in 1976) would have said approvingly: 'It's rock; it's not drippy music.'[5] And AC/DC's interests also extended beyond riff-boogie groups; Bob Daisley, the mainstay of a number of British metal groups in the 70s and 80s, remembers that future AC/DC members would come and see his Sydney group Kahvas Jute play in the early 70s: 'we were a musician's band.'

Because the writers of most books about AC/DC no doubt each spent a long hard week on them, and saw no need for any particular research into the band's background, readers are doled out ludicrous statements such as this one from Richard Bunton, who writes that at some unspecified time (presumably, the late 60s/early 70s):

> Australia was then at least 10 years behind Britain, and 20 years behind the States, in terms of social emancipation. The 'battles' that had had to be waged in the US and then in Europe, had yet to be fought.[6]

What this 'social emancipation' might involve remains unclear, perhaps because the 'battles' are also undefined (at least Bunton has the decency to put the word in inverted commas, to show he doesn't know what they are either). Social mores certainly varied from state to state and city to city, but Australia was nevertheless a western nation with a strong intellectual community and an awareness of the wider Anglophone world (in particular). There was vocal criticism of the slow pace of change towards progressive social policies – and justifiably so – but the nation already had a strong egalitarian ethos, for instance, that was comparatively lacking in countries such as the USA or even the UK, the nation Australia most commonly looked to but also defined itself against. Bunton – who shortly after the above statement tells us that John Paul Young is the brother of George, Malcolm and Angus Young[7] – apparently decided one 'battle' worth losing was the one with research and analysis, particularly since, he must have reasoned, the average AC/DC fan wouldn't require anything too complicated.

It is probably because most of the AC/DC books are British that they tend to begin in Glasgow on a dark, rainy night in 1953 with Malcolm Young's emergence into the world. As in so many Bee Gees narratives, Australia becomes merely a windswept Maralinga, a testing ground for the launching into reality of a plucky British rock group.

The best of the AC/DC books – so good, in fact, it should hardly be mentioned in such proximity to those of Huxley, Bunton, and other offenders such as Howard Johnson and Malcolm Dome – is Clinton Walker's *Highway to Hell,* though even Walker editorialises harshly regarding the state of Australian music before the mid 70s, for reasons known only to himself but which are certainly not the product of ignorance. Murray Engleheart and Arnaud Durieux's *AC/DC: Maximum Rock and Roll* is also a fine work, as is Mark Evans's insider memoir, *Dirty Deeds;* these three books cover the territory.

The problem faced by anyone writing about AC/DC, however, is that there is really remarkably little to say about the band. As personalities, the Youngs do not shine with celebrity vim, and whatever their virtues as players, the music they play is simply good (usually), solid, user-friendly rock. Their albums are not entirely interchangeable – at least, there is general consensus among users that some are worse than others, with *Fly on the Wall* at the bottom – but aside from the different voices of Dave Evans, Bon Scott and Brian Johnson, there's no marked change from record to record that fits the conventional notion of 'progression' or 'metamorphosis'. As Brian Johnson said in 1990, 'We've never swerved from the path ... there's been all these fads and fashions, and AC/DC and their brand of music never changed.'[8]

This is almost certainly the most important lesson that was passed on by George Young to his younger brothers, based on the Easybeats' experience. Like many lessons learnt by rote, it has surely been to the band's artistic detriment over the long haul. What George perceives as the Easybeats' mistakes (writing mini-operas like 'Heaven and Hell' and 'Come in You'll Get Pneumonia' instead of sticking to full-tilt rockers like 'Good Times') actually produced their *best* work. AC/DC's biggest decision before recording each album seems to have been who gets to produce it to achieve roughly the same result as before, or the marshalling of Angus and Malcolm's rusty lyrical skills in the late 1990s to get Brian Johnson over a writer's block.

If we place the Youngs at the heart of the AC/DC story, which seems fair, it begins with not one, but with several dark and rainy nights of Margaret Young bearing children in Glasgow, followed by relocation to Sydney in 1963. Angus played in a couple of Sydney bands in the early 70s; one was called Tantrum;[9] another was Kantuckee.[10] Malcolm was a member of the Velvet Underground, a Newcastle group who, like the New York band, had taken their name from Michael Leigh's 1963 book about 'the sexual corruption of our age'.[11] (The New York Velvet Underground were, as Jon Savage has pointed out, extremely obscure even amongst fans of Lou Reed's pop records at least until the mid 70s, by which time they – and the Newcastle group – had long since disbanded, so just like Don Walker's early 70s Adelaide group Queen, to take a random example, this doubling up of names is more a sign of Australians' immersion in the international pop gemeinschaft than anything else.) Dave Evans had been in a band called Django, and had joined the Velvet Underground[12] just after Malcolm Young left. When the Youngs joined forces in AC/DC – rumour has it that Angus Young actually *auditioned* for his brother's band – the group was barely more than a notion.

Howard Johnson's AC/DC biography quotes Dave Evans recalling, 'They asked me to come down for a jam so I went to Wilson Street on the corner of Urskinville Road in the Newton district.' Evans's memories battle to be heard through the lazy transcription of yet another under-researching author: Johnson means Erskineville Road, which is close to (though not in) the Sydney suburb of New*town*. Colin Burgess, formerly drummer for the Masters Apprentices, was also present at this audition; Malcolm Dome, author of yet another AC/DC potboiler, describes him as someone 'who had experience in several bands that never really achieved anything of note,'[13] which makes one wonder what an Australian band would have to have done beyond becoming one of the country's most successful and popular groups of the 60s to achieve something 'of note'. With the Youngs, Evans, Burgess, and random bassists, a group was born.[14] AC/DC had ten songs and made up two more during their debut, which took place on New Years Eve 1973 at Chequers. Their set included songs by Chuck Berry and Free; Malcolm wrote a song called 'The Old Bay Road'.

An important early AC/DC show was held in the open air in Victoria Park, a large space adjoining the University of Sydney where a swimming pool and (at that time) a bowling club were located. The group's receptiveness to musical experimentation was already probably heavily circumscribed, but they were still looking for a visual angle: unlike Skyhooks, who were aiming for something like parody, AC/DC 'decided we'd get some bizarre stage clothes' merely 'so we'd be remembered'. Angus's sister suggested he wear his school uniform (other sources suggest he was already doing this in his earlier bands, because he still *was* a schoolboy). Their bass player – whoever it was at that moment – wore a biker's outfit, the drummer – presumably Burgess at this time, though he only played in the band for a brief period – a clown costume; Malcolm was a parachutist, while singer Evans wore red platforms and 'trousers cut off at the knee.'[15] As well as his schoolboy outfit, Angus also occasionally wore a Zorro outfit onstage, but the uniform soon stuck: 'When I put it on,' he is quoted as saying, 'I felt such a monkey that I just had to keep moving onstage.'[16]

A few years after the group's emergence, *Rolling Stone* suggested that the Youngs had initially played up the 'bisexual connotations of their name' (one wonders how – by playing bisexual music?) but switched to heavy metal when that 'failed to inspire the masses'.[17] This sounds unlikely and indeed AC/DC were never really 'metal', just as they never really fitted the category of 'punk' that was unsuccessfully foisted on them at times.

Malcolm's Velvet Underground had recorded – they issued a cover of Jefferson Airplane's 'Somebody to Love' before he joined – but he and Angus do not seem to have entered the studio until the two of them were inducted to the Alberts way via

George Young and Harry Vanda's funky Marcus Hook Roll Band. Angus is also on record as saying: 'I did a few bits and bobs for my brother when he was producing some Stevie Wright stuff . . .'[18] But AC/DC was clearly already a viable entity in itself when Vanda and Young produced their first single, 'Can I Sit Next to You Girl', in January 1974. It was a bit of nihilistic music hall. Johnson's book quotes Evans as saying that the single 'got on a ten-minute rock show called . . . *GTK*. It was brilliant being on TV and really unusual for a rock band in those days'.[19] As we have seen in our story thus far, and will continue to see, being on TV was actually not at all uncommon for working groups in the capital cities; presumably it was Dave Evans's first time. Another Evans quote relayed by Johnson reveals the crux of the matter, however: 'Without George and Harry . . . Well, we'd only been together six weeks and we'd already recorded a single . . . That only happened because George was their brother.'[20]

There are probably those who prefer Brian Johnson (a capable singer and performer) to Bon Scott as a vocalist, and no doubt some who feel that Dave Evans didn't get the chance he deserved. Certainly, suggestions that Evans was too glam rock for the group seem farfetched when its mainstays were happy to garb up as Zorro and a parachutist (Mark Evans – no relation, incidentally, to Dave – suggests in *his* memoir that the band were still experimenting with fancy dress after releasing their first album).[21] But even knowing how dangerous hindsight can be, it is very hard to imagine AC/DC would have achieved the enormous success they did without the singer who took them to international fame.

It is said that AC/DC first made contact with Bon Scott through his former bandmate from the Valentines, Vince Lovegrove, who by 1974 was an Adelaide-based promoter for whom Scott did occasional jobs. AC/DC, with Evans singing, opened for another 'ex-Velvet Underground' act, Lou Reed (Stevie Wright was also on the bill) in August that year, and Scott was their driver while they were in Adelaide. Angus and Malcolm would of course have been aware of Scott from his days in the Valentines; Vanda and Young had written songs for them. Scott was hoping to become the Youngs' drummer; they responded that they were actually looking for a singer. They were heading for Perth, on the road; Scott told them 'if you make it back, come and look me up and I'll give you my answer'.[22] Huxley suggests that there was an attempt to bring John Paul Young into AC/DC as Evans's replacement,[23] and this may be true, although Stevie Wright without a drug problem would have been a better fit, had such a creature existed. In a strange way, Scott was a kind of parallel universe Wright: a former 60s pop singer gone to seed – though, in Scott's case, in a good way.

Scott's time as singer for Fraternity was mentioned in chapter 8: the group had found a rich benefactor and were working together in regional bliss outside Adelaide. Fraternity's Mick Jurd told *Daily Planet* that they made the move because 'we liked Adelaide, liked playing down here, and had the opportunity, with prices and everything, to get a place, as we have now. Also, we just wanted away from the rat race of Melbourne and Sydney.'[24] They already knew they were good, having won Battle of the Sounds; Scott told *Planet's* Brian Johnstone [!] he didn't think there was any particular glamour to that competition any more, but made it clear how much a part of the industry he still was: 'There once was [glamour], about three years ago. I think Doug Parkinson would have been the last one to gain any prestige from winning. The Flying Circus didn't get anything out of it except what we have, the prizes.'[25]

Scott was a natural for AC/DC; he had a good idea of the pop scene, and he had the moves. For a short time Evans and Scott took turns at singing with AC/DC, but Scott soon won out (he later re-recorded 'Can I Sit Next to You, Girl' on the second AC/DC album *TNT*). After that, it was all go. As Scott said in 1977, 'When you play as basic as us, it can only get tighter.'[26]

If you're not like Dome or Huxley et al., and so want to understand AC/DC's musical origins and the context of their work, you should listen not only to Buffalo, Buster Brown and the Coloured Balls, but also to some of the other records Vanda and Young produced for Alberts at this time. Stevie Wright's 'Black Eyed Bruiser' (the song and, to a lesser extent, the 1975 album of the same name) provides a template, while the Angels (not just in their new wave phase, such as 'Take a Long Line' on *Face to Face*, but also on their looser, bluesier debut) indicate where Vanda and Young and the demands of the times could take a band who were initially a million miles removed in feel and form from the Young brothers and their Chuck Berry riffs. Most importantly, Rose Tattoo on their first (self-titled) album sounded as AC/DC as AC/DC, if not more so. Rose Tattoo was composed of equal parts Buffalo and Buster Brown. The latter band had included a drummer who would later become central to AC/DC's attack: Phil Rudd, Burgess's successor, who also had Coloured Balls history in his background. The relentless, riff-based, almost mechanistic AC/DC sound is nothing if not a Vanda and Young sound and approach, and if it all springs originally from the Easybeats' 'Good Times', then we can only be grateful that at least something positive came out of that enterprise.

Mark Evans's memoir, specifically his observations about George Young's role in shaping the group's sound, sheds light on a second element of AC/DC's musical context. According to him, George not only had input into the components of the songs as they were recorded; he was also hands-on when it came to crafting finished work from elements contributed by the group in the studio. He also periodically played bass with the group in the period before Mark Evans joined.[27]

Curiously, Australians had been introduced to AC/DC's third vocalist, singing in what might arguably be an AC/DC style, before they ever heard Bon Scott do so. Brian Johnson's band Geordie toured Australia early in 1974, at the same time that AC/DC were recording their first single with Evans on vocals. *Go-Set's* Tony Walker described Johnson as owning a 'powerful, screeching voice somewhat reminiscent of Noddy Holder's'; the band appeared on *GTK*.[28] They also played at Sydney's Hordern Pavilion with Buffalo, Hush and Sherbet.[29] The 69ers were another band on the bill: they featured drummer Tony Currenti, who played on most of the first AC/DC album.[30] While that group's name must surely have had a sexual double entendre to it, its first entendre for many would have been a reference to the influx of Labor members who took office in 1969, when Whitlam almost won government: these people were known as the 69ers well into the 1970s.

AC/DC did not arrive at their classic sound/style fully formed; their second single, 'Baby Please Don't Go,' while soon to be a live favourite, suggests they still had a way to travel, but by the third, 'High Voltage' (released in June 1975), they're essentially there, with Scott's barking vocal style rounding it off beautifully. 'T.N.T.' and 'It's a Long Way to the Top (If You Wanna Rock 'n' Roll)' sound as fresh now as they did then and the group was turning out records at a breakneck pace. 'Jailbreak' and 'Dirty Deeds Done Dirt Cheap' were similarly stupendous.

It's surprising then – but also important – to see how reviled AC/DC were in the early to mid 70s – particularly in sectors such as the mainstream music press, where thirty years later they would be receiving endless praise. As the group with Scott began to make inroads in the USA (they had secured a contract with Atlantic), the eternally reactionary Australian *Rolling Stone* was happy to reprint their US parent's reviews of the group's albums, such as Billy Altman's of the hybrid *High Voltage* (the original *High Voltage* blended with its follow-up, *TNT*):

> Those concerned with the future of hard rock may take solace in knowing that with the release of the first U.S. album by these Australian gross-out champions,

the genre has unquestionably hit an all-time low. Things can only get better (at least I hope so) ... Stupidity bothers me. Calculated stupidity offends me.[31]

It is odd, too, to discover that in Australia and elsewhere AC/DC were occasionally lumped in with 'punk' bands. Vanda and Young defended them:

> AC/DC are not punk rockers as far as we are concerned, AC/DC is a rock band; they've been playing rock for the past three years, a good year and a half before the punk rock thing exploded onto the scene.[32]

Mark Evans writes at length about the scandal that accompanied his final tour with the group through regional Australia in 1976, largely due to Angus Young's stage behaviour; so perhaps it's not surprising in hindsight that AC/DC was so easily mixed up with 'punk'. 'High voltage rock 'n' roll,' is how the non-drinking Angus, with a Fanta in his fist, described his band to Australian *Rolling Stone's* Simon Grose. 'It's just really rock 'n' roll. We aren't here to confuse people.'[33] Soon the group were en route to Britain, where in 1976 it was reported they were poised for the 'biggest take-off for an Australian rock group in Britain since the Bee Gees in the 60s.'[34]

AC/DC's manager Michael Browning (he had taken over from former Sherbet singer Dennis Laughlin) had come through the Consolidated Rock booking agency in the early 70s. He knew Australian audiences, and it is peculiar now to read him opining in 1976 that the group that is now seen by Australians as so archetypically Australian were 'probably more suited to English audiences than Australian ones actually.'[35] For his part, Malcolm Dome believes the group are 'almost the quintessentially English Rock act ... The amazing thing is that for most people AC/DC are, and will always be, 'that Aussie band who made rather good!'[36] In 1990 Brian Johnson suggested – in a quip that feels scripted – that the group's origins were 'Palestinian, maybe – because none of us seem to have a homeland anymore.'[37] There is certainly a belief, adhered to almost intuitively amongst Australians of a certain age, that Bon Scott was the most Australian thing about AC/DC. Bob Hart, writing in *Spunky* in 1976, felt that Scott was 'about as Scottish as wallaby stew. He is a comic-book Australian.'[38] Angus was also of this opinion: 'You couldn't call Australia his adopted country. He was an Australian person.'[39] Scott died in February 1980; some may feel that his

death, from choking on his own vomit in a parked car – or at least the massive alcohol intake that led to it – was also very Australian.

Certainly the remaining members of AC/DC saw no reason to put the brakes on their enormous success. Like Dragon, who regrouped in a hurry after Neil Storey's death, they were in rehearsal almost immediately (three weeks) after losing a key long-term member. Angus Young intoned telegrammatically soon afterwards:

> We're a very close band. We really stick together. So we'll really miss Bon. He was a unique person. You can't really replace someone like that. All we can do for the future is get someone who is unique in themselves. Another image. Another personality.[40]

In fact, Angus was the only really inescapable part of their image. AC/DC's decision to carry on without Scott was rather more a tribute to his presumed expendability and the accidentally useful branding of the band in the shape of the schoolboy guitarist than anything else. Nevertheless, from a commercial perspective it was a brave move that could have blown up in their faces. Tasteless naming worked though and *Back in Black*, released less than six months after Scott's death sold 300,000 copies even before they toured, and became Australia's fourth biggest-selling album. Its commercial success notwithstanding, the album itself is truly horrible: Scott would surely have put its posturing and melodrama into perspective and spiced up its rowdy singalong drabness.

The *Back in Black* tour was also a huge success in Australia and the rest of the world; the album remains, ironically (if one can still find irony, with all that is true about popular music, in its enormous commercial success but complete lack of inherent value) the group's best-selling album and globally one of the top sellers of all time. At one show, Ed St John wrote in *Rolling Stone*:

> Backstage, members of the Easybeats, Sherbet, and characters like Ted Mulry, Lobby Loyde, Angry Anderson and Kerry Jacobsen, drank and partied like the old days. It was as if the old Bondi Lifesaver had been resurrected . . . The return of AC/DC was a rebirth because it made everyone proud, it gave them new confidence, and it reminded us where our roots are.[41]

Of course, part of AC/DC's 'roots' up until this point had been routine pillorying in the pages *Rolling Stone* – a magazine which has never shrunk from recalibrating its own history so that it appears to have always been on the cutting edge, when it very rarely is. AC/DC with Johnson would never recapture the cleverness or power of their 1970s work, though of course there is no way of knowing whether Scott would have saved them.

BOMBAY ROCK
'78 — SECOND COMING!

THE TOTAL
ENTERTAINMENT
COMPLEX

TWO FLOORS
FULLY LICENCED
8 pm — 3am

The Gigantic Opening Weekend

FRIDAY, MARCH 10
MOTHER GOOSE
ROSS WILSON
LAST CHANCE CAFE
$4-50

SATURDAY, MAR. 11
STARS
SPORTS
ONE NITE STAND
$4-50

MARCH 15
TEXAS
RESIDENT
+ SPECIAL GUEST
$3-00
WEDNESDAY

MARCH 16
NEW WAVE EXTRAVAGANZA!
JAB
TEENAGE RADIO STARS
BOYS NEXT DOOR
THE NEGATIVES
$3-00
THURSDAY

MARCH 17
RED HOT PEPPERS
DAVE WARNERS FROM THE SUBURBS
GLYN MASON
+ SURPRISE GUEST?
$4-00
FRIDAY

MARCH 18
KEVIN BORICH
ROSE TATTOO
X-RAY-Z
$4-50
SATURDAY

And then every Wed-Sat

BE THERE AND BE EARLY at the BOMBAY ROCK.

WE WILL GIVE YOU A CHOICE OF GREAT MEALS "FREE"
(included in your cover charge)

AND WE OFFER 'A LA CARTE' MENU AT CHEAP PRICES

After 1.00 a.m. admission only $3.00

After a season of bringing a new comprehension in music creativity to the heart of the city, Bombay Rock is spreading its concepts to the boundaries of Melbourne with its second coming at the city end of Brunswick.

In a new, larger venue which brings you the full scope of contemporary entertainment, Bombay Rock, a complete 3 a.m. licensed 2-storey entertainment complex, providing you with all forms of rock and media with top Australian talent, and supplying an avenue for international acts to perform a club concert atmosphere for you, the people of Melbourne.

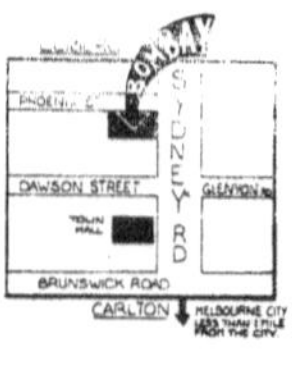

1 PHOENIX STREET, BRUNSWICK. PHONE: 380 9151
CITY END OF BRUNSWICK

11 Bending Corners

THE MID TO LATE SEVENTIES

> 1976 was the year Angus got his picture on the cover of England's *Sounds*, the year Sherbet scored a national number two hit single in England, the year Little River Band slugged their way into the American top-thirty singles charts. It's a predictable thing to say, and everyone's saying it, but '76 was the biggest year that Australian rock 'n' roll has ever had as far as overseas recognition goes . . . But don't you buggers get into a 'everything's rosy' attitude, 'cos there's still a way to go. There are a lot of young bands now emerging to fill in the void. Groups like Taste, Supernaut, Rabbit and the like who've got bags of enthusiasm and more than a little musical brains.[1]—Richard Guilliatt, *RAM*, 1977

Australian rock and pop music already had a sufficiently grand history up to the mid 1970s that many of its practitioners and proponents – even its consumers, to a certain degree – could justifiably feel smug. That said, the mid to late 70s were undoubtedly the time when many players in Australian rock music became key figures in the music scene worldwide, when Australian popular music demonstrated its ability to use core strengths (its varied cultural backgrounds, its capacity to develop local scenes-within-scenes, its relatively sophisticated and extensive electronic and print media) to innovate on – or, more commonly, insinuate itself into – the international scene. International standing is not the most important element for success in a *local* scene, but it does provide a valuable tool for self-assessment. If people in other parts of the world like your art, that's at least one gauge of its quality. It can also be financially beneficial, thus permitting greater professionalisation, though this is of course as problematic as it is advantageous.

In the 1960s international success came to Australian artists such as the Seekers and Rolf Harris, who could play up their 'Australianness' in Britain, where the notion of Australia as a rustic former colony continued to be prevalent. Australian performers battled distinct prejudices against Australians and the perception of Australia as second-rate and backward (particularly in Britain, where old tropes of racism were used with relative impunity against predominantly Anglo-Australian artists): Australianness could be promoted as a joke, but Australians could not be taken seriously as artists. Being Australian had become an even greater cause for ridicule after the *Monty Python* 'Bruces' sketch, first broadcast in late 1970 and subsequently rehashed in numerous different forms. The sketch – in which all Australians are called Bruce – had its roots in the humour of Barry Humphries' depiction of the boorish Australian male in the *Barry McKenzie* comic strip (the *McKenzie* films came slightly later).

In the USA, on the other hand, there was little awareness at all of Australia in a cultural or even geopolitical sense, and while this is in one sense regrettable, it also meant that Americans – unlike many British people – were less inclined to regard Australians as inherently inferior to any other foreigners. Artists like Air Supply, LRB, Rick Springfield and Olivia Newton-John – who was already a star in Britain, it's true, after her exposure on Cliff Richard's TV show and her 1974 Eurovision appearance (representing the UK) – could succeed in the US simply by being bright, accomplished, bland, catchy, hardworking, English-speaking, and white with nice teeth – anything they possessed beyond this was a bonus.

As cultural nationalism grew in strength in Australia in the 70s, however, an internationalist approach became less acceptable in the home market and, as we shall see, newer Australian artists who wished to make their mark in other countries would find it harder to combine local and international appeal.

Overlying this complicated environment was another phenomenon, the punk/new wave movement, which Australia embraced and to which it made very substantial contributions. Indeed, two of the five most important innovators amongst the world's first-generation 'punk' groups – Radio Birdman and the Saints – were Australian (the other three being Americans: the Ramones, Pere Ubu and Television). In acknowledgement of the fact that both bands were really a product of the earlier 70s, this chapter deals first with them and some of their punk affiliates, then discusses mainstream pop and its progenitors in the mid and late 70s, before returning to new wave and post-punk as the musical movement that would become most prominent in the 80s.

The economic, political and social context for this period is one of class and ideological division. A Liberal government, led by the stiff and patrician Malcolm Fraser, was in power at the federal level; the same conservative party also controlled most state governments. Fraser had plotted and effectively seized power from the Whitlam Labor government at the end of 1975, abetted by the Queen's representative, Governor-General John Kerr. This act inspired the formation of a truly strong republican movement in Australia, one which conservative politicians have since resorted to extremes of stealth and deception to thwart.

The second half of the 70s in Australia were also a time of economic hardship for many, although the legacy of Whitlam's free tertiary education remained, and unemployment benefits were relatively easy to obtain. 'The dole' was seen by many creative individuals as a de facto government grant system, and obtaining it under false pretences was hardly a major criminal act when unemployment was in any case high and the authorities accepted that a percentage of the population would not be able to find work no matter how much they tried. Like many Australian conservative leaders, Fraser was not strong on innovation, but for all his faults he was in many respects a genuine liberal (a 'small l' liberal), and he continued a number of Whitlam's cultural and social programs, including – importantly – the promotion of multiculturalism.

REAR VISION

One criticism often levelled at Australian punk rock is that it was a middle-class appropriation of the stylistic elements of a working-class British movement. Vikki Riley has exposed the myths involved in this claim, particularly myths regarding British 'working class' involvement in punk.[2] She also points out that when writing about Australian punk 'the Anglo-American music press viewed Australia as a colonial outpost whose subcultural activities mimicked its masters.'[3] While this misrepresentation was irrelevant to their day-to-day activities, it created difficulties for Australian musicians who wanted to expand their horizons overseas – a situation which worsened in the early 1980s.

The groups usually put forward as Australia's contributions to the international front line of punk rock – the Saints and Radio Birdman – are also perfect examples of why the "punk revolution" is largely a false construction, except inasmuch as the participants thought they were doing something revolutionary. Punk was clearly an inspiration to many – a panoply of now legendary players began their own histories with the punk rock experience. Yet it is plain that, just as anarchy itself longs for a spontaneous uprising that will overturn the established order, the punks of 1976-77 wanted to believe that they were formed by mutual, telepathically transmitted fed-upness, and they have since participated in the creation of a myth to prove it.

In fact, like many punk movements internationally, the Australian version came in three waves. One took the form of fragmented, apparently spontaneous and embryonic 'scenes' in unlikely suburban places in various cities; the most prominent of these were spearheaded in Sydney and Brisbane by the two bands discussed below, and they developed their own rules and styles. Another strand was inspired by punk movements elsewhere, but rather than being a straightforward appropriation, it was an adaptation of them, often tongue-in-cheek and also often less prescriptive than its northern hemisphere counterparts. It is significant – although it probably says more about Melbourne than it does about Australian punk – that the first Melbourne punk event was Punk Gunk, a commentary/conceptual event created by the art group →↑→ (pronounced with three clicks of the tongue and usually written Tch Tch Tch); Sydney and Brisbane, on the other hand, were able to sneer without feeling the need to smirk at the same time. The third strand was a punk 'revival' movement which began almost as soon as the original began to fade; it was all style and no substance, and only worth acknowledging as a bizarre phenomenon.

Though it looks ready for demolition in the film clip to the Saints' '(I'm) Stranded' and on the front cover of their *(I'm) Stranded* album, the Petrie Terrace house that the band christened 'Club 76'⁴ was merely undergoing a gentrification process like thousands of other Australian inner-city properties in the 70s. It later became a restaurant and then an IT outlet. What it *should* be, of course – as soon as Brisbane is able to fully embrace its 'police state' past and its status as a crucible of musical innovation – is the site of Australia's punk rock museum.

Visitors from around the world will be thrilled by relics – largely commercial consumables, though more visceral treasures might also be available – from the city's punk rock/new wave past: from the Saints, of course; the Fuckin' Leftovers; the Go-Betweens; the Grudge aka Neon Steal aka the Numbers aka the Riptides; and a special exhibit on the Corinda Boys, who were not a band exactly (though bands drew from it), but friends and relations of the Saints in this working-class Brisbane suburb. A small, partitioned section could focus on post-punk: the Poles, the Patients, Zero. That would be the Brisbane section. Upstairs the museum could go national, with a Radio Birdman room, a Boys Next Door/Birthday Party/Nick Cave room, a Victims/Geeks/Cheap Nasties/Scientists (and Hoodoo Gurus?) room, and general detritus from the years 1977 and 1978 in Australia – studded armbands, silkscreened posters, tabloid headlines, maybe even a video or two. There might even be paraphernalia relating to Ross Wilson's and David Pepperell's 1977 near-hit for Norman Gunston, 'I Might Be a Punk (But I Love You Baby)', which would doubtless fail to encompass the complex baggage of this genuine rarity, a novelty joke record that is also excellent in its own right.

Museums repackage the past and make their versions of it look unassailable by dint of selective accumulations of hard evidence. Of course, the Club 76 Australian Punk Museum™ would simply be consolidating myths that were firmly in place even by the end of the 70s: that punk strode in playing like the Pistols and with a safety pin in its nose, all snotty and undeniable, and destroyed everything in its path, for example. 'Our story begins with Sydney's Radio Birdman and Brisbane's the Saints,' declares Tim Pittman in the sleevenotes to his 2003 *Tales from the Australian Underground* double-CD compilation, 'pioneers both of the Australian independent single and the Australian underground scene.'⁵ If only it were so simple. In actuality, this reading of 'our story' (like the contents of the Australian punk rock museum) constitutes a convenient and entertaining shorthand version of what happened – but one that is so oversimplified as to be deceiving.

Pittman takes some of his cues from Clinton Walker, who, in his remarkable collection *Inner City Sound* suggests that the 'narrative' of the groups and scenes depicted in that book began in 1976 and ended in 1985: a nine-year period beginning with the international advent of punk rock (and Walker's own immediate engagement with it) and ending with the commercial and/or critical seal of approval granted to various groups made up of old punkers, such as the Hoodoo Gurus and Beasts of Bourbon. But this is just *a* reading of events – the conventional one which makes sense to most Australians who lived through that era. Many Australian music fans, and others all around the world, even those who weren't alive in the mid 70s, still get angry about the 'boring old farts' of the pre-punk years, even though in many cases they've rarely experienced, much less explored, the kind of variety that 'prog' actually offered. For such people, punk simply 'began' in 1976. This conventional reading always has punk 'beginning' with the rise of Radio Birdman and the Saints, even though both these groups had antecedents (Pittman terms them 'apprenticeships'[6]) going back to 1972 and 1973 respectively – and there were other earlier bands too, such as Pus in Perth, JAB in Adelaide or Judas and the Traitors in Melbourne. The conventional accounts also tend to agree that 'new wave', or what we now tend to call 'post-punk', ended sometime in the 1980s 'with every trajectory from punk reaching an impasse or petering out'.[7]

It is only in retrospect, and with big garish punky blinkers on, that we could come to believe that the punk rock revolution was so swift, so powerful and righteous – or indeed that punk 'began' at all. *Most* Australians – like *most* music consumers around the world – were only marginally aware of the principal musical exponents of punk rock/new wave at the time; it is only with hindsight, because of the artists it threw up or who used it as a springboard to fame, that it has come to be seen as so important. Back in the mid to late 70s, punk/new wave was one of many types and styles of music that one might enjoy, laugh at, marvel at or deride, and even most of those who enjoyed it a lot were unlikely to enjoy it exclusively: there just wasn't *enough* punk/new wave music for it to be the only music you liked. The majority – assuming they even thought about music in terms of trends, rather than catchy hit singles or individual artists – would probably have empathised with Craig Johnston from the progressive Australian-based New Zealand band Mother Goose, who said in 1980 that:

> Disco has come and gone, and new wave is in at the moment. I don't want to wear a black tee-shirt and dark glasses and sing in a lower-class English accent. Why should I? I'm just not going to bend corners.[8]

Johnston was right to describe new wave as a trend, but he was probably mistaken, from a professional standpoint, to dismiss it. Ultimately, many of its ideas and assumptions were simply incorporated into the passing show of rock music.

One question well worth asking, though, is this: what did Australian music gain – and lose – as a result of the gradual ascension of punk and new wave? We have already seen in chapter 8 how Captain Matchbox were as punk as any group could be without actually playing garage rock. Most importantly, their goal was to bypass the excesses of their peers and play something they saw as more direct, human and honest. When they sang 'My Canary Has Circles Under Its Eyes', they *meant* it – that is, they were highlighting the value of the everyday, the silly, and the non-transcendent, and they were not pompous, only self-important, in that they demanded to be heard. The Pelaco Brothers and the groups that sprang from them were doing the same thing: highlighting older, putatively more 'genuine' music, in a search for honesty that showed up the conceits (in both senses of the word) of both head music and, to a certain extent, sanitised 'international' music.

There was nothing automatically radical about a 'retro' *rock* message, either. The Masters Apprentices had espoused 50s rock in their hit 'Turn Up Your Radio' in 1970. This unbelievably awful song – which came with pretty much the stupidest of film clips – now sounds more like a portent of everything that was glib and pompous about glam rock than anything else, but it was clearly an attempt to reference a 1950s feel. This trend further manifested itself in Australia at this time through important cultural movements such as the sharpies, with their teddy-boy ambience; a renewed rise in the fortunes of Johnny O'Keefe; and of course the success of Daddy Cool – through to Sunbury '72, where seemingly everyone did an extended rock-out on Jerry Lee Lewis's 'Whole Lotta Shakin' Goin' On' (itself a cornerstone of the Coloured Balls' *Ball Power* album) or some other instantly recognisable 50s classic. Sha Na Na had started something at Woodstock, and the trend of embracing 50s rock and roll as if it were the font of all that was honest and valid in rock music came to fruition – or perhaps was laid to rest in a quiet but florid cul-de-sac – in the mid 70s in Australia with the commercial success of the band Ol' 55. In the same period, Bryan Ferry would act on a profound desire to 'recast the golden oldies',[9] the Band made *Moondog Matinee,* and John Lennon recorded his *Rock and Roll* album. Internationally, 50s nostalgia peaked with *American Graffiti, Grease* and *Happy Days,* all perpetuators of the 50s-in-the-70s fad. Australians were involved here, too: the film of *Grease,* produced by Robert Stigwood, would feature songs by John Farrar and gave a starring role to his friend Olivia Newton-John ('I trust John Farrar implicitly').[10] Neither Stigwood, Farrar nor Newton-John had been involved in any 1950s revival movements during their time in Australia – they were just working with the zeitgeist.

Ol' 55 were the biggest Australian group of 1976. They were managed and advised creatively by Glenn A. Baker, Australia's best-known rock historian (he was awarded the dubiously worded title of "Rock Brain of the Universe" in a BBC competition in 1985).[11] Ol' 55's biggest hit was the confusing single 'On the Prowl'. It's a confusing song because it's never quite clear what the main character in the song is actually doing when he's 'prowling with the boys on a Saturday night', though forty years on it all seems more *Scorpio Rising* than anything else. Their album *Take it Greasy* was a smash, praised and damned at the same time by Christie Eliezer in his *Juke* review as 'a series of perfectly executed caricatures.'[12] Their singer was Peter Bryan (or Brien),[13] who used the stage name Frankie J. Holden – a jokey reference to the F.J. Holden, the classic 1953 Australian-made car. Only a few years earlier the same model had been canonised by Daddy Cool in their song 'Love in an F.J.', celebrated by singer/JJ radio announcer Bob Hudson in his 'Newcastle Song',[14] and referenced in a peculiar psychosexual fantasy, 'A Fate Worse Than Death,' on Spectrum's *Milesago* album.

The original Ol' 55 was short-lived: Holden quit before the group's second studio album (though he has used the stage name ever since, not least in an impressive acting career). Main songwriter Jimmy Manzie was plainly itching to do something other than fifties-esque (more properly termed Daddy Cool-esque) cabaret pop; he subsequently moved on to film soundtrack work.

Their cabaret beginnings notwithstanding, Silver Studs were Ol' 55 lite. The group was formed by Lance Reynolds 'as a follow-on from a character', Rat Rearvision, 'he played in a Brisbane revue.'[15] Reynolds teamed up with Gino Latorre, a friend from the cast of *Hair* (he had won out over Jenny Brown for a part) and Paul Stevens (later replaced by Keith Reed) to deliver what a writer from the gay magazine *Campaign* felt he could 'only describe as a mini-play'[16] in live performance. The group presented themselves as the aforementioned Rearvision, along with Morrie Muffler and Spike Spoke.[17] Silver Studs were at least as much about theatre as they were about music – they had plans for a show called *The Last Air Raid Shelter* which involved King Kong's penis becoming stuck in Melbourne's Town Hall[18] – though they had a major hit with a cover of the theme tune to *Happy Days*, and not much else. Stevens would go on to replace Holden in the seemingly indestructible Ol' 55 under the stage name Mikey Raffone. Not only was this a bad pun, it was a derivative bad pun – Mic Conway had already renamed himself Microphone Conway the year before, for the 1975 Captain Matchbox album *Australia*.

50s pop/doo-wop, and 60s garage rock are, of course, worlds apart. Nevertheless, when British journalist Kieron Tyler published his laudatory assessment of the Saints in *Mojo* in 2004 on the occasion of the EMI box set based around their first three albums, and talked about the group having emerged in 'isolation, evolving with no peers, no context',[19] he was simply showing his British bias – and ignorance. The Saints had 'context' in spades – everything detailed in this book up to this point, for instance, but particularly such 60s groups as the Missing Links, the Throb, and the Purple Hearts. Tyler's judgment was also at odds with Chris Bailey's own earlier summary of his band's formative work as 'just Eddie Cochran riffs, tarted up by a bunch of yobs who couldn't play too good.'[20]

Radio Birdman had a number of ambitions; one that now seems almost quaint, not to mention cross-cultural, was the hope they would one day get 'the chance to blow Skyhooks' arse off the stage.'[21] To many in subsequent decades, this might seem a little like aspiring to snatch a senior citizen's walking frame. In the mid 70s, however, it was not by any means clear cut that Skyhooks represented the past and Radio Birdman were looking to the future – indeed, many would have thought quite the opposite. The same is true of a Skyhooks–AC/DC comparison, and AC/DC shared a similar hope to Radio Birdman: 'We believed we could out-rock any band in Australia', says Mark Evans.[22] For Radio Birdman as for AC/DC, the defining element was their 'back to basics' approach, in contrast to Skyhooks' arty observation. Deniz Tek and his compatriots were harnessing rough power from the

1960s to slogans and exhortations to action; Greg Macainsh's progressive (though never *prog*) group offered sophisticated and incisive narratives of contemporary society. Skyhooks pondered what had happened to the revolution; Radio Birdman proclaimed, of all things, a 'new race'! So who was old, and who was new?

The commercial success of Skyhooks, their enduring fame and the respect accorded them by their peers, had a number of important effects on the production of music by Australian artists. Skyhooks' Australianness was both the key to their success and, in a wider sense, also their undoing; they were a living example of exactly the kind of problem LRB strove successfully to avoid.

Musically, Radio Birdman was directly 'about' Detroit and the Stooges – an obscure interest at the time – but there were plenty of other ideas and flavours in the mix, including the Missing Links and the Masters Apprentices, whom the teenage Deniz Tek, born and raised in the Detroit area, had enjoyed in the late 60s when his family spent a year in Sydney before he made a more longterm move to Australia in 1972. The Saints were musically 'about' garage groups, 60s R&B, and even the expressionistic experimental music of bands like Can, and they were even more overt regarding their Missing Links connection, recording the earlier band's 'Wild About You' for their first LP. When he mailed out copies of the first Saints single in 1976, Ed Kuepper invited recipients who might want to know about them or 'Australian groups of the sixties' to write back to the band.[23] That said, whatever Kuepper and Bailey's own knowledge of 60s groups was, their choice of a close to generic 'bad boy' band name was probably *not* a deliberate steal from the Sydney group called the Saints who recorded eight singles and an album in the mid 60s.

Neither the Saints nor Radio Birdman were anti-intellectual. That may have been one reason for their lack of mass appeal, in fact, given the thuggish clichés that much early punk, particularly outside Australia, wallowed in. There was, however, a strong streak of anti-establishment attitude running through most rock music in Australia in the early 70s – just as there had been in the 60s – and it was often as aggressive as conventional punk rock. AC/DC might be said to fall into this category; certainly some ignorant commentators claimed they were Australia's answer to (or contribution to) punk rock once the phenomenon became known as such. What stopped AC/DC being truly countercultural was, arguably, their craftsmanlike approach and their demonstrable musicianship, their lack of interest in experimentation or 'progress' (for the sake of it – or otherwise) from album to album, and their willingness to be a part of the music industry: to have refused to take part in the Alberts/EMI process would, of course, have been a slap in the face to George Young. As we have seen, AC/DC were cultivated by the Youngs to hit the ground running in the Easybeats' footsteps, and then go further.

AC/DC were not the only pseudo-punkish hard rock band on the Alberts label in the late 70s – they weren't even necessarily the best. Rose Tattoo were more boisterous, and the Angels were musically more innovative and concise. Malcolm and Angus Young's career-driven approach showed with every step that they wanted to become very successful by *acting* like they meant it: their songs were calculated. Rose Tattoo and the Angels were, on balance, much more interesting, if messy, propositions.

IAN RILEN, ROSE TATTOO, AND X

In the early 70s Bendigo-born Ian Rilen had been bass player in the excellent Band of Light, though as we saw earlier he did not particularly enjoy Pam Key's lyrics for the band, which he later remembered as attempting to glorify the monogamous bliss between herself and husband Phil. This is not at all evident, incidentally, on the album that features Rilen.

Band of Light was the first foray into management for Sebastian Chase, who would play a significant part in the careers of many other groups from this era and had a major role in Rilen's career. Rilen left Band of Light because Key wouldn't let him perform the songs he'd written. Six years later he told Frank Brunetti from *Vox*:

> I screwed around with a few bands for a while. Boogie kings like Flake and Blackfeather. I did all that shit for a couple of years. Then about '76 Dragon came to Australia and fired their guitar player Ray Goodwin and we started writing songs together. We really got into it and then I started writing by myself.

Goodwin and Rilen were briefly part of Silver Studs' backing band[24] before forming their own group, Hot Cock. Whether because of its preposterous name or just general skittishness, little came of this, and went in a new direction:

> One day Sebastian Chase came around and said, 'we're gonna get this band together with you on bass, Peter Wells on lead and slide guitar, and Tony Lake on vocals', and that was the original Rose Tattoo. Then there was just me and Peter Wells and Lee Hamilton for a while and we went though a week of auditions looking for a drummer. Eventually we got this guy Stork. Then Angry and Mick Cocks joined the band, Stork was too out of it so Dallas came in on drums and we were away.[25]

Lake had been the singer in Flake and would soon join Madder Lake;[26] 'Stork' was Michael Vandersluys. Peter Wells, former Buffalo bassist, would later say he had 'formed the band in his head'[27] before he did so in real life. Rilen's wife at the time, Stephanie, recalls an afternoon of rehearsals in their home in Lewisham, Sydney, at which Anderson auditioned. In an early review of a Melbourne show late in 1977, Rebecca Batties wrote of Rilen that his hands looked 'as though he's used tarred roads in the same way boxers use punching bags. The veins protrude from his darkened skin as he goes through some fast and interesting rhythms'.[28]

Rilen could claim the distinction of composing the first and best Rose Tattoo hit, a riff-and-boogie workout titled 'Bad Boy for Love'. His 1981 interview with Brunetti suggests that the group's decision to replace Vandersluys with Dallas Royall was the reason he left, soon after the show Battie attended: 'As far as I was concerned Dallas didn't fit the band as well as Stork. But then I guess eventually I didn't fit in either.'[29] Rilen had been replaced by Geordie Leach by the time the band recorded their first album, produced by Vanda and Young. His chief contribution to Rose Tattoo was their sound – and 'Bad Boy for Love', which was a top-ten hit in late 1977, less than a year after the band's debut. 'Rosie Tatts' were legendary early; a 'farewell' show at the Bondi Lifesaver in June 1978 saw them attract special guests like John Swan, Johnny Dick, and Bob Spencer, as well as members of Cold Chisel and the Kevin Borich Express – close to Australian rock royalty.[30] As early as 1980, Eric Gradman's semi-underground group Man and Machine covered the first album's 'Nice Boys' – probably non-ironically – in their live set.[31] The 1978 'farewell' was ridiculously premature: the group has outlived Rilen, Royall, Cocks and Wells, releasing an album in 2007 which included a version of Vanda and Young's 'Black Eyed Bruiser' and demoing for another in 2011.

Rose Tattoo introduced themselves to the world as a 'hearty group of intra-urban survivors'.[32] 'We play it harder, faster, tighter, more aggressively, closer to its original form . . . than anyone else in the country', Anderson told Andrew McMillan from *RAM*, adding: 'we are obviously the most violent perpetrators of rock 'n' roll music in Australia.'[33] This did not mean everyone felt compelled to take Anderson seriously: in 1977 Rebecca Batties wrote:

> Angry Anderson with his chubby body, round face and shaved head looks like an elongated bouncing bambino. I guess some would call him cute but for reasons motivated by self preservation I'll call him Sir.[34]

Andrew McMillan's article on Rose Tattoo in *RAM* two years later did Anderson's dignity no favours: a typographical error (one presumes) led to him being quoted as professing a belief in 'fat and destiny'.[35] Anderson had his spiel down perfectly by the time he was interviewed by Toby Creswell for the banal *Big Australian Rock Book*:

> It's the dedication, the very heartfelt obligation of Rose Tattoo to appeal to everyone who has a heart and a soul, who lets life affect them on an emotional level. What about the kids who are being brought up in the suburbs today? They know from sixth grade that they're going to do four years of secondary school – for what? To qualify for the dole? . . . Society's turning a lot of people into desperados, and the numbers are growing. These are the people for whom Rose Tattoo speaks: the dispossessed.[36]

'It's like a romantic novel,' added Anderson (perhaps intending to temper the above fancy with a bit of wry humour, or perhaps not), 'where there are the five of us against the world.'[37] The question, of course, was always who the five were: Anderson was not an original member and he was to replace the entire band at least once, though Peter Wells was almost as permanent a fixture until his death in 2006, and there was a genuinely classic line-up, featuring Anderson, Wells, Leach, Robin Riley, and Dallas Royall on drums. Perhaps the most interesting – and essentially unheard – configuration was the one with Lobby Loyde on bass, which recorded a (to date) unreleased album in Los Angeles in 1979.[38] Anderson, an unabashed Sherbet fan,[39] would include a number of pitches to the pop charts in his chequered career over various Rose Tattoos, notably in the early 1980s with 'Branded' and 'We Can't Be Beaten'. Having survived a childhood of abuse from a violent father and others, he also developed his own bad taste showstopper (even more unacceptable at the time than Dragon's 'Miss Mercy') with the song 'Suicide City', at the end of which he would strangle himself with his microphone cord, loosening his grip only when he passed out.[40]

The first Rose Tattoo album is clearly Rilen's and Wells's baby, which the latter had been left holding, played by people who didn't understand (or understood but were alienated by) the vision it embodied. It also features a song called 'Stuck on You', a throwaway, Faces-esque track credited to all the group members who recorded that first album. One of Ian Rilen's later, career-making songs was a ballad with the same title that he co-wrote with Stephanie.

Rilen's subsequent activities built on his work in Rose Tattoo and exceeded it in terms of innovation, though not commercial success. In 1977, he assembled another band, which he called X (the Los Angeles band of the same name was formed the same year). The name X was, apart from anything else, easy to make posters for – Rilen could simply paint two large strokes on sheets of newspaper.[41] Having been responsible for the Rose Tattoo 'look' – black t-shirts, broken in by the band jumping on them, then nicked by Rilen with razorblades, and with sleeves and collars removed,[42] Rilen already made a vaguely punk impression. Stephanie  remembers taking in Rose Tattoo's jeans 'on an old treadle machine.' Using various connections, he plundered another group, Evil Roomers (also known as 'Evil Rumours),[43] to create his new band, featuring two Ians and two Steves: Rilen was on bass, Ian Krahe on guitar, Steve Cafiero on drums, and Steve Lucas on vocals. Recordings by Evil Roomers suggest that Krahe, in particular, was a punk rock talent at least the match of Rilen.

X remained in existence until 2012, with Steve Lucas the last living member of the original line-up. On June 13 of that year, during the group's farewell tour, he had a dream, which he detailed on Facebook:

> I was watching old X footage and out takes with a very young and healthy-looking Ian Rilen. We were sitting on a couch watching us sitting on a couch watching the screen etc . . . you know how dreams work. We were pointing at each other and laughing at ourselves and having a great time. At one stage I reached out to point out something on the screen and touched Ian's arm. really touched it. It was warm and he was alive. It was so moving I cannot begin to explain. I woke up and could still feel the warmth on my fingers. It was simultaneously overwhelmed by laughter and tears. A lot of people will tell stories of us hating each other and rivalries etc but I can tell you this, we made each other laugh like nobody else could. I miss the old bugger.[44]

In 1987, he told Christie Eliezer about the pair's first encounter: 'The first time I saw Ian [Rilen] I was totally intimidated, he had bright red spiky hair; he looked like he bit off children's heads for breakfast . . . weird and very frightening.'[45] Steve Cafiero was a Rose Tattoo fan 'who weighed about 18 stone and he was an amazing drummer', according to Rilen. Cafiero had also reputedly roadied for the Easybeats.[46] Rilen added:

> It all came together really well, it only took us six weeks to get our repertoire together, play our first gig at the Astra and get banned. We built up a good following really fast. We did it all ourselves.[47]

Getting banned was plainly an important element of the X story for Rilen, who – for reasons that are unclear – saw the group as being entirely outside the music 'machine' in a way that, notably, Rose Tattoo weren't. X refused to 'take any gigs whatsoever from within the industry'.[48] They played at places like the Grand, where another well-known punk band, Rocks, also played. The Grand had a PA which resembled washing machines and which was owned by Jeff Fatt,[49] later a member of the Cockroaches and the Wiggles.

Finally, the notorious Bondi Lifesaver offered them a large sum of money ($350) to play a Saturday night show. It was Krahe's last show. Rilen recalled:

> That was like a triumph for us and it really meant a lot to the band, so we did the gig and totally blew the place apart . . . Every couple of songs Ian was breaking a string and Steve would be lying down on the stage because he was so fucked, his style of singing was so energetic that it took a real lot out of him . . . As far as the band was concerned we'd totally succeeded in our aims. We'd upset the management to the point of no return, packed the place out, got our money and

run. As it turned out that was the last night that line-up ever played. Ian was a really unhealthy person who got pleurisy and asthma and all that, and that night he got really sick and had an asthma attack and died.[50]

Such tragic and meaningless events contributed to X's legend, as did the rumour that the group's music was 'so extreme it had . . . made people vomit and given them erections'.[51] An associate of the group described seeing them as 'an endless fuck'.[52]

Soon after Krahe's death the three surviving members of the band recorded a sensational punk album which even had a clever title – *X-Aspirations*. The group would subsequently persist, or recur, in a number of incarnations and reformations for close to 25 years. *X-Aspirations* was murky, fluid, and full of the catchiest pop-punk imaginable. Rilen later recalled that they had gone into the studio to make a single, but then 'Lobby Loyde, who was the only person game enough to take us into the studio, said, "Let's put 'em all down" . . . So we recorded all the tracks in about 5 hours.'[53]

Unusually, in a music world where the first line-up to make a record so often enjoys the highest status, the classic X line-up has come to be regarded as Rilen and Lucas with drummer Cathy Green, formerly of Canberra group *** *** (pronounced 'cough cough'), who did not join X until the mid 80s.

Like Loyde, Rilen quickly became a hero within the punk movement despite the fact that he had consorted with the enemy forces of prog and boogie in the early 70s, and there was recorded evidence (the first Band of Light album, and 'Bad Boy for Love', and possibly more) to prove it. In fairness to Rilen, he would never have done anything so contrived as to align himself with punk for personal gain – but neither did he resist being swept up in any 'movement' that came along, as evidenced by his early 80s forays with the brilliant Sardine V. Throughout their career, X both created their own legend and thwarted their opportunities. 'Seriously, you couldn't look for a bigger bunch of self-destructing idiots,' mused Lucas later. 'That's what we were. We just happened to play really well together when we weren't being idiots.'[54]

SAINTS NOT SAPS

Unlike Rilen, Ed Kuepper, Chris Bailey, Ivor Hay and Kym Bradshaw – the first line-up of the Saints to record and tour – were a punk band apparently without a history in 1977, even though they had been a rock band in one form or another since 1973.

Bailey had been a child hippie, and had participated in the 1970 Vietnam Moratorium marches at the age of 12, proudly wearing his anarchist badges.[55] Kuepper had been a guitar-playing Easybeats fan in primary school;[56] he and Bailey teamed up at Oxley High School. Kuepper, from a family of German migrants, claimed in '77 that with his unusual surname (pronounced 'Cooper') he received 'the migrant shit and the German shit' from his fellow students: 'I used to be called a nazi at school, which gave me the shits because I wasn't.'[57]

On leaving school both took on a series of ill-fitting jobs: Bailey worked as a fettler, in a foundry and as a storeman at a discount store; Kuepper 'worked at Astor Records for a good while ... storeman/casual labouring for a bit, maybe on the dole for about two weeks (paternal disapproval), then the public service for 6 months'.

In 1973 they formed a band with Ivor Hay called Kid Galahad and the Eternals, then changed their name to the Saints. For a short time, Jeffery Wegener – who was to play a crucial part in Kuepper's later career as the second immutable element of the Laughing Clowns – was their drummer. Hay played first piano and then bass before moving to drums. Kuepper says he 'had the idea for the band and asked the other two if they would like to join,' and that he 'wrote the bulk of the stuff – directed the band artistically (though I probably wouldn't have described it like that at the time)' and 'came up with the idea to record the band so yes, I was the band leader. This is not to diminish Chris and Ivor in any way. It wouldn't have happened without them – at least not in the same way. I will state, however, I would have had a band one way or the other. Not so sure about them.'

Hay later recalled the 'anti-war movement' as a key reason for forming a band: 'as a reaction to the oppressive police-state environment of Brisbane. We were teenagers who wanted to kick something.'[58] Since Australia was out of Vietnam by 1973, when the band began, the opposition to war must have been non-specific; the interest was surely musical as much as anything. Fourth Saint Kym Bradshaw saw the Saints shine out from 'the usual catalogue of shit' one Saturday afternoon at a rock show at the Queensland Academy of Music. 'They were just amazing.'[59] He joined in 1975, but seems to have been regarded by the others as less integral to the band and would only be a member for two years.

In 1994 Kuepper released an album of Saints live recordings from 1974 called *The Most Primitive Band in the World* – both to give enthusiasts some insight into their earliest period and, perhaps most importantly, to confirm the group's claim to have been innovators in the worldwide punk rock movement. Many have found the album unlistenable, but no-one can deny what it proves – the sound of the Saints, which they took to London four years later, was not formulated in response to anyone else's punk rock, even while it referenced 60s R&B. The groups who were the Saints' contemporaries by the time they released their first album, *(I'm) Stranded*, in 1977 – the Ramones in New York or the Sex Pistols in London, for example – had only existed as concepts when Kuepper wrote the song that gave the album its title. It was clearly punk rock which made the Saints stars, however; they were swept up in the worldwide enthusiasm for raw, gritty, fast rock music that seemed to strip away the pretentious curlicues of meditative early-70s rock and overly earnest, pretentiously smug singer-songwriters to offer naked, truthful angst.

Bradshaw and Hay lived in a 'fucking pigsty',[60] the wryly dubbed Club '76; Bailey crashed there on the weekend; Kuepper kept his distance, living in a flat with his girlfriend. Club '76 was an old shop front on the 'corner of a busy intersection, opposite the main police headquarters'[61] according to Hay. Brisbane was an oppressive and conservative place under the harrowingly hardline Bjelke-Petersen government, and the police force was notorious for its corruption and brutality.

The story of the Saints' next step is legendary in Australia. Their relative isolation in Brisbane, coupled with their status as innovators, has allowed the group to control their own myth perhaps more than would otherwise have been possible, but this much seems incontrovertible: they recorded '(I'm) Stranded' in a local jingle studio called Sunshine (unconnected to Ivan Dayman's recently defunct Sunshine record label) in mid 1976 and released it as a single.[62] Bailey was to claim, much later, that the song was unintentionally sped up in production.[63] Kuepper's response is that Bailey is 'talking through his arse':

> He gets confused because I seldom tuned to concert pitch. The guitar on the single was tuned up 2 semi tones. I would then use chords with open strings to achieve that ringing sound. This approach was continued on a lot of the material until *Prehistoric Sounds*, which I felt sounded better tuned down to concert pitch. I also stopped doing it live because I was breaking too many strings; eventually I just ended up using capos in my later ensembles when I needed that sound.

Kuepper recalled the circumstances of the record's release as follows:

> I was working at Astor Records as a storeman and noticed boxes of private pressings – mostly country tunes by truck drivers. Having our own label seemed like the sensible way to get a record out. We conducted a poll among our fans as to which songs would most likely become a hit and 'Stranded' got the most votes. I can't remember if we rigged the poll.[64]

The group called their label Fatal Records; they sent copies of the single to record labels and music magazines both in Australia and overseas. '(I'm) Stranded' was reviewed in the October 16, 1976 issue of British music weekly *Sounds* as the 'single of this and every other week'. Clinton Heylin – who patronizingly describes the single as an 'astonishing call from the wild' – claims that the group did not actually send their record to *Sounds* (which was, in truth, a poor cousin to the influential *New Musical Express* and *Melody Maker*), but that Caroline Coon at the *NME*, who *did* receive the record, alerted *Sounds'* Jonh Ingham to its existence, and played it to him over the phone.[65] It was released in Britain on the EMI-funded soul label Power

Exchange two months later.[66] The Saints tied in so conveniently with the punk scene that was developing in the UK that the British EMI label commanded its Australian subsidiary to sign this group, which EMI in Sydney (along with all the other mainstream Australian labels) had already rejected as unsuitable for the Australian market – a judgment that, it has to be said, was probably a fair reading of the commercial environment at the time.

Kuepper later told *Juke* journalist Susan Joy it was from 'a real funny source' that the group heard about the interest from abroad: 'A friend of ours heard on the ABC news about how it was causing a sensation, and we just thought it was a practical joke.'[67] Bradshaw 'went to a phone box and called ABC radio', where someone 'relayed the news item to him over the line'. Kuepper, Bradshaw says, 'felt justified; everything he was working for had found its way through the crap. It was all over the Aussie press; we heard from EMI within the week.'[68]

EMI put the Saints into the studio in Sydney with Rod Coe, who had been a member of Country Radio and the lesser-known band Australia. Coe had produced Carson's album *Blown* and the power-trio era La De Das (the *Rock and Roll Sandwich* LP and some singles); he'd also managed the latter group in the early 70s.[69] The Saints have praised Coe for his work – essentially, he let them get on with it – but as early as mid 1977 Kuepper was complaining that *(I'm) Stranded* had been 'recorded too late' – it was 'six months before it was released, and we'd been playing the songs for a long long time.'[70] Club '76 appeared in the video for '(I'm) Stranded' and on the cover of the album.

Punk was always problematic for the Saints, and of course the band was to prove problematic for punk, which in its purest form became ever more conservative and prescriptive as it lost its critical mass when the innovators and thinkers moved on to post-punk or mainstream rock/pop. Kuepper said he hated the idea that people 'thought they liked us 'cos we were the trend.'[71] In one of their earliest interviews with the mainstream press (for Australian *Rolling Stone*), Kuepper and Bailey reckoned they weren't interested in labels like punk, working-class rock, or 'dole queue rock' ('alcoholic rock'[72] was another) which the then left-wing critic (later right-wing revisionist) Keith Windschuttle had tossed around in *Nation Review*. 'I know the working class has to put up with bullshit,' said Kuepper – he would, being part of that class himself and coming from Corinda in Brisbane's south. 'But so does every class ... You've got to transcend that crap.'[73] Perhaps the t-shirt the group produced in early 1977 provides a key to this 'transcendence': 'IT'S BETTER TO BE A SAINT THAN A SAP.'[74]

The Saints only started to make an impact in the media once they began playing shows outside Brisbane. They were banned by Brisbane radio until pop station 4IP asked them for a chat, wherein Bailey used the expression 'pissed off', an unforgivable media transgression in the late 70s and one which proved to local radio that it had been right to exclude them all along.[75] It didn't matter too much to the band, who moved to Sydney soon afterwards to work with a management team of Chris Gilbey, previously vice-president of Albert's international music, and Rod Thomas, formerly an A&R man with Phonogram. Their first show in Sydney was at Chequers. Another band who played that venue on occasion in 1977 and would also have a considerable effect on Australian music and tastes in the 70s and beyond was Cold Chisel. Toby Creswell describes Chequers as a venue down on its luck:

> In the fifties and early sixties this room had been Sydney's most prestigious nightclub, featuring international performers direct from Las Vegas. Twenty years later, the velvet wallpaper was peeling badly and the lights were thankfully dim.[76]

Paul Comrie-Thomson took an elitist/racist stance that was not extraordinary in mid-70s *Rolling Stone* when describing how the sound of the Saints forced 'the sculptured, disco-loving, Mediterranean body builders who frequent the place into the dimmer corners or up and out onto the street.'[77] What really thrilled Comrie-Thomson was the music industry types who were there instead, mouths 'agape'; Australian *Rolling Stone*, like its American parent, has always found music industry excitement the most exciting thing imaginable. The Saints were a group who, according to another reviewer, projected the sense that they 'knew only one way to play – as fast as possible, as loud as possible'[78], though Kuepper blew a fuse in his amp eight minutes into the set; he then broke a string and put a new one on while continuing to play. Comrie-Thompson described Bailey amid the maelstrom as an 'embodiment of the young Brendan Behan'.[79] The Sydney sojourn was peculiar; Kuepper remembers that the band 'supported the Ritchie Family at the Hurstville Civic Centre – which was hilarious.'

The Saints would soon relocate to London for eighteen months of artistic triumph and commercial catastrophe: the short time they spent in the media spotlight after Brisbane and before Britain was a flash. It is part of the Saints' own mythology that they were hated and/or ignored by everyone in Australia and almost everyone everywhere else. Vivien Johnson's book on Radio Birdman suggests that Radio Birdman were bemused by the aggression the Saints displayed towards them. With typical use of slack punning, Bailey referred to the group and their fans as 'the Birdbrain club' in an interview two decades later; he claimed that clique 'really hated us because there was this really entrenched scene and I think we were viewed as kind of the hillbilly cousins from the north ... there was like this little war.'[80]

Kuepper maintains that the Saints received a 'completely negative' response from Australian press and radio[81] during his time in the band. Certainly, they did not have a hit record in Australia, though EMI was not entirely apathetic – for instance, their second single, 'Erotic Neurotic', was included on a volume of *Explosive Hits* (in between tracks by Showaddywaddy and Cliff Richard), providing them with exposure to the mainstream record-buying youth. (Richard Clapton had claimed the previous year that he 'made real money' when his hit 'Girls on the Avenue' was included on one of 'those bargain *Explosive Hits!* Series... they sell about 400,000 each time;'[82] Doug Ashdown told a similar story.[83]) '(I'm) Stranded' also appeared on a World Record Club's mail-order album, *Austrock 77*, and an EMI compilation called *Devastator*. What's more, the Australian press were often far from negative; they were intrigued and often laudatory. As indicated above, Australian *Rolling Stone* was uncharacteristically up-to-date and broad in its coverage of the band; a strong sign that the Saints had made an impact was their ability to kickstart *that* particular jalopy. More likely, the group members' unpleasant memories of 1977 come from the way their hearts were broken, first by their experiences in the UK, and then by their own breakup.

Certainly, Bailey had been exuberant about the group's likely success in early 1977, telling *Juke*: 'Sure, we'll appear on TV, the pop programs could be better, but we still love them, if they want us we'll be there to play for them. I personally love pop shows. We want the kids to see us.'[84] Pop hits were a goal, though Bailey's dry humour was often easy to misunderstand: that same year he claimed a fondness for John Paul Young because of Young's hormonal pull: 'lots of little girls have wet dreams over him and "the more sex in the world the better."'[85] However, the group ruled out compromise in pursuit of fame; their rejection of the 'Saints suit' designed for them by EMI UK, for example may have spelled the beginning of a long, drawn-out end to the relationship between label and band. The Saints didn't *look* like punks (nor did Radio Birdman): Bailey refused to get his hair cut 'or all the superficial trappings. Because it's pointless. That would be selling out.'[86] Yet success was Bailey's professed goal: 'The Saints are the Saints,' he told *Juke* in May 1977. 'If our records don't eventually make it big then this version of the Saints will probably cease to exist, break up.'[87] Twenty years later, in an interview with Steve Gardner, Bailey spoke of Kuepper and England in the same breath:

> I think he [Kuepper] expected us to be lauded as the sort of Lennon and McCartney of this new wave thing, and we were actually viewed as some kind of Australian joke. Because the English are very xenophobic and in those days Australia was viewed as the poor cousins.'[88]

The first two Saints albums are both flawed masterpieces, but in different ways (it might also be that the flaws make them even greater masterpieces – if only such a thing were possible). *(I'm) Stranded* is great songs played straight; it's something that had to be done as a launching pad for the group's career. *Eternally Yours* sees Bailey and Kuepper on a two-headed campaign against capitalism and consumerism, alongside crass nonsense like the anti-ocker 'Orstralia' (which these days comes across as trying to pander to British prejudice) and the utterly throwaway 'International Robots', neither of which should have made it onto a record. Kuepper and Bailey had stopped writing together by this time.[89] Most of the UK press, having feted the band in '76, hated them in '77: one review proclaimed: 'They sound like a very poor copy of the Ramones, with none of that band's virtues. They are between the old and new wave.'[90] The first statement was, of course, a historical impossibility, somewhat like saying the Beatles sounded like a copy of the Monkees, and also flagrantly untrue; the second was a badge of honour.

The third album, the decidedly flawless masterpiece *Prehistoric Sounds*, was Kuepper's baby. The band had failed to make it big and had, essentially, ceased to exist. But there was still a contractual obligation to EMI, so Kuepper wrote an album and persuaded a reluctant Bailey to sing on it. The title was superbly ironic; the Saints were perpetually irritated by punk's Year Zero approach (just as, perhaps, the Pelaco Brothers had been bothered by prog rock's ahistorical futurism, which denied Australian society, culture and background). *Prehistoric Sounds* is a miraculous snipe at everyone, starting with 'Swing for the Crime'; the song utilised horns in a far more sophisticated way than the singles from *Eternally Yours* had done.[91] The musicians sound gleeful at their break with punk tradition, as well they might. For no sensible reason (except perhaps as a statement of intent, although a punky reworking of an older song was hardly a new idea) EMI chose to release as a single their cover of Otis Redding's 'Security'. Oddly, this same song had been a well-publicised single for Jo Jo Zep and the Falcons eighteen months earlier in Australia; their version is the track preceding '(I'm) Stranded)' on EMI's *Devastator* compilation. A number of tracks on *Prehistoric Sounds* revisit the history of rock and roll: 'Save Me', for instance, is 'Jailbreak' crossed with 'Gloria'. 'Everything's Fine' sounds like Kuepper's recorded singing debut but, he says, it's actually 'Chris ... doing a good impersonation of my demo cassette recording.'

Bailey later claimed that parts of *Prehistoric Sounds* 'just went totally over my head. I guess it sounds stiff, or stilted, is the expression I have for that record ... it's very easy to tell that within a few months the whole thing is going to fall to pieces.'[92] In fact, it already had, although the band did subsequently record demos – a Kuepper song, 'Laughing Clowns', and a Bailey song – for the King Crimson-associated EG label, which was then being revived. The demos led nowhere. Kuepper returned to Australia early in 1979 and Bailey put together a new Saints line-up, whose sound, ironically, was a far more comfortable fit with the poppier elements of *Prehistoric Sounds* than with anything on *Eternally Yours*.

Kuepper has often expressed his disappointment that the Saints ended up looking to many people like also-rans rather than innovators. But perhaps he has cause to be grateful that the Saints had the punk movement to hitch a ride on, because his next move – his most inspired – was nowhere near as well received. The Laughing Clowns may have been the most misunderstood group of the post-punk era; they were surely the most brilliant.

If rock music is important enough to write books about, it is ludicrous that no-one has written a book about the Saints, especially when one considers the hack nonsense that has been peddled over and over again about Nick Cave or Michael Hutchence, for instance. The Ramones and the New York Dolls have been overanalysed in a series of egotistical and one-eyed studies, while Pere Ubu have forever been placed in the "too hard" category (also known as the "too-good" category). Fortunately, Radio Birdman are the subject of a undeniably excellent book by academic and art historian Vivien Johnson, who does not let two potentially fatal issues – she was an ardent follower of the band in their heyday, mixing with them socially, and she remains an almost entirely uncritical fan of their music – cloud her judgment in chronicling them. Her work renders an extensive account of the band superfluous here, although Radio Birdman's story has continued beyond Johnson's narrative, published in 1991, and on into the 21st century.

WHEN THE BIRDMEN FLEW

We have already seen the genesis of Radio Birdman in early 70s Sydney. Like the Saints, they pieced together an approach that avoided what they saw as the wasteful and decadent trappings of mainstream rock practice. Both bands were led by dedicated ascetics with a sense of history and each commanded a loyal fanbase. Chris Bailey said of Radio Birdman in 1977 that the Saints 'like a lot of their songs, but they're influenced by American 60s bands like the Stooges and the MC5 . . . Above all, we're Australian. Radio Birdman have an American and a Canadian in the band, so they're more American in feel and message . . . we're a high energy Australian rock band.'[93]

Johnson defends Radio Birdman against this perception of the band as 'copyists and colonists of a particular brand of American music', dismissing it as 'a predictable element in the mutual goading which audiences and performers engaged in at their gigs.'[94] She accepts it was an element of the band's music and approach, but claims that 'Radio Birdman took this tradition of rock and roll borrowing and turned it into a post-modernist strategy of plundering rock history for lyric and aural inspiration.'[95]

The Rats, TV Jones, and others from their small but dedicated Sydney scene have already been mentioned in chapter 7. Birdman vocalist Rob Younger, bassist Carl Rourke and drummer Ron Keeley had all been members of the Rats; guitarist Deniz Tek was a medical student from Ann Arbor, studying at the University of New South Wales, and had previously played in TV Jones. He and fellow medical student and keyboard player Pip Hoyle joined up with Younger, Keeley and Rourke in late 1974; Rourke was soon replaced by Warwick Gilbert, another former Rat. Two years later, Chris Masuak joined, initially as a replacement for Hoyle, although the latter rejoined in early 1978. Tek wrote the bulk of the group's material but there is little doubt that, as is the case with Cold Chisel, it's not the songs but the 'classic' line-up which provided the heart and soul of the band.

The group's rise to infamy in the days just before punk is well-known, at least in Australia. As Johnson relates, it was Lou Reed who laid the foundation for the group's renown in early 1975:

> [Reed] responded to Deniz Tek's gift of a Radio Birdman t-shirt at his pre-dawn press conference at Sydney airport for a 1975 tour with the line, 'I was in a local band once', and a promise to come and see them play that night. The manager of the Oxford Tavern in inner Sydney Darlinghurst gave them a gig on the strength of it. Lou Reed didn't show, but a packed house of local punters who had heard the story by word of mouth during the day did, and the band became regulars at the Oxford.[96]

The venue, once known as the hangout for Tully in the early 70s,[97] later became the Oxford Funhouse, and a mobilizing point for Radio Birdman followers.

Andy 'Mort' Bradley, Radio Birdman associate, journalist and sound technician, remembers their audiences as 'kids who were on the dole, who had no idea what they were going to do with their lives.' He told Ken Shimamoto:

> They either had terrible jobs and were working for minimum wage, or they had no jobs at all and were living on the dole, and they would relieve their hostilities by going to Birdman. All these angry kids ... Birdman would just engulf them in their blitzkrieg of music, and by the end of the night, the kids would leave with smiles on their faces. All the pent-up hostility from having no life ... the band were actually like their psychiatrists! The kids were able to let off all their excess energy and all their hostility by dancing up a sweaty storm. It was pretty amazing to watch.[98]

Johnson claims that Radio Birdman's militarism is overstated in most commentary;[99] it is certainly excessively imaginative, for instance, to interpret the logos and posters Warwick Gilbert created for the group as somehow "fascist." Some years after they disbanded, Peter Williams, of pop band the Particles, was still declaring himself disgusted by the Radio Birdman phenomenon, claiming that '100s of idiotic sheep going "Yeh hup, yey hup" at Birdman concerts' proved 'how easily people can be manipulated without any thought whatsoever.'[100] But the 'Yeah hup' catchcry was essentially surreal humour, and Birdmania – which was after all limited to a few thousand Australians – was hardly the Kiss Army, let alone the Hitler Youth. Tek's 'New Race' had nothing to do with eugenics and everything to do with providing an anthemic rallying cry for teenagers.[101] Just as country singer/comedian Chad Morgan's yodel was based on the wolf howl in a Tex Avery animated cartoon,[102] Radio Birdman – via the American Tek – took one key element from fluid, earthy Americana: he claimed that 'Yeah Hup' came from the archetypal bongo-playing 50s beatnik in a great R. Crumb comic.'[103] Detroit had produced a car of 'abnormal power', the Hupmobile, before the Second World War; it had been available in Australia in the early 20th century.[104] Radio Birdman were not opposed to jokes, after all: they had their own closed-shop, oblique humour, exemplified when Tek talked Rob Younger into wearing a clown suit for a major show.[105]

Though their rise was hardly swift – and, commercially speaking, not really much of a rise at all; like their competitors the Saints, they did not have any mainstream hits – Radio Birdman did gain validity in the local scene through the mid 70s. Within 18 months, the group were regularly appearing on television: an ABC program called *Rockturnal* filmed them doing five songs, for instance, and 'Channel 9 also did a series of interviews and allowed the band to choose some fave film clips for their *Rock-On-Sunday* programme.'[106] As with the Saints, the suggestion that Radio Birdman were ignored by the Australian media is essentially a fabrication, though it is certainly true they did not receive the attention their later legend might seem to have warranted.

Not unnaturally, by 1976-77 Radio Birdman began to be regarded by many as a punk group, a notion that was debated in a number of ways – whether they were, whether they weren't, whether describing them as such was a compliment or not. In October 1977 Andy Bradley wrote in *Juke* that a Radio Birdman show he'd seen had to his mind quashed 'the punk label that had been attached to their music. They proved once and for all during their performances that they weren't punks but tough rock and rollers.'[107] A bigger problem for the band – as remarkable as it might seem today – was the revelation by *RAM's* Anthony O'Grady in March 1978 that Tek, as a medical student, had no intention of becoming a professional musician. Radio Birdman were thus in O'Grady's eyes a 'part-time' band, and this status carried a negative connotation.[108] Tek's *real* career would later cause the group further problems, when their US record company Sire tried to insist he quit medicine and, additionally, sack the band's manager, George Kringas, who was essentially a member of the group.[109]

Ignoring interest from the industry – specifically, Michael Gudinski at Mushroom and Hush's manager Peter Rix[110] – Radio Birdman released an independent EP, *Burn My Eye*, which was sold via mail order. Recording at Trafalgar Studios in Sydney, they were signed by the studio to its label. Trafalgar was diverse and not particularly progressive: Radio Birdman were part of a roster that included the Ray Burton Band (as well as co-writing 'I Am Woman' with Helen Reddy, Burton had created the grotesque 'Love Gun' for Doug Parkinson, and his band opened for Queen in 1976);[111] Chariot, featuring Dennis Wilson, formerly of Kahvas Jute; and Barry Leef,[112] previously of Bakery and almost (but not quite) a member of the Mothers of Invention.[113] The first Radio Birdman album, *Radios Appear*, was released on Trafalgar in June 1977 and licensed to WEA. Eight months later, an album with a similar track listing (some remixes, some re-recorded songs, some new tracks but the same title) was issued by Sire in the US and UK. In early 1978 Radio Birdman flew to the UK to tour and record a second album, *Living Eyes*, which was released three years after their demise. It suffered the ignominy of having the same title as the Bee Gees' album of that year – or the other way around, depending on your perspective.

Like the Saints, Radio Birdman did not confirm to British ideas of a proper punk rock group, which was all anyone in the UK seemed to be interested in at the time. It would hardly have mattered in any case, because they were Australian – a good enough reason, as far as many were concerned, to dismiss them out of hand: one example quoted, unsourced, by Johnson refers to their music as 'Wallaby rock and its [sic] worse than the Godawful Saints'.[114] Hoyle's explanation for the group's lack of impact is straightforward, at least in relation to Britain as it was in the late 70s: 'There's a basic hatred of Australians in England. And if there's one thing they hate more than Australians, it's Americans. 'Cos we're rich.'[115]

When Radio Birdman split in Britain in June 1978, its members were already legends. As early as July 1979 they were offered $3000 each to play three shows; they refused,[116] and did not reappear for almost twenty years.

EVOLUTION/EXPLOITATION

Two compilation albums released within 18 months of one another reveal the complex transitions and contradictions of the late 70s period. *Long Live the Evolution* was a promotional record, not for general consumption or sale; copies made their way into the public's hands as free gifts to those who bought any Australian album at certain stores. *Lethal Weapons*, on the other hand, was a genuine sales proposition, although it probably shouldn't have been, and it was then re-released (twice), just to compound the problem of its existence.

Long Live the Evolution was produced by 2JJ, the ABC's 'youth' AM radio station, which was at that point based solely in Sydney. JJ had been formulated by the ABC under the Whitlam government, in response to the concern that pop radio stations were owned and managed by conservative forces which discriminated against both the left and minority interests.[117] Other stations, such as Brisbane's public radio broadcaster 4ZZ, were given licenses at the same time (always an FM station, ZZ became ZZZ or 'Triple Zed' in 1976).[118] This was a time when the 'democratisation of radio' (and the media generally) was seen as key to creating a progressive society.[119] The Whitlam government had lowered the voting age from 21 to 18; it pragmatically saw younger voters as an important part of Labor's support base, but many also sincerely believed in the value of democratic engagement by all sectors of society.

JJ's culture had various sources, including Chris Winter's early-70s ABC Radio 1 show *Room to Move*, and the RAM (Radio Action Movement – unconnected to *Rock Australia Magazine*), an ABC lobby group hoping to utilise the ABC's new FM transmissions in part at least for rock music; Winter was also a member of this group. Winter had dropped out of a university course in electrical engineering when he became involved in amateur drama; he became a soundman on *Hair* and *Jesus Christ Superstar*.[120] Unusually for the time, his show had featured whole album sides, and Winter was a laidback presenter. His producer on *Room to Move*, Ron Moss, became an early co-ordinator at JJ and Winter was a natural announcer for the station (though he was still performing as, for instance, a 'hippy dishwasher' in the TV drama series *Matlock Police*).

Opening on 19 January 1975 with the (ostensibly banned) Skyhooks song 'You Just Like Me 'Cos I'm Good in Bed', JJ soon commanded 22 percent of its target audience, much of it in Sydney's western suburbs,[121] part of Labor's heartland. In addition to playing music – much of it Australian and alternative – it was a launching pad for radical documentary, humour and drama programs. Other material was provided by Graeme Bond and Rory O'Donoghue (from *The Aunty Jack Show*) and Pip Proud, who created the science fiction *Vlort Phlitson* as a regular serial for the station: Harry Johnson wrote after Proud's death that he:

> had the pleasure of producing Pip's wonderful *Vlort Phlitson* on 2JJ. Vlort Phlitson was actually a play on words ... "A thought flits on" and was narrated by a Sydney composer known by the name Peter Thin. Vlort was broadcast on Sunday night's on 2JJ, and is probably the best example of Pip's mid-career writing.[122]

JJ's staff saw the station as self-renewing: Marius Webb believed the appropriate turnover time for staff was two years.[123] In 1977, consolidating its credentials as a home of vibrant Australian music, JJ (as Double Jay) produced the *Long Live the Evolution* album, featuring live performances recorded at various concerts and occasional in-studio appearances. That such an impressive selection of bands could be persuaded to contribute to the album is testament to JJ's high reputation even at this early stage of its existence and to the need it was filling,[124] although it also engaged in what from a 21st century viewpoint seem like less enlightened initiatives such as 'Squeeze a Bosom Day'.[125] It should be emphasised that stations like JJ and its later FM equivalent JJJ are not regarded as community radio stations; they are part of the Australian Broadcasting Corporation and are therefore primarily funded by taxpayers – as the ABC's listeners *and* its detractors never tire of pointing out in a way they don't often point out about, for instance, roadbuilding. Community radio,

on the other hand, is sponsored by subscribers and businesses, allowing listeners a strong stakeholder sense. JJ had a Melbourne counterpart, 3ZZ, which was a free-access station focused on ethnic diversity rather than youth and was nipped in the bud by the Liberal government in 1977, ostensibly for budget reasons.

Long Live the Evolution's sleeve notes claimed that JJ had 'dived headlong into the stagnant pool of Australian radio and tried, with varying degrees of success, to stir the water a bit for a while, to continue the metaphor, to avoid drowning.'[126] It also claimed that JJ had 'a lot of faith in Australian music, not just as a commercial product (good luck, get rich on it if you can) but as a continuing and developing part of all our lives.'[127] This was a relatively radical statement of intent for the time. What is perhaps more striking is the seamless nature of an album which might be seen by some as sounding the death knell for the old wave in the face of the new (as represented by Radio Birdman, whose 'Burn My Eye' – side 2, track 4 – sits between Tomlin's '65 Directory' and Feather's 'Free and Easy'. Skyhooks' 'Party to End All Parties' and AC/DC's 'Dirty Deeds Done Dirt Cheap' start off the two sides: each band is at its peak. Dragon's 'Blacktown Boogie' is also present. Jo Jo Zep and the Falcons, who would soon be seen to fit in perfectly alongside other pub rock/guitar pop luminaries such as the Sports as the acceptable face of the new wave, were also represented, in their earliest incarnations. Ariel, Mike Rudd's post-Spectrum group, and Finch, the band which would soon provide Skyhooks with a replacement for Red Symons in Bob Spencer, were included, along with a very souped-up Jeff St John and the only artist of them all who could be relied on not to launch into a boogie at any minute, Renée Geyer.[128]

The album was packaged to present these groups – some of them chart-toppers, others barely known – as a multi-faceted representation of a high-standard 'local' music scene. In that regard, it definitely succeeds; it also reveals as a myth the idea that pre-new wave Australian music was merely a lot of posturing, soloing and songs about Mama. Of course, Mama had a role to play (Coloured Balls, in particular, had favoured her), but she was not the whole story.

JJ would later grow into the JJJ 'youth network', with effects both positive and negative, but its spread across the entire country was over a decade away, even if transmitter quirks meant JJ could be picked up in parts of Tasmania and northern NSW in its early days.[129] Its development into a national station took long enough that each capital established strong community radio stations of its own, as did some smaller cities.

For a number of reasons, FM initially came to be aligned with esoteric rock music. Its signal was more limited than AM, but of a higher quality. 'FM suffers with far less interference from the weather and power sources', wrote Jules Lewicki in *On Dit*, adding that it 'provides as good a reproduction of sound as you would find in all but the most expensive players ... and for technical reasons unknown to me FM radio can broadcast in stereo ... Pop can hardly wait.'[130] There were many who were excited about public, as opposed to government-sponsored, radio. It was mooted as ideal for the '"experimental broadcaster"', who, as pioneering radio figure Peter Pockley predicted in 1974,

> would have the opportunity to do all kinds of creative things with sound – who experiments with form and style, who tries to extend the range of both the medium itself and the imagination of the listener ... The 'student or underground broadcaster', who unfortunately can't burrow too far underground given our restrictive libel laws but nonetheless will still have a channel of communication which we embryonically arthritic types might never touch.[131]

In almost all cases, these stations would come to be aligned with educational institutions (usually universities). Adelaide was an innovator in 1972 with 5UV (later Radio Adelaide), joined in 1979 by a new 'progressive music station', 5MMM (later 5DDD, after the commercial MMM network bought its name), which held a studio-warming in its ex-funeral parlour premises in Stepney.[132] Perth had the highly successful 6UWA (later UVS and then RTR); as mentioned, Brisbane had the radical and influential 4ZZZ from December 1975.[133] JJ in Sydney was joined by 2SER and the University of Sydney had its own, limited range, 2RSR. But it was in Melbourne – Australia's second large city but the one without the ABC's 'youth radio' patronage – that public radio really came into its own. The city gave rise to three public radio stations in addition to the original FM classical music station 3MBS: first came 3CR (like JJ, created by government decree just before Whitlam was deposed, but not government funded);[134] then 3PBS ('public broadcasting', dedicated primarily to minority/specialist music), and, most importantly for this history, 3RRR-FM. The 'RRR' (standing for reading, 'riting and 'rithmetic) indicated the station's original educational license, and the station was to make a magnificent impact on Melbourne once it moved on from its humble origins as 3RMT-FM[135] under the brief directorship of John Duigan, who was about to become one of Australia's best film directors.[136]

Although it came out two years later in 1978, *Lethal Weapons* is in many respects a parallel universe compilation to *Long Live the Evolution*. While not a RRR-initiated release,[137] it featured many groups (and groups containing people who would go on to form other groups) that would be championed by the station. RRR and Melbourne scenesters (though they would hate that label) such as Tch Tch Tch, or Clinton Walker and Bruce Milne and their zine *Pulp*, or the university newspapers, were already creating a myth around some of the acts, most notably the Boys Next Door but also Teenage Radio Stars and Jab, whose members went on to other more interesting things, often revolving around the Models. Milne (in partnership with Philip Morland) was planning to start his Au Go Go label, their intention being to release records by bands like the Babeez (they were soon to change their name to News) and Boys Next Door,[138] only to find himself effectively trumped by Barry Earl and Michael Gudinski's Suicide label. Earl had been a music industry stalwart in the early 70s, and the manager of Wendy Saddington, the Cleves and Spectrum; he and Gudinski's Mushroom Records now set up a 'new wave' record label that would be distributed by RCA (thus showing Mushroom's usual distributor, Festival, that it was not indispensable). Suicide, which boasted it was 'revving towards tomorrow today', would actually only ever manage one LP release, *Lethal Weapons*, but, as Bruce Milne told *Roadrunner's* Ross Stapleton the following year, the short-lived label had one indelible effect: it 'managed to split the punk scene down the middle.'[139]

Most of the groups involved with Suicide (Wasted Daze, X-Ray-Z, the Negatives and the Survivors were the others) seem to have come to regret it. The label's idea of assigning old rockers – "old" meaning in their late 20s if not early 30s – to produce the young upstarts didn't work out too well. It's unclear if this was intended as a mentoring system of some sort or was merely a manifestation of Suicide's fear of what young nihilists might produce if left to their own devices. Wasted Daze were hardly upstarts anyway; they had pedigrees stretching back to the early 70s. Greg Macainsh's production of the Boys Next Door's 'These Boots Are Made for Walking' – a pallid rendition of a live favourite, with roots in 70s pub rock, a 'punked-up' second verse, and a rave-up ending – is a bad impression of X-Ray Spex's 'Oh Bondage, Up Yours'. Another of the band's three songs on the album, 'Boy Hero', can be placed next to early Models to reveal common attitudes and approaches between these two groups, though by the time the Boys Next Door shared a giveaway single with the Models in 1979 the similarities were nowhere near as obvious.

Chris Walsh was – notoriously (perhaps apocryphally) – the first person in Melbourne to have a copy of *Never Mind the Bollocks*. For many this would be enough to give him a place in Australian new wave history, but his legacy is far more important: he left his simple but powerful stamp on several of the most interesting bands of the late 70s and early 80s. His involvement in the Negatives, together with Garry Gray, led to one track on *Lethal Weapons*, though the Negatives were almost certainly worth more than that. Their contribution, 'Planet on the Prowl', was produced by Eric Gradman, who added his own violin track to it without the group's permission; Gradman was an old school friend of Gudinski's and had introduced Gudinski to the music of Cream and Frank Zappa back at Melbourne High; he had also played in the Sharks with Joe Camilleri.[140] Walsh's connection to the Moodists (explored in greater detail in chapter 15) made them probably the best band of their Melbourne cohort – more musically adventurous than the Birthday Party, more dynamic than the leftover pub rockers, and far more consistent than soon-to-be-pop groups like Models. He was also – quite plainly to anyone who might care to compare them – a big influence on Hunters and Collectors in their 1981-83 incarnation: to give just one example, their first single proper, 'Talking to a Stranger', took everything the Moodists did (minus the singing, song structure and drumming style) and added extraneous percussion and other noises. This is not to say that Walsh should be held in any way responsible for the musical crimes committed either by Hunters and Collectors or the compilers of *Lethal Weapons*.

The packaging of *Lethal Weapons* effectively denied the bands their individuality; the track listing was separated from the bands' names, so it required detective work to match the songs to the artists. As if to accentuate their irrelevance in the scheme of things, the bands' photographs on the sleeve don't match the listed line-ups. The front cover is a cartoony drawing of a pistol with blood coming out of it, presumably referencing the label's name, but it makes no sense (the suicide of a gun?).

In his autobiography, James Freud freely admits that the Teenage Radio Stars' song 'Wanna Be Your Baby' was essentially a rewrite of the Vibrators' 'Baby Baby'; he also claims that producer Les Karski, onetime member of British group Supercharge (and soon to be the producer of the Models' second single 'Owe You Nothing'), played many of the group's parts on the recording.[141] The best song on the scrappy collection is undoubtedly X-Ray-Z's 'Three More Glorious Years', an anthemic protest against the 'puritan and Liberal rule' of the Fraser government and a beautiful melding of old-school activism and Saintsy drive.[142] As if to drive home the lesson of *Long Live the Evolution*, X-Ray-Z were a pre-punk band reconfigured for punk; they had previously been an Adelaide group, 'quite arty in its own little way',[143] known as Rufus Red.[144]

One of the most extraordinary aspects of the *Lethal Weapons* story is that Mushroom's 'alternative' White Label saw fit to reissue it five years later, presumably in acknowledgment of the compilation's status as a punk milestone by a label at the vanguard of Australian postpunk. Its reissue was made plausible by the involvement of the Boys Next Door, who by then had evolved into the much higher-profile Birthday Party; it could certainly not have been due to the record's intrinsic worth, for which it would be hard to mount any kind of case. The groups involved all but disappeared, though many key players had an impact with subsequent work. Freud allowed Barry Earl to fold him into another band, Colt, to form a new group, the Radio Stars,[145] with a view to traveling to England. Like much of Freud's career, what followed was a debacle that showed he had learnt nothing; it is examined in chapter 16.

The punk experience was replicated everywhere and, as mentioned, it combined spontaneous enthusiasm sparked by awareness of the international movement. Many punks in Australia read about punk in foreign magazines and imagined what it was like – even tried to replicate it – without actually having heard it. Of course, the imagined version was frequently better than the real thing, and usually blended well with it. Groups like Melbourne's the Virgins were, by all reports, too extreme for venues and allegedly banned from the three 'main alternative' clubs on the same day.[146] Like Lipp and the Double Decker Bros five years earlier, they appear to have left no recordings.

In 1976, the ABC-TV show *Weekend Magazine* – unusually for a cosy, newsreel-style Sunday evening program – presented a report on the Sex Pistols. Many young Australians, some of them already playing aggressive, simple music in makeshift groups, now saw the punk movement as a worldwide phenomenon. The Triffids' David McComb, for instance, was introduced to the idea of provocative, punky music for the first time via this one, brief, Sunday night report.

Perth already had a microscopic punk scene. A group posthumously named the Geeks (another mooted name was the Victims or the Cancer Victims), with a line-up that settled down as Ross Buncle on guitar, Lloyd P. as vocalist, Dave Cardwell on bass and James Baker on drums, were rehearsing in a scout hall in the Perth suburb of Wembley in 1977. Their first original song was 'I Like Iggy Pop'; the lyrics (by Baker) included 'I hate marijuana pendants, I hate disco junkies', with the title as the chorus. Other songs included 'I'm Flipped Out Over You', 'I Wanna Be Slick And Pick Up Chicks Like You', 'Disco Junkies' and 'High School Girls'. Baker had international punk rock experience: amongst other things, he had auditioned for the Clash in November 1976 ('But I failed'). He had also met and befriended Sid Vicious on a Chelsea bus.[147]

In 2005, writing on his website, perthpunk.com, Buncle recalled that 'James's lyrics were unique, often wistful, his observations witty and quirky, adolescent rather than tough-guy-punk, the musically simple choruses inbuilt with intuitive lyrical hooks'.[148] Baker already had experience drumming in local group the Slick City Boys, who were reputedly campy and aggressive – they antagonised audiences with extended versions of 'Louie Louie'. His father worked for the railways, and Baker himself worked as a clerk at the ABC, but he dressed and carried himself like someone from another time and place. The Geeks, though bolstered by a love for punk rock from the US Northeast, defined their own course early on. Rod Radalj, who was subsequently an early member of the Hoodoo Gurus (as was Baker), soon became a fellow traveler, and Baker made the acquaintance of Dave Faulkner (aka Dave Flick), who was playing at the time with the Beagle Boys, a local blues group which had emerged from the band Sid Rumpo.

The Cheap Nasties, who came together in 1976, performed their first show in front of a backdrop featuring a drawing of Nana Mouskouri (the Greek pop singer well-loved in Australia by an older generation), which they slashed as a finale.[149] The group had been formed by Kim Salmon and fellow art students, including guitarist Neil Fernandez, from the West Australian Institute of Technology's Faculty of Fine Art. Decades later Salmon recalled Perth at this time as harbouring 'a huge inferiority complex about what was referred to as the 'Eastern States': i.e. not some hierarchy of levels of enlightenment, but all that was to the east, in fact, everywhere in Australia!'

Faulkner had first spoken to Baker because he saw him wearing a Ramones t-shirt, and 'thought he might know something about music'.[150] The two soon became friends. Baker and Cardwell quit the Geeks – after Baker had unsuccessfully attempted to induct his new friend into the group – and, with Faulkner, they formed the Victims. Their first show was a party at their share house (their version of Club '76), Victim Manor, the bulk of their set comprised of Geeks songs that Baker had written with Buncle. This haphazard plagiarism was only resolved to everyone's satisfaction thirty years after the fact. It seems to be universally agreed that the Victims' best song was a genuine Baker-Faulkner composition, 'Television Addict', which the Victims released as a single, its recording and pressing paid for by a zealous fan. The group was 'primitive in the worst sense of the word', according to Lloyd P: 'Flick deliberately played the cheapest and shittiest-sounding guitar he could find'.[151] That said, the Victims were sufficiently 'together' to make records, and those show that they could also be primitive in the *best* sense of the word.

Kim Salmon quit the Cheap Nasties at the end of the following year to join another band, the Exterminators – who quickly became the Invaders – with Rod Radalj and Boris Sujdovic. They then became the Scientists (the name was a joke against education) in 1978, when Baker joined them on drums. Meanwhile the Cheap Nasties metamorphosed into the Veneers and then became the Manikins.[152] All these bands faced the problem of being ghettoised in the one venue that would accept them, a jazz club known as Hernando's Hideaway. 'The problem,' according to one unidentified Manikin interviewed for the UWA paper *Pelican*, 'was initially that the punk scene in Perth was a real clique.'[153] Faulkner briefly played in the Manikins with Fernandez and

then in Midget and the Farrellys; Bernard 'Midget' Farrelly was an internationally famous Sydney-born surfer of the 1960s. This was a group which attempted to appeal to multiple 'scenes': 'Dave kept up their credibility as a punk band,' according to the Manikins, 'then someone would change a guitar for a dulcimer to keep the hippies in, and so on through the whole range of surfies et al.'[154]

The Scientists' first single was 'Frantic Romantic', issued in 1979; they followed it with a self-titled EP in 1980, which they promoted with an eastern states tour that saw them invited to perform on *Countdown* (playing 'Last Night' from the EP). They played fast, simple, quirky 'teenage' songs; live, they covered the Undertones' 'Teenage Kicks'. Adrian Ryan, reviewing them in *Juke*, discerned in them 'the priceless quality of a genuine feel for teenage dance music.'[155]

Salmon would entirely revamp the group in the early 80s (he later claimed that the first Scientists was 'really James's direction')[156] and, like Faulkner, would travel east to make a further impact in Australia. The first incarnation of the group released a posthumous album that was funded by Kim Williams and Rob Samson and, according to Salmon, riddled with 'a million overdubs... and things that were all misunderstood.'[157] A decade on he recalled that 'We had a song called "Baby, You're Not For Sale"... an exercise in melodic noise, very hypnotic; we'd play these two chords with rising amounts of feedback towards the end, and it would finish with this big destruction.'[158]

The case of Dave Faulkner, in particular, demonstrates how difficult it is to characterize anyone as *hitching a ride* on punk rock. There was no guarantee, when 'Dave Flick' formed the Victims with James Baker, that this was the music of the future – although, as things turned out, it (or a watered-down version of it) arguably *was*. There was no guarantee that punk, new wave or anything similar would be anything more than a damp squib. Similarly, other bands, such as Midnight Oil or the Angels, who seemingly aligned themselves with some permutation of 'punk attitude', were at best hedging their bets, tapping into the mood of the moment, 'selling out', or expressing themselves, depending on who you consult.

In Perth, it would seem that it was all about boys (some would say it still is, everywhere): Beagle Boys, Slick City Boys, or Pus's fanbase, the Bori Boys. The name of Perth's biggest group of 1978, Boys, boiled this down to its essence. Boys began playing at Hernando's Hideaway in 1978, then packed larger venues such as the Shenton Park and the Civic. Singer Brent Lucanus reminisced seven years later that the group's 'only ambition was to become Perth's top band.' This was sealed when the evocatively named Paul McCarthy became the group's songwriter; McCarthy provided a hit single in Western Australia (and a minor hit nationally) with 'When You're Lonely' in 1980. The group's sound was power pop pure and simple, and though they lacked the quirkiness that Jeremy Oxley imparted to an east-coast 'boy band', the Sunnyboys, at around this time, Boys had no problem delivering pop-rock in a classic melodic vein. Lucanus was replaced by Wayne Green and the group moved to Sydney ('the capital of rock in Australia', according to Green). Thrown off a tour supporting Iron Maiden after three east coast shows for being 'new wave',[159] Boys split in early 1983, four months after releasing their second album, *In the Cage*.[160] Their story – biggest band in Perth tries their luck nationally only to be wrecked on the eastern seaboard – is a common one; their fate was replicated to some degree, for instance, by V Capri in the mid 80s.[161] This has perhaps happened less often since the rise of JJJ in the early 90s – Jebediah, the Sleepy Jackson, and San Cisco are merely three more recent groups who have benefited from the national station's inclination to give Perth groups, or at least the ones that JJJ finds appealing, a hotline to the mainstream. Perth's capacity in the late 20th century for growing bands that become too big for its audiences and then have to try their luck in the wider Australasian market make it similar in some ways to New Zealand; it is also, of course, a microcosm of Australasia's position within the international scene.

OILS

Art-rock, punk, and straight-ahead riff rock were combined by groups like Midnight Oil and the Angels. Midnight Oil's singer, Peter Garrett, had performed with an experimental electronic group called Devil's Breakfast in the early 70s in Canberra, while at the same time his future bandmates were playing on Sydney's northern beaches as the progressive group Farm.[162]

Garrett, born in 1953, claimed he had researched the role of rock star while he was studying law at ANU. This research included a trip to Sydney Showgrounds to see Rod Stewart 'fall out of a helicopter ... full of champagne and make a mess of himself',[163] an event which might have inspired many to follow in Stewart's footsteps, but motivated Garrett to take a different direction.

Midnight Oil – named by a briefly serving member and fusing beautifully the notions of work ethic, combustion and after-hours activity – came together as Jim Moginie on guitar, Rob Hirst on drums, Andrew James on bass and Garrett as vocalist (another guitarist, Martin Rotsey, joined in 1977); their music blended committed, even strident, left-wing politics, beefy guitar lines and singalong choruses. A 1977 review in *Juke* commented on the result:

> Midnight Oil don't appear to fit into any particular category. They're not your standard rock outfit like Finch or Feather, nor are they eccentric in the Mother Goose, Split Enz style, and neither are they punks, but New Wave in the true sense of the word, a unique and very original band ... truly original Australian Rock & Roll.[164]

When it came to musical differences Midnight Oil had it all, as far as drummer, songwriter and co-founder Rob Hirst was concerned: 'I don't like the singer's taste', he told Toby Creswell in 1980, 'and he doesn't like mine, and I hate the guitarist's. You're really putting together people who don't get on socially or musically.'[165]

Midnight Oil's early records, particularly their 1978 self-titled first album, its 1979 follow-up, *Head Injuries,* and the 1980 EP *Bird Noises,* predate their realisation that they had international ambitions, and served chiefly to establish their reputation as an exceptional live group in Sydney and then nationally. Even Sydney was too big a territory for them in their early days: they stayed mainly in the northern suburbs, Tully's home turf five years before, and were not an inner-city group, initially to their detriment. There is some similarity between Midnight Oil and Radio Birdman: both had putatively indie status (Midnight Oil's label was Powderworks, a successful independent with distribution relationships with majors), simple but effective imagery, and an unwillingness to compromise. It's an even bet that the two groups shared a fanbase in Midnight Oil's early days.

Almost two decades later, Garrett described the formative years of Midnight Oil in terms of 'loading black boxes into the back of vans, pasting your own posters, putting on your own shows, making a bond and building it with your audiences, learning by trial and error all of those aspects of what it takes to be a rock band not on the dole – contracts, promos, songwriting, sound and lights, cheap hotels, the Hume Highway, agencies' commissions, crappy recording contracts and indifferent radio.'[166]

Cold Chisel's Don Walker claims that his band 'despised the kind of success that Little River Band and Sherbet were having';[167] Midnight Oil despised LRB mostly for their irrelevance to the Australian condition. (Perhaps it was the pursuit of intangible dreams of relevance and integrity which led Garrett to participate in a ceremonial disco inferno – actually setting fire to a pile of records – at the Sydney suburb of Castle Hill in September 1979.[168]) In the mid 80s Garrett praised Skyhooks for 'using Australian references at a time when no one else did' and said that in their early incarnation Midnight Oil 'were more willfully Australian because there were so many other Australian groups, like Little River Band, who sang about America.'[169] Similarly Hirst has claimed that Greg Macainsh 'made it possible for you to write about, in his case, Carlton or Balwyn ... And then we've got this whole palette of Australian places we can use without a cringe factor.'[170]

So Midnight Oil's early songs were about surfing, the suburbs and public transport; their debut album blends this lyrical approach with hard rock that is sometimes closer to head rock. 'Surfing with a Spoon' – a song about working in an office but thinking about the beach, and probably the best track on the album – combines all the dynamics of, say, Kahvas Jute with the canny riffing of (for instance) Tully. *Head Injuries,* however, is the product of its exhilarating times (1979) and while it is by no means a punk or even a new wave record – Midnight Oil were always outside those kinds of movements and, frankly, not cool enough in the standard sense – it would have sat happily next to records by, say, the Clash or Stiff Little Fingers. 'Cold Cold Change' and 'Back on the Borderline', the two singles from *Head Injuries,* are urgent, frenetic pop. Three of the four songs on the EP of 'first and second takes',[171] *Bird Noises,* continued this trend, while a fourth

– the lavish surf instrumental 'Wedding Cake Island' – showed a delightful willingness to expand their scope. This last track reputedly had a scathing Garrett vocal which was deemed unreleasable, though it is hard to imagine how a vocal would fit the music, especially if, as is rumoured, the short snatch of Garrett's voice (he seems to be speaking) washing in on the breakers as the track ends are the remnants of his contribution. Hirst claims to have the only extant copy of the song with a vocal track.[172]

The group also began to expand their scope commercially, and set out to conquer Australia in the same manner they had taken Sydney. Rob Hirst's rather impolite assessment of Melbourne in 1979 as out of date – 'Rock and roll is dying down there. It's sort of Carlton 1965 vintage. There's no progress...'[173] – was prescient. Sydney could often lay claim to the best bands, the best venues, and the best attitude in the 80s. It was hardly good public relations, though: the group needed all the fans it could get. Midnight Oil played regularly around Australia and, importantly, curried favour with 3RRR for *Bird Noises*, a hit on the station.

By the time of *Bird Noises*, Midnight Oil were known for their anti-authoritarian, essentially green and left-leaning politics. Nevertheless, at this early stage, Garrett told *Roadrunner*'s Toby Cluechaz:

> I'm not here to talk as a politician, neither is the band. It's a band of Australian musicians, we write about political things that we feel strongly about. The politics are personal politics... we're not a fucking flag-waving band and we refuse to be turned into one.[174]

With two exceptional albums and a marvelous EP under their belt, Midnight Oil had enjoyed more than their fair share of success. Had the band broken up at this time, they would almost certainly have quickly acquired Birdman-style legendary status. As it transpired, they would take their greatest commercial strides in the 1980s, starting with 1981's *Place without a Postcard*. John Duigan's *One Night Stand* was not released until 1984, but the perfect bookend to this period of Midnight Oil's career is their key role in this flawed but captivating film, in which a group of teenagers spend a night in the Sydney Opera House awaiting a nuclear holocaust. Midnight Oil play a concert at the end of the film – and the end of the world. Playing on such themes, *Place without a Postcard* prefigured this, its cover depicting a science fiction-styled, post-apocalyptic Sydney Harbour.

NO WAY, GET FUCKED, FUCK OFF

Though today they would be regarded in Australia as two very different propositions, in the mid to late 70s the Angels and Midnight Oil seemed to inhabit a similar place. Bernard 'Doc' Neeson and Peter Garrett were both charismatic lead singers, though not band 'leaders' as such. Their groups produced driving, appealing, often edgy riff rock which appealed to critics and audiences alike. They also rose in conjunction with the 'new wave', while never really aligning themselves with that movement and possessing clear connections to the pre-punk era. The Angels were not, strictly speaking, a 'political' group like Midnight Oil, preferring to revel in tough-guy set pieces, but they were a million miles away from dumb and/or heavy metal.

In a short space of time, and under different names, the Angels passed through, and contributed to, all the retro musics of the early to mid 70s. The core of the group – including Rick and John Brewster and aspiring actor Neeson – had been playing as the Moonshine Jug and String Band in Adelaide between 1970 and early 74. Neeson, 'his head buried in a rubbish tin writing a thesis around the inside of a plastic rubbish tin'[175] shared a flat with John Woodruff, who managed the band. The Moonshine Jug and String Band had a hit record in Adelaide with a song called 'Keep On Dancin'' in 1974, but in May of the same year they 'made the switch' to an electric sound, losing a major portion of their audience in the process 'literally ... before our eyes', John Brewster later told *Juke*.[176] He was non-committal, remarking that 'This is just a phase in the progression of our respective music careers.'[177] As per the times, their new sound was 50s rock and roll, and their new name was the Keystone Angels; they toured backing Chuck Berry and received a great response at Sunbury '75. The following year saw them rework their sound again to fit with the punk/hard rock sound of the mid 70s, shorten their name, move to Sydney,[178] and create a record which would be associated with the Angels from this time onwards, despite the fact it only became a hit – in an inferior live version – over a decade later in 1988. 'Am I Ever Gonna See Your Face Again' was produced by Vanda and Young – AC/DC had recommended the Angels to them[179] – and released on Alberts. Woodruff claimed it was about a friend who had committed suicide;[180] other sources say a girlfriend,[181] and certainly it comes across as a love song. Beginning with a show in Mt Isa in north-western Queensland in the early 80s,[182] Australian audiences made it their own, replying to the song's title with the chanted response 'No way, get fucked, fuck off' – a feature the radio-friendly live single could only hint at.

Their first (self-titled) album was a disappointment, but a period of reflection led to their second album *Face to Face* becoming a milestone. Like Dragon's experience of being locked in an office for a weekend until they wrote a hit, the Angels were ordered by Woodruff to rehearse ceaselessly until they'd come up with a new, punky sound. They did this under a house in the Sydney suburb of Annandale, an experience alluded to in their video for the 1984 single 'Eat City.'

Nation Review's Ross Stapleton told his readers in 1979 that the album, released the previous year, had 'become the biggest-selling album by an Australian rock band in the last two years, with the dreaded exception of those Toorak cowboys who wail about hard nights on the road – the Little River Band.'[183] *Face to Face*, Stapleton enthused, took 'a more full-on, no fuss approach to its music, aided by a brace of riffy new songs'[184] – even if it took a while to start selling because, according to him, radio had been unwilling to play it. The story goes that it wasn't until white label versions of 'Take a Long Line' were given to radio stations that the Angels' radio exposure began to match their live success. It was played, apparently, only because DJs believed it was the new AC/DC record, although it was far too sophisticated to be so.

Doc Neeson – in Stapleton's view 'the most talented and interesting frontman' since Gerry Humphrys and a 'stylish singer at the peak of his powers'[185] – would reminisce shortly afterwards about the Angels' early lack of success in Melbourne, telling *Roadrunner's* Donald Robertson: 'When we first used to go down to Melbourne and play the Tiger Lounge ... people would be standing there saying, "Yes – but is it art?"'[186] As it happened, the band did possess an arty element in the form of guitarist Rick Brewster, who notoriously never moved on stage, joked that all his moves 'are strictly choreographed',[187] and collected telephone booths.[188] Perhaps Neeson, a Brecht enthusiast[189] and something of a thespian (he was cast in the role of Javo in the film of *Monkey Grip* but withdrew for the sake of an Angels tour), felt uneasy in what he saw as an artistic environment like the Tiger Lounge, or perhaps he just wanted some adulation and credit for the intensity and vigour of the band he fronted. 'Sydney bands are definitely more hard-hitting', he told Robertson, 'Melbourne bands ... right back to Daddy Cool, and even Skyhooks, the guitars were there but they were *light* guitars. And I think a lot of the difference has to be down to the audience. Sydney audiences, in general, are more responsive than audiences anywhere else.' [190] The Angels, like Cold Chisel, would place a premium on being heavy, loud and proficient live, believing this was their ticket to the wider world of rock stardom. Coincidentally (or not?) the Angels and Cold Chisel – like LRB – were essentially Adelaide bands.

'EAT THIS'

Much has been made of Adelaide's contribution to Australian popular music; some have suggested it punches above its weight in producing nationally successful artists, starting perhaps with the Masters' Apprentices, the Twilights and Zoot, and continuing through Paul Kelly and the Moodists to major names from the mid 90s such as the Superjesus. This perception is probably at least partly an eastern seaboard prejudice; Adelaide may be one of Australia's smaller capital cities, but it is a major centre. It serves as a conduit to the wider creative world for the people of South Australia and, to a lesser extent, the Northern Territory, so it is by no means the lightweight some take it for.

Much has also been made of Adelaide's substantial working-class and immigrant population, the argument being advanced that the area contained a seething populace of bored teens ready to rock. This might be part of the story, but it fosters a misleading narrative implying that great music emerges naturally from a 'hard knocks' mentality; an enlightened and empathetic Housing Trust, which settled thousands of new Adelaideans and sought to provide entertainment and recreation facilities, was a hugely important factor that is rarely mentioned in this context.

As we saw in chapter 2, the development of Elizabeth – a settlement 25 kilometres north of Adelaide that was half-way between an industrial suburb and a city in its own right – brought thousands of European migrants to post-war South Australia starting in the mid 1950s. We've already encountered major musicians who grew up there, from Doug Ashdown and Glenn Shorrock to Pip Proud and Doc Neeson, but Elizabeth's most famous son is arguably Glasgow-born Jimmy Barnes.

Cold Chisel, the band which brought Barnes fame, also featured hotshot guitarist Ian Moss, who had come to Adelaide from Alice Springs and answered a shop window advertisement;[191] keyboard player and principal songwriter Don Walker; bass player Phil Small and drummer Steve Prestwich. All would become credible and successful songwriters.

'Back in the seventies and early eighties,' writes Toby Creswell in his biography of Barnes (whose copyright is registered in the name of Barnes's own music publishing company, Dirty Sheets Music), 'Cold Chisel ruled Australian rock 'n' roll; they were a band noted for their volatile chemistry, for their off-stage partying, their uncompromising principles, and for reshaping Australian music.'[192] This summary only scratches the surface of their legend, which was substantially developed during this period but grew further in the 80s and 90s, long after they had ceased working together. Creswell's better-than-average (if almost completely uncritical) biography, *Too Much Ain't Enough*, is named after a Barnes hit; Barnes's very poorly written autobiography is the embarrassingly titled *Say It Loud*; the most insightful Cold Chisel book by far is former *RAM* editor Anthony O'Grady's *The Pure Stuff*, even though it too bears a title guaranteed to make you squirm once you think about it (is it a reference to drugs? Or to the redundant idea of integrity in rock and roll, which incidentally the book

does a lot to undermine in Cold Chisel's case?). O'Grady uses his time in the studio with a briefly re-formed Cold Chisel in 1999 to discuss the group's interactions, chemistry and craftsmanship, as well as, most importantly, their place within the music industry over time. It is certainly a contender for one of the best books about rock music, particularly in relation to the music industry. The following discussion of Cold Chisel and their exceptional impact on Australia draws on these books, and contemporary published interviews with band members.

Much of Barnes's early career seems to have played out in the shadow of older brother John Swan (magnanimously, Swan claimed in 1985 that the highlight of *his* career was 'watching my brother grow and develop'[193]). Despite their different surnames, the two are not, as often reported, half-brothers: Barnes and some of his siblings changed their surname when their mother remarried. In the early 70s Swan – later known as Swanee, perhaps partly in an obscure reference to the Gershwin/Caesar song but more likely because of difficulties in rendering the usual Australian diminutive ('Swannie' looks like it should rhyme with 'nanny') – played drums in a group called Queen with an erudite, middle-class Queenslander named Don Walker.[194] This was, of course, years before the rise of the well-known British band.

Swan was well known in Adelaide as both a drummer and a singer; his singing was sufficiently legendary by the end of the 70s that he was a strong contender to become the vocalist in AC/DC after Bon Scott's death, a role he was reputedly not offered because (!) of his drinking and drug use. He was apparently a decent drummer too (like Scott), but when he was offered a place in the next band Walker played in, Orange, he turned it down, recommending Prestwich instead.[195]

Orange was not Walker's band (yet). It had been assembled by bass player Les Kaczmarek, via an ad in a music shop. Kaczmarek also recruited guitarist Moss, a former electrician from Alice Springs[196] and, some time later, Jimmy Barnes. Walker was working in weapons research for the Defence Department,[197] and for the band's early life his professional advancement, much like Deniz Tek's medical commitments outside Radio Birdman, influenced the group's movements. As mentioned earlier, when he took up postgraduate studies at the University of New England in northern New South Wales, the group followed him. They relocated to Glen Innes, an hour's drive south, for the duration. Barnes's professional interests had an effect on Cold Chisel too, though his profession was singing: he was pursued by Mal Eastick to join the Adelaide band Stars,[198] and actually quit Cold Chisel for a brief period in 1975 to sing in Fraternity after Bon Scott left them to join AC/DC. Cold Chisel continued, with Moss taking over vocal duties, and even toured the east coast with this line-up. It was presumably at this time that the band submitted demos to Mushroom – Gudinski is adamant that the Cold Chisel demo he heard didn't have Barnes singing on it, and that this was the reason he didn't sign them.[199] The return of Barnes, the ousting of Kaczmarek, and the recruitment of bassist Phil Small cemented the line-up that was to become famous. Relocating to Sydney, Cold Chisel engaged a good manager in Rod Willis, who had been managing a band called Australia (featuring Ace Follington, once of Chain, and Rod Coe).[200] At his new employers' insistence, Willis let Australia go.

Cold Chisel signed with WEA on 9 September 1977.[201] The group already had a cache of original songs – Don Walker was acknowledged as the band's songwriting whiz, though he insisted the group itself was 'completely democratic'.[202] Peter Walker, former guitarist in Bakery, was enlisted to produce the band's first album. Walker, no relation to Don, had been an inspiration to the younger Moss[203] and the band had known him for some time.[204]

Their debut album's standout track – and the first of Cold Chisel's 'legendary' recordings – was undoubtedly the rollicking post-Vietnam story 'Khe Sanh'; at some point, WEA invested in a film clip of the group miming to the song in a live band configuration with a couple of sepia clips depicting them backstage at a show. Released as a single, the song did not receive airplay, ostensibly due to sex and drug references; today it is familiar to millions of Australians and regarded as a classic. The second album, *Breakfast at Sweethearts,* saw the group abandon its mid-70s light boogie predilection in favour of watered-down reggae with Barnes's powerful, shaggy blues stylings on top. The year after its release, Barnes proclaimed that '*Breakfast at Sweethearts* stunk and you can spell that f-u-c-k-e-d.'[205] WEA – who appear to have signed the band almost accidentally – might have wondered at this point what they'd invested in, even if Cold Chisel's reputation as a live act was unassailable. It was reinforced when Willis set up the Dirty Pool agency in 1978 along with two other managers, John Woodruff (the Angels) and Ray Hearn (Flowers, at that time a successful 'punk' covers band). In Willis's words, 'We had to create our own environment;'[206] Dirty Pool began using the leverage of three very successful bands to maximize their charges' opportunities. Cold Chisel were not a punk band, though their first EP, the stupidly titled *You're Thirteen, You're Beautiful and You're Mine* enlisted the worst of punk's imagery and rhetoric. Don Walker, having made himself aware of the 'agit-prop tactics' of new wave/punk, used these to promote Cold Chisel,[207] most controversially with the image of a monk burning to death for the shabbily punning 'Youth in Asia' tour of 1979.

Their third album, *East,* saw the group hit its stride; the record is acknowledged as one of the greats of its time, though O'Grady still whinges at the poor recording quality of this and other early Cold Chisel albums throughout *The Pure Stuff*. The hit single 'Choir Girl' is another classic, an oblique study of a woman terminating a pregnancy (so oblique, in fact, that the Catholic Church's pop station 2SM didn't 'get' it, and therefore played it).

Walker was beginning to come across like some kind of poet for the dispossessed, an image which many were quick to point out did not fit that well with his middle-class, university-educated real-life persona. He claimed he tried 'to keep in touch' with the seamier side of things but conceded that his songs could sound contrived:

> I can put a supreme effort into writing a song about living with very little money or being in gaol, but those people who are involved in it, the people who are in gaol can still say that I haven't got the faintest idea what I'm talking about, and they'd be right.[208]

Walker went on to profess his admiration for Ian Rilen, although the writer reporting this, Ed St. John, and/or his *Rolling Stone* copy editors, showed how little they knew (or cared) by misspelling 'Rilen' as 'Rylands':[209]

> He concentrates on writing good, simple lyrics, and his songs have a much more lasting value than all the overtly political songs in the world. Unfortunately it isn't something that comes naturally to me, and I have to work at it a lot, it's something worth aiming at.[210]

With the hugely successful *East* under their belts, Cold Chisel turned their attention to the wider world. With beautiful naiveté, Barnes expressed no doubts about the group's chances internationally. As early as 1977, he had opined that the American market was 'where our type of bands are.'[211] A few years later, he said of the group's impending US tour that 'we're all looking forward to it. From what I know of America and its audiences, I think it'll be easy. They'll love us.'[212] Plainly he knew nothing. *East* was repackaged for the US (the tracks 'Ita', about well-known Australian publisher and editor Ita Buttrose, and 'Four Walls' were replaced with a remixed 'Khe Sanh') and all was optimism. But their shambolic self-funded[213] tour and a dawning realisation of the enormous size of the US market saw the group return to Australia bloodied and perhaps even slightly humbled.[214] While they believed they had failed in part due to lack of interest from their record company, Elektra,[215] it is worth noting that in Mötley Crüe's notorious memoir *The Dirt*, Elektra's Tom Zutaut says that Elektra were dedicated to making Cold Chisel a success to the detriment of other acts, including new signing Mötley Crüe.[216] Whatever the reasons were, the group was unable to replicate its Australian success in the USA. Walker still seems to have been a little shell-shocked when he told Australian *Rolling Stone's* Jane Matheson:

> Our music appeals to the country where we grew up playing and doesn't necessarily appeal to American tastes. I know to most ears in this country we sound like an instantly accessible band but you have to be there and see us playing supports to American bands to see the vast difference between our music, which in Australian terms is quite mainstream, and theirs. Over there, we're right out of left field.[217]

Cold Chisel conceded that they'd failed, but did not accept any blame; they told Australia that it was America who had made the mistake. Manager Rod Willis claimed the US industry was 'confused' by any band doing 'more than one style of music.'²¹⁸ Walker blamed the American market's lack of adventurousness:

> Rock & roll, to the average young American, is Rush or Styx ... They've never heard of the Sex Pistols, or what we might consider to be classic New York groups. Everywhere we went we found hundreds of people who genuinely thought that Styx were the best band in the world.'²¹⁹

More interesting to Walker, however, was the way America responded to him as an Australian – or, rather, failed to respond:

> When you find yourself in a country [which has] been near the centre of your consciousness for all your life – you know so much about America before you get there – there's this underlying assumption that they're going to know the same things about where you come from. Suddenly the place you love and where you've spent your whole life, to everybody around you is not only insignificant but they're not even interested in finding out. It's like, suddenly, the first thirty years of your life is insignificant, because they've been spent in what is seen over there as a backwater.²²⁰

The next Cold Chisel album was particularly noteworthy for two reasons. Cold Chisel had embellished Walker's bare and uncomplicated tunes with tasteful intelligence over three albums, but now he was weary of carrying the group's songwriting alone and insisted that his colleagues contribute. More remarkably, *Circus Animals* was not an album that could have come from just about anywhere; it had significantly Australian themes and concerns. Walker's 'The Wild Colonial Boy' takes its title from an old bush ballad, but the lyrics are a reaction to his experiences in America:

> You start to grapple with things like national identity and stuff like that ... No, not national identity, that's a bit pretentious. When you're standing outside what's been your entire universe, you start to look for the first time at what your whole universe has been, and maybe try and get an atmosphere to a song, just banging a peg in the ground and saying, well, this is where I came from. I was just trying to get a feeling, in a set of lyrics, of space, not many people, a certain madness that seems to exist in the air in this country, a kind of delightful lunacy. I wouldn't say I was very successful ... Still, I'd love to hear it on American radio being played to Americans.²²¹

Ideas of 'space' and 'not many people' also carried over to the album's cover, in which the group is depicted in a vast, bare landscape. Walker explained:

> I wanted something that was Australian and couldn't be mistaken for anywhere else. And that people overseas might ask some questions about. There's nothing really like Lake Eyre over there. I just wanted a wide flat space with a caravan in it, and with the band sitting out front. I was thinking of doing it at Mascot airport, because that was the only wide flat space nearby and Rod said, 'Well, dammit, let's find the widest, flattest space around and do it properly.'

Perhaps disingenuously, Walker insisted the album's title had nothing to do with the music industry. 'I've just always liked sawdust and shows and, you know, when the agricultural show comes to town – sideshow alley and all that.'[222] Yet it is clear in hindsight that the group was rooted; if they'd peaked, and couldn't get anywhere outside Australia, the only way was down. Though in O'Grady's book they pass it off as a jape, their riotous diatribe at the *Countdown/TV Week* music awards in March 1981 (the year before *Circus Animals*) was a tantrum directed against a surfeit of local commercial success. Creswell says 'the band were worried about what they might be saying back at Largs Pier (Hotel)';[223] a venue that was to Cold Chisel what the Antler was to Midnight Oil or the Crystal Ballroom was to the Birthday Party (in his memoir *Shots,* Don Walker describes it as 'a low-ceiling room' where there's 'no student slump or apology').[224] 'We hated the whole idea of the industry wanking off and patting each other on the back,' Barnes said later, 'and the awards weren't even that representative of what was happening.'[225] What Jimmy Barnes thought was actually 'happening' is anyone's guess, but his angst was made clear by the tirade he delivered that night at the end of 'My Turn to Cry':

> *I never saw you at the Astra Hotel*
> *I never saw you at Largs Pier*
> *I never saw you down on Fitzroy Street*
> *Now you use my face to sell TV Week*
> *I never saw you*
> *I never saw you*
> *I've four minutes, ten seconds*
> *For one last shot*
> *At this media wank*
> *You want it hot*
> *So eat this*
> *Eat this*
> *EAT THIS!*

At which point the whole band smashed their instruments, to audience cheers and boos. O'Grady details the ways in which the performance ultimately did not stop the awards, or Molly Meldrum, in their tracks: Meldrum simply went on to the next item on the agenda.[226] The media later realised they were a little affronted, though obviously nowhere near as affronted as they would have been if Air Supply – or for that matter JAB – had done it.

Having established themselves as iconoclasts (or scallywags), Cold Chisel went on to act out the same story every band of their ilk eventually undergoes if they don't die trying. Hoping to garner an international profile via Europe, the group bought their way onto a German tour by British singer Roger Chapman, formerly of Family, who by this time was enjoying immense success in that country. The pressure of their lack of success outside Australia remained problematic. Barnes's increasingly high profile, his domestic life (he had married Jane Mahoney in mid 1981)[227] and the opportunities everyone assumed lay in store for him in a solo career – were all factors to be considered, one way or another. Presumably, these issues and the mere fact of their almost decade-long existence as a band made four-fifths of Cold Chisel decide they needed a scapegoat. On 12 June 1983 they sacked Steve Prestwich, whom Barnes in particular had often clashed with, and replaced him with two drummer's drummers (first Gary Young, then Ray Arnott) in quick succession.[228] Soon after, Barnes announced his decision to leave the band. Some would have considered a Barnes-less Cold Chisel to be a tantalising prospect – Moss has an excellent voice, makes for a charismatic frontman, and sang some of the group's best and most popular songs, like 'My Baby', 'Bow River' and 'Saturday Night'. When Marc Hunter, Paul Hewson and Robert Taylor reviewed the new singles for *RAM* in April 1984, they hit the nail on the head when describing this last song:

> This shows why Chisel are a top band – they're prepared to take chances. By doing the things they think are good they produce records that sound as if they are meant and not just constructed. Ian Moss sings superbly; the band plays with restraint but perfect taste ... Has to be a hit.[229]

It was, and it deservedly remains an acknowledged masterpiece.

Walker's voice is less versatile than that of Moss or Barnes, but his delivery can be heart-rending, as his solo albums show. As it turned out, no-one wanted to start up the band again – at least not for another 16 years. They recorded a final, masterful, album, *Twentieth Century*; Arnott plays on most of it, but Prestwich was invited back to round off the band's career and he and Walker contributed one of Cold Chisel's iconic songs, 'Flame Trees'. The key scene in Rowan Woods's 2005 film *Little Fish* sees Cate Blanchett's character Tracy Heart stumble inexplicably into a hall full of schoolchildren singing 'Flame Trees'. No explanation is offered for this event, nor is there any discussion of its effect on her subsequent decisions, but the whole scene is undeniably *right*. Certainly, it requires no stretch of the imagination to believe that children in a suburban hall might be singing a Cold Chisel song: the group's music has been ubiquitous in Australia since the mid 80s.

Cold Chisel played a series of extravagant and record-breaking farewell shows before scattering, some into relative obscurity and others to more low-key, though not insubstantial, careers. Barnes quickly built on the Cold Chisel legacy, following a predictable path of recording generally ill-considered albums with at least one eye on the US market. An early popular single (his fourth hit, in late 1985) was the teeth-gnashingly ghastly single 'Working Class Man', written and produced by Journey's Jonathan Cain, channeling a foetid, parallel universe Bruce Springsteen.

Midnight Oil, the Angels and Cold Chisel were probably the three biggest Australian groups in Australia in the late 70s/early 80s; certainly, their legacy looms large 35 years later. Midnight Oil's achievement is perhaps the most remarkable, gained as it was while sticking to firmly held principles and maintaining as much distance as possible from the conventional music industry 'machine', while the Angels' early albums were far from mindless metal or aggression, but it is Cold Chisel who are the most unlikely success story and remain the most beloved to this day (Dave Graney recalls that in mid-70s Adelaide, before they achieved any success, they seemed like an anachronism rather than the future of Australian pop-rock). The songs of Don Walker were at the core of the band's success, and they are lyrically often strikingly poignant and sharp – in fact, one almost suspects the tunes are kept as starkly simple as they are in order to keep the listener's attention focused on the words. In *Shots* Walker describes himself as a 'registered user' of science fiction, 'spaghetti westerns, soft porn, John Waters movies, comics and Eric Carmen singing "All By Myself" on the jukebox at the local pizzeria' – in other words, he wants to be thought of as lowbrow in his tastes, albeit with some quirks. Other members' compositions – like Barnes's 'You Got Nothing I Want', to take a good example of a great song – are far more musically adventurous than most of Walker's work. The group did not make artistic leaps, but they were always attentive to detail when it came to song dynamics. There is no doubt that their fine reputation is well deserved; uniquely, somehow, they have managed to break through the dross and become legendary figures to Australians who came of age long after the original band ceased trading on a regular basis.

Cold Chisel did not completely distance themselves from pop radio and television, even though their subsequent 'biographers' wish to pretend they did. Other groups, like the Angels, tried to straddle pop and the rock integrity through the late 70s and early 80s with some success (Doc Neeson's habit of signing autographs with '$E=MC^2$' can be seen as a critique of the pop process and a snook cocked at the fans he signed his name for, although Neeson *did* claim to have discovered a formula for energy and mass relating to rock music). But only Midnight Oil completely avoided *Countdown*, and ultimately made doing so something positive. For everyone else, *Countdown* was a must.

TINSEL FAECES

In 1979, on their second tour of the eastern states, during which they also backed Dave Warner,[230] Perth band the Dugites – whose first release had been an amusing independent single called 'Hit Single' – baffled, then delighted, their audience. Singer Linda Nutter proclaimed from the stage that she wanted to be on *Countdown,* after which the group launched into the song they claimed would be the hit that would get them there. But while the Dugites were giving it their all onstage, they produced no sound at all. 'Then a wave of understanding passed through the audience,' wrote *Roadrunner* reviewed David L. Langsam, 'until the uncomprehending caught on and started hooting and bleating.'[231] The group was making a number of statements at the same time: that the groups on *Countdown* weren't 'real', that they were miming when they performed, and that pop was nonsense. The point was well made (and if anyone present at any of those shows had asked the band for their money back the following year, once the Dugites were actually making regular appearances on *Countdown,* that would have been a point well made, too).

Countdown has been mentioned previously, because it straddled several eras: the show ran weekly on ABC television from November 1974 until July 1987; it was a staple of Sunday nights at 6 pm (its title was originally to be *Six O'Clock Still Rocks*)[232] and at its peak it was regularly the station's most popular program. It was, and is, legendary. As Donald Robertson wrote in the early 80s:

> Every week three million Australians tune into the ABC to watch the world's No. One Rock Show, *Countdown,* and the unconsciously side-splitting antics of its Talent Co-ordinator, Ian 'Molly' Meldrum. He loses the plot continuously, never uses cue cards or notes, conducts the most superficial and facile interviews possible, and is never less than superb entertainment.[233]

Any 70s rock trouper given a preview of what would be valorised as 'retro' two to three decades later would have been horrified by which elements of 70s music culture were later deemed worth celebrating, namely the glitz, dazzle and ephemeral gloss of Australian pop, what one *RAM* reader marvelously, and perfectly, described as 'tinsel faeces'.[234] The reversal of critical fortune in the way *Countdown* is regarded parallels the shift in ABBA's reputation: appropriately enough, since the show played such a key part in the group's (global) rise. The re-evaluation began with a series of clips rescued from the vaults and screened on *The Late Show,* a comedy program created by the team which later made the films *The Castle, The Dish* and *Any Questions for Ben.* It continued with *Glad All Over,* Peter Wilmoth's 1994 book celebrating the show, and was carried further by Brian Mannix's *Countdown: The Musical* in 1998. A touring concert series of big names associated with the show was launched in 2006, by which time entire episodes were being rerun on cable television. Though its innovation, creativity and nous have subsequently been overstated – in reality, it was often tawdry and mundane – *Countdown* has come to be associated with the rise of Australian pop music both locally and internationally. It is often compared to the BBC's *Top of the Pops* in the UK, but aside from the fact that both were weekly TV pop shows, there was little similarity. Despite its name's apparent promise, *Countdown* predicted what would be popular *next* as well as celebrating what was popular already; it also, initially at least, promised to be a 'visual top forty but including album tracks'.[235] It had a policy, often challenged, that it would not play anything it did not have first rights to: a song had to appear on *Countdown* first, or *Countdown* wouldn't play it.[236] A less rigidly enforced rule, for new singles by local acts, was that groups had to appear 'live' on *Countdown* before the show would play a video for the same record.

Since the demise of the *Happening* TV show in 1972, Ian Meldrum had continued to work in commercial television on short-lived programs such as *Do It*[237] and *Anything Can Happen*.[238] This would all change when *Countdown's* 'Council of Pop' convened at the Botanical Hotel in South Yarra, an upmarket but still almost bohemian area of Melbourne, in 1974. Producers Michael Shrimpton and Robbie Weekes are said to have been discussing possible talent scouts when Meldrum drove a car onto the pavement outside the hotel and fell out of it, at which point he was offered the job.[239] (According to Meldrum's autobiography, Weekes told Shrimpton: 'That's the cunt we need').[240] This is a beautiful story, though it is hard to imagine who they would have hired if it *hadn't* been Meldrum: as his conduit role throughout so much of this history to date has shown, he was ubiquitous. It was intended that he would operate strictly behind the scenes, and supposedly this was what he wanted, too. But he was to prove unhideable, for better and worse, and his visibility was his power – within a few months he was a regular presence in front of the cameras. As mentioned previously, Meldrum, a self-confessed 'band moll', had been given the nickname 'Molly' by DJ Stan Rofe. Rofe, apparently, gave women's names to anyone he didn't like (or perhaps just to men who weren't heteronormative); in any case, the name stuck. ABC management insisted that no-one was to refer to him as 'Molly' on air, but John Paul Young did so accidentally at one point, and ultimately Meldrum became better known as 'Molly' than under his real name. Resentment towards Meldrum – who came to be seen by many, particularly in the world of underground music, as a sycophantic corporate shill – often also took an anti-gay flavour (Meldrum is bisexual).

The patrician ABC's patronage of *Countdown* might have initially seemed a poor fit culturally; in fact it was a perfect one. As with 2JJ/Triple J, the ABC had a duty to provide quality programming to all Australians, not just the educated professional classes, although it is this minority group which has traditionally been its most consistent consumer. The 2002 documentary series *Love Is in the Air* suggests that *Countdown* was similar to a vaudeville show, and that international record companies used the show to road-test their new signings.[241] Evidence for this is scant, despite the oft-cited observation that ABBA were an immediate success in Australia via *Countdown*, forcing the reluctant RCA label to issue 'Mamma Mia' as a single before the rest of the English-speaking world (and beyond) cottoned on.[242] The testimony of Jon English that he observed big-name American bands coming on to *Countdown* 'and being terrible' because they had no TV experience[243] is plausible enough, although it does ignore the fact that hundreds of Australian acts had no trouble being terrible on *Countdown* as well. Despite the claims of the show's official histories, pop music was in no way absent from Australian television in the mid 70s until *Countdown* came along; there were numerous pop shows (for kids) and rock shows (for bigger kids) on commercial stations, and even on the ABC (there had also been a Queensland pop show called *Countdown* in the mid 60s). What was lacking after *Go-Set* stopped publishing was a national pop *institution*, and only the ABC could provide such a thing at this time because it was the only truly national network. Furthermore, the fact that *Countdown* was broadcast on the only non-commercial TV station was important; if the fact that it was not-for-profit did not ward off all claims that the show kowtowed to Mammon, it certainly tempered them.

In any case, Meldrum's insane enthusiasm for almost anything – coloured by his very occasional diatribes against records or artists he felt could have done better – put the show in a separate class. In the years since the program ended, many have forgotten that it also gave exposure to obscure up-and-comers: the Scientists in their 'teenage' phase, the Missing Link label's punk-pop hopefuls La Femme, or the independent art-rock band Mental as Anything, to name but three. Anyone who recalls *Countdown* as being merely a haven for pop dross needs to see the clip of Ian and Stephanie Rilen's Sardine V performing 'Sudan' in 1982.

It is worth reiterating that Meldrum was not the host of the program, though international writers, in their underresearched accounts of Australian popular music, often assume he was. The hosts were an ever-changing cavalcade of stars and wannabe stars, awkwardly reading bad jokes from an autocue and, if they had any integrity whatsoever, trying to look unimpressed. Once he was established as an on-screen presence, Meldrum was given his own segment, 'Humdrum'; he travelled the nation and the world conducting largely incomprehensible interviews which were run on the show in edited (but still incomprehensible) form.

The first six half-hour episodes of *Countdown* began screening in November 1974, shortly before the arrival of colour television.[244] It was a mishmash. It included Skyhooks, Sherbet, Stevie Wright, Daryl Braithwaite, Hush, Captain Matchbox Whoopee Band (who were about to have their one major hit record, 'Wangaratta Wahine'), Ray Burgess, Debbie Byrne and William Shakespeare. Such an all-Australian line-up would be unusual as *Countdown* went on; the show would tend to reflect international artists and hits as much as the charts themselves. Johnny Farnham was the host of the first real colour episode, in its more common one-hour format, in January 1975: the first song he introduced was Skyhooks' 'Horror Movie'.

Countdown loved it when local acts became successful, and it became the credo of the show that the mid to late 70s were the dawn of an era in which Australian talent was recognised on the world scene. Even consummate showmen like Peter Allen could make a comeback. He was first in the charts in 1960 as part of the Allen Brothers, with the song 'My Secret', and had long since been consigned to a sphere far outside 'pop'. Suddenly in 1977 he was celebrated by people who had long forgotten (or never knew) he'd been away, and having huge hits like 'I Go to Rio'.[245] But it was bands like LRB and Air Supply who were the shining examples of Australian pop talent as far as the industry and *Countdown* were concerned. Air Supply were a particularly unusual case, although like so many Australian pop successes of this era, their genesis lies in a rock opera.

HAIR SUPPLY

Graham Russell had joined the cast of *Jesus Christ Superstar* in April 1975; he formed a group with two fellow performers in the show, Russell Hitchcock and Chrissie Hammond, 'to fill in time on Sundays'.[246] Russell was born in England and had worked in music in the UK before coming to Australia and playing with Rob Mackenzie. Hitchcock was from the Melbourne suburb of Brunswick and had played drums from an early age, entertaining family friends 'by tapping out complicated rhythms on an upturned saucer for very small monetary rewards';[247] at Princes Hill High his classmate Chris Löfvén had asked him to join a band doing 'Johnny B. Goode style ... material'.[248] As *Superstar* performers the trio came with ready-made cachet; during the show's New Zealand season they made appearances at campuses and on radio and TV. Early in the piece, bass player and singer Jeremy Paul, formerly in a group with the grotesque name Soffrok who'd had a shortlived relationship with Alberts,[249] replaced Hammond, who later formed Cheetah (see chapter 8). The group made a demo of Russell's fulsome ballad 'Love and Other Bruises' on 'a small and primitive tape recorder in the pit of a St Kilda theatre,' but were turned down by every record company in Melbourne.[250]

Sydney-based Peter Dawkins had recently arrived at CBS from EMI as an A&R facilitator[251] and would soon make his name as a hotshot producer and hitmaker on the Australian rock scene; he helped Dragon reach the peak of their success in the late 70s, as we shall see in the next chapter. Dawkins was impressed with Air Supply's songs and approach, and offered the group a recording contract in September 1976.[252] The early results looked grim. A mere 917 copies of 'Love and Other Bruises' had been sold by the end of the year, at which point CBS and Dawkins must have been doubtful of their new signing's prospects (though some other bands' singles surely sold even fewer copies). But slowly the single gained airplay, first in Adelaide and then Brisbane. 'Straight after that,' Russell said in 1976, 'it just went zoom!'[253] A backing group was formed: Nigel Macara, once drummer for Ariel; guitarist Mark McEntee; and keyboard player Adrian Scott. A second single, 'Empty Pages', did not chart, despite being markedly superior to the first, perhaps because the group don't get to the chorus until three-quarters of the way through the song. This unusual format is the source of its genius, along with the fact that the song is a brilliant mélange of pomp and angst. The album *Love and Other Bruises* – 'a truly beautiful album' in the cod-sophisticate parlance of the CBS promo department[254] – went gold. The group appears on the front of the record in a bluestone alleyway, with Hitchcock holding up a large reflecting globe. This was even more pretentious than it initially appeared. According to Russell:

> We went into the alley simply to make people aware of where we came from, because we all come from the streets. The crystal ball signifies the music which is all white and pure, not aggressive at all. That's where we get all our inspiration from and we're looking to the crystal ball to find a way out.[255]

Within a few years they would find a pretty comprehensive 'way out', ultimately to the billion-selling Taiwanese market, via unprecedented success in the USA. They made it look simple. The first full-band line-up of Air Supply toured Australia extensively, playing any small-town hall they could fill, in what Hitchcock called 'sort of a meet-the-people thing'.[256] The following year they were clearly set to make it big: Rod Stewart was sufficiently threatened by them that he insisted they not be allowed to wear white on stage when they supported him,[257] though he did later gave them a US support slot. Jeremy Paul's departure in August 1977, leaving them as a duo, did little to slow them down. Paul later formed and briefly played bass in a band with McEntee that was first called Baton Rouge,[258] then Divinyls, but was ousted from that group after trying to replace Christina Amphlett with another singer.

Air Supply continued with Russell and Hitchcock up front[259] enlisting numerous well-known Australian musicians – including Ariel's Bill Putt, the aforementioned Peter Walker, and extra vocalists such Criston Barker, who had been in the Melbourne group Ash with LRB's Derek Pellicci – for touring and recording purposes. Their singles were usually sumptuous and syrupy; a rare exception was 1979's 'Just Another Woman', undoubtedly one of the lamest pieces of funk ever created, which was, mysteriously, promoted as a Russell Hitchcock solo release but subsequently included on an Air Supply album. By the beginning of the 1980s Air Supply had joined Steve Kipner, Russell Morris, Billy Thorpe, Daryl Cotton, Rick Springfield and Renée Geyer[260] as members of the California-based 'Gumleaf Mafia'.[261] The duo of Hitchcock and Russell – they utilized the Bee Gees' approach in distinguishing between 'core' and 'non-core' members – were one of the biggest groups in the USA, and while they were not forgotten in Australia, their sales there were disappointing by comparison. It was a common joke to refer to them as 'Hair Supply', which would have been funnier if their hairstyles had been markedly more elaborate than those of most young men of the mid to late 70s. The primary problem for Air Supply was that once the trend for sculpted, seamless, 'beautiful music' faded, their output started to seem awfully samey, however catchy some of those soaring choruses might be. The prevailing Australian attitude to them became one of slight embarrassment; they just seemed cheesy. Which, of course, they were.

CARLTON CALLING, PART ONE: THE SPORTS

The Pelaco Brothers, with their Pram Factory origins, or perhaps even Skyhooks, were what most people thought of when they thought 'Carlton bands'. Stephen Cummings recalls Russell Hitchcock complaining to him that people talked about 'Carlton bands' but that he, Hitchcock, was the only musician around who actually *came* from – meaning grew up in – Carlton; Cummings adds, however, that Gulliver Smith was another. In the mid 70s, new groups began to form from the original ones. Martin Armiger, who was born in England and moved to Elizabeth with his family, pursued musical visions for some time in Adelaide, where he formed Toads, Nightly, a 'performance art group pretending to be/wanting to be a rock band';[262] in 1974 he moved to Melbourne and, in addition to recording the soundtrack to the epic drug film *Pure Shit*, he put together a new version of his Adelaide band (usually known simply as Toads), featuring Jenny Keath, Jane Clifton, Eddie van Roosendael and Andrew Bell. In April 1977, Stephen Charlesworth scanned the Carlton scene for *Juke* and uncovered the Bleeding Hearts, 'distilled from vintage Carlton bands':

> Martin Armiger (guitar/vocals) came from a couple of years leading Toads, Eric Gradman (violin/vocals) came from much the same situation with Sharks, while Chris Worrall (guitar) served his apprenticeship with such notables as Pelaco Bros. and Captain Matchbox. Along with the recently recruited sax player Keith Shadwick, from Uncle Bob's Band, Bleeding Hearts play hard-edged, inner-city r and b ... it appears that people are looking beneath the tag of "Carlton Band" and seeing what makes this band tick the way they do. There is an ideological disposition within the band that would rule out any overnight success in the pop world.'[263]

Worrall was dropped from the line-up in April 1977 and joined Stiletto (another second-generation Carlton band that also included some Toads, discussed a little later in this chapter). Rick Grossman and Huk Treloar were added on bass and drums respectively; Charlesworth noted Armiger 'thrashing away at his white Strat' in live shows, when 'he would launch a song or finish it off in a crazed display of distortion.'[264] The Bleeding Hearts had the Carlton je ne sais quoi: one song title cited by Charlesworth was 'Love Is Just Like a Kick in the Bum in the Middle of the Night.'[265]

The Pelaco Brothers were one of those rare bands whose dissolution led to the emergence of three or four (perhaps, just possibly, better – certainly more resilient) new ones. Jimi Tomorrow and Carl Segnit started the Millionaires, who for a scant few seconds were regarded as 'the new Skyhooks',[266] showcasing songs about 'life in Brunswick',[267] the suburb to Carlton's immediate north. Johnny Topper and Peter Lillie were in a number of bands together and separately, including the Leisuremasters, the Autodrifters (who issued an EP on the Melbourne label Ralph, which was possibly named after Joe Camilleri's beagle),[268] Paul Madigan and the Humans, and the Relaxed Mechanics. Mark Ferrie played in the Leisuremasters and with Madigan. Stephen Cummings, who had precipitated the demise of the Pelaco Brothers by quitting the band, said in 1978 that:

> When the Pelacos first split, I was going to do something with Joe Camilleri and Wayne Burt but I had second thoughts. They could both sing, and I might have become redundant.[269]

Cummings says now that he quit simply 'to be getting my thing going, I guess':

> I thought, Well I'm a good singer – I wanted to be doing something. I'm ashamed to say I didn't have a thought in my head, really, I just wanted to be doing something, making some noise, I didn't really have any big ideas. That's something that's different now, a lot of groups that start, people have a plan. This was like – there was no plan. At all.

The Sports, as they were to become, were initially based around songs written by Cummings and guitarist Ed Bates, who had also been a Pelaco Brother. Robert Glover, a Sport from the beginning, had additionally been in a Carrl Myriad band called Myriad Rides Again.[270] Mark Ferrie, who played in another Myriad project – this one simply took the man's last name – recalls that playing with Myriad was 'a bit like doing your musical apprenticeship':

> A lot of people had gone through his group. Ed Bates, Rob Glover, who ended up in the Sports, Jeff Burstin, Jane Clifton. He started off as folky. That's what he was in the 60s. Playing coffee lounges with his wife, Janie who was one of the Conways [she is the sister of Mic and Jim Conway]. But they'd split up by that stage, and he'd turned to this more hard-bitten country stuff . . . It was where I first heard Hank Williams and Emmylou Harris, Gram Parsons. Carrl wrote songs himself, original stuff. The first gig I ever did with them was recorded and came out on this *Live at the Station Hotel* album that had bands like the Dingoes and Saltbush.

Ferrie's involvement in this scene was important as a bridge between the early-70s 'ockerbilly' scene and one that might have been considered more overtly 'new wave'; he also played on Peter Lillie solo records and did shows with his bandmate in the Models, Johnny Crash (Janis Freidenfelds). Peter Xeni, who had released the Autodrifters' EP, joined with Cummings to co-fund a Sports EP, which received positive reviews in UK magazines. Ross Wilson had produced some demos for the Pelaco Brothers, and now invited the Sports to record some tracks for the *Debutantes* album he was putting together for the Oz label; *Debutantes* was originally intended to be an annual affair but only one instalment appeared.[271] The Sports' three tracks fitted well with songs from Stiletto, Mark Gillespie, and Red Symons – who seems to have participated primarily out of a kind wish to use his celebrity as the former guitarist of Skyhooks to draw attention to the whole enterprise (his excellent song, surely his best by far, was a Todd Rundgren-esque piece called 'Only a Flipside', and was released as a single backed with a track by Stiletto, the group that starred his ex-bandmate in Scumbag, Jane Clifton). The Sports at this time were still in an R&B vein stemming from their leaders' days in the Pelaco Brothers; this would soon change. Unlike Jo Jo Zep and the Falcons, the Sports did not sign with Oz (Ross Wilson's label through EMI, which had released *Debutantes*); instead the band opted for Gudinski and Mushroom, thus ushering the label into its second and arguably best phase as the home of groups espousing new-wavey pop. Cummings says that to the Sports, Gudinski was 'like the enemy, really', but moving up to a major label was a pragmatic decision, as were other changes he made at the time:

> I realised there were other sorts of music I wanted to do ... people would get sick of you really quickly and I'd have to take this somewhere. All the other people in the Sports were good musicians, but I had the idea in my head of what I wanted to do ... So we got Andrew in the group – he was a really good guitar player – just to make it not so retro ... We put the record out and that punk/new wave thing happened and we were half dragged into that. We were different to what was happening at the time.

Like Glover, Andrew Pendlebury had been in a Carrl Myriad band: he appears alongside Mark Ferrie on the *Live at the Station* album. Pendlebury later said that he didn't think the Sports were 'a very good band. I was always attracted to Jo Jo Zep and the Falcons, 'cause they had a much more solid groove...'[272] Indeed, all ex-Sports seem to denigrate their own group – unfairly. The Sports produced some of the most vibrant and intelligent pop of late-70s Australia – quite an achievement in a field of extremely strong contenders: 'Brightness makes its own light, brilliance has its own reward', as David Pepperell wrote obliquely yet compellingly of the group in 1978.[273] In great part this was due to the way Cummings consolidated the Sports' frontline by sacking Ed Bates and inviting Martin Armiger from the Bleeding Hearts to join. (After Armiger left the Bleeding Hearts, Rick Grossman and Eric Gradman continued working together as Eric Gradman Man and Machine; Grossman quit in January 1980[274] to join Matt Finish, who are discussed further in chapter 16; Gradman was, according to *Roadrunner*, shortly to sign a deal with Michael Browning). Jim Niven was also essentially squeezed out of the Sports, like Bates a martyr to his 'retro' roots. Armiger told *Roadrunner* he'd been telephoning Niven to find out how to play particular keyboard lines and 'he's been good enough to tell me.'[275] A change of drummer, from Paul Hitchins to Iain McLennan (previously of Ariel and Mondo Rock) also took place at the start of 1980. They would have chosen Graham Perry of Man and Machine, but decided against it on the grounds that one should not steal from one's friends![276]

While Sidewinder (discussed later in this chapter) relished being described as 'sophisticated new wave', Maxwell Ross announced to *Juke's* readers in early 1977 that 'Sports qualify for the tag "sophisticated punks" because their music is more complex and interesting than the trash which sensation-thirsty Sunday papers have branded as punk rock.' Ross felt that, like Air Supply, the Sports came from a valid place: 'the streets':

> Sports' music is from the streets, and Cummings sings with a street-punk style that was in vogue in the early days of the Rolling Stones, Yardbirds and the Animals. The same style which has been poorly resurrected by such non-talents as the Sex Pistols.[277]

Such meaningless and reactionary sniping at the Sex Pistols on the Sports' behalf wasn't really doing anyone any favours, but given where they were headed – they were planning to be a pop band – it probably didn't matter. The Sports had clever ideas, based on their knowledge of popular music: they released a cover of 'When You Walk in the Room' as a single because Cummings had read it was 'famous because it was the first to use "nonchalant" in it. It was worth doing just for that.'[278] Their early self-penned hits – Cummings-Armiger compositions, for the most part – were better; they included the Cummings/Bates composition, 'Boys! (What Did the Detective Say?)'; the plaintive, witty and urgent 'Strangers on a Train'; and the catchy 'Don't Throw Stones'. Like many Australian records in the top forty at this time, these songs have had a post-chart life far out of proportion to their initial impact. 'The only group we really liked was Dragon,' Cummings says now. 'I felt they were really different, and they had really good pop songs. I liked pop music. That's why we were different to the Angels and Midnight Oil and all those bands we played with at the time.'

Gudinski, who would occasionally take on management duties with Mushroom groups he particularly cherished, drew up plans whereby the Sports would conquer both Britain and the USA. Britain – via the Stiff label – was to come first. Stiff arranged for them to use a British producer, Pete Solley, who had been a session musician and late-period (1977) member of Procol Harum.[279] Solley told Australian *Rolling Stone* that Stiff signed the Sports 'on condition that he'd get a producer to unAustralianise them . . . Stiff had wanted it to be super English, y'know, real rough sounding.'[280] Solley later produced Jo Jo Zep's *Hats Off Step Lively* album and Detroit band the Romantics' 'What I Like About You', a near-hit in the US but a chart-topper in Australia.

'In England,' Cummings said in 1978:

> Stiff started marketing the Sports as one thing – Australians. Usually that's enough to make the average English punter or critic laugh rather than listen. English racism against Australians exists on such an insidious level – they just don't want to take you THAT seriously. But they just have to admit that the Sports are OK.[281]

Cummings now says that the group were shocked, when they arrived in London, to discover that their first record on Stiff came in a sleeve with an early 70s picture of tennis player Evonne Goolagong, (or at least a lookalike) 'holding a koala.'

> They had a whole thing of 'Fosters night' there, and Johnny Rotten was in the audience. The English hated Australian people and Stiff's thing had gone the other way and totally pushed the Australianness. It was funny . . . Most of the guys that worked there were totally horrible English rock snobs.

The *NME* described the group as 'antiquated'; *Sounds* dismissed them as 'the Australian Rubinoos . . . as meaningless and passé as you'd expect'.[282] Cummings told *Juke* in May 1978 that 'we'd start off our set and we'd get cries of "FUCK OFF BRUCE", but by the end they'd really like us – especially at the smaller university gigs.'[283] The group recorded what Cummings described as 'rough and powerful' material 'with surging guitars and eunuch harmonies'[284] to augment songs from *Don't Throw Stones* for a British version of the album.

Their trips to the UK were little more than learning experiences; Cummings says he was continually expecting to discover that a mistake had been made and 'they'll send us home soon'. Stiff's Dave Robinson tried to make Cummings change his name to 'Steve Cochran' which Robinson believed would somehow serve as a response to Elvis Costello, but Cummings resisted. Names seemed to mean a lot to Stiff; the label had attempted to buy Lobby Loyde's name from him, believing it would be perfect for a manufactured pop star.[285] Image mattered too, of course: Robinson reputedly insisted the Sports get their hair cut *before* they arrived in the UK.[286]

As much as Britain welcomed the Sports – all told, not that much over two visits – their deal with Arista in the US seemed to hold more promise. Cummings says it was the biggest deal Mushroom had ever signed:

It was half a million bucks or something like that, which was pretty good for Gudinski because he was our manager, publisher and record label, and the records didn't cost much to make and they'd already gone gold in Australia.

The extremely catchy 'Don't Throw Stones' single cracked the top fifty in the USA,[287] which was a grand beginning, but Cummings essentially pulled the plug on everyone's global schemes for the band:

> I could just see this could take years. I'm just not built for it mentally, driving around through America for years playing club after club . . . I just sort of flipped out then. You'd be picked up by Gudinski and he'd be doing lines of coke in the taxi and talking a million miles a minute and I'd be like, Hey, what about some drugs for me? 'No, you're the singer, you'll ruin your voice.'

Martin Armiger later compared Gudinski and Cummings to Kerouac and Henry James, though without specifying which was meant to be which. The point, of course, was that the songwriter/singer and manager/record company could not understand each other. Rather than aim for infinite expansion, the group decided not to use the profits from the *Suddenly* album to fund further international touring; instead the group divided the money amongst themselves. Armiger, Cummings and Pendlebury used theirs to buy houses in Melbourne. Cummings's excellent second novel, *Stay Away from the Lightning Girl*, features a minor character called Harry McGinty, a record label entrepreneur/manager: 'He'd built an empire in Australia, but the lure of America and bigger and better deals was always eating away at him.'[288] Gudinski complained in 1990:

> I used to lose sleep over America. I used to get so frustrated . . . I used to hate England, I used to hate going there. They used to think that Australia had nothing to offer. They knew it all. Their press used to tear us apart.[289]

McGinty can't forgive *Stay Away from the Lightning Girl's* hero, Robert Moore, for 'abandoning' a push into the American market. But Gudinski continued to support the new, low-key Sports, who dug themselves into Melbourne even further by enlisting a couple of Skyhooks: first, Red Symons, who played keyboards with them for a tour; then Freddie Strauks in May 1980. Initially, Armiger and Cummings asked Strauks to play on some demos after McLennan contracted hepatitis; they then invited Strauks to join the Sports permanently (stealing, perhaps, from their friends). It was reported in the press at the time that Strauks's departure put an end to Skyhooks.[290]

While *Suddenly* might have sold well enough to fund house purchases, it wasn't as big a hit as its predecessors (Cummings claimed at the time, perhaps as an explanation of this, that 'It wasn't a superficial album'),[291] and the group's tour with Split Enz under the banner 'Sporting True Colours' saw them overshadowed by the unexpected chart success of their labelmates. Armiger told Australian *Rolling Stone* that it was their 'biggest grossing tour ever and we were terrible every night'.[292]

A few years after the Sports had broken up, Cummings claimed that the band had 'worked too hard . . . It was really stupid;'[293] in 1980, towards the end of the band's life, he had argued there was 'no point' in continuing a band 'if your record is stiffing overseas and you're stiffing here . . . We have always had a good thing going and it's important that we keep everything on the up and up.'[294] With Strauks, they recorded a final album that came close to perfect pop, the remarkable *Sondra* (1981). Named for the actress Sondra Locke (widely known in the early 80s as Clint Eastwood's girlfriend and frequent co-star alongside an orangutan named Clyde), it contained two incredible singles, 'Stop the Baby Talking' and 'How Come?' Inexplicably, neither was a major hit; the rest of the album is equally strong, particularly the more reflective and slow tracks, 'Black Stockings for Chelsea' and 'Last House on the Left'. The last Sports release was a novelty covers record, *Sports Sing Dylan (and Donovan)*, which Mushroom released as a 10-inch five-track EP. Stephen Cummings would go on to an acclaimed solo career, initially aided by Armiger.

CARLTON CALLING, PART TWO: STILETTO

In 1984 Jane Clifton recalled a time in the late 60s when she was an education student at Monash University, exposed to new theatre for the first time. 'I don't know if it because it was my first year at university . . . that made it so exciting, but it really was,' she told Damien Minton. Clifton was soon drawn into acting herself and, through that to 'offshoots which went more into rock 'n' roll.'

> The films being made around the Pram Factory at the time would always have a party scene, and I think I was in every party scene in every underground movie ever made in Carlton . . . I was on the sound track for one of them, *Pure Shit*.'[295]

This was the Bert Deling film whose musical soundtrack was written largely by Martin Armiger. The band Clifton sang with, Stiletto, was another Carlton group who – like the Pelaco Brothers – had roots in the Pram Factory scene and, at least initially, close contact with Ross Wilson as producer and mentor; they also featured Chris Worrall on guitar, straight from the Bleeding Hearts. For diverse reasons, however, Stiletto would not enjoy the same measure of success as the Sports or other of their contemporaries. While it would be easy to blame sexism on the part of the music industry and/or music fans for this – and sexism was of course prevalent – the group also suffered from the lack of a prolific central songwriter and frequent line-up changes.

Clifton would later achieve greater fame in the first half of the 80s playing Margo Gaffney in the TV series *Prisoner* (aka *Prisoner: Cell Block H* in the UK and USA), amongst other achievements in theatre, television, literature, and a solo music career. Stiletto's initial line-up also featured Andrew Bell and Janie Conway, who had reverted to her birth name after ending her relationship and performing career with Carrl Myriad. They first performed on 6 May 1976 when they 'put together a few songs for a supper show in the front theatre of Melbourne's Pram Factory. The rhythm section was Eddie van Roosendael and Marnie Sheehan . . . Stiletto was conceived.'[296] The 'supper show' was a one-off, but the group's artistic success was immediate and instantly recognised by the audience. Two years later, Clifton recalled 'that first night we played, Janie and I were quite convinced that if recording people came, we would be snapped up.'[297] Both Sheehan and Conway were single mothers of young children, which made their commitment to the band difficult; Conway left the following year because she was unhappy at being asked to take on the lead guitarist role. Celeste Howden replaced Sheehan as bass player in December of the same year. Like the Sports, Stiletto contributed three tracks to *Debutantes*; they utilised the undoubted talents of Helen Garner as lyricist on some of their songs. The group in Garner's first novel, *Monkey Grip* – played by Chrissie Amphlett and members of the Divinyls in the film of the book – are based on Stiletto, and Conway says she recognised everyone else in the novel; another character was based on Martin Armiger. Though Clifton was the focal point of Stiletto, particularly after Conway left the group, she contributed little to the songwriting. Bell was the most consistent songwriter, usually in collaborative arrangements with lyricists, notably Garner, with whom he shared a house at the time. In 1977 he told *Juke* about his songwriting process, managing to slip in a mention of a barely remembered Melbourne band of the time, Flying Tackle:

> The procedure normally is that someone comes to me and hands me a sheet of paper with some words scribbled on it and says, 'I want it to sound like a mixture of Steely Dan, the Rolling Stones and Flying Tackle.' I go and write something that's got nothing to do with that and they say 'That's great! Just what I wanted.' That's how it is with songs we write too. Someone will write the bones of a song and someone else will say, 'I can do this with that' and so on. The whole thing of crediting people with songs is very misunderstood.[298]

Clifton clearly felt that as a female singer in a rock band which also included female instrumentalists – though by the time Stiletto's only album, *Licence to*

Rage, was issued the only other woman in the band was Howden – she was either disadvantaged, or a disadvantage. Talking to Al Webb in 1978 she coined the idea of 'bloke bands' – a novel piece of terminology at a time when 'girl/ woman groups' were such a rarity.

> I get paranoid about being a girl singer because they're not becoming famous these days. It's all blokes! Bloke bands! I think maybe it's something to do with the high range you get vocally. Like, you don't hear that thrust that you get with Steve Cummings, or with Joe Camilleri, or even Braithwaite, they've all got meaty kibblets voices, and I don't have that sort of a voice.[299]

Produced by Peter Walker, *License to Rage* was a mixed bag. It comes off as fragmented, perhaps because it drew on seven songwriters, only three of whom were in the band; Martin Armiger wrote or co-wrote three tracks. *Rolling Stone's* reviewer Mark Butler felt it was the sound of Stiletto trying 'strenuously to play down the Carlton roots and aim for a wider audience.'[300] In her 1984 interview with Minton, Clifton says 'Stiletto initially was very popular with the sort of alternatives and feminists and as soon as we decided to keep going and actually make records and stuff like that, forget it Stella.'[301]

The album's title – and the cover, with the awkward-looking band outnumbered by manikins in a post-party netherworld, Worrall playing the joker by reading a magazine upside-down – has dated it. 'License to Rage' suggests a kind of call to arms for stolid rock-and-rolling; in fact, according to Worrall, the title song was about someone who's 'expected to have fun, expected to be glamorous, and to tear around the place and live out this whole thing, but he's got nothing. He doesn't live anywhere, he doesn't own anything, doesn't get anything back from it, yet it's this role he has to live out.'[302] The song was one of Armiger's, but someone – perhaps at Oz/EMI – clearly thought its title said everything that needed to be said about a new, smart rock band: they'd got their *license*. A half-hour documentary with the same title was also made about Stiletto; it seems to have been lost.

The album was not a commercial success, even if people would sing along to its songs in every 'out-of-the-way country town' they played in.[303] Worrall had told Webb that nobody was 'coming around and scratching their name in my door. I'm available for mobbing anytime!'[304] Perhaps this was the reason he continued his serial band member career by leaving Stiletto shortly after Oz/EMI dropped them;[305] he joined Paul Kelly and the Dots late in 1978.[306] Worrall's remark, in an article on the Dots, 'I'd read somewhere if you played a musical instrument, you'd be instantly popular,'[307] is funny but at the same time perhaps telling. Chris Dyson, formerly of the High Rise Bombers, replaced him.[308] On 5 January 1979, Stiletto officially broke up – at Clifton's initiative.[309] 'I dunno,' she told *RAM's* Andrea Jones, 'it just missed the mark somehow.'[310]

Van Roosendael and Dyson briefly joined the punk band News. Howden switched to drums to continue to work with Bell and Clifton in a musical by John Romeril called *Mickey's Moomba*.[311] Melbourne's Moomba Parade, a vapid event at the best of times, had been controversially headed up by the Disney character. Howden would later be a significant part of an all-female group called the Stray Dags, who released a stupendous swing single called 'Self-Attack' and a less successful EP, *Lemons Alive*. Stiletto's manager, Nathan Brenner, moved on to handle Split Enz.[312] Only Clifton would stay close to the former members of the early 70s 'Carlton scene' and continue to perform as one of them. Her subsequent career embraced jazz, pop, theatre, television, film and fiction. When she made the charts in 1983, it was in a duet with Joe Camilleri credited to 'Jo Jo Zep'.

CARLTON CALLING, PART THREE: JO JO ZEP AND THE FALCONS

Jo Jo Zep and the Falcons were yet another Carlton band featuring a former Pelaco Brother to develop under the influence of Ross Wilson; they lasted longer, and went through many more permutations, than any of their cohort. Elements of the band were drawn from Rock Granite and/or Pat Wilson's Marvels[313] and recorded a single, produced by Ross Wilson, under the stupid name Jo Jo Zep and his Little Helpers (rejecting even worse ones such as 'Joe Soap' and 'Jo Jo Zu Zu').[314] Wilson had wanted to form a band with Camilleri playing saxophone plus Jeff Burstin, Wayne Burt, Stephen Cummings on vocals, 'and a drummer'; Camilleri later recalled that Cummings 'came to a few rehearsals and couldn't get into it, and Wilson couldn't do it, so we decided to go ahead, with me singing. I didn't really want to.'[315] This was presumably not false modesty on Camilleri's part, yet he took to the band leader role with gusto: 'What I did in the Falcons,' he told Wendy Milsom, 'was fifteen years of everything I knew; I threw it all in and hoped for the best.'[316] He later said that he 'put a lot of hard work into it. I liked the Jo Jo Zep character.'[317]

This 'character' is a little hard to define. Jo Jo Zep and the Falcons – Camilleri with Jeff Burstin, Wayne Burt, John Power and Gary Young – bashed out two mid-70s rock/R&B albums, produced by Ross Wilson for his Oz label. The songs were a mixture of originals (by Burt or Young) and covers; the group recorded the mildly bawdy 'Beating around the Bush' for the first-rate soundtrack to Chris Löfvén's wonderful *Oz: A Rock'n'Roll Road Movie* and, as mentioned earlier, released a cover of Otis Redding's 'Security' as a single. Though he may have fallen accidentally into leading Jo Jo Zep and the Falcons, Camilleri – who had a family to support – took on the group as a project, and attempted to convince Glenn Wheatley to manage them, 'because he's real ruthless – *really* ruthless' – to the extent, it seems, that Wheatley was taking tips from Chaplin in *The Great Dictator*:

> Every time I would go to talk to him, he'd have the globe of the world and he would spin it around – he'd say we could go anywhere in the world. And all I wanted to know is if we were working next week.[318]

The first two Jo Jo Zep albums – only the debut featured Burt, who was then replaced by Tony Faehse, an Adelaide guitarist who'd once been a member of the preposterously titled Musick Express and had spent part of the early 70s in Britain playing with Alvin Stardust – were *Whip It Out* and *Don't Waste It*. They were accomplished and energetic, but in many ways too predicated on dated R&B, and while the band quickly became a successful live act, their records did not chart. They parted ways with Oz and EMI after a dispute over the retail price of their *So Young* EP – the record company wanted to charge $5.99, the band wanted $3.99 – and signed to Mushroom. Having failed to sign the Pelaco Brothers as a group, Gudinski was apparently now collecting members one by one. Elvis Costello, impressed by Jo Jo Zep on his first Australian tour, covered the song 'So Young'; Camilleri, impressed by Costello, was to create the album *Hats Off Step Lively* as a tribute to Costello's *Armed Forces*, though no-one seemed prepared to admit it at the time.

The signing to Mushroom merely formalised a process; Jo Jo Zep were already co-managed by Michael Gudinski (with Michael Roberts).[319] They acquired Ol' 55's Wilbur Wilde, who temporarily took on the ludicrous name Bad Youth Ivory,[320] as their saxophonist and reluctant polymoog player; Wilde had guested with the group as early as 1976.[321] They then embarked on a string of moderately successful and fondly regarded ska-flavoured hit singles, beginning with 'Hit and Run'. *Screaming Targets* was their first album to go gold[322] and also the first to explore the songwriting partnership of Camilleri/Burstin/Faehse; in addition, it featured a song by Paul Kelly, 'Only the Lonely Hearted'[323] – in order to give Kelly 'some credibility', or so Camilleri joked.[324] Camilleri's anxiety about balancing the group's financial return with artistic satisfaction is apparent in interviews he did at the time, whether he was satirically speculating about winning Tattslotto (the Victorian state lottery) so that he could subject the band members (and himself) to plastic surgery and make them as good-looking as LRB,[325] or opining:

> I reckon a band has about three years to make it in this country and then you've got to expand overseas ... Ultimately you've got to have that overseas stamp of approval.[326]

Ed St John noted Camilleri's tendency to criticise 'the band, the record company and (most often) himself';[327] the subtext of much of this criticism seems to be his belief that he was slightly older than much of his audience. He did not pretend otherwise, though he certainly did not look decrepit. Nevertheless, digs such as the *NME's* description of the group as 'ageing flabby flops' producing 'middle-aged, mildewed music'[328] would hardly have tickled.

Perhaps perversely, Jo Jo Zep and the Falcons records began to get younger in tone – lighter and more pop; Camilleri, in his role as 'Jo Jo', was less the pool-room Chico Marx-ish hustler of the early albums, more a sanitised, shallow pop singer. But on the whole, the records – *Screaming Targets, Hats Off Step Lively,* and the *Dexterity* EP – got better.

Jo Jo Zep and the Falcons were sufficiently mainstream and sufficiently credible at the same time that Camilleri was hired to record a track to celebrate the new commercial FM rock station EON-FM in 1980. But the group were in their death throes in 1981 when they released the single 'Sweet' – not only *their* best record, but possibly Camilleri's best ever from a large and varied assortment; it was certainly one of the finest releases of a very good year. 'Sweet' abandoned everything they'd preached about ska-inflected pop (except the value of a hook) and their earlier R&B style for a harder, more driving rock song. Camilleri switches between his usual vocal style and a falsetto; the band crashes down around him. Although Camilleri was now on the cusp of his third decade of genre-hopping, Jo Jo Zep and the Falcons' hit singles were his first mainstream work and radio programmers were seemingly made uneasy by the new direction. 'Sweet' was not the number one it should have been.

The group split up in mid 1981 in Tasmania,[329] and Camilleri switched direction yet again: disbanding the Falcons, he and Jeff Burstin made one more album in the original Jo Jo Zep series. *Cha* was primarily a Latin-styled dance record, and its hit single, 'Taxi Mary', featured Camilleri dueting with Jane Clifton, who was by now most famous as an actor. Camilleri later said of the song that it came at a time when 'we weren't looking too good on the charts, you know. I needed a hair transplant, I needed some work on my teeth, I needed platform shoes and to put my kids through university.'[330]

A version of the group toured until 1983, when Camilleri embarked on a European tour as saxophonist in Icehouse; he also played on that band's *Sidewalk* album. He then launched a new band, the Black Sorrows, which would ultimately be his most commercially successful project. He continued to be prolific and multifaceted in his output.

At the turn of the decade Camilleri briefly ran an independent label, Mighty Records, with the bizarre motto: 'Mr Ethnic reaches out for the Third World.'[331] In a nod to Carlton days, he produced a single for Janie Conway, and launched a second label, Spirit, with records by Jane Clifton, local singer Billy Baxter, and Nick Smith, who would play a major role in the rebooting of Camilleri's career in the late 80s. [332]

... AND THE SUBURBS BITE BACK

Australians tend to see the inner city and suburbia as very distinct places, though they don't always agree where one ends and the other begins: the dividing line is probably five kilometres from the city centre (three for hardliners). The unusual flipside to the Carlton bands' story was the rise of performers who – with varying degrees of irony – celebrated suburbia. As mentioned earlier, Skyhooks had made it okay to write about the Australian suburbs, but not necessarily okay to *like* them, regardless of the fact that they were clearly the heartland of Australian society, the place where the bulk of their audience lived and where almost all the band members themselves had grown up. The (formerly suburban) Boys Next Door's sarcastic name made fun of the notion of 'normal', but groups like Sydney's Mental as Anything – who began in the late 70s but flourished in the early 80s as an important and credible pop act – and Perth's Dave Warner's From the Suburbs were not frightened of suburbia, and indeed embraced it.

The members of Mental as Anything had met at art school in 1976 and were 'doing that punk scene really early',[333] playing at the Civic where bands like X and Wasted Daze also made their mark.[334] They displayed 'a certain gonzo humour';[335] from their first EP *Mental as Anything Plays at Your Party* onwards they were to celebrate Australiana in the classic sense and with extraordinary pop nous. *Plays at Your Party*, which the subsequently highly successful label Regular Records was set up to release, sold over 13,000 copies in two pressings[336] without the benefit of a conventional distribution arrangement. *RAM* writer Annie Burton told her readers in 1979 that Mental as Anything reminded her of 'activated garden gnomes'.[337] They are discussed in chapter 16 in the context of their commercial heyday in the 1980s.

Dave Warner, who briefly became nationally famous in the late 70s, has had an extraordinary career. He started out playing keyboards with a school group called Dreyfus, which practiced at his parents' house in Bicton; this was followed briefly by another group, the Umbrella Invasion, and a short-lived pop magazine called *Umbrella*, 'the paper that covers everything'.[338] Warner was still in his mid-teens. He had a short stint playing keyboards in a 'commercial' group known as Lupin Beck[339] which was followed in 1971 by a prog art-theatre group, Opus West, which had ambitions of playing original material in Perth's Swan Hotels, a chain of large, popular venues.[340] This group cut an album entitled *Dreyfus – Out of Beacon* at Souvenir Records of Bentley, but do not appear to have pressed, much less sold any copies.[341] Soon afterwards, Warner heard the Fugs and was inspired to form Pus, a band which attempted a different show every time they played.[342]

The name 'Pus' seems at first blush to be a crass play on 'Opus', but Warner associate Alan Howard – who wrote a memoir of Warner's early years, published in 1981 – implies that the similarity was a coincidence: Pus was merely preferred to the other main contender for the band's name, 'Pimple'. Group members changed their names to 'Grim Reaper' (Warner), 'Wild Scrote' (Howard), and

Captain Pimple (bass player and 'incorrigible eccentric'[343] Michael Feeney) so they would be 'playing parts, like a comic strip.'[344] Pus believed that only the local group Mud (later known as Crabs)[345] and Melbourne's Daddy Cool were their equals as entertainers:[346] their crowd-pleasing show closer was an anthem called 'Throbbing Knob.'[347]

Warner wrote his iconic song 'Suburban Boy' while driving to a psychology lecture at the University of Western Australia.[348] Pus's only studio recordings were made in mid 1975 when Warner had left for London; he added his vocals in a British studio.[349] Early the following year, having been joined in the UK by Feeney, he recorded some Pus songs with backing from members of the Albion Country Band. By October that year they were back, playing at fabled Perth entertainment venue the Octagon (not to be confused with the Elizabeth venue of the same name), billed as 'Dave Warner – From the Suburbs', along with a co-vocalist, Terry Serio.[350] Serio would go on to prominence as an actor and singer; other talented individuals, like Warner's UWA friend Bleddyn Butcher, would assist Pus and Warner. Butcher understood Warner's crafted vision of locally relevant music and was his promotional photographer.[351]

Warner and Feeny went on to consolidate their new group, which showcased Warner. His song 'From the Suburbs' became the band's name, which in turn became a dangerous statement: Dave Warner's From the Suburbs. The group's first album, *Mug's Game*, was half live, half studio recordings. 'Suburban Boy', which until now had been a violin-oriented song, was toughened up into something more contemporary that would stand up as a single.[352] Warner's vision – to celebrate the suburbs and perform for their residents – was not ironic, but he was smart enough to see it might play that way for many.[353]

Dave Warner's From the Suburbs
Meanwhile in the Suburbs

By the time the group were sufficiently known to be able to tour in the eastern states, they were rumoured to have a repertoire of ninety songs; Warner seemed almost serious when he suggested he could write four albums about a *door* as a manifestation of 'suburban rock'.[354] Live cassettes of their shows were available at 'certain hip record shops.'[355] Warner was unapologetically verbal: when the Carlton venue Martinis cut the power to make the band finish their set, an anonymous *Juke* writer reported, 'Warner continued on, without microphones, to the accompaniment of just the drummer and delivered a vicious, spontaneous rave about the management at Martinis and how they couldn't stop the people from hearing the music.'[356] Spontaneity seems to have been key: one writer praised his capacity for 'slabs of verbal content that makes these songs a new experience each time. The basic outline and concept remain the same, but the inner parts are always finely tuned so that these songs act... as one of the most scatological barometers available to the Australian culture.'[357]

Warner was outspoken at all times, his swimming against the tide fuelled only by passion. His records, he said, were 'an attempt to make something out of averageness; to invest some glamour into our otherwise boring lives.'[358] He told *Juke* there was only a 'handful of bands in Australia' of any value, 'and the rest of them are rip-offs, and second-rate rip-offs at that. Of the bands that I think deserve recognition are people like Skyhooks and Dragon. I like some of the material the Angels do.'[359] He later pointed out perceptively to *RAM* readers that Dragon 'came up with great pop songs without straining to model themselves on something overseas.'[360]

At the same time, Warner was upfront about his own motivations, admitting, 'I've never been able to sort out how I feel about my own experiences in life. Whether I was ever happy, angry or sad when I was being brought up in the suburbs.'[361]

What he was not, he was certain, was the Barry Humphries of rock 'n' roll:

> Humphries is a straight satirist anyway, whereas with my stuff I have a lot more sympathy for the suburbs. It's actually a great cultural identity that has been neglected... All of us have been told by artists or people connected with the arts for as long as I can remember since I was a kid, that culturally the worst thing to be is middle class. It's great if you're working class in the slums and you go around beating people up because you're a product of your environment and all that sort of thing.[362]

Warner hated punks; his song 'Suburban Rock' stated 'I'm not a punk rocker I've been there before / Anyway, punk rockers are really heads / They've only gone where the hippies led.'[363] But he wasn't afraid to mess with Australian pop icons, either, as in his epic fantasy 'Half Time at the Football', which imagined Sherbet's singer, Daryl Braithwaite, 'watching the action' – an orgy on a living room floor – 'from the television screen while *Countdown's* on.'[364]

Warner had a good head for business, and was commercially successful between the late 70s and early 80s.[365] 'Suburban Boy' – a once-heard, never-forgotten plea for understanding – is his greatest contribution to pop's pantheon. Its narrator is lonely and alone, and he's 'sure that it must be / easier for boys from the city'. The song made the top thirty in late 1978, and has remained in the 70s rock canon. Warner's first three mainstream albums, *Mug's Game*, *Free Kicks* and *Correct Weight*, were recorded live, completely or in part, and, importantly, all became truck-stop favourites on cassette for decades afterwards. *Correct Weight* was probably his best; it wasn't, he said in 1980, 'received with exceptional glee. But there's no doubt in my mind that it's the best Australian album out at the moment.'[366] Warner continued to turn out records sporadically but also wrote plays, and has more recently published books. He was never a hack performer, but his commissioned history of Mushroom Records, prepared for the label's 25th birthday, and his sleeve notes for the label's greatest hits CDs were unremarkable. His *Countdown* book of 2006 was somewhat better; his good-humoured, populist crime fiction is often quite fine.

WHAT LIVING'S ALL ABOUT

Warner was not the first, nor would he be the last, to single out Daryl Braithwaite as a symbol of bland, glitzy, almost himbo-fashion pop hollowness. Skyhooks' rendition of 'Big Bad Bruce' was surely not 'a dedication' to Braithwaite, as one dedicated *RAM* reader declared,[367] but it's clear that some people – particularly those who took sides in the Sherbet vs Skyhooks debate – thought this kind of abuse was appropriate. When Dave Graney won an ARIA 'Best Male Vocalist' award in 1996 and declared himself 'the King of Pop', he already had some years of Braithwaite-baiting behind him, most notably his extended fantasy, often expounded at live shows, that involved American film actor Warren Oates sitting in the Chat 'n' Chew, a seedy central Melbourne cafe, with Braithwaite's severed head in a bag beside him. Braithwaite certainly does not display anything resembling sardonic wit in his public appearances, though he is not averse to self-deprecating humour, as when he participated in a sight gag for the ABC's *Late Show* in which he was busking with an impossibly massive cap on the ground in front of him – a reference to temporary financial embarrassment.[368] The worst myth about Braithwaite is, undoubtedly, a prime example of rock establishment snobbery: according to the story, Bon Scott encouraged him to drink 'champagne' – actually, Scott's urine – from a roast chicken. As Braithwaite pointed out when confronted with this story, he and Scott were friends; what's more, unlike Braithwaite's detractors, Scott did not have that kind of cruel streak. In any case, the less we dwell on a world view in which the pinnacle of rock 'n' roll decadence is drinking alcohol (or bodily waste) from a small fowl's corpse the better.

Though they have always had their supporters – and while their run of 20 consecutive hit singles over the course of the 70s threw up some truly excellent recordings – Sherbet do seem, in hindsight, to have backed the wrong horse if they were trying for Australian rock 'n' roll immortality. Their songs were rarely uniquely Australian in content, because their collective eye was focused, through the prism of their manager Roger Davies, on the international market. Though they were not, as is often assumed, utterly pop- and teen-oriented, their pre-eminent skill lay in creating rousing, up-to-the-moment pop singles, and they were also good-looking young men (in satin bomber jackets, no less) who exploited their teen appeal without pushing any kind of overtly sexual angle in the way that Hush (or even the Ted Mulry Gang!) would do. For better or worse, there was a perception within the music industry that Sherbet owed their initial prominence to a cologne ad.[369] In short, all the elements that once served to make them successful now seem to condemn them; a January 2007 episode of the soap opera *Neighbours* in which the fortysomething lovers Steiger and Janelle enthuse over Sherbet concerts and paraphernalia – intrinsically 'daggy' obsessions – would not have rung true had it revolved around any other band.

Clive Shakespeare formed Sherbet in Sydney in 1969 from the ashes of his earlier group, the Downtown Roll Band. Alan Sandow replaced Sherbet's original drummer, Danny Taylor, three months after the band was launched, and line-up change became a frequent occurrence: when Shakespeare departed seven years later Sandow was the closest thing Sherbet had to an original member. Daryl Braithwaite replaced original vocalist Dennis Laughlin – who would become an early manager of AC/DC – in mid 1970. In their 'infancy',[370] Sherbet were a heavier, almost psychedelic group, and soon found work (a baptism by fire, really) in the form of an eight-month residency at Jonathan's discotheque which saw them play for seven hours a night four nights a week.

Individual members were expendable in a group whose early incarnation was later described as 'just another band of imageless young hopefuls hacking round the dives of Sydney back in '71'.[371] Organist Sammy See left to join Flying Circus and then Fraternity; his subsequent career in the 80s, when he went on to play with Jimmy Barnes and then John Farnham, proved to be a jobbing musician's dream run. Garth Porter replaced him and would become one half of Sherbet's songwriting goldmine. Early Sherbet hits were often covers, such as Barbara Keith's jaunty 'Free the People' in mid 1971, featuring soon-to-depart bassist Bruce Worrall on tuba, and Ted Mulry's 'You're All Woman' twelve months later (obtained, the group claimed, 'after spending a drunken evening' with Mulry).[372] In between those two hits, they engaged the services of manager Roger Davies,[373] who apparently saw no need to stop them releasing a genuinely toxic version of Leiber and Stoller's 'Hound Dog' 'especially for our Melbourne audience'.[374] But the Porter/Shakespeare songwriting team was on track by 1974, launching two brilliant singles that year: the dazzling glam of 'Slipstream' – which employed a theremin-style keyboard line and, excitingly for a generation about to become immersed in *Countdown*, a genuine rocket launch–style 10 to 1 count down – was followed by the jaunty, unapologetically cheesy ballad 'Silvery Moon'. The latter paved the way for Braithwaite's 'solo' career, which was not dissimilar in (lack of) value to Shirley Strachan's, although he was usually backed and supported by his band. Sherbet unleashed another 'Slipstream'-style basher, 'Summer Love', in March 1975; it was at this time that the group cannily took control of both the production and funding of their recordings, which they then leased to record companies – an unusual arrangement then as now.[375]

Sherbet were a strange group, but they had their pride. In the mid 70s Porter reflected on the way they always seemed to be pitted against bands many saw as more valid, or at least more rocking:

I remember when it was first starting to happen for us in Melbourne – in the promotion for the concerts at Festival Hall, it was made to look like a race. First it was Sherbet against Daddy Cool. Then it was us vs Billy Thorpe. Then there was the Madder Lake thing. Every time we went to Melbourne, a lot of the press would say 'Madder Lake are going to blow you off stage today.' Well it didn't quite happen like that. Then there was the Ariel thing. Which was promoted as good music against our teen appeal . . . as if we played basic three-chord music or something like that – which we never have. Then there was the Hush thing.[376]

Adrian Ryan was going against the grain in offering this later paean to the band:

'Summer Love' was rendered only slightly less than classic by dippy lyrics, but riding on thunderous drums, slashing power chords and great Braithwaite vocals, it deserves to be filed next to the best summer singles by the Beach Boys, Lovin' Spoonful and the Rascals. When Daryl sang 'Everyone's talking 'bout the summertime blues/but that ain't true', he was defiantly proclaiming a vision of Australian seasons in the sun as defined by a decade of TV commercials, and you knew he meant every word.[377]

At the end of 1975, Sherbet indulged in an 'incredibly left-field concept',[378] their aggressively experimental *Life . . . Is for Living* album. One writer likened the tracks to 'rejects from an advertising campaign for transcendental meditation';[379] according to Porter: 'It's not a concept album . . . It's just some of our views on life, what living's all about'.[380] *Life . . . Is for Living*, the working title for which had been *Life and Times, Words and Rhymes*,[381] is a superb mélange of prog and bubblegum; the band's telegrammatic yet clichéd lyrics let them down too often, and the yells of 'rock 'n' roll!' on the glam dirge 'Matter of Time' sound desperate, but the overall effect is nevertheless highly stimulating. The album begins with a sound collage history of Australia (didgeridoos and woodchopping give way to 1970s civilisation – missile launches, phones ringing) and a mellotron-driven instrumental; the title song, the first vocal track on the album, is a breathless, efficient, exhilarating piece that demonstrates exactly what made Sherbet a great band. They were musically adventurous, more than competent, and they had gumption.

Christie Eliezer was impressed in his unimpressedness:

Despite all the hoo-hah about *Life* being a concept album, musically it regurgitates the formula Sherbet have faithfully adhered to on their three studio albums . . . Technically Sherbet are by no means brilliant musicians. Their long-running consistency has rested instead on their eclectic and flexible nature as a collective unit, their ability in keeping their finger on the pulse of pop and anticipating trends and, most important of all, a naïve eagerness to random experimentation and exploration of other musical forms that is diluted by a massive sense of self-discipline.[382]

Felicity Surtees, writing in *RAM*, marveled at the group and its ambience:

> Sherbet's loyal fans have the dedication of Kamikaze pilots. Sherbet is not *just* a band and their music is not *just* music. In fact the actual music is often eclipsed by the fanatical adulation heaped upon the band members, their charisma, personalities, spunky bodies, pretty faces. And *that's* a pity – Sherbet's music is of a consistently high standard and it would be nice if some of the acclaim could be diverted in this direction.[383]

Few bands achieve complete personnel change. The group that peaked in 1976 were literally not the same group that had debuted in 1969. After a 'bummer of a tour' in Tasmania when their roadie, Geoff Cook, died in a road accident and bassist Tony Mitchell was busted for marijuana possession,[384] Sherbet parted ways with their founder. Clive Shakespeare told *RAM*'s Anthony O'Grady: 'I was ... whatever you want to call it ... dismissed, sacked.'[385] He recorded an impressive single ('I Realize') and planned a solo album – which never eventuated, perhaps in part because he (or record companies) feared confusion with William Shakespeare, whose monster Vanda and Young hits were only a few years in the past. Clive Shakespeare wished 'William Shakespeare would change his name or just disappear or something ... maybe even go back to his real name. It could get pretty confusing.'[386] He went on to start a recording studio, and in the process assisted in the recording of many of Sydney's great independent records of the 1980s and mainstream classics such as Paul Kelly's *Post*.

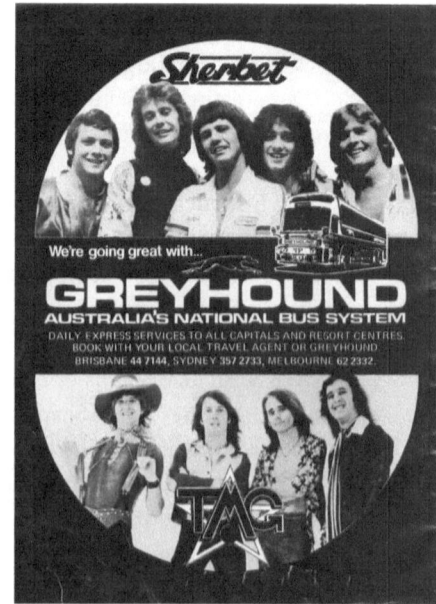

Clive Shakespeare was temporarily replaced in Sherbet by Ian 'Gunther' Gorman –'a real street punk guitarist'[387] Porter said at the time – who then returned to Richard Clapton's band, from which he had merely been borrowed. Harvey James was then brought in from putative rivals Ariel; he also replaced Shakespeare as half of Porter's songwriting team. 'Ambition above loyalty' was Mike Rudd's assessment of his bandmate's defection at the time,[388] though he now recognizes equivocally that James 'saw an opportunity and took it.'

The South Yarra-raised Braithwaite had been a primary school friend of Olivia

Newton-John, and it was reputedly at her insistence that Sherbet made an appearance on a program described as the *Olivia Newton-John – Glen Campbell TV Special*[389] which Porter described as 'so corny it would make you weep. Kangaroos leaping all over the place, koalas coming out of the woodwork. During our song there was even a cut to people bowling!'[390] These were lawn bowlers rather than cricketers, but Sherbet's next release was the extended cricket-metaphor romance 'Howzat', which would be their biggest hit. Porter later claimed the song had 'dumb lyrics',[391] but the concept of a girl who 'got my head undone' is a fine piece of naïve imagery, and indeed gave the great late-80s Melbourne band Head Undone its name.

Sherbet's manager Roger Davies had been pushing for international deals, but their overseas break came not from any deal struck by Davies, but rather by accident: the surprise involvement of an English 'promotions man' called Arthur Sheriff, who, Julia Orange told *Rolling Stone's* readers the following year, 'literally stumbled into Sherbet's studio, heard "Howzat" and brought the single to England, where it became top ten.'[392] Sheriff – more recently promotions manager for Aardman Animation – says that, rather than stumbling into it, he had been taken to the studio by Festival's promotions manager Peter Karpin; nevertheless, there is still an air of the haphazard to the story, as there so often is in pop. Sherbet duly travelled to the northern hemisphere, where Davies observed: 'there's this whole mystique about being Australian. The only thing that pisses us off is that everyone calls you Bruce.'[393] On returning, Braithwaite commented: 'Living in Australia is a privilege.'[394]

The follow-up to 'Howzat' was a piece of cabaret slop called 'Hollywood Dreaming'; in a rare display of mass audience taste, it failed to chart. The group's next effort, the absurd 'Rock Me Gently', was no better, yet it made the top ten. In their continued confusion as to why pop success apparently negated respect for their musicianship, Sherbet returned to their enthusiasm for concepts on their next album, *Photoplay*, the first release on their own label, Razzle. The album was to have been titled *Magazine* (the single was 'Magazine Madonna'), but Sherbet (or someone in their camp) feared that the existence of albums by the British new wave band Magazine might confuse consumers into thinking this was a Magazine album called *Sherbet* – an absurd notion. Their US label at the time, MCA, used the original title. The album's packaging was, Adrian Ryan recalled later in *Roadrunner*, 'outrageously over the top, with a twelve-page glossy booklet featuring photos by... Gered Mankowicz', but Ryan felt 'the music was vacuous, lush and forgettable.'[395] The single was certainly a dud – the usual false construction of womanhood. Why anyone believed that covering the Beatles' 'Nowhere Man' as a follow-up would fix the damage is unfathomable. Sherbet supported the Hollies on a US tour in 1978, and the band's genuine last gasp in Australia was the album *Sherbet*.

Sherbet's new US label, RSO (which signed them on the recommendation of their friends the Bee Gees[396]) insisted that the band change their name to

Highway.[397] This was apparently because RSO wanted them to be (or at least appear) 'heavier',[398] and it happened despite the fact the band had made a moderate impact in the US – the lower reaches of the album and singles charts – under their original name in the mid 70s. The *Sherbet* album, their seventh, was accordingly retitled *Highway 1* for US release and given a new cover depicting the band, and a car, on a highway. The new name did not go down well in Australia, where it seemed simply ludicrous, and Highway only released one further single. (In an amusing self-parody, the reformed Sherbet played warm-up shows around Sydney in 2006 as 'Daryl Braithwaite and Highway'.)

Sherbet split in March 1979, though they were not officially dropped by RSO in the US until August.[399] Whereas the Shakespeare debacle had been the product of internal tensions, this breakup came from a realisation that the group might have exchanged their Australian pop fanbase merely to jump through a series of hoops for uncaring international record companies who had no special insight into a global audience; although there was also, of course, the unassailable truth that teen audiences – actually, most audiences – move on. Porter blamed Davies:

> He was creating a big thing. He wanted us to have the biggest effect we possibly could. The marketing process was the shortest road to achieving that end ... From a creative standpoint, in terms of writing exactly how you felt, that never really happened. For some reason it was always more important to perpetuate the monster rather than make a personal statement.[400]

An interview with Anthony O'Grady of *RAM* exposed a genuinely baffled Braithwaite, who seemed lost amid the late-70s Australian musical landscape of new wave, pub rock, and minority-taste groups, asking:

> Why do you think the scene's so changed around? It's a totally different thing to the way we were brought up ... it just wouldn't be right for us to start blasting out powerchords. We're a different sort of band, but over the past year it just slipped away from us here ... Everything seems to have gone back to the pubs and clubs. And the audiences there want *angry* bands. Do you think that's because so many young people are unemployed?[401]

Harvey James published his home address in a *RAM* article, suggesting he was 'looking for good young players'[402] for his post-Sherbet music. Braithwaite tried to start a solo career and recorded an album, *Out on the Fringe*, in Los Angeles with session musicians.

This was not the real end of the band, however, just the preparation for a long drawn-out demise. By the end of the year, Porter and Shakespeare were writing together again.[403] Though Shakespeare did not reconvene with his former bandmates, the late-70s post-Shakespeare line-up used a common nickname[404] for themselves when they came together again as the Sherbs, 'a more familiar and credible alternative to attack the 80s with.'[405] Braithwaite was adamant they'd be true to themselves: 'What we're gonna do is just do our own thing and not be intimidated by what's happening or what people tell us we should be doing. It's just going to be *us*.'[406] But they were already going against earlier resolutions by blasting out power chords, as on their 1980 single 'Never Surrender', a credible piece of new-wave power pop which was, of course, not credible in anyone's mind at the time because it was being played by the archaic joke, one-time boy band Sherbet hiding behind the name 'the Sherbs'. 'No-one wants to let the Sherbet days alone,' said Garth Porter. 'It's really pathetic. We feel so strong, so positive about what we're doing now that we feel that Australia will only be incidental to our future career!'[407]

In 1984, having made no further impact on the charts, they broke up again. James and Shakespeare (who reconciled late in life with his former bandmates and participated in latter-day reunions) died within a year of one another in 2011 and 2012, both from cancer.

The legacy of Sherbet/Highway/the Sherbs continues to be reassessed – as indeed it should – largely in the band's favour. A fillip came in the form of a track on Daft Punk's 2013 album *Random Access Memories;* the album, undoubtedly one of the year's most successful (and best), included a track, 'Contact', substantially sampled from the Sherbs' 1982 non-hit 'We Ride Tonight'. It was rumoured to have been gestating as a Daft Punk idea since at least 2002,[408] and is the only track on that album that makes use of a sample. Mitchell, Porter and Braithwaite thus found themselves credited as three of six songwriters on the closing track of a multi-million selling album that won five major Grammys, thirty-one years after the original song's release. It would be naive to regard this as vindication of the Sherbs' vision, because part of the appeal of the original sample is its 'retro' nature, but it is important to recognise that much of the original song's mettle shows through in 'Contact'. Braithwaite – the only one of his 70s bandmates still touring regularly – did not introduce 'We Ride Tonight' into his live repertoire, though in his between-song banter at one 2014 show, at least, he did not shrink from making wry comments about the belated megasuccess of at least one small part of a project once considered a joke and a lost cause.

SINGER-SONGWRITERS

One thing that many of the biggest bands of the mid to late 70s in Australia had in common – Sherbet, Skyhooks, Dragon, Cold Chisel, and more – was that their primary songwriter(s) were not the lead singer and in most cases did not sing at all. This does not mean there was not a strong singer-songwriter strand in Australian music at the time. Unfortunately, it was often marked by the po-faced attitude that was a hallmark of the generation of coddled, self-righteous artistic men who came of age in the 70s.

Doug Ashdown was a notable exception. His ballad 'Winter in America', first released under the title 'Leave Love Enough Alone', was deservedly a substantial hit in 1976-77.[409] In an age of nascent pop nationalism, Ashdown was criticised for placing the word 'America' in his song's title, the inference being that he was trying to pass for an American; the same rebuke had been aimed earlier in the decade at groups like Mississippi and songs like 'Arkansas Grass.' Ashdown's hit album was maudlin, intelligent, well-crafted folk-pop. His wife, Carol, joined him and his white polo neck on the cover: she looked very much like a young child. His co-writer Jimmy Stewart was present in the subdued beggars' banquet depicted on the back cover. Future members of Little River Band played on the album; early 60s Melbourne folk singer Declan Affley contributed aeolian pipes. Stewart and Ashdown could be hokey, but they weren't without their arty side: they plotted to release a 'cult object' entitled *Ladies and Gentlemen* that would feature 'Palm Court music, drawn from the Edwardian era.'[410] Sadly this album – which brings to mind Paul McCartney's *Thrillington* project – does not appear to have emerged.

Richard Clapton's place in Australian music is legendary, though the bulk of his work is without doubt an acquired taste. Clapton's 2014 memoir fails to address his ethnic heritage, but in other media he has explained that his doctor father was 'distinctly Chinese looking', which can be taken to mean that in racist 60s-70s Australia Clapton hid his Asian heritage in plain sight for most of his career.[411] This is not to suggest duplicity; Marty Rhone, Samantha/Cheryl Sang, Les Gock and Rick Lum all addressed similar issues – their responses covering a spectrum between complete obfuscation and absolute embrace. Whatever name Clapton was born with, he definitely has not wanted it revealed; he took his rock name from his guitar hero Eric. Born in Sydney, he was a commercial art student[412] who returned to Australia in the earlier 70s after hanging out at Apple[413] and playing in seven 'terrible' groups in Britain[414] and in an 'off-the-wall' Berlin experimental scene (his band there, Sopwith Camel, were shot down in flames for the non-trivial if easily rectifiable reason that there was already a San Francisco rock group with the same name, though Clapton suggested in 1975 that their demise was due to 'company red tape').[415] Emerging from a Sydney folk scene centred on a 'trendy folk club' in the Kirk Gallery, a converted church building,[416] he briefly replaced Renée Geyer in the group Sun in 1973[417] but had a low-key relationship with the record-buying public until his top-ten hit of 1975, the laidback and chorus-less[418] 'Girls on the Avenue'. He claimed to have written the tune in half an hour, though he insisted it was not contrived; for many it was the catchy guitar lines of New Zealander Red McKelvie (formerly of Flying Circus) that sold the song.

That Clapton's career is based on strong songwriting talent is emphasized by his complete unsuitability, visually and temperamentally, for teen heartthrob status (*Spunky* columnist Mr. Cool tastefully suggested he had 'a face which hardly befits the word "pretty"'[419]). He has had a lasting presence in Australia, not just because the record industry continues to serve him up as a boutique taste for fiftysomething audiophiles, but in other, less expected ways too. He produced early records for INXS and, strange as it may now seem, gave them credibility in the industry (few others cared) simply by doing so. More extraordinarily, whether by default or design Chris Bailey of the Saints adopted all of Clapton's vocal mannerisms for twenty years of his music career after 1980 – an approach which benefited neither man.

Clapton manifestly grappled with the problem of communication with his audience, although it is difficult now to understand exactly why so much was expected of him. It is distinctly possible that simply because he looked so unlike a pop star, people (particularly journalists, but also perhaps other musicians – his backing bands were always a stellar collection of names) assumed he was a prophet. Ed St John coated the Clapton legend – such as it was – in a clingy Jesus-esque syrup when he told *Rolling Stone* readers that Clapton was, 'like most of us, a confused and perpetually disoriented man searching for a path to follow.'[420] Clapton himself mused:

> In the early Seventies my audience was limited to a few thousand people, most of them at University. Those people have now graduated and they have become doctors and dentists. They've grown up and become like everybody else, so how effective was it? Now I feel that if I'm not writing music which will be played on AM radio then I'm wanking. Somebody has got to put some sort of common-sense view to the public, and by common-sense I don't mean left-wing, because I'm not left-wing. I just mean a sane, rational view.[421]

Putting aside this naive view of a world in which everyone is like a doctor or a dentist, as well as the ridiculous idea of the songwriter as a propagandist for sane and rational views, the pedestal on which Clapton was placed is clearly visible and, to judge by much of his output, fairly preposterous. David Pepperell, always outspoken and thoroughly consistent, says he has 'always, since that first magic time I saw him at the Kingston in 1974, regarded him as this country's finest singer-songwriter and someone who has captured the Australian ethos more than any other music artist.'[422] Clapton ended the 70s with the album *Dark Spaces*, its title track addressed to Sylvia Plath as though she were some kind of seductive film actress (or indeed a 'girl' on an 'avenue'). 'Reading her poetry is much better than watching TV', he told St John and, through him, the doctors and dentists of Australia. Clapton utilised Dragon's drummer Kerry Jacobsen for the album, and claimed its 'spirit' was 'mine and Kerry Jacobsen's . . . He's the most human drummer I can think of.'[423]

In the 80s, as mentioned, Clapton would produce INXS and have the favour returned some time later when that band backed him on not one but two greatest hits live packages. Clapton has long asserted that rock music is, unfairly, too sexy and shallow. He has maintained a career in music for all his adult life.

Paul Kelly is only six years younger than Richard Clapton but seems to belong to an entirely different era – in some respects almost to an entirely different society. This may be, in part or even wholly, because of the way he has continued to experiment with sounds and styles, for instance on the buoyant self-titled 1999 album by Professor Ratbaggy. While Kelly's recorded output under his own name is far from perfect, he has contributed marvelous songs to the pop canon and engaged in a number of imaginative and inspired projects to boot.

Kelly began playing trumpet at the age of ten. Miranda Brown introduced him to *RAM* readers in 1979, telling them that at the age of 17:[424]

> He dropped out of a music/philosophy course to travel around Australia for several years working as a railways fettler, stage hand, brick layer, and foundry worker before returning to Adelaide to try playing music professionally.[425]

He also wrote bush balladry, published in Flinders University's *Empire Times*,[426] and helped run a literary magazine, *Another One for Mary*, which was published in Adelaide between 1976 and 1977.[427] Though Kelly's name did not appear under any of the magazine's stories, the curiously named Kiley Pale contributed tales of intense and lonely young men, including the 'backstairs musician' who mused:

> Six cans of beer plus a packet of cigarettes plus four hours equals one song. The best songs are written during heatwaves.[428]

In his memoir *How to Make Gravy*, Kelly does not mention Kiley Pale. Keith Shadwick, who co-founded the literary magazine *Dodo* and had a book of poetry, *Windows and Mirrors*, published in 1977, was also a contributor – of poems – to *Another One for Mary*. One of these, 'Rock/Roll Revolvers', is a musing on record reviews; 'ah, this is/the thinking and the taking/and I like the beat'.[429] Shadwick, whom we already encountered briefly in Carlton, was to become a well-regarded and prolific music writer in Britain, focusing particularly on jazz.

When Kelly moved to Melbourne in 1976, he became a member of the High Rise Bombers alongside saxophonist Shadwick, guitarists Martin Armiger and Chris Langman, and drummer John Lloyd, who went on to join Flowers in 1979. The High Rise Bombers split in mid 1978 (leaving behind a live cassette, sold at the Missing Link shop);[430] the following year Kelly formed Paul Kelly and the Dots with Langman and Lloyd. Their Tony Cohen-produced song 'Recognition' was issued with three live tracks as an EP in late 1979; they also considered releasing it as a single with a B side that was 'all voices and hand clapping, something they sing on the way to gigs'[431] – a loose, slightly hippyish notion that might not have gone down well with the new wavers Kelly was often lumped in with. Yet 'Recognition' itself is recognizably the template Kelly would often return to, musically: if a missing link had to be established between Young Modern and the Hoodoo Gurus – both are discussed in greater detail later in this history – this might be it, though the song lacks the loud power drumming of the latter, opting instead for a precise, clipped new-wave beat. Brown, one of Kelly's earliest supporters, saw him as 'part of the new breed/wave that slots in somewhere between the Borich/Mike Rudd/Thorpie generation and the youthful punks, rising rapidly and crashing in the exuberance of expressing themselves.'[432]

'The Dots are a powerful line-up', wrote Peter Mudd in *Roadrunner*.

> Dual guitar attack . . . with Kelly's chunky chording filling the sound out even more, and a Mack Truck solid rhythm section that drives hard, rushes at the right times and rocks in the right directions. Which way's that? You say. Round in circles like all established art forms, of course. With an unlimited number of tangents.[433]

These tangents were to develop further and wider as Kelly moved with increasing confidence in the 80s; the group signed to Mushroom early in the new decade and caused a minor sensation with the song 'Billy Baxter' that year.

GROWING UP AND GLAMMING UP IN THE SEVENTIES

Weekend, a short documentary made by Film Australia in 1977, is a colourful, impressionistic, slightly dark study of a group of teenagers living in the regional city of Lithgow in New South Wales. The kids muse on sex, dating, and their social life – on weekends they'll go to the pool room, the rollerskating rink or the Lithgow fun parlour. Older kids will 'chuck laps' in their cars in the main street ('there's lots of car smashes') or there'll be a big fight outside a pub. At one point in the film, the kids go to see a daytime concert featuring John Paul Young and the All Stars, and we see Young perform 'Standing in the Rain'. The frankly jealous testimony of one of the Lithgow boys appears on the soundtrack, imagining a girl's attitude to Young's clothing and appearance: 'When a girl sits there staring,' he says, you know she likes the way he moves.'[434] The relationship between teens and 'sexy' pop stars was long-known, but changing mores and particularly the changing way that teen sexuality was experienced and discussed altered the dynamic. Well might Les Gock of Hush have claimed his band 'appeal to an age group that's just discovering fucking.'[435]

John Paul Young's musical output was discussed in chapter 8; he was, in many respects, a performer on behalf of Vanda and Young, who provided him with most of his hits. He had been an apprentice sheet-metal worker when friends insisted he sing in their band, Elm Tree. British manager and entrepreneur Simon Napier-Bell, on a brief visit to Australia, recruited Young to sing over George Young's vocals[436] on a demo of a song Vanda and Young had co-written with actor David Hemmings; the result, 'Pasadena', was a minor hit.[437] Buoyed by this development,

Young went on to play Annas in *Jesus Christ Superstar* for two years. At this point, and up until his first album, he was known as John Young.

The All Stars had an even more unusual career. They could be said to have evolved from the La De Das minus Kevin Borich. Young essentially inherited them from Stevie Wright, whom they'd backed when he was touring to promote *Hard Road*; Young (who had by now added 'Paul' to distinguish him from Johnny Young, and was often known as JPY or 'Squeak'; his new nomenclature predated the two similarly named popes) would come onstage during those shows and sing a couple of songs.[438] Though their line-up fluctuated, by the mid 70s the All Stars included Ian Willy Winter, Ray Goodwin on lead guitar and vocals, Johnny Dick on drums and Ronnie Peel aka Rockwell T. James on bass and vocals;[439] Goodwin had formerly been a member of Dragon; a later member of the same band, Billy Rogers, would become the All Stars' saxophonist for a time at the end of the decade. Vince Melouney would also become a member. Warren 'Pig' Morgan, formerly of Chain and the Aztecs, was the band's most crucial component, and he would be Young's musical director for the remainder of the decade. The All Stars were, in effect, the Alberts house band.

John Paul Young became one of Australia's most successful pop artists in the late 70s and, like many others already mentioned, he enjoyed significant international success, although he left no lasting impression except in Australia, where he remains an iconic figure. A number of his records were successful in European territories and even – unfortunately – in the two countries in the world where apartheid was official policy, South Africa and Rhodesia; he toured both. On his return to Australia in 1978, he felt somewhat ignored: 'It's really weird when you do well overseas and you come back and no one gives a stuff,' he philosophised. 'It's a common thing though . . . look at the last Sherbet single.'[440] He was definitely entering a lean period. Ian Meldrum has often characterised him as irrationally unmotivated, and relates in his biography his horror on discovering that Young was lounging around a pool in the regional town of Swan Hill, Victoria instead of hotfooting it to the US to lend support to his song 'Yesterday's Hero', which had entered the charts there.[441] Though he later had minor hits with other writers (including himself) it is the Vanda and Young (and Alberts) connection that continues to define JPY's career. He found it revived in 1992 when a remixed version of 'Love Is in the Air', a Vanda and Young disco hit for him in 1977, was included on the soundtrack of Baz Lurhmann's first film *Strictly Ballroom*.

The Ted Mulry Gang, like the Angels, were not as loyal to Alberts as Young. Mulry's early songwriting forays have already been documented; he had been popular and inoffensive with songs like 'Julia' and 'Falling in Love Again' and (as Anthony O'Grady put it) had been on the 'teevee a fair bit, he looked a mite waifish, he looked a touch raffish.'[442] But his second album, *I Won't Look Back*, featured some of his pop-boogie material alongside more of the balladry that had originally made him famous, and 'Jump in my Car', his first hit with the Ted

Mulry Gang (TMG) – Herm Kovac and Les Hall, two members of Malcolm Young's old band the Velvet Underground, with Mulry on bass and vocals – has become legendary. They followed it up with an unlikely reworking of the pre-war hit 'Darktown Strutters' Ball', which Mulry explained 'was an old favourite of m'parents actually'.[443]

Like a number of artists on the Alberts label, the perception in the Mulry camp was that the label's resources were stretched too thin; its heavy concentration on the sheet music side of the industry might also have seemed something of a burden on its efficiency. TMG moved to Mushroom in April 1977, claiming that Alberts was not doing its best for the group.[444] Their subsequent career was impressively consistent, if undistinguished: though they had no hits after 1978, they continued to play live for 25 years until Mulry's death in 2001, proof that a few fondly remembered singles – especially a piece of lucky, silly doggerel like 'Jump in my Car' – can stand an artist in good stead for a lifetime. In an extraordinary twist, 'Jump in my Car' was a British top-ten hit in 2006 for the US television actor David Hasselhoff, a rare example of a song's silly retro quality remaining evident even when released in a country where very few would have heard the original.

There was a continual supply of what *Rolling Stone* witheringly called 'baby-faced spunk rock bands'.[445] Taste had at least one moment of artistic glory with the glam-rock wonder 'Tickle Your Fancy'; Finch veered between artiness and down-the-line rock. If TMG were a little bit Sid James, a little bit sweaty pop-rock, then Supernaut – who hit the charts in mid 1976 with 'I Like It Both Ways', about a boy called 'Johnny' (of course) who can't make up his mind about his sexuality – were positively challenging. 'I Like It Both Ways' is infectious in its over-the-top quality, particularly the almost Hitchcockian (Alfred, not Russell) telephone that rings in the build-up to the song's final chorus – reputedly an accident but left in the final version,[446] and in practice a tinpot version of the grandiose sound effects that producer Ian Meldrum had generated for 'The Real Thing' eight years earlier. Almost a decade after their debut, former Supernaut guitarist Chris Burnham (promoting his subsequent group, This is This), recalled that during their early days in Perth, Supernaut was 'a "shocking" band, treated like outcasts from the music scene ... We were a very unhip band.'[447]

After capturing the public's imagination, Supernaut celebrated their (or someone's) heterosexuality with 'Too Hot to Touch', a song in praise of a sexy woman. They were young and spotty, and on their self-titled debut album ground out a kind of patchy, pre-punk power pop with slightly prog overtones – the record was an early engineering job for a very young Tony Cohen who also at this time worked on a sci-fi epic, *Beyond Morgia*, by Lobby Loyde[448] – but Supernaut were not a bunch of yobs. Vocalist Gary Twinn, for instance, enjoyed touring regional Australia because it allowed him to pursue an interest in gold mines and ghost towns.[449] Supernaut's third single, 'The Kids Are Out Tonight' – another social study – included an extensive period of silence; they were forced to withdraw it and remix the track after the gap caused consternation at radio stations. Their second album was too long in the making, and the band drifted out of touch with their audience; by the time it was finished it was deemed old hat and shelved. *RAM* mocked their single 'Unemployed' as 'raw' and 'brooding',[450] and the group looked like they were already on the scrap heap in their early twenties. By early 1979 – in a strange parallel to Sherbet and the Sherbs – Supernaut had changed their name to the Nauts, a recognisable reference to their old incarnation but with a 'punky' resonance. They released a self-titled album[451] which did not do well, and traveled to the elephant's graveyard of the UK to disband. Gary Twinn became involved in a long line of groups playing 50s rock and featuring players with British punk credentials, including Twenty Flight Rockers and the International Swingers.

Another group who changed their name and sound in the name of new wave were the Radiators, 'two farm boys from Bega . . . together with another three lads from the country.'[452] Guitarist Steve 'Fess' Parker and vocalist Brian Nichol's first band was the Undecideds,[453] followed by Big Swifty; they took a big gamble – and, they said, an 80 per cent pay cut in their early 'new wave' days – when they decided to become the Radiators.[454] Their first single, 'Coming Home',[455] was Angels-style new wave, with the kind of ripper, crafted conclusion that begged you to play it again. Their anthem was a turgid work called 'Gimme Head' – it was issued as the B side of their second single, and this sentence is already more attention than it has ever deserved. Whatever the Radiators' ambitions, they were soon set on a course of eternal hard work, playing medium-sized venues around the nation and releasing albums that were far more melodic and adventurous than their 'Gimme Head' reputation indicates. Thirty years after their conception, the group retained their original line-up and, astonishingly, their focus; but it is clear that they had made the decision to stay at a certain level for their entire working lives.

The jury will probably be forever out on whether it is better to die young – at least, as a band. Hush was Keith Lamb's band, whoever he decided to put in them, though the best-known and charting version featured Lamb as vocalist, Les Gock on guitar, Rick Lum on bass and Smiley Pailthorpe on drums. Gock later opined that 'Hush was a band which came out of a period where bands were very serious and played twenty-minute guitar solos' – he sees the early 70s as a 'denimy, drugged-out' era which they reacted against: 'We just said, stuff this, we're going to have a great time.'[456] This is a somewhat disingenuous summary, especially given that the group's fifth album, *Touché*, was an attempt at a 'serious' record which failed commercially and led quite quickly to their demise.

What was perhaps most unusual about Hush in the early 1970s was the presence of two Chinese-Australians, Lum and Gock, in the group. In addition, though they were hardly rebels in any meaningful way, Hush were not 'nice': their second album, *Get Rocked*, contained a song with the same title that was naturally interpreted by their audiences as inspiration to yell 'get fucked' at the band, each other, and the world, during a pyrotechnical, karate kick–infused, glam and glitter spectacular. The group's music was, for the most part, basic and crafted; Lamb told *RAM*'s Annie Burton that 'If a song really turns 'em on, in the next one we'll put out even more energy, and so on until it's like a stone wall. We don't play down, we play straight at 'em – we want to make 'em feel how we feel. When we come off the stage, we're rooted – and so are they.'⁴⁵⁷

The group's appeal, according to their manager Peter Rix, was not mysterious; he cited their origins in Sydney's western suburbs: 'Hush was a backyard band in Seven Hills... They're not hotshit players and they don't pretend to be. Obviously the girls' feelings are sexual, but the boys can identify with the band and think, "Hey, I could do that some day too."'⁴⁵⁸

Interviewed by Burton, Les Gock claimed the group's 'raunchy' image was organic and unrehearsed:

> We can't change it. Nobody says, 'Alright Keith, here's your script for tonight': it just comes out of his mouth. Nobody says, Here are your moves, Les, I want you to shake your arse here, here and there. If the music and what we do on stage doesn't work, tough shit.⁴⁵⁹

Lamb was extremely unhappy with Hush's biggest hit, a glam reading of Larry Williams's 'Bony Moronie' produced by Robie Porter, which reached number one in September 1975. Two and a half years later, playing with an entirely different line-up of Hush, Lamb introduced the group's touchstone song as 'Phoney Baloney' and 'very unprofessionally' (according to Christie Eliezer, who covered one of the earliest shows by the very short-lived 'new Hush') 'tells the audience he's always hated the song'.⁴⁶⁰ Lamb was upfront with Eliezer, explaining that he'd 'hated it when I first heard it, I hated it when we recorded it because the band's producer insisted, I still hated it when it became the top-selling Australian single for 1975 and I still hate it.'⁴⁶¹ Lamb also apparently did not always care too much for Eliezer – perhaps the Australian music writer most immortalized in song – Lamb wrote a song about him entitled 'Number One.'⁴⁶² It is interesting to contemplate what Hush might have done with a song they *wanted* to cover, the Masters Apprentices' 'Undecided.' Unfortunately, Jim Keays refused to allow the group to record it, choosing to release what was to be the first in a series of substandard reworkings of his first hit under his own or the Masters Apprentices' name.⁴⁶³

Hush's manager, Peter Rix, obtained a major international deal for the band with Vertigo, and while this did not lead to anything for Hush, it was presumably a factor in Lamb's later songwriting work with Status Quo. When Burton commented to Gock that she'd heard Americans liked Hush's Australian sound, he responded: 'I don't think they would have been so knocked out if they'd known there were two Chinamen and a Pommie in the band.'[464] Even Les Gock was uncertain about what constituted an 'Australian'.

Gock and Lum were young adults in an Australia which had only recently abandoned active constraints on Asian immigration, and where there was still a very limited Asian presence. It was 'Get Rocked' – clearly another precursor to the Angels' audience's 'No way, get fucked' chant – that the press focused on as the 'controversial' element of the Hush story, rather than its 'two Chinamen', but it is remarkable, looking back at Hush's press coverage in the early 70s, to read the kind of jokes that Gock, in particular, made about race. Discussing the Chinese imagery in Hush's stage sets, he explained it as being testament to his and Lum's superior skills: 'These Westerners are too disorganized,' he told Anthony O'Grady in 1976, 'to even get close to superior Chinese intelligence.'[465] In another article by O'Grady from the same year, Rick Lum took the joke even further, extrapolating from a relatively serious discussion of Hush's chances in the lucrative Asian market:

> Japan is definitely the place for rock and roll. Millions and millions of yellow people go to concerts to see white people play rock. And the Japanese bands only play top-forty stuff. So imagine, with Asians in the band...
>
> Actually I've always believed the Asian race is the most inventive in the world. I can't imagine why we haven't made it big in rock and roll yet. We invented gunpowder, spectacles, the compass. We had civilization while the white men were living in caves. We built the Great Wall of China... The white man hasn't done anything like that.[466]

In the same interview, Gock picks up Lum's idea and runs with it, suggesting the Chinese are 'the Superior Race' who should be 'leading Rock and Roll.'[467]

Perhaps fittingly, the four members of the 'classic' Hush line-up went on to have successful careers in different creative professions: Chris 'Smiley' Pailthorpe is an architect; Lum is a graphic designer; Lamb, following a period of mental illness which saw him arrested and hospitalized after trying to draw on a cheque he wrote himself for four million dollars,[468] is a successful businessman; and Gock has long worked in advertising and commercial music.

SERIOUS

It is difficult, if not unfair, to categorise many of the bands of the late 1970s as too 'serious' when there still seems to have been an element of 'anything goes' to record company decision-making at the time, linked with a strong desire at almost all levels to progress artistically.

The Ferrets' Billy Miller had made repeated stabs at musical success; he had been both a cast member of *Hair* (and *Jesus Christ Superstar*, with some other future Ferrets) and a late period, fill-in member of Buster Brown. As shown by his *Elsternwick '69* album – a collection of songs he wrote as a teenager, but did not record and release until the late 90s – he has been an accomplished and dedicated musician with a craftsmanlike attitude from an early age. The Ferrets shared core members Miller, bass player Ken Firth, and guitarist Dave Springfield with the final Buster Brown line-up. They came to the attention of Ian Meldrum, who promoted them on *Countdown* and also undertook to produce their debut album (engineered by Tony Cohen and Ian MacKenzie) which became the Mushroom release *Dreams of a Love*. The Ferrets' jaunty, silly single 'Don't Fall in Love' (co-written by Firth with Ian Davis) was a number one hit even as Meldrum continued to labour over the mixing of the album; the group eventually wrested it away from him (he is credited as 'Willie Everfinish' on the sleeve) and completed it. The urgent demand for the album meant that Mushroom took the unusual step of issuing it in a temporary sleeve which purchasers would be able to swap for the finished product when it was ready (it took a long time, and many didn't bother). *Dreams of a Love* is elaborate and diverse; the title track – a rock opera of sorts with fluid strings, restrained, punctuated drumming by Rick Brewer, and versatile vocals from Miller – is a particular highlight. Tribulations over the delayed album and the sleeve fiasco aside, the Ferrets probably suffered as a result of being typecast by 'Don't Fall in Love', which was catchy but – as mentioned – silly. Their second album, with the maudlin title *Fame at Any Price*, did not sell, and the group split in 1979.

Ross Wilson had abandoned the final incarnation of Daddy Cool in late 1975; he launched Ross Wilson's Mondo Rock, as it was originally called, a year later, hot on the heels of his solo single 'Living in the Land of Oz', which was both on Oz Records, run by Wilson with Glenn Wheatley,[469] and on the soundtrack to Chris Löfvén's film *Oz*. (He was dismissive about the label later: 'Basically our taste was good, but our timing was off.'[470])

Wilson apparently intended Mondo Rock to be an occasional vehicle rather than a permanent group, and suspended the initial line-up in November 1976 to record a solo album (he didn't).[471] He imagined that when he revived Mondo Rock, it would include Ross Hannaford, the guitarist who had been his creative partner in Daddy Cool and earlier bands, even though he was leery of Hannaford's mystical pursuits: 'I was a bit reluctant because I thought he might wander off as he's done in the past, due to his devotion to his guru . . . [but] he assured me the band would come first . . . A couple of weeks later I had a Dear Ross letter.'[472]

As it transpired, Wilson would have a strong partner in the commercially very successful post-1980 version of Mondo Rock in the unlikely figure of Eric McCusker, who wrote many of the group's hits during this period. Before then, a late-70s version of the band recorded the first Mondo Rock album, *Primal Park*. A proto-new-wave rock record, it contained co-writes between Wilson, David

Pepperell, Kim Fowley, and band members Tony Slavich and Simon Gyllies; it also included a song by Gunther Gorman, who had briefly been a member. The cover art showed a confrontational close-up of a male figure in a studded leather jacket and a leather mask – a slight improvement, at least, on an earlier hard-boiled detective novel–style design featuring a possibly dead naked woman.[473] Wilson was clearly intent on making a clean break with his earlier work – but evidently even he wasn't sure where he was headed. He showed both wisdom and courage, however, in creating a vehicle to take him into the new decade.

His peers, notably Mike Rudd, already seemed to be taking a step backwards and rehashing their past career rather than sustaining a fruitful and ongoing one, although career decisions were made, of course, not merely with the aim of soaring as high as possible artistically but also so that the artists and their families could keep eating. Ariel's *Rock & Roll Scars* was a great-sounding, cheerful album mainly comprised of material that had previously been recorded by earlier Rudd bands; ostensibly it was made to introduce Ariel to the British market, though it sank without trace there, despite the support of John Peel. Ariel split in August 1977 after a great final album, *Goodbye Fiona,* and a song Peter Dawkins believed was Rudd's most commercial yet, 'I Can Do Anything', which nonetheless did not sell in great quantities.[474] Ariel released not one but two live albums of recordings from their farewell concert.

Rudd and Bill Putt subsequently formed Mike Rudd's Instant Replay, a group which did not record but which Rudd recalls as 'actually the most successful band we've ever had. We did mostly Australian covers, [such as] the Easybeats' "Women" – we had two versions of it. Mostly Australian covers, including ourselves.' They took on gems from the 60s by groups such as the Loved Ones, as well as Ross Wilson's 'Woman of the World', a highlight of Rudd and Wilson's Party Machine.[475]

Oz Records also released material by Stylus, a group ostensibly offering a 'musical backdrop of pounding black funk,'[476] although none of them were actually black. On the upside, they were all vegetarians. 'Although the vegetarian aspect of their collective beliefs is only a subsidiary theme on the new Stylus album *Where in the World* . . . it is nevertheless much in evidence in the lyrics', claimed Christie Eliezer, adding that 'the songs are the complete antithesis of the AC-DC/Hush/Skyhooks genre.'[477] Their early singles were catchy, smooth and soulful, and Stylus might perhaps have had a hope of following in the wake of a group like Air Supply into international markets – indeed, their third album, *Best Kept Secret,* was released by Motown in the USA. But their commercial success, such as it had been, faded, and lead singer Peter Cupples embarked on a solo career often derided for its single-minded blandness.

The daughter of Hungarian-born Jewish refugees (her mother had been in Auschwitz),[478] Renée Geyer has caused problems for the Australian music industry since first coming to prominence in the mid 70s with her version of 'It's a Man's Man's World'. Geyer, born in Sydney in the early 1950s, was a member of various early-70s groups: Dry Red, who rehearsed in their guitarist, Eric McCusker's, garage in Tamarama;[479] Sun, featuring Keith Shadwick, who sacked her after the album *Sun '72*;[480] Nine Stage Horizon;[481] and the 'Sydney soul band' (exponents of a genre, apparently) Mother Earth.[482] Mother Earth were relegated to backing band status on Geyer's first, self-titled solo album, recorded at Col Joye's studio[483] and containing a selection of the most unbelievably obvious covers possible. Yet it is already plain from this LP and its successor that Geyer was a highly impressive singer in search of appropriate material; the tragedy of her recording career – particularly in its early days – is that such material was often not readily available. Geyer's inspiration as a singer was Wendy Saddington, and the parallels are evident – indeed, Saddington might well have pointed to Geyer's recorded output as justification of why a female soul singer in Australia in the 70s was better off *not* recording extensively. In her memoir *Confessions of a Difficult Woman*, Geyer gives numerous examples of the ways she was marginalised and disregarded on the Australian rock scene: a mid-80s *Rolling Stone* book excluded her completely.[484] In this sense, she was most certainly 'difficult' for the industry – not just because she was a woman, but also because she did not work in conventional rock music.

Geyer was briefly a member of the ill-fated Sanctuary, Billy Green's group that grew out of his recording sessions for the soundtrack to *Stone*. By the time she came to record her third solo album, *Ready to Deal*, in 1975, Green had departed for the USA and the band had simply become the Renée Geyer Band. She began to write lyrics: 'I write 'em five minutes before I go and sing 'em in the studio', she said in 1976. 'It's pretty uncomplicated ... I'm not saying they're bullshit, they're just words I can write to fit the feel of the melody.'[485]

> I don't like people who don't take the business seriously, who treat it as a bludge. In America, the music business is huge, like cars or oil. If you're in the business here, you should really want to be, and be adequately qualified.[486]

'I'm demanding in that I don't want to do anything shitty,'[487] she said in the same *RAM* interview – and who does? Yet 'shitty' is a good word to describe many of the decisions and consequences of her career in the 70s. The worst of these decisions came in 1975, when she agreed to take a thousand dollars[488] to sing the Liberal party's election campaign advertisement, written by Mike Brady (his chief rival in the jingle business, Peter Best, a principled man as well as a musical talent, had refused to be involved). Most people with credibility in popular music were in any case left-leaning, and 1975, the year of the dismissal of the Whitlam government, was a particularly bad time to be associating with those who had usurped an elected government. Geyer quickly claimed that she had been completely ignorant of the purpose of the ad and was herself apolitical (in her memoir she fudges this in a number of ways, stating that it was the 1974 election, rather than the 1975 one, and that her manager should have told her there'd be ramifications).[489]

Setting aside this and other errors of judgment, 'Heading in the Right Direction' (1976) and 'Stares and Whispers' (1977) were stupendous ballads that put most of her competitors to shame. There were rumours by the late 70s that she would be signing to Motown.[490] In 1979 she released *Blues License*, 'a collection of blues trax' recorded with Kevin Borich and Tim Partridge.[491] Ian Meldrum once remarked that a recording session bringing Geyer and Borich together would put a studio engineer to sleep;[492] it was not this statement but probably something like it that incited Geyer to slap Meldrum live on the hundredth episode of *Countdown*,[493] an action she subsequently said was often required but in that instance was merely 'showbiz'.[494] She also later conceded that the Borich album was a contractual obligation: 'I didn't dig that at all.'[495]

Geyer would enjoy her biggest commercial success in Australia in the 80s; this decade would also see her voice and her pop sensibility channeled to the wider world as a session vocalist on often dreadful records by artists such as Sting. In the 70s, however, her uniqueness came with its own glass ceiling; she was not part of a cohort of singers, female or otherwise, working in a strong blues/soul tradition, while her poor business decisions further contributed to her marginalisation. Looking back over the past winners of the *TV Week* 'Queen of Pop' crown, for instance, and seeing the unimaginative performers who were given this, admittedly ridiculous, award, it seems extraordinary that Geyer was never a winner; but she was, in essence, ready made for the 'too hard' basket.

As mentioned, Geyer was shared between RCA and Mushroom for most of the 70s, an unusual arrangement which allowed Mushroom to vary its distribution options and not depend entirely on Festival – a similar scenario to that employed by the Suicide Records label, for which RCA was also distributor. Notably, Barry Earl was involved. Whatever its failings, Mushroom certainly threw its weight behind some difficult artists, in ways that only occasionally paid off. When it did pay off, however, it was in spades. New Zealanders Split Enz would ultimately become a major Mushroom success story, though this looked highly unlikely in the 70s, even while they were briefly a priority for their British label, Chrysalis.[496]

FINALLY CUTTING IT

Since 1980, when their *True Colours* album finally saw them not only produce their first consistently excellent LP but also garner commercial success for it, Split Enz have been accorded respect as a major group. They seem always to have been feted in New Zealand itself (in a way that Dragon, a very different group with approximately the same origins, are not), but in the late 70s, as they moved between Australia and Britain hoping to find some kind of toehold, few would have predicted a long-term future for them.

Apart from anything else, there was a period of time in which their harlequin-style appearance seemed like so much foolish, arty fluff; their claim that it was 'a reaction to living in a very conservative place like New Zealand'[497] may not have cut it in Australia, which was a different country altogether.

Having experienced a measure of success in their homeland, the group – centred primarily at this stage on the friendship/songwriting of Tim Finn and Phil Judd (Judd would effectively be replaced by Neil Finn in 1977) – passed through Australia. As Mushroom recording artists they recorded their first album, *Mental Notes* (1975), described by Tim Finn as having 'a certain lack of... presence',[498] and were soon on their way to Britain, where they re-recorded half of it as *Second Thoughts* (1976) with Phil Manzanera of Roxy Music producing. The band found Manzanera 'totally uninterested in commerciality', but this did not really faze them because – as Noel Crombie told *RAM* – 'we were just happy doing albums too.'[499] The albums *Dizrythmia* and *Frenzy* saw the group slowly attuning themselves to the times; this is particularly noticeable on a very 'new wave' (and very good) 1978 single written by Tim's newly arrived brother Neil, 'I See Red', a song which Tim Finn said was 'very much adapting to circumstances.'[500]

England did not really work out for Split Enz, however. Tim Finn told Anthony O'Grady:

> Y'see, *we* saw a continuous thread between us and bands who'd influenced us like the Beatles and the Kinks – we really did think we were an extension of that.
>
> Whereas in England, at the time, there seemed a desperate need for everyone to reassure themselves there was life in rock 'n' roll, 'cos at that time, in England, it did seem to be dead... So in many ways we were just too sophisticated... But now the New Wave thing is turning into a more sophisticated beast and a lot of the original bands haven't survived...[501]

In fact, it was much more a case of Split Enz changing than it was of Britain catching up to Split Enz; nevertheless, Finn was correct when he announced a new tweaking of roles in, and a style for the group:

> It's the best Enz line-up so far, the best talent... it feels very strong and we are just waiting for round two to start... TING![502]

A similar attitude was prevalent in Melbourne, where for instance the band Sidewinder were playing what they called 'sophisticated new wave' to a growing fanbase. The group's founder and chief songwriter, violinist Richard Lee, had come through 'stints in the ABC Showband [and] the National Youth Orchestra'[503] but decided 'it has to be rock 'n' roll', because 'I'm a real ham'.[504] He and Sidewinder singer David Castles had previously led the group Isaac Aaron, which made no records but can be seen playing during a very public sex scene in Tim Burstall's remarkable film *Petersen*.

Sidewinder's music was, Lee boldly asserted, 'the sort of music that a lot of people hoped New Wave would develop into. There was a lot of interest in New Wave as an academic and concise exercise, rather than filling people's heads with annihilistic [sic] music which was a response to sophistication in music.'⁵⁰⁵

Rebecca Batties was enthused when she saw a performance in early 1977 and wrote in *Juke*:

> If you don't get an immediate idea of what this band is about when you hear their first number, then your musical perceptions are blanketed. Sidewinder get straight to the musical point and it's a case of either liking or lumping it... 'Dead Meat Boogie', a Richard Lee composition, was one of their starters... Interestingly, Lee played vitar, an instrument which is similar in shape to the violin, but unlike it in that it has a fifth string, a bass like the viola... Sidewinder make an interesting and impressive alternative to the run of the mill rock band.⁵⁰⁶

Sidewinder can stand here for the innumerable groups who deserved hit records and wide acclaim, but which – for various reasons of fate and inter-band personality – did not quite manage to step up the requisite number of rungs. The history of Australian music is, naturally, riddled with such bands, from Home to Shadowfax.

The boundary between prog rock and new wave was even more porous for the Melbourne group Cybotron, whose albums *Cybotron*, *Colossus* and *Implosion* were predominantly synthesiser-based, often in the vein of early 70s German progressive music. Founder Steve Maxwell von Braund had lived in Europe during the early 70s and on his return to Melbourne recorded a solo album before starting Cybotron with Geoff Green; remarkably, the former Aztecs drummer Gil Matthews played on their third album, *Implosion* – working with a drummer was part of their 'Humanising Project'(!)⁵⁰⁷

Green, like Rob Mackenzie five years earlier, was at pains to outline the intent of his group's largely instrumental, often extended, tunes:

> Cybotron's music lets the listener get adjusted to it more fully, and when we do have a change, the change is more dramatic because they've become accustomed to the riff, the idea, and they can feel it, because the sounds, the emotions, the tensions of the band are all building up to that change, and when that change comes, it's so entirely different that, wham! It hits you like a sledgehammer. If things happen too quickly, people haven't got time to think about the progression. Even classical music works that way, where it slowly builds up to a dramatic climax or change.⁵⁰⁸

Other otherworldly individuals crept into the local scene, sometimes staying only for short periods. Geoff Duff, formerly (as Jeff Black) the singer for the (New) Avengers – a descendent of the Brisbane group – was the main instigator of the group Kush, and remained the only constant member throughout their initial two-year, two-album stint. Kush's theatricality overpowered whatever musical appeal they may have had, and Duff's 'outrageous combination of high camp frivolity, Lou Reed evil and decadent irresponsibility'[509] was presumably not always to the group's advantage. In 1975, for the cover of their second album, the stupidly titled *Nah, tellus wh't Kush means yer great sausage*, five of the band's members were depicted in the process of stringing up Duff to extract this important information from him (*RAM* told its readers that Kush was 'the Arabic equivalent for vagina').[510] Duff departed for England in 1977, by which time he had resumed spelling his first name 'Jeff', and using the name Duffo for his solo records. Michael Gudinski, traveling in Britain in the late 70s, commented that Duff was 'ruining the reputation of Australian rock;'[511] Duff, clearly offended by the lack of success Kush had received in Australia, referred to it in interviews as 'the other country.'[512] Duff claimed in mid 1975 that he was going to leave Kush (its remaining members intended to press on) and concentrate on 'his sausages', these being a book and a solo record.[513] In 1979 *Sounds* dismissed him as 'Just another basic Bruce stereotype,'[514] which is a ludicrous criticism (even if his single 'Give Me Back My Brain' was sung in an Australian accent). 'My publicist ... says he's never known an artiste to receive so much bad publicity in such a short time',[515] Duff told *RAM*; he had high hopes for his song 'Let Me Fuck Your Mind' which he described in terms of his own asexuality: 'that's the only way I can screw people, by screwing their minds.'[516]

Queenslander Chris Moriatis was another unique performer who recreated himself in early 1975 when he became the singer Mandu. The name 'came from nowhere, meant nothing and was intended simply to avoid placing needless attention on his typical background of progressing through bands and coffee shops.'[517] He later claimed to have discovered that the name actually meant 'starshine and moonshine' in an Aboriginal language. 'Unreal!' he told *RAM's* reporter 'Daisy Chain'. 'It just came to me in an awareness I had, which is part of everything I do and am.'[518] He evidently did not know – or chose not to mention – that a mandu is also a famous and delicious Korean dumpling.

Mandu's only solo album, *To the Shores of His Heaven*, was recorded with a number of Melbourne luminaries under the guidance of his manager, the former pop singer and *Uptight* presenter Jon Blanchfield. The album, which related the experiences of an alien on earth, was not particularly commercially successful (though it was reissued a number of times), and neither

was a remarkable cover of the Rolling Stones' 'Gimme Shelter'. Mandu later became the vocalist for Lobby Loyde's Southern Electric,[519] presumably as a result of Blanchfield's machinations; *Obsecration*, Loyde's 1976 album featuring Mandu as vocalist, was released on Blanchfield's Rainbird Records. Like much of Loyde's work in the 70s, while it still nodded periodically to trippy psychedelia and heavier – almost punkier – approaches of the 60s (the title track was reputedly from that era),[520] *Obsecration* was the product of a unique perspective. Portions of *Obsecration* and its follow-up, *Too Poor to Die*, also had jazz-rock leanings that put one in mind of the Laughing Clowns (particularly *Too Poor's* 'The Fist Falls'). When Richard Branson heard the album – Loyde travelled to Britain in 1976 – he was keen to release it there, but Blanchfield's label had gone into liquidation, and the original tapes were unavailable.[521] Blanchfield went on to have fingers in various quite different pies; by the early 80s he was managing Richard Clapton.[522]

It is interesting – and appropriate – that Lobby Loyde was present in the UK for the very early days of British punk rock, playing shows (as Southern Electric, with some of the musicians who had played on *Obsecration)* and working as live sound mixer for the group Doll by Doll. He would return to Australia in the middle of 1979 and become a highly accomplished producer and mentor to a diverse range of Sydney bands, including the Sunnyboys, Sardine V and the Machinations. Having been an innovator throughout the 70s, and having prefigured punk in a number of unusual ways, particularly with the Coloured Balls and Wild Cherries, he was perfectly placed to assist in the realisation of some of the best post-punk records of this era.

UP THERE CAZALY

In any broad history, there will be anomalies that just cannot be brought into the general flow. Mike Brady's 1979 hit, 'Up There Cazaly', had just one precedent, the Mojo Singers' 'C'mon Aussie C'mon', and while Brady's song gave rise to a style – the anthemic, putatively uplifting singalong – it was a style so strongly connected with Brady and television advertising that it was rarely used in pop again (although hugely successful records like John Farnham's 'You're the Voice' used a similar strategy: basing songs around gleefully soaring choruses and chants).

Both 'C'mon Aussie C'mon' and 'Up There Cazaly' were calculated, even cynical efforts to use jingles to promote sport: the former a particularly devious commercialized form of cricket, the latter Australian Rules football. Mojo was an advertising agency, and the single derived from the popular jingle was a poorly edited loop of the TV ad; it nevertheless sold extremely well. 'Up There Cazaly' was a far more crafted product, Brady's professionalism belying his complete lack of interest in the sport. Credited to the Two Man Band (Peter Sullivan was the other one), and urged on by Ron Tudor, who released the song on his Fable label, 'Up There Cazaly' was a major hit.[523] The song belongs to pop history, though it is of course an example of a record that owes a large part of its extraordinary success to the fact that it was bought mainly by people who don't usually buy pop records. Perhaps the most remarkable thing about it is its title, which is not explained in Brady's lyrics: he revealed to his biographer Noel Delbridge that he took the phrase from the Ray Lawler play *Kid Stakes* (part of Lawler's celebrated 'Doll Trilogy', of which *Summer of the Seventeenth Doll* was the first).[524] Roy Roy Cazaly was a Victorian footballer active in the early 20th century, noted for his height (and his ability to make spectacular 'marks'); the song has confirmed the legend of a man inducted into the Australian Football Hall of Fame 33 years after his death. Of course, one of the entrancing things about pop music – probably more so than most art forms – is that curious balance between moneymaking doggerel and truly inspired, one might even say progressive, cultural statement. The simple, catchy 'Australian' pop anthem, of which Mike Brady was a genius creator (see also Salvadore Smith's 'I'm an Aussie' from 1979), is nonetheless more artifact than anything else.

NEW WAVE

This chapter ends as it began, with a discussion of the new wave of forward-looking and experimental Australian rock musicians. It is almost impossible to do justice to the richness of the work created in this era, although Clinton Walker's edited collection *Inner City Sound* at the very least gives a good picture of the excitement and diversity of the times; immersed in the scene, Walker doesn't really see the big picture – unless, as may well be the case, the big picture is a collage that can only be appreciated by regarding the smaller pictures throughout.

The most important Australian music current of the late 1970s was arguably that of Melbourne's little bands – even if only in a contradictory way, given that the groups were designed to be ephemeral in nature. Initiated on a whim after a friendly argument Marcus Bergner and Marie Hoy had with Nick Cave at a show at the Prince of Wales, the first 'little band' was Too Fat To Fit Through the Door – Hoy, Bergner and a drum machine – who made their debut supporting the Boys Next Door in 1979. At around the same time, Dave Light put together a side project, the Leapfrogs, who opened a show for his principal band, the Primitive Calculators.[525] Soon Bergner, Hoy, the other members of the Primitive Calculators (Stuart Grant, Denise Rosenberg, and Frank Lovece), Ollie Olsen, Jules Taylor – in fact a whole host of local musicians, as well as artists and filmmakers – had spawned a scene that flourished through 1979 and into 1980.

It was performance-based, taking the form of a series of 'Little Band Nights' at which anyone who turned up could play; the participants usually used the Primitive Calculators' equipment. It was focused largely on Fitzroy's Champion Hotel, within spitting distance of the site of the discontinued T. F. Much Ballroom (which no doubt seemed to belong to a whole different generation). According to Grant, there were "a few basic rules" – little bands had to be "disposable," couldn't play more than two shows, and should have no more than three songs; people were also encouraged to play instruments they weren't familiar with.[526]

Many of the little bands – their number has been placed as high as 150 – were temporary vehicles for musicians experimenting outside their principal groups: Rosenberg of the Primitive Calculators was in Thrush and the Cunts, for example, while Lisa Gerrard took time out from her main group, Microfilm, to play in a little band called Junk Logic. For others, who perhaps didn't adhere to the disposability ethos, these events offered an opportunity to get their band started or gain exposure (the Pastel Bats, who became Shower Scene from Psycho, for instance, or the Jetsonnes, who later morphed into Hunters & Collectors). Bergner, who can claim to have sparked the whole thing, was active in art and film (and remains so). Jules Taylor's involvement with little bands (she was in Ronnie and the Rhythm Boys, Thrush and the Cunts, and others) came about when the groups began rehearsing in a space behind Climax Records, an import record shop where she worked and which was itself a meeting place for local musicians.

Some little bands, as well as the Primitive Calculators themselves – reformed several years later to be documented in Richard Lowenstein's 1986 film *Dogs in Space*. The inference some viewers might take from the film, that groups like the Ears and Whirlywirld were also 'little bands,' is inaccurate, though all were part of the same cultural environment.

Only a few years after the 'movement' came and went, *Vox* declared:

> Endless bitchings and theorizing continues about the movement even today, though little evidence of their existence is still about, save a few bitter and cynical survivors, several invaluable cassettes, a few energetic optimists and an eight-millimetre film primitively but clearly depicting the spontaneous excitement initially generated by the event, followed closely by the rapid decline through drugs that more than a few became entangled in.[527]

Many of these bands are today no more than a memory, or perhaps a photograph. The Take, Ronnie and the Rhythm Boys, Too Fat to Fit Through the Door, and Morpions were four little bands captured on an EP released in 1979. Soon afterwards a number of the participants temporarily relocated to London, where Taylor was given the job of trying to get Rough Trade interested in these legacy recordings: the UK's foremost outlet for independent music apparently found the record too unusual to work with.

The little bands were part comedy, part musical theatre, and part genuine nihilist statement: they were the perfect counter-argument to the excesses – and the ambitions – of the 1970s.

As mentioned, the Primitive Calculators were not themselves a 'little band', though they were at the heart of the scene. Their origins were in outer-eastern Springvale, a working-class Melbourne suburb which populated rapidly in the 60s. Grant recalls:

> When I was ten, I was listening to Brod Smith, I was listening to Carson . . . 1968. 1970, I was 12 . . . [sings] *'I'm a wolfman howling at the moon'* – *gdoong doong doong doong* . . . That was the sound of every fuckin' outer suburban hole in Melbourne. Every band that came and played at our school, Ida Mae Mack, Freeway . . . not only the bigger bands like Carson and Chain but the second tier and the third tier and the fourth tier. Everybody had a fuckin' SG, with reverb on it, playing pentatonic blues scales over a one-chord boogie groove. Everywhere in Melbourne, every fucking room, every corner, had someone doing that.

The Primitive Calculators combined Stockhausen, punk and disco ('the only pop music that's relevant today', Grant claimed in 1979)[528] with the early 70s boogie of Grant's youth to make their own unique racket: they were early adopters of a drum machine, using a Roland CR-78 drum machine to be as 'irritating and agitating' as they could. The group's self-titled debut album was a staggered release – the cover existed years before the record was ultimately pressed; its packaging adorned many a Melbourne share house living-room wall in the intervening years.

Punk had many manifestations in the late 70s. A casual flick through the teen magazine *Spunky* reveals numerous pointers to a punk future; the bemasked Maltese-Italian 'raw meat rock animals' Fat Daddy, for instance, whose bass player Boofhead (Mick Stila) told readers 'we hate everybody and everything.'[529] One of the best punk singles of the era was not by punks at all, although it was made by people who understood punk's 1960s origins. Norman Gunston was a well-loved comic creation of early to mid 70s Australian television. Played by the versatile actor Garry McDonald, Gunston was a parody of television's shabby glitz, and through him McDonald conducted some of the funniest interviews ever conducted for television. When British comedian Sacha Baron Cohen began conducting parodic interviews as Ali G in 2000, many Australians instantly saw the parallel with McDonald/Gunston; both played on the celebrity industry's propensity (and desire) to accept the dynamic of broadcast media at face value and to resist any challenges to their own validity as celebrities. Gunston was in this regard punkier than anyone, because he had access to the rich and famous, and the means – the hotline to their own vanity – to demolish them. In the tacky style of television 'all-rounders', Gunston would regularly perform songs on the show, usually 'acting out' the words charade-style for the section of the audience he claimed would be otherwise too stupid to understand them (for instance, in his rendition of 'My Way' he depicted the word 'career' by pretending to drive and then pointing to his bottom). Gunston had already had a hit record on Keith Glass's specially formed label Lamington Records in 1976 with a track entitled 'Salute to ABBA', ostensibly cashing in on that band's popularity; he had also released an album, *The Popular Ballad Animal*, on the same label.

When he recorded 'I Might Be a Punk (But I Love You Baby)', Gunston was in cultural commentator mode. The song was written by Ross Wilson ('whose origins', *Juke* reminded its readers, 'lie in mid-sixties punk rock') and 'famed journo-cum-record-label-proprietor' David Pepperell.[530] The two had actually written the song some time previously for an unrealized musical; they had also collaborated in writing 'Primal Park', the best song on the first Mondo Rock album. The idea behind Gunston doing 'I Might Be a Punk' was less to parody punk rock (though there was no reason not to) than it was to parody bandwagon-jumping. 'If it means fantastic royalties and adulation from the moronic masses', Gunston told *Juke*, 'then let's face it – it's worth it.'[531] The record was a gem, as rousing and amusing as a real punk record and, of course, far less po-faced.

Pepperell would soon show that he had a fairly broad notion of what constituted 'new wave'. In a report he wrote for *Juke* three months after the Gunston record – which was not a hit, though CBS's initial refusal to allow the accompanying album *Nylon Degrees* to directly parody Boz Scaggs's *Silk Degrees*, thus holding up its release, was probably a factor in this – Pepperell discussed his own observations of new wave music, with reference to the Wild Beaver Band, the Sports and KGB:

> The New Wave is alive and well and even blossoming in Melbourne which is as it should be I suppose – this town has always taken to any new movement with open arms and the whole punk/new wave thing is no exception ... not only is the new music much more than a passing fad but it is going to bring about the biggest breakout of new bands since the mod explosion of 1965.

KGB was the Keith Glass Band, in which Glass, temporarily rescinding his post-60s allegiance to country rock, brought together 'all the many streams of pop music ... like beads on one string'. Ross Wilson would sing 'Louie Louie' – his first recording with the Pink Finks – with them on occasion, and one night Pepperell himself 'was even moved enough to attempt "Gloria" – the attempt is still being judged as to its success or meaning.'[532] Pepperell would come to draw a distinction between new wave – which he saw as a simple music that referenced 60s pop – and punk, which was a lifestyle, look and fashion. That said, we would today probably not categorise any of the above bands as 'new wave' or even 'punk'.

Glass and Wilson, both products of the 60s Melbourne R&B scene and both from the southern beach suburbs of Melbourne, started the Missing Link label in 1978; its first release was 60s recordings by the Union, which had been fronted by Pepperell. The label was named after the band, naturally, and Glass changed the name of Archie and Jugheads, the import record shop he had started with Pepperell early in the decade (Pepperell, burnt out, left to run a highly successful t-shirt business) to Missing Link, too. Another release planned for early 1978 was Gerry Humphrys' version of Bo Diddley's 'Mona', but alongside this were some more recent recordings, such as a (12-inch) single by Eric Gradman Man and Machine, an EP by Ian Stephen's Schizophrenia called 'I'm Still in Two Minds about the Title', and records by the Romantics and News.[533] Crime and the City Solution, visiting Melbourne from Sydney, evidently saw Missing Link as their best option and gave Glass a demo (to no avail).[534] The label quickly came to be seen as a punk/new wave stronghold, though it continued to put out 'retro' releases, too: a various artists album with the self-explanatory title *The Autodrifters and the Relaxed Mechanics meet the Fabulous Nudes and the Pelaco Brothers;* a re-release of the mid-70s *Live at the Station;* and *The Melbourne Club,* featuring hitherto unreleased songs by legendary groups like Paul Kelly and Martin Armiger's High Rise Bombers. In 1978, News – the best-known of the first wave of Melbourne punk bands – were to release their Missing Link single posthumously;[535] as mentioned, their short-lived final line-up had featured Eddie Van Roosendael and Chris Dyson, formerly of Stiletto, an interesting blend of old and new Carlton bands.[536] What is clear in examining the early releases of the Missing Link label is that once again, as had been the case with the Saints and Radio Birdman, the Glass-Wilson-Pepperell pyramid was exploring late 70s punk as a 60s revival phenomenon.

Adelaide's Young Modern did something similar. John Dowler had been the singer in Spare Change, a three-piece band he formed with two locals in Amsterdam on a trip to Europe in the mid 70s. An Australian-based version of the group recorded a 'wimpy, lacklustre single' ('The Big Beat'/'Classified Ad') and an album that was released years after they'd split up.[537] Dowler's next band, Young Modern, took its name from the Adelaide magazine[538] and made its debut in November 1977 supporting Radio Birdman at Unley Town Hall.[539] Dowler's intention with Young Modern was 'to get music back on the right tracks – pop music.'[540] He told Jillian Burt of *Juke* that he was 'trying to write reasonably clever lyrics without them being too selfconsciously clever. Just sensible songs that mean something.' Burt wondered if Dowler could be 'on the way to becoming the Patrick White of pop?'[541] Their song titles included 'New Wave', 'Countdown' and 'Wanna be a Birdman' which was *not,* Dowler was at pains to point out, about *Radio* Birdman but about 'the illegitimate son of Howard Hughes.'[542]

Donald Robertson stated in *Roadrunner* that Young Modern had the most refreshing sound in Adelaide since the Twilights; 'If there is to be a renaissance in Australian Rock then my money is on Young Modern to be right there in the front line.'[543] Their shows began with a tape of their theme tune, Jack Nitzsche's 'The Lonely Surfer';[544] Stephen Cummings produced their first single, 'She's got the money'.[545] Relocating to Sydney, this jaunty, intelligent, power pop outfit found they'd already peaked; neither the music industry, nor audiences, liked them. They broke up in mid 1979.

Another Adelaide band for whom many had high hopes was JAB, formed in 1976 by Bohdan X, Boris, Janis Freidenfelds and Ash Wednesday. Bohdan, who has been known to claim to be unable to remember his real last name, says the band was formed 'the same time as the Sex Pistols – we were doing the same thing without even hearing about them, back in 1976.'[546] The band's name was a kind of acronym and didn't really account for the two Bs in the group, but luckily when Boris left the group in late 1977 he was replaced by Bobby Stopa, another 'B'. When he was in turn replaced by Pierre Voltaire the group collapsed under the strain of the tension between acronym and reality.[547] Their recorded legacy is two tracks on the Suicide compilation discussed earlier; the common impression that they metamorphosed into the Models by discarding Bohdan (who went on to work as an announcer on 3RRR, as well as in various bands and solo recording projects) is technically untrue, as will be seen in chapter 16.

Similarly to JAB, and like the Pelaco Brothers, the Young Charlatans are known today primarily because several members later joined unusual and interesting bands, though the complimentary reports of many who saw them suggest the Young Charlatans were of considerable interest in their own right. Bassist Janine Hall played with the Saints in the early 80s, and later in Weddings Parties Anything and Kings of the World; guitarist Rowland S. Howard would soon be a member of the Boys Next Door; keyboard player Ollie Olsen played in Whirlywirld and numerous other projects in a variety of musical styles; drummer Jeffery Wegener, arriving after a brief tenure in an early line-up of the Saints, would go on to be the only permanent member of Laughing Clowns other than Ed Kuepper. This, then, was a supergroup before the fact.

The Young Charlatans played what may have been their last show on New Wave Night at the University of Melbourne in mid 1978 with Proles and News; *Juke* journalist Stephen Charlesworth was not impressed: 'Their music doesn't have that stamp of instant recognisability about it, lying somewhere in the middle between the power chording and full-on energy of what is identifiably mainstream punk and nervous twitch riffing...'[548]

The elegant and articulate Howard shortly after became the hot new fifth member of the Boys Next Door, who at this point had released one single on Suicide and recorded an album, *Brave Exhibitions*, for that label. They cut a deal with Mushroom – their contract having reverted to the parent label following Suicide's demise – to use the least bad (in their opinion) of the *Brave Exhibitions*

tracks on one side of their debut LP, and record new material they felt was more representative of their current sound and style for the other side. Of the four new songs recorded for side two of *Door, Door*, three were by Howard – and one of them, 'Shivers', was destined to become an anthem.

The other Boys Next Door were Nick Cave, Mick Harvey, Tracy Pew and Phill Calvert. 'At around fifteen years of age,' Cave reminisced in the mid 90s, 'my friends and I formed a rock band and I gave up writing really bad poems and started writing really bad songs instead, and these songs were very much influenced by whatever the book was that I was reading at the time.'[549] The original four Boys Next Door had attended the privileged secondary school Caulfield Grammar. In earlier incarnations, they'd played 'These Boots Are Made for Walking', Alice Cooper's 'I'm Eighteen' and Bowie's 'Andy Warhol'.[550] In June 1978, interviewed for *Farrago*, they came across as bright, informative and aware. They also made no bones about their background:

> Cave: For a start we always admitted that we were um ... in the days when it was a problem whether you had "credibility" and whether you were poor or not, we were always –
> Phill: delighted by the fact that we were middle class ...
> Cave: the first to say we weren't [poor], and that we were educated properly etc.

Cave said they were going to change their name 'very soon,' adding 'I guess we were a punk group. I've always said that we weren't, but so many people said we were, I'm starting to believe them.'[551] Indeed, he volunteered that he had 'gobbed' on his audience at the very first Boys Next Door show:

> All those skinheads, Holmesglen skinheads, were sort of screaming at us 'Punks!' and stuff like that. And it suddenly occurred to me that we were punks, because everyone said that we were. So I just sort of thought, "What things do punks do? Will I fart, shit, gob, spit or whatever!"[552]

Punk or otherwise, the group was willing to appear on *Countdown* when asked – they mimed to 'These Boots . . .' Calvert, who would later be dismissed from the disintegrating band (by then renamed the Birthday Party) for being too pop-oriented, suggested he would do it because it was 'communication', adding:

> People use to sing vocals (live) and the only people who do that were – Well, Marc Hunter did it and I can't think of anyone else.[553]

Cave was already, at this very early stage of what has become a long and illustrious career, showing himself to be by turns self-aware, self-deprecating, canny and stand-offish: 'Nothing I write is totally from personal experience', he declared to the anonymous author of the *Farrago* story; 'it's really hard to write about anything I've experienced without becoming totally self-obsessed and indulgent . . . I generally write in the first person . . . the things I talk about are interesting, it's just that they're written in an unemotional way, as if I've got no contact with what I'm saying.'[554] Jillian Burt told *Juke* readers that:

> Visually the Boys Next Door are just stunning and riveting. Somewhere between the smouldering sensuality of Valentino and the brooding villainy of Vincent Price with a dash of the Chaplinesque tragic/comic – that's vocalist Nic Cave . . . he oozes with style, heaps of 1920sish matinee idol charisma.[555]

The best of the Cave biographers to date, the curiously (self-)named Robert Brokenmouth, suggests there was a German ambience to the Boys Next Door that derived from the post-war refugees in St Kilda, the suburb they soon became identified with.[556] The cover art of *Door, Door* was reputedly from a *Theatre Arts Monthly* poster advertising a 1930s Norwegian play.[557] The album reputedly sold less than 2000 copies at the time of its release,[558] though several factors might help explain this – the small size of the 'alternative' scene at the time; the record's release on a major label, Mushroom, which might have alienated some potential purchasers; and the fact that it is a bad record.

The worst of the Nick Cave books (though competition is fierce) is probably *The Life and Music of Nick Cave* by German journalist Maximilian Dax, who completely lacks any understanding of the group's context, apparently believing that Australian music before the Boys Next Door was a coterie scene of what he calls 'country-pop', perhaps of the Olivia Newton-John variety, though he also describes it as 'a simple rehash of chart hits.'[559] 'Unobserved by the music press,' Dax proclaims, 'a new musical culture had taken root in Australia that wasn't entrenched in the country-pop scene. For the first time, musicians were willing to go further than simply imitating chart-storming rock idols from America.'[560] But even then, he pontificates, Australian new wave lacked 'political content, its message watered down on its long journey from Europe.'[561] Dax's statements are not a matter of opinion or perspective; they are demonstrably false, the consequence of substituting lazy preconceptions for basic research. As a result, he gives a wholly inaccurate account of the Boys Next Door's environment in particular and of late 70s Australian music and culture in general; this is a common failing of books about Cave and the Birthday Party (and, as has been mentioned, of books about AC/DC and other artists successful enough outside their country of origin to elicit interest in an international market).

The Boys Next Door meandered for a period of time in the late 70s, some of them accumulating severe drug habits and all of them gaining in charisma. Tracy Pew adopted his cowboy look, Nick Cave his shock of black hair. Mick Harvey – the main talent behind the majority of Cave-oriented projects until the two parted in 2009 – came to the fore as an organiser, arranger, composer and player. The group obtained a manager in the form of Keith Glass, who plucked them from Mushroom and placed them on his own label, Missing Link. Numerous ideas were thrown about: one which gained considerable currency was that their second album, *Hee Haw*, would be released in the USA on the Residents' label, Ralph Records,[562] with whom Missing Link had cultivated a relationship.

By the time the group decided to go to England in 1980, they had won a place in many music writers' hearts (as the press coverage cited earlier indicates) and a certain following among music aficionados generally.

As they left – expecting, just like the Bee Gees when they mulled over changing their name to Rupert's World, that relocating would be like a rebirth – the Boys Next Door renamed themselves the Birthday Party. Their new name was taken from one of their songs, 'Happy Birthday', which signaled their new direction: more fractured and cacophonous, as well as a little funky in the manner of English groups like Bristol's the Pop Group (a personal favourite of Cave's). Like that band, the Birthday Party adopted a name that represented a grim-faced joke about niceness; they also – in major leaps forward like the splendid song 'Mr. Clarinet' – incorporated non-Western (and also non-melodic) styles into their rock music. Howard recalled in 1982, 'We got the name just before we left for England. And me and Nick were writing a song which turned out to be "Happy Birthday" but we decided to grab that for our name. There were numerous reasons: it was a non-depressing name, (unlike names) all the groups in England at that time had, and at the same time established images of ritual and some kind of celebration and things.'[563] The narrative of 'Happy Birthday' is simply a fantasy child's view of materialism and overstimulation, typical of the time: a denial of innocence and an acknowledgement of the sometimes venal world of childhood which was already being made much of by horror movie directors – and by a nascent goth scene that would soon take the Birthday Party to its bosom.

The Birthday Party's story unfolds in the early 80s and will be told in chapter 16. After their break-up in 1983, Mick Harvey and Rowland Howard – along with Harry Howard and sublime British drummer Epic Soundtracks – convened with Simon Bonney to form a third version of Crime and the City Solution, whose earlier incarnations are anchored in the late 70s. Bonney was the only constant member; the group's initial manifestations are obscure largely because they did not release anything. Mick Harvey had long been an admirer of Bonney's, and mused a decade later 'that the actual real influence that [the earlier] Crime and the City Solution had was probably on the music of the Birthday Party . . . I know that Rowland and myself had talked about it and were still emulating certain elements of their music right up to the end of the Birthday Party.'[564]

The first version of the group formed in Sydney in 1977. Simon Bonney had briefly and occasionally been the singer in the Particles; he and Particles drummer Don McLennan founded Crime and the City Solution as an early Sydney punk band. The following year McLennan and Bonney moved to Melbourne and formed a second version, which included Dan Wallace-Crabbe, later of the Laughing Clowns. (Bonney was much in demand: Dan's cousin Ben, who had also been in the Laughing Clowns, formed Upside Down House in 1981 to showcase him as singer, though Bonney inexplicably failed to show up for the group's first rehearsal, or thereafter – Upside Down House nevertheless had an impressive, if brief, career.[565]) 'Crime' rehearsals took place in what saxophone player Kim Beissel described as 'Wallace-Crabbe's grotty house in Fitzroy. Nick Seymour... came to one rehearsal but wasn't into it.'[566] In a short memoir written almost thirty years later, Beissel insisted that the group 'weren't a punk band' though they did indulge in 'posturing teen angst and introversion.'[567] Bass player Lindsay O'Meara, formerly of Voigt/465, moved down from Sydney to play with them, then returned there to play in Pel Mel, who are discussed further in chapter 16.[568] Crime and the City Solution's demise in early 1979, and their lack of any recorded legacy, meant that the Boys Next Door/Birthday Party were, as Harvey implies, free to take anything they wished from the group's sound and style; it is to Harvey's credit that he later facilitated the revival of Bonney's career.

Beissel had joined Crime and the City Solution version two after a chance meeting with Mick Harvey, who was recruiting members for the group on Bonney's behalf: the two met in the foyer of the Crystal (later Seaview) Ballroom – not that much of a chance meeting, since this was the venue where everybody in the nascent new wave scene in Melbourne went on the weekend. The venue – in a grand 19th-century hotel usually known as The George – was opened in 1978 (originally as the Wintergarden Room) by Dolores San Miguel for the benefit of audiences for bands like JAB and Teenage Radio Stars who were being ignored by the booking agencies. 'I felt there was a big need for them to be able to play somewhere,' she said, 'plus there was an audience, which hadn't been tapped.'[569] Maximilian Dax suggests that the venue was 'near the edge of town'[570] – just one more example of why it is a bad idea to write in an assured tone about something you know nothing about (and then foist it on the world); St. Kilda is part of Melbourne's 'inner city', and the building is opposite what was then St Kilda railway station on Fitzroy Street, 5 km from the city centre. Vikki Riley writes that:

The Crystal Ballroom functioned as an old hotel and residence that was used on the weekend as a venue. (It still had tenants who would sometimes pop in and out, trying hard to ignore what was going on.) Separate band rooms opened into each other like boudoirs in a brothel which you could wander between. Downstairs was a small room called the Star Club where supper was served at 10 pm and a strange chamber quartet carved out neat little repetitive tunes. Next to this room was the Paradise Lounge where other bands played, sometimes simultaneously with the main act upstairs – acts like Eric Gradman's Man Machine, Paul Kelly and the Dots, Two Way Garden, the Ears and the Models.[571]

Sydney had similar multi-roomed, multi-level venues, usually run from specific trade union clubs in the inner city rather than from large hotels; the Sydney Trade Union Club was probably the closest to the Crystal/Seaview in ambience at this time, though it was a much more modern building and did not fully come into its own until the following decade. Brisbane had Cloudland, the base for Ivan Dayman's operations in the 60s and a major music venue up until its unauthorized demolition in 1982, one more in the list of crimes against culture and the people committed by the inordinately corrupt Bjelke-Petersen government (Midnight Oil wrote a song about it – 'Dreamland'). The city also had suburban halls which, according to Andrew Stafford, 'were cheap to hire, and there were fewer questions to be answered.'[572] The Saints had debuted at Chelmer Hall, and the Go-Betweens made their first – unscheduled – appearance at Baroona Hall in April 1978.

I have written a book about the Go-Betweens and their late-70s Brisbane environment, so I'm well aware that attempting to contextualize a major group with its own rich world in the late 70s scene in a few paragraphs is difficult, however necessary. Andrew Stafford's *Pig City* offers an important and fascinating outline of the late 70s in Brisbane and also includes a very effective portrait of the Go-Betweens, as do Robert Forster's notes (written in the third person) for the 2015 box set of the band's first three LPs.

One illustration of the way in which Brisbaneites in the mid to late 1970s might have felt isolated and strange comes from the testimony of Robert Vickers, who was a member of the Go-Betweens and their early colleagues in Brisbane's 'new wave', the Numbers:

> I got out of Brisbane as soon as I could. I worked for 8 months in a Woolworths in Inala in order to go to Europe in 1977 and travel around, ending up in London. I heard the Saints on the radio there and decided to go back to Brisbane and get in a band. I didn't feel as desperate after that and was happy to spend time there learning to play. The next time I left was January 79, and I was much more able to cope with a different environment. I couldn't stay in London when I was 18 but I was able to deal with New York at 20.

[Before then] bands in Brisbane were all covers – metal, disco, glam, whatever. I wasn't aware of any original bands. In 1976 I did get interested in the folk scene a little and went to a folk club in the city. That scene seemed more creative than crappy covers bands in pubs. But I was saved by rock and roll. A friend from school pointed out some guys walking around a jazz festival one day and said they were called the Saints and had just a signed a record deal in England. A few months later I heard them in my dingy hotel room in London and I just wanted to do that. As I didn't know anyone in London to do it with, I got back on a plane for Brisbane.

Vickers joined the Numbers, also known as the Grudge and Neon Steal and later the Riptides. When he was fired from that band, he moved to New York, which would be his base thereafter.

The Numbers were highly motivated. They were architecture students, for the most part, who built their own PA, amongst other achievements. They claimed to be influenced by 'the last twenty years of AM radio' (an early press release noted that the Who started out as the High Numbers); they were ambitious and pop oriented in all the right ways. 'Our heart was in the right place,' leader Mark Callaghan says in a 1988 documentary on Brisbane music, 'but we didn't exactly have the credibility of living in a derelict squat like the guys from the Saints did, up on Petrie Terrace.' Callaghan's unwillingness to celebrate his own early work aside, the Numbers' EP *Sunset Strip* (later reissued under their new name, the Riptides) and the Riptides' single 'Tomorrow's Tears' are undeniable classics, and even better was to follow with a slew of remarkable pop singles, the best of which were 'Only Time' and the superb 'Hearts and Flowers', released in 1982, by which time the group was Sydney-based and Callaghan was the only remaining original member.

The Go-Betweens were founded in 1978 by two university friends with private school backgrounds – Robert Forster and Grant McLennan – who counted film, literature, art and other 'scenes' amongst their interests. Forster was a guitarist and songwriter; McLennan had only rudimentary guitar skills when Forster tutored him in bass for the express purpose of starting the band. They played fewer shows than their peers, to 'make each time you play important'.[573] They played an impromptu show within two months of forming; their first 'real' appearance was on a bill with the Numbers, with that group's drummer Denis Cantwell. They quickly developed a substantial repertoire of Forster's dashed-off pop songs and in May recorded a debut single, 'Lee Remick'/'Karen', once again with Cantwell. In the first of what would be many bizarre experiences with maverick record companies, the band was signed (for eight albums) by the UK branch of the British-American Beserkley label, whose star artist at this time was Jonathan Richman. The label planned to release the two songs from the Go-Betweens' first single as separate A sides, so the group recorded new songs with their first permanent drummer, Tim (he later reverted to his original name, Temucin) Mustafa and briefly recruited second guitarist Peter Walsh. The label went bankrupt shortly afterwards.

Undaunted, the three-piece Go-Betweens recorded a new single, 'People Say'/'Don't Let Him Come Back' which was released, like the first, on the group's own Able Label. In his memoir of the band, Forster indicates that Brisbane played a similar role for the Go-Betweens as it had for the Bee Gees fifteen years earlier: 'the town was like a laboratory, a place to mix ingredients'.[574] They traveled to Britain (without Mustafa, whose girlfriend made him quit), where they recorded a third single, 'I Need Two Heads'/'Stop Before You Say It' in April 1980 for the Scottish label Postcard, home to Aztec Camera, Josef K and Orange Juice. Postcard's owner, Alan Horne, was primarily concerned with promoting Orange Juice, but wished to create the impression of a roster of like-minded bands.

Forster returned to Australia before McLennan and was sufficiently swept up in the headiness of the band's progress, ability, and good fortune that he concocted a new four-piece line-up, which played one show in mid 1980 before collapsing at a time that roughly coincided with the return of a somewhat irate McLennan. Retracing their steps slightly, the Go-Betweens instead settled on a new third member in drummer Lindy Morrison, who had hitherto been in the edgy Zero. Missing Link's Keith Glass had licensed their 'I Need Two Heads'/'Stop Before You Say It' single directly from Postcard, and the group then began a relationship with the label. The first single to include Morrison was 'Your Turn, My Turn'/'World Weary', by which time the literary and pop-oriented McLennan was writing songs alongside Forster. The book accompanying the first instalment of a major box set series of Go-Betweens material reveals that McLennan was the artist behind many of the group's early record sleeves; a talent few suspected.

The Go-Betweens traveled to Melbourne in 1980 and by the following year had become a part of the local scene, though it was always understood they were en route to Britain again. They recorded a debut album, which was to become *Send Me a Lullaby*, at Richmond Recorders. Forster writes of the album's 'rough and dynamic charm': 'It was as if [producer] Tony Cohen had walked into the band's practice room and recorded exactly what the band had wanted to play that day'.[575] This time, Glass was not licensing material to release on Missing Link, but recording material to release himself and to license to others: the London-based Rough Trade label took on the first Go-Betweens album (in Australia, the album was, curiously, released as a mini-LP, with four fewer tracks than the UK version). The group's career was a continued upwards spiral hereafter, and their impact and influence would grow exponentially for decades, well into the 21st century.

The Baroona Hall show at which the Go-Betweens had formally debuted was headlined by the Numbers, who would go on to release records on the Able Label and who at this time featured Robert Vickers. At the beginning they would cover songs by the Saints, while 'Corinda Boys' band the Patients even contained a Saint's brother, Wolfgang Kuepper. But the Saints' influence on the nation's music at this time was not a patch on Australian (particularly Sydney) musicians' love affair in the late 70s with Radio Birdman, fostered in part by ex-members of the group who continued to play in various bands, and by those who were inspired by the group's live shows, or their records, or even just by seeing a picture of them, as was the case with Brisbane schoolboy Brad Shepherd. Shepherd read about them in *RAM*:

> There was a column that they used to have, kinda undiscovered bands, unsigned bands that they had in the back of *RAM*. And there'd be some silly group, and they had this picture of this band, 'Radio Birdman', and this picture of the singer. He had white hair down to his arse, black makeup running down his face and elbow length lurex gloves and, like, a snakeskin shirt! It was just the greatest thing I'd ever seen ... here were these guys in our own backyard. Deniz, playing a guitar I'd never seen before, at a time when unless you had a Les Paul or a Strat, you weren't a proper guitar player! And this guy's got this amazing looking guitar, he's got mirrored shades and leather pants! It just blew my mind.[576]

A little later, Shepherd formed the Fun Things, whose song 'When the Birdmen Fly' on their only EP was, unlike Young Modern's song, a tribute to the group; he then joined the Hitmen in 1981, a band whose only regular member was vocalist Johnny Kannis, but which had featured numerous former members of Radio Birdman. Kannis had earlier played guitar and sung in the Jackals with Chris Masuak, playing 50s and 60s classics alongside Masuak's songs; Masuak had been recruited from this band by Radio Birdman. Four members of Radio Birdman had backed Kannis on a 1978 single, a version of the Drifters' 'Under the Boardwalk', produced by Deniz Tek.[577] When Radio Birdman went overseas, Kannis formed another version of the Hitmen; Masuak and Warwick Gilbert were involved in the version which signed with WEA in 1979, as was the Saints' Ivor Hay (for a year).[578] The Hitmen were an inclusive, industry-friendly group; they aimed to play outside the inner-city stomping ground Radio Birdman had concentrated on. Tellingly, they included three men (Shepherd, Clyde Bramley and Mark Kingsmill) who would later join another avowedly anti-elitist group, the Hoodoo Gurus.

Numerous bands sprang up in the late 70s and into the

80s, particularly in Sydney, that owed a considerable amount – in varying degrees of sound, style, approach, attitude – to Radio Birdman. The Lipstick Killers were one of them. Mark Taylor ran a Sydney record shop called White Light and played in the Psychosurgeons alongside David Taylor (no relation). Peter Tillman, formerly a member of Filth, the two Taylors, and bass player Kim Giddy (from 'a Riverina band called Precious Little'[579]) formed the group and recorded a single produced by Deniz Tek, 'Hindu Gods of Love', in 1978.[580] Giddy addressed the notion that the Lipstick Killers had replaced Radio Birdman, suggesting that people thought that 'only because we play with the same sort of feel to the music. It's just that it's hard and fast'.[581] Certainly the group's interest in glam rock was at some remove from Radio Birdman-style austerity; Giddy also joked with Darcy Condon, in a story written for *RAM*, that the group would appear on *Countdown* if it weren't for the fact that 'we'd have to find William Shakespeare and borrow all his costumes.'[582] The Lipstick Killers moved to Los Angeles, where a live album, *Mesmerizer*, was recorded at Madam Wong's (described in *Rolling Stone* as a 'notorious punk nightclub'[583]) in November 1981. The band members later returned, separately, to Sydney; the album was released in 1984 on the Citadel label ('This is homage', Citadel's John Needham said at the time).[584] The album's artwork contained an advertisement for a book of poetry by band members entitled *Reflections upon a Golden Homosexual Statue*.[585]

Friends of Radio Birdman formed the Passengers in late 1978; the focus of the group was singer Angie Pepper, who had moved to Sydney from Newcastle, 120 km north, two years previously. Pepper later recalled a host of Radio Birdman-related groups:

> It was funny in those days because whereas before, all these friends became friends through going to Radio Birdman gigs, now all these friends had split off into different bands. And we all liked each other. It was fun. There was no competitiveness or jealousy between us, or aggression that you might come across.[586]

Pepper and Tek knew each other professionally and became friends when he was a doctor to her grandmother in a Newcastle Hospital; they married in 1981. At the same time, the Angie Pepper Band recorded an album with Clyde Bramley, later of the Hoodoo Gurus and former Saints drummer Ivor Hay.

The Thought Criminals made an important contribution to Sydney punk, not just through their records but also by founding an important record label, Doublethink. 'Much too modest for their own good,' claimed *RAM* in their 1979 survey of Sydney bands, 'their idealism provides the sort of positive inspiration that would make them heroic in a bus queue.'[587] Roger Grierson, who worked at White Light Records, started the band in 1977 because 'It seemed the thing to do. Punk was around so let's form a band . . . We put an ad up in the foyer of the Paris Cinema.' Guitarist Stephen Philip and, later, Ken Doyle joined the band; both had been in a group with the actor Bryan Brown. Early recordings such as 'I Won't Pay' ('for punk records') took a *Steal this book* attitude to music. They were committed, obnoxious, persecuted, and almost too clever. They played a benefit for Wendy Saddington at which they transformed the popular and famous late-19th-century poem by Banjo Patterson, 'Clancy of the Overflow', into 'Wendy of the Overdose'.[588]

The Thought Criminals became famous for their fierce independence, which was primarily, according to Grierson, 'because nobody wanted to help us.' At the same time, they seemed to take what they wanted in the name of their art:

> One of the very first posters we did, we broke into the poster-printing place at the Tin Sheds [on the University of Sydney campus] and printed them off in the middle of the night . . . this is just what you did . . . We used to break into the Last Words' rehearsal studio to rehearse. Use their gear, leave a mess and come back in the morning.[589]

Their usual venues were the Civic and the Stagedoor:

> You had the Angels/Mi-Sex nights, which were of course successful nights – but then the Wednesdays were the traditional punk bands . . . Thursdays were a bit more intellectual because it was with Tactics and the M Squared stuff, and Friday (or every other Friday) would be Popular Mechanics or the Thought Criminals, bands that were coming up. Sekret Sekret, I guess. And the same for the Civic. There was the usual crap like Mi-Sex, but there was a lot of stuff like the Mentals, Sekret Sekret and ourselves where a scene kinda formed around it.[590]

By 1981, the band members had moved on; Stephen Philip was a member of the extraordinary Do Re Mi, while Grierson had given up playing music, and was instead 'managing other bands. 'Cos I thought Tactics was a better band than we were. I'd be better playing the telephone than the bass.'[591] He also started the Green label with journalist Stuart Coupe, embarking on a career that took him to the highest echelons of the music industry; for instance, he was chairman of Festival Records in the late 1990s. Tactics released three albums on Green; the group is discussed in chapter 16.

The Last Words – the aforementioned victims of the Thought Criminals' easygoing attitude to property, with whom they also shared a member in Ken Doyle – were a short-lived but ambitious band. Their first single, 'Animal World', recorded at a time when there were only two members, motivated by 'boredom and desire to be stars', was released on their own Remand label. Perhaps hoping to emulate the Saints, they sent a copy to Stiff Records – and received 'a polite "get fucked" reply.'[592] They did, however, end up signing with the Wizard label, home to Hush and the Australian label for frontline British punk/new wave groups like the Buzzcocks and Public Image Limited. Wizard had them re-record 'Animal World' and put it out as a single again; Jeffery Wegener joined the band for a short time – long enough to appear in a video for the single – though he did not appear on the recording or accompany them to the UK, where Rough Trade also issued the re-recorded 'Animal World' as a single.[593] Last Words recorded and released an album in Britain in 1980 for the Armageddon label before petering out.

This chapter ends – a bang and not a whimper – with a short discussion of Sekret Sekret, another of the groups in the Thought Criminals' scene. Sekret Sekret are obscure to the extent that Ian McFarlane includes them in his generally very thorough *Encyclopedia of Australian Rock and Pop* only as a forerunner to the vastly inferior, but undeniably far more commercially successful group the Cruel Sea; guitarist Danny Rumour was a member of both. Sekret Sekret were of the late-70s punk scene, but it is hard to imagine a group who sound less like they belonged there. Their 'New King Jack' is one of those songs that, once heard, is never forgotten, yet is also undeniably lyrically meaningless (or at best entirely obscure) and a jaunty piece of folk rock sung in high voices. It would be difficult to come up with a song less befitting the feel, sound and style of late-70s punk/new wave, but the way it was instantly embraced  by that scene shows what a broad church 'the scene' had become. Listening to 'New King Jack' and the Triffids' 1984 single 'Beautiful Waste' one after the other, it is hard to believe that David McComb did not write the latter immediately after five plays of the former.

Martin Bishop, who ran Sekret Sekret's first record label, Basilisk, told *Rolling Stone* that 'Sekret Sekret just want to make beautiful music, and they can't understand why they aren't as big as Rod Stewart.'[594] To add to the mystery of Sekret Sekret's mastery of pop, it seems to have emerged quickly after a period of seeking in anti-music quarters; the group's two crucial members, Danny Rumour and David Virgin, had both been early members of a 1980s 'equivalent of 60s acid rock...'[595] – the industrial noise band SPK[596] – at a time when, Virgin later said, 'the theme of most of the songs was: having sex with a machine.'[597] Before that, at age 15, Virgin had been the oldest member of a 'really hot band' called the Broken Toys.[598] Sekret Sekret would go on to release two more excellent singles in the 80s, 'Just To Love You' and 'Girl with a White Stick'; these were closer to the spirit of Vanda and Young, or perhaps Marc Bolan, than to 'New King Jack'. Virgin and Rumour have periodically worked together over the ensuing years, but it is that one extraordinary song which has made their legend – a legend that should be a million times larger than it is.

MAKING A MODEL OF AUSTRALIA'S LATE SEVENTIES

A 3D model of the progress made by Australian popular music in the late 1970s would resemble a large diagonal line, increasing in width as the industry expanded and more participants became involved, and heading upwards: that represents the cultural impact of Australian music in Australia. This diagonal would be bisected by another widening but *horizontal* line, representing the impact of new wave music on Australian bands. Somehow, the model's designer would have to find a way to indicate within it the very real possibility that new wave, as much as it invigorated the 'scene' and inspired thousands more individuals (particularly enlightened and creative amateurs) to become musicians, may also have nipped in the bud the particular Australian sensibility of pre-punk practitioners such as Peter Lillie and the Carlton musicians – or at least reset the terms of the debate as to what constituted 'real' as opposed to airy-fairy 'head' music.

Another horizontal line would be required to represent the impact of music from overseas on the Australian variety. To suggest that this was simply a matter of one-way influence is, as we have seen, sheer nonsense – the word 'influence' is inherently inadequate, for that matter; other words need to be invented to encompass what actually occurred (and occurs). What's more, the idea that Australian groups found it necessary to go overseas to expand their horizons is invariably inaccurate. Joe Camilleri might justifiably have observed that three years was the maximum amount of time a band could keep going in Australia before expanding internationally; Jo Jo Zep and the Falcons, however, lasted for seven years (and have sporadically reconvened since), with international trips including a prestige spot at the Montreux Jazz Festival and yet no ensuing international 'seal of approval'. International travel additionally caused creative difficulties, with bands required to play older material to cater to markets who were catching up with their back catalogue.

It is valuable to contrast Camilleri's opinion with the slightly embittered view of the Dingoes' Broderick Smith: for him, having returned after maintaining the Dingoes for a lengthy period in the USA:

> Denver...is just like Ballarat...a country city. We just went in and walked all over them, although they didn't realise it at the time because they thought we were basically boys from the bush, that's the entire concept of Australia. Yet there are about six cities – like New York, Chicago, Detroit, Dallas... [DJ and television host] Lee Simon asked me what I thought of New York, I

just looked at him and said 'It reminded me of Brunswick' ... But it does. It's got that same cosmopolitan feel about it.[599]

Which is to say – what's so good about America, aside from the critical (often hypercritical) mass?

In any case, Australian music did not exist in a vacuum; not only was there a constant parade of international artists touring Australia, there was also a strong awareness of music from overseas as presented via radio, television, the music press and record releases. Australian music competed with music from elsewhere, in the Australian music market. Australian record buyers would buy records by both international and local artists. Australians were not confused about the potential of Australian music; if that was a problem, it was being worked out elsewhere in the world.

Our 3D model would need, somehow, to encompass these possibilities and issues. It would also need to reflect questions of popular music and politics; the rise of the independent music industry and its problematic status; and the changing modes of delivery of music to audiences.

All of this probably goes to explain why an excessively long book chapter offers a better representation of the reality of the late 70s in Australia than a 3D model could provide. The era was a gaggle of conflicting and contrasting voices, with varying levels of validity, integrity and justification.

The 70s ended with three of the decade's biggest names in mainstream Australian rock/pop – Sherbet, Dragon and Skyhooks – seemingly dead in the water, though Skyhooks would limp on for a few more months into 1980. As it transpired, Dragon would reform and enjoy their greatest commercial success in the new decade, and Sherbet (as the Sherbs) also reformed, but only to experience humiliatingly diminishing commercial returns for a number of years. Skyhooks, rather than reconstitute themselves as an ongoing entity, merely reformed as living legends for short gasps in the 80s and 90s.

The second line of 70s rock in Australia – Hush and Ted Mulry Gang for instance – were either gone or had found a level as good-time, outer-suburb rock outfits. The new breed – the Angels, Midnight Oil, Cold Chisel – pre-punk groups who had adapted their sound, style and look to new-wave templates – were to have their greatest success in the 80s. The *new* new breed – the genuine postpunk groups of the late 70s inner city – would, as will be seen, keep the excesses of the old 'dinosaurs' in check, while developing a few of their own (both excesses *and* dinosaurs). The 80s would be a riot.

12 Five Years of Fancy Cars
DRAGON

Dragon made for an unlikely soufflé – even before the band rose more than once. They enjoyed (or didn't) at least two top-forty heydays (1975-78 and 1982-86) with the same ingredients of brothers Marc and Todd Hunter. This chapter offers an abbreviated version of a complex, extraordinary story of excess and brilliance. It is structured around an interview with Robert Taylor, the group's guitarist from early 1975 on, and covers the group till the end of the 1980s; some of the rest of the band's story is detailed in chapter 16. It is a story that deserves much more than a superficial overview; the biography of Marc Hunter by Jeff Apter unfortunately goes only a certain way to doing justice to it.

Like so many people in this book, the members of Dragon were for the most part New Zealanders, although after Marc Hunter's temporary departure in 1979, Australians and other nationalities were invited into the mix. Most importantly, Australia has been Dragon's commercial base since May 1975, yet their New Zealand identity has never really deserted them, though New Zealanders do not clutch them to their collective bosom in the way they treasure Split Enz.

Dragon arrived in Australia from New Zealand with two remarkable albums, *Universal Radio* (1974) and *Scented Gardens for the Blind* (1975), under their belt, but were already metamorphosing into an entirely different band in sound and style. Those first two albums had been spirited and unpretentious prog rock on the Vertigo label, recorded when the band's average age was in the teens. They began in the New Zealand art-rock scene with a core of Graeme Collins, Todd Hunter, Neil Reynolds (quickly replaced by Neil Storey) and Ray Goodwin, and soon added Todd's brother Marc as vocalist and conga player; having previously sung in cabaret-style groups, he moved naturally into this role. Ivan Thompson, a keyboard player, was another important member of the New Zealand line-up; he left before there was any discussion about relocating. The Hunters were partly of Fijian ancestry, and Todd Hunter has said of the group's early work that 'they were South Pacific harmonies, basically.'[1]

Todd claimed in 2005 that the group had been very keen to 'get out of New Zealand; it drove us crazy, it was so parochial.'[2] Thirty years earlier, having just arrived in Australia, he had told *RAM*: 'We were the most consistently booked band in NZ and it was just too easy. You know, you tour the north, you tour the south, and then you turn around and do it all over again. You book venues and sell them out without looking.'[3] By the time they arrived in Australia in May 1975,[4] Dragon had already undergone numerous changes of personnel; their line-up was now the Hunter brothers, Goodwin, Storey and guitarist Robert Taylor. Taylor had been brought into the band from another major act, Mammal, at least in part for his songwriting skills, on the urging of Mammal's manager Graeme Nesbitt – the first of many authority figures who mentored the band. Todd claimed that Taylor's introduction meant 'It's got less head and more arse now.'[5]

Taylor recalls Dragon's days 'touring on the strength of *Universal Radio:*'

> They held down gigs in the top nightclubs in Auckland . . . they weren't totally original, they were doing things like Santana and Doors songs and things like that, but they were pretty focused. At that stage Marc Hunter was playing congas and I think a little bit of sax. Yeah, so they knew where they were going in their songwriting department, but at the same time they played what the Auckland club owners wanted to hear, too.
>
> When I'd been in Mammal, it was $18 a week wages but free food and accommodation. And Dragon I think offered me a hundred dollars a week, which was an enormous amount of money . . . So I was pretty startled by that. But within myself I felt as if I wanted to do bigger things and New Zealand, once you've done the country three or four times, you can get into a rut, which was what we were getting into, and they'd introduced some sort of new tax system in the live gig scene whereby the money was going to become ridiculous . . .
>
> A Maori chap came over from Sydney, Teddy, I can't remember his surname, and said, 'Well, I'll buy a truck and a roadie and everything. You guys come over and – there's only two top bands in Australia, there's Hush and Sherbet, you should be able to knock them off the top in a couple of weeks.' So that was the sort of crap that we headed off into.
>
> We had no idea. The Australian music scene in New Zealand was like – the only Aussie records we'd had to listen to was, obviously, the Easybeats, Doug Parkinson, Wendy Saddington, Jeff St John, we didn't know anything about bands out of Melbourne, things like that. So we didn't really know what we were walking into.
>
> We were told by Bruno Lawrence, the drummer and actor, that you had to go one of two ways in Australia – you either became a campus band or a pop band, and you had to make a choice, you couldn't do both. So we had no idea of the underground scene in Australia. And at that stage we were still doing songs like 'Spectrum' by Billy Cobham, you know, semi-jazz things like Van Morrison, and things like that. One of the first lessons we learnt when we came to Australia was to just minimalise whatever music you were playing. You had to have one single-minded direction. Four on the floor.

Like Brian Peacock ten years earlier (see chapter 5), Dragon were entering the Australian market willing to do what it took to become successful, but with only the slightest notion of what this might involve. New challenges – such as Australian customs impounding their equipment until an $8,000 bond was paid,[6] and soon afterwards the theft of that same equipment – hardened their resolve. Taylor remembers:

> There was some hassle with our gear. We came over, we brought our amps and guitars and things like that, which had to stay at customs until we could pay some sort of fee, to guarantee we weren't over here to sell our stuff. Because we were signed to Polygram in New Zealand, as a courtesy Polygram Australia gave us some support, mainly paying that excise on our gear. Two of the PR ladies from Polygram were friendly, as in they'd cook us dinner and things like that, when we first arrived. We went straight from the airport to a boarding house in Bondi Junction.
>
> I think our first gig was at the Coogee Bay Hotel, an afternoon session . . . after that it became very sporadic. Basically in those days the scene was run by roadies talking – word of mouth by roadies, 'these guys are worthwhile, they might become big' . . . The guy that was very big amongst the roadies was Ray Arnold, and he took a lot of interest in us, again taking us out to dinner and stuff like that, feeding us and encouraging us to go on.
>
> So we had to create a network in the first few months. But we still had plenty of time to rehearse. And after that a guy called Wayne de Gruchy became interested in us, he was John Paul Young's manager, and he could see the pop potential in us, and once he'd convinced us to stop playing Billy Cobham instrumentals, told Marc to stop playing the congas, be more of a frontman . . . It was strange: in those days, Ray Goodwin, Marc, Todd and I would [all] sing songs – Marc was more just one of the musos. It was de Gruchy who wanted him to go out and be the front man, he was a big influence on Marc in that area.

Vertigo funded a new single, 'Star Kissed', written by Goodwin. A far more boisterous and pushy effort than its predecessor, the bouncy and ruminating 'Education' (which had been sung by its composer, Taylor), 'Star Kissed' was not only a unabashed attempt at chart success, it was also a statement of intent, with the rallying cry 'Sooner or later, you know we're gonna get you'. In fact they did – and it would be sooner rather than later – but Goodwin, who'd been an important creative contributor since the group began, did not get to share the spoils: manager Wayne de Gruchy moved him sideways into another de Gruchy concern, John Paul Young's All Stars. 'Star Kissed' was Goodwin's final present to Dragon, and a better mid-70s single would be hard to imagine, but shortly before he left he gave them another important gift, one that would keep on giving – he brought Paul Hewson into the group. Because of his involvement in an Auckland band called

Cruise Lane,[7] keyboard player and songwriter Hewson had been a familiar figure to Dragon for some time. Legend has it that Goodwin enticed Hewson with a telegram declaring 'fame and fortune awaits'. Todd Hunter told *RAM* readers that Dragon's plans for the future were laid out in detail:

> Settle into the scene here. Tighten up. Gear . . . stage presentation . . . We're putting down a single on Vertigo at the moment . . . should be out in a couple of weeks. Then an LP . . . Then we take off for London with Wayne de Gruchy. If it works here, we move on . . . London's where we've got contacts. The second album, *Scented Gardens for the Blind*, has grabbed the interest of Phonogram in Europe and they're putting videos together and repackaging the LP for distribution in Paris . . . As for the States . . . well who wants to start out as a soul band in a Minneapolis beer hall?[8]

This is an interesting set of goals, even (or especially) given that almost none of them were realised. The group were hoping to use Australia as a stepping stone, but a combination of commercial success and drug dependence ultimately kept them anchored in their adoptive nation. *Scented Gardens for the Blind* had been pressed in Australia by Vertigo, who then opted to let it die with no commercial push;[9] after 'Star Kissed' flopped, the label released the group from their contract. Curiously, despite the contempt Todd Hunter had expressed regarding the US market, this was the one place outside Australasia that Dragon did set foot in the 70s – with catastrophic results, as will be seen.

Dragon were never a punk band in any ordinary sense, but there was an anger to them that contrasted strongly with the Australian penchant for laconic satire. They had an abiding interest in Lou Reed, and a version of 'White Light/White Heat' was part of their set for most of the 70s. Live reviews from the time include references to numerous songs that did not make it to record, including for instance in 1975 'a rather subversive little roller called "Spunk Drunk" climaxing in an all-voices raving of "spunkdrunk spunkdrunk SPUNKDRUNK spunkdrunk."'[10] Taylor remembers a song called 'Dance': 'our big show-stopper, it was an audience participation song, you know. Let's get a little bit quieter now, let's get a bit louder now, let's have a long instrumental passage here, it was a real showbiz song, that was one of Paul's first songs, and that was a real staple thing for us to use in our live performances.' Another unrecorded track, 'Club of Rome,' was a conspiracy-theory foray based on a *Penthouse* article.

Yet another song, which one reviewer called 'Rape' but the band referred to more commonly as 'Miss Mercy', may date from a later period; it was recorded for, but probably wisely omitted from, *O Zambezi*.[11] Taylor remembers it as 'a murder ballad, you know . . . sort of Rolling Stones type thing.' This song was a highlight of Dragon shows in the seventies, particularly after they had become known for their pop hits; Hunter would single out a young girl in the audience, bring her on stage and pretend to assault her (and then, as one reviewer described it, 'allow' her 'to hug him between choruses')[12]. It may have been a way to subvert the 'pop' elements of Dragon for a (usually, adult) audience. Lindy Allen, in a review of a Dragon show in 1978, wrote:

> Is it sexist to sing about how it feels to be a man, raping someone because you just can't help it? ... It was a bit dangerous simulating the thing onstage, a bit gross (but it's the gross what counts isn't it?) and it's not too good image-wise. I suspect a few fantasies were shattered here, but then, that's good too. I mean, you've got to be retarded to idolise a rock star anyway. Perhaps this is the point, a milestone of sorts, I reckon.[13]

A 1980 *RAM* article by Jenny Hunter-Brown – she had acquired the 'Hunter' by marrying Todd in June 1978[14] – about sexism in the music industry, entitled 'No Women Backstage' was accompanied by a picture of Marc Hunter straddling a young girl in front of an audience. To add to the surreal nature of this confronting image of a man who would become (if he wasn't already) a beloved entertainer, he is wearing a t-shirt advertising the Residents' *Duck Stab* album.[15] The photograph was almost certainly taken during a rendition of 'Miss Mercy'. Lindy Allen, analysing the song, suggested it 'epitomises the role of women in rock and roll':

> They're the suckers who buy the records, the ones who are getting fucked and they're stupid enough to love it, but I agree with the point of the song, though if they all woke up, who'd keep the machine going?[16]

When Ariel played with Dragon at a university show in Melbourne, Mike Rudd was so impressed he suggested to his long-term producer, Peter Dawkins, now at CBS Australia, that he investigate the band with a view to signing them to the new CBS label, Portrait. Rudd recalls that it was Neil Storey who needed the most convincing that Dawkins was an appropriate option for Dragon, saying (in Rudd's recollection): "'Oh no, we don't think we want to record with Peter, he's too poppy...'" And I said, "You should give him a go."'

The group's climb to commercial success was sordid – and tragic, too. They switched managers from de Gruchy (who went on to manage the Spaniards)[17] to Robert Raymond, whom Marc credited with the impetus for their first hit, two albums and five singles into their career:

> Raymond... used to let us practice in one of the rooms next to his office. One day he came in and said, 'stop farting about and write a pop song, a hit single.' So we decided to write a hit single. Paul Hewson started playing a chord pattern, I started singing a tune, Todd put in little feels – we all contributed to that song... it was done in about ten minutes.[18]

Different versions of this story abound. In one of them, Raymond locked the band inside the office for a weekend, refusing to free them until they came up with a hit (which took rather more than ten minutes); the resulting song was called 'This Time'. Other sources have suggested it was not so simple, and that the group actually wrote *too much* of a song, which they then split into two, the second half becoming one of Hewson's many songs about chess, 'The Dreaded Moroczy Bind'. That song was released as the B side of 'This Time'.

Three of the five members of Dragon – Marc Hunter, Hewson, and Storey – were by now associated with heroin selling and consumption in ways that are hard to characterize. The band is named in the 1983 *Royal Commission of Inquiry into Drug Trafficking*, largely because of its connection to one individual, Greg Ollard, a former accountancy student at Auckland University turned heroin dealer, who had a day job at EMI New Zealand. Ollard followed Dragon to Sydney in the mid 70s, where, according to the report, he supported the group 'financially and with heroin.'[19] 'The Commission has evidence', the report states, 'that Ollard supplied heroin to group members and that at least one member of the group sold heroin on Ollard's behalf'.[20] This 'one member' was Hewson, who had a family to support and an abiding interest in drug use, cultivated some say during a childhood filled with prescription medicines, treatment for curvature of the spine. Ollard was murdered in September 1977; his remains lay undiscovered in Ku-Ring-Gai Chase National Park for five years.

'This Time', jointly credited to all the band members and featuring another of Dawkins's signings, Air Supply, on backing vocals, was released in June 1976. By the time it peaked at no. 26 in the charts, Neil Storey was dead, having overdosed and died alone one night in September 1976 in the group's Edgecliff apartment. A much-loved and committed member of the group – and a spectacular musician – he veered between extremes, according to his bandmates: 'Neil used wipe himself out for two days and then get into vegetables the next,' Taylor told *Spunky* magazine in 1976.²¹ Storey's girlfriend Donna Shaw's testimony to the Royal Commission suggests that the 'entire band' was 'being supported by the sale of heroin' and that she and Storey were frequent (by inference, daily) users of the drug.²² Nor was Storey unaware of the dangers involved in frequent association with drug distribution: Shaw recalled a conversation in which Storey related a tale of a murder committed by Ollard: 'a girl had been thrown in Sydney Harbour by Greg with a concrete boot on her.'²³ Taylor relates these events:

> Neil went out one night; Paul and I didn't go with him. The three of us were like the Three Musketeers, we'd go out. Marc and Todd, they didn't enjoy going out to pubs or parties or anything like that, it wasn't part of their scene. For some reason Neil went out by himself and we had a band meeting scheduled the morning after this party he went to. Evidently he went to the party and took too much free heroin, and when Paul went down to wake him up for the meeting – we were all living in a boarding house in Edgecliff, and Neil was in a room where you wouldn't have heard him come home, it was like separate from the main building – Paul went in to wake him up and Neil wasn't breathing. We all went down, and my girlfriend at the time tried to give him artificial resuscitation, but he was at the stage he was turning blue – so he was gone. It was bloody horrendous.
>
> And that was just after we'd recorded 'This Time', with Peter Dawkins. I think we actually shot the film clip for 'This Time' about a week after Neil died, and you won't see any drummer in the clip . . . we all agreed we had to keep going, there wasn't any point in just fucking up. So we rang Graeme Nesbitt in Wellington and he got in touch with Kerry, who had been playing with a band called the Quincey Conserve. Kerry flew over, about a week after Neil died, and started touring, going out and promoting 'This Time'.
>
> It was very weird because Neil and I were very close . . . We were both country boys, and we were the ones that were sitting round late at night and listening to music, smoking dope and drinking together, and it was like losing a brother. Neil was a very loving man, and had no shit about him, he was just a bit of a greedy chap when it came to food, beer or anything that was put in front of him. And he certainly paid the cost big time. But as these things go, I knew Kerry Jacobsen very well, so it was like getting another brother to step in, so I was lucky in that way. And Kerry tried to fit in as quickly as possible. Although he soon ran into trouble with Marc and Todd because he wouldn't be bossed around by them. He had a bit of arrogance about him too, that added fire to the thing. So the fire was still there.

Dragon chose to interpret their decision to ride the wave of their newfound – and long-fought-for – commercial success as a tribute to Storey. Their third album, *Sunshine*, which to most Australians would have seemed like a debut, was dedicated to Storey. Marc Hunter later described the title track as 'the band's first recorded foray into cabaret music.' He felt it was 'a very Sydney song... it was really good to hear it on radio driving across the Harbour Bridge.'[24]

Sunshine, released in 1977, showed Jacobson settling apparently seamlessly into the group's well-rehearsed repertoire. Hewson was beginning to establish his reputation as a pop master: he was the sole author of the group's second hit, 'Get That Jive', which along with a number of other Dragon songs from this era has entered the Australian 70s pop canon. Todd Hunter, with no little wit, recast this song on a 21st-century Dragon album (he revived the group, with himself as the only original member, in 2006) in the style of 'Walk on the Wild Side'. Though it is quite non-specific, the song 'Blacktown Boogie' could have been seen by some as another rallying cry to the masses like 'Star Kissed'. Blacktown is a large western suburb of Sydney; when CBS's Dennis Handlin talked about target audiences he referred to them using names like 'Barry Blacktown'.[25]

Dragon were initially dismissed by a big wheel at 2SM as the 'most disgusting exhibition of no-talent I've ever seen'[26] – Taylor recalls a 2SM opinion-shaper breaking an early single over his knee in disgust – but the band's hard work paid off in commercial acceptance. Taylor remembers the redirection of the band:

> I think the importance of *Countdown's* got to come into play. And then if you do *Countdown*, in those days you'd have *TV Times* which would have a pinup, fold-out pin-up and a staple through your face, there was *RAM* magazine ... There was actually a bigger, ongoing media thing that, once you got onto it, once you got an article in *RAM*, and on *Countdown* and then a poster in *TV Week*, and then *Juke* magazine would have a look at you, and your relentless attempts to break into the Melbourne scene, which was like pretty hard to do, and then we'd sort of outflank Melbourne by becoming very popular in Geelong – we used to absolutely kill it down there. And word would spread up that 75 kilometres to Melbourne. Whereby we got some credibility in Melbourne. Because in those days there was bands in Melbourne like Jo Jo Zep, bands that I really loved, and we were just still incredibly poppy, but Jo Jo Zep would like us, because we'd do a few things that were funky, or whatever.
>
> So it's sort of a slow thing, and of course Marc and Seb [Sebastian Chase, the group's manager after Raymond] came up with the concept of Marc becoming the Prince of Pop, and Seb and Marc were prepared to go out and – Marc used to go to bloody country [i.e. agricultural] shows ... The record company of course was part of that. Marc and me – I used to cop a lot of the radio interviews, you'd do hours of radio interviews, and obviously it starts working. But then we started to get the young fans, the *Countdown* audience, they spread over to our school lunchtime concerts and that would become big, the screaming thing would become big, so we knew what was going on. But there was a lot of hard work where just any gig you'd do – we became really big in Wollongong, go down

there, we'd just have the place absolutely packed, and we always played better there, we always played harder there.

Nevertheless, Dragon could not escape the familiar scenario whereby acceptance by the masses leads to rejection by a clique – and this hit a craftsman like Taylor particularly hard:

> Once we became *Countdown* people, it was like – they turned against us, we'd become too poppy, I remember getting punched in the face by some aggravated fan, 'you guys just turned into wankers', and then they went out and smashed the front window of our roadie's truck, so he had to drive from Wollongong to Melbourne in freezing conditions and got stopped by the cops – this stupid prick didn't know what he'd done to our roadie, didn't hurt us. So there was that sort of thing, you become controversial, you become – 'are you anti-Dragon or are you –' it's like that silly crap.
>
> Marc Hunter said, 'Oh, we're an Aussie band now, nothing really happened for us in New Zealand' – and we get irritated New Zealand people saying, 'How you could disown your country?' What a load of shit! They didn't even know who we were in New Zealand. So that's when you know you're becoming a bit of a celebrity band, you get these factions that are agin you or for you. Or like, what was it, one of the rumours was: 'Dragon have gone straight'. What do you mean? 'Well they're not a poofter band'. Oh, OK! This sort of stuff. Then you realise the gossip goes on, you know you're making [inroads] into the public consciousness.

Perhaps the frustrations engendered by all the rumours and public fickleness account for some of their more antisocial behaviour; at one show, Marc Hunter attacked some girls on stage with a riding whip (as Taylor remembers it, this was because they had thrown the disposable flash cubes from their cameras at his face), and he punched another girl at a regular Dragon venue, the Bondi Lifesaver. The group was banned in the northern Victorian city of Mildura. Hunter didn't care, telling Christie Eliezer: 'Sometimes, man, you've gotta do something so outrageous for them to sit up and take interest. Some of these country people have no sense of humour at all. You feed them all these lines and they just sit there and look blankly at you.'[27]

The group's second Australian album, *Running Free*, was nowhere near as satisfying as its predecessor, though it did include the stupendous 'April Sun in Cuba', one of Hewson's greatest moments and soon so ubiquitous in Australian pop that the folk-protest group Redgum quickly made a live favourite of a song about *Countdown* set to its tune; ten years later, cabaret-pop group Captain Cocoa did something similar.[28] A remarkable 'cabaret' ballad, 'Since You Changed Your Mind' was another highlight. 'All their songs are sad songs (even happy songs about being sad),' noted Christie Eliezer, 'full of depressions, blues, shattered

idealisms, occasional reachings out for hope, mostly centred around the theme that You Don't Get Close to Anyone 'Cos In The End You Get Burned.'[29]

'Dragon have made it, and it shows,' wrote Jon Matthews in a review published in *Juke* at the end of 1977; 'their display of silk shirts and ties with finely tailored coats and pants reminded me more of a Mr John shop than a rock gig . . . Marc Hunter's cabaret-type vocals did little to innovate the songs.[30] They recorded another invigorating single, 'Konkaroo', which Marc Hunter dismissed thus:

> It was Easter, we had two days off and we had to have a single out. 'Cos we didn't have anything in the charts, which meant we didn't have an excuse to go on television and promote the tour . . . We just tossed it off to see what happened, and nothing did.'[31]

The next single was, however, another smash. According to Marc, it came from 'lots of work pressure, lots of sulking in the tour bus and playing no talkies with each other. To let off pressure we'd do things like fire guns in motel rooms and sometimes we'd write songs. "Are You Old Enough" was one of them'.[32]

Having survived both the association with selling and taking hard drugs, and having received little tangible controversy for the 'Miss Mercy' act, this untouchable band's next hit was essentially a paean to underage sex, perhaps even to pedophilia (another hit from the same time, 'Still in Love with You', also makes no bones about its narrator's sexual interest in a schoolgirl). A glowing, irresistible pop tune, sung delectably by Marc Hunter with uncredited backing vocals from Renée Geyer, it is a virtually flawless pop record, its subversive nature being an essential element of this status. It is a song told from the viewpoint of a man recently released after ten years in prison, interested in sex with the first girl he can find. Cleverly, Hewson also manages to work in references to Toulouse Lautrec, Neil Diamond and 'Walk on the Wild Side' in ways that evoke a passing show. Hewson said at the time:

> The story is basically about a guy who comes out of jail and meets a chick, but he's scared to get involved in case she's underaged and he'll be chucked back in the clink again.
>
> I mean, all guys basically worry about that when they make a pick up. Well, I do, anyway. You always ask 'how old are you?' We're very confident of it as a single.[33]

'Are You Old Enough' was Dragon's biggest hit of the 70s and remains one of their best songs, but it does not outshine anything else on their fifth, and best, album, *O Zambezi*. Robert Taylor's title track and Marc Hunter's 'Burn Down the Bridges' – a rare solo composition that warns about the brittleness of fame but also the dangers of fear – bookend a scintillating and exceptionally strong album. Two of its greatest moments, 'Politics' and 'Company', feature lyrics by Jenny Hunter-Brown; 'Politics', a sardonic summary of the Australian pop process, draws in particular on Hunter-Brown's experience as a music journalist observing the hypocrisies of the industry.

The tensions within the band were not merely those which naturally exist between wishing to be credible and wishing to sell records. Taylor gives his own views on the band's musical output as he recalls the impact of Chase as manager. Chase had previously managed Buffalo and Rose Tattoo; he replaced Robert Raymond, who quit because of disagreements with Peter Dawkins:

> Seb was very used to managing – how can I say it? – 'party animals'. He was fantastic, he came in and really centred us and got us happening after that. His idea was, just go out there and work, and work we did. He was the one who said, let's take you out to the western suburbs, 'cos that's where the population that's going to buy your stuff is, That's what we set out to do, so we were gigging, let's say, six nights a week after that – just an incredible workload.
>
> It had all sorted itself out, we were hot, we were on the go. We knew what we were doing. We knew what the people liked about Dragon . . . even if our records were a bit wimpy, they got a pretty solid entertaining rock show when they came along. We weren't just *Countdown* fodder. We had a little bit of muscle. And I don't think any of our records have ever captured that. I think that's my one regret about Dragon – and yet you can't lay the blame on Peter Dawkins . . .

> I think it was just how pop music was done in that era. There was none of the force... Skyhooks sound very tinny these days when you hear them – we were tinny too. We wanted to sound like AC/DC, but that never happened... Songs like 'April Sun in Cuba' especially – Paul always envisaged that as having a real AC/DC 'dunana da, da da da da'. By the time we did it, it came out like a tango. So there you go – what you hear of Dragon on vinyl wasn't really what the band wanted to be.

Numerous other Australian acts have expressed similar frustration with Dawkins's production work, but it was part and parcel of the hit machine of the era.[34]

Some of this frustration came out in the song 'Telephone', which was recorded for *Running Free* and, in the weeks leading up to the album's release, discussed as an integral part of it. The decision to omit it was made at the last minute, hence the yawning gap in the lyric sheet printed on the album's inner sleeve. It was, however, released as the B side to 'April Sun in Cuba', attributed to Dr. Agony; one writer described it as a 'punchy, new-wavey number which shows that Dragon can write good, solid songs.'[35] Marc Hunter recalled that the song 'was written in Queensland, all two chords of it. It was pretty manic actually. It was the band's punk rock experiment.'[36] 'Telephone' is a good demonstration of how great Dragon could be, as well as an illustration of band tensions; close listening reveals a textured guitar part from Taylor that was no doubt considered too sophisticated for such a blunt piece of work and therefore placed so low in the mix that it becomes merely a light tone. Additionally, though the group were as flamboyant as any pop group at their level, it is impossible to imagine any member of (for instance) Sherbet wearing, as Taylor did in 1978, a 'skin-tight snake print jersey and... wide leather belt with "ENNUI" spelt out in flat silver studs slung at a rakish angle around his angular hips.'[37] Jenny Hunter-Brown, who observed this fashion accoutrement of Taylor's, also noted Taylor 'playing like an absolute bitch.'[38]

Good bands can turn these difficulties to their advantage. The next cataclysmic event in Dragon's story – their disastrous US tour and the departure of Marc Hunter – led to a renewed artistic flowering, commercial disaster, and a few years later, commercial rebirth.

In late 1978 the group toured the United States opening for Johnny Winter, who was enjoying considerable prestige at the time, not least for his production work on Muddy Waters' albums. Dragon's albums since *Sunshine* had been released in the US on the prestige American label Portrait. Like so many Antipodean groups before and after them, it was plain that 'cracking' the American market would require an enormous amount of work for Dragon; and *this* Antipodean group happened to be plagued by internal conflict, drug addiction in a broad sense, and – according to participants and observers – an intra-band communications system based almost entirely on sarcasm. Nonetheless, there were encouraging signs. Marc Hunter considered Los Angeles 'a plastic shit-city' and New York 'so creative' with its 'champagne air';[39] Christie Eliezer reported that in Pasadena, Hunter spent three hours on commercial radio during which 'Are You Old Enough' was played alongside an instant fifty-phone-listener survey. 'Everyone liked the disc except for one cat who barked "Led Zeppelin!" and then slammed the phone down.'[40] But the group's show in Dallas ended the reign of Dragon's classic' 1970s line-up in an instant. Eliezer related in 1979:

> Dallas is real *Easy Rider* rednecksville, where men are men and the cattle are real anxious. They're totally into machismo, and they all wear regulation checked shirts and patched denims. They looked at Dragon in their skin-tight black leather pants and satin jackets and thought they were New York punks.
>
> At that particular show, Hunter was at his most obnoxious. In between songs he taunted the crowd, calling them 'faggots' and other livid insults, none of which are good for children and other living things. Predictably his audience manipulation evoked every inch of hostility from them.

Readers familiar with the Sex Pistols' history might see a parallel between that band's experience and Dragon's in the same year. Eliezer continues:

> Yapping and growling in rage they hurled everything they could get their paws on – shoes, glass jugs and mugs, light bulbs and fittings, chairs etc. Hunter kept aggravating them, leaping from table to table screaming more obscenities or standing onstage arms outstretched like a martyr. The rest of the band kept ducking and playing!

Marc later told Eliezer that his behaviour in Dallas was 'all calculated, an experiment in crowd control . . . I thought I'd take them to the extreme and gauge their reaction. What we got on was this amazing wall of hostility. I wanted a clear-cut reaction, and we got one!'[41] Two months later, he told *RAM's* Anthony O'Grady: 'I just freaked out, I didn't like Dallas, I didn't like Texas, I just fucked up there.'[42] Six months later he told *Juke* writer Allan Webster that the American trip had been 'very Zen':

> All the tricks I'd learnt in Australia weren't worth a damn thing . . . I realised that if I wanted the rewards usually associated with rock and roll then I'd have to keep on doing that for the next 10 years . . . just going round and round. All that just to be able to walk into a restaurant and get recognised. It's all bullshit.[43]

Taylor recalls that the band 'were all right into booze and drugs and I think that Marc was just becoming tired. Purely physically tired'. The singer recalled in mid 1979 that he 'slept for about a month' earlier in that year.[44] Taylor adds:

> If I didn't work in Dragon I was broke... If Marc said we had to go off the road for three months, the reality would be that I'd have to go and get a part-time job, which is not – you don't do that if you're a pop star.
>
> I don't know how long it went on, but it was discussed – obviously behind Marc's back... He was getting more and more irritable, not so much with the band but with people who were in the industry... roadies, managers, and radio station people.
>
> We'd run out of puff after the American tour, and once you've come back from America and you've achieved nothing, no sales, no 'We can't wait for you guys to come back', it was just like 'See ya later' – you look within yourself and you think, well what can we do now, we can change *this*... Eventually it came that... Todd sort of said, Well I think Marc'll have to go.

The band were cagey about their next move, and ultimately deceived each other and their new recruits. In early 1979 they announced they were adding Richard Lee, the violinist from Sidewinder who had played on *O Zambezi*, 'to punch more energy into their sound and stage presence.'[45] 'We felt we were in danger of getting a little rusty', Todd told *Rolling Stone*.[46] *Juke* reported that 'Lee will share the spotlight with Marc Hunter as their frontman', while Lee was candid about his ambitions within the group: 'I want to write a hit song!'[47] Lee and Marc Hunter never did lead Dragon together, though; instead Dragon now sacked the singer with whom, in many minds, the band was synonymous and recruited Billy Rogers to stand alongside Lee. They knew Rogers from the Perth group Last Chance Café, who they'd met in Perth while supporting Status Quo and who had been namechecked in Hewson's song 'Same Old Blues' on *Sunshine*; they kept in contact when the West Australians briefly relocated to Sydney in 1977. Chase now called Rogers in Perth and told him, 'We want you in the band if you're together'. Rogers wasn't, but says now, 'I wasn't going to let that spoil it.' He left his new band, Fremantle Doctor, literally halfway through their third show to get on a plane to Sydney.

Todd Hunter had been the only original member of Dragon since the departure of Ray Goodwin three years earlier. 'We've already had three totally different Dragons,' he told *RAM*'s Miranda Brown. 'There'll probably be more after this. The last one just happened to make it.'[48] The dismissal of Marc had not defused Dragon's internal tensions, however. Todd was opting for a sound that was closer to 'new wave' and art-rock, something his brother would have rejected (or at very least confined to album tracks); Todd saw the youthful, sophisticated Lee as a proponent of this sound. Taylor and Hewson were more interested in classic, crafted roots rock, and hoped to push the group in that direction through Rogers, who played saxophone and harmonica as well as being a viable vocalist. The recorded evidence suggests the 'roots' faction won, but in 1979 Dragon was a battlefield of ideas.

Seven years later, Marc decried the 'self-indulgence' of the 70s version of Dragon: 'Left to our own devices we became this horrible, degenerate sloppy thing that poured itself onstage every night . . . If I hadn't been fired, I don't know what would have happened: I would probably be dead.'[49] Bands, he said in 1979, are 'carnivorous, they eat people from time to time . . . I think perhaps I was indigestible so I came out as waste product.'[50] He would later claim that he was 'paid to say I wasn't fired . . . I owned the name with Todd but I've given him my half.'[51]

For all his talk of rejecting rock fame, Marc quickly launched himself into a solo career, and he was aided in this by Todd and other Dragon members. The mooted titles for his first album, ultimately known as *Fiji Bitter*, were *A Bad Weekend and a Double Chin* or *The Frog Prince Returns*.[52] 'It's all a matter of marketing,' he said; 'CBS are an incredibly creative company.'[53] Hunter was often heard to deride himself as a hack; his hit single, 'Island Nights', was a backing track originally intended as a single for the actor Tony Alvarez, who played Tony Garcia in the soap opera *The Young Doctors*. Alvarez couldn't 'reach the top notes' so Hunter volunteered[54] and was rewarded with a minor hit. He toured with a band called the Romantics but a Melbourne group of the same name threatened legal action so he changed it to the Pedantics.[55] The band included Harvey James, Terry Wilson and Peter Roberts of the La De Das and Chariot.[56] A letter to *Roadrunner* at this time suggests that solo Marc Hunter shows did not include any of the hits he'd very recently enjoyed with Dragon,[57] though other witnesses swear he included 'April Sun in Cuba', at the very least.

Meanwhile the new Dragon scaled down, playing pubs, universities and smaller venues more than pop-oriented tours. Some audience members, Simon Balderstone wrote in *Juke*, wanted 'just to stand and stare . . . disappointed M. Hunter has not honoured them with his presence – and others have got into the raging, the dancing. Taking, Todd says, "the music for what it is." There was a man at Macquarie Uni who kept screaming out "Marc has a hairy chest".[58] Christie Eliezer, long a fan and friend of the group, believed that Dragon 'developed into an even finer band' at this time.[59] Certainly the brief life of the Marc-less Dragon was extraordinary. Retaining Dawkins as their producer, and with CBS expressing only tentative faith in a group who had earned it millions in previous years, their first step was a conservative one – the recording of a favourite from their live set, Hewson's 'Love's Not Enough', for pop consumption. The single was a low-level hit. Five years after the fact, Taylor commented that the 1979 Dragon was 'in a lot of debt';[60] perhaps it was for this reason that Hewson arranged for Jacobson, Lee and Rogers to be credited with the B side, 'Four Short Solos', and thereby obtain some royalties from sales of what he justifiably thought was a sure-fire A side.

The album *Power Play* was recorded in mid 1979, and proudly boasted on its inner sleeve the slogan 'Last one for the seventies'. Continuity was carefully observed, with lyrics referring to previous Dragon songs. The group also wrote a song they called 'Son of Miss Mercy', yet another murder ballad in which retribution was exacted for the rape committed in the earlier song[61] (like the original, this did not make it to record). More extraordinary, however, was *Power Play*'s cover, which parodied the cover of *Running Free*. On the earlier album, the group were lined up facing the viewer, seen from behind when you turned the sleeve over; Marc Hunter was seen to have an empty wine glass behind his back. For *Power Play*, Todd insisted the group all wear black for the front cover picture, while on the reverse they were revealed to be holding various weapons (knives, a cleaver, a baseball bat and a chain). Taylor recalls that Hewson thwarted this plan somewhat:

> You look at the cover and yes, it's all pretty strange and of course, you know, the edict went out ... we were all to wear black. So Paul Hewson comes along with some Peruvian multicoloured jacket to wear. He was always the individual. That suited.
>
> The major difficulty we had with the shoot was coming up with suitable weapons. 'Cos we weren't into weapons. So the poor photographer and the art department had to come up with these cleavers and crap like that.

The album contained two singles ('Love's Not Enough', which wouldn't have fitted, was left out), including the first Todd Hunter/Jenny Hunter-Brown song to be pitched at the charts, 'Motor City Connection'. Neither this nor Hewson's atypically rocky 'Counting Sheep' were commercial successes. Another of Hewson's songs on the album, 'Crooked Highway', seems with hindsight to be a much more commercial proposition, but it certainly does not sound like the Dragon of the year before. Taylor says that 'Peter Dawkins was great with *Power Play*, he was really relaxed about it, and he completely supported.' Dawkins may have been feeling guilty: it was suggested soon afterwards that he had undermined any chance of US success for Dragon by telling Portrait executives about the group's drug problems.

Paul Hewson said of the *Power Play*–era Dragon: 'Musically the band was bloody good',[62] though Richard Lee – who had been invited into the group as a co-leader with Marc Hunter – had cause to be disappointed; his featured song live, 'Gans en farben', an instrumental modeled somewhat on his Sidewinder song 'M.S.O.', was really his only showcase on the album. Dragon travelled to New Zealand to tour at this time; a group less like the band who had left Auckland in 1975 would be harder to imagine. In some ways, their very name was a hindrance as much as a help when it came to audience expectations. According to Taylor:

> New Zealand didn't know what to think of us. We did a live broadcast to air in Auckland – my parents stayed up late to listen to it – and Billy Rogers actually told a member of the audience, 'Why don't you go and get fucked'. We were taken off air in seconds, and that's when we really knew we were in trouble, because

> Billy went through a lot of personal problems ... It was sort of the death of the band, I think, that last New Zealand tour. But people who came and saw us were knocked out, because we were still playing really well. It was a really good band, but as Marc Hunter said, we just didn't have the guts to keep going.

Taylor feels it was CBS's decision to drop Dragon – and put a lid on them by releasing a 'greatest hits' collection (including some songs that hadn't been hits, but omitting 'Love's Not Enough,' which had been) – that ended the band's first run.

> It comes down to this, when they have a marketing meeting at CBS, and they want to establish their point of sales things: 'All right, we've got the new Santana, the new Willie Nelson, the new Dolly Parton, um ... are we going to put Dragon in this rack? No we're not.' There wasn't anything conspicuously 'Let's get rid of Dragon'. I didn't feel any 'CBS are out to get us', it was just – it became apparent to them that we'd dealt our cards and we didn't have a winning hand. The main thing was when they had their business meeting and didn't put us on point of sale. I think Santana went up instead of us. You can't argue with that. And of course releasing the *Greatest Hits*, which is the death knell of any band ... We first heard the ads on 2SM as we were driving off to a gig. No consultation whatsoever.

The final Dragon show featuring Lee and Rogers took place at the Strata Hotel, Cremorne in December 1979.[63] Marc Hunter joined them for the last songs of the set, playing 'April Sun in Cuba' followed by a 'sardonic spontaneous blues construction that went under the title "Five Years"', featuring the lines 'Five years of fancy cars / Five years of big cigars', after which they launched into the old faithful, 'White Light/White Heat'.[64]

As it turned out, Dragon would have their biggest commercial success after they reformed two years later (see chapter 16). The tragedies and torments would, however, continue.

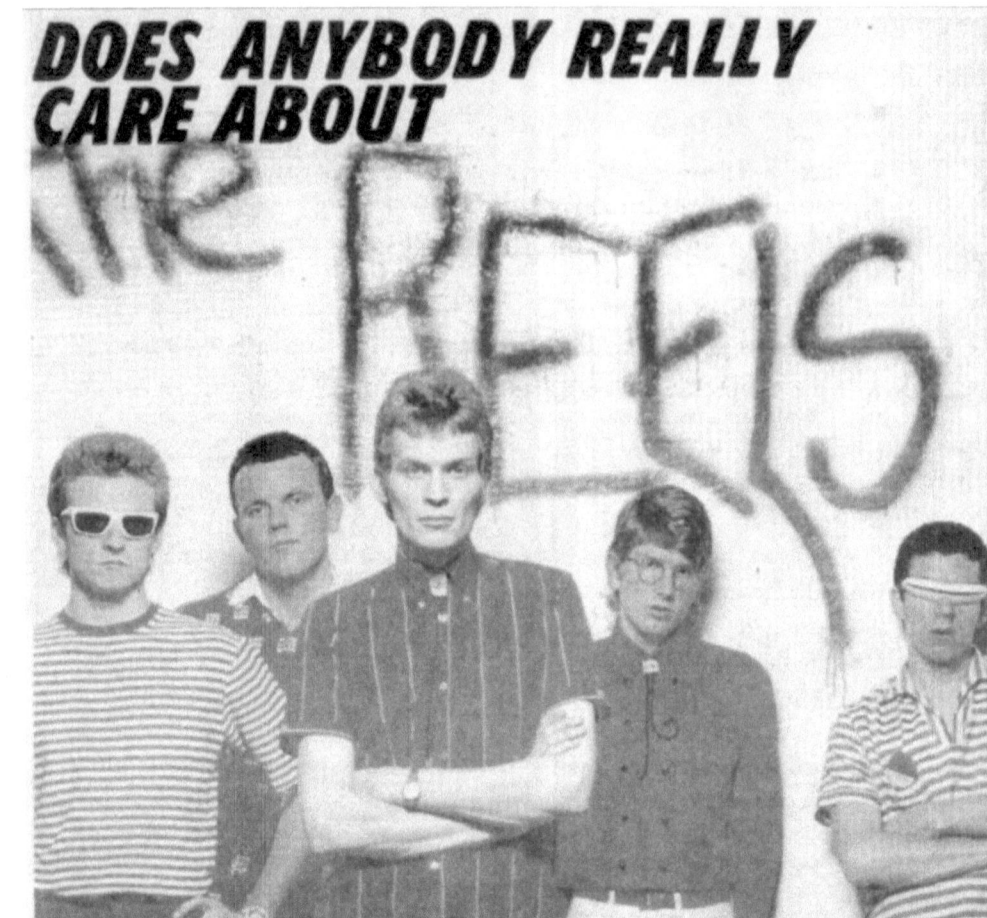

13 Happy/Sad Is a Really Fantastic Emotion
THE REELS

In their five incarnations between 1976 and 1993 the Reels demonstrated everything that was good about Australian pop music, both musically and politically. They were laconic, honest, pragmatic, technologically advanced, challenging and inventive. They had top-forty hits and at least one album, *Beautiful*, that was a major commercial success; it was also, like most of their other work, an artistic success. The group also received an unlikely accolade when 'Quasimodo's Dream', which was not a hit either time it was released as a single, was voted one of the ten best Australian songs of all time by a group of admittedly unrepresentative yet decidedly industry-oriented Australians (which made it all the more surprising, given the song's relative obscurity). The Reels' biggest hits were covers, but unlike many groups they placed a high premium on unusual and experimental arrangements which played with the material both structurally and in terms of instrumentation and rhythm. This chapter, drawing on archival material and conversations with founding members Craig Hooper and John Bliss as well as later arrivals Stefan Fidock and Karen Ansell, discusses the Reels' legacy and provides important insight into the way a good pop group could (and couldn't) fit into the mainstream commercial pop industry in the late 70s and early 80s.

The Reels formed in Dubbo, a regional centre in New South Wales, in 1976; Guitarist Craig Hooper and drummer John Bliss had earlier that year been playing in the New Gold Stars, a '50/50' band. The initial Reels line-up (under the name Native Sons) featured, in addition to Hooper and Bliss, keyboard player Colin 'Polly' Newham, singer Dave Mason, and bassist Tony Martin (replaced in 1978 by Paul Abrahams when the group moved to Sydney). In the early 80s Hooper surmised that part of the group's success 'and probably a lot of our individuality' was due to 'not having grown up in the major music centres of Australia':

> Coming fresh from the country – y'know, the only bands we used to see in Dubbo were Sherbet and John Paul Young, AC/DC came once, and that's all we saw of bands other than *Countdown*. And we never fitted into any of that, or somehow fitted into all of it.[1]

Native Sons changed their name to the Brucelanders in 1976 after playing a show at Nyngan RSL club at which, Hooper recalls, 'some actual native sons took exception to a bunch of white guys calling themselves that'. They played a 2JJ live-to-air early the following year under their new name, a rather tepid joke with its origins in the notorious *Monty Python* sketch. After waiting until Hooper finished high school, they relocated to Sydney at the end of 1977. Mason claimed in 1979 that 'we had to piss off to survive'.²

Mason, who was the group's singer and also their principal songwriter, rose to fame at the same time as his father, John, an Anglican minister and leader of the NSW Liberal Party between 1979 and 1982. 'I grew up in religion AND politics,' Mason claimed in 1980. 'It's a crazy world, but you learn. The politicians in Australia are fucked. They are all little boys, they really are. It's like an exclusive little boys club.'³ Dave Mason did not share his father's political outlook, and claimed (probably with his tongue in his cheek) that his own songs were 'sociologically political' and supportive of the downtrodden.⁴ The tabloid press occasionally drummed up a furore by describing the politician's son as a sexually profligate drug addict, publicity which Mason thought did the Reels 'the world of good for exposure, but it's a novelty, and that's how we treat it.'⁵ It is quite possible that his wayward son was the reason the Liberal Party did not allow John Mason to lead it to an election; after retiring from politics, he returned to the Anglican ministry.

The band changed their name to the Reels after booking agents refused to take them on as the Brucelanders, which apparently implied they were a bush band. 'The Reels was vague enough that nobody could find anything really wrong with it,' says Hooper, 'and it didn't really paint us as anything in particular.' Polygram signed the group in 1979.⁶ Their high standard of musicianship, and their strong belief in ongoing renewal, change and adventure, saw them constantly rearrange and rework their songs. Karen Ansell, who became a member of the Reels shortly after the release of their first (self-titled) album, notes: 'Polly is a classically trained musician arranger. Craig could read music and had great rhythm, John Bliss had played in orchestras, Paul was a beautiful tight bass player.' For Stefan Fidock, who replaced Bliss as drummer following the group's second album, *Quasimodo's Dream*, the group's approach and outlook followed Newham's vision:

> The Reels was actually his band. Polly was really interested in brass bands – he's a nut, he's a genius really, and he loved brass bands. To be able to achieve that, you've got to get all the notes falling down at the right time, all the beats have to be spot on, you play this part and we can put this part here in the middle of it, or we can play off this into a syncopation, you do the ups, you play the downs, and this that and the other, I'll play the accents – you can chop it all up like Bach. The only way that you can fit anything else into that part is for that part to be *that* precise ... The power of the Reels was precision, being repetitive and being

syncopated. There was no-one else engaged in putting music together in that way. No-one was as sophisticated as the Reels.

The Newham approach can best be appreciated by listening not to a Reels record – where he had too much competition – but to *What's a Quaver?* by Sydney synthesiser pop band Ya Ya Choral, recorded in 1981 in the brief period that Newham and Bliss were members of the group. The syncopated, rapid-fire rhythm of the music was appropriate for a time when rhythm machines and synthesisers, and increasingly computers, were being used in pop music, yet the approach was unique. Both men were hired soon afterwards to tour with the (Sydney) Numbers for their second album and they restructured many of that band's hits with new synthesiser lines and cunningly composed rhythms. While the Numbers' Chris Morrow claims that the band's music at this time was half inspired magnificence, half self-indulgence, he readily acknowledges Newham's genius.

That said, Fidock's suggestion that the Reels were 'Polly's band' is debatable. Hooper – along with Mason the only group member throughout its original formations (he refused to be involved in its 21st-century reincarnation) – has a slightly different view:

> Polly had lots of great ideas, and he was a perfectionist, so he would argue louder and longer than anyone else ... He also played more different instruments than anyone else, and he was also the oldest. He did have a lot of input into the bass lines and basic drum patterns, but ... the end result was very much a group effort. A lot of what ended up on records was the result of jamming for weeks on end, just trying different things and looking for new approaches. Even when we were touring we used to set up in the motel rooms and rehearse all day, often doing complete rearrangements of songs that we would then play on stage a few hours later.
>
> We all had a propensity to want to be terminally unique. The kiss of death to any musical idea during rehearsal or in the studio was for anyone to say 'Hey, that sounds a bit like ...' Whatever it was it would be instantly dropped, whether or not it even vaguely sounded like what the person said! We worked very hard to find a musical approach that was ours. And there were times when the terminal uniqueness was our worst enemy, because we would end up paralysed out of fear of being derivative. It used to annoy the crap out of us to be compared to, say, XTC or Devo – they were our contemporaries, not our influences. I remember going to see XTC at the Bondi Lifesaver and thinking 'that guy (Andy Partridge) plays guitar like me!'

Miranda Brown was both circumspect and celebratory when she wrote that 'the Reels play music that is simultaneously ominous and pop.'[7] Mason claimed a taste for 'all the old sixties hits ... especially the Australian ones.'

We're right into pop music, singles – basically what you hear on the radio, *hit* singles ... Todd Rundgren's one of our heroes ... We just basically write about trivia, we *love* trivia.[8]

'Trash', too, was a Mason enthusiasm. Always ready to spout ideas that rubbished notions of serious musicianship, he suggested that the group could have a US hit with a cover of Vanda and Young's "Lazy River", and that a Reels cartoon would popularize the group in that country: "America's culture is trash", he told *Rolling Stone*. "Trash is their heritage."[9] He also had a marketing concept in which the group's fans would encounter a Reels performance by entering through a tube and standing on a conveyor belt.

When you start off you just have one song, and you get a visual around you, and you just go through about twelve songs or however many are on the album. When you get out, you've got the video cassettes on one side and the LPs on the other; you've got us at the end to sign them, the cash register next to that, then off you go![10]

These ideas were remarkable, although much easier to talk about than execute. Fortunately, the Reels could usually be depended on to deliver the goods, too, on the rare occasions they were given the financing. Their music was intricately mapped and delineated, and while they may have poked fun at *Countdown's* required practice of miming in front of screaming girls, they clearly loved the scene.

'Love Will Find a Way' was a minor hit, and it sounded like nothing else anywhere, though many have inappropriately cited early XTC, or even ska pop, as a reference point. The follow-up single, 'Prefab Heart' (mistitled 'Hearts' on the sleeve) was superficially similar. And with their brightly coloured outfits, jerky dancy movements and choppy riffs, the group certainly could have appeared at first glance to be a classic new-wave outfit. Hooper said at the time that the band had evolved to their current state as 'a result of culture shock' after arriving in Sydney from their previous isolation in Dubbo: 'when the new wave hit, we were isolated from it. We knew something was happening, but we never really saw what was going on.'[11]

Newham added: 'Most popular bands are basically a rhythmic front with a modicum of melody or varying levels of lyric intensity, and most of them stress soloists. But for us the rhythm has become the medium.'[12] 'It *is* up and down music', Annie Burton confirmed for *RAM* readers.[13]

Money was a perennial problem for the Reels. They recorded their first album in Dubbo, in a mobile studio. Hooper explained that 'we tried most of the studios available in Sydney but we couldn't find any we were happy with, either in sound or atmosphere. The chance for a sixteen-track mobile came up, so we decided to go somewhere where we could create our own atmosphere and have plenty of leeway. Besides, it meant we had minimal accommodation costs.'[14] The album was 'one big single', according to Mason.[15]

Perhaps groups like the Reels were always meant to be falling apart at the seams; there were already powerful tensions when they inducted a sixth member in Karen Ansell. Mason believed that even though the group was based in Sydney, 'we're much more popular in Melbourne. That's because Sydney's still a heavy metal kingdom, everyone wants to hear Rose Tattoo or Led Zeppelin.'[16] And it was in Melbourne that they acquired two further members who would sculpt their refracted vision, first keyboard player Ansell and later, drummer Fidock. Both played in the Romantics (not to be confused, of course, with the Detroit power-pop group of the same period); their joint presence in the Reels overlapped long enough for both to work on one magnificent record, the commercially unsuccessful single 'No. 3' from late 1981.

Fidock places Ansell and another Romantics member, Uschi Flett, in the thick of things:

> Uschi and Karen had a clothes shop, it was the first shop in Melbourne to sell punk clothes; they sold clothes to Blondie. They also did costumes for Skyhooks.

Ansell says the Romantics had 'a floating population of musicians':

> Bob Starkie came through for a few gigs. Nick Seymour joined, I think he heard about us through word of mouth ... [Fidock says the group later asked Seymour to leave 'because he couldn't play properly.'] Nick Seymour and I started to hang together with some mutual love of disco meets the Sex Pistols in a dark wet Melbourne cobblestone alley. Stefan was the first drummer I knew who could play to a click track with feel – and that was getting important to me because I was starting to get deeper into the electronic music side of things, and wanted to free-range with some sounds while keeping a soulful feel ... The Romantics got on stage anywhere we could. Nick Rischbeith wore a suit made of rump steak that was starting to turn rancid under the lights after a couple of gigs – he threw it off and flattened a member of the audience. [Flett had previously made a 'fruit suit' for a member of Captain Matchbox[17]]. I had a penchant for lace stockings, nurse's uniforms and jungle boots as I recall.

When the Romantics opened for the Reels, Ansell made a musical impression, too:

> I had written a song in the Romantics called 'Dream Kitchen' – it had a kind of melancholy suburban feel to it. We played it when we supported the Reels at the Tiger Lounge. I think Dave Mason recognised something there. When I saw them, I recognised something in them too ... it was like I was hearing the

visuals of my experience growing up in Clayton. Dubbo and Clayton have a lot in common, I think. The alienation. There was a recognition there between us.

I think Dave was looking for a change too, after the first album. He was bored. We hung out, went to see each other's bands when they came to Melbourne. A couple of months later he asked me to audition. He liked what I was doing with the synths. It did have a great sound with that digital delay and the Lesley speaker, and as technically challenged as I was, I do have a good ear. I went to some rehearsal place in Moorabbin.

Now, I knew I was out of my depth musically. They were all trained, and they were road-conditioned. I walked in, this girl from the wilds of the Melbourne art scene, who could only play by ear, and I hung on by my fingertips.

Ansell immediately made a difference to the Reels. She worked with them on the video for their second single, 'Prefab Heart', though she did not appear in the clip (because she wasn't on the record), and for the next two years she was a major presence.

Mason told Elly McDonald in 1980 that the Reels had been 'a little boys club until we got Karen . . . I don't want to walk into dressing rooms anymore. I just can't . . . You don't know what it's like to be with all males, all the time, except for dumb groupies and shit who . . . have zero intelligence anyway.'[18]

The Reels' next single, 'After the News', was vibrant and sarcastic: Mason told *Juke* writer John Lethlean that he was 'pissed off' the record didn't sell better than it did, 'because to me, that was the ultimate in pop. Maybe the lyric content wasn't that crash hot but it was repetitive so it should have done alright.'[19] It was followed by an EP, *Five Great Gift Ideas from the Reels*, which marked the start of a trend that would later consume them, the cult of the cover version. Mason claimed that his own musical forays were 'Henry Mancini type musical themes for films' and that he told the rest of the band 'look I'm writing this shit at the moment and we can do it but if you don't want to, then we'll just do cover versions.'[20] The EP's featured track, a cover of Jim Reeves's country hit 'According to My Heart', was a hit single, and was accompanied by a jokey clip, filmed at a riding school and supermarket car park in Upper Hutt, New Zealand, that was entirely appropriate. There were better tracks on the EP, however, including a stomping version of 'Band of Gold' and one original, 'The Bombs Dropped on Xmas' (co-written by Ansell), which showed the group's slightly hippyish – in the way that British punk group Crass were hippies – anti-materialist stance.

Christmas, with its resonances of family, religion and consumerism, became one of Mason's bugbears during the Reels' existence; 'Christmas is fucked', he told the editorial staff at *Vox* in 1981 with 'great profundity.'[21] By the mid 80s, the group were performing a show entitled 'Reels by Candlelight', featuring covers of songs such as 'Snoopy's Christmas' and 'Six White Boomers'. ('The Reels create their own world of what entertainment is about', wrote a *Juke* journalist wonderingly.)[22]

Later in their career, Mason even insisted that the group had recorded a Christmas album, though this did not emerge.[23] 'According to My Heart' was a top-ten record, but fate taunted the Reels. Hooper recalls:

> We did a tour of New Zealand and ended up getting stuck there because of industrial action. We were at the airport, with our luggage and equipment, including our Bose PA, having gone through customs, when suddenly every flight was cancelled. 'According To My Heart' was in the top ten and we had our first really major tour in Australia that we had to cancel the first half of because we couldn't get out of NZ. It turned into a national strike across all of NZ. Eventually we had to hire a light plane to come out from Australia to get us and our road crew, but all our gear, including the PA, was stuck . . . It cost us a huge amount of money and despite having a #2 single we were looking at working for the next couple of years just to pay off our debts. This added hugely to existing tensions, and so first John, then Polly, then Karen, then Paul left over a period of about eight or nine months. Dave and I were left with the debt.

'According to My Heart' also highlighted the misunderstandings between the Reels and their label. Polygram 'forgot' to enter the song in the Australian Country Music Awards, which indicated to the group how little the company understood them. Their manager, who at this time was Sebastian Chase, initiator of Rose Tattoo and former manager of Dragon, told *Juke* that 'a Polygram representative claimed the company didn't think it released any local country records in 1981.' Mason

chipped in, with every justification: 'If a song sells 25,000 copies you would think it would be hard for a record company to forget. If Polygram hadn't bungled it, it would have been great exposure for Dubbo and it would have given us country credibility.'[24] Adding insult to injury, the label nonetheless insisted the group include the song on their second album. Its sleeve announced that 'According to My Heart' was present against their will.

The album was called *Quasimodo's Dream*; its working titles were *Comedy* and *Torture Garden*.[25] Seven of the thirteen tracks are credited solely to Mason, but Ansell disputes this. 'I know the writing credits don't reflect it, but the band wrote that album together,' she says:

> They were wild rehearsals. I was doing my synthesiser free-form, John was holding down the beat, we taped a lot of stuff and we jammed for hours. Some stuff must have sounded like primal scream therapy but there were moments we could all hear and we got interested in repeating those moments. We pulled sections that worked out of the whole mess and started to focus in. Dave would turn up with lyrical snatches of things that would trigger some soundscape in me, John and Paul would work up a feel and we'd explore. We kind of shook the whole thing apart and let it settle. It was risky. At the same time Dave and I were working up the visuals. He wanted to get away from the phallic microphone and guitar thing, and Harley, our sound guy, was investigating smaller Bose speakers, then we experimented with the head-set mics.

Perhaps Mason was adopting a similar approach to British film director Mike Leigh, who requires his actors to improvise their characters before he writes the script, yet one undeniable feature that supports Ansell's suggestion of group co-operation is the songs that feature multiple vocals: the boisterous 'Colorful Clothes', the stark 'Cancer', the bouncy 'For All We Know', the entrancing 'Shout and Deliver' and the frenetic 'Depression', which a student newspaper reviewer described as 'like a Russian work song but it's about Australia. It's weird.'[26] A slow, savage song, 'Dubbo Go Go', was multi-hued: Mason told *Roadrunner's* Elly McDonald:

> Dubbo IS Australia. In Dubbo, they take lots of polls and advertising things. It's like Glen Waverley as an entire town. They try all the experiments out in Dubbo because everybody there is just so fucking average; ordinary, everyday people. They should call Australia Dubbo![27]

Another track recorded for *Quasimodo's Dream*, 'Chemistry and Mystery', was not included on the album but instead donated to Marc Hunter to become the opening track on his second album, *Big City Talk*; Hunter's voice is generally discernible amidst the Reels' vocals. Two remarkable songs on *Quasimodo's Dream*, the title track and 'Kitchen Man', highlight Mason's talent as a balladeer. 'Recording my part for the song "Quasimodo's Dream", I kept my eyes low because of my tears,' recalls Ansell. 'There was palpable melancholy living right there deep in that song.' The video for the first proper single from the album, 'Shout and Deliver', showed the Reels fresh-faced and with exceptional hairstyles – that of Paul Abrahams is particularly stunning – their faces morphing into each other in a fashion similar to Godley and Creme's (much later) video for their song 'Cry'. This video marked the debut of Stefan Fidock, John Bliss having quit shortly before the album's release. He and Ansell were both in the band long enough to work on the so-called *Heavy Metal* EP[28] (also, possibly to have been titled *Comedy*), from which only one song was issued, the masterful 'No. 3,' a boisterous meditation on gender orientation. Fidock now says:

> I thought John Bliss was a very very good drummer, and completely different to me as well, and what [Ansell] didn't like about his drumming was what I liked – he was a really heavy metal background drummer, whereas I had a lighter touch . . . Karen really liked my drumming, and she wanted me in the band. The Reels was tough – I saw it myself – a hard band to stay in. You'd burn out very quickly, it was a very intense experience. For one reason or another John said, 'I'm leaving the band'. That provided the opportunity, and they auditioned [Matt Finish's drummer] John Prior. Then they rang me . . .
>
> I directly replaced John Bliss so that whole *Quasimodo's Dream* album had just been recorded. There was Paul Abrahams, Polly was still in there, Karen, Craig, Dave, so it was a six piece band. That's the band that went on tour. I joined the band and went on tour for ten months non-stop, and in that time the band reduced to three members! That's all we did, we just played six nights a week, endlessly, for $150 a week when we were on the road, and $125 when were off. They were the wages. It was always pretty shithouse.

The wholesale departures were extraordinary, but perhaps more extraordinary was the fact that, though gone, the absent Reels continued to exert a strong presence in the band. Paul Abrahams quit music ostensibly to become a soccer referee.[29] Newham was next: 'Polly told us on the Thursday that Saturday would be his last gig,' Hooper reminisced in 1984. 'We had Sunday off and had to play on Monday. We had one day's rehearsal. I had to learn to play keyboards with two hands.'[30] Fidock says that 'Polly and I didn't get on very well':

> He really missed Bliss, they were great mates . . . Massively talented, the most talented person I'd ever met in music, but that makes it very difficult to adjust to normal life. He just said 'I'm leaving' and he left. He and John Bliss went off and did something with the Numbers.

Newham was also rumoured to have created a band called Private Orchestra, who were 'doing some interesting things but ... it's very, very private.'[31] Ansell, who had rescued the Reels creatively and been as strong a partner to Mason in terms of the band's vision as Newham had been to their sound and approach, was dissatisfied. Fidock says 'there was a tremendous falling out between Karen and Dave, they'd been very close, it was nasty stuff. Who knows. They fell out badly.' For her part, Ansell recalls:

> Something had to give. I hadn't written credited songs, we were playing covers, we were tired, not communicating. I wanted to keep writing ... I was getting interested in electronic visuals, videos were coming into their own, computer animation was starting up ... We had a horrendous gig in Tamworth, big fight amongst the guys after the gig,
>
> I think I'd emotionally withdrawn from the tension by then, and I remember being on the bus driving back, half asleep, and visualizing music and computer animation, and I thought, I wouldn't have to tour if I pursued that, I could write, record and release the computer-generated visuals. I guess this was around 1982. I went back to Melbourne, presented a song I wrote and demo'ed on my home studio, and played it to Jenny Keath at Mushroom, who offered me a single deal. I asked Neil Finn to produce, with Nigel and Noel on rhythm and Neil and I on mandolin and keyboards. I played a little bit with Bang, with Nick Seymour and Oleh Witer, and thought it would be good to get them in to the studio for the flip side of my single.

That single, 'No Commotion', was to be her last major musical foray (she was not, as Crowded House biographer Paul Bourke assumes, Bang's singer);[32] since then Ansell has worked primarily in computer-generated animation.

After her departure, the Reels came up with a radical new concept in early 1982: The Act. This projected new band would have involved the amalgamation of the Reels and the Models, and would have been an extraordinary coup. 'What-if' historians might claim such a development would have robbed Australia of the delights of the Reels' later career, but the potential payoff would have been that the world was spared the horrors of 'Out of Mind, Out of Sight', 'Barbados', and similarly vile Models releases, many of which foregrounded James Freud.

From the Reels' perspective, it was a Mushroom conspiracy that prevented it from coming to fruition: 'We arranged it all and kept in contact with them for a few weeks,' Mason said at the time. 'They were going to finish off with the Models and then come up to Sydney for rehearsals. I spoke to them on Tuesday. On Thursday, Gudinski flew up to Sydney on business and told me it wasn't going to happen. Which is a horrible way to find out, I guess.'[33] Fidock remembers simply: 'That arsehole Gudinski said, No, you're not doing this', though he adds: 'I'm glad we didn't really, because it would have been short-lived.' Mushroom denied (via a telex that was reproduced in the pages of *Juke*) that it had thwarted the new band.³⁴ Instead, Freud helped Sean Kelly reconvene the Models; perhaps their plan to cover the Reels' 'Love Will Find a Way' on a bonus disc to be included with their *Models Media* album was a homage crossed with an apology, though that didn't happen either.³⁵ The Reels made a better move: they recorded an album for K-Tel.

It was time for Craig Hooper to come into his own. Hooper and Mason were populists (though Mason tempered his populism with wry and 'sick' humour). Hooper had done session work, playing on advertisements for Bacardi rum and a chocolate bar, Chokito, for example, as well as recording (with Kevin Borich) the station ID for Sydney FM radio's 2MMM ('There were times there where my session work was keeping a few of us alive').³⁶ Fidock remembers the *Beautiful* album as his idea:

> Where that record comes from is as simple as this: I used to listen to Burt Bacharach singles at 33, at the wrong speed. And so 'This Guy's in Love'. The reason why I used to listen to singles at the slower speed was so I could get the chords. And if you do that, you can hear how strong the melody is and what the chord progression is. So we just moved from that through to 'what about if we just approach all the music in a similar vein, where we're going to slow the tempos, put a lot of space between the chords and try and make it as beautiful as we can' – and it was honest about that, not in a sentimental or sickly way, we wanted to approach things and make them as beautiful as we could. Not everything would turn out that way on *Beautiful* but some did. 'Prefab Heart' worked out really well, and there's a couple of others. The other material – I think there's a bit of Jimmy Reeves on that, the other material we just sort of – I brought in 'La Mer', and then I wrote 'Cry', and I brought 'This Guy's in Love', and Dave some things, 'Where is the Love', the Chinese one.

Hooper, for his part, believes many of the song choices on *Beautiful* were his: 'Having come from a background of playing in 50/50 bands in RSL clubs in my early teens ... I had the most say in what we did.'

The album was comprised entirely of other people's songs except for two: a reworked slow version of 'Prefab Heart', and a new song, 'Return', about a drowning father, which Mason claimed was inspired musically by playing the song 'No. 3' backwards. The Reels' embrace of covers was, naturally, problematic – particularly given the high quality of their originals. Fidock says that even though Mason was entirely capable of writing songs off the cuff, he only presented an average of one a year to the band: 'Which is odd, because you'd say 'Dave, you've got to write a song', and he'd just get up and do it – literally get up, walk over and come up with something.' Mason would come to believe that audiences preferred the group to play covers, and certainly their cover versions sold better as singles than their originals – although they also had just as many cover versions that failed to sell. More contentious at the time was the arrangement to issue *Beautiful* that was worked out between the Reels, their new record company RCA, and the K-Tel organisation. Put simply, this was as subversive as anyone could be in pop music at this time. Fidock, the only member of the band who had played in a punk band, says it was 'a real comment on the industry.'

> It was K-Tel, and it was also in reaction to – there was a lot of snob stuff in the music industry, people who thought that Johnny Kannis and the Hitmen, Radio Birdman, the Boys Next Door were somehow more legit, and more real, and we were just this lightweight kind of thing, a little bit insipid or something, and we weren't using guitars and Marshalls, people still use that gear, and it was good gear, great sound, but we didn't want to do that because it had been done before, why bother? It's been done really well, actually, so let's just stay right out of that. We wanted to do a very Australian form of entertainment that was new, and wasn't going to refer to Marshalls or Les Pauls or America or an English sort of a sound, but was a really Australian approach to entertainment or music.

In 1980, Mason had told *Roadrunner* readers that the Reels were 'really straight, actually – we're middle-class people, just the same as they [radio programmers] are.'[37]

The single 'This Guy's in Love' from *Beautiful* was a top-twenty hit. Hooper, who Fidock describes with a mixture of admiration and dismissiveness as 'just sort of the egghead' in the group, later summed up *Beautiful* as 'an exercise … I was trying to see whether we could record successfully as a three-piece, with the musical weight on my shoulders. We were experimenting with a lot of things like the Fairlight, without making a definitive statement.'[38] Hooper responds that if he was an 'egghead' it was because he was now the only member of the three-piece group making 'any musical contribution':

> I had to spend most of my waking hours getting up to speed with the technology and a great deal of what became *Beautiful* was me sitting in a little room on my own with what was really quite primitive technology. The

early version of the Fairlight that we were using was a difficult thing to make sound good, and the 'feel' of drum machines and sequencers in those days was very mechanical. The minimalistic space and odd melancholy of 'This Guy's in Love' was something I worked very hard on, and I still think the anti-climax of the chorus is one of the best things we ever did. I wanted it to feel like you've just driven off a cliff into thin air. There was actually a long silence before the outro which re-emphasised it, but the record company made us cut it out because they thought that DJs would think it had finished and just stop it there.

Certainly, there were challenges in the production of the album, but the Reels had begun an inexorable shift into electronic music. Mason said of their computer, Pollyanna:

Once it's programmed there will be no problems. It'll be much better than a new member, you can be more certain it'll keep time and whatever – and really, I don't think I want to go through auditions again... The computer can not only play most instruments, but it can do our accounts.[39]

'The trouble with all the technology that's being used now,' said Hooper, 'is that it's still typewriter music... the number of records with really terribly programmed drum machines on them these days is frightening.'[40] He envisaged recording an album using the computer 'because the LP will virtually be half-recorded even before we enter the studio.'[41] Mason claimed the group's ambition at this point was to 'not sound like Icehouse.'[42]

The Reels also used tape machines on stage, and this was an issue for many; the idea of live musicians augmenting (or being augmented by) recorded music was one which, like so many of the Reels' innovations, had not yet 'arrived'.

As early as 1980 it had been suggested in the press that 'the Reels would like to put out albums which were rearranged versions of their first, so that there could be an indefinite number of albums all featuring the same songs.'[43] Certainly, as has been seen, arrangement meant much more to this group than it did to most, and rearrangement of their own songs, as well as others', was a constant in their career after *Quasimodo's Dream*. Indeed, the Reels released only six new original songs in the final five years of their existence. The *Pitt Street Farmers* EP featured four of these: after plotting to call at least two of their releases *Comedy*, a jaunty song with that title finally appeared; another track, 'Happiness' was one of their less successful compositions, drawing out the eastern European feel of 'Depression' but overemphasising a joyless sarcasm; 'My Family' followed from the ruminations on male domesticity on 'Kitchen Man'; the gothic 'Black and Damp' was co-written by Mason and Johanna Pigott. Presumably because they figured some of their fans had avoided the *Beautiful* album on principle, the group included a re-recorded 'Return' on the EP as well. Fidock is dismissive of the record, which he terms a 'dud':

> I thought 'My Family' was a pretty good song, 'Happiness' was a waste of time. 'Black and Damp' – we had so many goes at that song. I can't even remember, it was done in bits and pieces... We started doing *Pitt Street Farmers* with Tony Cohen [and then] the same guy who did the *Beautiful* record, Bruce Brown... It lacked a centre...I thought it was a really dumb title, and a really terrible record cover. I don't know what Dave was about, I told him it was stupid and I don't get it. I still don't get it.

A Pitt Street farmer is a wealthy Sydneyite who profits from rural interests without any hands-on participation. The cover showed the group in Pitt Street early one morning surrounded by sheep.

A re-mixed version of 'Quasimodo's Dream' ('I was furious,' says Hooper, 'I thought it was awful') was released as a single, backed with a version of the Beach Boys' 'Love Is Here Today' and accompanied by a stunning, textured and epic video showing the group in mediaeval habits on a river. The song was not a hit the second time around either, but was clearly gaining a profile; the Reels performed it in a specially created spot at the *Countdown Music Awards,* which seemed already to acknowledge it as a classic, and gave it exposure which would have guaranteed commercial success for almost anyone other than such an overly difficult band.

Adrian Ryan's review of a late 1982 Reels show at which they shared a bill with Stephen Cummings gives an insight into the band's self-presentation in the last days of their original existence:

> During the gothic doom of "Black and Damp" there's film of drummer Stefan Fidock dressed in nun's drag walking through a twilight cemetery... And after the final encore of "Bombs Dropped on Christmas", the credits roll up on the screen for sight, sound and management. Just like the movies, in fact, this is a night when all of Mason's theories of media exploitation are laid on the line.[44]

The Reels had shed members drastically over a short period of time, as we saw; they had also, in Fidock's words, 'worked our rings off':

> By the time you're finished, you're thoroughly sick and tired of music. You don't want to know about it, you never want to play again – you're not getting anything out of it.

RCA sent the group – now just Mason, Hooper, and Fidock – to the USA and Britain, where there was some suggestion at the time that they might tour, or record – in fact, neither of these things happened. From Fidock's account, the entire experience sounds absurd:

We went up to America and Dave was really really sick for about a week. We took his brother, who was our tour manager, to just drive us around. So Paul [Mason] and I sat in the front of the car and Dave and Craig sat in the back, and we'd just go to a town, check in, I'd go my way, Dave would stay in the hotel room. He was sick . . .

During this time Mason and Fidock hatched a scheme, slightly reminiscent of their plan to form the Act, to lure Mick Harvey into the Reels: 'We were going to get him out of the Birthday Party, get rid of Craig and . . . start again with Mick Harvey – and start quite differently. By the time we got to England Dave really started to turn on Craig'. He continues:

Our manager rented a house for us, and it was hugely expensive. We sent out our material to Mute and a number of record companies and none of them were particularly interested . . . [Mute] had Depeche Mode and all that sort of stuff, and they couldn't understand what the Reels was about – what is this weird shit? Too Australian, for a start.

We were sent there to do some shows, to go and live in England, and stay there and make a career, but the instruments never arrived, the shows were never booked. The Go-Betweens were in London, they used to hang around our house a bit . . . nothing was happening. I got sick of it, and I went on holidays in Europe, and I'd ring up and say 'has our gear arrived, have we got any shows yet?' Very little work had gone into keeping us there, and then the manager said, look, we've spent a lot of money, you've got to go back to Australia and earn, and pay off debts, so faced with the prospect of going on tour with only three of us in the band, with a tape machine, the band just bit the dust.

This was the end of the first phase of the Reels, although an *On the Street* review of a band called the Jelly Babies, playing at Sydney's Paddington Green hotel in March 1984 and running through covers of 'Sugar Sugar', the Particles' song 'Remington Rand', Mental as Anything's 'The Nips Are Getting Bigger', Kraftwerk's 'The Model' and Abba's 'Ring Ring', is plainly describing a three-piece (drummerless) manifestation of the Reels. [45]

Hooper was invited into the Mullanes with Paul Hester, Neil Finn and Nick Seymour in 1985; this was, of course, the band that would become Crowded House, though Hooper did not remain long. Fidock joined the Sacred Cowboys, alongside his former Romantics associate Nick Rischbeith and replacing the Models' former drummer, Janis Freidenfelds. Mason, suffering from hepatitis, did not embark on any new musical forays.

The group revived in 1986 and repeated the pattern of their previous career, if a little faster. Invited by INXS to support them on tour, the original band reformed, sans Abrahams. They released a single – a lively version of 'It Must Be Love', originally recorded by Etta James – and effectively became a unit again. Clearly nothing had been resolved, however: Bliss described the band in the studio as 'tension, tension, tension, bullshit. We punch each other out metaphysically.'[46] The group, which Hooper believes was only reformed at Bliss and Newham's suggestion after its old debts had disappeared, again shed members at intervals.

They were signed to Regular, a label which seemed content to indulge their one-single-a-year tendency. The second post-reformation Reels single – described by Mason as 'sort of adult entertainment for the thinking man or woman'[47] – was Creedence Clearwater Revival's 'Bad Moon Rising', slowed down in the style of the Reels' 'This Guy's in Love'. It was a top-twenty hit, their last. It was announced at this time that Paul Goldman was making a feature film in which Mason and Nick Cave would play drug dealers;[48] it was not made, but Mason did star alongside Cave in John Hillcoat's *Ghosts . . . of the Civil Dead,* playing the transvestite Lilly. Cave was one of the film's screenwriters. This was not Mason's first notable appearance in drag: he had apparently appeared onstage at a Jimmy and the Boys show 'dressed like Marlene Dietrich'; he then went on to 'act out sexual fantasies with J&B's lead singer Iggy Jones.'[49]

Their next step was a misstep, though it is hard in retrospect to see why. The group had always done thematic tours, such as the early-80s' "Reels by Rail" alongside the Particles (Mason: 'we believe in public transport and we want to encourage people to use it more,')[50] and "The Reels Go Primitive", for which they debuted their headset microphones.[51] In their second incarnation, they began by touring a Reels by Request show, during which they had forty songs, listed on printed sheets distributed to audiences, who would call out for their favourites: 'We play lots of songs that people know, also everything we've ever recorded.'[52] There was also an Australian songs-only variation of this request-show format. The following year, they performed 'a sort of cabaret show' in Sydney which included Mason dueting with Little Pattie; on other occasions, guest stars – such as Bongo Starkie or Ross Wilson – would perform on live versions of songs they themselves had made famous. Mason later mused on his wish to hear other Australian stars performing his songs, such as Chris Bailey performing 'No. 3', or Kate Ceberano singing 'My Family' alongside 'some other jazz songs we wrote in the early 70s and never recorded.'[53] Ceberano did go on to record 'Quasimodo's Dream' for her first album.

What in fact came to pass – and perhaps it developed out of some of these ideas, particularly the Australian request show – was the *Neighbors* album. In theory, it seemed like a great idea, particularly that of guest musicians like Steve Prestwich and the Go-Betweens' Amanda Brown playing on a spirited version of Prestwich's hit for Cold Chisel, 'Forever Now'. Hooper says:

> We spent a couple of solid weeks recording everything we had, then ran off some rough mixes to go away and listen to for a couple of weeks. When we came back

> to discuss what we were going to do I was the only one who had even listened to the tapes and they were appalling. I said it was it was a complete pile of shit and we should destroy all traces of it. But it had cost a lot of money, and I was out-voted, Martin Fabinyi (the head of Regular) talked us into spending more money to try to salvage it rather than just throw it away. So we went back into the studio, but Polly was becoming exceedingly erratic, and eventually left, leaving me to finish an album I didn't even want to do. There's a couple of songs that turned out OK but overall it was one of the worst periods of my life.

Despite the release of two singles – the abovementioned 'Forever Now' and a slow take on Dragon's 'Are You Old Enough?' – the album was a commercial disaster and in many respects an artistic one too.

The Reels' story does not have a particularly happy ending, although reunion tours after 2008 – featuring Mason, Bliss, Newham and Abrahams – were received positively. Hooper recalls:

> After *Neighbors* Dave and I carried on as a duo, with me doing pretty much everything – the music, management, even driving the truck. Because our costs were minimal we only had to do a few gigs a month to survive, and I was keen to try to find a new direction – hell, we'd done it several times before. But it was very one-sided, again. Eventually Dave wrote a new song, 'I Don't Love You Anymore', which I thought was musically great but would never be a hit because of the lyrics. The recording went pretty well. I thought it was encouraging that we could still make a record that sounded OK. After that Dave started writing again but the songs were half electronic and half folky acoustic songs, it was very schizophrenic. We did some demos but it really wasn't going anywhere musically. We decided to call it quits in early 1993 . . . After the last show we made a solemn oath to never, ever do a reunion tour, to just let the memories be what they were.

Mason spent the next three years in bed suffering from depression.[54] The new album had been provisionally titled *The Love Album*; it did not emerge. 'I Don't Love You Anymore' was one of their best recordings, a boisterously maudlin piece of work. Seven years earlier, Mason had said he wasn't a happy person: 'I can't write happy songs. And if I can write a happy *song*, I can't write fucking happy lyrics to go with it.'[55] Hooper's comment, from the same discussion, was even more pertinent: 'Happy/sad is a really fantastic emotion to try and capture.'[56]

The Triffids' founders David McComb and Alsy McDonald fiercely defended their West Australian origins, particularly against what they saw as eastern states (and later European, notably British) pretension. The list of music they covered in this 1984 one-off show ranges from the credible to the absurd. The group would apply the same range of influences to their last studio album, *The Black Swan*.

14 We Were Sixty Years Old When We Were Nineteen

THE TRIFFIDS

By the mid 80s, Perth group the Triffids had reached a creative peak they would sustain for another five years, creating a unique body of work that would spend a considerable period of time unnoticed and then return to prominence during the first decade of the 21st century. This chapter tells the story of the Triffids from their Perth origins in 1976 up to the release of their *Born Sandy Devotional* album in early 1986.

The Triffids was the final name given to a morphing series of groups that revolved around middle-class Perth schoolfriends David McComb and Alan (Alsy) MacDonald in the mid to late 1970s. David McComb was nothing if not an inveterate chronicler of his past and of his projected future; around 1978 he wrote a mock-epic history of his and MacDonald's musical world:

> On the night of November 27 1976 a tape was made by Alsy MacDonald, playing a single toy drum, and Dave McComb, playing acoustic guitar. The multimedia group 'Dalsy' had come into being.
>
> Dalsy went on to make several remarkable tapes mainly of original material – the Loft tapes, Rock n Roll Accountancy, Live at Ding Dong's, Bored Kids, Domestic Cosmos, People are Strange Dalsy are Stranger, Steve's, and the seminal punk work; Pale Horse Have a Fit. They obtained conventional electric instruments and employed the help of musical acquaintances Phil Kakulas, Andrew McGowan and Julian Douglas-Smith. They sang songs about cats, cheesecakes, hotels, gardens, and ruthlessly satirised everything they saw.[1]

According to McComb's narrative, the original Dalsy were 'immensely unpopular' and 'split up towards the end of 1977', at which point McComb, MacDonald and Kakulas bought new equipment 'totalling $1000' and became Blök Music, playing – amongst other things – the Leederville Punk Festival, 'alongside Perth's punk rock contingent'. Blök Music changed their name to Logic, then to the Triffids. This band developed what McComb jokingly referred to as 'connections', who included 'Dixie from Tune-In, Kim from Mark's, Dave Ellery from 6WF, Dave Flick (ex-Victim and current Farrelly), James Baker (ex-Victim and ex-Scientist),

R. E. Purvis (writer for the Music Section of the *Sunday Independent*) and other musical and non-musical persons.'[2] McComb later said, quite seriously, that 'punk bands like the Victims and the Scientists were a great inspiration.'[3]

The Triffids' activities always included recording; their first cassette album, indeed, predated the group itself in exactly the same way that Flowers did with *Icehouse*. It was credited to Logic and called *The Triffids*; only later did they adopt that title for the group's name. The band went on to record five more cassette albums – recorded live and produced in limited runs which, accompanied by oversized lyric sheets, were sold at Perth record shops – before they released anything on vinyl. The Triffids did not start the trend, but they certainly popularised the idea of cassette albums in Perth; so that, for instance, five years later another Perth group, Rabbits Wedding, was declaring they would 'be recording a tape quite soon.'[4]

The cliché about Perth is that it's 'the 'most isolated city on earth' (isolated, that is, from other large cities); these recordings show the workings of a highly creative and dexterous group who – far from operating in isolation – employed a magpie mentality, throwing everything they found into the mix and making it their own. Kakulas left the band to concentrate on his chemistry studies, though he remained a part of the Triffids' circle – he and McComb later reunited in the Blackeyed Susans in 1989 – and an important musician and songwriter in his own right. Other members included bass player Byron Sinclair and one of David's brothers, Robert, who had performed with local live groups such as the Tiger Mountain Band and was to become a permanent member. 'The new Triffids bought up big on new equipment (100 watt amps, etc.) and awaited their Easter '79 debut at Hernando's', according to McComb's history.

The group recorded their first single, 'Stand Up'/'Farmers Never Visit Nightclubs' in February 1981 with a line-up of David and Robert McComb on guitars and vocals, Will Akers on bass, Margaret Gillard on keyboards and vocals, and Mark Peters on drums. MacDonald had left the group briefly for the sake of his education, though he was playing in another group, the Real Dreamers, with Kakulas.

If any song deserves the term 'dinky', it is 'Stand Up', a shambling piece of bubblegum that is not indicative of anything the group would go on to do. McComb said many years later that the group preferred the single's B side because it was 'zany.' He also recalled that the band at the time had felt an affinity with American new wave:

> We felt a strong bonding with the New York bands that came out at the end of the 70s, people like Television and Talking Heads, who played guitar music in a totally 'un' rock and roll way. They just went about things as thought the whole history of rock music hadn't existed, so they could do songs about buildings on fire and doing their cleaning, or whatever. We did a song about farmers not being socially accepted at nightclubs.[5]

At the same time, *Roadrunner* readers were learning about 'The Real Dreamers... three ex-Triffids who play and more to the point sing slow Lou Reed/Velvets/ Only Ones type songs, not proficiently but with incredible vitality and youthful enthusiasm.'[6] They were the 'only band to challenge' the Triffids, but 'were largely former Triffids anyway.'[7] The group was short-lived and MacDonald returned in time to have his name (but not his drumming) on the Triffids' second record release, the exceptional EP *Reverie*.

'We started in '78, we didn't start playing live till '81,'[8] McComb claimed in the British press five years later; he was only telling half the truth. The group had been playing shows of various types (parties, school events) since the late 70s and in part what McComb was probably masking was his age – he was not old enough to enter a hotel until 1981. This was the year he also began studying journalism at what was then known as WAIT (West Australian Institute of Technology, now part of Curtin University). Late in that year C. C. Mitchell wrote in *Roadrunner*:

> A new air of optimism seems to be sweeping Perth, such a contrast to the dreary Winter blues we all had a few months back. Still, all is not well in the State of Excitement. Rockist bands like the Bargains, the Frames, the Eurogliders, the Essentials, the Riffs, the Rockets, the Manikins, Doris Day and so on and so on still dominate the city's civil servant and secretary scene. These bands are now really big at Adrians, a venue now totally out of hand ... Adrians is now totally bland and without any worthwhile character. It needs to be firebombed and the sooner the better.
>
> The Triffids ... to me they are what music should be – clever, earnest, non-professional, innovative, original and enjoyable. Their original drummer, Alsy MacDonald, is back with them sounding as good as ever.[9]

The group's third 7-inch, a single called 'Spanish Blue', was a sensational work: a short, sweet, damning yet affectionate assessment of their hometown which seems to show McComb grappling with a number of issues both musical and spiritual. The lyrics speak of a numbness that descends on someone who spends too long in a comfortable, hot place like Perth; songs from the same period, such as 'Too Hot to Move' and 'Hell of a Summer' explore the problem of writing about this environment in the western rock tradition. The music is reminiscent of a faster, clunkier but less hackneyed 'Spanish Harlem'; McComb was exceptionally aware of popular music history. One writer suggested that 'Spanish Blue' had 'a resonance that is uniquely Australian ... recalling such writers as Carey, Moorhouse and McQueen.'[10] The B side to the single, 'Twisted Brain', is a genre song in the style of the Birthday Party; this, too, would be a seam that the Triffids would work extensively ('Property Is Condemned' was a later one, as was 'Field of Glass').

While showing the group's versatility, and giving the lie to any accusation that they were overly twee (an impression that 'Farmers Never Visit Nightclubs' could easily convey), these were experiments in tone and third-person narrative. At the same time songs such as these took McComb into troubled territory, where he was swept up in an odd religiosity. The McComb family were practising Methodists; this is unlikely to be the reason David McComb was so keen on Catholic guilt. Dave Graney has flatly stated that 'anybody who grew up in a Catholic world would not use religious imagery in their songs',[11] though Stephen Cummings, reflecting on McComb's oeuvre, empathizes: 'For some who's grown up with no religion . . . I had an incredible amount of guilt.'[12] Most likely this earnest, self-flagellating narrative style was one more form that David McComb found fascinating.

Because he was so prolific and able to work in so many different musical forms, McComb became fearful of appearing a dilettante. In the mid 80s he told Toby Creswell:

> I guess lots of people feel, especially in adolescence, that emotions are false and that people just live out charades. I used to wonder how you aim for a true emotion, and one way is to have a detached narrator. I generally don't like writing confessional lyrics that are supposed to be completely honest, because I don't think you usually are very honest to yourself. However, you can't go on forever dealing in images of something; eventually you have to make music that touches the thing itself.[13]

'To some extent,' he said at the same time, 'I think we were sixty years old when we were nineteen. It's a process of unlearning hipness; we were very cynical teenagers.'[14]

The Triffids travelled east in 1982, the first of their many forays across the Nullarbor Plain. They lived in a room in Brunswick Street, Fitzroy, in the same 19th-century apartment block as Ash Wednesday (of JAB and then the Models), who hated the hippies in the building so much that when he went out for the day he would leave his synthesisers feeding back on each other.

The following year, the group relocated to Sydney to begin their Australian music careers in earnest. Sally Collins remembers that during her time at SCAM (see chapter 16), the band 'moved into the Shepherd Newman building, behind our offices in Yurong St, Darlinghurst':

> I was besotted with their music and did everything I could for them, putting them on a myriad of Sunnyboys supports, buying up all their Dungeon Tapes that I could and giving them to anyone who would listen. Incidentally so did Peter and Jeremy Oxley. They were amazed at the Triffids. I pushed them toward White Label, and very quickly realised that it was a mistake. If Mushroom/ White didn't cope with SCAM bands and understand our 'alternative' approach and nonconformity, how in the hell would they understand the Triffids and their 'cottage industry' approach to their career.

White reissued 'Spanish Blue' (which the group had initially released themselves) and then funded and issued a new EP, *Bad Timing And Other Stories* (like their earlier song 'Place in the Sun', the title was borrowed from cinema).

From an early age, David McComb had compiled lists and fantasy projections of the band's future development. Album track listings were agonized over; songs, in particular, were reworked and manipulated in numerous ways. While the Triffids was undoubtedly his group – with MacDonald an occasional songwriting contributor but more a supporter than a driver – there was an unusual strength and commitment between them. In 1983 the band moved to Sydney and began building their profile on the east coast. In the first of a series of pieces entitled 'Letter from Sydney' that were published in the University of Western Australia's magazine *Pelican*, McComb challenged the young people of Perth with firm pronouncements on the dangers of lionising other places as more urbane or creative than one's own town:

> The first prize theory we can lay to waste is that Sydney is any more exciting or worthwhile than Perth. There will always be somewhere hipper than wherever it is you are, and if it's not Sydney it's bound to be New York City or the Congo.
>
> The so-called 'art scene' here brims over with dilettantes, band-wagon-jumpers, hangers-on, charlatans and leeches; the quiffs are highly cultivated; the 'punks' are third generation imbeciles; and [every]one is drunk on self-congratulation. In short, at the risk of deflating hope, things are much the same as in Perth.[15]

McComb said later that the group felt they were 'quite ambitious within the confines of Australia':

> I think any band that has looked after their own career efficiently for that amount of time is potentially a little bit dangerous for a record company. It's obvious they've got too much of a mind of their own and their ambitions might not coincide with the company's. But it's not like we're us-against-them with the industry, we just want to have our own particular course of events rather than following other people's precedents.'[16]

Along with the McCombs – Robert McComb in particular played a very formative role in the group's sound in the early to mid 80s, with empathic and perfectly placed violin – and the solid, considered drumming of MacDonald, the band featured Martyn Casey, previously of the Nobodies, on bass; and on keyboards Jill Birt, whose musical experience had been limited to a Perth version of a 'little band', What Are Little Boys Made Of. Birt was no less dedicated to her instrument simply because her skills were at first basic; she kept an exercise book detailing the structure and notation of every song in the group's repertoire and more than held her own. Later she would develop another skill as an evocative singer, as well as co-writing songs for the band.

The group's repertoire at this time was an interesting blend of earlier, sillier songs ('My Baby Thinks She's a Train' was initially formulated on one of their cassette albums); the most recent examples of David McComb's pop songwriting ('Rosevel'); and the grandiose, structured epics which would become his trademark, 'Red Pony' being probably the best example of this. These last two songs, along with the aforementioned 'Hell of a Summer', formed the backbone of *Treeless Plain,* their first vinyl album (and their ninth in total, the six Perth cassette albums having been joined by two Sydney releases, *Dungeon Tape* and *Son of Dungeon Tape*).

The Triffids were now a leading light of Hot Records, the arrangement with White Label having not worked out (although it would later be revived in Australia in tandem with Hot, if only because the name White Hot seemed so workable). The band also came to be managed by Sally Collins (see chapter 16). She was able to use her knowledge of the music industry and its formulaic approach to marketing to the group's advantage; she made certain, for instance, that when they signed to Island in the UK the one part of 'the world' not covered by the deal was Australasia, where Mushroom would, she assumed, use its knowledge of their territory to promote a group who were conquering overseas markets.

Treeless Plain was the first and last Triffids LP to be simply a recording of the band's set as it stood at the time (the template, presumably, of the preceding cassette albums). 'I'm proud of it,' David McComb said at the time, though he qualified his statement: 'I can see some flaws there, I think we tried too many things, so there are too many varying moods, so it doesn't stand as a consistent piece throughout. That is a fault with most debut albums, anyway.'[17] McComb realized later, when he came to construct the group's last studio album, *The Black Swan,* that this was in any case not necessarily a fault. Later, he said of *Treeless Plain*: 'There were accusations that we really didn't know what to do with ourselves. We did. It's just that we wanted everything at once.'[18] Toby Cluechaz wrote this appreciation for *Roadrunner* in 1982:

> After listening to the Triffids I find myself confused by infatuation and trepidation. I have to become a miser with words to talk about their purity. I am sure my time would be more wisely spent if I just listened or danced to their music rather than write about it ... the pop music they play is not only infectious it's unusually smart: read as sweetness and a thumping rhythm section, lyrics as empathic as they are insidious, harmonies and other idiosyncrasies, humour ... a skin of dark shadow. And quavering emotion. David McComb's voice is the rich centrepiece . . . One sometimes wonders how bands of great feeling like the Triffids and Go-Betweens could ever form in Perth and Brisbane, amid all the reactionary cant and grubby money. But somehow they do, the resoluteness

gained from such an environment and the continuing will to play innovative music is enough to heave any band to the top of the scrap heap: if not, we the audience are to blame.[19]

The group were seen as very 'alternative' in the early 1980s. In 1983, an unnamed Triffid (probably David McComb) claimed:

> I think we used to secretly hope/suspect that we could have commercial success, cos we wrote pop songs; and we presumed they would be played on radio, TV, sung along to, etc. Now I see things aren't that simple. Now I can honestly say I don't care about large scale success at all. I really don't expect it to happen, we don't fit into to the pop industry scheme of things.[20]

In another 'Letter from Sydney' McComb mused on the music industry, which he was now seeing in close-up:

> Rock 'n' roll, like all other popular culture industries, cannot survive in mere stasis; it must generate more and more money, it must relentlessly expand. And members of rock 'n' roll bands themselves (old-fashioned creatures that they are) cannot bear the idea of 'getting smaller'. Their entourage of lighting and sound technicians, truck drivers, managers, secretaries, booking agents, promoters and miscellaneous lackeys, must swell until it reaches bursting point. If something is worth doing, they argue, it is worth overdoing.[21]

His joke frustration increased in a subsequent letter:

> 2SM or 6IX will play any record as long as it's a relatively bland three-minute pop song. The likes of 2JJJ, however, will play any record, be it a ten-minute dirge or two-minute disco as long as it is painfully fashionable. They, the very forces that prevent themselves from being the bastion of alternative CULTURE, thus fall pray to the most loathsome bourgeois hypocrisy. They give SUCK to whatever is in vogue.[22]

The Triffids, along with Tactics, Severed Heads and Great White Noise, had tracks on a double compilation album, *Beyond the Southern Cross,* released in Britain on Ink, an offshoot of the Red Flame label, in 1984. This label and another, Cherry Red, were interested in signing the group, 'but we've got no complaints about remaining in Australia,' said David McComb, who added: 'I entertain no romantic notions about going to London and starving in some grotty garret.'[23] There was also interest in the mainstream: 'when the CBS execs voted us the next big band at their convention,' he said in 1984, 'I thought that was laughable because we're furthest away from what they want.'[24]

The Go-Betweens made their mission statement with their second album, *Before Hollywood:* a benchmark record. The Triffids seemed uneasy about being pinned down with a major release. Their move after *Treeless Plain* was to dither: they released the remarkable Sekret Sekret-esque single, 'Beautiful Waste'; a 12-inch EP, *Raining Pleasure;* and the *Lawson Square Infirmary* EP. *Raining Pleasure,* with a cover showing a dilapidated house in Lawson Street, Redfern opposite the building where the group were living in 1983, included Birt's first Triffids vocal, the title track, which David McComb wrote specifically for her to sing, and 'Property Is Condemned', the B side of 'Beautiful Waste'; other tracks, like 'Everybody Has to Eat', were less well-formed. With their permission, McComb also adopted a cover of the traditional 'St James Infirmary' from another Hot group, the Lighthouse Keepers. The combination of a street name and a song title gave them the name for the next release: Lawson Square Infirmary was the name of the group and the 6-song record; all the Triffids except Birt played on it, along with a couple of other principals.[25] Dobro and guitar player Graham Lee had played on Paul Kelly's album *Post;* he met the Brisbane singer-songwriter John F. Kennedy through a newspaper advertisement and consequently James Paterson, Kennedy's bandmate in J.F.K. and the Cuban Crisis.[26] David McComb asked Lee and Paterson over to 'work on a few songs that wouldn't be for the Triffids'; Paterson remembers:

> That night I took the tape we made home and listened to it and was struck that into some small cassette player we could get something better than the JFK album, which had taken months of studio time. It was great. It was so instant, and I thought well I'd rather make a record like this ... So I said I'd put up the

money to record it. And on the Triffids' last Saturday night in Sydney we found a few free hours, so we rushed off and recorded it.

Graham's significance was that he was the only musician that had any experience at playing country music and therefore added the authenticity that gave it that extra something. In fact that's why we were so thrilled with it and decided to record it, because Graham made it stand out. It wasn't just a couple of people sitting around with guitars playing pseudo-country.[27]

Lee guested with the Triffids for a while, and was invited to join in 1985, becoming the band's only member without significant Perth experience. He was now part of a band which, in any case, was above all a vehicle for an outstandingly original songwriter who wanted to make fresh, individual observations but also fully understood, and always wanted to explore, the situation of the songwriter as someone who must analyse and synthesise the work of those who preceded him. David McComb would later claim that at this time:

I was a bit confused about what was imagery for its own sake and what was an honest depiction of how I felt. I don't want to write direct confessionals and I don't want total fantasy. I want to use my emotional experiences to write a story that will have resonances but be a story in its own right. Which is what any good writing is.[28]

The pursuit of the genuine – 'the thing itself' – was a continued concern of McComb's. 'You could never say we're caricatures, or we follow a precedent set by others,' he said in 1984. 'We don't want to become cartoon type rock and roll people. And we're not into kitsch.'[29]

The Triffids went to the UK in 1984 and were successful very quickly – to the chagrin of some of their peers, who felt – just as Derek Pellicci had claimed LRB prepared the ground for other Australian bands to succeed in America (see chapter 8) – that the way had been paved for them by those who had gone before. To add insult to injury, perhaps, the Triffids' middle-class connections meant that, far from starving in garrets like many of their cohort, they often had apartments and houses owned by friends of friends and family to stay in. Appearing on the cover of the *NME* almost as soon as they arrived in the UK, their experience was very different to that of almost every other Australian group to trouble Britain and Europe. David McComb looked back ten years later:

A grassroots following soon appeared and we proceeded to tour virtually every European country, finding specific pockets of popularity in the oddest of locations: Holland, Greece, Scandinavia, Ireland. And we realised we had been touched by the blessed hand of Spinal Tap when we found ourselves to be certifiably . . . big in Belgium (a mystery that endures to this day). We were introduced to the delights of the Summer Eurofestival circuit, performing at Glastonbury, Pinkpop, Waterpop, Seinojoke, Roskhilde (40,000), T&W Belgium (35,000) and den Haag's Parkpop (pushing 100,000).[30]

'It turned out really well for us,' he said in 1985, 'because we were in a place where we could make an impression at a time when no-one else was doing much.'[31] It has also been suggested by insiders that a good part of the Triffids' success resulted from the exertions of Hot, as the label battled to get established in Britain. The band recorded three songs for a Peel session, subsequently released as an EP under the title of the longest of the three tracks, 'Field of Glass'; McComb claimed it 'is still I guess the most aggressive and violent record that we have done. It gave us heaps of confidence.'[32] The song was an amalgam of two others that had briefly appeared in their Australian live set.

In an interview conducted towards the end of his life (he died in 1999) for the *Long Way to the Top* series, McComb made the curious claim that in his experience prior to recording *Born Sandy Devotional*, 'Australian records did not have atmosphere.'[33] 'I guess I've a longstanding admiration and fascination with Phil Spector, Shadow Morton and all the people, both male and female, who were involved in all the girl-group records,' he had told Tracee Hutchison in 1992, 'the really orchestrated girl-group records with sound effects. The whole record was done with a view to making it incredibly lush and incredibly listenable.'[34] The new album's title was 'the name of a song which didn't make it onto the record which is about someone called Sandy,'[35] and the cover was – appropriately yet strangely – an aerial photograph of the West Australian coastline.

Long Way to the Top describes 'Wide Open Road', the opening track on side two of *Born Sandy Devotional* which became the group's cornerstone song, as 'a subtle search for national identity'.[36] Most of the album's lyrics, however, revolve around a painful break-up:

> The writing was much more autobiographical than anything I'd done before, I felt quite close to the subject matter. I found myself almost following the idea of fidelity as a complete all-consuming faith, to give you some sort of direction or something. But then I realised that if you're going to look at human relationships very critically, then fidelity is just as irrational as religion is. Once you live with a person long enough, you notice that they're not such a great person, you start having arguments with them and things start breaking up. So what most people do, I'm sure, including myself, is you observe the idea rather than the person. You stay faithful to the idea of sticking with the person, I suppose, and of course when that starts to crumble it's just like when faith starts to crumble.[37]

'The Seabirds' dealt with an incident in which he nearly drowned while swimming, hungover, to an island; 'Chicken Killer' was 'about a village idiot'; while the album's penultimate song, 'Stolen Property', went through nine different versions.[38] As the novelist Tim Richards has pointed out, the final version could almost be a homage to Joy Division's 'Atmosphere', and its title might be a sly nod to this.

Born Sandy Devotional was an instant hit with critics and seems to have remained most fans' favourite Triffids recording. But it would be entirely inaccurate to even hint that they would struggle to recapture this quality in their later work; indeed, for this writer the best was to come in 1989 with *The Black Swan*.

We leave The Triffids with David McComb's reflections on *Born Sandy Devotional*. Here, it could be argued, he was a victim of the ahistorical nature of a musical environment like Perth's, where vibrant music scenes had ebbed and flowed for decades, with each new scene often not knowing or not caring about the groups that had come before, many of which may have seemed tawdry. Here was one of the numerous cities in which punk emerged before everywhere else in the world, in the early forays of James Baker, Kim Salmon and Dave Warner, and yet in which it could be suggested in 1978 that punk had just 'arrived'. Not having a network of support outside his own cohort – he was unlikely to have sat down with Billy Rogers or Peter Walker and discussed Perth's music scene earlier in the 70s – McComb looked back at his origins and saw a blank slate. Composing the songs was, he said, 'a matter of finding things that weren't contrived for me, because I think that would be the beginning of weakness for writing:'

> The images that seem to come up most readily and most honestly are things from early childhood, for me. You can't really lie about that. But it's a funny place to write about because not a lot has been written about it. Somewhere like Paris has been described 10 million times, and every time you walk down a street in Paris you get buried under the weight of every page that's ever been written about that street. In Australia, you honestly get a complete sense of just nothingness.[39]

THE MOODISTS
HONEYMOON IN GREEN
FERAL DINOSAURS

**ESPLANADE HOTEL
UPPER ESPLANADE
ST. KILDA
THURS SEPT. 2nd**

8pm to 1am. $4.00 each.

BEWARE! MOODISTS CAMP 100 km AHEAD

By Christie Eliezer

As cult figure Jim Foetus screams out, time and time again from the stage, "long live the new flesh/long live the new flesh".

New York's new flesh are a totally different breed. I'd always seen The Moodists — Mt. Gambier born, Melbourne bred and London nurtured — as a band that belonged to New York. Not necessarily in musical terms, but in terms of attitude, of a band that seemingly thrived on breaking out of sealed-and-air-conditioned environments, of harbouring no illusions about wanting to invade and profit from the ivory towers of the rock industry.

But then again, they've got different ideas.

"Personally I don't care where I live," shrugs Dave Graney, seated in an abode somewhere in inner city Carlton, sipping on a cup of coffee an hour before rehearsals start for the next Moodists LP (to be recorded through February in Melbourne before the band heads back overseas).

"I just want to create something worthwhile,

made such a big impact there that the next few bands from Australia seen in that light."

By now, Graney says, the initial towards Australian rock from the press has softened. "Some bad bands there, that's for sure," he suggests, when you had people like The Saints, Birdman, they started to change attitudes, though, caused so much concause they looked like they'd come from er planet, compared to what was happening in London at the time."

Graney doesn't take the UK rock seriously. They tend to be far too expecting bands to crack it in six months relegated to no-hoper status, and bands American band like Black Flag who respected (and feared) in America even they haven't released records for far Plus you have writers who pick out cities, insist that all the great music from there, and then discard those months later to the detriment of groups that might come from there after.

15 There's absolutely no art in the Moodists
THE MOODISTS

The Moodists were one of the most original rock groups of the late 70s and early 80s. Their stated references – early rock 'n' roll and television – were only fleetingly apparent in their records and live performances. The music they played was often repetitive and dressed with fragments of guitar hooks, rather than presented as realised songs – this is true particularly of their middle period, between the release of their lauded second single, 'Gone Dead', and their second-to-last, 'Take the Red Carpet out of Town'. Though he did not play on 'Take the Red Carpet' (he did help write it) or the subsequent, final, release, the key to this uniqueness was almost certainly bass player Chris Walsh.[1]

Walsh had been a member of the Negatives (who began as Judas Iscariot and the Traitors, then became the Reals with Ollie Olsen on guitar, Peter Cave (unrelated to Nick) on drums, and Garry Gray (much later of the Sacred Cowboys) on keyboards and vocals). The Negatives were an early punk outfit whose 'Planet on the Prowl' had appeared on the Suicide compilation *Lethal Weapons* in early 1978. However he was perhaps more influential in the pressure he applied – probably involuntarily – on the Birthday Party. Walsh's importance to that group may be deduced from the fact that in early 1982 he filled in for his childhood friend Tracy Pew while Pew rode out parking fines in prison, and is thanked for this on the group's best record, *Junkyard*. Walsh's playing is very basic, intelligent and driving. While bandmates Dave Graney and Clare Moore have had a lasting impact on the Australian music scene since the early 90s, Walsh knew he was the most important member when he jokingly asked Clinton Walker, in a 1983 interview, whether he had been 'aware of the Moodists' since 1977 – the group did not form until 1980.

They emerged from Adelaide band the Sputniks, which featured Clare Moore on drums, Steve Miller and Phillip Marks playing guitar, Liz Dealey on bass, and Dave Graney singing. This band's only single, 'Second Glance'/'Our Boys' is powerful and tuneful, and while the youthful Graney's trebly vocal style is almost unrecognisable when compared to his subsequent 35 years' output, the beginnings of his unusual blend of Austral-Americana are detectable. 'No light and shade,' complained Andrew McMillan in *RAM*, 'just a feeling of late sixties Oz psychedelia.'[2] Though it appeared in a plain white sleeve, some copies of the single came with a free badge which announced, hilariously, 'You cunt I love the

Sputniks'. The Graney-Miller-Moore triangle continued on to the Moodists; all three soon came, inexplicably, to disown this early single.

Dave Graney and Steve Miller had grown up in Mount Gambier, the second largest city in South Australia (after Adelaide), close to the border with Victoria. Graney would later say:

> South Australia's different, it's where I get my worldview from. Towns are far away from each other, it makes you a particular way, people are quite desperate there. Mt Gambier is an idyllic place, beautiful rolling green hills, and lakes and rivers. It's quite violent, too, like most South Australian places.[3]

A song Graney was later to write with Stephen Cummings, 'Three Dead Passengers in a Stolen Second-Hand Ford', problematically romanticises this world;[4] earlier songs with the Moodists, such as 'Swingy George' (about a playground voyeur) present an even grittier view; 'This Road Is Holy', from their first EP, was a story of rape (or at least violence) ending with a plea for better infrastructure planning ('this road needs to be lit'). A band member was later to observe that Graney only had two themes in his songs: Clare Moore and the life of a travelling musician; but there's also the perspective from a small-town South Australian world infused in many of his lyrics, in his Moodists recordings and many subsequent songs.

Miller, Moore, and Graney moved to Melbourne in 1980, at which time the people they met were still reeling from the impact – and recent departure – of the Birthday Party. Graney later recalled:

> When I went to Melbourne the Birthday Party's shadow was huge. I first got there in their absence, but they were incredibly charismatic. Melbourne [had] this atmosphere that someone had done something and gone away, and all these people there who were part of this larger story. It was attractive, full of enigmatic late teenage, early-twenties people who lived out these bohemian dramas.[5]

The new group was named the Moodists, and another single, 'Where the Trees Walk Downhill', was recorded with bassist Steve Carmen, who had been attracted by an advertisement placed in *Juke* for 'someone who likes to play bass guitar. Any age, any sex. Must be able to hum Sister Ray'[6] (though Graney later revealed that 'none of them could do it'[7]). Adelaidean Donald Robertson, writing in *Roadrunner*, claimed there was 'more than a hint of promise displayed on this jangling item of Victorian neo-psychedelia.'[8] Robertson was either being ironic, or ignorant, or referring to the Victorian *era*, since the group were largely fellow South Australians. The song is remarkably fine, as well as an early example of the unique humour of Graney's lyrics – not only do the trees walk downhill they 'hitch a ride to the city'. It was light rock-pop slightly reminiscent of Sekret Sekret. Graney would quickly come to dismiss it, like the Sputniks' record, as 'stilted and strident'.[9]

Chris Walsh was playing with another indie pop group, the Fabulous Marquises, led by Mr. Pierre (who had joined JAB when that band moved to Melbourne, and was soon afterwards the founding bass player in the Models). That group also featured guitarist Edward Clayton-Jones, later to be an important member of Plays With Marionettes, the Bad Seeds and the Wreckery. The Fabulous Marquises released one single – 'Holidays', a terrific example of that rare species, the mournful ditty – and, recognising Walsh's importance, split a week after he quit to join the Moodists.

The Moodists clicked with Walsh, who said in 1983 that he 'was sorta constantly running up to them after they finished playing and saying "Great! Great! You're a great band!"'[10] They had already written 'Gone Dead', which Walsh 'cut all the harmonic bullshit out of'[11] in time for it to be recorded by engineer/producer Victor Van Vugt; Graney later referred to this track as 'the blueprint for everything we've done . . . It's a two chord song, it has a strong flexible rhythm, the vocals and guitars are free to do whatever they like.'[12] The record's sleeve is a distorted polaroid portrait which band members were quick to insist was not a picture of any of them; beginning with a convincing, glam rock screech, the song was a dramatic, eccentric and highly effective announcement of new intent. There was no whimsy here; 'Gone Dead' was in some ways as clipped, relentless and funky as a no-nonsense disco record, Australian independent rock's equivalent of Donna Summer's 'I Feel Love'.

With Walsh, the Moodists developed a modus operandi by which they wrote songs from 'the most minuscule amounts of music you could imagine.'[13] According to Graney, 'I write the lyrics and some chords. The whole band writes all the songs. We do 'em quickly. We don't jam or anything like that.'[14] Clare Moore would later say that 'most of the songs started as a bassline . . . Me and Chris would figure out the rhythm for them, and the guitars were laid on top, and the vocals and lyrics were put on top of that. Generally they started as a bass and drums exercise.'[15] Graney told *Juke's* Christie Eliezer that he liked 'what hits you between your ears or eyes or whatever . . . There's absolutely no art in the Moodists.'[16] He was wrong about that, although what he probably meant by 'art' was 'self-indulgence', in which case he was right.

A mini-album called *Engine Shudder* was their third record for Au Go Go; the songs were all new – and many had been dropped from their live set by the time the record was released. Slightly more spacious, this record boded very well for the Moodists' future, and the group was determined to relocate to the UK. To fill out their sound, they recruited another guitarist, Mick Turner. Turner had played for a long time in the Sick Things (as Mick Sick) with singer Dugald Mackenzie, and more recently had been a member of a group that was much more 'his', Fungus Brains (since 1992 he has been a core member of the Dirty Three). Turner's contributions as guitarist are very noticeable in the Moodists' output during the two years he spent with the band: Graney has described the genesis of the song

'Runaway' as Turner coming 'to the rehearsal with two chords, E minor to C, and he just started playing them, and Mick plays the guitar in a very mysterious very confident sly way and gets a huge sound out of quite minimal movement... Chris was really great at hooking in between simple chords and finding a groove there... I was often acting in an arranger way.[17]

With a British record label interested and an American tour mooted, Graney could afford to be mercurial. He returned to the anti-art theme in an interview during the group's brief return to Australia in 1985:

> What I like about pop is that it's so artless. I know there are people who sell it on the premise that it's experimental, but I couldn't care less... Our music might seem experimental compared to the rest of the top ten – which is so contrived and sweet – but it certainly isn't in the league of, say, Throbbing Gristle. I see the Moodists as just a straight forward [sic] rock & roll band.[18]

The Moodists' live set at this time blended the best of their pop sensibility with the ideal instrumental interplay of Miller, whose guitar lines were fractured and chiming. Miller claimed he never played a song the same way twice; with typical self-deprecation he recast his skill as a failing: 'After years of doing that I sort of thought that might be my style.'[19] Walsh led and contributed the lion's share of the music; Graney sang over and through the instrumentalists, rather than with them, and Moore was and remains one of the country's best drummers, perhaps partly because she is not *just* a drummer but also an adept keyboard player and composer. She had been playing in front of large audiences at an early age: singing nun Sister Janet Mead (see chapter 8) had incorporated the teenage Moore into her band (though Moore did not play on Mead's records).

Although the Moodists were ambitious enough to step on the ladder to international success, they did not appear to have a game plan for their future. Graney claimed they had never 'set out to do anything consciously.'[20] They cultivated a public lifestyle of spending most of their time watching television and drinking beer. When they listened to music, apart from friends' bands, they opted for records that were (according to Graney) 'nothing like the music we played'; old country music, 50s R&B, and rockabilly.[21]

Their two years in Melbourne were not smooth. They did not attract large audiences, although paradoxly they played some major shows in Sydney, including the infamous Sedition festival (see chapter 16). They left for the UK in mid 1983, their British label Red Flame having recrafted *Engine Shudder* to incorporate the preceding 'Gone Dead' single. Red Flame's employees had no compunction selling the group (at least unofficially) as a second Birthday Party: for this, or some other reason, they appeared to disappoint the British. Graney claimed a few years later:

When we arrived in England, we encountered some confusion initially. The same sort of thing happened to the Saints when they first went there. People expected them to look like punks and when they saw them, they got confused. We'd had really great reviews for *Engine Shudder* but when we got there, our appearance, according to their preconceptions, didn't match up with the music we created. I don't know, I thought we actually looked pretty smart![22]

Graney said in 1994 that:

I've never sung any songs like Nick Cave, and I always knew it, so if anyone said it, I would never throw up the table and say "Fuck you!" No, I just knew I didn't. I've never, ever sung songs about little girls. I've never done any blues songs. I've always liked Nick Cave's stuff, he's a very dramatic singer [but] being compared to him was uncalled for. [And] I knew the true story would come out one day.'[23]

Comparisons were specious. The Moodists' musical references, entirely processed and distorted through their own composition process, were from just before rock – largely blues and country. Graney's lyrics were not particularly ethereal; they even contained jokes. In 1985 he said that most of the Moodists' songs were 'about pretty real sort of emotions and stuff':

They're not meant to be vague. I've always thought that the closest band to us was the Go-Betweens. Not the sound, but the fact that they did simple things which anybody could follow and yet they'd get looked at as being really odd because of it.[24]

The first Moodists album, *Thirsty's Calling*, is a disappointment mainly because in some strange way it was really their *second* album: arriving in Britain and given an adequate recording budget, they did not record their best and road-tested songs, merely their newest. Only 'Pure Gold Flesh' – a flashy highlight and a perverse exploration of teen bravado – derived from the band's earlier set. Few of the remaining tracks could match it, though 'Swingy George', 'Runaway' (the single drawn from the album), and 'Frankie's Negative' were superb. Van Vugt's production was epic; he had travelled to the UK with the band, much to their relief, so according to Moore they were assured of his presence 'in the control room making sure the engineer ... didn't fuck up our sound in any way or make us sound like whoever was the popular band at the time'.[25] The Laughing Clowns' Louise Elliot guested on the noir title track. 'Because we started getting a reputation for hard drinking,' Graney said in 1985, 'we had the choice of calling the album *No We Don't Drink*, which would have been a lie, and *Thirsty's Calling*, to play up the joke.'[26]

'The nice thing about England,' he added, 'is that we could play to a lot more people.'[27] The group played in Europe and America too, and found– in comparison to their experience of Australian music venues, at least – that touring was 'cushy'.[28] Walsh has said that the Moodists' career had 'no [puts on affected voice] "OK, what are we going to do next week," or "how do you see your career further down the track"... it was a totally intuitive gut feeling... we worked strictly from that.'[29]

The group had no manager, and while Red Flame were able to offer recording budgets, and had a relationship with the Virgin label (which released Moodists records in Australia at this time), they were not a major-league independent company. The group's dissatisfaction with the label is clear on the sleevenotes to their second mini-LP, *Double Life*, where for instance they note that they 'would have liked the opportunity to mix' the three new tracks included (the material that was released was originally intended to be part of the recordings for a second album).[30] These tracks, incidentally, are amongst their best. Graney has claimed that his songs were informed largely by crime novels from the 30s and 40s, and because of that the songs were 'kind of thrillers'.[31] *Double Life* was the first Moodists record to contain a lyric sheet, but it would have been clear in any case that this was a very wordy, funny and complex set of songs, particularly 'Six Dead Birds', a parody of the music business in the form of a Dashiell Hammett pastiche. Lyrics included the following:

> I hadn't seen any food for quite a while. He handed me a document which I put my name to. It looked good down there. He stuck it up his nose, got up, lay down and said, 'Look I dunno what you do, but you won't be doin' it for anybody else, call me on any one of these.'[32]

When they returned to Australia in late 1984 the Moodists lost Turner, who reformed Fungus Brains in Melbourne. In early 1985 Moore and Graney married, and the group went back to Britain. The single 'Justice and Money Too' was recorded as a one-off for the Creation label; it included Robert McComb singing and Mick Harvey playing piano. Walsh then left, and the group went into a slow but far from obvious metamorphosis into Dave Graney's 'solo' career (in reality, the subsequent career of Graney *and* Moore).

Walsh's replacement was David McClymont, a former member of the Scottish pop group Orange Juice. The Moodists recorded two further singles, for the T.I.M. label. 'Take the Red Carpet Out of Town' was a song that had been composed by the group when it included both Walsh and Turner; a video clip was made, the group's first, notable mainly for its excessive jump cuts and the prominence of McClymont, perhaps because he had been in a hit group less than two years earlier. Louise Elliott again contributed brass arrangement and saxophone; Mark Fitzgibbon, who would work with Graney and Moore in later decades, played piano. Fitzgibbon, and another former Orange Juice member, Malcolm Ross, appear on the final Moodists record, a self-titled 12-inch EP; the standout track was undoubtedly 'Hey Little Gary', which associates of the band believed to be a dig at Garry Gray, Chris Walsh's one-time bandmate in the Negatives (Graney denies this). McClymont is a consummate, melodic pop bass player – he would go on to play on Mick Harvey's two albums of Serge Gainsbourg songs and has recently produced a remarkable amount of music with Nick Currie – but Walsh's absence was tangible here. His ghost is still all over 'Take the Red Carpet', but these last Moodists recordings are closer to Dave Graney and Clare Moore's next record, *Dave Graney with the Coral Snakes at His Stone Beach*, than to anything else the Moodists created.

Graney went on to badmouth the Moodists' work; it was only in the early years of the new millennium that he began to reassess, and he and Moore incorporated some of those songs into their live set. In 2004 the Graney-Miller-Moore-Turner-Walsh line-up reconvened for shows in Sydney and Melbourne ('Three practices and we were right back into it,'[33] according to Walsh), and Miller's label W Minc issued a double CD, *Two Fisted Art*; the first CD compiled 19 of the Moodists' studio recordings, while the second offered a chance for the world to hear the full span of their pre-*Thirsty's Calling* live set. Despite vague suggestions that the group might write new material, these 2004 shows did not include any, though some shows featured a cover of the Scientists' 'We Had Love', on which Kim Salmon guested. The reunion was temporary, as intended.

The Moodists' legacy is hard to define, just as the band itself was a mysterious anomaly. Like many Australian acts before them – the Coloured Balls and X, for instance, were comparable in their unusual single-mindedness and dedication – the Moodists' blinkered determination to be unaware was staggering. This was a group who would talk to each other about anything but what they were doing together musically.

In the early 80s, the band were also seen as groundbreaking because of the presence of Moore – like the Go-Betweens' Lindy Morrison and Cathy Green from X, a female drummer was still a rarity anywhere in the world at this time. Moore and Graney were a couple from early in the Moodists' career, and their partnership, along with Graney and Miller's regional/rural laconic humour, gave the Moodists a slightly archaic, insular feel that was only accentuated by their preference for pre- or early rock 'n' roll music.

In a history of rock 'n' roll in Australia, it is clear that the Moodists represent a cul-de-sac less travelled (though some bands – Melbourne group These Future Kings, for instance – were taken by their sound). Like certain others featured prominently in this story, however, the fact that they can't be slotted into a continuous line of influence is not a reason to leave them out – quite the opposite. There has been nothing like them before or since. That critics so often tried to fit them into the Birthday Party mould is, perhaps, the lie that proves the truth of this. The importance of the Moodists to Australian music of the 1980s is largely to be found in their own work.

16 The Modern Song
THE EARLY TO MID EIGHTIES

There have always been stars in Australian popular music. Sometimes they were commercially successful acts; in other cases they were 'stars' because they made things happen and – such is the nature of human genius and/or foolishness – continued to make great records regardless of the fact there wasn't too much chance many people would hear them. However, the late 1970s and early 80s saw an upsurge in Australian rock and pop previously unmatched in scale and quantity. *Quality*, of course, was not guaranteed.

Sydney group the Numbers (not to be confused with the Brisbane band which changed its name to the Riptides) were a perfect example of crafted, stylish pop genius. They were also the epitome of an Australian band for the 80s, and though their music has not become part of the Australian rock canon of the 90s or beyond in the way that, for instance, the work of the Hoodoo Gurus or Hunters and Collectors has, they were nevertheless highly innovative. They embraced technology while striking a solid deal with the music of their own (still resonant) youth: power pop, glam, and even boogie. They featured a powerful singer, Annalisse Morrow, who also played bass. Her brother Christian wrote most of the group's songs and played guitar. A succession of drummers and other instrumentalists – some of them celebrities in their own right – challenged the conventional idea of the pop group line-up. The Numbers further subverted convention by reinventing themselves in the early 90s as the Maybe Dolls and touching the top forty again. All these things were, if not individually revolutionary, certainly elements of a package that spoke of changes in approach to mainstream success. Always song-based, the group's output is a beautiful example of lean, sculpted writing and production – indeed, they encountered flak for the brevity (less than half an hour) of their first, self-titled album ('You got in and you did your best, economy of everything', says Chris). They responded to this criticism by naming their second album *39.51* (its duration in minutes and seconds).

The routinely changing line-up of the group (eight members, some intended as stop-gaps and others as 'permanent', in a five-year lifespan up to the end of 1983) is testament to the Morrows' attempts to realise a singular vision while dealing with the financial difficulties inherent in being a pop group which only ever charted at the lower reaches of the top forty, and then only infrequently. In artistic terms, however, the Numbers were a resounding success, and if groups like LRB or Men at Work (discussed elsewhere in this chapter) were paving the way for Australian success internationally, the Numbers were developing new notions of what made a band. Chris Morrow's high-quality songwriting and the compact, economical scale of each iteration of the group were key to this.

The Morrows' idyllic childhood in a partially developed suburb ('We grew up playing cricket on the street and racing billy carts down the road', Annalisse recalls) in Thornleigh, in Sydney's north-west, included ad hoc musical experiments supported and encouraged by their parents. Dragon may have sung about Blacktown (perhaps responding to the urgings of CBS's Dennis Handlin and his mythical punter, 'Barry Blacktown'), but the Numbers – who had a song called 'Blacktown', too – knew the place firsthand. They became associated with the Blacktown Music Co-op, located more deeply in the west than their home suburb: the 'true north' northern suburbs of Sydney are typically upper-middle-class, but Thornleigh lies between those and other suburbs considered to be working-class. Chris explored the curious middle/working-class dichotomy of the area in which he grew up on the band's vibrant debut, the independently released single 'Govt. Boy' (the only Numbers A side on which he was the vocalist). In late 1979/early 1980 the group were inducted into the mainstream music world from the upmarket side of their milieu when they encountered high-profile music industry men in a North Sydney wine bar. Chris recalls:

> We had a residency at this place called the Alley Cat wine bar in North Sydney, and around the corner from that was Chris Murphy's. He'd just left Premier booking agency and set up his own agency MMA. He was looking for bands, and it was that kind of golden age of pub rock so there was money to be made just in playing live . . . He came around and saw us play at the Alley Cat, and started booking us. Previous to that we were doing support gigs for Mi-Sex and stuff like that. Michael Browning came back from America after splitting with AC/DC, wanted to start a label, met Chris Murphy, and at that stage we had a residency at the Civic Hotel in the city. Michael Browning came around and saw us and said yeah, he'd sign us.

Browning's Deluxe label would release two albums apiece by two remarkable Australian acts, the Numbers and the Dugites; an important album by one of New Zealand's finest late-70s groups, Toy Love; two great singles by the Voices; an album, *Twilight of Mischief*, by the metal band Heaven, and two albums by the overrated (particularly at this time) INXS. It is probable that the label's releases sold in inverse proportion to their quality.

Browning pushed Annalisse to the fore – it was decided she would now be the singer, rather than Chris; she also continued to play bass on recordings and in most of the live configurations of the group. The Numbers' two hits for Deluxe were the catchy, medium-paced 'Five Letter Word' and the shaggy 'The Modern Song'. 'Five Letter Word' was, readers of *Rolling Stone* may have been surprised to discover, about *two* five-letter words: 'death' and 'Chris'.[1] Chris Morrow now says he felt 'it was pretty obvious that's what the song was about, it's a nihilistic song about death . . . Most people just thought, "Oh isn't that lovely." Just play the record backwards!'

The experience of having a record out on Deluxe, backed by RCA's financial push, was 'exciting and weird', says Annalisse.

> When 'Modern Song' came out, we had great big billboard posters around the city and NSW – and that was the weirdest thing driving down the road and seeing this huge thing of you and your brother and Simon, and you just go, 'Oh my god'. So suddenly it's there, and it's real, and people have huge opinions about whether that was a good idea or not. It was a huge risk to take. Yes, you get all that attention, and although you've been working in the industry a few years before that and developing yourself, the audience and the people who listen to music . . . in the majority of cases it's the first time they've heard or seen you, so suddenly a lot of people are very interested in you, and you're not prepared for that. You want to be successful, and you want as many people as possible to listen to your music, because that's very important to you, but with that comes a whole lot of other things . . . They want to know you personally, and they want to know the band. But it was exciting, and it was great, yeah. And they're going to buy the records and love the music.

Like the Numbers, labelmates the Dugites had formed in 1978, but they were very different in almost every other way. Brian Peacock aided their pursuit of pop success; he'd been managing his own band with Matt Taylor, Western Flyer, in Perth. With industry contacts stretching back fifteen years and his experience road-managing the New Seekers as part of David Joseph's entertainment empire, Peacock was a good fit for a Perth group with some but not all the components for mainstream success. The Dugites' Peter Crosbie visited him in his Fremantle office 'for advice about record deals', Peacock recalls:

> They were getting a lot of interest out of the Eastern states . . . So I started going along to some of their gigs so I could advise them better. And before I knew it, I ended up managing them.

> I think I knew that it didn't really matter where you came from. And I'd allied that to New Zealand, leaving New Zealand. I realised you could stay wherever you came from and you didn't have to run off and uproot yourself from everything you knew.
>
> The rest of the band were all pretty intelligent people, who I got on well with. They had very firm ideas of what they wanted to do and where they wanted to go, which made it easy to work with them. I liked what they wanted to do myself. My management skills, if there were any, always came into play with a genuine admiration for the artist.

Songwriter and keyboard player Peter Crosbie had a Bachelor of Music degree from the University of Western Australia;[2] during an extended trip to Britain in the mid 1970s, he had also written songs with King Crimson's Peter Sinfield.[3] The group were inspired by their singer Lynda Nutter's earlier garage band, which played 60s-girl-group songs such as 'Leader of the Pack'. Nutter and Crosbie were married when the Dugites began, but their personal relationship did not last long into the band's career.[4]

Though the two women projected very differently, Nutter and Annalisse Morrow are both examples of a new type of female 'lead singer' in that they were clearly members of the band, not isolated or separate in some way. Additionally, like many women in bands at this time, Nutter found this to be a necessity. She told *Rolling Stone's* Jacky Hyams: 'I just don't agree with all that pouting and "look at me" . . . I have to be one of the boys – and I'm quite good at that – in order to avoid hassles all the time.'[5]

The Dugites' 'Hit Single' was self-released 'on their first birthday'; for the band it came at 'the end of Phase One', during which they had played in a number of different styles. Their parody of *Countdown* (see chapter 11) notwithstanding, the satirical 'Hit Single' (it declared, for instance, that pop stars never had 'to go to the toilet') marked, for them, the beginning of 'Phase Two'.

Deluxe enlisted Bob Andrews, from Graham Parker and the Rumour, to produce the first (self-titled) Dugites album.[6] Fans of the band were pleased to see Andrews rein in Peter Crosbie's 'overbearing self-indulgence on keyboards';[7] the extended, disco-esque jam on the musically excellent 'Gay Guys' is probably a vestigial example of Crosbie's druthers. This was the first song played on JJJ-FM after it converted from 2JJ into an FM station in 1984 (en route to the next level, national coverage). In retrospect the song's lyrics come across as nastily bitchy and populated with stereotypes, although at the time it seemed refreshingly sardonic. It is also a good example of a male songwriter (Crosbie) utilising a female persona to create a narrator who would, in most people's minds, critique the 'gay guys' in question not from a position of fear or desire, but from one of platonic affection.[8]

Their first single for Deluxe, the buoyant and fresh 'In Your Car' got the Dugites off to a great start, but it was a success which, for reasons that remain unclear, the band seemed unable to build on. After several singles and two albums for Deluxe, they moved to Mercury, for whom they recorded a third album, *Cut the Talking*, with English producer Carey Taylor, who went on to assemble Dragon's immensely successful album *Body and the Beat* and its attendant singles.[9] The Dugites' best song, among many gems, was perhaps the dark, synthesiser-dominated ballad 'Waiting', though the classic pop of 'Juno and Me' was more typical and highly appealing. The group were *Countdown* mainstays and perennially good-natured and a solid proposition live; they struggled, nonetheless, to reach commercial sales heights at the time.

By the mid 80s both the Numbers and the Dugites were gone, and for many forgotten (we will return to them occasionally throughout this chapter). Indeed, one of the many crimes perpetrated by commercial FM radio, whose insidious rise occurred during this period, was the predominance of men's voices in the newly designated category of 'Oz rock'. Chrissy Amphlett (discussed later) and Grace Knight are among the few exceptions.

Knight was the vocalist in Eurogliders, another band which developed under Peacock's aegis – they would be his biggest success and his biggest disappointment. The group was formed by Bernie Lynch and keyboard player Amanda Vincent (previously a bandmate of Bill Rogers) under the name Living Single.[10] Peacock was already managing the Dugites when he met Lynch and Vincent.

> They came and saw me as well. That led to a bit of conflict of interest with the Dugites, but I liked what they were doing too. I explained to the Dugites that I couldn't live on what I made with them. They didn't really have any right to expect me to just manage one artist. If I was going to be doing a good job for them, I could be doing it for another act as well. So I took on Living Single ... That was probably the act out of all them that I really had an absolutely integral part in transforming into a successful national artist. Right from the name. Living Single, while it was clever, I never felt was the name that was going to work for them. So that was the first thing that I had input into changing. I didn't actually come up with or pick Eurogliders, it sort of picked them.
>
> It was interesting that both these Perth-based acts had a common theme ... that both had partner-created nucleuses. Partners that had split up, no less. By the time I came along they'd both split up. And that was a pretty uncanny echo of the New Seekers experience that had taken so much out of me.

('The') Eurogliders would enjoy major success with singer Grace Knight in the mid 80s; they were to become an exemplar of the international capabilities of Australian groups later in the decade, notwithstanding (or perhaps including) their involvement in the payola scandals of the period.

A VEGEMITE SANDWICH

> Who would have thought that a song about chunder and vegemite would get to number one in America?[11]

As suggested above, an 80s sound required a reworking of attitude, inflection, approach, and dynamics when it came to songs, groups and recordings. This was not merely true of the new 'post-punk' groups; it was also the case for many more established (not necessarily older) artists who were forced – by the success of the new wavers, but also by the increase in world attention as Australia became more enmeshed in global markets – to reconsider their approach and output. The early 80s saw, very broadly speaking, a move from flabby boogie towards slicker, sharper sounds and styles. The discomfort this new reality occasioned in certain circles can be detected in studio band the Monitors' 1980 top-ten hit 'Singing in the 80s', whose chorus asks 'What will we be singing in the 80s' (Kim Durant's vocal is lip-synched in the video by the 14-year-old Blakeney twins – later known in Australia as actors – wearing Kiss makeup). At the same time, the 'old wave' was co-opting the new – by way of cheaper equipment including new synthesisers and other high-tech equipment – as comprehensively as it possibly could.

In her review of Mike Rudd and the Heaters' album *The Unrealist*, Elly McDonald described this phenomenon perfectly:

> Listening to output by Renée Geyer, Kevin Borich, Russell Morris and Mike Rudd over the last year or so, a vision arises of the ... old guard, lined up like miscreant school kids in front of a higher authority, being told in no uncertain terms to Get Modern.[12]

In the way it remoulded its established artists at the same time as it fostered the rise of thousands of new ones who were original or interesting to differing degrees, Australia is similar to other western countries that enthusiastically embraced the new wave at this time (most western countries, that is, except the more conservative USA). Older artists do not curl up and die in the face of new movements; and in this case the new movement essentially involved repackaging old ideas and bringing them to the fore.

In Australia, however, the new wave often came with an unusually high level of humour – and potential. In addition to the bands mentioned above, Mental as Anything brought a uniquely Australian timbre to the charts in a way that would previously only have been possible in novelty hits; Australian Crawl appealed across demographics with finely honed tunes and sardonic lyrics; the Laughing Clowns were uniquely innovative, creating a whole new, unprecedented genre; and the Reels threatened the pop charts – making some of the best pop music of the day – while restlessly pursuing unreachable goals. The new groups and the media fed off one another, and the music industry was going through changes.

At the same time, it should be remembered that rollicking ditties such as country stalwart Slim Dusty's 'Duncan' – one of the biggest hits of 1980 – sat side by side with other new releases in the nation's record stores. Part of the record's appeal could be traced to its open-endedness; Dusty could incorporate the names of local characters into a customised rendition of the song, as he did with Molly Meldrum on *Countdown*.[13] Hoary and simple, 'Duncan' was a piece of rollicking Australiana, once heard and never forgotten; like Dusty's 'Pub with No Beer' from two decades earlier, it was a bit of local silliness that could only translate to international markets as a novelty work.

Men at Work, whose peak occurred at the same time as 'Duncan', pushed the Australiana angle a little further. A Melbourne band, until they became the world's property, they were the most impressive Australian commercial success story of the early 80s. In fact, Colin Hay's talents as a songwriter notwithstanding, Men at Work were impressive largely *because* they were such a commercial success. Founded by guitarists Ron Strykert and Hay (who'd had a minor career as a singer-songwriter on the local scene) after the two met working on the stage production *Heroes*, the pub band signed to CBS Australia on the strength of some catchy tunes and a healthy live following to release the LP *Business As Usual* in 1981. Their first single for CBS, 'Who Can It Be Now', was derided (fairly) by Donald Robertson in *Roadrunner* as 'a pretty average rock song';[14] its successor, 'Down Under', was dismissed in the same paper as 'Jethro Marley' for its flute-flavoured ska silliness.[15]

For all that, 'Down Under' was lyrically complex. The group had already recorded and released an earlier version of this mildly parodic series of fables about Australians meeting their countrymen around the world, delivered exuberantly by Hay, as the B side of their independent single 'Keypunch Operator' in 1980. The reworked version was less languid, more streamlined, yet still on the same unlikely topic: Australians around the world recognizing each other and reveling in their Australianness. CBS in America turned down *Business As Usual* twice;[16] once the label finally agreed to release it, it found itself with the biggest debut album in the US since the Monkees. This was an impressive achievement, particularly since while Men at Work could be as catchy as the Monkees, with the exception perhaps of Greg Ham they were in no way *cute*; they were mature, jobbing musicians.

Men at Work sold 15 million records worldwide. Hay was levelheaded about it: 'What we have to offer,' he said in 1983, 'is by no means earth-shatteringly new, and we're not doing anything really that hasn't been heard before in some form.'[17] These words would seem particularly ironic almost three decades later in 2010, when Men at Work were successfully (if farcically) sued by the copyright owner of Marion Sinclair's 'Kookaburra Sits in the Old Gum Tree' – a famous Australian children's song – for incorporating part of the song's tune into Greg Ham's flute line in 'Down Under'. Much more sadly, the lawsuit seems to have led to Ham's suicide; 'I'm terribly disappointed that that's the way I'm going to be remembered', he said when the judgment was handed down, 'for copying something.'[18]

The delays in promoting Men at Work to the top of the charts internationally – particularly in the USA – meant the group's debut was still seen as 'new' (or at least insufficiently milked) when they released the follow-up, *Cargo*.[19] Accentuating the too much they'd had too soon, the best Men at Work song by a mile was the world-weary, vivid 'Overkill', the second single from the second album. All that was good about the group came together here: their strong sense of melody and pop song dynamics, along with Hay's cynical outlook. But the group's success was unsustainable. Hay reasoned their prominence was a 'once in a lifetime situation.'[20] Within two years they were down to a core of three – Hay, Ham, and Strykert – for the recording of *Two Hearts*. Hay later said he had quit by the end of 1983, and indeed he, Ham and Strykert considered taking a new name. Because they decided not to, when the others left Hay ended up as the last man standing in 'Men at Work'.[21] By this point the public hardly cared. Strykert, whose value to the group was particularly high in its early days, quit in disgust and retired, apparently traumatized, to relative obscurity in the US, from where to this day he issues bitter bulletins to the world regarding his former bandmates (he was also jailed, for threatening to kill Hay, in 2007).

Hay battled to shed the stigma of having written (with Strykert) 'Down Under', a satirical song he claimed few understood. Internationally it is seen as a novelty hit that could presumably have been just as successful had it been a collection of clichés about Mexico or Pakistan (except that being about white, rather than indigenous, Australia such a record might delve into the thorny world of racial, rather than cultural, stereotype), its initiation of a worldwide fascination with Vegemite notwithstanding. In Australia, its schticky status as an anthem – of the 'Up there Cazaly' variety – was aided by its constant presence in television coverage of the America's Cup, a boat race which Australia won in 1983. Many who lived through this time, an era of breast-beating patriotism stoked by charismatic Prime Minister Bob Hawke, recall 'Down Under', the America's Cup, and Hawke's laconic pronouncement that any boss who did not give a worker the day off after the victory was a 'bum', as three aspects of the same national celebration.

The importance of Men at Work to the Australian music industry in the 1980s cannot be overstated. In John Bois's account of the Dingoes' (commercial) failure during their mid-70s American sojourn, band members suggest that all Australian groups were destined to be 'Pharlaped' in the USA: like the famous racehorse Phar Lap who died in California in 1932, apparently of poisoning, Australians – however talented or capable – were jinxed. If anyone still clung to this fatalistic belief in the early 80s (which would have required ignoring the international forays of the Seekers, the Bee Gees, AC/DC, Little River Band, and even Joe Dolce's 'Shaddap You Face'), Men at Work's huge American success demonstrated what the possibilities were.

Men at Work were not just an inspiring example, either: just as they had prioritised their Australian market – probably to the detriment of their international career – by insisting on the release of *Cargo* before *Business As Usual* had properly 'peaked' overseas, they offered practical help to Australian groups by inviting them to ride on their coattails. Their support acts on international tours would always be Australian; this of course underlined one of their selling points as an Australian rock group with a hit record about Australia, but it was also an altruistic move – more so than LRB's grudgingly dedicated 'four-lane highway'. It was a time when the makers of Australian pop and rock music in both the commercial and non-commercial spheres were encouraged to see themselves on the world scene.

Colin Hay and Joe Dolce are both (immigrant) Melbournites from diverse backgrounds who emerged from the late 70s alternative pub circuit and went on to have major international hits in the early 80s that brought them a career and an income but not much respect. Dolce's hit, 'Shaddap You Face', was a ditty with novelty appeal that was helped to worldwide success with investment and assistance from Mike Brady. The Ohio-born Dolce was inspired by the cajoling, aggressive language of his Sicilian grandparents to write a song which echoed stereotypes in Australia (and the English-speaking world) of the 'Mediterranean temperament'. Ian Meldrum, in disguise, mimed playing the accordion when Dolce performed the song on *Countdown*. The original version credited to Joe Dolce Music Theatre sold six million copies,[22] as well as creating numerous cover versions in different languages and a version for the UK market by Andrew Sachs ('Manuel' from *Fawlty Towers*). Dolce recounts an exchange he had with Shirley Strachan after Strachan accused him indirectly of being a one-hit wonder; Dolce's response was that one 'phenomenon' was better than 'ten piddly hits like you've had'.[23] Dolce's bitterness – it might also be interpreted simply as self-preservation – has led him to make a number of pronouncements on the validity of the song and the character, 'Giuseppe', he created to perform it. Like Hay and 'Down Under', 'Shaddap You Face' has long since become detached from any intention its author may have had for it, and drifted into a generation's repository of loved/hated relics. However history may judge 'Shaddap You Face' and the songs of Skyhooks – and history tends to regard the first as excruciating, the second as golden magic – they have in common their origins in the Carlton music/theatre scene of the 1970s, as well as the uniquely Australian air of sardonic commentary, now often ignored, that pervades both.

CONTENT DELIVERY

There were a number of ways to explore new music (which included 'New Music', an amorphous term that tried to broaden or fudge the boundaries of the new wave) in the 80s. One way was to read about it. A writer for the university paper *Pelican* summed up the state of the mainstream papers well:

> *Juke* (weekly) used to be rather boring and horribly mainstream, big bucks etc. However, lately it's definitely improved, achieving a wider coverage. Also, it tends

to be well-written . . . *RAM* (fortnightly) is horrible now. It pretends to be more "alternative" than *Juke* but, in fact, it's petty and poorly written. One to avoid . . . *Rolling Stone* (monthly) is a combination of Australian articles and articles and reviews from its parent in the United States. Accordingly, it has all of American *Rolling Stone's* faults, i.e. it's consistently out of date, jaded and plain boring . . . *Roadrunner* (monthly) is probably the best of the Australian mags. The writing is good and its New Wave coverage is excellent.[24]

Juke benefited from using professional writers (often cadets or other journalists from Melbourne daily newspaper *The Age,* whose parent company published it). Australian *Rolling Stone* negotiated – as it still does today, though slightly more successfully – the tricky task of acting countercultural while being entirely dependent on major record company advertising. Adelaide's *Roadrunner* was without doubt a quality publication. Edited and published by Donald Robertson – the survivor from its founding co-operative – the paper attracted a number of important and interesting writers from around the country who recognised it as a valuable forum. *Roadrunner,* whose cover price was similar to that of the imported music magazines such as *NME* and *Melody Maker,* exhibited considerable bravery. It had no qualms about running a five-page exploration by Ross Stapleton of Michael Gudinski's extensive business interests. It also gave invaluable early coverage to new Aboriginal groups such as No Fixed Address, even before they made the classic film *Wrong Side of the Road* – indeed, it put them on its cover. That all of this was achieved from Australia's smallest mainland state capital is testament to the talent and dedication of Robertson and his writers.

Vox was Melbourne's equivalent to *Roadrunner,* although it didn't look as good, had less of a national focus, and often served to cover – if not curry favour with – slightly left-of-centre pop groups such as Hunters and Collectors (band and magazine came to prominence simultaneously) and Models. It was edited by Neil Bradbury, who would go on to operate the White Label, which signed Hunters and Collectors and a number of the other groups he'd very recently been covering in *Vox.* While *Vox* contained much of value, in retrospect it is most useful for tracking the music industry's changing focus of attention from Melbourne to Sydney – which is to say, it illustrates its own increasing irrelevance.

This era also saw the real arrival of the 'street paper'. There had been earlier ventures in this direction, such as *tagg* ('the alternative gig guide'), a pocket-sized, ad-funded fortnightly that published Melbourne and Sydney editions in the first half of the decade. Sydney's *On the Street* emerged in 1983 as a broad-ranging free music weekly, paid for by advertising, and often provided a forum for young or emerging writers to first see their names and opinions in print. This combination of the amateurish and the commercially minded – free, so-called 'street' magazines very rarely bite the advertising hand that feeds them by indulging in even slightly negative comment on artists or other elements of the industry – became the template for similar publications in every major city in Australia throughout the 80s and 90s. *On the Street's* status as beholden to the music industry makes it both useful and frustrating – the magazine's writers were often caught striving to be relevant and 'valid' while being essentially hindered in expressing themselves freely.

In 1984 James Manning – a music writer whose credits ranged from the communist weekly *Tribune* to *RAM* and *Juke* – acquired the license to publish an Australian version of the successful British pop magazine *Smash Hits*, which, like the local *Rolling Stone*, combined entire pages from its parent magazine with pages featuring specifically Australian content. Largely a vehicle for pin-up photos and hit song lyrics ('songwords'), *Smash Hits* nonetheless took an affectionately irreverent attitude to the stars it covered and was humorously cavalier in its approach. It was hated by 'serious' music consumers, and was an overnight success.

Another way of hearing 'about' new releases in pop music was to actually *hear* them – on the radio. Aside from a few television shows, commercial pop music was largely dependent on pop radio, and this medium was about to be shaken up considerably. Owen Johnston's short film *Radio Day*, made in 1982, paints the traditional picture of pop radio's power and process. It opens with a Melbourne family eating breakfast in their kitchen and people driving or traveling on trams to work and school to the sound of Mental as Anything's 'Come Around', Cold Chisel's 'Choir Girl' and Skyhooks' 'Love on the Radio'. The film focuses on the operations of 3XY, the city's prime pop radio station. Programmers are shown discussing the addition of the comedy monologue 'Australiana' by Austen Tayshus to their playlists; a focus group of two young girls choose a track by Choirboys, a Sydney band recently signed to Alberts, to provide a rock and roll counterweight to the station's ballads; the plodding reggae of Australian Crawl's 'Boys Light Up' is also heard. The film is to a certain extent an exposé of the casual and routine nature of pop radio's machinations – unusual given the insidious power of stations like 3XY at this time. Such power would not last out the decade, though, as FM radio took hold, particularly through what became the MMM organisation. This development would have important ramifications for the form and style of popular music, particularly later in the decade, when pop music all but disappeared from the airwaves.

The first Australian commercial FM radio stations were launched in 1980. The non-commercial (though not anti-commercial) station JJ became JJJ FM in January the following year; much of its spoken-word content – comedy, news and other talk – was dropped at this time.[25] Rock was back on TV with a vengeance after lulls in the 70s. Public radio continued to play a formative role far greater than that of commercial FM, which rarely 'broke' any new acts, merely chose from the smorgasbord put before it by public radio and the record companies (who also took a lot of cues from public radio, particularly where 'new music' was concerned, and within very conservative constraints).

As will be seen, rock and pop were also evident everywhere in Australian film, art, literature – and in and even more unlikely environments. This is not to say that anyone other than industry leeches were getting rich, but that should not detract from the scope and quality of much of the music being created at this time. Pop groups of various stripes were able to make commercial inroads – and become known to the mainstream – perhaps because of their adventurousness and diversity, rather than despite it. And that was just the *mainstream*, which is almost always less interesting than the underground. The underground itself in Australia was dazzling.

The late 70s had seen a slowly increasing flow of independent records. The music press, which had become used to considering the mere act of releasing a record as a tilt at the mainstream, found it difficult to get to grips with 'independence' as a broader phenomenon, and the notion that particular groups were comfortable with a low-key 'independent' status was, as always, hard for many to imagine – particularly because many independent records were singles rather than albums (generally for financial reasons), and ever since the early 70s singles had come to be considered as 'pop' (sellout!) rather than 'serious' artifacts. To add to the complexity of the situation, many acts considered their records to be art statements, or treated them as a kind of joke, rather than as genuine attempts to become famous or make money. Since the 1990s when it became relatively easy to burn CDs and market them commercially, and even more since the beginning of the 21st century, in which music can be marketed without needing to exist in any physical format whatsoever, it has become more difficult to keep in mind the status a vinyl record might have actually enjoyed in the 60s, 70s and 80s. At both the independent and the mainstream level, making a record was a commitment. Since almost all records were recorded in studios (unless they were live recordings, which usually still had to be mixed and/or overdubbed in studios and therefore often represented false economy), and printing covers was an additional expense on top of mastering and pressing costs, even a short-run single involved a considerable financial outlay.

There was no way to escape most of these costs except via public radio and, in the late 70s and early 80s, the audio cassette. Studio expenses were usually still involved, but the recorded music could either be kept on a readily accessible 'cartridge' at the station and played on public radio when the opportunity presented itself, or released as cassettes, which could be home-dubbed (tape-to-tape cassette machines were released in affordable models at this time) or duplicated cheaply by commercial or semi-amateur businesses.

Nothing reflects the ebullience of the 'underground' in this era better than *Fast Forward*, a bi-monthly magazine on audio cassette, edited by Bruce Milne and Andrew Maine and designed by Michael Trudgeon, 13 issues of which appeared between November 1980 and October 1982.²⁶ It was one of those innovations that was almost too simply brilliant for anyone to believe it hadn't been done before; there was some discussion of a British forerunner, Bill Furlong's *Audio Arts,* which began in 1973 and which was broadly art-focused.²⁷ Maine and

Milne were RRR presenters who had access to material via the station and Milne's Au Go Go/Missing Link label connections, as well as by the mere fact they were known about town. They had planned to publish a magazine with a flexidisc, until they heard that EMI's standard procedure for disposing of unsold pre-recorded cassettes was to bulk-erase them and sell them. The early *Fast Forwards* had new labels pasted over reused pre-recorded cassettes – the temporary or makeshift nature of them was part of the appeal. Milne told *Rolling Stone's* Andrea Jones in 1981: 'I don't see the music we put down on those tapes as being a permanent document like a record. We hope that people will hear the tape and then go out and see the bands.'²⁸ They also actively encouraged reuse of their tapes.

For a few weeks in the early 1980s the world saw a cassette magazine explosion – for instance, the British pop magazine *Mix,* and the US Pacific Northwest's *Sub Pop* (which alternated cassette and print issues and later evolved into the record label). Meanwhile, in the Pacific south east, Maine and Milne were producing what was effectively a purchasable radio show (not, as some have termed it, a 'compilation album'²⁹ – interviews and other spoken-word material were integral parts of the content). The packaging began as a simple one-sheet, 7-inch-single-size 'cover' in a plastic bag along with the cassette; later issues came in a silkscreened wallet with various leaflets and booklets in its pockets. Trudgeon explained his vision of an alternative to what was 'usually a small, miserably packaged object that has no intrinsic qualities.'³⁰ The most ambitious *Fast Forward* was probably the double issue: two 90-minute cassettes and extra print material. The music on the various *Fast Forwards* was largely of its time and, more often than not, marvelous; many casual purchasers around the world were no doubt first exposed to the Laughing Clowns, the Go-Betweens' demos for *Send Me a Lullaby,* Rowland Howard's 'Shivers' as performed by the Young Charlatans, Pel Mel's 'No Word from China' (the 'demo' recording that launched the Newcastle group on a two-album near-mainstream career), and much more via this miraculous modern periodical. As Jon Stratton has demonstrated, *Fast Forward* was not based on a notion of 'Australian music to the world' – unlike, say, Mark Dodshon's *Big Back Yard* show, which was distributed on CD to non-profit radio stations around the world in the late 80s. Nor was it exclusively Australian in content: it would feature music from anywhere, the main criterion being the editors' taste, with the proviso that it had not (yet) been released on vinyl. Maine and Milne ultimately fell out: Maine went on alone to relaunch *Fast Forward* as *Crowd*, a magazine-with-cassette which became print-only with its second issue and disappeared after the third.

The immediacy of the cassette format accounted for part of its appeal. Performer/producer Ron Rude recorded two songs, 'Cauldron of Rebirth' and 'Houseboat', with his band Piano Piano on Saturday, 19 September 1981. They finished recording by 5 p.m. and had a hundred cassettes ready two hours later; the group played a release show at Seaview Ballroom that night, making them, Rude proclaimed, 'the first rock band in the history of the universe to release their product on the same day as recording it.'[31]

Ideas for magazine-style audio product continued apace: Roger Grierson (formerly of the Thought Criminals) and journalist Stuart Coupe, who together had founded the Green label to release Tactics' album *My Houdini*, announced that they were about to produce '*Green the Magazine*, which is a long-playing record of spoken-word stuff and tapes by unreleased bands. We'd like to do albums of beat poets or anything that interests us as well as rock music.'[32] It didn't happen, but maybe that didn't matter too much; identities and themes were founded on such conceptualisations.

As is probably already clear from the above, the divide between indie and mainstream was great, and only a few could cross it. The early 80s began for many with an unfounded assumption that punk rock had created a Year Zero; key pre-punk figures like Ross Wilson might be tolerated – although barely, by some, and probably not at all by the young who did not fully comprehend or care about his importance – because he had entirely reshaped his image and attitude, while others, like his former bandmate Brian Peacock, were partially acceptable in non-musical roles such as manager to the Dugites, Wa Wa Nee and Eurogliders (except those bands were usually not acceptable to the 'hip crowd' either). Anomalies like Split Enz were able to recast themselves as 'new wave' partly by sleight of hand and partly because they were clearly out of place in the pre-punk era anyway.

THE CLOWNS ARE IN TOWN

There was a sense of momentousness about punk almost immediately, reinforced if not engendered by the clever record industry novelty of producing 'collectible' releases on coloured vinyl and in picture sleeves. By 1980 Radio Birdman, for instance, had the status – in Australia and particularly in Sydney – of something exceptional but long gone. In April 1981, New Race (former Birdman members Deniz Tek, Warwick Gilbert, and Rob Younger, with the addition of the Stooges' Ron Asheton and MC5's Denis Thompson,[33] toured, playing what Tek described as 'mostly Birdman songs, along with some newer stuff' as well as material by Asheton and Thompson's earlier bands.[34] WEA now took the opportunity to issue

Radio Birdman's hitherto unreleased *Living Eyes* album, to the discomfort of Tek and the new band.[35]

The Saints' story was and is more problematic because of Chris Bailey's continued use of the name for a band in which he has been the only constant presence. This has caused irritation in many quarters, peaking perhaps in 1999 with Ian McFarlane's decision in his *Encyclopedia of Australian Rock and Pop* to discuss incarnations of the Saints after Ed Kuepper's departure in the entry for Chris Bailey, rather than as part of the entry for the Saints.[36] After Kuepper, followed by Englishman Algy Ward (who had replaced Kym Bradshaw on bass before the recording of *Eternally Yours*), and lastly Ivor Hay (who returned very briefly in the mid 80s), Bailey claims to have turned the Saints into what he called 'some kind of radical feminist collective'.[37] This kind of absurdist in-joke is typical of his lackadaisical, oblique style; Bailey was perhaps referring to an early 80s line-up which featured Janine Hall on bass, but just as likely he was engaging in surreal satire. Kuepper was less jovial, though possibly also joking, when he mused much later that 'Chris was much happier after I left so he could get on with doing his campy vaudeville act.'[38]

Rumours of Kuepper rejoining the Saints go back as far as late 1981– only two years after he'd quit the band – when *Vox* reported his mooted return for a European tour.[39] He told Christie Eliezer he wasn't going to be asked, 'and I'd probably say no, anyway.'[40] Like Hay, he did return briefly later: he was hired as bass player in 1985 when the Saints toured in support of their successful, ostensibly Percy Grainger-inspired 'rustic'[41] album *A Little Madness to be Free*. Bailey later recalled that in the 80s,

> there was always this talk that Ed and I would get back together and we'd be the geniuses that I could never be or he could never be . . . He came back playing bass . . . because then we could maybe take it one step further. But everyone else in the group thought he was an incredible pig and couldn't stand him . . . Ed demands too much as a person.[42]

Since Bailey was the leader of the group – arguably he *was*, and remains, 'the group' since 1979, reformations including Kuepper and Hay in 2007-9 notwithstanding – this is a rather disingenuous explanation.

Other well-known 'alternative' stars – such as Tracy Pew, in his only major musical foray after the Birthday Party (he died in 1987) – had also played in the latter-day Saints the year before Kuepper toured with them. Pew appears in the video for one of their best singles, 'Ghost Ships', though he did not play on the record. Louise Elliott and Jeff Wegener of the Laughing Clowns were also briefly members in early 1985,[43] as was guitarist Richard Burgman, once of the Sunnyboys (who are discussed elsewhere in this chapter). Burgman says that line-up was 'in my humble opinion . . . one of the best line-ups Bailey ever had';[44] a version of this band recorded *All Fools Day* in 1986. Since that time, Bailey's Saints have tended not to trouble the Australian market – except for the minor hits 'Ghost Ships' and 'Just Like Fire Would' (which was covered, incidentally, by Bruce Springsteen in 2013) and a slot on the 1986/87 Australian Made tour – and he has made the Netherlands his home.

Since the original Saints split, Bailey has made some great records – the 2012 Saints album *King of the Sun* was one of the best releases of that year – but his work became, with some exceptions and in the nicest possible way, more craft than art. It was Kuepper who genuinely progressed after the Saints, making an extraordinary move into new territory. The Laughing Clowns, like the Saints in the mid to late 70s, played fresh, exotic, sensational music; their work between 1980 and 1985 is nothing short of spectacular.

Kuepper has said of the Saints-Laughing Clowns connection that 'if you listen to the first album, and then listen to the second... by the time you get [to] the third one, you kind of see a line developing towards the Laughing Clowns' first album';[45] indeed, in its later years the group would perform a version of 'Swing for the Crime' from *Prehistoric Sounds*. As early as 1979, Kuepper told Jane Matheson that the Laughing Clowns were, musically speaking, 'a worthy extension of the Saints' third album.'[46] That said, the Laughing Clowns' line-up resulted from relationships formed outside Kuepper's influence, even if they were within his orbit. Jeff Wegener had been an early Saints associate and moved from Brisbane to Melbourne in the late 70s to play in the Young Charlatans alongside Rowland Howard, Ollie Olsen and Janine Hall; when that band dissolved very quickly, he became involved in the Last Words and another short-lived group, the Love, which featured Ben Wallace-Crabbe, son of prominent Australian poet Chris Wallace-Crabbe. On Wegener's advice, Wallace-Crabbe hitchhiked to Brisbane to meet Kuepper.[47] Bob Farrell, another old friend of Kuepper's and a Saints insider, went to Brisbane from Sydney at the same time as Wegener 'in the hope of getting involved in Kuepper's next project';[48] the two met up at an informal welcome home party Bailey's sister threw for Kuepper. The new group played their first show five months later at the Local Inn, in the middle-ring Sydney suburb of North Ryde. They played a small amount of *Prehistoric Sounds*-era Saints material and the unrecorded Saints song 'The Laughing Clowns', which had come into being during the breakdown of the Kuepper-Bailey partnership. When it came to determining the Laughing Clowns' set, Kuepper believed the inclusion of well-known Saints songs 'would have been restrictive.'[49] He joked to *RAM's* Andrew McMillan that 'the real aim is to get back to England and record three albums'[50] – that is, to repeat the Saints all over again.

A quarter of a century after founding the Laughing Clowns, Kuepper suggested that his primary inspirations for the new group had been Archie Shepp, Tony Bennett's *The Beat of My Heart* album, the Walker Brothers and Jim Webb.[51] It was a moody, unusual and sensuous blend, some of it hovering just on the edge of pop. The Laughing Clowns' instruments, experimentalist outlook, and arguably even their slightly retro, slightly avant-garde sleeve designs, made people search for a term to describe them that included the word 'jazz' but was not 'jazz-rock' (because that was taboo and implied something laidback, pompous and self-indulgent). Kuepper demurred: 'We're not a bunch of crusaders taking the jazz message to the world, it's a fairly individual statement the band is trying to make.'[52]

Wegener suggested that the group's Australian location helped its members feel comfortable with a wide range of musics around the world, past and present, but he saw no need to 'tap in' to 'what was happening'. Australia's cultural diversity meant, for Wegener, that

> if you want to go out and listen to all this stuff that's really exhilarating, you can, and I find it really strange that because that accessibility is there for people, the less they are interested in it and they just produce bland stuff that doesn't say anything... a lot of rock groups actually just draw on what's been done a couple of months before.[53]

Towards the end of the group's life Kuepper mused that he had 'only ever wanted the Laughing Clowns to be a rock band,' and he had 'no real desire to be complex,' adding that he and his colleagues were 'not the sort of group that copies anything. We've always endeavoured to create our own identity.'[54] In that, they were successful.

Kuepper told Tracee Hutchison in 1992:

> I remember when we [Clowns] started playing there was hysteria, both positive and negative, because we were seen by some people as being a bit of a travesty. We were sort of traitors to the cause of punk rock... We were playing songs slowly, we had a saxophone in the band and things like that. It was kind of amusing. When the Clowns first started playing in 1979, the third Saints album, *Prehistoric Sounds*, hadn't been released in Australia, even though it had been out for a year in England, so I think most people found the leap from the first two albums to the first Clowns record a little bit too great.[55]

Kuepper is wrong to suggest that *Prehistoric Sounds* was not known to the Clowns' audience: it was available on import, and had received airplay on public radio. But the Laughing Clowns were difficult in other ways, too. The group had an unexpectedly stylish appearance, particularly the dapper Wegener, whose well-cut suits more than adequately befitted one of the most accomplished drummers of any early 80s rock band. More to the point, Kuepper's dry, droll lyrics (and voice) were not easily categorised.

After just over a year of existence came the first of a series of impeccable records, a self-titled six-track 12-inch on Missing Link. Transcending musical fashion, the Laughing Clowns played passionate, sophisticated, difficult yet compelling music.

'The Laughing Clowns' – the song – was surely *about* the Saints, both as visceral, showstopping entertainment and as a sad joke. Yet with the Laughing Clowns, Kuepper, Wegener and their colleagues had manifestly created a whole new musical style. There were kindred spirits around the world – the Contortions in New York, Essential Logic in London; but the group's sound was its own.

Five months after *The Laughing Clowns*, the group released a three-track 7-inch, *Sometimes the Fire Dance*, on their own label, Prince Melon, which Kuepper initially touted as 'totally controlled by the band... we keep our eyes and ears open for new talent.'[56] The label also released singles by Ollie Olsen and John Murphy's band Hugo Klang ('Grand Life for Fools and Idiots') and Peter Walsh's group Out of Nowhere ('No Resistance').

The Laughing Clowns' 'Sometimes (I Can't Live with Anyone)', an upbeat if misanthropic pop song, was the group's first real cult hit. If they were reviled, as Kuepper has claimed, they were also celebrated, even in song – the Go-Betweens' Robert Forster wrote 'The Clowns Are in Town' during his last days in Brisbane, before his own band moved to Melbourne en route to the UK.

By the end of 1980 the Laughing Clowns had suffered their first major line-up changes. Peter Doyle joined on trumpet, but Ben Wallace-Crabbe, whose funky bass had been so integral to the first two records, his pianist cousin Dan Wallace-Crabbe, who had joined early in the year, and saxophonist Farrell were all gone. Farrell was soon replaced by Louise Elliott (who, like Wegener – and, of course, Kuepper – would be present for the rest of the band's life), and Ben Wallace-Crabbe by Leslie Millar. The old line-up's last product was a mini-album called *3*, which featured another signature track, the paranoid-depressive 'Collapse Board'. The mere title of a parody of this song – 'Diving Board' by the Maudlin Intellectuals – on the Melbourne *Cults on C90* cassette gives some indication of how the Laughing Clowns were perceived by some. 'We laughed ourselves silly over that one', Kuepper dryly informed *Roadrunner's* Toby Cluechaz.[57] Yet even this was affectionate satire of a group that few could fault. *3* was later combined with the second release to make the group's first 'full' album, the sardonically titled *Reign of Terror/Throne of Blood*.

On seeing the Laughing Clowns play a show with the Tablewaiters and Sardine V in early 1982, *Roadrunner's* Linda Campbell wrote:

> Responding happily to an entranced audience, they literally blew into a set of searingly emotive sounds. Sax and trumpet dominated with a magnificent

brittleness; pushed, pulled and driven up, over, the blistering minefield of crackling guitar, bottomless trenches of the relentless power spilling pulse of drums, and electric stupor of a soaking double bass. And yet the shades are subtle, rising, falling, negative and positive meeting, clashing, spurring the intricacy of the spontaneous.[58]

Their *Mr Uddich Smuddich Goes to Town* was probably their most realised and consistent, yet difficult album: 'a blossom born out of five minds realizing precisely at the same time a common intent and achieving it via subjective intuition', as Craig N. Pearce put it.[59] Like the best Saints album, *Prehistoric Sounds*, it received limited release and attention at the time it was issued, and was difficult to find soon afterwards. Indeed, it was largely forgotten. The album's title, Kuepper said in 1982, 'has some significance but I wouldn't like to go into any detail',[60] though he flummoxed *Sounds* host Donnie Sutherland by asserting in a rare television appearance that the LP's name was entirely meaningless: 'just a name'. Another great pop song – the frenetic 'Theme from Mad Flies, Mad Flies' – was included on the album and even released as a single. The group relocated to Europe for a year and a half, enduring what Kuepper referred to as 'tours organised by the Marquis de Sade'[61]; during this period Elliott also played with a London-based high-life band – 'in order to stay alive', she said at the time.[62]

The Laughing Clowns recorded a John Peel session, tracks from which appeared soon after on a 12" EP on Prince Melon entitled *Everything That Flies*. An EP of the same name, but with different tracks, appeared in Britain. A British compilation album, *Laughter Round the Table*, was also produced. The rehashing of tracks on various Laughing Clowns releases would continue beyond the group's lifespan, consistent with Kuepper's own continual reconfiguring of recordings released under his own name.

Millar left, and two Brisbaneites sharing a flat in New York, Robert Vickers and Peter Walsh, got calls at the same time to aid old friends in London. They'd been playing together in Vickers's New York band the Colors, but Vickers would join the Go-Betweens, making them a quartet, and Walsh, hitherto a guitarist, replaced Millar as bassist in the Laughing Clowns. Two years after heeding the call, Walsh said:

> It was a job in one sense, in that the original proposal from Ed was purely on a tour basis . . . he rang me up and said they'd broken up, come over and do a European tour and an Australian tour and at that point I thought, 'I'll do those tours and then go back to New York.' But then we recorded an album while I was out here. And then we did a European tour. And then I thought I'd like to play the songs I played on the album live, because we came out here doing all material that no-one had ever heard before.[63]

Kuepper was the only songwriter for the Laughing Clowns (aside from the group composition 'Mister Uddich Smuddich . . .'); like many other passionate and intelligent creative people, he was rumoured to be difficult to work with. 'I suppose', he said in 1982, 'I'm a tyrant.'[64] One of the best later Laughing Clowns songs was the self-parodying 'New Bully in the Town'. Yet Walsh, not long after he left the group in 1984, insisted it functioned democratically. 'Both Jeffrey and LouLou are fairly assertive because it's their future. And they drive the material. The guts of the material's there, and the signature is a shared one. They've got strong identities – strong musical identities. It hangs to a certain extent on the songwriter because if there's no songs – what are they going to do?'[65]

The end was near (in fact, it had already come at least once, when the UK line-up of the band split, Kuepper has since said that '*Law of Nature* was almost not a Clowns record').[66] Kuepper considered a version of the band in which keyboards would replace brass;[67] he didn't act on this idea, but it presaged aspects of his solo career. In the group's concluding months, the Laughing Clowns became more accessible. Kuepper created one of his most resilient songs (and another pop classic), the searing single 'Eternally Yours'. The song's title was yet another Saints reference, re-using the name of that group's second album, though it was apparently a new composition. It included superb saxophone from Elliott (originally a Hammond organ line) and was accompanied by an amusing/amused video featuring a stop-frame animation of a desk lamp a decade before Pixar used the same device. The song slotted well into the more conventional album *Law of Nature*. New bassist Paul Smith replaced Walsh and Elliott's saxophone was augmented by Glad Reed and Dianne Spence on trombone and saxophone respectively. This line-up was a tight, cohesive unit in performance, though reputedly heroin use amongst some (not all) members was causing significant problems within the band. The Clowns split before *Ghosts of an Ideal Wife* was released in early 1985; this album featured not only an unrecorded pre-Saints Kuepper song, 'Winter's Way', but also a driving and magnificent title track.

Like many a dizzyingly repetitive and powerful pop song, the group elected to end this last track with a scalpel cut to the master tape; the band itself was similarly snipped off in its prime. Kuepper later said, 'I think the Clowns were out of sync with what was going on . . . I just wished I'd killed it earlier.'[68] The group's manager in its later years, Ken West, was also of the opinion that Kuepper's paranoid desire for control and what West believed was the band leader's inability to sing, were also important.[69] In fact Kuepper's voice is a remarkable and distinctive instrument, unlike anyone else's; it is also uniquely Australian.

Immediately after the Laughing Clowns' demise, Wegener, Elliott and Smith formed a short-lived rockabilly group, the Tapdancers, with Canberra singer Peter Blakely, then on the brink of a major if brief pop career. The volatile Wegener retreated into drug dependency. He was later jailed, but he and Kuepper successfully rekindled their partnership twenty years later. Elliott moved to London, played on a Moodists single, and in the mid 90s was working with Tactics' Dave Studdert.

Kuepper initially discussed ('over the kitchen table', he says) the formation of a new group with singer/pianist Louis Tillett and Penny Ikinger from the Wet Taxis, plus drummer Louis Burdett. 'In the new group,' Clinton Walker told *Rolling Stone* readers, 'Tillett will sing and play piano, Kuepper will play guitar and definitely not sing, and the pair will collaborate to write songs, in a projected rocky vein.'[70] This did not happen; Kuepper very quickly launched himself on a dedicated – and very successful – solo career.

While the Laughing Clowns were unusually good, they did not exist in a vacuum: Peter Walsh's post- (and pre-) Apartments group Out of Nowhere; Wildlife Documentaries, former Saints drummer Ivor Hay's band with the songwriting anthropologist (!) Howard Cairns;[71] and Ben Wallace-Crabbe's underrated, low-key outfit Upside Down House formed a coterie of related Sydney-based bands with some similarities in sound and approach. In Melbourne, Equal Local and various associated groups featuring double bass, brass and keyboards shared some of the same reference points. The exceptionally impressive Lindy Morrison (Zero, the Go-Betweens, and later Cleopatra Wong) and the masterful Jim White (People with Chairs up their Noses, Venom P. Stinger, the Dirty Three and numerous others) have both cited Wegener as an inspiration, as indeed his work would be to any drummer. Not only were the Laughing Clowns not forgotten; their work played a formative role in the future development of Australian popular music.

SEDITION

In early 1983 the new wave had its grand festival, which was a declaration of intent as well as an optimistic attempt to showcase what tended to be wrapped up in a bag labeled 'new music' – meaning, in others' eyes, arty and angular independent rock. Sedition was a 'three day independent music festival at the Sydney Trade Union Club' and declared itself to be 'an attempt to overcome the prejudices associated with inner city music.' Writer Mark Mordue reported it as:

> An attempt to burst a few bubbles, shake up some of the illusions that box it in as a closed, elitist fashion scene centred around music that is indigestible or of no interest to anyone else ... Sedition was an idea, a word, an act of revolt against some of the governing xenophobia we've just been talking about ... Peter Scammell (Go Broke Promotions) and Graeme Regan (Hot) with publicity push from Virginia Moncrieff – JJJ, performances/mixed media on 2nd floor; inc. Enmore Music Collective; video bank – Built In Ghosts.[72]

The bands present were a credible selection: the Celibate Rifles, the Scientists, Bring Phillip, the Same, Upside Down House, Kill the King, the Moodists, Hugo

Klang, Sound System One ('soon to change their name to Transworld Death Corporation'), the Benders and Great White Noise.[73] The event was, from all reports, a great success.

David Wall, writing in *Juke*, reported that 'the only band appearing ... that evoked that perpetually rediscovered newness of music was Hugo Klang; it is of no small significance that they were the band which 90% of the audience walked out on ... here's to newness.'[74] Wall's withering take on the Sedition audience's resistance to 'newness' is a testament to the speed of change at the time, but his praise of Hugo Klang showed excellent taste. The Laughing Clowns' international appeal was even more limited than their appeal to 'alternative' music fans in Australia, a fact related to the difficulty journalists had in pigeonholing them. As Australian legends in London (that is, with a status amongst a select Australian expatriate contingent, though none elsewhere), Hugo Klang played their first shows there supporting the Birthday Party – to 'dismally small' crowds, according to *RAM's* British correspondent at the time, Marie Ryan, who added that 'Hugo Klang songs are a complex mesh of discordant interpolations.'[75] It is worth noting that although the Young Charlatans themselves meant almost nothing to anyone in Melbourne in the late 70s, connections made in that band continued long into the 80s.

Murphy had an obscure pre-punk history but would become a legend in late 70s Melbourne and 80s Sydney with various edgy and anti-mainstream rock bands; he appears in two roles (acting and musical) in *Dogs in Space*, his own minor celebrity taking on a life of its own. In the early 80s in London he had a growing cachet as the drummer in the Associates during that Scottish pop band's most productive and entertaining period, when they recorded the singles compiled on what is probably their best album, *Fourth Drawer Down*.[76] Murphy was also asked to play with Matt Johnson's well-known and respected angsty pop group The The. Murphy gave the impression that these 'edgy' British acts were merely his bread and butter; he and Olsen entertained thoughts of releasing material on a new label, Code Information Systems, including 'a piece of music by Harry Zantey' (onetime guitarist in Crime and the City Solution) and some older Hugo Klang demos and rehearsal tapes.[77] When Olsen needed money, he would turn to the Norwegian fishing industry; he was able to work in that country due to his family background. The 'patriality' or work/citizenship status of Australians abroad at this time was often a significant issue; until the rules were changed in 1983, patriality (that is, having a British spouse, parents, or grandparents) gave Anglo-Australians "right of abode" in the UK. As squalid and dismal as Britain was in the early 80s (as the Moodists' Steve Miller rightly and disdainfully pointed out just before relocating there, television still shut down at midnight) the chance to reach large audiences – particularly in continental Europe – and the opportunity to record more cheaply, for longer, and in larger studios, and to be released on British or European labels with some distribution clout, were all drawcards. Once groups such as the Moodists, Scientists, Triffids, Go-Betweens, Birthday Party, and Crime and the

City Solution found touring possibilities in Europe, it was possible for them to make sufficient money to survive, more profitably if not wholly, from making music. There was also a support network of Australian expatriates. This was what it took for Australian groups at the less mainstream end of the spectrum to build an international 'profile', which may also have included trips across the Atlantic to North America, at least to the East coast.

Yet Australian groups were also very eager to deride Britain, in part for its cultural attitudes to its former colonies, as well as its fashion trends. Such attitudes can be discounted as bet-hedging on the part of resident Australian acts who might, at some stage, be persuaded to try and expand to an international audience, but who (like most) would probably not find lasting success, or any success at all; they were also a manifestation of the new patriotism of the times. In addition, they were, for many, justifiable and heartfelt: the live scene in London, for instance, wasn't a patch on that of any of the Australian capitals. Matt Moffitt, the dashing guitarist whose guitar-pop group Matt Finish were a popular signing to Peter Dawkins's Giant Recording Company label, summed up the prevailing view when he told Jenny Eather in a 1981 interview:

> Talk to anyone like Armiger who's been across there and they'll say it's fucked. You can't wait to get back here – like the Oils. We were round at Rob's and he was saying that they were going to do Reading [play at the Reading Festival] but they wanted to come back... Bands like Spandau Ballet, Visage – they have no relevance to Australia ... Their country is over 2000 years old, the cities are overcrowded. It's shitty weather, nobody's got any money. Dressing up is probably a good way to forget you've got no bread and butter. It's got nothing to do with Australia and anyone who walks around in a kilt is just a fucking idiot really. We've got our own bands ... a different climate, different people.[78]

'Armiger' is, of course, Martin Armiger of the Sports, and 'Rob' is Rob Hirst of Midnight Oil – two groups who made sure of management and industry connections before venturing into other territories. When they did so, it was in part merely because the alternative was to do one more tour of Australia, on a limited circuit, to diminishing audiences.

The Laughing Clowns' European forays, and the problems Australian groups as a whole experienced in the 1980s – balancing a local audience while fostering a global one – were the subject of a short discussion between Ed Kuepper, Louise Elliott, Donnie Sutherland and the Dugites' Lynda Nutter on Sutherland's laid-back, late-night, Sydney music show *After Dark* in early 1984:

> Sutherland (to Nutter): Darling, when are you going to take your band overseas?
> Nutter: As soon as our record company releases a record there and makes it worthwhile.

Sutherland: You wouldn't like to trot over . . .
Nutter: I don't think I could handle it.
Sutherland: It would be fairly uncertain . . .
Elliott: We've become experts on international desperate living.
Nutter: That's the thing about it, the desperateness of it. I just couldn't imagine myself starting at the bottom completely all over again. I don't think I'd have that much energy.
Kuepper: We thrive on challenge.
Elliott: Anything. As long as I don't have to carry out the P.A.
Nutter: (to Elliott) Did you used to have to? I did.
Kuepper: I insist on it.
Nutter: It was only a Peavey 400. Little six-channel one.[79]

A few chose to *begin* their careers overseas, two examples being Jim Thirlwell and Dead Can Dance. Thirlwell, who grew up in the middle-class Melbourne suburb of Camberwell, arrived in London in 1978, apparently having produced no music before that time. His records usually emerged under variations of the 'Foetus' name, notably You've Got Foetus on your Breath and Foetus under Glass. He played everything on his early, self-released recordings, joking many years later that he was like a latter-day Todd Rundgren;[80] he soon gathered a strong following in certain circles. Dead Can Dance, essentially the duo of Lisa Gerrard and former New Zealand punk rocker Brendan Perry, claimed in press releases many years later that they had only ever played one show in Melbourne, where they formed, before decamping to Britain; in fact, it appears there were more than a few. Be that as it may, the group certainly had almost no profile in Australia before they left in 1982. A rare review from this time, by Robert Lewis, captures their early sound and style – something that might have been described as 'goth' or even 'emo', had those terms existed at the time:

> Dead Can Dance hit the audience with an aural avalanche. Look out below! Watch your ears! Their horror show music and stage appearance has a power to disturb which I haven't encountered for quite a while. Somebody said to me, they were a partial Cure ripoff. No way. They're in separate worlds. The sonic violence of the Dead Can Dance is however bearable within certain limits. Meaning that not everyone's going to like them.[81]

A third approach was demonstrated by Tactics, who were unable to muster the energy, free themselves from rampant drug-taking, and overcome the setbacks inherent in group line-up changes to venture overseas; it appears that most of them were, in any case, not that fussed. The group's founder and leader, Dave Studdert, was a true original, and Tactics were an acquired taste, but even their strongest detractors could not deny that they had a unique approach (and they received support from unexpected quarters: Icehouse's Iva Davies, for instance, a star for the 80s from entirely the other end of the pop music spectrum, felt the group were 'always ... potentially excellent').[82] Formed in Canberra, Tactics briefly featured Steve Kilbey in an early line-up, but Kilbey and Studdert didn't get on (their association deserves the same kind of attention as Peter Walsh's two-week tenure with the Go-Betweens – mildly interesting but as irrelevant to subsequent work as if they had once shared a bottle of riesling at a party). Acquiring a manager in Marie Ryan, who had seen them play at Australian National University's union building, Tactics relocated to Sydney in the late 70s. In yet another example of the networking available at this time, Ryan, who had worked at public radio station 2XX in Canberra, obtained employment at JJ.

Tactics were a new-wave band because they were an unusual, guitar-oriented band with frenetic, intelligent and funny songs who existed around the time that 'new wave' was happening. But they could as easily have come together at any time. One of Studdert's musical passions was the American group Love, and he traced their 'juxtapositioning' against his own for *Roadrunner's* Tyrone Flex:

> Love were an incredible mixture of styles. The originality came from the juxtapositioning. They'd set off guitars against Tijuana brass, and I really like that Spanish thing. It's like, in LA, you see Spanish haciendas sitting in the middle of nowhere, and here you got haciendas sitting in the middle of an A V Jennings estate. It's got a similar feel ... In Australia, there's always this element of selfconsciousness in what we do. Love reminded me a lot of what life's like in the suburbs ... All we try and do is play exactly how we are.[83]

He was passionate that Australian bands should reflect the world around them in the present day. He told *RAM* writer Julia de Meyrick:

> What I like about the scene in Sydney is that there are actually *some* bands who are trying to write about how people feel in Australia in 1979, without singing about swagmen and shit like that. Trying to help other bands, trying to write about the future instead of playing out this great image role ... The Thought Criminals do it, Voigt used to do it, XL Capris, the Products do it ... I think it's the *bounden duty* of every Australian band – it's totally incomprehensible to me why people would want to write songs about anything else.[84]

The name Tactics appealed to Studdert because, he claimed, 'it didn't have any connotations . . .We didn't want to get put into any bags, boxes, plots – as in graves.'[85] However, the name could also have been seen as a play on Tic Tacs, the breath-freshening mint drops, as well as fitting well with the late 70s/early 80s practice of applying names entirely unrelated to music – names which would seem more appropriate in the titles of books on social theory – to rock bands. Studdert was not strident, though he was shifty. He told *Vox*'s Paul Merrick that groups who sang about the working class were 'mostly . . . middle class', whereas 'people sitting in the housing commissions they have something to be depressed about and I bet the last thing they want to hear is a song about depression . . . it's petty fascism.'[86]

The group's uncommercial nature was deliberate and unfixable, though many of their songs were very catchy. Like Ed Kuepper, Studdert was often criticised for his singing style. Merrick probably spoke for many when he lamented in 1981: 'I do wish he would occasionally use another octave to work in instead of the rasping parrot approach';[87] *RAM*'s Julia de Meyrick described Studdert's singing as 'like an empty 44-gallon drum being dragged across concrete';[88] *Roadrunner*'s Tyrone Flex used the term 'wailing banshee'.[89] Marie Ryan feels that 'Dave's voice was diabolical', but that 'they were doing something different'. However Studdert's voice was perceived at the time, early Tactics records are not grating; they're permanently exhilarating.

Tactics released some singles on their own Folding Chair label, then produced two albums for Green via the folk label Larrikin and EMI. The Larrikin connection emphasised the band's uniqueness, as though they were apart from other post-punk bands – which they were. As John Encarnacao later put it, Studdert had 'his own essentially Australian musical language.'[90] Their first album, *My Houdini*, begins with a poorly-recorded snatch from the 60s American TV series *Get Smart*, segueing into the jerky 'New York Reel'; a dip of the lid to trash culture not unlike X's imaginative morphing of one of their songs into the theme tune to *Batman*. Studdert later said that the originality of the first album was 'due to my ignorance and stupidity.'[91] Yet *My Houdini* was an album as manifestly original and brilliant as Pip Proud's *Adreniline and Richard* or Megan Sue Hicks's *Maranatha*. The follow-up, *Glebe* (named for what was then a down-at-heel suburb of Sydney) was even more glorious, a rich cavalcade and probably Studdert's finest moment to date, though the short time available to them in which to mix it was clearly a problem for many; the production problems were not rectified until a 2006 reissue. Plainly – despite the patronage of hotshot manager and longtime supporter Roger Grierson – the band were penniless; immediately after the recording of *Glebe*, Studdert got a job cleaning the naval warship HMAS Platypus.[92] Their later career was even shakier; a third Larrikin album, *The Bones of Barry Harrison*, sounded the death knell for their relationship with that label; it consisted of live material of varying recording quality. By the late 80s Tactics had briefly fruitful relationships with two of Sydney's best record labels, Waterfront (which released the single 'Fat Man') and Citadel (which put out the album *Blue and White Future Whale*). Studdert's vocals were now often less to the fore, and the group opted for joint vocalising and an agreeable, non-confrontational ambling pop sound; they often used a trumpet to drive the tunes and provide the hooks. Recordings from this era surfaced on a British compilation album, *Holden Interview*. Their swansong was *The Great Gusto*; Grierson facilitated a mainstream release on Regular and even a couple of excellent singles. There was, however, insufficient interest. Tactics' last incarnation was a ridiculous funky abomination, which fortunately never recorded. Studdert removed himself to Britain where he recorded a couple of albums with a new band, Mumbo Jumbo, but otherwise did not make a great musical impact. A briefly revived Tactics toured Australia in 2010.

HAUNTED, HUNTED, HOUNDED

One of the impressive aspects of Tactics' public persona was their refusal to pretend the Australian rock industry, or even merely its independent sector, was one big happy family. They often dismissed other groups with withering put-downs. A number of standout bands from the 80s – the Moodists were definitely another – took this tack. One target of Tactics' ire was Hunters and Collectors, who in their early days dressed above the height of current fashion, as Tactics' drummer Bob Whittle discovered. He told *Roadrunner's* reporter Tyrone Flex:

> They were quite friendly, but they were all dressed up in their 'new romantic' clothes and it was a very 'eye-make-up-hair-set-done-before-going-on-stage' kind o' thing, and I'm sure they looked at us and thought 'Oh, Fuck!' . . . I mean I walked in with my blue ocker singlet on and they found this a bit hard to take. The whole attitude's quite ridiculous. For us, it's mainly the music, for them it's mainly the image.'[93]

Dave Studdert's response in the same interview was that the group were 'just repressed Victorians'.[94] What is remarkable about this is that 'ocker singlets', along with flannel shirts, are exactly what Hunters and Collectors would soon become famous for. They would also go on to make the kind of solid, determinedly Australian(ist) statement that Tactics were unable to get across to the populace.

Mark Seymour and his brother Nick (later of Plays With Marionettes and Crowded House) were the sons of schoolteachers; Mark was also briefly a schoolteacher himself.[95] The Seymour brothers and their two sisters travelled through rural Australia as children, performing as the Seymour Family Singers, but Mark – clearly the intellectual brother; Nick was artier – was resolutely inner-city Melbourne by the late 70s, when he and other future members of Hunters and Collectors (Doug Falconer, Robert Miles, John Archer, and Ray Tosti-Gueira) formed the Jetsonnes, with Margot O'Neill on vocals. The group's song 'Newspaper' was released on a split single with the International Exiles in 1980, and a well-loved joke sub-instrumental, 'Brian Wears Lipstick', was placed on 'cart' (in-studio cartridge) at 3RRR. 'Newspaper' contains all the germs of H&C with a bit more pop. Seymour thought the Jetsonnes were 'dinky';[96] the group split in September 1980 and O'Neill went on to become a prominent journalist. The remaining Jetsonnes reconsidered; Mark formed a short-lived band with Nick, then began to write new material with Geoff Crosby, a core early member of Hunters and Collectors who had not been a Jetsonne.[97]

The new group created a buzz immediately, even before anyone had seen them play. Their supergroup status is clear from the fact that one of the earliest shows they played (if not the first), on 15 May 1981,[98] was a fundraiser to collect money for Snakefinger's medical costs.[99] Which is to say, from the outset they were a money-making attraction in their own right. (Snakefinger's abortive tour – the legendary San Francisco guitarist had played one show at the University of Melbourne and then collapsed after a heart attack – essentially spelled the end of the Missing Link label, which had funded his trip; together with the Birthday Party's studio excesses later in the year while recording *Junkyard*, the label had bitten off more than it could chew.)

Hunters and Collectors were initially a large, funky group; this led to them being paired in some people's minds with short-lived British new wave/new romantic/dance acts like Blue Rondo a la Turk. Jonathan Green described their sound at this time as 'a swamping tide of brooding clatter that didn't quite make the break to solid musical form.'[100] Vikki Riley felt they had 'a stale taste of contrivance about them and a lot of contempt for their audience.'[101] Clinton Walker thought (wrongly) that all their songs sounded the same.[102] Everyone was jealous and wanted a piece of the action.

The group's name was chosen by percussionist Greg Perano from a song on Can's 1975 album *Landed*, and their sound in the earliest days was an unusual marriage of gothic/swamp rock, disco – the opening strains of 'Alligator Engine' on their first album is a non-ironic appropriation of New York 70s funk – and new-wave pop. Like the Birthday Party, they owed a lot to the Moodists, particularly Chris Walsh's prominent loping basslines. The songs were complex and cumbersome, full of extraneous noise and simple rhythms that seemed in places to be an attempt to approximate the 'tribal' music of Australian Aboriginals and other indigenous southern hemisphere peoples. This author recalls being outside a Hunters and Collectors show at the University of Melbourne during their first year of existence and overhearing a drunk and outraged young white man denounce the band for having stolen their music 'from the black man'. A very popular live cassette bootleg from that era used a stock photograph of some pygmies on its cover. The group presumably had no involvement in this, but it surely indicates the way they were perceived by their audience – as exploring something tribal and primal. Seymour claimed in 1985 that the early group had 'plagiarised' overseas acts, though he was not specific and may not even have been telling the truth, as by this time he was keen to discredit the band's early work.[103]

Hunters and Collectors signed to Mushroom's new offshoot, White, via an arrangement which (it was reported at the time) was 'slanted in the band's favour... giving them artistic control over all forms of recordings and promotion', and 'limited to Australasia which gives them freedom to negotiate for overseas deals.'[104]

The White label was headed by Neil Bradbury, previously editor of *Vox*. The group's first EP, released at the beginning of 1982,[105] featured the song 'World of Stone', which seems to be an obscure denunciation of modern cities. The self-titled album that followed (it had the working title *Fuck God*)[106] was a lush package of two 12-inch discs, one playing at 33 1/3 and the other at 45,[107] and was not a huge success. *Hunters and Collectors* did contain their first genuine classic, 'Talking to a Stranger', the closing minutes of which showed off an important element of the group – a newly acquired brass section dubbed the Horns of Contempt. Seymour has said the song was influenced by Baudelaire and Michael Jackson.[108] Michael Gudinski – for whom Hunters and Collectors have clearly become an iconic Mushroom group – complained some years later that the group stood in the way of making the song a hit, saying: 'If they'd have let me put out the edit they put out in America, that would've been a top-ten hit. No problems.'[109] Furthermore, like Midnight Oil before them, the group refused to play on *Countdown*, feeling 'the show would present them in an unsuitable manner'.[110]

A second 12-inch EP, *Payload*, followed; with songs like 'Lumps of Lead' it shows the band already moving away from impressionistic sketches in the direction of songs about personal/domestic issues; the most remarkable thing about this particular song, however, is that eight months after its release in late 1982, the British band Genesis had their biggest (and arguably most excruciating) hit single with the very similar sounding 'Mama'. Hunters and Collectors visited Europe; their second album, *The Fireman's Curse*, saw the group realise a dream by working in Germany with Conny Plank. The end product was neither a critical nor a commercial success; drummer Doug Falconer later commented that the group 'were questioning our raison d'etre and that put a mood into the whole album.'[111] Hunters and Collectors were unceremoniously dropped by the 'incredibly arrogant'[112] Virgin label, which had signed them for the UK, and by their US label, A&M.

It was not just a musical issue with Virgin; there were cultural differences between the band and the English people they were trying to appeal to, as Seymour told his interviewers for *Long Way to the Top*:

> The whole attitude that the English had, the record company, there was a definite sense that we stunk – we were Australian men ... Even now it makes my blood boil, the attitude the English have to Australia. It's just this real intellectual snobbery. And a lot of it has to do with their own insecurity, the idea that a colonial society can emerge and develop a sense of itself.[113]

Seymour and key members of the band – notably percussionist Greg Perano, who'd been crucial to their early phase – parted company in what Seymour later called 'a really ugly scene'.[114] Seymour later suggested that had the group continued as they were, they would have come to 'resemble the Angels,'[115] a group who, the attentive reader will have noted, seem to be everyone's scapegoat. Perano moved to Sydney and formed Love Rodeo with Rod Radalj and Marc Scully. This comedic, improvisational group had a set which included a continuing 'rock n' roll soapie' about a troubled man called Harold and a girl called Maryanne.[116] Perano later formed the Deadly Hume.

Newly arrived guitarist Martin Lubran also left Hunters and Collectors at this time, but most of the remaining members decided to have one more stab at getting the balance right. White/Mushroom was more loyal than Virgin had been, and its dedication to the group, hard to fathom at the time, was rewarded by its third album, *The Jaws of Life*. While this album was also recorded in Germany at Can's studio and mixed by Conny Plank, it was seen by reviewers[117] as a distinctively Australian record, and their best by far. Heralded as a concept album, it ostensibly explored an August 1983 incident in which Douglas Crabbe deliberately drove his vehicle into a pub at the base of Uluru, killing five people; the album was released just over a year after the event. Beyond its specific subject matter, though, *Jaws of Life* is more broadly Hunters and Collectors' attempt to carve a niche as a suburban rock band that did not pander or posture but instead sang the Australian suburbs back to themselves. Doug Falconer told the New Zealand magazine *Rip It Up* that the band now had 'more credibility with straight [i.e. conventional] people than with artists. We attract workers, students, suburban unemployed: the audience is more diverse than trendy.'[118]

The new group – now with an ethos which presaged men's support groups – was very masculine, but prided itself on also being aware and sensitive. The first track on side two of *The Jaws of Life*, 'Betty's Worry or the Slab', can only be about cunnilingus, and makes a perfect companion piece (or counterpart) to the Radiators' 'Gimme Head' – both became instant pub rock classics.[119] At the same time, H&C's new direction ultimately precipitated the band's (and Seymour's) decline into mediocrity. This was to be the case with so many seemingly radical groups who signed with the self-proclaimed independent Mushroom (Models are another case in point): they made some extraordinary records, apparently with the label's blessing and encouragement, but ultimately found it necessary to knuckle down, become 'serious,' and craft a commercially acceptable sound.

Their mainly live 'video album', *The Way to Go Out,* shows Hunters and Collectors at their peak. The band funded the live filming themselves – it cost $40,000[120] – presumably to show the world, particularly the U.S. college radio set, how good they were. It also helped to show Australia how much Hunters and Collectors had changed. As he puts the group through a workout with only the slightest connection to their earlier incarnation, muscly and sweaty little Mark Seymour is evidently the central figure, as singer and guitarist, no longer just one element in a collective (although the band insisted to the end that they functioned as a democracy: it was a 'soul thing' as far as Seymour was concerned).[121] The live footage is interspersed with glimpses of Melbourne in 1984; night streetscapes, the beach at St Kilda, a few domestic scenes. The music is the best they ever produced, mainly material from *The Jaws of Life* but including their acknowledged classic ballad 'Throw Your Arms Around Me', their then-current single. The reconfigured band sang wry love stories about a heterosexual male that were calculated to appeal to suburban rock audiences. Wanda Jamrozik marvelled in 1985 that 'Hunnahs', 'so quintessentially boyish in most respects, are unafraid to perform such a smouldering torch song' as 'Throw Your Arms Around Me', 'so full of secret tenderness.'[122] Seymour told *Juke's* Christie Eliezer that he had 'come to the conclusion that there's no such thing as (a) non-sexist male'[123] but that didn't mean he was preaching misogyny.

At this time the group made much of their rejection of their earlier 'pretentious' or 'arty' incarnation, though their new version was at least as artificial; they were just as much a product of the inner city as the Slugfuckers. 'Throw Your Arms Around Me' is another example (like Rowland Howard's 'Shivers') of a hit single that never was, and may be a final example of the group's intransigence in the face of potential commercial success. At the same time as Gudinski bemoaned the poor presentation of 'Talking to a Stranger', he told Toby Creswell:

> If they would've let me get a producer in to record 'Throw Your Arms Around Me' properly that would have been a Number One hit, if not all over the world, then at least in Australia. But no, they went through a phase of everything sounding full of bottom end and recording it live on two-track.'[124]

The single was re-recorded and reissued a number of times, but was never a hit. In the late 80s, Crowded House – the band Nick Seymour was by then playing in – aspired to record it, but apparently didn't. Its legacy is probably stronger because it is not associated with a particular chart-oriented moment or a *Countdown* performance; instead it is a firm favourite with fans from many stopping points throughout the group's long tenure. It has become Australia's version of 'I Will Always Love You'.

Hunters and Collectors' 1986 studio album *Human Frailty* was deliberately commercial; the group saw this as a pragmatic move to consolidate their career.[125] Constant live performance made a difference to the way they were perceived among their peers; Spencer Jones told Toby Creswell that they had 'started off pretentious shitheads and . . . turned out to be a really good group.'[126] Over the next decade of their existence, Hunters and Collectors were highly successful as a performing act (more so than as a recording unit); Mushroom's Gudinski was evidently a firm supporter throughout.

"A SOLID WEB-LIKE FORTRESS": MUSHROOM RECORDS

Hunters and Collectors are one example of why, when it came to creative and individualistic mainstream music in Australia, the 1980s was the decade of Mushroom Records. Competing with both local and international acts on larger labels – some of them on the Festival label; Festival was also the distributor of Mushroom's releases (and those on the Regular label) – Mushroom's size and power made it unique. It liked to call itself an independent, particularly once that term became fashionable, but of course it had nothing in common with true independents such as M Squared or even Hot (though it came to have one thing in common with Hot: the boutique label White Hot). Even if Gudinski very occasionally came across as a David to the Goliath that was the rest of the industry, he always had many weapons at his disposal. Christine Camp described 'the Mushroom Records empire' in 1982 as 'a solid web-like fortress. There's the record company, booking agency, touring company, personal management, publishing company.' Kimble Rendall's 1997 documentary *Counting the Beat* suggests that of all Gudinski's enterprises, Mushroom Records was the least profitable, but the most beloved.

Having tried and then discarded the print medium with *(Daily) Planet* (see chapter 8), Gudinski switched his media focus to television, becoming involved in the late-night rock show *Nightmoves* from 1977. It did not always work well, for instance when 3XY DJ John Peters delivered a damning review of the Skyhooks album *Hot for the Orient* on *Nightmoves* in early 1980, and Gudinski – no doubt torn between loyalty to Skyhooks and the credibility of his media properties – felt compelled to intervene and force a retraction.[127] Gudinski should have learned from his earlier problems: he'd closed down *Planet* a decade earlier around the time it started publishing criticisms of Gudinski's organisation (it was 'as if your own army had turned against you', he commented a few years later), although the magazine's financial troubles forced that issue, perhaps fortuitously.[128] Such incidents were less common than they might have been. In the early 80s he also conceived a *'Countdown*-type' show with the ludicrous name of *WROK* (ludicrous mostly because it referenced American radio call letters, which barely meant anything in Australia) as well as a live concert broadcast entitled *Stereo Home Box Office*. These, said Camp, were 'another tentacle in Mushroom's vice-like grip on the local music industry.'[129] Mushroom's various sister companies were not only profitable in their own right, they also served as means of networking between key businesses and the media.

The confusion at Mushroom and in the wider music community over what the label represented musically is clear from the mooted line-up for its 1982 tenth anniversary concert:

> Early Mushroom bands who are confirmed to return for the concert are Chain, McKenzie [sic] Theory, Madder Lake . . . Ol '55 and the original line-up of the Sports . . . Lobby Lloyde [sic], who has given up performing in recent years in favor of producing bands like the Sunnyboys and Kevin Borich Express, is expected to perform with both bands . . . Dave Warner [will be] one of the comperes.[130]

Which is to say that Mushroom already had a long history stretching from prog and blues to modern pop groups like the Sunnyboys and the Tasmanian group MEO 245 (responsible for one sharp if grimly dystopian pop album), but like almost any label of its size it had no overall sound, style or credo.

Much as XTC enjoyed premium status on Virgin for years regardless of their broader commercial viability, Gudinski appears to have held on to some acts simply because he loved them, though it might also have been that groups whose records didn't make money were profitable as live acts, and vice-versa. He seems to have engaged others solely as money-spinners; the latter were, of course, often expelled when they failed to meet commercial requirements, though it is testament to the complexity of Gudinski's style and personality that even here the boundaries are blurred. Gudinski is an enigma: a man who claimed in 1990 that his favourite Mushroom release was *Toward the Blues* by Chain, an album that actually came out on another label (Infinity) a year before Mushroom was founded.[131]

While it is unfair to the artists – and, to a lesser extent, to the label – to typify the individual groups as owing anything specifically to the label (aside from a distinctive typeface that appears on the back sleeves of the records it released until late in the 1980s), it is nevertheless important to keep in mind Mushroom's influence within Australian music in the 80s. In some ways it functioned almost the way a government agency would: any 'act' that gained a certain level of prominence, particularly in Melbourne, would find itself summoned to an audience with Gudinski. Some chose not to take up an offer; others, like the Boys Next Door, did so, but were very pleased to get away when they could. The Triffids enjoyed an on-again, off-again relationship with the organisation. Mushroom's output was far from universally excellent, but it is impossible to deny that a lot of it was important.

THE SWINGERS: ONE-AND-A-HALF HIT WONDERS

When the Swingers made a triumphant appearance on *Countdown* in early 1981 to perform their perfect pop song 'Counting the Beat', one young attendee was severely disappointed: the adolescent Kylie Minogue failed to catch Buster Stiggs's drumstick, thrown from the stage, and was left feeling 'gutted'.[132] It certainly would have been a marvelous passing of the baton from Mushroom's most successful band of 1981 to the label's greatest success at the end of that decade. Ray Argall's short film from the time, *The Swingers: Staying Number One* perfectly illustrates the prizes and problems of being a hit band. More of a docudrama than it initially appears (it is revealed at the end of the film that its interviewer, Andrew Snoid, was not merely a presenter but had in fact *joined* the Swingers, so that much of the testimony of interviewee Bones Hillman had been 'faked' to appear contemporary and was delivered some time after the fact), it nevertheless tells a good story superbly well.

The Swingers were Phil Judd's post-Split Enz group, neatly dovetailing into New Zealand's new wave scene in much the same way as Split Enz's *True Colours* album did in Australia in 1980. They began writing songs as soon as they got together, 'Judd supplying the lyrics, the music being written by the group as a whole.'[133] Argall depicts an animated Gudinski as an angel blowing dollar signs through trumpets, luring the group, in Hillman's words (echoing Dragon's to Paul Hewson five years before) to 'whatever goes in Australia – fame and fortune, I guess'. The Swingers had a decent hit in New Zealand with 'One Good Reason', but 'Counting the Beat' was the kind of song most groups only come up with once in a lifetime – bouncy and catchy, once heard never forgotten.

Gudinski may have had complete faith in Judd's ability as a songwriter – after all, he alone among all humanity had never doubted Split Enz's commercial potential – but the number one hit actually proved to be a problem. According to Hillman in Argall's film, it 'happened all too quick'. Original drummer Buster Stiggs (aka Mark Hough)[134] quit after the single's release, while Judd was signed up to write songs for Gillian Armstrong's wonderful film musical *Starstruck* at the same time as the group were attempting to complete their first (and, it transpired, only) album, *Practical Jokers*. Another single, 'It Ain't What You Dance' was great, but not in the same league as 'Counting the Beat'; it had emerged from the band's relentless rehearsal of numerous permutations of 'The Beat Goes On' (a cover of which was later a hit for the comedy duo the Globos, on Mushroom's White Label, in April 1983). The single was only a minor chart hit, and shortly thereafter new drummer Ian Gilroy broke his arm, causing further delays.

Andrew Snoid (né McLennan) had been the leader of a New Zealand band called Pop Mechanix, who had signed to CBS only to be sued – unexpectedly, but arguably with some justification – over their name by the experimental Sydney group Popular Mechanics. After losing the case, the group chose possibly the worst conceivable replacement name, 'NZ Pop'. Snoid quit the band immediately after they completed their Eddie Rayner-produced[135] album, which had cost CBS $60,000,[136] and joined the Swingers as their new singer. What Judd (who is not interviewed in the Argall film) was thinking is anybody's guess, though clearly he, or whoever else was in control of the Swingers, was not making good decisions. *Roadrunner*'s Tim McGee was witness to the final days of the Snoid-led line-up. He was unimpressed:

> The Swingers sung from a beam on the ceiling, a rancid corpse of power-plop parading as peepshow poop. Yes, folks, this charade is on its last legs (knees). Pity too. They write catchy songs, construct admirably dynamic choruses, dress oh so sharp, even had a neat light show, AND I couldn't have cared less.[137]

As with many groups since defined by their one major hit, the Swingers' legacy is largely hidden behind that star. But *Starstruck* was a brilliant film, and the Swingers deserve some of the credit. Director Gillian Armstrong and designer Luciana Arrighi made *Starstruck* in part to prove – following the impressive *My Brilliant Career* – that they were not 'just lace and soft candlelight'.[138] Armstrong said the film was 'in praise of free spirits'.[139] Its scriptwriter, Stephen Maclean, had been a rock journalist;[140] Armstrong pushed strongly for Split Enz to be the favourite band of one of the film's protagonists, Angus. *Roadrunner's* Larry Buttrose derided the film:

> In a few words: Ginger Meggs meets Martin Sharp and they go shopping for primary colours at Flamingto [sic] Park. The actual plot is so simple that the treatment must have taken up a full paragraph . . . bright colours, luvly Sydney fashion, beautiful people and a few half developed sub plots.[141]

That anyone could dislike *Starstruck* after seeing the magnificent choreography and camera work of the scene set to Billy Miller's terrific 'I Want to Live in a House' (Ian Meldrum campaigned for the song's inclusion) is hard to believe. Not only are the film's storyline and appearance awesome, the new songs by Judd and the Swingers that it features are excellent. The film also included a tremendous rendition (by actor Jo Kennedy) of a rationalized version of Tim Finn's 'Body and Soul', which had originally appeared on Split Enz's *Frenzy*.

Mushroom released both the *Starstruck* soundtrack and the Swingers' *Practical Jokers*, but such a high profile, even in Australia, clearly did not suit Judd, whose on-and-off involvement with pop music was confusing in itself for the industry: he has since claimed that Gudinski 'forced me to break up the band due to our accumulated debt'. The biggest winner from the Swingers' debacle (if it can be called that) was 'Bones' Hillman (Wayne Stevens). After playing in Coconut Rough with Snoid, then losing out on the bassist position in Crowded House to Nick Seymour, Hillman was invited to join Midnight Oil – former Dragon and Sidewinder violinist Richard Lee having declined for the minor technical reason that he couldn't play bass – and subsequently prospered in that group for over fifteen years.

MODELS: THE LONGEST AND STEEPEST DOWNHILL SLIDE EVER

Models and the Swingers, both Mushroom artists, have two points of connection: The Swingers' first drummer, Buster Stiggs, was Models' second one; he switched from one group to the other on 20 December 1980. Ray Argall made a film about Models just before he made the one about the Swingers described above.

Models were a whole different prospect for Mushroom, however. For many people they were the great hope of Australian rock music in the early 80s, not least because of their apparent unwillingness to compromise with the music industry. But they – or rather, Sean Kelly, for he was the only remaining original member by the time of 1981's *Cut Lunch* – soon made a complete about-turn in this regard, and began mimicking the approach (though not the sound) of INXS, with whom they shared management.

In the mid 80s, Kelly – who was surely already bored with Models' creation myth – told Ian Meldrum:

> The first line-up was myself and three gentlemen from another Australian punk group called JAB, and they were Ash Wednesday, Johnny Crash [aka Janis Freidenfelds] and Mr. Pierre, and we rehearsed for about three or four months before we did any shows. We started doing some shows, Pierre left, we got Mark Ferrie in the group, Ash left, we got Andrew Duffield and we cut our first record.[142]

Over a decade later, Kelly told Tracee Hutchison that Models were formed an hour after he left Teenage Radio Stars and met Pierre (born Peter Sutcliffe, but variously known as Pierre Sutcliffe, Pierre Voltaire, and Mr. Pierre).[143]

It was nothing like that simple, of course. Though to an outsider the group may have appeared to be a natural continuation of the punk group Jab with one additional member, a more believable account has Models being assembled, through a process of auditioning, by Wednesday and his girlfriend Karen Marks, the new group's manager. Marks had been a journalist on teen magazines such as *Scream* in the mid 70s and had a close relationship with Ross Wilson at that time; Wilson had introduced her to the music industry in those just-pre-punk days.

Models (their records dispense with the definite article, although most people continue to use it)[144] were to go through eleven (at least) line-ups in nine years.[145] Pierre was replaced by Mark Ferrie after two months. Ferrie was an unusual but ideal choice, given his history in pub rock groups. More importantly, he had a songwriting style that owed more to the Peter Lillie/Pelaco Brothers school than to that of the new wavers; he was no born-again punker. It would be Ferrie and Wednesday who would go on to have the most consistent and interesting – if often low-key – careers of all the ex-Models. Ferrie says:

> When the Models started . . . I think as soon as they started playing they realised the bass player they had wasn't going to pan out. They wanted someone who could actually play. I'd played a fair bit with Johnny, so he got in contact with me and I went along and tried out, and it was all good. I didn't really understand what they were doing, but we all we knew, as soon as we started playing, that it kind of worked.
>
> Karen was very involved. When I first joined, she held all the purse strings and got the gigs and told you what to wear and things like that. Or advised . . . You could take notice of it if you wanted to.

Like so many important Australian groups, Models' quirks are often ignored by historians at all levels. The band was an unusual phenomenon even in their earliest stages: instantly successful as a live group, they played only originals (with the odd exception – for instance, 'All Tomorrow's Parties'). An early review, by David Langsam in *Juke* of a show at Bananas, observed:

> The P.A. is loud, reflecting the band's attitude, seen before in Gough Whitlam's style of 'Crash through or crash'. And that's what I like about both Whitlam and rock 'n' roll. It's one of those things that lies at the essence of rock. A challenge, a confrontation with the status quo. An attempt to produce something new. Something worthwhile [sic] knowing about.[146]

Christie Eliezer, writing in the late 80s about the early days of the band, recalled 'their glam-rock . . . [and] schlocky routines, their bemused smiles at being regarded as cult heroes when they were just bimbos in a rock and roll band fooling around trying to do what they wanted to.'[147] Although their music was high-quality, atmospheric pop, Models showed no particular inclination to record in 1978-79. Kelly later claimed:

> The group's attitude at that time was a very kind of casual one towards recording because we formed and existed essentially as a live performing group, and I think when we finally got into the studio, which was sometime after we actually formed... I think we were totally confused about the whole recording industry.[148]

In mid 1980 he put down the lack of early recording to 'bad management',[149] a backhander at Marks; perhaps more truthfully, the *Lethal Weapons* experience they'd undergone with their previous bands, Teenage Radio Stars and Jab, (see chapter 11) had put Kelly and Freidenfelds off being forced into the studio and doing something they might not enjoy having to live with. Models released two giveaway singles: the first of these was 'Early Morning Brain', which they shared with the Boys Next Door's 'Scatterbrain', in October 1979. The group was so embarrassed by 'Early Morning Brain' – a great song, incidentally – they briefly broke up in shame. Most of them were working together in a plastics factory when Alberts asked them to do some demos.[150] One song from these sessions was released on the next single with another demo they'd recorded for EMI: 'Owe You Nothing'/'Progressive Office Pools' was released in June 1980.[151] It was testament to their popularity that they were able to fund the pressing of a single based on ticket sales, and also that these singles were, soon after being given away, hot items amongst collectors.

Ferrie says of the group's attitude to recording:

> There was no policy. I'm sure if we could have got a record deal we would have taken it. There's this whole thing about the Models about being a bit shy about putting stuff out, but we actually were... Over the time I was in it, it went from being a band that drew this room full of cultish followers to quite a mainstream drawing act, without a whole lot of recorded stuff out, or without any mainstream chart success. It was all based on the live profile of the band. And we played all the time. Every week, a number of times. A level that's unthinkable now. And there was audiences to support it. The reason I think we didn't record is that record companies didn't know what to make of us... Guys in record companies just didn't understand the music we were playing. Whereas nowadays, if there was a band that was drawing that many people on that regular basis, record companies would be offering contracts left, right and centre.
>
> And I remember people coming to see us. I think Peter Dawkins, producer for CBS or something, and saying, 'Those guys smoke and drink on stage.' What does that mean? Their whole thinking was, 'We don't want a young band who we have to break in. We want Jon English or someone... Look, we had enough trouble taming Dragon. We don't want to go through all that again.' That was

how they thought. Which is the exact opposite of nowadays . . . The record companies aren't interested in anyone with any kind of experience. They just want new, naive talent that they can shove through the system. That whole thing has changed.

We were actually probably making enough money playing live. The whole thing that you had to put out a record to find an audience didn't occur to us, 'cause we had an audience.

The group continued to demo here and there. Wednesday and Marks left at the same time; Wednesday released the single 'Love by Numbers', which featured Janis Freidenfelds (as Johnny Crash), Robert Kretschmer on guitar, and Marks on backing vocals; he also co-wrote and produced a solo single for Marks, 'Cold Café'. Both releases were superb-sounding, catchy, brilliant electro-pop.

Marks was replaced as manager by Adrian 'Ada' Barker, who Ferrie says had "started off as a roadie for the Masters Apprentices. And then he ended up running a few different venues. He had a place called Garrison in Prahran, and Martinis in Carlton. When we met him, he was running a booking agency called Nucleus, that was kind of an alternative to Premier Artists, the Michael Gudinski franchise." Barker had also been a chef at Lily's restaurant in the late 60s and had roadied for Ram Jam Big Band and Max Merritt as well as the Masters Apprentices; he was later head of the Masters Apprentices' Drum booking agency[152] and briefly the manager of a group called Freeway.[153]

Wednesday's replacement in Models was Andrew Duffield, who had studied under composer and music critic Felix Werder and replaced Philip Jackson in Whirlywirld. The group recorded some tracks at Richmond Recorders which were ostensibly 'produced by no-one', although Tony Cohen, who already had a history with the band, had engineered.[154] The sessions included a number of classics but with the exception of 'Happy Birthday IBM', most of the songs were very new. For reasons that are now mysterious but perhaps related to Barker's influence, they made Mushroom their record label, and their sparse collection of demos became their debut album *AlphaBravoCharlieDeltaEchoFoxtrotGolf* (soon afterward referred to by Kelly as *'Alpha Demo'*). Tellingly, the album's plain sleeve features a map of the world with sonic waves emanating from Melbourne: this was a statement about international significance. *AlphaBravo* caused excitement at the time[155] and still sounds startlingly fresh and inspired. All members wrote material for it, and it was Freidenfelds – no longer using his Johnny Crash alias – who contributed one of a number of singles that never were, the ska-pop 'Uncontrollable Boy (I'm Just An)', another being Kelly's '2 People per Square Km'. Ferrie sings his own 'Pull the Pin', but overall the album is dominated by Kelly's fingernails-on-a-blackboard voice; it was around this time that he had an operation to remove nodules from his vocal cords. Some tracks are short instrumentals, and others (such as the aforementioned 'IBM') are hilarious epics. Ian Meldrum's autobiography relates an incident from 1980 during which Meldrum, spying Kelly driving in Chapel Street in the Melbourne suburb of Prahran, blocked traffic to berate him for not releasing it as a single – for it was the third (at least) of the album's sure-fire hits that were not to be.[156]

The group at this time was entirely unafraid to reference earlier Melbourne roots, as evidenced by Ferrie's own far more laconic, 70s Carlton–style tunes; Peter Lillie's 'Holiday House' was also part of Models' live set[157] and various Models backed Lillie on tracks that ended up on his 1980 LP, *Guitar Method*.

At the time *AlphaBravo* was released, Models participated in the making of Ray Argall's short film, *Pop Movie*.[158] *Pop Movie* makes it clear in an instant why Models were pretty much the coolest pop group in the world in 1980 – cleverer than Joy Division, snappier than Blondie – though it wasn't a competition, of course, (or at least not a fair one). The film shows them playing a brilliant set at Bombay Rock in Brunswick, after which three-quarters of the band and film crew go to Kelly's flat in St Kilda – graffiti about him and Mr. Pierre is scrawled on the walls outside; Ferrie says people who saw the film were 'astonished by the state of Sean's flat' – to see Duffield interviewed by Lee Simon on *Nightmoves*. Elsewhere in the film, Freidenfelds claims the band is 'in our blood'; the antagonism between him and Kelly is tangible even here, and Freidenfelds had left the group before the film was finished. He was replaced by the aforementioned Stiggs, who in Ferrie's words:

> wasn't a guy who practiced his drumming. Drumming's a very physical thing. If you don't do it, you fall to pieces. We want to England with him, he got a drum kit, he sold it, kept the drum cases, and filled them all up with clothes. That's what he took back to Australia. So that's where his head was at, you know?
>
> Great guy. Great fun to be around. And he was fantastic in England, 'cause he was the kind of guy who could go out and make friends with anyone. He was very affable, gregarious kind of guy. Which stood us in great stead over there.

Though it's really not a term that should be applied to anyone, because it's so overused, Kelly has always been a genuine enigma, whether he was forging an industry-unfriendly path, as he did up until the third Models album, *The Pleasure of Your Company*, or being a self-proclaimed pop star, or helping to record the worst album ever to be issued on Mushroom (or perhaps any label) with his fellow

Models under the name the Clampetts.[159] Although he was the central figure in Models, he seemed unwilling to control the band, though he made many bizarre and wilful decisions about line-ups and releases throughout its history. In the mid 1980s Kelly joked that the group didn't have 'any ego problems because my attitude is so good'.[160] Every line-up of Models was different and had its own unique dynamic, but the band was always recognisable – even when it was deteriorating.

After *AlphaBravo*, the group took part in Mushroom's brief experiment with 10-inch mini-albums (the Sports, Jo Jo Zep and Kevin Borich did the same), creating the mainly Tony Cohen–produced *Cut Lunch*, a six-track collection 'extended from studio demos based on jams and tossing fragments here and there.'[161] It might even be their best release, ranging from the very poppy 'Two Cabs to the Toucan' (the Toucan being 'the place you go after everywhere is closed in Adelaide'[162] – the group had recently toured that city) to the bizarre anti-song 'Germ'. Though they usually refused point blank to record or release older, pre-Mushroom material, they made an exception for their early live favourite 'Atlantic Romantic', 'a boy chase girl song'[163] which they had recorded for release as a single with Split Enz's Eddie Rayner producing, changing the songwriting credits to eliminate Ash Wednesday in the process. The single did not materialise, but the track was included on *Cut Lunch*. They produced a quirky, colourful publicity video for the 10-inch that sampled various tracks. Kelly has since stated that the *Cut Lunch* sessions were actually demos for their second album, but they were so pleased with them that they released them.[164] If this is so, it would mean the group would be three years – and four records – into their career before they actually recorded something *intending* to release it.

Mushroom were pleased with their property, and along with A&M, who had signed the band for the UK after a company employee saw them open for the Police on their 1980 tour, sent Models to Britain to record at Rupert Hine's Farmyard Studios, with Stephen Tayler producing. Here, and in London, they were able to indulge in 'boozing and rowdy behaviour' with their old friends the Birthday Party; that group and sundry hangers-on were even more pleased to booze rowdily with Models on A&M's tab. Kelly enthused to *Roadrunner's* Donald Robertson about a Birthday Party/Hugo Klang show he attended with a 'lot of Australians in the audience'.[165] Models also played a show at the Hope and Anchor, which Ferrie recollects as

> this tiny little corner bar in the East End of London . . . all these people from the record company came, and we'd been playing constantly for years, we were hot, and we blew their heads off. They thought, 'This band's fantastic!' Bands in London didn't play, you had to get a record out to get a gig. So where we were coming from was the complete opposite.

The result of the British sessions was *Local &/or General,* an even less commercial affair than its predecessors; the title track, released as a single, had a great singalong chorus and a perversely shambolic verse reminiscent of the Pop Group's 'She Is Beyond Good and Evil' crossed with Todd Rundgren's 'All the Children Sing'.[166] Kelly has claimed that the album was very influenced by reggae music they heard in London, which sounds like a poor excuse.[167] The album had one truly brilliant song: 'Drive and Reflex', which Kelly claimed was about masturbation. 'Unhappy', one of Ferrie's contributions to *Local &/or General* in the same laconic style as his earlier tracks, was released in Britain as the next Models single just as he was about to leave the group:

> Before we left for England, my daughter was born. It was literally weeks after that we left to go to England, for however many months it was. And it killed me. You have this really intense experience with the birth of your first kid. She got sick while I was away, and I'm over there feeling useless. That had a lot to do with it. We came back here and toured, and by that stage Sean had started to assume — I think the record company people all talked to him. Going from just another guy in the band, he became the focus of it. Buster wasn't really cutting it. So when we got back here he got a couple of his mates in the band. Graham Scott, who was a drummer, and John Rowell. And it kind of changed the whole dynamic of the group. Going from four-piece to five-piece.
>
> For me it wasn't the same kind of band anymore. I was having doubts about how much the band was encroaching on my personal life. While we were on this tour, my sister got married. We were in Queensland, and I said, 'Do you reckon I could have time off to go to my sister's wedding?' And the manager wouldn't do this. It was like, 'No, forget it. We can't blow out these things.' I bit my tongue and did it. And as it turns out, the day she got married, the gig blew out, so I was just sitting around. That really pissed me off. To me, the band was taking over my life.
>
> When this tour finished, I was, 'See you later guys.' I didn't leave, I just didn't stay.

Appropriately, considering his attitude, Mushroom released 'Unhappy' in Australia as a solo Mark Ferrie single; it was not a hit.

Scott and Rowell had been members of a St Kilda band called the Curse, which had been assembled around Nique Needles, soon to become an actor. At this point, Kelly's old bandmate James Freud lobbied to join Models. Freud had just returned from the UK, where he had recorded an (unreleased, unloved by Freud, and now partially lost) album produced by Gary Numan[168] and abandoned his group, the remnants of his 'Radio Stars' band latterly known as Berlin.[169] Freud's intervention scuttled an astonishing plan for Models to merge with the Reels in a new band called the Act (see chapter 13).[170]

Freud recalled a few years later:

> After I broke up James Freud and Berlin, I shaved my head and went and lived in this house in Richmond and recorded this arty kind of music that was really depressing... Everything went wrong for me... The day before I left to go to London, Sean played me the tapes for *Local &/or General*... I thought it was the best thing I'd ever heard.[171]

At first the inclusion of Freud seemed like a good decision. The new line-up created one of the most powerful, driving and strident pop records of the early 80s, the commercially unsuccessful single 'On', released in September 1982.[172] Lobby Loyde produced 'On', and it was no doubt this sound that Craig N. Pearce was raving about in a live review when he praised 'this new hybrid of Kellycharisma, Freudfingering and Rowelfavaging' – although in typically contrary fashion he described the band on the night in question as 'a paltry blast of shit.'[173] Rowell and Scott departed soon after to re-form the Curse without Needles, and including, on bass, future Mushroom solo artist Nick Barker.

By the time Models came to make the typically bizarre video for 'On', the line-up was Kelly, Duffield, Freud and new drummer Barton Price (another New Zealander). The video was one of the first to draw on what must have been an ongoing deal between Mushroom Records and a South Melbourne abattoir to ensure a ready supply of pigs' heads.

The transitional period between the version of Models that issued 'On' and the group who had their first hit with 'I Hear Motion' is confusing to say the least. The first seriously commercial Models album was *The Pleasure of Your Company*: Duffield claims to have written 'I Hear Motion' (which reached number 12 in 1983) while trying unsuccessfully to play Stevie Wonder's 'Superstition'. Apparently ashamed at having produced a commercially appealing dance track, Models then released another track from the album, Kelly's 'No Shoulders, No Head', an oblique and gloomy piece that indicated their continuing inability to gauge popular taste and Mushroom's complacent willingness to indulge their wallowing.

Exact details of the arrival and departure of band members at this time are hazy and probably unimportant. Duffield was in and out of the band for a while, but Freud was definitely *in*, and contributing. In time he was to lobby successfully for his former Radio Stars/Berlin bandmate Roger Mason to join as keyboard player. A three-piece Kelly-Freud-Price Models recorded yet another album's worth of demos with Tony Cohen; the group at least managed to break one old habit, because these recordings remain largely unreleased (although legendary). Other participants around this time included Gus Till, formerly of Beargarden and the Ears, who briefly replaced Duffield.

Friendships between Models and members of INXS began in the early 80s; Kelly would visit them in their hotel and 'drink their mini-bars and sit around jamming.' He would later credit their bass player, Garry Beers, with introducing the band to what Kelly called 'the Sydney music connection'.[174] This included INXS's management, MMA, who urged Models to take their commercial qualities seriously with a view to enlarging their fanbase.

Though *Pleasure of Your Company* was not a major success, Models' next album, *Out of Mind, Out of Sight*, was their 'breakthrough.' It featured the decent, sparky 'Big on Love', which was a top-thirty hit, and two major top-five singles, both of them unbelievably awful: Freud's title track, a piece of pseudo-sexy fluff featuring a section purloined from Hunters and Collectors' 'Holding Down a D',[175] and the disastrously trite Freud/Duffield composition 'Barbados'. Duffield had by this time been firmly ejected from the band. He recorded a solo album, *Ten Happy Fingers*, which he sold largely by mailorder, and found some solace in receiving half the royalties for penning a number one single without having to go on the road to support it.

The new pop Models were not to everyone's taste. Longtime fans were already dispirited by what the group had become: one diehard had compiled a three-cassette bootleg of earlier, unreleased songs, some of which were ultimately released two decades later as the album *Melbourne*. The word around the traps was: whatever Models had become, they had once been brilliant.

In 1985 and 1986, Models were at their commercial peak. They travelled to the UK again in mid '86, making little impact, and they were part of the Australian Made tour in December 1986 and January 1987, which brought together such diverse groups as Mental as Anything, I'm Talking, the Saints, the Triffids, Divinyls and INXS; Richard Lowenstein directed a film of the tour. For a brief period Models were probably the biggest Australian pop group in Australia (as opposed to those huge Australian pop groups, like INXS, who weren't in Australia any more). As is usually the case, Models' commercial rise correlates closely with their artistic decline, in great part due to Kelly's perversity; having helped create some of the most individualistic music of the late 70s and early 80s, he now seemed to aspire to a workmanlike facsimile of MOR pop and R&B. Freud, by now the co-leader of the group, was at best an amiable hack and (as he detailed in two volumes of autobiography) an alcoholic. He committed suicide in 2010, succumbing to what Gudinski described as the 'disease' of alcoholism.[176]

Some of the group's later work was passable; the slow and funky 'Evolution' wasn't bad, for example. The last really good Models song was the single 'King of Kings', a Kelly composition. Their two final releases signify the absolute dearth of ideas in the Models camp: a plodding cover of the Beatles' already woeful 'Oh Darling', released in late 1987, which was apparently recorded because their new US label Geffen couldn't hear a hit on the tracks assembled for *Models' Media*; and the aforementioned Clampetts album, a live covers record by the group's country and western alter egos.[177] James Valentine, who had joined the band as saxophonist in late 1984, at the same time Duffield was replaced by Mason, said a few years later that his decision to leave was not prompted by the 'writing on the wall' so much as a 'big neon [sign], flashing "This band is rooted/get out now."'[178]

When Models finally split (officially, it was 'certainly not The End'),[179] Kelly had brief further success with Absent Friends; they had a number one hit in 1986 (with Eddie Floyd's 'I Don't Wanna Be With Nobody But You'); members included Duffield, Valentine, INXS bassist Garry Beers, and singer Wendy Matthews. Kelly became stuck eternally threatening to make a solo album, which he first announced in February 1987.[180] When he did release an album under his own name, in 2005, it was made up of re-recordings of older songs.

Beginning in the early 2000s, there were numerous well-publicised Models reunions (of both the mid-80s and late-70s line-ups). Kelly had flagged this kind of activity much earlier: the shows on the 1987 tour had been structured chronologically and played 'as faithfully as possible to the original recording',[181] with a view to a live album that did not eventuate.

For most Australians, Models will remain the hit band of the late 80s that gave the world 'Barbados' and a children's TV host in James Valentine. Many Melbournites – and those who saw them on their numerous supports to international touring artists in their pre-Mushroom days – will have more profound or sentimental feelings. What Models never were – and this is testament to their fractured, obscure lyrics and bright pop – was 'serious' in the way that contemporaries like the Birthday Party or Duffield's earlier (brilliant) group Whirlywirld were. Their pop legacy reveals that; so does the fact that few remember the ghastly Third Reich fantasy of 'Tearing Hair Out' (on *Local &/or General*) or such lightweight bombast as 'God Bless America'. Some of those early Models songs, however, are almost too good to be true.

DIVINYLS: VERY CONFUSED, BUT ALL AMBITION

While Models tried and failed in Britain and America, a group like Divinyls, who probably underwent almost as many line-up changes and perverse career decisions (and even shared a member in drummer Barton Price) were ultimately rewarded with an international top-ten hit with 'I Touch Myself'. Like many Australian groups lauded in their own country as internationally famous (Midnight Oil, for instance) they are considered in most other countries to have been one-hit wonders – and, in the case of Divinyls, with a rather bizarre and tawdry song (Sean Kelly was particularly partial to writing songs about masturbation, but he couldn't make them stick with the general public).

The group's origins are unusual. Mark McEntee, their guitarist and one half of the essential Divinyls duo with Christina (Chrissy) Amphlett, was a member of Air Supply, as was early member Jeremy Paul;[182] both men feature on the cover of the first Air Supply album. Paul is generally credited with actually forming Divinyls, and he appears to have been its leader until he attempted, unsuccessfully, to sack Amphlett and was himself ejected instead. While McEntee was plainly a crucial member of the group, from the outset all attention was focused on Amphlett. 'What a pleasure it is to have a credible female singer in this country again,' Donald Robertson exclaimed in *Roadrunner* in 1981, though he spoilt the effect a little by calling Amphlett 'Chrissie Amphong.'[183]

Amphlett, born in the regional Victorian city of Geelong (and cousin to Little Pattie), was barely in her teens in the early 70s when she played with Daisy Clover and an 'interesting and ambitious' group called One Ton Gypsy,[184] which included Ronnie Peel, formerly of the Missing Links and the La De Das. At sixteen she was living on her own in Greville Street, Prahran, home of the notorious Station Hotel, Brian Peacock's bakery, and later, the highly regarded Greville Records shop.[185] Before her twentieth birthday she had scored a role in the all-nude, thrillingly named *Let My People Come* at the Total Theatre in Melbourne, and while one critic described the cast as 'not exactly beautiful in the fullest sense of the word,'[186] the experience was liberating for Amphlett – as was punk rock, which she considered 'very freeing for the female' (though the examples of 'punk' she gives, the Motels and Ian Dury, show it wasn't that close to her heart).[187] Before Divinyls, Amphlett told author Debbie Kruger, 'I was very confused, but all ambition.'[188]

Producer Mark Opitz heard Divinyls practicing daily from the petrol station in front of their rehearsal space and realised they were 'serious',[189] but it was surely the Air Supply connection, their involvement in the film *Monkey Grip* and, early in their career, the engagement of Vince Lovegrove, onetime co-lead singer of the Valentines alongside Bon Scott, later journalist and promoter, as their manager that sealed their acceptance within the record industry. Amphlett often presented herself as an ugly, gutsy, crass woman; her stage props were a plastic microphone stand containing a neon light (an invention of the *Monkey Grip* crew)[190] and a schoolgirl's uniform. This latter was perhaps a nod to Angus Young, but it was also a poke in the eye for any men entertaining fantasies of compliant, girly girls. When it came to the American market, Amphlett says in her 2005 autobiography, her image was decidedly problematic: 'Americans are obsessed with white, perfectly symmetrical teeth. They didn't understand that my buck teeth were as much a part of me as my voice and spirit.'[191] She also crafted a compelling, distinctive singing and speaking voice; her accent was a cross between Australian vernacular and cinematic cockney, which marked her out as definitively not American, and yet not 'ocker': this is just one more example of why Divinyls were a hard sell, yet an irresistible proposition.

The presentation of the Divinyls to the general public in Australia was confusing at first, primarily because their first single – 'Boys in Town', a hit and now an acknowledged classic – was taken from a mini-album called *Music from Monkey Grip*. Were they a group of musicians; or were they actors pretending to be musicians? 'A lot of people would have thought we were a movie band,' Amphlett said in 1983.[192] Most of the Divinyls appeared in this marvelous film, based on a book set in the early 70s but with the action updated to 1980. The unnamed group the Divinyls portrayed was based on Stiletto, for whom the book's author Helen Garner had written lyrics. Amphlett played the minor character Angela; Noni Hazelhurst, who played the film's protagonist Nora, had originally auditioned for the role. Both Mel Gibson and Doc Neeson had been proposed for the role of Nora's lover, Javo; Neeson cancelled because of an Angels tour,[193] and Colin Friels beat out Gibson for the part.

Rumours of rock stars playing at acting and actors playing rock stars inevitably swirled around *Monkey Grip*, but Divinyls was already a real band. It had grown out of an early group with the dreadful – and in their context, meaningless – name of Baton Rouge.[194] The actor Tracy Mann, a friend of Amphlett's who before long would be playing a singer-songwriter in the ABC series *Sweet and Sour*, had come up with the equally meaningless, but nevertheless memorable name Divinyls.[195] After the success of 'Boys in Town', the group embarked on fifteen years of debauchery, tantrums and terrible business decisions (if Amphlett's biography is to be believed even slightly, and there is no reason not to believe it). They also had some truly excellent musical moments. After Jeremy Paul was ousted, Rick Grossman – who already had impressive experience, including the legendary Melbourne pub rock-new wave bridge Bleeding Hearts and Matt Finish, but was, in his words, 'still learning to play bass'[196] – entered the group's ranks in 1982 and remained for most of the decade. Lovegrove initially signed the group to the international arm of Chrysalis Records, cutting out Australian record companies, though of course Divinyls would still have their records released in Australia, just as most Chrysalis acts did. While this was potentially an advantage when it came to their international ambitions, it created problems in their day-to-day life as a band. As Amphlett put it: 'We're over here recording, they're over there being a record company, and the result is this massive communication problem whereby everything takes a month to decide.'[197] McEntee add that with such an arrangement, 'even saying "get fucked" becomes a complicated procedure.'[198]

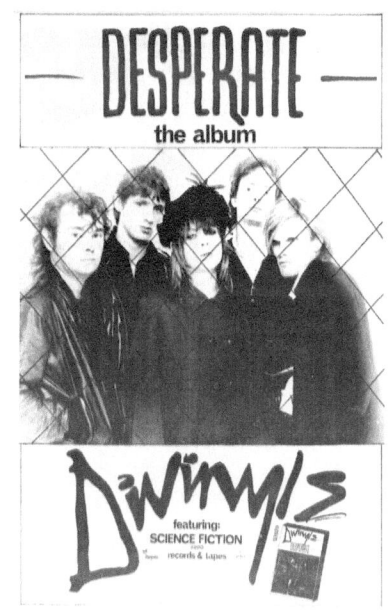

Luckily none of this stopped the group from making a few great records. Their 1983 single 'Siren', a top-forty hit in April, is compelling. Their 1985 single 'Pleasure and Pain' – despite its unusual genesis (Amphlett had tried to write songs with hitmaker Holly Knight but wasn't able to; so Knight wrote a song with producer Mike Chapman which Amphlett says 'felt right for me')[199] is another golden Divinyls moment, all angst and ennui. If anyone doubted Amphlett's grit, her jail term for failure to pay parking fines during Christmas 1985[200] may have put them right, though this could also be interpreted as merely a sign of someone dysfunctionally distanced from reality. Their best record was the 1988 *Temperamental* album, its standouts the plaintive 'Back to the Wall,' the title track, and 'Punxsie'. Their greatest commercial success was a self-titled album released in 1990, featuring the infamous 'I Touch Myself'.

WHAT'S MY SCENE?

By this time, Divinyls had lost the long-serving Grossman to the Hoodoo Gurus; after receiving treatment for heroin addiction, he joined them in 1988. The Hoodoo Gurus offer a further example of an Australian outfit with a distinctive, brilliantly colourful sound and style all their own, who were able to make inroads internationally – in their case, particularly on the US college circuit – by employing the Australian talent for providing an informed perspective on global western culture. Like Models (and, of course, innumerable other artists around the world) the group had difficulty extricating themselves from their original 'cult' fanbase and finding a place in the mainstream, and their subsequent output likewise came closer to a carefully crafted response to the pop marketplace.

Le Hoodoo Gurus were formed in Sydney in 1981 by Dave Faulkner and James Baker; both had been members of the Victims in Perth, but were now living in Sydney. The original line-up included Kimble Rendall, formerly a member of XL Capris and itching for a career as a film director, and Rod Radalj (sometimes also known as Roddy Ray'da and, by the time he and Baker reunited in the Adorable Ones in 1987, the Raj Radalj).[201] With Faulkner on vocals and guitar, Baker drumming, and Rendall and Radalj on guitar, the initially bass-less group was immediately a hit on the inner-city scene. As Le Hoodoo Gurus – a flamboyant and silly name that underscored the high-spirited good-naturedness of the whole enterprise – they released a glam racket of a single, 'Leilani' – sixties tiki-style camp and bluster. Oddly, the song had a recent precedent – 'Till the Beast Is Dead' by Adelaide-Melbourne group the Aliens had used the same rollicking beat in 1980. 'Leilani' came out on Phantom, a label which, like many independents, was associated with a record shop, in this case located in Pitt Street, Sydney; its name referenced the strange fascination Australians had for many decades with the American comic strip. A second single, the more straightforward rock-pop 'Tojo', soon followed, after which the group lost their 'Le' because it they felt it was too difficult for people.[202] This was the beginning of their move away from what Faulkner – increasingly leaning towards a more strategically crafted songwriting approach – saw as the flighty unreality of the inner city:

> We realized that you can get away with a lot more when you play at inner-city venues than you can in the suburbs. You can be really obscure or indulgent in that environment and people will get off on it. Out in the suburbs, people are less aware of different forms of music. They won't get the joke or pick up the obscure

reference, but they will appreciate a good song. They don't want to meditate on the delicacies of the songwriting, though. They want the rush that music with real impact can give you.[203]

Faulkner was, in effect, becoming an anti-snob snob – discriminating against people he considered snobs.

The pursuit of this approach saw the group soon afterwards pick up a bass player, Clyde Bramley, and bring in Brad Shepherd. Shepherd had been playing in the Hitmen but also, more importantly, in the good-humoured bubblegum band Super K ('a combination of odd balls from odd bands and places who formed to play less than 10 fabbo gigs of bubblegum classics'[204]) with Bramley. The invigorated, concertedly commercial group signed to Big Time Records, and had their first chart hit with 'My Girl', a ballad Faulkner originally considered 'just a pastiche': 'When we did it I wanted to make it more like a true sentiment as well as laughing at itself... this sap that's got left in the dance hall.'[205] Nevertheless, the video for the song suggested it was not about Faulkner and a girl (or, as he claimed in one interview, himself and a giraffe) – but about Faulkner and a champion greyhound, Defiant Lee.[206] Just before recording their first album, Bramley made the facetious remark in a press interview that the group 'wanna be Men at Work!' James Baker's response – 'I don't want that quote read anywhere'[207] – was funny, but also indicative of the tensions within the Hoodoo Gurus' dynamic.

Their original fanbase may have been able to swallow their heroes' foray into the mainstream, but Faulkner alienated a large proportion of it after the release of that album, the well-received *Stoneage Romeos*, when he ejected the iconic Baker from the band ('Bad taste on their behalf' said Baker).[208] After considering the Sunnyboys' Bil Bilson, Faulkner replaced Baker with Mark Kingsmill, formerly of the Hitmen. Baker was also a member of the Beasts of Bourbon and had played on that band's first album, *The Axeman's Jazz*, which was recorded in one day – the day before the Hoodoo Gurus began recording *Stoneage Romeos*. The Beasts of Bourbon retaliated on Baker's behalf by dismissing recent recruit Brad Shepherd from their band.

Faulkner's response to critics of his behaviour towards Baker was another song, 'Poison Pen', which he said was

> about everyone telling me what to do with my life. The things they were saying, no-one had a right to say. There was character assassination on a broad scale, which I resented... There are people in Penrith [a western suburb of Sydney] who have opinions about what the Gurus did or didn't do with James Baker and it's just fantasy, speculation and titillation.[209]

The Hoodoo Gurus survived the Baker controversy, with the solid Kingsmill and the versatile Shepherd proving vital ingredients in their continued success. Their second album, *Mars Needs Guitars* (working title *Zombie Jambouree*),[210] shook off most of their campy past.

One of the most important reasons for their widespread appeal was surely that Faulkner did not allow his cleverness as a writer to turn into clever-cleverness; he was appalled, for instance, by Mi-Sex's song 'Where Do They Go', which mused about the unknown lives of their suburban fans as though they were incomprehensible. 'I just don't wanna actually be writing songs that are about songs,' he told the *NME*'s Lynden Barber, 'I wanna write songs.'[211] Nor were the group 'revivalists', he insisted to Ed St John. 'We have no interest in fitting into other people's bags.'[212] By the end of 1984, the group was reminiscing fondly about an American tour during which they were able to coax not only Cyril Jordan and Roy Loney of the Flamin' Groovies onstage to sing with them, but also – at one show – Jello Biafra.[213]

CAN'T HELP MYSELF

In the main, the Australia of the early to mid 80s was about bands. They often had one (occasionally two) auteur songwriters; some, like Faulkner, constructed their ideal band over time from a more casually created prototype (the original Le Hoodoo Gurus were, at least from the outside, seemingly more of a democratic group, full of possibility); others, like Ed Kuepper, were always the founder and songwriter, even spokesperson, though they depended heavily on certain musicians (in Kuepper's case, Jeffrey Wegener and, later, Louise Elliott) to realise their vision.

Very few mainstream Australian musicians were brave (or foolish) enough to cast aside all pretence of a permanent line-up and release a succession of what were essentially solo albums and shows under a group name. Iva Davies was one such performer/writer, and was for a time extremely successful with this approach.

Born Ivor Davies in Wauchope, NSW, in 1955, his father was a forestry officer, and Davies grew up in Wagga. 'That was where I first heard the bagpipes', he told John O'Donnell in 1990, 'and it was all downhill from there.'[214] As it transpired it was the oboe, rather than the bagpipes, that took Davies on a scholarship to the Conservatorium in Sydney. Prodigies like Davies (others include Richard Lee and Cleis Pearce) were no doubt equally tempted by the glamour of rock in comparison with contemporary classical music.

Davies made a number of false and hazy moves into the pop arena in the mid 70s. In his last year of high school ('1972 or something'), he 'played all the folk traps'.[215] A stumbling block for him was his lack of inclination towards songwriting; he told O'Donnell in 1990 that his classical background, in which few wrote their own material, was to blame for this. He did, however, make records of some of his own songs under his own name in the early 1970s. His first single was 'Leading Lady', and the second, 'Back to California' ('a real Neil Young thing'), was credited to Iva Davies and Afghan. He took the name 'Iva' from that label misspelling; 'I kept it just to remind me that this is not the real world.²¹⁶ 'Back to California' was also a mispressing; the B side accidentally featured Cloud Nine (a precursor of Taste) performing 'Summertime Blues'.²¹⁷

Davies' early records were not hits, and he found employment in other areas of the music industry – scoring the charts for the *Ian Dury Songbook*, for instance.²¹⁸ His professionalism, musical ability, and willingness to prioritise the value of a song over the notion of a singer-songwriter's canon, led him to form the band Flowers, a punk rock showband, with friend Keith Welsh in 1978. Rather lamely, he told O'Donnell:

> Very early in the piece I got typecast as this ex-classical musician, which kind of tainted my credibility. The fact of the matter is that Flowers were a punk band and had pretty much the same credentials as any of the bands that were produced in that period, the Midnight Oils, the INXSs.²¹⁹

'Credentials' is an odd word to use, and neither of the bands Davies uses as examples were punk bands, which reveals his bluster for what it is; he has also admitted that Flowers were 'basically . . . a pub cover band'.²²⁰ If Flowers had any punk 'credibility' it came from some of the group's other members, such as drummer John Lloyd, who left Paul Kelly's Dots to join the group. Otherwise, it was a largely unimaginative but highly successful commercial enterprise: Davies and the band would play two sets, in which one song each by international 'new wave' acts like the Sex Pistols and Graham Parker would be played in the same order. Davies would later muse that:

> Australian audiences have a very low bullshit tolerance; they don't stand for much rubbish. That's what is so healthy about the pub circuit . . . There's not much scope for lyrical or musical pretentiousness in Australia.²²¹

There may be some truth to this argument, so often advanced by Australian groups who have gone on to large-scale international success when they're trying to explain their own resilience, but as a creative policy it leaves much to be desired.

Towards the end of Flowers' incarnation as a pub covers band, the group began to insert one Davies original in each set. Davies would claim in 1979 that he'd been sent into a 'shock state' by the failure of his solo singles, and only wrote songs when circumstances forced him to.²²² He also claimed it was a management initiative; 'I felt a bit of a phoney actually, because it's not as if I've always been bursting to communicate something to the world. I was put in a corner and had to cope with that situation.'²²³ There was sufficient buzz by the time Flowers signed a record deal with Regular Records that CBS, who had been hoping to sign the group themselves, sent a wreath to Davies' manager, Ray Hearn, on discovering the group had rejected them.²²⁴

The first song Davies wrote entirely on his own was 'Walls' – he later said that all the group's first original compositions (many were co-written with band member Michael Hoste) were on the group's first album, *Icehouse*. The band also recorded a version of Paul Kelly's 'Leaps and Bounds', which was not included on the album.[225] *Icehouse* is distinctly of its time and place, a fact consolidated by the presence of Greedy Smith (from Regular labelmates Mental as Anything) and Cold Chisel's Ian Moss on some tracks.[226] By far the best of the songs was the repetitive, shimmering new-wave disco song 'Can't Help Myself', composed by Davies (who had never been to a dance club) using a 'peculiar four-minute drum loop that John Lloyd invented'.[227] He bet label manager Martin Fabinyi that 'Can't Help Myself' would not reach the top forty.[228] As it transpired, both this song – released as a 10-inch and 7-inch single – and its follow-up, the bagpipe-tinged 'We Can Get Together', were hits. Davies began to understand celebrity 'when people started sleeping on the front lawn of the house [after] following me home.'[229]

It seemed plain to many in the music industry that Flowers had international potential, though it would first be necessary to change their name; Davies claimed soon afterwards that this was due to legal problems in the USA, though there was already a Scottish group called Flowers. A simple solution was to transpose the album title and the group's name, so the album *Icehouse* by Flowers became *Flowers* by Icehouse. (Donald Robertson presumably misheard Sean Kelly when Kelly told him on the phone from the UK that Flowers had changed their name to Ultraboost.[230] More likely Kelly was referring to a *Melody Maker* review that referred to the band as 'Ultrabruces',[231] meaning a cross between the *Monty Python* parody Australian 'Bruce' and the group Ultravox. This was typical of the level of humour and criticism of the British press at the time – and, of course, long before and long after.) For his part, Davies told Robertson he was 'expecting the British to be really critical. I'm not saying it's fair – it's just the way it is.'[232]

Perhaps appropriately for an album with as fey a name as *Flowers*, Davies remixed the tracks for the international market, giving the record a 'lighter/poppier mix'[233] than its more somber, clinical Australian original; Chrysalis issued it internationally as the eponymous album by Icehouse. Another single, 'Love in Motion', was 'widely touted' (according to Toby Creswell) as being overly similar to 'Rock On' by David Essex;[234] the general conceit of the song, as well, was a little close to 'Poetry in Motion' (and where Models were coming from with 'I Hear Motion' is anyone's guess).

'People say to me that I'm a fascist,' Davies told Creswell, 'because I want to control everything.'[235] Much as Kuepper was reputed to do within the Laughing Clowns, Davies exerted complete control over Icehouse and its personnel. While recording songs for the follow-up album, he appears to have decided it would be expedient to dismiss the entire band. For Davies, a band was a situation 'where you're seen as a unit and you're basically married to these people, to a situation where they feel trapped... Anybody can up and leave at any moment.'[236] That is to say, he made sure they couldn't quit by firing them.

Some of the songs for what was to become *Primitive Man* were written by Davies at the last minute in Giorgio Moroder's home studio in LA;[237] others owed their existence to 'that revolutionary Australian invention, the CMI Fairlight'[238] synthesiser, a sophisticated sampling keyboard hailed as revolutionary in the early 80s. It was named the Fairlight in tribute to the Sydney suburb in which its creators, Peter Vogel and Kim Ryrie, had perfected it. Perhaps disingenuously – it is hard to imagine him working so haphazardly – Davies claimed soon afterward:

> I didn't really mean to do the album on my own. My original intention was to put some demos on tape and get everyone to add bits, but when you're working with fully programmable instruments there's really no need for any assistance; you just set it all up, run the tape and out comes the song.[239]

Primitive Man – the title was of course ironic given the cutting-edge technology used in making the album – featured one iconic track, 'Great Southern Land', an imaginative pairing of the evocative possibilities of the Fairlight with a paean to landscape and history. This would be one of Davies' best moments; its boldness and capacity to tap into a strong early-80s nationalism – like the best patriotic songs, it said the right things to everyone, without really saying much at all – had tremendous appeal. Other Icehouse songs from this time, such as 'Street Café' and to a lesser extent 'Hey Little Girl', sound like Bryan Ferry, or perhaps a more animated David Sylvian, singing with a low-key Duran Duran. But 'Great Southern Land', like the remarkable 'Can't Help Myself' from the first album, is unique and shows Davies' songwriting strengths.

Davies told O'Donnell that 'although I keep attempting to write something of literary worth, really I'm probably just a craftsman of music. I still sit up and take note of the occasional Nick Cave song and think, "god, that's guy's a genius, where do these things come from?"'[240]

By the time of the fourth Icehouse album, *Measure for Measure,* the group was firmly established as a marketing name for Davies, though the record was almost entirely co-written with Robert Kretschmer. Later in the 80s – and Icehouse, in terms of its impact and commercial reign, was definitely an 80s phenomenon – the group would feature some notable recurring players, such as keyboardist Andy Qunta as well as guitarist Kretschmer, who had been a member of Eric Gradman Man and Machine in the late 70s and had played on Ash Wednesday's 'Love by Numbers' single.

OH NO, NOT YOU AGAIN

Icehouse's international status in the early 80s probably depended in part on a capacity for camouflage. The singles in particular – with the exception of 'Great

Southern Land' – had a sound and style that didn't seem out of place in, for example, the European pop scene at that time. In the eyes of many Australians, the need to adopt such camouflage was understandable and in some ways admirable. But other Australian bands took on a distinctive and unique sound which made them heroic figures at home – and in many respects spoilt their international chances almost immediately, although the best example of this kind of group, Australian Crawl, perhaps nipped their chances of world fame in the bud simply with their tell-all name, even before anyone overseas was required to tackle the distinctively acrobatic vocal style of singer James Reyne. This should not detract from the fact that Australian Crawl quickly became the yardstick by which other local bands' success (or failure) was measured in early 1980s Australia.

It has been claimed that the group emerged from a mid-70s outfit called Spiff Rouch – this name presumably a joke mangling of 'spliff' and 'roach' – who came from the fringe Melbourne beach suburb of Mt Eliza. They had been part of the Pelaco Brothers' Kingston Hotel coterie. Stephen Cummings recalls that Peter Lillie 'featured them in his comic books':

> The Frankston correspondent would be Kieron Sell, who became our roadie. He'd write silly surfer things, they'd write about beach culture. They had really wacky songs too, they'd come up to the Kingston and bring the Frankston crew with them. This was before James Reyne joined the band.

Spiff Rouch split into two groups, the Flatheads and Clutch Cargo, and then reorganized themselves again in 1978 as Australian Crawl; the name refers to a swimming stroke. Reyne was a good-looking, urbane young man who played guitar and sang; his brother David, later of the Chantoozies and more recently a TV host, was briefly the group's drummer. Like Iva Davies and, it would seem, most high-profile Australian pop musicians of the time, James Reyne cited the tough and basic crowds the group played to as its formative element:

> We played all our really early gigs to a surfing crowd, and obviously it was the sort of music they liked hearing. The music always had a big dance beat, because that's what's required, but mainly it was what I'd call rage music, very loud and full-on. Smoking bongs and getting drunk, going surfing and generally having a rage; that's what they're into.[241]

Reyne claims to have taken his cues from Skyhooks' Greg Macainsh and other earlier 70s bands such as Sid Rumpo, Kahvas Jute, Tamam Shud,[242] Carson, and 'all those Ross Wilson and Broderick Smith bands':[243] He felt one couldn't 'write songs about Highway 41'[244] in Australia. Similarly, perhaps, Tamam Shud had claimed that they played 'music for surfers, but not surfing music.'[245] When David Briggs, Little River Band's guitarist, saw Australian Crawl in May 1979, he was impressed by what he saw as the group's *lack* of international influences. 'Listen carefully,' he said, 'they're all Australian.'[246]

Ed St John claimed in 1985 that Australian Crawl was 'instantly at odds with the moody, introspective and highly trend-conscious Melbourne music scene of the day';[247] a typical *Rolling Stone* description that recasts a generalised perception into some kind of battle of mystic moods (*Rolling Stone* feared that which it did not understand, that is, anything in the present). Reyne kind of agreed:

> In these days of fads, we're incredibly unfashionable. We get a lot of criticism because of it. People at gigs put it on you and say, 'You guys are full of shit'. I think it's because we're not New Wave and can't be labeled.[248]

They weren't new wave, it's true, but they were distinctive enough to make it onto the soundtrack of the classic inner-city Sydney film *Going Down,* alongside groups like the Birthday Party. As it happened, many around Australia saw Australian Crawl as part of a Melbourne tradition: the Millionaires or even 'witty and intelligent'[249] cabaret punks Jimmy and the Boys were described as 'the new Skyhooks' because of their flamboyance, whereas Australian Crawl were given the same tag because of their wry, sardonic lyrics, and their debut album, *The Boys Light Up* (a title the group had agonised over!)[250] was declared by some to be 'the *Living in the 70s* of the Eighties'.[251] There were also suggestions, early in their career, that they sounded similar to the Sports.[252]

Australian Crawl's first single – a hit – was 'Beautiful People'; it had all the hallmarks of their work, particularly Reyne's vocal style, which had the same stridency and angularity as Peter Garrett's but was also garbled, making the words he was singing indecipherable. (Curiously, though, on their live album *Phalanx* Reyne articulates every word with care.) When the Reels covered 'Beautiful People' for their album *Neighbors,* many heard the lyrics clearly for the first time, and a few might have recognised at least one satirical couplet playfully purloined from the British musical comedy duo Flanders and Swann. Reyne claimed that if the cynicism was taken out of Australian Crawl's songs, 'you'd have some really nice chord progressions.'[253]

Reyne claimed that the original Australian Crawl was 'just mates who thought we'd mess around, and the thing got out of hand. It was like all the guys together, have a good time, go around Australia, meet girls.'[254] If this was indeed a founding principle of the band, it was soon cast aside; their machinations became legendary within the music industry. Glenn Wheatley became their manager.

The Boys Light Up was produced by David Briggs at the time that 'Beautiful People' was in the charts. Reyne made a splash by appearing on *Countdown* to perform the song with both his arms in plaster; he'd had a car accident. The album was keenly awaited, and the title track – which many assumed was a drugs reference (Reyne said not) – was another hit single, its veiled references to fellatio sufficiently oddly phrased to slip under commercial radio's radar. The album's closer, 'Hoochi Gucci Fiorucci Mama', was 'gauche' and 'irksome', Reyne came to believe,[255] and it certainly dates the product somewhat, as does its cover, which conformed to the empty glamour so prevalent in the early 80s: the band stand in shallow water in semi-darkness observing a naked woman on a beach, and no-one seems to think it is creepy or 'loserish'. 'Downhearted', also on the first album, was a well-received single; it was later re-recorded for their third album, *Sons of Beaches*, in the hope of exciting the American market.

The group's second LP, *Sirocco*, was a more successful proposition than *The Boys Light Up*, though a perception of Australian Crawl as ineffectual pretty boys unfortunately caused the group – which by now included extra guitarist and songwriter, Guy McDonough – to fill any space available in their songs with a spaghetti of leadenly expert lead guitar breaks. Guy McDonough had, it seems, been added into the group (his brother Bill was already a member) because he had some good songs – he'd co-written 'Downhearted' – and the band's instant success had prevented them from coming up with enough new material in time. *Sirocco*'s cover showed the six-piece as well-dressed young men good-humouredly putting up with a photo shoot. Produced by Peter Dawkins, it included some of their best songs, particularly 'Things Don't Seem' ('Beaty pub rocking, competently performed', said Donald Roberston in *Roadrunner*),[256] and Guy McDonough's truly brilliant 'Oh No Not You Again' (which he also sang), charting in the simplest terms the decline of a bourgeois relationship under the influence of heroin: if anything Australian Crawl produced approaches perfection, this is it.

Other songs covered the ways in which Reyne and his fellows were reeling from their huge success: 'Unpublished Critics', for instance, was about Christie Eliezer, who had written about Reyne's private life in his 'Barbed Wires' column in *Juke*, and who Reyne hoped to punch in the face.[257] The album also featured 'Errol', another McDonough song, about infamous Tasmanian film star Errol Flynn. Many consumers at the time assumed the narrator of the song's wish to be like Flynn was primarily related to Flynn's reputedly large penis, though the song's lyrics don't delve below the belt. The album was named for Flynn's yacht and played, to some small degree, on the group's reputation as high-flying rich boys, though Reyne was quick to point out whenever possible that, though they had all lived in high-rolling Mt Eliza, they were not rich – nor were they surfies.[258] In a 1981 profile, Brecon Walsh described the group as having emerged from the 'sun and surf milieu of Melbourne's answer to Bel Air: Mt Eliza', and summed up their second album thus:

> The themes covered on *Sirocco* vary from a kind of laconic lambast of the current suburban obsession with hedonistic abandon and terminal greed through to the cheapness of the nouveau riche in pursuit of the illusive 'good times' – ('Lakeside', 'Resort Girls' and 'Can I Be Sure'). Dark visions of the national

underbelly. Along with these concerns, Guy and James have steered the ketch into the unchartered waters of their own gung-ho romanticism. The lure of the mythic explorer, adventurer and Hollywood star – Errol Flynn. Conjuring visions of bush pilots, cargo cults and his own cinematic danse macabre – a suggestion of things archaic and chivalrous.[259]

'You end up saying you'll compromise there, and then somewhere else, and you're just contributing to the whole ridiculous nature of it all', Reyne claimed between *Sirocco* and *Sons of Beaches*.[260] There was some dissatisfaction within the group about their level of success, and their secondary position in the Wheatley organisation with a manager who might have been expected to be a hotline to international stardom for a relatively cool but still very mainstream band of 'spunks' but was instead tied up with the affairs of LRB (who at least by this time were rolled into a neat package with his other major concern, John Farnham), as well as forays into development of FM radio in Australia. The group split with Wheatley and chose their personal manager from within the Wheatley organisation, Sandra Robertson, to represent them. It was an arrangement they would eventually regret, and they later returned to Wheatley, but tension over the group's future was apparent.

Not surprisingly, most attention fell on Reyne throughout the band's career. He had cause for his outbursts against critics who regarded him as pretty and inconsequential: 'If people are going to write about us as beach gigolos then they can stick it . . . If anybody ever criticises us for writing "pop songs", if anyone ever says that to me – that's fucked', he told Toby Creswell (who groundlessly mused that most of the group's 'biting satire' was beyond the 'teenyboppers who besiege the band').[261]

Reyne's stab at acting was far more difficult to overcome. He appeared in the schlocky miniseries *Return to Eden* playing manipulative murderer Greg Marsden. Reyne had been to drama school, but he was picked for the role purely because a producer saw his picture on an album sleeve.[262] The series also featured members of the Yunipingu family, the backbone of the group Yothu Yindi, in minor roles. It was entertainingly silly, but probably not the best career move for a rock singer who felt he needed to be taken seriously for his work rather than his looks. Reyne claimed it drove him 'wild' to be seen as a 'spunky sort of guy . . . It's a nightmare. It's so ridiculous.'[263] Yet he had to grin and bear being voted *TV Week's* 'Most Popular Male Performer', claiming: 'They needed someone to make into their little sex symbol and I seemed the only person available. It was me or Jim Barnes and he drinks a lot of vodka, which is not quite right.'[264]

Australian Crawl continued to prosper; their albums always sold, even if their singles were often not hits. *Sons of Beaches*, from its title onwards, was evidently an attempt to sanitise and commercialise their sound for an international market; the re-recorded 'Downhearted' sounds a bit like the Eagles (though better). Guy McDonough died (from viral pneumonia, septicemia, AIDS or an overdose:

reports differ) in 1984, but the group soldiered on. A stripped-down version of the band, featuring temporary drummer Buzz Bidstrup, recorded the EP *Semantics*, which gave them their last really big hit, a spacious song called 'Reckless'; though very different from their previous work, it has become possibly their best-known track. Reyne's convoluted singing continued to be a source of wonder and ridicule; the 3RRR comedy series *Punter to Punter* satirised Reyne in a parody of 'Reckless'. He told Toby Creswell in *Rolling Stone*:

> Legally, they had to ask my permission to put it on record and they had to send me a copy of the song and the lyric. As if I was going to say no! If I did, they would have had even more ammunition. I thought they could've written better lyrics because there's so much scope. The only thing I can remember is the last line – 'Oh, please, James Reyne, don't bore me shitless.' It was quite funny. The recording was done live and the laughter from the crowd was really vicious. It was wild.[265]

He was parodied again in a similar way later in the 80s, on comedy team the D-Generation's single 'Five in a Row'.

Australian Crawl's last gasp (aside from their second live album) was the debacle of *Between a Rock and a Hard Place*, recorded with British producer Adam Kidron and featuring the funky single 'Two Can Play'. The band had created its own label, Freestyle, which then leased the recordings to EMI. They had invested everything in the album, and it sold poorly, even though it was not entirely below par. As a result, members of Australian Crawl were forced to perpetuate their working relationship far longer than they would have wished, touring to pay off debt.

At the group's demise in 1985, the future loomed bright for Reyne, who immediately threw himself into new projects, including writing music for an album for Lizzy Mercier Descloux, the French post-punk singer (they co-wrote her 1986 single 'Calypso Moguls')[266] and his own solo career. Australian Crawl's biggest hits continued to be a staple on FM radio for decades; a (possibly apocryphal) story from the late 80s has Reyne playing a show with his band in the same street as an Australian Crawl tribute band, who are enjoying a huge crowd while the 'real thing' plays to far fewer 'punters'. The group were no Cold Chisel, however, possibly in part because of their air of cynicism, and also the class nature of their material (broadly speaking, Cold Chisel's songs were about, or appeared to be about, hard-done-by folk in working-class suburbs and towns; Australian Crawl's were often about rich people with volition but no direction).

TOO FAST FOR YOU

The Church were labelmates of Australian Crawl on EMI, which is apparently the reason they were so often compared at this time – there surely could be no other, because two groups of men working within rock music and playing guitars could hardly be more different. Australian Crawl's music was calculated and slick, and referenced 70s sounds and styles with a frisson of 80s production; the Church – partly just because Marty Willson-Piper played a twelve-string – were considered by many to be working in a '60s style'.

Steve Kilbey, the Church's founder and primary singer and songwriter, had moved to Australia with his family from Britain as an infant. After some roaming the Kilbeys settled in Canberra, and Steven's early musical forays took place in his bedroom or in low-key groups playing locally. As mentioned above, he had also briefly been a member of Tactics. When Stephen O'Neil, then of punk group Guthugga Pipeline, met Kilbey in the late 70s at Canberra's local public radio station 2XX, where Kilbey co-hosted a punk show, he was taken aback by Kilbey's self-confidence and extensive future plans. Indeed, the Church signed to EMI after playing only five shows, after A&R man Chris Gilbey heard his second-in-command playing a demo tape through his office wall.[267] Kilbey might have initially celebrated, then – when relations with his first record company started to sour – cursed the thin partitions of the early 80s.

Kilbey notoriously wrote his lyrics for the Church in stream-of-consciousness style, 'being deliberately obscure right from the word go.'[268] He took the attitude that if a song didn't come together in half an hour it wasn't going to: 'It seems to me if you're working really hard on music, there's something going wrong. I feel it should just sort of flow out.'[269] Not surprisingly, this gave rise to an extremely uneven and occasionally even derivative output: the highs, however, were surely higher than they might otherwise have been.

The Church began as a three-piece, with Kilbey on bass and vocals, Peter Koppes on guitar, and Nick Ward on drums. Marty Willson-Piper had only been in Australia from Britain 'for six weeks when I joined the band. Six months later I was making an album.'[270] The first Church album, *Of Skins and Heart*, featured a single, 'The Unguarded Moment', which for many Australians remains the group's best-known song, their 1988 worldwide hit 'Under the Milky Way' notwithstanding. The Church's 'psychedelic' aspect was oft commented on, though Kilbey at this time was a long way from the hardcore drug use that would dog him throughout the 90s; a descent into a 'fucking rubbish world' he was mired in for over a decade thereafter through a whimsical choice enabled, in part, through his friendship with the Go-Betweens' Grant McLennan.[271]

So it was the trappings of an image that gave them their otherworldly feel in the early 80s: the Church's 'retro' nature was part of their appeal – paisley shirts, bootlace ties and clean long hair added to the feeling. 'Maybe it was exciting for people who thought the country was going to be bogged down with the Human League and Buggles for the whole decade, that someone had returned to something that was a little more organic or a little bit more traditional or retro, depending on how you look at it,' Kilbey told Tracee Hutchison in 1992.[272] He also put a good case for the group's Australian acceptance:

> I think if the Church had been in America we never would have got signed up, ever. I think the only reason we were successful was because we had success here. I think you are allowed to develop a sound here ... In Australia I still think there are more people who are willing to take a chance and therefore Australian music was slightly more idiosyncratic ... It's more forgiving here, it's not based on trends.[273]

A second album, *The Blurred Crusade*, followed less than a year later, by which time Richard Ploog, who had been in the Darwin group Exhibit A with Stuart Gray,[274] had replaced Ward. Similarly to the Smiths' theatrical release of Derek Jarman's promotional films for songs from their album *The Queen Is Dead* in 1986, or similar experimental work by the Cure, the Church planned a short film of songs from *The Blurred Crusade* that could run in place of 'documentaries on Tasmania', as Kilbey put it, before the main feature at the cinema.[275]

The Church were 'poorly received' when they supported Duran Duran on a 1982 tour of England; a number of their records, including the third album, *Séance*, were not big sellers. 'The Australian people didn't like *Séance*,' Willson-Piper told an anonymous interviewer for *Pelican*: 'Everybody went, "Oh God, it's really depressing."'[276] *Séance* contained one of their best singles, 'It's No Reason', and other songs that have come to be regarded as classics. In 1984, with the Reels in abeyance, Craig Hooper became a touring member of the Church, playing keyboards; as a friend of the band he was 'the obvious choice', said Kilbey,[277] though in fact he lasted less than a year. By 1985 the Church were worried about their ability to remain financially viable; Kilbey said that 'to maintain credibility we have to keep the band on a fairly big scale.'[278] What he meant by 'credibility' is anyone's guess, but comparisons to Australian Crawl were never far away. The group's EP *Remote Luxury*, for instance, was rumoured to have been a commercial flop; when quizzed about this Willson-Piper lured himself into the art-or-fame trap, and dropped a few cool names – of bands he admired – at the same time:

> Well, it sold 10,000 copies, which in comparison with Australian Crawl's mini-LP of 70,000 copies is a drop in the ocean. I think it justified its release, so did EMI. I mean, it didn't sell that well, but what does sell well in Australia? What does the Birthday Party sell? How well do the Moodists sell? How well do the Go-Betweens sell?[279]

For his part, Kilbey thought his band were 'a lot better looking than Australian Crawl' but that in comparison to that band, 'we're just a pin in the ocean'. (The Crystal Set, a band operated by Russell Kilbey, Steve's younger brother, released a single called 'A Drop in the Ocean' in 1985). On the subject of the group's broader status in Australia, Steve mused:

> Looking at it in the cosmic scheme of things, I guess Iva Davies filled that gap as "the glamorous pop star" before I did. The position has always been there for anyone with enough suss to do it . . . We've got Cold Chisel and Mental As Anything, but not since Skyhooks has there been any glamorous people in there. They're all rugged or humorous, blah blah blah.'[280]

At this early stage, the Church was an EMI band only in Australia; their records were issued (in numerous strange permutations) by independent and pseudo-independent labels in other territories. Early in its career, the group was having hits. But it's important to keep these things in perspective. In the first half of the 1980s the Church had three Australian top-forty singles; Australian Crawl had six; Mental as Anything, on the other hand, had *fourteen*.

BERSERK WARRIORS

Like Australian Crawl and the Church, Mental as Anything featured numerous songwriters and a number of members also contributed vocals. Yet Mental as Anything did not have an acknowledged leader or 'main man'. The band retained its popularity well into the 90s, and was still playing in some form in the second decade of the 21st century. In certain respects – their unabashed Australianness; lighthearted, prolix and parodic nature; and leaning towards rockabilly and other earlier rock 'n' roll forms – the group was a Sydney version of the Pelaco Brothers, a few years on. The artist Paul Worstead, who designed many of the Mentals' early posters and album art and ran a regular dance at the Settlement in Redfern at which the group performed, was a friend of Stephen Cummings', in fact, and Cummings recalls that members of Mental as Anything were in the audience when the Pelaco Brothers played on two trips to Sydney supporting Daddy Cool.

'Visually,' wrote Stephen Charlesworth, who saw Mental as Anything at a university show in 1978, 'the band is a conglomeration of tatty suitcoats (even an old school blazer worn by guitarist Martin Murphy) and assorted ties. There is in the band a certain gonzo humour ... it takes a certain amount of self-determination to go bananas before an audience that is standing still some distance away stuffing sandwiches into their little mouths.'[281] The group's dress sense was apparently worth comment: Smith later said that they were 'written up in the rock magazines as looking like the musical St Vincent de Paul.'[282]

Mental as Anything were art students who retained their love of creating art – they would paint 'fairly detailed'[283] landscapes when on tour. They came together in the late 70s as a joke group with joke names: Reg Mombassa (Chris O'Doherty), Wayne 'Bird' Delisle (David Twohill), Andrew 'Greedy' Smith, Martin Plaza (Murphy's stage name) and – not a joke, unless it's a punchline

– Peter O'Doherty, who did flirt with a stage name (Yoga Dog). They claimed in 1978 that they had been 'doing that punk scene really early... We played at this place called the Unicorn Pub every week and that was one of the first punk venues going... but then we started getting all sorts of different people coming along.'[284] They later described themselves as not new, but 'slightly soiled wave.'[285] They helped to found Regular Records with Martin Fabinyi to issue their first record, *Mental as Anything Plays at Your Party,* in 1979. One track from this 7-inch EP, 'The Nips Are Getting Bigger' was re-recorded and issued as a single; the group were invited onto *Countdown* under a new, briefly operational policy that allowed (or encouraged) independent bands, though by the time they appeared Regular had struck a deal with Festival, rendering it no longer independent. There was some objection to the word 'nips' in the media – regardless of whether it referred to Japanese people or to alcohol (it was the latter),[286] and 2SM – Sydney's premier pop station – initially denied the group airplay because of its name,[287] which was considered a dig at the handicapped.

Mental as Anything's first album was *Get Wet;* they held a swimming competition to publicise it in December 1979,[288] though presumably they were not extending a metaphor when they signed with the management agency Dirty Pool a few weeks later.[289] 'The Nips Are Getting Bigger' made it a moderate success, and despite the hiccup of a weak second album, *Espresso Bongo* (Smith later said 'We'd like to get all the copies of *Espresso Bongo* and recall them and redo them and send them back out – like you do faulty cars),[290] they were a frequent presence in the charts during the 80s. Despite Smith's claim that the band suffered from 'Oblomov's disease'[291] (chronic laziness), their third album, *Cats and Dogs,* appeared less than two years after the first, and was correctly described by him as 'Fifty, no, a hundred and fifty times better than the last one.'[292] Elvis Costello produced a single for them (the catchy 'I Didn't Mean to Be Mean'); the best track on *Cats and Dogs* was 'Berserk Warriors'. Smith told *RAM* readers that Mombassa, the song's author, had confided in him that "It's really an allegory about the break-up of Björn and Anna in ABBA". He was thrilled. That's about as close as he comes to being deep.'[293] Jimmy Barnes jammed with the group one night at Sydney University's Manning Bar under the name the Handsome Vikings.[294] The group's lyrical subjects were diverse: Smith contributed a song, 'Sad Poetry', to the album that he described

as a 'put down of Shakespeare, William Shakespeare, the famous Bard of Avon, not William Shakespeare the pop singer with the nice shoes. Anyway the song is basically criticizing the inclusion of Shakespeare in the English curriculum of Australian High Schools. It's fairly deeply disguised.'[295]

Mental as Anything enjoyed just one international hit record, in 1987: the single 'Live It Up', written by Andrew 'Greedy' Smith, was a top-ten hit in various European countries, including Britain. It was from their album *Fundamental*, produced by Richard Gottehrer. There was something karmic about Gottehrer's involvement with the group: his 1960s band, the Strangeloves (their biggest hit was 'I Want Candy'), had pretended to be Australian rather than face the drab reality of being New Yorkers. Sadly, 'Live It Up' was not one of Mental As Anything's best singles; musically, it merely chugged along, and was nowhere near as good as contemporary Australian hits 'Apocalypso', 'Spirit Got Lost', 'Brain Brain' or 'Date with Destiny'. It was perhaps its mindless cheer and atypical *lack* of quirkiness that made it acceptable UK chart fodder; the last thing the British wanted or needed (since they already had Madness) was a larrikin pop group like Mental as Anything.

YOU NEED A FRIEND

A group even more unjustly fated to miss out on international success was the Sunnyboys, whose work was unique and – at least in its first incarnation – superb. Their sound was firmly international, but singer/songwriter Jeremy Oxley had a vision which seems today to be completely Australian – both amusing and amused without being in the least obscurist. Contemporaries of (and equals to) Manchester's Buzzcocks, Derry's Undertones and New York's Blondie, the Sunnyboys were better at clever guitar pop than most and more consistent.

Richard Burgman had moved from his hometown of Wagga Wagga in 1973 to study at the University of NSW. He had briefly been in a covers band called Charlie with Chris Masuak; the group had showcased Masuak's talents for members of his next band, Radio Birdman. Whether Burgman was also considered for this band is not recorded, but of course the similarity of his own name to the group's would have made it too weird. Much later – between late 1979 and mid 1980 – Burgman found himself in a band with vocalist Penny Ward, drummer Michael Charles (later of the Screaming Tribesmen), and Peter Oxley on bass. Witnessing the Shy Imposters' first show at the Civic, Darcy Condon wrote in *RAM*: 'I think I've just seen history being made',[296] which was slightly true (the incident has, after all, been recorded in historical accounts).

Peter Oxley, his younger brother Jeremy, and drummer Richard 'Bil' Bilson, grew up in Kingscliff in northern New South Wales, close to the Queensland border. Both Oxleys surfed competitively; Jeremy was also a champion as an artist and wrote songs. The brothers – and Bilson – had a number of bands, including Wooden Horse and Golden Syrup.[297]

The Shy Imposters played only a handful of shows, and after their demise Burgman joined the Oxleys, Bilson and (briefly) Rob Younger in a new group. The Sunnyboys debuted in August 1980 with a sound and style premised on what Jeremy Oxley perceived as a gap in the 'scene' that his songs – many of them cheerful celebrations of his first proper romantic relationship – could fill. A quarter of a century later, Richard Burgman recalled:

> We played at Chequers nightclub on Goulburn St in downtown Sydney on August 15 1980. A scant two months after Shy Imposters had imploded. We were on the bill with the Flaming Hands and the Lipstick Killers. It was a wildly exciting night. Sydney was abuzz with bands everywhere, the gig was full, we played well, we got an enthusiastic response, and we went home happy. It really couldn't have been better.

The group were hard-working, but it was also a golden time – they were an instant hit. Their name came from Peter Oxley (a Sunnyboy being a cheap 'n' cheerful ice-based confection); Jeremy had wanted to call the band the Detectives.[298] Younger had been a founder member and the group originally played songs by both Younger and Jeremy Oxley. But Younger, playing the kindly facilitator role he would reprise soon after with Died Pretty, felt Jeremy was the most suitable to sing his own songs and he bowed out before the band played their first show. On the night of their debut, Jules Normington from Phantom Records told them their song 'Alone with You' had to be a single. The group were already in contact with Lobby Loyde, who was running a rehearsal space where they practiced; he produced their first, self-titled EP which included that song and was released on Phantom on the last day of 1980 – rush-released, because the band really wanted the record to come out that year. A thousand copies were sold in a fortnight; the band was 'by far the hottest potato on the Phantom label'.[299]

Jeremy Oxley (and others) made much of his youth; he was still a teenager when he wrote the songs that made the Sunnyboys legendary, and those early, happy songs were, he insisted, genuine and honest: 'The thing is, when I wrote those songs I was really in love,' he told 'T.C.', a *Roadrunner* journalist, in 1981, 'so I don't give a fuck what anybody says. I wrote exactly what I felt.'[300]

Neil Bradbury, the editor of *Vox*, suggested that before they took the rollercoaster ride:

> Perhaps the boys should sit down and have a long chat with someone like Steve Cummings and Martin Armiger. The Sports are a band which by their own admission see things in a somewhat bitter light. Dialogue between the two groups would do each a world of good.[301]

This was good advice, though there is no evidence the Sunnyboys acted on it. The Sports were long-standing Mushroom stalwarts; Bradbury would soon be in the label's employ; the Sunnyboys were recent signings. Mushroom had developed a distinct interest in Phantom's release schedule; they signed the Sunnyboys in early 1981, releasing their first single 'Happy Man' soon after. Jeremy Oxley later said 'We used to go out to lunch with a few people ... Then we went out with Michael Gudinski. We saw that Michael was a nice guy, and that we could place our hearts in his hands.'[302]

Burgman has since claimed that the group thought, weighing up the various good offers made to them, that Mushroom had the ability to give them commercial exposure. Lobby Loyde was to remain the group's producer and mentor, and their manager in tandem with Sally Collins in SCAM management; the Machinations and Sardine V also came under the SCAM umbrella. The generous and thoughtful Matt Moffitt was to say of Loyde:

> I think the best thing about Lobby is that he is a really warm guy with a lot of experience and not much of a chip on his shoulder. He's a pretty clear thinker. He's very warm. You can see that in the Sunnyboys. You can see they've got someone there who isn't a manager, who isn't a paternal sort of pushy character but who genuinely likes them and who is genuinely interested in their welfare. It shows, I think.[303]

The first (self-titled) album is a total success; it is rare to find a rock/pop album that is so perfect in almost every detail. There are numerous reasons for this but above all Jeremy Oxley's vision was concise and clear; pop music is hardly ever so intelligent and heartfelt at the same time. The album was a top-twenty hit (two singles, 'Alone with You' and 'Happy Man', were top thirty). Its stark, cool cover – the group against a yellow or blue backdrop, depending on which version you bought – and its amusing inner sleeve, depicting the Sunnyboys 'climbing the wall of life', were all enticing, but the fresh and exciting songs were the most important ingredient. 'I have no hesitation,' wrote David Pestorius in *Roadrunner*, 'in saying that this is the most complete debut album by an Australian band since the Sports' *Reckless*. Australian Crawl's *Boys Light Up* is utterly insignificant by comparison.'[304]

The follow up, *Individuals*, was embarked on within six months; the group recorded, again with Loyde, but in Auckland, as part of a Hawke government export initiative. There had been little time for Jeremy to write new material and, while they had a large number of older songs, the Sunnyboys understandably wanted to progress. Since its release in May 1982, the band – and many others – have regarded *Individuals* as a failure; they blamed Mushroom for releasing a record they were not happy with. In fact, *Individuals* is an excellent album, unfairly maligned, it seems, by everyone but Peter Oxley.[305] It features 'You Need a Friend', which might well be the best song Jeremy Oxley has written (to date); the remarkable video featured a montage similar to that in Greg Macainsh's sharpie film of ten years previously, depicting young – arguably alienated or marginal – people in public places. The creepy reprise of the song's 'Turn the people round' chorus at the end of the album hinted at disturbing events to come, but on the whole, *Individuals* is strong, centred and solid; it simply requires empathy and understanding.

Collins, looking back on the whole SCAM era, describes Lobby Loyde as 'a softy' who had great empathy with the musicians he was working with: 'He dearly loved those bands and being a left-of-centre musician himself, he could understand them from the inside out. He was blown away by Jeremy's ability and could see his fragility, and used to say to me, "Watch that one". I tried; ultimately I failed.' It was towards the end of her three-year tenure as manager of the Sunnyboys that Jeremy Oxley began to exhibit symptoms of mental illness, though it was some years before he was diagnosed. He became paranoid and violent and drank to excess; the group changed management, from SCAM to Loyde's associate Michael Chugg, who also managed the Church and who considered the Sunnyboys 'fucking magnificent'.[306] The group made a third album, *Get Some Fun*. Burgman later recalled of Jeremy:

> He used to drink so he wouldn't hear the 'voices', and Peter was doing his desperate best to shield him from the world. We all worked very hard on *Get Some Fun*. Jeremy was solid through it all, you can tell by his guitar playing and his singing. Especially his singing, he was getting better and better at that.
>
> There were incidents all along the way, most of which could be explained as eccentric or high-strung behaviour, not as schizophrenia per se. His disease claimed him gradually. It was more a gradual disintegration than a catastrophe.[307]

A mooted American tour with the Go-Gos, who were fans of the band, failed to occur. In 2004 Burgman said:

> We'd all had our hopes pinned on the second album, but it wasn't quite the calling card Mushroom was hoping for. After that it was a "wait for the third album and we'll see" situation. By the time the third album was done, it was too late. I think we might have gone down well, but who knows. We were released on independent labels in France, and they liked us in Scandinavia, but nothing ever happened in the USA.[308]

Get Some Fun had been recorded in the UK with the Motors' Nick Garvey – an inspired pairing, even if Peter Oxley later described Garvey as 'shithouse'.[309] – and the group played some well-received shows in Britain, but by this time it was clear that Jeremy's condition would make it impossible to continue. *Get Some Fun* sold poorly, but nevertheless featured some classic songs, particularly the hilariously strange 'Show Me Some Discipline', with its carefully choreographed video featuring the Sunnyboys in black polo-necks surrounded by very skinny dancers. Other singles –'Love in a Box', about (someone else's) drug use, and 'Comes As No Surprise' – offered ample evidence that however poor Jeremy's mental health, his talent as a songwriter continued to thrive. He spoke at the time of songs representing 'a young man crying out for order in a world which seems to be filled with chaos and disorder'.[310] In mid 1984 Bilson was offered the chance to join the Hoodoo Gurus to replace James Baker; after checking with his current group and being assured that the Sunnyboys were continuing, he declined – two weeks later, they announced their break-up,[311] which happened at the end of that year.

Two Sunnyboys (Bilson and Peter Oxley) joined the Sparklers with younger Oxley sister Melanie, Chris Abrahams, Mark Walker (who had been in the Sweet Nothings), and Ernie Finch, 'cult hero of Newtown.'[312] Jeremy Oxley formed the Chinless Elite, then Fishermen, and then a new band also called the Sunnyboys which recorded one album, *Wildcat*, for RCA, produced by Garth Porter. Soon after this group disbanded in 1990, the original line-up reconvened for a four-week tour promoting a compilation album entitled *Play the Best*; the possibility of recording new material was floated, but this did not happen.[313] Sporadic reunions have included a short set at the 1998 Mushroom Records celebration in Melbourne, and a 2012 appearance (under the name Kids in Dust) at the Hoodoo Gurus 'mini-fest' Dig It Up. Jeremy's condition having stabilized, the group has since embarked on a series of small but enormously popular tours. Their music – particularly their first album – retains a timelessness for Australians across generations; it is not necessarily nostalgic but continues to be relevant.

SCAM

The degree to which the Australian music industry at this time was dominated by a scant few individuals – mainly men, operating as a kind of network with associated connections dating back to the mid and late 60s – is difficult to assess fully. There is little doubt that a significant proportion of *Countdown*'s Australian schedule throughout the 70s and 80s consisted either of personal friends of Ian Meldrum dating back to his time at *Go-Set* or groups and artists under the aegis of Meldrum's friends. This is not to imply widespread corruption; it is rather an indication of how small, and in some respects conservative, the industry was. As long as Gudinski and Meldrum retained a mutual respect, each could aid the other in maximizing their opportunities. Few major players (and even many minor ones) were ever separated by more than a degree of two from one or the other of these figures, or both. Ross Wilson, for instance, was never a Mushroom artist, but he was mentor to and producer/publisher of Skyhooks, the archetypal Mushroom band of the 1970s. Similarly, Lobby Loyde only had one album, *Live with Dubs*, released on Mushroom in 1980, but his points of contact with Gudinski were numerous throughout the 70s and 80s. When Loyde wrote passionate screeds against the establishment that were published in *Planet*, he almost certainly went well beyond Gudinski's own views; at the same time, he was a useful iconoclast to have onside. Ten years later, he was a valuable supplier of new talent to the Mushroom stable.

Sally Collins is the perfect witness to all this. With qualifications in business, retail management and childcare, she was eminently qualified to work alongside Loyde in band management. When this started, she was working in a vegetarian restaurant, And Now For Something Completely Different, in the northern Sydney suburb of Chatswood. 'The Diff' doubled as a venue,[314] and her boyfriend at the time – Flowers' keyboard player, Anthony Smith (who, apparently to circumvent a 'boring' name, often called himself Adam Hall)[315] – introduced her to Loyde. Smith was clearly a major influence on Collins's future: he also happened to mention having seen the Triffids in Perth, and two years later, when the group toured Sydney for the first time, Collins made sure she was at the first show. She would later become their manager.

At Loyde's recommendation, Collins saw Sardine V play their first show in December 1980 and recalls: 'I was transfixed, hypnotised, an instant fan.' She arranged for them to play a New Year's Eve show at the restaurant; 'I had never promoted anything, but I promoted the crap out of that night,' she remembers, 'and it was huge.' She adds:

> So Lobby says to me the next day, 'Mate, I've been watching you, you are a bit of a fucking smart arse. I am about to start this management thing for Sardine V and a couple of others. We could do with a smart arse like you.' I replied that I was only really experienced with managing children, to which he replied 'perfect, musicians are just like children'. Next day I quit my job in day care and at the restaurant and started meeting with Lobby every day to plot and scheme about the management company.
>
> SCAM stood for Suss City Artist Management. There were four of us, with Lob at the helm. The other two were Bob Nimmo – Bob ran and owned Day Street Rehearsal Studios, which were not only rehearsal studios but a screen printing business – and an accountant (or so we were lead to believe), Clive Townsend. Our initial charges were Sardine V and Machinations. Then Local Product, the Traitors and Sunnyboys.

Nimmo had also been present for the legendary session at which Loyde engineered and produced X's *X-Aspirations* album in October 1979.[316]

Collins says that 'Lobby had a long-standing love/hate relationship with the music industry':

> He repeatedly said to me, while winking: 'Learn from them, but never trust the bastards. Always do your own thing and not what they tell you. Use them for you'...At the same time he loved those guys as well, admired their achievements, particularly Chuggy and Gudinski, and they loved him in return. They grew up together in a way, and while they became 'the establishment' Lobby remained a rebel.

Loyde, for his part, always had praise for Gudinski; decades after the SCAM era, and not long before his death, he remarked that 'Everything Michael's put out, he's loved.'[317]

Collins found herself a beneficiary of further mentorship from the old guard. Michael Chugg was, she says, 'like a silent partner of SCAM', and Loyde frequently sought advice from him. Similarly, Loyde arranged for Collins herself to be tutored in tour accounting by Philip Jacobsen. Loyde also recommended she read widely on topics related to the 'industry' side of the music business; biographies of Colonel Tom Parker, Brian Epstein and Albert Grossman, for instance, 'to understand representation and how artists had been ripped off by publishers and labels.'

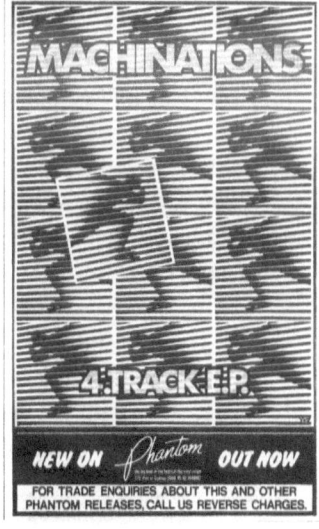

Loyde became manager of the Sunnyboys by default, while he was already producing their first records; Collins was drafted into managing a tour of Adelaide almost immediately. Twenty years later, Peter Oxley reminisced that the Sunnyboys 'used to play all the time. We used to go on the road all the time. We travelled the Deadly Hume [Highway] 20 times a year, probably more. So, it was sort of an endless run of playing shows.[318]

All the SCAM acts who were at the level of releasing records did so first through the independent label Phantom and then, in the case of chart acts Sunnyboys and Machinations, through Mushroom. Collins remembers:

> Lob acknowledged the need for our acts not to be bunched with all Mushroom acts, who were all primarily Melbourne-based. He felt Mushroom was a good progression for the Sunnyboys from Phantom, as they were crossing over. However Machinations and Sardine V had different sensibilities. So he hatched a scheme with Michael for Mushroom to launch a new label for new 'alternative' acts, a bit more sensitive, the White label. I'm sure Michael Gudinski remembers

this differently, however as I recall, Lob zapped down to Melbourne for chats with Gudinski, and the White Label started to evolve. Lob didn't think anyone of the existing staff should run it. We really liked *VOX* magazine, edited by Neil Bradbury (who showed real interest in our acts) and thought he might be a great label guy. Turned out he was, for a time.

Of course our love/hate relationship with Mushroom/White was born at the time of signing. There were some great people working there in the early '80's particularly, Michelle Higgins, a PR dynamo, who adored Lobby and our acts and did a fabulous job for us. Despite this the Australian music scene was full of 'big fish' in a small pond. It was a pervasive attitude and you could easily hit a brick wall. They wanted conformity. We had our own ideas.

Collins was a loyal supporter of Loyde's, seeing him as 'a creative genius being squashed into a business model. I would always do my best to cover for him. His answer was often to go AWOL and do things in his own time.' She was essentially the learner driver in an operation that was consolidated around Loyde, and saw SCAM attempt to expand in the manner traditional to the Australian music industry. She recalls that Loyde and Gudinski traveled to Los Angeles frequently between 1981 and 83, when artists from Mushroom's White label (notably Machinations and Hunters and Collectors) were being released on A&M. 'America was a different beast,' of course, as Collins and SCAM quickly discovered; for reasons now obscure, not only did A&M have little interest in promoting its Australian artists, but when Machinations did get in the Billboard R&B charts with 'Pressure Sway', she says, 'Mushroom would not financially support the band in its efforts to realise this good fortune.'

SCAM fought a good fight during its brief period of existence. Collins believes the organization rewrote some industry rules, creating a better model for future practices:

> 'We negotiated real change for our artists by refusing to sign publishing deals with retention periods "for life" or "75 years", [reducing them] to a manageable 25 years. Lob was determined that our acts would not sign 'jail terms' which encouraged laziness by publishers or labels. He was rightly convinced that short terms of contracts and short retention periods were better for artists, because labels and publishers had to work harder to keep their artists.'

However, SCAM was short-lived. Nimmo became a heroin addict, Townsend was 'less than useless', and 'Lobby, I think, became overwhelmed with the shit of it all and eventually disappeared to Melbourne.' Collins says that Loyde left her 'more or less holding the fort, with the accounts guys.'

> Too busy with Sunnyboys and poor Jeremy's increasingly bizarre behaviour, to have any control over the stuff at the office (I was too young still to fully appreciate what was happening to Jeremy and to cope) and without Lob's support, I wanted out too. I resigned from Sunnyboys, heartbroken. We took the Sunnyboys to Chuggy.
>
> I then hung around and tried to help Machinations, clean up their mess and get them going in the States. Spent a couple of weeks in a cheap dive hotel near A&M trying to get some attention over there. Machinations were charting, but our representative was out on tour with Mentals as they mowed people's lawns and did odd jobs. The only familiar face in that office was Michael Roberts, who was trying to get attention for Hunters. It was pathetic. In those days, nobody really spoke to each other, so we never banded together for our common good. I came home defeated and sick of it. With Fred Loneragan's dad, I took Machinations to Jeremy Fabinyi. And got out.

Looking back, Collins reiterates her respect for industry moguls like Chugg and Gudinski, while noting: 'The problem was, for me, that they treated acts generically.'

> For me each act deserved its individual marketing plan and approach. If a record didn't stick during its designated four-week promotional cycle, they lost interest and moved on to the next thing. I found this insulting and ridiculous. They weren't developing their artists. You could spend months making a great record, but they wouldn't spend more than 3 to 4 weeks working it. Ridiculous. Also they never delved into the psyche of their artists, to be sensitive enough to their needs. How could they ever understand the sensitivities of Ian Rilen, with his fuck you attitude, or Jeremy Oxley, as he began to break down, or David McComb, who without the support of the Triffids and the presence of management had a heart attack in New York? Mushroom dismissed him as a drug addict, not someone with a heart condition. They just thought he was wasting their money. Lobby and I could care for these people. We understood their sensibilities and tried to protect and nurture them, with support and humour. We were honest and had a 'duty of care'.

The tumultuous ménage a trois of business, art and craft is a perpetual motion machine; it keeps the music industry eternally moving forward, and at the same time makes it an eternally unsatisfactory and disturbing enterprise. The story of the Gudinski-Loyde relationship may well stand as an exemplar of the industry's dynamics – in Australia or anywhere else. Collins's last word on Loyde and Gudinski is highly revealing:

As frustrating as Michael G. found Lobby and our approach to the industry, they knew what a creative thinker he was and wanted to keep him near, within their fold. They learnt from Lobby, though they would deny it, such are the egos involved. He forced Michael to think, and to change they way they issued contracts and what was acceptable practice. I think many Mushroom acts benefited from Michael Gudinski's relationship with Lobby.

EXCESS

Anyone who expects art to triumph over tawdry commerce – ever – is fooling themselves; and in some ways it's probably better that it never does. Members of the Sunnyboys, Machinations, and even Sardine V may well have looked wistfully on as far less talented groups succeeded in Australia and worldwide. It is absurd to suggest that a group is too good to succeed: however, the formula for success, if there is a formula, is almost certainly nothing more than a balance between hard work and a willingness to keep hammering out variations on the same dull theme forever.

INXS supported the Sunnyboys in 1980; within a few years they had soared to implausible international success. Of course, INXS and the Sunnyboys are not otherwise particularly comparable groups, and whatever Jeremy Oxley's strengths as a songwriter and performer, he was an entirely different proposition to the lithe and sensational Michael Hutchence. From early on INXS were regarded by many – both supporters and detractors – as tailor-made for the international stadium circuit.

The story of INXS's rise to fame (and Hutchence's tragic, self-inflicted death, and the remainder of the group's tragic inability to accept that their use-by date was far behind them) is a core element of Australia's rock history. Listening to their cornerstone album *Kick*, from 1987, it's easy to detect many elements of Australian post-punk; those fuzz guitars, mechanistic rhythms, beautifully enunciated middle-class vocals, and attractively repetitive basslines would not have been out of place at the Seaview Ballroom in 1982, even if the group's slick production values and screaming fans would. Earlier work, like their self-titled debut, is even more in the post-punk vein – Jenny Hunter-Brown, a fan, called it 'mutant Austral skank'[319] – featuring ska inflections, mod moments and that unattractive bellowing/yelling style so common amongst groups who identified as 'pub rock'. In fact, Hutchence's 1990 foray with Ollie Olsen, the Max Q group-and-album which roped in many of Olsen's 70s/80s new-wave collaborators, is in many ways far more of an exploration of the world beyond Australian post-punk than INXS's best work is.

A key element of INXS dates back to more than a decade before the band first appeared: the Loved Ones' classic 1966 hit 'The Loved One'. INXS covered this song in 1981 to great effect and they recorded it again, in a vastly inferior version, in 1986 for *Kick*, at Tim Farriss's suggestion and because the band decided it would be 'interesting'.[320] What's more, the group's own 'Never Tear Us Apart' (on the same album) uses 'The Loved One' as a template; you can sing the earlier song to the later one. Gerry Humphrys was in no mind to complain; the royalty cheque he received for the INXS cover(s) 'bought me a car and a couple of pairs of shoes' and 'was perhaps the biggest royalty cheque I ever got in my life'.[321] The sexuality and seeming spontaneity of the 60s group were reflected in the latter one; for both, 'The Loved One' was a highlight of their recorded work and in performance, the difference being that the Loved Ones wrote it.

INXS began in Frenchs Forest, a northern suburb of Sydney, in the early 70s. They were known first of all as Guinness,[322] and based largely around the three Farriss brothers. The first song Andrew Farriss wrote with the group's singer Michael Hutchence was about how clever the Beatles had been.[323] Hutchence was the standout in the band from the outset, if only for his unusual background: though born in Sydney, he had spent much of his childhood in Hong Kong where he trained as a swimmer for two hours a day and formed a folk group performing 'café music'.[324] He had also spent a short period of his early life in Los Angeles. The group began calling themselves, unimaginatively and semi-truthfully, the Farriss Brothers, playing shows in 'chicken and mouse' costumes or, in Andrew Farriss's case, naked under a transparent yellow outfit – probably a postman's raincoat.[325] These days might have lasted forever had not Midnight Oil's manager Gary Morris taken them in hand and relabelled them with a very different, but equally terrible, name (what does 'INXS' mean? That there are too many of them? They lay it on too thick? Or does it punningly apply the same kind of meaningless meaning as Tactics' name?).[326]

The group famously moved to Perth in 1979 when youngest member John was forced to accompany the Farrisses' parents there: they were based in the suburb of Nedlands. Band mythology suggests they cut their teeth on the rough, tough beer barns of Western Australia – it's a quaint story. Tim Farriss reminisced three years later that the Farriss Brothers at that time were 'a small "unpretentiously pretentious" pub band'.[327] 'Perth might be very small,' Hutchence mused soon after, 'but there are a lot of eccentrics there.'[328] They returned to Sydney in 1980, signed to former AC/DC manager Michael Browning's Deluxe label[329] – where their labelmates were all much better than them (Eric Gradman Man and Machine, who produced an album's worth of demos for the label, also fall into this category) – and set about conquering the world.

INXS's self-titled album was produced by Duncan Maguire, once of jazz fusion group Ayers Rock. Hutchence told Ed St John in 1982: 'Our first album was a little like a pre-debut album. We thought, well, why not, because we'd been playing for a while. But I'm glad that we did it. We also dabbled a bit in the production, so parts of it didn't sound too good.'[330] Adrian Ryan, reviewing a live show for *Roadrunner* at this time, was unimpressed:

Despite the showmanship, the rhythms, the stuttering guitars and the occasional attempts to be eccentric (usually signaled by tentative avante-gardisms on the keyboards) INXS are trapped in a comfortable prison of their own making.[331]

Ryan is correct: the early forays of INXS sound uncomfortable and half-realised, as if the group were locked in the studio and would only be released on delivery of recordings. For the second LP, *Underneath the Colours*, Deluxe installed another rock stalwart – Richard Clapton – in the producer's seat; Hutchence suggested the attitude was that producer and band were like different chemicals, 'so let's see what happens'. For his part, Clapton claimed the relationship was happy because 'we'd sit around playing records all night and talking about music, and then we'd go into the studio and they'd do what I told them.'[332] Clapton believed that to produce the band he 'had to fully explore their musical influences, and their musical influences are really diverse ... I got into some pretty obscure stuff that I hadn't really gotten before.'[333] The mind boggles, particularly as he told another interviewer that he 'felt it was important for INXS to be untainted by outside influences.'[334] On business matters, he was far more sophisticated and less equivocal, telling St John:

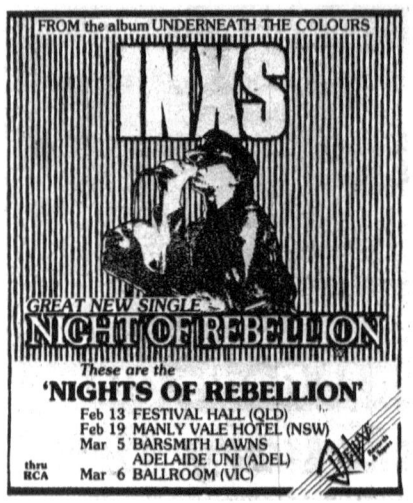

> We came to a realisation a while ago, that no matter what you're doing musically, whether you're farting into a bedpan or making perfect pop music, you should go for the best deal possible. That may sound simple, but most bands settle for less than that. We realised that we should try and make as much as possible, because that's all they're trying to get out of you.[335]

Once again, however, the results were not marvellous. One thing that could be said in early-period INXS's favour was that they always seemed about to do something good; the obvious criticism of them would be that they never really did.

Shabooh Shoobah, the band's third album, marked their slow move into international markets and the beginning of their move out of the 'alternative' world (prior to this – in 1982 – it could still be said that 'INXS always created interest on an "alternative" level ... well before commercial exposure',[336] though they were already playing to large crowds). Their music became more seamless and stylish; the group sounded a little less like it was uneasily hiding on the sidelines taking notes from 'new wave' groups it respected but didn't really understand. '*Shabooh Shoobah* was a very emotional record. *The Swing* was, by our standards, pretty political',[337] Hutchence said after the release of their fourth album, which included vocal contributions from Daryl Hall, Jenny Morris, Sean Kelly, Andrew Duffield and the Reels' Dave Mason (under the record-company-eluding name Dave Spinner). By this time INXS had figured out how to maximize what they had in the way of talent, though some of the album is still bizarrely clunky – the banal 'Face the Change', for instance. Its biggest single, 'Original Sin', was produced by Nile Rogers, who Hutchence found 'damned exuberant'.[338] A kind of faux-naif comment on racism as a bad thing, the song's video marked INXS's foray into the Japanese market – and their flirtation with Japanese imagery.

The INXS story has been explored in numerous books, most of them written after Hutchence's death in 1997, and the bulk of them laudatory of both man and band, though his brother Rhett's memoir does present some tangible evidence of Hutchence's frustrations within a band he had outgrown but felt he could not desert. *Kick* was their biggest hit album, and it was clear that their formula was only going to take them so far. More importantly, while the band were craftsmen, Hutchence was an artist, though whether he was a good one is hard to ascertain from the meagre evidence. His lyrics for INXS were reputedly drawn (literally) from a large garbage bag of disconnected lines, though this story may actually have been a product of his own self-deprecation. He was always at pains to make it clear that he was one part of a six-piece unit, and certainly other members of the group, for reasons unclear, had their fans too. *Rolling Stone* always liked to cite comparisons with the canon: 'a classic rock & roll beanpole twisting his frame into erotic, Jaggeresque body sculptures.'[339] Hutchence certainly didn't model himself on Jagger, or for that matter Jim Morrison, another individual who for no earthly reason he was often compared to (in the early 80s *Rolling Stone* seemed to use 'Jim Morrison' as a synonym for 'man singing').

One role in which Hutchence was successful was that of catalyst. His co-production with Andrew Farriss of the vigorous, provocative single 'Sex Symbol' for Flame Fortune was a fine example of this. The group assembled to record the song was an all-star cast of Australian pop – James Reyne, Rick Grossman and Buzz Bidstrup were all involved. Fortune (real name Heather Hogue) was a mystical young former child star from Los Angeles who had impressed Hutchence with her potential; the single was released in 1985. It was only a minor hit. 'At the risk of being called an idiot,' Kim Reed wrote in *On the Street*, 'this record isn't bad at all.'[340] A Sydney schoolgirl, Sybilla Vasali, was inspired by the song to begin a correspondence with Fortune; the group she helped form three years later, Matrimony, would be groundbreaking and, in an unexpected turnaround, Fortune herself would travel back to Sydney in 1990 to try to co-opt some of Matrimony's cool to restart her own career. She was smart to do so – Matrimony are now considered a forerunner, if not an instigator, of the riot grrl movement. Flame Fortune's own career went no further, though, and she died in tragic circumstances a few years later. The main guitar theme from 'Sex Symbol' would be co-opted for a Victorian bicycle safety advertisement, which featured a cartoon version of Molly Meldrum (no-one's idea of a sex symbol) cycling with children.

Hutchence's attraction to the Melbourne post-punk underground is telling. He claimed that on leaving school he had 'nosedived into the underground',[341] but Hong Kong folk coffee-houses aside, the only real scene he'd ever been a part of was INXS-related. Very daggily, Andrew Farriss describes Hutchence's interest in alternative music as an attraction to 'the dark side of the force', a *Star Wars*-Aleister Crowley metaphor mix which showed how little the other five-sixths of INXS understood their singer.[342] By the time Richard Lowenstein was making INXS videos he'd had a hit film with *Strikebound*, a political docudrama based on a book by his mother, Wendy. Lowenstein had once shared a house with members of the Ears and made videos for them (the Ears' Sam Sejavka had a minor role in *Strikebound*). Lowenstein had also made the filmclip to Hunters and Collectors' 'Talking to a Stranger', which Hutchence adored. He was therefore employed to do something similarly avant garde for INXS, and the two became close friends. On one now famous occasion, Lowenstein was pitching a detective thriller as his next film to a bored producer in Cannes, with Hutchence in the room, when he realised he was losing the money's attention and instead began extrapolating a film predicated on Hutchence being the star; Hutchence intuitively backed him up.

The result was *Dogs in Space*, a film notable in so many ways – and so difficult, too – that it has been too hard for many to digest. Yet it remains the best document of late-70s Australian rock culture you could hope to find, filmed only a few years after the times in which it is set – and in the same house (lovingly de-restored for the screen) that Lowenstein had lived in. The band the Ears was reconstituted as Dogs in Space – and misrepresented, too: the Ears on record, and live, were much more coherent than the rubbish band singing the truly horrid 'Golf Course'. Hutchence plays a man called Sam, with no last name, but Sam Sejavka was brought in for a short while as advisor on the character (in a 1985 interview Sejavka explained that he'd bumped into Richard Lowenstein "at this party last night. He was telling me he wanted to make a movie about my life ... I suspect he was winding me up or something ... I think he wants to go for a rags-to-riches story, haha'[343]), and Lowenstein has insisted that Hutchence's portrayal of a short-sighted, animalistic, impenetrable egotist is as near the truth as it could be.

Just as INXS would have been a shadow without Hutchence (which is in fact what they became in the late 1990s), *Dogs in Space* would never have been made without his presence: regardless of how one feels about his acting, one has to be grateful to him for that, at least. Other bands – including famous 'little bands' such as Thrush and the Cunts, as well as the highly impressive Primitive Calculators – reformed for the film. If Lowenstein wished to suggest the Ears were also a 'little band', though, he was messing with reality. They were a pop group with a regular line-up playing regular shows, with the tall, handsome and debonair Sejavka out front, occasionally being asked to sign their singles by cute girls from Noble Park.

Some former Ears proved their pop credentials by making good but unsuccessful records under the management of Sebastian Chase[344] as Virgin Australia's first signing, Beargarden (Hutchence was slated at one stage to produce them),[345] and Cathy McQuade was in the briefly excellent Deckchairs Overboard.

Lowenstein deftly navigates the difficulties of making a dirty little rock film starring a teen heartthrob. When Hutchence sings Ollie Olsen's sharp, harrowing, pristine 'Rooms for the Memory' over Anna's grave in the final sequence, the audience is left with a bunch of pregnant ideas. But that's just a slender tailpiece of the film: it's documentary, cultural critique, and humanist passion play all in one.

Ridiculously – and surely showing the chasm of misunderstanding that already existed between Hutchence and the rest of INXS – Andrew Farriss's response was to make a video about fishing, which he called *Fish in Space*. Some might say this was preposterous, but that would hardly take account of the strange dynamics within INXS.

REFINING THE OILS

INXS moved into the international market with ease: with hindsight, it looks like they were a shoo-in. Midnight Oil were a much less predictable candidate, yet in 1987 their single 'Beds Are Burning' would become a world-wide hit – top ten in Britain, top twenty in the USA and, curiously, number one in South Africa, six years before the end of apartheid. The campaign to gain wide acceptance for a group whose sound and style was uncompromising to many (although, as mentioned earlier, they certainly operated within a rock/pop format) was smart and determined.

In 1980 Midnight Oil worked hard to move from being popular in Sydney to commanding a national audience; they did this by gaining acceptance in Melbourne,[346] particularly via 3RRR and then 3EON-FM, its commercial imitator. The 12-inch EP *Bird Noises* was their first hit. *Place without a Postcard*, their third album, was recorded in London and yielded the hit single 'Don't Wanna Be the One'. Rob Hirst credits Nadia Anderson, a RRR announcer who was British producer Nick Launay's girlfriend (and later his wife) with introducing Midnight Oil to Launay;[347] he recorded *Red Sails in the Sunset* in 1984.

Hirst says that the albums *10 9 8 7 6 5 4 3 2 1* and *Red Sails* were a change of approach for the band – they stopped, at this point, trying to capture their live sound.[348] The band's future was threatened in 1984 when Garrett stood as a NSW Senate candidate for the Nuclear Disarmament Party.[349] He polled just under 10% of the vote, but narrowly missed out on a seat, and Midnight Oil had a reprieve for the time being. Twenty years later Garrett precipitated the band's demise when he was elected as a Labor MP, a move which many have found unforgivable, the compromises of mainstream politics seemingly at odds with the diehard left-wing stance of the lyrics Garrett had sung and even written in the past.

In vying for international success, Midnight Oil seemed aware of the ways in which it might change the group's output. As Peter Garrett explained, discussing Skyhooks in particular, 'When musicians actually travel overseas they have to universalise their lyrics and their approach ... A good example of that is a band like Skyhooks, who made no sense whatsoever to the Americans, and how could they?'[350] Iva Davies crowed that Midnight Oil was regarded as just another 'political punk band' in London,[351] but technology was perhaps more of an issue for the group. On their single 'Power and the Passion' (which is almost a rap), for instance, Rob Hirst felt compelled to make a point about the drum-machine track on which the song is based by playing a drum solo alongside – or perhaps even *over* – it. The group used all kinds of advertising imagery – sardonically – in the clip because, as the most prominent boycotters of *Countdown*, they would not need to delete commercial logos for the sake of the government broadcaster.

Midnight Oil stayed a steady course until 2002, when Garrett quit to enter politics again (he became the federal member for Kingsford Smith for nine years, serving in the never dull Labor government under two Prime Ministers – Kevin Rudd and Julia Gillard – between 2007 and 2013). The group is fondly remembered in Australia and still celebrated in many quarters; their leftist politics are always acknowledged as a core element.

FINN DE SIECLE

Unlike Midnight Oil, Split Enz had become virtually part of the scenery by the late 70s; their odd timings, vocalisings, and campy vaudeville stutterings were, if not universally admired, at least broadly accepted. Whereas Dragon had come to Australia intending it to be a stopover en route to the wider world, only to find success beyond Australasia elusive, Split Enz had realised many of their ambitions, using Australia as a stepping stone and gaining something of a profile in London (going so far as to claim credit for the mohawk), and finding a producer in Phil Manzanera. They were even quite well known in Canada.

The group had undergone considerable change by the end of the 70s, however. Their ostentatious craziness – always stagey – began to look forced, particularly when compared to the more theatrical of the punk/new wave scenesters. Tim Finn was now the group's leader, following the irrevocable (second) departure of Phil Judd (though Neil Finn was rising as a songwriting force); he felt their style was getting in the way and seemed gimmicky:[352] 'How can you communicate to an audience,' he wondered, 'when you look like a parrot?'[353] Finn was particularly unhappy with the fact that their 'rootin' tootin' Luton' demo had failed to turn into an equally impressive album (*Frenzy*, their third, produced by Mallory Earl). 'The sound comes at you from behind a pad of cotton wool,' he complained; '*Frenzy* is the last time we work with an American.'[354] The (separately recorded) hit single 'I See Red' and the 'lost' single 'Things' were harbingers of their future sound, although 'Things' failed to chart. *The Rootin' Tootin' Luton Tapes* were eventually released 28 years later.

When the group acted on their new resolve, choosing the young British producer David Tickle, who had produced 'I See Red', to create the stripped-down pop album *True Colours*, Michael Gudinski, their strongest supporter, was oddly nervous. Molly Meldrum – who has never had any compunction about telling others, particularly old friends, their business – reputedly banged on Gudinski's desk and insisted he dump the group from the label's roster.[355] The story at the time was that the disappointed Gudinski, feeling the record had no single, only pressed 6,000 copies,[356] though he has since said he simply wasn't sure *which* song to choose as the single. Either version of the story is surely an object lesson in how hard it is, for a group which has so boldly insisted on its right to be weird, to go 'straight'; Tickle was, as Eddie Rayner later said, 'very much a singles man. He wanted albums that were full of singles.'[357] Mike Chunn, in his definitive history/memoir of Split Enz, credits Tickle with a major role in limiting Rayner to synthesisers and mixing Noel Crombie's percussion completely out of the sound.

True Colours was certainly straightforward and of the moment; it contained not only the driving 'I Got You' but also 'I Hope I Never', 'Poor Boy' and the frenetic 'Shark Attack'. The album turned out to be by far the group's biggest commercial success to date; Mushroom's initial run sold out in three days after *Countdown* featured the group playing the first single, 'I Got You'. The album consolidated their position immeasurably – when it peaked, one in ten Australian households reportedly possessed a copy[358] – as well as introducing them to an entirely new audience that was much larger than their initial artier crowd. The Sports discovered this when they were 'overshadowed' by their labelmates on the 'Sporting True Colours' joint tour;[359] the one time Split Enz attempted to enforce the egalitarian ideal of the tour by insisting the Sports play last, audiences left after Split Enz's set.[360] Having manufactured a short initial run, Mushroom went on to release new versions of *True Colours* in sleeves with seemingly limitless colour combinations. They also issued a 'laser-etched' edition, for which the vinyl grooves were overlaid with variations on the basic shapes of the sleeve design; a light shone on the album as it was played in a darkened room would, purchasers were told, refract on the walls in a colourful display. It didn't work, but 22,000 people nevertheless became proud (or confused) owners of that edition alone.[361]

Split Enz became a permanent feature of the Australian musical landscape in the early 80s, as Chunn details in his memoir. The follow-up to *True Colours*, tokenistically titled with the Aboriginal word *Corroboree* in Australia but known everywhere else by the Maori name *Waiata*, was similar in style and sound to its predecessor, due in part to Tickle reprising his producer role and the band realizing they were onto a good thing. They completed a world tour in 1981, then took three months off for 'writing, rehearsing, holidaying and getting divorces',[362] according to Rayner. Unlike many of their contemporaries, they were happy to celebrate their past incarnations: they planned a tenth birthday 'reunion concert' in New Zealand, which was to feature all previous members of the band, playing songs and donning costumes chronologically:[363] a novel approach. As it transpired, many former members showed up, but not Phil Judd.

In 1983, with Crombie having been their drummer for 18 months (Nigel Griggs: 'Whatever you give Noel to do, he does')[364] the group recorded *Time and Tide*, which included the loping 'Dirty Creature', about Tim Finn's own 'more or less ... nervous breakdown'.[365] He, in particular, was having both artistic and personal issues. His solo album *Escapade* was issued in 1983 and sold almost as well in Australia as *True Colours*; the single 'Fraction Too Much Friction', which had been a reject from that earlier album, came with a Richard Lowenstein video that borrowed from New Five's 'Life without Lulu' (New Five was a pop band revolving around Gavin Quinn, once of News) and made Finn look like a cool guy with young friends – which he may well have been.

The next album, *Conflicting Emotions*, continued the introversion that had begun with *Time and Tide*, and Split Enz stopped caring about the northern hemisphere – the feeling may have been mutual. The fact that (according to Tim Finn) their manager Nathan Brenner spat in his American counterpart (and later CBS supremo) Tommy Mottola's face in Los Angeles in 1982[366] probably made this an easier choice. It was the north's loss – the ballad 'Message to My Girl' is surely Neil Finn's best song ever (or at least to date), amongst numerous jewels, and its video explored that most captivating of forms, the real-time mimed performance. Crombie was returned to his percussionist/designer role when the group added their first Australian in Paul Hester. Hester, who had formerly been in Melbourne's Cheks and the Sydney-based Deckchairs Overboard, had been set to trade music for acting; his stepping stone was his role as the drummer in the fictional group the Takeaways in Johanna Pigott and Tim Gooding's TV series *Sweet and Sour*.[367] But he abandoned this idea when he was offered the job in Split Enz.[368] Hester's good nature and comedic abilities proved a perfect fit for the final year of Split Enz as a functioning group. Envisaging a popular solo career, Tim Finn quit, leaving Crombie as the longest surviving Split Enz member – and even he wasn't an original. Neil resolved to keep the group going as his songwriting vehicle, then lost that resolve. The final album, *See Ya Round*, was thrown together from leftovers – originally envisaged as a 5-song EP, other songs were

drawn together as padding – and the group bowed out, with Tim returning for a final tour. He would not reach the commercial heights of *Escapade* again, except in further work with his brother while briefly a member of Crowded House for its third album *Woodface*, released in 1991.

Paul Hester's decision to opt for Split Enz rather than acting in *Sweet and Sour* may have been a smart one, though his skill as a drummer was at least matched by his quick wit and his comedic abilities, and *Sweet and Sour* would have been a good launching pad for such a career move.

SWEET AND SOUR AND JOHANNA PIGOTT

Gooding and Pigott based their TV show very loosely on the career of XL Capris, the band they had operated with limited success in the late 70s and early 80s.[369] Pigott had an architecture degree from the University of Sydney, but like Grahame Bond and Rory O'Donoghue before her, went into theatre and 'became an actress' before punk inspired her to become a bass player and vocalist.[370] Teaming with guitarist Gooding – who had written a play, *Rock Ola*,[371] and worked with Bond and O'Donoghue in TV comedy – and Kimble Rendall, as well as drummer Julie Anderson, she formed XL Capris. The band took on appropriately punky joke names (Gooding was Errol Cruz, Rendall was Däg Rattler, Anderson was Nancy Serapax and Pigott was Alligator Bagg). They recorded a single, 'Dead Budgies' backed with a tongue-in-cheek rendition of the cheesy, celebratory 'My City of Sydney'; it was released exactly a year after their first show in 1980. They probably thought they were doing something right when they read James Reyne dismiss them in *Roadrunner*: 'Sydney bands like the XL Capris, they're just so awful, so derivative, though I suppose I should be tolerant.'[372]

The group moved beyond the frenetic roughness of these tracks, however, to produce the slightly slicker album *Where's Hank?*; by this time Anderson had quit, replaced by Michael Farmer. Produced by Dragon's Todd Hunter, the album included songs parodying and ruminating on Australian history, including the recently dead Johnny O'Keefe and Juanita Nielsen, the Woolloomooloo newspaper editor/publisher who mysteriously disappeared, apparently murdered by crime magnates.[373] Its single paired a dirgey pop track, 'World War 3', with an upbeat discussion of Dusty Springfield's career and personal conflicts ('Dusty').

For Pigott, the 'heart and soul' of XL Capris had 'a lot to do with being ratbags. Any band who hasn't got that element, they might be very successful but they don't have the punch. It's one of the few things that can still do it and we've always wanted to keep that.'[374] Between *Where is Hank?* and its follow up, *Weeds*, the group lost Rendall to Le Hoodoo Gurus. His replacement was Todd Hunter ('I reckon,' Hunter said in 1981, 'change is divine')[375] who wrote half of *Weeds* with Pigott. Towards the end of the band's life, XL Capris also experimented with a duo of drummers.[376] According to Hunter, sales of *Where is Hank?* had been 'shithouse ... because the record company changed hands in the middle of it all ... Still as a great man once said, "It's not losing an album, it's gaining back catalogue."'[377]

Hunter had vast experience of pop success compared to his new bandmates, of course, but it had not sprung from his own songwriting. His work for Dragon at this point had been largely restricted to album tracks, many of them co-written with Jenny Hunter-Brown. Yet at the same time as Hunter was producing Toy Love's album and embracing the new wave, he and Pigott appear to have harboured a strong desire to create pop music. It didn't really work for XL Capris; in 1984 Pigott said that 'once we tried to jump horses mid-stream and try and turn the band into some sort of contender, then it collapsed.'[378] In another interview published the same week, she said:

> For Todd, bands were just things that you chopped and changed to make it the best it could be. For us it was this mysterious object that had come because four people had worked together. It got overbalanced: we went in the direction that Todd was suggesting, and it wasn't really the direction Tim and I wanted to go.[379]

The group split on the first day of 1982, exactly three years after its debut. With it went its label, Axle, and plans to release a single by 'Phil Lafferty and the Singing Dog.'[380]

Pigott and Hunter, a successful songwriting couple, would go on to compose a number of major hit singles, mainly for the resurrected Dragon but also famously John Farnham's 1988 hit 'Age of Reason'. In the immediate aftermath of XL Capris, Pigott took on a low-key role, replacing Phil Hall as bass player in Ian and Stephanie Rilen's group Sardine V. Within a few months she quit that band ('I was filling in for them', she said later,[381] though Stephanie recalls that Pigott went on holiday and was sacked by Ian, an act that upset both women). She and Gooding had, however, begun work on *Sweet and Sour*: she had already gained some experience from working on the soap opera *The Restless Years*.[382] A lighthearted drama series, *Sweet and Sour* followed an independent band, the Takeaways, through various tribulations; it starred Tracy Mann as guitarist-songwriter Carol Howard and David Reyne as guitarist Martin Kabel. Each episode included a humorous cameo from at least one well-known pop star, and more importantly, featured songs by a diverse range of writers, ranging from Sharon O'Neill (who contributed the show's theme), Reg Mombassa, Mark Callaghan, Buzz Bidstrup, Pigott and Hunter, and Jenny Hunter-Brown, to (more adventurously, given his 'indie' status) David McComb, who contributed the old Triffids songs 'Digging a Hole', 'Too Hot to

Move' and 'On the Street Where You Live'. Reyne, Mann and others in the series lip-synched to the voices of John Clifforth and Cathy McQuade of Deckchairs Overboard, or, in Mann's case particularly, to Deborah Conway of Do Re Mi.

While Paul Hester had opted out of appearing in *Sweet and Sour*, as mentioned above, his involvement at its inception is plain; he and Conway were in a relationship, and Deckchairs Overboard was his old band. It was Conway's voice that took the Takeaways into the top twenty with the first of two albums of music from the series (the second was less successful) and the 'Sweet and Sour' single. The 'real' band on the records was a group of interchangeable session musicians under the aegis of Martin Armiger. The name of the band was a mildly witty reference to the disposability of pop that chimed with one association of 'sweet and sour'; it was not appropriated from a Newcastle-based group of the period, although (and this would be a stunning coincidence, if true) Buzz Bidstrup is rumoured to have produced the 'real' Takeaways' single.

Bidstrup and Mark Callaghan's band GangGajang resulted directly from their experience with *Sweet and Sour*. The group's lasting legacy is their fourth single, 'Sounds of Then', a self-conscious evocation of a stereotypical Australian (and probably, Brisbane) experience of suburban life. It was a minor hit when released in late 1985, gained further currency in a Coca-Cola advertisement, and became iconic for a certain generation.

Deckchairs Overboard can be classified as one more example of a group who might well have been enormously successful had the record industry not, in effect, removed everything that made them remotely interesting for the purpose of producing a slick product. They emerged from a popular Melbourne dance/pop act, the Cheks; when Cathy McQuade joined, they took a more sophisticated, angular name (which, Clifforth snickered to *On the Street*, had 'no hidden meaning') and produced some good pop recordings, such as 'Shout' and 'That's the Way'. As described above, Paul Hester left in late 1983 and while the group engaged numerous notables as extra players – including Michael Hoste, once of Flowers, and Tim Brosnan – Deckchairs Overboard were essentially a duo of McQuade and primary songwriter (and doctor)[383] John Clifforth. In 1985 they made an album, assisted by Martin Armiger, and broke up almost immediately. The band's principals effectively disappeared from mainstream music, although Clifforth later played with Paul Hester again in his post-Crowded House band, Largest Living Things.

MONDO ROCK

If GangGajang were a peculiar blend of a former punk rocker (Callaghan, formerly of the Numbers/Riptides) and a hard rock drummer (Bidstrup) making pop music, a group like Mondo Rock was arguably even stranger. Somehow – although not by stealth, as he didn't try and would have looked ridiculous trying, given he was already so famous – Ross Wilson reinvented himself as leader of a new pop group called Mondo Rock. The first incarnation of the band had recorded the flawed *Primal Park* album in 1979 (see chapter 11). Like earlier Wilson forays, it was geared to appeal to an adult audience. Throughout the 1980s, however, Mondo Rock positioned itself as a singles band – aimed as much at teenagers as at their parents – with an international sound. The group that released the second Mondo Rock album, *Chemistry,* had no members in common with the Mondo Rock of *Primal Park* except Wilson. More importantly, it featured Eric McCusker, who wrote five tracks on *Chemistry* including the top-ten hit 'State of the Heart' (the video for which saw Wilson, the vocalist, display a bizarrely hypnotic hand movement throughout, reminiscent perhaps of a suckling kitten). The song was a lush, irresistible ballad, with the drumming of Gil Matthews (a stand-in for the session) a particular delight. McCusker had once played with Renée Geyer in Dry Red, with Jon English, Ross Ryan and Jeff St John, and in a late-70s version of (Captain) Matchbox. McCusker had given Wilson a tape of 'weird songs' he had recorded at home after a month spent in America riding Greyhound buses and reading Jung.[384] Writing in *Roadrunner* in 1981, Adrian Ryan described McCusker as 'literate, watchful, an obvious careerist intensely interested in the mechanics of his art'.[385] McCusker claimed the group was united by 'a feeling for black music which I think comes out in what we play.'[386] The slightly blue-beat 'Cool World', written by Wilson, was another top-ten hit, and subtly paraded Wilson's own unease about the changing face of popular culture: no-one went around with foxtails sticking out of the back of their pants anymore (though they would again, soon enough). A third ballad, 'Chemistry', keyboard-driven like its predecessors, was likewise clinically smooth. 'Summer of '81' was a great piece of disposable pop – its very title was its use-by date, at least until 2081. Wilson also wrote and produced a single, 'Bop Girl', for his wife Pat, which was a top-five hit in Australia in 1983, its video featuring a young Nicole Kidman as a cigarette-waving schoolgirl.

The third Mondo Rock album, *Nuovo Mondo,* contained no hits and had little appeal. The fourth, the oddly titled *Modern Bop* (1984), featured the group's most famous song, 'Come Said the Boy', a mildly prurient record which was banned by Catholic-owned 2SM in Sydney. Musically not too much more than a rewrite of 'Cool World', 'Come Said the Boy' would be the group's peak in Australia, though they continued to have minor hits in the latter half of the 80s.

MISSING LINK AND INDEPENDENTS

Wilson had meanwhile left his former partner in Missing Link Records, Keith Glass, to turn the label into something else entirely. Though Glass would describe Missing Link as 'a sort of "folksy" rock label'" in 1980,[387] he used it to bring a number of highly important names to the wider world. This was made easier in mid 1980 when Missing Link obtained distribution through 7 Records.[388] No longer functioning as a reissue label, Missing Link was instead a cutting-edge semi-independent, acting as an adjunct to the record shop of the same name (a similar combination to that operating in Sydney with the Phantom label). In the early 80s Bruce Milne, owner-operator of the Au Go Go label, worked in the Missing Link shop, which was now owned by Keith and Helena Glass, and their respective record labels were closely allied at this time. Decisions were made jointly about which releases would be on which label. Missing Link issued, for example, the Laughing Clowns' first EP, the first Go-Betweens album, a number of records by the Birthday Party, La Femme's one and only album, and Peter Lillie's first album, while Au Go Go's releases included records by Little Murders, Moodists, Scientists, and Hugo Klang.

Both Glass and Milne were affected by the desertion of groups whose recordings they had paid for. Glass's difficulties with the Birthday Party, particularly over the very expensive and initially slow-selling *Junkyard* album, were infamous. Keith and Helena Glass were ultimately compelled to sell the shop which had provided the base for the label; Keith also attempted to recoup some of the money he was owed by issuing a Birthday Party singles compilation on Missing Link. The track 'After the Fireworks', recorded by Birthday Party and Go-Betweens members and released as a single on Au Go Go under the name Tuff Monks, was purportedly donated by the band to help him in this effort, although his decision to release it with a B side 'remix' that was essentially the A side backwards, did not endear him to the Birthday Party. Another later project, the release of some early Go-Betweens demos as the *Very Quick on the Eye* LP, did not endear him to that band, either. Milne, for his part, found that Scientists, now recreated as a prototypical grunge (or 'swamp') group, had signed a deal with another label to release an album in Britain that Au Go Go had paid to record. His partner Greta Moon flew to London to retrieve the master tapes and, when the band refused to co-operate, Au Go Go issued their own version of the album, *Atom Bomb Baby*, which the group claimed was a 'bastardised distortion of the real thing.'[389] The British version was called, wryly, *You Get What You Deserve*.

It is almost always deceptive and unhelpful to discuss artists or groups in terms of their record label and declare a sound, style or mentality unique to any label, although some smaller independents certainly had a more intense focus. Tom Ellard, for instance, operated a largely cassette-based label called Terse Tapes (he characterised it much later, in 1991, as 'garbage'),[390] on which he showcased his group Severed Heads and a host of other noise and experimental bands. But even labels focusing on one sound or style, and with many of the same individuals involved within different groups – the early 80s Sydney label M Squared, with its primarily synthesizer-based sounds, is probably the best example of this – were far more diverse than they were commonly given credit for. M Squared was usually written about as if it were a group itself, rather than a studio concern which sometimes put out records. 'M Squared's music is as accessible as that which you hear in elevators and hotel lobbys. The difference is M Squared generally stimulates the senses instead of sending them off into a stupor,' wrote Craig N. Pearce.[391]

The label emerged from a group, of sorts. They were called the Barons, and they released a 5-song EP called *Greatest Hits*, which band member and M Squared co-founder Michael Tee remembered as 'probably the worst record ever made'[392] (there are, in fact, worse). This was on Doublethink, the Thought Criminals' label, as was 'Pulp Baby', a single created by Patrick Gibson under the name the Systematics. The Systematics then provided one of the first M Squared products, an EP called *Rural* which was, it was claimed, three-sided (the tracks on 'side three' were available to any interested party who sent the label a blank cassette), but the group only really became vital with the addition of two more members, Michael Filewood and later, Fiona Graham. This band would morph into Ya Ya Choral (which also included Michael Tee) and then, with the addition of John Bliss and Polly Newham from the Reels, briefly into Zeee Toons ('The songs are forced, the songs crack, they are shells of songs', blared one particularly harsh review of this shortlived group).[393] Retaining that line-up to record a second EP, they then reverted to the name Ya Ya Choral which – bizarrely – later mutated into a heavy metal-tinged rock/pop group.

The Makers of the Dead Travel Fast released two albums of crafted, esoteric pop on M Squared. Their first release, a track on an M Squared compilation, was an uncredited song entitled 'The Dead Travel Fast', and their intention was to continually rename their band as 'The Makers of' whatever their previous release was titled, but they stalled on their first name. Possibly the best of the M Squared releases – though the label almost immediately disowned it because of personal conflicts with the artist in question – was 'Just Not True' by EST, a solo performer using a band name. Like many truly great singles, 'Just Not True' was a minimalist masterpiece, with a reverbed vocal, limited but heartfelt electric-guitar chords, and an attention-grabbing synthesiser (?) solo.

In Melbourne, even stranger groups were happening. The Shower Scene from Psycho started up in 1982, led by Simon Grounds, formerly of the Pastel Bats. 'We're great fans of the Seekers,' he told *Juke*. 'In fact, when we started out there was a fourth member who played a 12-string guitar because we wanted to *sound* like the Seekers.'[394] The group played violently rearranged covers of songs typically considered bubblegum or otherwise crass, ranging from the Strangeloves' (and Johnny Young's) 'Cara-Lyn' to the Masters Apprentices' 'Turn up Your Radio'. They used a keyboard, a drum machine, a bass guitar and a fuzz guitar.

> The band was designed before it was made – we actually sat down and designed it . . . combining real garish ugly noises with very sweet sounds . . . When we formed this band, the three of us were totally disappointed with what rock music was offering – not only in this country but overseas.

> There's so much potential in electronic sound, the cheapness and the complexity, and the way you can virtually create something so original with it. But so much of that potential has been lost... I'd put it basically down to the conservatism of the capitalism system.[395]

Cheapness and convenience were becoming a hallmark of electronics, a fact often lost on those who continued to associate synthesisers with prog-rock excess. Tom Ellard had a Korg synth next to his bed: 'I really like the way I can lean out of bed, patch a few chords [sic] and achieve a totally fresh sound.' Severed Heads were Ellard and Stephen Jones, a 'video whizzkid'.[396]

Severed Heads were later to put their 'rhythms interlocking with each other'[397] to good use in something approximating dance music (as, indeed, did SPK). The Wet Taxis – who began in the late 70s as the Sydney Quads[398] – had an even more unusual trajectory. Louis Tillett recalls: 'There was us, bands like the Severed Heads who're still going, SPK etc. That's how it originally started. Very negative music, making sounds to bring out something negative in people, which it certainly did...'[399]

Whereas groups like the Shower Scene from Psycho (and sometimes the Reels) would take classic songs apart and reconstitute them as electronic bombast – the same approach taken by the British studio 'band' the Silicon Teens, but with more heart and bite – the Wet Taxis reconfigured themselves as a guitar-based 60s-garage covers band. Their first album, *From the Archives*, combined recordings by both their electro-noise and their garage punk incarnations. Tillett, who was a creditable pianist as well as a distinctive vocalist, then began writing songs of his own. He also formed another group, Paris Green, which was to include Jeffrey Wegener – keeping his hand in while the Laughing Clowns weren't playing – and a bass player, Raoul Hawkins.[400]

A MANIFESTATION OF A NEW SENSIBILITY

The Particles were contemporaries of the M Squared groups and had some stylistic similarities with them, though they were far better able to move between mainstream and 'alternative' spheres. They were ostensibly Sydney's longest-lasting punk group, though by the time they began recording (in 1979) they were drastically removed from punk in sound and style. Simon Bonney had been the Particles' vocalist in their early days, followed by Michael Wood, and Bob Farrell (later of the Laughing Clowns) was a founder member,[401] but when their first EP, *Colour In*, was issued, it featured the vocals of the recently recruited Astrid Spielman, whose sister Ingrid was the keyboard player in Tactics. The Particles had originally revolved around brothers Peter and Steven Williams on guitar and drums respectively; Steven became the group's manager in 1980, and a drum machine took his place in the band.

They were a pop group, but a highly original and inventive one; they were also – particularly in the period 1980-82 – very committed, and extremely modern. The *Roadrunner* journalist who praised them for 'the way they sang a song about a penguin and really meant it'[402] was not just joking. He was also conveying the spirit of a group that could be minimalist – which was one of their avowed aims ('stripping it back all the time to the point where eventually there's not going to be anything there except the entertainment, just pure'[403] according to Peter Williams) – but also very bold. Spielman was adamant that 'we could never dive up on stage and go grunge grunge grunge. That would have looked like a comedy act',[404] but the Particles were very forthright – and their modernity is undoubtedly demonstrated by Spielman's very early (1982) use of the word 'grunge'.

Astrid Spielman told *RAM* readers that same year that:

> Rock and roll is dead as far as I'm concerned. And there's something else starting to take its place. It's good for a nostalgia trip. It's great stuff, I can't deny that. But as a formula, it's past, because it's to do with ancient ways of looking at things. It's to do with men and a very masculine sort of philosophy.[405]

She was scathing about the Dugites, who she clearly (and in only one sense correctly – the Dugites had origins as a parody of the 60s 'girl group') saw as trivializing women in popular music:

> The Dugites aren't the Particles, right. They're looking at bands with women as lead singers as being a novelty which is going to pass. They don't see it as a manifestation of a new sensibility.[406]

The Particles only released three EPs, each containing three songs and showing a marked progression. The first had a sleevenote by Ray Medhurst, later to prove himself a pop master in the Rockmelons, and – more importantly – the EP featured a plaintive romance on the A side, 'Driving Me'. The second release, *Advanced Colouring*, featured the extremely cogent 'Truth about You'. The final, and best, of the three was an early release on the Waterfront label in 1982, *I Love Trumpet*. By this time, Spielman and Williams had been joined by Alex Hamilton (later replaced by Nicole Menzies) on the aforementioned trumpet and Stephen O'Neil as bassist. The Particles was the first of O'Neil's bands that was not based around his Canberra schoolfriends.

It is one of the tragedies of the early-80s Australian music scene that the Particles – who made such a strong impression on all those who saw them – did not thrive, but instead fell into disarray while making a belated debut album, the tapes of which were subsequently lost, at the same time that Spielman was musing in print that the band's anti-industry policies were working against them: 'Fuck that, we wanna have a number one hit.'[407]

A major part of the Particles story was their drive across Australia – a rarity even for major East coast bands, who traditionally do not play in Western Australia until they're sufficiently well-known that their tour budgets can pay for them to fly back and forth. This trip, in tandem with fellow Sydney band the Lighthouse Keepers (the two bands had some common members), included a show in the West Australian town of Norseman, where the group was shocked to discover that the venue would not admit Aboriginals. 'And having set up their gear,' Wanda Jamrozik relayed to the readers of *RAM*, 'they were sufficiently intimidated to carry on and play. They felt guilty and just plain stupid – city kids out of their depth on the treeless plain.'[408]

O'Neil was involved in both the Particles and the Lighthouse Keepers, a group which could trace its origins back to Guthugga Pipeline, which in various incarnations featured O'Neil, Greg Appel and Gavin Butler. The Lighthouse Keepers – Appel claimed in 1985 that the group bore 'the worst name he could think of at the time'[409] – centred largely around Appel's songs as sung by Juliet Ward; Michael 'Blue' Dalton played dobro and harmonica. O'Neil switched from drums to guitar and saxophone when Steven Williams joined the band as its drummer. The group's 1984 album, *Tales of the Unexpected*, was and remains an acknowledged classic. Later, Appel remarked that the group had been 'a bit of a small-time media baby . . . we couldn't break out of the press and audience image.'[410] This was a common complaint among the bigger fish in the small pool of independent/alternative music, and one which reflected poorly on mainstream media at the time.

The Lighthouse Keepers were one of the large cohort of acts regularly on hand at Sydney's Trade Union Club in the 1980s. Stuart Coupe told *Roadrunner* readers in 1981 that in that year 'the Trade Union Club quickly became the focal point of after-dark life. Three or four bands at weekends, reasonable prices, comfort, two floors, and a bar open till 5 a.m. Almost always good line-ups.'[411] Adelaide group Purple Gang wrote a song, 'Rocks in My Mouth' about the Trade Union Club and 'inarticulateness.'[412] The venue was on Fouveaux Street in Darlinghurst and operated for acts often described as 'alternative'. Groups like Scientists were in their element there, a far cry (yet only half an hour's drive) from the

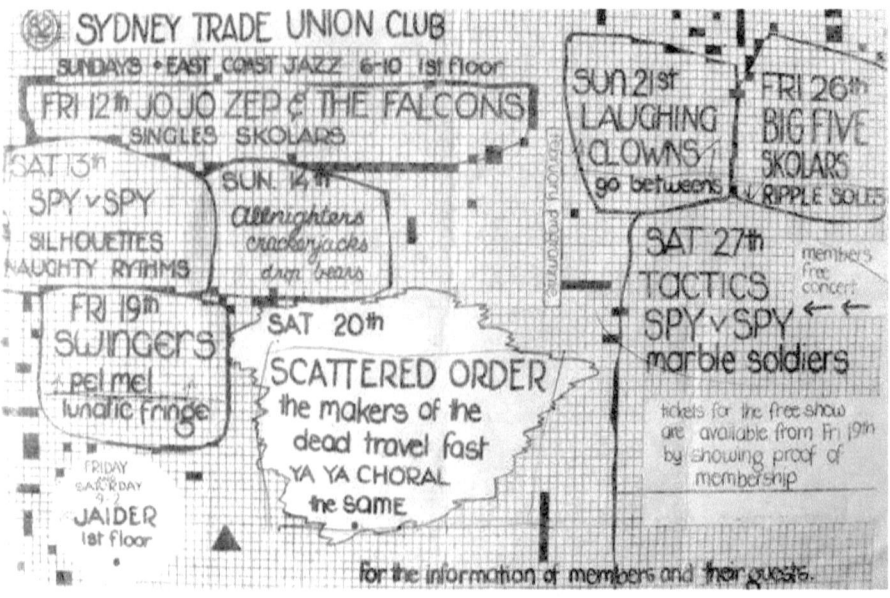

Parramatta Leagues Club where they opened for the Angels in 1983 – having been begged by Dirty Pool to take the support slot[413] – and were 'bottled off stage.'[414] Kim Salmon later claimed the bottle in question was a magnum of champagne, though this might have merely been wishful thinking; the group claimed to have written the song 'Nitro' about the experience, although how the two relate is not obvious to the casual listener.

Crime and City Solution played 'the Trade' on an Australian tour in 1985. After the band had broken up in 1979, Simon Bonney had spent some time in a psychiatric institution; he moved to London in 1983 with Bronwyn Adams, the mother of his children. Following the Birthday Party's split, Mick Harvey, well aware of the importance the original group had on his and Nick Cave's work, constructed a new Crime and the City Solution around Bonney, recruiting brothers Rowland and Harry Howard, then later British drummer Epic Soundtracks; Adams joined in 1986. The group shone briefly in Europe; they can be seen in Wim Wenders's *Wings of Desire* playing a Rowland Howard song, 'Six Bells Chime'. While their subsequent career is more of a story of the second half of the 1980s and beyond, the group's little-known origins and early networking continued to serve them into the 21st century.

CLIFTON HILL COMMUNITY MUSIC CENTRE MUSICIANS DID NOT ALL LIVE IN THE SAME HOUSE AND EAT THE SAME FOOD

In the early 1980s Sydney's music scene was as strong as Melbourne's, if not stronger. Melbourne began to seem more showy and shallow, whereas Sydney – particularly as vibrant networks began to be formed between 'grungy' scenes like those in Adelaide and Perth – became more attuned to 60s-styled rock, with bands like the Moffs and the Stems, both on the Citadel label. This label had been started as a hobby by John Needham, originally for the same purpose as Missing Link: to document groups which had disbanded.[415] The Stems were from Perth, the brainchild of Dom Mariani, and were resolutely power pop. The Moffs, led by Tom Kazas, were from Sydney's southern beaches and self-consciously 'psychedelic'.[416]

Melbourne's more stylish – if not stylised – approach to music caused resentment around the country, much of it focused on Hunters and Collectors' fine dressing and intellectual funk.

David McComb wrote in 1982:

> Alternative pop music seems especially prone to the process whereby each week someone comes out of their living room and screams, "hold everything, this is it, this is the one, everything else is just WANK!, our music is the ultimate, forget about everything you heard before, we have the answer." It is precisely this clammy environment that cherishes and mollycuddles [sic] bands like Hunters and Collectors and Tsk Tsk Tsk, the doyens of the Australian new funk. They claim to be challengers, but instead they merely maintain pretences.[417]

The kind of 'new funk' McComb hated became even more evident in the work of I'm Talking. This group emerged from arguably the strangest and most unlikely source: the Clifton Hill Community Music Centre at that suburb's Organ Factory. The improvisational Laughing Hands, comprising Ian Russell and Paul Schultz, were habitués of this small-scale experimental/art/drama centre in a quiet suburban street. They found, to their irritation, that certain assumptions about them reigned in Sydney, where 'everyone seems to think that Chesworth, Tch Tch Tch, Essendon Airport and Laughing Hands... all live in the same house and eat the same food.'[418] In fact, the Clifton Hill artists ranged from rock groups all the way through to academic musicians like Ron Nagorcka, who had founded the centre in the mid 70s. At Clifton Hill, it was 'well accepted that low-budget equipment helped to "shape" the music, not devalue it; there was no stigma attached to its use'; anyone could have the space for performance, and no money changed hands.

Some of the groups who played at Clifton Hill were released on Innocent Records, Philip Brophy's label on which he issued EPs by Tch Tch Tch, and various side-projects of that group, such as the Chocolate Grinders or Asphixiation. If Innocent had an overall sound, it was the blocky and flat, but character-laden sound of the four-track tape recorder at Latrobe University, where Brophy was employed. This was where Asphixiation, Tch Tch Tch's disco project, recorded their *What Is This Thing Called Disco?* album. Like the Hunters and Collectors debut, it was issued as two 12-inch discs, one playing at 45 and the other at 33⅓; the songs – particularly the two on the 45, as much of the 'album' was instrumental – were humorous ruminations on disco and sex (the joke of 'L'acrostique d'amour' was that its telegrammatic lyrics spelt the words 'fuck my arse'). When the group performed, they would actually mime to a tape.[419] McComb was disgusted by their attitude, which he saw as banal.[420]

Asphixiation and I'm Talking could not have been further apart from each other and still remain ostensibly disco outfits – yet both were intellectual in their approach. I'm Talking is as extraordinary an example as there is of crossover between the independent, experimental scene and the mainstream. It was directly descended from the duo Essendon Airport (not, as some might have imagined, a pun on the San Francisco psychedelic band but a reference to the genuine airport near Niddrie, where the group's original duo grew up). David Chesworth managed the Clifton Hill Community Music Centre and Robert Goodge was a crack guitarist who'd played in minor local bands since the mid 70s. They released an EP, *Sonic Investigations of the Trivial*, in 1979. The duo switched direction in the early 80s, adding a drummer who had never played before, Paul Fletcher, and a saxophonist, Ian Cox. Later Barbara Hogarth joined on bass. Goodge told Wendy Milsom in 1986:

> We naturally gravitated towards playing more in pubs because we stopped feeling like a pimple onstage. We made the music less minimal . . . the first time we played in a pub was with Midnight Oil and at that stage they had a reputation for having the "yobbiest" kind of audience, so we just thought, "We're going to get slaughtered." But I was surprised how polite people are in pubs, no one ever gets really irate unless you set out to confront them.[421]

Goodge later remarked that the group wrote a new song, 'General Hospital', to play at the show – ''cause that's where we thought we would end up.'[422] Essendon Airport's album, *Palimpsest* was recorded in December 1981. Like *What Is This Thing* . . . it was mainly instrumentals with a few dry spoken/sung vocals all with a funky leaning, and some humorous spoken-word samples, the band obviously railing against the limitations of the studio. *Palimpsest* had a beautiful silkscreened cover, for which the group suffered, having been 'asphyxiated by this incredibly pungent silk screening ink. It was terrible.'[423] Cox came to the fore at this point; he was often the lead instrumentalist, his saxophone almost taking the place of a vocal in many instances. One song, 'Re-funkt', featured a vocal fretting over the 'Fear of talking . . . fear of trying to get out a coherent sentence'.

David Chesworth left the band in 1982 and formed White Trash with Philip Jackson, a former member of Whirlywirld (five years later, he would also join I'm Talking in its dying days). Chesworth used White Trash's material in solo shows, then wrote 'some sort of opera' related to *Midsummer Night's Dream*.[424] Experimental opera would constitute a major part of his work from the mid 80s onward.

The remainder of the group began looking for a singer. They were imagining a male vocalist, but Cox instead came up with Kate (then often known as Katie) Ceberano, a teenager who waitressed by day at the Black Cat, a popular inner-city café. Cox later said he'd 'heard about Kate from people we knew. I went down to the Chevron and watched her in Exposay, a band she was in.'[425] Goodge had seven male singers ready to audition, but the group didn't bother once they decided to try and talk Ceberano into joining them. Exposay (or Expozay) were also attracting attention in their own right, though Ceberano – compared by one eager reviewer to both Chrissy Amphlett and Annalisse Morrow – was always the centre of attention.[426] The process of luring her into I'm Talking took two months, complicated by the fact that other bands were also competing for her attention.[427] I'm Talking also recruited a drummer, Cameron Newman, formerly of a band called Fun Fun Gyro Boat, and keyboard player Stephen Charlesworth, an occasional music journalist and previously in Artificial Organs.[428]

Ceberano had been singing in Melbourne soul and funk bands since the age of 14.[429] Michael Hutchence was already a fan.[430] The new group was named by Ceberano and Hogarth, because, Ceberano said, 'We decided it was a strong way of presenting something. When someone says "Hey, I'm talking!" it's like "Shut up."'[431] 'It's functionalism,' said Goodge, 'it's style, it's freshness... it wears its heart on its sleeve, it doesn't have pretensions to being deep and meaningful, it is just up front!'[432]

I'm Talking's first single was 'Someday', recorded as a piece of film music for Robert Randall and Frank Bendinelli,[433] a duo who had created video installations at the Organ Factory in the late 70s. Five hundred copies were pressed and sold out almost instantly: the band had played two shows at this point. As on future recordings by the group, the lyrics Ceberano sang here were written by Cox who, Clinton Walker later said, would 'invariably proffer pretentious intellectual theories on I'm Talking's generic location' whenever he encountered the press.[434]

I'm Talking became very big quickly; they were co-managed by Rob Waugh, manager of British pop groups Scritti Politti and ABC, and the Laughing Clowns' former manager Ken West,[435] who was involved with the band from an early stage and who Cox described as 'a bit like something from the nineteenth century, like a Barnum and Bailey circus guy'.[436]

Cox adjusted philosophically to his band's rise to fame:

> I can't see that anyone has a right to expect their music or whatever they're doing to be accepted or heard, especially in pop. Pop in a sense is more about failing than succeeding. The whole record industry works on the notion of overproduction. It just has no idea of what's going to sell, it just produces everything, it just throws it out there... I think failure is the norm; that's what rock is about, failure. It's bizarre actually succeeding.[437]

Fred Maher, the drummer in New York group Material and a recent recruit to another very slick pop act with extremely experimental origins, Scritti Politti, was engaged to produce I'm Talking's album, *Bear Witness*. It was adequate, but it wasn't a major success, and after a UK trip supporting teen dance act Five Star, the group began to fall apart. Absurd rumours began to circulate, such as 'Ceberano to record with [Jeff] Beck and [Malcolm] McLaren'[438]: while the musically incompetent McLaren was at least the putative author of some fine dance records, the idea of pairing Ceberano with the reclusive guitarist Beck was as nonsensical as Deborah Conway's contemporaneous career move of recording with Pete Townshend.

Ceberano quit I'm Talking; Zan Abeyratne, who had joined as a second vocalist, took over but the band did not last much longer. Of all the band members, only Ceberano has subsequently maintained a high public profile; Goodge went on to write jingles and in the early 21st century reformed the pre-funk Essendon Airport with Chesworth and a new member, former Triffid Graham Lee.

NO GUITARS

Like the M Squared groups, Essendon Airport and the Clifton Hill groups were taking advantage of an electronics and hardware revolution that had an impact on all contemporary music. Melbourne's Pseudo Echo were an unabashed synthesiser band whose early music appeared as demos played on 3RRR but who were undoubtedly chart material; Sam Sejavka called them 'a pile of pus'.[439] They did, nonetheless, ultimately gain a sense of irony – and a worldwide hit with a guitar-riddled version of Lipps Inc's Kraftwerk-styled disco hit 'Funkytown'. There were, however, many more interesting groups than Pseudo Echo, whose pop nous was often overtaken by an unjustified arrogance.

And An A, from Perth, produced epic and extensive melodramas (if their two self-funded and notoriously expensively recorded 12-inch singles are an indication). Their designation as an example of early 'goth' music is inappropriate pigeonholing. Local legend Nigel Harford was their bass player for three years.[440] Harford had been songwriter in the Stray Tapes at the same time as he played in And An A; an anonymous correspondent for *Roadrunner* commended his mettle, but bemoaned the likelihood of any success in the inner city areas of Perth where venue owners 'are tasteless and obtuse.'[441]

Another group a million miles removed from And An A (but ostensibly fitting the same 'electronic' category) was the Machinations, who came together in 1978 at St Leo's, a Catholic college on Sydney's north shore. Described by one writer as being 'an electronically oriented Go-Betweens' in their early days, they began with Tony Starr, Tim Doyle and a drum machine. Their minimalist 1980 single 'Average Inadequacy', released on Phantom, was a classic of its time. The group's singer Fred Loneragan – like so many in his position, considered by audiences to be synonymous with the band – deserted them halfway through the recording of their first album to follow his girlfriend to London. Showing great strength of character, the remainder went on tour as Machinations II with a 'large screen' and 'a tape of Fred's voice'.[442] When they regrouped, their manager Lobby Loyde produced their first few records.[443] Their eventual debut album, *Esteem* – described by Donald Robertson as 'an artfully and elaborately decorated piece of sound sculpture fashioned by Lobby Loyde and Paul Radcliffe using the raw material of the Machinations'[444] – was remembered fondly by Loyde as his best production work: a record less like his own music with the Coloured Balls or Purple Hearts would be hard to imagine. The Machinations' best pop record during their time on Mushroom was the punning 'Pressure Sway', from their first album. After this, their label made uninteresting attempts to refashion the group and market them as an epic pop act, bringing in producer Julian Mendelssohn and inveigling the group in substandard cod-feminist (?!) concoctions like 'No Say in It'. Loneragan, for all his talents as a lyricist and singer, was not the front man an aspirant mega group needed.

The comparison with Real Life is instructive in this regard. Improbably, this Melbourne group emerged from the last line-up of Jeff Duff's 70s group Kush, and singer David Sterry was just what the world thought the lead singer of a new-wave pop group should look like. Real Life began as the Wires, then changed briefly to A Private Life before they took on the name under which they made it big, and signed with Glenn Wheatley. They are probably still best known for the fairly pedestrian 'Send Me an Angel' (a top-thirty hit in the USA in late 1983), but it's the breathless and searing 'Catch Me I'm Falling', their third single, which was their once-in-a-lifetime perfect pop moment. The group asked the designer Katie Pye to 'make them a wardrobe' for the single's video (Sterry: 'someone had to do it or Australian musicians would forever wear Levis and t-shirts').[445] His bandmate Richard Zatorski was of the opinion that Real Life 'would be, critically, the most hated band in Australia.'[446] Yet, pragmatically at least, the band had no need to care. Their American success seemed assured at the end of 1983 – though Zatorski believed that 'if anyone in the band thought about the American thing, it'd be for a few minutes of the day, at the very most.'[447] With Wheatley and his FM interests, they were a classic early example of a band advocating for the safety of the conservative older consumer:

> If you look carefully, the radio stations that are playing the album are all AOR stations, the over-30s . . . it's not the young kids buying the album because it's hip to have synthesisers or because of the way we dress or whatever. We're getting to people on the strength of the MUSIC alone, and that really pleases me.[448]

At the same time, Zatorski embraced a fantasy future, suggesting that Real Life's second album 'will be written on the road . . . carrying around portable synth-packs.'[449] In fact, their second album *Flame* was a rushed and unsatisfactory job, and the group lost their momentum.

Electronics were not exclusively the province of young or first-time groups. Mike Rudd and Bill Putt, having enjoyed a reasonable amount of success as Mike Rudd and the Heaters, made the adventurous decision to throw out their back catalogue and cease trading on their Spectrum/Ariel past (and Rudd's name). Instead they came up with W.H.Y., a synthesiser-based audio-visual experience. Rudd recalls:

> W.H.Y was at the point where we went, Oh to hell with it, we'll do something completely different! And unfortunately [*laughs*] lost everything as a result of that. But it was kind of fun doing it. It was a huge investment, we borrowed all this money to get all this technology which of course almost immediately dropped in price.
>
> We had a video projector – first mistake – synced up to the world's first drum machine – another mistake. And then we'd film all our own material and sync it up with the drum machine which was the basis of...
>
> It was all very strictly choreographed to the drum machine which every so often used to go 'Blip! Forgotten everything' in the middle of a performance. Or worse, was out of sync from the start, so you were out of sync for the next hour and a half.

It was a bold move, and it proved disastrous. This was partly outside the group's control, though the songs that appear on W.H.Y.'s only album, *Present Tense*, are self-conscious and dwell too much on the superficiality of technology – a common concern at this time (the discussion of Percy Grainger in one song is prescient, however). 'It's the most 80s album you'll ever hear,' Rudd says now, with good reason: the album is heavily programmed and synthesiser-driven, though the extensive technology draws out Rudd's pop sensibilities to a much greater degree. Keyboard player John Capek – who had been an early member of Carson, amongst other things – produced the album, which was recorded in Germany for IC Records. In the same year, Capek did much the same thing for John Paul Young as he did for W.H.Y., except that Young's record, the album *One Foot in Front* which included the synth-pop single 'Soldier of Fortune', was commercially successful. The W.H.Y. story was not so happy for Rudd:

> John Capek lost control of it early on so we ended up producing it ourselves and we did the most hideous job, it was just awful. The only track that sounds any good is the one the engineer just dashed off... Everything else sounds like shit.
>
> Just trying to do something different. We thought it was our own idea, obviously there were other people around the world doing different things we just weren't aware of, and it was fairly adventurous for the time, just hideously costly.

The end result of that was we ended up back in Australia with nothing to show for it, and then put together a Spectrum tour to make money, which lost money, so we got Ray Arnott back on drums which wasn't a good move, and so I lost my house as a result of that because we had to pay back all those debts.

The market had sent Rudd a message. Spectrum reformed in earnest in February 1984. 'It was the bills that suggested it to me, actually,' Rudd told *RAM*.[450] Rudd and Putt then played together under the Spectrum name until Putt's death in 2013.

THE THIRD PARTY LOOKING BACK IN

Others had better luck reinventing themselves for the computer music generation. In 1979, Dragon watched as their producer and mentor Peter Dawkins embraced a new New Zealand group, Mi-Sex, which he and CBS saw as the way of the future. Mi-Sex signed to CBS in April 1979. They spent their first two weeks in Australia simply researching the market by going out to see other bands play. The group's singer, Steve Gilpin, had – like Marc Hunter – been a cabaret artist; the core of the band had – like Dragon – previously been a head group (they were called Father Thyme). Gilpin was focused:

> In that two weeks we threw out nearly all of our old material and came up with the songs we're doing now. They are more rhythmic and bouncy than the music of the Angels, designed specifically to make audiences move from side to side. It's the sort of music we wanted to but couldn't play in New Zealand.[451]

Their first single, 'High Class Dame'/'Straight Laddie', was released against their wishes; it dated from their New Zealand days.[452] But the mere fact that EMI, their previous label, saw fit to release it suggested there was already a buzz about the group. 'This is going to be our home,' Gilpin told Annie Burton. 'This *is* our home – Austral . . . Austral*asia*. Australasia is where we wanna work.'[453] As well as a new set of mildly futuristic and 'edgy' songs, Mi-Sex (whose name derived from the track 'My Sex' by the British group Ultravox) developed a light show that could spotlight a single person or even a hand gesture, which made their shows seem 'more like a theatrical production than a rock & roll show.'[454] The group lived together in a house in the salubrious Sydney suburb of Bellevue Hill[455] and played music together six nights a week. 'We work as a unit onstage and off,'[456] Gilpin told Miranda Brown.

Some of their song titles – 'Camera Kazi' springs to mind – were plain stupid. Their progressive leanings would sometimes show on this composition in particular, though: in live performance it sometimes 'built up into 30-minute workouts, into a swirling magnum opus.'[457] At the same time as they hoped to be seen as new and radical, the group was angsty about their lack of history. Guitarist Kevin Stanton complained to Burton, 'Nobody can see the background work we've done. Say with the Angels, they can see seven years of progression from one concept to another, one band to another band to another band.'[458] From a vantage point thirty years later, the most interesting aspect of this statement might be Mi-Sex's continuing obsession with the Angels, who seem to have been a bugbear – envied, hated, to be emulated – of almost every Australian musician.

In his early interviews, Gilpin comes across as a dunderhead trying to catch up with a new world he couldn't quite comprehend. 'We write from the third party looking back in,' he told *Rolling Stone's* Andrea Jones.

> We look at situations like graffiti on the wall. Even when we write a love song we write it from the third party. We never say George or Janet. It's the King of Spades meaning the male and the Queen of Hearts, the female. I don't see how you could write it any other way.[459]

The first Mi-Sex album, *Graffiti Crimes,* was a mixed bag; excellent power pop like 'I Wanna Be with You' rubbed shoulders with old rock like 'You Just Don't Care'. It was their single 'Computer Games' – a celebration of and commentary on a technological future which showed off Gilpin's versatility as a vocalist and the band's dexterity within a deceptively simple piece of futurist disco – that brought them international attention. Their attempt to ride this silliness with the album *Space Race* ('Space Race means universe,' said Gilpin)[460] and the nonsense sci-fi of 'People' showed they had less understanding of the reason for the appeal of 'Computer Games' than might have seemed the case at first.

A DARK, MALEVOLENT, DESTRUCTIVE FORCE

We last saw Dragon and Marc Hunter farewelling the 8-year-old band at the end of the 1970s. Since that time, Paul Hewson had played in Perth with Billy Rogers, and then returned to New Zealand to join the Pink Flamingos, whose mainstay Dave McArtney had been a member of infamous New Zealand rock group Hello Sailor. McArtney recalled Hewson as 'a self-destructive bastard – you take Paul at your risk.'

> He was an eccentric ... a true eccentric. He'd come on the road with us, he'd go and buy a new set of clothes and he wouldn't take them off for about a week, sleep in them. And he had a little blue suitcase which had all his medications in it, that was it. When the clothes would rot off him he'd go out and buy another silk jacket and shirt.

Hewson brought few songs to the Pink Flamingos; one, 'Lovesick', was a co-write with Jenny Hunter-Brown. The group recorded two brilliant albums; the first, *Dave McArtney and the Pink Flamingos,* was the kind of rock-pop only New Zealanders can do, the second, *We Never Close,* showed all of the pop spirit of late-70s Dragon. It was produced by Peter Dawkins, with whom Hewson had a cagey relationship.

It was rumoured that Marc Hunter, still handsome and charismatic, would star in a full-length feature film, but he did not.[461] Craig N. Pearce saw him play a solo show at Melbourne's Grainstore Tavern in late 1981 with a band who demonstrated 'clenched teeth-pelvic thrust guitar solos and . . . insipid posing.'[462] In March the following year, Hunter was arrested at St George Leagues Club, where he was appearing with Renée Geyer, for $4500 in unpaid parking fines. He described his cell at Kogarah Police Station as 'unbelievably filthy.' (There is an opportunity for further study here, given that Tracy Pew was arrested at the same time, for the same offence, in Melbourne,[463] and Chrissy Amphlett was also charged with this crime.)

It was not Marc Hunter's parking fines but other debts, dating back to the 70s, that inspired the classic Dragon line-up to reunite. The shows they played were so well received that they decided to stay together – or rather, in Hewson's words, 'the public decided. They were so enthusiastic. Even young kids.'[464]

Taylor remembers the return as 'fantastic. It wasn't over the top – we weren't doing really big venues, it was back to the pubs, but great – y'know. Everyone knew all the words and sang along, and – it was really easy.' The group's members each put in $3,000 of their own money to record a new single, 'Ramona', which Hewson later suggested 'was a really strong song . . . it was just a really bad recording.'[465] Marc Hunter hailed the new 'clean' days of Dragon: 'I don't miss vomiting on stage and being a general fuckwit.'[466] Hewson claimed that in the 80s 'we're much more efficient and economical.'[467] In fact, they weren't – various group members were still addicted to hard drugs – leading to what Taylor called 'a big clean-up' in 1984:

> We had a doctor that used to come to gigs with us and things like that. So it became really systematic – at this stage, Kerry had left, Paul and Marc had both given up heroin, and were on incredibly strong drugs to get them off it. That was hilarious, that was like – they couldn't believe their luck, everyone was really happy, we were on top of the world. That was just before we went into the studio to do *Body and the Beat.* Yes, so we were out to conquer the world then, because Paul and Marc were really healthy, I never went along with that, I was still drinking at a steady rate, this is when we had the drummer out of XTC, Terry Chambers, he became my beer-drinking buddy. Within the group there were some indulgences, but to the corporate world . . .

Dragon actually had their biggest commercial success at this time, with a new songwriting team: Johanna Pigott and Todd Hunter. The song 'Rain' – which Marc Hunter originally detested, even though (or until?) he was listed as co-writer – was perfect 1983 pop. Pigott said the song was 'written before Dragon even reformed. I didn't think it'd be a hit but Todd always thinks all his songs are hits. I actually did a version of it first, but it was too commercial for Scribble and I only half finished it. I think Dragon were the perfect vehicle for it.'[468] Others, such as 'Magic' (which Taylor co-wrote with Marc) and 'Cry' were similarly spectacular. Carey Taylor produced an album, *Body and the Beat*, which was perfect for the times. Hewson, formerly the group's songwriting saviour, had only one songwriting credit. Admittedly it was for one of the album's best songs – 'What Am I Going To Do?' – but he shared it with five other band members, including the new second keyboard player, Alan Mansfield, an American who had previously played with Robert Palmer; Hewson's first and last Dragon songs, from 'This Time' to 'What Am I Going To Do?' were thus full-band compositions.

Robert Taylor was in his final days with Dragon. 'Magic', he says, was 'my last chance of writing a hit'.

> When it first came out it went straight to number 17. I thought, 'Yes! At last I've written a song that's a hit,' because I've never written a hit. 'Yes!' and then the ironic thing was – in those days MMM ruled the airwaves, and we released it just close to Christmas, and MMM used to have a programming thing where they'd program three months of summer, and if you got on that list, you knew you had a hit – in this case they chose 'Come Said the Boy' by Mondo Rock instead of 'Magic', so I missed by that much. Yeah. So it never went any higher than 17.

In film clips for the *Body and the Beat*–period singles, Dragon look like a strange melange of old and new. The ill and decrepit Hewson seems ghostly, hovering in the background. Todd Hunter, a technophile, would sport headset microphones and use the newest equipment. Taylor was sacked from the group by their new manager, Steve White:

> Paul and I felt we weren't contributing much, and my technique, my guitar technique wasn't – I couldn't do the Eddie Van Halen and stuff like that which was state of the art, what you needed to do... You needed Tommy Emmanuel or someone like that to do the real busy big guitar parts, and I just didn't have it in me... My time with Dragon had sort of run out at that stage. I had to learn all the parts off the record to do them live, and things like that.

Hewson died a few months later, in early 1985, in New Zealand. He had previously made concerted efforts to give up drugs, including relocating to Perth in the late 70s.[469] Pigott, who recorded one of his later compositions in her band Scribble, recalled that 'Paul used to invite me to take heroin all the time, because he thought that this made you a better artist. You know, come hither little girl and have some heroin, 'cause you'll be a better songwriter.'[470] One irony among many is that Hewson wrote very little in the last years of his life; he contributed few songs to the Pink Flamingos and, apart from the reformation single 'Ramona', few to the reformed 80s version of the group which had made him successful. The night of his death, he confided in friends that he was quitting Dragon.[471] He had slept in his car with a friend, who then drove him to another friend's house in Henderson, by which time he was dead from an overdose.[472] Marc Hunter said:

> Dragon did not kill Paul Hewson although we might have been like a vehicle, and excuse, for certain behaviour. A band is just this name for all the energy put into it by the members. It's not responsible for what those members do with their lives. I don't subscribe to that vision of Dragon as a dark, malevolent, destructive force.[473]

Taylor recalls:

> Paul had real bad hassles with curvature of the spine. One shoulder was always higher than the other, and it was probably degenerating. He also had huge fingers and they were very badly arthritic, so he was having trouble playing. Before he went onstage he used to have to run his hands under almost boiling hot water. And he would have to drink three double scotches to get any warmth through... He was as strong as an ox, but it was creeping up on him, especially the arthritis in the fingers.

After the departure of Taylor and Jacobsen and the death of Hewson, Dragon became a Hunter brothers vehicle, with Mansfield usually involved. Virtuoso guitarist Tommy Emmanuel often featured too, as did – extraordinary as it may seem – Doane Perry, more frequently the drummer in Jethro Tull. But if any band could recruit a drummer from XTC then replace him with one from Jethro Tull, it was Dragon. Taylor's last words on the group bring their extraordinary story up to the mid 80s:

> I would run into Marc occasionally because I was flatting with his ex-girlfriend and his son, I lived with Annie Burton, sharing a place with her, for about a year, and Marc would come on the phone or he would come round to see the boy or whatever, but no, [I had] no real contact. I'd see Tommy Emmanuel, of course, run into him. He'd say, 'Oh, what string did you play on the third bar of such-and-such', and then proceed to do it with five fingers faster than I could ever do it.
> Probably the thing I regret the most is I'd always wanted to have Todd Rundgren as a producer. 'Cause I used to love *Something/Anything*, that Todd Rundgren LP, and I always thought he was a really good pop producer. And bugger me if they didn't go and do an LP, *Dreams of Ordinary Men*, with him, you know! I would have loved to have been on that one, but I knew in my heart I just didn't have the guitar technique to get away with it. You needed someone like

Tommy Emmanuel. So, yeah, I'd sort of made myself redundant by not keeping up with guitar trends and things.

'PAINFULLY AUSTRALIAN'

In commercial terms, Dragon did not expand beyond the normal parameters for an Australasian hit group. Some mainstream Australian groups, on the other hand, found a niche internationally with what seemed like ease, as well as maintaining strong support in Australia. Early in the new decade, Rose Tattoo went to the UK, touring there – they played two sold-out shows at London's Marquee – and then elsewhere in Europe. Mick Cocks left the band during this period, and Robin Riley was flown over from Sydney to replace him.[474] When Rose Tattoo came back from Britain in late 1981, Angry Anderson paid his band a compliment at the same time as deriding them, saying 'you could get up and shit on stage as long as you did it with style'. Anderson claimed the group had returned to Australia 'to eat some decent food, get some sun and record an album.'[475]

Rose Tattoo was already, somehow, a legendary outfit. Pete Wells mused to *Rolling Stone's* Jane Matheson: 'A band like Duran Duran – how long a lifespan will they have? But with us – well, Angry at fifty years old is going to *look* awful, but he's going to be better than he is today.'[476] Anderson saw 'being a Tatt' as 'a brotherhood thing,'[477] but this did not stop him from regularly losing and sacking members, or moving further away from the group and into the mainstream as a media figure, taking a job as a journalist for Ray Martin's *Midday Show* and acting in *Mad Max Beyond Thunderdome*.[478] Nor did it stop him from pursuing his interests as 'a narrow-minded, racist loudmouthed thug', as Christie Eliezer described him.[479] This, understandably, is an element of Anderson's personality he has since sought to play down, but his ramblings to Eliezer were unspeakable, or should have been:

> All these uni students go marching against apartheid, but wait 'til a Lebanese family or a Vietnamese family lives next door, start to throw their garbage on the back verandah, keeps zillions of goats and dogs ... We're talking about people who grew up in an entirely different situation to us; in a war situation where they learned to grab grab, take take.[480]

Rose Tattoo's 1984 album *Southern Stars* is infected with this strain of Anderson's racism-patriotism. 'I wanted to write and record something that was painfully Australian,'[481] he said; he achieved at least part of his goal. The song 'Freedom's Flame', for instance, was directly in the tradition of William Lane's late-19th-century racist dystopias, 'a science fiction scenario . . . basically about a seven-year war way into the future. There's only two sides, the western and the eastern . . .'[482] That the music industry – Eliezer honourably excepted – allowed him to prattle on with this ill-conceived drivel is a sign (ironically) of more innocent times and perhaps of excessive, uncritical respect for celebrity. There is little doubt, too, that Anderson is an intelligent, or at least quick-witted man, which some even today mistakenly believe entitles a person to make idiotic public pronouncements more commonly known (and criminalized) in Australia as 'hate speech'.

Other new Rose Tattoo songs, such as 'Saturday's Rage', were more interesting: they were sentimental and community-minded. Anderson mused:

> When I was a kid I had a special suit of clothes that I only wore at weekends. I never went out during the week . . . I might visit a couple of mates during the week but I'd never go out. That was Friday and Saturday nights. And Sunday, have a quiet one to get up for work in the morning. But Saturday night is the night. That's why I'm trying to get our management interested in doing big shows again. Saturday night shows out in the suburbs. Three-band line-up in a big hall. No piss or nothin', just kids crowded into a hall dancing their tits off, ya know? That's what 'Saturday's Rage' is all about.[483]

Alongside Rose Tattoo and his other interests, Anderson found employment in another venture, the Party Boys, a group that was the simplest concept of all. Bass player Paul Christie was sacked from Mondo Rock in 1981, and then: 'I had a dream':

> I actually dreamt of the Party Boys. In the dream, James Reyne, myself, Kevin Borich, Buzz Bidstrup and Ian Moss were playing live at Whale Beach Surf Club at a dance. The next morning I remembered the dream and called all the guys up. The only one who couldn't do it was Ian Moss, he was on the road with Cold Chisel at the time. But Harvey James was at his place, he answered the phone and I said, 'You'll do.'[484]

James had been a member of Sherbet. The Party Boys played contemporary covers and classics, releasing live albums commemorating the vocalist on each tour. Reyne sang on the first Party Boys tour, *Live at Several 21st's;* this was followed by one with the grammatically problematic but amusing title *Greatest Hits (of Other People),* with Richard Clapton as vocalist. *No Song Too Sacred* featured Shirley Strachan, who 'drank tea the whole time' he toured with the band. The fourth vocalist was Marc Hunter and the resulting album was *You Need Professional Help,* which also included Eagles guitarist Joe Walsh (who had a special ambition: 'Every day I look in the mirror to see if I've turned Australian yet. I hope I do').[485] Christie later opined, 'That was the "Lucky to Make It" tour . . . I sat around on the northern beaches for the next 10 months trying to recover.'[486] Angry Anderson then sang with the band for three tours. (Ideas were thin on the ground: the album from this period was *The Party Boys Rage Album*). An 'odd couple' tour was mooted, pairing Anderson with Ross Wilson. Roger Daltrey became a possibility and failing him, Jimmy Barnes, Swanee, or John Farnham. In the end John Swan phoned Christie.[487]

MUTINY

The media did not call Anderson on his racism, and neither did they call Nick Cave on his misogyny, or various other transgressions of thought perpetrated by the Birthday Party. Fortunately, Cave's explorations were humorous and intelligently conceived, even if they often misfired.

The Birthday Party relocated to Europe in 1980, though it was not a particularly happy change for the group. Whatever the motivation for the move, Cave told Matthew Hall in *Puncture* fifteen years afterwards that:

> We assumed we'd never be successful when we were living in Australia . . . We didn't have huge hopes, when we went to England, that the English would suddenly understand us . . . I don't think anything we did in Australia except 'The Friend Catcher' and 'Mr. Clarinet', those two singles, was worth anything at all. It was a load of crap basically . . . We were enraged by England – we were so pissed off by the place after a year of living there. We hated the place – we *hated* English people. That's what the spirit of the Birthday Party was: an intense, blind, boiling, hatred for England and English people. I don't feel that way anymore.[488]

Absurdly, and showing a ridiculous lack of historical awareness, Cave told Tracee Hutchison in 1992 that the Birthday Party 'were just one of the first groups to actually leave Australia.'[489] Although they had the pleasure of jamming with the Pop Group[490] and soon became a well-regarded, even idolised, participant in the British scene, some of them were appalled by the frippery of the overly glam London scene. Harvey hated 'all things English . . . especially the music press.'[491] 'It's a shithole,' he told *Party Fears* writer Effigy in the early 90s. 'You can play and get a reasonable amount of money in London, if you can discount the British audience problem being at its worst in London.'[492] Although Harvey and Cave continued their creative partnership to great success for close to 35 years (it came to an end in 2009), for much of that time there were thousands of miles between them – Cave has not lived in Australia since the early 80s, while Harvey is a Melbournite: 'One thing I've noticed is how many groups in Australia still seem to be able to follow their own path . . . there's still the potential for groups to be really good here, untainted somehow,'[493] he said in the mid 90s.

It was perhaps the fear of being a shortlived big fish in a suffocatingly tiny pond that had inspired the group to relocate to Europe. Cave had said in the early 80s:

There's been numerous cases of really great groups, groups who I've seen in Australia who worked on a completely underground level, were given no recognition by anybody and eventually just folded up, because they couldn't survive. These groups are just gnats, and there is this media who are a big fly swat that knocks them out of the sky one by one. They're not even given a chance.[494]

The intricacies of the Birthday Party's career have been well told elsewhere, in books by Ian Johnstone and a decent writer who calls himself Robert Brokenmouth. Suffice it to say that *Prayers on Fire*, their first 'real' album under their new name – a self-titled compilation featuring the marvellous 'Mr. Clarinet' and 'Friend Catcher' singles, B sides and other Boys Next Door–Birthday Party changeover-era songs was thrown together by Missing Link – shows the group continuing to forge the individual path they had finally marked out for themselves. It contained 'Nick the Stripper', an early entry in a delightful series of self-parodying songs by Cave, Though this song (released as a single) has not made it into the first tier of the Cave/Birthday Party canon – unlike, for instance, 'Release the Bats', their undeniably best moment of self-parody, described by Robertson in *Roadrunner* as 'the biteyest sound around'[495] – it was notable at the time for its humour. Other songs from the album, like 'Cry', 'King Ink' (also the title of a very well-received 1988 lyric book by Cave) and 'Capers' were similarly humorous and strange, filled with chanting, mumbling and the superior and empathic playing of the band (particularly Pew and Calvert on this album). There was something playful and fantastic (in the old sense), even pathetic (again, in the old sense) about these songs. 'I've created my own unique land,' Cave told Debbie Krueger, decades later. 'I think that's quite similar to a lot of Australian cinema, to Australian songwriting, Australian society. It's largely a kind of hybrid, mongrel society.'[496]

In 1982 Cave told Marie Ryan:

> I think our particular sense of humour and way of looking at things has a lot to do with the fact that most of us went to a rich private school (Caulfield Grammar) and that most of us felt fairly misfitted there. I think that kind of lifestyle is one reason why we have never had, and will never have any desire to make any politically angered statements about anything. They're all totally selfish, personal statements.[497]

A *Roadrunner* reader, Anna, rambled engagedly in a letter to the magazine about the group's show in Newcastle, NSW, on their 1982 tour:

> I've always preferred the Birthday Party method of violent repetition to get their songs across to those trying to get their dance worths out of an evening, but if it had to be spelled out, you did it more than adequately.

It was truly heartbreaking to see the crowds turn out for this year's Party 'shows'. Yes that's right – to see the performing animals go through the motions exactly you quick-minded people – just like the seals at the zoo. '... AND FOR HIS NEXT TRICK NICK WILL JUMP FROM THE MONITOR INTO THE CROWD', cue for much kicking into the personage on the floor.

That's why the Newcastle gig was so good. They refused to perform the tricks, and Nick sat down as did Tracy, hence the malevolent, spiteful cries "we want the real Birthday Party", "You didn't pay to see us", (oh but it's much more fun to see you react than for you to see us perform) and from the girls next to me 'Newcastle luves [sic] ya' – wrong band, girls, Australian Crawl were down the road.

I preferred Nick's classic 'Look I know we're boring, but we've all got headaches tonight, no one is allowed to touch the singer'. Cheeky boy.[498]

The selfish, personal, apolitical nature of the group was reflected in the fairly sizeable drug habits a number of them were now shouldering – particularly Cave and Howard. Some of the band's members did not take drugs at all: to Harvey, for instance, 'there was this backdrop of a whole lot of weird stuff; people with drug problems; people being really out of it, a lot of the time. That was just the territory I lived through in the eighties.'[499]

Ryan, a Canberran living in London and writing occasionally for the music press, outed Cave as a heroin addict in *RAM*, for which he berated and threatened her from the stage at a show in Sydney when the group came back to tour.

In 1982 the Birthday Party also released a live album (or half of one – it was shared with Lydia Lunch, with whom Howard recorded a version of 'Some Velvet Morning' released the same year) entitled *Drunk on the Pope's Blood*; another zany, meaningless name calculated to shock. Harvey claimed at the time that it was a recycled title which 'was actually the name of a Birthday Party album that came out on Missing Link about three years ago,' (that is, the early compilation). 'But for some strange reason, it never got on the cover,' added Howard.[500] Statements like this suggest the group's increasingly strained relationship with Keith and Helena Glass and the Missing Link label. This came to a head by the time the band were recording their second studio album (what would become *Junkyard*), as mentioned earlier. The evidence suggests two possible explanations: either the group were wasting money the Glasses couldn't afford by partying in the studio, or the Glasses were party poopers. Be that as it may, *Junkyard* was undoubtedly their best album, from its Ed 'Big Daddy' Roth cover art – yet another example of Australians embracing American culture and iconography, in the same way Daddy Cool had done with Ian McCausland's comic strip about the drive-in a decade earlier – to the murky brilliance of its constituent tracks.

Cave, Howard and Pew sacked Calvert when they discovered Harvey could play drums: like Cold Chisel, it was a case of blaming the drummer when the band wasn't working, and unfair on Calvert, whose playing in the Birthday Party had great merit. As with Glen Matlock's sacking from the Sex Pistols, it was suggested that Calvert was fired for liking the Beatles. Two EPs that were relics of the time they spent living in West Berlin, *The Bad Seed* and *Mutiny*, concluded the four-piece group's impressive if uneven output. *The Bad Seed* was every good idea they had, condensed into four epic tracks; 'Sonny's Burning' was a refined 'Release the Bats'. 'Wild World' was a parallel-universe Elvis Presley covering Cat Stevens; 'Deep in the Woods' was possibly their finest moment, though Cave's dozens of similar explorations of fictional isolated murders in song since 1983 dull its effect somewhat in retrospect. The second EP was less worthwhile. Cave has referred to it as 'this albatross of a record called *Mutiny* . . . it was a totally abortive attempt at recording, due to our own lack of communication and the dissension in the group at the time.'[501] The best track on *Mutiny* is easily Howard's blues ballad 'Say a Spell', reminiscent of the Loved Ones. When the group returned to Australia for a farewell tour, Harvey refused to go with them, and the drummer role was filled by Des Hefner. The Birthday Party played their last ever performance at the Seaview Ballroom in June 1983.

Cave claimed to Marie Ryan that "we dissolved mid-climb":

> But then everyone else was so many rungs below us it didn't matter anyway. I tended to find, towards the end particularly, that the audience became just an infringement on my own personal expression. I wished there was some way that we could have performed through a one-way mirror, where they could watch us but we would never have to see them – and they would still have to pay to get in.[502]

Much was made of the slew of Birthday Party 'copyists' who appeared to fill a gap left by their departure from Australia in the early 80s, though many of these were in fact more interesting than this lazy categorization would suggest.

Madroom, in Sydney, were filling a need (or was it just a desire?) for inner-city art rock; they debuted in July 1982 to promote their first release, an EP called *The Cruelty of Beauty*.[503] Their guitarist, Kevin Purdy, had played in a band called Aural Indifference, which had released material through M Squared and they also boasted a wire mannequin player in Susie Beauchamp. When JJJ released a *Live at the Wireless* album (originally conceived as a box set of singles)[504] of radio sessions by various 'indie' bands of the time – such as the Triffids, the Particles, the Hoodoo Gurus and Do Re Mi – it also issued a 12-inch EP of more 'difficult' music, which included Madroom, Severed Heads, and Bring Philip, an edgy and driven Sydney group who would later relocate to Berlin.

Melbourne's Plays with Marionettes were an equally promising proposition. In a 2014 memoir, the band's Hugo Race suggests that the early 80s were, for him and his friends, a dazzling and fragmented cacophony of ambition and spectacle:

> There is a lot of talk about who is cooler than whom. At eighteen, everything is really happening in the now. We're eggshell fragile, trying to act tough, growing thicker skins to protect our own egos and absurdity. We know almost nothing, yet think we know everything, even when we really know that we don't. Speeding all night, writing songs we think are masterpieces that in the cold comedown of morning all sound the same, running down chord changes in an orbit around E minor, the deepest, most open chord you can hit with two fingers. It floats through the scene like a cement graveyard angel, all gothic overtones and tremolo arm harmonics.[505]

A review of an early show in 1981, written by Andrew Maine in a deliberately experimental and humorous voice, gives not only a sense of the night in question but also the extreme style of the time:

> Word of Mouth. Second show. A 'Local' support. Good night? Comfortable crowd! (Furious Pig?) Sleepy Hollow comes alive! Command(ing) vocal performance. Ooozzzing Confidence. Stiff upper lip. *Maniccc cc c.* (Huh!) (hugo) sings, guitars, clarinets, squeels, shouts, soars (in tune). Hobbit meets Beefheart? COMICbook stories. Sleepy Hollow. (Brian) sax, alto and tenor, keyboards; a BIGGG G Brass sound, stands around. (Robyn) violins, keyboards, and a smashing good time. Hippy Dippy? Nopey Dopey. Music college; *the discipline factor?* Yes. (Dave) bass and horn. A graphic quaff. Self-consciousness moves over to enjoy. (Frank) drums. The beat. Can(t) dance (?) Beat, beat, baash, sh, shuh, beat. (aaaarrghhhh)beat(hhhuh), beat . . .[506]

The band's mainstay was Hugo Race, a handsome guitarist-vocalist reputed to have ranked first in the state (of Victoria) in English literature in his final year of secondary school. Plays with Marionettes also featured Robin Casinader, Edward Clayton-Jones (formerly of the Fabulous Marquises) and Nick Seymour, Mark's brother, later a member of Crowded House and seemingly a member of, or rejected by, almost every band Melbourne produced between 1978 and 1985. Shortly before their demise, Race claimed the group were turning pop:

> Our old songs used to be crammed, filled to the guts with ideas, objects and references and stuff and it's taken us this long to get wise to how small the collective mind of an audience is and how long it takes them to catch on to what we're doing. So now it's become simpler and easier to like and understand.[507]

One song, 'Buffalo Heart', was for Race 'about the most perfect example we've got of us clarifying one idea and distilling it over four minutes of music until it's perfectly apparent what's going on, and logically enough that's the song that gets the biggest response.'[508] Ironically, and to the group's dismay, it was pointed out to them by well-wishers that, far from being on the cutting edge of new music, one section of this song bore a strong resemblance to a boogie passage in Skyhooks' well-known hit 'Love on the Radio'. Race blamed Edward Clayton-Jones's country upbringing and his overexposure to pop radio (Clayton-Jones, raised in Melbourne's eastern suburbs, has refuted both charges).

In an unusual act of co-optation, Nick Cave invited Race to join his first post-Birthday Party band, Man or Myth, which soon morphed into the Bad Seeds. Rumour has it that his fellow Bad Seeds became so tired of Race they left him at a remote truckstop on their first US tour. The group Race had left behind in Australia 'eventually evolved into the Horla',[509] with Brian McMahon at its centre. A Horla was a 'vampire type creature or some kind of alien life force';[510] the group jammed the music and Casinader would then add lyrics. They did not last long, and when Race returned to Australia he, Clayton-Jones and Casinader formed the Wreckery.

Elsewhere, more first-generation late 70s punks were focusing their energies for a second go. Armed with their knowledge of what had gone before and whatever networking they could muster, they could take advantage of the burgeoning pub rock scene in the major capitals and perhaps even aspire to international travel and interest. The Sacred Cowboys were virtually a Melbourne underground supergroup, based around Garry Gray, who had been involved in early punk experiments with Chris Walsh and Tracy Pew in the early to mid 70s. After the fiasco of Suicide Records, Gray fled to Sydney for two years. Returning to Melbourne in 1982 he made a friend in Mark Ferrie, who invited him to a rehearsal of a new band he was forming. After Models, Ferrie recalls:

> I moved into a share house with John Clifforth and Paul Hester. They had a band called the Cheks, who used to support the Models. That was in St Kilda. I ran into Garry Gray. He was bursting to do something. Another guy from a share house that I lived in Carlton, Terry Doolin, when I was with the Models I lived in a house with him. He was a good guitar player and he wanted to do something. [That was] the first line-up of the Sacred Cowboys. And I got Johnny along.

'Johnny' was Johnny Crash, who during his Models days had reverted to his real name of Janis Freidenfelds.

> Garry was a pretty committed lyricist, but he didn't write music. So he needed music to work off. My vision for the Sacred Cowboys initially was for it to be a band that played one-chord songs. The Models, like I said, was all, 'take this

section here, then put on this section' it was all that kind of stuff. They were quite arranged pieces by the time we ended up doing them. Whereas the Sacred Cowboys was more like you play this one chord or this feel and Garry does his delivery over the top. So the songs weren't reliant on chord changes and that kind of arrangement. It was more like playing off a feel, where everyone had to really listen to each other. You had to listen to each other to play together rather than play a set arrangement. And that's how the Cowboys began.

Like the Models, it was this very exciting thing. As soon as we all got in a room together ... everyone just knew. As soon as we got on stage it was explosive.

The group quickly recorded a long, loping single, 'Nothing Grows in Texas', full of silly cowboy-isms. It was introduced by Ian Meldrum on *Countdown* with these typically abstruse words:

The next group that's about to hit the airwaves is a group that I referred to, um, after I saw them live, as the worst group I've seen in the last five years. They challenged me to have them on the program. I think the single 'Nothing Grows in Texas', ah, is pretty good, however I still think their live performance is pretty down the drain. But here they are, Sacred Cowboys with 'Nothing Grows in Texas'.

The Sacred Cowboys could not match the impact of this first single. A second line-up included two former Romantics, Nick Rischbeith and Stefan Fidock. Fidock was brought in at Rischbeith's suggestion:

It's not a style of music I really like. It's swamp rock, kinda Iggy Pop, all that sort of stuff ... I did it because it was nice to play some rock drums after the Reels stuff. The Reels were the same one night to the next, you can't change the feel, the same night after night after night, which was not what I was doing before I joined the Reels and not what I was doing after. I joined the Sacred Cowboys and there was a bit more freedom in the drumming.

Gray says he 'experienced "temporary engine failure", which took me out of the scene for a little while'[511] in the late 1980s; his drug and legal problems were well-known.

BEGINNINGS, ENDINGS, HAS-BEENS, NEVER-WERES AND ALWAYS-WILL-BES

'I'd like us to be considered a rock & roll band,' Little River Band's Glenn Shorrock told US *Rolling Stone's* David Fricke in 1980, 'but I can see reasons why we aren't.'[512] Shorrock – true to his showman leanings – impressed Fricke by imitating Hitler entering Czechoslovakia during a Park Avenue car ride; he also joked 'I sort of fancy myself as a rock & roll Columbo.'⁵¹³ Shorrock and former LRB member David Briggs both appeared on Mike Brady's album *Invisible Man,* which came soon after the success of his advertisement-turned-hit-record 'Up there Cazaly'. Brady's album cover, showing him unobserved in a girls' changing room, 'wasn't meant for erotic stimulation', he said.⁵¹⁴ The album – and Shorrock and Briggs's presence on it – was a stab at the adult market, where groups like LRB were meant to excel.

LRB were still a megasuccess in the early 1980s and seemed unstoppable, but there were stresses – perhaps more from within than without: essentially, the members hated one another. Shorrock left in 1982 and Glenn Wheatley saw a chance to meld his two greatest enthusiasms by replacing him with the man now known as John Farnham (it took at least a decade for Australians to forgive him for having once been 'Johnny'). Farnham had already (in 1980) recorded an album of Graeham Goble songs, *Uncovered;* however, he had no profile or experience outside Australia, where his star had quietly faded under unimaginative managerial decisions before Wheatley took him on. *The Net,* the first LRB album with Farnham as vocalist, is desperately upbeat and modern, with precise drums and prominent synthesisers courtesy of David Hirschfelder, who would soon be invited into the group. *The Net* was the last LRB album to yield top-forty singles, and the group began a long, slow petering out. One of their last interesting acts was to replace Derek Pellicci with Cold Chisel's former drummer Steve Prestwich in early 1984, although even the most patient reader of this history will probably feel this involves an extreme redefinition of the term 'interesting'.

The Sydney group Do Re Mi seemed much more like the future than aged crooners like Farnham and LRB; as it turned out, they weren't. The group was formed by two Melbournites, drummer Dorland Bray and singer-guitarist Deborah Conway, who had both been members of Melbourne group the Benders, with guitarist Stephen Philip and bass player Helen Carter. After some independent releases in Melbourne, they moved to Sydney where they spent three years between 1982 and 1985 preparing for Do Re Mi's debut album.⁵¹⁵ Initially it seemed worth it: the debut single 'Man Overboard' charted, and broke an important barrier by being – at last! – a mainstream hit that referred to pubic hair (on a pillow, no less). Carter was later philosophical about the band's demise following their second album and in the midst of preparing for a third, saying 'I think the record company thought that we were going to turn into this mega pop band with the beautiful lead singer with her underpants on and we fiercely fought that, to the point where everything got confused.'⁵¹⁶ The important elements of the Do Re Mi story happened outside the timeframe covered by this history.

Asleep at the Wheel, a compilation LP released by Au Go Go in 1985, captures a moment in Melbourne music that is due for reassessment, and which can perhaps be seen as an attempt to move beyond the shadow of the Birthday Party (which is overemphasised in discussions of Melbourne at this time; the shadow of Pseudo Echo was at least as dark and bold). Groups such as Harem Scarem, Spring Plains

and the Olympic Sideburns featured prominently, playing a cacophonous R&B music that was described by compiler Gavan Purdy as a reaction to 'video package bands experimenting with clothes and haircuts'. Harem Scarem's extraordinary powerful 'Love Attraction' and Spring Plains' 'American Hymn' are probably the two best tracks, though other bands would go on to great things later in the 1980s, in Spring Plains' case, under a different name: after jettisoning singer Steven Morrow (no relation to the Numbers), they became the Cosmic Psychos. The Huxton Creepers'
'King of the Road' was track one, side one of *Asleep at the Wheel*; their first single was produced by Rob Younger, who also produced the Lime Spiders' '25th Hour' (one of the cornerstone singles of the early 80s), Died Pretty, and his own band the New Christs. They signed to Big Time, the Hoodoo Gurus' record label, via the recommendation of Dave Faulkner.[517] Like the Hoodoo Gurus, the Huxton Creepers hoped to 'kinda throw "cool" out the window and bring in dagginess in a sense and try to communicate to the audiences a bit more and make it part of the show, sort of like Painters and Dockers, although they're more extreme.'[518]

Painters and Dockers were another group on *Asleep at the Wheel*. Formed as a one-off joke in the early 80s for a benefit – their name referenced a well-known and controversial union but was also, of course, cocking a snook at Hunters and Collectors – they 'spent a year doing supports, with an audience of three and us falling off the stage pissed.'[519] They knew their rock history: they would play, for instance, a cover of the Saints' 'Know Your Product'. The group's mundane twist was that during the song the band's brass players would drop their pants.[520] In 1987 they released the single 'Basia', a somewhat conservative but definitely positive response to the host of a television music show launched in 1982, *Rock around the World*. This program was a feature of the new Special Broadcasting Service television station that resulted from a Whitlam government scheme, for broadcasting in languages other than English, subsequently pursued by the Fraser government. Basia Bonkowski was a knowledgeable and personable presenter of a show that was largely comprised of video clips of non-English speaking new-wave groups from Europe. She was one of the first women to be the permanent host of a music television program (she was succeeded by Geeling Ng, hosting a new show, *Kulture Schock*, in 1985). SBS was not the only station where women hosted rock shows: the ABC-TV program *Rock Arena*, hosted by Suzanne Dowling, was a late-night, 'adult' music show reminiscent of commercial television's *Nightmoves*.[521]

The marvellous musical comedy *Starstruck* has already been discussed in this chapter. A darker music-related film was Hayden Keenan's *Going Down*. The director said in 1983 that the film was 'about a group of people who discover Pel Mel, Mental as Anything and New Christs before JJJ hears about it. Those girls, that crowd, are the vanguard of taste, they go out and discover them.' The Divinyls, XL Capris, X, and the Laughing Clowns were all filmed during the production but not used in the final film; the script – which had to be radically reworked in the final stages of editing due to a death among the cast – was by 'four girls' including Julie Barry and Moira Maclaine-Cross, who starred in the film. Keenan's description of his intended audience is telling:

> I think it's not that piss weak that the inner city kids are going to hate it, but I think it's glittery, dangerous, foreign enough for the kids out west who have a couple of mandies, half a bottle of scotch and go up to the Cross.

This desire to attack elitism and the western suburban divide harks back to the early days of JJ, if not before; Keenan even considered touring pubs with the film on a huge video screen.[522]

Going Down included music by both Australian Crawl and the Birthday Party, which would be enough on its own to make it an unusual artefact. A group like Pel Mel, however, could easily fit with either of those groups, and appeared in the film itself. The group were considered 'too interesting for the program directors, and insufficiently avant-garde for the superhip;'[523] at least this was Ed St. John's assessment in a *Rolling Stone* book.

From Newcastle, Pel Mel were signed to the Gap label, whose purpose, according to founder Andrew Penhallow, 'was to get behind music that I particularly liked.'[524] In most cases, this meant licensing material originally issued in the UK by groups like Cabaret Voltaire, the (US/UK) Red Crayola, Joy Division and the Durutti Column. Pel Mel were far more commercial than any of these bands: it beggars belief now (as it did in 1983) that singles like 'Shoes Should Fit' and 'Blind Lead the Blind' were not chart hits. These appeared on the group's first album *Out of Reason;* their second, *Persuasion,* was an even more concerted bid for commercial success. 'We're underground not necessarily by choice,' said the group's Graham Dunne, 'but that shouldn't matter, like when Essendon Airport were around, they were experimental but they should have been able to make it in mainstream circles.'[525] The band – at least, their saxophonist/singer Judy McGee – was memorialised in a mural on the outside wall of a large car park in Sydney's Domain.

Phil Turnbull recalls that period in Newcastle:

There were two big houses at either end of Commonwealth Street, near Central Station, where most of Pel Mel, Wild West and associated friends lived in each other's pockets. If you didn't actually live there then you went there all the time anyway. Influenced by the 'little bands' idea from Melbourne, small bands would be formed on any evening after a few unsteady jams in cluttered rooms.

The group's late-period drummer Dave Weston was unequivocal about Newcastle on *After Dark*: 'it's boring. There's no major outlet . . . it was necessary to do something else. Perhaps other people thought the same thing . . .' Pel Mel had plans to travel overseas,[526] but instead they broke up.

As should by now be clear, the first half of the 1980s was an extraordinarily rich period in the development of Australian pop and rock music. This chapter, excessively long as it is, nevertheless barely scratches the surface of this important time. It does not, for instance, give adequate space to important phenomena such as the 'Citadel groups' (in fact a rather amorphous collection, in terms of sound). What is interesting and worthy of note here – in the way that it reflects the changing focus of the Australian scene on certain cities – is label founder John Needham's pronouncement in 1986 that:

> Music here in Australia is a thriving enterprise, it's a more healthy scene here musically than most parts of the world . . . I can find better bands in Sydney or Adelaide or Perth, but not Brisbane or Melbourne, just about any night of the week compared to places like London or large American cities.[527]

Similarly, truly superb, short-lived groups like the Sydney band Grooveyard require acknowledgement for their perfect guitar pop single 'Avalanche of Love', recorded in September 1983[528] and released on Stuart Coupe and Roger Grierson's Green label.

Wollongong's Sunday Painters were a low-key outfit. Their leader Peter Raengel claimed that the group formed as a result of 'just being at school, and wanting to play music. I was just really bored.'[529] They started by trying to cover Blue Oyster Cult, 'But we were always interested in the avant-garde as well, we used to listen to ABC-FM.'[530] Raengel began a band called Art Throbs with Bruce Ellis, and then Winged Death; this high school band became the Sunday Painters.[531]

Their first album was called *Something to Do*; Raengel told Clinton Walker (without apparent irony) that putting out records 'just gives us something to do'[532] and that his band were 'a good opportunity to do some screaming at least.'[533]

The Celibate Rifles' singer, Damien Lovelock, had a similarly laconic outlook to Raengel's. Lovelock could, with grim humour, say of the band's second, self-titled album: '*The Celibate Rifles* is about precisely what the title says'.[534] The group were formed by guitarist Kent Steedman in 1979 when he was living on 'a diet of Birdman, Saints and Stooges'[535] Steedman played an Epiphone that had been Chris Masuak's.[536] Lovelock claimed that in the first year of the band, 'Our claim to fame was that we'd knocked back a Midnight Oil support. Then we took off like a rocket . . .'[537] Despite their name – a joke on 'the Sex Pistols' that was so laboured many failed to pick it up – the group were more straightahead rock and roll than punk. Lovelock, slightly older than the rest of the group, provided wordy and worthy lyrics.

Being Sydney-based, the Celibate Rifles were at least in a position to reject the patronage of bigger bands. Groups like Darwin's Exhibit A seem to have had to create a scene for themselves. *Roadrunner* reported in 1981 that:

> Founder member Peter Brat had started a weekly 'new Music' page in the independent *Star* newspaper, and secured an hour show, *Alternative Chartbusters*, on the newly-opened 8TOP FM radio station. Naturally, these outlets were utilized to propagandize the activities of Exhibit A, both real and fantasized.
>
> Seeking to overcome the problem of lack of suitable venues, Exhibit A enlisted the aid of the Darwin Theatre Group to put on a series of 'multimedia extravaganzas' in the town's only theatre, Brown's Mart. Climaxing with 'Revenge of the Dolls', these concert/dances featured the band plus other acts, including dancers, a 'mad poet', video, feminist guerrilla theatre, and acoustic music, further enhancing Exhibit A's reputation for innovation.[538]

Exhibit A featured Stuart Gray, better known as Stu Spasm, who would be a feature of the Sydney music scene later in the 80s as the instigator and only constant member of Lubricated Goat; Exhibit A also had, as mentioned earlier, a drummer in Richard Ploog.

An individual who might have been seen in the same light as Gray in the mid to late 80s, but has gone on to have a very different career, is Greg 'Tex' Perkins. A common anecdote has Perkins's entree to music coming about purely because Greg and Ian Wadley, fellow Brisbaneites with a particularly idiosyncratic, humorous but also generally enthused attitude to musical activity, approached him at a party on the grounds that he looked like someone who could be in a band. Soon he was living up to his appearance, though the Wadleys deny any responsibility.

The band Perkins was in was given the deliberately stupid name of Tex Deadly and the Dum Dums; they included not only both Wadley brothers but also Mark (Marko) Halstead, who had played in a number of 'cowpunk' groups, such as the

Hilltop Hollow Bluegrass Band, and a punk-punk band, the Disposable Fits. By the time they arrived in Sydney the group's public persona relied on forced and silly cowboy humour; for instance, Halstead's stated ambition to 'write a country song about chartered accountants and juggling figures . . . Nothing to do with trains, divorce, engines, truck drivers.'539 Perkins had become 'Tex Deadly', and was, according to Halstead, a 'real Jekyll and Hyde when this critter gets loose onstage.'540

With the demise of the Dum Dums, Perkins started up the Beasts of Bourbon, a group that could be regarded as a Sydney independent/underground supergroup. As well as Perkins, it included guitarist Spencer Jones, drummer James Baker, and Scientists Kim Salmon and Boris Sujdovic. Like X, the band recorded their first album, *The Axeman's Jazz*, in one day. James Baker later recalled that it was:

> on a bleary Sunday afternoon. We just went in with about 4 cartons of beer and a couple of bottles of whiskey with Tony Cohen . . . We started at midday and by 6 pm the whole album was done . . . We were going to do one more track but Spencer passed out before we did it . . . We did the Hoodoo Gurus album the next day and that was so painfully slow, and so much time spent on each track, and it didn't sound as good.541

The group played what was definitely not their 'last show ever' – though it was advertised as such – on 22 February 1985. 542

Spasm, with Lachlan McLeod and Martin Bland both from Adelaide, Kim Salmon and Tex Perkins all passed through the band Salamander Jim.543 'I think Salamander Jim are great,' Perkins proclaimed in 1985, 'but they're never going to get anywhere. The bottom half of music, bands like us, just get put under the boot, pressed down and held down.'544 He was evidently disillusioned with Sydney music, but retained illusions about his chances elsewhere: he was about to go to UK to form a new band, Fur Bible, which turned out to be a debacle.545

At the other end of the music industry spectrum – or at least amongst acts considered playable on mainstream radio and television – certain groups showed more promise than they delivered. The Electric Pandas was a songwriting vehicle for Lin Buckfield, a Hong Kong-born, London-raised songwriter who pinched her group's name from London band Exotic Pandas. In early 1985, Buckfield claimed the public thought of the group as 'just a pop band . . . there are not too many who are catering for the young kids, who don't like to be frightened by their rock bands . . . '546 As it transpired the public didn't think of them much at all: they had one top-ten hit, 'Big Girls' in mid 1984, and petered out.

Groups such as Samurai Trash were even less commercially successful. Mark Foster, originally from Perth's punk scene and a filmmaker as well as a guitarist,547 had started the group as the Quiet Achievers in 1982.548 Virgin Records had found them by accident and contacted them via a 'flattering telegram'.549 Foster did not begin his pop career well by being represented as having a chip on his shoulder before it began: he claimed, for instance, that Samurai Trash's demos weren't liked by independent labels: 'I think it was a bit straight for them or something... there weren't any out-of-tune saxophones on them.' Similarly, he complained that the group's 'Samurai Stomp,' which appeared on *Live at the Wireless*, had been subjected to a remix which 'ruined it.'[550] Samurai Trash, along with Beargarden – a group with connections to the Ears – and Do Re Mi were signed to Virgin's new Australian arm in 1983. The label was also persuaded (or compelled) to release the Moodists' records in Australia while the band was recording for the UK's Red Flame label. Only Do Re Mi were really successful for Virgin Australia, and then only briefly.

The Dynamic Hepnotics, with their charismatic singer Continental Robert Susz, were another live favourite. The Sydney group originally recorded for Johnny Topper's Mambo label, after which Ross Wilson recorded the single 'Hepnobeat' for Missing Link. The band included Bruce Allen, who had gone by the name 'Tangles' when a member of Ol' 55.[551] The band's Andrew Silver outlined the Dynamic Hepnotics' situation in the music industry with considerable wisdom:

> Once you go beyond the really small level band, where you can make a fair bit of money just by gigging around, the next level is really the most expensive, once you get into the stage of hiring a PA system for yourself, the overheads go through the roof... I was actually making more money before we became a really big touring attraction.
>
> This is the middle level – the next step for the really big money is hard, only INXS, Australian Crawl and a couple of others are in that class in Australia, you have to think about going overseas, or back to the low level and just gig around forever.[552]

SPIRIT OF PLACE

Despite the wide variety of styles and personalities on offer, the Australian music industry had come to assume that the national spirit could really only be captured by a male singer-songwriter with a guitar. Enter Paul Kelly, the right guy in the right place at the right time.

We have already encountered Kelly as a prose writer and guitarist/songwriter in various Adelaide and Melbourne groups. There are elements of the 60s (or earlier) folk balladeer in Kelly's approach, though he usually seems to be operating in a guitar-pop vein. His biggest chart hits, such as 'To Her Door' and 'From St Kilda to Kings Cross', were often not that big at the time but – like Hunters and Collectors' best-known songs – enjoyed a huge afterlife on FM radio.

Kelly came up in mid 70s, pre–new wave pub rock with groups like the High Rise Bombers, then his own group Paul Kelly and the Dots. Their hit single 'Billy

Baxter', about a mid-70s musician and cult figure, with backing vocals from the Numbers' Annalisse Morrow, seemed at the time to revive Baxter's own fortunes (he gained indie prominence later in the 80s with the Hollowmen and as a 3RRR presenter). But it was not until Kelly abandoned the Dots and created another backing group, the Coloured Girls and later the Messengers (which of the two names is more awful?), that he hit his stride. His singles 'Before Too Long' and the abovementioned 'From St Kilda ...' are certainly classic and influential (you can hear echoes of 'Before Too Long' in the Go-Betweens' 'Streets of Your Town', for instance). 'From St Kilda ...', with its old echoes of the Sydney-Melbourne rivalry already explored in Skyhooks' 'This is My City', comes down heavily on St Kilda's side (and the cover of one edition of Kelly's published lyrics show him strolling the promenade of that prominent seaside suburb, which the song praises as worth 'all of Sydney Harbour'.)[553] 'Leaps and Bounds' (written with Chris Langman) references more Melbourne landmarks.[554] 'Darling It Hurts ('to see you down Darlinghurst tonight'[555]) sees Kelly once more responding to Greg Macainsh's important innovation – the use of Australian geography. Kelly has said that the local inclination of his third album, *Post*, came from 'listening to a lot of Chuck Berry songs. I've always like the way that Chuck Berry sort of lists things and is full of really concrete details.'[556] The previous year he'd surmised that 'being in Sydney is not that important. Except that it's given me some new place names to work with!'[557]

Kelly released three albums during the period 1980-85: *Talk*, *Manila* and *Post*. He has largely disowned the first two; the enormous amount of reworking that went into *Talk* is clear from detailed jottings on its inner sleeve, which include mention of songs that were not used in the finished product. With tracks produced by Martin Armiger and Joe Camilleri, it was a year in the making[558] and, said Kelly perhaps disingenuously (he had been writing songs for ten years), 'a lot of the tracks are the first songs I wrote.'[559] The album also marked the demise of Kelly's band partnership with songwriter/guitarist Chris Dyson, who wrote one song on *Talk* and was 'reluctant to leave the band.'[560]

Kelly had wanted the Clash's Joe Strummer and Mick Jones to produce his second album.[561] That didn't happen and instead the group recorded *Manila* in the city of that name. Kelly conceded that it 'wasn't the kind of record that was going to make it on the radio'[562] and indeed it did not sell. The self-funded *Post* was recorded at Clive Shakespeare's studio in 1985; Ian Rilen played bass on one track and otherwise recording was undertaken by Kelly and his creative partner of this period, Steve Connolly.[563] They began recording at a flat Kelly shared with Paul Hewson.[564] The album's title came from its concept: convinced he no longer had commercial possibilities, Kelly was planning to sell it as a mail-order product but when he licensed it to Mushroom, this marked the true beginning of a long and illustrious partnership between artist and label, ending only when Mushroom forgot to renew its contract.

The Go-Betweens, along with the Birthday Party and the Laughing Clowns (and, later, the Triffids), were seen in the early 80s as the vanguard of Australian new music that presented a distinctively Australian image to the world. The group recorded their first album, *Send Me a Lullaby*, in 1980 in Melbourne, where they lived for a brief period before they returned to Britain as a three-piece with Lindy Morrison as drummer. This first album soon came to be regarded by members of the band with some dismay: 'Don't put that one on during breakfast', joked Grant McLennan in 1983; Robert Forster, who was responsible for most of the album's songs, agreed: 'You won't get out of the house.'[565] McLennan commented that on their second LP, *Before Hollywood*, 'Robert and I have learnt to sing a bit more in tune'.[566] It features yet another genuinely iconic Go-Betweens song, the single 'Cattle and Cane', a McLennan song made particularly distinctive by Morrison's unique drum pattern. A late cancellation saw the Go-Betweens invited to play the song on *Countdown*: it was nevertheless not a chart hit. Despite its title referencing American culture, the album was regarded by many as expatriates looking back at Brisbane or Australia. The next album – also recorded in Europe, this time at Studio Miraval in the south of France – was very specifically Brisbane-oriented: it was named *Spring Hill Fair*. It featured a fourth Go-Between in Robert Vickers and saw the group begin to develop further their stylised romanticism, with McLennan ('Bachelor Kisses') and Forster ('Part Company') each penning a single that seemed to challenge typical assumptions about gender roles in heterosexual relationships. Although both Forster and McLennan were pop songwriters, McLennan was the one more likely to advocate chart success as a logical pursuit: 'It is important for me to get onto the charts because the band is doing melodic, rhythmic, enjoyable music and there is a need on the charts for that type of music.'[567]

In the mid 80s, a woman who would soon be a major piece in the Go-Betweens puzzle, violinist Amanda Brown, was playing in the experimental/improvisational group Climbing Frame, described in *On the Street* as 'a climax of sympathetic textures that tug and tease at your limbs.'[568] The group's name was taken from a phrase discovered in a magazine: 'the praiseworthy struggle against the climbing frame in arts playground'.[569]

Goanna made their name and reputation with their 1982 album *Spirit of Place*, though the group had existed (originally as the Goanna Band) since 1976. Produced by Trevor Lucas (who also worked wonders with Redgum's 'I Was Only 19', the album was focused on one particularly powerful song – almost grandiose in its structure and strength – about Aboriginal dispossession, 'Solid Rock'. Whereas

Ross Wilson had proclaimed 'the blacks are dead' in his 'Living in the Land of Oz' in 1976, Goanna were identifying Aboriginals as a wronged but resilient race and inviting the majority of Australians to consider justice. Goanna's leader, Shane Howard, reasoned that it was 'probably right for people to accept what the song was saying at that point in time. It struck a chord somehow . . .'[570] The song went to number one; the group were awarded a *Countdown* Award for best debut single and album and the Johnny O'Keefe Award for best new talent.[571] Howard claimed that the album:

> was a semi-conscious attempt to define a style of contemporary music that was distinctively Australian. The Dingoes made contributions to that, Richard Clapton made great contributions . . . Midnight Oil. In one sense we were one part of an Australian musical continuum and I think we had a consciousness about how we should exist. You are a function of what's been before you.[572]

To a degree, however, he got ahead of himself: 'Who in the future is going to be listening to Madonna singing, "I'm a material girl in a material world"?' he asked Toby Creswell. 'I don't think that will hold up over time.'[573]

The band's follow-up album was *Oceania* in 1985; unlike their debut it was not a blockbuster. Howard claimed: 'We weren't really all that comfortable with the success that *Spirit of Place* enjoyed. It was a little unexpected and it brought with it its internal pressures. We wanted to take a long time . . . to get this industry out of our system and get back to simply music.'[574]

I HATE YOU

The rise and (as it transpired, temporary) demise of X was outlined in chapter 11. Yet another great Ian Rilen group to add to a long list of diverse and extraordinary agglomerations took shape as Sardine V, the band he maintained between 1980 and 83 with his wife, Stephanie (now Stephanie Falconer). The two had been a couple since the late 60s – when Ian was still learning the bass – and had three young children.

The story of the beginning of Sardine was that Ian had bought a small keyboard for his children, and overheard Stephanie picking out notes on it; it was a eureka moment, and drummer Greg Skehill and bass player Phil Hall – also often found in lively pop group the Dropbears – were quickly rounded up to form a new band. Stephanie was a trained pianist, but she told Jenny Eather in 1981:

> I never played until a couple of months before Sardine began. I just started playing on an organ that Ian and I bought for the children and out of the blue we wrote a few songs. I was always very nervous about it and never wanted to play live. But when Phil and Greg played with us one day I found it really exciting and thought, why not?[575]

Hall – who had previously played with Lobby Loyde – was threatening to return to New Zealand; Ian wrote four good songs to 'trap' him.[576] These formed the basis of Sardine V. Stephanie says now that although Ian was always going out – ostensibly to do research – he would never listen to music. He claimed in 1981, 'I think I get more influence from songs my mother sang to me as a kid than going to someone's place and listening to a record player.'[577]

Stephanie's time in Sardine V seems to have been mostly frenetic, as she tried to balance the demands of home life with a music career:

> Line-up changes were frequent, it was fraught. It was pretty hairy. Ian wasn't the easiest person – but he was the one with drive. He just said, 'Come on, we're rehearsing', and there were children coming in and saying, 'Mummy, can I wash my teddy bear?' . . . It was a great job; I could be home with the kids because they were small, 3 to 7, and then I could go out at night and leave them with Ian's mother. We didn't get much sleep. Three nights a week, we'd play – often.

Sardine V introduced a sartorial aspect to music that was a million miles from the 'street' look of Rose Tattoo or X. Stephanie says:

> It was just a statement – everyone's looking all messy, were going to dress up. The $5000 advance we got – Ian used it, I didn't have any say in it – the $5000 advance went to a Chevy and those three suits the boys wore. So that was that gone! And he found me a Farfisa. He had an amazing connection with the world, whatever he set himself to seemed to eventuate.

Though Stephanie appropriately describes Sardine as representing the 'beautiful side' of Ian Rilen's musical personality, some also justifiably felt that the group was eerie or strident. Eather wrote in a 1981 live review:

> A tall, thin bespectacled man leant over my shoulder, 'You know, if I ever had to go to war I'd go with Sardine on my walkman. They're abrupt . . . abrupt, like a big confrontation. In fact, they're catastrophic.'[578]

Others were more decidedly negative. Linda Campbell reviewed the group in early 1982 for *Roadrunner*:

> No style to even think of categorizing. Life's far too short to be wasting on garbage like this. Emotionless untreated sewage. Just bad music, ya know?[579]

The group's first single was 'Sudan', written by Stephanie and produced by Lobby Loyde. 'Lobby put that out without consulting the band,' says Stephanie. 'He mixed it and pressed it without asking anyone. I think he thought Ian wouldn't want my song on the single.' The group were given a spot on *Countdown*, she says, because 'Molly was an Egyptophile.' She adds that 'I wrote that song after seeing a midday movie about the damming of the Nile, by Jacques Cousteau. People would say they'd been transported by that music.' The B side of the single was 'Sabotage'; 'one of their most autobiographical songs', according to Sally Collins: 'Ian constantly shot himself in the foot when things were going well'.

Sardine V's second release was a 5-track 12-inch EP, which included two of their greatest songs, the up-tempo 'I Hate You' and the mournful 'Stuck on You'. By this time the line-up had changed considerably: Stephanie quit Sardine V in 1983 to save her marriage, which nonetheless crumbled shortly afterwards. Ian revived X, which recorded the superb album *At Home with You*, riddled with songs about a bad relationship. A group called 'Some of Us Sardines' played the Sydney Chevron in April 1985, though Ian was probably not involved, since his band of ex-Rose Tattoo members, Illustrated Man, were playing the same night.[580]

'Stuck on You' has, curiously, become known as a song by X. Hunters and Collectors' Mark Seymour chose to cover it (and the band's drummer, Doug Falconer, married Stephanie Rilen). The seven songs Sardine V released during their existence show a meeting of minds that only scratched the surface of their musical possibilities.

HERE IT IS. ADELAIDE

Near the beginning of this book there is a discussion of Adelaide in the early 60s, its folk cafes and jazz clubs. Twenty-five years later, how had Adelaide changed?

As is the case with all smaller capitals, many who'd been born there were now expatriates; Ash Wednesday, for instance, who had decamped to Melbourne with Jab, helped formulate the sound and style of Models, and then embarked on numerous unusual forays, including two albums by the group the Metronomes that also featured journalist, scriptwriter and musician Al Webb and former X-Ray-Zed member Andrew Picoleau. Wednesday's greatest pop moment might prove to have been his single 'Love by Numbers', one of the funniest records of the 80s: in a mechanised voice Wednesday counts to just past 100 over a repetitious (but, perhaps because of the pop abilities of Robert Kretschmer, catchy) tune; at a certain point he pauses to have Karen Marx sing 'Ooh, it must be love'. Like the Ramones or some of Brian Eno's best work, it was simultaneously exceptionally dumb and extremely smart.

Wednesday also aided other expat Adelaideans. The briefly successful Aliens were escapees from an earlier time: formed by members of 5KA Battle of the Bands-winning group Gold, Danny Johnson and Geoffrey Stapleton created the Aliens two months after they'd moved to Melbourne in early 1978 to play power pop. Stapleton had already tasted fame as a member of Captain Thunder, a group signed – like Fraternity – to Adelaide's Raven label.[581] Perhaps more usefully for his later period in Melbourne, he had previously had Adrian Barker as the agent for his progressive theatrical group Ova. Greg Perano introduced them to keyboard player Graham Lewis, and they rehearsed using a drum machine belonging to their flatmate, Wednesday, before finding a drummer. The Aliens signed to Mushroom the following year and recorded a single, 'Confrontation', with Charles Fisher in August 1979, while they were touring with the Sports. Their album *Translator* was produced by David Tickle; line-up changes included the incorporation in October 1980 of Pierre Baroni, who later created his own group, the Pony, and later still was Mushroom Records' graphic designer. A final single 'I Don't Care' was recorded in May 1981 and released through the group's own label.[582]

Adelaide proper certainly seems to have had a sense of its value to the nation. For every disdainful reference to Adelaide – like the song Paul Kelly included on *Post*[583] – there are many who make a positive case, such as Ken Sykes from the Screaming Believers:

> It's good really, Because it's small, you have to constantly change all the time, otherwise people get sick of you, so you've got to vary your act. There's only a small amount of people that are going to come to see you, especially if you're an underground band...[584]

Or Terry Bradford from the group July 14:

> What it means is being rather like a clogged up sewer, and the Eastern states look upon themselves as being free, fast-flowing, creative bodies of water: you've got to leave Adelaide to do anything – that's the theory anyway – that's bullshit. I mean what happens is you get good musicians, who have to work really hard to try and make a living in Adelaide, go across to Sydney or Melbourne; most probably the band they go across with break up but they establish themselves in Sydney or Melbourne...[585]

Sykes's and Bradford's groups were among those released on Greasy Pop, a successful independent label with character operating out of Adelaide in the early 80s. Part of its success may have been due to public radio station 5MMM, a 'catalyst for a resurgence in Adelaide music' at this time.[586] However it is probably more appropriately attributed to the spirit of Doug Thomas and the Dagoes.

Dave Graney notes that 'in the 70s, Radio Birdman's shadow was big in Adelaide.'[587] Thomas would agree: 'Radio Birdman changed my life,' he said in the mid 80s.

I saw them balanced on the balcony at the Tivoli Hotel. Bought a guitar about three days later, joined the Dagoes that week, which was really Tony Rome's band. The Dagoes were started out to be a parody of everything possible. The original Dagoes . . . all five members were working in record stores and everybody saw the total shit that we were selling, or should I say, what people were buying. The cabaret music that had just been forced upon people through radio, ridiculous requests that behind a record counter everybody gets.[588]

The Dagoes Sell Soul was the first release on Thomas's Greasy Pop label, in 1980. It contained a version of Roky Erickson's 1965 song for the Spades, 'We Sell Soul,' plus two originals by vocalist Tony Rome. This was one more example of a group's record – and a label – born from a wish to commemorate something that was over. The Dagoes had in fact broken up, but Rome (real name Richard Cant) 'wanted to have a legacy so he got the band back together to record.'[589]

The money the group made from selling 600 copies was ploughed into a second release, a double EP this time – the Dagoes stayed together because they enjoyed recording so much.[590] Thomas says the Dagoes progressed 'from a garage-thrash band playing Easybeats, Ramones, stuff like that, to a pop band; it was still a grunge pop band, with people like me and the Turk in, your rank amateurs . . .'[591]

In early 1983, Thomas, fellow Dago 'The Turk' and Ian List released a record they had recorded in January 1982 as the Assassins. The song 'Assassination' had a message, said Thomas: 'Kill Malcolm Fraser – he's an arsehole.'[592]

Alf Omega – a punk musician who for a time seemed to be trying to cast himself as the Nick Cave of Adelaide – had tried out for singer of the Dagoes.[593] In the mid 70s, Ash Wednesday had met Bohdan X while the latter was busking in Rundle Mall; this was also the way Omega met Mick Brown, with whom he formed the Silver Trains, later the Spell, who went to Sydney.[594]

The blarney between Omega and Harry Butler, the editor of Adelaide's resilient, trainspotterish but good-humoured fanzine *DNA* at this time is scintillating.

In Sydney Mick Brown lived in the Strawberry Hills hotel in Darlinghurst, "cause that's where all the bands were and people:'[595] it was the centre of a rock universe at that time. Yet Eloise McAnulty, a journalist with *On the Street*, thought Adelaide worthy of a pilgrimage; her survey of the city made many Sydney-oriented comparisons:

Lark 'n Tinas – as close to the Manzil as you'll get outside of Springfield Ave. Rockhouse – the adolescent playground with post-puberty pretensions. Toucan

Club – trying to be cool but succeeding at only lukewarm. And the Princes Berkley – bigger and better than the Strawberry Hill but don't the faces look familiar?[596]

It is not clear whether McAnulty's last remark was suggesting there was such cross-fertilisation between Adelaide and Sydney that the actual 'punters' were familiar, or that Adelaide was, like Sydney, full of 'types'. Either interpretation is possible. What is perhaps most telling in her account is that Melbourne is largely bypassed in this intercity scene.

It should also be said, however, that Sydney seemingly only had room for those Adelaide bands who fitted its particular style of loud, fast 70s rock or the kind of music that would soon be known as 'grunge' – which 'began' in the swamp or psychobilly scenes of, for instance, the group Grong Grong (a name not a million miles away from the word 'grunge', but taken in fact from a small town in New South Wales; it supposedly means 'bad camping ground'), led by Michael Farkas and his half-brother Charlie Tolnay.[597]

'Adelaide Techno-poppers' Nuvo Bloc[598] seemed more suited to Melbourne, and the group Speedboat – formed from two bands, the Lounge and Systems Go, by Arnold Strals – enjoyed currency and exposure on 3RRR. Strals had the distinction of having been the arranger of Sister Janet Mead's 'The Lord's Prayer'. His group, wrote Eva Beauclerk in *Roadrunner,* used '"performance pieces" such as the breaking of an umbrella or a game of tennis to entertain and enhance the visual effect.'[599]

While these bands helped further Adelaide's sense of its uniqueness – Brisbane, Perth and other smaller cities had similarly advanced conceptions of their sound, style and scene by this stage – it was perhaps Adelaide's status as the crucible of Aboriginal rock music that was its most lasting and important contribution to the music of this era.

WE PLAY WHAT WE FEEL

Ned Lander's 1981 film *Wrong Side of the Road,* set in Adelaide and rural South Australia, is one of the most compelling and important films of the period. Its importance derives only partly from its status as a film about Aboriginal musicians; it also introduced many non-indigenous Australians to the story of the stolen generations, as well as highlighting the stresses and prejudice experienced by indigenous Australians in an urban context. It won the Jury Prize at the Australian Film Awards in1981[600] and launched the bands Us Mob and No Fixed Address into mainstream Australia. The film is a mixture of documentary and drama; its actors were encouraged to explore their own experience in fictionalised settings using improvised dialogue.

No Fixed Address were primarily a reggae band. John Castles, exploring the resurgence of Aboriginal music, locates the introduction of Adelaide Aboriginal groups to reggae at a concert Bob Marley played there in 1979, though Marley's songs and those of other reggae groups had of course been heard on mainstream radio long before that time. Castles also praises the role played by programs carried out by CASM – the Centre for Aboriginal Studies in Music, at the University of Adelaide – in the creation of Aboriginal rock: 'CASM was instrumental in the formation of many of the king bands to emerge in the 80s', he says, including No Fixed Address, Coloured Stone and Scrap Metal in this category.[601]

Once again, Donald Robertson and the Adelaide-based *Roadrunner* led the charge in favour of Aboriginal rock. 'For a whole lot of reasons, political, historical and musical,' wrote Robertson, 'No Fixed Address are probably the most important new group in this country today.'[602] The group featured Bart Willoughby on drums, Ricky Harrison on rhythm guitar, Les Graham playing lead, John Miller as bassist and Veronica Rankine on backing vocals. Willloughby and Miller were from the western South Australia town of Ceduna, Graham from the other side of the state in Murray Bridge. Their manager, Graham Isaacs had been a member of Captain Matchbox between 1976 and 77. He and Lander obtained a $40,000 grant from the Australian Film Commission towards the cost of producing a film about No Fixed Address and Us Mob.

Peter Dawkins had decided not to sign No Fixed Address to CBS because they weren't slick enough, but the band did open for acts as diverse as Mi-Sex and Taj Mahal (who considered them the 'Best Black Band in Australia'). Willoughby claimed in 1980 that there were twenty black bands in Australia, including Coloured Stone ('all my cousins').[603]

Coloured Stone's debut album *Koonibba Rock,* – recorded for $500 and, like the Beasts of Bourbon's first LP, in five hours[604] – came from the name of a settlement near Ceduna; leader Buna Lawrie described their music as 'between rock and reggae, and country . . . all sort of mixed . . . we play what we feel.'[605] Their 1984 single 'Black Boy', released on Imparja Records, based in Alice Springs, and Hot, was extremely successful not only in Australia but also in unusual territories such as Fiji. A second album, *Island of Greed,* was recorded in Perth and Alice Springs the following year.[606]

In 1985 the first Aboriginal radio station in Central Australia, 8-KIN, began broadcasting in five languages.[607] Media outlets such as these were important in reinforcing the value of indigenous cultures and providing a creative outlet for local artists. In the wider world, what had perhaps been less predictable was the way Aboriginal rock was embraced by the inner-city music world. In mid 1983 Murri Jama National Aboriginal Week was celebrated with a series of shows at Sydney's Gaelic Club;[608] a 12-hour radiothon was held on JJJ.[609] It must be presumed that *On the Street*'s cover in November 1984, announcing 'When Three Tribes Come to Town', was making a humorous reference to Frankie Goes to Hollywood's 'Two Tribes' single, released earlier that year. But it rests on the rather crass assumption that there was a connection between tribes and rock groups. The 'tribes' in question were No Fixed Address, the Warumpi Band, and Coloured Stone. No Fixed Address were returning from time in Britain; the Warumpi Band, another group associated with the Imparja label, were praised for their 'naïve good humoured music'.⁶¹⁰ While patronizing, this assessment also served to let white audiences know that going to see an Aboriginal band was not going to necessarily lead to a dose

of guilt. Warumpi Band would tour extensively with Midnight Oil in 1986. Their first 7", 'Jailanguru Pakarnu', was released by Hot under license from CAAMA, who'd previously put out a cassette release; Coloured Stone also released material through the hip inner-city label.

THE FUTURE

Hardware was an important consideration to many in the music industry in the early to mid 80s. The Walkman – a portable, high-quality cassette player listened to through earphones – was a huge success. Units cost $200 apiece at first, and Sony sold half a million in the first year of production. 'Simply, it was the right product at the right time,' as one writer put it. ⁶¹¹ Issues of portability continued to be important, not least with the arrival of the compact disc, which 'burst on the scene' in 1983 as 'a musical revelation and a prestigious toy'.⁶¹² Compact disc players initially cost a thousand dollars, though they were cut to a third of that within a year: 'The cheapest models,' *Rolling Stone* assured its readers, 'sound as spectacular – noise-free and unrestrained in dynamics and frequency response – as their costlier counterparts.'⁶¹³

The industry saw CDs in part as a way to counter piracy – which at this time took the form of home taping (that is, making cassette recordings of borrowed records). Harry Gett, a sales manager at WEA, claimed that 'the decline in the sales of records and the huge jump in blank tapes is obviously co-related . . . we are trying to arrest the rise of home taping.' It was claimed that the record industry at this time was losing $440.8 million as a result of home taping, though *Juke* reported a survey which 'revealed that 50% of the tapers would not buy the album if they could not tape it,' and that 65% of all home taping was done by people who already owned the record they were recording. *Juke* continued:

> To combat the cassette, Philips and Sony will be releasing a laser record in England in March.
> Called the Compact Disc, it is a 5" diameter piece of plastic. While not indestructible, it's impervious to minor scratches and sticky finger marks. It is

played by a laser system player and can contain about an hour's worth of playing on its one playing side.'⁶¹⁴

Music consumers probably only now realised how constrained they had been by the modes of music delivery previously available to them; though the conventional formats ('single', 'album', even 'EP') would remain in place – decided largely by price and length – the size, usability and durability of releases would change considerably. An anonymous advocate in the Perth street magazine *X-Press* praised the 'new big little thing' while acknowledging a common audiophile objection:

> You can play them in cars. With the new Sony (Walkman-sized) portable you can play them in planes or even on the end of a parachute.
> These rainbow-tinted discs are definitely the way to go – you can even throw them round the room at a party ... The reproduction? Well the stalwart aficionados of the black vinyl say that the sound is too clinical and sterile – got no warmth. To my ears ... the sound is immaculate.⁶¹⁵

As is so often the case, the middle of the decade saw a crisis of confidence about the direction of popular music, whether the participants were entirely aware of this crisis or not. New CBS signings, such as Boy Rocking (featuring Harry Brus and expatriate New Zealander Mark Williams, described in *On the Street* as 'pathetic in his semi-punk outfit'), Full Marks, the Tribe, and Arvo (featuring soap opera actor Deborah Gray) ⁶¹⁶ were not encouraging. The major labels – particularly but not exclusively CBS – would continue with their apparently safe, if obtuse, signing practices for years to come. These would provoke responses such as the compilation cassette issued in 1984 by Sydney public radio station 2SER's Demo Show; entitled *Xmas '89*, it included the groups PSI, Wrong Kind of Stone Age, Urban Guerillas and These Cars Collide. Co-compiler the Norm barked:

> You wanna know why it's called *Xmas '89*? 'Cos it'll be around then that the record companies wake up from their coked-out haze long enough to realise what's happening here in Oz. But of course that'll be way too late.'⁶¹⁷

Festivals such as Narara '84, on the outskirts of Sydney, signalled the kinds of groups considered crowd-pullers – amongst teenagers, in particular – at this time: the line-up included Eurogliders, Models, Real Life, Mondo Rock, the Johnnys, Kids in the Kitchen, Hoodoo Gurus, Machinations, INXS, Mental as Anything, Dropbears, Deckchairs Overboard, Dynamic Hepnotics, Little Heroes, a briefly reformed Sherbet, the Sunnyboys, the Radiators, Australian Crawl, Celibate Rifles and Avion, alongside an international contingent made up of the Pretenders, Eurythmics, Simple Minds, Talking Heads and Def Leppard.⁶¹⁸ The early 1985 concert 'The Big Swing' at Sydney's Heathcote Oval pulled together some of the same groups (INXS, Hoodoo Gurus, Dynamic Hepnotics, Celibate Rifles, the Tribe) and added the Cockroaches and I'm Talking.[619]

Australian *Smash Hits'* predictions for 1985 arguably give a good indication of the way the future landscape was being plotted: groups named were Beargarden, Electric Pandas, DD Smash, the Tribe, No Nonsense, QED, John Justin, Machinations, Dropbears, the Flaming Hands, Uncanny X-Men, the Triffids, Le Club Foote, Kam Sha (a shortlived Brian Peacock-managed project) and Corpse Grinders.[620] All bar the Triffids, the Flaming Hands and the Corpse Grinders were mainstream (and the Triffids were certainly mainstream-friendly) pop acts who took care to dress in fashion and project an upbeat outlook.

The last word should be left to Tracee Hutchison and Richard Kingsmill, two JJJ presenters who have since distinguished themselves as writers and media personalities. After looking back on 1985, they tried to extrapolate from this to a vision of Australian music's future development. They began with a rallying cry often heard in the past; it is in a sense a version of Lobby Loyde's pronouncement from the early 70s (see the opening of chapter 8):

> The most distinguishing feature of 1985 was the profound development of an Australian consciousness in our music. This year more than any other saw local artists not afraid of writing and singing about their own environment and culture.[621]

The authors then hedged their bets as they continued:

> The punk and grunge movements seem to be slowly grinding to a halt, having (for the moment at least) explored themselves to their fullest capacities. Sixties music has plagued Sydney this year (and surprisingly Melbourne as well), but the sight of too much paisley has begun to make people feel slightly nauseous. Too many of these bands are simply stuck in the time warp, and have failed to realise that since the 60s there has been such a thing as the 70s and 80s. Rockabilly, too, was fine when still a novelty, but when taken too seriously it becomes merely another means of escapism...
>
> INXS and Mental as Anything have continued to provide worthwhile examples of modern pop; the Hoodoo Gurus and the Church have kept the 60s sound progressing in the 80s; while Ed Kuepper, X and the Triffids have generated music filled with intensity and diversity.
>
> Exactly who will follow in their footsteps is difficult to predict. Many bands have released great singles this year – the Hipslingers, the Happy Hate Me Nots, Eastern Dark, Statues Cry, Arctic Circles, 21 Faces, Chad's Tree, John Kennedy's Love Gone Wrong, Ups and Downs, Huxton Creepers – but it's just a matter of time before we see who survives and carries on with promise.[622]

Richard Ford, 'Stars of 79', published in USU Recorder, vol. 9, no. 3 (14–28 Nov 1979)

Afterword

WHAT'S IT LIKE OUT THERE?

The comic strip on the facing page is a remarkable document of the Australian music scene just as it began an unprecedentedly strong period of internationalism. The first eight frames satirise John Paul Young – alongside Molly Meldrum ('Deafy Eardrum') – for not being 'authentically' Australian, for making disco records (obviously, these two crimes are related), and for making commercial inroads into minor global territories. The single-panel parodies that follow depict, in order, Ted Mulry (mocked for being mundane, apparently); Daryl Braithwaite (Sherbet, it is implied, have a generic international sound); Renée Geyer (presumably, the criticism is similar – that Geyer sounds American); Mark Holden (at this time a shallow, flash-in-the-pan pop star, although the parodist is perhaps unaware that Holden, if nothing else, was a songwriter); and Kevin Borich; the others are self-explanatory.

The artist/critic, Richard Ford, is expressing frustrations that were commonly voiced at the time, but from a present-day perspective one is moved to ask, 'What did Australians *want* from their pop stars in the 80s?' It is not helpful that Ford, while possessing a fine satirical pen, can only describe the positives in Australian music as 'good'. But the implications are evident: Australians should appeal to Australian audiences (both artist and consumer have obligations in this regard); their music ought to be recognizably Australian (as we have seen many times throughout this history, this was always a contentious topic: was the Australianness a matter of lyrical content, was it inherent in the music itself, was it in the accent, or did it more generally entail limiting one's ambition to work in and for the Australian market?); and it was not possible to be 'good' and 'commercial' at the same time (although this too was often a matter of dispute). Similar thoughts are expressed, for example, by Dave Warner in his contemporaneous pronouncements on Shorrock and Braithwaite (see pages 214 and 310).

This strip is rich in content, yet only the slightest traces of such attitudes survive today; indeed, they were already 'on the way out' in the mid 1980s, when this narrative ends. International success for Australian groups increasingly became, if not de rigueur, then certainly less remarkable. Perhaps this was in part because Australians began to gain perspective not only on the extended history of Australian acts in the international arena, but it also happened because – now that the recorded music market had become larger, broader, and more sophisticated – it was possible for Australian music consumers to draw more nuanced conclusions about measures of 'success' and the quality and standards of music being produced within Australia. Melbourne's 'little bands' – hardly a nationally known phenomenon – are a valuable marker at this time, when music professionalism, and the career trajectory of a musician broadening her or his fanbase leading to a strike at the international market, ceased to be the *only* option for a 'credible' musician. Indeed, the indicators for credibility of the kind enjoyed by Air Supply or LRB (that selling a lot of records in the USA must necessarily be a good or honourable thing) gave way, in the minds of many tastemakers, to a diametrically opposite set of markers.

In the preceding pages I may have accentuated the pallidness of LRB's and Air Supply's pan-Pacific sounds, but there is undeniable skill involved in creating crafted pop; at the right moment, each band could be very good indeed. With all respect to the subjectivity of individual musical tastes, it's a rare musical artist who creates nothing of value, especially when they get far enough along the track to produce records for an audience. Yet there has always been a divide between what is deemed worthy and what is dismissed as unworthy, even if the dividing line is drawn differently by each consumer. As countless examples in this book have shown – Stefan Fidock's description of the criticism the Reels received for their *Beautiful* album (page 384) offers a fine example – the notion of 'credibility' is essentially a product of nothing more than pompous, half-understood pretension. Sadly, this is a lesson many have yet to learn.

The TV miniseries *Molly*, produced by Michael Gudinski and created from Meldrum's 2014 memoir (which is itself a pastiche of numerous attempts involving different ghostwriters), showed a very 2016 view of the 1970s, an era correctly recognized as formative in the development of Australian rock and pop – but in what ways? Even allowing for some unusual poetic license – above all the dubious dream sequence in which the eight-year-old Meldrum is shown composing the melody to Johnny Young's song 'The Real Thing' on his childhood piano in Quambatook, but also the late-20s Meldrum's conception of *Countdown* as a means of allowing kids to see live Australian music on television (as if *that* was ever a dream of the show's producers in 1974) and the depiction of him as reluctant and nervous about appearing in front of the cameras, something he'd been doing for almost a decade previously – the show was a success. The entire drama is depicted as a dream sequence unfolding in Meldrum's head following his real-life fall from a ladder while adjusting Christmas decorations late in 2011. If in his traumatised brain he imagines that he composed 'The Real Thing', that's perhaps just his pleasant fantasy.

What *Molly* showed was that Australians (particularly those of a certain age) wanted to celebrate their nation's pop history of forty years ago in earnest. Readers will recall a discussion of the *Late Show's* unearthing of *Countdown* tidbits in the early 90s in order to expose them to general ridicule as an unsophisticated atrocity (page 291). In 2016 *Countdown* is celebrated as a glamorous spear to the heart of conservative fuddy-duddyism.

More importantly, what the celebration of *Molly* among a certain demographic showed is that for many people popular music is a canvas on which their own memories, dreams and resentments are played out. Associations were freely made on social media in 2016 about *Countdown* as a hotline (if not a lifeline) to the mainstream, and as the source of lifelong musical love affairs. Then there was the eternal debate over whether Meldrum himself facilitated exposure of good and/or Australian music, through his passion and knowledge, or whether he was an impediment to same. The answer, as so often in these cases, is that he was probably both. Comments made about *Molly* during the week reveal the range of responses from people who were 'there' – as consumers, or even music industry insiders – in the 1970s. One unhappy viewer complained about 'the unmitigated dribble [sic] masquerading itself as the script for this pantomime confection'; another felt that Meldrum 'is a clever, intelligent man with a great love for popular music. This biopic is an insult to everything he has done with his life.' There were almost as many opinions on the show as there were viewers (one tenth of the nation's population watched the first episode), but all were a reflection on the times and the man who, seemingly accidentally, was the curator at the heart of them.

Ian Meldrum and John Farnham were two of Australian pop music's most recognizable faces in the 70s and 80s. I remember an awkward conversation with my septuagenarian maternal grandparents in the late 1980s in which they completely conflated Farnham and Meldrum – the two men's fame being more important to that conversation than any individual 'output'. Yet it's notable that neither man was known for strong songwriting or instrumental skills; each was an interpreter or facilitator of the work of others. The glass-half-full view of this would celebrate their versatility and adaptability; the half-empty interpretation would mutter darkly about a culture that rewards mediocrity.

The introduction to this work made noises about not offering a comfortable history for baby boomers, and this may have led some readers to expect a thrill ride of cock-snooking and general blowing-up of reputations. Whether anything resembling that was delivered is obviously in the eye of the beholder, but it is my assumption that a certain number of readers will in fact just go through the index and then check to see if I got things 'right' – for instance, that I gave appropriate prominence to a band they like. If they like Chain, for example, they're out of luck – with all due respect to Chain, there just wasn't room for them in the main story. I feel no compunction at expressing disregard for those potential readers here, particularly since if you are reading these words you are clearly not one of them.

Shows like *Molly* aside, the world of popular music history is for most just a happy retro trip, as much about clothes and kissing one's first boy- or girlfriend as it is about drum sounds, guitar riffs, and catchy tunes, indeed probably more so. Ian McFarlane, one of the great men of Australian rock history, largely (but not solely) for his *Encyclopedia of Australian Rock and Pop* (he also gave valuable feedback on the final draft of this book), has spoken to me of the many times people have confused his book with another extraordinary masterwork, Chris Spencer's *Who's Who of Australian Rock!* (co-compiled in its latest and presumably last edition with Zbig Nowara and Paul McHenry).[1] Some will no doubt end up confusing this book with one or both of those works, neither of which, by its very format, attempts to offer an overarching narrative thread. The *Who's Who* is, in some respects, the most forthright – Spencer, Nowara and McHenry only editorialize to the extent of providing a brief, often quoted, description of the band or artist in question; otherwise, they give a straight catalogue of personnel, releases and release dates. These are all very different books, and while I'm not going to put forward any more of a case for the value of this one than I already have, I do want to say that both the *Who's Who* and the *Encyclopedia* are well worth owning and using.

That said, in the grand scheme of things none of this detail matters in and of itself: only if it can be related to social, cultural and political change can anything be gleaned or learned. I am reminded of a conversation – it sailed close to an argument – I had with two colleagues in late 2015 about the documentary *Stranded*, which screened on the ABC in mid-September. To my mind it was an ill-thought-through fairytale, marred by elisions that oversimplified the fascinating world of Brisbane and the Saints in the late 1970s and thus distorted it. Because the show's producers raced through the story, they delivered an account that was simply black-and-white, devoid of nuance, and therefore ahistorical. My companions, who are not historians but are highly intelligent people aware of history's importance, had enjoyed the program. I protested that it was full of inaccuracies. 'But,' one of them said, *'you know a lot about music.'* I took this to mean: as an expert, it was inappropriate for me to try and impose my greater knowledge of and interest in popular music *and* social history on people who were simply trying to engage with some visceral infotainment. I appreciate that mine is a trainspotter's lament, but it's also an example of the issues facing any historian working in popular culture: there's a lot of love in the room, but only if the story has a happy ending.

As the writing of this book drew to a close, almost a decade after it began, two things happened. The Brisbane-derived three-piece Small World Experience, one of my favourite bands, toured Melbourne ahead of the release of a new album (their third or fourth, depending on what you count as an album); and Jane Gazzo published a biography of John Farnham. These events resonated together for me particularly because a previous version of this conclusion was a meandering and unresolved rumination on the first SWE album *Shelf Life* (1994) and Farnham's 'comeback' album of 1986, *Whispering Jack*.

The world will never have to know what I was trying to say about SWE (or the ridiculous way I tried to tie this, and Farnham, into discussion of the Aints' album *Ascension*), but the greater point about *Whispering Jack* (discussed briefly earlier) is that in many ways it was the culmination of much of the tower of babel that is this history. With *Whispering Jack*, Australian music finally produced its own uber-successful record which was, in effect, *only really a massive hit in Australia* (yes, Skyhooks had racked up hitherto unprecedented sales to a mostly younger audience a decade earlier, but by the mid 80s pop records could appeal to people in their sixties). There was a captivating back story to *Whispering Jack*, too: Farnham and Glenn Wheatley, by now Farnham's manager, had invested considerable amounts of their own money in the recording sessions – an act of faith at a time when Farnham appeared a has-been, to say the least.

Gazzo's book, straightforward and upbeat, is a treat, not because Farnham himself is a marvellous character – charming as he can be, he often seems little more than a cipher – but because his story is the 'Everyman' story of Australian popular music. He's as ordinary as any very wealthy man whose adult life has been largely public can be. Success has also failed to spoil his down-to-earth attitude, though Gazzo does not shy from detailing some of Farnham's foibles, such as his refusal to reconnect with his old Strings Unlimited bandmates at a special show in the Victorian town of Cohuna, in 2002, to commemorate his 'discovery' by Darrel Sambell.[2] Commercial, often bland, yet in its own way an especially skillful negotiation, Farnham's career, with its ups and downs, provides a perfect entrée into the story of Australia's pop music (just as Small World Experience's story encapsulates the story of uncommercial music, as I outlined so skillfully in the earlier version of this conclusion which you will never read). The loyal Wheatley is still regarded affectionately too, his lapses – such as his 2007 jail term for tax fraud – largely forgiven.[3]

Gazzo also makes connections that I haven't in this work, sometimes because I wasn't aware of them (April Byron and John Farnham went out together?!)[4] but also because, as mentioned, sometimes one just has to pursue a line to tell a story, even when (*particularly* when) the story is just one of a hundred that weave in and out of one other. In writing this narrative of a twenty-five year period of Australian popular music – during which music, but also the nation as a cultural entity, is often said to have 'come of age' – it has become increasingly clear to me that if I have accomplished anything at all it is simply to lay down a base for further thought and discussion.

Each example opens up more options for further study. Hundreds of the people mentioned in this text would be worthy of greater investigation, and those still alive have extraordinary stories to tell. Their expectations, achievements and disappointments are worthy of analysis in themselves, for the light they shine on Australian society and its beliefs. As the country became more affluent in the 1950s, and as the teenager became a recognized cultural type (and a recognized market), and as musical endeavour, technological advancement, and the availability of hardware (for both recording and audio or audiovisual reproduction) became less problematic, there was bound to be considerable expansion of the musical field. There was cross-fertilisation, too, as artists and audiences entered and exited, moving from and to different types of expression and consumption. The number of groups playing in the clubs and (particularly) pubs of the major capitals on any given night increased to a staggering extent throughout the 70s. The *ex*-teenager quickly became a market too, and indeed Daddy Cool was already playing on this in the early 70s, as a 'retro' band which celebrated a past that was alien to many Australians but which nonetheless recognized there was no longer any room for non-ironic innocence in teenagedom, remembered or presently experienced.

As I discussed earlier, this narrative's starting point of 1960 and end point in 1985 are of course completely artificial. There is nothing magical about either of those years (there might be something slightly 'magical' about beginning a new decade, because people often tend to think in such periods, but that only means that expectations were aroused in 1960, not that any particularly bright or new ideas were necessarily engendered in that year). With all due respect to the talented and skilled artists who produced good work in Australian music in the early 1960s, from a 21st-century perspective little of great value or appeal seems to have been produced musically before the middle of that decade. Once the Bee Gees hit their stride and the Easybeats began producing hits, Australian music was a goldmine, and it has remained so since, with the obvious caveat that a goldmine does not contain pure gold, but rather gold that is accessible only after great effort and the removal of a lot of dross.

As I write these words in early 2016, the television is playing an episode of the overnight video show *Rage*, now in its 27th year. Like *Countdown*, *Rage* has guest hosts; Sydney four-piece Royal Headache are programming tonight's episode. Their own music is excellent, and so is their musical taste and their appreciation of the Australian musical past. International acts like the Who, the Jesus and Mary Chain, Suzanne Vega, Carly Simon and the Minutemen are present alongside a good cross-section of the rich history of Australian music and the many acts covered in this book, including the Easybeats, the Sunnyboys, Tactics, XL Capris, Mental as Anything, the Riptides and the Go-Betweens. Just as a good writer, artist, filmmaker, ceramicist – in fact any creative person at all, of any stripe – has to know her or his context and background, so too a good musician seeks to understand and appreciate the past: not just for what it produced, but for its milieu and its shifting tectonic plates of influence, perceived value and lack thereof. This is at least as true for consumers.

If this book contributes anything to that knowledge, and especially if it leads to further research and discussion, I'll be pretty happy.

Acknowledgments

Dig is the product of almost a decade of writing, rewriting, reflection and calculated procrastination. Over this time many, many, *many* people have been extraordinarily helpful and engaged with the writing of the book. My chief informants – people I directly interviewed for this work - were (alphabetically) Karen Ansell, Martin Armiger, Jen Jewel Brown, Janie Conway, Stephen Cummings, Stephanie Falconer, Wil Greenstreet (aka Billy Green), Mark Ferrie, Stefan Fidock, Megan Sue Hicks, Bruce Milne, Annalisse and Chris Morrow, Brian Peacock, Cleis Pearce, Pip Proud, Mike Rudd, John Topper and Ross Wilson. I did not formally interview Craig Hooper and Ed Kuepper, but both provided extensive written feedback and/or corrections on my narrative, which was then incorporated into the revised text.

Others who were helpful (once again, alphabetically): Stewart Anderson, Greg Appel, Guy Blackman, Annabel Bleach, Andrew Bonnici, Carla Bruce Lee, Francesca Bussey, Gavin Butler, Danny Butt, Michelle Cannane, Helen Carter, David Castles, Simon Castles, David Chesworth, Kathryn Clarke, Penny Coad, Stuart Coupe, Saul Cunningham, Sophie Cunningham, Vera di Campli San Vito, John Durr, Duke Dinh, Barry C. Douglas, Peter Doyle, James Dutton, Toby Dutton, Frances Gibson, Keith Glass, Christopher Gorman, Fiona Graham, Dave Graney, Sadie Grant Butler, Stuart Grant, Roger Grierson, Simon Grounds, Peter Hogg, Harry Howard, Naomi Howe, Renate Howe, Philip Jackson, Neil Kelly, Caroline Kennedy, Tom Kristensen, David Laing, Randall Lee, Ted Lethborg, Darren Levin, Nici Lindsay, Cameron Logan, Bren Luke, Suzie Luke, Elizabeth McCarthy, Thomas Barry 'Bazza' McCulloch, Ian McFarlane, Stewart McFarlane, Iain McIntyre, Rob McKenzie, Bernard McMahon, Paul McHenry, Jonathan Michell, Mary Mihelakos, Steve Miller, Clare Moore, Shane Moritz, Guy Morton, Ben O'Connor, Claire O'Meara, Stephen O'Neil, Amanda Peacock, David Pepperell, Sophie Perillo, Miranda Picton-Warlow, Johanna Pigott, Edwina Preston, Andrew Ramadge, Keir Reeves, Casey Rice, Donald Robertson, Art Rush, Eddy Sarafian, Mia Schoen, Nick Seymour, Kate Shaw, Helen Slonek, Elizabeth Taylor, Sarah Taylor, Julian Teakle, Megan Tudor, Jennifer Turrell, Michael Van Vliet, Greg Wadley, Ian Wadley, Clinton Walker, Sari Wawn, Melissa Webb, Ash Wednesday, Julian Williams, Simon Williams, John Willsteed, Pat Wilson, Oleh Witer, Carmel Zappia.

Of the above, Stuart Coupe, Ian McFarlane and Eddy Sarafian deserve a second namecheck for their assistance with visual material used herein.

The staff at the National Library of Australia and the State Libraries of New South Wales, South Australia, Victoria and Western Australia were all immensely helpful and this book – like another couple of thousand published this year and every year – demonstrates how invaluable state and national libraries are to the intellectual life of the Australian nation and the globe. The staff at the University of Melbourne, Latrobe University and Deakin University libraries also provided assistance, and a special shout-out should go to the remarkable Hume Learning Centre library in Broadmeadows, one of the best local libraries I have known.

Katherine Spielmann and Steve Connell commissioned this book from me in or around 2006 and I am indebted to them for their innovative and committed approach to quality history and writing, be it about music or anything else! Steve's dedication to keeping a wayward and unwieldy manuscript on course has been extraordinary.

It's been a long slog to get *Dig* to its current state, and knowing my mind the way I do, I have to assume I've forgotten to thank some very important people. If that's you, let me know how I can make it up to you.

David Nichols

Notes

Chapter 1: Wild Beat Overture

1. Anon., foreword to Ken Taylor, *Rock Generation: The Inside Exclusive* (Melbourne: Sun Books, 1970), 5.
2. Taylor, *Rock Generation*, 69.
3. Taylor, *Rock Generation*, 60.
4. Clinton Walker, 'Before the Big Bang', *Meanjin* 65:3 (2006), 12.
5. Walker, 'Big Bang', 13.
6. Taylor, *Rock Generation*, 29.
7. Taylor, *Rock Generation*, 30.
8. Taylor, *Rock Generation*, 29.
9. John Bird, *Percy Grainger* (Sydney: Currency Press, 1998), 275.
10. *Passion*, dir. Peter Duncan (1999).
11. Bird, *Grainger*, 6-7.
12. Bird, *Grainger*, 5.
13. See Malcolm Gillies, 'Grainger and Race', in Kate Darian-Smith and Alessandro Servadei (eds.), *Talking Grainger: Perspectives on the Life, Music and Legacy of Percy Grainger* (Parkville: The Australian Centre/Grainger Museum, University of Melbourne, 1998), 9-14.
14. Bird, *Grainger*, 49.
15. Bird *Grainger*, 235.
16. Percy Grainger, 1949-54, quoted in Bird, *Grainger*, 49.
17. Bird, *Grainger*, 231.
18. Bird, *Grainger*, 239.
19. Bird, *Grainger*, 240.
20. Bird, *Grainger*, 241.
21. Bird, *Grainger*, 274.
22. Grainger, 1936, quoted in Bird, *Grainger*, 248.
23. Bird, *Grainger*, 273.
24. Bird, *Grainger*, 277.
25. 'Rock 'n' Roll Has Its Place – Prof.', *Farrago* (11 Apr 1958), 3.
26. *The Bulletin* (23 Oct 1957), 9
27. *The Bulletin* (28 Aug 1957), 40.
28. Taylor, *Rock Generation*, 24.
29. Taylor, *Rock Generation*, 26.
30. Taylor, *Rock Generation*, 13.
31. Ian Meldrum, 'Rolf Harris has been on top of the English charts for 6 weeks', *Go-Set* (14 Feb 1970), 7.
32. Debbie Kruger, *Songwriters Speak: Conversations about Creating Music* (Balmain: Limelight Press, 2005), 36-7.
33. Kruger, *Songwriters Speak*, 36-7.
34. 'Bed of a Thousand Struggles', *Long Way to the Top*, Episode 1, ABC-TV (2001).
35. Walker, 'Big Bang', 5.
36. Walker, 'Big Bang', 6.
37. Walker, 'Big Bang', 7.
38. Les Welch, quoted in Walker, 'Big Bang', 8
39. John 'Catfish' Purser, quoted in Sylvie Leber and Euan Mitchell, *History and Styles of Rock Music in Australia*. Videocassette. (Port Melbourne: Ausmusic, 1995).
40. John Sangster, *Seeing the Rafters: The Life and Times of an Australian Jazz Musician* (Ringwood: Penguin, 1988),19.
41. Sangster, *Rafters*, 21.
42. Walker, 'Big Bang', 9.
43. 'Bed of a Thousand Struggles', *Long Way to the Top*.
44. Slim Dusty and Joy McKean, *Another Day, Another Town* (Sydney: Pan Macmillan, 1996), 122-4.
45. Dusty and McKean, *Another Day*, 121.
46. 'Bed of a Thousand Struggles', *Long Way to the Top*.
47. 'The Col Joye story... He's here on March 24!' *Young Modern* (hereafter *YM*) (1 Mar 1962), 4-5.
48. Taylor, *Rock Generation*, 31.
49. 'Bed of a Thousand Struggles', *Long Way to the Top*.
50. 'Bed of a Thousand Struggles', *Long Way to the Top*.
51. Peter Doyle, 'Signs and Wonders', *Meanjin* 65:3 (2006), 16.
52. 'Bed of a Thousand Struggles', *Long Way to the Top*.
53. Marianne Renate, *Off the Record: Life with and without Johnny O'Keefe* (Sydney: Pan Macmillan, 1998), 155.
54. Taylor, *Rock Generation*, 39.
55. *History and Styles of Rock Music in Australia*.

Chapter 2: A Funny Buzz

1. Helen Garner, 'Other People's Children', in *Honour and Other People's Children* (Ringwood: Penguin, 1982), 79.
2. Joe Boyd, *White Bicycles* (London: Serpent's Tail, 2006), 91.
3. Lawrence Zion, 'Disposable Icons: Pop Music in Australia, 1955-63', *Popular Music* 8/2 (1989), 165.
4. Raymond Evans, 'Rock 'n' Roll, Youth Culture and Law 'n' Order' in John Murphy and Judith Smart (eds.), *The Forgotten Fifties*, special issue of *Australian Historical Studies*, 109 (1997), 108.
5. Christie Eliezer, *High Voltage Rock 'n' Roll* (London: Omnibus Press, 2007), 97.
6. 'Low Down on Young Modern', *YM* (18 Mar 1964), 5.
7. 'It's Not Democracy – It's Dictatorship!', *YM* (21 Jun 1962), 7-8.
8. 'Paul Brand: Folksinger Idealist Bohemian', *YM* (21 Jun 1962), 16.
9. 'Paul Brand releases LP', *YM* (8 Nov 1962), 28.
10. 'Paul Brand: Folksinger', 16
11. 'YM goes on a Coffee Lounge Crawl', *YM* (11 Oct 1962), 10-11, 30.
12. 'Paul Brand: Folksinger', 15.
13. 'Folk centre in Brisbane', *Australian Tradition* (May 1964), 5.
14. Sue Collins, 'Paul Marks', *Jazz Notes* 105 (no date), 5-6.
15. 'The Mid-Atlantic Boomerang', *TV Week* (22 Feb 1975), 30.
16. 'Paul Brand: Folksinger', 16.
17. C J Koch, *The Doubleman* (London: Chatto and Windus, 1985), 93.
18. Martyn Wyndham-Reade, quoted in *Australian Tradition* (Mar 1966), 27.
19. 'Kicks and Kisses', *TV Week* (7 Jan 1960), 52.
20. R. J. Deeble, 'Folk and Jazz Scene', *YM* (19 May 1965), 8.
21. Deeble, 8.
22. *Gerry Humphrys: The Loved One*, dir. Nigel Buesst (Sunrise Picture Co., 2000).
23. Humphrys, interviewed in *Gerry Humphrys: The Loved One*.
24. *Gerry Humphrys: The Loved One*.
25. *Gerry Humphrys: The Loved One*.
26. *Gerry Humphrys: The Loved One*.
27. Ross Hannaford, interviewed in *Gerry Humphrys: The Loved One*.
28. *Gerry Humphrys: The Loved One*.
29. *Gerry Humphrys: The Loved One*.
30. *Gerry Humphrys: The Loved One*.
31. Koch, *The Doubleman*, 198.
32. 'YM goes on a Coffee Lounge Crawl', 30.
33. Jane Matheson, 'The La De Das Story', Australian *Rolling Stone* (hereafter *ARS*) #182 (13 Mar 1975), 37.
34. <http://progrock.homestead.com/DaevidAllenInterview.html>, accessed 12 Dec 2008.
35. <http://www.planetgong.co.uk/maze/blurbs/daevid.shtml>, accessed 12 Dec 2008.
36. Ian Peel, *The Unknown Paul McCartney: McCartney and the Avant-garde* (London: Reynolds and Hearne, 2002), 31.

37   <http://www.richieunterberger.com/allen.html>, accessed 12 Dec 2008.
38   <http://www.richieunterberger.com/allen.html>, accessed 12 Dec 2008.
39   Peel, *McCartney*, 31.
40   'Let's Have It! (Letters)', *YM* (3 Jun 1963), 21.
41   'Hi There, Over There!', *YM* (8 Apr 1963), 3.
42   John Sinclair, 'Folk Music Boom, *YM* (29 Apr 1964), 15.
43   Boyd, *White Bicycles*, 229.
44   'Trevor Lucas Makes Good in England', *Go-Set* (13 Jun 1970), 'Core' section.
45   Bill Haesler, 'The 16th Australian Jazz Convention: Impressions from the Bar at the Norwood Pub', *Jazz Notes* 111 (Jun 1962), 2.
46   Graham Simpson, *Colours of My Life: The Judith Durham Story* (Milsons Point: Random House Australia, 1998), 9.
47   Simpson, *Colours of My Life*, 31.
48   Simpson, *Colours of My Life*, 26.
49   Durham, quoted in Simpson, *Colours of My Life*, 29.
50   <http://www.milesago.com/Artists/seekers.htm>, accessed 28 Dec 2006.
51   Simpson, *Colours of My Life*, 38.
52   Simpson, *Colours of My Life*, 39.
53   Simpson, *Colours of My Life*, 41.
54   Simpson, *Colours of My Life*, 45.
55   Simpson, *Colours of My Life*, 45.
56   Simpson, *Colours of My Life*, 51.
57   Dusty Springfield, quoted in Jon Savage, *Time Travel* (London: Vintage 1996), 248.
58   'Pat Wins Contest with Mood Melody Line', *YM* (22 Nov 1962), 4.
59   'Pat Aulton "One of State's Finest Jazz Voices", *YM* (15 Mar 1962), 23.
60   'Pat wins contest'.
61   David Day/Tim Parker, *SA Great: It's Our Music 1956-1986* (Glandore: Pagel/Wakefield Press, 1987), 37.
62   Jim Keays, *His Master's Voice* (St Leonards: Allen and Unwin, 1999), 35.
63   'Youth Centres Need Youth', *YM* (27 May 1964), 16.
64   Keays, *His Master's Voice*, 41.
65   Day and Parker, *SA Great*, 35.
66   'Let's Have It! (Letters)', *YM* (30 Oct 1962), 28.
67   'Levis Smith Clefs stay in Sydney', *Go-Set* (7 Feb 1968), 5.
68   *YM* (21 Mar 1963), 35.
69   Helen Barrett, 'Ashdown Down Home Down Under', *Juke* (27 Aug 1975), 6.
70   'Low Down on YM', 5.
71   'SA 15-Year-Old Slates J. O'Keefe: "He Gave My Song to Another Singer"', *YM* (5 Jul 1962), 13.
72   'April Signs Contract', *YM* (16 Aug 1962), 14.
73   *YM* (27 May 1964), 35.
74   Patricia Amphlett, interviewed by Peter Thompson, *Talking Heads* (12 Feb 2007), transcript from <www.abc.net.au/talkingheads/txt/s1838867.htm>, accessed 18 Aug 2008.
75   Amphlett, *Talking Heads*.
76   Amphlett, *Talking Heads*.
77   Amphlett, *Talking Heads*.
78   Renate, *Off the Record*, 209.
79   Noel McGrath, *Australian Encyclopaedia of Rock and Pop* (Collingwood: Outback Press, 1978), 18.
80   Eliezer, *High Voltage Rock 'n' Roll*, 58.
81   Dean Mittelhauser, *The Atlantics* (Golden Square: Moonlight Publishing, n.d.), 2.
82   Keays, *His Master's Voice*, 22.
83   Day/Parker, *SA Great*, 59.
84   Day/Parker, *SA Great*, 59.
85   Keays, *His Master's Voice*, 1.
86   Col Joye, interviewed by Peter Thompson on *Talking Heads* (25 Sep 2006), transcript at <http://www.abc.net.au/talkingheads/txt/s1745834.htm>, accessed 20 Aug 2008.
87   Col Joye, *Talking Heads*.
88   Louis Cooper, 'Rock Man Reckons He's under a Jinx', *TV Week* (5 Jan 1961), 24.
89   Renate, *Off the Record*, 95.
90   Renate, *Off the Record*, 97.
91   Renate, *Off the Record*, 128.
92   Damian Johnstone, *The Wild One: The Life and Times of Johnny O'Keefe* (Crows Nest: Allen and Unwin, 2001), 72.
93   Johnstone, *The Wild One*, 56.
94   Iggy Pop, quoted in Patrick Donovan, 'Iggy pops in to help Jet go wild about Johnny', *The Age* (10 Apr 2008), 3.
95   'Kicks and Kisses', *TV Week* (7 Jan 1961), 53.
96   'Are They South Australia's Greatest J. O'K fans?', *YM* (24 May 1962), 8.
97   'Did Adelaide Tame the Wild One?', *YM* (26 Apr 1962), 4.
98   Johnstone, *The Wild One*, 42.
99   Renate, *Off the Record*, 124.
100 Johnstone, *The Wild One*, 108.
101 'Johnny Plans a Super Rock Show', *TV Week* (28 Jan 1960), 19.
102 'Teletype News', *TV Week* (31 Mar 1960), 4.
103 Johnstone, *The Wild One*, 100.
104 Johnstone, *The Wild One*, 102.
105 McGrath, *Australian Encyclopaedia of Rock and Pop*, 26-27.
106 Taylor, *Rock Generation*, 72.
107 Johnstone, *The Wild One*, 96.
108 Renate, *Off the Record*, 129.
109 Johnstone, *The Wild One*, 96.
110 Koch, *The Doubleman*, 166.
111 Denise Young, 'Six O'Clock Rock', *Meanjin* 65:3 (2006), 27.
112 Johnny O'Keefe, quoted in Johnstone, *The Wild One*, 107.
113 'Johnny Plans a Super Rock Show', 18.
114 'Johnny Plans a Super Rock Show'.
115 Renate *Off the Record*, 140.
116 'Teletype News', *TV Week* (3 Mar 1960), 4.
117 Johnny O'Keefe, quoted in George McCadden, 'Johnny Tells ... Us All About It!', *TV Week* (10 Mar 1960), 12.
118 'Kicks and Kisses', *TV Week* (24 Mar 1960), 53.
119 'Teletype News', *TV Week* (7 Apr 1960), 4.
120 Johnstone, *The Wild One*, 125.
121 Renate, *Off the Record*, 141.
122 Johnstone, *The Wild One*, 122.
123 Renate, *Off the Record*, 141.
124 Renate, *Off the Record*, 150.
125 Peter McDonald, 'I'm Almost Flat Broke, Says Johnny', *TV Week* (14 Jul 1960), 11.
126 Renate, *Off the Record*, 167-8.
127 Renate, *Off the Record*, 170.
128 Renate, *Off the Record*, 179.
129 Billy Thorpe, *Sex and Thugs and Rock 'n' Roll* (Sydney: Macmillan, 1996), 373.
130 Renate, *Off the Record*, 193.
131 Renate, *Off the Record*, 200.
132 Renate, *Off the Record*, 203.
133 'Teen View', 'Kicks and Kisses', *TV Week* (17 Mar 1960), 52.
134 'Kicks and Kisses', *TV Week* (7 Apr 1960), 20.
135 *TV Week*, (28 Apr 1960), 41.
136 'We Don't Get a Fair Go', *TV Week* (2 Jun 1960), 20-21.
137 Col Joye, *Talking Heads*.
138 Johnstone, *The Wild One*, 56.
139 McGrath, *Australian Encyclopaedia of Rock and Pop*, 10-11.
140 'Judy's New Charges', *The Mercury*, Hobart (5 Nov 1964), 22.
141 Jimmy Little, interviewed by Peter Thompson, *Talking Heads* (29 Apr 2005), transcript at <http://www.abc.net.au/talkingheads/txt/s1352846.htm>, accessed 20 Aug 2008.
142 'Jimmy Little Rates Adelaide Audiences As the GREATEST', *YM* (19 Jul 1962), 27.
143 'Teletype News', *TV Week* (6 Oct 1960), 4.
144 'DJs: Behind the Behind', *Farrago* (20 Jul 1964), 10.
145 John Dix, *Stranger Than Paradise* (Auckland: Paradise Publications, 1988), 51.
146 Dave Dawson, 'Max Merritt', *Beat* (24 Aug 2004), 56.
147 'Oz Fights Back Appeal Announced', *Farrago* (12 Oct 1964), 1.
148 '12,000 Miles – Sealed in Wooden Box', *The Mercury*, Hobart (7 Nov 1964), 1.
149 Jack Ayling, 'I Love Lucky ... Says Cheryl', *TV Week* (23 Jun 1960), 7.
150 Diana Trask, quoted in 'Random Is Not Censored', *TV Week* (3 Nov 1960), 24-25.
151 Nona Teller, 'Hollywood', *TV Week* (8 Sep 1960), 28-29.
152 'Teletype News', *TV Week* (13 Apr 1961), 3.
153 'Teletype News', *TV Week* (1 Jun 1961), 4.
154 Frank Ifield, interviewed by Peter Thompson, *Talking Heads* (15 Oct 2007), transcript at <http://www.abc.net.au/talkingheads/txt/s2056978.htm>, accessed 20 Aug 2008.
155 Sleeve note to *Frank Ifield's Greatest Hits* (Columbia).
156 Jan Smith, *An Ornament of Grace* (Melbourne: Sun Books, 1966), 145.
157 Smith, *Ornament of Grace*, 145-6.
158 Joye, *Talking Heads*.

NOTES

159 Paul McHenry, *Thorpie!* (Golden Square: Moonlight Publishing, 1994), 3.
160 McHenry, *Thorpie*, 3.
161 McHenry, *Thorpie*, 3.
162 McHenry, *Thorpie*, 3.
163 McHenry, *Thorpie*, 3.
164 Thorpe, *Sex and Thugs*, 27-8.
165 Thorpe, *Sex and Thugs*, 116.
166 Lee Dillow, 'Billy Thorpe "Changes"', *Daily Planet* (27 Aug 1971), 6-7.
167 Thorpe, *Sex and Thugs*, 156.
168 Thorpe, *Sex and Thugs*, 248.
169 Dillow, 'Billy Thorpe "Changes"', 6-7.
170 McHenry, *Thorpie*, 4.
171 McHenry, *Thorpie*, 6.
172 Dillow, 'Billy Thorpe "Changes"', 6-7.
173 Tony Barber, interviewed by Dean Mittelhauser, 'Billy Thorpe and the Aztecs', in *The Livin' End* (1 Sep 1983), 6.
174 Normie Rowe, interviewed by Peter Thompson, *Talking Heads* (13 Feb 2006), transcript at <http://www.abc.net.au/talkingheads/txt/s1565435.htm>, accessed 20 Aug 2008.
175 Ed St. John, 'Happiness Is a Black Sorrow'. *ARS* # 448 (1990), 50-53, 96.
176 Joe Camilleri, quoted in Ed St. John, 'Joe Camilleri: The Boss Steps Out', *ARS* #321-2 (1988), 31.
177 Joe Camilleri, quoted in Andrew McMillan, 'Jo Jo Zep and the Falcons: Finally, This Could Be Their Year', *RAM* (10 Aug 1979), 25.
178 Joe Camilleri, quoted in Wendy Milsom and Helen Thomas, *Pay to Play: Tales of the Australian Rock Industry* (Ringwood: Penguin Books, 1986), 128.
179 'Who's for Big Time . . . in 1964?', *YM* (22 Jan 1964), 16.
180 'YM Moves into Record Field', *YM* (18 Sep 1963), 10.
181 'Change in Policy', *YM* (27 May 1964), 3.
182 'Wanted – New People', *YM* (16 Jun 1965), 3.

Chapter 3: I Feel As Good As If I Were Dead

1 Vernon Joynson, *Dreams, Fantasies and Nightmares from Far Away Lands: Canadian, Australasian and Latin American Rock and Pop 1963-75* (Wolverhampton: Borderline, 1999), 198.
2 'Barry Gibb – "They Say Cairo Is Very Kinky"', *Go-Set* (22 Jan 1969), 3.
3 Bill Casey, 'Mr. Can-Do meets Mr. Make-Do', <http://lmg.hurstville.nsw.gov.au/Nat-Kipner-and-The-Bee-Gees.html>, accessed 17 Aug 2012.
4 Kim Stevens, *The Bee Gees* (New York, Scholastic, 1978), 16.
5 'Bed of a Thousand Struggles', *Long Way to the Top*.
6 'Irene', letter to *Go-Set* (3 Jan 1968), p. 5.
7 David English and Alex Brychta, *The Legend: The Illustrated Story of the Bee Gees* (London: Quartet, 1983), 15.
8 Jeff Jenkins, *Ego Is Not a Dirty Word: The Skyhooks Story* (Clifton Hill: Kelly & Withers, 1994) 17.
9 Ian D. Marks and Iain McIntyre, *Wild About You: The Sixties Beat Explosion in Australia and New Zealand* (Portland: Verse Chorus Press, 2010), 149-150.
10 Glenn A. Baker, 'Bee Gees: Early Days in Oz', *Juke* (25 Feb 1978), 5.
11 English and Brychta, *The Legend*, 26.
12 Jacobsen, quoted in Baker, 'Bee Gees', 6.
13 Baker, 'Bee Gees', 5.
14 Baker, 'Bee Gees', 6.
15 Bill Casey, *Spin Dried: A Complete and Annotated Discography of Australia's Spin Record Label 1966-1974* (Castlemaine: Moonlight Publications, 2007), 3.
16 Casey, *Spin Dried*, 4.
17 Baker, 'Bee Gees', 6.
18 Christie Eliezer, 'Will the Real Samantha Sang Please Stand Up . . .', *Juke* (8 Apr 1978), 13.
19 Casey, *Spin Dried*, 30.
20 'Bed of a Thousand Struggles', *Long Way to the Top*.
21 David N. Meyer, *The Bee Gees: The Biography* (North Sydney: Random House, 2013), 20.
22 Bill Casey, 'The One-eyed Fan in the Butcher's Storeroom', <www.hurstville.nsw.gov.au/beegees/ossie_byrne.htm>, accessed 30 Jul 2008.
23 Casey, *Spin Dried*, 27.
24 Casey, *Spin Dried*, 28.
25 'All Eyes Are on "Spicks and Specks"', *Everybody's* (19 Oct 1966), 15.
26 Baker, *Spin Dried*, 6.
27 Baker, *Spin Dried*, 6.
28 'All Eyes Are on "Spicks and Specks."'
29 Lillian Roxon, *Rock Encylopedia* (New York: Grosset & Dunlap, 1969), 40.
30 Casey, *Spin Dried*, 35.
31 Meyer, *The Bee Gees*, 20.
32 Meyer, *The Bee Gees*, 51.
33 Lee Dillow, 'Vince Melouney At Last!', *Daily Planet* (20 Oct 1971), 16
34 Quoted in Casey, *Spin Dried*, 45.
35 Dillow, 'Vince Melouney At Last!', 16.
36 Dillow, 'Vince Melouney At Last!', 17.
37 'Bee Gees: "We Love Australia"', *Go-Set* (10 Jan 1968), 7.
38 'Bee Gees Ill', *Go-Set* (17 Jan 1968), 4.
39 Ian Meldrum, 'Bee Gee Barry Home to Find Talent', *Go-Set* (8 Jan 1969), 9.
40 John Halsey, 'Ex Bee Gee Forms Production Co.', *Juke* (16 Jul 1977), 4.
41 'The Continuing Story of the Bee Gees Family Rumpus . . . Barry says Robin "Extremely Rude"', *Go-Set* (17 May 1969), 3.
42 'Barry Gibb for Pop Poll Show', *Go-Set* (6 Jun 1970), 7.
43 'Bee Gees Australian Details Tour', *Planet* (19 Jan 1972), 3.
44 Alistair Jones, 'The Return of the Bee Gees', *Planet* (18 Feb 1972), 4.

Chapter 4: We Weren't Exactly Keeping a Low Profile

1 This chapter is an expanded version of an article I wrote in 2000, on the occasion of the reissue of the entire Missing Links back catalogue on one CD by Sydney label Half A Cow. All quotes from Peter Anson and Andy Anderson here originally appeared in that article: David Nichols, 'The Missing Links: Prime Movers', *Puncture* 47 (2000), 56-60.
2 'C.G., 4th Year', 'Big Beat', *The Student* (Scarborough, WA) (Nov 1965), 66.
3 Jane Matheson, 'The La De Das Story', *ARS* #182 (13 Mar 1975), 37.
4 Doug Ford, quoted in 'The Missing Links', <http://www.3cr.org.au/way/content_03.html>, accessed 22 Nov 2008.
5 'Dossier: Doug Ford', *Go-Set* (4 Apr 1970), 9.
6 Maggie Makeig, 'Australian Beat', *Everybody's* (4 May 1966), 19.

Chapter 5: The Snap and Crackle of Pop

1 Koch, *The Doubleman*, 292.
2 Peter Weir, quoted in Sue Mathews, *35mm Dreams: Conversations with Five Directors about the Australian Film Revival* (Ringwood: Penguin, 1984), 82.
3 Sheila Whiteley, *The Space Between the Notes: Rock and the Counter-Culture* (London: Routledge, 1992), 69.
4 Dave Mason, quoted in Gavin Waller, 'One Day at a Picture Exhibition', *Juke* (14 Mar 1987), 17.
5 *Nation* (8 Apr 1967), 7.
6 Patrick White, *The Vivisector* (London: Jonathan Cape, 1970), 603.
7 Martin Huxley, *AC/DC: the World's Heaviest Rock* (London: Boxtree, 1996), 31-32.
8 Craig MacGregor, *Profile of Australia* (London: Hodder and Stoughton, 1966), 280.
9 Howard Lindley, 'Ross Hannaford', *Daily Planet* (27 Oct 1971), 5.
10 Robert Wolfgramm, 'City in the Self: Melbourne (1968-70) as seen from the margins', in Seamus O'Hanlon and Tanja Luckins (eds.), *Go! Melbourne in the Sixties* (Beaconsfield: Circa, 2005), 38-9.
11 Lindley, 3.
12 'Fab-gas-wild-groovy Party Machine!!', *Go-Set* (28 Feb 1968), 7.
13 David Elfick, 'Party Machine Split', *Go-Set* (2 Apr 1969), 21.
14 <http://www.milesago.com/industry/dayman.htm>, accessed 7 Jul 2012.
15 Normie Rowe, 'I'm No Sinner: His Own Frank Story', *Everybody's* (30 Mar 1966), 20-23.
16 Joe Camilleri, quoted in Wendy Milsom and Helen Thomas, *Pay to Play: Tales of the Australian Rock Industry* (Ringwood: Penguin ,1986), 130.
17 Marcie Jones, *Runs in the Blood* (Greensborough: NCS, 2008), 201.
18 Jones, *Runs in the Blood*, 207.

19 Graham Simpson *Colours of My Life: the Judith Durham Story* (Milsons Point: Random House Australia, 1998 edition), 104.
20 Glenn A. Baker, sleevenotes to Normie Rowe and the Playboys, *Shakin' All Over* (Raven, 1998).
21 Donald Robertson, 'It's Your Fault, Molly!', *Roadrunner* (4 May 1982), 12.
22 'Ronnie Burns Really Speaks Out!' *Go-Set* (28 Feb 1968), 12.
23 Paul Culnane, letter to *Go-Set* (3 Jan 1968), 5.
24 Ian Meldrum, 'Ian Meldrum Looks Thru Keyholes', *Go-Set* (10 Jan 1968), 6.
25 'Ronnie's Own Show', *Go-Set* (6 Jun 1970), 2.
26 McGrath, *Australian Encyclopaedia of Rock and Pop*, 11.
27 McGrath, *Australian Encyclopaedia of Rock and Pop*, 12.
28 Lee Dillow, 'Billy Thorpe "Changes"', *Daily Planet* (27 Aug 1971), 6-7.
29 Dillow, 'Billy Thorpe "Changes"'.
30 Dillow, 'Billy Thorpe "Changes"'.
31 Maggie Makeig, 'Tassie must get a better deal', *Everybody's* (25 May 1966), 22-3.
32 Keays, *His Master's Voice*, 88.
33 Joynson, *Dreams, Fantasies and Nightmares*, 219.
34 Joynson, *Dreams, Fantasies and Nightmares*, 318.
35 Andrew Jach, 'Brisbane Your Balls Have Burnt Off', *Holocaust* 2 (1970), pages not numbered.
36 Keays, *His Master's Voice*, 80.
37 Keays, *His Master's Voice*, 81.
38 Lobby Loyde quoted in Patrick Donovan, 'Lobby Loyde Tribute', *The Age* (23 Jun 2006), EG section, 5.
39 Thank you to Ian McFarlane for this information.
40 Keays, *His Master's Voice*, 61.
41 Philip Frazer quoted in Iain McIntyre (ed.), *Tomorrow Is Today: Australia in the Psychedelic Era 1966-1970* (Kent Town: Wakefield Press, 2007), 26.
42 Anon, 'Popping up', *The Bulletin* (27 Jan 1968) 4-7.
43 Keays, 61
44 Joynson, *Dreams, Fantasies and Nightmares*, 213.
45 'After Dark', *The Bulletin* (28 Feb 1970) 17.
46 Keays, *His Master's Voice*, 60.
47 Keays, *His Master's Voice*, 56.
48 Unsourced ad reproduced in Paul McHenry, *Hans Poulsen: Troubadour* (Golden Square: Moonlight Publishing, 1996) 6.
49 Keays, *His Master's Voice*, 112-3.
50 Keays, *His Master's Voice*, 124.
51 Jillian Birt, 'Instant Replay', *Juke* (12 Jul 1978), 20.
52 *Gerry Humphrys The Loved One*, dir. Nigel Buesst.
53 McIntyre, *Tomorrow Is Today*, 34.
54 Humphrys interviewed in *Gerry Humphrys The Loved One*.
55 Rob Lovett interviewed in *Gerry Humphrys The Loved One*.
56 See second rendition of 'The Loved One' in *Gerry Humphrys The Loved One*.
57 Kim Lynch interviewed in *Gerry Humphrys The Loved One*.
58 Untitled interview with Gerry Humphries, *Planet* (1 Mar 1972),12-14.
59 Peter Walsh, 'Gerry Humphries', *Daily Planet* (13 Oct 1971), 3.
60 'Loved Ones Re-form', *Go-Set* (31 Jan 1968), 4.
61 Barry Dickins, 'Fond Memories of an Ever-Lovin' man', *The Age* (10 Dec 2005), 17.
62 Dickins, 'Fond memories'.
63 Keays, *His Master's Voice*, 36.
64 Anon, 'Popping Up', *The Bulletin* (27 Jan 1968), 4.
65 Joynson, *Dreams, Fantasies and Nightmares*, 233.
66 Christie Eliezer, 'Burton Ain't Hurtin': He's Firin!', *Juke* (11 Mar 1978), 4.
67 Joynson, *Dreams, Fantasies and Nightmares*, 187.
68 Meldrum, '1969 Battle Sensation – It's . . . Doug Parkinson In Focus!', *Go-Set* (9 Aug 1969), 2.
69 David Elfick, 'Doug Looks Back', *Go-Set* (2 Aug 1969), 5.
70 Lee Dillow, 'Parko: The Large One', *Daily Planet* (22 Sep 1971), 7.
71 'Questions Break-up and Re-form', *Go-Set* (17 Jan 1968), 4.
72 Loyde interviewed in Marks and McIntyre, *Wild About You!*, 149.
73 Mick Hadley quoted in The Barman, 'Mick Hadley and his Purple Hearts Past', <http://www.i94bar.com/ints/mickhadley.html>, accessed 9 Apr 2012.
74 'Purple Hearts Are Full of Pep', *Everybody's* (5 Jan 1966), 13.
75 'Meteors at Maximum Speed', *Spunky no.* 2 (1976), 13.
76 Dave Dawson 'Max Merritt', *Beat* (24 Aug 2004), 56.
77 'Great Merritt', *Spunky no.* 4 (1976), 19.
78 Clark Forbes, *Whispering Jack* (Milsons Point: Hutchinson Australia, 1989), 11.
79 Forbes, *Whispering Jack*, 14.
80 Forbes, *Whispering Jack*, 26.
81 'Stan Rofe's Tonic', *Go-Set* (21 Feb 1968), 3.
82 Keays, *His Master's Voice*, 105.
83 Forbes, *Whispering Jack*, 17.
84 Forbes, *Whispering Jack*, 76.
85 Keays, *His Master's Voice*, 174.
86 Forbes, *Whispering Jack*, 31.
87 Richard Neville, *Playpower* (London: Jonathan Cape, 1970) 23.
88 Michael Morris, 'The Truth about the Daylights', *Farrago* (12 Jul 1974), 20.
89 Morris, 'Truth about the Daylights'.
90 See Tony Palmer, *The Trials of Oz* (Manchester: Blond & Briggs, 1971) or, more briefly, Jonathan Green, *A Day in the Life* (London: Minerva, 1988), 382-400.
91 Neville, *Playpower*, 172-3.
92 Robert Burns, 'The Quant-Jagger World', *Nation* (17 Apr 1971), 7.
93 Norman Bartlett, '"The Hairy Image": Underground in London', *Meanjin Quarterly no.* 3 (1970), 383.
94 Lee Dillow, 'Phillip Frazer: The Invisible Man', *Planet* (23 Feb 1972), 8-9.
95 Dillow, 'Phillip Frazer'.
96 Seamus O'Hanlon, '"Where All the Action Is, Man": Youth Culture in Melbourne in the 1960s', in O'Hanlon and Luckins (eds.), *Go! Melbourne in the Sixties* (Beaconsfield: Circa, 2005) 46.
97 McIntyre, *Tomorrow Is Today*, 26.
98 Keays, *His Master's Voice*, 51.
99 McIntyre, *Tomorrow Is Today*, 31.
100 'Big Changes in Go-Set Next Week', *Go-Set* (28 Mar 1970), 2.
101 McIntyre, *Tomorrow Is Today*, 25.
102 Naomi Manuell, 'Molly's Stardust', *Meanjin* 65:3 (2006), 99.
103 Eliezer, *High Voltage Rock 'n' Roll*, 138.
104 Meldrum quoted in Manuell, 'Molly's Stardust', 97.
105 Meldrum quoted in Manuell, 'Molly's Stardust', 97.
106 Eliezer *High Voltage Rock 'n' Roll*, 138.
107 Eliezer *High Voltage Rock 'n' Roll*, 139.
108 Meldrum quoted in Manuell, 'Molly's Stardust', 98.
109 Meldrum quoted in Manuell, 'Molly's Stardust', 99.
110 Manuell, 'Molly's Stardust', 99.
111 Eliezer *High Voltage Rock 'n' Roll*, 141.
112 Meldrum, quoted in Manuell, 'Molly's Stardust', 102.
113 Dean Moriarty, 'Will the Real Tony Perkins Please Lie Down: Interview Part 1, Ian Meldrum' *Planet* (9 Feb 1972), 7.
114 'Real Thing is Real Hit', *Go-Set* (2 Apr 1969), 21.
115 'Dossier: Doug Ford' *Go-Set*, (4 Apr 1970), 9.
116 Eliezer *High Voltage Rock 'n' Roll*, 137.
117 Meldrum quoted in David Groenewegen, *The Real Thing? The Rock Music Industry and the Creation of Australian Images* (Golden Square: Moonlight Publishing, 1997) 45.
118 Ern Rose quoted in Brian Cadd, *From This Side of Things* (Sydney: New Holland, 2010), 248.
119 Cadd, *From This Side of Things*, 133.
120 'Ian Meldrum Looks Through Keyholes', *Go-Set* (17 Jan 1968), 7.
121 Lee Dillow, 'Russell Morris', *Daily Planet* (29 Sep 1971), 6.
122 Russell Morris in *History and Styles of Rock Music in Australia* (videocassette).
123 Russell Morris quoted in Toby Creswell, 'Russell Morris Comes Back Through The In Door', *ARS* (6 Mar 1980), 24.
124 Kruger, *Songwriters Speak*, 156.
125 Keays, *His Master's Voice*, 148.
126 Dillow, 'Russell Morris'.
127 Dillow, 'Russell Morris'.
128 Morris quoted in Creswell, 'Russell Morris Comes Back'.
129 Dillow, 'Russell Morris'.
130 Paul McHenry, *Hans Poulsen: Troubadour* (Golden Square: Moonlight Publishing, 1996) 4.
131 Bob Staines in 1966, quoted in McHenry, *Hans Poulsen*, 4.
132 Glass quoted in McHenry, *Hans Poulsen*, 5.
133 Ian Meldrum, 'The Makings and Ramblings of Hans Poulsen' *Go-Set* (23 May 1970) 5.
134 Woodley quoted in Kruger, 48.

NOTES

135   Ed Nimmervoll and David Elfick, 'The Ourimbah Pop Piligrmage: Birth of something beautiful!' *Go-Set* (4 Feb 1970) 'Core' section.
136   McHenry *Hans Poulsen*,13.
137   McHenry *Hans Poulsen*,13.
138   Angus Young interviewed in *Long Way to the Top*, ABC-TV, DVD, extras disc 2.
139   Thaddeus Goldbank IV, 'Johnny Young Collapse', *Go-Set* (24 Jan 1968), 3.
140   Ian Meldrum, 'Meldrum: Ian Meldrum Speaks his Mind', *Go-Set* (13 Jun 1970), 4.
141   Johnny Young quoted in 'I Want to Tell the Truth', *Go-Set* (7 Feb 1968), 8.
142   Jean Gollan, 'Lionel Rose: Australia's New Pop Hero!', *Go-Set* (4 Feb 1970), 4.
143   Eliezer, *High Voltage Rock 'n' Roll*, 148.
144   Joynson, *Dreams, Fantasies and Nightmares*, 335.
145   Ian Meldrum, 'Here Comes the Star', *Go-Set* (13 Sep 1969), 2.
146   Ross D. Wylie on Shed TV, 5 Apr 2011, accessed on YouTube 21 Jul 2011.
147   Meldrum, 'Here Comes the Star'.
148   Samantha, 'Herman's Hermits Take It Easy', *Go-Set* (12 Jul 1969), 23.
149   David Day and Tim Parker, *SA Great: It's Our Music 1956-1986* (Glandore: Pagel/Wakefield Press, 1987), 70.
150   Neeson quoted in Day and Parker, *SA Great*, 68.
151   Birtles interviewed by David Kilby, ABC Canberra (17 Oct 1999), from Milesago website.
152   'The Zoot Raps', *Empire Times* (11 Mar 1969), 6.
153   Day and Parker, *SA Great*, 76.
154   Day and Parker, *SA Great*, 64.
155   'Stan Rofe's Tonic', *Go-Set* (3 Jan 1970), 12.
156   Jean Gollan, 'Zoot Preparing for their New Single', *Go-Set* (4 Apr 1970), 7.
157   Birtles interviewed by Kilby.
158   'Valentines Break-up: Last of the "Teeny" Groups?', *Go-Set* (13 Jun 1970), 5.
159   'Valentines Pop Scene Rebels', *Go-Set* (9 May 1970), 4.
160   'Valentines Pop Scene Rebels'.
161   'Valentines back in Melbourne', *Go-Set* (2 May 1970), 20.
162   Mitch, 'Album Out Soon for Flying Circus', *Go-Set* (9 Aug 1969), 6.
163   Keays, *His Master's Voice*, 23.
164   Keays, *His Master's Voice*, 20.
165   Day and Parker, *SA Great*, 67.
166   Keays, *His Master's Voice*, 31.
167   Keays, *His Master's Voice*, 32.
168   Keays, *His Master's Voice*, 33.
169   Keays, *His Master's Voice*, 34.
170   Keays, *His Master's Voice*, 37.
171   Day/Parker, 107.
172   Day/Parker, 110.
173   Max Pepper quoted in Day/Parker, 106.
174   Keays, *His Master's Voice*, 49.
175   Day/Parker, 61.
176   Keays, *His Master's Voice*, 64.
177   Keays, *His Master's Voice*, 65.
178   Keays, *His Master's Voice*, 65.
179   Keays, *His Master's Voice*, 73.
180   Keays, *His Master's Voice*, 89.
181   Keays, *His Master's Voice*, 97.
182   Colin Burgess quoted in 'We'll Kill Them!', *Go-Set* (31 Jan 1968), 3.
183   Keays, *His Master's Voice*, 105.
184   Ian Meldrum, 'MASTERS SAY "Turn Up Your Radio!"', *Go-Set* (2 May 1970), 9.
185   Keays, *His Master's Voice*, 154.
186   Jones, *Runs in the Blood*, 144.
187   Keays, *His Master's Voice*, 177.
188   Keays, *His Master's Voice*, 201.
189   Keays, *His Master's Voice*, 28.
190   Michael Smith, 'Two for the Show', *Juke* (25 Apr 1987), 25.
191   Ian Meldrum, 'Terry Britten, the Little "Big" Pop Star', *Go-Set* (12 Mar 1969), 16.
192   'The Stars' New Years Resolutions', *Go-Set* (10 Jan 1968), 11.
193   Cadd, *From This Side of Things*, 80.
194   'Group Parts: Sun Sets on the Twilights', *The Age* (18 Jan 1969), 2.
195   Ian Meldrum, 'Avengers Team Up with Ex-Twilight', *Go-Set* (19 Feb 1969), 9.

196   Lindy, 'When Is a Supergroup Not a Supergroup?', *Go-Set* (2 Aug 1969), 5.
197   Ian Meldrum, 'The Brisbane Avengers Talk about the New Zealand Avengers and Their Own Future', *Go-Set* (12 Mar 1969), 16.
198   Cadd, *From This Side of Things*, 49.
199   Ian Meldrum, 'Pop World in Turmoil', *Go-Set* (10 May 1969), 5.
200   Meldrum, 'Pop World in Turmoil'.
201   Lindy, 'The Continuing Saga of the Axiom', *Go-Set* (9 Aug 1969), 5.
202   Cadd, *From This Side of Things*, 85.
203   Lindy, 'The Continuing Saga'.
204   Lindy, 'When Is a Supergroup Not a Supergroup?', 5.
205   Lindy, 'When Is a Supergroup Not a Supergroup?'
206   Jean [Gollan], 'Axiom Comes to Call', *Go-Set* (14 Mar 1970), 7.
207   Ed Nimmervoll, 'Record Review', *Go-Set* (14 Mar 1970), 14.
208   Ross Stapleton, 'Axiom or Fool's Gold?', *Go-Set* (4 Apr 1970), 'Core' section.
209   'A Letter from the Axiom', *Go-Set* (9 May 1970), 5.
210   Jean Gollan, 'Axiom Say Goodbye to Australia', *Go-Set* (4 Apr 1970), 3.
211   Gollan, 'Axiom Say Goodbye'.
212   Ed Nimmervoll, 'Record Review', *Go-Set* (18 Apr 1970), 7.
213   Cadd, *From This Side of Things* 94.
214   McGrath, *Australian Encyclopaedia of Rock and Pop*, 22.
215   *Alvin Purple*, dir. Tim Burstall (1974). See also McGrath, *Australian Encyclopaedia of Rock and Pop*, 56; Anon., *Alvin Purple* (Sydney: Scripts Publishing, 1974), 74.
216   Birtles quoted in Day and Parker, *SA Great*, 78
217   Helen Barrett, 'Ashdown Down Home Down Under', *Juke* (27 Aug 1975), 6
218   Barrett, 'Ashdown Down Home'.
219   Doug Ashdown quoted in Malcolm Maiden, 'Ashdown & Stewart: An Appeal to the English Speaking World', *ARS* (19 Jun 1975), 47.
220   'Melbourne's Seekers Come Home', *Go-Set* (14 Feburary 1966), 3.
221   'Ronnie to England to Record with Maurice Gibb', *Go-Set* (24 Jan 1970), 2.
222   Jean Gollan and David Elphick, 'Future Plans for Russell and Ronnie', *Go-Set* (28 Feb 1970), 3.
223   'English tour put off for Ronnie Burns', *Go-Set* (4 Apr 1970), 4.
224   'Olivia Newton-John to Join "Monkee Group"', *Go-Set* (19 Feb 1969), 9.
225   'Olivia's Dream Comes True!', *TV Week* (30 Mar 1974), 20.
226   Phil Key quoted in Jane Matheson, 'The La De Das Story', *ARS* (13 Mar 1975), 37.
227   Key in Matheson, 'The La De Das Story', 37.
228   Key in Matheson, 'The La De Das Story', 37.
229   Matheson, 'The La De Das Story', 37.
230   David Elphick, 'The La De Das are back!', *Go-Set* (4 Apr 1970), 10.
231   Joe Camilleri quoted in Ed St. John, 'Happiness is a Black Sorrow', ARS # 448 (1990), 96.
232   Joe Camilleri quoted in Milsom and Thomas, *Pay to Play*, 130.
233   Joe Camilleri quoted in Milsom and Thomas, *Pay to Play*, 130.
234   Lindy, 'Wendy Only Wants to Be in It up to Her Waist', *Go-Set* (7 Jun 1969), 3.
235   'Beat 'n' Tracks become the Chain', *Go-Set* (8 Jan 1969), 5.
236   Lindy, 'Wendy Only Wants'.
237   Lindy, 'Wendy Only Wants'.
238   Lindy, 'Wendy Only Wants'.

Chapter 6: Falling off the Edge of the World

1   David Elfick, 'The Easybeats in England and the U.S.', *Go-Set* (30 Aug 1969), 7.
2   Vanda quoted in Kruger, *Songwriters Speak*, 61.
3   Young quoted in Glenn Baker, '13 Years of Rock and Roll: George Young remembers the Easybeats', *ARS* (15 Jul 1976), 42.
4   Clinton Walker, *Highway to Hell: The Life and Times of AC/DC Legend Bon Scott* (Portland: Verse Chorus Press, 2001), 117
5   Kruger, *Songwriters Speak*, 56.
6   Young in Baker, '13 Years of Rock and Roll', 42.
7   Vanda quoted in Kruger *Songwriters Speak*, 59.

8   Young in Baker, '13 Years of Rock and Roll', 42.
9   Stevie Wright, 'I Was Broke, but I Could Still Laugh', *Everybody's* (8 Jun 1966), 18-24.
10 Angus Young interview, *Long Way to the Top*, ABC-TV. DVD, extras disc 2.
11 Vanda quoted in Kruger *Songwriters Speak*, 59.
12 Quoted in Robert Milliken, *Lillian Roxon: Mother of Rock* (Melbourne: Black Inc, 2002), 137.
13 George Young quoted in Glenn A Baker's sleevenotes to *The Shame Just Drained* (Alberts, 1977).
14 'Batman's Melbourne: As Conspicuous As a Negro at a KKK Picnic', *The Bulletin* (27 May 1967), 5.
15 John Tait, *Vanda and Young: Inside Australia's Hit Factory* (Sydney: New South, 2010), 39.
16 Young in Baker, '13 Years of Rock and Roll', 43.
17 Young in Baker, '13 Years of Rock and Roll', 42.
18 Maggie Makeig, 'How the Easybeats Stumbled on a Great Big Hit', *Everybody's* (20 Apr 1966), 18.
19 'Postbox', *Go-Set* (23 Mar 1966), 2.
20 Vanda quoted in Kruger, *Songwriters Speak*, 61.
21 Vanda quoted in Kruger, *Songwriters Speak*, 60.
22 Vanda interviewed in Christobel Manson and Michael Foster, 'Chasing Beats', *Canberra Times* (11 Oct 1969), 17.
23 Wright interviewed by Andrew Probyn, 29 May 2001 <http://www.milesago.com/interviews/stevie-interview.htm>.
24 The Easybeats, *The Shame Just Drained* (Alberts, 1977).
25 Vanda quoted in Kruger, *Songwriters Speak*, 61.
26 Young in Baker, '13 Years of Rock and Roll', 43
27 Simon Reynolds, *Rip It Up and Start Again: Postpunk 1978-1984* Faber and Faber, London 2005, 300
28 Young in Baker, '13 Years of Rock and Roll', 43.
29 Young in Baker, '13 Years of Rock and Roll', 43.
30 Young in sleevenotes to *The Shame Just Drained*.
31 'Batman's Melbourne', 5.
32 'Batman's Melbourne'.
33 'Batman's Melbourne'.
34 Quoted in sleevenotes to *The Shame Just Drained*.
35 Young in Baker, '13 Years of Rock and Roll', 43.
36 Glenn A. Baker (ed. & annotated), *Australian Made: Gonna Have A Good Time Tonight, the Authorised Documentary of the Event* (Sydney Fontana/Collins, 1987), 18; Young in Baker, '13 Years of Rock and Roll', 43.
37 Quoted in sleevenotes to *The Shame Just Drained*.
38 Vanda quoted in Kruger, *Songwriters Speak*, 63.
39 Vanda quoted in Kruger, *Songwriters Speak*, 65.
40 Young in Baker, '13 Years of Rock and Roll', 43.
41 Young in Baker, '13 Years of Rock and Roll', 44.
42 Vanda quoted in Kruger, *Songwriters Speak*, 64-5.
43 Vanda in Manson and Foster, 'Chasing Beats', 17.
44 Tait, *Vanda and Young*, 195.
45 Wright quoted in Ed Nimmervoll, 'One of the Boys', *Juke* (14 May 1975), 10.
46 Matheson, 'The La De Das Story', 37.
47 'Australian Notes', *ARS* #157 (28 Mar 1974), 18.
48 Nimmervoll, 'One of the Boys', 10.
49 Toby Creswell, *Too Much Ain't Enough* (Milsons Point: Random House, 1993), 197.

Chapter 7: Knights in Yellow Armour

1   Pip Proud, undated letter (c. 1967) to Michael Hobbs.
2   Troy D. Colvin, 'Turn it up: Lobby Loyde Did It First and He Did It Loudest', *Mess + Noise* 09 (Sep/Oct 2006), 53.
3   Pip Proud, biographical entry dated 'Edgecliff, NSW September 1969' in Thomas Shapcott (ed.), *Australian Poetry Now* (Melbourne: Sun Books, 1970), 195.
4   David Hajdu *Positively 4th Street: The Lives and Times of Bob Dylan, Joan Baez, Mimi Baez Farina, and Richard Farina* (New York: Farrar Straus Giroux, 2001), 193.
5   Pip Proud, undated letter (c. mid 1968) to Michael Hobbs.
6   Garry Shead, letter to Michael Hobbs, 3 Feb 1968.
7   Pip Proud, undated (c. 1967?) letter to Michael Hobbs.
8   Pip Proud, undated letter (c. 1967) to Michael Hobbs.
9   Quoted in Kate Keavney, 'He's Running Away from Success', *Australian Women's Weekly* (31 Dec 1969), 9.
10 Thanks to Ian McFarlane for this information.
11 Jim Oram, 'Hip, Pip, Pip: Genius, or Oddball?', *Pix* (19 Oct 1969), 7-8.
12 Pip Proud, undated letter (c. Jul 1969) to Michael Hobbs.
13 Gil Wahlquist, 'The Quiet Originality of Pip Proud', *Sun Herald* (13 Oct 1968), 99.
14 'Poetic monologue', *Go-Set* (2 Oct 1968), 9.
15 Anon, 'Popping Up', *The Bulletin* (27 Jan 1968), 4.
16 Pip Proud, undated letter (c. 1967) to Michael Hobbs.
17 Pip Proud quoted in Oram, 'Hip, Pip, Pip', 7-8.
18 Pip Proud, undated letter (c. 1967) to Michael Hobbs.
19 Pip Proud, undated letter (c. Mar 1968) to Michael Hobbs.
20 Pip Proud, undated letter (c. Mar 1968) to Michael Hobbs.
21 Pip Proud, undated letter (c. Mar 1968) to Michael Hobbs.
22 David Elfick, 'Pip Proud Offers $1,000 reward', *Go-Set* (12 Feb 1969), 11.
23 Pip Proud, undated letter (c. Mar 1968) to Michael Hobbs.
24 Elfick, 'Pip Proud Offers', 11.
25 Anon, 'Casting', *The Bulletin* (8 Mar 1969), 43.
26 Michael Symons, 'Where are you, Pip?' Item in scrapbook belonging to Alison Burns.
27 A one-sided LP by a new Pip Proud Group was released in the mid 1990s, with the present author (and, of course, Proud) involved.
28 Proud quoted in Elfick, 'Pip Proud Offers', 11.
29 Pip Proud, undated letter (c. 1969) to Michael Hobbs.
30 'Win a One-Way Ticket Anywhere', *Go-Set* (2 Oct 1968), 10.
31 Keavney, 'He's Running Away from Success', 9.
32 'News on Pip', *Go-Set* (8 Nov 1969), 9.
33 Pip Proud, undated letter (c. 1970) to 'Mater'.
34 Pip Proud, undated letter (c. 1970) to 'Mater'.
35 Pip Proud, undated letter (c. 1979) to Michael Hobbs.
36 Joynson, *Dreams, Fantasies and Nightmares*, 296.
37 Proud, biographical entry in Shapcott, *Australian Poetry Now*, 195.

Chapter 8: It's a Flash!

1   Lobby Loyde, 'Lob's', *Daily Planet* (Aug 13 1971), 2.
2   Loyde, 'Lob's', 2.
3   See, for instance, 'Injudicious', *Nation* (22 Jan 1972), 3-4; 'Mr. McMahon for Keeps', *Nation* (18 Mar 1972), 5.
4   Pete Steedman, interview with author, 5 Dec 2002.
5   Leonard Radic, '"Cuckoos" Stake a Claim to Land', *The Age* (24 Feb 1972), 8; Radic, 'Leases, but No Freehold Land', *The Age* (25 Feb 1971), 9; Michael Richardson, 'Tragic Irony of Reserves', *The Age* (27 Feb 1971), 8.
6   Michelle Grattan, 'Native "Embassy" Pulled Down Again', *The Age* (31 Jul 1972), 3.
7   Don McPhee, 'Guns for Human Rights', *Farrago* (10 Mar 1972), 5.
8   '"White Stirrers" in Natives' City Protest', *The Age* (15 Jul 1972), 5.
9   Ian Turner, 'The Vietnam Moratorium', *Meanjin Quarterly* 2 (1970), 243; Alan Ward, 'The Second Vietnam Moratorium: Reflections of a Melbourne Participant', *Meanjin Quarterly* 4 (1970), 501-502.
10 Greg Quill, 'The Moratorium in Sydney', *Revolution* (1 Jun 1970), 4.
11 'Stand Fast Against the Plastic Wombats', *Go-Set* (9 May 1970), 23.
12 'Stand Fast', 23.
13 Michael Matteson, 'Escape from Gore Hill and Where to Find Me Next Time', *Nation* (19 Feb 1972), 5-6.
14 Bradley quoted in Barney Hoskyns, *Glam! Bowie, Bolan and the Glitter Rock Revolution* (London: Faber, 1998), 36.
15 Keays, *His Master's Voice*, 133.
16 'Local Boy Makes Good: Clinton Kramer Talks with Frank Thring', *Campaign* (11 Aug 1975), 29-30, 43.
17 Jean Gollan, 'Zoot Preparing for Their New Single', *Go-Set* (4 Apr 1970), 7.
18 Forbes, *Whispering Jack*, 36.
19 'Gay Lib Grows Angry at ABC', *The Age* (13 Jul 1972), 13.
20 Claude Forell, 'Time for Liberation of the "Gay" People', *The Age* (29 Jul 1972), 8.
21 Andrea Jones, 'Keith Glass: Pioneer Goes Public', *ARS* #327 (1980), 23.
22 Roger Aldridge, 'The Strange Years Ahead', *The Age* (1 Jan 1970), 6.
23 Wally Young, 'A Pop Picnic', *The Bulletin* (7 Feb 1970), 37.
24 Ed Nimmervoll and David Elfick, 'The Ourimbah Pop Pilgrimage: Birth of Something Beautiful!', *Go-Set* (4 Feb 1970), 'Core' section.
25 Robert Drewe, 'Hippiness and Happiness Ends the Great Pop Show', *The Age* (25 Jan 1970), 3.
26 Wendy Saddington, 'Not Just a Dream', *Go-Set* (4 Feb 1970), 'Core' section.

NOTES

27 Paul Conn, *2000 Weeks* (Golden Square: Moonlight Publishing, 1996) 37.
28 'Happier Day at Myponga', *The Age* (1 Feb 1971), 2.
29 'Happening under Canvas Now', *The Age* (31 Dec 1970), 2.
30 *Planet* (17 May 1972), 4.
31 Charles Buckmaster, "An End to Myth" in *Collected Poems* (St Lucia: University of Queensland Press, 1989), 106.
32 'Aquarius Festival', *Farrago* (27 Apr 1973), 11.
33 'Aquarius Festival', 12.
34 Clinton Walker, 'Where Cowpunks Dare to Sing', *The Age* (16 Jan 1987), EG section, 5.
35 Ian Meldrum, 'Sunbury '74', *Go-Set* (2 Feb 1974), 16.
36 Alastair Jones, 'Sunbury '74: Of Tents, Tits, Rubber Thongs and Two Big Brothers', *ARS* #154 (14 Feb 1974), 30-31.
37 Jones, 'Sunbury '74', 30-31.
38 Jonathan Green, 'Portrait of the Festival as a Viable Proposition', *Juke* (22 Jan 1983), 7.
39 Jonathan Green, 'Most People I Know Think That I'm an American Citizen', *Juke* (5 Feb 1983), 12.
40 'They Sold Us LSD: Police', *The Age* (30 Jan 1973), 4.
41 'Sunbury Two Gaoled for Selling LSD', *The Age* (31 Jan 1973), 2.
42 Natalia Chikovsky, 'When Pop Is Like Pot', *The Age*, TV-Radio Guide (19-25 Feb 1971), 2.
43 'I'm Prude, Teetotaller, Says Cass', *The Age* (26 Feb 1971), 10; original text has misspelling 'Teetoller'.
44 '"Pot" Should Be Legal, Says Cass', *The Age* (22 Feb 1971), 5.
45 Wendy Arnott, 'Pop Scene Is Really Popping', *The Age* (2 Jan 1972), 6.
46 Mic Conway in *The Rock Scene 1974*, dir. Bert Deling and Gary Martyn, National Film and Sound Archive.
47 'Reviews', *Daily Planet* (15 Sep 1972), 20. Yes, the band is plainly fictitious, a joke on the part of *Daily Planet* staff. The joke is repeated here as an experiment to see (1) if anyone reads these endnotes, and (2) if any further Cranberry Junglepuss factoids emerge as a result of this paragraph.
48 Angry Anderson quoted in Karen Dewey, *Angry: Scarred for Life* (Chippendale: Ironbark, 1994), 70.
49 John Pinder in *The Rock Scene 1974*.
50 At this point working under her nickname and maiden name of Cleo Calvo.
51 Beth Stanbury, 'Superdisc for the Singing Nun!', *TV Week* (6 Apr 1974), 20.
52 'Dean Plans Rock Mass in Cathedral', *The Age* (11 Dec 1970), 2.
53 Ian McFarlane, *Encyclopedia of Australian Rock and Pop* (St Leonards: Allen and Unwin, 1999), 38.
54 Ken Quinnell, 'Stork and Other Birds', *Nation* (29 Apr 1972), 19.
55 Bryan Patterson, 'Rockers and Crooners, They Seek Superstar Billing', *The Age* (13 Jan 1973), 2.
56 Roger Davies, 'Superstar Taking Shape', *Planet* (27 Mar 1972), 3.
57 Greg Taylor, 'English Twistery', *RAM* #121 (16 Nov 1979), 20-23.
58 'Superstar Opening Blows Up. Sabotage or Rushed Job', *Planet* (17 May 1972), 5.
59 Conn, *2000 Weeks*, 30.
60 John Larkin, 'Just Living Here Brings Grist to the Miller', *The Age* (10 Feb 1970), 1.
61 Mitch, 'Sven-gali', *Go-Set* (20 Jul 1974), 14.
62 Neville, *Playpower*, 255.
63 Stuart Macintyre, 'Under the Dictatorship of the Wizard!', *Farrago* (11 Jun 1971), 9.
64 Conn, *2000 Weeks*, 27.
65 See 'To Pay or Not to Pay: Radio's Big Decision', *The Bulletin* (2 May 1970), 58-9.
66 'To Pay or Not to Pay', 59.
67 Ian Meldrum, 'Where Have All the Records Gone?', *Go-Set* (23 May 1970), 3.
68 'Radio Ban on Local Records', *Go-Set* (18 Apr 1970), 2.
69 Stephen Maclean, 'How High Can Russell Fly?', *Go-Set* (13 Jun 1970), 6.
70 McFarlane, *Encyclopedia of Australian Rock and Pop*, 422.
71 'Around the Traps', *ARS* (10 Mar 1977), 53.
72 'The Fable Stable', advert in *Go-Set* (30 May 1970), 5.
73 Tony Johnston, 'Silver Record for the Trump Card', *The [Melbourne] Herald* (15 Jun 1970), 2.
74 A misspelling of dulcimer?
75 'Yet More Folkies Turn to Pop', *Go-Set* (30 May 1970), 21; Ed Nimmervoll, 'Carrl and Janie Myriad: Will They Ever Get a Chance?', *Go-Set* (13 Jun 1970), 'Core' section.

76 Mitch, 'Brian Cadd Did It for Alvin Purple', *Go-Set* (19 Jan 1974), 5.
77 Wendy Arnott, 'Pop Scene Is Really Popping', 6.
78 McGrath, *Australian Encyclopaedia of Rock and Pop*, 56.
79 Craig Mathieson, *Hi Fi Days: The Future of Australian Rock* (St Leonards: Allen and Unwin, 1996), 87.
80 Stuart Coupe, *Gudinski: The Godfather of Australian Rock 'n' Roll* (Sydney: Hachette Australia, 2015), 29.
81 Christie Eliezer, 'Gudinski: Mr. Mushroom', *ARS* #187 (22 May 1975), 50-53.
82 Eliezer, *High Voltage Rock 'n' Roll*, 19.
83 Keays, *His Master's Voice*, 202.
84 Eliezer *High Voltage Rock 'n' Roll*, 20.
85 Conn, *2000 Weeks*, 32.
86 Michael Browning quoted in Ian 'Molly' Meldrum with Jeff Jenkins, *The Never, Um, Ever Ending Story* (Crows Nest: Allen and Unwin, 2014), 283.
87 Coupe *Gudinski*, 18.
88 See for instance *Daily Planet* (5 Nov 1971), 19.
89 Ken Quinnell, 'John Paul Young: Today's Reluctant Hero' *ARS* (4 Nov 1976), 45-6.
90 Jonathan Green, 'Portrait of the Festival', 7.
91 Coupe, *Gudinski*, 26
92 'The Bright Lights Revealed', *Farrago Free Press*, supplement to *Farrago* (5 Oct 1973), 4.
93 Michael Morris, 'The Truth about the Daylights', *Farrago* (12 Jul 1974), 20.
94 Lee Dillow, 'Phillip Fraser: The Invisible Man', *Planet* (23 Feb 1972), 8-9.
95 Rob Pascoe, 'Where Do We Go from Here? Alternative Alternatives', *Farrago Free Press*, supplement to *Farrago* (5 Oct 1973), 4
96 'Announcing! A marriage ... Revolution-Rolling Stone', advert in *Go-Set* (13 Jun 1970), 18.
97 Stephen Charlesworth, Peter Poynton, and Paul Du Ve, 'Out in the Suburbs with Gra-Gra, Mick and the Boys', *Farrago* (8 Aug 1975), 17.
98 Pascoe, 'Where We Do Go', 4.
99 'Garbed Lawyers and Naked Women: *Thorunka* and the Clash of Sub Cultures', *Nation* (4 Mar 1972), 12-13.
100 Wendy Bacon, 'Silverwater Days', *Nation* (20 Mar 1972), 9.
101 Steedman interviewed by author.
102 This didn't stop Charles Buckmaster from slandering Steedman and his *Broadside*: 'worth noting: broadside (and probably pete steedman also) is a capitalist plot!! dont buy it', in *The Great Auk* (6 Apr 1969), 1.
103 Steedman interviewed by author.
104 Patrick Flanagan, 'Liberating the Elite', *Nation* (6 Feb 1971), 21.
105 Germaine Greer, *The Female Eunuch* (London: MacGibbon & Kee, 1970).
106 Greer, *The Female Eunuch*, 272.
107 Bob Ellis, 'In a Cultural Sewer', *Nation* (1 Apr 1972), 19.
108 Anon, 'Popping Up', *The Bulletin* (27 Jan 1968), 4.
109 See E. G. Whitlam, 'The Relevance of the Whitlam Government Today' in Jenny Hocking and Colleen Lewis, *It's Time Again* (Melbourne: Circa, 2003), 11.
110 Tudor quoted in Ken Quinnell, 'The Music Industry Inquiry: Iac Asks: But Is It Really Necessary' *ARS* #215 (17 Jun 1975), 52.
111 Bob Ellis, 'At the Chunder Party', *Nation* (20 Feb 1971), 22.
112 A. W. Sheppard (letter), *Nation* (6 Mar 1971),16.
113 'The New Seekers', *Go-Set* (21 Mar 1970), 11.
114 Still referred to as such today: see <http://www.lynpaulwebsite.org/NS-Potger.htm>, accessed 8 Jul 2012.
115 'The Carnival May Not Be Over', *Go-Set* (16 Feb 1974), 14.
116 <http://www.milesago.com/Artists/seekers2.htm>, accessed 28 Dec 2006.
117 One worked in theatre and felt compelled to use her maiden name to avoid the confusion; she is now a museum director. The other appeared regularly on *Uptight* and *Happening '70*, apparently as a dancer.
118 David Day and Tim Parker, *SA Great*, 189.
119 Editors of Rolling Stone, *The Big Australian Rock Book* (Neutral Bay: Megabooks, 1985).
120 Doubters please see Dave Jones's film *Yakety Yak* (1974).
121 Kruger, *Songwriters Speak*, 43, 52.
122 One of their set pieces was a version of 'Surfin' USA', which they rendered as 'Serving USA' to parody Prime Minister Malcolm Fraser's kowtowing to the US.

123 Pete Farndon quoted in Kurt Loder, 'Pretenders: The leather love songs of all-American Chrissie Hynde and her hot British band' *ARS* 29 May 1980 12-16.
124 Ian Meldrum, 'Wave Your Flags ... Captain Australia and the Honky Tonk Have Arrived', *Go-Set* (16 May 1970), 7.
125 Mic Conway interviewed by John Broughton <http://www.milesago.com/interviews/conway-iview.htm>, accessed 7 Jun 2005.
126 Mic Conway in *The Rock Scene 1974*.
127 This is included on the DVD *Peter Weir Short Film Collection* (Umbrella, 2004), the packaging of which identifies it as *Three Directions in Pop Music*. The title as it appears within the film itself is *3 Directions in Australian Pop Music*.
128 *Stork*, dir. Tim Burstall (1971).
129 Not that they couldn't be both – but they're not. Incidentally, in the film's credits as given on the 2003 DVD the band is incorrectly credited as 'The Captain Matchbox Whoopy Band'.
130 Alastair Knox, *We Are What We Stand On: A Personal History of the Eltham Community* (North Blackburn: Adobe Press, 1980), 71.
131 'Matching Up to Whoopee', *Juke* (14 May 1975), 2.
132 Charlesworth et al., 'Out in the Suburbs with Gra-Gra, Mick and the Boys', 16-17. Mic Conway – the 'Mic' ostensibly short for 'microphone' – is referred to as 'Mick' throughout.
133 Charlesworth et al, 'Out in the Suburbs', 17. Worrall actually refers to Conway as 'Michael' (rather than Mic or Mick) in this section.
134 Advert in *Planet* (9 Mar 1972), 20.
135 Alistair Jones, 'Captain Matchbox Whoopee Band: Hock Is Still a Dirty Word', *Planet* (9 Feb 1972), 2, 5.
136 See Philip Heyward, *Music at the Borders: Not Drowning, Waving and Their Engagement with Papua New Guinean Culture 1986-96* (Sydney: John Libbey, 1998), 73.
137 'Saddington Returns', *Planet* (17 May 1972), 2.
138 Bryan Patterson, 'Jeannie Lewis Comes Home', *The Age* (6 Jul 1972), 17.
139 David N. Pepperell, 'Much More Ballroom – You Me and Who?', *Planet* (10 May 1972), accessed at <http://milesago.com/Features/muchmoreballroom.htm>.
140 Greg Macainsh famously made a short film about sharpies in 1974 when he was a student at Swinburne Film and Television School.
141 'Charts', *Juke* (14 May 1975), 11.
142 The band was actually called the *Coloured Balls*; however *The Age*'s style was (and is) the more rational 'American' spelling of such words.
143 Arnott, 'Pop Scene Is Really Popping', 6.
144 'Mr. Cool's Scratch Pad', *Spunky* no. 2 (1976), 11.
145 Dean Moriarty, 'It Flew Away', *Planet* (19 Jan 1972), 4.
146 Margaret Macintyre, 'No Stone Unturned: the Ayers Rock Dossier', *ARS* #190 (3 Jul 1975), 41; Coupe, *Gudinski*, 40.
147 Margo Huxley, 'McKenzie Theory: Music for Everyone', *Daily Planet* (25 Dec 1971), 5.
148 Huxley, 'McKenzie Theory', 5.
149 Rob McKenzie quoted in Jenny Brown, 'McKenzie Theory: Close Your Eyes and I'll Bend You', *Planet* (10 May 1972), 11.
150 'McKenzie Theory: Guaranteed to Be 1972's Top Band', *Go-Set* (Jan[?] 1972), 7.
151 McKenzie quoted in Brown, 'McKenzie Theory', 11.
152 Eliezer, *High Voltage Rock 'n' Roll*, 22.
153 Gudinski quoted in Eliezer, *High Voltage Rock 'n' Roll*, 24.
154 'The Millionth Mushroom', *Juke* (11 Aug 1989), 13.
155 See Ed Nimmervoll, *Under the Covers: The Music Graphics of Ian McCausland, Graeme Webber and Steve Malpass* (Melbourne: Electronic Pictures, 1998), 24.
156 'MacKenzie Theory', *Semper*, cutting from scrapbook in possession of Cleis Pearce.
157 Richard Lee, 'McKenzie Theory's out of the Blue', *Farrago* (20 Jul 1973), 11.
158 Lee, 'McKenzie Theory's out of the Blue'.
159 Kevin Johnson quoted in Terry Durack, 'Kevin Johnson covers up', *ARS* #188 (5 Jun 1975), 44-45.
160 Clinton Walker, 'Crossing the Boundaries of Jazz with Women and Children First', *ARS* #386 (1985), 21.
161 Peter Lillie, 'Monarto' in *Monarto and My Brilliant Career in the Music Industry* (Elwood: Poetry and Western, 1999), 6-7.
162 Joe Camilleri in Milsom and Thomas, *Pay to Play*, 130.
163 Peter Lillie and Cosmo Topper, *Gone to See a Man about a Dog*, manuscript held in Fryer Library, University of Queensland, 3.
164 'Around the Traps', *ARS* (2 Dec 1976), 46.

165 'Kicks and Kisses', *TV Week* (28 Apr 1960), 21.
166 Mark Evans *Dirty Deeds: My Life inside and outside of AC/DC* (Crows Nest: Allen and Unwin, 2011), 212.
167 Joe Camilleri in Milsom and Thomas, *Pay to Play*, 131.
168 Camilleri in Milsom and Thomas, *Pay to Play*, 131.
169 'Around the traps', *ARS* #220 (26 Aug 1976), 46.
170 Ross Wilson quoted in *Daddy Cool*, dir. Bob Weis (1972), included on *The Complete Daddy Cool* (Aztec Music, 2005), DVD.
171 Rock Granite and the Profiles segment in *Daddy Cool* (1972).
172 Jenny Brown, 'Rock Granite and the Profiles', *ARS* #169 (12 Sep 1974), 13.
173 'The Making of Bob Weis' Daddy Cool', included on *The Complete Daddy Cool* (Aztec International, 2005), DVD.
174 Brown, 'Rock Granite and the Profiles', 13.
175 'Random notes', *ARS* #215 (19 Jun 1975), 54.
176 Quoted in Stephen MacLean and Peter Xeni, 'Rock Granite Hang up Their Rock 'n Roll Shoes', *Juke* (25 Jun 1975), 7.
177 Margo Huxley, 'Lipp and the Double Decker Bros', *Daily Planet* (28 Dec 1971), 7.
178 'Anna Keys', 'They Called It Carlton', *RAM* (11 Jan 1980), 35.
179 Jenny Brown 'Lambs and jams, Three Pound Hams Watch Your Step ... ?', *Planet* (26 Jan 1972), 7.
180 Colin Talbot, 'Split Lipp', *Go-Set* (19 Feb 1972), 18.
181 Keays, *His Master's Voice*, 190.
182 Non-Australian readers who recall the *Neighbours* characters Janelle and Kim Timmins might wonder about the connection between the sharpie movement and the otherwise relatively peaceful west Victorian town of Colac: for instance, the episode that aired in Australia on 15 Dec 2005, in which the pair indulged in what they called 'Sharpie dancing' and claimed to have been the sole 'sharps' in Colac. This is all whimsy on the part of the *Neighbours* storyliners. Nell Feeney, who played Janelle, had a role in Vincent Giarrusso's marvellous film *Mallboy*, in which she played a former sharpie: presumably the fondness of her *Neighbours* character for this scene was inspired by her earlier role. In *Mallboy* she dances to 'Can the Can'.
183 Glenn Wheatley, 'Stateside '70 tour Rocks On', *Go-Set* (7 Mar 1970), 14.
184 Keays, *His Master's Voice*, 194.
185 Adrian Barker, 'Masters Rock-On!' [interview with Glenn Wheatley], *Daily Planet* (17 Nov 1971), 23.
186 'Masters Write', *Planet* (26 Jan 1972), 2.
187 Barker, 'Masters Rock-On!', 23.
188 Adrian Barker, 'Jim Keays Now That It's Over', *Daily Planet* (1 Dec 1971), 7.
189 McFarlane, *Encyclopedia of Australian Rock and Pop*, 397.
190 McGrath, *Australian Encyclopaedia of Rock and Pop*, 191.
191 Brown, 'Lambs and Jams', 7.
192 Ed Nimmervoll, 'Gulliver is Slatzilvania', *Revolution* (Jan 1971), 21.
193 'Gully – Solo LP', *Planet* (26 Jan 1972), 2.
194 'Much More Ballroom February Concert Details', *Planet* (26 Jan 1972), 2.
195 'Co. Caine Give It Up', *Juke* (20 Aug 1975), 19.
196 Jim Sharman, *Blood and Tinsel* (Melbourne: Miegunyah Press, 2008), 141.
197 Sharman, *Blood and Tinsel*, 134.
198 Sharman, *Blood and Tinsel*, 136.
199 Richard Lockwood quoted in David Nichols, 'I Had Found Beauty', *Mess + Noise* (Jan 2013), <http://www.messandnoise.com/articles/4549511>.
200 Ian Rilen quoted in Frank Brunetti, 'Ian Rilen: Sardine V', *Vox Muzpaper* (Nov 1981), 8-9. Brunetti misspells Kain as Caine, perhaps because Kain went on to be a member of Company Caine.
201 Brunetti, 'Ian Rilen', 8-9.
202 'A. O'G', 'Just in Case You're Wondering about Buffalo', *RAM* (17 May 1975), 18-19.
203 Thorpe quoted in Wendy Saddington, 'Wendy Saddington Makes a Plea for More Free Blues Concerts: Listen to the Bands', *Go-Set* (3 Jan 1970), 8.
204 'Australian Notes', *ARS* #157 (28 Mar 1974), 18.
205 'Aztecs Record', *Planet* (26 Jan 1972), 2.
206 Rudd interviewed in 'The Making of ...', included on *The Complete Daddy Cool*, DVD.
207 Conn interviewed in *2000 Weeks*, p. 31. The track did however appear on an LP that year – *Go-Set Pop Poll 71*, along with Chain, the Masters Apprentices and Zoot. As Conn points out this represents something of 'a resurgence in pop music' (27).

208 Rob Smyth, 'A Prodigal Son Returns to His Vegetal Mother', *Revolution* (1 Jul 1970), 19.
209 'In fact', says the ever-helpful Noel McGrath (*Australian Encyclopaedia of Rock and Pop*, 213), 'Murtceps is Spectrum spelt backwards'.
210 Rudd interviewed in 'The Making of . . .', included on *The Complete Daddy Cool*, DVD.
211 'Inedible Crumpets at Sebastian's', *Planet* (17 May 1972), 2.
212 'Spectrum', *Farrago* (6 Apr 1973), 2.
213 Richard Lee, review of Ariel's *A Strange Fantastic Dream*, *Farrago* (5 Apr 1974), 15.
214 Mike Rudd, sleevenotes to Ariel, *The Jellabad Mutant* (Rare Vision, 2002).
215 Rudd quoted in Helen Barrett, 'It's Not What You Hear but What You Think', *Go-Set* (2 Feb 1974), 11.
216 Mike Rudd, quoted in Paul Culnane, 'We're Here Because We're Here, of Course', *Foffle* no. 19, 62.
217 Rudd in Culnane, 'We're Here', 63.
218 Conn, *2000 Weeks*, 32.
219 This may seem unnecessarily harsh, but it is not intended as a criticism of the musicians themselves, rather of the industry they work in.
220 Greg Quill, 'Executives Become Inner Sense', *Go-Set* (21 Feb 1970), 14.
221 Gil Wahlquist, 'Blown up by Music', *Sun-Herald* (4 Feb 1973), 86.
222 Advertisement in *Campaign* no. 8 (Apr 1975), 43.
223 Keays, *His Master's Voice*, 171.
224 Dave Dawson, 'Max Merritt', *Beat* (24 Aug 2004), 56.
225 George Young quoted in Kruger, *Songwriters Speak*, 73.
226 McGrath (*Australian Encyclopaedia of Rock and Pop*, 210) suggests that this album was recorded for and released solely in the USA. I have an Australian-released copy which puts the lie to at least part of this assertion. In addition, it is suggested here (and elsewhere) that Mulry also issued a British single, a frankly throwaway Vanda/Young composition called 'Ain't It Nice', under the wretched rock name of Steve Ryder.
227 Adrian Ryan, 'The Rise and Fall of Sherbet', *Roadrunner* (9 Oct 1981), 31.
228 Greg Quill, 'Ted Mulry Zooms into the National Charts', *Go-Set* (18 Apr 1970), 10.
229 'Mulry Talking', *Spunky* no. 2 (1976), 18-20.
230 McGrath, *Australian Encyclopaedia of Rock and Pop*, 211.
231 'Mulry Talking', 20.
232 <http://www.limboclub.com/forum/archive/index.php/t-78512.html>, accessed 2 Jan 2012.
233 Appallingly, perhaps – it certainly doesn't do Mulry's legacy much of a service, though it might help his estate – American television star David Hasselhoff recorded a cover of 'Jump in My Car', produced by Harry Vanda, in 2005. See John Mangan and Suzanne Carbone, 'The Age Diary', *The Age* (26 Dec 2005), 24.
234 'Mulry Talking', 19.
235 'Mulry Talking', 20.
236 'Ex-Easybeats Make Another Smash – This Time with Bowie', *Go-Set* (26 Jan 1974), 15.
237 Young quoted in Glenn Baker, '13 Years of Rock and Roll: George Young Remembers the Easybeats', *ARS* (15 Jul 1976), 40-44.
238 Clinton Walker, *Highway to Hell: The Life and Times of AC/DC Legend Bon Scott* (Portland: Verse Chorus Press, 2001), 117.
239 'Ex-Easybeats Make Another Smash', 15.
240 Paul Comrie Thomson, 'From Easybeats to AC/DC: Does the Tour Go On Forever?', *ARS* (18 Dec 1976), 50.
241 'Mr. Cool's Scratch Pad', *Spunky* no. 4 (1976), 11.
242 Andy Bradley, 'A Conversation with Vanda Young [sic]', *Juke* (30 Jul 1977), 7.
243 Stephen Phillips, 'John Paul Young Enters His Third Life', *Juke* (14 Apr 1984), 7.
244 John Paul Young quoted in Helen Barrett, 'John Paul Young', *Juke* (28 May 1975), 10.
245 Christie Eliezer, 'De Gruchy Dies', *Juke* (1 Jun 1985), 3.
246 Bob Granger, 'William Shakespeare', *RAM* no. 11 (26 Jul 1975), 13.
247 John Cabe quoted in Granger 'William Shakespeare', 13.
248 It appears on *Party Mix: Classic Australian Pop Clips and Countdown Performances from the 70s and 80s* (ABC, ca. 2003), DVD.
249 William Shakespeare interviewed by Steve Maclean on *GTK*, 1 Jan 1975.
250 <www.smh.com.au/entertainment/music/shakespearean-tragedy-bright-star-of-pop-cut-short-by-scandal-and-alcohol-20101007-169w2.html>, accessed 2 Jan 2012.
251 'Ex-Easybeats', 15.
252 Bradley, 'Conversation with Vanda Young', 7.
253 Toby Creswell, 'Stevie Wright: Facing the Music Again', *ARS* (9 Dec 1982), 26.
254 Creswell, 'Stevie Wright', 26.
255 Shane Nichols, 'Cheetah: Not Standing Too Close', *ARS* (8 Jan 1981), 13.
256 'Another great Australian record' *Planet* 23 Feb 1972, 2.
257 Untitled interview with Gerry Humphries, *Planet* (1 Mar 1972), 12-14. Interview subsequently revealed to have been written by Alistair Jones; see *Planet* (9 Mar 1972), 3.
258 *Gerry Humphrys The Loved One*, dir. Nigel Buesst.
259 McFarlane, *Encyclopedia of Australian Rock and Pop*, 246.
260 Mike Edwards interviewed in *Gerry Humphrys The Loved One*.
261 Peter Walsh, 'Gerry Humphries', *Daily Planet* (13 Oct 1971), 3.
262 Walsh, 'Gerry Humphries', 3.
263 Gerry Humphries, 'Gerry's Rave: Adelaide: the City of What?', *Planet* (17 May 1972), 8.
264 Jean Gollan, 'A Few Words from the Valentines', *Revolution* (1 Jun 1970), 13.
265 Clinton Walker, *Highway to Hell*, 79.
266 Day and Parker, *SA Great*, 126.
267 Walker *Highway to Hell*, 87.
268 Day and Parker, *SA Great*, 178.
269 Day and Parker, *SA Great*, 179. Tarkus had the bad taste to name themselves after an Emerson Lake and Palmer album, but at least it was a *great* Emerson Lake and Palmer album.
270 Anthony O'Grady, *Cold Chisel – The Pure Stuff* (Crows Nest: Allen and Unwin, 2001), 2.
271 Day and Parker, *SA Great*, 179.
272 O'Grady, *Cold Chisel*, 3.
273 Don Walker quoted in O'Grady, *Cold Chisel*, 2.
274 Quoted in Ed St John, 'Mental as Anything': 'This Chair is Eating My Trousers', in Clinton Walker (Ed.), *The Next Thing* (Kenthurst: Kangaroo Press, 1984), 73-80; see 75. The sentence preceding this quote is: 'I first saw Rob Younger about thirteen years ago, and he looked pretty well the same as he does now.'
275 Vivien Johnson, *Radio Birdman* (St Kilda: Sheldon Booth, 1990), 2.
276 Grossman quoted in Chrissy Amphlett with Larry Writer, *Pleasure and Pain: My Life* (Sydney: Hachette Australia, 2005), 89.
277 Wendy Saddington, 'Johnny for Uptight Chair?', *Go-Set* (10 Jan 1970), 3.
278 *Uptight* for Saturday Jan 10, 1970 ran from 8:00 am to noon on ATV-0 and was listed as a 'locally produced teenage musical programme, compered by Ross D. Wyllie, with Jon Blanchfield, Tony Healy, Leon Kamer, David Bland, Cecil Sterk, Trevor Spry, Megan Hicks and guests Johnny Chester, Aesops Fables, The Mixtures.' Viewers could then switch to the apparently much more adult *Everybody's In* on HSV-7 from noon to 1 pm, a 'Brisbane produced teenage music program, compered by Greg Jeffrey, with guests Marty Rhone, The Iguana, the Beaumen, Wendy Saddington, the Sect, the Groop, Jeff St. John and the Copperwine. Songs inc. Goin' Out of My Head, Just for Tonight, Good Morning Starshine, Such a Lovely Way.' This show was off-air by mid January. At 6:30 each Saturday night GTV-9 presented *The Best of Bandstand*, which it listed as a 'repeat of musical series hosted by Brian Henderson with guests: Anne and Johnny Hawkere, Kamahl, Ross D. Wyllie, Magaret Keller, Hans Poulsen, Cheryl Assang, For Kinsmen, Princetons'. *The Age TV-Radio Guide* (8 Jan 1970), 6.
279 J. Fangio, 'Bandstand – A Question of Validity', *Planet* (27 Mar 1972), 8.
280 3AK advertisement in *Daily Planet* (Aug 13 1971), 24.
281 Wendy Saddington, 'Wendy: a New Column in Core Each Week', *Go-Set* (4 Feb 1970), 'Core' section.
282 Ian Meldrum, 'Here Comes the Star', *Go-Set* (13 Sep 1969), 2.
283 McFarlane, personal communication, Jan 2015.
284 Jean Gollan, 'The Amazing Johnny Young', *Go-Set* (21 Mar 1970), 2.
285 Wendy Milsom, 'Boom's Natural Death', *The Age* (1 Jan 1971), 6.
286 'Mess Media', *Daily Planet* (13 Aug 1971), 4.
287 Bob Hill, 'Chain Record', *Planet* (19 Jan 1972), 4.

288 Lee Dillow, 'Billy Thorpe: Changes Part 2', *Daily Planet* (3 Sep 1971), 6-7.
289 *The Age TV-Radio Guide* (7-13 Jul 1972), 7.
290 'Metamorphosis of a Star ... Meet the New Colleen Hewett', *Go-Set* (26 Jan 1974), 7.
291 'Enough's Enough Johnny' [letter], *Go-Set* (26 Jan 1974), 23.
292 Colin Talbot, 'GTK: Hassling for More Time', *Go-Set* (19 Feb 1972), 17.
293 Jim Keays, *His Master's Voice*, 195.
294 Rory O'Donoghue and Graeme Bond, interview extras on *Love Is in the Air* (ABC), DVD.
295 See Sally Stockbridge, 'Rock 'n' Roll Television', in Albert Moran (Ed.), *Stay Tuned: An Australian Broadcasting Reader* (North Sydney: Allen and Unwin, 1992), 136. A different version of this article appears in Philip Hayward, *From Pop to Punk to Postmodernism* (North Sydney: Allen and Unwin, 1992). Stockbridge erroneously claims in the Moran volume that *Flashez* began in 1976; it was 1975.
296 'Flashez of Burgess', *Spunky* no. 5 (1976), 18-20.
297 'Shake, Rattle and Foxtrot', *TV Times* (11 Jan 1975), 8.
298 'Rock Is Back – Despite Knocks', *TV Times* (8 Feb 1975), 6.
299 Milsom, 'Boom's Natural Death', 6.
300 John Larkin, 'Huggy Bear Doug Has Re-grouped', *The Age* (12 Jan 1971), 2.
301 McFarlane, *Encyclopedia of Australian Rock and Pop*, 210.
302 Lee Dillow, 'Parko: the Large One', *Daily Planet* (22 Sep 1971), 7.
303 Lee Dillow, 'Vince Melouney At Last!', *Daily Planet* (20 Oct 1971), 17.
304 Mitch, 'The Grass is Green-er on the Other Side', *Go-Set* (20 Jul 1974), 7.
305 Adrian Rawlins, 'Oz's Bob Dylan' [letter], *Nation Review* (4-10 May 1973), 875.
306 'Around the Traps', *ARS* # 220 (26 Aug 1976), 46.
307 Jon Farris, 'Dingoes in Excess' [letter] *ARS* #477 (Dec 1992), 6.
308 'Random Notes', *ARS* #181 (27 Feb 1975), 43.
309 'Metamorphosis of a star', 7.
310 'I love the Music', *Spunky* no. 1 (1976), 18-20.
311 Al Webb, 'Lost Somewhere Beyond an Image', *Juke* (28 May 1975), 8.
312 Kevin Johnson quoted in Terry Durack, 'Kevin Johnson Covers up', *ARS* #188 (5 Jun 1975), 44-45.
313 Rick Springfield interviewed by Garry Hyde on GTK, YouTube clip accessed 22 Jun 08.
314 Springfield interviewed by Hyde.
315 Springfield interviewed by Hyde.
316 Derek Pellicci quoted in Bruce Elder, 'Little River Band', in *The Big Australian Rock Book*, (Neutral Bay: Megabooks, 1985), 96-97.
317 Wheatley, interviewed in *History and Styles of Rock Music in Australia* (videocassette).
318 A review of the first LRB album in *Campaign* states: 'The Little River Band used to be called "Mississippi"'; Peter French, 'Records', *Campaign* no. 4 (Dec 1975), 21. This suggests that the continuation of the name was part of the publicity for the band at the time. French's review also confusingly recommends the album thus: 'If you love heavy rock you'll really dig their sound'.
319 Drummond was a band name to which a number of recordings commissioned by Fable label owner Ron Tudor were credited, so while Allison Gros were the Drummond who recorded 'Daddy Cool', Drummond were not always Allison Gros. See Paul McHenry, 'Recording Oddity: Lost Bulldog Track?', *The Australian Music Museum* no. 21 (Dec 2000), 9.
320 No. 5 in August 1972, but with a much longer life than many of its contemporaries.
321 By 'drama' I mean tempo changes and rousing, rather than merely harmonious choruses – that is, both 'Kings of the World' and the Allison Gros song 'If I Ask You' (which was compiled on a Fable album with the cool title *Collectors' Item*).
322 In the mid 70s Fable issued an album credited to Shorrock, Birtles and Goble under the title *Beginnings*, with the sub-title 'Before: Little River Band'. Comprising Axiom and Mississippi recordings from the two bands' albums, it is remarkably cohesive, though all the Axiom material was composed by Cadd and Mudie.
323 This story is recounted in the short film *The Never Ending Apprenticeship*, dir. John Dick (Pepper Audio Visual, 1979). Kruger (*Songwriters Speak*, 210) suggests the incident happened in June 1972, but since Mississippi had another hit in September 1973, that does not seem plausible.
324 Bruce Elder, 'Little River Band', in *The Big Australian Rock Book*, 96-97.
325 'A web-interview with Mr. Pellicci' (31 May 1997), <http://www.lrb.net/pellicci/>, accessed 25 Feb 2015.
326 Goble quoted in Elder, 'Little River Band', *The Big Australian Rock Book*, 96-97.
327 Hunter quoted in Christie Eliezer, 'Riots, Rednecks and Rave Reviews', *Juke* (27 Jan 1979), 9.
328 Quoted in 'Scandal! Shock! Horror! Dave Warner Attacks Sacred Cows!', *Juke* (22 Jul 1978), 15.
329 Beeb Birtles interviewed by David Kilbey on ABC Canberra (17 Oct 1999). Transcript from Milesago website, accessed 9 Jun 2005. 'Witchery' reached no. 39 in August 1977.
330 Denise A. Austin with George McArdle, *The Man from Little River: The Story of George McArdle, Former Bass Player for the Little River Band* (North Sydney: Ark House, 2009), 74.
331 Austin/McArdle, *The Man from Little River*, 85.
332 Austin/McArdle, *The Man from Little River*, 89.
333 'It's a Long Way to the Top' entered the charts in January and reached no. 17. 'It's a Long Way There' reached no. 33 in December.
334 Beeb Birtles, interviewed by David Kilbey.

Chapter 9:

1 David Pepperell, 'Dr. Pepper's Hot Sauce', *Juke* (21 May 1975), 17.
2 Rob Smyth, 'A Prodigal Son Returns to His Vegetal Mother', *Revolution* (1 Jul 1970), 19.
3 Leadbelly had two songs with these words in the title, neither of which sounds remotely like Wilson's 'Eagle Rock'.
4 Pat Wilson interviewed in *The Story of Daddy Cool*, dir. Ron V. Brown, included on *The Complete Daddy Cool*, DVD.
5 David N. Pepperell, 'A Creative Musician's Dilemma' [interview with Jerry Noone], *Planet* (17 May 1972), 6-7.
6 Pepperell, 'A Creative Musician's Dilemma', 6-7.
7 Gary Young interviewed in *The Story of Daddy Cool*.
8 'Adrian', 'Someone Different ... Issy Di: "I Haven't Got Any Musical Convictions"', *Daily Planet* (22 Dec 1971), 15.
9 Young interviewed in *The Story of Daddy Cool*.
10 Ross Wilson, 'Rice Revival: Is Rice Coming Back?', *Revolution* (Jun 1971), 9.
11 Ross Wilson interviewed in *The Story of Daddy Cool*.
12 Conn, *2000 Weeks*, 31.
13 *Daddy Cool*, dir. Bob Weis (1972), included on *The Complete Daddy Cool*, DVD.
14 In Bob Weis's *Daddy Cool* film, for instance, Wilson satirically implores the audience: 'Don't pick on any teenagers'.
15 Greg Macainsh, 'The Fender L', *Meanjin* 65:3 (2006), 183.
16 *Daddy Cool*, dir. Bob Weis.
17 'The Making of Bob Weis' Daddy Cool'.
18 Ross Wilson quoted in Adrian Ryan, 'The Sons of the Father', *Roadrunner* (7 Aug 1981), 11.
19 Brian Wise, 'The Return of the Cool', *Rhythms* (Sep 2006), 39.
20 Young interviewed in *The Story of Daddy Cool*. Here the time taken to record this first album is stated as being between 12 and 60 hours.
21 Greg Macainsh interviewed in *The Story of Daddy Cool*.
22 McIntyre, *Tomorrow Is Today*, 29.
23 'Two's Company: Pat and Ross Wilson', *Smash Hits Yearbook* (1985), 6.
24 Jules Lewicki, 'Rock and Roll', *Farrago* (22 Jul 1971), 11.
25 Alastair Jones, 'Daddy Cool in America: But it Ain't Been Easy', *Planet* (17 May 1972), 11-13.
26 Wise, 'The Return of the Cool', 39.
27 Pepperell, 'A Creative Musician's Dilemma', 6-7.
28 McFarlane, *Encyclopedia of Australian Rock and Pop*, 154.
29 'Mighty Kong split', *Go-Set* (26 Jan 1974), 4.
30 '"Hanna, Can I Join the Band?"', *Juke* (14 May 1975), 8.
31 '"Hanna, Can I Join the Band?"', 8.
32 Toby Creswell, 'Gary Young and the Five Minute Song', *ARS* #356, 19, 21.
33 Ross Hannaford interviewed in *The Story of Daddy Cool*.
34 Ross Wilson quoted in Kruger, *Songwriters Speak*, 135.
35 Jeff Jenkins, *Ego Is Not a Dirty Word: The Skyhooks Story* (Clifton Hill: Kelly & Withers, 1994), 24.

NOTES

36 Some vinyl copies of *Living in the 70's* (mine, for example) are a 1983 pressing which adds 1983 live versions of 'Saturday Night' and 'Why Don't You All Get'.
37 As can be seen on *The Complete Daddy Cool* DVD.
38 Greg Macainsh interviewed by Michael Butler, <http://www.americanheartbreak.com/rnrgeekwp/rock-and-roll-geek-show-226-skyhooks-interview/>, accessed 8 Jul 2012.
39 John Sangster, *Seeing the Rafters*, 37.
40 Tim Burstall cited in Alastair Knox, *We Are What We Stand On: A Personal History of the Eltham Community* (North Blackburn: Adobe Press, 1980) 76.
41 Knox, *We Are What We Stand On*, ix.
42 Maree Barkla, *Skyhooks: The Other Side* (Newstead: Maree Publications, 1990) 63.
43 Jenkins, *Ego Is Not a Dirty Word*, 7.
44 Jenkins, *Ego Is Not a Dirty Word*, 9.
45 Jenny Brown *Million Dollar Riff* (Collingwood: Dingo, 1975), 4-5.
46 Jenkins, *Ego Is Not a Dirty Word*, 11.
47 Jenkins, *Ego Is Not a Dirty Word*, 11.
48 Macainsh, 'The Fender L', *Meanjin* 65:3 (2006), 180.
49 'Research Supershow', *Daily Planet* (15 Sep 1971), 2.
50 Brown *Million Dollar Riff*, 10.
51 Jenkins, *Ego Is Not a Dirty Word*, 14; Brown, *Million Dollar Riff*, 9.
52 Greg Macainsh, 'The Fender L', 181.
53 Jenkins, *Ego Is Not a Dirty Word* 14.
54 Jenkins, *Ego Is Not a Dirty Word* 15.
55 Strachan quoted in Brown, *Million Dollar Riff*, 11.
56 Macainsh, 'The Fender L', 181.
57 James McCaughey, 'Drama – from Carlton to the Desert', *Farrago* (27 Jul 1973), 13.
58 'Steve Hill: Keyhole to Skyhooks Past', *Juke* (21 May 1975), 9.
59 'Steve Hill', 9; see also Jenkins, *Ego Is Not a Dirty Word*, 23.
60 For instance, Jenkins suggests that Macainsh was *inspired* by Gary Glitter (*Ego Is Not a Dirty Word*, 23). Glitter's first Australian hit, 'Rock and Roll, Part 1', entered the charts in August 1972.
61 Barkla, *Skyhooks*, 12.
62 Jenkins, *Ego Is Not a Dirty Word*, 22.
63 Canberra Film Centre, *Bulletin* (Dec 1959), 1.
64 Jenkins, *Ego Is Not a Dirty Word* 23.
65 Ross Wilson quoted in Brown, *Million Dollar Riff*, 17.
66 A group featuring Joe Camilleri, who had also been a member of Lipp and the Double Decker Brothers and was shortly to form Jo Jo Zep and the Falcons. McFarlane, *Encyclopedia of Australian Rock and Pop*, 328.
67 Jenkins, *Ego Is Not a Dirty Word*, 33.
68 Ingliss, Hannaford, Strauks and Duncan – a pleasing amalgam of Daddy Cool and Skyhooks members – all feature on Paul Madigan's 1979 album *Paul Madigan and the Humans*.
69 Jenkins, *Ego Is Not a Dirty Word*, 19.
70 Red Symons, *Revenge* (Melbourne: Text, 2000), 292.
71 Ed Nimmervoll, 'Red', *Juke* (28 May 1975), 14.
72 Symons *Revenge*, 292.
73 Jenkins, *Ego Is Not a Dirty Word*, 18.
74 Red Symons, interview extras on *Love is in the Air* DVD.
75 Red Symons quoted in Nimmervoll, 'Red', 14.
76 Brown, *Million Dollar Riff*, 25.
77 Symons *Revenge* 292; Barkla, *Skyhooks*,17.
78 Brown, *Million Dollar Riff*, 26.
79 'Shirley: "The Bigger You Get, the Harder It Gets"', *Juke* (14 May 1975), 13.
80 'Shirley', 13.
81 '7. Uschi Flett', *Juke* (20 Aug 1975), 17.
82 Gudinski quoted in Brown, *Million Dollar Riff*, 22.
83 Ross Wilson quoted in Ryan, 'The Sons', 11.
84 *History and Styles of Rock Music in Australia* (videocassette).
85 Greg Neighbour, 'The 200 Greatest Australian Albums of All Time', *Foffle* no. 19 (2004), 41 This article may have been written by Ian D. Marks – it's hard to tell.
86 Terry Durack, '... Then There Was This Voice ...' *ARS* #184 (10 Apr 1975), 51.
87 Credited as 'Neils' on the 1984 reissue.
88 See Ed Nimmervoll, *Under the Covers: The Music Graphics of Ian McCausland, Graeme Webber and Steve Malpass* (Melbourne: Electronic Pictures, 1998), 2.
89 'Part Two of the Shirley Strachan Interview', *Juke* (17 Feb 1979), 10.
90 Warning: this footnote contains a spoiler. The 'horror movie' in question was television news.

91 Dave Warner, *Countdown: The Wonder Years 1974-87* (Sydney: ABC, 2006).
92 *History and Styles of Rock Music in Australia* (videocassette).
93 Strachan quoted in 'Shirley', 13.
94 *History and Styles of Rock Music in Australia* (videocassette).
95 Anon., 'Hey Shirl! Pass Me Panties, the Mayor's Comin' ...', *Campaign* no. 8 (Apr 1976), 23.
96 Adrian Ryan, 'The Rise and Fall of Sherbet', *Roadrunner* (9 Oct 1981), 31-2.
97 'Around the Traps' *ARS* (8 Apr 1976), 47.
98 Jenkins, *Ego Is Not a Dirty Word*, 96-7.
99 Symons *Revenge*, 293.
100 'Hey Shirl!', 23.
101 Quoted in Jenkins, *Ego Is Not a Dirty Word*, 97.
102 Jenkins, *Ego Is Not a Dirty Word*, 99.
103 Jenkins, *Ego Is Not a Dirty Word*, 115.
104 'Around the Traps', 47.
105 Jenny Brown 'Skyhooks Un-American Activities Part 1' *RAM* no. 32 (21 May 1976), 24.
106 Quoted in Jane Mathieson, 'Skyhooks in America; Red Symons in Focus', *ARS* (22 Apr 1976), 73
107 Quoted in Mathieson, 'Skyhooks in America', 73.
108 Jenkins, *Ego Is Not a Dirty Word*, 115.
109 'David Maclean's World of Pop', *Campaign* no. 14 (Oct/Nov 1976), 30.
110 McFarlane, *Encyclopedia of Australian Rock and Pop*, 580.
111 Symons *Revenge*, 293.
112 'Random Notes', *ARS* #215 (19 Jun 1975), 54.
113 Jenkins, *Ego Is Not a Dirty Word*, 125.
114 'The Hooks in Kiwiland', *Juke* (18 Feb 1978), 5.
115 McFarlane, *Encyclopedia of Australian Rock and Pop*, 581.
116 Red Symons, interview extras on *Love Is in the Air* DVD.
117 'Part Two of the Shirley Strachan Interview', 10.
118 'Part Two of the Shirley Strachan Interview', 10.
119 'Part Two of the Shirley Strachan Interview', 10.
120 Jenkins, *Ego Is Not a Dirty Word*, 135. It is not recorded what Garrett's response would have been, but it is unlikely to have been particularly positive, even though he is a Skyhooks fan.
121 If this was a serious consideration, Jane Clifton was surely the most likely candidate. Clifton was part of the Carlton 'scene', not least via Stiletto, who had split up in early 1979.
122 'Shirley Confirms – New Singer for Skyhooks', *RAM* no. 102 (9 Feb 1979), 3.
123 Jenkins, *Ego Is Not a Dirty Word*, 134.
124 Anthony O'Grady, 'The Mighty Hooks Rise Again', *RAM* no. 23 (Mar 1979), 13.
125 Mark Goulding and Peter Green, *Wings off Flies: 25 Years of Rock Photography* (Prahran: Rocket Pocket Books, 2002), 9.
126 Jenkins, *Ego Is Not a Dirty Word*, 140.
127 'The New 'Hook', *Juke* (3 Feb 1979), 3.
128 Christie Eliezer, 'Gearing Up for the Skyhooks' Next', *Juke* (9 Feb 1980), 3.
129 Jenkins, *Ego Is Not a Dirty Word*, 146; Andrea Jones, 'Skyhooks' Stormy R.I.P.' *ARS* #321, 21.
130 Greg Macainsh interviewed by Michael Butler, <http://www.americanheartbreak.com/rnrgeekwp/rock-and-roll-geek-show-226-skyhooks-interview/>, accessed 8 Jul 2012.
131 Jones, 'Skyhooks' Stormy R.I.P.', 21.
132 Young interviewed in *The Story of Daddy Cool*.
133 Jenkins, *Ego Is Not a Dirty Word*, 153.
134 Jenkins, *Ego Is Not a Dirty Word*, 160.
135 McFarlane, *Encyclopedia of Australian Rock and Pop*, 582.
136 *ARS* #660 (Jan 2007), 20.
137 Wise, 'The Return', 41.

Chapter 10: We Aren't Here to Confuse People

1 Brian Johnson quoted in Christie Eliezer, 'Blue Denim Hell', *Juke* (7 Nov 1992), 9.
2 Martin Huxley, *AC/DC: The World's Heaviest Rock* (London: Boxtree, 1996) 14.
3 Huxley, *AC/DC*, 32.
4 Huxley, *AC/DC*, 32.
5 Quoted in Simon Grose, 'AC/DC Farewell the Suburban Circuit: Next Stop London', *ARS* (8 Jun 1976), 42-43.
6 Richard Bunton, *AC/DC: 'Hell Ain't No Bad Place To Be!'* (London: Omnibus, 1994), 7.
7 Bunton, *AC/DC*, 7.
8 Brian Johnson quoted in Clinton Walker, 'Back with Attack', *ARS* #451 (1990), 33-34.
9 Malcolm Dome (Ed.), *AC/DC: The World's Most Electrifying Rock'n' Roll Band!*, (London, Virgin Books, 1995), 17.

10 Howard Johnson, *Get Your Jumbo Jet out of My Airport: Random Notes for AC/DC Obsessives* (Pewsey: Black Book Company, 1999), 18.
11 See Jon Savage, *Time Travel* (London: Vintage, 1996), 324.
12 Johnson, *Get Your Jumbo Jet*, 18.
13 Dome, *AC/DC*, 17.
14 Dave Evans interviewed in Johnson, *Get Your Jumbo Jet*, 18.
15 Johnson, *Get Your Jumbo Jet*, 18.
16 Angus Young quoted in Mark Putterford, *AC/DC: Shock to the System* (London: Omnibus, 1992), 13.
17 Grose, 'AC/DC Farewell', 42-43.
18 Angus Young quoted in Scott Howlett, 'No Celebrity Golf… for AC/DC', *X-Press* no. 65 (11 Dec 1987), 9.
19 Dave Evans interviewed in Johnson, *Get Your Jumbo Jet*, 21.
20 Dave Evans interviewed in Johnson, *Get Your Jumbo Jet*, 23.
21 Mark Evans *Dirty Deeds: My life inside and outside of AC/DC* (Crows Nest: Allen and Unwin, 2011), 65.
22 Angus Young interviewed in *Long Way to the Top* (ABC), DVD.
23 Huxley, *AC/DC*, 44.
24 Brian Johnstone, 'Fraternity', *Daily Planet* (13 Oct 1971), 16-17.
25 Johnstone, 'Fraternity', 16-17.
26 'Around the Traps', ARS (10 Mar 1977), 53.
27 Mark Evans *Dirty Deeds*, 96.
28 Tony Walker, 'Geordie Showed 'Em How It's Done', *Go-Set* (2 Mar 1974), 21.
29 'Geordie Bawdy and Geordie Brash, Geordie Music and Geordie Flash', *Go-Set* (9 Mar 1974), 6-7.
30 Murray Engleheart with Arnaud Durieux, *AC/DC: Maximum Rock & Roll* (Pymble: HarperCollins, 2006), 92.
31 Billy Altman, review of *High Voltage*, ARS (16 Dec 1976), 48.
32 Andy Bradley, 'A Conversation with Vanda and Young', *Juke* (30 Jul 1977), 7.
33 Quoted in Simon Grose, 'AC/DC Farewell', 42-3.
34 Geraldine Doogue, 'AC-DC Blow the British Fuses', *Spunky* no. 2 (1976), 2-4.
35 Michael Browning quoted in Doogue, 'AC-DC', 4.
36 Dome, *AC/DC*, 11.
37 Brian Johnson quoted in Walker, 'Back with Attack', 33.
38 Bob Hart, 'Jolly Good Show Lads', *Spunky* no. 9 (1976), 41.
39 Angus Young quoted in Bruce Elder, 'AC/DC: Angus Young Looks Forward', *ARS* #316 (1 May 1980), 21.
40 Angus Young quoted in Elder, 'AC/DC', 21.
41 Ed St John, 'The Triumphant Return of AC/DC', *ARS* #338, 22.

Chapter 11: Bending Corners

1 Richard Guilliatt in Anthony O'Grady et al., 'At last! The Last 1976 Show', *RAM* (11 Feb 1977), 16-17.
2 Vikki Riley, 'Death Rockers of the World Unite! Melbourne 1978-80 – Punk Rock or No Punk Rock?', in Philip Heyward, *From Pop to Punk to Postmodernism* (North Sydney: Allen and Unwin, 1992), 113-126.
3 Riley 'Death Rockers', 113.
4 Also known as the '76 Club'. See Andrew McMillan, 'The Saints versus the World, Part One', in Clinton Walker (Ed.), *Inner City Sound* (Portland: Verse Chorus Press, 2005), 11.
5 Tim Pittman, liner notes to *Tales from the Australian Underground: Singles 1976-1989* (Feel Presents, 2003), 2CD.
6 Pittman *Tales*.
7 Simon Reynolds, *Rip It Up and Start Again: Postpunk 1978-1984* (London: Faber, 2005), 517.
8 Graham Simpson, 'The Price of Originality', *Juke* (19 Jan 1980), 7.
9 Barney Hoskyns. *Glam! Bowie, Bolan and the Glitter Rock Revolution* (London: Faber, 1998), 66.
10 'Giving up the Baby Food Image', *Go-Set* (24 Aug 1974), 5.
11 Peter Walsh, 'Brainy Baker', *Juke* (7 Jan 1985), 4.
12 Christie Eliezer, review of Ol' 55, *Take It Greasy*, ARS (7 Oct 1976), 50.
13 'Mr. Cool's Scratch Pad', *Spunky* no. 11 (1976), 11.
14 'Random Notes', ARS #215 (19 Jun 1975), 54.
15 'Gene Pierson's Little Rave', *Campaign* no. 10 (Jun 1975), 29.
16 'Gene Pierson's Little Rave', 29.
17 Felicity Surtees, 'Silver Studs – '76, the year of Campoid 50s Kitsch', *RAM* (12 Mar 1976), 11.
18 Surtees, 'Silver Studs', 11.
19 Kieron Tyler, 'It Came from Down Under!', *Mojo* (Nov 2004), 49-52.
20 Chris Bailey quoted in Clinton Walker, 'Chris Bailey: A Saint Repents', in Walker (Ed.), *The Next Thing*, 23.
21 Vivien Johnson, *Radio Birdman* (St Kilda: Sheldon Booth, 1990), 107.
22 Mark Evans, *Dirty Deeds*, 101.
23 Undated letter signed 'The Saints' (attributed to Kuepper), which accompanied a gratis copy of their '(I'm) Stranded' single, <http://www.collectorscum.com/wyft/saints.html>, accessed 10 Jan 2006.
24 'Mr. Cool's Scratch Pad', 11.
25 Ian Rilen quoted in Frank Brunetti, 'Ian Rilen: Sardine V', *Vox Muzpaper* (Nov 1981), 8-9.
26 'The Calm Before the Storm?', *Spunky* no. 5 (1976), 16-17.
27 Andrew McMillan, 'Mmmmmenaccce', *RAM* (23 Feb 1979), 27.
28 Rebecca Batties, 'Rose Tattoo' (live review, London Tavern, Caulfield), *Juke* (22 Oct 1977), 16.
29 Rilen quoted in Brunetti, 'Ian Rilen', 8.
30 Roger Crothwaite, 'Tired Tatts', *Juke* (17 Jun 1978), 16.
31 Richard Guilliat, 'Man and Machine Lose a Man', *Roadrunner* (8 Feb 1980, though page 2 says 'Nov 1979'), 7.
32 'Around the Traps', ARS (10 Feb 1977), 46.
33 Angry Anderson quoted in McMillan, 'Mmmmmenaccce', 27.
34 Batties, 'Rose Tattoo', 16.
35 McMillan, 'Mmmmmenaccce', 27.
36 Anderson quoted in Toby Creswell, 'Rose Tattoo', in Editors of Rolling Stone, *The Big Australian Rock Book*, (Neutral Bay: Megabooks, 1985), 95-96.
37 Anderson in Creswell, 'Rose Tattoo', 95-96.
38 'Live with Dubs: Guitar God Lobby Loyde', <http://www.i94bar.com/ints/lobbyloyde.html>, accessed 31 Dec 2006.
39 Karen Dewey, *Angry: Scarred for Life* (Chippendale: Ironbark, 1994) 97.
40 Dewey, *Angry*, 104.
41 Toby Creswell, 'X: Doing What Comes Naturally', ARS #392, 18.
42 Dewey, *Angry*, 88.
43 Steve Lucas quoted by 'The Barman' (2000), <http://www.i94bar.com/ints/x.html>, accessed 29 Dec 2006.
44 Steve Lucas (14 Jun 2012), <http://www.facebook.com/Slxaus77>, accessed 6 Jul 2012.
45 Steve Lucas quoted in Christie Eliezer, 'Cross to Bear', *Juke* (9 May 1987), 9.
46 Steve Lucas in 'The Barman'.
47 Rilen quoted in Brunetti, 'Ian Rilen', 8-9.
48 Rilen quoted in Brunetti, 'Ian Rilen', 9.
49 Roger Grierson quoted in 'The Barman', 'You Only Think Twice: Return of the Thought Criminals', <http://www.i94bar.com/ints/thoughtcriminals.html>, accessed 31 Aug 2006.
50 Rilen in Brunetti, 'Ian Rilen', 9.
51 Christie Eliezer, 'Cross to Bear', 9.
52 Dan Morphett, 'X – the Magnificent Survivors?', *RAM* (22 Feb 1980), 9.
53 Gavan Purdy, 'X', *Distant Violins* no. 16 (1984), 8-9.
54 Lucas quoted in 'The Barman'.
55 Paul Comrie-Thomson, 'The Saints Go South: Holy Rollers Baptise Sydney', *ARS* (5 May 1977), 44-47.
56 Ed Kuepper quoted in Clinton Walker, 'Exile from Main Street', *ARS* (Mar 1992), 57-59, 96.
57 Comrie-Thomson, 'The Saints Go South', 45.
58 Tyler, 'It Came from Down Under!', 50.
59 Tyler, 'It Came from Down Under!', 50.
60 Tyler, 'It Came from Down Under!', 50.
61 Tyler, 'It Came from Down Under!', 50.
62 Andrew McMillan, 'Club 76 and All That', *Meanjin* 65:3 (2006), 111-117.
63 Bailey interviewed by Steve Gardner for *Foster Child* 'fanzine' (Feb 1998), reprinted at <http://www.nkvdrecords.com/saints.htm>, accessed 10 Jan 2006.
64 Tyler, 'It Came from Down Under!', 51.
65 Clinton Heylin, *Babylon's Burning: From Punk to Grunge* (London: Viking, 2007), 52.
66 Tyler, 'It Came from Down Under!', 49-52; Eliot Tiegel, 'New Horizons Sought by Barnum; Will Acquire Soul Acts for EMI', *Billboard* (9 Nov 1974), 4.
67 Kuepper quoted in Susan Joy, 'Saints: No Countdown Ban, Mixed Reaction in London', *Juke* (16 Jul 1977), 4.
68 Tyler, 'It Came from Down Under!', 51.
69 Jane Matheson, 'The La De Das Story', ARS (13 Mar 1975), 37.

NOTES

70 Kuepper in Joy, 'Saints: No Countdown Ban', 4.
71 Kuepper quoted in Joy, 'Saints: No Countdown Ban', 4.
72 Peter Poynton, Letter, *Juke* (12 Feb 1977), 14.
73 Comrie-Thomson, 'The Saints Go South', 45.
74 Poynton, Letter, *Juke* 12 Feb 1977, 14.
75 McMillan 'Club 76' 117.
76 Toby Creswell, *Too Much Ain't Enough* (Milsons Point, Random House, 1993) 50.
77 Comrie-Thomson, 'The Saints', 44.
78 Allan Webster 'Saints' (review of Tiger Room show) *Juke* 14 May 1977, 13.
79 Comrie-Thomson, 'The Saints Go South', 45.
80 Bailey interviewed by Gardner (2006).
81 Tyler, 'It Came from Down Under!', 51.
82 Christie Eliezer, 'Clapton Capers: Upbeat on Main Street', *ARS* (23 Sep 1976), 41-43.
83 Doug Ashdown quoted in Malcolm Maiden, 'Ashdown & Stewart: An Appeal to the English-Speaking World', *ARS* (19 Jun, 1975), 47-49.
84 'Saints Speak Out', *Juke* (14 May 1977), 8.
85 Michael Porteus, 'Saints', *Juke* (20 Aug 1977), n.p.
86 Porteus, 'Saints', n.p.
87 'Saints Speak Out', 8.
88 Bailey interviewed by Gardner (1998).
89 Tracee Hutchison, *Your Name's on the Door*, (Sydney: ABC, 1992),12.
90 Sandy Robertson in Joy, 'Saints: No Countdown Ban', 4.
91 Steven Herrick, 'The Apartments, Laughing Clowns and Hot Records' *On the Street* (21 Nov 1984), 28.
92 Bailey interviewed by Gardner (1998).
93 'Saints Speak Out', 8.
94 Johnson *Radio Birdman*, 6.
95 Johnson, *Radio Birdman*, 7.
96 Johnson, *Radio Birdman*, 3.
97 Anthony O'Grady, 'Radio Birdman', *RAM* (27 Feb 1976), 23-25.
98 Ken Shimamoto, 'Mort Bradley: A Birdman View from the Inside', *I-94 Bar*, <http://www.i94bar.com/ints/mort.html>, accessed 8 Jul 2012.
99 Johnson *Radio Birdman*, 110.
100 Peter Williams (1978) quoted in Scott Matheson, 'Tinkle, Tinkle Light And Fast', *Roadrunner* (3 Apr 1982), 7.
101 McFarlane, *Encyclopedia of Australian Rock and Pop*, 507.
102 Chad Morgan, interviewed in *Love Is in the Air*, DVD.
103 Johnson, *Radio Birdman*, 186.
104 See 'Revolutionary' (advertisement), *The Argus* [Melbourne], (15 Jan 1930), 12.
105 Johnson, *Radio Birdman*, 111.
106 Andy Bradley, 'Birdman Blitz', *Juke* (29 Oct 1977), n.p.
107 Bradley, 'Birdman Blitz', n.p.
108 *RAM* (Mar 24, 1978), 9; Johnson, *Radio Birdman*, 145.
109 Johnson, *Radio Birdman*, 135.
110 O'Grady, 'Radio Birdman', 23-25.
111 'Mr Cool's Scratch Pad', 11.
112 'Around the Traps', *ARS* (10 Feb 1977), 46.
113 John Dix, *Stranded in Paradise* (Wellington: Paradise Publications, 1988), 90.
114 Johnson, *Radio Birdman*, 139.
115 Johnson, *Radio Birdman*, 142.
116 Andrew McMillan, 'Radios Disappear', *RAM* (7 Sep 1979), 25.
117 See Sandra Hall, *Supertoy: 20 Years of Australian Television*, (South Melbourne: Sun Books, 1976), 57; and Susan Forde, Michael Meadows, Kerrie Foxwell, *Culture Commitment Community: the Australian Community Radio Sector* (Brisbane: Griffith University, 2002), 15.
118 Andrew Stafford, *Pig City: From the Saints to Savage Garden*, (St Lucia: University of Queensland Press, 2004), 26-7.
119 David Griffiths, 'Democratising Radio' in *Papers Presented to Public Radio Broadcasting Conference, 3 and 4 July 1974*, (Canberra: Department of Media,1974), 8-9.
120 Maro Owen, 'Head Radio's Pioneer: The Chris Winter Interview' *ARS* (18 Dec 1975), 50-52.
121 Ken Inglis (assisted by Jan Brazier), *This Is the ABC* (Carlton: Melbourne University Press, 1983), 376-377.
122 'harryjay' comment ca. 2010 on <www.messandnoise.com/articles/3900077>, accessed 27 Feb 2015.
123 Owen, 'Head Radio's Pioneer', 51.
124 Forde et al., *Culture Commitment*, 11-13; Peter Pockley, 'The Concept and Character of Public Broadcasting', in *Papers Presented to Public Radio Broadcasting Conference*, 2.

125 Ken Wark, '2JJJ-FM: Ten Years Old, Ten Years On', *Stiletto* no. 20, 50-51.
126 Anon., sleevenotes to *Long Live the Evolution*, no label, circa 1977. The original text as quoted here ends in a parenthesis, but no opening parenthesis precedes it.
127 Anon., sleevenotes to *Long Live the Evolution*.
128 The only group I haven't named here is Pantha. To do so would be to simply pander to the anxious possibility, always entertained by a historian of times within living memory, that someone will feel left out. Some poor ex-Pantha member will be reading this and perhaps the only thing standing between vindication and despair is the possibility that Pantha is discussed in the text as 'promising' or a 'lost gem'. Actually, their 'Rushcutter Bay Heartbeat Reggae' *is* a pretty fascinating piece, perhaps partly because of the local Sydney namecheck in the title, and the evidence of a mid-70s Sydney reggae movement to contrast with Melbourne's, under the stewardship of Ross Hannaford.
129 Ed St John, '2JJJ's Great Leap Forward', *ARS* #338, 27.
130 Jules Lewicki, 'tooFMuch', *Empire Times* no. 4 (9 Jul 1972), 7. Reprinted from *On Dit* (1970).
131 Pockley, 'Concept and Character of Public Broadcasting', 3.
132 'Malicious Gossip', *Roadrunner* (15 May 1979), 2.
133 'FM Radio: Something's in the Air in Brisbane', *RAM* (23 Apr 1976), 13.
134 Phillip McCarthy, 'City to Get Fourth New Radio Station', *The Age* (11 Oct 1975), 2.
135 Like Sydney's public radio FM station 2SER-FM, 3RRR-FM originated not with a university but with a College of Technology; both these institutions are now (confusingly?) universities, however.
136 John Duigan interviewed in Sue Mathews, *35mm Dreams: Conversations with Five Directors about the Australian Film Revival* (Ringwood: Penguin, 1984), 191.
137 Nor was it a 'live sampler', as it is characterised in Maximilian Dax, *The Life and Music of Nick Cave: An Illustrated Biography*, trans. Ian Minock (Berlin: Die Gestalten Verlag, 2000), 16.
138 Andrea Jones, 'Going It Alone: The Independent Labels', *ARS* (16 Apr 1981), 8-10.
139 Bruce Milne quoted in Ross Stapleton, 'The Rise and Rise of Michael Gudinski', *Roadrunner* (15 May 1979), 8-11.
140 Jeff Jenkins, *Ego Is Not a Dirty Word*, 20-21.
141 James Freud, *I Am the Voice Left from Drinking* (Pymble: HarperCollins, 2002) 29-31.
142 Clinton Walker wrote at the time that 'XRayZ are truly horrific, the less said about them the better.' He believed the Boys Next Door were by far the best of the Suicide groups. See Walker, 'Sign to Suicide or Suicide to Sign?' in *Inner City Sound*, 40.
143 Stephen Charlesworth, 'X-Ray-Z' (live review of 3RMT concert), *Juke* (18 May 1978), 16.
144 Allan Webster, 'X Ray Z: New Music', *Juke* (19 Nov 1977), 5.
145 John Rockwell and Derek Johnson, 'The Melbourne Band Explosion', *RAM* (13 Jul 1979), 22-23.
146 Harry Butler, 'The Virgins', *DNA* (Jun-Aug 1986), 20.
147 Dave Faulkner and James Baker interviewed by Donnie Sutherland on *After Dark*, replayed 17 Jun 1985.
148 <http://www.perthpunk.com/Geeks%20Story.htm>, accessed 13 Jun 2007.
149 <http://www.perthpunk.com/Geeks%20Story.htm>.
150 Dave Faulkner and James Baker interviewed by Donnie Sutherland on *After Dark*.
151 <http://www.perthpunk.com/Lloyd's%20Perth%20punk%20memoirs.htm>.
152 Peter Reeves, 'The Manikins: An Interview', *Pelican* 50:6 (1979), 16.
153 Reeves, 'The Manikins', 16.
154 Reeves, 'The Manikins', 16.
155 Adrian Ryan, 'The Scientists' (live review, Champion Hotel, Fitzroy), *Juke* (19 Jan 1980), 18.
156 David Gerard, 'Kim Salmon', *Party Fears* (Autumn 1989), 11-13.
157 Gerard, 'Kim Salmon', 11-13.
158 Gerard, 'Kim Salmon', 11-13.
159 Les Giesler, 'Boys Strike Back', *On the Street* (8 Dec 1983), 8.
160 Niel Scott, 'Band Business', *The Xpress* (Jul 1985), 14-15.
161 Jonathan Digby, 'V. Capri signed by Mushroom', *X-Press* no. 4 (2 Aug 1985), 10.
162 Walker, *Inner City Sound*, 9.
163 Garrett quoted in Jason Koutsoukis, 'Song Remains the Same', *The Age* (19 Nov 2005), 12.

164 Jon Matthews, 'Dragon/Midnight Oil' (live review, Avalon RSL) *Juke* 31 Dec 1977, 16.
165 Rob Hirst quoted in Toby Creswell, 'Midnight Oil: Dancing to It's [sic] Own Tune', *ARS* (20 Mar 1980), 26.
166 Peter Garrett, 'The Future of Rock', *Juice* (Jun 1994), 55.
167 Don Walker quoted in Kruger, *Songwriters Speak*, 278.
168 'Dirt', *RAM* (19 Oct 1979), 3.
169 Quoted in 'Midnight Oil', in Editors of Rolling Stone, *The Big Australian Rock Book*, 43.
170 Rob Hirst quoted in Kruger, *Songwriters Speak*, 303.
171 Hirst quoted in Tracee Hutchison, *Your Name's on the Door*, 3.
172 Hirst quoted in Hutchison, *Your Name's on the Door*, 3.
173 Quoted in Simon Balderstone, 'Burnin' the Midnight Oil', *Juke* (8 Jan 1979), 12.
174 Toby Cluehaz [should be Cluechaz], 'Peter Garrett: Relax with Max', *Roadrunner* 4:11/12 (1981), 26-27.
175 John Woodruff quoted in Greg Taylor, 'Brent Eccles Manages His "Fever"', *ARS* (Apr 1992), 27.
176 John Brewster quoted in Christie Eliezer, *High Voltage Rock 'n' Roll*, 101.
177 'The Keystone Angels', *RAM* (3 May 1975), 3.
178 Tony Lewis, 'The Angels Get Their Wings', *RAM* (23 Apr 1976), 13.
179 Eliezer, *High Voltage*, 101.
180 David Day and Tim Parker, *SA Great: It's Our Music 1956-1986* (Glandore: Pagel/Wakefield Press, 1987), 160.
181 Eliezer, *High Voltage*, 102.
182 Eliezer, *High Voltage*, 103.
183 Ross Stapleton, 'Climbing the Ivory Stairs', *Nation Review* (28 Jun 1979), 664.
184 Stapleton, 'Climbing', 664.
185 Stapleton, 'Climbing', 664.
186 Donald Robertson, 'Angels on a Pinhead', *Roadrunner* 4:11/12 (1981), 34-35.
187 Richard McGregor, 'The Angels: After Face to Face There Is No Exit', *ARS* (Jun 28 1979), 50.
188 Eliezer, *High Voltage*,108.
189 Jane Gardiner, 'The Angels Give Warning: They're Back with a Vengeance', *ARS* #385 (1985), 14
190 Donald Robertson, 'Angels on a Pinhead', 34-35.
191 Scott Howlett, 'Ian Moss Returns', *On the Street* (26 Nov 1986), 19.
192 Creswell, *Too Much* , 4.
193 John Swan quoted in Mark Carey, 'John's Swan Song', *On the Street* (24 Apr 1985), 3.
194 Creswell, *Too Much*, 34.
195 Creswell, *Too Much*, 34.
196 Creswell, *Too Much*, 35.
197 Creswell, *Too Much*, 42.
198 Creswell, *Too Much*, 42.
199 Eliezer, *High Voltage*, 40.
200 'Gene Pierson's Little Rave', *Campaign* (Jun 1975), 29.
201 Creswell, *Too Much*, 65.
202 Don Walker quoted in Christie Eliezer, 'The Chisels Come in from the Cold', *Juke* (13 May 1978), 9.
203 Creswell, *Too Much*, 69.
204 Eliezer, 'The Chisels Come in from the Cold', 9.
205 Creswell, *Too Much*, 74.
206 Creswell, *Too Much*, 82-3.
207 Creswell, *Too Much*, 80.
208 Walker quoted in Ed St John, 'At the Top with Cold Chisel: Great Rock & Roll for Here and Now', *ARS* (19 Mar 1981), 16-19.
209 McMillan, 'Mmmmmenaccce', 27.
210 Walker quoted in St John, 'At the Top', 16-19.
211 Christie Eliezer, 'Cold Chisel Fall into Place', *Juke* (26 Nov 1977), 7.
212 Barnes quoted in St John, 'At the Top' 16-19.
213 Creswell, *Too Much*, 179.
214 Jane Matheson. 'Cold Chisel: Risk-Taking Is Part of the Game', *ARS* #354, 14-18.
215 Creswell, *Too Much*, 123
216 Tommy Lee, Mick Mars, Vince Neil, Nikki Sixx with Neil Strauss, *Motley Crue: The Dirt* (New York: Regan Books, 2001) 87.
217 Matheson, 'Cold Chisel', 18.
218 Rod Willis quoted in Donald Robertson, 'Chisel in America: Daunted but Resolute', *Roadrunner* (Oct 1981), 5.
219 Don Walker quoted in 'Cold Chisel', in Editors of Rolling Stone, *The Big Australian Rock Book*, 56.
220 Don Walker quoted in Donald Robertson, 'New Rhythm Kings', *Roadrunner* (Mar 1982), 16-18.
221 Matheson, 'Cold Chisel', 14-18.
222 Walker in Robertson, 'New Rhythm Kings', 18.
223 Creswell, *Too Much*,119.
224 Don Walker, *Shots* (Melbourne: Black Inc, 2009), 71-2.
225 Barnes quoted in Hutchison, *Your Name's on the Door*, 27.
226 Anthony O'Grady, *Cold Chisel: The Pure Stuff* (Crows Nest: Allen and Unwin, 2001), 73-75.
227 'Congratulations Jane and Jimmy', *Roadrunner* (Jun 1981), 3.
228 Creswell, *Too Much*, 149.
229 Paul Hewson, Marc Hunter, Robert Taylor, 'Torture by Numbers', *RAM* (27 Apr 1984), 25.
230 Elly McDonald, 'Dugites ssssnakey rhythms', *Roadrunner* (Aug 1980), 10.
231 David L. Langsam, 'Dugites', *Roadrunner* (Feb 8 1980), 17.
232 Ian 'Molly' Meldrum with Jeff Jenkins, *The Never, Um, Ever Ending Story* (Crows Nest: Allen and Unwin, 2014), 7.
233 Donald Robertson, 'It's Your Fault, Molly!', *Roadrunner* (4 May 1982), 12.
234 D. Cowell '& Meldrum', letter, *RAM* (7 Sep 1979), 3.
235 Ian Meldrum quoted in 'The Lowdown on Countdown', *Juke* (14 May 1975), 6.
236 Sally Stockbridge, 'Rock 'n' Roll Television', in Albert Moran (Ed.), *Stay Tuned: An Australian Broadcasting Reader* (North Sydney: Allen and Unwin, 1992),138.
237 Eliezer, *High Voltage*, 154.
238 'TV's pop pedlars', *Spunky* no. 1 (1976), 32-33.
239 As detailed in *Love Is in the Air* (ABC), DVD.
240 Meldrum with Jenkins, *The Never, Um, Ever Ending Story*, 1.
241 The premise of *Love Is in the Air*, third episode (ABC), DVD.
242 Carl Magnus Palm, *Bright Lights Dark Shadows: The Real Story of ABBA* (London, Omnibus Press, 2001), 269-73.
243 As detailed in *Love Is in the Air* (ABC), DVD disc 3.
244 Stockbridge in Moran (Ed.), *Stay Tuned*, 139.
245 McGrath, *Australian Encyclopaedia of Rock and Pop*, 13.
246 Ed St John 'Air Supply Breezes to Overnight Success; Now for the Hard Work', *ARS* (10 Mar 1976), 52.
247 Russell Hitchcock quoted in Jillian Burt, 'Air Supply: Winds of Fortune', *Juke* (19 Feb 1977), 9.
248 Burt, 'Air Supply', 9.
249 Burt, 'Air Supply', 9.
250 St John, 'Air Supply', 52.
251 'Around the Traps', *ARS* (18 Sep 1980), 83.
252 St John, 'Air Supply', 52.
253 Quoted in St John, 'Air Supply', 52.
254 *ARS* (16 Dec 1976), 7.
255 Graham Russell quoted in Burt, 'Air Supply', 9.
256 Quoted in St John, 'Air Supply', 52.
257 'Around the Traps', *ARS* (10 Mar 1977), 53.
258 Christina Amphlett, *Pleasure and Pain*, 71-2.
259 McGrath, *Australian Encyclopaedia of Rock and Pop*, 9-10.
260 Brian Cadd, *From This Side of Things* (Sydney: New Holland, 2010) 171.
261 Simon Balderstone, 'Burnin' the Midnight Oil', 12.
262 Martin Armiger, 'Pool of Echoes', *Meanjin* 65:3 (2006), 70.
263 Stephen Charlesworth, 'And the Rise of the Underground', *Juke* (9 Apr 1977), 7.
264 Stephen Charlesworth, 'Bleeding Hearts' (live review), *Juke* (21 Apr 1977),16.
265 Charlesworth, 'Bleeding Hearts', 16.
266 Charlesworth, 'And the Rise of the Underground', 7.
267 Armiger, 'Pool of Echoes', 72.
268 Andrew McMillan, 'Jo Jo Zep and the Falcons: Finally, This Could Be Their Year', *RAM* (10 Aug 1979), 25.
269 Cummings quoted in Al Webb, 'We Don't Take It All That Seriously', *Juke* (6 May 1978), 9.
270 Maxwell Ross, 'Sports', *Juke* (26 Feb 1977), 16.
271 Chris Gough, 'Ross Wilson Mondo Rocks On', *Juke* (24 Dec 1977), 8.
272 Pendlebury quoted in Greg Taylor, 'The Good Sport', *ARS* (Jun 1992), 21.
273 David Pepperell, 'The New Wave in Melbourne', *Juke* (13 Aug 1977), 16.
274 'Eric Gradman Man and Machine' (live review, Stockade Hotel, Carlton), *Juke* (26 Jan 1980), 16.
275 'Malicious Gossip', *Roadrunner* (Feb 8 1980), 3.
276 Donald Robertson, 'New Year, New Album, New Line-Up', *Roadrunner* (Feb 8 1980), 5.
277 Maxwell Ross, 'Sports', *Juke* (26 Feb 1977), 16.
278 Cummings in Webb, 'We Don't Take It', 9.
279 Ross Gardiner, 'Pete Solley: Veteran Wizard', *ARS* (1 May 1980), 11.

280 Solley quoted in Gardiner, 'Pete Solley', 11.
281 Michael Porteus, 'The Sports: Learning to Play the English Style', *Juke* (5 May 1978), 11.
282 Nigel Burnham, 'Sports Battle the Cultural Cringe', *RAM* (1 Jun 1979), 21.
283 Cummings quoted in Porteus, 'The Sports, 11.
284 'Sports Play Fair in England', *RAM* (18 May 1979), 3.
285 See Ian McFarlane and Glenn Terry, sleevenotes to Lobby Loyde, *Obsecration* reissue (Aztec Music, 2006).
286 Stuart Coupe, 'Sports Go Overseas', *RAM* (9 Feb 1979), 11.
287 Andrea Jones, 'The Sports Light Up', ARS (18 Sep 1980), 23.
288 Stephen Cummings, *Stay away from Lightning Girl* (Milsons Point: Random House, 1999), 39.
289 Michael Gudinski quoted in Toby Creswell, 'The Godfather', *ARS* #452, 94-98, 128.
290 Andrea Jones, 'Skyhooks' Stormy R.I.P.', , 21.
291 Cummings quoted in Toby Creswell, 'The Sports: playing Less and Enjoying It More', *ARS* #341, 20.
292 Armiger quoted in Creswell, 'The Sports: Playing Less', 20.
293 'Stephen Cummings', Editors of Rolling Stone, *The Big Australian Rock Book*, 51.
294 Cummings quoted in Jones, 'The Sports Light Up', 23.
295 Jane Clifton quoted in Damien Minton, 'From Carlton to the Loungerooms of the Nation', *On the Street* (8 Aug 1984), 14-15.
296 David Langsam 'Stiletto: The Final Performance', *Juke* (10 Feb 1979), 18.
297 Jane Clifton quoted in Al Webb, 'Stiletto', *Juke* (13 May 1978), 7.
298 'Stiletto', *Juke* (20 Aug 1977), 4.
299 Jane Clifton quoted in Al Webb, 'Stiletto – A Sharp Debut Album', *Juke* (18 Sep 1978), 9.
300 Mark Butler, 'Stiletto', ARS (8 Feb 1979), 56.
301 Clifton quoted in Damien Minton, 'From Carlton', 14-15.
302 Chris Worral in Webb, 'Stiletto – A Sharp Debut', 9.
303 Langsam, 'Stiletto', 18.
304 Worral in Webb, 'Stiletto', 9.
305 Andrea Jones, '"Patti Smith Would Never Make It in Australia"', *RAM* (9 Mar 1979), 11.
306 Langsam, 'Stiletto', 18.
307 Miranda Brown, 'Join the Dots for Fun', *RAM* (9 Feb 1979), 11.
308 Langsam, 'Stiletto', 18.
309 Jones, '"Patti Smith Would Never Make It"', 11.
310 Clifton in Jones, '"Patti Smith Would Never Make It"', 11.
311 Langsam, 'Stiletto, 18.
312 Greg Taylor, 'The Concerned Wheeler-Dealer' *RAM* (24 Jun 1983), 13.
313 Kruger, *Songwriters Speak*, 135.
314 Andrew McMillan, 'Jo Jo Zep and the Falcons', 25.
315 Ed St.John, 'Joe Camilleri: The Boss Steps Out', ARS #321, 30-32.
316 Joe Camilleri quoted in Milsom and Thomas, *Pay to Play*, 131-132.
317 Joe Camilleri quoted in Christie Eliezer, 'Belief is a Beauty Thing', *Juke* (20 Jun 1987), 31.
318 Joe Camilleri quoted in Milson and Thomas, *Pay to Play*, 132.
319 *RAM* (23 Feb 1979), 5.
320 St.John, 'Joe Camilleri', 31.
321 Ross Stapleton, 'Jo Jo Zep: The Maltese Falcon Turns Gold', *ARS* (13 Nov 1979), 23.
322 'Dirt', *RAM* (19 Oct 1979), 3.
323 Adrian Ryan, 'Paul Kelly Beats the Cult Curse', *RAM* (19 Oct 1979), 7-8.
324 Joe Camilleri quoted in McMullan, 'Jo Jo Zep', 25.
325 'Jo Jo Zep: Don't Waste It', *Juke* (5 Feb 1977), 6.
326 Toby Creswell 'Zep Unzips', *ARS* (3 May 79), 52.
327 Camilleri quoted in St.John, 'Joe Camilleri', 31.
328 'London Notes', *ARS* #323, 49.
329 Scott Howlett, 'Honeydrippin", *On the Street* (14 Mar 1984), 15.
330 Clifton quoted in Hutchison, *Your Name's on the Door*, 46.
331 Mighty Records advertisement, *Roadrunner* (Aug 1980), 19.
332 Mark Carey and Peter Holder, 'Spirits in a Musical World', *On the Street* (20 Feb 1985), 14-15.
333 Stephen Charlesworth, 'Mental as Anything', *Juke* (5 May 1978), 16.
334 Annie Burton, 'Those Who Sweat Also Get Wet', *RAM* (14 Dec 1979), 16-17.
335 Charlesworth, 'Mental as Anything', 16.
336 Burton, 'Those Who Sweat', 16-17.
337 Burton, 'Those who Sweat', 16-17.
338 Alan Howard, *Dave Warner: Suburban Boy* (Perth: Creative Research, 1981), 24.
339 Howard, *Dave Warner*, 27.
340 Howard, *Dave Warner*, 41.
341 Howard, *Dave Warner*, 43.
342 Reek Havoc and Virgil Posse, 'Mug's Game', *The 1978 Orientation Pelican* (Mar[?] 1978), 14.
343 Havoc and Posse, 'Mug's Game', 8.
344 Warner quoted in Howard, *Dave Warner*, 86.
345 Howard, *Dave Warner*, 84.
346 Howard, *Dave Warner*, 63.
347 Howard, *Dave Warner*, 127-8.
348 Howard, *Dave Warner*, 109-110.
349 Howard, *Dave Warner*, 142-3.
350 Howard, *Dave Warner*, 153.
351 Howard, *Dave Warner*, 123.
352 Havoc and Posse, 'Mug's Game', 10-11.
353 Havoc and Posse, 'Mug's Game', 32.
354 Havoc and Posse, 'Mug's Game', 14.
355 'Scandal! Shock! Horror! Dave Warner attacks sacred cows!', *Juke* (22 Jul 1978), 15, 20.
356 'Scandal! Shock! Horror!', 20.
357 Ross Stapleton, 'Dave Warner', *Juke* (18 Jun 1979), 18.
358 D. R. Warner, 'Dave Warner defends himself', *Juke* (5 Jan 1980), 17.
359 'Scandal! Shock! Horror!', 15.
360 Dave Warner quoted in Anthony O'Grady, 'Thoughts of Chairman Dave', *RAM* (1 Jun 1979), 15-17.
361 'Scandal! Shock! Horror!, 20.
362 'Scandal! Shock!' Horror!, 20.
363 'Scandal! Shock! Horror!, 20.
364 'Scandal! Shock! Horror!, 20.
365 Havoc and Posse, 'Mug's Game', 43.
366 Jane Matheson, 'Around the traps', ARS (Jan 1980), 93.
367 Jenni, 'Hooks (Again)' [letter], *RAM* (9 Feb 1979), 2.
368 <http://www.tandarra.com/thelateshow/s1ep18.htm>, accessed 29 Jan 2007.
369 'Sherbet on the Go', *Spunky* no. 2 (1976), 24-25, 30.
370 Daryl Braithwaite, interview extras on *Love is in the Air* (ABC), DVD.
371 Adrian Ryan, 'The Rise and Fall of Sherbet', *Roadrunner* (Oct 1981), 31.
372 Sleevenotes to *Sherbet's Greatest Hits* (Infinity Recs., 1975).
373 Anthony O'Grady, 'The Mighty SHERBET Firm Flexes It's [sic] Muscles', *RAM*, 13, 14-15.
374 Sleevenotes to *Sherbet's Greatest Hits*.
375 O'Grady, 'The Mighty SHERBET', 14-15.
376 Anthony O'Grady, 'Sherbet: The New Streamlined International Look', *RAM* (17 May 1975), 12-13.
377 Adrian Ryan, 'The Rise and Fall of Sherbet', 31.
378 Garth Porter quoted in Kruger, *Songwriters Speak*, 221. Porter is discussing 'Arrival', the opening track on Sherbet's album *Life . . . Is for Living*.
379 Ryan, 'The Rise and Fall of Sherbet', 32.
380 Garth Porter quoted in O'Grady, 'The mighty SHERBET', 15.
381 O'Grady, 'Sherbet: The New Streamlined International Look', 12-13.
382 Christie Eliezer, 'Versatile Sherbet's Crowd-Pleasing Panache: Life Is a Formula', *ARS* (26 Jan 1976[?]), 78.
383 Felicity Surtees, 'Sherbet, Hordern Pavilion', *RAM* (30 Jan 1976), 23.
384 Anthony O'Grady, 'The Clive Shakespeare Story', *RAM* (7 May 1976), 14-15.
385 Clive Shakespeare quoted in O'Grady, 'The Clive Shakespeare Story', 14.
386 Shakespeare quoted in O'Grady, 'The Clive Shakespeare Story', 15.
387 Garth Porter quoted in Anthony O'Grady, 'Why Isn't Clive Shakespeare in Sherbet Any More? The Inside Story', *RAM* (13 Feb 1976), 11.
388 Christie Eliezer, 'Life with/without Harvey', *ARS* (8 Apr 1976), 46.
389 'Mr Cool's Scratch Pad', *Spunky* no. 1 (1976) ,11.
390 Quoted in Julia Orange, 'Sherbet: Home Is Where The Fans Are', *ARS* (24 Mar 1977), 15.
391 Garth Porter interviewed in *Love is in the Air* (ABC), DVD.
392 Orange, 'Sherbet', 15.
393 Orange, 'Sherbet', 15.
394 Orange, 'Sherbet', 15.
395 Ryan, 'The Rise and Fall of Sherbet', 31-32.

396 Christie Eliezer, 'Highway: Braving the Rocky Road', *Juke* (25 Aug 1979), 8.
397 Jane Matheson, 'Around the Traps', *ARS* (22 Mar 1979), 45.
398 Eliezer, 'Highway', 8.
399 Richard Rezeille, 'Now It's Just Sherbs with No Stigmawood attached', *Juke* (12 Jan 1980), 9.
400 Garth Porter quoted in John Di Mase, 'Sherbs: Skilled As Always' *ARS* #333/334, 22.
401 Daryl Braithwaite quoted in Anthony O'Grady, '"No-one Can Deny It's Been a Dream Run"', *RAM* (20 Apr 1979), 22-23.
402 O'Grady, '"No-one Can Deny"', 22.
403 Rezeille, 'Now It's Just Sherbs', 9.
404 See front cover of *Spunky* no. 11 (ca. 1976).
405 Michael Smith, 'Say Goodbye to Sherbet, Tread the Highway No More . . .', *RAM* (8 Feb 1980), 9.
406 Daryl Braithwaite quoted in Smith, 'Say Goodbye', 9.
407 Garth Porter quoted in Michael Delaney, 'Naked in the Danger Zone', *Juke* (23 Jan 1982), 9.
408 <http://soundisstyle.com/2013/05/daft-punk-contact-2002-demo-version.html>, accessed 26 Feb 2015.
409 'Around the Traps', *ARS* (12 Aug 1977), 73.
410 Ashdown in Maiden, 'Ashdown & Stewart', 41.
411 Richard Clapton interviewed by Peter Thompson, ABC-TV (10 May 2008,) transcript at <abc.net.au>, accessed 17 Dec 2014.
412 Helen Barrett, 'Going Places', *Go-Set* (12 Jan 1974), 8-9.
413 Richard Clapton, *The Best Years of Our Lives* (Sydney: Allen and Unwin, 2014), 34.
414 Helen Barrett, 'Going Places', 8-9.
415 Christie Eliezer, 'Clapton Capers: Upbeat on Main Street', *ARS* (23 Sep 1976), 41-43; Ed Nimmervoll, 'Richard Clapton', *Juke* (11 Jun 1975), 18.
416 Clapton, *The Best Years*, 34.
417 Clapton, *The Best Years*, 81.
418 Clapton, *The Best Years*, 98.
419 'Mr. Cool's Scratch Pad', *Spunky* no. 4 (1976), 17.
420 Ed St John, 'Richard Clapton: the Rolling Stone Interview', *ARS* #325/6 (1980), 37-39.
421 Clapton quoted in Ed St John, 'Richard Clapton', 37.
422 David Pepperill, Facebook status (29 Aug 2014), accessed 17 Dec 2014.
423 Clapton in St John, 'Richard Clapton', 37.
424 Andrew McMillan, *Talking Smack: Honest Conversations About Drugs* (St Lucia: University of Queensland Press, 2014), 70-71.
425 Miranda Brown, 'Join the Dots for Fun', *RAM* (9 Feb 1979), 11.
426 Paul Kelly, 'The Web', *Empire Times* (Jul 1972), 15; 'Jonathan Brown', *Empire Times* 5:2 (1973) 13.
427 Richard McGregor, 'Paul Kelly and the Dots: Poetic Battles and Hard Rock', *ARS* (6 Mar 1980), 38.
428 Kiley Pale, 'A Night in the Life of a Backstairs Musician', *Another One for Mary* (Apr 1977), 6-8.
429 Keith Shadwick, 'Rock/Roll Revolvers' in *Windows and Mirrors* (Bundeena: Island Press, 1977), 48.
430 'Malicious Gossip', *Roadrunner* (5 May 1979), 2.
431 Brown, 'Join the Dots, 11.
432 Brown, 'Join the Dots', 11.
433 Peter Mudd, 'Heart and Soul', *Roadrunner* (Oct 1981), 35.
434 Uncredited interviewee, *Weekend* (Film Australia, 1977).
435 Les Gock quoted in Annie Burton, 'Hush on the Road Again but Who Knows Where To?', *RAM* (21 May 1976), 18-19.
436 Stephen Phillips, 'John Paul Young Enters His Third Life', *Juke* (14 Apr 1984), 7.
437 Ken Quinnell, 'John Paul Young: Today's Reluctant Hero', *ARS* (4 Nov 1976), 45-6.
438 Quinnell, 'John Paul Young', 46.
439 Quinnell, 'John Paul Young', 45.
440 John Paul Young quoted in Christie Eliezer, 'John Paul Young: Love (and Success) Is in the Air', *Juke* (3 Jun 1978), 9.
441 Meldrum with Jenkins, *The Never, Um, Ever Ending Story*, 98.
442 Anthony O'Grady, 'Right You Lot, Line up and Flash Yer Bums', *RAM* (12 Mar 1976), 14-15.
443 Ted Mulry quoted in O'Grady, 'Right You Lot', 14.
444 'TMG join Mushroom', *Juke* (9 Apr 1977), 5.
445 Michael Gormly, review of Taste, 'Tickle Your Fancy', *ARS* (23 Sep 1976), 45.
446 Tony Cohen quoted in Meldrum with Jenkins, *The Never, Um, Ever Ending Story*, 55.
447 Chris Burnham quoted in Mark Carey, 'This Goes with This and That's That', *On the Street* (1 May 1985), 5.
448 See Ian McFarlane and Glenn Terry, sleevenotes to Lobby Loyde, reissue of *Obsecration* (Aztec Music, 2006).
449 'Recapturing Home Grounds', *Juke* (11 Jun 1977), 4.
450 Harry Kolatas, 'Supernaut' *RAM* (23 Feb 1979), 10.
451 Jane Matheson, 'Around the Traps', *ARS* (3 May 79), 51.
452 Scott Howlett, 'You're Only As Good As Your Last Gig', *Juke* (26 Apr 1987), 11.
453 Greg Taylor 'Puns are Odious but These Guys Are on the Boil', *RAM* (19 Oct 1979), 21.
454 'The Sydney Band Explosion', *RAM* (29 Jun 1979), 20-21.
455 Christie Eliezer, 'No Puns Please, We're the Radiators', *Juke* (12 Jan 1980), 9.
456 Les Gock interviewed by Simon Marnie (25 Jun 2006), <http://www.abc.net.au/sydney/stories/s1671260.htm>, accessed 28 Jan 2007.
457 Annie Burton, 'Truckin' Down the Highway with Hush', *RAM* (3 May 1975), 12-14.
458 Rix quoted in Burton, 'Truckin' Down', *RAM* (3 May 1975), 12-14.
459 Les Gock quoted in Annie Burton, 'Hush on the Road', 18.
460 Christie Eliezer, 'Hush: Still in There and Still Fighting', *Juke* (13 May 1978), 4.
461 Keith Lamb quoted in Eliezer, 'Hush: Still in There', 4.
462 Eliezer, 'Hush: Still in There', 4.
463 Al Webb, 'Jim Keays: Hello, Hello I'm Back Again', *Juke* (24 Jun 1978), 18.
464 Burton, 'Truckin' Down', 12.
465 Anthony O'Grady, 'The Further Dragon Flight Adventures of Hush', *RAM* (2 Jan 1976), 19.
466 Rick Lum quoted in Anthony O'Grady, 'By Jove, There's Some Controversy in this Article', *RAM* (6 Sep 1975), 15.
467 Les Gock quoted in O'Grady, 'By Jove', 15.
468 David Dawson, 'Lamb Flew Over the Cuckoo's Nest', *Juke* (11 Mar 1987), 5.
469 'Around the Traps', *ARS* (9 Sept 1976), 73.
470 Ross Wilson quoted in Adrian Ryan, 'The Sons of the Father', *Roadrunner* (Aug 1981), 11.
471 'Around the Traps', *ARS* (2 Dec 1976), 46.
472 Chris Gough, 'Ross Wilson Mondo Rocks On', *Juke* (24 Dec 1977), 8.
473 'Dirt', *RAM* (6 Oct 1979), 5.
474 'Mr. Cool's Scratch Pad', *Spunky* no. 2 (1976) 11.
475 Jillian Birt, 'Instant Replay' (live review of show at Arkaba Top Room, Adelaide), *Juke* (12 Jul 1978), 20.
476 Christie Eliezer, 'Stylus – It's All in the Game', *ARS* (Jan 26 1976), 44.
477 Eliezer, 'Stylus', 44.
478 Renée Geyer and Ed Nimmervoll, *Confessions of a Difficult Woman: The Renée Geyer Story* (Pymble: HarperCollins, 2000), 1, 18.
479 Geyer and Nimmervoll, *Confessions*, 29.
480 Geyer and Nimmervoll, *Confessions*, 30, 34.
481 Geyer and Nimmervoll, *Confessions*, 37.
482 Geyer and Nimmervoll, *Confessions*, 38.
483 Geyer and Nimmervoll, *Confessions*, 39.
484 Geyer and Nimmervoll, *Confessions*, 57.
485 Peter Olszewski, 'Renée Geyer – No More the Dreaded Pub Gig', *RAM* (2 Jan 1976), 9.
486 'Geyer's Going Great', *Spunky* no. 9 (1976), 18-20.
487 Olszewski, 'Renée Geyer', 9.
488 Geyer and Nimmervoll, *Confessions*, 77.
489 Geyer and Nimmervoll, *Confessions*, 76-77.
490 'Around the traps', *ARS* (13 Jan 1979), 84.
491 'Geyer/Borich Record', *RAM* (9 Feb 1979), 5.
492 Miranda Brown, 'Renée and Kevin Sing the Blues', *RAM* (20 Apr 1979), 23.
493 Meldrum with Jenkins *The Never, Um, Ever Ending Story*, 77.
494 Geyer and Nimmervoll, *Confessions*, 124.
495 Michael Delaney, 'So Lucky To Be an Australian', *Juke* (13 Mar 1982), 14-15.
496 'Around the Traps', *ARS* (26 Aug 1976), 46.
497 Neil Finn quoted in Hutchison, *Your Name's on the Door*, 15.
498 Tim Finn quoted in Mike Guthrie, 'Split Enz: Out on a Limb – up the Ladder', *RAM* (4 Oct 1975), 11.
499 Noel Crombie quoted in Michael Smith, 'Enz Wrap up Old Era', *RAM* (8 Feb 1980), 11.
500 Anthony O'Grady, 'Ting! Split Enz Start Round Two', *RAM* (9 Feb 1979), 13.
501 O'Grady, 'Ting!', 13.
502 Tim Finn quoted in O'Grady, 'Ting!', 13.
503 Simon Balderstone, 'The New Dragon: "Less Spectacle and More Music"', *Juke* (21 Apr 1979), 9.

NOTES

504 Richard Lee quoted in Balderstone, 'The New Dragon', 9.
505 Richard Lee quoted in Christie Eliezer, 'The Sidewinder Screenplay Starring Richard Lee', *Juke* (9 Sep 1978), 11.
506 Rebecca Batties, 'Sidewinder' (review of Martinis show), *Juke* (14 May 1977), 13.
507 Al Webb, 'The New, "Humanised" Cybotron' *Juke* (5 Aug 1978), 13.
508 Webb, 'The New, "Humanised" Cybotron', 13.
509 Neil Jameson, untitled Kush story, *RAM* (31 May 1975), 19.
510 Jameson, 19.
511 Gudinski quoted in Nigel Burnham, 'Sports Battle the Cultural Cringe' *RAM* (1 Jun 1979), 21.
512 Nigel Burnham, 'Nigel Burnham Is Totally Bemused by Duffo in London', *RAM* (19 Oct 1979), 27.
513 'Kush Push On', *Juke* (25 Jun 1975), 3.
514 Burnham, 'Nigel Burnham Is Totally Bemused', 27.
515 Burnham, 'Nigel Burnham Is Totally Bemused', 27.
516 Burnham, 'Nigel Burnham Is Totally Bemused', 27.
517 Daisy Chain, 'Mandu: Skinhead Cosmic Rocker Finds Nirvana', *RAM* (28 Jun 1975), 21.
518 Mandu quoted in Chain, 'Mandu', 21.
519 Pat Odanahue 'The sci-fi Plot That Ate Wagner', *RAM* (23 Apr 1976), 25.
520 'Mr. Cool's Scratch Pad', *Spunky* no. 4 (1976), 11.
521 See McFarlane and Terry, sleevenotes to *Obsecration*.
522 Donald Robertson, 'Richard Clapton', *Roadrunner* (Mar 1982), 5.
523 Noel Delbridge, *Up There Mike Brady* (Port Melbourne: Coulomb Communications, 2004), 163-186.
524 Delbridge, *Up There*, 170.
525 *We're Livin' on Dog Food*, dir. Richard Lowenstein (Ghost Pictures, 2009).
526 *We're Livin' on Dog Food*.
527 Untitled article, *Vox Muzpaper* (Dec 1981), 15.
528 Stuart Grant quoted in Alan Bamford, *The North Brunswick Beat* (ca. 1980).
529 'Fat Daddy and the Ugh! Shock Rock', *Spunky* no. 4 (1976), 38-39.
530 'Gunston – Punk Single', *Juke* (9 Apr 1977), 5.
531 'Norman Gunston', *Juke* (14 May 1977), 8-9.
532 David Pepperell, 'The New Wave in Melbourne', *Juke* (13 Aug 1977), 16.
533 Al Webb, 'At Last! The Missing Link!', *Juke* (17 Feb 1979), 13.
534 Kim Beissel, 'Crime and the City Solution #2 – Melbourne', *No Night Sweats*, <http://www.users.bigpond.com/pturnbul/nns_memoirs_kb.htm>, accessed 31 Jul 2006.
535 'Barbed Wires', *Juke* (5 Jan 1980), 4.
536 Al Webb, 'At last! The Missing Link!', 13.
537 Jillian Burt, 'Young and Modern', *Juke* (27 Jun 1978), 22.
538 Stuart Coupe, 'In-tro-ducing ... YM', *RAM* (9 Feb 1979), 19.
539 Coupe, 'In-tro-ducing', 19.
540 John Dowler quoted in Burt, 'Young and Modern', 22.
541 Burt, 'Young and Modern', 22.
542 Coupe, 'In-tro-ducing', 19.
543 Burt, 'Young and Modern', 22.
544 Coupe, 'In-tro-ducing', 19.
545 Coupe, 'In-tro-ducing', 19.
546 Bohdan X quoted in Mark Phillips, *Radio City: The First 30 Years of 3RRR* (Carlton North: Vulgar Press, 2006) 38-9.
547 The author feels it necessary to confirm this statement is, indeed, a kind of joke.
548 Stephen Charlesworth, 'Young Charlatans' (live review), *Juke* (24 Jun 1978), 18.
549 Nick Cave, 'The Flesh Made Word (for BBC Radio 3, July 1996)', *King Ink II* (London: Black Spring Press, 1997), 138.
550 Jillian Burt, 'Boys Next Door' (review of show at Highway Inn, Adelaide), *Juke* (20 May 1978), 16.
551 Nick Cave quoted in Anon, 'Boys Next Door ... Alien Tales', *Juke* (15 Jul 1978), 13.
552 Cave in Anon, 'Boys Next Door', 13.
553 Cave in Anon, 'Boys Next Door', 13.
554 Cave in Anon, 'Boys Next Door', 13.
555 Burt, 'Boys Next Door', 16.
556 Robert Brokenmouth, *Nick Cave: The Birthday Party and Other Epic Adventures* (London: Omnibus Press, 1996), 27.
557 Jane Matheson, 'Around the Traps', *ARS* (14 Jun 1979), 46.
558 Helen Gillman, 'Boys Next Door: Monument in the Making', *ARS* (6 Mar 1980), 33.
559 Dax, *The Life and Music of Nick Cave*, 14.
560 Dax, *The Life and Music of Nick Cave*, 15.
561 Dax, *The Life and Music of Nick Cave*, 16.
562 Clinton Walker, 'Last "Hee Haw" from the Boys Next Door?', *RAM* (22 Feb 1980), 7; 'Around the Traps', *ARS* (20 Mar 1980), 92.
563 Rowland Howard quoted in Ashley Crawford, 'It's Their Party, and They'll Try If They Want To', *Juke* (30 Jan 1982), 14.
564 Mick Harvey quoted in Mick Geyer, 'Bleak in the Face of Beauty', *Juke* (27 Jun 1987), 13.
565 Kathleen Stewart, 'Perfumed Farts', *Meanjin* 65:3 (2006), 132-137.
566 Beissel, 'Crime and the City Solution #2 – Melbourne'.
567 Beissel, 'Crime and the City Solution #2 – Melbourne'.
568 Beissel, 'Crime and the City Solution #2 – Melbourne'.
569 Andrea Jones, 'Melbourne: Post Punk Revival', *ARS* #323, 13.
570 Dax, *The Life and Music of Nick Cave*, 17.
571 Riley, 'Death Rockers', 119-20.
572 Stafford, *Pig City*, 48.
573 Unnamed Go-Between quoted in David Pestorius, 'What Goes On Between Two Heads?' *Roadrunner* (unknown date), 13.
574 Robert Forster, 'Anthology Notes', *G Stands For Go-Betweens Volume One 1978-1984* (Domino, 2014), 18.
575 Forster, 'Anthology Notes', 36.
576 Brad Shepherd quoted in The Barman, 'Doing the Regal Rock', <http://www.i94bar.com/ints/bradshepherd.html>, accessed 30 Dec 2006.
577 Andrew Bradley, 'Johnny Kannis: A Star Is Born?', *Juke* (17 Jun 1978), 7.
578 Andrew McMillan, 'Radios Disappear', *RAM* (7 Sep 1979), 25.
579 Darcy Condon, 'It's a Smear Campaign for the Lipstick Killers!', *RAM* (2 Nov 1979), 9.
580 Frank Brunetti, review of *Mesmerizer*, *ARS* #385, 92.
581 Kim Giddy quoted in Condon, 'It's a Smear Campaign', 9.
582 Kim Giddy quoted in Condon, 'It's a Smear Campaign', 9.
583 Brunetti, review of *Mesmerizer*, 92.
584 M.A., 'Lipstick Killers Live', *On the Street* (20 Feb 1985), 5.
585 M.A., 'Lipstick Killers Live', 5.
586 Angie Pepper quoted in 'Angie Pepper interview', <http://www.divinerites.com/in_pa1.htm>, accessed 28 Jan 2007.
587 'The Sydney Band Explosion', 22.
588 Sleevenotes to the Thought Criminals, *Chrono-logical* (Doublethink 2CD, 2005).
589 Roger Grierson quoted in 'The Barman', 'You Only Think Twice: Return of the Thought Criminals', <http://www.i94bar.com/ints/thoughtcriminals.html>, accessed 31 Aug 2006.
590 Grierson quoted in 'The Barman', 'You Only Think Twice'.
591 Grierson quoted in 'The Barman', 'You Only Think Twice'.
592 Malcolm Baxter quoted in Stuart Coupe, 'The First Word about the Last Words', *RAM* (9 Feb 1979), 10.
593 Coupe, 'The First Word, 10.
594 Martin Bishop quoted in Ed St. John, 'Basilisk's Radical Ambitions', *ARS* #340, 18.
595 David Nerlich, 'S.P.K.', *On the Street* (25 Jan 1984), 17.
596 Vikki Riley, 'System Planning Korporation' [album review], *Vox Muzpaper* (Aug 1981), 22; see also 'Blackmail' [letters page], *Vox Muzpaper* (Sep 1981), 2.
597 David Virgin quoted in Lindsay Jones, 'Psst ... Wanna Know a Sekret?', *On the Street* (27 Jun 1984), 9.
598 Jones, 'Psst' ... Wanna Know a Sekret?'
599 Christie Eliezer, 'Broderick Smith Cases the Promised Land', *Juke* (16 Jan 1982), 8-9.

Chapter 12: Five Years of Fancy Cars

1 Debbie Kruger, *Songwriters Speak: Conversations about Creating Music* (Balmain: Limelight Press, 2005), 457.
2 Todd Hunter quoted in Kruger, *Songwriters Speak*, 465.
3 Todd Hunter quoted in Sara Lee, 'Dragon', *RAM* (26 Jul 1975), 6.
4 Ed St John, 'After Sunshine, the Dragon Mutates', *ARS* (5 May 1977), 44-45.
5 Hunter quoted in Lee, 'Dragon', 6.
6 'Mr. Cool's Scratch Pad', *Spunky* no. 12 (1976), 11.
7 It will probably amuse any Australian who may associate Dragon and John Paul Young as purveyors of 70s pop to be told that Cruise Lane's first single was called 'Death Is in the Air'. <http://www.sergent.com.au/music/cruiselane.html>, accessed 28 Feb 2015. Red McKelvie was the guitarist in Cruise Lane at the time this record was made.

8. Hunter in Lee, 'Dragon', 6.
9. 'Mr. Cool's Scratch Pad', *Spunky* no. 12 (1976), 11.
10. Lee, 'Dragon', 6.
11. 'Dragon to Marry . . . New Album Soon', *Juke* (1 Jul 1978), 3.
12. Adrian Ryan, 'Dragon, Sports' (live review, Princes Park, Carlton), *Juke* (13 Jan 1977), 17.
13. Lindy Allen, 'Dragon' (live review), *Juke* (18 Apr 1978), 16.
14. 'Dragon to Marry', 3.
15. Jenny Hunter-Brown, 'No Women Backstage', *RAM* (22 Jan 1980), 20-21.
16. Allen, 'Dragon', 16.
17. Christie Eliezer, 'De Gruchy Dies', *Juke* (1 Jun 1985), 3.
18. Marc Hunter, 'Dragon's Greatest Hits Vol. 1' (review), *RAM* (18 May 1979), 29.
19. *Royal Commission of Inquiry into Drug Trafficking* (Canberra: Australian Government Printing Service, 1983), 127.
20. *Royal Commission of Inquiry*, 95.
21. Taylor quoted in Mr. Cool, 'Bad Luck Dogs Dragon'. *Spunky* no. 3 (1976), 44.
22. *Royal Commission of Inquiry*, 194.
23. Shaw quoted in *Royal Commission of Inquiry*, 137.
24. Hunter, 'Dragon's Greatest Hits', 29.
25. Christie Eliezer, *High Voltage Rock 'n' Roll* (London: Omnibus Press, 2007), 64.
26. Anthony O'Grady, 'Marc Hunter: Troubled Times for the Lizard Prince', *RAM* (23 Mar 1979), 18-21.
27. Christie Eliezer, 'On the Road with the Rock and Roll Zoo . . . Finch and Dragon', *Juke* (22 Apr 1978), 9.
28. Ian 'Molly' Meldrum with Jeff Jenkins, *The Never, Um, Ever Ending Story* (Crows Nest: Allen and Unwin, 2014), 289.
29. Eliezer, 'On the Road', 9.
30. Jon Matthews, 'Dragon/Midnight Oil' (Avalon RSL live review), *Juke* (31 Dec 1977), 16.
31. Hunter, 'Dragon's Greatest Hits', 29.
32. Hunter, 'Dragon's Greatest Hits', 29.
33. Hewson quoted in Brian Jones, 'Exclusive Preview of Dragon's *O Zambezi*', *Juke* (28 Aug 1978), 8.
34. See for instance Mark Evans, *Dirty Deeds: My life inside and outside of AC/DC* (Crows Nest: Allen and Unwin, 2011), 258.
35. Matthews, 'Dragon/Midnight Oil', 16.
36. Hunter, 'Dragon's Greatest Hits', 29.
37. Jenny Brown, 'Flying Fingers and Nerves of Steel – Dragon's Robert Taylor', *Juke* (8 May 1978), 13.
38. Brown, 'Flying Fingers', 13.
39. Hunter quoted in Christie Eliezer, 'Riots, Rednecks and Rave Reviews', *Juke* (27 Jan 1979), 9.
40. Eliezer, 'Riots', 9.
41. Eliezer, 'Riots', 9.
42. Hunter quoted in O'Grady, 'Marc Hunter', 19.
43. Hunter quoted in Allen Webster, 'Marc Hunter Takes Over the Controls', *Juke* (14 Jul 1979), 7.
44. Hunter quoted in Webster, 'Marc Hunter', 7.
45. Willie Fixit, 'Dragon Add Violinist', *Juke* (17 Feb 1979), 5.
46. Jane Matheson, 'Around the Traps', *ARS* (22 Feb 1979), 46.
47. Fixit, 'Dragon add', 5.
48. Todd Hunter, quoted in Miranda Brown, 'The boys in the band' *RAM* 23 Mar 1979, 21.
49. Marc Hunter quoted in Ed St John, 'Dragon' in Editors of Rolling Stone, *The Big Australian Rock Book* (Neutral Bay: Megabooks, 1985), 100-101.
50. Hunter quoted in O'Grady, 'Marc Hunter', 19.
51. Marc Hunter quoted in Stuart Coupe, 'Marc Hunter: Island Knight', *ARS* (7 Feb 1980), 26.
52. Coupe, 'Marc Hunter', 26.
53. Hunter quoted in Coupe, 'Marc Hunter', 26.
54. Coupe, 'Marc Hunter', 26.
55. Coupe, 'Marc Hunter', 26.
56. Coupe, 'Marc Hunter', 26.
57. 'More letters', *Roadrunnner* (Nov 1981), 6.
58. Simon Balderstone, 'The New Dragon: "Less Spectacle and More Music"', *Juke* (21 Apr 1979), 9.
59. Christie Eliezer, 'Dragon Split After All', *Juke* (5 Jan 1980), 3.
60. Robert Taylor quoted in Scott Howlett, 'The Body of the Beat', *On the Street* (25 Jul 1984), 12-13.
61. Hunter quoted in Balderstone, 'The New Dragon', 9.
62. Paul Hewson quoted in Howlett, 'The Body', 12.
63. Eliezer, 'Dragon Split', 3.
64. Anthony O'Grady, 'The Last Rites of Dragon', *RAM* (25 Jan 1980), 11.

Chapter 13 : Happy/Sad Is a Really Fantastic Emotion

1. Craig Hooper quoted in Clinton Walker and Richard Guilliat, 'Reels: Melancholia in Plastic', in Clinton Walker, (Ed.), *The Next Thing* (Kenthurst: Kangaroo Press, 1984) 106-113.
2. Miranda Brown 'Reely and Trooly Now', *RAM* (19 Oct 1979), 7.
3. Elly McDonald, 'Reel Australia', *Roadrunner* (Sep 1980), 7.
4. Heather, 'The Reels', *Tharunka* (5 May 1980), 11.
5. Heather, 'The Reels', 11.
6. Jane Matheson, 'Around the Traps', *ARS* (22 Mar 1979), 45.
7. Brown 'Reely and Trooly Now', 7.
8. 'David' Mason quoted in Annie Burton, 'Happiness Is Being from Dubbo, Neurotic and Enthusiastic', *RAM* (18 May 1979), 12.
9. Dave Mason quoted in Ed St John, 'The Reels: Always on the Move', *ARS* (8 Jan 1981), 20.
10. McDonald, 'Reel Australia', 7.
11. Craig Hooper quoted in Bill Massen, 'Reels: Country Punk', *ARS* (10 Jan 1980), 21.
12. Colin Newham quoted in Massen, 'Reels: Country Punk', 21.
13. Burton, 'Happiness Is Being from Dubbo', 12.
14. Hooper quoted in Massen, 'Reels: Country Punk', 21.
15. Heather, 'The Reels', 11.
16. 'Reels Run Hot and Cold', *Juke* (19 Jan 1980), 8.
17. '7. Uschi Flett', *Juke* (20 Aug 1975), 17.
18. McDonald, 'Reel Australia', 7.
19. Mason quoted in John Lethlean, 'Dave Mason: Reelin' and Dealin', *Juke* (17 Jan 1981), 13.
20. Mason quoted in Lethlean ,'Dave Mason', 13.
21. 'Dave's Xmas Message', *Vox* (Dec 1981), 3.
22. Mark Cromelin, 'The Reels' (live review, Tracks, Sydney), *Juke* (17 Jan 1984), 24.
23. Dave Mason quoted in Gavin Waller, 'One Day at a Picture Exhibition', *Juke* (14 Mar 1987), 17.
24. David Dawson, 'Reels, Models to Merge?', *Juke* (30 Jan 1982), 3.
25. St John, 'The Reels', 20.
26. Heather, 'The Reels', 11.
27. McDonald 'Reel Australia', 7.
28. Ed St John, 'The Reels' in *The Big Australian Rock Book*, 98-99.
29. Christie Eliezer, 'The Reels Play Computer Games', *Juke* (27 Feb 1982), 15.
30. Craig Hooper quoted in Walker and Guilliat, 'Reels: Melancholia', 109.
31. Earl Grey 'Hunchback Heaven', *Roadrunner* (Nov 1981), 28.
32. Chris Bourke, *Crowded House: Something So Strong* (Sydney: Pan Macmillan, 1997), 43.
33. Dave Mason quoted in Eliezer, 'The Reels Play', 15.
34. Dawson, 'Reels, Models to Merge?', 3.
35. David Nichols, 'The Reels', *Distant Violins* no. 21 (1986), 10.
36. Grey, 'Hunchback', 28.
37. McDonald, 'Reel Australia', 7.
38. Hooper quoted in St John, 'The Reels', 98-99.
39. Mason quoted in Eliezer, 'The Reels Play', 15.
40. Hooper in Walker and Guilliat, 'Reels: Melancholia', 109.
41. Mason quoted in Eliezer, 'The Reels Play', 15.
42. Mason in Walker and Guilliat, 'Reels: Melancholia', 111.
43. 'Around the Traps', *ARS* (18 Sep 1980), 83.
44. Adrian Ryan, 'Stephen Cummings/The Reels', *Juke* (1 Jan 1983), 22.
45. Mark Fraser, 'The Reel Thing?', *On the Street* (7 Mar 1984), 23.
46. 'The Reels Go Rock', *ARS* (Oct 1986), 20.
47. Mason quoted in Waller, 'One Day', 17.
48. Waller, 'One Day', 17.
49. 'Malicious Gossip', *Roadrunner* (Feb 8 1980), 3.
50. 'Around the Traps', *ARS* #321-322, 96.
51. Dave Mason quoted in St John, 'The Reels', 20
52. Mason quoted in Nichols, 'The Reels', 10.
53. Mason quoted in Waller, 'One Day', 17.
54. Peter Lalor, 'From the Reels to Real-Life Depression', *The Australian* (24 May 2007), 7.
55. Mason in Walker and Guilliat, 'Reels: Melancholia', 113.
56. Hooper in Walker and Guilliat, 'Reels: Melancholia', 109.

NOTES

Chapter 14: We were sixty years old when we were nineteen

1. David McComb, <http://thetriffids.com>, accessed 4 Dec 2008.
2. David McComb, <http://thetriffids.com>.
3. McComb quoted in Tracee Hutchison, *Your Name's on the Door* (Sydney: ABC, 1992) 20.
4. 'Rabbits Wedding', *Gonzo* 69 no. 13 (1985).
5. McComb quoted in Hutchison, *Your Name's on the Door*, 19.
6. C. C. Mitchell, 'Spring in Perth', *Roadrunner* (Nov 1981), 32.
7. Mitchell, 'Spring in Perth', 17.
8. McComb quoted in Adam Sweeting, 'Desert Songs', *Melody Maker* (2 Aug 1986), 14-15.
9. Mitchell, 'Spring in Perth', 32.
10. Beau Rimshot, 'Decaying Splendour', *On the Street* (27 Mar 1985), 17.
11. Dave Graney quoted in Mark Dapin, 'Purple Reign', *The Age (Good Weekend)* (8 Novembr 1997), 17-22.
12. Stephen Cummings quoted in Kruger, *Songwriters Speak*, 296.
13. David McComb quoted in Toby Creswell, 'The Triffids: A Shot in the Arm and a New EP', *ARS* (Mar 1985), 27.
14. McComb quoted in Creswell, 'The Triffids', 27.
15. David McComb, 'Letter from Sydney', *Pelican* no. 1 (1982).
16. McComb quoted in Sweeting, 'Desert Songs', 14.
17. McComb quoted in Christie Eliezer, 'The Triffids in Perth', *Juke* (18 Feb 1984), 9.
18. McComb quoted in Creswell, 'The Triffids', 27.
19. Toby Cluechaz, 'The Triffids' (review), *Roadrunner* (Mar 1982), 29.
20. 'The Triffids', *Distant Violins* no. 8 (1983).
21. McComb, 'Letter from Sydney', 30.
22. David McComb 'Sydney Set Swings Out', *Pelican* no. 5 (1982), 34.
23. McComb quoted in Eliezer, 'The Triffids in Perth', 9.
24. McComb quoted in Eliezer, 'The Triffids in Perth', 9.
25. Casey plays on it (and a few contemporaneous Triffids releases) under the childhood pseudonym of Daubney Carshott.
26. Liz Ackerman, 'The Graham Lee Expose', *On the Street* (15 May 1985), 5.
27. James Paterson quoted in Steven Herrick, 'Lawson Square: Raining Treasure', *On the Street* (12 Dec 1984), 10-11.
28. David McComb quoted in Clinton Walker, 'The Triffids Keep Moving', *ARS* #408, 14.
29. McComb quoted in Eliezer, 'The Triffids in Perth', 9.
30. <http://thetriffids.com/sitefiles/HMbio.shtml>, accessed 9 Dec 2008.
31. McComb quoted in Creswell, 'The Triffids', 27.
32. McComb quoted in Hutchison, *Your Name's on the Door*, 87.
33. McComb in *Long Way to the Top* episode 5 (ABC), DVD.
34. D. McComb in Hutchison, *Your Name's on the Door*, 146.
35. McComb in Sweeting 'Desert Songs', 15.
36. *Long Way to the Top* episode 5.
37. McComb in Sweeting, 'Desert Songs', 15.
38. McComb in Sweeting, 'Desert Songs', 15.
39. McComb in Sweeting, 'Desert Songs', 15.

Chapter 15: There's Absolutely No Art in the Moodists

1. I am indebted to Harry Butler's *DNA* fanzine, issue 48, for much of the information that appears in this chapter, though a draft of the chapter (and its structure) was completed before I chanced upon this material.
2. Andrew McMillan, 'Singles', *RAM* (8 Feb 1980), 39.
3. Dave Graney quoted in David Nichols, 'He's Just Too Hip, Baby', *Juice* (Jun 1994), 76.
4. Dave Graney, *It is Written, Baby* (Milsons Point: Random House, 1997), 78.
5. Graney in Nichols, 'He's Just Too Hip', 76.
6. The ad, dated 6 Dec 1980, is reprinted in *DNA* no. 48. See also Clinton Walker, 'Their Spirit Is Eternal', in Walker (Ed.), *The Next Thing* (Kenthurst: Kangaroo Press, 1984), 93-98.
7. Dave Graney quoted in Christie Eliezer, 'The Moodists Ponder the Walls of Art Ache', *Juke* (12 Feb 1983), 21.
8. Donald Robertson, 'Singles', *Roadrunner* (Nov 1981), 29.
9. Colin Hubert, 'Who Plays Synthesiser?', *On the Street* (21 Nov 1984), 10.
10. Walsh quoted in Walker, 'Their Spirit Is Eternal', 93-98.
11. Walsh quoted in Walker, 'Their Spirit Is Eternal', 93-98.
12. Hubert, 'Who Plays Synthesizer?', 10.
13. Walsh quoted in Walker, 'Their Spirit Is Eternal', 93-98.
14. Graney quoted in Eliezer, 'The Moodists Ponder', 21.
15. Clare Moore interviewed by David Nichols, *Moodists Live in London 1984* (Umbrella Music, 2004), DVD.
16. Graney in Eliezer 'The Moodists ponder', 21.
17. Dave Graney interviewed by David Nichols, *Moodists Live in London*.
18. Graney quoted in Clinton Walker and Ed St John, 'The Moodists', in Editors of Rolling Stone, *The Big Australian Rock Book* (Neutral Bay: Megabooks, 1985), 88-89.
19. Steve Miller interviewed by David Nichols, *Moodists Live in London*.
20. Graney quoted in Walker and St John, 'The Moodists', 88-89.
21. Dave Graney interviewed by David Nichols, *Moodists Live in London 1984*.
22. Dave Graney quoted in Frank Brunetti, 'The Moodists: More Extreme and More Direct', *ARS* #383, 14.
23. Graney quoted in Nichols, 'He's Just Too Hip', 76.
24. Graney quoted in Walker and St John, 'The Moodists', 88-89.
25. Clare Moore interviewed by David Nichols, *Moodists Live in London 1984*.
26. Dave Graney quoted in Christie Eliezer, 'Beware! Moodists Camp 100 Km Ahead', *Juke* (26 Jan 1985), 10.
27. Graney quoted in Eliezer, 'Beware! Moodists Camp', 10.
28. Clare Moore interviewed by David Nichols, *Moodists Live in London 1984*.
29. Chris Walsh interviewed by David Nichols, *Moodists Live in London 1984*.
30. Hubert, 'Who Plays Synthesizer?', 10.
31. Dave Graney interviewed by David Nichols, *Moodists Live in London 1984*.
32. Dave Graney, 'Six Dead Birds', *Double Life* EP (Red Flame 1985).
33. Chris Walsh interviewed by David Nichols, *Moodists Live in London 1984*.

Chapter 16: The Modern Dance

1. Shane Nichols, 'The Numbers: Three Who Dare', *ARS* #327, 22.
2. Lynda Nutter interviewed by Donnie Sutherland, *After Dark* (21 Apr 1984).
3. Greg Taylor, 'Beware the Dugite Bite', *RAM* (6 Oct 1979), 9.
4. Jacky Hyams, 'Dugites' Lynda Nutter Plays It Straight', *ARS*, 20.
5. Hyams, 'Dugites' Lynda Nutter', 20.
6. Shane Nichols, 'The Dugites: Not Snake Away', *ARS* #321-322, 22.
7. Kim Williams, review of *The Dugites*, *Roadrunner* (Aug 1980), 21.
8. 'The Dugites ... "Cut the Talking", Let's Dance', *On the Street* (11 Apr 1984), 22.
9. Nutter interviewed by Sutherland, *After Dark*.
10. Christie Eliezer, 'The Second Bite Could be the Sweetest', *Juke* (14 Jan 1984), 9.
11. Nathan Brenner quoted in Greg Taylor, 'The Concerned Wheeler-dealer', *RAM* (24 Jun 1983), 13.
12. Elly McDonald, review of *The Unrealist*, *The Record* (Mar 1982), 19.
13. Slim Dusty and Joy McKean, *Another Day, Another Town* (Sydney: Pan Macmillan, 1996), 234.
14. Donald Robertson, 'Singles', *Roadrunner* (Jun 1981), 23.
15. Donald Robertson, 'Singles', *Roadrunner* (Nov 1981), 7.
16. Ed St John, 'Men at Work', in Editors of Rolling Stone, *The Big Australian Rock Book*, (Neutral Bay: Megabooks, 1985), 60.
17. Colin Hay quoted in Greg Taylor, 'After Lunch ... the World!', *RAM* (10 Jun 1983), 16-17.
18. Greg Ham quoted in Patrick Donovan, 'Men at Work Flautist Has Heard the Thunder', *The Age* (7 Jul 2010), 9.
19. Ed Nimmervoll, *Friday on my Mind* (Rowville: Five Mile Press, 2004), 141.
20. Hay quoted in Taylor, 'After Lunch', 17.
21. Penny Harding, 'Colin Hay Strips Back the Gears' *Juke* (7 Mar 1987), 10.
22. Noel Delbridge, *Up There Mike Brady*, (Port Melbourne: Coulomb Communications, 2004), 206.
23. Joe Dolce in Delbridge, *Up There*, 207.
24. M. M., 'Grubby Rags, and Music Mags', *Pelican* (Aug/Sep 1982), 26.
25. Ed St John, '2JJJ's Great Leap Forward', *ARS* #338, 27; John Potts, 'Heritage Rock: Pop Music on Australian Radio', in

Philip Hayward (Ed.), *From Pop to Punk to Postmodernism* (North Sydney: Allen and Unwin, 1992), 65.
26 Paul McHenry and Chris Spencer, *The Australian Various Artist on Cassette 1978-96* (Golden Square: Moonlight Publishing, 1996), 19-23.
27 Tyrone Flex, 'C-30, C-60, C-90 Go! Go!! Go!!!', *Roadrunner* (Nov 1981), 8.
28 Andrea Jones, '"Fast Forward" fills the Gap between Magazine and LP', *ARS* #340, 18.
29 Philip Hayward, *Music at the Borders: Not Drowning, Waving and their Engagement with Papua New Guinean Culture* (Sydney: John Libbey, 1998), 26.
30 Flex, 'C-30, C-60, C-90', 8.
31 'News', *Vox* (Nov 1981), 3
32 Andrea Jones, 'Going It Alone: The Independent Labels, Part 1: Sydney', *ARS* #338, 23-25.
33 Vivien Johnson, *Radio Birdman* (St Kilda: Sheldon Booth 1990), 7.
34 Johnson, *Radio Birdman*, 9.
35 Toby Creswell, 'New Race: Connecting with the Force', *ARS* #331, 12.
36 McFarlane, *Encyclopedia of Australian Rock and Pop*, 36-38.
37 Bailey quoted by Steve Gardner for *Foster Child* 'fanzine' (Feb 1998), reprinted at <http://nkvdrecords.com/saints.htm>, accessed 10 Jan 2006.
38 <http://guestlisted.blogspot.com.au/2011/09/ed-kuepper-interview-2011.html>, accessed 9 Apr 2012.
39 'Well Now – Dig This', *Vox* (Dec 1981), 3.
40 Ed Kuepper quoted in Christie Eliezer, 'Ha! Ha! Said the Clowns', *Juke* (27 Mar 1982), 20.
41 Bailey in Gardner, *Foster Child*.
42 Bailey in Gardner, *Foster Child*.
43 Mark Carey, 'Bathloads of Custard', *On the Street* (27 Mar 1985), 15.
44 <http://www.i94bar.com/ints/richardburgman.html>, accessed 9 Mar 2006.
45 <http://www.grindonline.com.au/2011/08/ed-kuepper-interview/>, accessed 9 Apr 2012.
46 Jane Matheson, 'Around the Traps', *ARS* (31 May 79), 46.
47 Andrew McMillan, 'No Saints in the Laughing Clowns', *RAM* (6 Oct 1979), 10-11.
48 McMillan, 'No Saints', 10.
49 Ed Kuepper, quoted in McMillan, 'No Saints', 10.
50 McMillan, 'No Saints', 10.
51 Paul Pottinger, sleevenotes to Laughing Clowns compilation, *Cruel But Fair* (Hot, 2005).
52 Kuepper quoted in Toby Cluechaz, 'Laughing Clowns', *Roadrunner* (Mar 1982), 12.
53 Craig N. Pearce, 'The Laughing Clowns', *Roadrunner* (Oct 1981), 13.
54 Kuepper quoted in Ed St John, 'Laughing Clowns', in *The Big Australian Rock Book*, 90-91.
55 Kuepper quoted in Tracee Hutchison, *Your Name's on the Door*, 12.
56 Kuepper in Cluechaz, 'Laughing Clowns', 12.
57 Kuepper in Cluechaz, 'Laughing Clowns', 12.
58 Linda Campbell, 'Tablewaiters, Sardine, Laughing Clowns' (live review), *Roadrunner* (Apr 1982), 19.
59 Craig N. Pearce, 'Mr Uddich Smuddich' (review), *Roadrunner* (Apr 1982), 28.
60 Kuepper quoted in Cluechaz, 'Laughing Clowns', 12.
61 Ed Kuepper interviewed by Donnie Sutherland, *After Dark* (21 Apr 1984).
62 Louise Elliott interviewed by Donnie Sutherland, *After Dark* (21 Apr 1984).
63 David Nichols, 'The Apartments', *Distant Violins* no. 16 (1984), 12.
64 Craig N. Pearce, 'The Laughing Clowns', *Roadrunner* (Oct 1981), 13.
65 Nichols, 'The Apartments', 12.
66 Kuepper quoted in Andrew McMillen, 'Songwriters: Ed Kuepper', *Mess + Noise* <http://www.messandnoise.com/articles/4222171>, accessed 9 Apr 2012.
67 Peter Lawrance, 'Laughing Clowns; the Best of All That Conviction' *Tension* no. 1 (1983), 34-36.
68 Ed Kuepper quoted in Clinton Walker, 'Exile from Main Street', *ARS* (Mar 1992), 57-59, 96.
69 Walker, 'Exile from Main Street', 58.
70 Clinton Walker, 'The Laughing Clowns Break Up', *ARS* (Mar 1985), 28.
71 Toby Creswell, 'Wildlife Documentaries Search for Freshness', *ARS* #356, 18.
72 Mark Mordue, 'Sedition', *Tension* no. 1 (1983), 8-10.
73 Mordue, 'Sedition', 8-10.
74 David Wall, 'Sedition', *Juke* (14 May 1983), 22.
75 Marie Ryan, 'Down and Out: Melbournites in London', *Vox* (Dec 1981), 8-9.
76 Simon Reynolds, *Rip It Up and Start Again: Postpunk 1978-1984* (London: Faber, 2005), 357.
77 Ryan, 'Down and Out', 9.
78 Matt Moffitt in Jenny Eather, 'Matt Finish: Hard, Durable and Built to Last', *Roadrunner* (Oct 1981), 17.
79 Louise Elliott interviewed by Donnie Sutherland, *After Dark* (21 Apr 1984).
80 Reynolds, *Rip It Up*, 483.
81 Robert Lewis, 'Bohemians/League of Honour/Dead Can Dance' (live review), *Vox* (Dec 1981), 4.
82 Iva Davies quoted in Donald Robertson, 'Icehouse in Motion', *Roadrunner* (Nov 1981), 19.
83 Dave Studdert quoted in Tyrone Flex, 'Tactics without Manoeuvres – Housewives without Hoovers', *Roadrunner* (Dec 1982), 38.
84 Dave Studdert quoted in Julia de Meyrick, 'The Tactical Hunger', *RAM* (19 Oct 1979), 8.
85 Studdert quoted in de Meyrick, 'The Tactical Hunger', 8.
86 Studdert quoted in Paul Merrick, 'Tactics', *Vox* (Aug 1981), 20.
87 Merrick, 'Tactics', 20.
88 De Meyrick, 'The Tactical Hunger', 8.
89 Tyrone Flex, 'Tactics Progress Report', *Roadrunner* (Oct 1981), 6.
90 John Encarnacao, review of Tactics' album *The Great Gusto*, *ARS*, 102.
91 Studdert in Merrick, 'Tactics', 20.
92 'The Drum', *Roadrunner* (Nov 1981), 5.
93 'Bob' quoted in Flex, 'Tactics without Manoeuvres', 38.
94 Studdert quoted in Flex, 'Tactics without Manoeuvres', 38.
95 Vicki Abraham, 'Hunters and Collectors', *Party Fears* (Autumn 1989), 26-27.
96 Abraham, 'Hunters and Collectors', 26-27.
97 David Harlock interview with Ray Tosti-Guerra in *HSVII* (1982).
98 Harlock interview with Tosti-Guerra.
99 Stuart Coupe, *The Promoters* (Sydney: Hodder, 2003), 17.
100 Jonathan Green, *Juke* (6 Oct 1984), reprinted at < http://humanfrailty.com.au/?page_id=3546>. It is worth noting that Green came up with this description as a comparison with the post-*Fireman's Curse* version of the group.
101 Vikki Riley, 'Nuvo Bloc, Hunters and Collectors, Equal Local, Laughing Clowns' (live review), *Vox* (Aug 1981), 5.
102 Clinton Walker, 'Hunters and Collectors Come Out at Night', in Walker (Ed.) *Inner City Sound* (Portland: Verse Chorus Press, 2005), 145-6.
103 Ed St John, 'Hunters and Collectors', in *The Big Australian Rock Book*, 110-111.
104 John di Mase, 'Hunters and Collectors: Weathering a High Profile Adolescence', *The Record* (Mar 1982), 2.
105 'Hunter's [sic] debut', *Juke* (16 Jan 1982), 3.
106 Andrew Maine, 'Sorry, Couldn't Keep His Mouth Shut!', *Vox* (Dec 1981), 3.
107 In his *Encyclopedia of Australian Rock and Pop*, Ian McFarlane refers to this a mini-album, presumably based on the number of songs featured, though the overall length of the record exceeds 60 minutes. Clinton Walker makes the same mistake in *Inner City Sound*, 182.
108 See Debbie Kruger, *Songwriters Speak*, 476.
109 Michael Gudinski quoted in Toby Creswell, 'The Godfather', *ARS* #452, 94-98, 128.
110 Di Mase, 'Hunters and Collectors', 2.
111 Quoted in Mark Everton, 'Houses in Commotion', *Rip it Up* (Nov 1983), 4.
112 Mark Seymour quoted in Richard Guilliat, 'Hunters and Collectors: In Search of Motion' in Clinton Walker (Ed.), *The Next Thing* (Kenthurst: Kangaroo Press, 1984) 54.
113 Mark Seymour interviewed in *Long Way to the Top* episode 5 (ABC), DVD.
114 Jonathan Green, *Juke* (6 Oct 1984), reprinted at < http://humanfrailty.com.au/?page_id=3546>.
115 C. L., 'Hunting and Collecting', *Pelican* (8 Oct 1983).
116 Peter Holder, 'Love Rodeo: Halfway There ... but Fun', *On the Street* (21 Nov 1984), 7.
117 See for instance 'L E D' review of *Jaws of Life*, *Pelican* no. 8, (1984).
118 Doug Falconer quoted in Everton, 'Houses in Commotion', 4.

NOTES

119 'Gimme Head' got another reading/response when Kellie Sutherland and Genevieve Blackmore sang it in their part-time group Your Wedding Night in 2004. Radio favoured a more straightforward 70s *Puberty Blues*-styled pastiche, 'Lachlan'.
120 Jonathan Green, *Juke* (6 Oct 1984), reprinted at < http://humanfrailty.com.au/?page_id=3546>.
121 Mark Seymour quoted in Guilliat, 'Hunters and Collectors', 56.
122 Wanda Jamrozik, *RAM* (27 Mar 1985), reprinted at <http://humanfrailty.com.au/?page_id=3921>.
123 Mark Seymour quoted in Christie Eliezer, 'Hunters and Collectors' *Juke* 3 Jan 1987, 14.
124 Michael Gudinski quoted in Creswell, 'The Godfather', 97.
125 Hutchison, *Your Name's on the Door*, 113.
126 Jones quoted in Toby Creswell, 'The Johnnies Thrive on Paradox', *ARS* #401, 20.
127 'Around the Traps', *ARS* (29 May 1980), 90.
128 Christie Eliezer, 'Gudinski: Mr. Mushroom', *ARS* (May 1975), 50-53.
129 Christine Camp, 'Rock on the Small Screen', *Juke* (20 Mar 1982), 7.
130 'Big Name for Show', *Juke* (16 Jan 1982), 3.
131 Michael Gudinski quoted in Creswell, 'The Godfather', 97.
132 Ian 'Molly' Meldrum with Jeff Jenkins, *The Never, Um, Ever Ending Story* (Crows Nest: Allen and Unwin, 2014), 383.
133 Jane Matheson, 'If You Can't Beat Them . . . The Swingers Join the Real World', *ARS* #339, 25.
134 John Dix, *Stranded in Paradise* (Wellington: Paradise Publications, 1988), 209-210.
135 Donald Robertson, 'One Step Forward', *Roadrunner* (Apr 1982), 4.
136 'Warning! This Man Is Unstable!', *Vox* (Dec 1981), 3.
137 Tim McGee, 'Two Nights in Heaven or Hell', *Roadrunner* (Apr 1982), 19.
138 Gillian Armstrong interviewed in Sue Mathews, *35mm Dreams: Conversations with Five Directors about the Australian Film Revival* (Ringwood: Penguin, 1984) 153.
139 Armstrong quoted in Mathews *35mm Dreams*, 151.
140 Armstrong quoted in Mathews *35mm Dreams*,.149.
141 Larry Buttrose, 'Starstruck' (review), *Roadrunner* (May 1982), 21.
142 Sean Kelly and James Freud interviewed by Ian Meldrum, *The Meldrum Tapes Best Of* (ABC, 1986), videocassette.
143 Hutchison, *Your Name's on the Door*,11. Kelly refers to Pierre as 'Pierre Pop'.
144 See James Freud, *I Am the Voice Left from Drinking* (Pymble: HarperCollins, 2002), 116.
145 The booklet to the 2000 CD release *Melbourne*, collecting various Models classics preceding their major label debut, features a listing of all members.
146 David Langsam, *Juke*.
147 Christie Eliezer, 'Brain Freud Music', *Juke* (14 Feb 1987), 16. Original text reads 'folling' for 'fooling'.
148 Sean Kelly and James Freud interviewed by Ian Meldrum.
149 Shane Nichols, 'The Models: Recovering', *ARS* #323, 100.
150 Nichols, 'The Models', 100.
151 See Walker, *Inner City Sound*, 96.
152 Jim Keays, *His Master's Voice*, (St Leonards: Allen and Unwin, 1999), 146.
153 'Random notes', *ARS* (19 Jun 1975), 54.
154 Ian McFarlane, sleevenotes to Models' *Melbourne* (Shock, 1999).
155 See Adrian Ryan', 'Model Pop', in Walker (Ed.), *Inner City Sound*, 94-98.
156 Meldrum with Jenkins, *The Never, Um, Ever Ending Story*, 101.
157 Nichols, 'The Models'. 100.
158 Ray Argall (dir.), *Pop Movie* (Musical Films,1986).
159 For a print indication of how terrible this project really was, see Hopalong Hoss, 'Ham on the Range', *Juke* (23 May 1987), 10-11.
160 Sean Kelly and James Freud interviewed by Ian Meldrum.
161 Craig N. Pearce, 'Doing the Perverted Pop Hop', *Roadrunner* (Dec 1981), 40.
162 Donald Robertson, 'Singles', *Roadrunner* (Aug 1981) 19.
163 Sean Kelly quoted in Donald Robertson, 'Subject: Sean Kelly', *Roadrunner* (Aug 1981), 7.
164 Hutchison, *Your Name's on the Door*, 26.
165 Robertson, 'Subject: Sean Kelly', 7.
166 But nowhere near as good as either of those records.
167 Hutchison, *Your Name's on the Door*, 26.
168 'Around the Traps', *ARS* #321-322, 96.
169 'Around the Traps', *ARS* (18 Sep 1980), 83.
170 Christie Eliezer, 'The Reels Play Computer Games', *Juke* (27 Feb 1982), 15.
171 Kelly and Freud interviewed by Ian Meldrum.
172 The session is detailed in Freud, *I Am the Voice*, 116-7.
173 Craig N. Pearce, 'Sardine V, Models' (review), *Roadrunner* (May 1982), 22.
174 Sean Kelly quoted in John O'Donnell, 'Band of Gypsies', *ARS* #446, 43-46.
175 He seems to have failed to realize this himself. See Freud, *I Am the Voice*, 145-7.
176 Daile Pepper and Andrew Murfett, 'Models' Frontman Tragedy: James Freud Takes Own Life", *Sydney Morning Herald* (4 Nov 2010), 7.
177 Narelle Wilson recalls seeing Models in Canberra in the late 80s and being told it was essential that she see the support band, who were 'really good'. She didn't realise it was Models in disguise, but she did realise they weren't really good.
178 James Valentine quoted in O'Donnell, 'Band of Gypsies', 44.
179 Susan Ryan, 'Out of Mind, Out of Sight or Just Evolution?', *On the Street* (6 May 1987), 19.
180 Scott Howlett, 'Kelly's Solo LP', *Juke* (27 Feb 1987), 5.
181 Sean Kelly quoted in Ryan, 'Out of Mind', 19.
182 'Divinyls', in *The Big Australian Rock Book*, 72-73.
183 Donald Robertson, 'Singles', *Roadrunner* (Nov 1981), 29.
184 Chrissy Amphlett with Larry Writer, *Pleasure and Pain: My Life* (Sydney, Hodder, 2005), 33-34.
185 Amphlett, *Pleasure and Pain*, 35.
186 B.B., 'Doing What Comes Naturally', *Campaign* (Dec 1975), 35.
187 Amphlett quoted in Kruger, *Songwriters Speak*, 450.
188 Amphlett quoted in Kruger, *Songwriters Speak*, 450.
189 Hutchison, *Your Name's on the Door*, 23.
190 David Nichols, 'Chrissie Amphlett', *Smash Hits* Australia (11 Mar 1985).
191 Amphlett, *Pleasure and Pain*, 193.
192 Amphlett quoted in Wendy Milsom and Helen Thomas, *Pay to Play: Tales of the Australian Rock Industry* (Ringwood: Penguin Books, 1986) 139-140.
193 Patricia Lovell, *No Picnic* (Sydney: Pan Macmillan 1995) 261.
194 Amphlett, *Pleasure and Pain*, 72.
195 Amphlett, *Pleasure and Pain*, 82.
196 Grossman in Amphlett, *Pleasure and Pain*, 89.
197 Amphlett quoted in Ed St John, 'The Divinyls' True Grit', *ARS* #392, 14-15.
198 McEntee quoted in St John, 'The Divinyls' True Grit', 15.
199 Amphlett, *Pleasure and Pain*, 173
200 Amphlett in Milsom and Thomas, *Pay to Play*, 148.
201 Zeb Olsen; 'Let Me Present to You . . . the Adorable Ones', *On the Street* (7 Oct 1987), 7.
202 Hutchison, *Your Name's on the Door*, 70.
203 Faulkner quoted in Ed St John, 'Hoodoo Gurus', in *The Big Australian Rock Book*, 82-83.
204 Stuart Coupe, 'Sydney', *Roadrunner* (Nov 1981), 15.
205 Dave Faulkner quoted in Lynden Barber, 'Marsupials Bagged', *New Musical Express* (16 Nov 1985), 21.
206 Hutchison, *Your Name's on the Door*, 71.
207 Quoted in Shayne Collier, 'The Hoodoo Gurus Ride the Hayride to Success', *On the Street* (26 Oct 1983), 6.
208 James Baker quoted in Ken Wark, 'How the Ramones Changed My Life', *On the Street* (3 Oct 1984), 12.
209 Dave Faulkner quoted in Toby Creswell, 'The Hoodoo Gurus: Combining the Commercial and the Hip', *ARS* #389, 12-13.
210 David Nichols, 'Much Hoodoo about Gurus', *Smash Hits* Australia (22 Apr 1985), 38-39.
211 Faulkner quoted in Barber, 'Marsupials', 21.
212 Faulkner quoted in St John, 'Hoodoo Gurus', in *The Big Australian Rock Book*, 82-83.
213 Peter Holder, 'Yankee Guru Dandy', *On the Street* (19 Dec 1984), 23.
214 Iva Davies quoted in John O'Donnell, 'Shades of Blue', *ARS* #452, 52-57.
215 Davies quoted in O'Donnell, 'Shades of Blue', 55.
216 Davies quoted in O'Donnell, 'Shades of Blue', 55.
217 O'Donnell, 'Shades of Blue', 55.
218 'The Sydney Band Explosion', *RAM* (29 Jun 1979), 20-21.
219 Davies in O'Donnell, 'Shades of Blue', 52.
220 Iva Davies interviewed by Ian Meldrum, *The Meldrum Tapes Best Of* (ABC, 1986), videocassette.

221 Iva Davies quoted in Bruce Elder, 'Icehouse', in *The Big Australian Rock Book*, 22
222 Richard McGregor, 'Flowers: Pressing Originals between the Covers', *ARS* (9 Aug 1979), 42.
223 Iva Davies quoted in Donald Robertson, 'Welcome to the Icehouse', *Roadrunner* (Sep 1980), 12-13.
224 'Malicious Gossip', *Roadrunner* (Feb 8 1980), 3.
225 Toby Creswell, 'Paul Kelly's Other Voices, Other Rooms', *ARS* #402, 18-19.
226 'Around the Traps', *ARS* (18 Sep 1980), 83.
227 Davies quoted in Robertson, 'Welcome to the Icehouse', 13.
228 Hutchison, *Your Name's on the Door*, 16.
229 Iva Davies interviewed by Ian Meldrum, *The Meldrum Tapes*.
230 Robertson, 'Subject: Sean Kelly', 8.
231 'News', *Vox* (Nov 1981), 3.
232 Davies quoted in Robertson, 'Icehouse in Motion', 19.
233 Robertson, 'Icehouse in Motion', 19.
234 Toby Creswell, 'Iva Davies' Icehouse: An Anti-Classicist Reworks the Old to Create the New', *ARS* #358, 11; see also Andy Maine, 'Love in Motion' (review), *Vox* (Nov 1981), 25.
235 Davies in Creswell, 'Iva Davies' Icehouse', 11.
236 Davies quoted in O'Donnell, 'Shades of Blue', 54.
237 Creswell, 'Iva Davies' Icehouse', 11.
238 Bruce Elder, 'Icehouse', *The Big Australian Rock Book*, 22.
239 Iva Davies quoted in Elder, *The Big Australian Rock Book*, 22.
240 Davies quoted in O'Donnell, 'Shades of Blue', 54.
241 Ed St. John, 'Australian Crawl', in *The Big Australian Rock Book*, 17.
242 James Reyne in the extras to *Love Is in the Air*, episode 4 (ABC), DVD.
243 James Reyne quoted in Christie Eliezer, 'Australian Crawl Show Their Strokes', *Juke* (8 Sep 1989), 7.
244 James Reyne in the extras to *Love Is in the Air*, episode 4.
245 'The Tamam Shud Man Cometh', *Juke* (30 Jul 1977), 6.
246 David Briggs quoted in Eliezer, 'Australian Crawl Show Their Strokes', 7.
247 Ed St John, 'Australian Crawl', *The Big Australian Rock Book*, 46.
248 James Reyne quoted in Ross Gardiner, 'Australian Crawl: Surfing into the Charts', *ARS* (1 May 1980), 39.
249 Ed St John, 'Jimmy & the Boys: Perverse Vaudevillians' ,*ARS* (Jan 1980), 11.
250 'Crawl, Enz off the Road', *Juke* (12 Jan 1980), 3.
251 Miranda Brown, 'Australian Crawl: Encountering the Hidden Depths of Success', *ARS* #341, 15-16.
252 Eliezer, 'Australian Crawl Show Their Strokes', 7.
253 James Reyne quoted in Toby Creswell, 'Australian Crawl: The Party's Over', *ARS* #388, 14.
254 Reyne quoted in Creswell, 'Australian Crawl', 14.
255 James Reyne in the extras to *Love Is in the Air*, episode 4.
256 Donald Robertson, 'Singles', *Roadrunner* (Jun 1981), 23.
257 Brown, 'Australian Crawl', 15-16.
258 Brown, 'Australian Crawl' 15.
259 Brecon Walsh, 'Adventures in Paradise with Australian Crawl', *Roadrunner* (7 Aug 1981), 10.
260 Reyne quoted in Ed St John, 'Australian Crawl', *The Big Australian Rock Book*, 46.
261 Reyne quoted in Toby Creswell, 'Australian Crawl: The Boys Toughen Up', *ARS* #357, 22.
262 Reyne interviewed in 2001 in the extras for *Return to Eden*, DVD release.
263 Reyne quoted in Toby Creswell, 'Australian Crawl: The Party's Over', 14.
264 Reyne quoted in Brown, 'Australian Crawl', 15.
265 Reyne quoted in Toby Creswell, 'Australian Crawl: The Party's Over', 14.
266 Creswell 'Australian Crawl: The Party's Over', 14.
267 John Doe, 'Oh Ye of Little Faith', *Roadrunner* (Jun 1981), 13.
268 Kilbey quoted in Doe, 'Oh Ye of Little Faith', 13.
269 John O'Donnell, 'Steve Kilbey', *ARS* (May 1992), 70-73.
270 Anon., 'Martydom', *Pelican* no. 6.
271 Kilbey quoted in Andrew McMillan, *Talking Smack: Honest Conversations About Drugs* (St. Lucia: University of Queensland, 2014), 13.
272 Kilbey quoted in Hutchison, *Your Name's on the Door*, 22.
273 Kilbey quoted in Hutchison, *Your Name's on the Door*, 206.
274 Leigh Leyland 'Darwin: Territorians Are Worth Enslaving?', *Roadrunner* (Nov 1981), 19.
275 Steve Kilbey quoted in Andrea Jones, 'The Church and Their Blurred Crusade', *Juke* (13 Feb 1982), 8-9.
276 Marty Willson-Piper quoted in Anon., 'Martydom'.

277 Kilbey in Stephen Phillips, 'The Church Re-focus on the Crusade', *Juke* (10 Mar 1984), 7.
278 Bruce Elder, 'The Church', in *The Big Australian Rock Book*, 57.
279 Marty Willson-Piper, quoted in Anon, 'Martydom'.
280 Kilbey quoted in Jones, 'The Church', 8-9.
281 Stephen Charlesworth, 'Mental as Anything', *Juke* (5 May 1978), 16.
282 Greedy Smith quoted in Andrea Jones, 'The Difference in Being Mental', *Juke* (27 Feb 1982), 11.
283 Smith quoted in Jones, 'The Difference in Being Mental', 11.
284 Charlesworth 'Mental as Anything', 16.
285 Jones, 'The Difference in Being Mental', 11.
286 Miranda Brown, 'Mental as Anything Encounter the Local Culture Gap', *RAM* (10 Aug 1979), 13.
287 Jane Matheson, 'Around the Traps', *ARS* (22 Feb 1979), 46.
288 Annie Burton, 'Those Who Sweat Also Get Wet', *RAM* (14 Dec 1979), 17.
289 'Mentals Play Dirty Pool', *Juke* (19 Jan 1980), 3.
290 Smith in Jones, 'The Difference in Being Mental', 11.
291 Greedy Smith quoted in 'Blow winds and crack your cheeks! rage! blow! You cataracts and hurricanes, spout til you have drench'd our steeples, drown'd in cats & dogs', *Roadrunner* (Oct 1981), 15.
292 Smith in 'Blow winds and crack your cheeks!', 15.
293 Smith in 'Blow winds and crack your cheeks!', 15.
294 Christie Eliezer, 'Barbed Wires', *Juke* (2 Jan 1982), 5.
295 Smith in 'Blow winds and crack your cheeks!', 15.
296 Darcy Condon, 'Shy Imposters Debut' *RAM* (19 Oct 1979), 10.
297 Tim Pitman and Murray Engleheart, sleevenotes to *This Is Real: Singles/Live/Rare* (Feel Presents, 2004).
298 T.C., 'Sunnyboys De-mythologise' *Roadrunner* (Aug 1981), 12-13.
299 M. Majors, 'Bubbling with Potential, Sunnyboys Still to Get the Mixture Right', *ARS* #339, 28.
300 Jeremy Oxley quoted in T.C., 'Sunnyboys', 13.
301 Neil Bradbury, 'Sunnyboys', *Vox* (Nov 1981), 16-17.
302 T.C., 'Sunnyboys', 12.
303 Jenny Eather, 'Matt Finish: Hard, Durable and Built to Last', *Roadrunner* (Oct 1981), 17.
304 David Pestorius, review of *Sunnyboys*, *Roadrunner* (Oct 1981), 42.
305 Mark Goodwin, 'The Big Wave', *On the Street* (19 Dec 1984), 21.
306 Michael Chugg quoted in Pitman and Engleheart, sleevenotes to *This Is Real: Singles/Live/Rare*.
307 'This Is Real: Sunnyboys Guitarist Richard Burgman Recounts Days Past', <http://www.i94bar.com/ints/richardburgman.html>, accessed 9 Mar 2006.
308 'This Is Real', <http://www.i94bar.com/ints/richardburgman.html>.
309 Peter Oxley quoted in Mark Goodwin, 'The Big Wave', 21.
310 Jeremy Oxley quoted in Pitman and Engleheart, sleevenotes to *This Is Real: Singles/Live/Rare*.
311 Pitman and Engleheart, sleevenotes to *This Is Real: Singles/Live/Rare*.
312 'New Group Strikes Sparks', *ARS* #388, 11.
313 'Random Notes', *ARS* #462 (Oct 1991), 17.
314 <http://www.andnowforsomethingcompletelydifferent.com.au/>, accessed 9 Apr 2012.
315 <http://www.spellbound-icehouse.org/storynew6.html>, accessed 9 Apr 2012.
316 <http://i94bar.com/ints/x-aspirations.html>, accessed 9 Apr 2012.
317 <http://www.i94bar.com/ints/lobbyloyde.html>, accessed 9 Apr 2012.
318 <http://www.fasterlouder.com.au/features/1064/>, accessed 9 Apr 2012.
319 Ed St John, 'INXS: Austral Skank', *ARS* #331-2, 38.
320 Kirk Pengilly quoted in Hutchison, *Your Name's on the Door*, 140.
321 Humphrys interviewed in *Gerry Humphrys The Loved One*, dir. Nigel Buesst (Sunrise Picture Co., 2000).
322 Mike Gee, *The Final Days of Michael Hutchence* (London: Omnibus Press, 1989), 14.
323 Kruger, *Songwriters Speak*, 405.
324 Ian Birch, 'This Is Your Life, Michael Hutchence', *Smash Hits Australia* ,vol. 1, no. 6 (1985), 8-10.
325 Birch, 'This Is Your Life, Michael Hutchence', 10.

326 Gee, *The Final Days*, 22. Gee suggests that Morris's original concept was that the group make themselves 'inaccessible' to the press and audiences.
327 Tim Farriss quoted in Craig Reardon, 'In Access to INXS', *X Campus (Pelican* no. 8), 29.
328 Birch, 'This Is Your Life, Michael Hutchence', 10.
329 Jane Matheson, 'Mushroom Ten Years On', *ARS* (1 Feb 1982), 58-69.
330 Ed St John, 'INXS: Staying Young, Getting Smarter', *ARS* (9 Dec 1982), 27.
331 Adrian Ryan, 'INXS, Beargarden' (review), *Roadrunner* (May 1982), 23.
332 Toby Creswell, 'Richard Clapton Escapes from His Past', *ARS* (15 Apr 1982), 15, 30.
333 Donald Robertson, 'Richard Clapton: The Great Escape', *Roadrunner* (Mar 1982), 5.
334 Robertson, 'Richard Clapton: The Great Escape', 5.
335 Ed St John, 'INXS: Staying Young, Getting Smarter', 27.
336 Reardon, 'In Access to INXS', 29.
337 Toby Creswell, 'INXS: On the Borderline', *ARS* (Oct 1985), 7, 11-12.
338 Birch, 'This Is Your Life, Michael Hutchence', 8-10.
339 'INXS', in Editors of Rolling Stone, *The Big Australian Rock Book*, 49
340 Kim Reed, 'Record Reviews', *On the Street* (15 May 1985), 6.
341 Creswell, 'INXS: On the Borderline', 11-12.
342 Farriss quoted in Kruger, *Songwriters Speak*, 412.
343 Sejavka quoted in Robbie Grounds, 'Beargarden: All Hands on Deck', *Juke* (2 Feb 1985), 7.
344 Sejavka quoted in Coates, 'Beargarden' 7.
345 Adrian Ryan, 'INXS, Beargarden', 23.
346 Hutchison, *Your Name's on the Door*, 3.
347 Hutchison, *Your Name's on the Door*, 35.
348 Rob Hirst quoted in Toby Creswell and Michael White, 'Midnight Oil: The Rolling Stone Interview' *ARS* #397, 44-51, 84-85.
349 'Garrett to Head Nsw Senate Ticket for 'No Nukes' Party, *On the Street* (10 Oct 1984), 4.
350 Peter Garrett quoted in Ashley Crawford, 'They Did It Theeeeiiiiirrr Waaaaaayyyy', *Juke* (2 Jan 1982), 8.
351 Davies quoted in Hutchison, *Your Name's on the Door*, 16.
352 Hutchison, *Your Name's on the Door*, 15.
353 Finn quoted in David Fricke, 'Taking Split Enz Seriously', *ARS* (16 Oct 1980), 20.
354 Tim Finn quoted in Ross Gardiner, 'Split Enz Paint Their True Colours', *ARS* (6 Mar 1980), 26-27.
355 Craig Mathieson, 'The Enz Are Nigh', *The Age* (2 Jun 2006), 2-3.
356 Fricke, 'Taking Split Enz Seriously', 20.
357 Rayner quoted in Donald Robertson, 'One Step Forward', *Roadrunner* (Apr 1982), 4.
358 Mike Chunn, *Stranger Than Fiction* (Auckland: GP Publications, 1992), 190.
359 Stephen Cummings quoted by Andrea Jones, 'The Sports Light Up', *ARS* (18 Sep 1980), 325-6.
360 Chunn, *Stranger Than Fiction*, 177.
361 Chunn, *Stranger Than Fiction*, 188.
362 Robertson 'One Step Forward', 4.
363 Robertson 'One Step Forward', 4.
364 Nigel Griggs in *Spellbound*, dir. Bruce Sheridan (1993).
365 Tim Finn in *Spellbound*.
366 Mathieson, 'The Enz', 2-3.
367 Chris Bourke, *Crowded House: Something So Strong* (Sydney: Pan Macmillan, 1997) 25.
368 Toby Creswell, 'Deckchairs Overboard Redefine Funk with a Pop Twist', *ARS* #391, 23.
369 Clinton Walker, 'Johanna Pigott's Artful Pop', *ARS* #402, 20.
370 Steve Phillips, 'Johanna Pigott Comes in from the Cold', *Juke* (18 Feb 1984), 10; Walker, 'Johanna Pigott's Artful Pop', 20.
371 Toby Creswell, 'XL Capris', *Vox* (Dec 1981), 7.
372 Adrian Ryan, 'Gold for Australian Crawl', *Roadrunner* (Sep 1980), 5.
373 Toby Creswell, 'XL Capris', 7.
374 Piggott quoted in Creswell, 'XL Capris', 7.
375 Todd Hunter quoted in Creswell, 'XL Capris', 7.
376 Creswell, 'XL Capris', 7.
377 Creswell, 'XL Capris', 7.
378 Johanna Pigott quoted in Phillips, 'Johanna Pigott Comes in from the Cold', 10.
379 Johanna Pigott quoted in Greg Taylor, 'Vision of Johanna', *RAM* (17 Feb 1984), 9.
380 Jones, 'Going It Alone', 24.
381 Pigott quoted in Taylor, 'Vision of Johanna', 9.
382 Kruger, *Songwriters Speak*, 456.
383 Creswell, 'Deckchairs Overboard', 23.
384 Andrea Jones, 'Mondo Rock Deliver the goods at Home; Now International Success Is Crucial', *ARS* #355, 10-11.
385 Adrian Ryan, 'The Sons of the Father', *Roadrunner* (Aug 1981), 11.
386 McCusker quoted in Ryan, 'The Sons of the Father', 11.
387 Andrea Jones, 'Keith Glass: Pioneer Goes Public', *ARS* #327 (1980), 23.
388 Jones, 'Keith Glass', 23.
389 'Scientists Lash "Illegal" Album', *Juke* (8 Jun 1985), 3.
390 David Gerard, 'And Remember: No-one Ever Lost Their Job Buying Severed Heads', *Party Fears* (Summer 1991-92), 2-3.
391 Craig N. Pearce, 'Soul of the City: M² Come out from Hiding', *Roadrunner* (Mar 1982), 19.
392 Pearce, 'Soul of the City', 19.
393 Dermot Browne, 'Suppose They Had an M² benefit and No-one Came', *On the Street* (29 Feb 1984), 8.
394 Simon Grounds quoted in Brian Jones, 'God Bless Judith Durham!', *Juke* (2 Feb 1985), 9.
395 Grounds quoted in Jones, 'God Bless Judith Durham!', 9.
396 Ed St John, 'Severed Heads: A Thirst for the New', *ARS* (Dec 1985), 7, 20-21.
397 Tom Ellard quoted in Colin Hubert, 'Severed Heads: Forging in the Junkyard', *On the Street* (6 Mar 1985), 8-9.
398 Richard Fielding, 'Memoirs of a Baby Squid, Part 1', *No Night Sweats*, <http://www.users.bigpond.com/pturnbul/nns_memoirs_rfl.htm>, accessed 31 Jul 2006.
399 Meera Atkinson, 'Clearing up Six Months of Rumours with Louis Tillet [sic]', *On the Street* (19 Dec 1984), 13.
400 Meera Atkinson, 'Black Boots, White Fruits', *On the Street* (12 Sep 1984), 7.
401 Colin Hubert, 'Particals of Pop', *On the Street* (29 Aug 1984), 16-17.
402 Scott Matheson, 'Mental as Anything, The Particles, The Big S, Macquarie University, Sydney' (live review), *Roadrunner* (Oct 1981), 34-35.
403 Peter Williams quoted in Scott Mathieson, 'Tinkle, Tinkle, Light and Fast', *Roadrunner* (Apr 1982), 7.
404 Spielman quoted in Mathieson, 'Tinkle, Tinkle', 7.
405 Spielman quoted in Mathieson, 'Tinkle, Tinkle', 7.
406 Spielman quoted in Mathieson, 'Tinkle, Tinkle', 7.
407 Spielman quoted in Hubert, 'Particals of Pop', 17.
408 Wanda Jamrozik, 'Particles Take a New Shape', *RAM*, (27 Apr 1984), 9.
409 Mumbles Minton, 'Lighthouse Keepers', *X-Press* (16 Aug 1985), 1.
410 Juliet Ward quoted in David Gerard, 'Widdershins', *Party Fears* (Autumn 1989), 22-23.
411 Stuart Coupe, 'Sydney', *Roadrunner* (Nov 1981), 15.
412 Tim Kelton, *Underground in the City of Churches: Rock Music in South Australia* (Adelaide: WAV Publications, 1986), 27.
413 David Gerard, 'Kim Salmon', *Party Fears* (Autumn 1989), 11-13.
414 Dave Graney quoted in Michael Dwyer, 'Living Like a Refugee, *The Age* EG section (16 Jun 2006), 2.
415 Dawn Bailey and Julie Conroy, 'Citadel Records', *Party Fears* no. 5 (late 1986), 11.
416 Patrick Emery, 'The Moffs', *Beat* (17 Sep 2008), 34.
417 David McComb, 'Sydney Set Swings Out', *Pelican* no. 5 (1982), 34.
418 Ashley Crawford, 'Laughing in a Hand-me-down World', *Juke* (20 Mar 1982), 8.
419 James Manning, 'Asphyxiation' (live review), *Juke* (30 Jan 1982), 32.
420 David McComb, 'Sydney Set Swings Out', 34.
421 Robert Goodge quoted in Milsom and Thomas *Pay to Play*, 168.
422 Robert Goodge quoted in David Whittaker, 'Charisma and the Ability to Persuade without the Use of Logic', *On the Street* (24 Oct 1984), 12.
423 Ian Cox quoted in Milsom and Thomas, *Pay to Play*, 170.
424 C.W., 'David Chesworth Tackles Shakespeare', *ARS* (Jan/Feb 1985), 12.
425 Cox quoted in Milsom and Thomas, *Pay to Play*, 174.
426 James Manning, 'Expozay', *Juke* (22 Jan 1983), 22.
427 Jonathon Digby, 'I'm Talking', *Xpress* no. 4 (2 Aug 1985), 6-7.
428 Ashley Crawford, 'I'm Talking: Function *and* Style', *Juke* (17 Mar 1984), 18.

429 Lynne O'Donnell, 'Shout to the Top', *Smash Hits* Australia vol. 1, no. 7 (1985), 11.
430 O'Donnell, 'Shout to the Top', 11.
431 Toby Creswell, 'I'm Talking: Not Sitting Around', *ARS* #383, 18.
432 Robert Goodge quoted in Crawford, 'I'm Talking', 18.
433 Crawford, 'I'm Talking', 18.
434 Clinton Walker, 'Talking to the Top' *ARS* #400, 22.
435 Walker, 'Talking to the Top', 22.
436 Cox quoted in Milsom and Thomas, *Pay to Play*, 167.
437 Cox quoted in Milsom and Thomas, *Pay to Play*, 176.
438 Scott Howlett, 'Ceberano to Record with Beck and McLaren', *Juke* (14 Mar 1987), 3.
439 Sejavka quoted in Coates, 'Beargarden', 7.
440 Alan White, 'Do You Believe?', *On the Street* (10 Jun 1987), 25.
441 'Perth', *Roadrunner* (Apr 1982), 5.
442 Donald Robinson, 'I Was a Teenage Wombat (and still Am)', *RAM* (24 Jun 1983), 11.
443 'Machinations: Built in Sydney, Designed for Melbourne', *Vox* (Dec 1981), 5.
444 Donald Robinson, 'Well-moulded Machs', *RAM* (10 Jun 1983), 25.
445 Toby Creswell, 'Real Life Get Tough on "Flame"', *ARS* (Nov 1985), 14-15.
446 Richard Zatorski quoted in Damien Minton, 'Real Life', *On the Street* (18 Jan 1984), 17.
447 Richard Zatorski quoted in Christie Eliezer, 'Like Real Life Do', *Juke* (11 Feb 1984), 7.
448 Zatorski quoted in Eliezer, 'Like Real Life Do', 7.
449 Zatorski quoted in Eliezer, 'Like Real Life Do', 7.
450 'Spectrum to Reform' *RAM* (17 Feb 1984), 3.
451 Steve Gilpin quoted in Miranda Brown, 'Mi-Sex: More New Zealanders on the Make', *ARS* (14 Jun 1979), 44.
452 Stuart Coupe, 'Mi-Sex is a Spark of Electroflash, Geared for Synchro-mash', *RAM* (23 Mar 1979),. 7.
453 Steve Gilpin quoted in Annie Burton, 'Mi-Sex: Technological Criminals Work Horribly Hard at Making Rock 'N' Roll an Occupation, a Job, a Career And a Game', *RAM* (19 Oct 1979), 19.
454 Brown, 'Mi-Sex', 44.
455 Andrew McMillan, 'Mi-Sex and Images for Sale', *RAM* (24 Aug 1979), 7.
456 Steve Gilpin quoted in Brown, 'Mi-Sex', 44.
457 McMillan 'Mi-sex', 7.
458 Annie Burton 'Mi-sex: technological criminasl work horribly hard at making rock 'n' roll an occupation, a job, a career and a game' *RAM* 19 Oct 1979, 19.
459 Gilpin quoted in Andrea Jones, 'Mi-Sex: A Band on the Run', *ARS* (1 May 1980), 20.
460 Gilpin quoted in Jones, 'Mi-Sex', 20.
461 'Around the traps', *ARS* (Jan 13 1979), 84.
462 Craig N. Pearce, 'Marc – My Word!' *Roadrunner* (Oct 1981), 34.
463 'Jailhouse Rock', *The Record* (Mar 1982), 3.
464 Paul Hewson quoted in Scott Howlett, 'The Body of the Beat', *On the Street* (25 Jul 1984), 12-13.
465 Hewson quoted in Howlett, 'The Body of the Beat', 13.
466 Marc Hunter quoted in Ed St. John, 'Dragon: Drugs, Death and Tales of Ordinary Men', *ARS*, 16-17.
467 Hewson quoted in Howlett, 'The Body of the Beat', 13.
468 Pigott quoted in Phillips, 'Johanna Pigott', 10.
469 Christie Eliezer, 'Hewson's Death under a Cloud', *Juke* (26 Jan 1985), 3.
470 Johanna Pigott quoted in Kruger, *Songwriters Speak*, 457.
471 Eliezer, 'Hewson's Death', 3.
472 Eliezer, 'Hewson's Death', 3.
473 Marc Hunter quoted in St. John, 'Dragon: Drugs, Death', 17.
474 Jane Matheson, 'Rose Tattoo: Bearing the Scars of Rock & Roll', *ARS* #356, 10-11.
475 Angry Anderson quoted in Matheson, 'Rose Tattoo', 11.
476 Pete Wells quoted in Matheson, 'Rose Tattoo', 10.
477 Donald Robertson, 'Tatts to Play Shock!', *Roadrunner* (Mar 1982), 5.
478 Scott Howlett, 'A Rose by Another Name?', *Juke* (17 Jan 1987), 14.
479 Christie Eliezer, 'Mirror'd Image', *Juke* (8 Jun 1985), 7.
480 Anderson quoted in Christie Eliezer, 'Mirror'd Image', 7.
481 Anderson quoted in Karen Dewey, *Angry: Scarred for Life* (Chippendale: Ironbark, 1994) 152.
482 Anderson quoted in Scott Howlett, 'The Aussie Tattoo', *On the Street* (31 Oct 1984), 12.
483 Anderson quoted in Howlett, 'The Aussie Tattoo', 12.
484 Paul Christie quoted in Scott Howlett, 'The Party Boys – The Stuff Dreams Are Made Of?', *On the Street* (10 Jun 1987), 11.
485 Quoted in Scott Howlett, 'A New Party Boy', *On the Street* (12 Dec 1984), 21.
486 Howlett, 'The Party Boys', 11.
487 Howlett, 'The Party Boys', 11.
488 Nick Cave quoted in Matthew Hall, 'Nick Cave: The Thirtysomething Years', *Puncture* no. 24 (May 1992), 22-27.
489 Cave quoted in Hutchison, *Your Name's on the Door*, 9.
490 Ed St. John, 'The Birthday Party's Trenchant Return', *ARS* (8 Jan 1981), 20.
491 Sue Denim, 'Confessions of a Rubbish Rock Hack', *Frankie* (Aug/Sept 2005), 88.
492 Effigy 1 + 2, 'Mick Harvey', *Party Fears* no. 9 (Summer 1998-99), 5-7.
493 Effigy 1 + 2, 'Mick Harvey', 5-7.
494 Giles Barrow, 'King Cave Bat Returns', *Roadrunner* (Dec 1981), 25.
495 Donald Robertson, 'Singles', *Roadrunner* (Oct 1981), 37.
496 Cave quoted in Kruger, *Songwriters Speak*, 445.
497 Cave quoted in Marie Ryan, 'The Birthday Party', in Editors of Rolling Stone, *The Big Australian Rock Book*, 70-71.
498 'Anna', Letter, *Roadrunner* (May 1982), 30.
499 Harvey quoted in McMillan, *Talking Smack*, 96.
500 Mick Harvey and Rowland Howard quoted in Ashley Crawford, 'It's Their Party, and They'll Try If They Want To', *Juke* (30 Jan 1982), 14.
501 Cave quoted in Frank Brunetti, 'My Hands Just Went Limp', *RAM* (27 Apr 1984), 12-13.
502 Cave quoted in Marie Ryan, 'The Birthday Party'.
503 Goose quoted in Colin Hubert, 'Madroom – What's Wrong with a Bit of Serious Fun?', *On the Street* (11 Apr 1984), 24-25.
504 Liz Ackerman, 'Cooking with George and Especially ARNOLD', *On the Street* (19 Dec 1984), 17.
505 Hugo Race, 'The Crystal Blitz', *Overland* (Spring 2014), <https://overland.org.au/previous-issues/issue-216/feature-hugo-race/>, accessed 1 Mar 2015.
506 Andrew Maine, 'Plays With Marionettes' (live review), *Vox Muzpaper* (Dec 1981), 4.
507 Hugo Race quoted in Jonathan Green, 'Marionettes play with the strings' *Juke* 30 Apr 1983, 9.
508 Race quoted in Jonathan Green, 'Marionettes Play with the Strings', *Juke* (30 Apr 1983), 9.
509 Megan Edwards, 'Horla', *Distant Violins* no. 16 (1984), 3.
510 Edwards, 'Horla', 3.
511 Garry Gray, quoted in <http://www.indevelopment.org/2008/cowboys/garrygray-04.htm>, accessed 12 Dec 2008.
512 David Fricke, 'Little River Band Searches for an Image', *ARS* (Jan 1980), 14.
513 Glenn Shorrock quoted in Fricke, 'Little River Band', 14.
514 Shane Nichols, 'Mike Brady: The Invisible Man Steps Out', *ARS* (7 Feb 1980), 22.
515 Ed St John, 'Do Re Mi Are Ready for Action', *ARS* (Jun 1985), 19.
516 Carter quoted in Hutchison, *Your Name's on the Door*, 89.
517 Mara Smarrelli, 'Partners in Crime', *Juke* (4 May 1985), 11.
518 Rob Craw quoted in Smarrelli, 'Partners in Crime', 11.
519 Paul Stewart quoted in Peter Lawrance, 'Painters and Dockers: The Good, the Bad and the Horrible', *ARS* (Apr 1985), 22.
520 Lynne O'Donnell, 'The Painters and Dockers Report', *Juke* (5 Jan 1985), 13.
521 Basia Bonkowski quoted in Rob Miller, 'The Mild Enigma of Basia Bonkowski', *On the Street* (27 Feb 1985), 14-15.
522 Damien Minton, 'Going Down, Going Down . . . Down, Down, Down, Down, Down', *On the Street* (6 Jul 1983), 17.
523 Ed St John, 'Pel Mel', in *The Big Australian Rock Book*, 76-77.
524 Shayne Collier, 'The Powers of Persuasion', *On the Street* (29 Feb 1984), 10.
525 Dunne quoted in Ashley Crawford, 'And Now for an Alternative, Pel Mel Seek a Hit', *Juke* (14 Apr 1984), 9.
526 Dave Weston interviewed by Donnie Sutherland, *After Dark* (10 Mar 1984).
527 Dawn Bailey and Julie Conroy, 'Citadel Records', 11-12.
528 Shayne Collier, 'Feelin' Groovy – I Don't Think So', *On the Street* (18 Jan 1984), 6.

NOTES

529 Peter Raengel quoted in Clinton Walker, 'Sunday Painters: The Sound of Chloroform', in Walker (Ed.), *The Next Thing*, 131.
530 Raengel quoted in Walker, 'Sunday Painters', 132.
531 Clinton Walker, 'Sunday Painters', 131.
532 Raengel quoted in Walker, 'Sunday Painters', 133.
533 Raengel quoted in Walker, 'Sunday Painters', 134.
534 Quoted in Clinton Walker, 'Celibate Rifles', in *The Big Australian Rock Book*, 122-123.
535 David Swift, 'Ballistic Kisses', *New Musical Express* (4 Jul 1987), 26.
536 Kelton, *Underground in the City of Churches*, 47.
537 Quoted in Clinton Walker, 'Celibate Rifles', 122-123.
538 Leyland, 'Darwin: Territorians are Worth Enslaving?', 19.
539 Mark Halstead quoted in Arch Brown, 'Deep in the Heart of Tex', *Juke* (2 Jul 1983), 13.
540 Halstead quoted in Brown 'Deep in the Heart of Tex', 13.
541 Baker in Wark, 'How the Ramones Changed My Life', 12.
542 'The Beasts of Bourbon – It's the Last Show Ever!', *On the Street* (20 Feb 1985), 3.
543 Colin Hubert, 'Salamander Jim', *On the Street* (10 Oct 1984), 11.
544 Tex Perkins quoted in Hubert, 'Salamander Jim', 11.
545 Eloise McAnulty, 'Lorn [sic] Green Shares His Precious Fluids', *On the Street* (20 Feb 1985), 10.
546 Christie Eliezer, 'Nobody Here but Us Electric Pandas', *Juke* (12 Jan 1985), 11.
547 Simon Maynard 'Who Took the T(h)rash out of the Samurai?', *Juke* (6 Mar 1985), 8.
548 Lindsay Jones, 'Samurai Trash', *On the Street* (4 Apr 1984), 9.
549 Jones, 'Samurai Trash', 9.
550 Mark Foster quoted in Michael Roberts, 'Trash and Treasure', *On the Street* (12 Dec 1984), 12.
551 Michael Smith, 'Hepnotics on Higher Perches', *Juke* (8 Jun 1985), 11.
552 Silver quoted in Ross Clelland, 'Dynamic Hepnotics', *Smash Hits Australia*, vol. 1, no. 12 (1985), 16-17.
553 Paul Kelly, *Don't Start Me Talking: Lyrics 1984-2004* (Crows Nest: Allen and Unwin, 2004).
554 Kelly, *Don't Start Me Talking*, 22.
555 Kelly, *Don't Start Me Talking*, 38.
556 David Gerard, 'Paul Kelly', *Party Fears* no. 5 (late 1986), 5.
557 Kelly quoted in Adrian Ryan, 'Paul Kelly Takes Control', *Juke* (2 Feb 1985), 8.
558 Toby Creswell, 'Paul Kelly Talks', *ARS* #340, 21.
559 Kelly quoted in Creswell, 'Paul Kelly Talks', 21.
560 Adrian Ryan, 'Paul Kelly', *Roadrunner* (ca. 1979 clipping in the possession of S. O'Neil, 14.
561 Ryan, 'Paul Kelly', 14.
562 Kelly quoted in Ryan, 'Paul Kelly Takes Control', 8.
563 Ryan, 'Paul Kelly Takes Control', 8.
564 Frank Brunetti, 'Paul Kelly Takes the Solo Option', ARS #385 (1985), 21.
565 Damien Minton, 'The Go-Betweens', *On the Street* (6 Jul 1983), 6.
566 Minton, 'The Go-Betweens', 6.
567 Minton, 'The Go-Betweens', 6.
568 Wanda Jamrozik, 'Climbing Frame/PSI/Death in Vegas', *Juke* (26 Jan 1985), 20.
569 Rob Miller, 'Climbing Frame Climbing Up', *On the Street* (10 Oct 1984), 9.
570 Howard quoted in Hutchison, *Your Name's on the Door*, 42.
571 'Rock's Night of Nights', *Juke* (30 Apr 1983), 7.
572 Howard quoted in Toby Creswell, 'With True Grit and Blind Faith, Goanna Finally Delivers Second Album', *ARS* #387, 18-19.
573 Howard quoted in Creswell, 'With True Grit', 18-19.
574 Howard quoted in Creswell, 'With True Grit', 18.
575 Stephanie Rilen quoted in Jenny Eather, 'Sardine V', *Roadrunner* (Nov 1981), 15.
576 Frank Brunetti, 'Ian Rilen: Sardine V', *Vox* (Nov 1981), 8-9.
577 Ian Rilen quoted in Eather, 'Sardine V', 15.
578 Eather, 'Sardine V', 15.
579 Linda Campbell, 'Tablewaiters, Sardine, Laughing Clowns' (live review), *Roadrunner* (Apr 1982), 19.
580 Richard Kingsmill, 'Songs of the Pre-war Era', *On the Street* (17 Apr 1985), 12.
581 <http://www.gangajang.com/histyhed.htm>, accessed 21 Sep 2008.
582 <http://www.gangajang.com/geofpgs/aliens/aliens.htm>, accessed 21 Sep 2008.
583 Tracee Hutchison and Richard Kingsmill, 'Australian Music: 1985 in Review', *On the Street* (18 Dec 1985), 12-13.
584 Ken Sykes quoted in Kelton, *Underground in the City of Churches*, 73.
585 Terry Bradford quoted in Kelton, *Underground in the City of Churches*, 105.
586 Kelton, *Underground in the City of Churches*, 10.
587 Graney in Nichols, 'He's Just Too Hip', 76.
588 Thomas quoted in Kelton, *Underground in the City of Churches*, 20.
589 Kelton, *Underground in the City of Churches*, 10.
590 Kelton *Underground in the City of Churches*, 11.
591 Thomas quoted in Kelton, *Underground in the City of Churches*, 21.
592 Thomas quoted in Kelton, *Underground in the City of Churches*, 22.
593 Kelton, *Underground in the City of Churches*, 31.
594 Kelton, *Underground in the City of Churches*, 26.
595 Mick Brown in Kelton, *Underground in the City of Churches*, 27.
596 Eloise McAnulty, 'Untrained Observer in Adelaide', *On the Street* (20 Feb 1985), 13.
597 'Grong Singer Shock', *Juke* (2 Feb 1985), 5.
598 'The Drum', *Roadrunner* (Oct 1981), 5.
599 Eva Beauclerk, 'Speedboat', *Roadrunner* (Oct 1981), 6.
600 Hutchison, *Your Name's on the Door*, 21.
601 John Castles, 'Tjungaringanyi: Aboriginal Rock', in Hayward (Ed.), *From Pop to Punk*, 28-29.
602 Donald Robertson, 'No Fixed Address: Original Aboriginal Reggae', *Roadrunner* (Aug 1980), 12-13.
603 Robertson, 'No Fixed Address', 12-13.
604 Clinton Walker, 'Coloured Stone Aim for Black and White', *ARS* (Mar 1985), 28.
605 Buna Lawrie quoted in Clinton Walker 'Coloured Stone Aim for Black and White', 28.
606 Henry Pepper, 'Coloured Stone', *On the Street* (29 Jan 1986), 11.
607 'Invitation to the Red Centre for a Black Celebration', *On the Street* (24 Apr 1985), 5.
608 Elinor Boyd, 'Murri-Music', *On the Street* (6 Jul 1983), 1.
609 Andrew Garton, 'Black Radio', *On the Street* (6 Jul 1983), 4.
610 'When Three Tribes Come to Town', *On the Street* (7 Nov 1984), 7.
611 Richard Morgan, 'Hip Pocket and Street Pack: A Guide to Portable Sound', *The Record* (Mar 1982), 22.
612 Hans Fantel, 'CD Grows Up: An Expensive Toy Becomes a Sound Investment', *ARS* (Jan/Feb 1985), 39.
613 Fantel, 'CD Grows Up', 39.
614 Simon Maynard, '3 blows for Home Taping', *Juke* (8 Jan 1983), 3.
615 Anon., 'The New Big Little Thing', *X-Press* no. 6 (30 Aug 1985), 6.
616 Michael Roberts, 'New Music 1985', *On the Street* (20 Feb 1985), 17.
617 The Norm, 'Early Zmas for 2SER Compilation Cassette', *On the Street* (25 Apr 1984), 13.
618 *On the Street* (18 Jan 1984), 1-3 passim.
619 Heather Prain, 'INXS/The Models/Hoodoo Gurus/Dynamic Hepnotics/The Cockroaches/ I'm Talking/Celibate Rifles/The Tribe', *Juke* (19 Jan 1985), 23.
620 'Fifteen for 85', *Smash Hits Yearbook 1984*, 12-13, 76-77.
621 Hutchison and Kingsmill, 'Australian Music: 1985 in Review', 12.
622 Hutchison and Kingsmill, 'Australian Music': 1985 in Review, 13.

Afterword

1 Chris Spencer, Zbig Nowara, and Paul McHenry, *Who's Who of Australian Rock!*, fifth edition (Noble Park: Five Mile Press, 2002).
2 Jane Gazzo, *John Farnham: The Untold Story* (North Sydney: Ebury Press, 2015), 313.
3 Gazzo, *John Farnham*, 332.
4 Gazzo, *John Farnham*, 104.

Index

The term 'EP' ('extended play') is used herein to denote any record of more than two songs that does not amount to a full-length album; 'author' refers to a journalist or other writer – with the obvious caveat that many musicians are also authors of this kind and various others.

*** **** 259
→ ↑ ⇌ see Tch Tch Tch
0-10 Network [TV network] 72
10 9 8 7 6 5 4 3 2 1 [album] 487
'12lb Toothbrush' [song] 184
18th Century Quartet 72, 103
'2 People Per Sq. Km' [song] 449
2000 Weeks [book] 157; *2000 Weeks* [film] 113; '2000 Weeks' [song] 113
21 Faces 540
'25th Hour' [song] 522
2JJ [radio station] 269, 272, 374, 414, 421, 435; *see also* 2JJJ
2JJJ [radio station] 278, 398, 414, 421, 431, 523, 539; *see also* 2JJ
2MMM [radio station] 383, 510
2RSR [radio station] 272
2SER [radio station] 272
2SM [radio station] 33, 285, 362, 398, 472, 494
2UW [radio station] 96, 125
2XX [radio station] 435
3 [EP] 428
3 Directions in Australian Pop [film] 168, 170
39.51 [album] 411
3AK [radio station] 168, 202
3CR [radio station] 272
3DB [radio station] 24
3EON 307, 487
3KZ [radio station] 44
3MBS [radio station] 272
3PBS [radio station] 272
3RRR [radio station] 272, 340, 438, 487
3UZ [radio station] 98
3XY [radio station] 89, 421, 442
3ZZ [radio station] 270
4 Corners [TV show] 96
4IP [radio station] 262
4ZZZ [radio station] 269
5DDD [radio station] 272
5KA [radio station] 533
5MMM [radio station] 272, 534
5UV [radio station] 272
'65 Directory' [song] 271
69 [fictional character] 207
69ers, The 243
6IX [radio station] 398
6RTR [radio station] 272
6UWA [radio station] 272
6WF [radio station] 391
7 Records [record label] 494
8TOP [radio station] 525

A Sound, the 92
A&M [record label] 439, 451, 480
ABBA 291, 292, 387, 472
Abbey Road [studio] 112-3, 191
ABC (Australian Broadcasting Commission/Corporation) 18, 270, 275
ABC [band] 503
Aberfan (UK) 55
Abeyratne, Zan 504
Aboriginal Australians 3, 35, 38-9, 53, 59, 102, 105, 147, 179, 420, 438, 499, 529-30, 535-6

Abrahams, Chris 477
Abrahams, Paul 373-4, 381, 387
Absent Friends 455
Absolute Anthology [album] 132
AC/DC 70, 109, 111, 132, 145, 159, 195, 197, 215, 237-245, 253-4, 271, 284, 312, 328, 342, 366, 373, 418, 483
AC/DC: Maximum Rock 'n' Roll [book] 239
AC/DC: The World's Heaviest Rock [book] 237
Accent on Youth [TV show] 37
'According to my Heart' [song] 378, 380
Act, the 382, 452
Adams, Bronwyn 500
Adderley Smith Blues Band, the 65, 178
Adelaide (SA) 20, 29, 39, 70, 85, 99, 111, 155, 184, 200, 241, 281, 294, 320, 404, 524, 533; Hills 200
Adreneline and Richard [album] 139, 141, 436
Adrian's [Perth venue] 393
Advanced Colouring [EP] 498
Aesop's Fables 93
Affley, Declan 318
Africa [play] 226
African-Americans 53
After Dark [TV show] 433
After Dinner Moose [fictional character] 169
'After the News' [song] 378
Age of Mouse, The [album] 117
'Age of Reason' [song] 492
Age, The [newspaper] 420
'Ain't It Nice' [song] 194
Aints, the 547
'Air on the G String' [song] 128
Air Supply 198, 208, 248, 286, 294, 299, 328, 360, 456, 544
Akers, Will 392
Albert Park (Vic) 9, 19
Albert, Ted 125, 194, 196
Alberts [music publisher/record label] 43, 61, 125, 193, 198, 240, 254, 263, 294, 322-3, 421, 448
Alberts Archives [album] 133
Albion Country Band 309
Alice Springs (NT) 283, 536
Aliens, the 533
'All By Myself' [song] 290
All Fools Day [album] 426
All I Wanna Do Is Rock [album] 222
'All My Friends are Getting Married' [song] 228
'All My Loving' [song] 106
'All the Children Sing' [song] 452
'All Tomorrow's Parties' [song] 447
'All You Need Is Love' [song] 114
'All You Want to Do Is Dance' [song] 155
Allen Brothers, the 294
Allen, Bruce ('Tangles') 527
Allen, Daevid (Christopher Allen) 24, 109
Allen, Johnny ('Kaptain Kulture') 152
Allen, Laurie 84
Allen, Lindy [author] 359

Allen, Peter 37, 294
Allen, Wally 195
Alley Cat [Sydney venue] 412
Allison Gros 157-8, 212
Almond [play] 137, 141
'Alone With You' [song] 474-5
Alpha and Omega [film] 155
AlphaBravoCharlieDeltaEchoFoxtrotGolf [album] 449, 451
Alta Mira 213
Altman, Billy [author] 243
Altona North 120
Alvarez, Tony 369
Alvin Purple [film] 116
'Am I Ever Gonna See Your Face Again' [song] 195, 281
AMBO [agency] 159
American Bandstand [TV show] 35
American Graffiti [film/album] 252
'American Hymn' [song] 522
Amphlett, Christina (Chrissy) 295, 415, 455-6, 503, 509
Amphlett, Patricia *see* Little Pattie
'An Old Servant' [song] 138
And An A 504
Anderson, Andy (aka Andy James) 62-5, 90
Anderson, Angry (Gary Anderson) 154, 245, 255-7, 512, 514
Anderson, Julie (aka Nancy Serapax) 491
Anderson, Nadia 487
Andrew, Peter 221
Andrews, Bob 414
'Andy Warhol' [song] 341
Angela [fictional character] 457
Angels, the 20, 107, 126, 167, 242, 254-5, 277-8, 281, 290, 299, 310, 350, 353, 440, 500, 508; *Angels, The* [album] 281
Angie Pepper Band *see* Pepper, Angie
'Animal World' [song] 350-1
Animals, the 299
Ann Arbor 267
Annas [fictional character] 322
Another One for Mary [magazine] 320
Ansell, Karen (aka Karen Ansel) 373-5, 377, 379, 381-2
Ansett, Reg 78
Anson, Cliff 60
Anson, Peter 59, 60
Ant, Janet [fictional character] 156
'Anthem' [song] 79
Anthony, Julie 165
Any Questions for Ben [film] 291
Anything Can Happen [TV show] 292
Anzac (Australian and New Zealand Army Corps) 199
apartheid 322
'Apocalypso' [song] 473
Appel, Greg 499
Apple [record label] 142, 318
Approximately Panther [film] 89
'April Sun in Cuba' [song] 363, 366, 369
Apter, Jeff [author] 355
Aquarius Festival 152
Archer, John 437

575

Archie and Jugheads [record shop] 72, 149-150, 185, 339
Archies, the 220
Arctic Circles, the 540
'Are You Old Enough' [song] 364, 367, 389
Arena, Tina (Filippina Arena) 106
Argall, Ray [film director] 444-6, 450
Ariel 181, 190-1, 271, 299, 313, 328, 359, 506
Arista [record label] 192, 300
'Arkansas Grass' [song] 115, 318
Arlberg (Vic) 225
Armageddon [record label] 351
Armchairs, the 181
Armiger, Martin 28, 296, 299-304, 320, 339, 433, 474, 493, 528
Armstrong, Gillian [film director] 444
Armstrong's [studio] 111, 207, 220
Arnhem Land (NT) 12
Arnold, Ray 356
Arnott, Ray 190, 289
Arnott, Wendy [author] 171
Arrighi, Luciana 445
Art Throbs 524
Arthur, Jack 91
Artificial Organs 503
Arvo 538
Ascension [album] 547
Ash [Australian band] 295
Ashdown, Carol 318
Ashdown, Doug 28, 117, 264, 283, 318
Asheton, Ron 424
Ashton's Circus 151
Asian-Australians 326
Asleep at the Wheel [album] 521
Asphixiation 501
Assang, George 13
Assange, Julian 13
'Assassination' [song] 534
Assassins, the 534
Associates, the 432
Astor [record label] 111, 260-1
Astra [Sydney venue] 258, 286
At Home With You [album] 532
'Atlantic Romantic' [song] 451
Atlantics, the 31
'Atmosphere' [song] 401
ATN-7 [television station] 91
Atom Bomb Baby [album] 495
Au Go Go [record label] 405, 423, 495
Auckland (NZ) 39, 370
Audio Arts [magazine] 423
Aulton, Pat 28, 75-6, 91, 161, 186
Aunty Jack [TV show] 205, 270
Aural Indifference 517
Auschwitz 328
Austerica 18
Austin, Ward 87, 96, 119
Australian Country Music Awards 379
Australian Crawl 6, 416, 421, 464, 468-9, 470-1, 475, 516, 523, 539
Australian Entertainment Exchange 159
Australian Film Awards 536
Australian Idol [TV show] 164
Australian Made [tour] 426, 454
Australian Motor Industries (Hawthorn, Vic) 45
Australian National University (ANU) 278, 435
Australian Performing Group 169, 226
Australian Performing Rights Association (APRA) 132, 157
Australian Poetry Now! [book] 143
'Australiana' [monologue] 421
Austrock '77 [album] 264
Autodrifters, the 178, 235, 297-8
Autodrifters and the Relaxed Mechanics meet the Fabulous Nudes and the Pelaco Brothers, The [album] 339
'Avalanche of Love' [song] 524
Avantis, the 84
Avengers, the [Brisbane band] 93, 114; [NZ band] 114
'Average Inadequacy' [song] 504

Avery, Tex 268
Avion 539
Axeman's Jazz, The [album] 459, 526
Axiom 109, 114, 116, 213
Axle [record label] 492
Ayers Rock 172, 205, 483
Ayers, Kevin 24-5, 132
Aztec Camera 347
Aztecs, the 42, 84, 145; see also Billy Thorpe
Baba, Meher (Merwan Sheriar Irani) 187
Babeez, the 273
'Baby I'm a Coming' [song] 127
'Baby Let Me Bang Your Box' [song] 219
'Baby Please Don't Go' [song] 243
'Baby, Baby' [song] 274
Bach, Johann Sebastian 374
Bacharach, Burt 383
'Bachelor Kisses' [song] 529
Back in Black [album] 245; [tour] 245
'Back on the Borderline' [song] 279
'Back to California' [song] 460-1
'Back to the Wall' [song] 458
'Backlash Blues' [song] 121
'Bad Boy for Love' [song] 256, 259
Bad Companions, the 185
'Bad Moon Rising' [song] 388
Bad Seed, The [EP] 517
Bad Seeds, the 405, 519
Bad Timing and Other Stories [EP] 395
Bagg, Alligator; see Pigott, Johanna
Baigent, Col 42
Bailey, Chris (Red Angel Panic/the Angels) 167
Bailey, Chris (the Saints) 167, 253-4, 259-66, 319, 388
Baker, Glenn A. [author/manager/rock brain] 51-2, 54, 78, 252
Baker, James 275-7, 391, 401, 458, 526
Bakery 155, 269, 285
Balderstone, Simon [author] 369
Ball Power [album] 252
Ballad of Oz [EP] 233
Ballarat (Vic) 352
Balmer, Lori 53
Balwyn (Vic) 228, 279
Balwyn Boys Club 228
'Balwyn Calling' [song] 228
Bamford, John 186
Bananas [Melbourne venue] 447
'Band of Gold' [song] 378
Band of Hope 194
Band of Light 187-8, 255, 259
Band, the 252
Bandstand [Australian TV show] 32, 37, 52, 202
Bang 382
'Bang Bang (Shot Full of Love)' [song] 198
Bankstown (NSW) 63
'Barbados' [song] 382, 454-5
Barber, Keith 24
Barber, Lynden [author] 460
Barber, Tony 43-4
'Barefoot Boy' [song] 34
'Barefootin'' [song] 121
Bargains, the 393
Barker, Adrian 'Ada' 159, 449, 533
Barker, Black Allen 139
Barker, Criston 295
Barker, Nick 453
Barnard, Lance 161
Barnes, Helen 92
Barnes, Jane (Jane Mahoney) 289
Barnes, Jimmy (aka Jim) 28, 133, 136, 200-1, 283, 312, 467, 472, 514
Barnes, Mark 72
Barnes, Syd 92
Baroni, Pierre 533
Barons, the 496
Baroona (Queensland) Hall 345, 348
Barrett, Helen [author] 191
Barry McKenzie Holds His Own [film] 163
Barry, Julie 523
'Basia' [song] 522

Basilisk [record label] 351
Bass, Fontella 76
Bassendean (WA) 11
Bassey, Shirley 76
Bates, Ed 297-8
Batley, Noeline 34
Batman [TV show] 436
Baton Rouge [band] 295, 457
Battersea 222
Batties, Rebecca [author] 255-6, 332
Baudelaire, Charles 439
Baxter, Billy 307, 528
Bay City Rollers 192
Bay City Union 112
Be Bop Deluxe 213
Beach Boys, the 19, 313, 386
Beach House [Sydney venue] 42
Beach Hut [Sydney venue] 125
Beachcomber [Hobart venue] 84
Beagle Boys 275
Bear Witness [album] 504
Beargarden 453, 487, 527, 539
Beasts of Bourbon 250, 459, 526, 536
Beat Basement [Adelaide venue] 110
'Beat Goes On, The' [song] 445
Beat of My Heart, The [album] 426
Beat Preachers, the 84
Beat'n Tracks 121
Beathoven 5
'Beating Around the Bush' [song] 182
Beatle Village [Sydney venue] 125
Beatlemania 46
Beatles, the 2, 5, 17, 27, 40-41, 47, 55, 62, 68, 70, 90, 93, 99, 106, 108-9, 121, 207, 265, 315, 331, 483, 517
Beauchamp, Susie 517
Beauclerk, Eva [author] 535
Beaumaris (Vic) 71; Community Centre 72, 87; Yacht Club 23
Beaumen, the (aka the Bowmen) 29
Beautiful [album] 373, 383, 386, 544
'Beautiful People' [song] 465
'Beautiful Waste' [song] 351, 398
'Because I Love You' [song] 112, 183
Beck, Jeff 56, 109, 504
'Beds are Burning' [song] 487
Bee Gees 1st [album] 54, 69
Bee Gees Sing and Play 14 Barry Gibb Songs, The [album] 52
Bee Gees, the vii, 30, 44, 45, 49-57, 94, 105, 113, 117, 123, 145, 238, 244, 269, 295, 315, 343, 347, 418, 548
Beers, Garry ('Gary "Gary" Beers) 454-5
Before Hollywood [album] 398, 529
'Before Too Long' [song] 528
Bega (NSW) 324
Behan, Brendan 263
Beissel, Kim 344
Bel Air 466
Belgium 400
Bell, Andrew 296, 303, 305
Bell, Avril 182
Bell, Chris 37
Bell, Graeme 13
Bell, John 124
Bellevue Hill (NSW) 507
Benders, the 432, 521
Bendigo (Vic) 187
Bendinelli, Frank 503
Bennett, Tony 426
Bentley (WA) 308
Bergner, Marcus 335
Berlin [band] 452; [city] 514, 517
Berry, Chuck 33, 60, 124, 240, 242, 281, 528
'Berserk Warriors' [song] 472
Bertie's [Melbourne venue] 107, 149, 199, 221
Best Kept Secret [album] 328
Best, Peter 329
'Betty's Worry or the Slab' [song] 440
Between a Rock and a Hard Place [album] 468
Beyond Morgia [album] 323

INDEX

Beyond the Southern Cross [album] 398
Biafra, Jello 460
Bicton (WA) 308
Biddell, Kerrie 159
Bidstrup, Buzz 468, 485, 492-3, 513
Big Australian Rock Book [book] 256
Big Back Yard [radio show] 423
'Big Bad Bruce' [song] 311
'Big Beat' [song] 339
Big City Talk [album] 380
'Big Girls' [song] 526
'Big on Love' [song] 454
Big Swifty 324
Big Time [record label] 459, 522
'Billie's Bikey Boys' [song] 108
'Billy Baxter' [song] 321, 528
Bilson, Bill 459, 473-4, 477
Bird in the Engine, A [album] 141
Bird Noises [EP] 279-80, 487
Bird, John [author] 9
Birt, Jill 395, 398
Birthday Party, the 274, 342, 393, 403-4, 406, 409, 432, 438, 451, 455, 470, 514, 521, 523, 529; *see also* Boys Next Door
Birtles, Beeb (Gerard Birtlekamp) 95, 107, 109, 111, 117, 212
Birtles, Bob 94-5
Bishop, Martin 351
Bitter Lemons, the 84
Bjelke-Petersen, Mick 232, 345
'Black and Blue' [song] 189, 203
'Black and Damp' [song] 385-6
'Black Boy' [song] 536
Black Eyed Bruiser [album] 132, 242; [song] 195, 242, 256
Black Orchid [Adelaide venue] 24
Black Sabbath 108, 186
Black Sorrows, the 45, 177, 307
'Black Stockings for Chelsea' [song] 302
Black Swan, The [album] 396, 401
Black, John 141
Blackboard Jungle, The [film] 10
Blackeyed Susans, the 392
Blackfeather 171, 255
Blackman, Charles 78
Blacktown (NSW) 362, 412; Music Co-op, 412
'Blacktown' [song] 412
Blacktown, Barry [fictional character] 362, 412
'Blacktown Boogie' [song] 271, 362
Blackwell, Chris 159
Blair, Linda 211
Blakely, Peter 430
Blakeney, Gayle 416
Blakeney, Gillian 416
Blanchfield, Jon 333-4
Bland, Martin 526
Bleeding Hearts, the 296, 298, 302, 457
'Blind Lead the Blind' [song] 523
Bliss, John 373-5, 379-81, 388, 496
Blök Music 391
bloke bands 304
Blondie 377, 450, 452
Blood, Captain (Dr. Peter Blood) [fictional character] 158
Blown [album] 262
Blue and White Future Whale [album] 437
'Blue Day' [song] 43
'Blue Jeans' [song] 231
Blue Oyster Cult 524
Blue Rondo a la Turk 438
'Blue Roundabout' [song] 113
Bluegum, Billie 23
Blues Club [Brisbane venue] 94
Blues License [album] 330
Blues Rags 'n' Hollers 110
Blurred Crusade, The [album] 470
Bobby and Laurie 46, 70, 84, 218
'Body and Soul' [song] 446
Body and the Beat [album] 415, 509
Bois, John 209, 418
Bolan, Marc 351
'Bombora' [song] 31

'Bombs Dropped on Christmas, The' [song] 378, 386
Bon Voyage [album]
Bond, Grahame 205, 270, 491
Bondi Junction (NSW) 356
Bondi Lifesaver [Sydney venue] 245, 256, 258, 363, 375
Bones of Barry Harrison, The [album] 436
'Boney Moronie' [song] 325
Bonkowski, Basia 522
Bonney, Simon 343-4, 497, 500
'Bonnie, Bonnie, Bonnie – Na Na Hey Kiss Him Goodbye' [song] 83
Bonzo Dog Doo Da Band 161, 168
Booker T and the MGs 77
'Boom Sha La La Lo' [song] 103, 158
Boomerang Club [Adelaide venue] 28
Bootleg [record label] 115, 158
Bootleg Family Band 159
'Bop Girl' [song] 182
'Boppin' the Blues' [Blackfeather song] 171
Bored Kids [album] 391
Borich, Kevin 119, 256, 321-2, 330, 383, 416, 451, 513, 543; *see also* Kevin Borich Express
Boris 340
Born Sandy Devotional [album] 400-1
Bourke, Paul [author] 382
'Bow River' [song] 289
Bower, Mick 109-11
Bowie, David 33, 341
Box Hill (Vic) 149
Boy from the Stars [album/show] 153, 184
'Boy Hero' [song] 273
Boy Rocking 539
Boyd, Joe [record producer/ author] 10, 18, 26
Boyd, Robin [architect/author] 18
Boyne, Dave 60
Boys [band] 277
'Boys in Town' [song] 456
Boys Light Up, The [album] 465, 475
'Boys Light Up, The' [song] 421
Boys Next Door, the 180, 230, 250, 273, 308, 335, 340-2, 384, 444; *see also* the Birthday Party
'Boys! What Did the Detective Say' [song] 299
Bradbury, Neil [author/editor] 420, 439, 474-5, 480
Bradford, Terry 533
Bradley, Andy 'Mort' 267
Bradley, Andy [author] 195, 268
Bradshaw, Kym 259, 262, 425
Brady, Bob 63
Brady, Brian [fictional character] 22
Brady, Mike 108, 329, 334, 419
Brady, Tony 50
'Brain Brain' [song] 473
Braithwaite, Daryl 293, 304, 310, 312, 316, 543
Bramley, Clyde 348-9, 459
Brand, Paul 21
'Branded' [song] 257
Branson, Richard 159, 334
Brat, Peter 525
Brave Exhibitions [album] 340
Bray, Dorland 521
Breakfast at Sweethearts [album] 285
Brecht, Bertolt 282
Brenner, Nathan 305, 490
Brett, Lily 98
Brewer, Rick 107, 109, 218, 327
Brewster, John 167, 281
Brewster, Rick 167, 281-2
'Brian Wears Lipstick' [song] 437
Briggs, David 464, 520-1
Bright, Bobby 14, 29; *see also* Bobby and Laurie
Brighton (Vic) 71; North Brighton (Vic) 8
Bring Philip 431, 517
Brisbane (Qld) 76, 85, 176, 188, 260, 294, 535; Festival Hall 125; Folk Centre 21
'Brisbane Your Balls Have Burnt Off' [poem] 85

Britten, Terry 112-4, 164
Broadmeadows (Vic) 149; Town Hall 87
Broadsheet [magazine] 161
Broken Toys, the 351
Brokenmouth, Robert [author] 342, 515
Bronze [record label] 112
Brosnan, Tim 493
'Brother Sun, Sister Moon' [song] 155
'Brown Rice' [song] 219
Brown, Amanda 388, 529
Brown, Bob [comedian/musician] 170
Brown, Bruce 386
Brown, Bryan 350
Brown, Jenny (aka Jenny Hunter-Brown, Jen Jewel Brown) 159, 176, 182-4, 224, 225, 230, 253, 359, 366, 370, 482, 492-3, 508
Brown, Mick 534-5
Brown, Miranda [author] 320, 375
Brown, Ray and the Whispers 37, 42
Browning, Michael 149, 159-60, 244, 299, 412, 483
Browns, the 207
Brucelanders, the 374
Brunetti, Frank [author/musician] 255
Brunswick (Vic) 294, 297, 353
Brus, Harry 539
Bryant, Bix and the Raiders 45
Brychta, Alex [author] 49, 51
Bubblegum (music) 106, 109-10
Buckfield, Lin 526
Buckmaster, Charles [author] 152
Buesst, Nigel [film director] 19, 22, 88, 198
Buffalo 188, 238, 242-3, 255
'Buffalo Heart' [song] 519
Buggles, the 469
Built in Ghosts 431
Bull, Ted 178
Bulletin, The [magazine] 10, 38, 86, 92, 141, 157
Buncle, Ross 275-6
Bunton, Richard [author] 238
Bunyip (Vic) 95
Burgess, Baby John 96
Burgess, Colin 111, 184, 240
Burgess, Denny 184
Burgess, Ray 205, 293
Burgman, Richard 425, 473-5
'Buried and Dead' [song] 111
Buried Treasure [album] 170
'Burn Down the Bridges' [song] 365
Burn My Eye [EP] 268, 271
Burnham, Chris 323
Burns, Alison 138, 142
Burns, Hilary 142
Burns, Ronnie 44, 53, 70, 78, 84, 99, 101-2, 113, 117-8, 129, 148, 157, 217
Burstall, Tim [film director] 103, 113, 148
Burstin, Jeff 223, 297, 305
Burt, Jillian [author] 339, 342
Burt, Wayne 182, 296, 305
Burton, Annie [author] 308, 325, 376, 507, 511
Burton, Ray 92, 192, 210, 269
Burwood (NSW) 237
Burwood (Vic) 237
Bushwackers, the 166
Business as Usual [album] 417, 419
Buster Brown 154, 238, 242-3, 327
Butcher, Bleddyn 309
Butler, Gavin 499
Butler, Harry [author/editor] 534
Butler, Harry [naturalist] 11-12
Buttrose, Ita 286
Buttrose, Larry 445
Buzzcocks 351, 473
'Bye Bye Baby' [song] 32
Byrne, Debbie 293
Byrne, Ossie 52, 55
Byron, April (April Potts) 4, 29, 547
Bywaters, John 110

'C'mon Aussie C'mon' [song] 334

Cabaret Voltaire 523
Cadd, Brian (aka Brian Caine) 85, 101, 111, 113-4, 158-9
Caesar, Irving 284
Caesar's In Place [Sydney venue] 87, 115
Caesar's Palace [Sydney venue] 87, 115, 206
Cafiero, Steve 257
Cahill, Tony 129
Cain, Jonathan 290
Cairns, Howard 431
Callaghan, Mark 346, 492-3
Calvert, Phill 341, 515
'Calypso Moguls' [song] 468
Cam-Pact 72, 114, 148, 220
Camera Kazi' [song] 507
Camilleri, Joe 45, 75, 119, 178, 215, 274, 297, 304-5, 352, 528; see also Jo Jo Zep and the Falcons
Camp, Christine [author] 442
Campaign [magazine] 229, 231, 253
Campbell, Linda [author] 428
Can 254, 438
'Can I Be Sure' [song] 466
'Can I Sit Next To You Girl' [song] 241-2
'Can't Help Myself' [song] 462
Can't Stop Myself From Loving You [album] 197; [song] 197
'Can't Wait for September' [song] 192
Canada 110, 209, 211, 488
Canberra (ACT) 79-80, 259, 430, 435, 469
Cancer Victims, the 275
'Cancer' [song] 380
Cannon, Judy 51
Cantwell, Denis 346
Capek, John 506
'Capers' [song] 515
Capitol Theatre [Perth venue] 37
Captain Australian and the Honky Tonk 167
Captain Beefheart 46, 221, 223, 225
Captain Cocoa 363
Captain Goodvibes [fictional character] 167
Captain Matchbox Whoopee Band 103, 158, 160, 167-70, 172, 178, 181, 190, 209, 219, 224, 251, 293, 296, 377, 536
Captain Pimple; see Feeney, Michael
Captain Thunder 533
'Captain Zero' [song] 167
Cardwell, Dave 275
Carey, Peter [author] 393
Cargo [album] 418-9
'Carlton (Lygon Street Limbo)' [song] 228
Carlton (Vic) 121, 169, 224, 226, 228, 235, 279-80, 296, 302, 305, 308, 352, 419
Carmen, Eric 290
Carmen, Steve 404
Caropus Room [Sydney venue] 92
Carroll, Pat 119, 130
Carson (aka Carson County Band) 171, 262, 337, 506
Carter, Helen 521
Casey, Martin 395
Casinader, Robin 518-9
Casino (NSW) 63
Cason, Buzz 110
Cass, Moss 153
cassette tape 68, 265, 309-10, 320, 336, 392, 396, 399, 422-4, 428, 438, 454, 495-6, 537-8
Castaways, the 86
Castle, The [film] 291
Castles, David 331
Castles, John 536
Catacombs [Adelaide venue] 24
'Catch Me I'm Falling' [song] 505
Catcher, The [Melbourne venue] 88, 120
'Cathy Come Home' [song] 113
Cats and Dogs [album] 472
'Cattle and Cane' [song] 529
'Cauldron of Rebirth' [song] 423
Caulfield (Vic) Grammar School 341, 515

Cave, Nick 70, 237, 250, 266, 335, 341, 388, 407, 463, 500, 514-5
Cave, Peter 403
Cazaly, Roy 335
CBS [record label] 294-5, 371, 398, 417, 445, 448, 461, 507, 536, 539
Ceberano, Kate (Katie) 388, 503
Ceduna (SA) 536
Celibate Rifles, The [album] 524
Celibate Rifles, the 431, 524, 539
Cellar, The [Adelaide venue] 24
Central Sound Studios 129
Centre for Aboriginal Studies in Music (CASM) 536
Chad's Tree 540
Chain (aka the Chain) 87, 93, 121, 145, 152, 189, 202-3, 213, 322, 337, 443, 545
Chain Live [album] 87
Chain, Daisy [author] 333
Chamberlain, Lindy 208
Chambers, Terry 509
Channel 7 [TV network] 84
Channel 9 [TV network] 46
Channell, Ian 156
Chantoozies, the 464
Chants R&B 72
Chaos + Co 84
Chaplin, Charlie 305, 342
Chapman, Roger 289
Chariot 269, 369
Charles, Michael 473
Charles, Ronnie 114, 157, 167
Charlesworth, Stephen [author/musician] 296, 471, 503
Charlie 473
Chase, Sebastian 255, 362, 365, 379, 487
Chatswood (NSW) 478
Cheap Nasties, the 250, 276
Checker, Chubby 52
Cheetah 198, 294
Cheks, the 490, 493, 519
Chelmer (Qld) Hall 345
Chelsea (UK) 80, 275
Chelsea (Vic) 103
Chelsea Records [record label] 158
Chemistry [album] 493; [song] 494
'Chemistry and Mystery' [song] 380
Chequers [Sydney venue] 76, 221, 240, 263, 474
Cherry Red [record label] 398
Chesworth, David 501-2
Chevron Hotel [Sydney venue] 532
Chicago [band] 110
Chicago (Illinois) 352
'Chicken Killer' [song] 401
Chicken Shack 186
'Chickenshit' [song] 191
Children of the Sun [album] 188
Children's Bach, The [book] 160
Chinless Elite, the 477
Chocolate Grinders, the 501
Choice Cuts [album] 70, 183
'Choir Girl' [song] 285, 421
Choirboys 421
Chokito 383
Christ, Jesus [fictional character] 36, 155, 191
Christchurch (NZ) 39, 72
Chrysalis [record label] 330, 457
Chugg, Michael 132, 153, 159, 476, 479
Chunn, Michael 489
Church, the 468-9, 476, 540
Circus Animals [album] 286
Citadel [record label] 349, 437, 501, 524
Civic Hotel [Sydney venue] 308, 350, 412, 473
Clampetts, the 451, 454
'Clancy of the Overflow' [poem] 350
Clapton, Eric 56, 81, 207, 318
Clapton, Richard 264, 314, 318, 334, 484, 530
Claptrap 224
Clarion [record label] 104, 109
Clarke, Bruce 24
Clash, the 143, 275, 279, 528

'Classified Ad' [song] 339
Clayton (Vic) 378
Clayton-Jones, Edward 405, 518
Clelia Adams 155
Cleopatra Wong 431
Clevedonairs; see Cleves
Cleves, the 82-3 206, 210, 273
Clifforth, John 493, 519
Clifton Hill (Vic, aka Clifton Hole) 501
Clifton, Jane ('Janie') 178-9, 182, 226, 296-8, 302, 304-5, 307
Climax 5, the 91-2
Climax Records [record shop] 336
Climbing Frame 529
Clockwork Oringe 85
Cloud Nine 461
Cloudland [Brisbane venue] 76, 94, 345
Clovelly (NSW) 87
'Clowns Are In Town, The' [song] 428
Club 17 [TV show] 104
Club of Rome' [song] 358
Cluechaz, Toby [author] 280, 396, 428
Clyde [orangutan] 302
Clyne, Ian 88-9
'Coalman' [song] 53
Cobham, Billy 356
Coca-Cola 93, 105
Cochran, Eddie 33, 253
Cocker, Joe 113
Cockroaches, the 258, 539
Cocks, Mick 255-6, 512
'Cocky Song, The' [song] 113
Coconut Rough 446
Coe, Rod 119, 262, 285
coffee 24; coffee lounge 26
Cohen, Sacha Baron 337
Cohen, Tony 320, 323, 327, 347, 386, 449, 453, 526
Cohuna (Vic) 547
Colac (Vic) 183
'Cold Café' [song] 449
Cold Chisel 201, 256, 263, 267, 279, 282-90, 317, 353, 388, 421, 468, 471, 513
'Cold Cold Change' [song] 279
'Collapse Board' [song] 428
Collins, Graeme 355
Collins, Sally 394, 396, 475-6, 478, 532
Colors, the 429
Colossus [album] 332
Colour In [EP] 497
Coloured Balls 145, 152, 170-1, 238, 243, 252, 271, 409, 505
Coloured Stone 536-7
'Colourful Clothes' [song] 380
Colt [band] 275
'Come and See Her' [song] 126
'Come Around' [song] 421
'Come Back Again' [song] 221
'Come In, You'll Get Pneumonia' [song] 130, 239
'Come On' [Atlantics song] 31; [Rolling Stones song] 111
'Come On and Take My Hand' [song] 38
'Come Said the Boy' [song] 494, 510
'Come Together' [song] 119
'Comedy' [song] 385
'Comes As No Surprise' [song] 477
Comic Book Heroes [album] 211
'Coming Home' [song] 324
Commodores, the 180
compact discs 537-8
'Company' [song] 365
Company Caine (aka Co. Caine) 148, 172, 184-5, 218, 222
Complete Daddy Cool, The (DVD) 233
Complex, the 87
'Computer Games' [song] 508
Comrie-Thomson, Paul [author] 263
Condon, Darcy [author] 349, 473
Confessions of a Difficult Woman [book] 329
Conflicting Emotions [album] 490
'Confrontation' [song] 533
Congo, the 395
Conn, Paul [author] 157, 212

INDEX

Connolly, Steve 528-9
Conservatorium of Music (Sydney) 63, 460
Consolidated Rock [agency] 159, 175, 244
'Contact' [song] 317
Conway, Deborah 493, 504, 521
Conway, Janie (Janie Myriad; Janie Conway-Herron) 158, 297, 303, 307
Conway, Jim 168, 297
Conway, Mick (Mic Conway; Microphone Conway) 168, 253, 297
Conyngham, Peter 96, 171
Coogee Bay Hotel [Sydney venue] 356
Cook, Geoff 314
Cool Cats [TV show] 36
'Cool World' [song] 494
Cooley, Bob 138-9
Cooma (NSW) 83
Coon, Caroline [author] 261
Cooper, Alice 229
Corinda (Qld) 262
Corinda Boys 250, 348
Corpse Grinders 539
Correct Weight [album] 310
Corroboree (aka *Waiata*)[album] 489
Cosmic Psychos 522
Costello, Elvis 300, 306, 472
Cotton, Darryl 107, 109, 117, 295
Count Bishops, the 188
'Countdown' [song] 339
Countdown [60s TV show] 85; [70s-80s TV show] 83, 197, 205, 229, 277, 286, 290, 311, 330, 349, 362-3, 365, 373, 415, 439, 442, 444, 472, 477, 529, 544, 548
Countdown Music Awards 386
Countdown: the Musical 291
Countdown/TV Week Awards 286
'Counting Sheep' [song] 370
Counting the Beat [film] 442
'Counting the Beat' [song] 444
'Country Gardens' [song] 8
Country Radio [band] 262
Coupe, Stuart [author] 159, 350, 424
Covent Garden (UK) 161
Cox, Danny 62
Cox, Ian 502
Cox, Jimmy 121
Crabbe, Douglas 440
'Craise Finton Kirk Royal Academy of Arts' [song] 55
Cranberry Junglepuss's Fourteenth Tree Group 154
Crash, Johnny; *see* Freidenfelds, Janis
Crass 378
'Crazy' [song] 194-5
Cream [band] 56, 274
Creedence Clearwater Revival 388
Cremorne (NSW) 371
Creswell, Toby [author] 102, 256, 278, 283, 394, 462, 467, 530
Crewe, Bob 158
Cribb Island (Qld) 50
Crime and the City Solution 339, 343, 432, 500
'Crocodile Rock' [song] 221
Crombie, Noel (Geoffrey Crombie) 331, 382, 489
Cronulla Surf Club [Sydney venue] 92
'Crooked Highway' [song] 370
Crosbie, Peter 413-4
Crosby, Geoff 438
Crowd [magazine] 423
Crowded House 382, 387, 437, 441, 446, 491, 518
Crowley, Aleister 486
Cruelty of Beauty, The [EP] 517
Cruise Lane 357
Crumb, Robert 169, 268
Cruz, Errol; *see* Gooding, Tim
'Cry' [Birthday Party song] 515; [Dragon song] 510; [Godley and Creme song] 381; [Reels song] 383
Crystal Ballroom (aka Seaview Ballroom, The George) [Melbourne venue] 180, 286, 343-4, 424, 517

Crystal Set, the 470
Cucumber Castle [film] 57
Culnane, Paul [author] 79
Cults on C90 [album] 428
Cummings, Stephen 177, 215, 224, 296-301, 304-5, 339, 386, 394, 464, 471, 474
Cupples, Peter 328
Cure, the 434, 470
Currie, Nick 409
Curse, the 452
Curtin University 393
Curtin, Peter 74
Cut Lunch [EP] 446, 451
Cut the Talking [album] 415
Cybotron [album] 332
Cybotron 332

D Generation 468
Daddy Cool [band] 5, 23, 82, 146, 161, 170, 182, 189, 198-9, 205, 217, 219-221, 230, 234, 252, 282, 309, 313, 471, 516, 548
'Daddy Cool' [song] 158, 212
Daddy Who? Daddy Cool [album] 212, 220
Daft Punk 317
Dagoes, the 534; *Dagoes Sell Soul, The* [EP] 534
Daily Planet [magazine] 89, 145, 173, 202-3, 241, 442; *see also* Planet
'Daily Planet' [song] 145
Daily Telegraph (Sydney) 92
Daisley, Bob 186, 238
Daisy Clover 456
Dalby, Erl 192
Daley, Babs 182
Dallas (Texas) 352, 367
Dalsy 391
Dalton, Michael 'Blue' 499
Daltrey, Roger 514
'Dance' [song] 358
Dandelion [record label] 142
Danny's World 54
Dapto [band] 205
Darin, Bobby 33
Dark Spaces [album] 319
'Darktown Strutters' Ball' [song] 194, 323
Darling Harbour (NSW) 23
Darlinghurst (NSW) 394, 499
'Date with Destiny' [song] 473
Dave Graney with the Coral Snakes at His Stone Beach [EP] 409
Dave McArtney and the Pink Flamingos [album] 508
Dave Warner's From the Suburbs 234, 291, 308
Davies, Iva (Ivor) 435, 460-3, 471, 488
Davies, Ray 73
Davies, Roger 159, 311, 315-6
Davis, Mac 211
Dawkins, Peter 294, 328, 359-60, 365, 433, 448, 466, 507, 509
Dax, Maximillian [author] 342, 344
Day, David [author] 110-1
'Day in the Life, A' [song] 101
Dayman, Ivan 14, 75-6, 85, 137, 261
Days of our Lives [TV show] 31
DD Smash 539
De Da De Dum [album] 137; [song] 138
De Gruchy, Wayne 107, 196, 357, 360
De Meyrick, Julia [author] 435-6
'Dead Budgies' [song] 491
Dead Can Dance 434
Dead End Kids 185
Dead Forever [album] 188
'Dead Meat Boogie' [song] 332
Deadly Hume, the 440
Dealey, Jim 403
'Dear Prudence' [song] 5, 93
Debutantes [album] 298, 503
Deckchairs Overboard 487, 490, 493, 539
Dee Jays (group) 7
'Deep in the Woods' [song] 517
Deep Purple 153, 167, 180
Def Leppard 539
DeGennaro, Matt 10

Del Rios, the 46
Del-Aires, the 20
Delbridge, Noel [author] 335
Deling, Bert [film director] 154, 302
Delisle, Wayne 'Bird' (David Twohill) 471
Deluxe [record label] 412, 414-5
Denny, Sandy 26
Denver (Colorado) 352
Depeche Mode 387
'Depression' [song] 380, 385
Descloux, Lizzy Mercier 468
'Destiny Song, The' [song] 187
Detroit (Michigan) 254, 268, 300, 352, 377
Devastator [album] 264-5
Devil's Disciples 93
Devlin, Johnny 14, 34
Devo 375
Diamantina Cocktail [album] 214
Diamond, Neil 365
Diamonde, Dick (Dingeman Vandersluis or Van der Slujis) 124
Dick, Johnny 84, 93, 205, 256, 322
Dickins, Barry 89
Diddley, Bo 339
Died Pretty 474, 522
Diesel, Johnny and the Injectors 211
Dietrich, Marlene 388
Dig We Must [TV show] 84
Digger [magazine] 160
'Digging a Hole' [song] 493
Dillow, Lee [author/promoter] 42, 55, 84, 92, 98, 103, 160, 206
DiMera, Andre [fictional character] 31
Dingo [magazine] 160
Dingoes, the 178, 191, 208, 297, 352, 418, 530
Dingoes' Lament, The [book] 209
'Dingoes' Lament, The' [song] 209
'Dirty Creature' [song] 490
Dirty Deeds [book] 239
'Dirty Deeds Done Dirt Cheap' [song] 243, 271
Dirty Pool [agency] 285, 472, 500
Dirty Three, the 405, 431
'Disco Dilemma' [song] 192
'Disco Junkies' [song] 275
Dish, The [film] 291
Disposable Fits, the 525
'Diving Board' [song] 428
Divinyls 295, 454-8, 523
Divinyls [album] 458
Dix, John 4
Dizrythmia [album] 331
'Dizzy Miss Lizzy' [song] 37
Django 239
Do It [TV show] 292
Do Re Mi 350, 493, 517, 521, 527
Dobie, Gordon 23
Dodshon, Mark 423
Dogs in Space [film] 179, 336, 432, 486
Dolce, Joe 418-9
Doll by Doll 334
Dome, Malcolm [author] 239, 242, 244
Domestic Cosmos [album] 391
Domino, Fats 124
'Don't Fall in Love' [song] 327
'Don't It Make You Sick' [song] 74
'Don't Let Him Come Back' [song] 347
Don't Let It Get To You [film] 75
'Don't Throw Stones [album] 300;' [song] 299-300
'Don't Wanna Be the One' [song] 487
Don't Waste It [album] 306
Donovan 155
Doo Dah Music [music publisher] 223
Doolin, Terry 519
Door, Door [album] 341
Doors, the 166, 356
Doris Day [band] 393
Double Bay (NSW) 192
Double Life [EP] 408
Doubleman, The [book] 18, 35, 67
Doublethink [record label] 349, 496
Doug Parkinson In Focus 92, 108, 208
Douglas-Smith, Julian 391

Dover, UK 25
Dowler, John 20, 47, 339
Down the Line 107, 167
'Down Under' [song] 417-8
'Downhearted' [song] 466-7
Downs, Mike 84
Downtown Roll Band 312
Doyle, Ken 350
Doyle, Peter [author] 12
Doyle, Peter 76, 163-4, 428
Doyle, Tim 504
Dr Kandy's Third Eye 146, 184
Draft Resister's Union 151
Dragon 166, 177, 181, 245, 255, 257, 271, 294, 299, 310, 317, 319, 322, 353, 355-71, 379, 389, 412, 415, 444, 448, 488, 492, 507-10
Drake, Dr. Noah (fictional character) 211
Dransfield, Michael 136, 142
'Dreaded Moroczy Bind, The' [song] 360
'Dream Kitchen' [song] 377
Dreams of a Love [album] 327
Dreams of Ordinary Men [album] 511
Drewe, Robert [author] 150
Dreyfus [band] 308; *Dreyfus – Out of Beacon* [album] 308
Drifters, the 348
'Drifting' [song] 189
'Drive and Reflex' [song] 452
'Driving Me' [song] 498
'Driving Me Insane' (aka 'You're Driving Me Insane') [song] 64-5
Drollies, the 46, 119
Dropbears, the 530, 539
'Drop in the Ocean, A' [song] 471
Drummond 158, 212
Drummond, Pete 166
Drunk on the Pope's Blood [album] 516
Dry Red 329, 494
Dubbo (NSW) 75, 373, 376, 378
'Dubbo Go Go' [song] 380
Duck Stab [album] 359
Duff, Jeff (aka Jeff Black) 332-3, 505; see also Duffo
Duffield, Andrew 446, 449, 455
Duffield, Hurtle (fictional character) 68
Duffo 333
Dugites, the 291, 412, 415, 424, 498
Duigan, John [film director] 273, 280
Duncan, Peter 8
Duncan, Wayne 218-9, 223, 234
'Duncan' [song] 417
Dungeon Tape [album] 394, 396
Dunne, Graham 523
Dunstan, Don 20
Dunston, Graeme ('Superfest') 152
Dural (NSW) Memorial Hall 40
Duran Duran 463, 470, 512
Durant, Kim 416
Durham, Judith (Judith Cock) 26, 163
Durieux, Arnaud [author] 239
Durutti Column 523
Dury, Ian 456
Dust and Ashes 110
Dusty, Slim 12, 217, 417
Dutch-Australians 104, 123
Dy, Issi 157, 218
Dylan, Bob 64, 69, 119, 121, 136, 208
Dynamic Hepnotics 181, 527, 539
Dyson, Chris 304, 339, 528

'Eagle Rock' [song] 82, 218, 220-22, 233
Eagles, the 214
Eardrum, Deafy *see* Meldrum, Ian
Earl, Barry 210, 273-4
Earl, Mallory 488
Ears, the 336, 345, 453, 486
East [album] 285
East Hills (NSW) 13
Eastern Dark, the 540
Eastick, Mal 284
Eastlakes (NSW) 30
Eastwood, Clint 302
Easy Rider [film] 367

Easybeats, the 2, 62, 70, 84, 104, 109, 113, 120, 123-133, 193, 239, 245, 254, 258, 356, 534, 548
Easybeats Special [TV show] 131
Easyfever 125-6
'Eat City' [song] 281
Eather, Jenny [author] 433, 530-1
ECN8 [television station] 95
Edels [record shop] 60, 91
Edgecliff (NSW) 361
Edwards, Mike 199
Edwards, Tony 167
Effigy [author] 514
EG [record label] 265
Egan, Ted 12
Ego Is Not a Dirty Word [album] 229; [song] 229
Eight O'Clock Rock [fictional TV show] 35
'Eleanor Rigby' [song] 108
Electric Pandas, the 526, 539
Elektra [record label] 286
'Elevator Boogie Blues' [song] 12
'Elevator Driver' [song] 111
Elfick, David [author] 98, 123, 139-41, 167
Eliezer, Christie [author] 252, 258, 313, 325, 328, 363, 405, 425, 441, 447, 512-3
Elizabeth (SA) 28, 110, 135, 200-1, 282, 296, 309
Ellard, Tom 495, 497
Ellery, Dave 391
Ellington, Duke 9
Elliott, Louise 407-8, 425, 430-1, 460
Ellis [fictional character] 141
Ellis, Bob [author] 163
Elm Tree 196, 321
Eltham (Vic) 224, 228
EMI [record label] 107, 112, 138, 189, 261-2, 265, 304, 436, 468-9; EMI New Zealand 360
'Emma' [song] 116, 214
Emmanuel, Tommy 510-12
Empire State Building 35
Empire Times [magazine] 320
'Empty Pages' [song] 294
Encarnacao, John [author] 436
Encyclopedia of Australian Rock and Pop [book] 351, 425
Engine Shudder [EP] 405-7
England, Buddy 164
Engleheart, Murray [author] 239
English, David [author] 49, 51
English, John 155, 448, 494
Enmore Music Collective 431
Eno, Brian 533
Epics, the 45
Epstein, Brian 54, 479
Equal Local 431
Erdman, Martin (producer) 155
'Erotic Neurotic' [song] 263
'Errol' [song] 466
Erskineville (NSW) 240
Escapade [album] 490
Escorts, the 27
Esperanto [band] 116
Espresso Bongo [album] 472
Essendon Airport [airport] 19, 90, 502; [band] 24, 501-2, 523
Essentials, the 393
Essex, David 462
EST 496
Eternally Yours [album] 264
'Eternally Yours' [song] 430
Eurogliders, the 393, 415, 424, 539
Eurovision [TV show] 248
Eurythmics 539
Evans, Dave 239, 241
Evans, Mark 239, 243, 245, 253
Evans, Ray 159, 175
Evans, Raymond [author] 20
Evans, Rod 167
Evans, Sandy 177
Evening Standard (London) 97

Everage, Edna [fictional character] 163
Everfinish, Willie; see Meldrum, Ian
'Everlovin' Man' [song] 88, 90
'Every Christian Lion Hearted Man Will Show You' [song] 55
Everybody's [magazine] 52, 94, 98
Everybody's [record label] 47, 52
'Everyday of my Life' [song] 195
Everything that Flies [EP] 429
'Everything's Fine' [song] 265
'Evie' [song] 195
Evil Roomers (aka Evil Rumours) 257
'Evolution' [song] 454
Executives, the 91, 162, 192, 210
Exhibit A 470, 525
Exotic Pandas, the 526
Explosive Hits [album] 263
Exposay aka Expozay 503
Exterminators, the 276
Extradition 187

Fabinyi, Martin 389, 462, 472, 480
Fable [record label] 103, 115, 157-8, 161, 334
Fabulous Marquises 405, 518
Fabulous Nudes 181
'Face the Change' [song] 485
Face to Face [album] 281
Faehse, Tony 306
Fairlie, Peter 141
Fairlight (NSW) 463
Fairlight (synthesizer) 385, 463
Fairlight Festival 151
Fairport Convention 26
Falconer, Doug 437, 439
Falcons, the 84
Falling in Love Again [album] 193; [song] 131, 193-4, 322
'Falling off the Edge of the World' [song] 130
Fame at Any Price [album] 327
Family [band] 289
Fang 200
Fanny Adams [band] 56, 93-4, 205-7
Fanta 244
'Farewell Aunty Jack' [song] 205
Farkas, Michael 535
Farm [band] 278
Farmer, Michael 491
'Farmers Never Visit Nightclubs' [song] 392, 394
Farmyard [recording studio] 451
Farndon, Pete 166
Farnham, Johnny (aka John) 69, 95, 102, 110, 149, 202, 212, 233, 293, 312, 334, 492, 514, 521, 545
Farrago [magazine] 161, 177, 341-2
Farrar, John 78
Farrell, Bob 426, 428, 497
Farrelly, Bernard 'Midget' 277
Farriss, Andrew 483, 485, 487
Farriss, John 209, 483
Fast Forward [magazine] 422-3
Fat Black Pussy Cat [Melbourne venue] 24
Fat Daddy 337
'Fat Man' [song] 436
Fatal Records [record label] 261
'Fate Worse Than Death, A' [song] 252
Father Thyme 507
Fatt, Jeff 258
Faulkner, Dave (aka Dave Flick) 275-6, 391, 458-9, 522
Fauves, the [60s group] 71
Fawdon, Michelle 155
Feather 271, 278
Federation of Australian Radio Broadcasters 157
Feeling Folk Blues [album] 21
Feeney, Michael 309
Fellini, Federico 226
Fernandez, Neil 276
Ferrets, the 109, 327
Ferrie, Mark 296, 446-7, 519

INDEX

Ferry, Bryan 252, 463
Festival [record label/distributor] 8, 32, 34, 43, 50-2, 91-2, 106, 157, 159
Fidock, Stefan 373-87, 520, 544
'Field of Glass' [song] 393, 400
Fiji Bitter [album] 369
Filewood, Michael 496
Finch 232, 271, 278, 323
Finch, Ernie 477
Finlay, John 46
Finn, Neil 331, 382, 387, 488
Finn, Tim (Brian Finn) 331, 446, 488, 490-1
Firemans's Curse, The [album] 439
Firth, Ken 327
Fish in Space [film] 487
Fisher, Charles 533
Fishermen, the 477
'Fist Falls, The' [song] 334
Fitzgibbon, Mark 408
Fitzroy (Vic) 149, 172, 394
Five Great Gift Ideas from the Reels [EP] 378
'Five in a Row' [comedy song] 468
'Five Letter Word' [song] 413
Five Star 504
'Five Years' [song] 371
Flake 255
'Flame Trees' [song] 289
Flaming Hands 474, 539
Flanagan, Patrick (161)
Flanders and Swann 465
Flash and the Pan 197
Flashez [TV show] 198, 205
Fleet Studios 129
Fleet, Gordon 'Snowy' 124, 129
Fleetwood Mac 221
Fletcher, Paul 502
Flett, Dave 120, 226
Flett, Uschi (Ursula) 226, 377
Flex, Tyrone 435-6
Flinders University 166-7, 320
Flowers 320, 391, 461; see also Icehouse
'Flowers in the Rain' [song] 79
Floyd, Eddie 77
Fly on the Wall [album] 239
'Flying' [song] 108
Flying Circus 110, 165, 242, 312
Flying Tackle 303
Flynn, Errol 466-7
Flynn, Mick 158
Folding Chair [record label] 436
Folk music 9
Folk Three, the 46
Follington, Ace 210, 285
Fools Gold [album] 116
Footscray (Vic) 120
'For All We Know' [song] 380
'For My Woman' [song] 125
Ford, Doug 63-5, 101, 109, 111, 184
Ford, Richard 543
Ford, Sue 23
'Forever Now' [song] 388-9
Formby, George 53, 95
Formyula, the 103
Forster, Robert 345-6, 428, 529
Fortune, Flame (aka Heather Hogue) 485
Foster, Mark 526
'Four Short Solos' [song] 369
Fourth Drawer Down [album] 432
Fowley, Kim 221, 328
'Fraction Too Much Friction' [song] 490
Frame 224-5, 228
Frames, the 393
Frankel, Dick 21
Frankie Goes to Hollywood 537
Frankie's Negative' [song] 407
Fraser, Malcolm 248, 534
Fraternity 109, 199, 241, 284, 312, 533
Frazer, Philip 85, 98
'Freak, The' [song] 108
'Fred the Fish' [song] 25
Free 240
'Free and Easy' [song] 271

Free Kicks [album] 310
free music 10
'Free the People' [song] 312
'Freedom's Flame' [song] 512
Freestyle [record label] 468
Freeway 337
Fremantle Doctor 368
Frenchs Forest (NSW) 483
Frenzy [album] 331, 446
Freud, James (Colin McGlinchey) 274-5, 383, 452
Fricke, David [author] 520
'Friday Night, Saturday Morning' [song] 128
'Friday on My Mind' [song] 123
Freidenfelds, Janis (Johnny Crash) 298, 340, 387, 446, 448, 519
Friels, Colin 457
'Friend Catcher, The' [song] 514
Friends [album] 131
Friends [band] 172
Friends aka *Frendz* [magazine] 160
Frieze 109, 116
'From St Kilda to Kings Cross' [song] 527
From the Archives [album] 497
From this Side of Things [book] 113
Fuckin' Leftovers, the 250
Fugs, the 308
Full Marks 538
Fun Fun Gyro Boat 503
Fun Radio [film] 19
Fun Things 348
Fundamental [album] 473
Fungus Brains 405, 408
'Funkytown' [song] 504
Fur Bible 526
Furber, Mike 76, 110
Furlong, Bill 423
Fusions [TV show] 186
'Future of Our Nation' [song] 184

G, Ali [fictional character] 337
Gable, Howard 101
Gaelic Club [Sydney venue] 537
Gainsbourg, Serge 409
Galbraith, Alastair 9
Gamba [studio] 110
GangGajang 493
'Gans en Farben' [song] 370
Gap [record label] 523
Gardner, Steve [author] 264
Garland, Judy 37
Garner, Helen 17, 160, 303
Garrison [Melbourne venue] 90, 449
Garvey, Nick 477
Gas [magazine] 99
Gates, Bill [disc jockey] 51
'Gay Guys' [song] 414
gay liberation 148-9
Gayden, Mac 110
Gaze, Tim 171, 186, 190
Gazzo, Jane 546
Gebert, Bobby 187
Geelong (Vic) 213, 362, 456
Geeks, the 250, 275-6
Geffen [record label] 454
'General Hospital' [song] 502
Genesis 439
Geordie 243
'Germ' [song] 451
Gerrard, Lisa 336, 434
Gerry and the Joy Band 198
Gerry Humphrys: The Loved One [film] 22
Gershwin, George 284
'Get Ready for Love' [song] 194
Get Rocked [album] 324
'Get Rocked' [song] 324, 326
Get Smart [TV show] 436
Get Some Fun [album] 476-7
'Get That Jive' [song] 362
Get Wet [album] 472
Gett, Harry 537
Getting Back to Nothing [album] 103; [film] 207

Geyer, Renée 120, 205, 207, 271, 295, 328, 365, 416, 494, 509, 543
'Ghost Ships' [song] 425-6
Ghosts of an Ideal Wife [album] 430; [song] 430
Ghosts... of the Civil Dead [film] 388
Giant Recording Company [record label] 433
Gibb, Andy 49
Gibb, Barry 42, 49, 104, 118; see also Bee Gees
Gibb, Hugh 54
Gibb, Lesley 51, 57, 124
Gibb, Maurice 49, 117-8; see also Bee Gees
Gibb, Molly (Molly Hullis) 55, 57
Gibb, Robin 49, 55; see also Bee Gees
Gibson, Mel 457
Giddy, Kim 349
Gilbert, Warwick 267, 348, 424
Gilbey, Chris 263, 469
Gillard, Julia 488
Gillard, Margaret 392
Gillespie, Mark 298
Gilpin, Steve 507
Gilroy, Ian 445
'Gimme Head' [song] 324, 440
'Gimme Shelter' [song] 334
'Girl That I Love, The' [song] 101, 135
'Girl With a White Stick' [song] 351
'Girls on the Avenue' [song] 264
Gisborne (Vic) 164
Giuseppe [fictional character] 419
'Give Me Back My Brain' [song] 333
Glad All Over [book] 291
Glasgow 123, 238-9
Glass, Helena 72, 495, 516
Glass, Keith 8, 59, 65, 71-2, 103, 149, 185-6, 338, 342, 347, 494, 516
Glastonbury Festival 400
Glebe [album] 436
Glen Innes (NSW) 201, 284
Glen Waverley High School 120
Glenelg (SA) 110, 219
Glenroy (Vic) 24
Glitter, Gary 204, 223
Globos, the 445
'Gloria' [Ray Brown song] 37; [Them song] 265, 338
Glover, Robert 297
Go Broke Promotions 431
Go-Betweens, the 336, 345, 387, 397, 407, 423, 428-9, 431-2, 435, 469, 470, 495, 504, 529, 548
Go-Go's, the 476
Go-Set [magazine] 50, 79, 83, 85, 90, 98, 100, 104, 108-9, 116, 139, 155, 160, 165, 191, 202, 293, 477
Go!! Show, The [TV show] 44, 75, 84, 118, 125, 163
Goanna 529
Gobbles [Perth venue] 180
Goble, Graeham 117, 212-3, 521
Gock, Les 318, 321, 324
'God Bless America' [song] 455
Godburst (musical) 183
Godley and Creme, 381
Goffin, Jerry 208
Goffin, Louise 208
Going Down [film] 465, 522
Gold 533
'Golden Miles' [song] 213
Golden Syrup 473
Goldman, Paul [film director] 388
'Golf Course' [song] 486
Gollan, Jean [author] 108, 116
Gomelsky, Giorgio 25
'Gone Dead' [song] 403, 405-6
Gone to See a Man About a Dog (play) 178-9
Gong 25
Good Friday [album] 128
'Good Morning (How Are You?)' [song] 210
Good Times [album] 129; [song] 130, 133, 195, 239, 242

Goodbye Fiona [album] 328
'Goodbye Lollipop' [song] 175, 184, 189
Goode, Bill 51
Goode, Robert 24, 502-3
Gooding, Tim (aka Errol Cruz) 490, 491-2
Goodwin, Ray 188, 255, 322, 355
Goolagong, Evonne 300
Gordon, Lee 13, 33, 52
Gordon, Trevor 53
Gorman, Gunther (Ian Gorman) 182, 223, 314
Gorton, John 67, 147
Gosford (NSW) 150
Gottehrer, Richard 473
'Govt. Boy' [song] 412
Gradman, Eric 256, 274, 296, 298, 339, 345, 463
Graffiti Crimes [album] 508
Graham, Fiona 496
Graham, Les 536
Grainger, Percy 8-10, 425, 506; Grainger Museum 10
Grainstore Tavern [Melbourne venue] 509
'Grand Life for Fools and Idiots' [song] 428
Grand, The [Sydney venue] 258
Graney, Dave 290, 311, 394, 403-409, 534
Grant, Peter 119
Grant, Stuart 335
Grass (show) 156
Gray, Deborah 538
Gray, Garry 202, 403, 409, 519
Gray, Stuart 470, 525
Grease (show/film/album) 252
Greasy Pop [record label] 533
Great Dictator, The [film] 305
Great Gusto, The [album] 437
'Great Southern Land' [song] 463
Great White Noise 177, 398, 432
Greatest Hits [EP] 496
Greatest Hits (of Other People) [album] 513
Green [record label] 350, 424, 524
Green the Magazine [magazine] 424
Green, Billy (Wilhelmus Groenevegen) 5, 42, 45, 92-3, 103-4, 131, 193, 198, 205, 211
Green, Cathy 259, 409
Green, Geoffrey 332
Green, Wayne 277-8
Greenan, Jan 35
Greenan, John (Johnny) 7, 35
Greenstreet, Sydney 209
Greenwich Village (NY) 82
Greer, Germaine [author] 81, 97, 161, 204
Grendel [record label] 136
Grey, Cheryl (aka Cheryl Sang; Samantha Sang) 53, 95
Grierson, Roger 349-50, 424, 436-7, 524
Griffin, Trevor 78, 218
Griggs, Nigel 382, 490
Grong Grong (NSW) 535
Groop, the 70, 92, 99, 101, 113, 167
Grooveyard 524
Grose, Simon [author] 244
Grossman, Albert 479
Grossman, Rick 202, 296, 298, 457-8, 485
Groves, Steve 117
Grudge, the 250, 346
GTK [TV show] 121, 197, 204, 211, 229, 241, 243
Gudinski, Michael 159, 181, 226-7, 232, 268, 273, 284, 298-9, 306, 333, 382, 420, 439, 446, 449, 454, 475, 477-9, 482, 489, 544
Guilliatt, Richard [author] 247
Guilty Until Proven Insane [album] 232
Guitar Method [album] 450
Gumleaf Mafia 295
Gumnut Gully (fictional town) 113
Gunston, Norman [fictional character] 250, 337
Guthugga Pipeline 499
Guy, Athol 27, 164
Gyllies, Simon 328

Hackney (SA) 21
Hadley, Mick 94
Haffy's Whiskey Sour 194
Hague, The 123
Hair (musical) 115, 156, 253, 270, 327; 'Hair' [song] 93
Haley, Bill 35
'Half Time at the Football' [song] 310
Hall, Daryl 485
Hall, Janine 340, 425-6
Hall, Les 193, 323
Hall, Phil 492, 530-1
Halstead, Mark (Marko) 525-6
Ham, Greg 417
Hamer, Rupert 150
Hamilton, Alex 498
Hamilton, Lee 187, 255
Hammersmith Odeon [London venue] 77
Hammett, Dashiell 408
Hammond, Chrissie 198, 294
Hammond, Lyndsay 198
Hampstead 119
Handlin, Denis 362, 412
Handsome Vikings, the 472
'Handyman' [song] 101
'Hanging Round the House' [song] 235
Hannaford, Ross 23, 71-3, 218-9, 222-4, 234, 327
Happening [TV show] 292; *Happening '70* 108, 203; *Happening '72* 204
'Happiness' [song] 385-6
'Happy Anniversary' [song] 214
'Happy Birthday' [Boys Next Door song] 343
'Happy Birthday IBM' [song] 449
Happy Days [TV show] 252-3
Happy Hate Me Nots, the 540
'Happy Man' [song] 475
Harbutt, Sandy [film director] 207-8
Hard Road [album] 132
Hard Rock Theatre [band] 184
Hardy, Mary 113
Harem Scarem 521-2
Harford, Nigel 504
Harlequin (LP) 33
Harmon, Gaye 83, 206
Harrah's [Tahoe venue] 39
Harrigan, John 42-3, 60-1
Harris, Emmy-Lou 297
Harris, Jim 61
Harris, Rolf 11, 39, 47, 247
Harrison, George 119
Harrison, Mike 210
Harrison, Ricky 536
Harrison, Yuk 95
Hart, Bob [author] 244
Harvest [record label] 189
Harvey, Mick 24, 341, 387, 408-9, 500, 516
Hasselhoff, David 194
Hats Off Step Lively [album] 300
Havoc [record label] 145, 159, 184, 188
Hawaiian Eye [Sydney venue] 87
Hawke, Bob 418, 476
Hawkins, Raoul 497
Hay, Colin 417
Hay, Ivor 259-60, 348-9, 425, 431
'Hayride' [song] 110
'He's My Blonde-Headed, Stompie Wompie, Real Gone Surfer Boy' [song] 30
'He's My Michael' [song] 29
Head [band] 188
Head Injuries [album] 279
Head Undone 315
'Heading in the Right Direction' [song] 330
Headlines [album] 198
Healing Force 213
Hearn, Ray 285, 461
'Heart' [song] 30
'Hearts and Flowers' [song] 346
Heaven 412
'Heaven and Hell' [song] 129-30, 239
Hedley, Tom [author] 148

Hee Haw [album] 343
Hefner, Des 517
'Hell of a Summer' [song] 393, 396
Hello Sailor 209, 508
'Hello, How Are You' [song] 130-1
'Hello' [song] 44, 78, 106
'Help Is on its Way' [song] 116, 214
Hemmings, David 321
Henderson (NZ) 511
Henderson, Brian 32, 37
Hendry, Toni 46
Henry, Hamish 200
Herbs, the 213
Here (aka The Here) [Sydney venue] 86, 115
Herman's Hermits 53, 106
Hernando's Hideaway [Perth venue] 276, 392
Heroes (musical) 417
Herrmann, Bernard 9
Hester, Paul 387, 490, 519
Hewett, Colleen 204, 210
Hewson, Paul 181, 289, 357-8, 360, 362-3, 365, 368-70, 444, 508-11, 529
Hey Hey It's Saturday [TV show] 234
'Hey Little Gary' [song] 408
'Hey Little Girl' [song] 463
'Hey Pinky' [song] 108
'Hey St Peter' [song] 197
Heylin, Clinton [author] 261
Hi Fi Club [TV show] 36
'Hi Honey Ho' [song] 221
Hicks, Megan 166
Hicks, Megan Sue 154-5, 165-6
Higgins, Michelle 480
'High Class Dame' [song] 507
High Numbers, the 346
High Rise Bombers 304, 320, 339, 527
'High School Girls' [song] 275
High Voltage [album] 243
'High Voltage' [song] 195, 243
Highway 315; *see also* Sherbet
Highway 1 [album] 315
Hill, Steve 152, 178; 225-6
Hillman, Bones (Wayne Stephens) 444, 446
Hilltop Hollow Bluegrass Band 525
'Hindu Gods of Love' [song] 349
Hine, Rupert 451
Hines, Marcia 155, 186
Hipslingers, the 540
Hirschfelder, David 521
Hirst, Rob 278-80, 433, 487
His Master's Voice [book] 85
'Hit and Run' [song] 306
'Hit Single' [song] 291, 414
Hitchcock, Alfred 323
Hitchcock, Russell 294-6, 323
Hitchens, Paul 299
'Hitchhiker' [song] 84
Hitler, Adolf 101, 520
Hitmen, the 348, 384, 459
HMAS *Platypus* [ship] 436
Hoadley's (National) Battle of the Sounds 92, 112, 200
Hobart (Tas.) 18, 84-5
Hobbs, Michael 136
Hoff, Ray 60; Ray Hoff and the Offbeats 84
Hogan, Paul 152
Hogarth, Barbara 502-3
'Hold On' [Max Merritt song] 37
Holden Interview [album] 437
Holden, Frankie J. (Peter Brian, Brien or Bryan) 234, 252-3
Holden, Mark 543
Holder, Noddy 243
'Holding Down a "D"' [song] 454
Holdridge, Cheryl (Cheryl Phelps) 39
'Holiday House' [song] 349
'Holiday' [song] 55
'Holidays' [song] 405
Hollies, the 107, 113, 194, 315
Holly, Buddy 7, 33, 198
'Hollywood Dreaming' [song] 315

INDEX

Hollywood Palace [TV show] 56
Holmesglen (Vic) 341
Holocaust [magazine] 85
Holt, Harold 67, 147
Holy Fin [dolphin] 104
Home 332
'Home on Monday' [song] 214
Homicidal Idol 171
Hong Kong 483, 486, 526
'Hoochie Gucci Fiorucci Mama' [song] 466
Hood, Peter 31
Hoodoo Gurus (aka Le Hoodoo Gurus) 250, 275, 321, 348-9, 411, 458, 477, 491, 517, 526, 539-40
Hooper, Craig 373-88, 470
Hooper, Helen 89
Hope and Anchor [London venue] 451
Hopkin, Mary 157-8
Hordern Pavillion [Sydney venue] 243
Horla, the 519
Horne, Alan 347
'Horror Movie' [song] 229, 293
Hoskyns, Barney [author] 148
Hoste, Michael 462, 493
Hot Cock 188, 255
Hot for the Orient [album] 442
Hot Mummas, the 221
Hot Records [record label] 396, 400, 431, 442
Hough, Mark; *see* Stiggs, Buster
Hound [magazine] 178
'Hound Dog' [song] 312
Housden, Steve 213
'Houseboat' [song] 424
'How Come?' [song] 302
'How I Lied' [song] 37
How to Make Gravy [book] 320
Howard, Alan [author] 308
Howard, Carol [fictional character] 492
Howard, Harry 343, 500
Howard, Phil 25
Howard, Rowland S. 340, 423, 426, 441, 500, 516
Howard, Shane 530
Howden, Celeste 303
Howe, Bruce 200
'Howzat' [song] 315
Hoy, Marie 335
Hoyle, Pip 267, 269
Hudson, Bob [singer/radio announcer] 252
Hugg, Mike 80
Hughes, Howard 339
Hugo Klang 428, 431-2, 451, 495
Human Frailty [album] 442
Human League 469
Hume Highway ('Deadly Hume') 279, 479
Hume Hotel (Yagoona, NSW) 83
Humphries, Barry 161, 179, 310
Humphrys, Gerry 22, 88-9, 198, 282, 339, 483
Hunter River (NSW) 14
Hunter, Marc 214, 289, 341, 355-7, 359-71, 507-11, 513
Hunter, Todd 355-62, 368-70, 491-2, 509-10
Hunters and Collectors 3, 274, 336, 411, 420, 437, 481, 486, 501, 522, 527
Hunters Hill (NSW) 87
Hupmobile 268
Hurley, Jade (John) 34, 37
Hurstville (NSW) 52-3; Civic Centre 263
Hush 229, 243, 293, 311, 313, 321, 324, 328, 351, 353, 356
Hutchence, Michael 266, 380, 482, 484-7, 503
Hutchence, Rhett [author] 485
Hutchens, Baden 64
Hutchinson, Niels 228
Hutchison, Tracee [author] 427, 446, 470, 514, 539
Huxley, Margot 173
Huxley, Martin [author] 70, 237, 242

Huxton Creepers 522, 540
Hyams, Jacky [author] 414
Hyde, Gary 211

'I Am Australian' [song] 166
'I Am Woman' [song] 210, 269
'I Belong With You' [song] 120
'I Can Do Anything' [song] 328
'I Can Hear the Grass Grow' [song] 67
'I Don't Care' [song] 533
'I Don't Love You Anymore' [song] 389
'I Don't Think All Your Kids Should Be Virgins' [song] 74
'I Don't Wanna Be With Nobody But You' [song] 455
'I Feel Love' [song] 405
'I Found a New Love' [song] 38
'I Get A Kick Out of You' [song] 21
'I Go To Rio' [song] 294
'I Got You' [song] 489
'I Hate the Music' [song] 196
'I Hate You' [song] 532
'I Hear Motion' [song] 453
'I Hope I Never' [song] 489
'I Like Iggy Pop' [song] 275
'I Like It Both Ways' [song] 323
'I Listen to my Heart' [song] 40
I Love Trumpet [EP] 498
'I Might Be a Punk (But I Love You Baby)' [song] 250, 338
(I'm) Stranded [album] 260
'(I'm) Stranded' [song] 261
'I Need Two Heads' [song] 347
'I Realize' [song] 314
'I Remember You' [song] 40
'I See Red' [song] 331, 488
'I Touch Myself' [song] 455, 458
'I Wanna Be Slick and Pick Up Chicks Like You' [song] 275
'I Wanna Be With You' [song] 508
'I Want Candy' [song] 473
'I Want to Live in a House' [song] 445
'I Was a Lover, a Leader of Men' [song] 50
'I Was Only 19' [song] 529
'I Was Yesterday's Hero, Now I'm a Heartbroken Clown' [song] 196
'I Will Always Love You' [song] 442
I Won't Look Back [album] 193, 322
'I Won't Pay' [song] 350
'I'd Like to Teach the World to Sing' [song] 106
'I'll Be Gone' [song] 157, 189
'I'll Be Where You Are' [song] 112
'I'm an Aussie' [song] 335
'I'm Eighteen' [song] 341
'I'm Flipped Out Over You' [song] 275
'I'm So Ashamed' [song] 33
I'm Still Alive [album] 35
I'm Still in Two Minds about the Title [EP] 339
'I'm Talking 454, 501-2, 539
'I'm the Sea (Stop Killing Me)' [song] 145
'I've Been Everywhere' [song] 75
'I've Got to Get a Message to You [Fanny Adams song] 205
Ian Dury Songbook [book] 461
Ian Stephen's Schizophrenia 339
IC [record label] 506
Icehouse [album] 462
Icehouse 225, 307, 391, 435
Id, the 141
Ida Mae Mack 337
Idea [album] 56
'If Not For You' [song] 118
'If She Finds Out' [song] 112
Ifield, Frank 39-40, 47
Iguana, the 107, 114
Ikinger, Penny 431
Illustrated Man 532
Imparja [record label] 536-7
Implosion [album] 332
'In a Broken Dream' [song] 132
'In My Book' [song] 126
In the Cage [album] 278
In Too Deep [album] 132

'In Your Car' [song] 414
Inala (Qld) 345
Indelible Murtceps, the 171, 189-91
Individuals [album] 475-6
Inedible Crumpets, the 190
Infinity [record label] 443
Inga (Inge de Koster) 198
Ingham, Jonh [author] 261
Ingliss, Peter 225, 234
Ink [record label] 398
Inner City Sound [book] 250
Inner Sense 192
Innocent Records [record label] 501
Instant Replay 88
International Exiles 437
'International Robots' [song] 264
International Swingers, the 324
Introducing the Seekers 27
Invaders, the 77, 276
INXS 69, 133, 201, 209, 237, 319, 387, 412, 446, 453-4, 461, 482, 539-40
Ioannou, Johnny 46
Ireland 400
Iron Maiden 232, 278
Isaac Aaron 177, 331
Isaacs, Graham 536
Island [record label] 159, 396
'Island Nights' [song] 369
Island of Greed [album] 536
'It Ain't Necessarily So' [song] 44
'It Ain't What You Dance' [song] 444
It Flew Away 171, 190, 219
'It Must Be Love' [song] 388
It's a Gas [TV show] 84
'It's a Long Way There' [song] 214
'It's a Long Way to the Top (If You Wanna Rock 'n' Roll)' [song] 195, 214, 243
'It's a Man's Man's World' [song] 329
It's All Happening [TV show] 84
It's All Rock 'n' Roll to Me [album] 234
'It's Almost Summer' [song] 188
'It's Alright' [song] 37
It's Magic [TV show] 203
'It's No Reason' [song] 470
'It's Only a Matter of Time' [song] 103
'It's Time' [song] 146
'Ita' [song] 286
Italian-Australians 188
Iva Davies and Afghan 460; *see also* Davies, Iva

JAB 202, 251, 273, 286, 340, 344, 394, 405, 446, 448
Jach, Andrew [author] 85
Jackals, the 348
Jacks, Terry 211
Jackson 5 213
Jackson, Michael 439
Jackson, Philip 449, 502
Jacobsen, Colin *see* Joye, Col
Jacobsen, Kerry 319, 361, 509-11
Jacobsen, Kevin 13, 14, 30, 31, 51, 53
Jacobsen, Philip 159, 190, 209, 479
Jagger, Mick 97, 209, 485
'Jailanguru Pakarnu' [song] 537
'Jailbreak' [song] 195, 243, 265
'Jake the Peg' [song] 11
'Jamaica Rum' [song] 194
'Jamaican Farewell' [song] 190
James Taylor Move 121
James, Andrew 278
James, Etta 388
James, Harvey 191, 314, 316, 369, 513
James, Henry 301
James, Rockwell T.; *see* Ronnie Peel
James, Sid 323
'Jamie' [song] 96
Jamrozik, Wanda [author] 441
Jandakot (WA) 129
Jarman, Derek [film director] 470
Javo [fictional character] 282, 457
Jaws of Life, The [album] 440
Jazz Notes [magazine] 26
Jebediah 278
Jefferson Airplane 240

Jellabad Mutant, The [album] 191
Jelly Babies, the 387
Jennings, A V [builder] 435
Jesus and Mary Chain, the 548
Jesus Christ Superstar [album/show] 132, 155, 196, 198, 270, 294, 327
Jet [band] 34
Jetsonnes, the 336, 437
JFK and the Cuban Crisis 398
Jimmy and the Boys 388
Jo Jo Zep and the Falcons 177, 181-2, 265, 271, 298, 300, 305, 352, 362, 451; and His Little Helpers 305
Joe Dolce Music Theatre; *see* Dolce, Joe
John Justin 539
John Kennedy's Love Gone Wrong 540
John, Elton 210, 221
Johnnies, the 539
'Johnny B. Goode' [song] 294
Johnny O'Keefe Show, The [TV show] 36
Johns, Neale 171
Johnson, Brian 237, 239, 241, 243-4
Johnson, Danny 533
Johnson, Harry 141, 270
Johnson, Howard [author] 239-40
Johnson, Kevin 177, 210
Johnson, Vivien [author] 202, 263, 266
Johnston, Craig 251
Johnston, Owen [film director] 421
Johnstone, Brian [author] 242
Johnstone, Ian [author] 515
Jonathan's [Sydney venue] 87, 312
Jones, Alistair [author] 57, 169
Jones, Andrea [author] 304, 423, 508
Jones, Davy 106
Jones, Grace 131, 198
Jones, Iggy (aka Ignatius Jones, Juan Trapaza) 388
Jones, John 62-3
Jones, Marcie 75-6, 112
Jones, Mick 528
Jones, Paul 161
Jones, Peter 107
Jones, Spencer 526
Jones, Tom 106
Jordan, Cyril 460
Josef K 347
Joseph, Bill 154
Joseph, David 76-9, 164, 184, 413
Journey 290
Joy Boys 13, 37
Joy Division 450, 523
Joy, Susan [author] 262
Joye, Col (Colin Jacobsen) 13, 16, 18, 30-1, 37-8, 41-2, 44, 51, 53, 95, 161, 211, 329
Joynson, Vernon [author] 49, 143
Judas Iscariot and the Traitors 202, 251
Judd, Phil 331, 444, 488, 490
'Judgment' [song] 203
Juice [magazine] 283
Juke [magazine] 99, 195, 232, 252, 264, 268, 277, 299-300, 303, 309-10, 338, 362, 378, 419, 421, 441, 538
'Jukebox in Siberia' [song] 233
'Julia' [song] 193, 322
'Juliette' [song] 110
July 14 533
Jumbo's Tea Party [album] 154
'Jump in My Car' [song] 193, 195, 322-3
Jungle [Sydney venue] 119
Junk Logic 336
Junkyard [album] 403, 438, 516
'Juno and Me' [song] 415
Jurd, Mick 242
'Just Another Woman' [song] 295
'Just Like Fire Would' [song] 426
'Just Like Tom Thumb's Blues' [song] 121
'Just Not True' [song] 496
'Just to Love You' [song] 351
'Justice and Money Too' [song] 408

K-tel [record label] 383-4
Kabel, Martin [fictional character] 492
Kaczmarek, Les 200, 284
Kahvas Jute 185, 238, 279, 464

Kain, Dave 187
Kakulas, Phil 391
Kalamunda (WA) 104
Kalgoorlie (WA) 233
Kam Sha 539
Kane, Eden 83
Kannis, Johnny 348, 384
'Karen' [song] 346
Karpin, Peter 315
Kaye, Janice 46
Kazas, Tom 501
Keath, Jenny 226, 229, 296, 382
Keays, Jim 31, 65, 85, 90, 96, 99, 107-8, 110-12, 113, 149, 153, 183-4, 200, 325
Keeley, Ron 266-7
Keenan, Haydn [film director] 522
'Keep On Dancin'' [song] 281
'Keep the Junk in America' [song] 233
Keith Potger and the New Seekers [album] 164
Keith, Barbara 312
Kelly, Paul 282, 306, 314, 320, 339, 462; and the Dots 304, 320, 345, 461, 527; and the Coloured Girls 528; and the Messengers 528
Kelly, Sean 383, 446, 448, 485
Kempsey (NSW) 35
Kenett, Joan 34
Kennedy, Graham 149, 186
Kennedy, Jo 446
Kennedy, John F. [Brisbane musician] 398
Kennedy, Mark 207
Kennedy, Michelle 218
Kerouac, Jack 301
Kerr, John 248
Kevin Borich Express 256, 443
Kew (Vic) 149
Key, Pam 187, 255
Key, Phil 119, 187-8, 255
'Keypunch Operator' [song] 417
Keys, Anna [fictional character] 183
Keystone Angels, *see* the Angels
KGB (Keith Glass Band) 338
'Khe Sanh' [song] 285-6
Kick [album] 482
Kid Galahad and the Eternals 202, 260
Kid Stakes (play) 335
Kidman, Nicole 182, 494
Kidron, Adam 468
'Kids Are Out Tonight, The' [song] 323
Kids in the Kitchen 539
Kilbey, Russell 470
Kilbey, Steve 435, 469-70
Kill the King 431
Kinetics, the 102
King Bees, the 46, 75, 178, 225
King Crimson vii, 265, 414
King Harvest 172
King Ink [book] 515; [song] 515
'King of Kings' [song] 454
'King of the Road' [song]
King of the Sun [album] 426
King Street Studio 194
King, Brian 192
King, Carol 192
King, Carole 208
King, Jonathan 211
King Kong [fictional character] 253
Kings Cross (NSW) 60, 75, 77, 125
Kings of the World 340
'Kings of the World' [song] 213
Kingscliff (NSW) 473
Kingsmill, Mark 202, 348, 459
Kingsmill, Richard 539
Kingston Hotel [Melbourne venue] 319, 464
Kingston Trio, the 156
Kinks, the 127, 331
Kinney Corporation 164
Kinsellas [Sydney venue] 113
Kipner, Nat 52-3
Kipner, Steve 52, 117, 295
Kirk Gallery [Sydney venue] 318
Kirkpatrick, Gordon (Slim Dusty) 13
Kirshner, Don 118

Kiss 231-2, 416; Kiss Army 268
'Kitchen Man' [song] 381, 385
Kite 222
KJ Quintet 32
Knight, Anthony [author] 80
Knight, Grace 415
Knight, Holly 457
'Knock Knock, Who's There' [song] 158
Know Your Product [album] 425; [song] 522
Knowles, Karen 165
Koch, Christopher [author] 18, 22, 23, 34, 67
Kodiaks, the 106
Kogarah (NSW) Police Station 509
Kommotion [TV show] 100
'Konkaroo' [song] 364
'Kookaburra Sits in the Old Gum Tree' [song] 417
Koonibba Rock [album] 536
Koppes, Peter 469
Kovac, Herm 193, 323
Krahe, Ian 257-9
Kravats, the 84
Kretschmer, Robert 449, 463, 532
Kringas, George 268
Krishna [fictional character] 187
Kristian, Marty 163
Kruger, Debbie [author] 127, 131, 456
Ku-Ring-Gai Chase (NSW) 360
Kuepper, Ed 254, 259-63, 425, 433-4, 460, 462, 540
Kuepper, Wolfgang 348
Kulture Shock [TV show] 522
Kush 333, 505
Kyabram (Vic) 99

'L'acrostique D'Amour' [song] 501
La Cantina [Adelaide venue] 24
La De Das, the 70, 119, 238, 262, 322, 369, 456
La Femme 293, 495
'La La' [song] 110
La Mama Theatre 178
'La Mer' [song] 383
La Perouse (NSW) 35
Labor Party (ALP) 146, 162, 270
Ladies and Gentleman [album] 318
'Lady Scorpio' [song] 103
Lady Slick [fictional character] 182
Lafferty, Phil and the Singing Dog 492
Lake Tahoe (California) 39
Lake, Tony 255
Lakes Entrance (Vic) 99
'Lakeside' [song] 466
Lamb, Alan 9
Lamb, Keith 324-5
Lamb, Tony L. [film director] 90
Lamington Records [record label] 338
Landed [album] 438
Lander, Ned [film director] 535
Lane, William [author] 512
Langdon, Chris 124
Langford Lever 172, 190
Langman, Chris 320
Langsam, David L. [author] 291, 447
Largest Living Things 493
Largs Pier Hotel [Adelaide venue] 286
Lark and Tina's [Adelaide venue] 24, 535
Larrikin [record label] 436
Larry's Rebels 103, 129
Las Vegas [Adelaide venue] 24
Las Vegas (Nevada) 263
Last Air Raid Show, The [projected review] 253
Last Chance Café 180, 368
'Last House on the Left' [song] 302
'Last Night' [song] 277
'Last Saturday (We Fell in Love)' [song] 158
Last Words, the 350, 426
Late Show, The (Australian television show) 291, 545
'Latin Version' [song] 136
Latorre, Gino 253

INDEX

585

Latrobe University 166
Laughing Clowns, the 260, 334, 340, 344, 407, 416, 425-8, 432-3, 495, 523, 529; *Laughing Clowns* [EP] 427-8; 'Laughing Clowns' [song] 265, 426, 428
Laughing Hands 501
Laughlin, Denis 244, 312
Laughter Round the Table [album] 429
Launay, Nick 487
Launching Place (Vic) 151
Lavery, Doug 109, 208
Law of Nature [album] 430
Lawler, Ray [author] 335
Lawrence, Bruno 356
Lawrie, Buna 536
Lawson Square Infirmary [EP] 398
Lawson, Henry 217
Lawton, Tina 46
Laycock, Peter 26
'Lazy River' [song] 376
Le Club Foote 539
Lea, Laurel 30
Leach, Geordie 256-7
Leadabrand, Mike 172, 176
Leadbelly 60
'Leader of the Pack' [song] 414
'Leading Lady' [song] 460
Leapfrogs, the 335
'Leaps and Bounds' [song] 462, 528
'Leave Love Enough Alone' [song] 318
Led Zeppelin 119, 202, 204, 210, 367, 377
'Lee Remick' [song] 346
Lee, Albert 33
Lee, Defiant [greyhound] 459
Lee, Dinah 54, 77, 83
Lee, Graham 398-9, 504
Lee, John 191
Lee, Lonnie 38
Lee, Richard 177, 191, 331, 368, 370, 446, 460
Leederville Punk Festival 391
Leedon [record label] 30, 37
Leeds Music 91
Leef, Barry 269
Legend, The [book] 49
Leiber, Jerry 312
Leigh, Michael [author] 239
Leigh, Mike [film director] 380
'Leilani' [song] 458
Leisuremasters 297
Lemons Alive [EP] 305
Lennon, John 81, 101, 252, 264
Lennons Hotel (Brisbane) 129
Leo and Friends 172
Let It Be [agency] 159
'Let Me Fuck Your Mind' [song] 333
Let My People Come [stage show] 456
Lethal Weapons [album] 269, 274, 403, 448
Lethlean, John [author] 378
Levi Smith's Clefs 186, 200
Levin, Benny 83
Lewicki, Jules [author] 272
Lewis, Jerry Lee 7, 60, 80, 252
Lewis, Kevin 106
Lewis, Robert [author] 434
Lewisham (NSW) 255
Libaek, Sven 31, 93, 156
Liberal Party (national) 329; (NSW) 374
Liberty [record label] 35
Librettos 75, 77
License to Rage [album] 303-4
'Life Without Lulu' [song] 490
Life... Is for Living [album] 313
Light, Dave 335
Lightfoot, Gordon 210
Lighthouse Keepers, the 499
Lightnin' Hopkins 60
Lillie, Peter 169, 177, 181, 215, 235, 297, 352, 447, 450, 464, 495
Lilly [fictional character] 388
Limb, Bobby 161
Lime Spiders 522
Linda Lee [record label] 42
Lindon, Adrian 'Avatar' 156

Lindsay, Reg 217
Lipp and the Double Deckers (aka Lipp and the Double Decker Brothers) 178, 182, 225, 275
Lipps Inc 504
Lipstick Killers, the 349, 474
List, Ian 534
Lithgow (NSW) 321
little bands 335-6, 395-6
Little Feat 221
Little Fish [film] 289
Little Gulliver 120; and the Children 184; *see also* Smith, Gulliver
Little Heroes 539
Little Madness to be Free, A [album] 425
Little Murders 495
Little Pattie (Patricia Amphlett) 30, 161, 228, 388, 456
'Little Ray of Sunshine, A' [song] 115
Little Richard (Richard Penniman) 14, 33, 46, 124
Little River Band (LRB) 113, 116, 145, 195, 209, 212, 247-8, 253, 279, 282, 294, 306, 318, 412, 418, 464, 467, 520, 544
Little Rock Allen 42; *see also* Billy Thorpe
Little, Jimmy 38
Live at Ding Dong's [album] 391
Live at Several 21sts [album] 513
Live at the Station Hotel [album] 297-8, 339
Live at the Wireless [album] 517, 527
'Live It Up' [song] 473
Livestock [album] 200
Living Daylights, The [magazine] 96, 159
Living Eyes (Bee Gees album) 269
Living Eyes (Radio Birdman album) 269, 424
'Living in a Child's Dream' [song] 111
'Living in the Land of Oz' [song] 327, 530
Living in the 70's [album] 227-8, 231, 465
Living Single 415
Lloyd, John 320, 461
Lloyd's World 54
Local &/or General [album] 452-3
Local Inn [Sydney venue] 426
Local Product 478
Locke, Sondra 302
Lockwood, Richard 186-7
Löfvén, Chris [film director] 65, 168, 233, 294, 305
Logan, Mal 207
Loggins and Messina 159
Logic 391-2
Lomax, Alan 60
London (UK) 5, 39, 54, 71, 81, 345, 398, 451, 505, 514, 526
'Lonely Surfer, The' [song] 339
Loneragan, Fred 481, 504
Loney, Roy 460
Long John Baldry 55
Long Live the Evolution [album] 269-70, 274
Long Tan (battle) 30
Long Way to the Top [TV show] 50, 400, 440
'Looking Through a Tear' [song] 96
'Lord's Prayer, The' [song] 27, 155, 535
Los Angeles 220, 366, 480
Lost and Found, Coming Home the Wrong Way Round [album] 103
Lost Boys, The [film] 133
Lost Somewhere Beyond Harmony [album] 210
Lot's Wife [magazine] 98, 161
Lothlorien Festival 152
Lotus 187
Loughlin George 10
'Louie, Louie' [song] 275, 338
'Louisiana Lady' [song] 194
Love [US band] 435
Love, the [Australian band] 426
Love 200 [orchestral/rock piece] 186
Love Album, The 389
Love and Other Bruises [album] 295; [song] 294

'Love Attraction' [song] 522
'Love By Numbers' [song] 449, 463, 532
'Love Gun' [song] 269
Love In [Melbourne venue] 121
'Love in a Box' [song] 477
'Love in an F. J.' [song] 252
'Love in Motion' [song] 462
'Love Is Here Today' [song] 386
Love Is in the Air [TV show] 293
'Love Is in the Air' [song] 322
'Love Is Just Like a Kick in the Bum in the Middle of the Night' [song] 296
'Love Is the Drug' [song] 230
'Love Makes Sweet Music' [song] 109
'Love On the Radio' [song] 226, 421, 519
Love Rodeo 440
'Love Will Find a Way' [song] 376, 383
'Love's Not Enough' [song] 369-71
Lovece, Frank 335
'Loved One, The' [song] 88, 482
Loved Ones, the 70, 88-90, 328, 482, 517
Lovegrove, Vince 109, 200, 241, 456
'Lovesick Blues' [song] 40
'Lovesick' [song] 508
Lovett, Rob 88
Lovin' Spoonful, the 313
Loving Is Hard [album] 187
Lowenstein, Richard [film director] 26, 336, 454, 486, 490, 515
Lowenstein, Wendy [author] 26
Loyde, Lobby (Barry Lyde) vii, 42, 51, 59, 73, 85, 90, 93-4, 135, 145, 154, 185, 188, 245, 257, 259, 323, 334, 443, 453, 474, 478, 482, 505, 539
LSD 153
Lubran, Martin 440
Lucas, Steve 188, 257-8
Lucas, Trevor 26, 529
Lucky Dog 223
Luhrmann, Baz [film director] 196, 322
Lum, Rick 318, 324, 326
'Lumps of Lead' [song] 439
Lumsden, David 26
Lunch, Lydia 516
Lunn, Don 19
Lupin Beck 308
Lynch, Bernie 415
Lynch, Kim 22, 88-9

M Squared (aka M²) [record label] 350, 495-6, 517
'M.S.O.' [song] 370
Mabel's Dream 222
Macainsh, Greg 182, 217-8, 220, 223-34, 254, 273, 279, 464, 476, 528
Macainsh, Noel 224
Macara, Nigel 171, 190, 294
Machinations 334, 478, 504, 539
MacKenzie Theory 171-7, 183, 215, 443
Mackenzie, Dugald 405
MacKenzie, Rob 172-4, 208, 215, 332
Maclaine-Cross, Moira 523
Maclean, Stephen [author/screenwriter] 182, 445
Macquarie University 369
macrobiotics 82
Mad Max Beyond Thunderdome [film] 512
Madder Lake 175, 184, 189, 255, 313, 443
'Made My Bed, Gonna Lie In It' [song] 128
Madigan, Paul 226; and the Humans 297
Madness 473
Madonna 530
Madrid [fictional character] 141
Madroom 517
Maessen, Liv 157
Magazine [album] 315
Magdalene, Mary [fictional character] 198
'Magic' [song] 510
Magical Mushroom Mansion 175
Maguire, Duncan 92, 207, 483
Mahal, Taj 536
Maher, Fred 504
Mahoney, Jane; *see* Barnes, Jane
Maine, Andrew [author/editor] 423, 518

'Make the World Go Away' [song] 30
'Make Your Stash' [song] 82, 189, 222
Makeig, Maggie [author] 65, 84
Makers of the Dead Travel Fast 496
Malta, 45; Maltese-Australians, 46
'Mama' [song] 439
'Mama Keep Your Big Mouth Shut' [song] 64
'Mama Mia' [song] 293
Mammal 356
Man and Machine (Eric Gradman Man and Machine) 256, 299, 339, 463, 483
Man or Myth 519
'Man Overboard' [song] 521
Man, Isle of (UK) 49, 51
Manchester (UK) 49, 51
Mancini, Henry 378
Mandu (aka Chris Moraitis) 333
Manfred Mann [band] 80
Manfred Mann's Earth Band 112
Manikins, the 276, 393
Manila [album] 528
Mankowicz, Gered 315
Manly Pacific Hotel [Sydney venue] 86
Mann, Tracy 457, 492-3
Manning, James [author/editor] 421
Manning, Phil 203
Mannix, Brian 291
Mansfield, Alan 510
Mantra 74
Manuel [fictional character] 419
Manzanera, Phil 331, 488
Manzie, Jimmy 253
Manzil Room [Sydney venue] 535
Maralinga (SA) 238
Maranatha [album] 165-6, 436
Marcus Hook Roll Band 194-5, 241
marijuana 184
Marks, Fred 52
Marks, Karen 447-9, 532
Marks, Paul 21
Marks, Philip 403
Marley, Bob 536
Maroubra (NSW) 30
Marquee [London venue] 82
Mars Needs Guitars [album] 460
Marsden, Greg [fictional character] 467
Martin, George 12, 40
Martin, Tony 373
Martinis [Melbourne venue] 309
Marx, Chico 307
Marxism 173
Mascot Airport 286; *see also* Sydney Airport
'Mashed Potato' [song] 43
Mason, Dave 68, 373, 376-87, 485
Mason, John 374
Mason, Paul 387
Mason, Roger 453
Masters Apprentices 28, 69-70, 96, 99, 102, 107, 109, 145, 148, 183, 204, 212, 217, 252, 254, 282, 325, 496
Masuak, Chris 348, 473, 525
Matelot Club [Adelaide venue] 28
'Material Girl' [song] 192
Matheson, Jane [author] 286, 426
Mathews, Jon [author] 364
Matlock Police [TV show] 270
Matlock, Glen 517
Matrimony 485
Matt Finish 298-9, 381, 433, 457
Matters, Graham 65
Matteson, Michael 148
Matthews, Gil 159, 332, 494
Matthews, Wendy 455
Maudlin Intellectuals, the 428
Mavericks, the 95
Max Q 482
Maybe Dolls 411
MC5 266, 424
McAnulty, Eloise [author] 535
McArdle, George 214
McArtney, Dave 508
McAskill, Barry 29
McCallum, Alison 146, 162, 194

McCarthy, Paul 277
McCartney, Paddy 107, 112, 115
McCartney, Paul 25, 30, 81, 101, 113, 130, 264, 318
McCausland, Ian 185, 220, 516
McClymont, David 408-9
McComb, David 275, 351, 391, 481, 492, 501-2
McComb, Robert 392, 395, 408
McCusker, Eric 327, 329, 494
McDonald, Alsy (Alan) 391-5
McDonald, Elly [author] 378, 380
McDonald, Garry 337
McDonough, Bill 466
McDonough, Guy 466-7
McEntee, Mark 294, 455
McFarlane, Ian [author] 203, 351, 424, 546
McGee, Brownie 60
McGee, Judy 523
McGee, Tim [author] 445
McGinty, Harry [fictional character] 301
McGowan, Andrew 391
McGregor, Craig [author] 70, 93
McHenry, Paul 546
McIntyre, Iain [author] 88, 94
McKelvie, Red 318
McKenzie, Barry [fictional character] in film, 163, 248; in comic strip 248
McKenzie, Ian 327
McLaren, Malcolm 504
McLean, Jean 147
McLennan, Don 343
McLennan, Grant 346, 469, 529
McLennan, Iain 299
McLeod, Lachlan 526
McMahon, Brian 519
McMahon, Julian 147
McMahon, William 'Billy' 146
McMillan, Andrew [author] 256, 403, 426
McQuade, Betty 34
McQuade, Cathy 487, 493
McQueen, Humphrey [author] 393
Mead, Sister Janet 155, 406, 535
Meade, Mike 205
Measure for Measure [album] 463
Mechanics in a Relaxed Manner [play] 178
Medhurst, Ray 498
Medlin, Brian 166
Meggs, Ginger [fictional character] 445
'Melanie Makes Me Smile' [song] 158
Melbourne (Vic) 4, 43, 76, 85, 90, 111, 362, 377; Festival Hall 313; General Cemetery 36; Grammar School 120; High School 226; New Orleans Jazz Band 21; Olympics (1956) 40; Town Hall 231, 253
Melbourne [album] 454
Melbourne Club, The [album] 339
Melbourne Velodrome 107
Meldrum, Ian ('Molly') 69, 78-9, 85, 99, 104, 106-7, 111, 114, 149, 159-60, 198, 204, 286, 291, 322-3, 327, 330, 417, 446, 449-50, 477, 486, 489, 532, 543-4
Melody Maker [magazine] 261, 420, 462
Melouney, Vince 42, 50, 54, 93, 205, 322
Men at Work 412, 417-8, 459
Mendelssohn, Julian 505
Mendes, Sergio 87
Mental as Anything 293, 308, 350, 387, 421, 454, 471, 481, 523, 539-40, 548; *Mental as Anything Plays at Your Party* [EP] 308, 472
Mental Notes [album] 331
Menzies, Nikki 498
Menzies, Robert 37, 67, 147, 219
MEO 245 443
Mercury [record label] 79-80
Mermen, the 107
Merrick, Paul [author] 436
Merritt, Max 449; and the Meteors 37, 39, 71, 77, 84, 91, 94-5, 192
Mesmerizer [album] 349
'Message to my Girl' [song] 490
Mexico 418

Meyer, David N. [author] 53
Mi-Sex 350, 412, 460, 507-8
Miami (Florida) 157
Michael Turner in Session 184
Mickey's Moomba (musical) 305
microfilm 336
Midday Platter Chatter [radio show] 51
Midday Show [TV show] 512
Midget and the Farrellys 277, 391
Midnight Oil 201, 215, 232, 277-9, 290, 299, 345, 353, 433, 446, 461, 487, 502, 525, 530, 537
'Midnight Special' [song] 60
Midsummer Night's Dream (play) 502
Mighty Kong 190, 222-3, 225
Mighty Records [record label] 307
Mildura (Vic) 363
Miles, Barry 68
Miles, Robert 437
Milesago [album] 189, 252; [website] 79
Miller, Billy 326, 445
Miller, Harry M. 60, 137, 155-6
Miller, John 536
Miller, Richard [fictional character] 18
Miller, Steve 403, 404, 432
Miller's Pubs 60
Millionaires, the 297
Milne, Bruce 273, 422, 495
Milsom, Wendy [author] 203, 205, 305, 502
Minogue, Dannii (Danielle) 106
Minogue, Kylie 11, 444
Minton, Damien [author] 302, 304
Minutemen, the 548
'Miss Mercy' [song] 257, 358
Miss Universe 171, 190
Missing Link [record label] 293, 338, 342, 423, 427, 494, 501, 515 [record shop] 320, 339
Missing Links, the 43, 59-65, 91, 111, 125, 141, 253-4, 338, 456
Mission: Magic [TV show] 211
Mississippi 115, 117, 157, 159, 212, 318
'Mister Uddich Smuddich Goes to Town' [song] 430
Mitchell, C. C. [author] 393
Mitchell, Tony 314, 317
Mittagong, NSW 151
Mittelhauser, Dean [author] 44
Mix [magazine] 423
'Model, The' [song] 387
Models 3, 273, 298, 345, 382, 394, 405, 420, 446, 458, 519-20, 532, 539
Models Media [album] 383
'Modern Song, The' [song] 413
Moffitt, Matt 433
Moffs, the 501
Moginie, Jim 278
Moir Sisters, the 210
Mojo [magazine] 253
Mojos, the 124
Mombassa, Reg (Chris O'Doherty) 202, 471, 492
Momento [album] 155
'Mona' [song] 339
Monash University 98, 184, 302
Moncrieff, Virginia 431
Mondo Rock (aka Ross Wilson's Mondo Rock) 234, 299, 327, 493, 510, 539
Monitors, the 416
Monkees, the 265, 417
Monkey Grip [book] 160, 303; [film] 282, 303, 456
'Monster's Back, The' [song] 214
Montez, Chris 64
Montreux Jazz Festival 352
'Monty and Me' [song] 103, 107
Monty Python's Flying Circus [TV show] 247, 374, 462
Moodists, the vii, 274, 282, 403, 431-2, 437, 470, 495, 527
Moodists, The [EP] 408
Moon, Greta 495

INDEX

Moon, Keith 77
Moondance 194
Moondog Matinee [album] 252
Mooney, Brian 26
Moonshine Jug and String Band 167, 281
Moorabbin (Vic) 378
Moore, Clare 403-9
Moore, Robert [fictional character] 301
Moorhouse, Frank [author] 393
Mora, Philip [film director] 81
Moraitis, Chris; *see* Mandu
Mordue, Mark [author] 431
More Arse Than Class [album] 188
Morgan, Chad 268
Morgan, Graham 207
Morgan, Warren 'Pig' 198, 322
Morland, Philip 273
Morning of the Earth [album] 186
Moroder, Giorgio 463
Morpions 336
Morris, Gary 483
Morris, Jenny 485
Morris, Russell 68-9, 101-3, 157, 295, 416; and the Rubes 103
Morrison, Jim 485
Morrison, Lindy (Belinda) 147, 197, 347, 409, 431, 529
Morrison, Rick 110
Morrison, Van 356
Morrow, Annalisse 411-4, 503, 528
Morrow, Chris (Christian) 375, 411-2
Morrow, Steven 522
Morton, Janet [author] 203
Moss, Ian 201, 462
Moss, Ian 283-5, 289, 513
Moss, Ron 270
'Most People I Know Think That I'm Crazy' [song] 188
Most Primitive Band in the World, The [album] 260
Motels, the 456
Mother Earth 329
Mother Goose [band] 251, 278
Mother's Choice [album] 188
Mothers of Invention 269
Motley Crue 286
'Motor City Connection' [song] 370
Motors, the 477
Motown [record label] 328, 330
Mott the Hoople 132
Mottola, Tommy 490
Mouldie Fygges, the 13
Mouskouri, Nana 276
Move, the 68
MPD Ltd 70, 108
'Mr. America' [song] 103
'Mr. Clarinet' [song] 343, 514, 515
'Mr. Songwriter' [song] 108
Mr. Uddich Smuddich Goes to Town [album] 429; [song] 430
Mt Buller (Vic) 225
Mt Eliza (Vic) 464, 466
Mt Gambier (SA) 404
Mt Isa (Qld) 281
Mt Waverley (Vic) 224
Much More Ballroom [Melbourne venue] 153, 170, 183, 222
Mud [Perth band] 309
Mudie, Don 114-5
Muffler, Morrie 253
Mug's Game [album] 309
Mullanes, the 387
Mulry, Ted 131, 193, 245, 312; *see also* Ted Mulry Gang
multi-track recording 68
multiculturalism 3
Mumbo Jumbo 437
Mungo Jerry 158, 186
Murdoch, Rupert 157
Murphy, Chris 412
Murphy, John 428, 432
Murphy, Kevin 207
Murray Bridge (SA) 536
Murri Jama National Aboriginal Week 537

Mushroom [record label] 159, 172, 175, 181, 227, 284, 298, 300, 311, 323, 330, 340, 342, 394, 442, 445, 453, 455, 475, 529
Music from Michael [EP] 83
'Music Goes Round My Head, The' [song] 130
Musick Express 306
Mustafa, Tim (Temucin) 347
Mustangs, the 31, 110
Mute [record label] 387
Mutiny [EP] 517
'My Aim Is to Please You' [song] 92
'My Baby' [song] 289
'My Baby Thinks She's a Train' [song] 396
My Brilliant Career [film] 445
'My Canary Has Circles Under His Eyes' [song] 168, 251
'My City of Sydney' [song] 491
'My Family' [song] 385-6, 388
My Houdini [album] 436
'My Little Angel' [song] 197
'My Old Man's a Dustman' [song] 53
'My Secret' [song] 294
'My Sex' [song]
'My Turn to Cry' [song] 286
'My Way' [song] 338
Myriad Rides Again 297
Myriad, Carrl 158, 297-8, 303
Myriad, Janie; *see* Conway, Janie

Nagorcka, Ron 501
Nah, tellus wh't Kush means yer great sausage [album] 333
Naked Bunyip, The [film] 105
Napier-Bell, Simon 194, 321
Narara Festival 159, 539
Narrabeen Antler [Sydney venue] 92, 286
Nashville 117; Antipodean Nashville 200
Nathalia (Vic) 115
Nation [magazine] 97, 159, 161
Nation Review [magazine] 159, 208, 262, 282
National Film and Sound Archive 202
national identity 286
Native Sons 373-4
Natural High [album] 103
Nauts, the; *see* Supernaut
Neale, Lee 190
Nedlands (WA) 483
Needham, John 349, 501, 524
'Needle in a Haystack' [song] 113
Needles, Nique (Cornelius Delaney) 452
Neeson, Bernard 'Doc' 28, 107, 136, 167, 281, 283, 290, 457
Negatives, the 273-4
Neighbors [album] 388-9, 465
Neighbour, Greg [author] 227
Neighbours [TV show] 312
Nelson, Willie 371
Neon Steal 250, 346
Nerk, Fred [fictional character] 29
Nesbitt, Graeme 356, 361
Net, The [album] 521
Netherlands, 45, 107, 400
Never Ending Apprenticeship [film] 212
Never Mind the Bollocks... Here's the Sex Pistols [album] 227-8, 273
'Never Tear Us Apart' [song] 483
Neville, Richard [author/editor] 39, 81, 96, 160-1
New Avengers, the 332
'New Bully in the Town' [song] 430
New Christs, the 522-3
New Cool, The [album] 234
New Five 490
New Gold Stars 373
'New King Jack' [song] 351
New Musical Express (NME) [magazine] 261, 320, 492
New Orleans (Louisiana) 35
New Race 424
New Seekers, the 77, 103, 106, 163-5, 413, 415

new wave (1960s) 37, 111; (1970s/80s) 2
New Wave on Stage [TV show] 37
'New Wave' [song] 339
New York (NY) 82, 117, 345, 352, 366, 395
New York Dolls 266
'New York Mining Disaster, 1941' [song] 55
'New York Reel' [song] 436
New York University 9
New Zealand 37, 39, 101, 156, 210, 278, 294, 331, 355, 363, 379, 414, 444; New Zealanders 71, 355
Newcastle (NSW) 185, 237, 515-6, 523-4
Newcastle (UK) 237
'Newcastle Song, The' 252
Newham, Colin 'Polly' 373-5, 379, 388-9, 496
Newman, Cameron 503
Newman, Randy 231
News [band] 273, 339-40, 490
'Newspaper' [song] 437-8
Newton-John, Olivia 70, 118, 130, 145, 248, 314-5, 342
Newton, Bert (Albert) 36, 161, 232
Newton, Dobe 166
Newton, Wayne 52
Newtown (NSW) 240
Ng, Geeling 522
'Nice Boys' [song] 256
Nice, the 186
Nichol, Brian 324
'Nick the Stripper' [song] 515
Nickleodeon [album] 184
Nico 166
Niddrie (Vic) 502
Nielsen, Juanita [publisher/editor] 491
Night in Rio, A (play) 226
Nightmoves [TV show] 442, 450
Nimbin (NSW) 152
Nimmervoll, Ed [author] 99, 116, 132
Nimmo, Bob 478, 480
'Nips are Getting Bigger, The' [song] 387, 472
'Nitro' [song] 500
Nitzsche, Jack 339
Niven, Jim 299
NME; see *New Musical Express*
'No Commotion' [song] 382
No Fixed Address 420, 536, 537
No Nonsense 539
'No Resistance' [song] 428
'No Say In It' [song] 505
'No Shoulders, No Head' [song] 453
No Song Too Sacred [album] 513
'No Word From China' [song] 423
'No. 3' [song] 377, 381, 383
Noble Park (Vic) 486
Nobodies, the 395
'Nobody Knows You (When You're Down and Out)' [song] 121
Nomads, the 124
Noone, Jeremy (Jerry) 148, 222
Nora [fictional character] 457
Norm, the 538
Normington, Jules 474
Norseman (WA) 499
North Ryde (NSW) 426
North Sydney 412
Northcote (Vic) 126
Northern Territory 201, 282
'Nothing Grows in Texas' [song] 520
'Now I'm Together' [song] 185
Now Voyager [film] 57
Nowara, Zbig 546
'Nowhere Man' [song] 315
NowSound [TV show] 84
Nuclear Disarmament Party 487
Nucleus [agency] 449
Nullarbor Plain 394
Numan, Gary 452
'Number One' [song] 325
Number 96 [TV show] 72
Numbers, The [album] 411

INDEX

Numbers, the [Queensland band] 250, 345, 348; [Sydney band] 375, 382, 411, 415, 493
Nuovo Mondo [album] 494
Nutcracker Suite, The 89
Nutter, Lynda 414, 433-4
Nutwood Rug Band 141, 148, 150, 152
Nuvo Bloc 535
Nylon Degrees [album] 338
Nyngan (NSW) RSL 374
NZ Pop 445

O Zambezi [album] 358, 365
O'Doherty, Peter (aka Yoga Dog) 472
O'Donnell, John [author] 460
O'Donoghue, Rory 205, 270, 491
O'Grady, Anthony [author] 268, 283-4, 286, 316, 326, 331, 367
O'Hanlon, Seamus [author] 98
O'Keefe, Johnny vii, 7, 12-14, 18, 19, 29, 30, 32-35, 38, 42, 104, 113, 194, 252, 491; Award for Best New Talent 530
O'List, Davey 186
O'Meara, Lindsay 344
O'Neil, Stephen 469, 498, 499
O'Neill, Margot 437-8
O'Neill, Sharon 492
Oates, Warren 311
Obsecration [album] 334
Oceania [album] 530
Octagon [Adelaide venue] 28, 110
Octagon [Perth venue] 309
'Odessa' [song] 56
Odetta 121
Of Skins and Heart [album] 469
Ogden's Nut Gone Flake [album] 114
'Oh Bondage, Up Yours' [song] 273
'Oh Darling' [song] 454
'Oh No Not You Again' [song] 466
Ol' 55 252-3, 306, 527
'Ol' Hound Dog' [song] 100
Ol' Skydaddys 234
'Old Bay Road, The' [song] 240
'Old Man Emu' [song] 158
Oldham, Andrew Loog 139
Olinda (Vic) Golf Course 176
Olivia Newton-John – Glen Campbell TV Special [TV show] 315
Ollard, Greg 360
Olsen, Ollie 335, 340, 403, 426, 428, 482
Olszewski, Laurel 161
Olszewski, Peter (aka JJ McRoach) 161
Olympic Sideburns 521
Omega, Alf 534
'On' [song] 453
On Dit [magazine] 272
'On the Prowl' [song] 252
'On the Road Again' [song] 64
On the Street [magazine] 420-1, 493, 535, 538
'On the Street Where You Live' [song] 493
Once Upon a Twilight [album] 113
One Foot in Front [album] 506
'One Good Reason' [song] 444
One Ton Gypsy 456
'Only a Flipside' [song] 298
Only Ones, the 393
'Only Time' [song] 346
Only Want You For Your Body [album] 188
Ontario 209
Op Pop [Sydney venue] 86
Operation Starlift 102
Opitz, Mark 456
Opus West 308
Oram, James [author] 138
Orange [band] 284
Orange (NSW) 45
Orange, Julia [author] 315
Orange Juice [band] 347, 408
Orbison, Roy 19
Orbost (Vic) 99
Organ Factory [Melbourne venue] 501
Original Bushwackers and Bullockies Band, the; *see* Bushwackers
'Original Sin' [song] 485

Ormond (Vic) RSL 23
Ornament of Grace, An [book] 40
'Orstralia' [song] 264
Osborne [fictional character] 141
Osbourne, Ozzy 186
Others, the 110
'Our Boys' [song] 403
'Our Love of Long Ago' [song] 28
Ourimbah (NSW) 150
Ourimbah Festival 103, 150-1, 186
'Out of Mind, Out of Sight [album] 454; [song] 3, 382
Out of Nowhere 428, 431
Out of Reason [album] 523
Out of the Blue [album] 176-7
Out on the Fringe [album] 316
Outlaws, the 124
Ova (theatre group) 533
'Over the Border' [song] 232
'Over the Rainbow' [song] 18, 43, 188
'Overkill' [song] 418
'Owe You Nothing' [song] 448
Owens, Dave 7
Oxford Club [Adelaide venue] 112
Oxford Tavern [Sydney venue] 267
Oxley High School 259
Oxley, Jeremy 277, 394, 473-4, 481
Oxley, Melanie 477
Oxley, Peter 394. 473-4, 476
Oz (Australian magazine) 39-40, 60, 97, 137, 159 (British magazine) 97-8, 159
Oz [record label] 298, 304-5, 328
Oz: the Rock 'n' Roll Road Movie [film] 65
Ozzy Osbourne's Blizzard of Oz 186

P., Lloyd 275-6
P. A. Club [Sydney venue] 86
Packer, Clive 52
Packer, Frank 52
Paddington (NSW) 202; Town Hall 34
Paddington Green Hotel [Sydney venue] 387
Page, Peter 34
Pailthorpe, Chris 'Smiley' 324, 326
Paintbox 194
Painters and Dockers 522
Pakistan 418
Palace [Melbourne venue] 87
Pale, Kiley 320
Pale Horse Have a Fit [album] 391
Palimpsest [album] 502
Palmer, Robert 510
Panther, Douglas L. [author/presenter] 90, 98
'Papa's in the Vice Squad' [song] 82
'Paranoid' [song] 108
Paris Green 497
Paris (France) 25, 401
Parker, Colonel Tom 479
Parker, Graham and the Rumour 414, 461
Parker, Robert 121
Parker, Steve 'Fess' 324
Parker, Tim [author] 110-1
Parkinson, Doug 5, 45, 157, 205-6, 242, 269, 356; *see also* Questions, Doug Parkinson In Focus
Parlophone [record label] 43, 62, 125
Parramatta Leagues Club 500
Parsons, Don 29
Parsons, Gordon 13
Parsons, Gram 297
'Part Company' [song] 529
Part One – 806 [film] 168
'Part Three: Into Paper Walls' [song] 68, 101
Particles, the 267, 343, 387, 388, 497-9, 517
Parton, Dolly 371
Partridge, Andy 375
Partridge, Tim 330
Party Boys 513-4
Party Boys Rage Album, The [album] 514
Party Fears [magazine] 514
Party Machine 71-3, 81-2, 189, 220, 328
Party to end all Parties 271

Pasadena (California) 367
'Pasadena' [song] 194, 321
Passengers, the 349
Passion [film] 8
Pastel Bats, the 336, 496
Pat Wilson's Marvels 305
'Paternosta Row' [song] 113
Paterson, James 398
Patients, the 250, 348
Paul, Jeremy 294-5, 455
Payload [EP] 439
Peacock, Brian 4, 71-81, 164, 184, 192, 199, 356, 413, 424, 456, 539
Pearce, Cleis 172-5, 215, 460
Pearce, Craig N. [author] 429, 453, 496, 509
Peek, Kevin 164
Peel Sessions 400, 429
Peel, Ian [author] 24
Peel, John 142, 191, 328; *see also* Peel Sessions
Peel, Ronnie (aka Rockwell T. James) 60, 322, 456
Pel Mel 344, 423, 523
Pelaco Brothers, the 160, 168, 172, 177-9, 181, 215, 235, 251, 265, 296-7, 302, 340, 447, 464, 471
Pelaco Inquest [TV show] 179
Pelaco Playboys 181
Pelican [magazine] 395, 419, 470
Pellicci, Derek 212-3, 295, 399, 521
Pendlebury, Andrew 298, 301
'Penelope' [song] 78, 106
Penglis, Theo (aka Thaao) 31
Penhallow, Andrew 523
'Penny Lane' [song] 90
Penrith (NSW) 459
Penthouse [magazine] 358
People are Strange Dalsy are Stranger [album] 391
'People' [song] 508
'People Say' [song] 347
People With Chairs Up Their Noses 431
Pepper, Angie 349
Pepper, Max 110
Pepper's [Melbourne venue] 149
Pepperell, David (aka Dr. Pepper) [author/lyricist] 65, 72, 149, 170, 185, 217, 298, 319, 327-8, 338
Perano, Greg 438, 440
Pere Ubu 248, 266
Perkins, Carl 171
Perkins, Tex (Greg; aka Tex Deadly) 525-6
Perry, Brendan 434
Perry, Doane 511
Perry, Graham 299
Persuasion [album] 523
Perth (WA) 39, 43, 47, 85, 155, 180, 242, 368, 395, 483, 524, 526, 535
Pest, Beat 181
Pestorius, David [author] 475
Pete Best Beatles 181
Peter, Paul and Mary 165
Peters (icecream company) 198
Peters, Lance [film director/presenter 91
Peters, Mark 392
Petersen [film] 331
Peterson, Colin 50, 56, 106
Pew, Tracey 341, 403, 425, 509, 519
Phalanx [album] 465
Phantom [record label] 458, 474
Phar Lap 418
Philip, Stephen 350, 521
Philips [record label] 63, 79, 82, 109, 138, 139, 141, 538
Phillips, Jeff 204
Phillips, Stephen [author] 196
Phonogram [record label] 59, 138, 188, 263
Photoplay [album] 315
Piano Piano 424
Picadilly's [Melbourne venue] 73
Piccadilly Circus (UK) 161
Pickwick [record label] 50
Picoleau, Andrew 532

INDEX

Pig City [book] 345
Pigott, Johanna (aka Alligator Bagg) 385, 490, 491-2, 509-10
Pilgrimage for Pop Festival 150
Pilkington, Mary 'Doody' Scott 226
Pinder, John 154, 170, 172
Pink Finks, the 71, 120, 338
Pink Flamingos 508, 510
Pinkpop Festival 400
Pirate radio 55
Pitt Street Farmers [EP] 385-6
Pittman, Tim [author] 250-1
'Place in the Sun' [song] 393
Place without a Postcard [album] 280, 487
Planet [magazine] 57, 84, 156, 159, 169, 185, 206, 442, 478; *see also* Daily Planet
'Planet on the Prowl' [song] 274
Plank, Conny 439
Plath, Sylvia 319
Play the Best [album] 477
Playboys, the 44, 71, 78; *see also* Normie Rowe
Playpower [book] 96
Plays With Marionettes 405, 437, 518
Plaza, Martin (Martin Murphy) 471
'Please Please America (Hear My Plea)' [song] 222
'Pleasure and Pain' [song] 457
Pleasure of Your Company [album] 450, 454
Ploog, Richard 470, 525
Pockley, Peter [author] 272
'Poetry in Motion' [song] 462
Point Leo (Vic) 99
Poison Cyanide Gas Mafalda [fictional character] 185
'Poison Ivy' [song] 43
'Poison Pen' [song] 459
Poles, the 250
Police, the 451
'Politics' [song] 365
Pollyanna [computer] 385
Polydor [record label] 77, 138
Polygram [record label] 357, 374
'Poor Boy' [song] 489
pop festivals 115
Pop Group, the 343, 452, 514
Pop Mechanix 445
Pop Movie [film] 450
Pop, Iggy 7, 33, 275, 520
Popular Ballad Animal, The [album] 338
Popular Mechanics 350, 445
Port Macquarie (NSW) 60, 63
Porter, Cole 21
Porter, Garth 312, 316-7, 477
Porter, Robie 220-1, 325
Portrait [record label] 366, 370
Post [album] 314, 398, 528
Postcard [record label] 347
Potger, Keith 27, 163-4
Potts, April *see* Byron, April
Poulsen, Hans (Bruce Poulsen) 8, 72, 96, 102-3, 107, 111, 158, 207
Powderworks [record label] 279
'Power and the Passion, The' [song] 488
Power Exchange [record label] 261
Power Play [album] 369
Power, John 305
Practical Jokers [album] 444, 446
Prahran (Vic) 209, 450, 456
Pram Factory (Theatre) 178, 226, 296, 302-3
Prayers on Fire [album] 515
Precious Little 349
'Prefab Heart(s)' [song] 376, 378, 383
Prehistoric Sounds [album] 261, 265, 426, 428
Premier Artists [agency] 449
Present Tense [album] 506
Presley, Elvis 32, 36, 44, 106, 517
'Pressure Sway' [song] 505
Preston Piss Pointer 179
Prestwich, Steve 283-4, 289, 388, 521
Pretenders, the 166, 539
'Pretty Girl' [song] 128

Price, Barton 453, 455
Price, Vincent 342
Primal Park [album] 327, 493
'Primal Park' [song] 338
Primitif [Brisbane venue] 94
Primitive Calculators 335-7, 486
Primitive Man [album] 463
Prince Melon [record label] 428
Prince of Wales Hotel [Melbourne venue] 335
Princes Berkley [Adelaide venue] 535
Prior, John 381
Prisoner (aka *Prisoner: Cell Block H*) [TV show] 303
Private Eye [magazine] 161
Procession 44, 69, 71, 74-5, 79, 189, 218;
  Procession Live at Sebastian's [album] 80
Procol Harum 299
Product of a Broken Reality, A [album] 185
Products, the 435
Professor Ratbaggy 320
Proles, the 340
'Progressive Office Pools' [song] 448
'Property Is Condemned' [song] 393
Proud, Geoffrey 135
Proud, Pip 28, 63, 67-8, 74, 135-43, 148, 197, 270, 283
Pryor, Laurie 113-4
Pseudo Echo 504
PSI 538
Psychedelia 2, 68, 111; 'psychedelic bubblegum' 73
'Pub With No Beer' [song] 417
Public Image Limited 351
Puckett, Alan 195
'Pull the Pin' [song] 449
'Pulp Baby' [song] 496
Punk Gunk (event) 249
Punter to Punter [radio show] 468
'Punxsie' [song] 458
Purdy, Gavan 522
Purdy, Kevin 517
'Pure Gold Flesh' [song] 407
Pure Shit [film] 296, 302
Pure Stuff, The [book] 283, 285
'Purple Boy Gang' [song] 139
Purple Gang 499
Purple Hearts, the 93, 129, 229, 253, 505
Purple Spirit [Melbourne venue] 149
Purser, John 'Catfish' 13
Purvis, R. E. [author] 392
Pus 180, 202, 251, 308-9
'Pushbike Song, The' [song] 158, 162
Pussyfoot 158
Putt, Bill 190, 295, 328
Pye, Katie 505
Pyrmont Bridge (NSW) 24
Python Lee Jackson 132

Q Club [Melbourne venue] 149, 199
QED 539
Quant, Mary 97
Quasimodo's Dream [album] 374, 380, 385, 388; [song] 373, 380-1, 386
'Que Sera Sera (Whatever Will Be, Will Be)' [song] 18, 44
Queen [Adelaide group] 239, 284
Queen [London group] 153, 269, 284
Queen Is Dead, The [album] 470
Queensland 51, 75, 104, 186, 232, 452
Queensland Academy of Music 260
Questions, the (aka Doug Parkinson and the Questions) 45, 86, 92
Quiet Achievers, the 526
Quill, Greg 98, 148, 209
Quincey Conserve 361
Quinn, Gavin 490
Qunta, Andy 463

Rabbit 247
Rabbits Wedding 392
Race, Hugo 518
Radalj, Rod (aka Roddy Radar, Roddy Ray'da, the Raj Radalj) 275, 440, 458
Radar, Roddy; *see* Rod Radalj

Radcliffe, Paul 505
Radiators, the 324, 440, 539
Radio Action Movement 270
Radio Adelaide [radio station] 272
radio ban 156
Radio Birdman 202, 235, 248-51, 253-4, 266, 271, 279, 339, 348-9, 384, 424-5, 473, 524, 534
Radio Caroline 128
Radio Day [film] 421
Radio London 128
Radio Luxembourg 128
Radio Stars 275
Radio Theatre [studio] 125
Radio With Pictures [TV show] 205
Raengel, Peter 524
Raffone, Mikey 253
Rage [TV show] 7, 548
Ragtime 9
'Rain' [song] 509
'Raindrops Keep Falling on my Head' [song] 96
Raining Pleasure [EP] 398; 'Raining Pleasure' [song] 398
Ralph [Australian record label] 297
Ralph [US record label] 343
RAM (*Rock Australia Magazine*) 230, 256, 291, 308, 310, 331, 333, 348-9, 355, 362, 403, 420-1, 426, 435, 516
Ram Jam Big Band (aka Ram Jam) 115, 449
'Ramona' [song] 509-10
Ramones, the 248, 260, 265-6, 276, 533, 534
Rampling, Charlotte 220
Randall, Robert 503
Randell, Lynne 37, 46, 95-6, 99
Random Access Memories [album] 317
Randwick (NSW) 31
Rankine, Veronica 536
'Rape' [song] 358
Raphael, Peter 192
Rascals, the 313
Rats [magazine] 160
Rats, the 202, 266
Rattler, Däg; *see* Rendall, Kimble
'Rave On' [song] 198
Rawlins, Adrian 23, 119, 180, 208
Ray Burton Band 269
Ray, Johnny 19
Ray, Ken 27
Raymond, Robert 360, 362, 365
Rayner, Eddie 445, 489
Rays, the 212
Razzle [record label] 315
RCA [record label] 330, 384, 386, 413, 477
're-funkt' [song] 502
Ready to Deal [album] 329
Real Dreamers, the 392-3
Real Life 505, 539
'Real Thing, The' [song] 68, 101, 105, 544
'Real Wild Child' [song] 7; *see also* 'The Wild One'
'Really and Sincerely' [song] 55
Reals, the 403
Rearvision, Rat [fictional character] 253
Rebb, Johnny 31
Reckless [album] 475
'Recognition' [song] 320
Red Angel Panic 167
'Red Chair Fade Away' [song] 55
Red Crayola, the (aka The Red Krayola) 523
Red Flame [record label] 398, 408
Red Onions, the (aka the Red Onions Jazz Band) 22, 88
Red Orb [Brisbane venue] 85
'Red Pony' [song] 396
Red Sails in the Sunset [album] 487
Redcliffe (Qld) 50; Speedway 51
Redding, Otis 77, 121, 265, 305
Reddy, Helen 192, 210, 269
Redfern (NSW) 398, 471
Redgum 166, 363, 529

Reed, Glad 430
Reed, Keith 253
Reed, Kim [author] 485
Reed, Lou 239, 241, 267, 333, 358, 393
Reels, the 3, 68, 373-89, 416, 452, 465, 470, 485, 496-7, 520, 544; *Reels, The* [album] 376
Reeves, Jim (Jimmy) 378, 383
Reflections Upon a Golden Homosexual Statue [book] 349
Regan, Graeme 431
Regent Theatre [Melbourne venue] 149
Regular Record [record label] 308, 388-9, 437, 461, 472
Reigate (UK) 81
Reign of Terror/Throne of Blood [album] 428
Relaxed Mechanics, the 178, 297
'Release the Bats' [song] 515
Remand [record label] 350
'Remember Sam' [song] 128
'Remington Rand' [song] 387
'Reminiscing' [song] 214
Remote Luxury [EP] 470
Rendall, Kimble (aka Däg Rattler) 442, 458, 491
Renée Geyer Band; *see* Geyer, Renée
'Rescue Me' [song] 76
Research (Vic) 224; Fire Brigade Hall 224; Super Shows 224, 232
Residents, the 359
'Resort Girls' [song] 466
Restless Years, The [TV show] 492
Return to Eden [TV show] 467
'Return' [song] 383
Reuben Tice (aka Reuben Tice Memorial Band) 224, 232
Reverie [EP] 393
Review [magazine] 159
Revolution [band] 121
Revolution [magazine] 99, 160, 218
Revolution Club [London venue] 81
Reyne, David 492-3
Reyne, James 464, 485, 491, 513
Reynolds, Lance 253
Reynolds, Neil 355
Reynolds, Simon 128
Rhodesia 322
Rhone, Marty 69, 96, 318
Rice, Tim 155
Richard, Cliff 19, 113, 248, 263
Richards, Dig (Digby) 18, 33, 196
Richards, Keith 202
Richards, Laurie 180
Richardson, Harley 380
Richman, Jonathan 347
Richmond Recorders [studio] 449
Richmond (Vic) 188
Riffs, the 393
Rilen, Ian 187-8, 255-8, 286, 293, 481, 528, 530
Rilen, Stephanie (Stephanie Falconer) 188, 255, 257, 293, 530
Riley, Robin 257, 512
Riley, Vikki [author] 249, 344, 438
'Ring, Ring' [song] 387
Ringwood (Vic) 73
Rip It Up [magazine] 440
Ripped Family Marches 184-5
Riptides, the 250, 346, 411, 492, 548
Risby, Col 84
Rischbeith, Nick 377, 387, 520
Rising Sons, the 71
Ritchie Family, the 263
Riverina region (NSW) 349
Rix, Peter 268, 325
RoadKnight, Margaret 198
Roadrunner [magazine] 282, 299, 339, 369, 380, 384, 393, 420, 435, 445, 451, 466, 474-5, 483, 491, 498, 536
Rob E. G. 220
Robb, Tom 230
Roberts, Michael 306, 481
Roberts, Peter 369

Robertson, Donald [author/editor] 282, 291, 339, 404, 417, 420, 451, 462, 466, 505, 515, 536
Robertson, Sandra 467
Robinson, Dave 300
Robinson, John 171
Rock 'n' Roll [album] 252
Rock n Roll Accountancy [album] 391
Rock 'n' Roll Ballroom of the Air [TV show] 205
'Rock and Roll Boogie' [song] 131
Rock and Roll Sandwich [album] 119, 262
Rock & Roll Scars [album] 191, 328
'Rock 'n' Roll Woman' [song] 222
Rock and Roll Women [album] 198
Rock Arena [TV show] 522
Rock Around the World [TV show] 522
Rock Australia Magazine (RAM) 99
Rock Encyclopedia [book] 55
Rock Generation [book] 10, 12
Rock Granite and the Profiles (aka Rock Granite) 182, 305
Rock Mass for Love [album] 155
'Rock Me Gently' [song] 315
Rock Ola [play] 491
'Rock On' [song] 462
Rock Scene 1974, The [film] 154, 168
Rock-on-Sunday [TV show] 268
Rocka [album] 133, 195
Rockets, the 393
Rockhouse [Adelaide venue] 535
Rockin' Roll Train [touring show] 42
Rocking Emus, the 223
Rockmelons, the 498
Rocks [band] 258
'Rocks in my Mouth' [song] 499
Rockturnal [TV show] 268
Rofe, Stan 44, 100, 107, 126, 157, 293
Roger Rocket and his Millionaires 226
Rogers, Billy 322, 368, 370-1, 401, 415, 508
Rogers, Bob 93
Rogers, Mick 78, 82, 112, 207
Rolling Stone [Australian magazine] vii, 160, 179, 198, 209, 240, 243, 262, 264, 286, 299, 302, 315, 323, 413-4, 420-1, 423, 465, 485
Rolling Stones, the 2, 17, 60, 90, 119, 299, 303, 334
Romantics, the [Australian band] 339, 369, 377
Romantics, the (US band) 300
Rome, Tony (Richard Cant) 534
Rommel and the Desert Rats 29
Rondells, the 46
Ronnie and the Rhythm Boys 336
Room to Move [radio show] 270
'Rooms for the Memory' [song] 487
Rose Tattoo 188, 196, 242-3, 254-5, 258, 377, 379, 512, 531
Rose, Ern 101
Rose, Lionel 105
Rosenberg, Denise, 335-6
'Rosevel' [song] 396
Roskhilde Festival 400
Ross, Malcolm 408
Ross, Max 99
Ross, Maxwell 299
Roth, Ed 'Big Daddy' 516
Rotsey, Martin 278
Rotterdam (Netherlands) 104
Roue, Norm 187-8
Rough Trade [record label/distributor] 336, 347
Rourke, Carl 266-7
Rowe, Doug 165
Rowe, Normie 18, 44, 46, 65, 70, 71, 75-6, 90, 98, 106, 120, 157
Rowell, John 452-3
Roxburgh Richard 8
Roxon, Lillian 52, 55, 98, 125, 161
Roxy Music 186, 230
Royal Commission of Inquiry into Drug Trafficking 360
Royal Headache 548

'Royal Telephone' [song] 38
Royall, Dallas 'Digger' 187, 255-7
RSO [record label] 49, 315
Rubinoos, the 300
Rudd, Kevin 488
Rudd, Mike 4, 60, 71, 73, 80, 87, 148, 152, 161, 189, 217, 314, 321, 328, 359, 506; Mike Rudd's Instant Replay 328; Mike Rudd and the Heaters 416
Rudd, Phil 243
Rude, Ron 423
'Rufus Red' [song] 274
Rumour, Danny 351
'Runaway' [song] 406-7
Rundgren, Todd 298, 376, 452, 511
Running Free [album] 363, 369
Running Jumping Standing Still 65, 90, 111
Rupert's World 54, 343
Rural [EP] 496
Rush [Australian band] 93; [Canadian band] 286
Russell, Graham 294
Russell, Ian 501
Ruth [fictional character] 141
Ryan, Adrian [author] 220, 277, 386, 483
Ryan, Marie [author/manager] 432, 435-6, 515-7
Ryan, Ross 494
Ryrie, Kim 463

'Sabotage' [song] 532
Sabrino, Vic (George Assang) 13
Sachs, Andrew 419
Sacred Cowboys 387, 403, 519
Sacred Games [album] 104
'Sad and Lonely and Blue' [song] 126
Sad Poetry [song] 473
Saddington, Wendy 98, 120, 148, 150, 170, 190, 202, 273, 329, 350, 356
'Sadie (the Cleaning Lady)' [song] 95, 101
Saints, the [Brisbane group] 65, 248-51, 253-4, 269, 339, 345-6, 350, 407, 425, 454, 522, 524, 546; [Sydney group] 254
Salamander Jim 526
Salisbury (SA) 28, 29; Youth Centre 28
Salmon, Kim 276, 401, 409, 500, 526
Saltbush 297
'Salute to ABBA' [song] 338
Sam and Dave 77
Sambell, Daryl 69, 95, 107, 111, 149, 547
'Same Old Blues' [song] 368
Same, the 431
'Samurai Stomp' [song] 527
Samurai Trash 526-7
San Cisco 278
San Francisco 231
San Miguel, Dolores 344
Sanctuary 329
Sandow, Alan 312
Sang, Samantha aka Cheryl Sang 53, 318
Sangster, John 13, 224
Santana 356, 371
Sapphires, the 29
Sardine V 259, 293, 334, 428, 478, 492, 530
'Satisfaction' [song] 79
'Saturday Night' [song] 223, 289
Saturday Night Fish Fry [EP] 12
Saturday Party [TV show] 84
Saturday Stomp [TV show] 84
'Saturday's Rage' [song] 512
Satyricon [film] 226
Savage, Jon [author] 239
Savage, Roger 111
'Save Me' [song] 265
'Say a Spell' [song] 517
Say It Loud [book] 283; [song] 283
Sayers, John 176
SCAM (Suss City Artist Management) 94, 394, 476, 478
Scammell, Peter 431
Scandinavia 400
Scented Gardens for the Blind [album] 355, 358

INDEX

Schauble, Tony 98
Schultz, Paul 501
Schumacher, Joel (director) 133
Schumann, John 166-7
Scientists, the 250, 276-7, 391-2, 409, 431-2, 495
Scorpio Rising [film] 252
Scott, Adrian 294
Scott, Bon (Ronald) 70, 104, 109, 132, 194, 200, 237, 241, 244, 284, 311, 456
Scott, Graeme 452-3
Scrap Metal 536
Scream [magazine] 447
Screamin' Lord Sutch 129
Screaming Believers, the 533
Screaming Tribesmen 473
Scribble 510
Scritti Politti 503
Scrote, Wild; *see* Howard, Alan
Scully, Marc 440
Sculthorpe, Peter 186
Scumbag 226, 298
Sea of Joy [film/album] 187
'Seabirds, The' [song] 401
Seagull Jobbies' [song] 183
Séance [album] 470
'Seasons of Change' [song] 171
Sebastian Hardie 155
Sebastian's [Melbourne venue] 80, 87, 149, 190, 199, 225
'Second Glance' [song] 403
Second Thoughts [album] 331
Sect, the 157
'Security' [song] 265, 305
Sedaka, Neil 84
Sedition Festival 406, 431
See Ya Round [album] 490
See, Sammy 312
Seeing the Rafters [book] 13
Seekers, the 24, 27, 47, 77, 103, 117, 163, 247, 418, 496
Segnit, Carl 297
Seinojoke Festival 400
Sejavka, Sam 486, 504
Sekret Sekret 350-1, 398, 404
'Self-Attack' [song] 305
Sell, Kieron 464
Sellers, Peter 33
Semantics [EP] 468
Semper [magazine] 176
Send Me a Lullaby [album] 347, 529
'Send Me an Angel' [song] 505
Serapax, Nancy; *see* Anderson, Julie
Sergeant Pepper's Lonely Hearts Club Band [film] 57; [album] 114
Serio, Terry 33, 309
Seven Days [TV show] 91
Seven Hills (NSW) 325
Severed Heads 398, 495, 497, 517
Sex Pistols 250, 260, 275, 286, 299, 340, 367, 377, 461, 525
Sex, Dope and Rock and Roll: Teenage Heaven [album] 185, 189
Sex, Dope and Violence in Daily Life [book] 185
Seymour, Mark 437-441, 532
Seymour, Nick 344, 377, 382, 387, 437, 441, 446
Sha Na Na 177, 215, 252
Shabooh Shoobah [album] 484
'Shaddap You Face' [song] 418-9
Shadowfax 332
Shadows, the 13, 31
Shadwick, Keith 296, 320, 329
Shakespeare, Clive 312, 316, 528
Shakespeare, William (aka Johnny Cabe, Johnny Cave(s)) 197, 293, 314, 349, 473
Shame Just Drained, The [album] 129, 132
'Shark Attack' [song] 489
Sharkmouth [album] 103
Sharks, the 274, 296
Sharman, Jim 137
Sharp, Martin (artist) 39, 60, 81, 160, 445
sharpies 65, 73, 171, 228, 252, 476
Shaw, Donna 361

'She Is Beyond Good and Evil' [song] 452
'She Taught Me How to Yodel' [song] 40
'She's Got the Money' [song] 339
'She's My Baby' [song] 35
'She's So Fine' [song] 125
'She's the Ginchiest' [song] 14
Shead, Gary 136
Shearston, Gary 21
Sheehan, Greg 177
Sheehan, Marnie 303
Shelf Life [album] 546
Shenton Park (WA) 277
Shepherd [band] 176
Shepherd, Bill 130
Shepherd, Brad 348, 459
Shepp, Archie 426
Sherbet 229, 243, 245, 247, 257, 279, 293, 311, 322-3, 353, 356, 366, 373, 513, 539, 543
Sherbet [album] 315
Sherbs, the 316, 323; *see also* Sherbet
Sherriff, Arthur 315
Shimamoto, Ken [author] 267
Shirl's Neighbourhood [TV show] 232
'Shivers' [song] 341, 423, 441
'Shoes Should Fit' [song] 523
Shorrock, Glenn 28, 113, 115-6, 136, 212, 283, 520, 543
'Shot in the Head' [song] 194
Shots [book] 290
'Shout' [Johnny O'Keefe] 7; [Deckchairs Overboard song] 493
'Shout and Deliver' [song] 380-1
Shout! The Story of Johnny O'Keefe [TV show] 33
'Show Me Some Discipline' [song] 477
'Show No Mercy' [song] 196
Showaddywaddy 263
Shower Scene from Psycho 336, 496
Shrimpton, Michael [TV producer] 292
Shy Imposters 473-4
'Sick and Tired' [song] 43
Sick Things, the 405
Sid Rumpo [band] 275, 464
Sidewalk [album] 307
Sidewinder 299, 331, 368, 446
Sidney Myer Music Bowl [Melbourne venue] 117
Silhouettes, the 84
Silicon Teens, the 497
Silk Degrees [album] 338
'Silver People' [song] 111
Silver Studs 253
Silver Trains 534
Silver, Andrew 527
silverchair 20, 211
'Silvery Moon' [song] 312
Simon, Carly 548
Simon, Lee 352, 450
Simone, Nina 121
Simple Minds 199
Simpson, Graham [author] 27
Sinatra, Frank 60, 214
'Since You Changed Your Mind' [song] 363
Sinclair, Byron 392
Sinclair, Marion 417
Sinfield, Peter 414
Sing Along With Mitch [TV show] 39
Sing, Sing, Sing [TV show] 36, 118
'Singing in the 80s' [song] 416
Sire [record label] 268
'Siren' [song] 457
Sirocco [album] 466-7
'Sister Ray' [song] 441
'Sitting on Top of the Room' [song] 205
'Six Bells Chime' [song] 500
'Six Dead Birds' [song] 408
Six O'Clock Rock [TV show] 34, 36, *see also* 291
'Six White Boomers' [song] 378
Skehill, Greg 530
Skiathitis, Jim 31
Sky Hook [film] 225

Skyhooks 146, 166, 169, 171, 215, 217, 224, 253-4, 270-1, 279, 282, 293, 296-8, 301-2, 308, 310-11, 317, 328, 353, 366-7, 419, 421, 442, 464-5, 471, 478, 488, 492, 519, 528
Slatzilvania [fictitious nation] 185
Slavich, Tony 328
Slay, Frank 158
Sleepy Jackson 278
Slick City Boys 275
'Slipping Away' [song] 192
'Slipstream' [song] 312
Slugfuckers, the 441
Small World Experience 546
Small, Phil 283
Smash [record label] 80
Smash Hits [magazine] vii, 421
'Smiley' [song] 44, 78, 102, 105-6, 118, 148
Smith, Anthony (aka Adam Hall) 478
Smith, Bessie 26, 121
Smith, Broderick 178, 337
Smith, Freddy 129
Smith, Greedy (Andrew Smith) 462, 472
Smith, Gulliver ('Little Gulliver') 59, 120, 146, 182, 184, 296
Smith, Jan [author] 40, 68
Smith, Nick 307
Smith, Paul 430
Smith, Russell 74, 172
Smith, Salvadore 335
Smiths, the 470
Smoke Dreams [album] 168
Snake Gully [fictional town] 29
Snakefinger 437
Snap and Crackle of Pop, The [film] 91-96
Snoid, Andrew (Andrew McLennan) 444-6
'Snoopy's Christmas' [song] 378
Snowy Mountains (NSW) 83, 136
'So You Want to be a Pop Singer' [song] 69
So Young [EP] 306; [song] 306
Soapbox Circus 169
Soffrok 294
Soft Machine, the 25, 109, 132
'Soldier of Fortune' [song] 506
'Solid Rock' [song] 530
Solley, Peter 299
'Some Kind of Fun' [song] 64
Some of Us Sardines 532
'Somebody to Love' [song] 240
Somebody's Image 102, 105-6
'Someday' [song] 503
'Something Easy' [song] 72
'Something Strange' [song] 117
Something to Do [album] 524
Something/Anything [album] 511
'Sometimes (I Can't Live With Anyone)' [song] 428
Sometimes, The Fire Dance [EP] 428
Son of Dungeon Tape [album] 394, 396
'Son of Miss Mercy' [song] 369
Sondra [album] 302
Sonic Investigations of the Trivial [EP] 502
'Sonny's Burning' [song] 517
Sons of Beaches [album] 466-7
Sons of the Vegetal Mother 71, 82, 189, 217, 219
Sony 537-8
Sopwith Camel 318
Soul Agents, the 24
sound lounges 76
Sound Pump 224
Sound System One 432
Sounds (aka *Sound Unlimited*) [TV show] 428
Sounds [magazine] 247, 261, 300, 333
'Sounds of Then' [song] 493
Soundtracks, Epic 343, 500
South Africa 322
South Australia 9, 282
South Australian Housing Trust 283
South Melbourne 453
South Yarra (Vic) 24, 292, 314
Southampton (UK) 82

Southern Electric; *see* Lobby Loyde
Southern Stars [album] 512
Southern Talent Services (SA) 46
Souvenir Records [studio] 308
Space 187
Space Race [album] 508
Spandau Ballet 433
Spaniards, the 360
'Spanish Blue' [song] 393, 395
'Spanish Harlem' [song] 393
Spare Change 339
Spare Parts 224
Sparkes, Ken 100, 220
Sparklers, the 477
Sparmac [record label] 198, 223
Sparrow, Eddie 132
Spastic Centre, the 33
'Speak to the Sky' [song] 211
Specials, the 128
Spectrum 74, 82, 145, 151, 157, 172, 189-90, 252, 273, 506-7
Spectrum Part One [album] 151-2, 189
'Spectrum' [song] 356
Spedding, Chris 194
Speedboat 535
Speer, Stewie 94-5, 192
Spektors, the 109
Spence, Dianne 430
Spencer, Bob 232, 256, 271
Spencer, Chris 546
'Spend the Night' [song] 198
'Spicks and Specks' [song] 50-1, 54
Spielman, Astrid 497-8
Spielman, Ingrid 497
Spiers, Reg 39
Spiff Rouch 464
Spin [record label] 52
Spinal Tap [film] 191, 399
Spinetti, Morris 170
Spinning Wheels, the 46
Spirit [record label] 307
'Spirit Got Lost' [song] 473
Spirit of Place [album] 529
SPK 351, 497
Split Enz 181, 278, 305, 330, 355, 444-5, 488
Spoke, Spike 253
Spooky Tooth 210
'Sporting Life, The' [song] 232
Sporting True Colours [tour] 302, 489
Sports, the 177, 181, 271, 297-8, 338, 443, 451, 465, 474-5, 533
Sports Sing Dylan (and Donovan) [EP] 302
Spring Plains 521-2
Springfield, Dave 327
Springfield, Dusty (Mary O'Brien) 27, 491
Springfield, Rick 108-9, 145, 211, 248, 295
Springfield, Tom (Dion O'Brien) 27
Springsteen, Bruce 290, 426
Springvale (Vic) 337
'Spunk Drunk' [song] 358
Spunky! [magazine] 244, 318, 337, 361
Sputniks, the 403
St Aloysius College 155
St Clair (SA) 25
St Clair Recording Studio (Hurstville, NSW) 52, 54
St George Leagues Club [Sydney venue] 509
St Ives (NSW) 87
St John, Ed [author] 306, 319, 460, 465, 483, 523
St John, Jeff 157, 271, 356, 494; and the Id 62
St Jude's Church Hall 225
St Kilda 78, 99, 120, 294, 342, 344, 450; St Kilda East 23
'St Louis' [song] 131, 195
St Vincent de Paul 91
Stacpool, Les 207
Stafford, Andrew [author] 345
Stagecoach [Sydney venue] 87
Stagedoor [Sydney venue] 350
'Stand Up' [song] 392

'Standing in the Rain' [song] 196
Stanley, Bob [author] 17
Stanshall, Vivian 161
Stanton, Kevin 507
Stapleton, Geoffrey 533
Stapleton, Ross [author] 282, 420
'Star Kissed' [song] 357-8
Star Wars [film] 486
'Star, The' [song] 105-6
Stardust, Alvin 306
Stares and Whispers' [song] 330
Starfighters, the 124
Starkie, Bongo (Bob) 225-7, 233-4, 377, 388
Starkie, Peter 121,182, 225-6, 234
Starr, Lucky (Leslie Morrison) 39, 75
Starr, Tony 504
Stars [band] 284
Starstruck [film] 444-6, 522
'State of the Heart' [song] 494
Stateside 70 [tour] 183
Station Hotel [Melbourne venue] 209, 297, 456
'Statue of Liberty' [song] 116
Statues Cry 540
Status Quo 326, 368
Stax-Volt [record label] 77
Stay Away from the Lightning Girl [book] 301
Stead, Colin 53-4
Stebbing, Eldridge 119
Steedman, Pete 161
Steele, Kevin 29
Steely Dan 303
Steiger, Allan [fictional character] 312
Stems, the 501
'Step Back' [song] 104
Stephen, Ian 181, 339
Stepney (WA) 272
Stereo Home Box Office [TV show] 443
Sterry, David 505
Steve's [album] 391
Stevens, Cat 517
Stevens, Paul 253; *see also* Mikey Raffone
Stewart, Jimmy 117, 318
Stewart, Kaye 34
Stewart, Rod 132, 194, 278, 295
Stewart, Rodney 192
Stiff [record label] 299, 350
Stiff Little Fingers 279
Stiggs, Buster (Mark Hough) 444, 446
Stigwood, Robert 52, 54, 252
Stila, Mick (aka Boofhead) 337
Stiletto 296, 298, 302-3, 339, 457
'Still in Love With You' [song] 364
Stobart, Tim 180
Stock and Station Journal 20
Stockhausen, Karlheinz 337
Stockley, Chris 72
'Stolen Property' [song] 401
Stoller, Mike 312
Stomp City [Sydney venue] 42
'Stomping at Maroubra' [song] 30, 228
Stone [film] 207-8
Stone Class of Distinction, A (musical) 185
Stone, Judy 161
Stoneage Romeos [album] 459
Stonehenge [Melbourne venue] 72, 87
Stooges, the 254, 266, 424, 524
'Stop Before You Say It' [song] 347
'Stop the Baby Talking' [song] 302
Stopa, Bobby 340
Storey, Neil 355, 359. 360-1
Stork [film] 103, 148, 158, 168
Stork; *see* Vandersluys, Michael
Storm, Roland and the Statesmen 42, 45
Strachan, Graeme ('Shirley') 153, 224, 227, 312, 419, 513
Straight in a Gay Gay World [album] 231
'Straight Laddie' [song] 507
Strals, Arnold 155, 535
Stranded (TV documentary) 546
Stranded in Paradise [book] 4
Strange Fantastic Dream, A [album] 191

Strangeloves, the 473
'Strangers on a Train' [song] 299
Strangers, the 158
Strata Hotel [Sydney venue] 371
Stratton, Jon [author] 423
Strauks, Freddy (Imants Strauks) 166, 224-7, 230, 234-5, 301-2
Stray Dags 305
Stray Tapes 504
Streep, Meryl 208
'Street Café' [song] 463
Strictly Ballroom [film] 196
Strikebound [film] 486
Strings and Things 92
Strings Unlimited 95, 547
Strummer, Joe 528
Strykert, Ron 417-8
'Stuck on You' [Ian Rilen song] 257; [Rose Tattoo song] 257; [Sardine V song] 532
Studdert, Dave 431
Stylus 328
Styx 286
Sub Pop [magazine/record label] 423
'Suburban Boy' [song] 309-10
'Suburban Rock' [song] 310
suburbia 308
'Such a Shame' [song] 55
'Sudan' [song] 293, 532
Suddenly [album] 301
'Sugar Sugar' [song] 387
Suicide [record label] 273, 330, 340
'Suicide City' [song] 257
Sujdovic, Boris 276, 526
Sullivan, Barry 207
Sullivan, Ed 56
Sullivan, Peter 334
'Summer Love' [song] 312-3
'Summer of '81' [song] 494
Summer of the Seventeenth Doll (play) 335
Summer, Donna 405
'Summertime Blues' [song] 461
'Sun Arise' [song] 11
Sun-Herald 139, 192
Sunbury (Vic) 152
Sunbury Festival 152-3, 159, 182, 188, 199, 222, 252, 281
Sunday Independent 392
Sunnyboys, the 277, 334, 443, 481, 539, 548
Sunrise [agency] 159
Sunsets, the 186
Sunshine [album] 361
Sunshine [record label] 76-7, 164, 261; Sunshine Review (touring show) 75, 85
Sunshine (Vic) 111, 149
Super K 459
Superdroop [fictional character] 113, 116
'Superman' [song] 146
Supernaut 247, 323
'Superstition' [song] 453
Surf City [Sydney venue] 42, 45, 75, 125
Surfing with a Spoon' [song] 279
Surprises [album] 105
Surtees, Felicity [author] 314
Survivors, the 273
Susz, 'Continental' Robert 527
Sutherland, Donnie 83, 429, 433
Suttons [Melbourne music store] 45
Suzie Wong's [Sydney venue] 60-2, 75
Swaggie [record label] 21
Swan Hill (Vic) 322
Swan, John ('Swanee') 28, 200, 256, 283-4, 514
Swanee *see* Swan, John
'Swanee' [song] 283
Sweaty Betty 85
Sweet and Sour [TV show] 457, 490-2;
'Sweet and Sour' [song] 493
Sweet Nothings, the 477
'Sweet Song of Summer' [song] 57
'Sweet' [song] 307
Swinburne College of Technology (aka Swinburne Technical College) 225, 230
Swing, The [album] 484

INDEX 593

'Swing for the Crime' [song] 426
Swingers, the 444
Swingers: Staying Number One, The [film] 444
Swingle Singers, the 128
'Swingy George' [song] 404, 407
Sydney, NSW 41, 42, 43, 68, 75-6, 104, 184, 188, 281, 339, 376, 395, 524; Airport (aka Mascot Airport) 267, 286; beaches 67; Harbour 14, 204, 361-2; Opera House 280; Public library 141; Symphony Orchestra 186; Town Hall 129
Sydney Morning Herald 60
Sykes, Ken 533
Sylvian, David 463
Symons, Michael [author] 141
Symons, Red (Redmond) 51, 226-7, 229-31, 234, 271, 298, 301
Syssys, the 110, 135
Systematics, the 496

T. C. [author] 474
T. F. Much Ballroom [Melbourne venue] 149, 151, 170, 178, 199, 219, 335
T.V.'s Countdown [album] 85
Tablewaiters, the 428
Tactics 350, 398, 424, 431, 434, 469, 483, 548
Tagg (aka *the alternative gig guide*) [magazine] 420
Tait, John [author] 131
'Take a Long Line' [song] 242, 282
'Take Action' [song] 113
Take It Greasy [album] 252
'Take the Red Carpet Out of Town' [song] 403, 408-9
Take, the 336
Takeaways, the 490, 493
Tales from the Australian Underground [album] 250
Tales of Old Grand-Daddy [album] 195
Tales of the Unexpected [album] 499
Talk [album] 528
Talking Heads [band] 392, 539
Talking Heads [TV show] 32
'Talking to a Stranger' [song] 274, 439, 441, 486
'Tall Timber' [song] 233
Talmy, Shel 127
Tamam Shud 185, 190, 464
Tamarama (NSW) 329
Tamworth, (NSW) 95, 152, 382; Country Music Festival 152
Tantrum 239
Tapdancers, the 430
Tarax [soft drink] 99
Tarkus [band] 200
Tasmania 184, 271, 307, 314, 335, 443, 466, 470
Taste 247, 323
Taupin, Bernie 221
Tavern, The [Adelaide venue] 24
'Taxi Mary' [song] 307
Tayler, Stephen [producer] 451
Taylor, Carey 415
Taylor, Danny 312
Taylor, David 349
Taylor, Jules 335-6
Taylor, Ken [author/A&R person] 7, 10, 14, 34
Taylor, Mark 349
Taylor, Matt 59, 203, 413
Taylor, Robert [member of Dragon] 289, 355-6, 365, 509-10
Taylor, Robert [member of Tully] 186
Tayshus, Austen 421
Tch Tch Tch (→↑→; aka Tsk Tsk Tsk) 249, 273, 501
TCS [studio] 188
'Tearing Hair Out' [song] 455
Ted Mulry Gang 311, 322-3, 353
Tee, Michael 496
Teen Scene [TV show] 44

Teenage Hour [TV show] 36
'Teenage Kicks' [song] 277
Teenage Radio Stars 273-4, 344, 446, 448; see also Radio Stars
Tek, Deniz 202, 253-4, 266, 284, 348-9, 424
'Telephone' [song] 366
Television [band] 248, 392
'Television Addict' [song] 276
Temperamental [album] 458
Ten Happy Fingers [album] 454
Tenth Avenue [Sydney venue] 72-3
Terry, Sonny 60
Terse Tapes [record label] 495
Tex Deadly and the Dum Dums 525
'That's the Way' [song] 493
The, the 432
Theatre Arts Monthly [magazine] 342
'Theme from "Mad Flies, Mad Flies"' [song] 429
'These Boots Are Made for Walking' [song] 273, 341
These Cars Collide 538
These Future Kings 409
'They Built the Ute' [song] 235
'They'll Never Know' [song] 52
'They're All Losers, Honey' [song] 205
Thin, Peter 270
'Things' [song] 488-9
'Things Don't Seem' [song] 466
'Things to Do' [song] 96
Thirlwell, Jim 434
Thirsty's Calling [album] 407
This Day Tonight [TV show] 148
'This Guy's in Love' [song] 383-5, 388
'This Is My City' [song] 528
'This Road Is Holy' [song] 404
'This Time' [song] 360-1, 510
'This Town Is Boring' [song] 232
Thomas and the Rhymers [fictional band] 18, 24
Thomas, Robyn 131
Thomas, Rod 263
Thomasetti, Glen [author] 26
Thomastown (Vic) 179
Thompson, Denis 424
Thompson, Ivan 355
Thornleigh (NSW) 412
Thorpe, Billy ('Thorpie') 313, 321; and the Aztecs vii, 18, 42, 60, 84, 113, 125, 133, 146, 150, 152, 154, 172, 182, 188, 203, 238, 295, 322
Thorunka (aka *Tharunka*) [magazine] 160
Thought Criminals, the 349, 424, 435, 496
'Three Dead Passengers in a Stolen Second-Hand Ford' [song] 404
Three to Go [film] 83
Thrillington [album] 318
Thring, Frank 99, 149
Throb, the 124-5, 133, 253
Throbbing Gristle 406
'Throbbing Knob' [song] 309
'Throw Your Arms Around Me' [song] 3, 441
Thrush and the Cunts 336, 486
Thumpin' Tum [Melbourne venue] 88, 90, 149
Thunderbirds (group) 13, 44
Tice, Dave 187
Tice, Reuben 224
'Tickle Your Fancy' [song] 323
Tickle, David 489, 533
'Tie Me Kangaroo Down Sport' [song] 11
Tiger Lounge [Melbourne venue] 180, 282, 297
Tiger Mountain Band 392
Tilbrook, Peter 111
'Till the Beast Is Dead' [song] 458
Till, Gus 453
Tillett, Louis 431, 497
Tillman, Peter 349
Time and the Forest Flower 184
Time and Tide [album] 490
Time the Musical [album] 103

Timmins, Janelle [fictional character] 312
Tin Tin 117
Tivoli Hotel [Adelaide venue] 534
TNT [album] 242; 'TNT' [song] 243
'To Her Door' [song] 527
'To Love Somebody' [song] 55
To the Shores of His Heaven [album] 333
Toads (aka Toads, Nightly) 296
Toast to Panama Red, A [album] 183
Todd, Kevin 30
Toi, Teddy 84, 205
'Tojo' [song] 458
Tokyo (Japan) 37
Tolhurst, Kerryn 59, 178
Tolnay, Charlie 535
Tomlin 271
Tomorrow Is Today [book] 88
'Tomorrow Never Knows' [song] 121
Tomorrow, Jimi 297
'Tomorrow's Tears' [song] 346
Too Fat to Fit Through the Door 335-6
'Too Hot to Move' [song] 393, 493
'Too Hot to Touch' [song] 323
Too Much [TV show] 104
Too Much Ain't Enough [book] 283
'Too Much Ain't Enough' [song] 283
Too Poor to Die [album] 334
Toomorrow 118
Toorak Cowboy 228
Toorak (Vic) 149
Tooting Bec (UK) 36
Toowoomba (Qld) 76
Top of the Pops [TV show] 113, 292
Top Ryde (NSW) 60
Topper, Johnny (John) 120, 169, 178-80, 297
Tosti-Gueira, Ray 437
Toucan Club [Adelaide venue] 535
Touché [album] 324
Toulouse-Lautrec, Henri 365
Toward the Blues [album] 443
Townsend, Clive 478, 480
Townshend, Pete 70, 504
Toy Love 412, 492
Tracks [magazine] 167
'Tracks of My Tears' [song] 232
Trade Union Club [Sydney venue] 345, 431, 499-500
Trafalgar [album] 57
Trafalgar (studio/record label) 268
Traitors, the 478
Tramp 194
Tranmere (SA) 29
Trans-Australian Airlines (TAA) 95
Translator [album] 533
Transworld Death Corporation 432
Trask, Diana 39
Treble Clef, The [Melbourne venue] 27
Treeless Plain [album] 396
Treloar, Huk 296
Tremaine, Ron 20, 29, 47
Tribe [theatre group] 170, 178, 225
Tribe, the [band] 538-9
Tribune [newspaper] 421
Triffids, the 275, 351, 391-401, 432, 444, 454, 478, 493, 517, 529, 539, 540; *Triffids, The* [album] 392
Trocadero [Sydney venue] 114
Trolls, the 84
Trouble in Molopolis [film] 81
Trudgeon, Michael 423
True Colours [album] 330, 444, 489
'Truth about You' [song] 498
Tsk Tsk Tsk *see* Tch Tch Tch
Tudor, Ron 27, 157-8, 161, 212, 334
Tuff Monks 495
Tully 150, 185, 267, 279
Tully in Space 187
Tumahai, Charlie 213
Turk, the 534
Turkey 56
'Turn Up Your Radio' [song] 112, 252, 496
'Turn Your Head' [song] 108
Turnbull, Phil 523

Turner, Ian [author] 147
Turner, Mick (aka Mick Sick) 8, 405-8
Turpie, Ian 84, 119
TV Disk Jockey [TV show] 37
TV Jones 202, 266-7
TV Week [magazine] 22, 33, 34, 35, 36, 37, 39, 118, 286, 330, 362, 467
Twentieth Century [album] 289
Twenty Flight Rockers 324
Twilight of Mischief [album] 412
Twilights, the 29, 70, 107, 110, 112-14, 116, 129, 199, 213, 282, 339
Twinn, Gary 323-4
'Twisted Brain' [song] 393
Twisties [snack] 229
'Two Cabs to the Toucan' [song] 451
'Two Can Play' [song] 468
Two for the Show (cabaret) 113
Two Hearts [album] 418
'Two Little Boys' [song] 11
Two Man Band 334
'Two Tribes' [song] 537
Two Way Garden 345
Two-Fisted Art [album] 409
Tyler, Kieron [author] 253

Ubu Collective 138
Ugly Duckling, The [pantomime] 30
Ultravox 462, 507
Uluru 440
Umbrella [magazine] 308
Umbrella Invasion 308
Uncanny X-Men 539
Unchained (EP) 59
Uncle Bob's Band 296
'Uncontrollable Boy (I'm Just an)' [song] 449
Uncovered [album] 521
'Undecided' [song] 110, 325
Undecideds, the 324
'Under the Boardwalk' [song] 348
'Under the Milky Way' [song] 469
Underneath the Colours [album] 484
Undertones, the 277, 473
'Unguarded Moment, The' [song] 469
'Unhappy' [song] 452
Unicorn [Sydney venue] 472
Union, the 338
Universal Radio [album] 355
University Jazz Band (Melbourne) 26
University of Adelaide 536
University of Auckland 360
University of Melbourne 10, 177, 438
University of New England (NSW) 284
University of New South Wales 156
University of Queensland 176
University of Sydney 240, 472
University of Western Australia 309, 414
Unknown Blues 91
Unley (SA) Town Hall 339
Unterberger, Richie [author] 24
'Up There Cazaly' [song] 334, 418
Upper Hutt (NZ) 378
Ups and Downs 540
Upside Down House 344, 431
Uptight [TV show] 79, 85, 106, 139, 199, 202, 333
Uptight Party Team 79
Uptight Party Time [album] 79
Urban Guerillas 538
Uriah Heep 112, 186, 230
Us Mob 536

V Capri 278
Valentine, James 454-5
Valentines, the 93, 102, 109, 131, 159, 207, 237, 241
Valentino, Rudolph 342
Valenvengers, the [fictional band] 114
Van Diemen [record label] 85
Van Halen, Eddie 510
van Roosendael, Eddie 296, 303, 339
Van Vugt, Victor 405, 407

Vanda and Young 96, 192-9, 217, 244, 256, 321, 351, 376; *see also* Harry Vanda, George Young
Vanda, Harry (Hendrickus Vandenburg) 2, 104, 123-133, 194, 241
Vandenburg, Pam 126
Vandersluys, Michael ('Stork') 255-6
Vasali, Sybilla 485
Vaughan, Mike 125, 132
Vectormen, the 29
Vega, Suzanne 548
Vegemite 416
Velvet Underground, The [book] 239
Velvet Underground, the [Newcastle (NSW) band] 193, 239-40
Velvet Underground, the [New York band] 239, 241, 393
Veneers, the 276
Venom P. Stinger 431
Vertigo [record label] 188, 325, 355
Very Quick on the Eye [album] 495
Vibratones, the 42; *see also* Aztecs, Billy Thorpe
Vibrators, the 274
Vicious, Sid 275
Vickers, Robert 345, 348, 429, 529
Victims, the 250, 275-7, 391-2, 458
Vidale, Simon 413
Vietnam 83, 108; Vietnam War 44, 54, 78, 90, 111, 115, 139, 147-8, 161, 166, 199, 229-30, 259-60
'Vietnam Rose' [song] 194
Village Green, The (aka Village Green Hotel) [Melbourne venue] 181, 224
Villawood Migrant Hostel 123
Vincent, Amanda 415
Vincent, Gene 32, 33
Vintner Girls School 228
Virgil Brothers 163, 172
Virgin Records [record label] 159, 408, 439, 443, 526
Virgin, David 351
Virgins, the 275
Visage 433
Vishdungarius [fictional character] 185
Vivisector, The [book] 68
Vlort Phlitson [radio show] 143, 270
Vogel, Peter 463
Voices, the 412
Voigt/465 344, 435
Volcanic Rock [album] 188
Voltaire, Pierre (aka Peter Sutcliffe; Pierre Sutcliffe; Mr Pierre) 340, 405, 446, 450
Von Braund, Steve Maxwell 332
Vox (aka *Vox Muzpaper*) [magazine] 255, 336, 420, 425, 435

W Minc [record label] 409
W.H.Y. 506
W&G [record label] 27, 88-9, 157
Wa Wa Nee 424
Wadley, Greg 525
Wadley, Ian 525
Wagga Wagga (NSW) 75, 460, 473
Wagstaff, Stuart 149
Wahlquist, Gil [author] 139, 192
Waiata; see *Corroboree* [album]
'Waiting' [song] 415
'Waiting for a Train' [song] 198
'Walk on the Wild Side' [song] 362, 365
Walker Brothers, the 426
Walker, Clinton [author] 12, 194, 200, 239, 250, 273, 335, 403, 431, 438, 503
Walker, Denis 147
Walker, Don 201, 239, 283-4
Walker, Mark 477
Walker, Peter 285, 295, 304, 401
Walker, Rhett H. 168
Walker, Tony [author] 243
'Walking in the Rain' [Vanda/Young song] 131, 197; [Mann/Spector/Weill song] 198
Walkman 537
Wall, David [author] 432

Wallace-Crabbe, Ben 344, 426, 428, 431
Wallace-Crabbe, Chris 426
Wallace-Crabbe, Dan 344, 428
Wallacia (festival) 206
'Walls' [song] 462
Walsh, Brecon [author] 466
Walsh, Chris 202, 273, 403, 405, 519
Walsh, Joe 164, 513
Walsh, Mike 84, 169
Walsh, Peter 428-9, 431, 435
Walsh, Richard [author/editor] 96
'Waltzing Matilda' [song] 10, 40, 231
'Wangaratta Wahine' [song] 293
'Wanna be a Birdman' [song] 339
'Wanna Be Your Baby' [song] 274
Ward Austin's Jungle [Sydney venue] 87
Ward, Algy 425
Ward, Juliet 499
Ward, Nick 469
Ward, Penny 473
Ward, Ted 109
Warner Brothers [record label] 164, 210
Warner, Dave (aka Grim Reaper) 214, 308, 401, 443, 543; *see also* Dave Warner's From the Suburbs
Warrnambool (Vic) 120
'Wars or Hands of Time' [song] 111
Warumpi Band 537
Warwick, Dionne 103
Wasted Daze 273, 308
Waterfront [record label] 436
Waterpop Festival 400
Waters, Muddy 366
Watson, John 42
Wauchope (NSW) 460
Waugh, Rob 503
'Way That You Do It, The' [song] 158
Way to Go Out, The [album/video] 441
'Wayward Wind, The' [song] 40
'We 2 Should Live' [song] 62
'We Are Indelible' [song] 192
'We Can Get Together' [song] 462
'We Can't Be Beaten' [song] 257
'We Had Love' [song] 409
We Never Close [album] 508
'We Ride Tonight' [song] 317
WEA [record label] 285, 348, 424, 537
Webb, Al [author/musician] 304, 532
Webb, Jimmy (Jim) 214, 426
Webb, Marius 270
Webber, Andrew Lloyd 155
Webber, Graeme [photographer] 176
Webster, Allan [author] 367
'Wedding Cake Island' [song] 280
'Wedding Ring' [song] 126
Weddings, Parties, Anything 340
Wednesday, Ash 340, 394, 446, 449, 451, 463, 532, 534
Weeds [album] 491
Weekend [film] 321
Weekend Magazine [TV show] 275
Weekes, Robbie [TV producer] 292
Wegener, Jeffrey 260, 340, 351, 425-7, 430, 460, 497
Weir, Peter [film director] 67, 83, 149, 168, 190
Welch, Les 12
Wellington, NZ 361
Wells, Peter 188, 255-7, 512
Welsh, Keith 461
Wembley (WA) 275
Wenders, Wim [film director] 500
'Wendy of the Overdose' [song] 350
Werder, Felix 449
Wesley College 99
Wesley Trio, the 99
West Australian Institute of Technology 276, 393
West Heidelberg (Vic) 120
West, Carol 96
West, Ken 430, 503
Western Australia 191
Western Flyer 413
Weston, Dave 523

INDEX

Wet Taxis, the 497
'What Am I Going to Do?' [song] 510
What Are Little Boys Made Of [band] 395
'What I Like About You' [song] 300
What Is a Question [album] 92
What Is This Thing Called Disco? [album] 501-2
*What the F**k Is Happening on Planet Earth?* [musical] 185
'What Would the Children Think' [song] 211
What's a Quaver? [EP] 375
'What's the Matter' [song] 226
'Whatever Happened to the Revolution?' [song] 229
Wheatley, Glenn 96, 112, 164, 184, 212, 217, 305, 327, 465, 467, 505, 547
'When the Birdmen Fly' [song] 348
'When You Walk in the Room' [song] 299
'When You're Lonely' [song] 277
'Where Do They Go?' [song] 460
Where in the World [album] 328
'Where Is the Love' [song] 383
'Where the Trees Walk Down Hill' [song] 404
Where's Hank? [album] 491
Whip It Out [album] 306
Whirlywirld 336, 340, 449, 455, 502
Whisky A Go Go [Los Angeles venue] 221
Whisky A Go Go [Sydney venue] 87; aka 'the Whisky' 29
Whispering Jack [album] 233, 546
White Elephant [Melbourne venue] 87, 149
White Forest, The [book] 142
White Hot [record label] 396, 442
White Label [record label] 274, 394, 439, 445, 479
White Light [record shop] 349
'White Light/White Heat' [song] 358, 371
White Trash 502
White, Jim 431
White, Patrick [author] 68, 339
White, Steve 510
White, Trevor 155
'Whiter Shade of Pale, A' [song] 114
Whitlam, Gough 146-7, 161-2, 170, 243, 248-9, 269, 329, 447
Whittle, Bob 437
'Who Can It be Now' [song] 417
Who the Hell Is Judy in Sydney [book] 96
'Who Walks Out When I Walk In' [song] 168
Who, the 77, 127, 210, 346, 548
'Who'll Be The One' [song] 128
'Whole Lotta Shakin' Going On' [song] 252
Whoopee the Wonder Dog 170
'Why Do Little Kids Have to Die' [song] 117
'Why Don't You All Get Fucked' [song] 233
Whyalla (SA) 110
Wickedy Wak 108
Wide Open [album] 186
Widmer, Harry 83, 92, 96, 161
Wiggles, the 258
Wild about You [book] 51
'Wild About You' [song] 64-5, 254
Wild Beaver Band 338
Wild Cherries, the 24, 73, 91, 93, 107
'Wild Colonial Boy, The' [Cold Chisel song] 286
Wild Colonials, the 46
'Wild One, The' [song] 33
Wild Red Onions [album] 88
Wild West 523
'Wild World' [song] 517
Wildcat [album] 477
Wilde, Wilbur (aka Bad Youth Ivory) 234, 306
Wildlife Documentaries 431
William St (Sydney) 29
Williams, Hank 297

Williams, Larry 325
Williams, Mark 196, 538
Williams, Peter 267
Williams, Peter 497-8
Williams, Steven 497
Williams, Tony 232
Williamson, John 158
Willis, Rod 285-6
Willoughby, Bart 536
Willson-Piper, Marty 469-70
Wilmoth, Peter [author] 291
Wilson, Brian 131
Wilson, Daniel 220
Wilson, Dennis D. 269
Wilson, Murry 54
Wilson, Pat (Pat Huggins) 82, 182, 218, 305, 494
Wilson, Ross 8, 59, 65, 71-3, 80, 82, 113, 120, 182, 189, 217, 219, 223-4, 226, 233, 234, 250, 298, 302, 305, 327, 338, 388, 424, 447, 478, 493-4, 514, 527
Wilson, Terry 187
Wilson, Terry 369
Windschuttle, Keith [author] 262
Windsor, Margaret 57
Winged Death 524
'Wings of an Eagle' [song] 102
Wings of Desire [film] 500
'Winter in America' [song] 318
Winter, Chris 270
Winter, Ian Willy 322
Winter, Johnny 366
'Winter's Way' [song] 430
Winztons, the 109
Wires 505
Wisseling, Louisa 165
'Witchery' [song] 214
Witer, Oleh 382
Withers, Tony 33
'Without You' [song] 93
Witzig, Paul [film director] 187
Wizard [record label] 350
Wolfgramm, Robert [author] 73
Wollongong (NSW) 362-3
'Woman of the World' [song] 220, 328
'Woman You're Breaking Me' [song] 114
'Women (Make You Feel Alright)' [song] 126, 328
Women and Children First 177
'Women in Uniform' [song] 232
Women's Weekly, Australian 138
Wonder, Stevie 453
Wood, Michael 497
Wood, Roy 231
Wooden Horse 473
Woodface [album] 491
Woodies Teentime (television program) 28
Woodley, Bruce 27, 103, 107, 166, 207
Woodruff, John 20, 281, 285
Woods, Rowan [film director] 289
Woodstock [festival] 252
'Working Class Man' [song] 290
'World Goes On, The' [song] 103
'World of Stone' [song] 439
'World War 3' [song] 491
'World Weary' [song] 347
Worrall, Barrie 312
Worrall, Chris 168, 296, 302, 304
Worstead, Paul 471
Wreckery, the 405, 519
Wright, 'Little' Stevie 124, 159, 195-6, 198, 241, 293, 322
Wrinkly Show [TV show] 202
WROK [TV show] 442
Wrong Kind of Stone Age 538
Wrong Side of the Road [film] 420, 535
Wyatt, Robert 24-5
Wyllie, Eileen 202
Wyllie, Ross D. 79, 85, 157, 202
Wyndham-Reade, Martin 22, 26

X [Australian band] 257, 308, 409, 436, 530-1, 540
X [Los Angeles band] 257

X, Bohdan 340, 534
X-Aspirations [album] 259, 478
X-Press [magazine] 538
X-Ray Spex 273
X-Ray-Z 273, 532
Xeni, Peter 298
XL Capris 435, 458, 491, 523, 548
Xmas '89 [album] 538
XTC 233, 375-6, 443, 509

Y?4, the 110
Ya Ya Choral 375, 496
Yagoona (NSW) 83
Yardbirds, the 24, 299
Yates, Steve 207
'Yeah Howard' [song] 232
'Yeah Tonite' [song] 192
'Yes Sir, That's My Baby' [song] 38
'Yesterday's Hero' [song] 131, 196, 322
Yorke Peninsula (SA) 110
Yothu Yindi 467
You Get What You Deserve [album] 495
'You Got Nothing I Want' [song] 290
'You Just Don't Care' [song] 508
'You Just Like Me 'Cos I'm Good in Bed' [song] 270
'You Need a Friend' [song] 476
You Need Professional Help [album] 513
'You're the Voice' [song] 334
You're Thirteen, You're Beautiful and You're Mine [EP] 285
Young Charlatans 340, 423, 426, 432
Young Doctors, The [TV show] 92, 192
'Young Girl' [song] 113
Young Man and His Music, A [album] 106
Young Modern [band] 321, 339, 348
Young Modern [magazine] 20-30, 75, 98; [record label] 47
Young, Alex 132
Young, Angus 104, 124, 194, 196, 237-42, 244-5, 247, 255
Young, Denise [author] 35
Young, Gary 218-9, 222-3, 233, 289, 305
Young, George 2, 123, 193-4, 196, 239, 241, 254, 321
Young, John Paul (aka John Young) 132, 155, 159, 194, 196, 210, 238, 242, 264, 293, 357, 373, 506, 543 and the All Stars 321, 358
Young, Johnny (John de Jong) 44, 54-5, 60, 70, 84, 101, 104, 107, 111, 118, 135, 153, 157, 196, 496, 544; as 'Johnnie Young', 55
Young, Malcolm 124, 193-5, 237-40, 242, 254-5, 323
Young, Neil 460
Younger Set, the [charity organisation] 33
Younger, Rob 202, 266-7, 424
'Your Mama Don't Dance' [song] 159
'Your Turn, My Turn' [song] 347

Zantey, Harry 432
Zappa, Frank 274
Zatorski, Richard 505
Zeee Toons 496
Zero aka Xero, Xiro 250, 347, 431
Zion, Laurence [author] 19
Zoot 72, 102-3, 107-9, 149, 167, 282
Zorro (Don Diego de la Vega) [fictional character] 240-1
Zutaut, Tom 286

ABOUT THE AUTHOR

David Nichols is a historian focusing on Australian urban cultures. His previous books include *The Go-Betweens* (2003) and *The Bogan Delusion* (2011). He is the co-author of *Pop Life* (2011) and *Trendyville: The Battle for Australia's Inner Cities* (2014), and co-editor of *Community: Building Modern Australia* (2010).

Nichols began writing about music in his fanzine, *Distant Violins*, in 1980 and has subsequently contributed to *Rolling Stone*, *The Age*, *Meanjin*, *Smash Hits Australia* (where he was features editor from 1983 to 1991), and many other publications. He lives in Clifton Hill and teaches at the University of Melbourne.

www.ingramcontent.com/pod-product-compliance
Lightning Source LLC
Chambersburg PA
CBHW021049080526
44587CB00010B/189